ABORIGINAL LAW

PURICH'S ABORIGINAL ISSUES SERIES

THIRD EDITION

ABORIGINAL LAW

COMMENTARY, CASES AND MATERIALS

Thomas Isaac
B.A., M.A., LL.B., LL.M.
of the Bars of
British Columbia, New Brunswick,
Northwest Territories,
and Nunavut

Purich Publishing Ltd.
Saskatoon, Saskatchewan
Canada

Purich Publishing Ltd.
Box 23032, Market Mall Post Office
Saskatoon, SK Canada S7J 5H3
Phone: (306) 373–5311   Fax: (306) 373–5315
Email: purich@sasktel.net
Website: www.purichpublishing.com

National Library of Canada Cataloguing in Publication

Isaac, Thomas F. (Thomas Francis), 1966–
        Aboriginal law : commentary, cases and materials / Thomas Isaac. — 3rd ed.

(Purich's aboriginal issues series)
Previously publ. under title: Aboriginal law: cases, materials and commentary.
Includes bibliographical references and index.
ISBN 1-895830-23-0

        1. Native peoples—Legal status, laws, etc.—Canada. 2. Native peoples—Legal status, laws, etc.—Canada—Cases. I. Title. II. Series.

KE7708.5.I73 2003   342.71'0872   C2003-
907203-7
KF8204.5.I73 2003

Cover design by NEXT Communications Inc., Saskatoon, Saskatchewan.
Editing, design and layout by Roberta Mitchell Coulter, Saskatoon, Saskatchewan.
Printed in Canada by Houghton Boston, Saskatoon on acid-free paper.

The publisher acknowledges the financial assistance of the Cultural Industries Development Fund, Saskatchewan Culture, Youth and Recreation towards publication of this book.

Readers will note that words like Aboriginal, Native, and Indigenous have been capitalized in this book. In recent years, many Aboriginal people have argued that such words should be capitalized when referring to specific people, in the same manner that European and American are capitalized. We agree.
The Publishers

URLs for websites contained in this book are accurate to the time of writing to the best of the author's knowledge.

CONTENTS

CHAPTER 1 – ABORIGINAL RIGHTS AND TITLE

CHAPTER 2 – TREATY RIGHTS

CHAPTER 3 – FEDERAL, PROVINCIAL, AND TERRITORIAL POWERS AND DUTIES

CHAPTER 4 – THE MÉTIS AND INUIT

CHAPTER 5 – TAXATION

CHAPTER 6 – ABORIGINAL RIGHTS AND THE *CONSTITUTION ACT, 1982*

CHAPTER 7 – SELF-GOVERNMENT

CHAPTER 8 – ABORIGINAL WOMEN

TABLE OF CASES

PREFACE

Canadian law relating to the rights of Aboriginal people is becoming increasingly clear in its meaning and application. Subsection 35(1) of the *Constitution Act, 1982*[1] cannot be referred to as an "empty box."[2] Prior to 1982, Aboriginal and treaty rights were part of the federal common law and subject to unilateral modification or extinguishment by the federal Crown. This vulnerability changed in 1982 with the enactment of the *Constitution Act, 1982*, which recognizes and affirms Aboriginal and treaty rights, including Aboriginal title.

A number of Supreme Court of Canada decisions, including *R. v. Sparrow*,[3] *Delgamuukw* v. *B.C.*,[4] *R.* v. *Marshall*,[5] *Mitchell* v. *Min. of Nat. Revenue*,[6] and *Wewaykum Indian Band* v. *Canada*,[7] have provided meaning and importance to the constitutional recognition and affirmation of existing Aboriginal and treaty rights. These and other decisions also demonstrate that Aboriginal legal issues relating to rights and land are extremely complex; they are usually dependent upon historical evidence and require an unpredictable and cumbersome but necessary case-by-case analysis. However, more importantly, these decisions also demonstrate a reliance upon, and comfort with, general legal principles in Canadian law by the Supreme Court of Canada when adjudicating cases respecting the rights of Aboriginal people. While some aspects of Aboriginal law are necessarily unique to the area, generally speaking, the normal laws applicable to Canada and the common law generally provide a solid basis to understand and interpret the meaning of subsection 35(1) of the *Constitution Act, 1982*.

With the exception of the 1973 Supreme Court of Canada decision of *Calder* v. *B.C.*,[8] it is only in the last two decades that Canada's courts have begun to fully explore Canadian law relating to Aboriginal and treaty rights. *R.* v. *Guerin*[9] marked the beginning of the Supreme Court of Canada's analysis of Aboriginal and treaty rights in the post–*Constitution Act, 1982* era. One commentator described the Court's treatment of Aboriginal law to date as follows:

> Let it be said that the Supreme Court has fared well in its initial ventures. Little-known areas have been brought to light and apocryphal seas dispelled. We now know broadly what

---

[1] *Constitution Act, 1982*, R.S.C. 1985, App. II, No. 44, being Sched. B to the *Canada Act 1982* (U.K.), 1982, c. 11, as am. by the *Constitution Amendment Proclamation, 1983*, R.S.C. 1985, App. II, No. 46 [am. s. 25(b) and add. ss. 35(3), 35(4), 35.1, 37.1 and 54.1].

[2] See Bryan Schwartz, *First Principles: Constitutional Reform With Respect to the Aboriginal Peoples of Canada 1982–1984*, (Kingston: Institute of Intergovernmental Relations, Queen's University, 1986) and David Hawkes, *Aboriginal Peoples and Constitutional Reform: What Have We Learned?*, (Kingston: Institute of Intergovernmental Relations, Queen's University, 1989).

[3] *R.* v. *Sparrow*, [1990] 1 S.C.R. 1075.

[4] *Delgamuukw* v. *B.C.*, [1997] 3 S.C.R. 1010.

[5] *R.* v. *Marshall*, [1999] 3 S.C.R. 456 and [1999] 3 S.C.R. 533 (reconsideration refused).

[6] *Mitchell* v. *Min. of Nat. Revenue*, [2001] 1 S.C.R. 911.

[7] *Wewaykum Indian Band* v. *Canada*, [2002] 4 S.C.R. 245.

[8] *Calder* v. *B.C.*, [1973] S.C.R. 313.

[9] *R.* v. *Guerin*, [1984] 2 S.C.R. 335.

is *terra firma* and what is not, and the monsters have been largely tamed or banished to the decorative margins.[10]

Recognizing that Aboriginal law forms a part of broader Canadian law provides guidance in respect of future issues in the relationship between the Crown and Aboriginal people. While areas of uncertainty remain in Canadian aboriginal law, there is a well-established body of law that provides a basis for certainty respecting Aboriginal and treaty rights.

This third edition is intended to provide an introduction to, and an overview of, the major themes that have developed in Canadian Aboriginal law over the past two hundred years. There are a number of areas where the book deliberately does not venture, notably those relating to justice, Aboriginal customary law, international law, and a detailed analysis of some aspects of the *Indian Act.*[11]

One of the most significant legal developments in recent years has been the judicial focus applied to the Crown's duty to consult and accommodate Aboriginal people when an act, decision, or statute of the Crown interferes and infringes existing Aboriginal and treaty rights. This development is not surprising but, rather, is a natural evolution of understanding the meaning of subsection 35(1). Although courts have struggled with the full meaning of adequate Crown consultation with Aboriginal people, it is clear that the Crown's duty to consult and accommodate Aboriginal people, at its core, requires a focused application of the duty to be fair, both procedurally and substantively. In many ways, consultation and accommodation serve as balancing mechanisms between existing Aboriginal and treaty rights on the one hand, and federal and provincial legislative authority on the other.

While the evolution of Aboriginal law over the past two decades in Canada has been extraordinary, it has developed within the context of existing Canadian constitutional law and Anglo-Canadian common law. Although not writing for the majority in *Mitchell* v. *Min. of Nat. Revenue*, the following statement by Mr. Justice Binnie is indicative of how the Supreme Court of Canada has attempted to *balance* and *reconcile* the rights of Aboriginal people with the rights of other Canadians and the federal and provincial governments: "The *Constitution Act, 1982* ushered in a new chapter but it did not start a new book."[12] The constitutional recognition and affirmation of Aboriginal rights in subsection 35(1) did not fundamentally alter Canada's constitutional structure, but did add another important element to it, including subjecting federal and provincial legislation to the scrutiny of being justified when infringing existing Aboriginal and treaty rights.

In the terms of Binnie J., the real issue for Aboriginal people will be how the "rest of the book" meshes with this new chapter. For example, how will the laws governing Canada's natural resources, over which *all* Canadians have an interest, interact with existing Aboriginal and treaty rights? For Aboriginal people, the question remains when and how governments will recognize and affirm their rights in a justifiable and consistent manner. The resource industry and Canadians in general also have an interest in the answer to the second question. These questions are being played out and, to some degree, answered in various parts of Canada. *R.* v. *Sparrow*, *R.* v. *Delgamuukw*, and *R.* v. *Marshall*, among other decisions, seem to support solutions between the Crown and Aboriginal people that are negotiated, practical, and fair.

The term "Aboriginal" is used in this text to describe those persons who come within

---

[10] Brian Slattery, "Making Sense of Aboriginal and Treaty Rights", [2000] Vol. 79 Can. Bar Rev. 196 at 197.
[11] *Indian Act*, R.S.C. 1985, c. I-5.
[12] *Supra* note 6 at para. 115.

the meaning of subsection 35(2) of the *Constitution Act, 1982*, namely the Indian, Inuit, and Métis peoples of Canada. When the term "Indian" is used alone, it refers to those persons identified and registered as Indians within the meaning of the *Indian Act*.[13] The term "first nation" is used sparingly because its legal definition is less well defined than the term "Indian band." However, more Indian bands are using the term to describe themselves, as is Parliament, for example, in the *First Nations Land Management Act*.[14]

Citations used in decision excerpts and commentary in chapters have been limited to one or two case reports. In most instances, multiple-decision citations have been deleted from the excerpts. Comprehensive decision citations can be found in the Table of Cases. Where applicable, paragraph numbers have been deleted from decision excerpts, with the exception of recent Supreme Court of Canada decisions. Footnotes have either been deleted or incorporated into the text of the excerpted decisions. All Canadian decisions include the names of members of the court giving judgment and the date of the decisions. Selected bibliographies at the end of each chapter identify materials that provide further guidance respecting the subject. Additional materials are also noted in the footnotes.

Cases and materials for this third edition have been reduced in order to provide additional commentary. However, the content removed is available on the internet. The following list contains some useful on-line aboriginal-related materials:

1. University of Saskatchewan, Resources for Aboriginal Studies, on-line: Canadian Native Law Cases <http://www.library.usask.ca/native/cnlch.html>: This website provides access to historic Aboriginal law cases, covering the period 1763–1978. The cases were compiled and indexed by the Native Law Centre at the University of Saskatchewan.

2. Indian and Northern Affairs Canada, on-line: <http://www.ainc-inac.gc.ca/index_e.html>. Treaties, self-government agreements, claims agreements, land governance agreements, and implementation plans are listed at <http://www.ainc-inac-gc.ca/pr/agr/index_e.html>. Aboriginal-related legislation may be found at <http://www.ainc-inac.gc.ca/pr/leg/lgis_e.html>. For more formal reference purposes the official Acts as passed by Parliament should be referred to.

3. Supreme Court of Canada, on-line: <http://www.scc-csc.gc.ca>.

I wish to thank all those who provided comments on the first and second editions, either by letter, review, or otherwise. I thank Don Purich and Karen Bolstad of Purich Publishing for their support and assistance in the preparation of this edition. I also wish to acknowledge the support of my colleagues at McCarthy Tétrault LLP and, in particular, Tony Knox, with whom I have worked closely on making practical solutions in this area more accessible. I also acknowledge my assistant, Trish Dick, who ably applied her skills to the production of this text. Finally, I thank my wife, Christine Tetrault, for her support and assistance, and to whom this book is lovingly dedicated.

---

[13] *Supra* note 11.
[14] *First Nations Land Management Act*, S.C. 1999, c. 24.

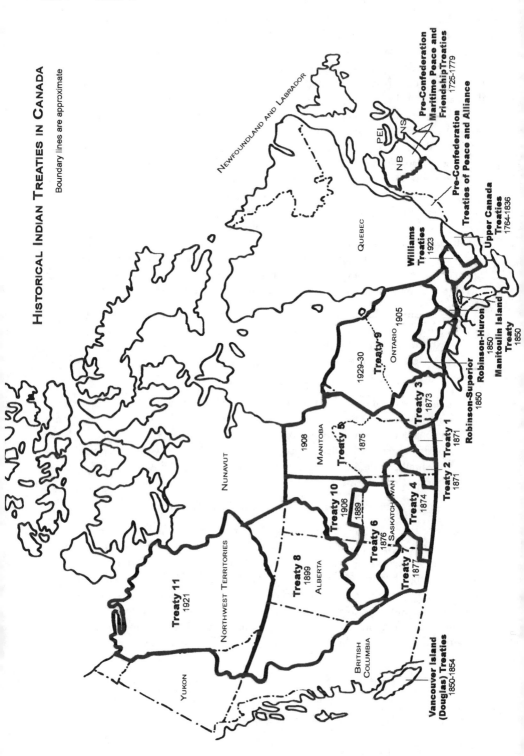

HISTORICAL INDIAN TREATIES IN CANADA

Boundary lines are approximate

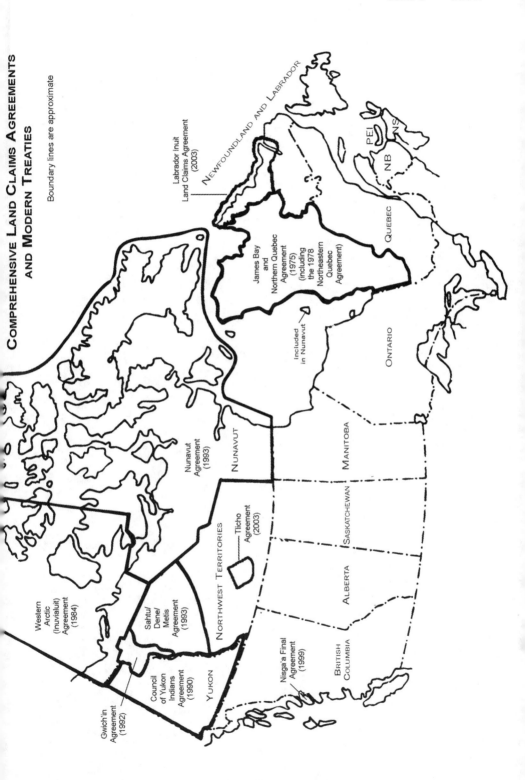

COMPREHENSIVE LAND CLAIMS AGREEMENTS
AND MODERN TREATIES

Boundary lines are approximate

Labrador Inuit
Land Claims Agreement
(2003)

NEWFOUNDLAND AND LABRADOR

PEI

NB

NS

QUEBEC

James Bay
and
Northern Quebec
Agreement
(1975)
(including
the 1978
Northeastern
Quebec
Agreement)

Included
in Nunavut

ONTARIO

Nunavut
Agreement
(1993)

NUNAVUT

MANITOBA

Tlicho
Agreement
(2003)

NORTHWEST TERRITORIES

SASKATCHEWAN

Western
Arctic
(Inuvialuit)
Agreement
(1984)

Sahtu/
Dene/
Metis
Agreement
(1993)

ALBERTA

Council
of Yukon
Indians
Agreement
(1990)

YUKON

Nisga'a Final
Agreement
(1999)

BRITISH
COLUMBIA

Gwich'in
Agreement
(1992)

Chapter 1

ABORIGINAL RIGHTS AND TITLE

INTRODUCTION

Throughout the history of Canada, Aboriginal people have sought to have their rights recognized and respected. Even after the signing of treaties in the eighteenth, nineteenth, and early twentieth centuries, Aboriginal and treaty rights were vulnerable to unilateral federal modification or extinguishment. The federal, provincial, and territorial governments did little to recognize Aboriginal rights, and to some extent, even went so far as to obstruct Aboriginal peoples' access to the legal protection of their rights.[1] Aboriginal and treaty rights existed in a vacuum; their status was vulnerable and not completely understood.

The *Constitution Act, 1982*[2] filled this legal vacuum by recognizing and affirming existing Aboriginal and treaty rights and by incorporating such rights into the Constitution of Canada. Aboriginal people have come to rely upon the courts to recognize and affirm their rights in the lands that they traditionally used and occupied. Constitutional recognition and affirmation provides Aboriginal and treaty rights protection from infringements by governments. Initiatives such as the British Columbia treaty process, the Royal Commission on Aboriginal Peoples (RCAP), and the federal comprehensive land claims and specific claims processes seek to deal with the claims and rights of Aboriginal people in a meaningful way.

Federal and provincial laws that infringe existing Aboriginal and treaty rights are of no force or effect, except where such laws can be justified. The courts have confirmed that the meaning attributed to these rights must be balanced with existing federal and provincial legislative authority.

Aboriginal law is a relatively new and rapidly evolving legal area. Although the Supreme Court of Canada has rendered a number of decisions regarding Aboriginal legal issues, as Lamer C.J. noted in *Delgamuukw* v. *B.C.*,[3] "the content of common law Aboriginal title . . . has not been authoritatively determined by this Court."[4]

Historically, Aboriginal people had their own forms of government, social organization, and economies. The presence of Aboriginal people in North America prior to Euro-

---

[1] For example, beginning in 1927 and remaining in force until the 1952 *Indian Act*, R.S.C. 1952, c. 149, it was illegal for any person to provide money to Indians for the pursuit of their claims. Section 141 of the *Indian Act*, R.S.C. 1927, c. 98 stated:

> Every person who, without the consent of the Superintendent General expressed in writing, receives, obtains, solicits or requests from any Indian any payment or contribution . . . for the purpose of raising a fund or providing money for the prosecution of any claim which the tribe or band of Indians . . . for the recovery of any claim or money for the benefit of the said tribe or band, shall be guilty of an offence. . . .

[2] *Constitution Act, 1982*, R.S.C. 1985, App. II, No. 44, being Sched. B to the *Canada Act 1982* (U.K.), 1982, c. 11, as am. by the *Constitution Amendment Proclamation 1983*, R.S.C. 1985, App. II, No. 46 [am. s. 25(b) and add. 35(3), 35(4), 35.1, 37.1 and 54.1].

[3] *Delgamuukw* v. *B.C.*, [1997] 3 S.C.R. 1010.

[4] *Ibid.* at para. 75.

1

pean contact is the basic premise upon which the doctrine of Aboriginal rights and title has developed. As the Supreme Court of Canada confirmed in *R. v. Van der Peet*:[5]

> The doctrine of Aboriginal rights exists, and is recognized and affirmed by s. 35(1) because of one simple fact: when Europeans arrived in North America, Aboriginal peoples *were already here,* living in communities on the land, and participating in distinctive cultures, as they had done for centuries.[6] [emphasis in original]

The RCAP noted:

> Aboriginal peoples' experience with the law of Aboriginal title has been premised on promises and has resulted in frustration. The law of Aboriginal rights, including rights associated with Aboriginal title, provides a bridge between Aboriginal nations and the broader Canadian community. . . . The law of Aboriginal title thus acknowledges that societies and cultures evolve and transform over time and that legal recognition of Aboriginal rights is premised on continuity, not conformity, with the past. . . . [C]urrent jurisprudence cannot . . . accomplish all that is required to protect Aboriginal lands and resources. . . . [T]he law of Aboriginal title serves as a backdrop to complex nation-to-nation negotiations concerning ownership, jurisdiction and co-management.[7]

The RCAP's comments are noteworthy particularly with respect to the role that Aboriginal title can play to support broader-based negotiations that involve self-government, as evidenced by the treaty negotiations underway in British Columbia.

ABORIGINAL RIGHTS

In *Van der Peet,* the Supreme Court of Canada clarified the relationship between Aboriginal title and rights. Although *Van der Peet* concerned Aboriginal rights, Lamer C.J., for the majority, affirmed that "Aboriginal title is a sub-category of Aboriginal rights which deals solely with claims of rights to land."[8] Thus, Aboriginal rights can exist independently of Aboriginal title.[9] Although the sub-categorization of Aboriginal title from Aboriginal rights may be a useful legal concept, some Aboriginal people argue that such a distinction does not reflect their historical relationship with and connection to the land.

Aboriginal rights are the legal embodiment of Aboriginal peoples' claims to their traditional lands and their ability to engage in traditional activities and customs. Aboriginal rights relate to activities that are an element of a practice, custom, or tradition integral to the distinctive culture of the Aboriginal group claiming the right.[10] The European settlement of Canada did not terminate Aboriginal peoples' interest in land. This interest and Aboriginal customary law are presumed to have survived the assertion of Crown sovereignty and were incorporated into the common law. The exceptions to such incorporation are where such rights are:

- incompatible with the assertion of sovereignty by the Crown;

---

[5] *R. v. Van der Peet,* [1996] 2 S.C.R. 507.

[6] *Ibid.* at para. 30.

[7] Royal Commission on Aboriginal Peoples, *Report of the Royal Commission on Aboriginal Peoples,* vol. 2 (Ottawa: RCAP, 1996), 559, 561, 562.

[8] *Van der Peet, supra* note 5 at para. 74.

[9] In *R. v. Adams,* [1996] 3 S.C.R. 101 at para. 27, the Supreme Court of Canada stated: "To understand why Aboriginal rights cannot be inexorably linked to Aboriginal title it is only necessary to recall that some Aboriginal peoples were nomadic, varying the location of their settlements with the season and changing circumstances."

[10] *Van der Peet, supra* note 5 at para. 46.

- voluntarily surrendered by Aboriginal people by way of treaties; or

- extinguished by the federal Crown.[11]

The common law status of Aboriginal rights made them vulnerable to unilateral modification or extinguishment by the federal Crown until the constitutional recognition and affirmation of such rights in the *Constitution Act, 1982* on April 17, 1982.

ABORIGINAL TITLE

Lamer C.J. provided a general meaning to the concept of Aboriginal title in *Delgamuukw*:

> Aboriginal title is a right in land and, as such, is more than the right to engage in specific activities which may be themselves Aboriginal rights. Rather, it confers the right to use land for a variety of activities, not all of which need be aspects of practices, customs and traditions which are integral to the distinctive cultures of Aboriginal societies.[12]

Aboriginal title is the special legal interest that Aboriginal people possess in lands based on their historic occupation and relationship to those lands. It is a right "to the land itself."[13] Aboriginal title is also a burden on the Crown's underlying title to the land.[14] Aboriginal title encompasses the right to exclusive use and occupation of the land held pursuant to that title for a variety of purposes, and that those purposes must not be irreconcilable with the nature of the Aboriginal group's attachment to that land.[15] In *Calder* v. *A.G.(B.C.)*,[16] Judson J. of the Supreme Court of Canada stated: "the fact is that when the settlers came, the Indians were there, organized in societies and occupying the land as their forefathers had done for centuries. This is what Indian title means."[17]

While the connection to land by many Aboriginal people is important, the courts have confirmed that Aboriginal and treaty rights can exist independently of Aboriginal title. Aboriginal title is not essential to proving the existence of Aboriginal rights.[18] In *R.* v. *Adams*[19] the Supreme Court of Canada stated the following, based on its analysis of *Van der Peet*:[20]

> [W]hile claims to Aboriginal title fall within the conceptual framework of Aboriginal rights, Aboriginal rights do not exist solely where a claim to Aboriginal title has been made out. Where an Aboriginal group has shown that a particular practice, custom or tradition taking place on the land was integral to the distinctive culture of that group then, *even if they have not shown that their occupation and use of the land was sufficient to support a claim of title to the land*, they will have demonstrated that they have an Aboriginal right to engage in that practice, custom or tradition. . . . To understand why Aboriginal rights cannot be inexorably linked to Aboriginal title it is only necessary to recall that some Aboriginal peoples were nomadic.[21] [emphasis in original]

---

[11] *Mitchell* v. *Canada (Min. of National Revenue)*, [2001] 1 S.C.R. 911 at para. 10.
[12] *Delgamuukw, supra* note 3 at para. 111.
[13] *Ibid.* at para. 140.
[14] *Ibid.* at para. 145.
[15] *Ibid.* at para. 117.
[16] *Calder* v. *A.G.(B.C.)*, [1973] S.C.R. 313.
[17] *Ibid.* at 328.
[18] *Delgamuukw, supra* note 3 at paras. 137–39 and *R.* v. *Côté*, [1996] 3 S.C.R. 139 at para. 41.
[19] *R.* v. *Adams*, [1996] 3 S.C.R. 101.
[20] *Van der Peet, supra* note 5 at para. 74.
[21] *Adams, supra* note 19 at paras. 26–27.

This statement supports the view that Aboriginal people who are not covered by the terms of a treaty may be able to make claims for Aboriginal rights distinct from claims relating to Aboriginal title.

The Supreme Court of Canada confirmed the common law basis of Aboriginal title in *Roberts* v. *Canada*,[22] which also affirmed that Aboriginal title is within the jurisdiction of the Federal Court of Canada. In *R.* v. *Côté*, Lamer C.J. summarized *Roberts* by stating that "the law of Aboriginal title represents a distinct species of federal common law rather than a simple subset of the common or civil law or property law operating within the province."[23] In *R.* v. *Smith*,[24] the Supreme Court of Canada held that once Aboriginal title was surrendered, the rights associated with Aboriginal title also disappeared and the land became like other Crown land and not land necessarily "reserved" for Indians as contemplated under subsection 91(24) of the *Constitution Act, 1867* (s.91(24)).[25]

The Supreme Court of Canada affirmed the existence of Aboriginal title in *Calder*, reaffirmed it in *R.* v. *Guerin*,[26] and extensively expanded the understanding of the concept in *Delgamuukw*.

Royal Proclamation of 1763

Aboriginal title is recognized in the Royal Proclamation of 1763[27] issued by King George III of Great Britain on October 7, 1763, following the British conquest of New France and its resulting cession to Great Britain in the Treaty of Paris. The Proclamation:

- consolidated Great Britain's dominion over North America;

- set aside a huge tract of land as land reserved for the Indians "as their hunting grounds";

- prohibited grants, purchases, and settlement of reserved Indian land without Crown authorization;

- required that all non-Indians who had settled on non-ceded land vacate such land; and

- required a licence for all trade with Indians.

The Proclamation recognized the rights of Indians to unceded lands in their possession and provided that Indians may only cede such lands to the Crown. The Proclamation noted that "great Frauds and Abuses have been committed in purchasing Land of the Indians" and prohibited the purchasing of Indian lands by settlers. The Crown possessed the sole right to acquire lands from Indians.[28] The Supreme Court of Canada stated that the objective of the Proclamation was:

> [T]o provide a solution to the problems created by the greed which hitherto some of the English had all too often demonstrated in buying up Indian land at low prices. The situation was causing dangerous trouble among the Indians and the Royal Proclamation was meant to remedy this.[29]

[22] *Roberts* v. *Canada*, [1989] 1 S.C.R. 322.
[23] *Côté, supra* note 18 at para. 49.
[24] *R.* v. *Smith*, [1983] 1 S.C.R. 554.
[25] *Constitution Act, 1867* (U.K.), 30 & 31 Vict., c. 3, reprinted in R.S.C. 1985, App. II, No. 5.
[26] *R.* v. *Guerin*, [1984] 2 S.C.R. 335.
[27] *Royal Proclamation of 1763*, R.S.C. 1985, App. II, No.1.
[28] See B. Slattery, *The Land Rights of Indigenous Canadian Peoples as Affected by the Crown's Acquisition of their Territories* (Saskatoon: University of Saskatchewan Native Law Centre, 1979), 191–345.
[29] *R.* v. *Sioui*, [1990] 1 S.C.R. 1025 at 1064.

Thus, the Proclamation sought to put into place a set of rules and procedures to provide a land base for Indians and to protect their interests in such land.

The *Quebec Act*[30] repealed the procedural elements of the Indian land cession requirements of the Proclamation in Quebec, but did not alter existing rights, titles or possessions involving Aboriginal rights.[31] Much debate has surrounded the geographic application of the Proclamation. It appears not to apply to Rupert's Land,[32] to have a limited application in Quebec,[33] and to have no application in British Columbia.[34] Based on its terms, the Proclamation most likely applies to Nova Scotia and New Brunswick. Brian Slattery writes: "it is submitted that the Proclamation presumptively applied to any American territories acquired after 1763 which satisfied the terms of that instrument, so long as it remained in force."[35] To some extent, the Proclamation's application may be moot in so far as it *confirms* the existence of Aboriginal title, but does not *create* Aboriginal title.[36] The Proclamation describes the "Indian Territories" as those lands lying west of the Appalachians, except those within Quebec, East Florida, West Florida, and Rupert's Land. These Indian Territories were reserved for the use of Indians and were closed to settlement "for the present." The Proclamation also required the removal of all persons who settled within the Indian Territories and ". . . upon any other Lands, which not having been ceded to or purchased by Us, are still reserved for the said Indians. . . ." This latter clause clearly covers lands outside of the Indian Territories and provides protection to unceded Indian lands claimed by the Crown in North America. Finally, the Proclamation refers to the great frauds and abuses that were committed when Indian lands were purchased. In order to prevent such further frauds and abuses, the Proclamation forbids any person purchasing "any Lands reserved to the said Indians, within those Parts of Our Colonies where, We have thought proper to allow settlement." This provision is not restricted to "Indian Territories" but rather to all colonial lands, thereby reinforcing the interpretation that the Proclamation applies broadly throughout North America. Thus, the precise geographic application of the Proclamation continues to remain uncertain.

Although reversed on another issue by the Supreme Court of Canada, the Federal Court of Appeal in *R. v. Smith*[37] concluded that the Proclamation applied in New Brunswick: "[I]ts [the Proclamation's] terms . . . are on the whole broad enough to include the territory that became New Brunswick." In *R. v. Sec. of State for Foreign and Commonwealth Affairs*,[38] the English Court of Appeal, in considering the legality of Canada patriating its Constitution, agreed with the Nova Scotia Supreme Court in *R. v. Isaac*[39] when it stated that "the provisions of the Royal Proclamation did and do extend to the provinces of Nova Scotia and New Brunswick."

[30] *Quebec Act, 1774* (U.K.), 14 Geo. III, c. 83.

[31] *A.G. (Ont.) v. Bear Island Foundation et al.,* [1989] 2 C.N.L.R. 73 at 85 (Ont. C.A.).

[32] *Sigeareak v. The Queen,* [1966] S.C.R. 645 at 650.

[33] *R. v. Côté,* [1994] 3 C.N.L.R. 98 at 106–108 (Que. C.A.).

[34] See Judson J. in *Calder, supra* note 16 at 323; *R. v. White and Bob* (1964), 50 D.L.R. (2d) 613 (B.C.C.A.), aff'd [1965] S.C.R. vi (S.C.C.).

[35] Slattery, *supra* note 28 at 361.

[36] See *Delgamuukw, supra* note 3 at 1082; *Guerin, supra* note 26 at 377.

[37] *R. v. Smith,* [1980] 4 C.N.L.R. 29 at para. 59 (F.C.A.), rev'd [1983] 1 S.C.R. 554.

[38] *Re R. v. The Secretary of State for Foreign and Commonwealth Affairs, ex parte the Indian Association of Alberta, Union of New Brunswick Indians, Union of Nova Scotia Indians, Note from Appeal Committee of the House of Lords,* [1982] 3 C.N.L.R. 195, [1982] 2 All E.R. 118 (H.L.), aff'g [1981] 4 C.N.L.R. 86 at 116, [1982] 1 Q.B. 892 (C.A.).

[39] *R. v. Isaac* (1975), 13 N.S.R. (2d) 460 at 478 (N.S.S.C., A.D.); see also *R. v. Marshall,* [2001] 2 C.N.L.R. 256 (N.S. Prov. Ct.) wherein Curran Prov. Ct. J., at para. 107, concurred that the Proclamation applies to Nova Scotia. ·

Although not a constitutional document, the Proclamation has the force of law in Canada and is "an Executive Order having the force and effect of an Act of Parliament."[40] Section 25 of the *Canadian Charter of Rights and Freedoms*[41] reads in part:

> The guarantee in this Charter of certain rights and freedoms shall not be construed as to abrogate or derogate from an aboriginal, treaty or other rights or freedoms . . . including . . . any rights or freedoms that have been recognized by the Royal Proclamation of October 7, 1763.

Cession of land only to the Crown, as provided for by the Proclamation, served as the basis for the Crown to enter into treaties with Aboriginal people. In *R. v. Sparrow*,[42] the Supreme Court of Canada wrote the following about the nature of the Proclamation vis-à-vis Aboriginal title:

> It is worth recalling that while British policy towards the native population was based on respect for their right to occupy their traditional lands, a proposition to which the Royal Proclamation of 1763 bears witness, there was from the outset never any doubt that sovereignty and legislative power, and indeed the underlying title, to such lands vested in the Crown.[43]

Thus, Aboriginal title can be said to come from the historic use and occupation of certain lands, evidenced by the Proclamation,[44] and from the common law. It is a burden on the Crown's title.[45] Although Aboriginal title was recognized by the Proclamation, it arises from the prior occupation of Canada by Aboriginal people.

Early Aboriginal Title and Rights Decisions

Two leading American decisions, *Johnson and Graham's Lessee* v. *M'Intosh*[46] and *Worcester* v. *Georgia*,[47] which discussed the origins of Aboriginal title have been frequently cited by Canadian courts, including the Supreme Court of Canada. Both decisions were written by Chief Justice Marshall and confirm that the basis for Aboriginal title is derived from

[40] *Calder, supra* note 16.

[41] Part I of the *Constitution Act, 1982, supra* note 2.

[42] *R.* v. *Sparrow,* [1990] 1 S.C.R. 1075.

[43] *Ibid.* at 1103.

[44] In "Making Sense of Aboriginal and Treaty Rights", (2000) 79:2 Can. Bar Rev. 196 at 203, Brian Slattery noted:

> The Court clearly assumes that the common law governing these subjects is uniform and does not vary from place to place. . . . This uniformity means that for many purposes there is no need to determine precisely which territories are covered by the Indian provisions of the *Royal Proclamation of 1763*. While there is reason to think that the *Proclamation's* basic provisions apply across Canada, the question is rendered moot by the fact that the common law principles reflected in the *Proclamation* are in force throughout the entire country.

[45] In *Haida Nation* v. *B.C.*, [1998] 1 C.N.L.R. 98 (B.C.C.A.); leave to appeal to S.C.C. refused May 8, 1998 (No. 26394), the British Columbia Court of Appeal considered a petition from the Haida Nation to have s. 28 of the *Forestry Act* (R.S.B.C. 1979, c. 140, now 1996, c. 157) interpreted in a manner so as to recognize Aboriginal title as an encumbrance to be considered when issuing a tree farm licence. The Court of Appeal agreed with the Haida Nation and found: (*a*) that Aboriginal title would constitute an encumbrance on Crown title, (*b*) Aboriginal title can include an interest in standing timber, and (*c*) the terminology "otherwise encumbered" used in the *Forestry Act* includes any such encumbrance found in Aboriginal title.

[46] *Johnson and Graham's Lessee* v. *M'Intosh* (1823), 8 Wheat. 543 (U.S.S.C.); The United States Supreme Court confirmed that the ultimate title to the land at issue rested with the United States, and not with the State of Illinois or Piankeshaw Indian Nations.

[47] *Worcester* v. *Georgia* (1832), 31 U.S. 530 (U.S.S.C.); The laws of Georgia were held not to apply to Cherokee Indian territory. This decision is cited frequently by Canadian courts as jurisprudential support of Indian tribes being self-governing, and was cited with approval by the Supreme Court of Canada in *Sioui, supra* note 29 at 1053–54.

the Proclamation. Both decisions struggle with the issue of how the Crown assumed sovereignty over North America and conclude that either conquest (Indian tribes as a "conquered people") or discovery (Indians did not possess recognizable forms of law and governance) form a sound basis to limit Aboriginal title as being a burden on the Crown's title.

Connolly v. *Woolrich*[48] was one of the few early Canadian judicial decisions that took the same expansive approach to interpreting Indian rights outlined in *Worcester* v. *Georgia*. The decision concerned whether the common law recognized a Cree customary marriage. Monk J. concluded that the customary marriage was recognizable at common law and therefore valid. This conclusion was based, in part, on the premise that Indian laws, customs, and political and legislative rights were in full force and applicable. Although the appeal court upheld the verdict, they did not affirm to the same extent as the trial court the degree to which Indian laws were applicable.

The Judicial Committee of the Privy Council held in *St. Catherine's Milling and Lumber Co.* v. *R.* that Indians possessed a "personal and usufructuary right, dependent upon the good will of the Sovereign"[49] over which they enjoyed Indian title, but did not explain what the phrase "personal and usufructuary" meant.

Calder v. *A.G.(B.C.)* (1973)

In *Calder*[50] the Supreme Court of Canada considered an application by the Nisga'a in British Columbia for a declaration that their claim of Aboriginal title over their asserted traditional lands was not extinguished. The Nisga'a had been unsuccessful in the lower courts.[51] The Supreme Court of Canada held four to three that the Nisga'a's Aboriginal rights with respect to their traditional lands were extinguished. Pigeon J. (among the four) decided against the Nisga'a claim on procedural reasons, thus leaving the Supreme Court of Canada split on the substantive issue.

The majority judgment of Pigeon, Judson, Martland, and Ritchie JJ. and the minority judgment of Hall, Spence and Laskin JJ. elaborated on the origins, recognition, and nature of Aboriginal title in British Columbia. Both judgments held that Aboriginal title did not originate with the Proclamation,[52] although the majority decision, given by Judson J., held that it did not apply to British Columbia,[53] while the minority decision, given by Hall J., held that it did apply.[54] Judson J. defined Aboriginal title as follows:

> [I]t is clear that Indian title in British Columbia cannot owe its origin to the Proclamation of 1763, the fact is that when the settlers came, the Indians were there, organized in societies and occupying the land as their forefathers had done for centuries.[55]

Hall J. described the nature of Aboriginal title as follows:

> The exact nature and extent of the Indian right or title does not need to be precisely stated in this litigation. . . . This is not a claim to title in fee but is in the nature of an equitable title or interest . . . a usufructuary right and a right to occupy the lands and to enjoy the

[48] *Connolly* v. *Woolrich* (1867), 11 L.C. Jur. 197 (Que. S.C.), aff'd in result in *Johnstone* v. *Connolly*, 17 R.J.R.Q. 266 (Que. C.A. (Q.B.)).
[49] *St. Catherine's Milling and Lumber Co.* v. *R.* (1888), 14 A.C. 46 at 54 (J.C.P.C.).
[50] *Calder, supra* note 16.
[51] *Calder* v. *A.G.(B.C.)* (1969), 8 D.L.R. (3d) 59 (B.C.S.C.), (1971), 13 D.L.R. (3d) 48 (B.C.C.A.).
[52] *Calder, supra* note 16 at 395; Proclamation, *supra* note 27.
[53] *Calder, supra* note 16 at 323.
[54] *Ibid.* at 395.
[55] *Ibid.* at 328.

fruits of the soil, the forest and of the rivers and streams which does not in any way deny the Crown's paramount title. . . . Possession is of itself at common law proof of ownership. . . . Unchallenged possession is admitted here.[56]

Calder affirmed that Aboriginal title is not dependent on the Proclamation[57] or any other instrument for its existence, but rather is a common law right. Judson J. defined Aboriginal title in terms of the Nisga'a's use and occupancy of the lands at issue for centuries, and that it was embodied in the communal structure of the Nisga'a people. Hall J. defined Aboriginal title as being a usufructuary right based in the common law.

R. v. Guerin (1984)

The Supreme Court of Canada also dealt with the nature of Aboriginal rights respecting reserve land in *Guerin*.[58] In October 1957, the Musqueam Indian Band of British Columbia surrendered 162 acres of reserve land situated in the City of Vancouver to the federal Crown pursuant to ss. 37–41 of the *Indian Act*.[59] The surrender enabled the Crown, on behalf of the Musqueam, to secure a lease with a golf club. The terms and conditions of the lease were not part of the surrender but rather were discussed between federal officials and the Musqueam. The Crown executed the lease on terms less favourable than the terms originally agreed upon verbally with the Musqueam. The Crown did not have the Musqueam's permission to change the terms of the lease and did not provide a copy of the lease to the Musqueam until 1970. The Musqueam initiated an action against the Crown based on breach of trust.

Guerin consists of three distinct sets of reasons by the eight judges taking part in the decision. Dickson J. held that Indian (Aboriginal) title comes from two sources: (1) Indians' historical occupation and possession of their lands, and (2) the Proclamation.[60] Seven of the eight judges held that the Crown has a fiduciary duty respecting Indian lands. Dickson J. wrote:

> [T]he nature of Indian title and the framework of the statutory scheme established for disposing of Indian land places upon the Crown an equitable obligation, enforceable by the courts, to deal with the land for the benefit of the Indians. This obligation does not amount to a trust in the private law sense. It is rather a fiduciary duty. If however, the Crown breaches this fiduciary duty it will be liable to the Indians in the same way and to the same extent as if such a trust were in effect.[61]

This enforceable, equitable, and fiduciary obligation has placed a high onus on the Crown when acting or making decisions on behalf of Indians. In *Guerin*, the Supreme Court of Canada noted that Aboriginal title has also been interpreted to encompass a "beneficial interest" in lands.[62] *Guerin* summarized the nature of Aboriginal title as follows:

> Indians have a legal right to occupy and possess certain lands, the ultimate title to which is in the Crown. While their interest does not, strictly speaking, amount to beneficial owner-

---

[56] *Ibid.* at 352 and 368.

[57] *Proclamation, supra* note 27.

[58] *Guerin, supra* note 26.

[59] *Indian Act,* R.S.C. 1952, c. 149; now R.S.C. 1985, c. I-5.

[60] *Guerin, supra* note 26 at 377.

[61] *Ibid.* at 376.

[62] *Ibid.* at 382. With respect to beneficial interest, the Supreme Court of Canada cited *A.-G. Canada v. Giroux,* (1916), 53 S.C.R. 172; *Cardinal v. A.-G. Alberta,* [1974] S.C.R. 695; and *Western Int. Contractors Ltd. v. Sarcee Development Ltd.,* [1979] 2 C.N.L.R. 107 (Alta. C.A.).

ship, neither is its nature completely exhausted by the concept of a personal right. It is true that the *sui generis* interest which the Indians have in the land is personal in the sense that it cannot be transferred to a grantee, but it is also true, . . . that the interest gives rise upon surrender to a distinctive fiduciary obligation on the part of the Crown to deal with the land for the benefit of the surrendering Indians. . . . The nature of the Indians' interest is therefore best characterized by its general inalienability, coupled with the fact that the Crown is under an obligation to deal with the land on the Indians' behalf when the interest is surrendered. Any description of Indian title which goes beyond these two features is both unnecessary and potentially misleading.[63]

The Supreme Court of Canada summarized the two essential characteristics of Aboriginal title as being: (1) its inalienability, except to the Crown, and (2) the Crown's fiduciary duty relating to issues surrounding the alienation of the Indian interest in their lands.

Recent Case Law

Delgamuukw v. *British Columbia* (1997)

Delgamuukw[64] was a landmark Supreme Court of Canada decision in its treatment of oral histories as meeting the evidentiary rules of court and Aboriginal title generally.[65] *Delgamuukw* reaffirmed the Supreme Court of Canada's discussion of the rules of evidence in *Van der Peet*[66] in that trial courts must consider evidentiary rules in light of the special and *sui generis* nature of Aboriginal claims.[67] In *Van der Peet*, the Supreme Court of Canada stated that when courts adjudicate Aboriginal rights cases, they should approach the rules of evidence and interpret the evidence that exists in light of the difficulties in proving a right originating in times when there were no Aboriginal written records. Courts must not undervalue the evidence presented by Aboriginal claimants simply because that evidence does not conform precisely with the evidentiary standards that would be applied in, for example, a modern torts case.[68]

Writing for the majority, Lamer C.J. stated that since the respondents (British Columbia) suffered some prejudice due to the fact that the appellants did not amend their pleadings to amalgamate the individual claims brought by the fifty-one Gitksan and Wet'suwet'en Houses into two collective claims, the Court was prevented from considering the merits of the appeal and, therefore, a new trial would be an appropriate remedy.

Delgamuukw affirmed that oral histories rejected by the trial court must be considered in decisions involving Aboriginal rights. The laws of evidence must accommodate Aboriginal oral history and place it "on an equal footing with the types of historical evidence that courts are familiar with."[69] The trial judge in *Delgamuukw* rejected the argument that the Gitksan and Wet'suwet'en people had the required extent of occupation necessary for ownership of the lands in question. Much of the oral history presented as evidence dealt with the historical nature of the use and occupation of the lands in question. The finding by the Supreme Court of Canada that this evidence is admissible and must

---

[63] *Guerin, supra* note 26 at 382.

[64] *Delgamuukw, supra* note 3.

[65] The history of Aboriginal title in British Columbia, especially within the context of *Delgamuukw*, can be found in D. Culhane, *The Pleasure of the Crown: Anthropology, Law and First Nations* (Burnaby: Talon Books, 1998).

[66] *Van der Peet, supra* note 5 at paras. 42, 49, 50, and 68.

[67] *Delgamuukw, supra* note 3 at para. 82.

[68] *Van der Peet, supra* note 5 at para. 68.

[69] *Delgamuukw, supra* note 3 at para. 87.

be considered will continue to be useful for Aboriginal people in litigation respecting Aboriginal title.

In *Delgamuukw*, Lamer C.J. also discussed the *sui generis* nature of Aboriginal title and its various dimensions: (*a*) it is inalienable; (*b*) its source arises from the prior occupation of Canada by Aboriginal people; and (*c*) it is held communally.[70]

Aboriginal title includes the right to exclusive use and occupation of the land for an array of purposes, not limited to Aboriginal practices, customs, and traditions integral to distinct Aboriginal cultures. The use of the land cannot be irreconcilable with the Aboriginal occupation of the land, and it is the relationship the Aboriginal group in question had with the land that gives rise to the Aboriginal title in the first place.[71] Aboriginal title is a right to land being claimed. Aboriginal rights are activities that must be an element of a practice, custom, or tradition integral to the distinctive culture of the Aboriginal people claiming the right.[72] Aboriginal title is a distinct variation of Aboriginal rights, which are recognized and affirmed in s. 35(1) of the *Constitution Act, 1982* (s. 35(1))[73] and is an "interest" that attaches to the Crown's underlying title to land.[74]

Delgamuukw affirmed that Aboriginal title confers the right to use land for a variety of activities, including activities that are aspects of practices, customs, and traditions integral to the distinctive cultures of the Aboriginal people concerned. Those activities that are not integral aspects of practices, customs, and traditions are parasitic on the underlying Aboriginal title.[75] Aboriginal title includes mineral rights and the right to exploit the land for oil and gas.[76] However, these rights are not absolute and must be balanced with the rights of others, particularly those persons holding fee simple title. Lands subject to Aboriginal title cannot be used in a manner irreconcilable with the intent of Aboriginal title. In practical terms, the scope of Aboriginal rights and title, including irreconcilable land uses, remains incomplete and uncertain.[77]

Aboriginal title, as a component of Aboriginal rights, is recognized and affirmed by s. 35(1). In *Delgamuukw*, the Supreme Court of Canada described Aboriginal rights as being on a spectrum. At one end are those Aboriginal rights that are practices, customs, and traditions integral to the distinctive culture of the group claiming a right. These activities have constitutional protection, but the occupation and use of the land where the activities are occurring is not sufficient to support a claim of Aboriginal title to the land. In the middle of the spectrum there are activities that, out of necessity, take place on land and might be intimately related to a particular parcel of land. While an Aboriginal group may not be able to prove Aboriginal title, it may be able to prove a site-specific Aboriginal right to engage in a particular activity. At the other end of spectrum, there is Aboriginal title itself, and all the attributes associated with it.[78]

The differences between Aboriginal title and other forms of land title can be summarized as follows:

---

[70] *Ibid.* at paras. 113–15.

[71] *Ibid.* at paras. 117 and 128.

[72] *Ibid.* at para. 140; *Van der Peet, supra* note 5 at para. 46.

[73] *Delgamuukw, supra* note 3 at para. 2.

[74] Section 109 of the *Constitution Act, 1867* provides that the Crown's title is subject to "any interest" other than that of a province. Aboriginal title constitutes such an interest. See *Delgamuukw, supra* note 3 at para. 175.

[75] *Ibid.* at para. 111.

[76] See also *Blueberry River Indian Band v. Canada*, [1995] 4 S.C.R. 344.

[77] *Delgamuukw, supra* note 3 at para. 128.

[78] *Ibid.* at para. 138.

1. Aboriginal title finds its roots in pre-sovereignty occupation, as opposed to post-sovereignty Crown grants;

2. Aboriginal title is inalienable, except to the Crown (thus placing the Crown in the position of acting as an intermediary between Aboriginal people and third parties, and imposing a fiduciary duty upon the Crown), whereas other forms of land title (e.g., fee simple) are alienable;

3. Aboriginal title gives rise to exclusive use and occupation by the Aboriginal group holding the title and the right to engage in an array of activities, whereas other forms of land tenure need not necessarily be exclusive;

4. Aboriginal title is held communally, not individually; and

5. Aboriginal title is constitutionally protected as an existing Aboriginal right within the meaning of s. 35(1) and is, therefore, part of the supreme law of Canada.

Osoyoos Indian Band v. *Oliver (Town)* (2001)

In *Osoyoos Indian Band* v. *Oliver (Town)*[79] the Supreme Court of Canada discussed the nature of reserve lands vis-à-vis Aboriginal title: "[a]lthough the two interests are not identical, they are fundamentally similar."[80] In *Osoyoos*, the Court said that Aboriginal title and the Aboriginal interest in reserve land are similar in that both are inalienable except to the Crown, they are rights of use and occupation, they are held communally, and they are distinct from normal proprietary interests.[81] Aboriginal title may attach to Indian reserve lands where it can be shown that reserve lands fit the court-enunciated indicia of "Aboriginal title." The likelihood of reserve lands being subject to Aboriginal title in British Columbia is high given the lack of treaties in most of that province and in consideration of the questions concerning the original methodology used in allocating reserves to Indians there. While Aboriginal title has a communal aspect to it, individuals can hold reserve lands by way of Certificates of Possession.[82] In addition, reserve lands can be added to and surrendered absolutely.

ABORIGINAL TITLE IN THE MARITIMES

Aboriginal title remains an outstanding issue in the Maritime provinces. In *Warman* v. *Francis*,[83] the New Brunswick Supreme Court considered the application of Aboriginal title to New Brunswick and found that the Mi'kmaq were prevented from entering upon private property, in part, because they could not prove Aboriginal title. The Court concluded that the Proclamation applied to the Atlantic provinces, and that the Mi'kmaq never surrendered their Aboriginal rights.

Commenting on the status of the cession of Indian land, MacKeigan C.J.N.S. of the

---

[79] *Osoyoos Indian Band* v. *Oliver (Town)*, [2001] 3 S.C.R. 746.
[80] *Ibid.* para. 41. See *Guerin, supra* note 26 at 379, Dickson J. (as he then was); *Delgamuukw, supra* note 3 at paras. 116–21, Lamer C.J.
[81] *Osoyoos, supra* note 79 at para. 42; see *St. Mary's Indian Band* v. *Cranbrook (City)*, [1997] 2 S.C.R. 67 at para. 14.
[82] See s. 20(2) of the *Indian Act*, R.S.C. 1985, c. I-5, which states: "The Minister may issue to an Indian who is lawfully in possession of land in a reserve a certificate, to be called a Certificate of Possession, as evidence of his right to possession of the land described therein."
[83] *Warman* v. *Francis* (1958), 20 D.L.R. (2d) 627 (N.B.S.C.).

Nova Scotia Court of Appeal stated in *R. v. Isaac*: "No Nova Scotia treaty has been found whereby Indians ceded land to the Crown, whereby their rights on any land were specifically extinguished, or whereby they agreed to accept and retire to specified reserves."[84] MacKeigan C.J.N.S. also commented that "neither the French nor British had extinguished the Indian rights in Nova Scotia."[85]

In *Peter Paul* v. *R.*,[86] the New Brunswick Court of Appeal considered an appeal from the Crown regarding Peter Paul, a registered Mi'Kmaq Indian, who was charged with unlawfully removing timber from Crown lands without a licence. Paul argued that he was exempt from the requirement of obtaining a licence because he possessed a treaty right to harvest timber on Crown lands, both under the Treaty of 1726 and based on Aboriginal title. At trial, Arsenault J. held that Paul's activities were within the terms of the Treaty of 1726 and that small-scale harvesting of timber for commercial purposes was a "lawful occasion" within the terms of the treaty.

The Court of Queen's Bench upheld Arsenault J.'s decision, while the Court of Appeal overturned the lower court's decision. The Court of Appeal concluded that since the arguments of counsel and the evidence tendered were not directed to the issue of Aboriginal title, the Court could not properly assess any claim of Aboriginal title. The Court also rejected Arsenault J.'s interpretation of the treaty since there was insufficient historical evidence presented at trial regarding the intentions of the parties to the treaty and, in particular, no evidence to support the conclusion that commercial tree harvesting was "a lawful occasion" contemplated by the treaty.

In another New Brunswick decision concerning a partial defence of Aboriginal title to support a claim of treaty rights to harvest forest products commercially, Lordon Prov. Ct. J. stated:

> There was no evidence of capacity to retain exclusive control and, given the vast area of land and the small population they did not have the capacity to exercise exclusive control. . . . [A]ccording to the evidence of Chief Augustine, the Mi'kmaq had neither the intent nor the desire to exercise exclusive control, which, in my opinion, is fatal to the claim for Aboriginal title.[87]

The New Brunswick Court of Appeal, in a 2–1 decision, overturned the trial court decision.[88]

If Aboriginal title exists in the Maritimes, political negotiations would be essential. Without a negotiated settlement, governments and Indian bands would have to utilize the courts extensively as a case-by-case analysis would be required to ascertain the precise scope and meaning of Aboriginal title to a particular area of a province.[89]

---

[84] *R. v. Isaac, supra* note 39 at 479.

[85] *Ibid.* at 482.

[86] *Peter Paul* v. *R.*, [1998] 3 C.N.L.R. 221 (N.B.C.A.).

[87] *R. v. Bernard*, [2000] 3 C.N.L.R. 184 at 213 (N.B.Prov.Ct.), aff'd [2002] 3 C.N.L.R. 141. Savoie J. of the Court of Queen's Bench stated at para. 38: "The trial judge in his well reasoned ruling on the matter of occupation came to the conclusion that the Mi'kmaqs did not have exclusive occupation of the Sevogle area at the time of sovereignty in 1759 and have not had it since then. That conclusion was not unreasonable. On a review of the evidence, I agree with him."

[88] *R. v. Bernard*, 2003 N.B.C.A. 55, [2003] 4 C.N.L.R. 48 (N.B.C.A.).

[89] B. Slattery, "Some Thoughts on Aboriginal Title" (1999) 48 U.N.B.L.J. 19 at 40, has stated:

> [T]he question of aboriginal title in New Brunswick and Nova Scotia is very much alive and will continue to preoccupy the courts of those provinces for some years to come. Perhaps the governments of New Brunswick and Nova Scotia would be wise to read the judicial writing on the wall and take steps to resolve the matter by timely negotiations.

A case-by-case analysis was conducted in *R. v. Marshall*.[90] This decision considered thirty-five Mi'kmaq charged with cutting timber on, and removing timber from, Crown land without authorization, contrary to Nova Scotia's *Crown Lands Act*. The Mi'kmaq offered as a defence that they possessed Aboriginal title to all of Nova Scotia and that the Treaties of 1760–61 include a right to harvest forest products for sale. Curran Prov. Ct. J. extensively reviewed the history of the Mi'kmaq but spent little time in analyzing the Aboriginal title claim according to the test outlined in *Delgamuukw*.[91] Nevertheless, he arrived at the following conclusions:

1. The Mi'kmaq of the eighteenth century were moderately nomadic and maintained communities generally in the same area on mainland Nova Scotia;

2. The Mi'kmaq historically used bays, rivers and nearby hunting grounds intensively. However, there was a lack of evidence to deduce precisely where this use occurred. It did not encompass all of mainland Nova Scotia but was site specific;

3. There was a lack of evidence to conclude that the Mi'kmaq occupied for any substantial period Cape Breton, to the extent required to prove Aboriginal title; and

4. The Mi'kmaq of the eighteenth century probably had Aboriginal title to specific sites on mainland Nova Scotia, particularly around there local communities.[92]

The weakness in the trial judge's analysis is most apparent in not directly linking the *Delgamuukw* test to the evidence provided. While considerable evidence was presented at trial and noted by the trial judge, relatively little discussion directly and explicitly linked the evidence to the conclusions by the trial judge. Using the Supreme Court of Canada's *R. v. Marshall*[93] decision and its reconsideration[94] the trial judge also concluded that the treaties at issue do not provide a basis for claiming a right to harvest wood.[95] The Treaties of 1760–61 could not be used as a defence, he ruled, stating that there was "no evidence the Mi'kmaq sold or traded timber up to the time of the treaties and no reason to believe they did."[96] He also dismissed using Belcher's Proclamation as the source for a treaty right to log since it did not apply to the cutting sites in question. This decision underscores the onus on Aboriginal groups to prove Aboriginal title, and the corresponding onus on the courts to consider that evidence carefully and refer to it appropriately when considering the merits of a case.

A number of factors suggest that Aboriginal title remains outstanding in the Maritimes. First, although Aboriginal title does not find its source in the Royal Proclamation of 1763, it is nevertheless a powerful piece of evidence. The Proclamation likely applies to the Maritimes. Since no land was ceded and little land was purchased, the Proclamation arguably confirms the continued existence of Aboriginal title in the Maritimes.

Second, in *Delgamuukw* the Supreme Court of Canada laid out the three criteria required to make a claim for Aboriginal title. First, prior to the British assertion of sovereignty, the land must have been occupied by the ancestors of the Aboriginal group claiming title. While the onus of proving Aboriginal title rests with those making the claim, it is clear that the Mi'kmaq and Maliseet have occupied various parts of the Maritimes (the Mi'kmaq in New Brunswick, Nova Scotia, and Prince Edward Island and the Maliseet in

[90] *Marshall, supra* note 39.
[91] *Ibid.* see paras. 136–42.
[92] *Ibid.* at paras. 142–43.
[93] *R. v. Marshall*, [1999] 3 S.C.R. 456.
[94] *R. v. Marshall* (reconsideration), [1999] 3 S.C.R. 533.
[95] *Marshall, supra* note 39 at paras. 90, 93–95.
[96] *Ibid.* at para. 92.

New Brunswick). Second, the continuity between existing and pre-sovereignty occupation must be demonstrated, when the existing occupation of the lands in question is being offered as proof of pre-sovereignty occupation.[97] Third, at the time of sovereignty, the occupation by the Aboriginal group must have been exclusive. As previously noted, the exclusivity that is required is not necessarily the exclusion of other Aboriginal groups in the area; a case-by-case analysis of the extent to which the Aboriginal group making the claim for title used and/or occupied a particular area of land is required.

Fourth, the potential coexistence of treaty rights with Aboriginal title in the Maritimes would be unique in Canada in that the existing treaties do not include the cession of land and some of the corresponding rights associated with it. Taken alone, the fact that these treaties do not include any reference to the cession of land does not prove the existence of Aboriginal title. However, combined with the broad and liberal interpretation *Marshall* gave to interpreting the Treaties of 1760–61, these treaties could support the continued existence of Aboriginal title in the Maritimes.

What are the implications to the Maritimes if Aboriginal title is deemed to continue to exist? The first practical implication is that both sides, Aboriginal and the Crown, would have a strong incentive to negotiate comprehensive treaties. This mode of determining the content and meaning of Aboriginal rights and title is strongly supported and endorsed by the Supreme Court of Canada. Negotiations in this area involve complex legal, governance, and resource management issues, the historical rights of Aboriginal people, and the constitutional legislative authority of the federal and provincial governments. To this end, on June 7, 2002, the Governments of Canada and Nova Scotia and thirteen Mi'Kmaq Chiefs of Nova Scotia signed an umbrella agreement to continue the existing Mi'Kmaq–Nova Scotia–Canada Tripartite Forum. The agreement also initiated discussions regarding a framework agreement for more formal negotiations to deal with the outstanding issues surrounding Mi'Kmaq rights in Nova Scotia.

ABORIGINAL TITLE AND PRIVATE PROPERTY

The impact of Aboriginal title on private land is a matter of great interest to those seeking certainty in private land transactions. Some Aboriginal people have argued that Aboriginal title is an encumbrance on fee simple title that could result in possession by the Aboriginal group concerned. However, the nature of Aboriginal title is inconsistent with the essential attributes of fee simple title, thereby likely excluding the possible remedy of possession in the face of an Aboriginal title claim.

The fee simple estate is as close to absolute ownership in respect of land as is possible in Canada. Theoretically, the only higher form of land ownership would be the sovereign, absolute, or underlying title held by the Crown, which supports all land title in Canada. Oosterhoff and Rayner describe fee simple title as follows:

> The estate in fee simple is the largest estate or interest known in law and is the most absolute in terms of the rights which it confers. It permits the owner to exercise every conceivable act of ownership upon it or with respect to it. . . . While technically the owner holds of the Crown under the doctrine of tenure, in practice his ownership is the equivalent of the absolute dominion a person may have of a chattel. . . .[98]

[97] The Supreme Court of Canada considered this matter to some extent in *R. v. Simon*, [1985] 2 S.C.R. 387 at 407 concerning the Treaty of 1752 and confirmed that the present day Mi'kmaq could possess rights signed by their ancestors.

[98] A.H. Oosterhoff & W.B. Rayner, *Anger and Honsberger Law of Real Property*, 2d ed. (Aurora, Ont.: Canada Law Book Inc., 1985), 98–99.

In *Delgamuukw,* Lamer C.J. noted that Aboriginal title encompasses the right to "exclusive use and occupation,"[99] a description that, on its face, directly contradicts the attributes associated with fee simple title in Canadian law. Lamer C.J. also noted that Aboriginal title can only be alienated to the Crown and is inalienable to third parties.[100]

The Supreme Court of Canada has expressly stated that Aboriginal title is an encumbrance on the Crown's underlying title to land to which Aboriginal title applies.[101] Because of the inalienable nature of Aboriginal title, it cannot shift from being a burden on the Crown's underlying title to other title holders, such as those holding fee simple title.

In *Delgamuukw,* the Supreme Court of Canada set out an implicitly clear and reasonable legal analysis on how to deal with the apparent conflict between Aboriginal title and fee simple title:

1. The Crown's grant of a fee simple title is a justifiable infringement of Aboriginal title.

2. The fee simple title holder acquires "good title" from the Crown insofar as the encumbrance of Aboriginal title does not attach to the fee simple title but, rather, remains with the Crown's underlying title.

3. The Supreme Court of Canada confirmed that the Crown can infringe Aboriginal title, whether justified or unjustified.

4. The Supreme Court of Canada has confirmed that the appropriate remedy for breach of Aboriginal title is compensation from the Crown.[102]

5. The issue of whether the Crown can justify an infringement of Aboriginal title, that is, the granting of a fee simple interest, is relevant with respect to the amount of compensation payable by the Crown to the Aboriginal group holding such Aboriginal title.

6. On the issue of justification, the Supreme Court of Canada expressly set out a broad array of valid legislative objectives that could justify an infringement of Aboriginal title which include: the development of agriculture, forestry, mining, hydroelectric development, general economic development, protection of the environment or endangered species, building of infrastructure, and settlement of foreign populations.[103] The settlement of foreign populations is akin to the homesteading practices of the early history of Canada's development.

7. With respect to consultation, the Supreme Court of Canada expressly stated that the degree of consultation that has occurred will have a direct impact upon the extent of compensation that is payable by the Crown as a result of the infringement.[104]

8. The Crown likely has limited duties to consult Aboriginal people respecting Aboriginal title on land held by fee simple title because the Aboriginal title has already been infringed by the granting of the fee simple interest. The Aboriginal group

---

[99] *Delgamuukw, supra* note 3 at para. 117.

[100] *Ibid.* at para. 113.

[101] *Ibid.* at para. 145.

[102] *Ibid.*; see also *Chippewas of Sarnia Band* v. *Canada (A.G.)* (2000), 51 O.R. (3d) 641, 195 D.L.R. (4th) 135, (Ont. C.A.), leave to appeal dismissed, [2001] SCCA 63 (S.C.C.).

[103] *Delgamuukw, supra* note 3 at para. 165.

[104] *Ibid.* at para. 169.

cannot obtain any possessory remedy or accommodation of the type that can be sought prior to infringement. The limited nature of the Crown's duty to consult on private property likely extends to adjacent Crown land or downstream effects, as the case may be.

The law respecting the application of Aboriginal rights on private property is likely consistent with the jurisprudence respecting private property and existing treaty rights. The Supreme Court of Canada considered the relationship between existing treaty rights and private property in *R. v. Badger*[105] whereby the "visible, incompatible use" test was applied. This test provides that where private property is put to a use visibly incompatible with the exercise of treaty rights, then such private property may not be used to exercise treaty rights, such as hunting. Conversely, where private property is not put to a visible incompatible use, then Aboriginal people may utilize such property in the exercise of their existing treaty rights. In *Badger,* the Supreme Court of Canada stated:

> Where lands are privately owned, it must be determined on a case-by-case basis whether they are "other lands" to which Indians had a "right of access" under the Treaty. If the lands are occupied, that is, put to visible use which is incompatible with hunting, Indians will not have a right of access. Conversely, if privately owned land is unoccupied and not put to visible use, Indians, pursuant to Treaty No. 8, will have a right of access in order to hunt for food.[106]

In *R. v. Alphonse*[107] the British Columbia Court of Appeal considered an appeal by an Indian charged under the *Wildlife Act*.[108] One issue confronting the Court was whether Aboriginal rights could be exercised on private lands and whether provisions allowing hunting on what is essentially unoccupied private land as set out in the *Trespass Act*[109] and *Wildlife Act*[110] were applicable. Macfarlane J.A. stated:

> The land on which Mr. Alphonse was hunting was not cultivated land. It was not subject to a Crown granted grazing lease, and it was not occupied by livestock. . . . [T]he land in question was not "enclosed land." . . . Applying the Trespass Act to the circumstances of this case, there was no prohibition with respect to hunting on the lands in question. That being so, it was not unlawful to hunt on those lands. Thus, it was not unlawful to exercise an Aboriginal right on those lands.[111]

When read together, *Badger* and *Alphonse* confirm that existing Aboriginal and treaty rights may be exercised on unoccupied private land; where private property is occupied and visibly used, it may not be accessed by Aboriginal people to exercise their rights. The existence of such rights cannot, however, be used to prevent private landowners from lawfully using their land. Once private property is put to a visible, incompatible use, Aboriginal rights are no longer exercisable on private property.

The relationship between the Crown's duty to consult and accommodate Aboriginal people and private property is unclear. The Crown's duty to consult is likely limited to effects of actions taken on, or uses made of, private property that may have an impact on Aboriginal rights that are exercised on Crown land adjacent to, or downstream of, private property, but not *on* private property.

[105] *R. v. Badger*, [1996] 1 S.C.R. 771.
[106] *Ibid.* at para. 66.
[107] *R. v. Alphonse*, [1993] 4 C.N.L.R. 19 (B.C.C.A.).
[108] *Wildlife Act*, S.B.C. 1982, c. 57, ss. 27(1)(c) and 34(2).
[109] *Trespass Act*, R.S.B.C. 1979, c. 411, ss. 1 and 4(1).
[110] *Wildlife Act, supra* note 108.
[111] *Alphonse, supra* note 107 at paras. 26, 34.

In the Ontario Court of Appeal decision of *Chippewas of Sarnia Band* v. *Canada (A.-G.),*[112] leave to appeal to the Supreme Court of Canada dismissed, the Court considered a claim by the Chippewas of Sarnia Band of ownership of a parcel of land located in Sarnia, Ontario. Malcolm Cameron purchased the land in question (approximately ten square kilometres) from the Band in 1839. The lands were conveyed to Cameron by Crown patent in 1853. The present occupants of the land traced their title back to the patent. The Band claimed that their ancestors never surrendered the disputed lands and, therefore, they continue to hold Aboriginal title to the land.

The Court confirmed the need for certain procedures to be followed in order to effect a proper surrender of Aboriginal title. The Crown believed a surrender of the lands had occurred but, in fact, no legal surrender took place. Cameron, with the approval of the Crown, negotiated the transaction with three chiefs of the Chippewas and reached an agreement, approved by the Crown. However, the Chippewas as a group were not asked to approve the surrender to the Crown. Consequently, the formal surrender process was not followed. In the twenty years following the transaction, those Chippewas affected by the agreement acknowledged and accepted the transaction and regarded the lands as no longer part of their reserve. The repudiation of the patent by the Chippewas and their claim that they retained interests and rights in the lands occurred some 140 years after the Cameron transaction when it was discovered that there was no documentation confirming the surrender of the lands by the Chippewas to the Crown.

The Court noted that members of the public rely upon the apparently valid acts of public officials in planning their affairs and official documents are taken at face value.[113] In this case, a Crown patent that apparently grants fee simple title to land provides a good example of an official act that is relied upon by innocent third parties. The Court noted that it "would plainly be wrong" to deny a remedy that would support a claim for Aboriginal title on the grounds that the affirmation of such a claim might be "troublesome" to others.[114] However, the Court confirmed that Aboriginal rights are part of the broader Canadian legal landscape and do not exist in a vacuum: "In the Canadian legal tradition, no right is absolute, not even constitutionally protected Aboriginal rights."[115]

The Court concluded that the interests of innocent third parties who have relied upon the apparent validity of the patent must prevail over any remedy that would set aside the patent. This conclusion, however, does not preclude or limit the right of the Band to proceed with a claim for damages against the Crown.

Chippewas provides insight into the Court's comfort with balancing the rights of Aboriginal people with the rights of innocent third parties. This approach was affirmed by the Supreme Court of Canada in *R.* v. *Marshall,*[116] wherein the Supreme Court of Canada reinforced its earlier decisions that stressed the need for a balanced approach to interpret existing Aboriginal and treaty rights with the rights of other Canadians.

Chippewas confirms that where a surrender has not occurred, the appropriate remedy is at the discretion of the court and must be balanced with competing interests: those of Aboriginal title itself, as confirmed in *Delgamuukw*[117] and those of the innocent third

---

[112] See *Chippewas, supra* note 102; see P. Perell & J. Cowan, "In Defence of *Chippewas of Sarnia Band* v. *Canada*" (2002) 81:3 Can. Bar Rev. 727.

[113] *Ibid.* at para. 258.

[114] *Ibid.* at para. 262.

[115] *Ibid.* at para. 263.

[116] *Marshall, supra* note 93 and *Marshall* (reconsideration), *supra* note 94.

[117] *Delgamuukw, supra* note 3.

party purchaser, as discussed in *Chippewas*. *Chippewas* is also consistent with the British Columbia Court of Appeal decision in *Skeetchestn Indian Band* v. *B.C. (Reg. of Land Titles)*,[118] which affirmed a decision of the Registrar of Land Titles to refuse to register a certificate of pending litigation on fee simple title. The Court held that a claim of Aboriginal title is not a registrable interest under the *Land Title Act*. In *Uukw* v. *B.C.*[119] Macdonald J.A. for the British Columbia Court of Appeal wrote:

> It is enough to observe that Aboriginal title can have no place in a Torrens system which has the primary object of establishing and certifying the ownership of indefeasible titles and simplifying transfers thereof. I conclude that s.213 requires the claim of a registrable estate or interest in land and what is claimed in this case is not registrable.

GOVERNMENTAL DUTIES

In the absence of negotiated settlements, it is clear that governments must change the way they regulate activities that have an impact on Aboriginal and treaty rights. Whatever form the rights of Aboriginal people take, either as Aboriginal or treaty rights or as Aboriginal title, governments have been given clear directions to change the way they have traditionally conducted themselves with respect to Aboriginal people and their rights. Dealing with Aboriginal people and their interests is simply a cost of doing business for governments in Canada.

Governments in Canada appear uncertain as to what effect this new legal regime will have on their regulatory and legislative authority. *Marshall,* for example, provides a helpful and clear articulation of the extent to which governments may justifiably regulate Aboriginal and treaty rights, including Aboriginal title. This was supported by other Supreme Court of Canada decisions, namely *Delgamuukw, Sparrow, Badger,* and *Van der Peet.* It requires a fundamental shift in focus and additional resources to ensure that Aboriginal people are consulted and their rights are properly considered respecting decisions or activities that may have an impact on Aboriginal and treaty rights, including Aboriginal title.

PROOF OF ABORIGINAL TITLE

Proving Aboriginal title can be a difficult task for Aboriginal people.[120] Prior to *Delgamuukw*, the test used by Canadian courts to determine the existence of Aboriginal title was that set out in *Hamlet of Baker Lake* v. *Min. of Indian Affairs and Northern Dev.*[121]

---

[118] *Skeetchestn Indian Band* v. *B.C. (Reg. of Land Titles)*, [2000] 10 W.W.R. 222 (B.C.C.A.), aff'g [2000] 2 C.N.L.R. 330 (B.C.S.C.).

[119] *Uukw* v. *B.C.*, [1988] 1 C.N.L.R. 173 at 186, 187 (B.C.C.A).

[120] In *Mitchell* v. *Canada (Min. of National Revenue)*, [2001] 1 S.C.R. 911, the Supreme Court of Canada considered whether the Mohawks of Akwesasne possessed an Aboriginal right to bring goods across the Canada–United States border for the purposes of trade. Writing for the majority, McLachlin C.J. concluded that the federal trial court made a "palpable and overriding error" (para. 51) in the treatment of the evidence provided on behalf of the Mohawks. The Court held that the evidence suggested the opposite of what the Mohawks and the trial and appeal courts held; that is, the evidence did not support the existence of such a right. While a generous and liberal approach must be taken in considering evidence in Aboriginal rights cases, this approach must be *balanced* with the continued application of "general evidentiary principles." (para. 38) The Court reflected this perspective in *Marshall, supra* note 93 at para. 14: "'Generous' rules of interpretation should not be confused with a vague sense of after-the-fact largesse." For commentary on *Mitchell*, see Thomas Isaac, "The Meaning of Subsection 35(1) of the *Constitution Act, 1982*: A Comment on *Mitchell* v. *Min. of National Revenue*" (Nov. 2002) 60:6 *The Advocate* 853.

[121] *Hamlet of Baker Lake* v. *Min. of Indian Affairs & North. Dev.*, [1979] 3 C.N.L.R. 17 (F.C.T.D.).

This decision was modified and refined in *Delgamuukw*, discussed below. The four principles necessary to prove Aboriginal title outlined in *Baker Lake* are:

1. membership in an organized society;

2. occupation by the organized society of the specific territory over which Aboriginal title is being claimed;

3. occupation by the organized society was to the exclusion of other organized societies; and

4. occupation was an established fact at the time English sovereignty was asserted.

Calder established that possession of land is proof for the existence of Aboriginal title and that once established, Aboriginal title is presumed to continue until extinguished. In *Kruger and Manuel* v. *R.*,[122] the Supreme Court of Canada considered the rights of non-treaty Indians in British Columbia to hunt without a permit. Although the Court held that the provincial legislation applied to Indians, *Kruger* also affirmed that in establishing and dealing with the issue of Aboriginal title, the unique situation of each community must be considered individually.

In *Delgamuukw*, Lamer C.J. laid out the criteria to prove Aboriginal title:[123]

1. prior to the British assertion of sovereignty, the land must have been occupied by the ancestors of the Aboriginal group claiming title;

2. continuity between existing and pre-sovereignty occupation must be demonstrated when existing occupation of the lands in question is being offered as proof of pre-sovereignty occupation; and

3. at the time of sovereignty, the occupation by the Aboriginal group must have been exclusive.[124]

Exclusivity of occupation does not mean that other Aboriginal groups were not present; the context of the Aboriginal society at sovereignty must be taken into account. The Supreme Court of Canada stated that exclusive occupation can be shown even though other Aboriginal groups were present or frequented the lands in question. In those circumstances, exclusivity could be established by demonstrating that the group claiming title had the intent and capacity for exclusive control.[125] Lack of proving exclusivity does not prevent the Aboriginal group from establishing Aboriginal rights beyond Aboriginal title.

Noticeably missing from the *Delgamuukw* test is *Baker Lake*'s reference to the need for an "organized society." This may be an implicit recognition by the Supreme Court of Canada not to judge the nature of pre-contact Aboriginal governance structures. Occupation, continuity, and exclusivity are enough to make an Aboriginal title claim. The Supreme Court of Canada relied on Australia's *Mabo*[126] decision to conclude that the "substantial maintenance of the connection" between the people and the land is a critical relationship when proving Aboriginal title.[127]

---

[122] *Kruger and Manuel* v. *R.*, [1978] 1 S.C.R. 104 at 108–9.
[123] *Delgamuukw*, *supra* note 3 at paras. 140–59.
[124] *Ibid.* at para. 143.
[125] *Ibid.* at para. 156.
[126] *Mabo* v. *Queensland*, [1992] 5 C.N.L.R. 1 (H. Ct. Aust.).
[127] *Delgamuukw*, *supra* note 3 at para. 153.

JUSTIFYING AN INFRINGEMENT OF ABORIGINAL TITLE

The federal and provincial governments may infringe Aboriginal rights, including Aboriginal title, where such infringements can be justified.[128] In *Delgamuukw*, Lamer C.J. summarized the law in this regard. First, the infringement of an Aboriginal right must be in pursuit of a valid legislative objective that is compelling and substantive. Agricultural development, forestry, mining, hydroelectric development, economic development generally, protection of the environment and of endangered species, and infrastructure development are objectives consistent with a valid legislative objective capable of justifying an infringement of Aboriginal title.[129] It is noteworthy that most of these objectives fall within provincial jurisdiction. In *Gladstone*,[130] the Supreme Court of Canada stated that compelling and substantial objectives are those that strike at the purposes behind the recognition and affirmation of Aboriginal rights in s. 35(1). These purposes are "the reconciliation of Aboriginal prior occupation with the assertion of the sovereignty of the Crown."[131]

The second element of the test to justify an infringement of Aboriginal title is a determination of whether the infringement is in keeping with the Crown's fiduciary relationship with Aboriginal people. The nature of this relationship depends on the "legal and factual context" of each particular case.[132]

While the *Sparrow* justification analysis applies to Aboriginal title cases, a number of other factors peculiar to Aboriginal title are relevant, namely:

1. Aboriginal title is a right to the exclusive use and occupation of land;

2. Aboriginal title provides to the holders of the title the right to choose how the land may be used, subject to the land not being used for purposes that would destroy the land for future generations of Aboriginal people; and

3. the lands to which Aboriginal title apply invariably have an economic element integral to them.

Lamer C.J.'s majority decision in *Delgamuukw* reaffirmed that litigation is not necessarily the best route to find solutions to such broad issues as how Aboriginal and non-Aboriginal people are to live together in Canada:

> By ordering a new trial, I do not necessarily encourage the parties to proceed to litigation. . . . [U]ltimately, it is through negotiated settlements, with good faith and give and take on all sides, reinforced by the judgments of this Court, that we will achieve . . . a basic purpose of s. 35(1)—"the reconciliation of the pre-existence of aboriginal societies with the sovereignty of the Crown." Let us face it, we are all here to stay.[133]

The conclusion of Lamer C.J. is revealing in its theme of reconciliation and is consistent with the Supreme Court of Canada's approach to other matters of a political and public policy nature.[134] Indeed, as in *Sparrow*, the Court placed s. 35(1) into a much broader political and public policy realm by suggesting that it "at the least, provides a

---

[128] *Ibid.* at para. 160.
[129] *Ibid.* at para. 165.
[130] *R. v. Gladstone,* [1996] 2 S.C.R. 723.
[131] *Ibid.* at para. 72, as cited in *Delgamuukw, supra* note 3 at para. 161.
[132] *Ibid.* at para. 56, as cited in *Delgamuukw, supra* note 3 at para. 162.
[133] *Delgamuukw, supra* note 3 at para. 186.
[134] For example, see *Reference re Amendment of the Constitution of Canada*, [1981] 1 S.C.R. 753 [the Patriation case], wherein the Supreme Court of Canada balanced constitutional convention with strict jurisprudence and

solid constitutional base upon which subsequent negotiations can take place."[135] Negotiated settlements will become all that much more important in British Columbia, and perhaps New Brunswick and Nova Scotia, where the issue of Aboriginal rights and title remains outstanding.

REMEDIES

Indian bands have been successful in obtaining injunctive relief to prevent encroachment upon their Aboriginal title.[136] However, injunctive relief is a discretionary remedy of the courts and when the evidence presented to the courts has been inadequate for the purposes of granting an injunction, the courts have refused the application.[137] A number of decisions from British Columbia show some reluctance by the courts to issue injunctions in Aboriginal title cases.[138]

As noted earlier, a claim for Aboriginal title is not an interest in land that can be registered under the British Columbia *Land Title Act*[139] but may be registrable under the British Columbia *Forestry Act*.[140] As for compensation, Lamer C.J. noted in *Delgamuukw* that:

> In keeping with the duty of honour and good faith on the Crown, fair compensation will ordinarily be required when Aboriginal title is infringed. The amount of compensation payable will vary with . . . the nature and severity of the infringement and the extent to which Aboriginal interests were accommodated.[141]

The issue of compensation for breach of Aboriginal title has not yet been fully litigated. However, compensation and its potential impact on the Governments of Canada and British Columbia, for example, could be immense. It also underscores the importance of governments attempting to reach negotiated settlements where Aboriginal title remains an outstanding issue.

Delgamuukw also held that if Aboriginal title is found to exist, activities such as forestry could continue and justify an infringement of Aboriginal title.[142] However, governments must also accommodate proven Aboriginal title and this can be accomplished in areas such as forestry by ensuring that Aboriginal people participate in resource development by way of leases and licences, and negotiate forms of impact and benefit agreements with Aboriginal people or by Crown compensation.[143]

---

recommended a more conciliatory approach to federal–provincial relations, resulting in the *Constitution Act, 1982.*

[135] *Sparrow, supra* note 42 at 1105.

[136] For example, see *Baker Lake* v. *Min. of Indian Affairs & Nor. Dev.*, [1979] 1 F.C. 487 (F.C.T.D.); *MacMillan Bloedel Ltd.* v. *Mullin (sub nom., Martin* v. *R. (B.C.))*, [1985] 3 W.W.R. 577 (B.C.C.A), leave to appeal to S.C.C. refused, [1985] 5 W.W.R. lxiv; and *Westar Timber Ltd.* v. *Ryan*, [1989] B.C.W.L.D. 1863 (B.C.C.A).

[137] For example, see *Tlowitsis Nation* v. *MacMillan Bloedel Ltd.*, [1991] 2 C.N.L.R. 164 (B.C.S.C.), leave to appeal to B.C.C.A. refused, [1991] B.C.W.L.D. 004, aff'd [1991] 4 W.W.R. 83, 53 B.C.L.R. (2d) 69 (B.C.C.A.); and *Eel Ground Indian Band* v. *New Brunswick*, [1999] 3 C.N.L.R. 72 (N.B.Q.B.).

[138] See *KitKatla Band* v. *B.C. (Min. of Forests)*, [1999] 2 C.N.L.R. 156 (B.C.S.C.), aff'd [1999] 2 C.N.L.R. 170 (B.C.C.A.), aff'd 2002 S.C.C. 31 (S.C.C.); *Chemainus First Nation* v. *B.C. Assets and Land Corp.*, [1999] 3 C.N.L.R. 8 (B.C.S.C.).

[139] *Land Title Act*, R.S.B.C. 1996, c. 250; *Skeetchestn Indian Band* v. *B.C.*, [2000] 2 C.N.L.R. 330 (B.C.S.C.), aff'd [2001] 1 C.N.L.R. 310 (B.C.C.A.); see also *Uukw* v. *B.C.*, [1988] 1 C.N.L.R. 173 (B.C.C.A.).

[140] *Haida Nation* v. *B.C., supra* note 45.

[141] *Delgamuukw, supra* note 3 at para. 169. See also *Chemainus, supra* note 138; see R. Mainville, *An Overview of Aboriginal and Treaty Rights and Compensation for their Breach* (Saskatoon: Purich Publishing Ltd., 2001).

[142] *Delgamuukw, supra* note 3 at para. 165.

[143] *Ibid.* at para. 167.

EXTINGUISHMENT OF ABORIGINAL TITLE

Aboriginal rights and title may be extinguished in three ways:

1. by voluntary surrender by Aboriginal people to the Crown;

2. prior to 1982, by federal, not provincial, legislation; and

3. after 1982, by constitutional amendment, altering s. 35 of the *Constitution Act, 1982.*

The precise means by which Aboriginal title can be extinguished, other than by express means on the part of Aboriginal people or the federal Crown, remain unclear. As the Proclamation states, Indians' interest in their lands cannot be extinguished without their "consent." Indian lands are reserved for Indians until the Indians "should be inclined to dispose of the said lands." In *St. Catherine's*, the Judicial Committee of the Privy Council stated that Aboriginal title is "dependent upon the good will of the Sovereign."[144] Steele J. of the Ontario High Court adopted this reasoning in *Bear Island* when he wrote that Aboriginal title "exists solely at the pleasure of the Crown."[145] In *R. v. Howard*,[146] the Supreme Court of Canada held that a treaty (other than an international treaty) is one means by which the Crown can extinguish Aboriginal title. An international treaty cannot serve to restrict or extinguish rights protected under s. 35.

The distinction between extinguishing Aboriginal title and Aboriginal rights was exemplified in *Adams*.[147] In *Adams*, the Government of Quebec argued that since it flooded a key fishing area to create a canal in 1845 and the Mohawks surrendered the lands around the area in 1888, the Aboriginal right to fish was extinguished. Lamer C.J. stated that:

> While these events may be adequate to demonstrate a clear and plain intention in the Crown to extinguish any Aboriginal *title to the lands* of the fishing area, neither is sufficient to demonstrate that the Crown had the clear and plain intention of extinguishing the appellant's Aboriginal *right to fish for food* in the fishing area. . . . The surrender of lands, because of the fact that title to land is distinct from the right to fish in the waters adjacent to those lands, equally does not demonstrate a clear and plain intention to extinguish a right.[148]
> [emphasis in original]

A careful examination of the facts and intentions of the parties is required when either making a claim for, or defending a claim of, extinguishment of Aboriginal title or Aboriginal rights.

In *Delgamuukw*, Lamer C.J., writing for the majority, considered the issue of whether the province of British Columbia had the power to extinguish Aboriginal rights after 1871, either by way of its own jurisdiction or by the application of s. 88 of the *Indian Act*.[149] Lamer C.J. stated that the federal government has the exclusive jurisdiction to legislate with respect to "Indians and lands reserved for Indians" pursuant to s. 91(24), and within that authority is the exclusive power to extinguish Aboriginal title and Aboriginal rights.[150] Lamer C.J. dealt only with British Columbia's authority to extinguish

---

[144] *St. Catherine's, supra* note 49.
[145] *Bear Island Foundation v. A.-G. of Ontario*, [1985] 1 C.N.L.R. 1 at 28 (Ont. S.C.).
[146] *R. v. Howard*, [1994] 2 S.C.R. 299.
[147] *Adams, supra* note 19 at 130.
[148] *Ibid.* at 130, para. 49.
[149] *Delgamuukw, supra* note 3 at paras. 172–82.
[150] *Ibid.* at para. 173; see also *Taku River Tlingit First Nation v. B.C.*, [2002] 2 C.N.L.R. 312 at para. 146 (B.C.C.A.).

Aboriginal rights after 1871 when it joined Canada. The issue of whether British Columbia had the authority, as a colonial power, *prior* to 1871 is not expressly considered. This raises the question of how a provincial law could be justified over an area—Aboriginal title—that is at the core of "Indianness" within the parameters of s. 91(24).[151]

ALTERNATIVES TO EXTINGUISHMENT

Traditionally, treaties have required that Indians "cede, release and surrender" (or extinguish) their rights and interests in the land to the Crown in return for specified rights and interests as outlined in a treaty. Although such a provision might achieve a key goal of governments in securing certainty over rights and title in treaties, this language has been a point of contention for Indian bands, primarily because Indian bands do not consider it in their best interests to "sign-off" on their rights for future generations and without fully understanding what rights currently exist.

In December 1994 the Minister of Indian and Northern Affairs appointed the Honourable A.C. Hamilton as an independent fact-finder to analyze alternatives to extinguishment and other means of providing certainty through land claims agreements.[152] Hamilton reported back in June 1995 with his report *Canada and Aboriginal Peoples: A New Partnership*.[153] His report provided a number of recommendations on how to limit the need for extinguishment by way of treaty. Hamilton suggests that treaties could recognize that an Aboriginal group possesses Aboriginal rights and that the treaties detail, to the best extent possible, the land and resource rights associated with the land in question. A critical aspect of Hamilton's recommendations is the inclusion of "mutual assurance" clauses in new treaties, which would state that the parties to the treaty would abide by the treaty and exercise their rights associated with the land affected according to the treaty. A dispute-resolution mechanism would also be included in the treaty to allow the parties to resolve their disputes quickly and outside judicial processes.

Under this approach Aboriginal rights would be kept intact and certainty would be provided to the Crown that the rights would be exercised in a particular manner. It would, however, require a fundamental shift in the current and long-standing approach of the federal Crown, which is to extinguish Aboriginal rights when settling a treaty. The RCAP also favoured a more flexible approach to treaty making and extinguishment.[154]

The Nisga'a Final Agreement dealt with alternatives to extinguishment by focusing on the "certainty" that the treaty provides.[155] The agreement is the "full and final settlement in respect of the Aboriginal rights (and title)" of the Nisga'a (s. 22), the exhaustive setting out of Nisga'a rights contained in s. 35 of the *Constitution Act, 1982* (s. 23), the embodiment of modifying Nisga'a Aboriginal title (ss. 24 and 25), and, finally, the Nisga'a release of British Columbia and Canada from any Aboriginal rights and title that did exist outside those rights modified in the agreement (ss. 26 and 27). This modification model is

---

[151] K. McNeil, "Aboriginal Title and the Division of Powers: Rethinking Federal and Provincial Jurisdiction" (1998) 61:2 Sask. L. Rev. 431; K. McNeil, "Aboriginal Title and Section 88 of the *Indian Act*" (2000) 34:1 U.B.C. Law Rev. 159.

[152] See also M. Asch & N. Zlotkin, "Affirming Aboriginal Title: A New Basis for Comprehensive Claims Negotiations" in M. Asch, ed., *Aboriginal and Treaty Rights in Canada* (Vancouver: U.B.C. Press, 1997) 208.

[153] A.C. Hamilton, *Canada and Aboriginal Peoples: A New Partnership* (Ottawa: Public Works and Government Services Canada, 1995).

[154] See RCAP, *supra* note 7 at 44–47.

[155] L. Dufraimont, "Continuity and Modification of Aboriginal Rights in the Nisga'a Treaty" (2002) 35:2 U.B.C. L. Rev. 455–509.

reinforced in the *Nisga'a Final Agreement Act*[156] both for Aboriginal rights (s. 7(1)) and Aboriginal title (s. 7(2)). The Nisga'a approach is a novel alternative to the traditional "cede, release and surrender" terminology. It appears to achieve the objective of providing the necessary certainty to governments that it is the sole source of Aboriginal rights for the Nisga'a Nation and that it sets out these rights fully, finally, and exhaustively. Nevertheless, the precise boundaries of Nisga'a jurisdiction remain outstanding. It remains to be seen how the courts will interpret the treaty vis-à-vis federal and provincial legislative authority. This is a key uncertain element of modern treaties and land claims agreements.

UNRESOLVED ABORIGINAL TITLE AND TREATIES

In general, the issue of Aboriginal title is outstanding in those areas where treaties have not been signed or where the issue of extinguishment of Aboriginal title is still in question. For example, much of British Columbia is not covered by treaty and is therefore open to claims based on Aboriginal title. Of course, the use and occupancy of land continue to be important issues with respect to determining whether Aboriginal rights exist. As in British Columbia, Aboriginal title will also likely become a dominant issue in the Maritimes,[157] particularly after the Supreme Court of Canada's *Marshall* (1999) decisions.[158] Like the rest of Canada, where comprehensive treaties that deal with the question of Aboriginal title have been negotiated, New Brunswick and Nova Scotia in particular would be well served to examine their options and develop their policy frameworks respecting such negotiations.

In some cases, land claims agreements have been ratified to meet the Crown's obligations to deal with outstanding claims of Aboriginal title. Among these agreements is the 1975 James Bay and Northern Quebec Agreement,[159] which permitted the government of Quebec to proceed with the James Bay hydroelectric project. Land claims agreements have also been concluded in the Yukon Territory, the Northwest Territories and Nunavut. The Nisga'a Final Agreement, British Columbia's first modern treaty, was initialled on August 4, 1998 and proclaimed into law on April 13, 2000. Subsection 7(2) of the *Nisga'a Final Agreement Act* provides:

> For greater certainty, the aboriginal title of the Nisga'a Nation anywhere that it existed in Canada before the effective date of the Nisga'a Final Agreement is modified and continues as the estates in fee simple to those areas identified in that Agreement as Nisga'a Lands or Nisga'a Fee Simple Lands.[160]

The purpose of this clause is to limit the interpretation of Aboriginal title (i.e., the nature of the Nisga'a Aboriginal title has been "modified") to those lands identified in the agreement. This is important from the perspective of the federal and provincial governments because it both limits the rights contained within the agreement and confines them to a defined geographical area. For the Nisga'a it ensures that this final settlement is constitutionally protected for now and for future generations.

---

[156] *Nisga'a Final Agreement Act*, S.C. 2000, c. 7.

[157] See *Bernard, supra* note 88.

[158] *Marshall, supra* note 93; *Marshall* (reconsideration), *supra* note 94.

[159] James Bay and Northern Quebec Agreement, (Quebec: Editeur official du Quebec, 1976), en. by the *James Bay and Northern Quebec Native Claims Settlement Act*, S.C. 1976–77, c. 32.

[160] *Nisga'a Final Agreement Act, supra* note 156.

AUSTRALIA AND THE *MABO* DECISION

Relying heavily upon Canadian jurisprudence, the High Court of Australia in 1992 recognized a form of Aboriginal title that, subject to being extinguished, continues to exist in Australia.[161] *Mabo* overturned the earlier decision in *Milirripum* v. *Nabalco*[162] that Aboriginal title did not survive British settlement of Australia. *Mabo* concerned a claim by the Merriam people of the Murray Islands that they possessed unextinguished Aboriginal title and affirmed that the Crown retained the underlying title and that the Aboriginal land interest can only be alienated to the Crown.

Australia responded to *Mabo* with the enactment of the *Native Title Act 1993*. The Act recognizes native title rights and establishes the National Native Title Tribunal to deal with uncontested native title claims and compensation. Contested title must be dealt with in the federal courts. The Act provides a regime to determine whether native title exists over particular areas of land or waters, for validating certain past acts of government, and for regulating future acts that may affect Aboriginal rights in land.

The *Native Title Act 1993* was amended in 1998 to allow for greater government intervention in native title determination and registration. Amendments included: (*a*) the validation of government grants from January 1, 1994 to the *Wik* decision[163] (discussed below), (*b*) native title was confirmed to be extinguished regarding exclusive tenures granted before January 1, 1994, and (*c*) impediments to the provision of government services on land where native title was still attached were removed, among other amendments.

In *Wik Peoples* v. *Queensland*,[164] the High Court of Australia considered a claim by the Wik Peoples of native title in land on the Cape York Peninsula in Queensland. This same land included pastoral leases issued by the Queensland Government. The Wik Peoples, joined by the Thayorre People, who have an overlapping claim over the area, argued that the pastoral leases did not extinguish their native title but rather, their native title co-exists with the leaseholders' interests. A majority of the High Court held that the pastoral leases did not confer exclusive possession of the leased land on the grantees and did not necessarily extinguish native title rights and interests that may continue to be possessed by the Wik and/or Thagorre Peoples. Native title rights and the leases can co-exist, and where an inconsistency arises between native rights and pastoral rights, the pastoral rights take precedence.

In *Western Australia* v. *Ward*,[165] the High Court of Australia confirmed that the Aborigines involved in the case did not establish any "native title right to or interest in any mineral or petroleum."[166] The Court also held that while mining and farming leases granted by government did not necessarily extinguish Aboriginal title, the leases did prevail over Aboriginal title in any conflict between the two.

---

[161] *Mabo* v. *Queensland*, *supra* note 126; see also *Ben Ward* v. *State of Western Australia*, [1999] 1 C.N.L.R. 33 (Fed. Ct. Aust.).

[162] *Milirripum* v. *Nabalco* (1971), 17 F.L.R. 141 (N. Terr. Sup. Ct.).

[163] *Wik Peoples* v. *Queensland* (1996), 141 A.L.R. 129 (H. Ct. Aust.).

[164] *Ibid.*; see Graham Hiley, ed., *The Wik Case: Issues and Implications* (Sydney: Butterworths, 1997).

[165] *Western Australia* v. *Ward*, [2002] H.C.A. 28 (H. Ct. Aust.).

[166] *Ibid.* at para. 22.

CONCLUSION

A major issue for Aboriginal people has been their claim that Canadian courts are Eurocentric in their perspective and have legitimized non-Aboriginal occupation and "ownership" of their traditional territories. Although the Constitution of Canada has afforded constitutional recognition and affirmation to existing Aboriginal and treaty rights, these rights are not absolute and remain subject to justifiable infringement by the Crown. *Delgamuukw* affirmed that Aboriginal oral history, which until recently had an uncertain status in Canadian evidentiary law, is admissible as evidence in Aboriginal rights and title cases. This broader approach to Aboriginal legal issues will undoubtedly bring about change as the Canadian legal system attempts to further define and clarify the rights of Aboriginal people. However, an equally important question remains: How will the courts, Aboriginal people, and public governments, through negotiations, reconcile Aboriginal title (and other Aboriginal rights) with the rights and interests of other Canadians?

Despite more than one hundred years of Canadian jurisprudence regarding Aboriginal title, some questions remain unanswered. To ascertain the nature of Aboriginal title on a case-by-case basis, the particular facts and circumstances at issue must be considered. While *Delgamuukw* assisted in clarifying the meaning of Aboriginal title, it did not deal with the nature of the full spectrum of Aboriginal rights and the practical issues of what to do with Aboriginal title in a modern capitalist society. Rather, the Supreme Court of Canada sent the issue back to trial, which will delay resolution and cost considerable time, money, and resources for all parties. *Delgamuukw* and other decisions of the Supreme Court of Canada have created a body of law that is extremely complex and, in some instances, appears to send conflicting messages. However, a careful review of the case law suggests that the Supreme Court of Canada has crafted a carefully balanced and reasonable approach to deal with Aboriginal title which much be applied thoughtfully and on a case-by-case basis.

CASES AND MATERIALS

ABORIGINAL TITLE

Royal Proclamation of 1763
R.S.C. 1985, App. II, No. 1, October 7, 1763.

By the King, A Proclamation
George R.

And whereas it is just and reasonable, and essential to our Interest, and the security of our Colonies, that the several Nations or Tribes of Indians with whom We are connected, and who live under our protection, should not be molested or disturbed in the Possession of such Parts of Our Dominions and Territories as, not having been ceded to or purchased by Us, are reserved to them or any of them, as their Hunting Grounds—We do therefore, with the Advice of our Privy Council, declare it to be our Royal Will and Pleasure, that no Governor or Commander in Chief in any of our Colonies of Quebec, East Florida, or West Florida, do presume, upon any Pretence whatever, to grant Warrants of Survey, or pass any Patents for Lands beyond the Bounds of their respective Governments, as described in their Commissions; as also that no Governor or Commander in Chief in any of our other Colonies or Plantations in America do presume for the present, and until our further Pleasure be Known, to grant warrants of Survey, or pass Patents for any Lands beyond the Heads or Sources of any of the Rivers which fall into the Atlantic Ocean from the West and North West, or upon any Lands whatever, which, not having been ceded to or purchased by Us as aforesaid, are reserved to the said Indians, or any of them.

And We do further declare it to be Our Royal Will and Pleasure, for the present as aforesaid, to reserve under our Sovereignty, Protection, and Dominion, for the use of the said Indians, all the Lands and Territories not included within the Limits of Our Said New Governments, or within the Limits of the Territory granted to the Hudson's Bay Company, as also all the Lands and Territories lying to the Westward of the Sources of the Rivers which fall into the Sea from the West and North West as aforesaid:

And We do hereby strictly forbid, on Pain of our Displeasure, all our loving subjects from making any Purchase or Settlements whatever, or taking Possession of any of the Lands above reserved, without our especial leave and Licence for the Purpose First obtained.

And, We do further strictly enjoin and require all Persons whatever who have either wilfully or inadvertently seating themselves upon any Lands within the Countries above described, or upon any other Lands which, not having been ceded to or purchased by Us, are still reserved to the said Indians as aforesaid, forthwith to remove themselves from such Settlements.

And Whereas Great Frauds and Abuses have been committed in purchasing Lands of the Indians, to the Great Prejudice of our Interests, and to the Great Dissatisfaction of the said Indians; In Order, therefore, to prevent such Irregularities for the future, and to the End that the Indians may be convinced of our Justice and determined Resolution to remove all reasonable Cause of Discontent, We do, with the Advice of our Privy Council, strictly enjoin and require, that no private Person do presume to make any Purchase from the said Indians of any Lands reserved to the said Indians, within those parts of our Colonies where, We have thought proper to allow Settlement; but that, if at any Time any of the said Indians should be inclined to dispose of the said Lands, the same shall be Purchased only for Us, in our Name, at some public Meeting or Assembly of the said Indians, to be held for the Purpose of the Governor or Commander in Chief of our Colony respectively within which they shall lie; and in case they shall lie within the limits of any Proprietary Government, they shall be purchased only for the Use and in the name of such Proprietaries, conformable to such Directions and Instructions as We or they shall think proper to give for the Purpose; And We do, by the Advice of our Privy Council, declare and enjoin, that the Trade with the said Indians shall be free and open to all our Subjects whatever, provided that every Person who may incline to Trade with the said Indians do take out a Licence for carrying on such Trade from the Governor or Commander in Chief of any of our Colonies respectively where such Person shall reside, and also give Security to observe such Regulations as We shall at any Time think fit, by ourselves or by our Commissaries to be appointed for this Purpose, to direct and appoint for the Benefit of the said Trade:

And We do hereby authorize, enjoin, and require the Governors and Commanders in Chief of all our Colonies respectively, as well those under Our immediate Government as those under the Government and Direction of Proprietaries, to grant such Licences without Fee or Regard, taking especial care to insert therein a Condition, that such Licence shall be void, and the Security forfeited in the case the Person to whom the same is granted shall refuse or neglect to observe such Regulations as We shall think proper to prescribe as aforesaid.

And We do further expressly enjoin and require all Officers whatever, as well Military as those Employed in the Management and Direction of Indian Affairs, within the Territories reserved as aforesaid for the Use of the said Indians, to seize and apprehend all Persons whatever, who standing charged with Treason, Misprisons of Treason, Murders, or other Felonies or Misdemeanors, shall fly from Justice and take Refuge in the said Territory, and to send them under a proper Guard to the Colony where the Crime was committed of which they stand accused, in order to take their Trial for the same.

Given at our Court at St. James's the 7th Day of October, 1763, in the Third Year of our Reign.
GOD SAVE THE KING

St. Catherine's Milling and Lumber Company v. *R.* (1888)

14 App. Cas. 46 (J.C.P.C.). The Earl of Selborne, Lord Watson, Lord Hobhouse, Sir Barnes Peacock, Sir Montague E. Smith, and Sir Richard Couch, December 12, 1888.

The judgment of their Lordships was delivered by LORD WATSON:—On the 3rd of October, 1873, a formal treaty or contract was concluded between commissioners appointed by the Government of the Dominion of Canada, on behalf of Her Majesty the Queen, of the one part, and a number of chiefs and headmen duly chosen to represent the Salteaux tribe of Ojibbeway Indians, of the other part, by which the latter, for certain considerations, released and surrendered to the Government of the Dominion, for Her Majesty and her successors, the whole right and title of the Indian inhabitants whom they represented, to a tract of country upwards of 50,000 square miles in extent. By an article of the treaty it is stipulated that, subject to such regulations as may be made by the Dominion Government, the Indians are to have right to pursue their avocations of hunting and fishing throughout the surrendered territory, with the exception of those portions of it which may, from time to time, be required or taken up for settlement, mining, lumbering, or other purposes.

Of the territory thus ceded to the Crown, an area of not less than 32,000 square miles is situated within the boundaries of the Province of Ontario; and, with respect to that area, a controversy has arisen between the Dominion and Ontario, each of them maintaining that the legal effect of extinguishing the Indian title has been to transmit to itself the entire beneficial interest of the lands, as now vested in the Crown, freed from incumbrance of any kind, save the qualified privilege of hunting and fishing mentioned in the treaty.

Acting on the assumption that the beneficial interest in these lands had passed to the Dominion Government, their Crown Timber Agent, on the 1st of May, 1883, issued to the appellants, the St. Catherine's Milling and Lumber Company, a permit to cut and carry away one million feet of lumber from a specified portion of the disputed area. The appellants having availed themselves of that licence, a writ was filed against them in the Chancery Division of the High Court of Ontario, at the instance of the Queen on the information of the Attorney-General of the Province, praying—(1) a declaration that the appellants have no rights in respect of the timber cut by them upon the lands specified in their permit; (2) an injunction restraining them from trespassing on the premises and from cutting any timber thereon; (3) an injunction against the removal of timber already cut; and (4) decree for the damage occasioned by their wrongful acts. . . .

The territory in dispute has been in Indian occupation from the date of the proclamation until 1873. During that interval of time Indian affairs have been administered successively by the Crown, by the Provincial Governments, and (since the passing of the British North America Act, 1867), by the Government of the Dominion. The policy of these administrations has been all along the same in this respect, that the Indian inhabitants have been precluded from entering into any transaction with a subject for the sale or transfer of their interest in the land, and have only been permitted to surrender their rights to the Crown by a formal contract, duly ratified in a meeting of their chiefs or head men convened for the purpose. Whilst there have been changes in the administrative authority, there has been no change since the year 1763 in the character of the interest which its Indian inhabitants had in the lands surrendered by the treaty. Their possession, such as it was, can only be ascribed to the general provisions made by the royal proclamation in favour of all Indian tribes then living under the sovereignty and protection of the British Crown. It was suggested in the course of the argument for the Dominion, that inasmuch as the proclamation recites that the territories thereby reserved for Indians had never "been ceded to or purchased by" the Crown, the entire property of the land remained with them. That inference is, however, at variance with the terms of the instrument, which shew that the tenure of the Indians was a personal and usufructuary right, dependent upon the good will of the Sovereign. The lands reserved are expressly stated to be "parts of Our dominions and territories;" and it is declared to be the will and pleasure of the sovereign that, "for the present," they shall be reserved for the use of the Indians, as their hunting grounds, under his protection and dominion. There was a great deal of learned discussion at the Bar with respect to the precise quality of the Indian right, but their lordships do not consider it necessary to express any opinion upon the point. It appears to them to be sufficient for the purposes of this case that there has been all along vested in the Crown a substantial and paramount estate, underlying the Indian title, which became a plenum dominium whenever that title was surrendered or otherwise extinguished.

By an Imperial statute passed in the year 1840 (3 & 4 Vict. c. 35), the provinces of Ontario and Quebec, then known as Upper and Lower Canada, were united under the name of the Province of Canada, and it was, inter alia, enacted that, in consideration of certain annual payments which Her Majesty had agreed to accept by way of civil list, the produce of all territorial and other revenues at the disposal of the Crown arising in either of the united Provinces should be paid into the consolidated fund of the new Province. There was no transfer to the Province of any legal estate in the Crown lands, which continued to be vested in the Sovereign; but all moneys realized by sales or in any other manner became the property of the Province. In other words, all beneficial interest in such lands within the provincial boundaries belong to the Queen, and either producing or capable of producing revenue, passed to the Province, the title still remaining in the Crown. That continued to be the right of the Province until the passing of the British North America Act, 1867. Had the Indian inhabitants of the area in question released their interest in it to the Crown at any time between 1840 and the date of that Act, it does not seem to admit of doubt, and it was not disputed by the learned counsel for the Dominion, that all revenues derived from its being taken up for settlement, mining, lumbering, and other purposes would have been the property of the Province of Canada. The case maintained for the appellants is that the Act of 1867 transferred to the Dominion all interest in Indian lands which previously belonged to the Province.

The Act of 1867, which created the Federal Government, repealed the Act of 1840, and restored the Upper and Lower Canadas to the condition of separate Provinces, under the titles of Ontario and Quebec, due provision being made (sect. 142) for the division between them of the property and assets of the United Province, with the exception of certain items specified in the fourth schedule, which are still held by them jointly. The

Act also contains careful provisions for the distribution of legislative powers and of revenues and assets between the respective Provinces included in the Union, on the one hand, and the Dominion, on the other. The conflicting claims to the ceded territory maintained by the Dominion and the Province of Ontario are wholly dependent upon these statutory provisions. In construing these enactments, it must always be kept in view that, wherever public land with its incidents is described as "the property of" or as "belonging to" the Dominion or a Province, these expressions merely import that the right to its beneficial use, or to its proceeds, has been appropriated to the Dominion or the Province, as the case may be, and is subject to the control of its legislature, the land itself being vested in the Crown.

Sect. 108 enacts that the public works and undertakings enumerated in Schedule 3 shall be the property of Canada. As specified in the schedule, these consist of public undertakings which might be fairly considered to exist for the benefit of all the Provinces federally united, of lands and buildings necessary for carrying on the customs or postal service of the Dominion, or required for the purpose of national defence, and of "lands set apart for general public purposes." It is obvious that the enumeration cannot be reasonably held to include Crown lands which are reserved for Indian use. The only other clause in the Act by which a share of what previously constituted provincial revenues and assets is directly assigned to the Dominion is sect. 102. It enacts that all "duties and revenues" over which the respective legislatures of the United Provinces had and have power of appropriation, "except such portions thereof as are by this Act reserved to the respective legislatures of the Provinces, or are raised by them in accordance with the special powers conferred upon them by this Act," shall form one consolidated fund, to be appropriated for the public service of Canada. The extent to which duties and revenues arising within the limits of Ontario, and over which the legislature of the old Province of Canada possessed the power of appropriation before the passing of the Act, have been transferred to the Dominion by this clause, can only be ascertained by reference to the two exceptions which it makes in favour of the new provincial legislatures.

The second of these exceptions has really no bearing on the present case, because it comprises nothing beyond the revenues which provincial legislatures are empowered to raise by means of direct taxation for Provincial purposes, in terms of sect. 92(2). The first of them, which appears to comprehend the whole sources of revenue reserved to the provinces by sect. 109, is of material consequence. Sect. 109 provides that "all lands, mines, minerals, and royalties belonging to the several Provinces of Canada, Nova Scotia, and New Brunswick, at the union, and all sums then due or payable for such lands, mines, minerals, or royalties, shall belong to the several Provinces of Ontario, Quebec, Nova Scotia, and New Brunswick, in which the same are situate or arise, subject to any trusts existing in respect thereof, and to any interest other than that of the Province in the same." In connection with this clause it may be observed that, by sect. 117, it is declared that the Provinces shall retain their respective public property not otherwise disposed of in the Act, subject to the right of Canada to assume any lands or public property required for fortifications or for the defence of the country. A different form of expression is used to define the subject-matter of the first exception, and the property which is directly appropriated to the Provinces; but it hardly admits of doubt that the interests in land, mines, minerals, and royalties, which by sect. 109 are declared to belong to the Provinces, include, if they are not identical with, the "duties and revenues" first excepted in sect. 102. . . .

Had its Indian inhabitants been the owners in fee simple of the territory which they surrendered by the treaty of 1873, *Attorney-General of Ontario* v. *Mercer* (8 App. Cas. 767) might have been an authority for holding that the Province of Ontario could derive no benefit from the cession, in respect that the land was not vested in the Crown at the time of the union. But that was not the character of the Indian interest. The Crown has all along had a present proprietary estate in the land, upon which the Indian title was a mere burden. The ceded territory was at the time of the union, land vested in the Crown, subject to "an interest other than that of the Province in the same," within the meaning of sect. 109; and must now belong to Ontario in terms of that clause, unless its rights have been taken away by some provision of the Act of 1867 other than those already noticed.

In the course of the argument the claim of the Dominion to the ceded territory was rested upon the provisions of sect. 91(24), which in express terms confer upon the Parliament of Canada power to make laws for "Indians, and lands reserved for the Indians." It was urged that the exclusive power of legislation and administration carried with it, by necessary implication, any patrimonial interest which the Crown might have had in the reserved lands. In reply to that reasoning, counsel for Ontario referred us to a series of provincial statutes prior in date to the Act of 1867, for the purpose of shewing that the expression "Indian reserves" was used in legislative language to designate certain lands in which the Indians had, after the royal proclamation of 1763, acquired a special interest, by treaty or otherwise, and did not apply to land occupied by them in virtue of the proclamation. The argument might have deserved consideration if the expression had been adopted by the British Parliament in 1867, but it does not occur in sect. 91(24), and the words actually used are, according to their natural meaning, sufficient to include all lands reserved, upon any terms or conditions, for Indian occupation. It appears to be the plain policy of the Act that, in order to ensure uniformity of administration, all such lands, and Indian affairs generally, shall be under the legislative control of one central authority.

Their Lordships are, however, unable to assent to the argument for the Dominion founded on sect. 92 (24). There can be no *a priori* probability that the British Legislature, in a branch of the statute which professes to deal only with the distribution of legislative power, intended to deprive the Provinces of rights which are expressly given them in that branch of it which relates to the distribution of revenues and assets. The fact that the power of legislating for Indians, and for lands which are reserved to their use, has been entrusted to the Parliament of the Dominion is not in the least degree inconsistent with the right of the Provinces to a beneficial interest in these lands, available to them as a source of revenue whenever the estate of the Crown is disencumbered of the Indian title.

By the treaty of 1873 the Indian inhabitants ceded and released the territory in dispute, in order that it might be opened up for settlement, immigration, and such other purpose as to Her Majesty might seem fit, "to the Government of the Dominion of Canada," for the Queen and Her successors for ever. It was argued that a cession in these terms was in effect a conveyance to the Dominion Government of the whole rights of the Indians, with consent of the Crown. That is not the natural import of the language of the treaty, which purports to be from beginning to end a transaction between the Indians and the Crown; and the surrender is in substance made to the Crown. Even if its language had been more favourable to the argument of the Dominion upon this point, it is abundantly clear that the commissioners who represented Her Majesty, whilst they had full authority to accept a surrender to the Crown, had neither authority nor power to take away from Ontario the interest which had been assigned to that province by the Imperial Statute of 1867.

These considerations appear to their Lordships to be sufficient for the disposal of this appeal. The treaty leaves the Indians no right whatever to the timber growing upon the lands which they gave up, which is now fully vested in the Crown, all revenues derivable from the sale of such portions of it as are situate within the boundaries of Ontario being the property of that Province. The fact, that it still possesses exclusive power to regulate the Indians' privilege of hunting and fishing, cannot confer upon the Dominion power to dispose, by issuing permits or otherwise, of that beneficial interest in the timber which has now passed to Ontario. Seeing that the benefit of the surrender accrues to her, Ontario must, of course, relieve the Crown, and the Dominion, of all obligations involving the payment of money which were undertaken by Her Majesty, and which are said to have been in part fulfilled by the Dominion Government. There may be other questions behind, with respect to the right to determine to what extent, and at what periods, the disputed territory, over which the Indians still exercise their avocations of hunting and fishing, is to be taken up for settlement or other purposes, but none of these questions are raised for decision in the present suit.

Their Lordships will therefore humbly advise Her Majesty that the judgment of the Supreme Court of Canada ought to be affirmed, and the appeal dismissed.

Calder v. *A.G.(B.C.)* (1973)

[1973] S.C.R. 313 (S.C.C.). Martland, Judson, Ritchie, Hall, Spence, Pigeon, and Laskin JJ., January 31, 1973.

MARTLAND J., concurs with JUDSON J.

JUDSON, J.:—The appellants sue, as representatives of the Nishga Indian Tribe, for a declaration "that the aboriginal title, otherwise known as the Indian title, of the Plaintiffs . . . has never been lawfully extinguished." The action was dismissed at trial. The Court of Appeal rejected the appeal. The appellants appeal from both decisions. . . .

Any Canadian inquiry into the nature of the Indian title must begin with *R.* v. *St. Catherine's Milling & Lumber Co.* v. *The Queen* (1888), 14 App. Cas. 46. . . .

The decision throughout was that the extinction of the Indian title enured to the benefit of the Province and that it was not possible for the Dominion to preserve that title so as to oust the vested right of the Province to the land as part of the public domain of Ontario. It was held that the Crown had at all times a present proprietary estate, which title, after Confederation, was in the Province, by virtue of s. 109 of the *B.N.A. Act*. The Indian title was a mere burden upon that title which, following the cession of the lands under the treaty, was extinguished.

The reasons for judgment delivered in the Canadian Courts in the *St. Catherine's* case were strongly influenced by two early judgments delivered in the Supreme Court of the United States by Chief Justice Marshall—*Johnson* v. *M'Intosh* (1823), 8 Wheaton 543, and *Worcester* v. *State of Georgia* (1832), 6 Peters 515. In *Johnson* v. *M'Intosh* the actual decision was that a title to lands, under grants to private individuals, made by Indian tribes or nations north-west of the river Ohio, in 1773 and 1775, could not be recognized in the Courts of the United States. In *Worcester* v. *Georgia*, the plaintiff, who was a missionary, was charged with residing among the Cherokees without a licence from the State of Georgia. His defence was that his residence was in conformity with treaties between the United States and the Cherokee nation and that the law under which he was charged was repugnant to the constitution, treaties and laws of the United States. The Supreme Court made a declaration to this effect. Both cases raised the question of aboriginal title to land. The following passage from 8 Wheaton at pp. 587–8 gives a clear summary of the views of the Chief Justice:

> The United States, then, have unequivocally acceded to that great and broad rule by which its civilized inhabitants now hold this country. They hold, and assert in themselves, the title by which it was acquired. They maintain, as all others have maintained, that discovery gave an exclusive right to extinguish the Indian title of occupancy, either by purchase or by conquest; and gave also a right to such a degree of sovereignty, as the circumstances of the people would allow them to exercise.
>
> The power now possessed by the government of the United States to grant lands, resided, while we were colonies, in the crown, or its grantees. The validity of the titles given by either has never been questioned in our Courts. It has been exercised uniformly over territory in possession of the Indians. The existence of this power must negative the existence of any right which may conflict with, and control it. An absolute title to lands cannot exist, at the same time in different persons, or in different governments. An absolute, must be an exclusive title, or at least a title which excludes all others not compatible with it. All our institutions recognise the absolute title of the crown, subject only to the Indian right of occupancy, and recognise the absolute title of the crown to extinguish that right. This is incompatible with an absolute and complete title in the Indians.

The description of the nature of Indian title in the Canadian Courts in the *St. Catherine's* case is repeated in the reasons delivered in the Privy Council. . . .

There can be no doubt that the Privy Council [in the *St. Catherine's* case] found that the *Proclamation of 1763* was the origin of the Indian title—"Their possession, such as it was, can only be ascribed to the . . . royal proclamation in favour of all Indian tribes then living under the sovereignty and protection of the British Crown."

I do not take these reasons to mean that the Proclamation was the exclusive source of Indian title. The territory in the *St. Catherine's* appeal was clearly within the geographical limits set out in the Proclamation. It is part of the appellants' case that the Proclamation does apply to the Nishga territory and that they are entitled to its protection. They also say that if it does not apply to the Nishga territory, their Indian title is still entitled to recognition by the Courts. These are two distinct questions. . . .

Following the Treaty of Paris, General Murray was appointed the first Governor of Quebec. By Royal Proclamation, dated October 7, 1763 . . . , which accompanied his commission, he was directed with respect to Indians that he should "upon no account molest or disturb them in the possession of such parts of the said province as they at present occupy or possess".

The Crown created four distinct and separate Governments, styled, respectively, Quebec, East Florida, West Florida and Grenada, specific boundaries being assigned to each of them. Upon the recital that it was just and reasonable that the several nations and tribes of Indians, who lived under British protection, should not be molested or disturbed in the "Possession of such Parts of Our Dominions and Territories as, not having been ceded to or purchased by Us, are reserved to them or any of them, as their Hunting Grounds", it is declared that no Governor or Commander-in-Chief in any of the new Colonies of Quebec, East Florida or West Florida, do presume on any pretence to grant warrants of survey or pass any patents for lands beyond the bounds of their respective Governments or, "until our further Pleasure be Known," upon any lands whatever which, not having been ceded or purchased as aforesaid, are reserved to the said Indians or any of them. It was further declared "to be Our Royal Will and Pleasure, for the present as aforesaid, to reserve under our Sovereignty, Protection, and Dominion, for the use of the said Indians, all the lands and Territories not included . . . within the Limits of the Territory granted to the Hudson's Bay Company". The Proclamation also provides that no private person shall make any purchase from the Indians of lands reserved to them within those Colonies where settlement was permitted, and that all purchases must be on behalf of the Crown, in a public assembly of the Indians, by the Governor or Commander-in-Chief of the Colony in which the lands lie.

It is clear, as the British Columbia Courts have held, and whose reasons I adopt, that the Nishga bands represented by the appellants were not any of the several nations or tribes of Indians who lived under British protection and were outside the scope of the Proclamation. . . .

As to the establishment of British sovereignty in British Columbia in 1818 by a Convention of Commerce between His Majesty and the United States of America, the British Crown and the United States settled the boundary to the height of land in the Rockies, referred to in the Convention as the "Stoney Mountains". The boundary was the 49th parallel of latitude. The Convention provided for the joint occupancy of the lands to the west of that point for a term of 10 years. This Convention was extended indefinitely by a further Convention in 1827.

The area in question in this action never did come under British sovereignty until the Treaty of Oregon in 1846. This treaty extended the boundary along the 49th parallel from the point of termination, as previously laid down, to the channel separating the Continent from Vancouver Island, and thus through the Gulf Islands to Fuca's Straits. The Oregon Treaty was, in effect, a treaty of cession whereby American claims were ceded to Great Britain. There was no mention of Indian rights in any of these Conventions or the treaty. . . .

When the Colony of British Columbia was established in 1858, there can be no doubt that the Nishga territory became part of it. The fee was in the Crown in right of the Colony until July 20, 1871, when the Colony entered Confederation, and thereafter in the Crown in light of the Province of British Columbia, except only in respect of those lands transferred to the Dominion under the Terms of Union. . . .

Although I think that it is clear that Indian title in British Columbia cannot owe its origin to the *Proclamation of 1763*, the fact is that when the settlers came, the Indians were there, organized in societies and occupying the land as their forefathers had done for centuries. This is what Indian title means and it does not help one in the solution of this problem to call it a "personal or usufructuary right". What they are asserting in this action is that they had a right to continue to live on their lands as their forefathers had lived and that this right has never been lawfully extinguished. There can be no question that this right was "dependent on the goodwill of the Sovereign".

It was the opinion of the British Columbia Courts that this right, if it ever existed, had been lawfully extinguished, that with two societies in competition for land—the white settlers demanding orderly settlement and the Indians demanding to be let alone—the proper authorities deliberately chose to set apart reserves for Indians in various parts of the territory and open up the rest for settlements. They held that this had been done when British Columbia entered Confederation in 1871 and that the Terms of Union recognized this fact. . . .

From what I have already said, it is apparent that before 1871 there were no treaties between the Indian tribes and the Colony relating to lands on the mainland. From the material filed, it appears that on Vancouver Island there were, in all, fourteen purchases of Indian lands in the area surrounding Fort Victoria. These are the ones referred to in the correspondence between James Douglas and the Colonial Office. In 1899, Treaty 8 was negotiated and certain tribes of northeastern British Columbia were grouped with the Cree, Beaver, Chipewyan, Alberta and Northwest Territories' tribes, and included in the treaty. The area covered by this treaty is vast—both in the Northwest Territories and northeastern British Columbia. There can be no doubt that by this treaty the Indians surrendered their rights in both areas. . . .

In my opinion, in the present case, the sovereign authority elected to exercise complete dominion over the lands in question, adverse to any right of occupancy which the Nishga Tribe might have had, when, by legislation, it opened up such lands for settlement, subject to the reserves of land set aside for Indian occupation. . . .

For the foregoing reasons I have reached the conclusion that this action fails and that the appeal should be dismissed. . . .

I would dismiss the appeal. . . .

RITCHIE J., concurs with JUDSON, J.

HALL, J. (dissenting):—This appeal raises issues of vital importance to the Indians of northern British Columbia and, in particular, to those of the Nishga tribe. The Nishga tribe has persevered for almost a century in asserting an interest in the lands which their ancestors occupied since time immemorial. The Nishgas were never conquered nor did they at any time enter into a treaty or deed of surrender as many other Indian tribes did throughout Canada and in southern British Columbia. The Crown has never granted the lands in issue in this action other than a few small parcels later referred to prior to the commencement of the action. . . .

The assessment and interpretation of the historical documents and enactments tendered in evidence must be approached in the light of present-day research and knowledge disregarding ancient concepts formulated when understanding of the customs and culture of our original people was rudimentary and incomplete and when they were thought to be wholly without cohesion, laws or culture, in effect a subhuman species. This concept of the original inhabitants of America led Chief Justice Marshall in his otherwise enlightened judgment in *Johnson and Graham's Lessee v. M'Intosh* (1823), 8 Wheaton 543, which is the outstanding judicial pronouncement on the subject of Indian rights to say [8 Wheaton 590], "But the tribes of Indians inhabiting this country were fierce savages, whose occupation was war. . . ." We now know that assessment was ill-founded. The Indians did in fact at times engage in some tribal wars but war was not their vocation and it can be said that their preoccupation with war pales into insignificance when compared to the religious and dynastic wars of "civilized" Europe of the 16th and 17th centuries. Chief Justice Marshall was, of course, speaking with the knowledge available to him in 1823. Chief Justice Davey in the judgment under appeal [13 D.L.R. (3d) 64,74 W.W.R. 481], with all the historical research and material available since 1823 and notwithstanding the evidence in the record which Gould, J. [8 D.L.R. (3d) 59, 71 W.W.R. 81], found was given "with total integrity", said of the Indians of the mainland of British Columbia [p. 66]:

> . . . they were undoubtedly at the time of settlement a very primitive people with few of the institutions of civilized society, and none at all of our notions of private property.

In so saying this in 1970, he was assessing the Indian culture of 1858 by the same standards that the Europeans applied to the Indians of North America two or more centuries before. . . .

In enumerating the indicia of ownership, the trial Judge overlooked that possession is of itself proof of ownership. *Prima facie*, therefore, the Nishgas are the owners of the lands that have been in their possession from time immemorial and, therefore the burden of establishing that their right has been extinguished rests squarely on the respondent.

What emerges from the foregoing evidence is the following: the Nishgas in fact are, and were from time immemorial a distinctive cultural entity with concepts of ownership indigenous to their culture and capable of articulation under the common law having, in the words of Dr. Duff, "developed their culture to higher peaks in many respects than in any other part of the continent north of Mexico". A remarkable confirmation of this statement comes from Captain Cook who, in 1778, at Cape Newenham claimed the land for Great Britain. He reported having gone ashore and entered one of the native houses which he said was 150 ft. in length, 24 to 30 ft. wide and 7 to 8 ft. high and that "there were no native buildings to compare with these north of Mexico". The report continues that Cook's officers were full of admiration for the skill and patience required to erect these buildings which called for a considerable knowledge of engineering.

While the Nishga claim had not heretofore been litigated, there is a wealth of jurisprudence affirming common law recognition of aboriginal rights to possession and enjoyment of lands of aborigines precisely analogous to the Nishga situation here. . . .

The dominant and recurring proposition stated by Chief Justice Marshall in *Johnson* v. *M'Intosh* is that on discovery or on conquest the aborigines of newly-found lands were conceded to be the rightful occupants of the soil with a legal as well as a just claim to retain possession of it and to use it according to their own discretion, but their rights to complete sovereignty as independent nations were necessarily diminished and their power to dispose of the soil on their own will to whomsoever they pleased was denied by the original fundamental principle that discovery or conquest gave exclusive title to those who made it. . . .

Paralleling and supporting the claim of the Nishgas that they have a certain right or title to the lands in question is the guarantee of Indian rights contained in the Proclamation of 1763. This Proclamation was an Executive Order having the force and effect of an Act of Parliament and was described by Gwynne, J., in *St. Catherine's Milling* case at (1887), 13 S.C.R. 577 at 652 as the "Indian Bill of Rights"; see also *Campbell* v. *Hall*. Its force as a statute is analogous to the status of Magna Carta which has always been considered to be the law throughout the Empire. It was a law which followed the flag as England assumed jurisdiction over newly-discovered or acquired lands or territories. It follows, therefore, that the *Colonial Laws Validity Act*, 1865 (U.K.), c. 63, applied to make the Proclamation the law of British Columbia. That it was regarded as being the law of England is clear from the fact that when it was deemed advisable to amend it the amendment was affected by an Act of Parliament, namely the *Quebec Act* of 1774 [1774 (U.K.) (14 Geo. III), c. 83].

In respect of this Proclamation, it can be said that when other exploring nations were showing a ruthless disregard of native rights England adopted a remarkably enlightened attitude towards the Indians of North America. The Proclamation must be regarded as a fundamental document upon which any just determination of original rights rests. Its effect was discussed by Idington, J., in this Court in *Province of Ontario* v. *Dominion of Canada* (1909), 42 S.C.R. 1 at pp. 103–4 [affd [1910] A.C. 637], as follows:

> A line of *policy* begotten of prudence, humanity and justice adopted by the British Crown to be observed in all future dealings with the Indians in respect of such rights as they might suppose themselves to possess was outlined in the *Royal Proclamation of 1763*

erecting, after the Treaty of Paris in that year, amongst others, a separate government for Quebec, ceded by that treaty to the British Crown.

That policy adhered to thenceforward, by those responsible for the honour of the Crown led to many treaties whereby Indians agreed to surrender such rights as they were supposed to have in areas respectively specified in such treaties.

In these surrendering treaties there generally were reserves provided for Indians making such surrenders to enter into or be confined to for purposes of residence.

The history of this mode of dealing is very fully outlined in the judgment of the learned Chancellor Boyd in the case of *The Queen v. St. Catherine's Milling Co.*, 10 O.R. 196 (affirmed 13 O.A.R. 148). [Italics added.]

The question of the Proclamation's applicability to the Nishgas is, accordingly, relevant in this appeal. The point has been before provincial Courts in Canada on a number of occasions but never specifically dealt with by this Court. . . .

The wording of the Proclamation itself seems quite clear that it was intended to include the lands west of the Rocky Mountains. . . .

The only territories not included were: (1) Those within the limits of the three new Governments; and (2) within the limits of the territory granted to the Hudson's Bay Company. The concluding sentence of the paragraph just quoted, "as also all the Lands and Territories lying to the Westward of the Sources of the Rivers which fall into the Sea from the West and North West as aforesaid; shows clearly that the framers of the paragraph were well aware that there was territory to the west of the sources of the rivers which ran from the west and north-west. . . .

This important question remains: were the rights either at common law or under the Proclamation extinguished? Tysoe, J.A., said in this regard at p. 95 [13 D.L.R. (3d) 59] of his reasons: "It is true, as the appellants have submitted, *that nowhere can one find express words extinguishing Indian title* . . ." (emphasis added).

The parties here agree that if extinguishment was accomplished, it must have occurred between 1858 and when British Columbia joined Confederation in 1871. The respondent relies on what was done by Governor Douglas and by his successor, Frederick Seymour, who became Governor in 1864. . . .

The appellants rely on the presumption that the British Crown intended to respect native rights; therefore, when the Nishga people came under British sovereignty (and that is subject to what I said about sovereignty over part of the lands not being determined until 1903) they were entitled to assert, as a legal right, their Indian title. It being a legal right, it could not thereafter be extinguished except by surrender to the Crown or by competent legislative authority, and then only by specific legislation. There was no surrender by the Nishgas and neither the Colony of British Columbia nor the Province, after Confederation, enacted legislation specifically purporting to extinguish the Indian title nor did Parliament at Ottawa. . . .

It would, accordingly, appear to be beyond question that the onus of proving that the Sovereign intended to extinguish the Indian title lies on the respondent and that intention must be "clear and plain". There is no such proof in the case at bar; no legislation to that effect.

The Court of Appeal also erred in holding that there "is no Indian Title capable of judicial interpretation . . . unless it has previously been recognized either by the Legislature or the Executive Branch of Government" [see 13 D.L.R. (3d) 59 at 70]. Relying on *Cook et al. v. Sprigg*, [1899] A.C. 572, and other cases, the Court of Appeal erroneously applied what is called the Act of State Doctrine. This doctrine denies a remedy to the citizens of an acquired territory for invasion of their rights which may occur during the change of sovereignty. English Courts have held that a municipal Court has no jurisdiction to review the manner in which the Sovereign acquires new territory. The Act of State is the activity of the Sovereign by which he acquires the property. Professor D. P. O'Connell in his work *International Law*, 2nd ed. (1970), at p. 378 says:

> This doctrine, which was affirmed in several cases arising out of the acquisition of territory in Africa and India, has been misinterpreted to the effect that the substantive rights themselves have not survived the change. In fact English courts have gone out of their way to repudiate the construction, and it is clear that the Act of State doctrine is no more than a procedural bar to municipal law action, and as such is irrelevant to the question whether in international law change of sovereignty affects acquired rights.

The Act of State doctrine has no application in the present appeal for the following reasons: (a) It has never been invoked in claims dependent on aboriginal title. An examination of its rationale indicates that it would be quite inappropriate for the Courts to extend the doctrine to such cases: (b) It is based on the premise that an Act of State is an exercise of the Sovereign power which a municipal Court has no power to review: see *Salaman* v. *Secretary of State in Council of India*, [1906] 1 K.B. 613 at pp. 639–40; *Cook* v. *Sprigg, supra,* at p. 578. . . .

Once it is apparent that the Act of State doctrine has no application, the whole argument of the respondent that there must be some form of "recognition" of aboriginal rights falls to the ground.

On the question of extinguishment, the respondent relies on what was done by Governors Douglas and Seymour and the Council of British Columbia. The appellants, as I have previously mentioned, say that if either Douglas or Seymour or the Council of the Colony of British Columbia did purport to extinguish the Nishga title that any such attempt was beyond the powers of either the Governors or of the Council and that what, if anything, was attempted in this respect was *ultra vires*. . . .

If in any of the Proclamations or actions of Douglas, Seymour or of the Council of the Colony of British Columbia there are elements which the respondent says extinguish by implication the Indian title, then it is obvious from the Commission of the Governor and from the Instructions under which the Governor was required to observe and neither the Commission nor the Instructions contain any power or authorization to extinguish the Indian title, then it follows logically that if any attempt was made to extinguish the title it was beyond the power of the Governor or of the Council to do so and, therefore, *ultra vires*. . . .

Having reviewed the evidence and cases in considerable detail and having decided that if the Nishgas ever had any right or title that it had been extinguished, Tysoe J.A., was inexorably driven to the conclusion which he stated as follows [13 D.L.R. (3d) 59 at 94]:

> As a result of these pieces of legislation the Indians of the Colony of British Columbia *became in law trespassers* on and liable to actions of ejectment from lands in the Colony other than those set aside as reserves for the use of Indians. (Emphasis added.)

Any reasoning that would lead to such a conclusion must necessarily be fallacious. The idea is self-destructive. If trespassers, the Indians are liable to prosecution as such, a proposition which reason itself repudiates. . . .

I would, therefore, allow the appeal with costs throughout and declare that the appellants' right to possession of the lands delineated in ex. 2 with the exceptions before mentioned and their right to enjoy the fruits of the soil, of the forest, and of the rivers and streams within the boundaries of said lands have not been extinguished by the Province of British Columbia or by its predecessor, the Colony of British Columbia, or by the Governors of that Colony.

SPENCE, J., concurs with HALL, J.

PIGEON, J.:— . . . I have to hold that the preliminary objection that the declaration prayed for, being a claim of title against the Crown in the right of the Province of British Columbia, the Court has no jurisdiction to make it in the absence of a fiat of the Lieutenant-Governor of that Province. I am deeply conscious of the hardship involved in holding that the access to the Court for the determination of the plaintiffs' claim is barred by sovereign immunity from suit without a fiat. However, I would point out that in the United States, claims in respect of the taking of lands outside of reserves and not covered by any treaty were not held justiciable until legislative provisions had removed the obstacle created by the doctrine of immunity. In Canada, immunity from suit has been removed by legislation at the federal level and in most Provinces. However, this has not yet been done in British Columbia.

I would therefore dismiss the appeal. . . .

LASKIN, J., concurs with HALL, J. . . .

Delgamuukw v. *British Columbia* (1997)

[1997] 3 S.C.R. 1010 (S.C.C.). Lamer C.J., and LaForest, L'Heureux-Dubé, Sopinka (took no part in judgment), Cory, McLachlin, and Major JJ., December 11, 1997.

LAMER, C.J. (CORY, MCLACHLIN AND MAJOR JJ. concurring):

1   This appeal is the latest in a series of cases in which it has fallen to this Court to interpret and apply the guarantee of existing Aboriginal rights found in s. 35(1) of the *Constitution Act, 1982*. Although that line of decisions, commencing with *R.* v. *Sparrow*, [1990] 1 S.C.R. 1075, proceeding through the *Van der Peet* trilogy (*R.* v. *Van der Peet*, [1996] 2 S.C.R. 507, *R.* v. *N. T. C. Smokehouse Ltd.*, [1996] 2 S.C.R. 672, and *R.* v. *Gladstone*, [1996] 2 S.C.R. 723), and ending in *R.* v. *Pamajewon*, [1996] 2 S.C.R. 821, *R.* v. *Adams*, [1996] 3 S.C.R. 101, and *R.* v. *Côté*, [1996] 3 S.C.R. 139, have laid down the jurisprudential framework for s. 35(1), this appeal raises a set of interrelated and novel questions which revolve around a single issue—the nature and scope of the constitutional protection afforded by s. 35(1) to common law Aboriginal title.

2   In *Adams*, and in the companion decision in *Côté*, I considered and rejected the proposition that claims to Aboriginal rights must also be grounded in an underlying claim to Aboriginal title. But I held, nevertheless, that Aboriginal title was a distinct species of Aboriginal right that was recognized and affirmed by s. 35(1). Since Aboriginal title was not being claimed in those earlier appeals, it was unnecessary to say more. This appeal demands, however, that the Court now explore and elucidate the implications of the constitutionalization of Aboriginal title. The first is the specific content of Aboriginal title, a question which this Court has not yet definitively addressed, either at common law or under s. 35(1). The second is the related question of the test for the proof of title, which, whatever its content, is a right in land, and its relationship to the definition of the Aboriginal rights recognized and affirmed by s. 35(1) in *Van der Peet* in terms of activities. The third is whether Aboriginal title, as a right in land, mandates a modified approach to the test of justification first laid down in *Sparrow* and elaborated upon in *Gladstone*.

3   In addition to the relationship between Aboriginal title and s. 35(1), this appeal

also raises an important practical problem relevant to the proof of Aboriginal title which is endemic to Aboriginal rights litigation generally—the treatment of the oral histories of Canada's Aboriginal peoples by the courts. In *Van der Peet*, I held that the common law rules of evidence should be adapted to take into account the *sui generis* nature of Aboriginal rights. In this appeal, the Court must address what specific form those modifications must take.

4   Finally, given the existence of Aboriginal title in British Columbia, this Court must address, on cross-appeal, the question of whether the province of British Columbia, from the time it joined Confederation in 1871, until the entrenchment of s. 35(1) in 1982, had jurisdiction to extinguish the rights of Aboriginal peoples, including Aboriginal title, in that province. Moreover, if the province was without this jurisdiction, a further question arises—whether provincial laws of general application that would otherwise be inapplicable to Indians and Indian lands could nevertheless extinguish Aboriginal rights through the operation of s. 88 of the *Indian Act*, R.S.C., 1985, c. I-5. . . .

A. Do the pleadings preclude the Court from entertaining claims for Aboriginal title and self-government?

73   In their pleadings, the appellants, 51 Chiefs representing most of the houses of the Gitksan and Wet'suwet'en nations, originally advanced 51 individual claims on their own behalf and on behalf of their houses for "ownership" and "jurisdiction" over 133 distinct territories which together comprise 58,000 square kilometres of northwestern British Columbia. On appeal, that original claim was altered in two different ways. First, the claims for ownership and jurisdiction have been replaced with claims for Aboriginal title and self-government, respectively. Second, the individual claims by each house have been amalgamated into two communal claims, one advanced on behalf of each nation. However, there were no formal amendments to the pleadings to this effect, and the respondents accordingly argue that claims which are central to this appeal are not properly before the Court. Furthermore, the respondents argue that they have suffered prejudice as a result because they might have conducted the defence quite differently had they known the case to meet.

74   I reject the respondents' submission with respect to the substitution of Aboriginal title and self-government for the original claims of ownership and jurisdiction. Although it is true that the pleadings were not formally amended, the trial judge, at p. 158, did allow a de facto amendment to permit "a claim for Aboriginal rights other than ownership and jurisdiction". Had the respondents been concerned about the prejudice arising from this ruling, they could have appealed accordingly. However, they did not, and, as a result, the decision of the trial judge on this point must stand. . . .

76   However, no such amendment was made with respect to the amalgamation of the individual claims brought by the 51 Gitksan and Wet'suwet'en Houses into two collective claims, one by each nation, for Aboriginal title and self-government. Given the absence of an amendment to the pleadings, I must reluctantly conclude that the respondents suffered some prejudice. . . .

77   This defect in the pleadings prevents the Court from considering the merits of this appeal. However, given the importance of this case and the fact that much of the evidence of individual territorial holdings is extremely relevant to the collective claims

now advanced by each of the appellants, the correct remedy for the defect in pleadings is a new trial, where, to quote the trial judge at p. 368, "[i]t will be for the parties to consider whether any amendment is required in order to make the pleadings conform with the evidence". Moreover, as I will now explain, there are other reasons why a new trial should be ordered.

B. What is the ability of this Court to interfere with the factual findings made by the trial judge?

(1) General Principles

78   I recently reviewed the principles governing the appellate review of findings of fact in *Van der Peet, supra*. As a general rule, this Court has been extremely reluctant to interfere with the findings of fact made at trial, especially when those findings of fact are based on an assessment of the testimony and credibility of witnesses. Unless there is a "palpable and overriding error", appellate courts should not substitute their own findings of fact for those of the trial judge. The leading statement of this principle can be found in *Stein* v. *The Ship "Kathy K"*, [1976] 2 S.C.R. 802, *per* Ritchie J., at p. 808:

> These authorities are not to be taken as meaning that the findings of fact made at trial are immutable, but rather that they are not to be reversed unless it can be established that the learned trial judge made some palpable and overriding error which affected his assessment of the facts. While the Court of Appeal is seized with the duty of re-examining the evidence in order to be satisfied that no such error occurred, it is not, in my view, a part of its function to substitute its assessment of the balance of probability for the findings of the judge who presided at the trial.

The same deference must be accorded to the trial judge's assessment of the credibility of expert witnesses: see *N.V. Bocimar S.A.* v. *Century Insurance Co. of Canada*, [1987] 1 S.C.R. 1247.

79   The policy reason underlying this rule is protection of "[t]he autonomy and integrity of the trial process" (*Schwartz* v. *Canada*, [1996] 1 S.C.R. 254, at p. 278), which recognizes that the trier of fact, who is in direct contact with the mass of the evidence, is in the best position to make findings of fact, particularly those which turn on credibility. Moreover, *Van der Peet* clarified that deference was owed to findings of fact even when the trial judge misapprehended the law which was applied to those facts, a problem which can arise in quickly evolving areas of law such as the jurisprudence surrounding s. 35(1).

80   I recently held, in *Van der Peet*, that these general principles apply to cases litigated under s. 35(1). On the other hand, while accepting the general principle of non-interference, this Court has also identified specific situations in which an appeal court can interfere with a finding of fact made at trial. For example, appellate intervention is warranted "where the courts below have misapprehended or overlooked material evidence": see *Chartier* v. *Attorney General of Quebec*, [1979] 2 S.C.R. 474, at p. 493. In cases involving the determination of Aboriginal rights, appellate intervention is also warranted by the failure of a trial court to appreciate the evidentiary difficulties inherent in adjudicating Aboriginal claims when, first, applying the rules of evidence and, second, interpreting the evidence before it. As I said in *Van der Peet*, at para. 68:

> In determining whether an aboriginal claimant has produced evidence sufficient to demonstrate that her activity is an aspect of a practice, custom or tradition integral to a distinctive aboriginal culture, *a court should approach the rules of evidence, and interpret*

the evidence that exists, with a consciousness of the special nature of aboriginal claims, and of the evidentiary difficulties in proving a right which originates in times where there were no written records of the practices, customs and traditions engaged in. *The courts must not undervalue the evidence presented by aboriginal claimants simply because that evidence does not conform precisely with the evidentiary standards that would be applied in, for example, a private law torts case.* [Emphasis added.]

81   The justification for this special approach can be found in the nature of Aboriginal rights themselves. I explained in *Van der Peet* that those rights are aimed at the reconciliation of the prior occupation of North America by distinctive Aboriginal societies with the assertion of Crown sovereignty over Canadian territory. They attempt to achieve that reconciliation by "their bridging of Aboriginal and non-Aboriginal cultures" (at para. 42). Accordingly, "a court must take into account the perspective of the aboriginal people claiming the right . . . while at the same time taking into account the perspective of the common law" such that "[t]rue reconciliation will, equally, place weight on each" (at paras. 49 and 50).

82   In other words, although the doctrine of Aboriginal rights is a common law doctrine, Aboriginal rights are truly *sui generis*, and demand a unique approach to the treatment of evidence which accords due weight to the perspective of Aboriginal peoples. However, that accommodation must be done in a manner which does not strain "the Canadian legal and constitutional structure" (at para. 49). Both the principles laid down in *Van der Peet*—first, that trial courts must approach the rules of evidence in light of the evidentiary difficulties inherent in adjudicating Aboriginal claims, and second, that trial courts must interpret that evidence in the same spirit—must be understood against this background.

83   A concrete application of the first principle can be found in *Van der Peet* itself, where I addressed the difficulties inherent in demonstrating a continuity between current Aboriginal activities and the pre-contact practices, customs and traditions of Aboriginal societies. As I reiterate below, the requirement for continuity is one component of the definition of Aboriginal rights (although, as I explain below, in the case of title, the issue is continuity from sovereignty, not contact). However, given that many Aboriginal societies did not keep written records at the time of contact or sovereignty, it would be exceedingly difficult for them to produce (at para. 62) "conclusive evidence from pre-contact times about the practices, customs and traditions of their community". Accordingly, I held that (at para. 62):

> The evidence relied upon by the applicant and the courts may relate to aboriginal practices, customs and traditions *post-contact*; it simply needs to be directed at demonstrating which aspects of the aboriginal community and society have their origins *pre-contact*. [Emphasis added.]

The same considerations apply when the time from which title is determined is sovereignty.

84   This appeal requires us to apply not only the first principle in *Van der Peet* but the second principle as well, and adapt the laws of evidence so that the Aboriginal perspective on their practices, customs and traditions and on their relationship with the land, are given due weight by the courts. In practical terms, this requires the courts to come to terms with the oral histories of Aboriginal societies, which, for many Aboriginal nations, are the only record of their past. Given that the Aboriginal rights recognized and affirmed

by s. 35(1) are defined by reference to pre-contact practices or, as I will develop below, in the case of title, pre-sovereignty occupation, those histories play a crucial role in the litigation of Aboriginal rights. . . .

Oral accounts of the past include a good deal of subjective experience. They are not simply a detached recounting of factual events but, rather, are "facts enmeshed in the stories of a lifetime". They are also likely to be rooted in particular locations, making reference to particular families and communities. This contributes to a sense that there are many histories, each characterized in part by how a people see themselves, how they define their identity in relation to their environment, and how they express their uniqueness as a people. . . .

87   Notwithstanding the challenges created by the use of oral histories as proof of historical facts, the laws of evidence must be adapted in order that this type of evidence can be accommodated and placed on an equal footing with the types of historical evidence that courts are familiar with, which largely consists of historical documents. This is a long-standing practice in the interpretation of treaties between the Crown and Aboriginal peoples: *Sioui, supra*, at p. 1068; *R. v. Taylor* (1981), 62 C.C.C. (2d) 227, at p. 232. To quote Dickson C.J., given that most Aboriginal societies "did not keep written records", the failure to do so would "impose an impossible burden of proof" on Aboriginal peoples, and "render nugatory" any rights that they have (*Simon v. The Queen*, [1985] 1 S.C.R. 387, at p. 408). This process must be undertaken on a case-by-case basis. I will take this approach in my analysis of the trial judge's findings of fact. . . .

(2) Application of General Principles . . .

89   The general principle of appellate non-interference applies with particular force in this appeal. The trial was lengthy and very complex. There were 318 days of testimony. There were a large number of witnesses, lay and expert. The volume of evidence is enormous. . . .

90   It is not open to the appellants to challenge the trial judge's findings of fact merely because they disagree with them. I fear that a significant number of the appellants' objections fall into this category. Those objections are too numerous to list in their entirety. The bulk of these objections, at best, relate to alleged instances of misapprehension or oversight of material evidence by the trial judge. However, the respondents have established that, in most situations, there was some contradictory evidence that supported the trial judge's conclusion. The question, ultimately, was one of weight, and the appellants have failed to demonstrate that the trial judge erred in this respect. . . .

92   . . . [T]he appellants have alleged that the trial judge made a number of serious errors relating to the treatment of the oral histories of the appellants. Those oral histories were expressed in three different forms: (i) the adaawk of the Gitksan, and the kungax of the Wet'suwet'en; (ii) the personal recollections of members of the appellant nations, and (iii) the territorial affidavits filed by the heads of the individual houses within each nation. The trial judge ruled on both the admissibility of, and the weight to be given to, these various forms of oral history without the benefit of my reasons in *Van der Peet*, as will become evident in the discussion that follows. . . .

93   The adaawk and kungax of the Gitksan and Wet'suwet'en nations, respectively, are oral histories of a special kind. They were described by the trial judge, at p. 164, as a "sacred 'official' litany, or history, or recital of the most important laws, history, traditions

and traditional territory of a House". The content of these special oral histories includes its physical representation totem poles, crests and blankets. The importance of the adaawk and kungax is underlined by the fact that they are "repeated, performed and authenticated at important feasts". . . .

94   It is apparent that the adaawk and kungax are of integral importance to the distinctive cultures of the appellant nations. . . .

98   Although he framed his ruling on weight in terms of the specific oral histories before him, in my respectful opinion, the trial judge in reality based his decision on some general concerns with the use of oral histories as evidence in Aboriginal rights cases. In summary, the trial judge gave no independent weight to these special oral histories because they did not accurately convey historical truth, because knowledge about those oral histories was confined to the communities whose histories they were and because those oral histories were insufficiently detailed. However, as I mentioned earlier, these are features, to a greater or lesser extent, of all oral histories, not just the adaawk and kungax. The implication of the trial judge's reasoning is that oral histories should never be given any independent weight and are only useful as confirmatory evidence in Aboriginal rights litigation. I fear that if this reasoning were followed, the oral histories of Aboriginal peoples would be consistently and systematically undervalued by the Canadian legal system, in contradiction of the express instruction to the contrary in *Van der Peet* that trial courts interpret the evidence of Aboriginal peoples in light of the difficulties inherent in adjudicating Aboriginal claims.

(c) Recollections of Aboriginal life . . .

101   In my opinion, the trial judge expected too much of the oral history of the appellants, as expressed in the recollections of Aboriginal life of members of the appellant nations. He expected that evidence to provide definitive and precise evidence of pre-contact Aboriginal activities on the territory in question. However, as I held in *Van der Peet*, this will be almost an impossible burden to meet. Rather, if oral history cannot conclusively establish pre-sovereignty (after this decision) occupation of land, it may still be relevant to demonstrate that current occupation has its origins prior to sovereignty. This is exactly what the appellants sought to do. . . .

102   Finally, the trial judge also erred in his treatment of the territorial affidavits filed by the appellant chiefs. Those affidavits were declarations of the territorial holdings of each of the Gitksan and Wet'suwet'en houses and, at trial, were introduced for the purposes of establishing each House's ownership of its specific territory. Before this Court, the appellants tried to amalgamate these individual claims into collective claims on behalf of each nation and the relevance of the affidavits changed accordingly. I have already held that it is not open to the appellants to alter fundamentally the nature of their claim in this way on appeal. Nevertheless, the treatment of the affidavits is important because they will be relevant at a new trial to the existence and nature of the land tenure system within each nation and, therefore material to the proof of title.

103   The affidavits rely heavily on the declarations of deceased persons of use or ownership of the lands, which are a form of oral history. But those declarations are a kind of hearsay and the appellants therefore argued that the affidavits should be admitted through the reputation exception to the hearsay rule. . . .

104   I am concerned by the specific reasons the trial judge gave for refusing to apply

the reputation exception. He questioned the degree to which the declarations amounted to a reputation because they were largely confined to the appellants' communities. The trial judge asserted that neighbouring Aboriginal groups whose territorial claims conflicted with those of the appellants, as well as non-Aboriginals who potentially possessed a legal interest in the claimed territory, were unaware of the content of the alleged reputation at all. Furthermore, the trial judge reasoned that since the subject-matter of the affidavits was disputed, its reliability was doubtful. Finally, the trial judge questioned, at p. 441, the "independence and objectivity" of the information contained in the affidavits, because the appellants and their ancestors (at p. 440) "have been actively discussing land claims for many years".

105   Although he regretted this finding, the trial judge felt bound to apply the rules of evidence because it did not appear to him (at p. 442) "that the Supreme Court of Canada has decided that the ordinary rules of evidence do not apply to this kind of case". The trial judge arrived at this conclusion, however, without the benefit of *Van der Peet*, where I held that the ordinary rules of evidence must be approached and adapted in light of the evidentiary difficulties inherent in adjudicating Aboriginal claims.

106   Many of the reasons relied on by the trial judge for excluding the evidence contained in the territorial affidavits are problematic because they run against this fundamental principle. The requirement that a reputation be known in the general community, for example, ignores the fact that oral histories, as noted by the Royal Commission on Aboriginal Peoples, generally relate to particular locations, and refer to particular families and communities and may, as a result, be unknown outside of that community, even to other Aboriginal nations. Excluding the territorial affidavits because the claims to which they relate are disputed does not acknowledge that claims to Aboriginal rights, and Aboriginal title in particular, are almost always disputed and contested. Indeed, if those claims were uncontroversial, there would be no need to bring them to the courts for resolution. Casting doubt on the reliability of the territorial affidavits because land claims had been actively discussed for many years also fails to take account of the special context surrounding Aboriginal claims, in two ways. First, those claims have been discussed for so long because of British Columbia's persistent refusal to acknowledge the existence of Aboriginal title in that province until relatively recently, largely as a direct result of the decision of this Court in *Calder, supra*. It would be perverse, to say the least, to use the refusal of the province to acknowledge the rights of its Aboriginal inhabitants as a reason for excluding evidence which may prove the existence of those rights. Second, this rationale for exclusion places Aboriginal claimants whose societies record their past through oral history in a grave dilemma. In order for the oral history of a community to amount to a form of reputation, and to be admissible in court, it must remain alive through the discussions of members of that community; those discussions are the very basis of that reputation. But if those histories are discussed too much, and too close to the date of litigation, they may be discounted as being suspect, and may be held to be inadmissible. The net effect may be that a society with such an oral tradition would never be able to establish a historical claim through the use of oral history in court.

(e) Conclusion
107   The trial judge's treatment of the various kinds of oral histories did not satisfy the principles I laid down in *Van der Peet*. These errors are particularly worrisome because oral histories were of critical importance to the appellants' case. . . . Had the trial judge

assessed the oral histories correctly, his conclusions on these issues of fact might have been very different.

108   In the circumstances, the factual findings cannot stand. However, given the enormous complexity of the factual issues at hand, it would be impossible for the Court to do justice to the parties by sifting through the record itself and making new factual findings. A new trial is warranted, at which the evidence may be considered in light of the principles laid down in *Van der Peet* and elaborated upon here. In applying these principles, the new trial judge might well share some or all of the findings of fact of McEachern C.J.

C. What is the content of Aboriginal title, how is it protected by s. 35(1), and what is required for its proof?

109   The parties disagree over whether the appellants have established Aboriginal title to the disputed area. However, since those factual issues require a new trial, we cannot resolve that dispute in this appeal. But factual issues aside, the parties also have a more fundamental disagreement over the content of Aboriginal title itself, and its reception into the Constitution by s. 35(1). In order to give guidance to the judge at the new trial, it is to this issue that I will now turn.

110   I set out these opposing positions by way of illustration and introduction because I believe that all of the parties have characterized the content of Aboriginal title incorrectly. The appellants argue that Aboriginal title is tantamount to an inalienable fee simple, which confers on Aboriginal peoples the rights to use those lands as they choose and which has been constitutionalized by s. 35(1). The respondents offer two alternative formulations: first, that Aboriginal title is no more than a bundle of rights to engage in activities which are themselves Aboriginal rights recognized and affirmed by s. 35(1), and that the *Constitution Act, 1982*, merely constitutionalizes those individual rights, not the bundle itself, because the latter has no independent content; and second, that Aboriginal title, at most, encompasses the right to exclusive use and occupation of land in order to engage in those activities which are Aboriginal rights themselves, and that s. 35(1) constitutionalizes this notion of exclusivity.

111   The content of Aboriginal title, in fact, lies somewhere in between these positions. Aboriginal title is a right in land and, as such, is more than the right to engage in specific activities which may be themselves Aboriginal rights. Rather, it confers the right to use land for a variety of activities, not all of which need be aspects of practices, customs and traditions which are integral to the distinctive cultures of Aboriginal societies. Those activities do not constitute the right per se; rather, they are parasitic on the underlying title. However, that range of uses is subject to the limitation that they must not be irreconcilable with the nature of the attachment to the land which forms the basis of the particular group's Aboriginal title. This inherent limit, to be explained more fully below, flows from the definition of Aboriginal title as a *sui generis* interest in land, and is one way in which Aboriginal title is distinct from a fee simple.

(2) Aboriginal Title at Common Law
(a) General features

112   The starting point of the Canadian jurisprudence on Aboriginal title is the Privy Council's decision in *St. Catherine's Milling and Lumber Co.* v. *The Queen* (1888), 14 A.C. 46, which described Aboriginal title as a "personal and usufructuary right" (at p. 54). The

subsequent jurisprudence has attempted to grapple with this definition, and has in the process demonstrated that the Privy Council's choice of terminology is not particularly helpful to explain the various dimensions of Aboriginal title. What the Privy Council sought to capture is that Aboriginal title is a *sui generis* interest in land. Aboriginal title has been described as *sui generis* in order to distinguish it from "normal" proprietary interests, such as fee simple. However, as I will now develop, it is also *sui generis* in the sense that its characteristics cannot be completely explained by reference either to the common law rules of real property or to the rules of property found in Aboriginal legal systems. As with other Aboriginal rights, it must be understood by reference to both common law and Aboriginal perspectives.

113   The idea that Aboriginal title is *sui generis* is the unifying principle underlying the various dimensions of that title. One dimension is its inalienability. Lands held pursuant to Aboriginal title cannot be transferred, sold or surrendered to anyone other than the Crown and, as a result, is inalienable to third parties. This Court has taken pains to clarify that Aboriginal title is only "personal" in this sense, and does not mean that Aboriginal title is a non-proprietary interest which amounts to no more than a licence to use and occupy the land and cannot compete on an equal footing with other proprietary interests: see *Canadian Pacific Ltd.* v. *Paul*, [1988] 2 S.C.R. 654, at p. 677.

114   Another dimension of Aboriginal title is its source. It had originally been thought that the source of Aboriginal title in Canada was the *Royal Proclamation, 1763*: see *St. Catharines Milling*. However, it is now clear that although Aboriginal title was recognized by the Proclamation, it arises from the prior occupation of Canada by Aboriginal peoples. That prior occupation, however, is relevant in two different ways, both of which illustrate the sui generis nature of Aboriginal title. The first is the physical fact of occupation, which derives from the common law principle that occupation is proof of possession in law: see Kent McNeil, *Common Law Aboriginal Title* (1989), at p. 7. Thus, in *Guerin, supra*, Dickson J. described Aboriginal title, at p. 376, as a "legal right derived from the Indians' historic occupation and possession of their tribal lands". What makes Aboriginal title *sui generis* is that it arises from possession before the assertion of British sovereignty, whereas normal estates, like fee simple, arise afterward: see Kent McNeil, "The Meaning of Aboriginal Title", in Michael Asch, ed., *Aboriginal and Treaty Rights in Canada* (1997), 135, at p. 144. This idea has been further developed in *Roberts* v. *Canada*, [1989] 1 S.C.R. 322, where this Court unanimously held at p. 340 that "aboriginal title pre-dated colonization by the British and survived British claims to sovereignty" (also see *Guerin, supra*, at p. 378). What this suggests is a second source for Aboriginal title—the relationship between common law and pre-existing systems of Aboriginal law.

115   A further dimension of Aboriginal title is the fact that it is held communally. Aboriginal title cannot be held by individual Aboriginal persons; it is a collective right to land held by all members of an Aboriginal nation. Decisions with respect to that land are also made by that community. This is another feature of Aboriginal title which is sui generis and distinguishes it from normal property interests.

(b) The content of Aboriginal title
116   Although cases involving Aboriginal title have come before this Court and Privy Council before, there has never been a definitive statement from either court on the content of Aboriginal title. In *St. Catharines Milling*, the Privy Council, as I have mentioned, described the Aboriginal title as a "personal and usufructuary interest", but de-

clined to explain what that meant because it was not "necessary to express any opinion on the point" (at p. 55). Similarly, in *Calder, Guerin*, and *Paul*, the issues were the extinguishment of, the fiduciary duty arising from the surrender of, and statutory easements over land held pursuant to, Aboriginal title, respectively; the content of title was not at issue and was not directly addressed.

117   Although the courts have been less than forthcoming, I have arrived at the conclusion that the content of Aboriginal title can be summarized by two propositions: first, that Aboriginal title encompasses the right to exclusive use and occupation of the land held pursuant to that title for a variety of purposes, which need not be aspects of those Aboriginal practices, customs and traditions which are integral to distinctive Aboriginal cultures; and second, that those protected uses must not be irreconcilable with the nature of the group's attachment to that land. For the sake of clarity, I will discuss each of these propositions separately.

Aboriginal title encompasses the right to use the land held pursuant to that title for a variety of purposes, which need not be aspects of those Aboriginal practices, cultures and traditions which are integral to *distinctive Aboriginal cultures*.

118   The respondents argue that Aboriginal title merely encompasses the right to engage in activities which are aspects of Aboriginal practices, customs and traditions which are integral to distinctive Aboriginal cultures of the Aboriginal group claiming the right and, at most, adds the notion of exclusivity; i.e., the exclusive right to use the land for those purposes. However, the uses to which lands held pursuant to Aboriginal title can be put are not restricted in this way. This conclusion emerges from three sources: (i) the Canadian jurisprudence on Aboriginal title, (ii) the relationship between reserve lands and lands held pursuant to Aboriginal title, and (iii) the *Indian Oil and Gas Act*, R.S.C., 1985, c. I-7. As well, although this is not legally determinative, it is supported by the critical literature. In particular, I have profited greatly from Professor McNeil's article, "The Meaning of Aboriginal Title", *supra*.

(i) Canadian jurisprudence on Aboriginal title
119   Despite the fact that the jurisprudence on Aboriginal title is somewhat underdeveloped, it is clear that the uses to which lands held pursuant to Aboriginal title can be put is not restricted to the practices, customs and traditions of Aboriginal peoples integral to distinctive Aboriginal cultures. In *Guerin*, for example, Dickson J. described Aboriginal title as "an interest in land" which encompassed "a legal right to occupy and possess certain lands" (at p. 382). The "right to occupy and possess" is framed in broad terms and, significantly, is not qualified by reference to traditional and customary uses of those lands. Any doubt that the right to occupancy and possession encompasses a broad variety of uses of land was put to rest in *Paul*, where the Court went even further and stated that Aboriginal title was "more than the right to enjoyment and occupancy" (at p. 688). Once again, there is no reference to Aboriginal practices, customs and traditions as a qualifier on that right. Moreover, I take the reference to "more" as emphasis of the broad notion of use and possession.

(ii) Reserve land
120   Another source of support for the conclusion that the uses to which lands held under Aboriginal title can be put are not restricted to those grounded in practices, customs and traditions integral to distinctive Aboriginal cultures can be found in *Guerin*, where Dickson J. stated at p. 379 that the same legal principles governed the Aboriginal

interest in reserve lands and lands held pursuant to Aboriginal title:

> It does not matter, in my opinion, that the present case is concerned with the interest of an Indian Band in a reserve rather than with unrecognized aboriginal title in traditional tribal lands. *The Indian interest in the lands is the same in both cases.* [Emphasis added.]

121   The nature of the Indian interest in reserve land is very broad, and can found in s. 18 of the *Indian Act.* . . . The principal provision is s. 18(1), which states that reserve lands are held "for the use and benefit" of the bands which occupy them; those uses and benefits, on the face of the *Indian Act,* do not appear to be restricted to practices, customs and traditions integral to distinctive Aboriginal cultures. The breadth of those uses is reinforced by s. 18(2), which states that reserve lands may be used "for any other purpose for the general welfare of the band". The general welfare of the band has not been defined in terms of Aboriginal practices, customs and traditions, nor in terms of those activities which have their origin pre-contact; it is a concept, by definition, which incorporates a reference to the present-day needs of Aboriginal communities. On the basis of *Guerin,* lands held pursuant to Aboriginal title, like reserve lands, are also capable of being used for a broad variety of purposes.

(iii) Indian Oil and Gas Act

122   The third source for the proposition that the content of Aboriginal title is not restricted to practices, customs and traditions which are integral to distinctive Aboriginal cultures is the *Indian Oil and Gas Act.* The overall purpose of the statute is to provide for the exploration of oil and gas on reserve lands through their surrender to the Crown. The statute presumes that the Aboriginal interest in reserve land includes mineral rights, a point which this Court unanimously accepted with respect to the *Indian Act* in *Blueberry River Indian Band* v. *Canada (Department of Indian Affairs and Northern Development),* [1995] 4 S.C.R. 344. On the basis of *Guerin,* Aboriginal title also encompass mineral rights, and lands held pursuant to Aboriginal title should be capable of exploitation in the same way, which is certainly not a traditional use for those lands. This conclusion is reinforced by s. 6(2) of the Act, which provides:

> 6 . . . (2) Nothing in this Act shall be deemed to abrogate the rights of Indian people or preclude them from negotiating for oil and gas benefits in those areas in which land claims have not been settled. . . .

The areas referred to in s. 6(2), at the very least, must encompass lands held pursuant to Aboriginal title, since those lands by definition have not been surrendered under land claims agreements. The presumption underlying s. 6(2) is that Aboriginal title permits the development of oil and gas reserves. . . .

124   In conclusion, the content of Aboriginal title is not restricted to those uses which are elements of a practice, custom or tradition integral to the distinctive culture of the Aboriginal group claiming the right. However, nor does Aboriginal title amount to a form of inalienable fee simple, as I will now explain.

(c) Inherent limit: Lands held pursuant to Aboriginal title cannot be used in a manner that is irreconcilable with the nature of the attachment to the land which forms the basis of the group's claim to Aboriginal title

125   The content of Aboriginal title contains an inherent limit that lands held pursuant to title cannot be used in a manner that is irreconcilable with the nature of the claim-

ants' attachment to those lands. This limit on the content of Aboriginal title is a manifestation of the principle that underlies the various dimensions of that special interest in land—it is a *sui generis* interest that is distinct from "normal" proprietary interests, most notably fee simple.

126   I arrive at this conclusion by reference to the other dimensions of Aboriginal title which are *sui generis* as well. I first consider the source of Aboriginal title. As I discussed earlier, Aboriginal title arises from the prior occupation of Canada by Aboriginal peoples. That prior occupation is relevant in two different ways: first, because of the physical fact of occupation, and second, because Aboriginal title originates in part from pre-existing systems of Aboriginal law. However, the law of Aboriginal title does not only seek to determine the historic rights of Aboriginal peoples to land; it also seeks to afford legal protection to prior occupation in the present-day. Implicit in the protection of historic patterns of occupation is a recognition of the importance of the continuity of the relationship of an Aboriginal community to its land over time.

127   I develop this point below with respect to the test for Aboriginal title. The relevance of the continuity of the relationship of an Aboriginal community with its land here is that it applies not only to the past, but to the future as well. That relationship should not be prevented from continuing into the future. As a result, uses of the lands that would threaten that future relationship are, by their very nature, excluded from the content of Aboriginal title.

128   Accordingly, in my view, lands subject to Aboriginal title cannot be put to such uses as may be irreconcilable with the nature of the occupation of that land and the relationship that the particular group has had with the land which together have given rise to Aboriginal title in the first place. As discussed below, one of the critical elements in the determination of whether a particular Aboriginal group has Aboriginal title to certain lands is the matter of the occupancy of those lands. Occupancy is determined by reference to the activities that have taken place on the land and the uses to which the land has been put by the particular group. If lands are so occupied, there will exist a special bond between the group and the land in question such that the land will be part of the definition of the group's distinctive culture. It seems to me that these elements of Aboriginal title create an inherent limitation on the uses to which the land, over which such title exists, may be put. For example, if occupation is established with reference to the use of the land as a hunting ground, then the group that successfully claims Aboriginal title to that land may not use it in such a fashion as to destroy its value for such a use (e.g., by strip mining it). Similarly, if a group claims a special bond with the land because of its ceremonial or cultural significance, it may not use the land in such a way as to destroy that relationship (e.g., by developing it in such a way that the bond is destroyed, perhaps by turning it into a parking lot.)

129   It is for this reason also that lands held by virtue of Aboriginal title may not be alienated. Alienation would bring to an end the entitlement of the Aboriginal people to occupy the land and would terminate their relationship with it. I have suggested above that the inalienability of Aboriginal lands is, at least in part, a function of the common law principle that settlers in colonies must derive their title from Crown grant and, therefore, cannot acquire title through purchase from Aboriginal inhabitants. It is also, again only in part, a function of a general policy "to ensure that Indians are not dispossessed of their entitlements": see *Mitchell* v. *Peguis Indian Band*, [1990] 2 S.C.R. 85, at p. 133.

What the inalienability of lands held pursuant to Aboriginal title suggests is that those lands are more than just a fungible commodity. The relationship between an Aboriginal community and the lands over which it has Aboriginal title has an important non-economic component. The land has an inherent and unique value in itself, which is enjoyed by the community with Aboriginal title to it. The community cannot put the land to uses which would destroy that value.

130   I am cognizant that the *sui generis* nature of Aboriginal title precludes the application of "traditional real property rules" to elucidate the content of that title (*St. Mary's Indian Band* v. *Cranbrook (City)*, [1997] 2 S.C.R. 657, at para. 14). Nevertheless, a useful analogy can be drawn between the limit on Aboriginal title and the concept of equitable waste at common law. Under that doctrine, persons who hold a life estate in real property cannot commit "wanton or extravagant acts of destruction" (E.H. Burn, *Cheshire and Burn's Modern Law of Real Property* (14th ed. 1988), at p. 264) or "ruin the property" (Robert E. Megarry and H.W.R. Wade, *The Law of Real Property*, 4th ed. (1975) at p. 105). This description of the limits imposed by the doctrine of equitable waste capture the kind of limit I have in mind here.

131   Finally, what I have just said regarding the importance of the continuity of the relationship between an Aboriginal community and its land, and the non-economic or inherent value of that land, should not be taken to detract from the possibility of surrender to the Crown in exchange for valuable consideration. On the contrary, the idea of surrender reinforces the conclusion that Aboriginal title is limited in the way I have described. If Aboriginal peoples wish to use their lands in a way that Aboriginal title does not permit, then they must surrender those lands and convert them into non-title lands to do so.

132   The foregoing amounts to a general limitation on the use of lands held by virtue of Aboriginal title. It arises from the particular physical and cultural relationship that a group may have with the land and is defined by the source of Aboriginal title over it. This is not, I must emphasize, a limitation that restricts the use of the land to those activities that have traditionally been carried out on it. That would amount to a legal straitjacket on Aboriginal peoples who have a legitimate legal claim to the land. The approach I have outlined above allows for a full range of uses of the land, subject only to an overarching limit, defined by the special nature of the Aboriginal title in that land.

(d) Aboriginal title under s. 35(1) of the Constitution Act, 1982
133   Aboriginal title at common law is protected in its full form by s. 35(1). This conclusion flows from the express language of s. 35(1) itself, which states in full: "[t]he *existing* aboriginal and treaty rights of the aboriginal peoples of Canada are hereby recognized and affirmed" (emphasis added). On a plain reading of the provision, s. 35(1) did not create aboriginal rights; rather, it accorded constitutional status to those rights which were "existing" in 1982. The provision, at the very least, constitutionalized those rights which Aboriginal peoples possessed at common law, since those rights existed at the time s. 35(1) came into force. Since Aboriginal title was a common law right whose existence was recognized well before 1982 (e.g., *Calder, supra*), s. 35(1) has constitutionalized it in its full form.

134   I expressed this understanding of the relationship between common law Aboriginal rights, including Aboriginal title, and the Aboriginal rights protected by s. 35(1) in *Van der Peet*. While explaining the purposes behind s. 35(1), I stated that "it must be

remembered that s. 35(1) did not create the legal doctrine of Aboriginal rights; Aboriginal rights existed and were recognized under the common law" (at para. 28). Through the enactment of s. 35(1), "a pre-existing legal doctrine was elevated to constitutional status" (at para. 29), or in other words, s. 35(1) had achieved "the constitutionalization of those rights" (at para. 29). . . .

136   I hasten to add that the constitutionalization of common law Aboriginal rights by s. 35(1) does not mean that those rights exhaust the content of s. 35(1). As I said in *Côté, supra*, at para. 52:

> [s]ection 35(1) would fail to achieve its noble purpose of preserving the integral and defining features of distinctive aboriginal societies if it only protected those defining features which were fortunate enough to have received the legal recognition and approval of European colonizers.

I relied on this proposition in *Côté* to defeat the argument that the possible absence of Aboriginal rights under French colonial law was a bar to the existence of Aboriginal rights under s. 35(1) within the historic boundaries of New France. But it also follows that the existence of a particular Aboriginal right at common law is not a *sine qua non* for the proof of an Aboriginal right that is recognized and affirmed by s. 35(1). Indeed, none of the decisions of this Court handed down under s. 35(1) in which the existence of an Aboriginal right has been demonstrated has relied on the existence of that right at common law. The existence of an Aboriginal right at common law is therefore sufficient, but not necessary, for the recognition and affirmation of that right by s. 35(1).

137   The acknowledgment that s. 35(1) has accorded constitutional status to common law Aboriginal title raises a further question—the relationship of Aboriginal title to the "aboriginal rights" protected by s. 35(1). I addressed that question in *Adams, supra*, where the Court had been presented with two radically different conceptions of this relationship. The first conceived of Aboriginal rights as being "inherently based in aboriginal title to the land" (at para. 25), or as fragments of a broader claim to Aboriginal title. By implication, Aboriginal rights must rest either in a claim to title or the unextinguished remnants of title. Taken to its logical extreme, this suggests that Aboriginal title is merely the sum of a set of individual Aboriginal rights, and that it therefore has no independent content. However, I rejected this position for another—that Aboriginal title is "simply one manifestation of a broader-based conception of aboriginal rights" (at para. 25). Thus, although Aboriginal title is a species of Aboriginal right recognized and affirmed by s. 35(1), it is distinct from other Aboriginal rights because it arises where the connection of a group with a piece of land "was of a central significance to their distinctive culture" (at para. 26).

138   The picture which emerges from *Adams* is that the Aboriginal rights which are recognized and affirmed by s. 35(1) fall along a spectrum with respect to their degree of connection with the land. At the one end, there are those Aboriginal rights which are practices, customs and traditions that are integral to the distinctive Aboriginal culture of the group claiming the right. However, the "occupation and use of the land" where the activity is taking place is not "sufficient to support a claim of title to the land" (at para. 26). Nevertheless, those activities receive constitutional protection. In the middle, there are activities which, out of necessity, take place on land and indeed, might be intimately related to a particular piece of land. Although an Aboriginal group may not be able to demonstrate title to the land, it may nevertheless have a site-specific right to engage in a

particular activity. I put the point this way in *Adams*, at para. 30:

> Even where an aboriginal right exists on a tract of land to which the aboriginal people in question do not have title, that right may well be site specific, with the result that it can be exercised only upon that specific tract of land. For example, *if an aboriginal people demonstrates that hunting on a specific tract of land was an integral part of their distinctive culture then, even if the right exists apart from title to that tract of land, the aboriginal right to hunt is nonetheless defined as, and limited to, the right to hunt on the specific tract of land.* [Emphasis added.]

At the other end of the spectrum, there is Aboriginal title itself. As Adams makes clear, Aboriginal title confers more than the right to engage in site-specific activities which are aspects of the practices, customs and traditions of distinctive Aboriginal cultures. Site-specific rights can be made out even if title cannot. What Aboriginal title confers is the right to the land itself.

139   Because Aboriginal rights can vary with respect to their degree of connection with the land, some Aboriginal groups may be unable to make out a claim to title, but will nevertheless possess Aboriginal rights that are recognized and affirmed by s. 35(1), including site-specific rights to engage in particular activities. As I explained in *Adams*, this may occur in the case of nomadic peoples who varied "the location of their settlements with the season and changing circumstances" (at para. 27). The fact that Aboriginal peoples were non-sedentary, however (at para. 27) does not alter the fact that nomadic peoples survived through reliance on the land prior to contact with Europeans and, further, that many of the practices, customs and traditions of nomadic peoples that took place on the land were integral to their distinctive cultures.

(e) Proof of Aboriginal title
(i) Introduction
140   In addition to differing in the degree of connection with the land, Aboriginal title differs from other Aboriginal rights in another way. To date, the Court has defined Aboriginal rights in terms of activities. As I said in *Van der Peet* (at para. 46):

> in order to be an aboriginal right an activity must be an element of a practice, custom or tradition integral to the distinctive culture of the aboriginal group claiming the right.

Aboriginal title, however, is a right to the land itself. Subject to the limits I have laid down above, that land may be used for a variety of activities, none of which need be individually protected as Aboriginal rights under s. 35(1). Those activities are parasitic on the underlying title.

141   This difference between Aboriginal rights to engage in particular activities and Aboriginal title requires that the test I laid down in *Van der Peet* be adapted accordingly. I anticipated this possibility in *Van der Peet* itself, where I stated that (at para. 74):

> *Aboriginal rights arise from the prior occupation of land, but they also arise from the prior social organization and distinctive cultures of aboriginal peoples on that land. In considering whether a claim to an aboriginal right has been made out, courts must look at both the relationship of an aboriginal claimant to the land and [emphasis in original] at the practices, customs and traditions arising from the claimant's distinctive culture and society. Courts must not focus so entirely on the relationship of aboriginal peoples with the land that they lose sight of the other factors relevant to the identification and definition of aboriginal rights.* [Emphasis added.]

Since the purpose of s. 35(1) is to reconcile the prior presence of Aboriginal peoples in North America with the assertion of Crown sovereignty, it is clear from this statement that s. 35(1) must recognize and affirm both aspects of that prior presence—first, the occupation of land, and second, the prior social organization and distinctive cultures of Aboriginal peoples on that land. To date the jurisprudence under s. 35(1) has given more emphasis to the second aspect. To a great extent, this has been a function of the types of cases which have come before this Court under s. 35(1)—prosecutions for regulatory offences that, by their very nature, proscribe discrete types of activity.

142   The adaptation of the test laid down in *Van der Peet* to suit claims to title must be understood as the recognition of the first aspect of that prior presence. However, as will now become apparent, the tests for the identification of Aboriginal rights to engage in particular activities and for the identification of Aboriginal title share broad similarities. The major distinctions are first, under the test for Aboriginal title, the requirement that the land be integral to the distinctive culture of the claimants is subsumed by the requirement of occupancy, and second, whereas the time for the identification of Aboriginal rights is the time of first contact, the time for the identification of Aboriginal title is the time at which the Crown asserted sovereignty over the land.

(ii) The test for the proof of Aboriginal title

143   In order to make out a claim for Aboriginal title, the Aboriginal group asserting title must satisfy the following criteria: (i) the land must have been occupied prior to sovereignty, (ii) if present occupation is relied on as proof of occupation pre-sovereignty, there must be a continuity between present and pre-sovereignty occupation, and (iii) at sovereignty, that occupation must have been exclusive.

The land must have been occupied prior to sovereignty

144   In order to establish a claim to Aboriginal title, the Aboriginal group asserting the claim must establish that it occupied the lands in question at the time at *which the Crown asserted sovereignty over the land subject to the title*. The relevant time period for the establishment of title is, therefore, different than for the establishment of Aboriginal rights to engage in specific activities. In *Van der Peet*, I held, at para. 60 that "[t]he time period that a court should consider in identifying whether the right claimed meets the standard of being integral to the aboriginal community claiming the right is the period prior to contact. . . ." This arises from the fact that in defining the central and distinctive attributes of pre-existing Aboriginal societies it is necessary to look to a time prior to the arrival of Europeans. Practices, customs or traditions that arose solely as a response to European influences do not meet the standard for recognition as Aboriginal rights.

145   On the other hand, in the context of Aboriginal title, sovereignty is the appropriate time period to consider for several reasons. First, from a theoretical standpoint, Aboriginal title arises out of prior occupation of the land by Aboriginal peoples and out of the relationship between the common law and pre-existing systems of Aboriginal law. Aboriginal title is a burden on the Crown's underlying title. However, the Crown did not gain this title until it asserted sovereignty over the land in question. Because it does not make sense to speak of a burden on the underlying title before that title existed, Aboriginal title crystallized at the time sovereignty was asserted. Second, Aboriginal title does not raise the problem of distinguishing between distinctive, integral Aboriginal practices, customs and traditions and those influenced or introduced by European contact. Under common law, the act of occupation or possession is sufficient to ground Aboriginal title and it is

not necessary to prove that the land was a distinctive or integral part of the Aboriginal society before the arrival of Europeans. Finally, from a practical standpoint, it appears that the date of sovereignty is more certain than the date of first contact. It is often very difficult to determine the precise moment that each Aboriginal group had first contact with European culture. . . . For these reasons, I conclude that Aboriginals must establish occupation of the land from the date of the assertion of sovereignty in order to sustain a claim for Aboriginal title. McEachern C.J. found, at pp. 233–34, and the parties did not dispute on appeal, that British sovereignty over British Columbia was conclusively established by the Oregon Boundary Treaty of 1846. This is not to say that circumstances subsequent to sovereignty may never be relevant to title or compensation; this might be the case, for example, where native bands have been dispossessed of traditional lands after sovereignty. . . .

147   This debate over the proof of occupancy reflects two divergent views of the source of Aboriginal title. The respondents argue, in essence, that Aboriginal title arises from the physical reality at the time of sovereignty, whereas the Gitksan effectively take the position that Aboriginal title arises from and should reflect the pattern of land holdings under Aboriginal law. However, as I have explained above, the source of Aboriginal title appears to be grounded both in the common law and in the Aboriginal perspective on land; the latter includes, but is not limited to, their systems of law. It follows that both should be taken into account in establishing the proof of occupancy. Indeed, there is precedent for doing so. In *Baker Lake, supra*, Mahoney J. held that to prove Aboriginal title, the claimants needed both to demonstrate their "physical presence on the land they occupied" (at p. 561) and the existence "among [that group of] . . . a recognition of the claimed rights . . . by the regime that prevailed before" (at p. 559).

148   This approach to the proof of occupancy at common law is also mandated in the context of s. 35(1) by *Van der Peet*. In that decision, as I stated above, I held at para. 50 that the reconciliation of the prior occupation of North America by Aboriginal peoples with the assertion of Crown sovereignty required that account be taken of the "aboriginal perspective while at the same time taking into account the perspective of the common law" and that "[t]rue reconciliation will, equally, place weight on each". I also held that the Aboriginal perspective on the occupation of their lands can be gleaned, in part, but not exclusively, from their traditional laws, because those laws were elements of the practices, customs and traditions of Aboriginal peoples: at para. 41. As a result, if, at the time of sovereignty, an Aboriginal society had laws in relation to land, those laws would be relevant to establishing the occupation of lands which are the subject of a claim for Aboriginal title. Relevant laws might include, but are not limited to, a land tenure system or laws governing land use.

149   However, the Aboriginal perspective must be taken into account alongside the perspective of the common law. Professor McNeil has convincingly argued that at common law, the fact of physical occupation is proof of possession at law, which in turn will ground title to the land: *Common Law Aboriginal Title, supra*, at p. 73; also see Cheshire and Burn, *Modern Law of Real Property, supra*, at p. 28; and Megarry and Wade, *The Law of Real Property, supra*, at p. 1006. Physical occupation may be established in a variety of ways, ranging from the construction of dwellings through cultivation and enclosure of fields to regular use of definite tracts of land for hunting, fishing or otherwise exploiting its resources: see McNeil, *Common Law Aboriginal Title, supra*, at pp. 201–202. In con-

sidering whether occupation sufficient to ground title is established, "one must take into account the group's size, manner of life, material resources, and technological abilities, and the character of the lands claimed": Brian Slattery, "Understanding Aboriginal Rights", at p. 758.

150   In *Van der Peet*, I drew a distinction between those practices, customs and traditions of Aboriginal peoples which were "an aspect of, or took place in" the society of the Aboriginal group asserting the claim and those which were "a central and significant part of the society's culture" (at para. 55). The latter stood apart because they "made the culture of that society distinctive . . . it was one of the things which truly made the society what it was" (at para. 55). The same requirement operates in the determination of the proof of Aboriginal title. As I said in *Adams*, a claim to title is made out when a group can demonstrate "that their connection with the piece of land . . . was of central significance to their distinctive culture" (at para. 26).

151   Although this remains a crucial part of the test for Aboriginal rights, given the occupancy requirement in the test for Aboriginal title, I cannot imagine a situation where this requirement would actually serve to limit or preclude a title claim. The requirement exists for rights short of title because it is necessary to distinguish between those practices which were central to the culture of claimants and those which were more incidental. However, in the case of title, it would seem clear that any land that was occupied presovereignty, and which the parties have maintained a substantial connection with since then, is sufficiently important to be of central significance to the culture of the claimants. As a result, I do not think it is necessary to include explicitly this element as part of the test for Aboriginal title.

If present occupation is relied on as proof of occupation pre-sovereignty, there must be a continuity between present and pre-sovereignty occupation.

152   In *Van der Peet*, I explained that it is the pre-contact practices, customs and traditions of Aboriginal peoples which are recognized and affirmed as Aboriginal rights by s. 35(1). But I also acknowledged it would be "next to impossible" (at para. 62) for an Aboriginal group to provide conclusive evidence of its pre-contact practices, customs and traditions. What would suffice instead was evidence of post-contact practices, which was "directed at demonstrating which aspects of the Aboriginal community and society have their origins pre-contact" (at para. 62). The same concern, and the same solution, arises with respect to the proof of occupation in claims for Aboriginal title, although there is a difference in the time for determination of title. Conclusive evidence of pre-sovereignty occupation may be difficult to come by. Instead, an Aboriginal community may provide evidence of present occupation as proof of pre-sovereignty occupation in support of a claim to Aboriginal title. What is required, in addition, is a continuity between present and pre-sovereignty occupation, because the relevant time for the determination of Aboriginal title is at the time before sovereignty.

153   Needless to say, there is no need to establish "an unbroken chain of continuity" (*Van der Peet*, at para. 65) between present and prior occupation. The occupation and use of lands may have been disrupted for a time, perhaps as a result of the unwillingness of European colonizers to recognize Aboriginal title. To impose the requirement of continuity too strictly would risk "undermining the very purposes of s. 35(1) by perpetuating the historical injustice suffered by Aboriginal peoples at the hands of colonizers who failed to respect" Aboriginal rights to land (*Côté, supra* at para. 53). In *Mabo, supra*, the High

Court of Australia set down the requirement that there must be "substantial maintenance of the connection" between the people and the land. In my view, this test should be equally applicable to proof of title in Canada.

154   I should also note that there is a strong possibility that the precise nature of occupation will have changed between the time of sovereignty and the present. I would like to make it clear that the fact that the nature of occupation has changed would not ordinarily preclude a claim for Aboriginal title, as long as a substantial connection between the people and the land is maintained. The only limitation on this principle might be the internal limits on uses which land that is subject to Aboriginal title may be put, i.e., uses which are inconsistent with continued use by future generations of Aboriginals.

At sovereignty, occupation must have been exclusive

155   Finally, at sovereignty, occupation must have been exclusive. The requirement for exclusivity flows from the definition of Aboriginal title itself, because I have defined Aboriginal title in terms of the right to exclusive use and occupation of land. Exclusivity, as an aspect of Aboriginal title, vests in the Aboriginal community which holds the ability to exclude others from the lands held pursuant to that title. The proof of title must, in this respect, mirror the content of the right. Were it possible to prove title without demonstrating exclusive occupation, the result would be absurd, because it would be possible for more than one Aboriginal nation to have Aboriginal title over the same piece of land, and then for all of them to attempt to assert the right to exclusive use and occupation over it.

156   As with the proof of occupation, proof of exclusivity must rely on both the perspective of the common law and the Aboriginal perspective, placing equal weight on each. At common law, a premium is placed on the factual reality of occupation, as encountered by the Europeans. However, as the common law concept of possession must be sensitive to the realities of Aboriginal society, so must the concept of exclusivity. Exclusivity is a common law principle derived from the notion of fee simple ownership and should be imported into the concept of Aboriginal title with caution. As such, the test required to establish exclusive occupation must take into account the context of the Aboriginal society at the time of sovereignty. For example, it is important to note that exclusive occupation can be demonstrated even if other Aboriginal groups were present, or frequented the claimed lands. Under those circumstances, exclusivity would be demonstrated by "the intention and capacity to retain exclusive control" (McNeil, *Common Law Aboriginal Title, supra*, at p. 204). Thus, an act of trespass, if isolated, would not undermine a general finding of exclusivity, if Aboriginal groups intended to and attempted to enforce their exclusive occupation. Moreover, as Professor McNeil suggests, the presence of other Aboriginal groups might actually reinforce a finding of exclusivity. For example, "[w]here others were allowed access upon request, the very fact that permission was asked for and given would be further evidence of the group's exclusive control" (at p. 204).

157   A consideration of the Aboriginal perspective may also lead to the conclusion that trespass by other Aboriginal groups does not undermine, and that presence of those groups by permission may reinforce, the exclusive occupation of the Aboriginal group asserting title. . . .

158   In their submissions, the appellants pressed the point that requiring proof of exclusive occupation might preclude a finding of joint title, which is shared between two or more Aboriginal nations. The possibility of joint title has been recognized by American

courts: *United States* v. *Sante Fe Pacific Railroad Co.*, 314 U.S. 339 (1941). I would suggest that the requirement of exclusive occupancy and the possibility of joint title could be reconciled by recognizing that joint title could arise from shared exclusivity. The meaning of shared exclusivity is well-known to the common law. Exclusive possession is the right to exclude others. Shared exclusive possession is the right to exclude others except those with whom possession is shared. There clearly may be cases in which two Aboriginal nations lived on a particular piece of land and recognized each other's entitlement to that land but nobody else's. However, since no claim to joint title has been asserted here, I leave it to another day to work out all the complexities and implications of joint title, as well as any limits that another band's title may have on the way in which one band uses its title lands.

159   I should also reiterate that if Aboriginals can show that they occupied a particular piece of land, but did not do so exclusively, it will always be possible to establish Aboriginal rights short of title. These rights will likely be intimately tied to the land and may permit a number of possible uses. However, unlike title, they are not a right to the land itself. Rather, as I have suggested, they are a right to do certain things in connection with that land. If, for example, it were established that the lands near those subject to a title claim were used for hunting by a number of bands, those shared lands would not be subject to a claim for Aboriginal title, as they lack the crucial element of exclusivity. However, they may be subject to site-specific Aboriginal rights by all of the bands who used it. This does not entitle anyone to the land itself, but it may entitle all of the bands who hunted on the land to hunting rights. Hence, in addition to shared title, it will be possible to have shared, non-exclusive, site-specific rights. In my opinion, this accords with the general principle that the common law should develop to recognize Aboriginal rights (and title, when necessary) as they were recognized by either *de facto* practice or by the Aboriginal system of governance. It also allows sufficient flexibility to deal with this highly complex and rapidly evolving area of the law.

(f) Infringements of Aboriginal title: the test of justification . . .
160   The Aboriginal rights recognized and affirmed by s. 35(1), including Aboriginal title, are not absolute. Those rights may be infringed, both by the federal (e.g., *Sparrow*) and provincial (e.g., *Côté*) governments. However, s. 35(1) requires that those infringements satisfy the test of justification. . . .

(ii) General Principles
161   The test of justification has two parts, which I shall consider in turn. First, the infringement of the Aboriginal right must be in furtherance of a legislative objective that is compelling and substantial. I explained in *Gladstone* that compelling and substantial objectives were those which were directed at either one of the purposes underlying the recognition and affirmation of Aboriginal rights by s. 35(1), which are (at para. 72):

> the recognition of the prior occupation of North America by aboriginal peoples or . . . the reconciliation of aboriginal prior occupation with the assertion of the sovereignty of the Crown.

I noted that the latter purpose will often "be most relevant" (at para. 72) at the stage of justification. I think it important to repeat why (at para. 73) that is so:

> Because . . . distinctive Aboriginal societies exist within, and are part of, a broader social, political and economic community, over which the Crown is sovereign, there are cir-

cumstances in which, in order to pursue objectives of compelling and substantial importance to that community as a whole (taking into account the fact that Aboriginal societies are part of that community), some limitation of those rights will be justifiable.
*Aboriginal rights are a necessary part of the reconciliation of Aboriginal societies with the
broader political community of which they are part; limits placed on those rights are, where
the objectives furthered by those limits are of sufficient importance to the broader community
as a whole, equally a necessary part of that reconciliation.* [Emphasis added; "equally" emphasized in original.]

The conservation of fisheries, which was accepted as a compelling and substantial objective in *Sparrow*, furthers both of these purposes, because it simultaneously recognizes that
fishing is integral to many Aboriginal cultures, and also seeks to reconcile Aboriginal
societies with the broader community by ensuring that there are fish enough for all. But
legitimate government objectives also include "the pursuit of economic and regional fairness" and "the recognition of the historical reliance upon, and participation in, the fishery
by non-aboriginal groups" (para. 75). By contrast, measures enacted for relatively unimportant reasons, such as sports fishing without a significant economic component (*Adams,
supra*) would fail this aspect of the test of justification.

162   The second part of the test of justification requires an assessment of whether the
infringement is consistent with the special fiduciary relationship between the Crown and
Aboriginal peoples. What has become clear is that the requirements of the fiduciary duty
are a function of the "legal and factual context" of each appeal (*Gladstone, supra*, at para.
56). *Sparrow* and *Gladstone*, for example, interpreted and applied the fiduciary duty in
terms of the idea of priority. The theory underlying that principle is that the fiduciary
relationship between the Crown and Aboriginal peoples demands that Aboriginal interests be placed first. However, the fiduciary duty does not demand that Aboriginal rights
always be given priority. As was said in *Sparrow, supra*, at pp. 1114–15:

> The nature of the constitutional protection afforded by s. 35(1) *in this context* demands
> that there be a link between the question of justification and the allocation of priorities
> in the fishery. [Emphasis added.]

Other contexts permit, and may even require, that the fiduciary duty be articulated in
other ways (at p. 1119):

> Within the analysis of justification, there are further questions to be addressed, depend-
> ing on the circumstances of the inquiry. These include the questions of whether there
> has been as little infringement as possible in order to effect the desired result; whether, in
> a situation of expropriation, fair compensation is available; and, whether the aboriginal
> group in question has been consulted with respect to the conservation measures being
> implemented.

Sparrow did not explain when the different articulations of the fiduciary duty should be
used. Below, I suggest that the choice between them will in large part be a function of the
nature of the Aboriginal right at issue.

163   In addition to variation in the form which the fiduciary duty takes, there will also
be variation in degree of scrutiny required by the fiduciary duty of the infringing measure
or action. The degree of scrutiny is a function of the nature of the Aboriginal right at
issue. The distinction between *Sparrow* and *Gladstone*, for example, turned on whether
the right amounted to the exclusive use of a resource, which in turn was a function of
whether the right had an internal limit. In *Sparrow*, the right was internally limited, be-

cause it was a right to fish for food, ceremonial and social purposes, and as a result would only amount to an exclusive right to use the fishery in exceptional circumstances. Accordingly, the requirement of priority was applied strictly to mean that (at p. 1116) "any allocation of priorities after valid conservation measures have been implemented must give top priority to Indian food fishing".

164   In *Gladstone*, by contrast, the right to sell fish commercially was only limited by supply and demand. Had the test for justification been applied in a strict form in *Gladstone*, the Aboriginal right would have amounted to an exclusive right to exploit the fishery on a commercial basis. This was not the intention of *Sparrow*, and I accordingly modified the test for justification, by altering the idea of priority in the following way (at para. 62):

> . . . the doctrine of priority requires that the government demonstrate that, in allocating the resource, it has taken account of the existence of aboriginal rights and allocated the resource in a manner respectful of the fact that those rights have priority over the exploitation of the fishery by other users. This right is at once both procedural and substantive; at the stage of justification the government must demonstrate both that the process by which it allocated the resource and the actual allocation of the resource which results from that process reflect the prior interest of aboriginal rights holders in the fishery.

After *Gladstone*, in the context of commercial activity, the priority of Aboriginal rights is constitutionally satisfied if the government had taken those rights into account and has allocated a resource "in a manner respectful" (at para. 62) of that priority. A court must be satisfied that "the government has taken into account the existence and importance of [Aboriginal] rights" (at para. 63) which it determines by asking the following questions (at para. 64):

> Questions relevant to the determination of whether the government has granted priority to aboriginal rights holders are . . . questions such as whether the government has accommodated the exercise of the aboriginal right to participate in the fishery (through reduced licence fees, for example), whether the government's objectives in enacting a particular regulatory scheme reflect the need to take into account the priority of aboriginal rights holders, the extent of the participation in the fishery of aboriginal rights holders relative to their percentage of the population, how the government has accommodated different aboriginal rights in a particular fishery (food versus commercial rights, for example), how important the fishery is to the economic and material well-being of the band in question, and the criteria taken into account by the government in, for example, allocating commercial licences amongst different users.

(iii) Justification and Aboriginal title

165   The general principles governing justification laid down in *Sparrow*, and embellished by *Gladstone*, operate with respect to infringements of Aboriginal title. In the wake of *Gladstone*, the range of legislative objectives that can justify the infringement of Aboriginal title is fairly broad. Most of these objectives can be traced to the *reconciliation* of the prior occupation of North America by Aboriginal peoples with the assertion of Crown sovereignty, which entails the recognition that "distinctive aboriginal societies exist within, and are a part of, a broader social, political and economic community" (at para. 73). In my opinion, the development of agriculture, forestry, mining, and hydroelectric power, the general economic development of the interior of British Columbia, protection of the environment or endangered species, the building of infrastructure and the settlement of foreign populations to support those aims, are the kinds of objectives that are consistent

with this purpose and, in principle, can justify the infringement of Aboriginal title. Whether a particular measure or government act can be explained by reference to one of those objectives, however, is ultimately a question of fact that will have to be examined on a case-by-case basis.

166   The manner in which the fiduciary duty operates with respect to the second stage of the justification test—both with respect to the standard of scrutiny and the particular form that the fiduciary duty will take—will be a function of the nature of Aboriginal title. Three aspects of Aboriginal title are relevant here. First, Aboriginal title encompasses the right to exclusive use and occupation of land; second, Aboriginal title encompasses the right to choose to what uses land can be put, subject to the ultimate limit that those uses cannot destroy the ability of the land to sustain future generations of Aboriginal peoples; and third, that lands held pursuant to Aboriginal title have an inescapable *economic component*.

167   The exclusive nature of Aboriginal title is relevant to the degree of scrutiny of the infringing measure or action. For example, if the Crown's fiduciary duty requires that Aboriginal title be given priority, then it is the altered approach to priority that I laid down in *Gladstone* which should apply. What is required is that the government demonstrate (at para. 62) "both that the process by which it allocated the resource and the actual allocation of the resource which results from that process reflect the prior interest" of the holders of Aboriginal title in the land. By analogy with *Gladstone*, this might entail, for example, that governments accommodate the participation of Aboriginal peoples in the development of the resources of British Columbia, that the conferral of fee simples for agriculture, and of leases and licences for forestry and mining reflect the prior occupation of Aboriginal title lands, that economic barriers to Aboriginal uses of their lands (e.g., licensing fees) be somewhat reduced. This list is illustrative and not exhaustive. This is an issue that may involve an assessment of the various interests at stake in the resources in question. No doubt, there will be difficulties in determining the precise value of the Aboriginal interest in the land and any grants, leases or licences given for its exploitation. These difficult economic considerations obviously cannot be solved here.

168   Moreover, the other aspects of Aboriginal title suggest that the fiduciary duty may be articulated in a manner different than the idea of priority. This point becomes clear from a comparison between Aboriginal title and the Aboriginal right to fish for food in *Sparrow*. First, Aboriginal title encompasses within it a right to choose to what ends a piece of land can be put. The Aboriginal right to fish for food, by contrast, does not contain within it the same discretionary component. This aspect of Aboriginal title suggests that the fiduciary relationship between the Crown and Aboriginal peoples may be satisfied by the involvement of Aboriginal peoples in decisions taken with respect to their lands. There is always a duty of consultation. Whether the Aboriginal group has been consulted is relevant to determining whether the infringement of Aboriginal title is justified, in the same way that the Crown's failure to consult an Aboriginal group with respect to the terms by which reserve land is leased may breach its fiduciary duty at common law: *Guerin*. The nature and scope of the duty of consultation will vary with the circumstances. In occasional cases, when the breach is less serious or relatively minor, it will be no more than a duty to discuss important decisions that will be taken with respect to lands held pursuant to Aboriginal title. Of course, even in these rare cases when the minimum acceptable standard is consultation, this consultation must be in good faith, and with the intention of substantially addressing the concerns of the Aboriginal peoples

whose lands are at issue. In most cases, it will be significantly deeper than mere consultation. Some cases may even require the full consent of an Aboriginal nation, particularly when provinces enact hunting and fishing regulations in relation to Aboriginal lands.

169   Second, Aboriginal title, unlike the Aboriginal right to fish for food, has an inescapably economic aspect, particularly when one takes into account the modern uses to which lands held pursuant to Aboriginal title can be put. The economic aspect of Aboriginal title suggests that compensation is relevant to the question of justification as well, a possibility suggested in *Sparrow* and which I repeated in *Gladstone*. Indeed, compensation for breaches of fiduciary duty are a well-established part of the landscape of Aboriginal rights: *Guerin*. In keeping with the duty of honour and good faith on the Crown, fair compensation will ordinarily be required when Aboriginal title is infringed. The amount of compensation payable will vary with the nature of the particular Aboriginal title affected and with the nature and severity of the infringement and the extent to which Aboriginal interests were accommodated. Since the issue of damages was severed from the principal action, we received no submissions on the appropriate legal principles that would be relevant to determining the appropriate level of compensation of infringements of Aboriginal title. In the circumstances, it is best that we leave those difficult questions to another day.

D. Has a claim to self-government been made out by the appellants?

170   . . . The errors of fact made by the trial judge, and the resultant need for a new trial, make it impossible for this Court to determine whether the claim to self-government has been made out. . . .

E. Did the province have the power to extinguish Aboriginal rights after 1871, either under its own jurisdiction or through the operation of s. 88 of the Indian Act? . . .

172   For Aboriginal rights to be recognized and affirmed by s. 35(1), they must have existed in 1982. Rights which were extinguished by the sovereign before that time are not revived by the provision. In a federal system such as Canada's, the need to determine whether Aboriginal rights have been extinguished raises the question of which level of government has jurisdiction to do so. In the context of this appeal, that general question becomes three specific ones. First, there is the question whether the province of British Columbia, from the time it joined Confederation in 1871, until the entrenchment of s. 35(1) in 1982, had the jurisdiction to extinguish the rights of Aboriginal peoples, including Aboriginal title, in that province. Second, if the province was without such jurisdiction, another question arises—whether provincial laws which were not in pith and substance aimed at the extinguishment of Aboriginal rights could have done so nevertheless if they were laws of general application. The third and final question is whether a provincial law, which could otherwise not extinguish Aboriginal rights, be given that effect through referential incorporation by s. 88 of the *Indian Act*.

(2) Primary Jurisdiction

173   Since 1871, the exclusive power to legislate in relation to "Indians, and Lands reserved for Indians" has been vested with the federal government by virtue of s. 91(24) of the *Constitution Act, 1867*. That head of jurisdiction, in my opinion, encompasses within it the exclusive power to extinguish Aboriginal rights, including Aboriginal title.

"Lands reserved for the Indians"

174   I consider the second part of this provision first, which confers jurisdiction to the federal government over "Lands reserved for the Indians". The debate between the parties centred on whether that part of s. 91(24) confers jurisdiction to legislate with respect to Aboriginal title. The province's principal submission is that "Lands reserved for the Indians" are lands which have been specifically set aside or designated for Indian occupation, such as reserves. However, I must reject that submission, because it flies in the face of the judgment of the Privy Council in *St. Catherine's Milling*. One of the issues in that appeal was the federal jurisdiction to accept the surrender of lands held pursuant to Aboriginal title. It was argued that the federal government, at most, had jurisdiction over "Indian Reserves". Lord Watson, speaking for the Privy Council, rejected this argument, stating that had the intention been to restrict s. 91(24) in this way, specific language to this effect would have been used. He accordingly held that (at p. 59):

> . . . the words actually used are, according to their natural meaning, sufficient to include all lands reserved, upon any terms or conditions, for Indian occupation.

Lord Watson's reference to "all lands" encompasses not only reserve lands, but lands held pursuant to Aboriginal title as well. Section 91(24), in other words, carries with it the jurisdiction to legislate in relation to Aboriginal title. It follows, by implication, that it also confers the jurisdiction to extinguish that title.

175   The province responds by pointing to the fact that underlying title to lands held pursuant to Aboriginal title vested with the provincial Crown pursuant to s. 109 of the *Constitution Act, 1867*. In its submission, this right of ownership carried with it the right to grant fee simples which, by implication, extinguish Aboriginal title, and so by negative implication excludes Aboriginal title from the scope of s. 91(24). The difficulty with the province's submission is that it fails to take account of the language of s. 109, which states in part that:

> 109. All Lands, Mines, Minerals and Royalties belonging to the several Provinces of Canada . . . at the Union . . . shall belong to the several Provinces . . . subject to any Trusts existing in respect thereof, and to any Interest other than that of the Province in the same.

Although that provision vests underlying title in provincial Crowns, it qualifies provincial ownership by making it subject to the "any Interest other than that of the Province in the same". In *St. Catherine's Milling*, the Privy Council held that Aboriginal title was such an interest, and rejected the argument that provincial ownership operated as a limit on federal jurisdiction. The net effect of that decision, therefore, was to separate the ownership of lands held pursuant to Aboriginal title from jurisdiction over those lands. Thus, although on surrender of Aboriginal title the province would take absolute title, jurisdiction to accept surrenders lies with the federal government. The same can be said of extinguishment—although on extinguishment of Aboriginal title, the province would take complete title to the land, the jurisdiction to extinguish lies with the federal government.

176   I conclude with two remarks. First, even if the point were not settled, I would have come to same conclusion. The judges in the court below noted that separating federal jurisdiction over Indians from jurisdiction over their lands would have a most unfortunate result—the government vested with primary constitutional responsibility for securing the welfare of Canada's Aboriginal peoples would find itself unable to safeguard one of the most central of native interests—their interest in their lands. Second, although

the submissions of the parties and my analysis have focused on the question of jurisdiction over Aboriginal title, in my opinion, the same reasoning applies to jurisdiction over any Aboriginal right which relates to land. As I explained earlier, *Adams* clearly establishes that Aboriginal rights may be tied to land but nevertheless fall short of title. Those relationships with the land, however, may be equally fundamental to Aboriginal peoples and, for the same reason that jurisdiction over Aboriginal title must vest with the federal government, so too must the power to legislate in relation to other Aboriginal rights in relation to land.

"Indians"

177   The extent of federal jurisdiction over Indians has not been definitively addressed by this Court. We have not needed to do so because the *vires* of federal legislation with respect to Indians, under the division of powers, has never been at issue. The cases which have come before the Court under s. 91(24) have implicated the question of jurisdiction over Indians from the other direction—whether provincial laws which on their face apply to Indians intrude on federal jurisdiction and are inapplicable to Indians to the extent of that intrusion. As I explain below, the Court has held that s. 91(24) protects a "core" of Indianness from provincial intrusion, through the doctrine of interjurisdictional immunity.

178   It follows, at the very least, that this core falls within the scope of federal jurisdiction over Indians. That core, for reasons I will develop, encompasses Aboriginal rights, including the rights that are recognized and affirmed by s. 35(1). Laws which purport to extinguish those rights therefore touch the core of Indianness which lies at the heart of s. 91(24), and are beyond the legislative competence of the provinces to enact. The core of Indianness encompasses the whole range of Aboriginal rights that are protected by s. 35(1). Those rights include rights in relation to land; that part of the core derives from s. 91(24)'s reference to "Lands reserved for the Indians". But those rights also encompass practices, customs and traditions which are not tied to land as well; that part of the core can be traced to federal jurisdiction over "Indians". Provincial governments are prevented from legislating in relation to both types of Aboriginal rights.

(3) Provincial Laws of General Application

179   The vesting of exclusive jurisdiction with the federal government over Indians and Indian lands under s. 91(24), operates to preclude provincial laws in relation to those matters. Thus, provincial laws which single out Indians for special treatment are *ultra vires*, because they are in relation to Indians and therefore invade federal jurisdiction: see *R. v. Sutherland*, [1980] 2 S.C.R. 451. However, it is a well established principle that (*Four B Manufacturing Ltd.*, *supra*, at p. 1048):

> The conferring upon Parliament of exclusive legislative competence to make laws relating to certain classes of persons does not mean that the totality of these persons' rights and duties comes under primary federal competence to the exclusion of provincial laws of general application.

In other words, notwithstanding s. 91(24), provincial laws of general application apply *proprio vigore* to Indians and Indian lands. Thus, this Court has held that provincial labour relations legislation (*Four B*) and motor vehicle laws (*R. v. Francis*, [1988] 1 S.C.R. 1025), which purport to apply to all persons in the province, also apply to Indians living on reserves.

180   What must be answered, however, is whether the same principle allows provincial

laws of general application to extinguish Aboriginal rights. I have come to the conclusion that a provincial law of general application could not have this effect, for two reasons. First, a law of general application cannot, by definition, meet the standard which has been set by this Court for the extinguishment of Aboriginal rights without being *ultra vires* the province. That standard was laid down in *Sparrow, supra*, at p. 1099, as one of "clear and plain" intent. In that decision, the Court drew a distinction between laws which extinguished Aboriginal rights, and those which merely regulated them. Although the latter types of laws may have been "necessarily inconsistent" with the continued exercise of Aboriginal rights, they could not extinguish those rights. While the requirement of clear and plain intent does not, perhaps, require that the Crown "use language which refers expressly to its extinguishment of aboriginal rights" (*Gladstone*, supra, at para. 34), the standard is still quite high. My concern is that the only laws with the sufficiently clear and plain intention to extinguish Aboriginal rights would be laws in relation to Indians and Indian lands. As a result, a provincial law could never, *proprio vigore*, extinguish Aboriginal rights, because the intention to do so would take the law outside provincial jurisdiction.

181   Second, as I mentioned earlier, s. 91(24) protects a core of federal jurisdiction even from provincial laws of general application, through the operation of the doctrine of interjurisdictional immunity. That core has been described as matters touching on "Indianness" or the "core of Indianness" (*Dick, supra*, at pp. 326 and 315; also see *Four B, supra*, at p. 1047 and *Francis, supra*, at pp. 1028–29). The core of Indianness at the heart of s. 91(24) has been defined in both negative and positive terms. Negatively, it has been held to not include labour relations (*Four B*) and the driving of motor vehicles (*Francis*). The only positive formulation of Indianness was offered in *Dick*. Speaking for the Court, Beetz J. assumed, but did not decide, that a provincial hunting law did not apply *proprio vigore* to the members of an Indian band to hunt and because those activities were "at the centre of what they do and who they are" (*supra*, at p. 320). But in *Van der Peet*, I described and defined the Aboriginal rights that are recognized and affirmed by s. 35(1) in a similar fashion, as protecting the occupation of land and the activities which are integral to the distinctive Aboriginal culture of the group claiming the right. It follows that Aboriginal rights are part of the core of Indianness at the heart of s. 91(24). Prior to 1982, as a result, they could not be extinguished by provincial laws of general application.

(4) Section 88 of the Indian Act
182   Provincial laws which would otherwise not apply to Indians *proprio vigore*, however, are allowed to do so by s. 88 of the *Indian Act*, which incorporates by reference provincial laws of general application. . . . [I]n Professor Hogg's words, . . . s. 88 does not "invigorate" provincial laws which are invalid because they are in relation to Indians and Indian lands (*Constitutional Law of Canada* (3rd ed. 1992), at p. 676; . . . What this means is that s. 88 extends the effect of provincial laws of general application which cannot apply to Indians and Indian lands because they touch on the Indianness at the core of s. 91(24). For example, a provincial law which regulated hunting may very well touch on this core. Although such a law would not apply to Aboriginal people *proprio vigore*, it would still apply through s. 88 of the *Indian Act*, being a law of general application. Such laws are enacted to conserve game and for the safety of all. . . .

I see nothing in the language of the provision [s. 88] which even suggests the intention to extinguish Aboriginal rights. Indeed, the explicit reference to treaty rights in s. 88 suggests that the provision was clearly not intended to undermine Aboriginal rights.

VI. Conclusion and Disposition

184   For the reasons I have given above, I would allow the appeal in part, and dismiss the cross-appeal. Reluctantly, I would also order a new trial.

185   I conclude with two observations. The first is that many Aboriginal nations with territorial claims that overlap with those of the appellants did not intervene in this appeal, and do not appear to have done so at trial. This is unfortunate, because determinations of Aboriginal title for the Gitksan and Wet'suwet'en will undoubtedly affect their claims as well. This is particularly so because Aboriginal title encompasses an exclusive right to the use and occupation of land, i.e., to the exclusion of both non-Aboriginals and members of other Aboriginal nations. It may, therefore, be advisable if those Aboriginal nations intervened in any new litigation.

186   Finally, this litigation has been both long and expensive, not only in economic but in human terms as well. By ordering a new trial, I do not necessarily encourage the parties to proceed to litigation and to settle their dispute through the courts. As was said in *Sparrow*, at p. 1105, s. 35(1) "provides a solid constitutional base upon which subsequent negotiations can take place". Those negotiations should also include other Aboriginal nations which have a stake in the territory claimed. Moreover, the Crown is under a moral, if not a legal, duty to enter into and conduct those negotiations in good faith. Ultimately, it is through negotiated settlements, with good faith and give and take on all sides, reinforced by the judgments of this Court, that we will achieve what I stated in *Van der Peet*, *supra*, at para. 31, to be a basic purpose of s. 35(1)—"the reconciliation of the pre-existence of Aboriginal societies with the sovereignty of the Crown". Let us face it, we are all here to stay. . . .

PROOF OF ABORIGINAL TITLE

Delgamuukw v. *British Columbia* (1997)
[1997] 3 S.C.R. 1010 (S.C.C.).

See paragraphs 142–159 at pages 54–58.

St. Catherine's Milling and Lumber Company v. *R.* (1887)
13 S.C.R. 577 (S.C.C.). This SCC decision was affirmed by the J.C.P.C. (1888), 14 A.C. 46.

STRONG J.:— . . . It thus appears, that in the United States a traditional policy, derived from colonial times, relative to the Indians and their lands has ripened into well established rules of law, and that the result is that the lands in the possession of the Indians are, until surrendered, treated as their rightful though inalienable property, so far as the possession and enjoyment are concerned; in other words, that the *dominium utile* is recognized as belonging to or reserved for the Indians, though the *dominium directum* is considered to be in the United States. Then, if this is so as regards Indian lands in the United States, which have been preserved to the Indians by the constant observance of a particular rule of policy acknowledged by the United States courts to have been originally enforced by the crown of Great Britain, how is it possible to suppose that the law can, or rather could have been, at the date of confederation, in a state any less favorable to the Indians whose lands were situated within the dominion of the British crown, the original author of this beneficent doctrine so carefully adhered to in the United States from the days of the colonial governments? Therefore, when we consider that with reference to Canada the uniform practice has always been to recognize the Indian title as one which could only be dealt with by surrender to the crown, I maintain that if there had been an entire absence of any written legislative act ordaining this rule as an express positive law, we ought, just as the United States courts have done, to hold that it nevertheless existed as a rule of the unwritten common law, which the courts were bound to enforce as such, and consequently, that the 24th sub-section of section 91, as well as the 109th section and the 5th sub-section of section 92 of the *British North America Act*, must all be read and construed upon the assumption that these territorial rights of the Indians were strictly legal rights which had to be taken into account and dealt with in that distribution of property and proprietary rights made upon confederation between the federal and provincial governments. . . .

Ontario (A.G.) v. *Bear Island Foundation* (1991)

[1991] 2 S.C.R. 570 (S.C.C.). Lamer C.J., La Forest, Gonthier, McLachlin, and Stevenson JJ., August 15, 1991.

PER CURIAM:— . . . Steele J. [Ontario Supreme Court] . . . found that the appellants had no aboriginal right to the land, and that even if such a right had existed, it had been extinguished by the Robinson-Huron Treaty of 1850, to which the Temagami Band was originally a party or to which it had subsequently adhered. These findings were essentially factual, and were drawn from the mass of historical documentary evidence adduced over the course of 130 days of trial. Steele J. also dismissed the counterclaim. . . .

An appeal to the Ontario Court of Appeal ([1989] 2 C.N.L.R. 73) was dismissed. On the assumption that an aboriginal right existed, the court held that right had been extinguished either by the Robinson-Huron Treaty or by the subsequent adherence to that treaty by the Indians, or because the treaty constituted a unilateral extinguishment by the sovereign.

This case, it must be underlined, raises for the most part essentially factual issues on which the courts below were in agreement. On such issues, the rule is that an appellate court should not reverse the trial judge in the absence of palpable and overriding error which affected his or her assessment of the facts: . . . The rule is all the stronger in the face of concurrent findings of both courts below. . . . We do not take issue with the numerous specific findings of fact in the court below, and it is, therefore, not necessary to recapitulate them here.

It does not necessarily follow, however, that we agree with all the legal findings based on those facts. In particular, we find that on the facts found by the trial judge the Indians exercised sufficient occupation of the lands in question throughout the relevant period to establish an Aboriginal right; . . .

It is unnecessary, however, to examine the specific nature of the aboriginal right because, in our view, whatever may have been the situation upon the signing of the Robinson-Huron Treaty, that right was in any event surrendered by arrangements subsequent to that treaty by which the Indians adhered to the treaty in exchange for treaty annuities and a reserve. It is conceded that the Crown has failed to comply with some of its obligations under this agreement, and thereby breached its fiduciary obligations to the Indians. These matters currently form the subject of negotiations between the parties. It does not alter the fact, however, that the aboriginal right has been extinguished.

For these reasons, the appeal is dismissed.

R. v. *Sparrow* (1990)

[1990] 1 S.C.R. 1075 (S.C.C.). Dickson C.J., Lamer, Wilson, La Forest, L'Heureux-Dubé, McIntyre (took no part in the judgment), Sopinka JJ., May 31, 1990.

PER DICKSON C.J. and LA FOREST J.:— . . . The word "existing" makes it clear that the rights to which s. 35(1) applies are those that were in existence when the *Constitution Act, 1982* came into effect. This means that extinguished rights are not revived by the *Constitution Act, 1982*. A number of courts have taken the position that "existing" means being in actuality in 1982: . . .

As noted by Blair J.A., academic commentary lends support to the conclusion that "existing" means "unextinguished" rather than exercisable at a certain time in history. Professor Slattery, "Understanding Aboriginal Rights" (1987), 66 *Can. Bar Rev.* 726, at pp. 781–82, has observed the following about reading regulations into the rights:

> This approach reads into the Constitution the myriad of regulations affecting the exercise of aboriginal rights, regulations that differed considerably from place to place across the country. It does not permit differentiation between regulations of long-term significance and those enacted to deal with temporary conditions, or between reasonable and unreasonable restrictions. Moreover, it might require that a constitutional amendment be enacted to implement regulations more stringent than those in existence on 17 April 1982. This solution seems unsatisfactory. . . .

It is this progressive restriction and detailed regulation of the fisheries which, respondent's counsel maintained, have had the effect of extinguishing any aboriginal right to fish. The extinguishment need not be express, he argued, but may take place where the sovereign authority is exercised in a manner "necessarily inconsistent" with the continued enjoyment of aboriginal rights. For this proposition, he particularly relied on *St. Catherine's Milling and Lumber Co.* v. *The Queen* (1888), 14 App. Cas. 46 (P.C.); *Calder* v. *Attorney-General of British Columbia*, [1973] S.C.R. 313; *Baker Lake (Hamlet)* v. *Minister of Indian Affairs and Northern Development*, [1979] 3 C.N.L.R. 17, (F.C.T.D.); and *Attorney-General of Ontario* v. *Bear Island Foundation, supra*. The consent to its extinguishment before the *Constitution Act, 1982* was not required; the intent of the sovereign could be effected not only by statute but by valid regulations. Here, in his view, the regulations had entirely displaced any aboriginal right. There is, he submitted, a fundamental inconsistency between the communal right to fish embodied in the aboriginal right, and fishing under a special licence or permit issued to individual Indians (as was the case until 1977) in the discretion of the Minister and subject to terms and conditions which, if breached, may result in cancellation of the licence. The *Fisheries Act* and its regulations were, he argued, intended to constitute a complete Code inconsistent with the continued existence of an aboriginal right.

At bottom, the respondent's argument confuses regulation with extinguishment. That the right is controlled in great detail by the regulations does not mean that the right is thereby extinguished. The distinction to be drawn was carefully explained, in the context of federalism, in the first fisheries case, *Attorney-General for Canada* v. *Attorney-General for Ontario*, [1898] A.C. 700. There, the Privy Council had to deal with the interrelationship between, on the one hand, provincial property, which by s. 109 of the *Constitution Act, 1867* is vested in the provinces (and so falls to be regulated *qua* property exclusively by the provinces) and, on the other hand, the federal power to legislate respecting the fisheries thereon under s. 91(12) of that Act. The Privy Council said the following in relation to the federal regulation (at pp. 712–13):

... the power to legislate in relation to fisheries does necessarily to a certain extent enable the Legislature so empowered to affect proprietary rights. An enactment, for example, prescribing the times of the year during which fishing is to be allowed, or the instruments which may be employed for the purpose (which it was admitted the Dominion Legislature was empowered to pass) might very seriously touch the exercise of proprietary rights, and the extent, character, and scope of such legislation is left entirely to the Dominion Legislature. The suggestion that the power might be abused so as to amount to a practical confiscation of property does not warrant the imposition by the Courts of any limit upon the absolute power of legislation conferred. The supreme legislative power in relation to any subject-matter is always capable of abuse, but it is not to be assumed that it will be improperly used; if it is, the only remedy is an appeal to those by whom the Legislature is elected.

In the context of aboriginal rights, it could be argued that, before 1982, an aboriginal right was automatically extinguished to the extent that it was inconsistent with a statute. As Mahoney J. stated in *Baker Lake, supra*, at p. 568 [p. 55 C.N.L.R.]:

Once a statute has been validly enacted, it must be given effect. If its necessary effect is to abridge or entirely abrogate a common law right, then that is the effect that the courts must give it. That is as true of an aboriginal title as of any other common law right.

See also *Attorney-General of Ontario* v. *Bear Island Foundation, supra*, at pp. 439–40 [pp. 80–81 C.N.L.R.]. That in Judson J.'s view was what had occurred in *Calder, supra*, where, as he saw it, a series of statutes evinced a unity of intention to exercise a sovereignty inconsistent with any conflicting interest, including aboriginal title. But Hall J. in that case stated (at p. 404) that "the onus of proving that the Sovereign intended to extinguish the Indian title lies on the respondent and *that intention must be 'clear and plain'*" (emphasis added). The test of extinguishment to be adopted, in our opinion, is that the Sovereign's intention must be clear and plain if it is to extinguish an aboriginal right.

There is nothing in the *Fisheries Act* or its detailed regulations that demonstrates a clear and plain intention to extinguish the Indian aboriginal right to fish. The fact that express provision permitting the Indians to fish for food may have applied to all Indians and that for an extended period permits were discretionary and issued on an individual rather than a communal basis in no way shows a clear intention to extinguish. These permits were simply a manner of controlling the fisheries, not defining underlying rights.

We would conclude then that the Crown has failed to discharge its burden of proving extinguishment. In our opinion, the Court of Appeal made no mistake in holding that the Indians have an existing aboriginal right to fish in the area where Mr. Sparrow was fishing at the time of the charge. This approach is consistent with ensuring that an aboriginal right should not be defined by incorporating the ways in which it has been regulated in the past. ...

SELECTED BIBLIOGRAPHY

Ayers, N. "Aboriginal Land Rights in the Maritimes" [1984] 2 C.N.L.R. 1.
Clark, B. *Indian Title in Canada* (Toronto: Carswell, 1987).
Culhane, D. *The Pleasure of the Crown: Anthropology, Law and First Nations* (Burnaby: Talon Books, 1998).
Cumming, P.A. & N.H. Mickenburg, eds. *Native Rights in Canada*, 2d ed. (Toronto: General,

1972).

Elliot, D. "Aboriginal Title" in B. Morse, ed. *Aboriginal Peoples and the Law: Indian, Metis and Inuit Rights in Canada* (Ottawa: Carleton University Press, 1985).

————. "Baker Lake and the Concept of Aboriginal Title" 18 Osgoode Hall L.J. 653.

Foster, H. "The Saanichton Bay Marina Case: Imperial Law, Colonial History and Competing Theories of Aboriginal Title" (1989) 23 U.B.C. L. Rev. 34.

————. "Aboriginal Title and the Provincial Obligation to Respect It: Is *Delgamuukw* v. *B.C.* 'Invented Law'?" (March 1998) 56 Advocate 221.

Hurley, J. "The Crown's Fiduciary Duty and Indian Title: *Guerin* v. *The Queen*" (1985) 30 McGill L.J. 559.

Isaac, T. *Aboriginal and Treaty Rights in the Maritimes. The Marshall Decision and Beyond* (Saskatoon: Purich Publishing, Ltd., 2001) 71–103.

Lloyd, S. & M.A. Perry. *Australian Native Title Law* (Australia: LBC Information Services, 2000).

Lysyk, K. "The Indian Title Question in Canada: An Appraisal in the Light of *Calder*" (1973) 51 Can. Bar Rev. 450.

Macklem, P. "What's Law Got to Do With It? The Protection of Aboriginal Title in Canada" (Spring 1997) 35 Osgoode Hall L.J. 125.

McLeod, C. "The Oral Histories of Canada's Northern People, Anglo-Canadian Evidence Law, and Canada's Fiduciary Duty to First Nations: Breaking Down the Barriers of the Past" (1992) 30 Alta. L. Rev. 1276.

McMurtry, W.R. & A. Pratt. "Indians and the Fiduciary Concept, Self-Government and the Constitution" [1986] 3 C.N.L.R. 19.

McNeil, K. *Common Law, Aboriginal Title* (Oxford: Clarendon Press, 1989).

————. "The Meaning of Aboriginal Title" in M. Asch, ed. *Aboriginal and Treaty Rights in Canada* (Vancouver: U.B.C. Press, 1997).

————. *Emerging Justice: Essays on Indigenous Rights in Canada and Australia* (Saskatoon: University of Saskatchewan Native Law Centre, 2001).

Royal Commission on Aboriginal Peoples. *Report of the Royal Commission on Aboriginal Peoples*, vol. 2. (Ottawa: RCAP, 1996) 44–47 and 559–89.

Slattery, B. *The Land Rights of Indigenous Canadian Peoples as Affected by the Crown's Acquisition of their Territories.* D.Phil. Thesis, Oxford University. (Saskatoon: University of Saskatchewan Native Law Centre, 1979).

————. "Understanding Aboriginal Rights" (1987) 66 Can. Bar Rev. 727.

————. "The Legal Basis of Aboriginal Title" in F. Cassidy, ed. *Aboriginal Title in British Columbia: Delgamuukw v. The Queen* (Lantzville, B.C.: Oolichan Books, 1992).

————. "Some Thoughts on Aboriginal Title" (1999) 48 U.N.B.L.J. 19.

Chapter 2

TREATY RIGHTS

INTRODUCTION

Treaty rights are those rights expressly set out in treaties and agreements, or subsequently inferred as a result of judicial interpretation,[1] between Aboriginal people and the Crown. Treaties and land claims agreements are the formal mechanisms that outline Crown-Aboriginal relations, and broadly speaking, the promises made to Aboriginal people by the Crown's representatives. They document concessions made by Aboriginal people[2] and vary considerably in their terms.[3] In some cases, unilateral declarations by the Crown[4] have been interpreted as being treaties. In many treaties, the Crown acknowledged that Aboriginal people possessed some interest in the land.[5] In other cases, there is evidence suggesting that the Crown did not negotiate in good faith and that the Indians did not fully comprehend the Crown's intent behind signing treaties.[6]

Existing treaty rights are constitutionally "recognized and affirmed" in s. 35(1) of the *Constitution Act, 1982* ("s. 35(1)").[7] The existing treaty rights referred to in s. 35(1) are not absolute and can be infringed by the federal and provincial governments, if such infringement can be justified. Prior to 1982, treaty rights were expressly protected from interference by provincial, but not federal, laws by s. 88 of the *Indian Act*.[8] Since 1982, treaty rights can no longer be altered unilaterally by the federal Crown,[9] they are binding on the Crown and are legally enforceable.[10] Federal, provincial, and territorial governments have an interest in seeing modern treaties negotiated because they can clarify the nature of the Aboriginal burden on the Crown's title to land and can assist in providing certainty to promote land, resource, and economic development.

---

[1] See *R. v. Marshall*, [1999] 3 S.C.R. 456; In *Marshall*, the Supreme Court of Canada held that the Treaties of 1760–61 contained the right for the Mi'kmaq to hunt, fish, gather, and trade for necessaries, even though there was no express reference to such rights within the text of the treaty.

[2] *R. v. Simon*, [1985] 2 S.C.R. 387 at 408–9; *R. v. Sioui*, [1990] 1 S.C.R. 1025 at 1035–45.

[3] *R. v. Sundown*, [1999] 1 S.C.R. 393 at para. 25.

[4] For example, see *Sioui, supra* note 2, wherein the Supreme Court of Canada held that a brief document signed only by the Governor of Quebec in 1760 outlining certain rights for the Huron Indians constituted a treaty.

[5] Lamer J. (as he then was) wrote in *Sioui, ibid.* at 1043: "There is no reason why an agreement concerning something other than a territory, such as an agreement about political or social rights, cannot be a treaty within the meaning of s. 88 of the *Indian Act*."

[6] For example, see R. Fumoleau, *As Long As This Land Shall Last: A History of Treaty 8 and Treaty 11* (Toronto: McClelland & Stewart, 1973); see also D. Hall, "'A Serene Atmosphere'? Treaty 11 Revisited," in S. Corrigan & J. Sawchuk, eds., *The Recognition of Aboriginal Rights* (Brandon, Manitoba: Bearpaw Publishing, 1996).

[7] *Constitution Act, 1982*, Sched. B to the *Canada Act 1982* (U.K.), 1982, c. 11, as am. by *Constitution Amendment Proclamation 1983*, R.S.C. 1985, App. II, No. 46, adding ss. 35(3) and 35(4).

[8] *Indian Act*, R.S.C. 1985, c. I–5: Section 88 provides that provincial laws of general application apply to Indians "subject to the terms of any treaty."

[9] See *R. v. Moosehunter*, [1981] 1 S.C.R. 282 at 293; see also text accompanying note 46.

[10] *Simon, supra* note 2 at 408–9; *Sioui, supra* note 2 at 1063; *R. v. Badger*, [1996] 1 S.C.R. 771 at 793–94.

PRE-CONFEDERATION TREATIES

Treaties made with the British Crown before Confederation are now considered to be treaties with the Crown in right of Canada.[11] Some of the pre-Confederation treaties include the Murray Treaty of September 1760, which recognized the Quebec Hurons' customary and religious practices, along with trading rights with the British; this is the subject of the *Sioui* decision of the Supreme Court of Canada.[12] At well, from 1764 to 1862 a series of land surrender treaties were signed in what is now Ontario, including the Manitoulin Island Treaty (1862), the Robinson-Huron Treaty (1850), and the Robinson-Superior Treaty (1850).[13] Finally, from 1850 to 1854 Governor James Douglas negotiated fourteen land surrender treaties on Vancouver Island. Many of the Indian bands involved in these treaties ceded their lands in return for a lump-sum payment, reserve lands, and hunting and fishing rights.

EARLY MARITIME PEACE AND FRIENDSHIP TREATIES[14]

The earliest treaties made between Indians and settlers were the peace and friendship treaties in eastern North America in the seventeenth and eighteenth centuries. These treaties guaranteed hunting, fishing and other rights to Indians in return for peaceful relationships and military alliances with the settlers. Unlike later treaties, they did not include the cession of land by the Indians,[15] and therefore in the Maritimes, Aboriginal rights and Aboriginal title may co-exist with treaty rights.[16] This situation is perhaps unique in Canada.

Between 1713 and 1763 much political instability existed in eastern North America. The Maritimes were central to the struggle between the French and the English over control of North America, with the Mi'kmaq and Maliseet in the middle of this conflict. From 1713, when the British acquired sovereignty over the Maritimes, until the Proclamations of 1762 and 1763, a series of peace and friendship treaties were signed between the British and the Mi'kmaq[17] and Maliseet peoples in what is now New Brunswick and Nova Scotia. The primary goal of these treaties was to solidify peaceful relations with the Mi'kmaq and Maliseet and to end hostilities between them and the British. In return for agreeing to keep the peace and respect British law, the Crown promised the Mi'kmaq and Maliseet rights to hunt, fish, and trade. Unlike other treaties in Canada, these treaties did

---

[11] *R. v. Secretary of State*, [1981] 4 C.N.L.R. 86 (Eng. C.A.).

[12] *Sioui, supra* note 2.

[13] A copy of this treaty can be found at p. 179.

[14] See Thomas Isaac, *Aboriginal and Treaty Rights in the Maritimes: The Marshall Decision and Beyond* (Saskatoon: Purich Publishing Ltd., 2001).

[15] *Simon, supra* note 2.

[16] See Brian Slattery, "Making Sense of Aboriginal and Treaty Rights" [2000] 79 Can. Bar Rev. 197 at 210, with respect to the relationship between Aboriginal and treaty rights:

> What is the relationship between treaty rights and aboriginal rights? Clearly, the relationship may vary, depending on the precise terms of the treaty and the overall context. In some cases, the treaty may recognize and guarantee certain existing aboriginal rights. In other instances, it may alter aboriginal rights, as by consolidating them, redefining them, sharing them, ceding them, or reshaping them in some other fashion. Where a treaty recognizes and guarantees aboriginal rights, it does not convert them into treaty rights, in the absence of very clear language to that effect. Treaty rights throw a protective mantle over aboriginal rights, providing an extra layer of security. The latter become "treaty-protected aboriginal rights."

[17] See W. Wicken, "The Mi'kmaq and Wuastukwiuk Treaties" (1994) 44 U.N.B.L.J. 241.

not involve the cession of land and did not expressly extinguish Aboriginal title.[18]

One of the first treaties between Aboriginal people and the English in the Maritimes was the 1725 "Submission and Agreement of the Delegates of the Eastern Indians" signed in Boston, Massachusetts,[19] ratified later by the Mi'kmaq and possibly the Maliseet.[20] On December 15, 1725, the Treaty of Boston[21] was signed ending the English-Indian War. In this treaty, the Indians acknowledged British jurisdiction and sovereignty over Nova Scotia, agreed to cease all hostilities, and agreed to use the Crown's courts to settle disputes. The Indians were also granted the "privilege of fishing, hunting, and fowling as formerly."

Many of the articles in these early Maritime treaties are similar because they were modelled on the Treaty of 1725, including:

1. A recognition of the Crown's jurisdiction and dominion over territory covered, including Nova Scotia and Acadia;

2. Conflicts between the Indians and settlers would be adjudicated according to English law;

3. Indians would not "molest" English subjects who had already established settlements or who would do so in the future; and

4. The English would not "molest" the Indians with respect to their hunting, fishing, planting and fowling.

The treaties of 1726 and 1749 conferred hunting and fishing rights[22] on the Maliseet[23] as did the treaties of 1725 and 1760. The Treaty of 1778 did not guarantee any hunting or fishing rights to the Indians of New Brunswick,[24] except noting that the Indians would be allies against the United States of America.[25] These treaties are discussed in detail in *Marshall*.[26] In addition to the Mi'kmaq and Maliseet communities in the Maritimes, there are a number of Mi'kmaq and Maliseet Indian bands in the Gaspé region of Quebec that are also most likely covered by the terms of the 1760–61 treaties.

The Treaties of 1760–61[27] were the focus of *Marshall*,[28] where the Supreme Court of Canada quoted the trial judge as follows:

> The 1760–61 treaties were the culmination of more than a decade of intermittent hostilities between the British and the Mi'kmaq. Hostilities with the French were also prevalent in

---

[18] P.A. Cumming & N.H. Mickenberg, *Native Rights in Canada*, 2d ed. (Toronto: General Publishing Ltd., 1972) at 98.

[19] *Ibid.* at 95.

[20] *Ibid.*; see also D.M. Hurley, *Report on Indian Land Rights in the Atlantic Provinces* (Ottawa: National Museum of Canada, 1962).

[21] See *R. v. Perley*, [1982] 2 C.N.L.R. 185 (N.B.Q.B.) and *Simon*, *supra* note 2, upholding the applicability of the Treaty of 1725.

[22] *R. v. Paul*, [1981] 2 C.N.L.R. 83 (N.B.C.A.); *R. v. Polchies*, [1988] 4 C.N.L.R. 107 (N.B.Q.B.).

[23] *Polchies, ibid.*

[24] *Ibid.*

[25] *R. v. Polchies*, [1983] 3 C.N.L.R. 131 (N.B.C.A.).

[26] *Marshall, supra* note 1.

[27] In *R. v. Marshall*, [1997] 3 C.N.L.R. 209 at 216 (N.S.C.A.), the Nova Scotia Court of Appeal described the Treaties of 1760–61 as follows:

> The Treaties of 1760–61 comprise several separate treaties, entered into by the British with each Mi'kmaq Sakamow (Chief). . . . It was hoped that at some future time there would be a grand re-affirmation of all of these treaties. That never happened. The trial judge found that the documents were indeed treaties and that all of the Mi'kmaq treaties were "materially the same."

[28] *Marshall, supra* note 1.

Nova Scotia throughout the 1750's, and the Mi'kmaq were constantly allied with the French against the British. . . . The British wanted peace and a safe environment for their current and future settlers.[29]

POST-CONFEDERATION TREATIES

As the settlement of Canada moved west, so did the treaty-making process. In 1850 the Robinson Treaties (Lake Huron and Lake Superior) were signed, followed by eleven numbered treaties between 1871 and 1921.[30] The numbered treaties cover most of the land in northwestern Ontario and the prairie provinces. Treaty No. 11 and part of Treaty No. 8 apply to the Northwest Territories. Even after last of the numbered treaties was signed in 1921 (Treaty No. 11), large amounts of Canadian territory continued to have no treaties in place, including Newfoundland and Labrador, northern Quebec, the Yukon, and parts of the Northwest Territories and British Columbia.

All the numbered treaties contain similar provisions, including reserve lands, monetary payments, new suits of clothing every three years for chiefs and headmen, allowances for education, and, with the exception of Treaties No. 1, No. 2, and No. 9, annual ammunition and twine payments. Treaty No. 6 provided for medical treatment in case of "pestilence or famine."

SUI GENERIS NATURE OF TREATIES

Governments and courts in Canada have historically viewed treaties with Aboriginal people from a positivist, literal perspective, while many Aboriginal people see treaties as being more holistic and sacred documents. For many Aboriginal people, the historical and modern treaties are significant not only for what they contain, but also for what they represent: solemn agreements and commitments among groups of independent and sovereign peoples. Harold Cardinal has written:

> To the Indians of Canada, the treaties represent an Indian Magna Carta. The treaties are important to us, because we entered into these negotiations with faith, with hope for a better life with honour. . . . The treaties were the way in which the white people legitimized in the eyes of the world their presence in our country. It was an attempt to settle the terms of occupancy on a just basis, legally and morally to extinguish the legitimate claims of our people to title to the lands in our country.[31]

The differences between Aboriginal and non-Aboriginal people regarding the significance and meaning of treaties has resulted in a novel interpretation of treaties in Canadian law. Canadian courts have held that treaties are unique, or *sui generis*.[32] Indian treaties are neither international-like agreements between nation-states,[33] nor are they simple contracts.[34] Relying primarily on *Sioui*[35] and *Simon*,[36] Peter Hogg provides a succinct

[29] *Ibid.* at para. 23.
[30] A collection of the texts of many treaties can be found in *Consolidated Native Law Statutes, Regulations and Treaties 2003* (Toronto: Carswell, 2003); Treaty Nos. 1 and 2 (1871), 3 (1873), 4 (1874), 5 (1875), 6 (1876), 7 (1877), 8 (1899), 9 (1905), 10 (1906), and 11 (1921).
[31] Harold Cardinal, *The Unjust Society: The Tragedy of Canada's Indians* (Edmonton: Hurtig, 1969) 28–29.
[32] See *Simon, supra* note 2, at 404, and *Sioui, supra* note 2 at 1043.
[33] *R. v. Francis*, [1956] S.C.R. 618.
[34] *Pawis* v. *R.*, [1979] 2 C.N.L.R. 52 (F.C.T.D.) and *Hay River* v. *R.*, [1979] 2 C.N.L.R. 101 (F.C.T.D.).
[35] *Sioui, supra* note 2.
[36] *Simon, supra* note 2.

summary of the characteristics of a valid Indian treaty:

1. The parties to the treaty must be the Crown on the one side, and an Aboriginal nation on the other.

2. The signatories to the treaty must have the authority to bind their principals, namely, the Crown and the Aboriginal nation.

3. The parties must intend to create legally binding obligations.

4. The obligations must be assumed by both sides, so that the agreement is a bargain.

5. There must be "a certain measure of solemnity."[37]

In *Sioui*, Lamer J. identified five factors that are useful in determining the intent of the parties to enter into a treaty. The factors are not exhaustive and originate from the Ontario Court of Appeal decision in *R. v. Taylor and Williams*:[38]

1. continuous exercise of a right presently, and in the past;

2. the reasons as to why the Crown made a commitment;

3. the situation prevailing at the time when the document was signed;

4. evidence regarding mutual respect and esteem between the negotiators; and

5. the subsequent conduct of the parties.[39]

Most of these factors seek to go beyond the text of treaty itself and focus on the intentions of the parties in the negotiations leading up to the final text.

SECTION 88, *INDIAN ACT*[40]

The application of provincial laws to treaties has been a subject of ongoing judicial interpretation. In *R. v. Dick*,[41] the Supreme Court of Canada held that provincial laws of general application neither affect the status or capacity of Indians nor their "Indianness," but could apply *ex proprio vigore* (of their own effect). The *Indian Act* adds to this confusion by providing that provincial laws of general application that apply to Indians are subject to the terms of any treaty. Section 88 of the Act outlines the relationship between treaty rights and provincial legislation:

> Subject to the terms of any treaty and any other Act of Parliament, all laws of general application from time to time in force in any province are applicable to and in respect of Indians in the province, except to the extent that those laws are inconsistent with this Act or any order, rule, regulation or by-law made thereunder, and except to the extent that those laws make provision for any matter for which provision is made by or under this Act.

Section 88 of the Act ensures that: (*a*) provincial legislatures do not stray into federal jurisdiction with respect to Indians, (*b*) there is no legislative vacuum respecting Indians, and (*c*) provincial laws of general application are subject to the terms of any treaty.[42]

---

[37] Peter Hogg, *Constitutional Law of Canada*, 4th ed. (Toronto: Carswell, 1997), 27.6(c), 691.

[38] *R. v. Taylor and Williams* (1982), 34 O.R. (2d) 360 (Ont. C.A.).

[39] *Sioui, supra* note 2 at 1045.

[40] *Indian Act, supra* note 8.

[41] *R. v. Dick*, [1985] 2 S.C.R. 309; see also *Derrickson v. Derrickson*, [1986] 1 S.C.R. 285 and *R. v. Francis*, [1988] 1 S.C.R. 1025.

[42] See *R. v. White and Bob* (1965), 52 D.L.R. (2d) 481 (S.C.C.); *Simon, supra* note 2; *Sioui, supra* note 2.

Treaty rights are recognized and affirmed in s. 35(1) and, therefore, can impair provincial legislation that infringes treaty rights, unless such legislation can be justified. Section 88 incorporates by reference provincial laws of general application (those laws that are "provincial in scope"[43] and that are not in relation to one class of citizens, such as "Indians"[44]) into federal law, subject to the terms of any treaty.[45]

Although "Indians and lands reserved for Indians" are within Parliament's exclusive jurisdiction, provincial laws of general application can apply to Indians and their lands by two methods:

1. of their own effect (*ex proprio vigore*), so long as they do not interfere with Parliament's jurisdiction over Indians and their lands and are not inconsistent with any other federal law; and

2. by way of s. 88 of the Act, whereby provincial laws of general application can apply to Indians, even though they affect "Indianness," so long as they are not contrary to the *Indian Act* or any other federal legislation.

Until treaty rights were recognized and affirmed in the *Constitution Act, 1982*, their legal status was fluid and vulnerable. Prior to April 17, 1982, treaty rights could be unilaterally modified or extinguished by the federal Crown. In *R. v. Moosehunter*, the Supreme Court of Canada succinctly stated this vulnerability: "The Government of Canada can alter the rights of Indians granted under treaties (*Sikyea* v. *R.*). Provinces cannot."[46] In *Simon*, the Supreme Court of Canada stated:

> Under s. 88 of the *Indian Act*, when the terms of a treaty come into conflict with federal legislation, the latter prevails, subject to whatever may be the effect of s. 35 of the *Constitution Act, 1982*.[47]

The vulnerability of treaty rights prior to 1982 was also illustrated in *Sikyea* v. *R.*[48] In *Sikyea* the Supreme Court of Canada held that the *Migratory Birds Convention Act* applied to Indians notwithstanding that their hunting rights were guaranteed by Treaty No. 11. The Court affirmed this result in both *R. v. George*[49] and *Daniels v. White*.[50]

In *R. v. Francis*, the Supreme Court of Canada held that the term "treaty" in s. 88 of the Act refers only to treaties made with Indians, not international treaties such as the Jay Treaty, a 1794 treaty between Great Britain and the United States proposing a duty exemption for Indians who crossed what is now the U.S./Canada border.[51] While not trea-

---

[43] *R. v. George*, [1966] 2 S.C.R. 267 at 281.

[44] *Kruger and Manuel* v. *R.*, [1978] 1 S.C.R. 104 at 110. The term "Indian" is used to refer to those Aboriginal people coming within the meaning of "Indian" for the purposes of s. 91(24) of the *Constitution Act, 1867* and s. 35(2) of the *Constitution Act, 1982*.

[45] See *R. v. Dick*, *supra* note 41 at 326, 327, where Beetz J. stated:

> I believe that a distinction should be drawn between two categories of provincial laws. There are, on the one hand, provincial laws which can be applied to Indians without touching their Indianness, like traffic legislation; there are on the other hand, provincial laws which cannot apply to Indians without regulating them *qua* Indians. . . . [I]t is to the laws of the second category that s. 88 refers.

[46] *Moosehunter, supra* note 9 at 293.

[47] *Simon, supra* note 2 at 411.

[48] *Sikyea* v. *R.*, [1964] 43 D.L.R. (2d) 150 (N.W.T.C.A.), aff'd [1964] S.C.R. 642.

[49] *George, supra* note 43.

[50] *Daniels* v. *White*, [1968] S.C.R. 517.

[51] *R. v. Francis*, [1956] S.C.R. 618. For a commentary of *Francis* see K. Lysyk, "The Unique Constitutional Position of the Canadian Indian" (1967), 45 Can. Bar Rev. 513 at 527–28. In *R. v. Jacobs*, [1999] 3 C.N.L.R. 239 (B.C.S.C.), the Court dismissed an application by a number of members of the Sto:lo Indian Nation who claimed a right to import tobacco from the United States without reporting to Canadian customs authorities

ties for the purposes of s. 35(1), treaties such as the Jay Treaty can be useful historical documents to illustrate the treatment of Aboriginal people when the treaty was signed.[52] Although they are not international treaties and were not formally implemented in Canadian law, except to the extent that they are mentioned in s. 88 of the Act, Indian treaties are nevertheless enforceable (both before and after 1982).[53] Modern treaties and land claims agreements are incorporated into Canadian law by way of complementary legislation.[54]

INTERPRETATION OF TREATY RIGHTS

The imbalance in bargaining power that existed in some early treaty negotiations has not gone unnoticed by the courts. In *R. v. Battisse*,[55] Bernstein J. wrote that where the terms of a treaty seem unfair or where the bargaining power of one party greatly outweighs that of the other

> [t]he courts must not assume that His Majesty's Commissioners were attempting to trick or fool the Indians into signing an agreement under false pretences. . . . [A]mbiguity should be resolved in favour of the Indian.[56]

The courts must show flexibility when determining the legal nature of documents recording transactions with Indians.[57] In *Simon*, the Supreme Court of Canada held that Indian treaties must be liberally construed and uncertainties resolved in favour of the Indians.[58] In an earlier Supreme Court of Canada decision, *Nowegijick v. R.*,[59] Dickson J. stated:

> In *Jones v. Meehan*, 175 U.S. 1 (1899), it was held that Indian treaties "must be construed, not according to the technical meaning of [their] words, . . . but in the sense in which they would naturally be understood by the Indians."[60]

The *Nowegijick* principle—that Indian treaties must be construed as they would have been understood by the Indians of the time the treaty was signed—remains in place.

In *Taylor and Williams*[61] the Ontario Court of Appeal set out a number of factors to be used when interpreting treaties. The Court held that although fishing and hunting were

---

and without paying duties based, in part, on Article III of the Jay Treaty of 1794. The Court relied upon the reasoning of McKeown J. in *Mitchell v. Min. of Nat. Rev.*, [1997] 4 C.N.L.R. 103 (F.C.T.D.), who made reference to the Ontario of Court of Appeal decision of *R. v. Vincent*, [1993] 2 C.N.L.R. 165. *Vincent* held that the Jay Treaty is no longer in force and that even if it were, it applied only to the trading of goods for personal or community goods on a non-commercial scale.

[52] *Mitchell, ibid.*

[53] See *R. v. Wesley*, [1932] 4 D.L.R. 744 (Alta. C.A.) and *R. v. Prince and Myron*, [1964] S.C.R. 81. In *R. v. Agawa*, [1988] 3 C.N.L.R. 73, the Ontario Court of Appeal held that Indian treaties are not like international treaties, they are *sui generis* and are not self-executing. Treaties acquire the force of law in Canada when they are protected by statute or by the constitution.

[54] For example, Canada enacted the *Nisga'a Final Agreement Act*, S.C. 2000, c. 7, to bring into effect the Nisga'a Final Agreement.

[55] *R. v. Battisse* (1978), 84 D.L.R. (3d) 377 (Ont. Dist. Ct.); see also *Re Paulette*, [1973] 39 D.L.R. (3d) 45, 42 D.L.R. (3d) 8 (N.W.T.S.C.).

[56] *Ibid.* at 385.

[57] *Sioui, supra* note 2 at 1036.

[58] *Simon, supra* note 2 at 402; *R. v. Horseman*, [1990] 1 S.C.R. 901 at 906–7; *Sioui, supra* note 2 at 1068; *Claxton v. Saanichton Marina Ltd.*, [1989] 3 C.N.L.R. 46 (B.C.C.A.).

[59] *R. v. Nowegijick*, [1983] 1 S.C.R. 29.

[60] *Ibid.* at 36.

[61] *Taylor and Williams, supra* note 38.

not guaranteed by the written terms of Treaty No. 20 (1818), the minutes from the negotiation of the treaty revealed that these rights were discussed and were meant to be included. Oral portions of a treaty are as much part of the treaty as the written portions.
The Court stated that it is important to consider the history and oral traditions of the
tribes concerned. Treaties should be interpreted in a manner that: (a) upholds the honour
of the Crown, (b) avoids the appearance of "sharp dealings," (c) resolves any ambiguity in
favour of the Indians, and (d) considers the parties' understanding of the terms of the
treaty when it was signed. In *Marshall*,[62] the Supreme Court of Canada reaffirmed these
interpretive principles.

In *R. v. Horse*,[63] the Supreme Court of Canada held that extrinsic evidence, such as
minutes of treaty negotiation meetings, cannot be used as an aid in interpreting a treaty
in the absence of ambiguity or where the result would be to alter the terms of the written
agreement.[64]

Treaty rights must be interpreted in an evolutionary manner.[65] For example, in *Simon*,
the Supreme Court of Canada considered the treaty phrase "it is agreed that the said Tribe
of Indians shall not be hindered from, but have free liberty of Hunting and Fishing as
usual":

> I do not read the phrase "as usual" as referring to the types of weapons to be used by the
> Micmac and limiting them to those used in 1752. Any such construction would place upon
> the ability of the Micmac to hunt an unnecessary and artificial constraint out of keeping
> with the principle that Indian treaties should be liberally construed. Indeed, the inclusion
> of the phrase "as usual" appears to reflect a concern that the right to hunt be interpreted in
> a flexible way that is sensitive to the evolution of changes in normal hunting practices.[66]

The British Columbia Court of Appeal summarized the principles applicable to treaty
interpretation in *Claxton* v. *Saanichton Marina Ltd.*:[67]

1. The treaty should be given a fair, large, and liberal construction in favour of the
   Indians;

2. Treaties must be construed, not according to the technical meaning of their words
   but in the sense that they would naturally be understood by the Indians;

3. As the honour of the Crown is always involved, no appearance of "sharp dealing"
   should be sanctioned;

4. Any ambiguity in wording should be interpreted as against the drafters and should
   not be interpreted to the prejudice of the Indians if another construction is reasonably possible; and

5. Evidence of conduct or otherwise as to how the parties understood the treaty is of
   assistance in giving it content.

The Northwest Territories Supreme Court held in *Re Paulette*[68] that Aboriginal rights,

---

[62] *Marshall, supra* note 1 at para. 51; see also para. 14.
[63] *R. v. Horse*, [1988] 1 S.C.R. 187.
[64] *Ibid.* at 201.
[65] See *R. v. Ireland*, [1991] 2 C.N.L.R. 120 (Ont. Ct. J. (Gen.Div.)); *R. v. Norn*, [1991] 3 C.N.L.R. 135 (Alta.
Prov. Ct.); *Marshall, supra* note 1 at para. 59; *R. v. Badger, supra* note 10 at 799.
[66] *Simon, supra* note 2 at 402.
[67] *Claxton* v. *Saanichton Marina Ltd., supra* note 58.
[68] *Re Paulette, supra* note 55.

such as those contained in Treaty Nos. 8 and 11, constitute an interest in land and that the *Royal Proclamation of 1763* did not create Aboriginal rights, but rather confirmed their existence. The Court doubted whether Treaty Nos. 8 and 11 extinguished Aboriginal title to the land in question:

> Unless, therefore, the negotiation of Treaty 8 and Treaty 11 legally terminated or extinguished the Indian land rights or aboriginal rights, it would appear that there was a clear constitutional obligation to protect the legal rights of the indigenous people in the area covered by the proposed caveat, and a clear recognition of such rights.[69]

This liberal approach to treaty interpretation and the evidentiary treatment of oral history preceded the Supreme Court of Canada's decision in *Delgamuukw* v. *B.C.*[70] regarding the flexible approach required when considering Aboriginal historical evidence.

PRE-1982 TREATY RIGHTS DECISIONS

Before they were constitutionally recognized and affirmed, treaty rights were vulnerable to unilateral federal modification or extinguishment. Prior to 1982, the impact of treaty rights on federal legislative authority and decision-making was minimal. The following judicial decisions provide an overview of early treaty rights law.

R. v. *Syliboy*[71] is an example of the narrow approach employed by courts to interpret treaty rights in the early part of the twentieth century. The Nova Scotia County Court considered the appeal of the conviction of the Grand Chief of the Mi'kmaq for the unlawful possession of furs. The Treaty of 1752 between the British and the Mi'kmaq of Nova Scotia was used as a defence. It allowed Indians to hunt and trap at all times. The Court concluded that it was not a real treaty because it was not made between competent contracting parties—it was made with a smaller group of Mi'kmaq not associated with the accused.

In *R.* v. *White and Bob,*[72] the Supreme Court of Canada affirmed that provincial game laws could be superseded by treaty provisions, however vague, by virtue of s. 88 of the *Indian Act*. *White and Bob* affirmed the legal status of treaties in Canadian law and emphasized the importance of the honour of the Crown. It is also the origin of a broad and liberal approach to treaty interpretation and to the rules governing what constitutes a treaty.

In *R.* v. *Francis,*[73] the New Brunswick Court of Appeal upheld the conviction of a Mi'kmaq charged with fishing salmon without a licence. The Court adopted the reasoning in *Syliboy* by stating that the Treaty of 1752 was not made with the Mi'kmaq Nation as a whole, but only with a smaller group of Mi'kmaq. The Court also made reference to *R.* v. *Simon* (1958), which held that the Treaties of 1725 and 1752 do not provide a defence since it could not be shown that they applied to the appellant, and that the Treaty of 1779 applied to the Mi'kmaq in the Richibucto area. However, any rights to fish contained in the 1779 treaty were overridden by the *New Brunswick Fishery Regulations* and the *Fisheries Act*. The Court cited *Sikyea*[74] as authority that laws made by Parliament

---

[69] *Ibid.* at 30.

[70] *Delgamuukw* v. *B.C.*, [1997] 3 S.C.R. 1010.

[71] *R.* v. *Syliboy*, [1929] 1 D.L.R. 307 (N.S. Co. Ct.).

[72] *White and Bob, supra* note 42.

[73] *R.* v. *Francis* (1969), 10 D.L.R. (3d) 189 (N.B.S.C.App.Div.).

[74] *Sikyea, supra* note 48.

are not qualified or made unenforceable by treaty rights.

In *R. v. Cope*,[75] the Nova Scotia Court of Appeal considered an appeal of a Mi'kmaq convicted under the *Fisheries Act*. He argued that he was not subject to the fishery regulations because the Treaty of 1752 conferred a right to fish and hunt on all Mi'kmaq in Nova Scotia. The Court held that even if the Treaty of 1752 conferred the special rights that the Mi'kmaq claimed, those rights could be extinguished by federal legislation. The Court also stated that the treaty did not grant the Mi'kmaq special rights, but rather merely affirmed their Aboriginal rights to hunt and fish. Finally, the Court held that the treaty was not made with the Mi'kmaq Nation as a whole but only with a small group of Mi'kmaq inhabiting the eastern part of what is now Nova Scotia. The Supreme Court of Canada refused to hear the appeal on the basis that this issue was already decided in *R. v. Derricksan*.[76] In *Derricksan*, the Supreme Court of Canada had held that Aboriginal rights to fish are subject to regulation as set out in the federal *Fisheries Act*. Later, in *Marshall*, the Supreme Court of Canada made reference to *Cope* when it noted approvingly that "peace and friendship" treaties with the Mi'kmaq did not extinguish Aboriginal hunting and fishing rights.[77]

While some earlier lower court decisions such as *White and Bob*[78] and *Taylor and Williams*[79] were helpful in expanding the interpretive regime for treaty rights, prior to 1982, treaty rights generally existed at the pleasure of the federal Crown and federal and provincial regulation. It is important to recognize that early judicial reasoning reflected commonly held beliefs about Aboriginal people. The impact and effect of Aboriginal and treaty rights, and indeed attitudes, to some extent, changed dramatically with the constitutional recognition and affirmation afforded to existing Aboriginal and treaty rights in the *Constitution Act, 1982*.

POST-1982 TREATY RIGHTS DECISIONS

The enactment of s. 35(1) had a profound impact on treaty rights. Constitutional "recognition and affirmation" means that treaty rights can no longer be unilaterally modified or extinguished by the federal Crown and that federal and provincial laws must be "justified" if they interfere with and infringe upon existing treaty rights. Section 25 of the *Canadian Charter of Rights and Freedoms*[80] (Charter) ensures that treaty rights cannot be abrogated or derogated by rights and freedoms guaranteed in the Charter. Treaty rights, like Aboriginal rights, are to be interpreted flexibly and evolutionarily, and in a manner sensitive to the changing times.[81] The following Supreme Court of Canada decisions highlight the changes in this area of the law.

R. v. Horseman—Treaty No. 8 and Treaty Interpretation

In *R. v. Horseman*,[82] the Supreme Court of Canada affirmed that the onus to prove the extinguishment of a treaty right rests with the Crown and that ambiguities in treaties must be resolved in favour of the Indians. The case concerned a Treaty No. 8 Indian,

---

[75] *R. v. Cope*, [1982] 1 C.N.L.R. 23 (N.S.C.A.).
[76] *R. v. Derricksan*, [1976] 2 S.C.R. v.
[77] *Marshall*, *supra* note 1 at para. 42.
[78] *White and Bob*, *supra* note 42.
[79] *Taylor and Williams*, *supra* note 38.
[80] Part I of the *Constitution Act, 1982*, *supra* note 7.
[81] *Simon*, *supra* note 2 at 402–3; *Sundown*, *supra* note 3 at para. 32; and *Marshall*, *supra* note 1 at para. 53.
[82] *Horseman*, *supra* note 58.

Horseman, charged with unauthorized hunting contrary to Alberta's *Wildlife Act*.[83] Horseman's original acquittal was restored. The relevant provisions of the *Wildlife Act* were applicable to Treaty No. 8 Indians only to the extent that Indians engaged in sport or commercial hunting. Prior to the enactment of the *Constitution Act, 1982,* the federal government had the exclusive authority to modify treaty rights,[84] as evidenced by the *Constitution Act, 1930,*[85] in which the Natural Resources Transfer Agreement (NRTA) unilaterally "merged and consolidated" Treaty No. 8 hunting rights. The NRTA also recognized that the federal government required provincial land in order to fulfil its legal obligations to provide land to Indians under treaties.

R. v. Sioui—Nature of a Treaty

In *Sioui,*[86] the Supreme Court of Canada considered the rights of the Huron Indians under a treaty made in 1760 to exercise their cultural and traditional activities within the boundaries of Jacques-Cartier Park. As with *Simon,* the Court affirmed that treaties are *sui generis* and require a liberal, generous interpretation favouring Aboriginal people. The Court held that s. 88 of the *Indian Act* affirmed the validity of the treaty in question to exempt the Huron Indians from the application of provincial park regulations. The document was brief and signed only by the Governor of Quebec, but was nonetheless deemed to be a treaty because it contained assurances and promises to the Hurons. The Court also affirmed that at the time the treaty was made, Indian nations were regarded by the Europeans as "independent nations" capable of making treaties. Treaty rights are in addition to rights recognized by the *Royal Proclamation of 1763*. They cannot be extinguished simply because they have not been used for a long period of time.

R. v. Badger—Treaty No. 8 and Treaty Interpretation

The interpretive regime within which treaty rights are to be analyzed was made clearer with the 1996 Supreme Court of Canada decision in *Badger*.[87] *Badger* concerned whether the beneficiaries of Treaty No. 8 possessed the treaty right to hunt on privately owned land within Treaty No. 8 territory, whether treaty hunting rights were extinguished or modified by the NRTA,[88] and the degree to which legislation requiring hunting licences applies to registered Indians. The Court held that the treaty right to hunt for food was not extinguished by the NRTA, but that the right was limited geographically using the concept of "visible, incompatible use." This concept requires a case-by-case analysis and means that if privately owned land is occupied or put to a visible use, Indians do not have a right to access. If the land is unoccupied and not being put to visible use, Indians will have a right to access, pursuant to Treaty No. 8. The Court held that in this case, the requirement of hunting licences is a *prima facie* infringement of treaty rights that must be justified. A new trial was ordered for one of the appellants to deal with the issue of justification, while the other two appellants' claims were dismissed because they were hunting on occupied land. *Badger* affirmed that Treaty No. 8 rights have been subsumed by the NRTA and that the NRTA is the *sole* source for claiming a right to hunt.[89]

---

[83] *Wildlife Act*, R.S.A. 1980, c. W-9.

[84] *Horseman, supra* note 58 at 934.

[85] *Constitution Act, 1930*, R.S.C. 1985, App. II, No. 26 (20 & 21 Geo. V, c. 26 (U.K.)).

[86] *Sioui, supra* note 2.

[87] *Badger, supra* note 10. Application of the *Badger* analysis can be found in many treaty rights decisions since 1996, including *R. v. Gladue*, [1996] 1 C.N.L.R. 153 (Alta. C.A.), and *Marshall, supra* note 1.

[88] Natural Resources Transfer Agreement, *Constitution Act, 1930, supra* note 85.

[89] In *Badger, supra* note 10 at para. 8, Sopinka J. noted: "The Treaty may be relied on for the purpose of

Badger also included a summary of the applicable principles of treaty interpretation:[90]

(1) A treaty represents an exchange of solemn promises between the Crown and Indians and the nature of this agreement is sacred.

(2) The honour of the Crown is always at stake when dealing with Indian people, and it is always to be assumed that the Crown intends to fulfil its promises. The integrity of the Crown must be maintained when interpreting statutes or treaties that affect Aboriginal and treaty rights. The appearance of "sharp dealing" is not sanctioned.

(3) When interpreting a treaty or document, any ambiguities or doubtful expressions in wording must be resolved in favour of the Indians. Any limitations that restrict Indian treaty rights must be narrowly construed.

(4) The onus of proving the extinguishment of a treaty right lies with the Crown. Strict proof of the extinguishment is required, as is a clear and plain intention to do so.

Badger also affirmed that the *Sparrow* justificatory analysis (used to determine whether Crown infringement of Aboriginal rights under s. 35(1) is justified) is to be applied in cases respecting treaty rights:[91]

> [J]ustification of provincial regulations enacted pursuant to the NRTA should meet the same test for justification of treaty rights that was set out in *Sparrow*. The reason for this is obvious. The effect of para. 12 of the NRTA is to place the Provincial government in exactly the same position which the Federal Crown formerly occupied. Thus the provincial government has the same duty not to infringe unjustifiably the hunting right provided by Treaty 8 as modified by the NRTA. Paragraph 12 of the NRTA provides that the province may make laws for a conservation purpose, subject to the Indian right to hunt and fish for food. Accordingly, there is a need for a means to assess which conservation laws will if they infringe that right, nevertheless be justifiable. The *Sparrow* analysis provides a reasonable, flexible and current method of assessing conservation regulations and enactments.[92]

By applying the *Sparrow* analysis to treaty rights cases, the Supreme Court of Canada has attempted to provide a degree of consistency to s. 35(1) analysis and to ensure a balancing between treaty rights and the rights of other Canadians. *Badger* is significant because it applies the principle of co-existence on Crown lands, developed in *Sioui*, to private lands. *Badger* also uses oral history as a basis for interpreting treaty rights and stresses the importance of such history in understanding the context surrounding the signing of a treaty.[93]

The *Badger* approach to unoccupied land was applied in *R. v. Peeace*.[94] In *Peeace*, the Saskatchewan Court of Appeal held that Treaty No. 4 hunting rights can be exercised when private land can be shown to be abandoned and "unoccupied." Land that is visibly used as agricultural lands is not unoccupied and, therefore, Treaty No. 4 hunting rights

---

assisting in the interpretation of the *NRTA*, but it has no other legal significance."

[90] *Ibid.* at para. 41.

[91] *R. v. Sparrow*, [1990] 1 S.C.R. 1075; the *Sparrow* analysis was also applied in *R. v. Little*, [1996] 2 C.N.L.R. 136 (B.C.C.A.), when it examined whether the Douglas Treaties (1854) protected fishing rights. The Court held that the B.C. fisheries regulations did not infringe on the Indian fishing rights as little as possible and that the Indian food fishing requirements were not given priority over the commercial and sport fisheries.

[92] *Badger, supra* note 10 at para. 96.

[93] *Ibid.* at para. 45.

[94] *R. v. Peeace*, [2000] 2 C.N.L.R. 228 (Sask. C.A.); see also *R. v. Peeace*, [1999] 3 C.N.L.R. 286 (Sask. Prov. Ct.).

do not apply. In another decision from Alberta, mining is a "visible, incompatible use" of the land[95] and treaty rights do not apply.

R. v. Sundown—Incidental Treaty Rights

In *R. v. Sundown*[96] the Supreme Court of Canada considered the Crown's appeal of the quashing of a Treaty No. 6 Cree's conviction for constructing a structure within a provincial park, contrary to provincial regulations. The shelter constructed was part of a long-standing tradition of the respondent's Indian band when hunting or fishing:

> A hunting cabin is, in these circumstances, reasonably incidental to this First Nation's right to hunt in their traditional expeditionary style. . . . A reasonable person apprised of the traditional expeditionary method of hunting would conclude that for this First Nation the treaty right to hunt encompasses the right to build shelters as a reasonable incident to that right. . . . It has evolved to the small log cabin, which is an appropriate shelter for expeditionary hunting in today's society.[97]

Sundown is interesting in light of the "reasonably incidental" analysis it outlines and will surely provide Indian bands with a useful tool respecting a liberal and generous approach to interpreting treaties, since a wide array of potential incidental rights could attach to the treaty rights of hunting, fishing, and trapping.

R. v. Marshall—Treaty Rights in the Maritimes

The 1999 Supreme Court of Canada decisions of *R. v. Marshall* affirmed the Mi'kmaq treaty right to hunt, fish, gather, and trade for necessaries. The first *Marshall*[98] decision dealt with the substantive matter under review, while the second decision[99] considered an intervener's application for a rehearing. Donald Marshall Jr., a Mi'kmaq, was convicted of selling eels and fishing without a licence and fishing during a closed season with illegal nets under the *Fisheries Act*.[100] The Court examined whether such acts could be justified by Marshall's claim to a right to catch and sell fish under treaties signed in 1760 and 1761. The crux of the claim was in a restrictive covenant contained within the 1760 treaty, which reads:

> [W]e will not traffick, barter or exchange any commodities in any manner but with such persons or the managers of such Truck houses as shall be appointed or Established by His Majesty's Governor at Luncnbourg or elsewhere in Nova Scotia or Accadia.

A majority of the Court concluded that while the above clause appeared to restrict the Mi'kmaq to trade at "truck houses," it actually reflected the Mi'kmaq demand for trade. The written terms of the 1760 treaty did not contain the entire agreement reached between the British and the Mi'kmaq. The majority reversed the Nova Scotia Court of Appeal's upholding of the trial court conviction. Binnie J., on behalf of the majority, noted that although the text of the March 10, 1760 treaty did not, by itself, support the

---

[95] *R. v. Brertton*, [1998] 3 C.N.L.R. 122 (Alta. Q.B.), aff'd [2000] 1 C.N.L.R. 201 (Alta. C.A.), leave to appeal to S.C.C. dismissed, [2000] 2 C.N.L.R. iv (S.C.C.).

[96] *Sundown, supra* note 3.

[97] *Ibid.* at para. 33.

[98] *Marshall, supra* note 1. See Thomas Isaac, *supra* note 14; Thomas Isaac, "The Courts, Government, and Public Policy: The Significance of *R. v. Marshall*" (2000) 63:2 Sask. Law Rev. 137; and K. Coates, *The Marshall Decision and Native Rights* (Montreal & Kingston: McGill-Queen's University Press, 2000).

[99] *R. v. Marshall* (reconsideration), [1999] 3 S.C.R. 533.

[100] *Fisheries Act*, R.S.C. 1985, c. F-14.

appellant's position, the extrinsic evidence surrounding the negotiations supported the parties' general intention at the time the treaty was signed. The Court first focused on the issue of the use of extrinsic evidence and affirmed its use in appropriate circumstances:[101]

(1) even in the commercial context, extrinsic evidence may be used to demonstrate that a written document does not contain all the terms of an agreement;[102]

(2) even in a document that is purported to contain all the terms of an agreement, extrinsic evidence, of a cultural or historical significance, may be considered if it assists in understanding the context of the treaty, even if there is no apparent ambiguity;[103] and

(3) in the case where the Crown's representatives put into written form only a portion of the verbal agreement with Indians, it would be unconscionable for the Crown to ignore the verbal terms while only relying on that which is written.[104]

The majority held that the British-drafted treaty did not accurately reflect the British-drafted minutes of the negotiating sessions and other evidence.[105] The Supreme Court of Canada found that the Court of Appeal erred by distinguishing between land cession treaties and treaties of peace and friendship (the 1760 treaty) in that the same rules of interpretation must apply to both. Since the Mi'kmaq were largely dispossessed of their lands by 1760, the purpose of a land cession treaty would have been moot.

The Supreme Court of Canada stated that the "honour of the Crown is always at stake in its dealings with Aboriginal people."[106] Binnie J. summarized the Court's interpretation of the events leading up to the 1760 treaty by stating that an interpretation "that turns a positive Mi'kmaq trade demand into a negative Mi'kmaq covenant is [not] consistent with the honour and integrity of the Crown."[107] The lower courts' interpretation of the truck house clause left the Mi'kmaq with "an empty shell of a treaty promise."[108]

Finally, the Supreme Court of Canada affirmed that the test for infringement under s. 35(1) is the same for both Aboriginal and treaty rights. The Court also focused on the discretionary authority of the Minister of Fisheries and Oceans, as set out in the *Maritime Provinces Fishery Regulations,* the *Aboriginal Communal Fishing Licenses Regulations,* and the *Fisheries Act,* which imposed no obligation on, or direction to, the Minister to explain how the Minister should exercise their discretionary authority in a way that respects treaty rights.[109]

---

[101] In *Delgamuukw, supra* note 70 at paras. 82, 84, 87, the Supreme Court of Canada stated:
> Both the principles laid down in *Van der Peet*—first, that trial courts must approach the rules of evidence in light of the evidentiary difficulties inherent in adjudicating Aboriginal claims, and second, that trial courts must interpret that evidence in the same spirit—must be understood against this background. . . . [T]his requires the courts to come to terms with the oral histories of Aboriginal societies, . . . the laws of evidence must be adapted in order that this type of evidence can be accommodated and placed on an equal footing with the types of historical evidence that courts are familiar with, . . . historical documents.

See also *R. v. Van der Peet,* [1996] 2 S.C.R. 507 at para. 68.

[102] *Marshall, supra* note 1 at para. 10.

[103] *Ibid.* at para. 11; see *R. v. Taylor and Williams,* [1981] 3 C.N.L.R. 114 at 123 (Ont. C.A.), leave to appeal refused, [1981] 2 S.C.R. xi; cited with approval in *Delgamuukw, supra* note 70 at 1069 and *Sioui, supra* note 2 at 1050.

[104] *Marshall, ibid.* at para. 12; see also *R. v. Guerin,* [1984] 2 S.C.R. 335.

[105] *Marshall, ibid.* at paras. 19–20.

[106] *Ibid.* at para 49.

[107] *Ibid.* at para. 52.

[108] *Ibid.*

[109] *Ibid.* at paras. 62–64

The Court concluded that, in this case, the charge of fishing and selling eels without a licence constituted *prima facie* infringements of Marshall's treaty rights and such infringements were not justified according to the *Badger* test. Marshall was acquitted of selling fish during the closed season because there "'can be no limitation on the method, timing and extent of Indian hunting under a treaty' . . . apart . . . from a treaty limitation to that effect."[110]

McLachlin J. (and Gonthier J.) dissented and focused on the trial judge's conclusion that the historical evidence strongly suggested that there was no guarantee of a general treaty right to trade (and no treaty right to hunt or fish), but rather simply a "right to bring goods" to truck houses. This right eventually terminated when the exclusive trading and truck house regime ended. McLachlin J. concluded that the trial judge made no error of law and, therefore, the Supreme Court of Canada should not interfere with the trial court's judgment.

The West Nova Fishermen's Coalition, an intervener in the first (September 17, 1999) decision, applied for a rehearing with respect to the federal government's regulatory authority regarding fisheries and, if granted, a stay in the judgment until the rehearing was complete. The Coalition also sought a new trial to determine whether the Crown, on the basis of conservation or some other ground, could justify licensing and closed seasons. The Coalition's application was part of a vocal reaction by non-Aboriginal fishers to *Marshall* and to members of some Indian Bands who set lobster traps during the closed season.

Courts may consider a rehearing based on an intervener's submission in exceptional circumstances. The Supreme Court of Canada, in its second *Marshall* decision, held that no such circumstances existed in this case. Furthermore, the Crown, Marshall, and other interveners were opposed to a new trial.[111] The request for a rehearing was, as the Court put it, "a basic misunderstanding of the scope of the Court's majority reasons."[112] In rejecting the application for a rehearing, the Court provided a useful reiteration of the law relating to treaty rights, their regulation, and justifiable infringement by the Crown.

Marshall is another example of the Supreme Court of Canada attempting to balance Aboriginal and treaty rights with the rights of other Canadians, including the authority of governments to regulate the exercise of those rights within justified limits. Ultimately, the onus rests with governments to enact laws and regulations as a matter of good public policy. Such laws and regulations should not only respect existing Aboriginal and treaty rights, but also enable governments to govern with the public interest in mind.

In both *Marshall* decisions, the Supreme Court of Canada stressed that treaty rights are not absolute but, in this case, limited to hunting, fishing, gathering, and trading for necessaries. The limitations outlined in the *Marshall* decisions are many. Treaty rights are always subject to regulation by the Crown[113] and are limited to securing "necessaries." "Necessaries" is defined by the Court as being equal to that of a moderate livelihood and does not include "the open-ended accumulation of wealth."[114] Even where regulations do infringe upon treaty rights, those regulations can be justified if they meet the *Badger* justification test.[115] The treaties at issue and their benefits are local in nature and, unless a

---

[110] *Ibid.* at para. 65; see also *Badger, supra* note 10 at para. 90.

[111] *Marshall* (reconsideration), *supra* note 99 at para. 11.

[112] *Ibid.* at para. 11.

[113] *Marshall, supra* note 1 at para. 4.

[114] *Ibid.* at para. 7.

[115] See *Badger, supra* note 10 at paras. 96 and 97, wherein Cory J. affirmed the application of the *Sparrow* justificatory analysis.

new agreement with the Crown is reached, the exercise of these treaty rights is limited to the area traditionally used by the local community. "[T]he treaty rights do not belong to the individual, but are exercised by authority of the local community to which the accused belongs."[116]

The Supreme Court of Canada also noted in *Marshall* (reconsideration) that certain unjustified assumptions were made by the Native Council of Nova Scotia regarding its interpretation of *Marshall* and in a so-called economic treaty right on forestry, minerals, and natural gas deposits offshore. The Union of New Brunswick Indians suggested that any gathering contemplated in *Marshall* included harvesting of resources from the sea, forest, and the land. The Supreme Court of Canada held that this interpretation of "gathering" was not considered by the Court in its September 17, 1999 decision and that negotiations with respect to resources such as lumber, minerals, or offshore natural gas deposits would extend beyond the subject matter of *Marshall:* "While treaty rights are capable of evolution within limits, ... their subject matter (absent a new agreement) cannot be wholly transformed."[117]

The Supreme Court of Canada defined what it meant by the treaty right being limited, such as catch limits that would produce a moderate livelihood for an individual Mi'kmaq at present day standards that could be established by regulation and enforced without violating any treaty rights.[118] Regulations could accommodate the treaty right and these regulations would not constitute an infringement that would have to be justified under the *Badger* test.[119] Running through these limitations and much of what the Court held is that there is a high onus on government to put its house in order with respect to the regulation and enforcement of fisheries and other regulations so that they can accommodate and consider Aboriginal and treaty rights.

The *Marshall* decisions also underscore the onus placed on the Crown to determine how it is going to manage Aboriginal and treaty rights. Since *Sparrow,* federal, provincial, and territorial governments have not developed a sophisticated and comprehensive scheme to ensure that their laws take into account existing Aboriginal and treaty rights. While this may seem a high onus, the Supreme Court of Canada has been clear that a failure to do so will usually result in a regulation, statute, or act not being justified. The Court noted that it was "always open to the Minister . . . to seek to justify the limitation on the treaty right because of the need to conserve the resource in question or for other compelling and substantial public objectives"[120] and also suggested that ministerial discretionary authority must be expressed in a manner that provides some direction to the Minister on how to exercise such authority in a way that respects treaty rights.[121]

---

[116] *Marshall* (reconsideration), *supra* note 99 at para. 17.

[117] *Ibid.* at para. 19; see also *Marshall, supra* note 1 at para. 58.

[118] *Marshall, supra* note 1 at para. 61.

[119] *Marshall* (reconsideration), *supra* note 99 at para. 36.

[120] *Ibid.* at para. 19; also, in *Badger,* for example, the Crown chose not to put arguments forward justifying their regulations. See *Badg*er, *supra* note 10 at para. 98.

[121] *Marshall, supra* note 1 at para. 64. In *R. v. Adams,* [1996] 3 S.C.R. 101 at para. 52, Lamer C.J. noted: "In this instance, the regulatory scheme subjects the exercise of the appellant's Aboriginal rights to a pure act of Ministerial discretion, and sets out no criteria regarding how that discretion is to be exercised." At para. 54 Lamer C.J. wrote:

> Parliament may not simply adopt an unstructured discretionary administrative regime which risks infringing Aboriginal rights in a substantial number of applications in the absence of some explicit guidance. If a statute confers an administrative discretion which may carry significant consequences for the exercise of an Aboriginal right, the statute or its delegate regulations must outline specific criteria for the granting or refusal of that discretion which seek to accommodate the existence of Aboriginal rights.

The Supreme Court of Canada has clearly outlined the types of legislative objectives that governments can use to justify infringing Aboriginal and treaty rights. These objectives include conservation and resource management[122] and must be for a "compelling and substantial" purpose.[123] In *Gladstone* (1996), the Court affirmed that there is a broad range of objectives that can justify the infringement of an existing Aboriginal right:

> Because, however, distinctive Aboriginal societies exist within, and are a part of, a broader social, political and economic community, over which the Crown is sovereign, there are circumstances in which, in order to pursue objectives of compelling and substantial importance to that community as a whole (. . . Aboriginal societies are a part of that community), some limitation of those rights will be justifiable. . . . [L]imits placed on those rights are, where the objectives . . . are of sufficient importance to the broader community . . . *equally* a necessary part of that reconciliation.[124]

The Supreme Court of Canada also stated that objectives such as economic and regional fairness and the historical reliance of non-Aboriginal people on the fishery, for example, satisfy the *Sparrow* justificatory standard.[125]

CONSULTATION[126]

The Crown must consult with Aboriginal people when Crown decisions or legislation impact upon Aboriginal and treaty rights. This duty to consult is incorporated in the justificatory analysis of s. 35(1), originally outlined in *Sparrow* and confirmed by *Badger* as applying to treaty rights cases. The Crown's duty to consult is discussed in detail in chapter 3.

The practical application of the duty to consult is problematic. For example, as noted by Gilbert J. of the Alberta Provincial Court in *R. v. Rodgers*:[127]

> The final issue raised is whether the Provincial Government should have consulted with the Treaty Chiefs prior to the enactment of the reporting condition. While I believe that the better practice is that contact and consultation should occur unless there is some infringement of their treaty rights, however small, the requirement of consultation does not arise. The matter of contact and consultation with the Aboriginals whose treaty rights are or may be affected is important when the matter of justification is at issue but would not normally arise where no infringement has been found.[128]

This excerpt illustrates the confusion around governments possessing a duty to consult where treaty rights are infringed, but not knowing if, in law, an infringement has actually occurred without proceeding to litigation. In essence, governments and their counsel must make a judgment call on: (*a*) whether consultation is required (Is there a right? Is there a *prima facie* right?[129] Is that right being infringed?), and (*b*) the extent of the consultation required.

In *R. v. Stump*,[130] the British Columbia Provincial Court considered night hunting

[122] See *Sparrow, supra* note 91 at 1113.
[123] *Ibid.*, and *R. v. N.T.C. Smokehouse Ltd.*, [1996] 2 S.C.R. 672 at para. 97.
[124] *R. v. Gladstone*, [1996] 2 S.C.R. 723 at para. 73.
[125] *Ibid.* at para, 75.
[126] T. Isaac & T. Knox, "The Crown's Duty to Consult Aboriginal People" (2003) 41:1 Alta. L. Rev. 49–77.
[127] *R. v. Rodgers*, [1999] 3 C.N.L.R. 295 (Alta. Prov. Ct.).
[128] *Ibid.* at para. 9.
[129] *Taku River Tlingit First Nation* v. *Ringstad*, [2002] 2 C.N.L.R. 312 (B.C.C.A.); *Haida Nation* v. *B.C. (Min. of Forests)*, [2002] 2 C.N.L.R. 121 (B.C.C.A.), rev'g [2001] 2 C.N.L.R. 83 (B.C.S.C.).
[130] *R. v. Stump*, [2000] 4 C.N.L.R. 260 (B.C. Prov. Ct.).

charges against a number of Chilcotin Indians and whether the government was justified in restricting night hunting. The Court held that government regulation regarding night hunting was a valid safety objective. On the issue of the lack of consultation respecting the regulation, the Court noted:

> I conclude that while consultation may have been desirable, in all the circumstances of this case, the lack of evidence of consultation does not destroy the Crown's justification of the infringement. This case is distinguishable from *Halfway* and *Noel* where justification was of utmost importance in the context of those cases—each involving a specific Aboriginal group and specific land over which the group had a treaty right. Factors I have looked at in arriving at in finding the Crown has proven justification include the province-wide prohibition on night-hunting, the long time the legislation has been in existence in one form or another, and the major role safety plays in the legislation.[131]

Stump contradicts the prevailing view that the Crown's duty to consult Aboriginal people, in addition to being a central component of the justification analysis for an infringement of s. 35(1), also arises from the special relationship between the Crown and Aboriginal people. Thus, while a legislative objective may be justified, the lack of adequate consultation with Aboriginal people concerning the impact of legislation upon them may render that portion of the infringing legislation unjustified.

Treaty No. 8—*Mikisew Cree First Nation* v. *Canada*

The Federal Court of Canada, Trial Division decision of *Mikisew Cree First Nation* v. *Canada (Min. of Can. Heritage)*[132] concerned an application for judicial review of a decision by the Minister of Canadian Heritage to approve construction of a winter road through Wood Buffalo National Park. The road had been approved on the basis that it would not cause a significant environmental impact, pursuant to the *Canadian Environmental Assessment Act*.[133] The Mikisew Cree First Nation argued that the winter road would have a negative impact on their rights under Treaty No. 8 and claimed that the Minister's decision was made without adequate consultation with the Band or its members. The Crown argued that the Band's treaty rights in the Park had been extinguished, that consultation was not required, and, alternatively, any infringement of the Band's rights resulting from the operation or construction of the road could withstand scrutiny under s. 35(1).

The Court concluded that Treaty No. 8 constitutionally protects treaty rights to hunt, fish, and trap in the Park, and that such rights were not extinguished by the establishment of the Park or by subsequent legislation. The treaty rights are subject to two internal limitations:

1. the geographic limitation that the rights could be exercised "throughout the tract surrendered . . . saving and excepting such tracts as may be required or *taken up* from time to time, for settlement, mining, lumbering, trading or other purposes" (emphasis added); and

2. that the rights could be limited by government regulations adopted for conservation purposes.

The standard established and the meaning attributed to "taken up" by the Supreme

---

[131] *Ibid.* at para. 53.
[132] *Mikisew Cree First Nation* v. *Canada (Min. of Can. Heritage)*, [2001] F.C.J. No. 1877 (F.C.T.D.).
[133] *Canadian Environmental Assessment Act*, S.C. 1992, c. 37.

Court of Canada in *Badger* was the "visible, incompatible land use" test.[134] The Court concluded that the Park does not constitute a "visible, incompatible land use" and should not, by itself, restrict the exercise of treaty rights. Interestingly, the Court did not make reference to the NRTA, which, among other things, modified Treaty No. 8 by limiting the right to hunt for food purposes only and extending the geographic application of the treaty right to hunt, trap, and fish to all of Alberta.[135]

The Court stated that the Crown "taking up" lands would result in the "extinguishment of the treaty right in the area taken up."[136] However, this may not be an accurate characterization of what actually occurs upon a "taking up." Aboriginal rights were already extinguished by Treaty No. 8 and replaced with specified treaty rights. After 1982, treaty rights cannot be modified or extinguished without the express consent of the Aboriginal people involved. The "taking up" of land is an inherent component of the rights contained in Treaty No. 8. As land is being "taken up," the treaty right to hunt for food is simply having additional geographic limitations placed upon it, as explicitly contemplated by Treaty No. 8, and is not actually being extinguished.

The Court may have mischaracterized the treaty rights contained in Treaty No. 8. The treaty rights recognized and affirmed included the terms relating to government regulation contained in Treaty No. 8 and the NRTA. Treaty No. 8 is the sum of *all* its terms. For this reason, the "taking up" of lands under the "taken up" provision of Treaty No. 8 does not require justification since no treaty right would be infringed.

The Court also discussed the adequacy of the Minister's consultation with the Band and concluded that since the consultation was part of a broader public consultation process and not distinct to the Band, that adequate consultation did not occur. The application for judicial review was allowed by the Court and the Minister's decision was set aside.

The Court stated that if the road amounts to "taking up" land, it would make the 1982 constitutional protection of treaty rights meaningless. This conclusion does not consider that all that is occurring is that the geographic boundaries of the treaty rights are being further limited, not extinguished, and that the authority of the federal government to effect this limitation is expressly contemplated in the terms of Treaty No. 8. The Supreme Court of Canada, in its 1980 decision of *R. v. Mousseau*,[137] cited with approval by the Court in *Badger*, confirmed that a public highway is "occupied Crown land" and, therefore, "taken up."[138]

The rights set out in Treaty No. 8 are not absolute in that they are internally limited by the terms of Treaty No. 8, and may be infringed by the Crown if such infringement is justified by the analysis to be used under s. 35(1). Treaty No. 8 expressly states that the rights of the Aboriginal parties to Treaty No. 8 to hunt, trap, and fish are "subject to such regulations as may from time to time be made by the Government," and do not apply to "such tracts as may be required or taken up from time to time for settlement, mining, lumbering, trading or other purposes." In *Mikisew*, the creation of a winter road by the Crown falls within the express authority of the Crown to take up land for public purposes. Therefore, such "taking up" cannot constitute an infringement of a treaty rights since no treaty rights exist within the terms of Treaty No. 8 that prevent Crown "taking

---

[134] *Badger, supra* note 10.
[135] *Ibid.* at para. 45.
[136] *Mikisew, supra* note 132 at para. 59.
[137] *R. v. Mousseau*, [1980] 2 S.C.R. 89 at 97.
[138] *Badger, supra* note 10 at para. 62.

up" of lands for settlement, mining, lumbering, trading, or other purposes.

In *Badger*, Cory J., for the majority, confirmed the ability of the Crown to "take up" land for public purposes and "regulate" land for conservation purposes without infringing the rights created by Treaty No. 8.[139]

Mikisew reaffirms the need for governments to ensure that their consultation processes and practices are consistent with the courts' direction to date, including providing some means of distinct consultation for the Aboriginal people affected. This includes allocating sufficient resources to enable procedural fairness through a consistent, thorough, and sensitive consultation scheme and ensuring that government actions and decisions can withstand a challenge under s. 35(1).

GOOD FAITH NEGOTIATIONS

Although the Crown is not obligated to enter into treaty negotiations with Aboriginal people, once it chooses to do so, the Crown must negotiate in good faith.[140] The issue of good faith was raised in a number of decisions, including *Gitanyow First Nation* v. *Canada*[141] and *Haida Nation* v. *B.C.*[142] The Court noted that any fiduciary relationship and the principle of the honour of the Crown between the Crown and the Gitanyow is not displaced simply because these parties have entered into negotiations respecting Aboriginal rights and title.[143] The Court also found that the reference to the Crown in the phrase "honour of the Crown" and fiduciary responsibility includes both the Crown in right of Canada and the Crown in right of the provinces.[144] The Court stated that although a declaratory proceeding is not the proper forum to outline the Crown's duty to negotiate in good faith, such duty must include: (*a*) the absence of any "sharp dealing,"[145] (*b*) disclosure of relevant factors, and (*c*) negotiation absent "oblique motive."[146] The Court of Appeal issued the following declaration:

> The Crown in Right of Canada and the Crown in Right of British Columbia in undertaking to negotiate with the Gitanyow within the framework of the British Columbia treaty process and in proceeding with those negotiations *are obliged to negotiate in good faith with the Gitanyow*, and all representatives of the Crown in Right of Canada and the Crown in Right of British Columbia are bound by such duty.[147] [emphasis added]

Presumably, if a good faith requirement exists once a government agrees to negotiate treaties, there is also a requirement of good faith if a government plans to exit the treaty negotiation process.

The Court's conclusion in *Gitanyow* that the "honour of the Crown" and fiduciary relationship applies to both the federal and provincial governments is consistent with the jurisprudence. However, the origin of the fiduciary relationship between the federal Crown and Aboriginal people has an additional element; namely federal responsibility flowing

---

[139] *Ibid.* at para. 37.
[140] *Gitanyow First Nation* v. *Canada*, [1999] 3 C.N.L.R. 89 (B.C.S.C.), at para. 70, the Court writes: ". . . I can find nothing that obliges the Crown to negotiate a treaty. The B.C. treaty process is voluntary."
[141] *Ibid.*
[142] *Haida Nation* v. *B.C. (Minister of Forests)*, [2001] 2 C.N.L.R. 83 (B.C.S.C.).
[143] *Ibid.* at para. 40.
[144] *Ibid.* at para. 53.
[145] *Ibid.* at para. 74; *Badger, supra* note 10 at 794.
[146] *Ibid.*; see *Chemainus First Nation* v. *B.C. Assets and Lands Corporation*, [1999] 3 C.N.L.R. 8 (B.C.S.C.) at para. 26.
[147] *Gitanyow, supra* note 140 at para. 75.

from s. 91(24) of the *Constitution Act, 1867.*[148] Additionally, the "honour of the Crown" and the Crown's fiduciary relationship with Aboriginal people are distinct concepts. The Supreme Court of Canada's imposition of a duty to negotiate in good faith is best understood as an approach similar to that taken in understanding the meaning of s. 35(1) by the Court—a balancing of interests. Courts appear to be going to great lengths to ensure that the ground rules and principles regarding treaty negotiations are fair, but also emphasize that negotiations are voluntary.[149] *Gitanyow* emphasizes that governments must be diligent in establishing processes that are fair, transparent, and that hold all parties accountable.

SPECIFIC CLAIMS

Specific claims are those claims made by Indians against governments relating to "the administration of land and other Indian assets and to the fulfilment of Indian treaties."[150] Examples of specific claims are treaty land entitlement, a breach of an obligation under the Act or other statutes, a breach of an obligation arising from government administration of Indian funds or assets, or an illegal disposition of land. Noncompensation for reserve lands taken or damaged by the Government of Canada, and fraud in connection with the disposition or acquisition of reserve lands by federal employees or agents, may also give rise to a specific claim.[151]

In 1991 the Government of Canada established the Indian Claims Commission (ICC) as an independent body to hold public inquiries into specific land claims disputes. The ICC holds inquiries at the request of Indian bands, where the federal government has rejected a claim or where a dispute has arisen over the compensation criteria being applied to settle a claim. The ICC has also assisted in mediating disputes between the government and Indian bands.[152] The ICC can only make recommendations to the government.

On June 13, 2002, Parliament introduced Bill C-60, the *Specific Claims Resolution Act,* the object of which is to replace the current ICC with the Canadian Centre for the Independent Resolution of First Nations Specific Claims. The Centre would facilitate the settlement of specific claims across Canada in a cooperative manner, but would also make available a tribunal to adjudicate claims where no agreement was reached. The creation of a tribunal that could make decisions binding on the Crown would be a significant development in this area. The Act was passed on November 7, 2003, and, at the time of writing, was waiting for Royal Assent.

TREATY LAND ENTITLEMENT

There are outstanding claims under some treaties that remain unfulfilled. A claim for treaty land entitlement arises when an Indian band did not receive all of the land that it was entitled to receive under the terms of the applicable treaty. For example, Treaty Nos. 1, 2, and 5 allowed for 160 acres of land to be provided to each family of five (32 acres per person). Treaty Nos. 3, 4, 6, and 10 allowed for 640 acres of land to be provided for each family of five (128 acres per person). In some instances, these requirements were not met.

---

[148] *Constitution Act, 1867* (U.K.), 30 & 31 Vict., c. 3 (U.K.), reprinted in R.S.C. 1985, App. II, No. 5.

[149] See note 140.

[150] *Outstanding Business: A Native Claims Policy* (Ottawa: DIAND, 1982) 19.

[151] *Ibid.* at 20.

[152] The Indian Claims Commission website may be found at: <www.indianclaims.ca>.

Saskatchewan

An example of a treaty land entitlement being fulfilled is the September 22, 1992, Saskatchewan Treaty Land Entitlement Framework Agreement between the Governments of Saskatchewan and Canada and the chiefs of twenty-two treaty land entitlement bands in Saskatchewan.[153] The agreement is the fulfilment of Saskatchewan's obligation to provide land to the federal government, and the federal government's obligation to provide lands to treaty Indians to satisfy the terms of the treaties applicable to Saskatchewan. The agreement provided approximately $450 million over twelve years to Saskatchewan Indian bands to purchase land and mineral rights. The bands are entitled to purchase a maximum of 1.67 million acres of land as reserve land.

In *Lac La Ronge Indian Band* v. *Canada*,[154] the Saskatchewan Court of Appeal held that the population figures to be used when determining treaty land entitlement for the Lac La Ronge Indian Band were as of 1889, adjusted for late adherents. This resulted in the Band being entitled to 27,400 hectares of land, rather than the 310,00 hectares of land granted by the lower court using the current population of the Band. The matter was sent back to the Court of Queen's Bench for a determination of the amount of damages, if any, owed by the Crown to the Band resulting from the loss of opportunity of use of the reserve lands, and for a determination of the amount of compensation owing to the Band for twine and ammunition, as provided for in the terms of Treaty No. 6.

In *One Arrow First Nation* v. *Saskatchewan*,[155] the Saskatchewan Court of Queen's Bench considered a dispute between the One Arrow First Nation and the Government of Saskatchewan regarding the Saskatchewan Treaty Land Entitlement Framework Agreement. One Arrow wanted to purchase provincial Crown land pursuant to the agreement. The provincial government was prepared to sell the land subject to several conditions precedent, including that One Arrow obtain the written consent of six livestock owners who held annual grazing permits for the land. One Arrow was unable to get the consent of all of the permit holders and, in the meantime, the government continued to issue new grazing permits.

The Court held that Saskatchewan did not breach the Saskatchewan Treaty Land Entitlement Framework Agreement. Subsection 4.05(d)(iii) of the agreement states that Saskatchewan can continue to create new third-party interests on land during the eighteen month period following its offer to sell, so long as the new interests have a term of less than one year. As for the condition precedent, the Court noted that the requirement of consent had a cost for One Arrow which reduced the value of the land to One Arrow, thereby being inconsistent with the Saskatchewan Treaty Land Entitlement Framework Agreement. However, if Saskatchewan adjusted its offer to recognize the adverse effects of the condition precedent, no breach of the agreement would occur.

On March 22, 2002 the *Claim Settlements (Alberta and Saskatchewan) Implementation Act*[156] was proclaimed law. The Act assists in the implementation of treaty and entitlement and specific claim settlements by, for example, providing expanded authority to Indian bands to accommodate third-party interests and facilitate on-reserve economic activity.

---

[153] *The Saskatchewan Treaty Land Entitlement Act*, S.C. 1993, c. 11 does not incorporate the Saskatchewan Treaty Land Entitlement Framework except in relation to specific clauses. See *Thomas* v. *Peace Hills Trust Co.*, [2001] 4 C.N.L.R. 335 (F.C.T.D.).

[154] *Lac La Ronge Indian Band* v. *Canada*, [2001] 4 C.N.L.R. 120 (Sask. C.A.), rev'g [2000] 1 C.N.L.R. 245 (Sask. Q.B.).

[155] *One Arrow First Nation* v. *Saskatchewan*, [2000] 1 C.N.L.R. 162 (Sask. Q.B.).

[156] *Claim Settlements (Alberta and Saskatchewan) Implementation Act*, S.C. 2002, c. 3.

Manitoba

In 1977, the Treaty Land Entitlement Committee of Manitoba was established to examine the settlement of treaty land entitlement issues in that province. This process eventually led to the signing of an agreement in principle on June 21, 1996 by nineteen Indian bands and the Governments of Canada and Manitoba, resulting in the Manitoba Treaty Land Entitlement Framework Agreement being signed on May 29, 1997.[157] The agreement provides for the transfer of 445,754 hectares of land to reserve status for the nineteen Indian bands involved in the process. Manitoba will provide 399,008 hectares of Crown land and Canada will provide $76 million so that land may be purchased from private owners (on a willing seller/willing buyer basis).

Other

In the Northwest Territories, the Government of Canada, and the Treaty No. 8 Dene Indian bands initialled the Northwest Territories Treaty 8 Treaty Entitlement Negotiations Protocol Agreement in November 1994. The Salt River First Nation and the Governments of Canada and the NWT initialled the Final Treaty Land Entitlement Settlement Agreement on November 15, 2001 to settle outstanding reserve land entitlements for the Salt River First Nation arising from Treaty No. 8. Its purpose is to initiate negotiations between the two parties for a formal treaty entitlement settlement.

Alberta has settled seven treaty land entitlement claims, with another sixteen either in negotiations or being reviewed by the Government of Canada.

SUBSECTION 35(3) AND MODERN TREATIES/ LAND CLAIMS AGREEMENTS

Introduction

Treaties are not only historical documents, but also include modern land claim agreements and treaties between Aboriginal people and the Crown. Subsection 35(3) of the *Constitution Act, 1982* states: "For greater certainty, in subsection (1) 'treaty rights' includes rights that now exist by way of land claims agreements or may be so acquired."

The federal government's willingness to negotiate comprehensive claims[158] was influenced by a number of judicial decisions made in the mid-1970s, most notably *Calder.*[159] In *Calder,* the Supreme Court of Canada, in a split decision, confirmed the existence of Aboriginal title. It set the stage for the federal government's recognition that comprehensive claims must be addressed. To date, Aboriginal people have found the courts a successful tool to achieve recognition of their rights.

Comprehensive land claims are those claims by Aboriginal peoples that are based on their traditional use and occupation of land not otherwise dealt with by treaties. The Government of Canada's Comprehensive Land Claims Policy can be traced back to 1973 when the Minister of the Department of Indian Affairs and Northern Development issued a policy statement outlining the federal government's willingness to negotiate compensation and other benefits in return for the Aboriginal interest in lands over which no

---

[157] See also *Manitoba Claim Settlements Implementation Act,* S.C. 2000, c. 33.
[158] For a discussion of the development of the comprehensive land claims policy see the *Report of the Royal Commission on Aboriginal Peoples,* vol. 2 (Ottawa: RCAP, 1996), 527–57.
[159] *Calder* v. *A.G.(B.C.),* [1973] S.C.R. 313.

treaties apply. The Government of Canada has accepted a limited number of claims in areas affected by treaties. For example, the Treaty No. 8 and No. 11 claims of the Dene and the Métis in the Northwest Territories were accepted on the basis that the land entitlement provisions of these treaties had not been implemented. Under this policy, the Government of Canada required complete finality with respect to the Aboriginal claim and the extinguishment of all Aboriginal rights.[160] The James Bay and Northern Quebec Agreement (1975) and the Northeastern Quebec Agreement (1978) were finalized under the policy.

The federal government reiterated its Comprehensive Land Claims Policy in its 1981 booklet entitled "In All Fairness."[161] The 1984 Inuvialuit Final Agreement was finalized under this policy. The most recent version of the federal government's policy on land claims can be found in its Comprehensive Land Claims Policy of 1987.[162] Its objectives are summarized as follows:

> The purpose of settlement agreements is to provide certainty and clarity to ownership and use of land and resources in those areas of Canada where aboriginal title has not been dealt with by treaty or superseded by law. . . . [T]he claimant group will receive defined rights, compensation and other benefits in exchange for relinquishing rights relating to the title claimed over all or part of the land in question.[163]

The 1987 amendments to the Comprehensive Land Claims Policy were extensive. The new policy attempted to improve the negotiation process, provided clarity to the subjects to be negotiated, and allowed for a broader range of options regarding land tenure. Until 1990, the federal government had a limit of six negotiations ongoing at any one time. Under the federal government's 1995 Inherent Right Policy, self-government arrangements may be negotiated along with the claim settlement, such as those negotiations ongoing between the Dogrib and the federal and Northwest Territories governments.

The Supreme Court of Canada has not made a clear distinction between "historic" treaties (early twentieth century and earlier) and "modern" treaties (within the past thirty years). The Federal Court, Trial Division held that the federal Crown has a duty to consult Aboriginal people regarding the creation of a national park in an area under land claims agreement negotiations.[164] Although the precise degree to which all of the interpretive principles surrounding treaties apply to land claims agreements is uncertain, the rights contained in land claims agreements and modern treaties are constitutionally recognized and affirmed in s. 35(1). Although these modern treaties play a role in the governance of significant portions of Canada's northern territories, the understanding of the effect of these agreements on land management and governance is limited.

The 1992 Charlottetown Accord[165] proposed extensive changes to existing constitu-

---

[160] Canada, Department of Indian Affairs and Northern Development, News Release/Communiqué 1-7339 (8 August 1973).

[161] Canada, Department of Indian Affairs and Northern Development, *In All Fairness: A Native Claims Policy—Comprehensive Claims* (Ottawa: Supply and Services, 1981).

[162] Comprehensive Land Claims Policy (Ottawa: DIAND, 1987); see also *Living Treaties: Lasting Agreements; Report of the Task Force to Review Comprehensive Claims Policy* (Ottawa: DIAND, 1985).

[163] *Ibid.*, Comprehensive Land Claims Policy, 9.

[164] *Nunavik Inuit* v. *Canada (Min. of Canadian Heritage)*, [1998] 4 C.N.L.R. 68 (F.C.T.D.).

[165] See chapter 8; see also Thomas Isaac, *An Analysis of the Aboriginal Self-Government Provisions of the 1992 Charlottetown Accord: Self-Government in the Post-Charlottetown Era* (LL.M. Thesis, University of Saskatchewan College of Law, 1993); S. Venne, "Treaty Indigenous Peoples and the Charlottetown Accord: The Message in the Breeze" (1993) 4:2 Constitutional Forum 43.

tional provisions affecting Aboriginal people. The Accord recognized the inherent right of self-government and proposed that this right be interpreted in a manner consistent with the recognition of Aboriginal governments constituting one of three orders of government in Canada. Treaty rights were guaranteed an interpretation that would be "just, broad and liberal" and consider the "spirit, intent and the context" of treaty negotiations. Self-government agreements would have the force of law and create treaty rights within the meaning of s. 35(1). Although the Charlottetown Accord was rejected in a national referendum, it remains a relevant document in that it details the possibilities for a broader approach to constitutionally entrenching treaty rights and self-government.

Interpreting Modern Treaties

The future course of modern treaties as a mechanism for implementing Aboriginal self-government has yet to be determined. Certainly, the British Columbia treaty process will most likely set the agenda for modern comprehensive treaty negotiations. Federal, provincial, and territorial governments are likely to continue the "treaty-making" approach to settle land claims, treaty entitlement, and claims to self-government (as is the case with the treaty process in British Columbia). Relatively little case law exists respecting the interpretation of modern land claims agreements. A number of these decisions are discussed below.

The issue of the exercise of ministerial discretionary authority under the Nunavut Land Claims Agreement[166] was considered in *Nunavut Tunngavik Inc.* v. *Canada (Min. of Fisheries and Oceans)*[167] and *Nunavik Inuit*.[168] In *Nunavut Tunngavik* the issue concerned the decision of the Minister of the Department of Fisheries and Oceans (the "Minister") regarding turbot quotas affecting an area within the Nunavut Land Claims Agreement. Nunavut Tunngavik Inc. argued that the Minister failed to consider the advice of the Nunavut Wildlife Management Board (NWMB), which is constituted under the agreement. Campbell J. held that the reference to consultation in the agreement must be "meaningful inclusion of the NWMB in the Governmental decision-making process before any decisions are made."[169] Campbell J. held that the Minister cannot simply receive and examine the advice and recommendations given by the NWMB, but that the relationship between the Minister and the NWMB was "intended to be mandatory, close, cooperative and highly respectful."[170] The Court affirmed that government must take a proactive stance when considering Aboriginal interests and advice with respect to decisions and actions that may adversely affect Aboriginal people.

The Federal Court of Appeal, while agreeing with the trial court's conclusion to set aside the Minister's decision, referred the matter back to the Minister for reconsideration. The Court of Appeal focused on whether the Minister gave special consideration to the adjacency and economic dependence principles required by the Nunavut Land Claims Agreement or misconstrued these principles. The Court of Appeal also rejected a number of the trial judge's conclusions respecting the interpretation of the relevant provisions of the agreement. The Court stressed that it will not "second guess" the Minister,[171] but balanced this by noting that "the Minister's discretion in section 7 of the *Fisheries Act* is

---

[166] Nunavut Land Claims Agreement (1993), en. by the *Nunavut Land Claim Agreement Act*, S.C. 1993, c. 29.

[167] *Nunavut Tunngavik Inc.* v. *Canada (Min. of Fisheries and Oceans)*, [1997] 4 C.N.L.R. 193 (F.C.T.D.).

[168] *Nunavik Inuit, supra* note 164.

[169] *Nunavut Tunngavik, supra* note 167 at 211.

[170] *Ibid.* at 210.

[171] *Nunavut Tunngavik Inc.* v. *Canada (Min. of Fisheries and Oceans)*, [2000] 3 C.N.L.R. 114 at 132 (F.C.A.).

no longer absolute when the exercise of that discretion affects the wildlife and the marine areas of the [Nunavut Settlement Area] and the wildlife management."[172]

Nunavut Tunngavik Inc. again challenged the authority of the Minister in *Nunavut Tunngavik Inc. v. Canada (Min. of Fisheries and Oceans).*[173] In that decision, Blais J. dismissed a similar application that the Minister erred in failing to apply the principles set out in the Nunavut Land Claims Agreement.

The difference from the earlier decision was the substantial evidence that the Minister took into account the advice and recommendations of the NWMB together with all of the relevant considerations, and it was clear that such consideration occurred. Additionally, there was a clear paper tail of the Minister receiving and considering the applicable advice. The Federal Court of Appeal affirmed the trial court's decision. Leave to appeal application to the Supreme Court of Canada was dismissed.

In *Nunavik Inuit,*[174] Richard A.C.J. dealt with a request for a declaration by the Nunavik Inuit that the Minister of Canadian Heritage ought not to establish a national park, the proposed boundaries of which would form 80 percent of the territory then under treaty negotiations between the Nunavik Inuit and the federal government. The Court held that the Government of Canada had a duty to consult with the Nunavik Inuit prior to establishing a park reserve in Northern Labrador and that such a duty to consult includes both a duty to inform and to listen. The government also has a duty to consult and to negotiate in good faith with Nunavik Inuit with respect to its claims to Aboriginal rights in certain parts of Labrador prior to the establishment of a national park in Northern Labrador. The Court concluded that if an agreement between the Governments of Canada and Newfoundland and Labrador to establish a national park is reached before a final treaty is settled with the Nunavik Inuit, those lands are to be set aside as a national park reserve pending land claim negotiations.[175]

Although dealing with a modern treaty in Nunavut, these decisions[176] shed some light on judicial reasoning respecting the interpretation of land claims agreements and the onus being placed on governments to seriously consider treaty rights when making decisions. These decisions clearly indicate that when governments put effort into changing their administrative and decision-making processes to expand transparency and reasonableness, then regulatory and discretionary decisions can withstand judicial scrutiny.[177]

In *Eastmain Band v. Canada,*[178] the Federal Court of Appeal held that although the principle of interpreting treaties "liberally" applies to modern treaties, the principle of

---

[172] *Ibid.* at 122.

[173] *Nunavut Tunngavik Inc. v. Canada (Min. of Fisheries and Oceans),* [2000] 3 C.N.L.R. 136 (F.C.T.D.), aff'd [2001] 1 C.N.L.R. iv (F.C.A.); leave to appeal dismissed, 19 October 2001 (S.C.C.).

[174] *Nunavik Inuit, supra* note 164.

[175] *Ibid.* at para. 128.

[176] See also *Kadlak v. Nunavut (Min. of Sustainable Development),* [2001] 1 C.N.L.R. 147 (Nun. Ct.J.), where an Inuit sought judicial review of the decision by the Minister of Sustainable Development to disallow the decision of the Nunavut Wildlife Management Board related to hunting polar bears. The Minister's decision was quashed and the matter was referred back to the Minister. Kilpatrick J. stated at para. 22: "Section 35(1) . . . does not promise that the rights under the Nunavut Land Claims Agreement will be immune from all forms of government regulation. It does require the Territorial and Federal Crown to justify any decision that impacts adversely upon the promises made and rights conferred in the Land Claims Settlement." Like the *Nunavut Tunngavik* and *Nunavik* decisions, the Court clearly placed the onus on government to be prepared to justify its regulations.

[177] The procedural fairness of the Nunavut Water Board was the focus in *QiKiqtani Inuit Assn. v. Canada (Minister of Indian Affairs and Nor. Dev.),* [1999] 3 C.N.L.R. 213 (F.C.T.D.).

[178] *Eastmain Band v. Canada,* [1993] 3 C.N.L.R. 55 (F.C.A.).

doubtful expressions being construed in favour of the Indians does not apply. Decar J.A. wrote:

> We must be careful, in construing a document as modern as the 1975 [James Bay] Agreement, that we do not blindly follow the principles laid down by the Supreme Court in analyzing treaties entered into in an earlier era. The principle that ambiguities must be construed in favour of the Aboriginals rests, in the case of historic treaties, on the unique vulnerability of the Aboriginal parties, who were not educated and were compelled to negotiate with parties who had a superior bargaining position. When it is modern treaties that are at stake, the Aboriginal party must now, too, be bound by the informed commitment that it is now in a position to make. No serious and lasting political compromise . . . can be entered into in an atmosphere of distrust and uncertainty.[179]

This statement clearly confirms that the interpretation of modern treaties requires a degree of modification from the interpretive principles governing historic treaties.

Modern treaties may also have an ancillary impact on the division of federal and provincial legislative powers. An outstanding issue is how the courts will interpret provisions of modern treaties that do not contain the language of "rights," i.e., a right to fish as opposed to the reference to a truckhouse (see *Marshall*) that is interpreted as affirming a right to fish. The term "right" is not used extensively in the modern treaties, and the question must therefore be posed as to what is actually constitutionally protected? Some may argue that only those "substantive" provisions of an agreement receive constitutional protection. But as decisions such as *Nunavut Tunngavik* (1997 and 2000)[180] have demonstrated, those provisions that may simply be "advisory" or "administrative" in nature, can still hold a government to a substantive degree of accountability, all within the ambit of having constitutional protection. The same can be said for self-government provisions that may appear to be delegated in nature, but the extent to which they may supersede federal and provincial laws remains uncertain. Also, as "rights," do the provisions in modern treaties still require the requisite "consultation," the same degree of fiduciary responsibility by the Crown, and do they invoke, to the same extent as historic treaties, the honour of the Crown when interpreted?

While on its face, the effect of s. 35(3) of the *Constitution Act, 1982* ensures that rights contained in modern treaties are covered by the application of s. 35(1), the precise meaning of this constitutional protection remains unclear. For example, does the liberal and generous interpretive scheme required by s. 35(1) and applied to historical treaties also apply to modern treaties? It is also unclear what is deemed to be a "right" within a land claim agreement. Are all sections of an agreement constitutionally protected, such as those creating advisory boards? If so, what is the impact on the existing division of powers and constitutional authority of federal and provincial governments? There are many outstanding questions relating to the impact and meaning of s. 35(3) of the *Constitution Act, 1982*, with little by way of judicial or academic commentary to reference.[181] The term "right"

---

[179] *Ibid.* at 61 and 64.

[180] In *Nunavut Tunngavik, supra* note 167, and *Nunavut Tunngavik, supra* note 173, the Federal Court considered the impact of the Nunavut Land Claims Agreement on the discretionary authority of the Minister of Fisheries and Oceans to set turbot quotas. See text accompanying notes 168 to 177.

[181] In Thomas Isaac, "The *Constitution Act, 1982* and the Constitutionalization of Aboriginal Self-Government in Canada: *Cree-Naskapi of (Quebec) Act*", [1991] 1 C.N.L.R. 1, the author argues that s. 35(3) of the *Constitution Act, 1982* implicitly recognizes and constitutionally protects the contingent form of self-government, to the extent that self-governing provisions are contained in land claims agreements. In particular, self-government legislation flowing from constitutionally protected land claims agreements, such as the *Cree-Naskapi Act* (from the 1975 James Bay and Northern Quebec Agreement) may have quasi-constitutional

probably does not need to be present in every provision of a land claim agreement in order for it to be considered a "right" for the purposes of s. 35(1). In *Cree School Board* v. *Canada*,[182] Croteau S.C.J. held that the Cree school board created under the James Bay and Northern Quebec Agreement enjoys constitutional status, even though the creation of the school board was not phrased as a "right" *per se*. Although s. 35(3) of the *Constitution Act, 1982* has existed for almost twenty years, there continues to be little understanding about what it means in practical terms. Modern treaties and land claims agreements have the potential to be powerful instruments that may directly affect the Constitution of Canada and the existing authority of federal and provincial governments.

James Bay and Northern Quebec Agreement (1975) and the Northeastern Quebec Agreement (1978)

The first modern treaty[183] to be signed was the 1975 James Bay and Northern Quebec Agreement.[184] Since then a number of other land claims agreements have been signed. The James Bay Agreement was signed by the governments of Canada and Quebec and the Cree, Inuit, and subsequently the Naskapi Indians[185] and allowed for the development of the James Bay hydroelectric project in northern Quebec. In return for ceding most of their land, the Cree, Inuit, and subsequently the Naskapi received certain rights related to the regulation of their lands, environment, and governance. The rights to governance are outlined in the *Cree-Naskapi (of Quebec) Act*.[186] The Cree received 5,544 square kilometres and the Inuit 8,151 square kilometres of Category I lands, 69,995 square kilometres (Cree) and 81,596 (Inuit) of Category II lands, and more than 1,000,000 square kilometres in shared Category III lands. Its implementation has been a matter of much discussion and concern over the past two decades.[187] The Naskapi signed the Northeastern Quebec Agreement with Canada and Quebec in 1978, and the James Bay agreement was amended to integrate the Naskapi.

On October 23, 2001, the Government of Quebec and the Grand Council of the Crees signed an agreement ensuring that the Cree will receive at least $3.5 billion over fifty years, including $139 million before 2004. In return, the Cree have agreed to two new hydroelectric facilities worth approximately $3.8 billion, both of which remain subject to environmental review, and have also agreed to drop $3.6 billion in claimed damages and legal proceedings.

On October 25, 2002, representatives of the Makivik Corporation (who represent the Nunavik Inuit) and the federal government signed the Nunavik Inuit Marine Region

---

status. See also *Eastmain Band* v. *Gilpin*, [1987] 3 C.N.L.R. 54 (Que. Prov. Ct.) and *Waskaganish Band* v. *Blackned*, [1986] 3 C.N.L.R. 168 (Que. Prov. Ct.).

[182] *Cree School Board* v. *Canada*, [1998] 3 C.N.L.R. 24 (Que. Sup. Ct.).

[183] See K. Coates, ed., *Aboriginal Land Claims Agreements: A Regional Perspective* (Toronto: Copp Clark Pitman, 1997).

[184] James Bay and Northern Quebec Agreement (Quebec: Editeur official du Quebec, 1976); enacted by the *James Bay and Northern Quebec Native Claims Settlement Act*, S.C. 1976–77, c. 32; with corresponding provincial legislation, *James Bay Agreement*, S.Q. 1976, c. 32; see *Cree Regional Authority* v. *Robinson*, [1991] 3 C.N.L.R. 82 (F.C.A.).

[185] The Naskapi signed a similar agreement in 1978, the Northeastern Quebec Agreement. The Cree and Inuit number approximately 12,100 and 8,600 people respectively. The Naskapi number approximately 660 people in total.

[186] S.C. 1984, c. 46; see Thomas Isaac, "Aboriginal Self-Government in Canada: *Cree-Naskapi (of Quebec) Act*" (1991) 7:2 Native Studies Rev. 69.

[187] For example, see W. Moss, *Practically Millionaires* (Ottawa: National Indian Brotherhood, 1981), and R. Salisbury, *A Homeland for the Cree* (Montreal: McGill-Queen's University Press, 1986).

Agreement in Principle. The Nunavik Inuit's claims to the mainland of northern Quebec were dealt with in the 1975 James Bay agreement. The Nunavik Marine Region, covered by the Nunavik Inuit Marine Region Agreement in Principle, comprises islands and waters in the Hudson Bay, Hudson Strait, and Ungara Bay. The agreement in principle provides that the Nunavik Inuit will own approximately 80 percent of the claimed islands in fee simple, including surface and subsurface resources and will receive $50 million and a share of the resource royalties accruing as a result of development activities in the Nunavik Marine Region. The Nunavik Inuit also have an outstanding claim to the on and offshore of Labrador.

Northwest Territories

There are four settled land claims in the Northwest Territories. The Inuvialuit Final Agreement[188] was signed on June 5, 1984, and included approximately 2,500 Inuvialuit beneficiaries who live in the northwestern region of the Northwest Territories (namely the communities of Inuvik, Aklavik, Sachs Harbour, Tuktoyaktuk, Paulatuk, and Holman). The agreement includes title to 91,000 square kilometres of land (including 13,000 square kilometres of subsurface mineral rights), $152 million (1984 dollars), a one-time payment of $10 million to an economic enhancement fund, and $7.5 million to a social development fund. The total Inuvialuit settlement area exceeds 400,000 square kilometres. The Inuvialuit also received preferential and exclusive hunting and harvesting rights in the settlement area.

The Inuvialuit and the Gwich'in (discussed below) have initialled a self-government agreement in principle with the federal and territorial governments. To support their right to engage in self-government negotiations with Canada and the Government of the Northwest Territories, the Inuvialuit have relied on s. 4(3) of the Inuvialuit Final Agreement, which reads:

> Canada agrees that where restructuring of the public institutions of government is considered for the Western Arctic Region, the Inuvialuit shall not be treated any less favourably than any other native groups or native people with respect to the governmental powers and authority conferred on them.

The agreement in principle was initialled on October 3, 2001 and applies to the Beaufort-Delta region of the Northwest Territories. The agreement in principle provides for one regional public government serving all residents of the region but also guarantees representation for the Inuvialuit and the Gwich'in. Under a final agreement, eight public community governments would replace the eight existing municipal councils in the Beaufort region, also with guaranteed representation for the Inuvialuit and the Gwich'in. The agreement in principle also establishes a Gwich'in government to replace the existing band councils and an Inuvialuit government.

On April 22, 1992, the Gwich'in Dene and Métis and the federal and territorial governments signed the Gwich'in Final Agreement.[189] With approximately 2,300 beneficiaries, the Gwich'in claim included a $75-million financial component (1990 dollars) payable over fifteen years and gave the Gwich'in a share of resource royalties in the western Arctic. They also received a fifteen-year subsidy on property taxes on certain Gwich'in municipal lands, title to more than 22,000 square kilometres of land in the Northwest

---

[188] Inuvialuit Final Agreement (1978), en. by the *Western Arctic (Inuvialuit) Claims Settlement Act,* S.C. 1984, c. 24.

[189] Gwich'in Final Agreement (1992), en. by the *Gwich'in Land Claim Settlement Act,* S.C. 1992, c. 53.

Territories and approximately 1,500 square kilometres of land in the Yukon Territory (including more than 5,000 square kilometres of subsurface mineral rights), and an exclusive licence to conduct commercial wildlife activities on Gwich'in lands. All of the parties agreed to pursue self-government negotiations with the Gwich'in which, along with the Inuvialuit, are underway.

The Sahtu Dene and Métis Land Claim Agreement was signed on September 6, 1993[190] and came into effect on June 23, 1994. It affected approximately 2,000 beneficiaries. Like the Gwich'in agreement, the Sahtu Dene and Métis agreement included a $75-million financial component (1990 dollars) payable over fifteen years and a share of resource royalties in the western Arctic. They received title to more than 41,000 square kilometres of land (including 1,813 square kilometres of subsurface mineral rights). Like the Gwich'in, the Sahtu can enter into self-government negotiations with the federal and territorial governments. One of the five Sahtu communities has initiated community-based self-government discussions with both the federal and territorial governments.

Unlike most Aboriginal groups in Canada (with the exception of the Nisga'a in British Columbia), the Dogrib (also known as the Tlicho) of the lower Mackenzie Valley, Northwest Territories, negotiated both self-government and their land claim concurrently with the both the federal and NWT governments. On August 25, 2003 the Dogrib Treaty II Council and the Governments of Canada and the Northwest Territories signed the Tlicho Agreement. Under the agreement, the Dogrib own a single block of land consisting of approximately 39,000 square kilometres of land, including subsurface resources surrounding the four Dogrib communities. This land base will not be Indian reserve land as defined in the *Indian Act*. The Dogrib will also receive approximately $100 million, in addition to royalties collected from development in the Mackenzie Valley.[191]

The Deh Cho First Nations, who are signatories to Treaty No. 11, live primarily on the southern shores of Great Slave Lake. They and the federal government have agreed to enter into a two-stage discussion process: first, interim measures and funding agreements will be negotiated, followed by land, resources, and self-government agreements. The South Slave Metis Tribal Council signed a framework agreement with the federal and territorial governments on August 29, 1996. Negotiations are ongoing.

Nunavut Land Claims Agreement (1993)

Dividing the Northwest Territories into two territories was discussed in the early 1950s, but did not gain momentum until the mid-1970s. In the 1970s, Aboriginal groups in the western part of the Northwest Territories submitted proposals for Aboriginal self-government there: the Inuvialuit sought a strong regional government, while the Dene and Métis sought their own territory, Denendeh.

The creation of Nunavut, in the eastern half of Canada's North, is the result of the May 23, 1993 Nunavut Land Claims Agreement[192] between the Governments of Canada and the Northwest Territories and the Inuit represented by the Tunngavik Federation of Nunavut, now Nunavut Tunngavik Inc. The agreement, which affects more than 17,000

---

[190] Sahtu Dene and Metis Land Claim Agreement (1993), en. by the *Sahtu Dene and Metis Land Claim Settlement Act*, S.C. 1994, c. 27.

[191] In *Paul* v. *Canada*, [2003] 1 C.N.L.R. 107, the Federal Court, Trial Division dismissed an application by the North Slave Metis Alliance who claimed that the Dogrib were not entitled to negotiate their land claim agreement without district Métis representation. The Court held that to grant such relief would be to cause the Dogrib to be harmed disproportionately and dismissed the application.

[192] *Supra* note 166.

Inuit living in the eastern Arctic, resulted in the transfer of approximately 351,000 square kilometres of land (including approximately 37,000 square kilometres of subsurface mineral rights) to the Inuit. The total settlement area is almost 2 million square kilometres, with a cash compensation of more than $1 billion to be paid over fourteen years. It is the largest land claim in Canadian history and led to the creation of a new third territory in Canada on April 1, 1999.

Article 4 of the Nunavut Land Claims Agreement required Canada to recommend to Parliament legislation to establish Nunavut with its own legislative assembly and public government separate from the existing government of the Northwest Territories. The *Nunavut Act,*[193] which in some ways is a modernized version of the *Northwest Territories Act,*[194] was proclaimed in June 1993.

Iqualuit on Baffin Island was declared the capital of Nunavut following a plebiscite. The Government of Nunavut is decentralized to deal with the unique needs of its twenty-eight communities. The Nunavut Legislative Assembly has nineteen members. Although the Inuit form the majority of residents in Nunavut and the creation of Nunavut is a direct result of the Nunavut Land Claims Agreement, Nunavut does not, strictly speaking, represent Inuit self-government. Nunavut has a public government, albeit one that will have a majority Inuit representation.

In the western Northwest Territories, self-government discussions have focused on exclusive Aboriginal government arrangements, similar to those in existence in southern Canada (for example, Indian reserve-style governments) and on combined public–Aboriginal government systems.

The Nunavut Land Claims Agreement establishes structures with responsibilities and authority in the Nunavut Settlement Area relating to wildlife, land, resource management, and environmental protection. Article 5 of the agreement establishes the Nunavut Wildlife Management Board. Articles 11 to 13 provide for the creation of the Nunavut Planning Commission, the Nunavut Impact Review Board, and the Nunavut Water Board. Finally, article 21 provides for the establishment of a Surface Rights Tribunal if requested by the Inuit or as an initiative of the Government of Canada. With the exception of the Wildlife Management Board, these other institutions are to be established by legislation with their powers, functions, and objectives set out by statute. The *Nunavut Waters and Nunavut Surface Rights Tribunal Act*[195] established the Nunavut Water Board and the Nunavut Surface Rights Tribunal. Section 35 of this Act states that the objective of the Nunavut Water Board is to "provide for the conservation and utilization of waters in Nunavut, except in a national park, in a manner that will provide the optimum benefit from those waters for the residents of Nunavut, in particular in Canadians in general." These institutions are the direct result of the Nunavut Land Claims Agreement and provide the Inuit with an important voice in resource management in Nunavut.

Yukon Agreements

On May 29, 1993 Canada, the Yukon Territory, and the Council for Yukon Indians signed the Umbrella Final Agreement, which serves as the basis to negotiate final agreements to settle outstanding claims of individual Indian bands. Section 2.2.1 of the agreement states: "Settlement Agreements shall be land claims agreements within the meaning

---

[193] *Nunavut Act,* S.C. 1993, c. 28.
[194] *Northwest Territories Act,* R.S.C. 1985, c. N-27.
[195] *Nunavut Waters and Nunavut Surface Rights Tribunal Act,* S.C. 2002, c. 10.

of section 35 of the *Constitution Act, 1982*."

On the same date, four Indian bands signed final and self-government agreements, including the Vuntut Gwitchin First Nation, the First Nation of Nacho Nyak Dun, the Champagne and Aishihik First Nations, and the Teslin Tlingit Council.[196] On July 21, 1997 final and self-government agreements were signed with Little Salmon/Carmacks and Selkirk First Nations, both coming into effect on October 1, 1997. On July 16, 1998, final and self-government agreements were signed with the Tr'ondëk Hwëch'in, coming into effect on September 15, 1998. On January 13, 2002 the Ta'an Kwacha'n Council, along with the federal and Yukon governments, signed final and self-government agreements and implementation plans.

To date, eight out of fourteen Yukon First Nations have completed and signed final land claims and self-government agreements. Although the claims agreements are "treaties" within the meaning of s. 35 of the *Constitution Act, 1982*, the self-government agreements are not. The eight completed final agreements provide the approximately 4,400 beneficiaries with almost 41,600 square kilometres of land, of which more than 25,000 square kilometres includes mines and minerals. The financial component of these agreements totals more than $146 million (1989 dollars).

Four other Yukon First Nations—Carcross/Tagish, Luane, Kwanlin dun, and White River—formally concluded negotiations on their final and self-government agreements on April 1, 2002. These agreements must still be ratified. They provide the four First Nations with approximately 4,000 square kilometres of land and approximately $77 million. The Ross River Dena Council and the Liard First Nation have not yet concluded final self-government negotiations.

In *Carcross/Tagish First Nation* v. *Canada*,[197] the Federal Court of Appeal held that the Umbrella Final Agreement has no legal significance of its own; it is essentially an agreement to negotiate an agreement:

> (a) . . . [T]he UFA [Umbrella Final Agreement] is essentially a collective agreement of a preliminary nature signifying the intention of each First Nation to negotiate a Final Agreement on an individual basis, (b) that, being essentially an agreement to negotiate an agreement, the UFA "does not create or affect any legal rights" and (c) that a Final Agreement relates to one First Nation only, is negotiated by that First Nation alone and is comprised of both the provisions of the UFA and the specific provisions that are applicable to that First Nation alone.
>
> There is no suggestion anywhere in the UFA that it might have a life of its own. It begins its life as a non–legally binding step in a collective negotiating process and ends it as an integral, necessary part of an individual Final Agreement. Unless and until it is incorporated in a Final Agreement, it has no legal significance except as an agreement to negotiate.[198]

On June 5, 2001 a working group representing Yukon First Nations and the Governments of Canada and the Yukon Territory released a report reviewing the first five years of implementing the Yukon land claims agreements. Areas of concern included the pace of implementation and the extensive amount of time required early on in the implementation phase to establish new processes. The working group also suggested the development

---

[196] Yukon Final Agreement (1993), en. by the *Yukon First Nations Land Claims Settlement Act,* S.C. 1994, c. 34; *Yukon First Nations Self-Government Act,* S.C. 1994, c. 35; *Yukon Surface Rights Board Act,* S.C. 1994, c. 43.
[197] *Carcross/Tagish First Nation* v. *Canada,* [2001] 4 C.N.L.R. 49 (F.C.A.).
[198] *Ibid.* paras. 26, 27.

of consultation protocols regarding forestry and the review of funding for Renewable Resource Councils.

British Columbia Treaty Negotiations

Two historic elements are linked to the current lack of resolution and uncertainty involving Aboriginal rights to land in British Columbia: the inconsistency of the reserve land policy in British Columbia, and the premature cession of treaty making. All of the British colonies followed the policy of extinguishing Aboriginal title, including the early colonial government that settled treaties on Vancouver Island. Under the Douglas treaties, reserve creation began there in the 1850s. In response to the peculiar geographic and political nature of British Columbia, however, the colonial government on the mainland did not follow the policy of making treaties. Instead, the government initially reserved as much land as the Indians requested. A more conservative approach was followed by successive British Columbia governments and federal representatives. The Royal Commission on Aboriginal Peoples noted:

> By national standards, reserves in British Columbia remained small, and they were to get even smaller. Another joint federal-provincial Royal Commission (McKenna-McBride), appointed in 1912 to deal with the long-standing Indian land question, recommended that 19,000 hectares, including areas long coveted by settlers, be eliminated from existing Indian reserves and communities as surplus to their requirements.[199]

With few exceptions (including the pre-Confederation and geographically limited Douglas treaties on Vancouver Island, Treaty No. 8, part of which is applicable to northeastern British Columbia, and the Nisga'a Final Agreement) treaties were not negotiated in British Columbia. As a result, existing Aboriginal rights and title were left unextinguished and undefined, and the extent and meaning of Aboriginal interests within British Columbia are uncertain.

Until recently, the position of the Government of British Columbia was that colonial legislation had extinguished all Aboriginal rights. This position was abandoned after it was held to be incorrect by *Delgamuukw.* The confusion over British Columbia's reserve policy added to this problem and has led to litigation relating to various reductions in reserves after 1912.

Many of the matters presently under negotiation in the British Columbia treaty process concern areas of provincial jurisdiction, including land and the land tenuring regime, forest resources, access rights, wildlife, environmental protection, and numerous other issues relating to governance such as health and education. The federal government could negotiate a wide array of arrangements on Indian reserve lands, including delegated self-government, but it may not be able to address adequately those matters within provincial jurisdiction. The provincial government could offer a great deal of practical assistance, expertise, and guidance in negotiating such arrangements. Additionally, if one of the objectives of the treaty process is to allow for greater self-sufficiency and independence of Indian bands in British Columbia, including better economic circumstances, then allowing Indian bands to have a degree of consistency and integration into the broader provincial system seems logical.

In order to understand British Columbia's need for treaties, an understanding of the legal history of the province is imperative. The former colony of British Columbia was

---

[199] *Report of the Royal Commission on Aboriginal Peoples, supra* note 158 at 478.

admitted into Canada under the *British Columbia Terms of Union*[200] in 1871. The terms of union contain no express provision requiring the province of British Columbia to engage in treaty negotiations with Indians and to provide public lands to assist the federal government to fulfil its treaty or other obligations. Paragraph 13 does, however, affirm that the British Columbia government shall provide to the federal government "tracts of land of such extent as it has hitherto been the practice of the British Columbia Government to appropriate for that purpose [reserved for Indians' use and benefit]."

Compare this to the Natural Resources Transfer Agreements of 1930, which impose obligations on the provinces of Alberta, Saskatchewan, and Manitoba to provide land to Canada so that Canada could fulfil its obligations under the treaties there The applicable provision of the Natural Resources Transfer Agreements states:

> [T]he province will from time to time, upon the request of the Superintendent General of Indian Affairs, set aside, out of unoccupied Crown lands hereby transferred to its administration, such further areas as the said Superintendent General may, in agreement with the Minister of Mines and Natural Resources of the Province, select as necessary to enable Canada to fulfil its obligations under the treaties with the Indians of the Province. . . .[201]

Paragraph 10 of the *British Columbia Terms of Union* makes the *Constitution Act, 1867* applicable to British Columbia as if it had been an original signatory. Paragraph 1 provides that the federal government shall be liable for the debts and liability of British Columbia existing at the time of union. Additionally, s. 109 of the *Constitution Act, 1867* provides that all lands belonging to the provinces before union shall continue to belong to them after union, subject to any interest other than the provinces' interests. The Supreme Court of Canada confirmed that Aboriginal title is such an interest. Section 109 of the *Constitution Act, 1867* states:

> All Lands, Mines, Minerals, and Royalties belonging to the several Provinces of Canada, Nova Scotia, and New Brunswick at the Union, and all Sums then due or payable for such Lands, Mines, Minerals, or Royalties shall belong to the several Provinces of Ontario, Quebec, Nova Scotia, and New Brunswick in which the same are situate or arise, subject to any Trusts existing in respect thereof, and to any Interest other than that of the Province in the same.

Paragraphs 10 and 1 of the British Columbia Terms of Union, when read together, are clear that Canada assumes all the responsibilities for Indians and any encumbrances or liabilities associated with Indians, including Aboriginal title. Section 109 of the *Constitution Act, 1867* confirms that British Columbia owns provincial Crown lands, subject to Aboriginal title.

This is confirmed by the Supreme Court of Canada in *Delgamuukw*. In *Delgamuukw*, the Court affirmed that since 1871, the exclusive power to legislate in relation to "Indians, and Lands reserved for Indians" has rested with Parliament under s. 91(24). Although Parliament has the authority to legislate with respect to Indians and their lands, British Columbia holds the underlying title to Crown lands.[202]

In *Dominion of Canada* v. *Province of Ontario* (1910),[203] the Judicial Committee of the Privy Council identified the dual roles that the federal and provincial governments play

---

[200] *British Columbia Terms of Union*, R.S.C. 1985, App. II, No. 10.

[201] *Supra* note 85 at para. 11 (Manitoba) and para. 10 (Alberta and Saskatchewan).

[202] *Delgamuukw, supra* note 70 at para. 175.

[203] *Dominion of Canada* v. *Province of Ontario*, [1910] A.C. 637 at 645 (J.C.P.C.), aff'g (1909), 42 S.C.R. 1.

in treaty-making:

> The Crown acts on the advice of ministers in making treaties, and in owning public lands holds them for the good of the community. When differences arise between the two Governments in regard to what is due to the Crown as maker of treaties and from the Crown as owner of public lands they must be adjusted as though the two Governments were separately invested by the Crown with its rights and responsibilities as treaty maker and as owner respectively.

The authority to conclude treaties with Indians that concern the surrender or extinguishment of Aboriginal title rests exclusively with Parliament. Similarly, although Parliament holds the authority to receive a surrender or extinguishment of Aboriginal title, British Columbia continues to own provincial Crown lands, subject to the Aboriginal title interests that may be held by Indians. This dichotomy of roles and responsibilities between the federal and provincial governments results in a situation where only the federal government may deal substantively with obtaining the legal certainty (a key objectives of the treaty process), and only the provincial government can provide the substantial land base necessary to conclude treaties. Securing a land base is a central objective of the Indian bands involved in the treaty process. Although British Columbia may not legally be required to conclude treaties, its involvement in treaty negotiations is critical so long as provincial Crown land remains encumbered with the possible existence of Aboriginal title.

This situation creates tension between the federal and provincial governments, but the net result of this unique situation is that the objectives of both governments are probably best served by working together.

In 1990, British Columbia, Canada, and the British Columbia First Nations Summit created the British Columbia Claims Task Force to recommend a process for negotiating treaties. The three parties accepted all nineteen of the Commission's recommendations contained in its report released in June, 1991. One of these recommendations led to the September 21, 1992 signing of the British Columbia Treaty Commission Agreement by the First Nations Summit and the Governments of British Columbia and Canada. The commission will oversee the treaty negotiation process and monitor the progress of the negotiations.[204] In its 2002 Annual Report, the commission stated that 122 Indian bands were involved in forty-two sets of negotiations, representing approximately two-thirds of the almost 200 Indian bands in British Columbia. Significantly, British Columbia's treaty process includes not only a land and compensation package, similar to historical land claims agreements, but also governance provisions. As of 2002, the British Columbia Treaty Commission has allocated $222 million in negotiations support funding to First Nations, including $177 million in loans.[205]

The British Columbia treaty process has not yet resulted in a final agreement (the Nisga'a Final Agreement was not technically part of this process). The expectations of the Indian bands involved are increasing, and there is growing pressure from economic, resource, and local government interests to resolve the issue, but government mandates are limited by the need to maintain a balance of reasonable governance and fiscal pressures. As a result, the process will likely take many years to complete. Nevertheless, there is increasing awareness of the importance of resolving this issue among all British

---

[204] *British Columbia Treaty Commission Act,* S.C. 1995, c. 45, and the *Treaty Commission Act,* R.S.B.C. 1996, c. 461.
[205] British Columbia Treaty Commission, Annual Report 2002 (Vancouver: BCTC, 2002) 22.

Columbians.[206] One agreement in principle has been signed with the Sechelt First Nation. In March 2001, the Nuu-chah-nulth Tribal Council and the Sliammon First Nation initialled agreements-in-principle with the federal and British Columbia governments.

The British Columbia treaty process is voluntary. There is no legal requirement to negotiate.

On August 27, 2001 the Liberal government in British Columbia empowered the Select Standing Committee on Aboriginal Affairs to examine and make recommendations regarding all matters and issues the government intends to submit to voters regarding treaty negotiation principles in the form of a province-wide referendum. The Committee released its report on November 30, 2001.[207] It recommended a referendum ballot concerning sixteen issues such as the transparency of treaty negotiations, local government involvement, access to land for all British Columbians, negotiating Aboriginal governments with the characteristics and legal status of local governments, the phasing out of existing Indian tax exemptions, and the continuing application of provincial-wide standards for resource management and environmental protection.

On July 3, 2002 the results of the referendum were released. Of more than 2,100,000 referendum ballot packages, approximately 760,000 ballots were returned, or 36 percent of the total registered voters. Only eight of the original sixteen proposed questions were on the ballot. All eight principles received strong "yes" endorsements ranging from 84.5 percent to 94.5 percent. While the Government of British Columbia may have resolved key issues with respect to its mandates at the various treaty tables, the referendum has caused anxiety among many Aboriginal people in the province. The real test for the referendum will be if the Government of British Columbia's new certainty concerning its mandate results in any substantive progress in a treaty negotiation process that has not yet delivered any treaties.

Nisga'a Final Agreement (1999)

On August 4, 1998, the Governments of Canada and British Columbia and the Nisga'a Tribal Council initialled the Nisga'a Final Agreement.[208] The first modern treaty in British Columbia and the most recent in Canada, it was over twenty years in the making, beginning with the 1973 Supreme Court of Canada decision in *Calder*. The agreement was ratified by the Nisga'a in November, 1998, and the Governments of Canada[209] and British Columbia[210] enacted the settlement legislation in April 1999. The agreement represents the full and final settlement between the Nisga'a and the governments of Canada and British Columbia regarding Nisga'a Aboriginal rights and title.

The agreement marks a significant turn in Aboriginal relations in British Columbia. *Delgamuukw* caused confusion for governments, Aboriginal people, and the general public, particularly in British Columbia. By recognizing that Aboriginal title exists in parts of British Columbia and affirming that it is a burden on the Crown's title to the land, *Delgamuukw* increased substantially the expectations of Indian bands there. The Nisga'a Final Agreement may mark the end to this period of uncertainty and fear. It and future treaties

---

[206] *Ibid.* at 1: "Treaty making is a legal, economic and increasingly, political necessity in British Columbia."

[207] British Columbia, Legislative Assembly, Select Standing Committee on Aboriginal Affairs, *Revitalizing the Provincial Approach to Treaty Negotiations: Recommendations for a Referendum on Negotiating Principles* (Victoria: Legislative Assembly, 2001).

[208] Nisga'a Final Agreement, en. by *Nisga'a Final Agreement Act, supra* note 54.

[209] *Ibid.*

[210] *Nisga'a Final Agreement Act,* S.B.C. 1999, c. 2.

will not only provide certainty and scope to Aboriginal interests in the province, they will also offer a degree of political and economic stability in a province that is largely dependent upon the resource sector.

The Nisga'a Final Agreement is a lands claims agreement and a treaty within the meaning of s. 35(3) of the *Constitution Act, 1982* and provides that the Charter will apply to Nisga'a government. The former Nisga'a Indian reserves (fifty-six in total, including four villages) will no longer be governed by the *Indian Act* but rather by the Nisga'a Final Agreement.

The Nisga'a Nation (population approximately 5,500) holds a total of 1,992 square kilometres of land in the lower Nass River area. Under the agreement, the Nisga'a Nation own the forest resources and will develop regulations and standards to govern forest practices on their lands, while at a minimum meeting provincial standards. The Nisga'a Nation holds its land in fee simple and must allow public access to these lands for non-commercial and recreational purposes, including hunting, fishing, and public transportation corridors. With respect to fishing, the Nisga'a are guaranteed an allocation of salmon returning to Canadian waters. In making the allocation, the Crown must consider conservation and equitable distribution. Canada and British Columbia continue to manage the fisheries as they relate to the Nisga'a. In return for their undefined Aboriginal right to hunt, the Nisga'a receive a portion of the total allowable harvest for wildlife such as moose and grizzly bear in the Nass Wildlife Area. The Nisga'a Nation remains subject to provincial laws governing conservation, public health, and safety. The Nisga'a will have an increased role in the management of the Nass Wildlife Area.

The Nisga'a Final Agreement affirms that the Nisga'a Nation has the right to self-government and the authority to make laws. There is a central Nisga'a Lisims government, along with four Nisga'a village governments. The Nisga'a also have a constitution, which sets out rules and procedures related to a democratic government. Non-Nisga'a residents on Nisga'a lands have the right to participate in Nisga'a public institutions that directly affect them, such as school boards or health boards, and the right to be consulted regarding decisions that directly affect them. In general, the Nisga'a Nation governance model is a combination of municipal-style governmental authorities, authorities currently provided for in the *Indian Act,* and new powers such as environmental assessment, wills and estates, and post-secondary education.

The Nisga'a Final Agreement also allows the Nisga'a to provide full policing services on Nisga'a lands, using provincial standards in police training, conduct, and qualifications. A Nisga'a court may also be established to deal with Nisga'a laws on Nisga'a lands.

The Nisga'a will receive $190 million to be paid out over fifteen years. Additionally, the Nisga'a will receive $11.5 million to purchase commercial fishing vessels and licences. The agreement calls for five-year agreements to be negotiated between Canada, British Columbia, and the Nisga'a regarding the funding of public services and programs on Nisga'a lands. A central principle for these agreements is that the level of public programs and services provided on Nisga'a lands will be at a level generally comparable to those delivered by other local and regional governments in northwestern British Columbia. The *Indian Act*'s s. 87 income tax exemption for reserve-based income will be phased out over a twelve-year period.

An outstanding national issue that may have finally been settled by the Nisga'a Final Agreement is the issue of the "cede, release and surrender" language found in many older treaties. The purpose of this terminology was to ensure that any outstanding Aboriginal rights were replaced with treaty rights and that the First Nations involved ceded, released, and surrendered any interests in the land to the Crown. First Nations have found this language particularly distasteful and have sought flexible, more sensitive language. At the same time, public governments at the treaty table have been concerned that without such strong language, the certainty and finality that they seek cannot be achieved. The Nisga'a Final Agreement appears to have solved this problem. Sections 23 to 27 clearly state that all the Aboriginal and treaty rights of the Nisga'a are contained within the agreement. Section 22 reads: "This Agreement constitutes the full and final settlement in respect of the aboriginal rights, including aboriginal title, in Canada of the Nisga'a Nation." Section 26 states:

> If, despite this Agreement and the settlement legislation, the Nisga'a Nation has an aboriginal right, including aboriginal title, in Canada, that is other than, or different in attributes or geographical extent from, the Nisga'a section 35 rights as set out in this Agreement, the Nisga'a Nation releases that aboriginal right to Canada to the extent that the aboriginal right is other than, or different in attributes or geographical extent from, the Nisga'a section 35 rights as set out in this Agreement.

In *Campbell et al.* v. *B.C.*,[211] the British Columbia Supreme Court considered an application seeking an order that the Nisga'a Final Agreement is in part inconsistent with the Constitution of Canada and therefore of no force or effect. The applicant argued that the agreement was inconsistent because it purports to bestow upon the governing body of the Nisga'a Nation legislative authority inconsistent with the division of powers granted to Parliament and the Legislative Assemblies of the Provinces by ss. 91 and 92 of the *Constitution Act, 1867*.[212] The Court held that the assertion of sovereignty by the British Crown did not necessarily extinguish the right of Aboriginal people to govern themselves. Any Aboriginal right to self-government could be extinguished after Confederation and before 1982 by federal legislation or it could be replaced or modified by the negotiation of a treaty. After 1982, such rights could not be extinguished but may be defined and given meaning by way of a treaty. The Nisga'a Final Agreement defined the content of Aboriginal self-government expressly. The *Constitution Act, 1867* did not distribute all legislative power to the Parliament and the provincial Legislatures. It did not end what remains of the royal prerogative or Aboriginal and treaty rights, including the diminished but not extinguished power of self-government which remained with the Nisga'a in 1982. Section 35 of the *Constitution Act, 1982* guaranteed the limited form of self-government that remained with the Nisga'a after the assertion of sovereignty; the Nisga'a Final Agreement and settlement legislation gave that limited right definition. The Nisga'a government is subject to both the limitations set out in the Nisga'a Final Agreement itself and to the limited guarantee of rights in s. 35 of the *Constitution Act, 1982*.

Labrador Inuit Land Claims Agreement (2003)

After the signing of the framework agreement in 1990, negotiations between the Labrador Inuit Association, which represents approximately 5,300 Inuit, the federal government, and the government of Newfoundland and Labrador have resulted in the Labrador Inuit Land Claims Agreement. The agreement was initialed on August 29, 2003 and provides for a settlement area of approximately 72,520 square kilometres of land and 48,690 square kilometres of ocean within Canada's twelve mile limit. The Inuit will have the most rights and benefits within 15,800 square kilometres of the settlement area in

---

[211] *Campbell et al.* v. *B.C.*, [2000] 4 C.N.L.R. 1 (B.C.S.C.).
[212] *Constitution Act, 1867, supra* note 148.

lands owned by the Inuit. The agreement also provides for the establishment of the Torngat Mountains National Park Reserve of approximately 9,600 square kilometres located within the settlement area. The agreement provides for Inuit self-government, with the creation of a central Inuit government, five Inuit community governments, and Inuit community corporations. The Inuit will receive $140 million (capital transfer) from the federal government, as well as $156 million designated for implementation.

Other Claims

In addition to those mentioned above, the following claims are currently under negotiation across Canada: the Atikamekw and Montagnais (Quebec and Labrador), Makivik (off and on shore in Nunavut, Quebec, and Labrador), the Innu Nation Claim (central Labrador and Québec), Manitoba Dene Negotiations North of 60 degrees (Nunavut and Northwest Territories), Saskatchewan Athabasca Denesuline (northern interests), Crees of Quebec Offshore Islands (James Bay, Nunavut, and Quebec), and the Algonquins of Eastern Ontario.

EXTINGUISHMENT OF TREATY RIGHTS

Like Aboriginal rights, treaty rights may be extinguished in three ways:

(1) by voluntary surrender by Aboriginal people to the Crown;[213]

(2) prior to 1982, by federal—not provincial—legislation;[214] and

(3) after 1982, altering s. 35 of the *Constitution Act, 1982* by way of a constitutional amendment.

Non-exercise of treaty rights does not equate to extinguishment.[215] As with Aboriginal rights, a "clear and plain intention" is required to extinguish treaty rights.[216] Treaties are one mechanism by which Aboriginal rights can be extinguished.[217]

CONCLUSION

The Supreme Court of Canada has, on numerous occasions, emphasized the usefulness and practicability of treaty negotiations. In *Sparrow*, the Court stated that "Section 35(1), at the least, provides a solid constitutional base upon which subsequent negotiations can take place."[218] In *Delgamuukw*, Lamer C.J. made reference to the above-noted passage from *Sparrow* and stated:

> Ultimately, it is through negotiated settlements, with good faith and give and take on all sides, that we will achieve . . . "the reconciliation of the pre-existence of aboriginal societies with the sovereignty of the Crown."[219]

---

[213] In *Sioui, supra* note 2 at 1063, Lamer C.J. stated that prior to 1982, "a treaty cannot be extinguished without the consent of the Indians concerned." This was the case in *R. v. Howard*, [1994] 2 S.C.R. 299, where fishing rights were extinguished by treaty.

[214] In *Simon, supra* note 2 at 411, Dickson C.J. noted: "It has been held to be within the exclusive power of Parliament under s. 91(24) of the *Constitution Act, 1867* to derogate from rights recognized in a treaty agreement made with the Indians."

[215] *Sioui, supra* note 2 at 1066.

[216] See *Sparrow, supra* note 91 at 1099.

[217] *Howard, supra* note 213.

[218] *Sparrow, supra* note 91 at 1105.

[219] *Delgamuukw, supra* note 70 at 1123–24.

Finally, the Supreme Court of Canada stated in *Marshall:*

> As this and other courts have pointed out on many occasions, the process of accommodation of the treaty right may best be resolved by consultation and negotiation of a modern agreement for participation in specified resources by the Mi'kmaq rather than by litigation. . . . The various governmental, Aboriginal and other interests are not, of course, obliged to reach an agreement. In the absence of a mutually satisfactory solution, the courts will resolve the points of conflict as they arise case by case.[220]

Governments must deal with the practical, social, and economic impacts of not having settled the outstanding Aboriginal interests. Although both levels of government may have, as their primary objective, the settlement of treaties for the purpose of achieving legal certainty, they also want to achieve what could be called "pragmatic certainty." Treaties alone cannot guarantee healthy relationships between Aboriginal people and government, stable and productive Aboriginal communities, and the prevention of threats of direct action when the process fails. Mechanisms outside of treaty processes that support the objective of creating a stable legal and economic climate are also necessary. These mechanisms could include the federal, provincial, and territorial governments and Indian bands moving forward on practical initiatives toward achieving a reconciliation of government and Aboriginal interests. These mechanisms need not be encumbered by treaty processes, but their goals should include supporting the treaty process. Mechanisms that seek to ensure access to resources by all are beyond any one treaty and will require carefully crafted, innovative, and pragmatic solutions, as directed by the Supreme Court of Canada decisions referenced above.

As to the future, the courts may be of limited practical value in determining these issues. While decisions such as *Sparrow, Marshall,* and *Delgamuukw* have provided substantive insight into what s. 35(1) means, it appears that, but for a radical shift in perspective, the courts have already given a clear indication of what should and can occur: governments and Aboriginal people, working together, by way of treaties and other mechanisms, to achieve some lasting reconciliation.

CASES AND MATERIALS

R. v. *Simon* (1985)

[1985] 2 S.C.R. 387 (S.C.C.). Dickson C.J., Beetz, Estey, McIntyre, Chouinard, Wilson, and Le Dain JJ., November 21, 1985.

DICKSON C.J.:—This case raises the important question of the interplay between the treaty rights of native peoples and provincial legislation. The right to hunt, which remains important to the livelihood and way of life of the Micmac people, has come into conflict with game preservation legislation in effect in the province of Nova Scotia. The main question before this Court is whether, pursuant to a Treaty of 1752 between the British Crown and the Micmac, and to s. 88 of the *Indian Act*, R.S.C. 1970, c. I-6, the appellant, James Matthew Simon, enjoys hunting rights which preclude his prosecution for offences under the *Lands and Forests Act*, R.S.N.S. 1967, c. l63. . . .

---

[220] *Marshall* (reconsideration), *supra* note 99 at paras. 22–23.

Was the Treaty of 1752 Validly Created by Competent Parties?
The respondent raised the issue of the capacity of the parties for two reasons which are stated at p. 8 of the factum:

> The issue of capacity is raised for the purpose of illustrating that the Treaty of 1752 was of a lesser status than an International Treaty and therefore is more easily terminated. The issue is also raised to give the document an historical legal context as this issue has been raised in previous cases.

The question of whether the Treaty of 1752 constitutes an international-type treaty is only relevant to the respondent's argument regarding the appropriate legal tests for the termination of the treaty. I will address this issue, therefore, in relation to the question of whether the Treaty of 1752 was terminated by hostilities between the British and the Micmac in 1753. . . .

The treaty was entered into for the benefit of both the British Crown and the Micmac people, to maintain peace and order as well as to recognize and confirm the existing hunting and fishing rights of the Micmac. In my opinion, both the Governor and the Micmac entered into the treaty with the intention of creating mutually binding obligations which would be solemnly respected. It also provided a mechanism for dispute resolution. The Micmac Chief and the three other Micmac signatories, as delegates of the Micmac people, would have possessed full capacity to enter into a binding treaty on behalf of the Micmac. Governor Hopson was the delegate and legal representative of His Majesty the King. It is fair to assume that the Micmac would have believed that Governor Hopson, acting on behalf of His Majesty the King, had the necessary authority to enter into a valid treaty with them. I would hold that the Treaty of 1752 was validly created by competent parties.

Does the Treaty Contain a Right to Hunt and What is the Nature and Scope of this Right?
Article 4 of the Treaty of 1752 states, "it is agreed that the said Tribe of Indians shall not be hindered from, but have free liberty of hunting and Fishing as usual . . .". What is the nature and scope of the "liberty of hunting and Fishing" contained in the treaty? . . .

The fact that the right to hunt already existed at the time the Treaty was entered into by virtue of the Micmac's general aboriginal right to hunt does not negate or minimize the significance of the protection of hunting rights expressly included in the treaty.

Such an interpretation accords with the generally accepted view that Indian treaties should be given a fair, large and liberal construction in favour of the Indians. This principle of interpretation was most recently affirmed by this Court in *Nowegijick* v. *The Queen*, [1983] 1 S.C.R. 29, [1983] 2 C.N.L.R. 89. I had occasion to say the following at p. 36 [p. 94 C.N.L.R.]:

> It is legal lore that, to be valid, exemptions to tax laws should be clearly expressed. It seems to me, however, that treaties and statutes relating to Indians should be liberally construed and doubtful expressions resolved in favour of the Indians. . . . In *Jones* v. *Meehan*, 175 U.S. l, it was held that "Indian treaties must be construed not according to the technical meaning of their words, but in the sense that they would naturally be understood by the Indians."

Having determined that the treaty embodies a right to hunt, it is necessary to consider the respondent's contention that the right to hunt is limited to hunting for purposes and by methods usual in 1752 because of the inclusion of the modifier "as usual" after the right to hunt.

First of all, I do not read the phrase "as usual" as referring to the types of weapons to be used by the Micmac and limiting them to those used in 1752. Any such construction would place upon the ability of the Micmac to hunt an unnecessary and artificial constraint out of keeping with the principle that Indian treaties should be liberally construed. Indeed, the inclusion of the phrase "as usual" appears to reflect a concern that the right to hunt be interpreted in a flexible way that is sensitive to the evolution of changes in normal hunting practices. The phrase thereby ensures that the treaty will be an effective source of protection of hunting rights.

Secondly, the respondent maintained that "as usual" should be interpreted to limit the treaty protection to hunting for non-commercial purposes. It is difficult to see the basis for this argument in the absence of evidence regarding the purpose for which the appellant was hunting. In any event, article 4 of the treaty appears to contemplate hunting for commercial purposes when it refers to the construction of a truck house as a place of exchange and mentions the liberty of the Micmac to bring game to sale: see *R. v. Paul*, [1981] 2 C.N.L.R. 83 (N.B.C.A), at p. 563, per Ryan J.A., dissenting in part. . . .

In my opinion, it is implicit in the right granted under article 4 of the Treaty of 1752 that the appellant has the right to possess a gun and ammunition in a safe manner in order to be able to exercise the right to hunt. Accordingly, I conclude that the appellant was exercising his right to hunt under the treaty. . . .

It seems clear that, at a minimum, the treaty recognizes some hunting rights in Nova Scotia on the Shubenacadie Reserve and that any Micmac Indian who enjoys those rights has an incidental right to transport a gun and ammunition to places where he could legally exercise them. In this vein, it is worth noting that both parties agree that the highway on which the appellant was stopped "is adjacent to the Shubenacadie Indian Reserve" and "passes through or by a forest, wood, or other resource frequented by moose or deer".

The respondent tries to meet the apparent right of the appellant to transport a gun and ammunition by asserting that the treaty hunting rights have been extinguished. In order to succeed on this argument it is absolutely essential, it seems to me, that the respondent lead evidence as to where the appellant hunted or intended to hunt and what use has been or is currently made of those lands. It is impossible for this Court to consider the doctrine of extinguishment 'in the air'; the respondent must anchor that argument in the bedrock of specific lands. That has not happened in this case. In the absence of evidence as to where the hunting occurred or was intended to occur, and the use of the lands in question, it would be impossible to determine whether the appellant's treaty hunting rights have been extinguished. Moreover, it is unnecessary for this Court to determine whether those rights have been extinguished because, at the very least, these rights extended to the adjacent Shubenacadie reserve. I do not wish to be taken as expressing any view on whether, as a matter of law, treaty rights may be extinguished. . . .

The appellant, Simon, as a member of the Shubenacadie Indian Brook Band of Micmac Indians, residing in Eastern Nova Scotia, the area covered by the Treaty of 1752, can therefore raise the treaty in his defense. . . .

Is the Treaty a "Treaty" Within the Meaning of s. 88 of the Indian Act?
Section 88 of the *Indian Act* stipulates that, "Subject to the terms of any treaty . . . , all laws of general application from time to time in force in any province are applicable to and in respect of Indians in the province. . . ."

. . . In my view, Parliament intended to include within the operation of s. 88 all agreements concluded by the Crown with the Indians that would otherwise be enforceable treaties, whether land was ceded or not. None of the Maritime treaties of the eighteenth century cedes land. To find that s. 88 applies only to land cession treaties would be to limit severely its scope and run contrary to the principle that Indian treaties and statutes relating to Indians should be liberally construed and uncertainties resolved in favour of the Indians.

Finally, it should be noted that several cases have considered the Treaty of 1752 to be a valid "treaty" within the meaning of s. 88 of the *Indian Act* (for example, *R. v. Paul, supra*; and *R. v. Atwin and Sacobie*, [1981] 2 C.N.L.R. 99 (N.B. Prov. Ct.). The Treaty was an exchange of solemn promises between the Micmacs and the King's representative entered into to achieve and guarantee peace. It is an enforceable obligation between the Indians and the white man and, as such, falls within the meaning of the word "treaty" in s. 88 of the *Indian Act*.

Do the Hunting Rights Contained in the Treaty Exempt the Appellant from Prosecution under s. 150(1) of the Lands and Forests Act?
As a result of my conclusion that the appellant was validly exercising his right to hunt under the Treaty of 1752 and the fact he has admitted that his conduct otherwise constitutes an offence under the *Lands and Forests Act*, it must now be determined what the result is when a treaty right comes into conflict with provincial legislation. This question is governed by s. 88 of the *Indian Act*, which, it will be recalled, states that "Subject to the terms of any treaty, all laws of general application . . . in force in the province are applicable to . . . Indians". . . .

Under s. 88 of the *Indian Act*, when the terms of a treaty come into conflict with federal legislation, the latter prevails, subject to whatever may be the effect of s. 35 of the *Constitution Act, 1982*. It has been held to be within the exclusive power of Parliament under s. 91(24) of the *Constitution Act, 1867*, to derogate from rights recognized in a treaty agreement made with the Indians. See *R. v. Sikyea* (1964), 43 D.L.R. (2d) 150, *R. v. George, supra, R. v. Cooper, supra; R. v. White and Bob, supra*, at p. 618.

Here, however, we are dealing with provincial legislation. The effect of s. 88 of the *Indian Act* is to exempt the Indians from provincial legislation which restricts or contravenes the terms of any treaty. In *Frank v. The Queen*, [1978] 1 S.C.R. 95, the Court held, at p. 99:

> The effect of this section is to make applicable to Indians except as stated, all laws of general application from time to time in force in any province, including provincial game laws, but subject to the terms of any treaty and subject also to any other Act of the Parliament of Canada.

Similarly, in *Kruger v. The Queen*, [1978] 1 S.C.R. 104, the Court held, at pp. 111–12:

> However abundant the right of Indians to hunt and to fish, there can be no doubt that such right is subject to regulation and curtailment by the appropriate legislative authority. Section 88 of the Indian Act appears to be plain in purpose and effect. In the absence of treaty protection or statutory protection, Indians are brought within provincial regulatory legislation.

and at pp. 114–15 the Court held in reference to Indian treaties and s. 88:

> The terms of the treaty are paramount; in the absence of a treaty, provincial laws of general application apply.

Therefore, the question here is whether s. 150(1) of the *Lands and Forests Act*, a provincial enactment of general application in Nova Scotia, restricts or contravenes the right to hunt in article 4 of the Treaty of 1752. If so, the treaty right to hunt prevails and the appellant is exempt from the operation of the provincial game legislation at issue. . . .

In my opinion, s. 150 of the *Lands and Forests Act* of Nova Scotia restricts the appellant's right to hunt under the treaty. The section clearly places seasonal limitations and licensing requirements, for the purposes of wildlife conservation, on the right to possess a rifle and ammunition for the purposes of hunting. The restrictions imposed in this case conflict, therefore, with the appellant's right to possess a firearm and ammunition in order to exercise this free liberty to hunt over the lands covered by the treaty. As noted, it is clear that under s. 88 of the *Indian Act* provincial legislation cannot restrict native treaty rights. If conflict arises, the terms of the treaty prevail. Therefore, by virtue of s. 88 of the *Indian Act*, the clear terms of article 4 of the treaty must prevail over s. 150(1) of the provincial *Lands and Forests Act*.

Several cases have particular relevance. These also deal with charges similar to those in the present case where Indians were accused of unlawful possession of certain objects without the permit required under provincial legislation. In each case, the accused Indians raised their treaty rights in defence and it was held that they should be acquitted because they were not bound by the terms of the provincial statutes: See *R. v. White and Bob, supra*; *R. v. Paul, supra*; *R. v. Atwin and Sacobie, supra*; *R. v. Paul and Polchies, supra*; *R. v. Batisse* (1978), 84 D.L.R. (3d) 377 (Dist. Ct.); *R. v. Taylor and Williams*, [1981] 3 C.N.L.R. 114 (Ont. C.A.); *R. v. Moses* (1969), 13 D.L.R. (3d) 50 (Ont. Dist. Ct.); *R. v. Penasse and McLeod* (1971), 8 C.C.C. (2d) 569 (Ont. Prov. Ct.); *Cheeco v. R.*, [1981] 3 C.N.L.R. 45 (Ont. Dist. Ct.).

I conclude that the appellant has a valid treaty right to hunt under the Treaty of 1752 which, by virtue of s. 88 of the *Indian Act,* cannot be restricted by provincial legislation. It follows, therefore, that the appellant's possession of a rifle and ammunition in a safe manner, referable to his treaty right to hunt, cannot be restricted by s. 150(1) of the *Lands and Forests Act*.

I would accordingly quash the convictions and enter verdicts of acquittal on both charges. . . .

To summarize:

1. The Treaty of 1752 was validly created by competent parties.

2. The treaty contains a right to hunt which covers the activities engaged in by the appellant.

3. The treaty was not terminated by subsequent hostilities in 1753. Nor has it been demonstrated that the right to hunt protected by the treaty has been extinguished.

4. The appellant is a Micmac Indian covered by the treaty.

5. The Treaty of 1752 is a "treaty" within the meaning of s. 88 of the *Indian Act*.

6. By virtue of s. 88 of the *Indian Act*, the appellant is exempt from prosecution under s. 150(1) of the *Lands and Forests Act*.

7. In light of these conclusions, it is not necessary to answer the constitutional question raised in this appeal.

I would, therefore, allow the appeal, quash the convictions of the appellant and enter verdicts of acquittal on both charges.

R. v. Sioui (1990)

[1990] 1 S.C.R. 1025 (S.C.C.). Dickson C.J., Lamer, Wilson, La Forest, L'Heureux-Dubé, Sopinka, Gonthier, Cory, and McLachlin JJ., May 24, 1990.

LAMER J.:— . . . The four respondents were convicted by the Court of Sessions of the Peace of cutting down trees, camping and making fires in places not designated in Jacques-Cartier park contrary to ss. 9 and 37 of the *Regulation respecting the Parc de la Jacques-Cartier* (Order in Council 3108-81 of November 11, 1981, (1981) 113 O.G. II, 3518), adopted pursuant to the *Parks Act*, R.S.Q. 1977, c. P-9. . . .

The respondents are Indians within the meaning of the *Indian Act*, R.S.C., 1985, c. I-5 (formerly R.S.C. 1970, c. I-6), and are members of the Huron Band on the Lorette Indian reserve. They admit that they committed the acts with which they were charged in Jacques-Cartier park, which is located outside the boundaries of the Lorette reserve. However, they alleged that they were practising certain ancestral customs and religious rites which are the subject of a treaty between the Hurons and the British, a treaty which brings s. 88 of the *Indian Act* into play and exempts them from compliance with the regulations. . . .

The appellants are asking this Court to dispose of the appeal solely on the basis of the document of September 5, 1760 and s. 88 of the *Indian Act*. The following constitutional questions were stated by the Chief Justice:

> 1. Does the following document, signed by General Murray on 5 September 1760, constitute a treaty within the meaning of s. 88 of the *Indian Act* (R.S.C. 1970, c. I-6)?
>
>> THESE are to certify that the CHIEF of the Huron tribe of Indians having come to me in the name of His Nation, to submit to HIS BRITANNICK MAJESTY, and make Peace, has been received under my Protection, with his whole Tribe; and henceforth no English Officer or party is to molest, or interrupt them in returning to their Settlement at LORRETTE; and they are received upon the same terms with the Canadians, being allowed the free Exercise of their Religion, their Customs, and Liberty of trading with the English:—recommending it to the Officers commanding the Posts, to treat them kindly.
>>
>> Given under my hand at Longueil, this 5th day of September, 1760.
>>
>> By the Genl's Command,
>> JA. MURRAY
>> JOHN COSNAN,
>> Adjut. Genl.
>
> 2. If the answer to question 1 is in the affirmative, was the "treaty" still operative on 29 May 1982, at the time when the alleged offence were committed?
>
> 3. If the answers to questions 1 and 2 are in the affirmative, are the terms of the document of such a nature as to make ss. 9 and 37 of the *Regulation respecting the Parc de la Jacques-Cartier* (Order in Council 3108-81, *Gazette officielle du Québec*, Part II, November 25, 1981, pp. 3518 et seq.) made under the *Parks Act* (R.S.Q., c. P-9) unenforceable in respect of the respondents? . . .

Our courts and those of our neighbours to the south have already considered what distinguishes a treaty with the Indians from other agreements affecting them. The task is not an easy one. In *Simon v. The Queen*, [1985] 2 S.C.R. 387, [1986] 1 C.N.L.R. 153 this Court adopted the comment of Norris J.A. in *R. v. White and Bob* (1964), 52 W.W.R. 193, 50 D.L.R. (2d) 613 (B.C.C.A.) (affirmed in the Supreme Court (1965), 52 D.L.R. (2d)

481), that the courts should show flexibility in determining the legal nature of a document recording a transaction with the Indians. In particular, they must take into account the historical context and perception each party might have as to the nature of the undertaking contained in the document under consideration. To the question of whether the document at issue in *White and Bob* was a treaty within the meaning of the *Indian Act*, Norris J.A. replied (at pp. 648–49 D.L.R.):

> The question is, in my respectful opinion, to be resolved not by the application of rigid rules of construction without regard to the circumstances existing when the document was completed nor by the tests of modern day draftsmanship. In determining what the intention of Parliament was at the time of the enactment of s. 87 [now s. 88] of the Indian Act, Parliament is to be taken to have had in mind the common understanding of the parties to the document at the time it was executed.

As the Chief Justice said in *Simon, supra,* treaties and statutes relating to Indians should be liberally construed and uncertainties resolved in favour of the Indians (at 410) [p. 174 C.N.L.R.]. In our quest for the legal nature of the document of September 5, 1760, therefore, we should adopt a broad and generous interpretation of what constitutes a treaty.

In my opinion, this liberal and generous attitude, heedful of historical fact, should also guide us in examining the preliminary question of the capacity to sign a treaty, as illustrated by *Simon* and *White and Bob.*

Finally, once a valid treaty is found to exist, that treaty must in turn be given a just, broad and liberal construction. This principle, for which there is ample precedent, was recently reaffirmed in *Simon.* The factors underlying this rule were eloquently stated in *Jones* v. *Meehan,* 175 U.S. 1 (1899), a judgment of the United States Supreme Court, and are I think just as relevant to questions involving the existence of a treaty and the capacity of the parties as they are to the interpretations of a treaty (at pp. 10–11):

> In construing any treaty between the United States and an Indian tribe, it must always . . . be borne in mind that the negotiations for the treaty are conducted, on the part of the United States, an enlightened and powerful nation, by representatives skilled in diplomacy, masters of a written language, understanding the modes and forms of creating the various technical estates known to their law, and assisted by an interpreter employed by themselves; that the treaty is drawn up by them and in their own language; that the Indians, on the other hand, are a weak and dependent people, who have no written language and are wholly unfamiliar with all the forms of legal expression, and whose only knowledge of the terms in which the treaty is framed is that imparted to them by the interpreter employed by the United States; and that the treaty must therefore be construed, not according to the technical meaning of its words to learned lawyers, but in the sense in which they would naturally be understood by the Indians.

The Indian people are today much better versed in the art of negotiation with public authorities than they were when the United States Supreme Court handed down its decision in *Jones.* As the document in question was signed over a hundred years before that decision, these considerations argue all the more strongly for the courts to adopt a generous and liberal approach. . . .

C. Legal nature of the document of September 5, 1760

1. Constituent elements of a treaty

In *Simon* this Court noted that a treaty with the Indians is unique, that it is an agreement *sui generis* which is neither created nor terminated according to the rules of international law. In that case the accused had relied on an agreement concluded in 1752 between Governor Hopson and the Micmac Chief Cope, and the Crown disputed that this was a treaty. The following are two extracts illustrating the reasons relied on by the Chief Justice in concluding that a treaty had been concluded between the Micmacs and the British Crown (at pp. 401 and 410) [at pp. 166 and 174 C.N.L.R.]:

> In my opinion, both the Governor and the Micmac entered into the Treaty with the inten-
> tion of creating mutually binding obligations which would be solemnly respected. It also
> provided a mechanism for dispute resolution.
> . . . The Treaty was an exchange [of] solemn promises between the Micmacs and the
> King's representative entered into to achieve and guarantee peace. It is an enforceable obli-
> gation between the Indians and the white man and, as such, falls within the meaning of the
> word "treaty" in s. 88 of the *Indian Act*.

From these extracts it is clear that what characterizes a treaty is the intention to create obligations, the presence of mutually binding obligations and a certain measure of solemnity. . . .

The decision of the Ontario Court of Appeal in *R. v. Taylor and Williams*, [1981] 3 C.N.L.R. 114, also provides valuable assistance by listing a series of factors which are relevant to analysis of the historical background. In that case the Court had to interpret a treaty, and not determine the legal nature of a document, but the factors mentioned may be just as useful in determining the existence of a treaty as in interpreting it. In particular, they assist in determining the intent of the parties to enter into a treaty. Among these factors are:

1. continuous exercise of a right in the past and at present,

2. the reasons why the Crown made a commitment,

3. the situation prevailing at the time the document was signed,

4. evidence of relations of mutual respect and esteem between the negotiators, and

5. the subsequent conduct of the parties. . . .

While the analysis thus far seems to suggest that the document of September 5 is not a treaty, the presence of a clause guaranteeing the free exercise of religion, customs and trade with the English cannot but raise serious doubts about this proposition. It seems extremely strange to me that a document which is supposedly only a temporary, unilateral and informal safe conduct should contain a clause guaranteeing rights of such importance. As Bisson J.A. noted in the Court of Appeal judgment, there would have been no necessity to mention the free exercise of religion and customs in a document the effects of which were only to last for a few days. Such a guarantee would definitely have been more natural in a treaty where "the word of the white man" is given. . . .

As this Court recently noted in *R. v. Horse*, [1988] 1 S.C.R. 187 at 201, [1988] 2 C.N.L.R. 112 at 124, extrinsic evidence is not to be used as an aid to interpreting a treaty in the absence of ambiguity or where the result would be to alter its terms by adding words to or subtracting words from the written agreement. This rule also applies in determining the legal nature of a document relating to the Indians. However, a more flexible approach is necessary as the question of the existence of a treaty within the meaning of s. 88 of *Indian Act* is generally closely bound up with the circumstances existing when the document was prepared (*White and Bob, supra*, at pp. 648–49, and *Simon, supra,* at pp. 409–10 [p. 173–74 C.N.L.R.]). In any case, the wording alone will not suffice to determine the legal nature of the document before the Court. On the one hand, we have before us a document the form of which and some of whose subject-matter suggest that it is not a treaty, and on the other, we find it to contain protection of fundamental rights which supports the opposite conclusion. The ambiguity arising from this document thus means that the Court must look at extrinsic evidence to determine its legal nature. . . .

[W]e can conclude from the historical documents that both Great Britain and France felt that the Indian nations had sufficient independence and played a large enough role in North America for it to be good policy to maintain relations with them very close to those maintained between sovereign nations.

The mother countries did everything in their power to secure the alliance of each Indian nation and to encourage nations allied with the enemy to change sides. When these efforts met with success, they were incorporated in treaties of alliance or neutrality. This clearly indicates that the Indian nations were regarded in their relations with the European nations which occupied North America as independent nations. The papers of Sir William Johnson (*The Papers of Sir William Johnson*, 14 vol.), who was in charge of Indian affairs in British North America, demonstrate the recognition by Great Britain that nation-to-nation relations had to be conducted with the North American Indians. As an example, I cite an extract from a speech by Sir Johnson at the Onondaga Conference held in April 1748, attended by the Five nations:

> Brethren of the five Nations I will begin upon a thing of a long standing, our first *Brothership*. My Reason for it is, I think: there are several among you who seem to forget it; It may seem strange to you how I a *Foreigner* should know this, But I tell you I found out some of the old Writings of our Forefathers which was thought to have been lost and in this old valuable Record I find, that our first *Friendship* Commenced at the Arrival of the first great Canoe or Vessel at Albany . . . [Emphasis added.]

> (*The Papers of Sir William Johnson*, vol. 1,1921, at p. 157)

As the Chief Justice of the United States Supreme Court said in 1832 in *Worcester* v. *State of Georgia*, 31 U.S. (6 Pet.) 515 (1832), at pp. 548–49, about British policy towards the Indians in the mid-eighteenth century:

> Such was the policy of Great Britain towards the Indian nations inhabiting the territory from which she excluded all other Europeans; such her claims, and such her practical exposition of the charters she had granted: *she considered them as nations capable of maintaining the relations of peace and war: of governing themselves, under her protection: and she made treaties with them, the obligation of which she acknowledged.* [Emphasis added.]

Further, both the French and the English recognized the critical importance of alliances with the Indians, or at least their neutrality, in determining the outcome of the war between them and the security of the North American colonies.

Following the crushing defeats of the English by the French in 1755, the English realized that control of North America could not be acquired without the co-operation of the Indians. Accordingly, from then on they made efforts to ally themselves with as many Indian nations as possible. The French, who had long realized the strategic role of the Indians in the success of any war effort, also did everything they could to secure their alliance or maintain alliances already established (Jack Stagg, *Anglo-Indian Relations in North America to 1763* (1981); "Mr. Nelson's Memorial about the State of the Northern Colonies in America," September 24, 1696, reproduced in O'Callaghan ed., *Documents relative to the Colonial History of New York* (1856), vol. VII, at p. 206; "Letter from Sir William Johnson to William Pitt," October 24, 1760, in *The Papers of Sir William Johnson*, vol. III, 1921 at pp. 269 et seq.; "Mémoire de Bougainville sur l'artillerie du Canada," January 11, 1759, in *Rapport de l'archiviste de la Province de Québec pour 1923–1924* (1924), at p. 58; *Journal du Marquis de Montcalm durant ses campagnes en Canada de 1756(1759* (1895), at p. 428).

England also wished to secure the friendship of the Indian nations by treating them with generosity and respect for fear that the safety and development of the colonies and their inhabitants would be compromised by Indians with feelings of hostility. One of the extracts from Knox's work which I cited above reports that the Canadians and the French soldiers who surrendered asked to be protected from Indians on the way back to their parishes. Another passage from Knox, also cited above, relates that the Canadians were terrified at the idea of seeing Sir William Johnson's Indians coming among them. This proves that in the minds of the local population the Indians represented a real and disturbing threat. The fact that England was also aware of the danger the colonies and their inhabitants might run if the Indians withdrew their co-operation is echoed in the following documents: "Letter from Sir William Johnson to the lords of Trade," November 13, 1763, reproduced in O'Callaghan ed., op. cit., at pp. 574, 579 and 580; "Letter from Sir William Johnson to William Pitt," October 24, 1760, in *The Papers of Sir William Johnson,* vol. III at pp. 270 and 274; Ratelle, *Contexte historique de la localisation des Attikameks et des Montagnais de 1760 (nos jours* (1987); "Letter from Amherst to Sir William Johnson," August 30, 1760, in *The Papers of Sir William Johnson,* vol. X, 1951, at p. 177; "Instructions from George H to Amherst," September 18, 1758, National Archives of Canada (MG 18 L 4 File 0 20/8); C. Colden, *The History of the Five Indian Nations of Canada* (1747), at p. 180; Stagg, op. cit., at pp. 166–67; and by analogy Murray, *Journal of the Siege of Quebec, supra,* entry of December 31, 1759, at pp. 15–16.

This "generous" policy which the British chose to adopt also found expression in other areas. The British Crown recognized that the Indians had certain ownership rights over their land, it sought to establish trade with them which would rise above the level of exploitation and give them a fair return. It also allowed them autonomy in their internal affairs, intervening in this area as little as possible.

Whatever the similarities between a document recording the laying down of arms by French soldiers or Canadians and the document at issue, the analogy does not go so far as to preclude the conclusion that the document was nonetheless a treaty.

Such a document could not be regarded as a treaty so far as the French and the Canadians were concerned because under international law they had no authority to sign such a document: they were governed by a European nation which alone was able to represent them in dealings with other European nations for the signature of treaties affecting them. The colonial powers recognized that the Indians had the capacity to sign treaties directly with the European nations occupying North American territory. The *sui generis* situation in which the Indians were placed had forced the European mother countries to acknowledge that they had sufficient autonomy for the valid creation of solemn agreements which were called "treaties," regardless of the strict meaning given to that word then and now by international law. The question of the competence of the Hurons and of the French or the Canadians is essential to the question of whether a treaty exists. The question of capacity has to be examined from a fundamentally different viewpoint and in accordance with different principles for each of these groups. Thus, I reject the argument that the legal nature of the document at issue must necessarily be interpreted in the same way as the capitulations of the French and the Canadians. The historical context which I have briefly reviewed even supports the proposition that both the British and the Hurons could have intended to enter into a treaty on September 5, 1760. I rely, in particular, on Great Britain's stated wish to form alliances with as many Indians as possible and on the demoralizing effect for the French, the Canadians and their allies which would result from the loss of this long–standing Indian ally whose allegiance to the French cause had until then been very seldom shaken. . . .

Lastly, the Court was asked to consider the subsequent conduct of the parties as extrinsic evidence of their intent to enter into a treaty. I do not think this is necessary, since the general historical context of the time and the events closely surrounding the document at issue have persuaded me that the document of September 5, 1760 is a treaty within the meaning of s. 88 of the *Indian Act.* The fact that the document has allegedly not been used in the courts or other institutions of our society does not establish that it is not a treaty. Non–use may very well be explained by observance of the rights contained in the document or mere oversight. Moreover, the subsequent conduct which is most indicative of the parties' intent is undoubtedly that which most closely followed the conclusion of the document. Eleven days after it was concluded, at the conference to which I have just referred, the parties gave a clear indication that they had intended to conclude a treaty.

I am therefore of the view that the document of September 5, 1760 is a treaty within the meaning of s. 88 of the *Indian Act.* At this point, the appellant raises two arguments against its application to the present case. First, he argues that the treaty has been extinguished. In the event that it has not been, he argues that the treaty is not such as to render ss. 9 and 37 of the *Regulation respecting the Parc de la Jacques-Cartier* inoperative. Let us first consider whether on May 29, 1982, the date on which the respondents engaged in the activities which are the subject of the charges, the treaty still had any legal effects. . . .

Neither the documents nor the legislative and administrative history to which the appellant referred the Court contain any express statement that the treaty of September 5, 1760 has been extinguished. Even assuming that a treaty can be extinguished implicitly, a point on which I express no opinion here, the appellant was not able in my view to meet the criterion stated in *Simon* regarding the quality of evidence that would be required in any case to support a conclusion that the treaty had been extinguished. That case clearly established that the onus is on the party arguing that the treaty has terminated to show the circumstances and events indicating it has been extinguished. This burden can only be discharged by strict proof, as the Chief Justice said at pp. 405–6 [p. 170 C.N.L.R.]:

> Given the serious and far-reaching consequences of a finding that a treaty right has been extinguished, it seems appropriate to demand strict proof of the fact of extinguishment in each case where the issue arises.

The appellant did not submit any persuasive evidence of extinguishment of the treaty. He argues, first, that the treaty had become obsolete because the *Act of Capitulation* of Montreal replaced all other acts of capitulation, thereby extinguishing them. This argument is based on article 50 of the *Act of Capitulation,* which reads as follows:

> The present capitulation shall be inviolably executed in all its articles, and bona fide, on both sides, notwithstanding any infraction, and any other pretence, with regard to the *preceding capitulations,* and without making use of reprisals. [Emphasis added.]

As I have concluded that this is a peace treaty and not a capitulation, art. 50 has no application in this case, so far as extinguishment of the treaty of September 5 is concerned. That article was designed to ensure that the signatories would comply with the *Act of Capitulation*, in spite of the existence of reasons for retaliation which the parties might have had as the result of breaches of an earlier act of capitulation. Article 50 can only apply to preceding acts signed on behalf of France, such as the *Act of Capitulation of Québec* in late 1759. I see nothing here to support the conclusion that this article was also intended to extinguish a treaty between an Indian nation and the British.

The appellant also cites art. 40 of the *Act of Capitulation* of Montreal, which provides that:

> *The Savages or Indian allies* of his most Christian Majesty, shall be maintained in the Lands they inhabit, if they chuse to remain there; they shall not be molested on any pretence whatsoever, for having carried arms, and served his most Christian Majesty. They shall have, as well as the French, liberty of religion, and shall keep their missionaries. [Emphasis added]

France could not have claimed to represent the Hurons at the time the *Act of Capitulation* was made, since the latter had abandoned their alliance with the French some days before. As they were no longer allies of the French, this article does not apply to them. In my opinion, the article can only be interpreted as a condition on which the French agreed to capitulate. Though the Indian allies of the French were its beneficiaries, it was fundamentally an agreement between the French and the British which in no way prevented independent agreements between the British and the Indian nations, whether allies of the French or of the British, being concluded or continuing to exist. Further, I think it is clear that the purpose of art. 40 was to assure the Indians of certain rights, not to extinguish existing rights.

It would be contrary to the general principles of law for an agreement concluded between the English and the French to extinguish a treaty concluded between the English and the Hurons. It must be remembered that a treaty is a solemn agreement between the Crown and the Indians, an agreement the nature of which is sacred: *Simon, supra,* at p. 410 [p. 173–74 C.N.L.R.], and *White and Bob, supra,* at p. 649. The very definition of a treaty thus makes it impossible to avoid the conclusion that a treaty cannot be extinguished without the consent of the Indians concerned. Since the Hurons had the capacity to enter into a treaty with the British, therefore, they must be the only ones who could give the necessary consent to its extinguishment.

The same reasoning applies to the appellant's argument that the Treaty of Paris of February 10, 1763 between France and England terminated the treaty of September 5, 1760 between the Hurons and the English. England and France could not validly agree to extinguish a treaty between the Hurons and the English, nor could France claim to represent the Hurons regarding the extinguishment of a treaty the Hurons had themselves concluded with the British Crown.

The appellant then argued that it follows that the Royal Proclamation of October 7, 1763 extinguished the rights arising out of the treaty of September 5, 1760, because it did not confirm them. I cannot accept such a proposition: the silence of the Royal Proclamation regarding the treaty at issue cannot be interpreted as extinguishing it. The purpose of the Proclamation was first and foremost to organize, geographically and politically, the territory of the new American colonies, namely Quebec, East Florida, West Florida and Grenada, and to distribute their possession and use. It also granted certain important rights to the native peoples and was regarded by many as a kind of charter of rights for the Indians: *White and Bob, supra,* at p. 636; *Calder v. Attorney-General of British Columbia,* [1973] S.C.R 313 at 395, (Hall J., dissenting); *R. v. Secretary of State for Foreign and*

Commonwealth Affairs, [1982] 2 All E.R 118 at 124–25, [1981] 4 C.N.L.R. 86 at 91 (C.A.) (Lord Denning). The very wording of the Royal Proclamation clearly shows that its objective, so far as the Indians were concerned, was to provide a solution to the problems created by the greed which hitherto some of the English had all too often demonstrated in buying up Indian land at low prices. The situation was causing dangerous trouble among the Indians and the Royal Proclamation was meant to remedy this: . . .

I see nothing in these passages [of the Royal Proclamation] which can be interpreted as an intention on the part of the British Crown to extinguish the treaty of September 5. The Proclamation confers rights on the Indians without necessarily thereby extinguishing any other right conferred on them by the British Crown under a treaty.

Legislative and administrative history also provides no basis for concluding that the treaty was extinguished. In 1853, 9,600 acres of land located outside the territory at issue were ceded to the Hurons by the Government of Lower Canada. These lands were within the boundaries of the lands frequented by the Hurons when the treaty of September 5 was concluded. In 1903 the Hurons again ceded these 9,600 acres, without reserving the rights that had been granted to them under the treaty of September 5. The Attorney General of Quebec considers that by making this cession without reservation, the Hurons indicated beyond all doubt that this document was not a source of rights so far as they were concerned. This argument cannot stand. Assuming that the 9,600 acres ceded were initially the subject of the treaty, the absence of any reservation in the deed ceding this territory clearly cannot be interpreted as a waiver of the benefits of the treaty in the territory which was not the subject of the cession, whatever the effect of the absence of such a reservation may be with respect to the territory ceded.

The appellant further argues that by adopting the *Act to establish the Laurentides National Park*, S.Q. 1895, 58 Vict., c. 22, and by making the territory in question a park, the Quebec legislator clearly expressed his intention to prohibit the carrying on of certain activities in this territory, whether or not such activities are protected by an Indian's treaty.

Section 88 of the *Indian Act* is designed specifically to protect the Indians from provincial legislation that might attempt to deprive them of rights protected by a treaty. A legislated change in the use of the territory thus does not extinguish rights otherwise protected by treaty. If the treaty gives the Hurons the right to carry on their customs and religion in the territory of Jacques-Cartier park, the existence of a provincial statute and subordinate legislation will not ordinarily affect that right.

Finally, the appellant argues that non-use of the treaty over a long period of time may extinguish its effect. He cites no authority for this. I do not think that this argument carries much weight: a solemn agreement cannot lose its validity merely because it has not been invoked to, which in any case is disputed by the respondents, who maintain that it was relied on in a seigneurial claim in 1824. Such a proposition would mean that a treaty could be extinguished merely because it had not been relied on in litigation, which is untenable.

In view of the liberal and generous approach that must be adopted towards Indians rights and the evidence in the record, I cannot conclude that the treaty of September 5 no longer had any legal effect on May 29, 1982.

The question that arises at this point is as to whether the treaty is capable of rendering ss. 9 and 37 of the Regulations inoperative. To answer this it will now be necessary to consider the territorial scope of the rights guaranteed by the treaty, since the appellant recognizes that the activities with which the respondents are charged are customary or religious in nature. . . .

Accordingly, I conclude that in view of the absence of any express mention of the territorial scope of the treaty, it has to be assumed that the parties to the treaty of September 5 intended to reconcile the Hurons' need to protect the exercise of their customs and the desire of the British conquerors to expand. Protecting the exercise of the customs in all parts of the territory frequented when it is not incompatible with its occupancy is in my opinion the most reasonable way of reconciling the competing interests. This, in my view, is the definition of the common intent of the parties which best reflects the actual intent of the Hurons and of Murray on September 5, 1760. Defining the common intent of the parties on the question of territory in this way makes it possible to give full effect to the spirit of conciliation, while respecting the practical requirements of the British. This gave the English the necessary flexibility to be able to respond in due course to the increasing need to use Canada's resources, in the event that Canada remained under British sovereignty. The Hurons, for their part, were protecting their customs wherever their exercise would not be prejudicial to the use to which the territory concerned would be put. The Hurons could not reasonably expect that the use would forever remain what it was in 1760. Before the treaty was signed, they had carried on their customs in accordance with restrictions already imposed by an occupancy incompatible with such exercise. The Hurons were only asking to be permitted to continue to carry on their customs on the lands frequented to the extent that those customs did not interfere with enjoyment of the lands by their occupier. I readily accept that the Hurons were probably not aware of the legal consequences, and in particular of the right to occupy to the exclusion of others, which the main European legal systems attached to the concept of private ownership. Nonetheless I cannot believe that the Hurons ever believed that the treaty gave them the right to cut down trees in the garden of a house as part of their right to carry on their customs.

Jacques-Cartier park falls into the category of land occupied by the Crown, since the province has set it aside for a specific use. What is important is not so much that the province has legislated with respect to this territory but that it is using it, is in fact occupying the space. As occupancy has been established, the question is whether the type of occupancy to which the park is subject is incompatible with the exercise of the activities with which the respondents were charged, as these undoubtedly constitute religious customs or rites. Since, in view of the situation in 1760, we must assume some limitation on the exercise of rights protected by the treaty, it is up to the Crown to prove that its occupancy of the territory cannot be accommodated to reasonable exercise of the Hurons' rights.

The Crown presented evidence on such compatibility but that evidence did not persuade me that exercise of the rites and customs at issue here is incompatible with the occupancy. . . .

For the exercise of rites and customs to be incompatible with the occupancy of the park by the Crown, it must not only be contrary to the purpose underlying that occupancy, it must prevent the realization of that purpose. First, we are dealing with Crown lands, lands which are held for the benefit of the community. Exclusive use is not an essential aspect of public ownership. Second, I do not think that the activities described seriously compromise the Crown's objectives in occupying the park. Neither the representative nature of the natural region where the park is located nor the exceptional nature of this natural site are threatened by the collecting of a few plants, the setting up of a tent using a few branches picked up in the area or the making of a fire according to the rules dictated by caution to avoid fires. These activities also present no obstacle to cross-country recreation. I therefore conclude that it has not been established that occupancy of the territory of Jacques-Cartier park is incompatible with the exercise of Huron rites and customs with which the respondents are charged. . . .

For all these reasons, I would dismiss the appeal with costs.

I would dispose of the constitutional questions stated by the Chief Justice as follows:

1. Does the following document, signed by General Murray on 5 September 1760, constitute a treaty within the meaning of s. 88 of the Indian Act (R.S.C. 1970, c. 1-6)? . . .

Answer: Yes.

2. If the answer to question 1 is in the affirmative, was the "treaty" still operative on 29 May 1982, at the time when the alleged offences were committed?

Answer: Yes.

3. If the answer to questions 1 and 2 are in the affirmative, are the terms of the document of such a nature as to make ss. 9 and 37 of the Regulation respecting the Parc de la Jacques-Cartier . . . made under the Parks Act (R.S.Q., c. P-9) unenforceable in respect of the respondents?

Answer: Yes.

R. v. *Horseman* (1990)

[1990] 1 S.C.R. 901 (S.C.C.). Dickson C.J., Lamer, Wilson, La Forest, L'Heureux-Dubé, Gonthier, and Cory JJ., May 3, 1990.

CORY J. (LAMER, LA FOREST AND GONTHIER JJ., concurring):—At issue on this appeal is whether the provisions of s. 42 and s. 1(s) of the *Wildlife Act*, R.S.A. 1980, c. W-9, apply to the appellant, whose forebears were members of one of the Indian bands party to Treaty 8 signed in 1899 which guaranteed substantive hunting rights to certain Indian people. . . .

The sole defence raised on behalf of Horseman was that the *Wildlife Act* did not apply to him and that he was within his Treaty 8 rights when he sold the bear hide. Nothing is to turn on the killing of the bear in self-defence. Nor is it argued that Horseman was induced into a mistake of the law by the words of an official of the government. Rather, it is the appellant's position that he can, at any time, on Crown lands or on lands to which Indians have access, kill a grizzly bear for food. Further, it is said that he can sell the hide of any grizzly bear he kills in order to buy food. . . .

I am in complete agreement with the finding of the trial judge that the original treaty right clearly included hunting for purposes of commerce. The next question that must be resolved is whether or not that right was in any way limited or affected by the Transfer Agreement of 1930.

The Effect of the 1930 Transfer Agreement

At the outset two established principles must be borne in mind. First, the onus of proving either express or implicit extinguishment lies upon the Crown. See *Simon* v. *The Queen*, [1985] 2 S.C.R. 387, [1986] 1 C.N.L.R. 153; *Calder* v. *Attorney-General of British Columbia*, [1973] S.C.R. 313. Secondly, any ambiguities in the wording of the treaty or document must be resolved in favour of the native people. This was expressed by Dickson J., as he then was, speaking for the Court in *Nowegijick* v. *The Queen*, [1983] 1 S C.R. 29

at 36, [1983] 2 C.N.L.R. 89 at 94, in these words:

> ... treaties and statutes relating to Indians should be liberally construed and doubtful expressions resolved in favour of the Indians. ...

[P]ara. 12 of the 1930 Transfer Agreement was carefully considered and interpreted by Chief Justice Dickson in the three recent cases of *Frank* v. *The Queen*, [1978] 1 S.C.R. 95; *R.* v. *Sutherland*, [1980] 2 S.C.R. 451; and *Moosehunter* v. *The Queen*, [1981] 1 S.C.R. 282. These cases dealt with the analogous problems arising from the Transfer Agreements with Manitoba and Saskatchewan which were worded in precisely the same way as the Transfer Agreement with Alberta under consideration in this case. These reasons constitute the carefully considered recent opinion of this Court. They are just as persuasive today as they were when they were released. Nothing in the appellant's submission would lead me to vary in any way the reasons so well and clearly expressed in those cases.

It is also clear that the Transfer Agreements were meant to modify the division of powers originally set out in the *Constitution Act, 1867* (formerly the *British North America Act*, 1867). Section 1 of the *Constitution Act, 1930* is unambiguous in this regard. "The agreements ... shall have the force of law notwithstanding anything in the Constitution Act, 1867. ..."

In addition, there was in fact a *quid pro quo* granted by the Crown for the reduction in the hunting right. Although the Agreement did take away the right to hunt commercially, the nature of the right to hunt for food was substantially enlarged. The geographical areas in which the Indian people could hunt was widely extended. Further, the means employed by them in hunting for their food was placed beyond the reach of provincial governments. For example, they may hunt deer with night lights and with dogs, methods which are or may be prohibited for others. Nor are the Indians subject to seasonal limitations as are all other hunters. That is to say, they can hunt ducks and geese in the spring as well as the fall, just as they may hunt deer at any time of the year. Indians are not limited with regard to the type of game they may kill. That is to say, while others may be restricted as to the species or sex of the game they may kill, the Indians may kill for food both does and bucks; cock pheasants and hen pheasants; drakes and hen ducks. It can be seen that the *quid pro quo* was substantial. Both the area of hunting and the way in which the hunting could be conducted was extended and removed from the jurisdiction of provincial governments.

The true effect of para. 12 of the Agreement was recognized by Laskin J., as he then was, in *Cardinal* v. *A.-G. Alta.*, [1974] S.C.R. 695 at p. 722, where he wrote:

> [Section 12] is concerned rather with Indians as such, and with guaranteeing to them a continuing right to hunt, trap and fish for food regardless of provincial game laws which would otherwise confine Indians in parts of the Province that are under provincial administration. *Although inelegantly expressed s. 12 does not expand Provincial legislative power but contracts it.* Indians are to have the right to take game and fish for food from all unoccupied Crown lands (these would certainly not include Reserves) and from all other lands to which they may have a right of access. There is hence, by virtue of the sanction of the *British North America Act, 1930*, a limitation upon provincial authority regardless of whether or not Parliament legislates. [Emphasis added.]

This effect of para. 12 of the Agreement was also recognized by Dickson J., as he then was, in *Myran* v. *The Queen*, [1976] 2 S.C.R. 137 at 141:

> I think it is clear from *Prince and Myron* that an Indian of the Province is free to hunt or trap

game in such numbers, at such times of the year, by such means or methods and with such contrivances, as he may wish, provided he is doing so in order to obtain food for his own use and on unoccupied Crown lands or other lands to which he may have a right of access.

It is thus apparent that although the Transfer Agreement modified the treaty rights as to hunting, there was a very real *quid pro quo* which extended the native rights to hunt for food. In addition, although it might well be politically and morally unacceptable in today's climate to take such a step as that set out in the 1930 Agreement without consultation with and concurrence of the native peoples affected, nonetheless the power of the federal government to unilaterally make such a modification is unquestioned and has not been challenged in this case.

Further, it must be remembered that Treaty 8 itself did not grant an unfettered right to hunt. That right was to be exercised "subject to such regulations as may from time to time be made by the Government of the country." This provision is clearly in line with the original position of the Commissioners who were bargaining with the Indians. The Commissioners specifically observed that the right of the Indians to hunt, trap and fish as they always had done would continue with the proviso that these rights would have to be exercised subject to such laws as were necessary to protect the fish and fur bearing animals on which the Indians depended for their sustenance and livelihood. . . .

In summary, the hunting rights granted by the 1899 Treaty were not unlimited. Rather they were subject to governmental regulation. The 1930 Agreement widened the hunting territory and the means by which the Indians could hunt for food thus providing a real *quid pro quo* for the reduction in the right to hunt for purposes of commerce granted by the Treaty of 1899. The right of the federal government to act unilaterally in that manner is unquestioned. I therefore conclude that the 1930 Transfer Agreement did alter the nature of the hunting rights originally guaranteed by Treaty 8.

Section 42 of the Wildlife Act

At the outset it must be recognized that the *Wildlife Act* is a provincial law of general application affecting Indians not *qua* Indians but rather as inhabitants of the province. It follows that the Act can be applicable to Indians pursuant to the provisions of s. 88 of the *Indian Act* so long as it does not conflict with a treaty right. It has been seen that the Treaty 8 hunting rights have been limited by the provisions of the 1930 Transfer Agreement to the right to hunt for food, that is to say, for sustenance for the individual Indian or the Indian's family. In the case at bar the sale of the bear hide was part of a "multi-stage process" whereby the product was sold to obtain funds for purposes which might include purchasing food for nourishment. The courts below correctly found that the sale of the bear hide constituted a hunting activity that had ceased to be that of hunting "for food" but rather was an act of commerce. As a result it was no longer a right protected by Treaty 8, as amended by the 1930 Transfer Agreement. Thus the application of s. 42 to Indians who are hunting for commercial purposes is not precluded by s. 88 of the *Indian Act*.

The fact that a grizzly bear was killed by the appellant in self-defence must engender admiration and sympathy, but it is unfortunately not relevant to a consideration of whether there has been a breach of s. 42 of the *Wildlife Act*. Obviously if it were permissible to traffic in hides of grizzly bears that were killed in self-defence, then the numbers of bears slain in self-defence could be expected to increase dramatically. Unfortunate as it may be in this case, the prohibition against trafficking in bear hides without a licence cannot admit of any exceptions.

Neither, regrettably, can it be relevant to the breach of the s. 42 that the appellant in fact obtained a grizzly bear hunting permit after he was in the possession of a bear hide. The granting of a permit does not bring a hunter any guarantee of success but only an opportunity to legitimately slay a bear. The evidence presented at trial indicated that the limitations placed upon obtaining a licence and the limited chance of success in a bear hunt resulted in the success rate of between 2 and 4 per cent of the licence holders. This must be an important factor in the management of the bear population. Wildlife administrators must be able to rely on the success ratio and proceed on the assumption that those applying for a permit have not already shot a bear. The success ratio will determine the number of licenses issued in any year. The whole management scheme which is essential to the survival of the grizzly bear would be undermined if a licence were granted to an applicant who had already completed a successful hunt.

As well, s. 42 of the *Wildlife Act* is consistent with the very spirit of Treaty 8 which specified that the right to hunt would still be subject to government regulations. The evidence indicates that there remain only 575 grizzly bears on provincial lands. This population cannot sustain a mortality rate higher than 11 per cent per annum if it is even to maintain its present numbers. The statistics indicate that the population will decline if death resulting from natural causes, legal hunting and poaching (and indications are that levels of poaching match legal takings) reached a total of more than 60 bears in a year. The grizzly bear requires a large range and is particularly sensitive to encroachment on its habitat. This magnificent animal is in a truly precarious position. All Canadians and particularly Indians who have a rich and admirable history and tradition of respect for and harmony with all forms of life, will applaud and support regulations which encourage the bears' survival. Trafficking in bear hides, other than pursuant to the provisions of the Wildlife Act, threatens the very existence of the grizzly bear. The bear may snarl defiance and even occasionally launch a desperate attack upon man, but until such time as it masters the operation of firearms, it cannot triumph and must rely on man for protection and indeed for survival. That protection is provided by the *Wildlife Act*, but if it is to succeed it must be strictly enforced.

Section 42 of the *Wildlife Act* is valid legislation enacted by the government with jurisdiction in the field. It reflects a bona fide concern for the preservation of a species. It is a law of general application which does not infringe upon the Treaty 8 hunting rights of Indians as limited by the 1930 Transfer Agreement.

Disposition

In the result, I would dismiss the appeal. The constitutional question posed should be answered as follows:

> *Question*:
> Between February 1, 1984 and May 30, 1984, was section 42 of the *Wildlife Act,* R.S.A. 1980, c. W-9, constitutionally applicable to Treaty 8 Indians in virtue of the hunting rights granted to them under the said Treaty? In particular, were the hunting rights granted by Treaty 8 of 1899 extinguished, reduced or modified by paragraph 12 of the Alberta Natural Resources Transfer Agreement, as confirmed by the Constitution Act, 1930?

> *Answer*:
> The answer to both queries framed in the Question should be in the affirmative. The *Wildlife Act* applied to the appellant and Horseman is guilty of violating s. 42 of

the Act. Nonetheless he did not seek out the bear and shot it only in self-defence. The trial judge found that he acted in good faith when he obtained the licence to hunt bear. He was in financial difficulties when he sold the bear hide in an isolated transaction. He has provided the means whereby the application of the *Wildlife Act* to Indians was explored. If it were not for statutory requirement of a minimum fine, in the unique circumstances of the case, I would vary the sentence by waiving the payment of the minimum fine. Nevertheless, in light of the circumstances of the case, and the time that has elapsed, I would order a stay of proceedings. There should be no order as to costs.

WILSON J., dissenting (DICKSON C.J. and L'HEUREUX-DUBÉ J., concurring): I have had the advantage of reading the reasons of my colleague Justice Cory and must respectfully disagree with his conclusion that the appellant's conduct is caught by s. 42 of the *Wildlife Act*, R.S.A. 1980, c. W-9.

While my colleague has reviewed the facts of this appeal and the decisions of the lower courts, I believe it is important to emphasize that all parties were agreed and the trial judge so found that Mr. Horseman was legitimately engaged in hunting moose for his own use in the Treaty 8 area when he killed the bear in self-defence. Mr. Horseman did not kill the bear with a view to selling its hide although he was eventually driven to do so a year later in order to feed himself and his family. The sale of the bear hide was an isolated act and not part of any planned commercial activity. None of this is in dispute.

The narrow question before us in this appeal then is whether the isolated sale for food of a bear hide obtained by the appellant fortuitously as the result of an act of self-defence is something that the government of Alberta is entitled to penalize under the *Wildlife Act*. In my view, the answer to this question requires a careful examination of the terms of Treaty 8 and the wording of para. 12, of the Natural Resources Transfer Agreement, 1930 (Alberta) (the "Transfer Agreement"). . . .

The interpretive principles developed in *Nowegijick*, [1983] 1 S.C.R. 29, [1983] 2 C.N.L.R. 89, and *Simon*, [1985] 2 S.C.R. 387, [1986] 1 C.N.L.R. 153, recognize that Indian treaties are *sui generis* (per Dickson C.J. at p. 404 [p. 169 C.N.L.R.] of *Simon, supra*). These treaties were the product of negotiation between very different cultures and the language used in them probably does not reflect, and should not be expected to reflect, with total accuracy each party's understanding of their effect at the time they were entered into. This is why the courts must be especially sensitive to the broader historical context in which such treaties were negotiated. They must be prepared to look at that historical context in order to ensure that they reach a proper understanding of the meaning that particular treaties held for their signatories at the time.

But the interpretive principles set out in *Nowegijick* and *Simon* were developed not only to deal with the unique nature of Indian treaties but also to address a problem identified by Norris J.A. in *R. v. White and Bob* (1964), 50 D.L.R. (2d) 613 at 649 (B.C.C.A.) (aff'd [1965] S.C.R. vi, 52 D.L.R. (2d) 481):

> In view of the argument before us, it is necessary to point out that on numerous occasions in modern days, rights under what were entered into with Indians as solemn engagements, although completed with what would now be considered informality, have been whittled away on the excuse that they do not comply with present day formal requirements and with rules of interpretation applicable to transactions between people who must be taken in the light of advanced civilization to be of equal status.

In other words, to put it simply, Indian treaties must be given the effect the signatories obviously intended them to have at the time they were entered into even if they do not comply with today's formal requirements. Nor should they be undermined by the application of the interpretive rules we apply today to contracts entered into by parties of equal bargaining power.

In my view, the interpretive principles set out in *Nowegijick* and *Simon* are fundamentally sound and have considerable significance for this appeal. Any assessment of the impact of the Transfer Agreement on the rights that Treaty 8 Indians were assured in the treaty would continue to be protected cannot ignore the fact that Treaty 8 embodied a "solemn engagement." Accordingly, when interpreting the Transfer Agreement between the federal and provincial governments we must keep in mind the solemn commitment made to the Treaty 8 Indians by the federal government in 1899. We should not readily assume that the federal government intended to renege on the commitment it had made. Rather we should give it an interpretation, if this is possible on the language, which will implement and be fully consistent with that commitment. It is appropriate, therefore, to begin the analysis of the issues in this appeal with a review of the nature of the "solemn engagement" embodied in Treaty 8. . . .

In my view, it is in light of this historical context, one which did not, from the Indians' perspective, allow for simple distinctions between hunting for domestic use and hunting for commercial purposes and which involved a solemn engagement that Indians would continue to have unlimited access to wildlife, that one must understand the provision in Treaty 8 that reads:

> And Her Majesty the Queen HEREBY AGREES with the said Indians that they shall have *the right to pursue their usual vocations of hunting, trapping and fishing* throughout the tract surrendered as heretofore described, *subject to such regulations as may from time to time be made by the Government of the country*, acting under the authority of Her Majesty, and saving and excepting such tracts as may be required or taken up from time to time for settlement, mining, lumbering, trading or other purposes. [Emphasis added.]

If we are to remain faithful to the interpretive principles set out in *Nowegijick* and *Simon*, then we must not only be careful to understand that the language of Treaty 8 embodied a solemn engagement to Indians in the Treaty 8 area that their livelihood would be respected, but we must also recognize that in referring to potential "regulations" with respect to hunting, trapping and fishing the government of Canada was promising that such regulations would always be designed so as to ensure that the Indians' way of life would continue to be respected. To read Treaty 8 as an agreement that was to enable the government of Canada to regulate hunting, fishing and trapping in any manner that it saw fit, regardless of the impact of the regulations on the "usual vocations" of Treaty 8 Indians, is not credible in light of oral and archival evidence that includes a Commissioners' report stating that a solemn assurance was made that only such laws "as were in the interest of the Indians and were found necessary in Order to protect the fish and fur-bearing animals would be made."

In other words, while the treaty was obviously intended to enable the government of Canada to pass regulations with respect to hunting, fishing and trapping, it becomes clear when one places the treaty in its historical context that the government of Canada committed itself to regulate hunting in a manner that would respect the lifestyle of the Indians and the way in which they had traditionally pursued their livelihood. Because any regulations concerning hunting and fishing were to be "in the interest" of the Indians, and because the Indians were promised that they would he free to hunt, fish and trap "after the treaty as they would be if they never entered into it," such regulations had to be designed to preserve an environment in which the Indians could continue to hunt, fish and trap as they had always done.

Natural Resources Transfer Agreement

When the province of Alberta was created in 1905 its government did not receive the power to control natural resources in the province. Control over natural resources in Alberta remained in the hands of the federal government until 1930 when Canada and Alberta entered into the Transfer Agreement which placed Alberta on the same footing as the other provinces. Mindful of the government of Canada's responsibilities under a series of numbered treaties with Indians, the parties to the Transfer Agreement inserted a paragraph dealing with the Indians' treaty rights to hunt, fish and trap. Paragraph 12 of the Transfer Agreement stated:

> *In order to secure to the Indians of the Province the continuance of the supply of game and fish for their support and subsistence,* Canada agrees that the laws respecting game in force in the Province from time to time shall apply to the Indians within the boundaries thereof, provided, however, that *the said Indians shall have the right, which the Province hereby assures to them, of hunting, trapping, and fishing game and fish for food* at all seasons of the year on all unoccupied Crown lands and on any other lands to which the said Indians may have a right of access. [Emphasis added.] . . .

The proposition that para. 12 of the Transfer Agreement was formulated with a view to protecting Treaty 8 rights and that it is therefore quite proper to look at Treaty 8 in order to understand the meaning of para. 12 of the Transfer Agreement has been emphasized on a number of occasions. For example, in *R. v. Smith*, [1935] 3 D.L.R. 703 at 705–6, Turgeon J.A. (Mackenzie J.A. concurring) stated:

> As I have said, it is proper to consult this treaty in order to glean from it whatever may throw some light on the meaning to be given to the words in question. *I would even say that we should endeavour, within the bounds of propriety, to give such meaning to these words as would establish the intention of the Crown and the Legislature to maintain the rights accorded to the Indians by the treaty.* [Emphasis added]

Similarly, in *R. v. Strongquill* (1953), 8 W.W.R. (N.S.) 247, (Sask. C.A.) (a case relied upon by this Court in *Frank v. The Queen*, [1978] 1 S.C.R. 95 at 100) McNiven J.A. stated at p. 269 [W.W.R.]:

> I have already said that whatever rights with respect to hunting were granted to the Indians by the said treaty were merged in par. 12 of the *Natural Resources Agreement, supra. I have only referred to the treaty for such assistance as its terms may give in interpreting the language used in par. 12 for we must attribute to parliament an intention to fulfil its terms.* It is also a cardinal rule of interpretation that words used in a statute are to be given their common ordinary and generally accepted meaning. *Statutes are to be given a liberal construction so that effect may be given to each Act and every part thereof according to its spirit, true intent and meaning.* [Emphasis added.]

The view expressed in *Smith* and in *Strongquill* to the effect that one should assume that Parliament intended to live up to its obligations under treaties with the Indians was subsequently approved by this Court in *Prince and Myron v. The Queen*, [1964] S.C.R. 81. Hall J. (for the Court) adopted the following passage from *R. v. Wesley*, [1932] 2 W.W.R. 337 in which McGillivray J.A. had commented at p. 344:

> I think the intention was that in hunting for sport or for commerce the Indian like the

white man should be subject to laws which make for the preservation of game but, in hunting wild animals for the food necessary to his life, the Indian should be placed in a very different position from the white man who, generally speaking, does not hunt for food *and was by the proviso to Sec. 12 reassured of the continued enjoyment of a right which he has enjoyed from time immemorial.* [Emphasis added.]

More recently, in *Frank* v. *The Queen, supra,* this Court reiterated that para. 12 was in part designed to ensure that the rights embodied in Treaty 8 were respected. Dickson J. stated at p. 100:

It would appear the overall purpose of para. 12 of the Natural Resources Transfer Agreement was to effect a merger and consolidation of the treaty rights theretofore enjoyed by the Indians *but of equal importance was the desire to re-state and reassure to the treaty Indians the continued enjoyment of the right to hunt and fish for food.* See *R.* v. *Wesley: R.* v. *Smith: R.* v. *Strongquill.* [Emphasis added.]

In my view, the decisions in *Smith* and *Wesley,* cases that were decided shortly after the Transfer Agreement came into force, as well as later decisions in cases like *Strongquill* and *Frank,* make clear that, to the extent that it is possible, one should view para. 12 of the Transfer Agreement as an attempt to respect the solemn engagement embodied in Treaty 8, not as an attempt to abrogate or derogate from that treaty. While it is clear that para. 12 of the Transfer Agreement adjusted the areas within which Treaty 8 Indians would thereafter be able to engage in their traditional way of life, given the oral and archival evidence with respect to the negotiation of Treaty 8 and the pivotal nature of the guarantee concerning hunting, fishing and trapping, one should be extremely hesitant about accepting the proposition that para. 12 of the Transfer Agreement was also designed to place serious and invidious restrictions on the range of hunting, fishing and trapping related activities that Treaty 8 Indians could continue to engage in. In so saying I am fully aware that this Court has stated on previous occasions that it is not in a position to question an unambiguous decision on the part of the federal government to modify its treaty obligations: *Sikyea* v. *The Queen,* [1964] S.C.R. 642; *R.* v. *George,* [1966] S.C.R. 267; and *Moosehunter* v. *The Queen,* [1981] 1 S.C.R. 282 at 293, [1981] 1 C.N.L.R. 61 at 68. We must, however, be satisfied that the federal government did make an "unambiguous decision" to renege on its Treaty 8 obligations when it signed the 1930 Transfer Agreement. . . .

In *Moosehunter* v. *The Queen, supra,* a case that involved a treaty Indian who had killed deer in Manitoba, Dickson J. did have occasion to consider the nature of the dividing line created by the term "for food" in somewhat more detail. He observed at p. 285 [pp. 62–63 C.N.L.R.]:

The reasons or purpose underlying paragraph 12 was to secure to the Indians a supply of game and fish *for their support and subsistence* and clearly to permit hunting, trapping and fishing for food at all seasons of the year on all unoccupied Crown lands and lands to which the Indians had access. The Agreement had the effect of merging and consolidating the treaty rights of the Indians in the area and restricting the power of the province to regulate the Indians' right to hunt for food. *The right of Indians to hunt for sport or commercially could be regulated by provincial game laws but the right to hunt for food could not.* [Emphasis added.]

In my view, the distinction that Dickson J. drew in *Moosehunter* between hunting for "support and subsistence," and hunting for "sport or commercially" is far more consistent with the spirit of Treaty 8 and with the proposition that one should not assume that the legislature intended to abrogate or derogate from Treaty 8 hunting rights than the respondent's submission that in using the term "for food" the legislature intended to restrict Treaty 8 hunting rights to hunting for direct consumption of the product of the hunt. And if we are to give para. 12 the "broad and liberal" construction called for in *Sutherland*, a construction that reflects the principle enunciated in *Nowegijick* and *Simon* that statutes relating to Indians must be given a "fair, large and liberal construction," then we should be prepared to accept that the range of activity encompassed by the term "for food" extends to hunting for "support and subsistence" i.e. hunting not only for direct consumption but also hunting in order to exchange the product of the hunt for other items as was their wont, as opposed to purely commercial or sport hunting.

And, indeed, when one thinks of it this makes excellent sense. The whole emphasis of Treaty 8 was on the preservation of the Indian's traditional way of life. But this surely did not mean that the Indians were to be forever consigned to a diet of meat and fish and were to have no opportunity to share in the advances of modern civilization over the next one hundred years. Of course, the Indians' hunting and fishing rights were to be preserved and protected; the Indians could not have survived otherwise. But this cannot mean that in 1990 they are to be precluded from selling their meat and fish to buy other items necessary for their sustenance and the sustenance of their children. Provided the purpose of their hunting is either to consume the meat or to exchange or sell it in order to support themselves and their families, I fail to see why this is precluded by any common sense interpretation of the words "for food". It will, of course, be a question of fact in each case whether a sale is made for purposes of sustenance or for purely commercial profit.

If we are to be sensitive to Professor Ray's observation that the distinction between hunting for commerce and domestic hunting is not one that can readily be imposed on the Indian hunting practices protected by Treaty 8, and if we are to approach para. 12 as a proviso that was intended to respect the guarantees enshrined in Treaty 8 (which I think we must do if at all possible), then para. 12 must be construed as a provision conferring on the province of Alberta the power to regulate sport hunting and hunting for purely commercial purposes rather than as a provision that was to enable the province to place serious and invidious restrictions on the Indians' right to hunt for "support and subsistence" in the broader sense.

When the phrase "for food" is read in this way para. 12 of the Transfer Agreement remains faithful to the Treaty 8 Commissioners' solemn engagement that the government of Canada would only enact "such laws as to hunting as were in the interest of the Indians and were found necessary in order to protect the fish and fur-bearing animals . . ." and that Treaty 8 Indians "would be free to hunt and fish after the treaty as they would be if they never entered into it". While Treaty 8 Indians and the government of Canada may not have foreseen in 1899 that limits would one day have to be placed on the extent to which people could engage in commercial and sport hunting, such restrictions are obviously necessary today in order to preserve particular species. Provided such restrictions on commercial and sport hunting are imposed in order to preserve species that might otherwise be endangered, the government would appear to be acting in the interests of the Indians in maintaining the well-being of the environment that is the pre-condition to their ability to pursue their traditional way of life. Such restrictions are entirely consistent with the spirit and language of Treaty 8. What is not consistent with the spirit and language of Treaty 8 is to restrict the ability of the Indians to hunt for "support and subsistence" unless this restriction also is required for the preservation of species threatened with extinction.

In summary, it seems to me that the term hunting "for food" was designed to draw a distinction between traditional hunting practices that the Indians were to be free to pursue and sport hunting or hunting for purely commercial purposes. And if we are to avoid paying mere lip-service to the interpretive principles set out in *Nowegijick* and *Simon*, principles that require us to resolve ambiguities with respect to the language of statutes like the Transfer Agreement in favour of the Indians, then any uncertainties regarding the nature of the boundary between purely commercial or sport hunting and the Indians' traditional hunting practices must be resolved by favouring an interpretation of para. 12 of the Transfer Agreement that gives the province of Alberta the power to regulate commercial and sport hunting but that leaves traditional Indian hunting practices untouched.

My colleague, Cory J., takes a different view. He concludes that para. 12 of the Transfer Agreement was designed to "cut down the scope of Indian hunting rights" and that there was a "quid pro quo" granted to the Indians by the Crown for the reduction in hunting rights. Describing this "quid pro quo," Cory J. suggests that the "area of hunting and the way in which the hunting could be conducted was extended and removed from the jurisdiction of provincial governments." But in my view the historical evidence suggests both that the Indians had been guaranteed the right to hunt for their support and subsistence in the manner that they wished some four decades before the Transfer Agreement was ratified and that it is doubtful whether the provinces were ever in a legitimate constitutional position to regulate that form of hunting prior to the Transfer Agreement. As a result, I have difficulty in accepting my colleague's conclusion that the Transfer Agreement involved some sort of expansion of these hunting rights. Moreover, it seems to me somewhat disingenuous to attempt to justify any unilateral "cutting down of hunting rights" by the use of terminology connoting a reciprocal process in which contracting parties engage in a mutual exchange of promises. Be that as it may, I see no evidence at all that the federal government intended to renege in any way from the solemn engagement embodied in Treaty 8. . . .

I would allow the appeal, set aside the order of the Court of Appeal, and restore the acquittal. I would answer the constitutional question as follows:

Question:
Between February 1, 1984 and May 30, 1984, was section 42 of the *Wildlife Act*, . . . constitutionally applicable to Treaty 8 Indians in virtue of the hunting rights granted to them under the said Treaty? In particular, were the hunting rights granted by Treaty 8 of 1899 extinguished, reduced or modified by paragraph 12 of the Alberta Natural Resources Transfer Agreement, as confirmed by the *Constitution Act, 1930*?

Answer:
Section 42 of the *Wildlife Act* was applicable to Treaty 8 Indians only to the extent that they were engaged in commercial or sport hunting. The Treaty 8 hunting rights were neither extinguished nor reduced by paragraph 12 of the Alberta Natural Resources Transfer Agreement. The territorial limits within which they could be exercised were, however, modified by paragraph 12.

R. v. *Badger* (1996)

[1996] 1 S.C.R. 771 (S.C.C.). Lamer C.J., La Forest, L'Heureux-Dubé, Sopinka, Gonthier, Cory, and Iacobucci JJ., April 3, 1996.

1   SOPINKA J. (LAMER C.J. concurring)—I have had the benefit of reading the reasons for judgment prepared in this appeal by my colleague, Justice Cory, and I am in agree-

ment with his disposition of the appeal and with his reasons with the exception of his exposition of the relationship between Treaty No. 8, the Natural Resources Transfer Agreement, 1930 (*Constitution Act, 1930*, Schedule 2) (*NRTA*), and s. 35 of the *Constitution Act, 1982.*

2   In my view, the rights of Indians to hunt for food provided in Treaty No. 8 were merged in the *NRTA* which is the sole source of those rights. While I agree that the impugned provision of the *Wildlife Act*, S.A. 1984, c. W-9.1, infringes the constitutional right of Indians to hunt for food, I disagree that this constitutional right is one covered by s. 35(1) of the *Constitution Act, 1982*. I agree, however, that the constitutional right to hunt for food must be balanced against the right of the province to pass laws for the purpose of conservation and that this balancing may be carried out on the basis of the principles set out in *R. v. Sparrow*, [1990] 1 S.C.R. 1075.

3   There is no disagreement that the *NRTA*:
   a) duplicated the right of Indians to hunt for food which was contained in Treaty No. 8;
   b) widely extended the geographical area to include the whole of the province rather than being limited to the tract of land surrendered;
   c) shifted responsibility for passing game laws from the federal government to the provinces;
   d) eliminated the right to hunt for commercial purposes;
   e) is a constitutional document and the Treaty is not, although the Treaty receives constitutional protection by virtue of s. 35(1) of the *Constitution Act, 1982.*

4   In these circumstances, I am of the view that it was clearly the intention of the framers to merge the rights in the Treaty in the *NRTA*. To characterize the *NRTA* as modifying the Treaty is to treat it as an amending document to the Treaty. This clearly was not the intent of the *NRTA*. In enlarging the area in which hunting for food was permitted to extend to the whole of the province, it could not be suggested that the *NRTA* extended the Treaty to all of the province. Rather, the right to hunt for food was extended by the *NRTA* to the whole of the province, including the area covered by the Treaty. An Indian hunting on land outside the Treaty lands could not claim to be covered by the Treaty. If the *NRTA* merely modified the Treaty, an Indian hunting on Treaty lands could claim the right under the Treaty while an Indian hunting in other parts of the province could claim only under the *NRTA*. This would invite bifurcation of the rights of Indians hunting for food in the province.

5   Similarly, the provisions which transferred to the province the power to pass gaming laws for the purpose of conservation could not have been intended simply to amend the Treaty. As an amendment to the Treaty, this provision would have no constitutional force and could not alter the constitutionally entrenched division of powers. It might be suggested that the *NRTA* both amended the Treaty and, as an independent constitutional document, amended the Constitution. If this were the intent, it is difficult to understand why all the terms of the Treaty relating to the right to hunt for food were replicated in *NRTA*. It must have been the intention to merge these rights in the *NRTA* so that they could be balanced with the power of the provinces to legislate for conservation purposes. In order to achieve a reasonable balance between them, it was important that they both appear in one document having constitutional status.

6   I can suggest no reason why the framers of the *NRTA* would have wanted to main-

tain any aspects of the Treaty except as an interpretative tool. They surely did not do so in order to allow these rights to be recognized under s. 35(1) of the *Constitution Act, 1982* which appears to be the sole present justification for preserving the Treaty. However, even that justification loses any force when considered in light of the fact that the *NRTA* is itself a constitutional document and recognition under s. 35(1) is unnecessary for the protection of these important Indian rights.

7   From the foregoing, I conclude that it was the intention of the framers of para. 12 of the *NRTA* to effectuate a merger and consolidation of the Treaty rights. This was the view of Dickson J. (as he then was), speaking for the Court, in *Frank* v. *The Queen*, [1978] 1 S.C.R. 95, at p. 100:

> It would appear that the overall purpose of para. 12 of the Natural Resources Transfer Agreement was to effect a merger and consolidation of the treaty rights theretofore enjoyed by the Indians but of equal importance was the desire to re-state and reassure to the treaty Indians the continued enjoyment of the right to hunt and fish for food.

As pointed out, these rights were restated in the *NRTA* and their preservation was assured by being placed in a constitutional instrument.

8   If this was the intention, and I conclude that it was, then the proper characterization of the relationship between the *NRTA* and the Treaty rights is that the sole source for a claim involving the right to hunt for food is the *NRTA*. The Treaty rights have been subsumed in a document of a higher order. The Treaty may be relied on for the purpose of assisting in the interpretation of the *NRTA*, but it has no other legal significance.

9   The fact that the source of the appellants' rights to hunt and fish for sustenance is found within the provisions of the *NRTA* does not alter the analysis that has previously been employed in the interpretation of treaty rights. The key interpretative principles which apply to treaties are first, that any ambiguity in the treaty will be resolved in favour of the Indians and, second, that treaties should be interpreted in a manner that maintains the integrity of the Crown, particularly the Crown's fiduciary obligation toward aboriginal peoples. These principles apply equally to the rights protected by the *NRTA*; the principles arise out of the nature of the relationship between the Crown and aboriginal peoples with the result that, whatever the document in which that relationship has been articulated, the principles should apply to the interpretation of that document. I find support for this reasoning in the prior decisions of this Court concerning the interpretation of the *NRTA*. In *R.* v. *Sutherland*, [1980] 2 S.C.R. 451, for example, this Court specifically stated, at p. 461, that the *NRTA* should be given a "broad and liberal construction", and, at p. 464, that any ambiguity should be "interpreted so as to resolve any doubts in favour of the Indians". Moreover, this position is compatible with the concept that the *NRTA* constitutes a merger and consolidation of treaty rights, and with the view that it was through the enactment of the *NRTA* that the "federal government attempted to fulfil their treaty obligations" (see *Moosehunter* v. *The Queen*, [1981] 1 S.C.R. 282, at p. 293).

Validity of the provisions of the Wildlife Act

10   In light of my conclusion that the right of Indian persons to hunt for food is constitutional in nature, the issue remaining for determination is whether the provisions of the *Wildlife Act* under which the appellants were convicted are constitutionally permissi-

ble. On the bare wording of para.12 of the *NRTA*, it appears as though such an issue could never arise. The *NRTA* grants legislative power over "gaming" subject to the Indians' right to hunt for food, apparently suggesting that the province has no jurisdiction to legislate in relation to those rights. This interpretation arises out of the mandatory language used in para.12, wherein the legislative power is granted to the province, but qualified by the statement that the power exists "provided, however, that the said Indians shall have the right. . . ."

11   The reasoning in *R. v. Horseman*, [1990] 1 S.C.R. 901, informs us that such a formalistic interpretation of the language of the *NRTA* is incorrect. At the time the treaties that preceded the *NRTA* were signed, there was already in place legislation enacted for conservation purposes which affected the Indians' rights. Indeed, there existed total bans on the hunting of certain species. As a result, at the time the treaties were signed and, even more so, at the time that the *NRTA* was agreed to by the provinces and the federal government, it would have been clearly understood that the rights of Indians pursuant to either document would be subject to governmental regulation for conservation purposes. The rights protected by the *NRTA* thus cannot be viewed as being constitutional rights of an absolute nature for which governmental regulation is prohibited.

12   How, then, is the governmental regulation permitted by the *NRTA*, and the extent of the protection of the appellants' rights in the face of such regulation, to be assessed? Cory J. has taken the position that the standard against which the validity of the *Wildlife Act* is to be assessed is s.35(1) of the *Constitution Act, 1982*, and the test set out in *Sparrow, supra*. I am unable to agree with my colleague on this point. Section 35(1) was intended to provide constitutional protection for aboriginal rights and treaty rights that did not enjoy such protection. It cannot have been intended to be redundant and provide constitutional protection for rights that already enjoyed constitutional protection. Moreover, para. 12 of the *NRTA* is a constitutional provision and, as such, s.35(1) has no direct application to it. Infringements of constitutional rights cannot be remedied by the application of a different constitutional provision. As Estey J. stated in *Reference Re Bill 30, An Act to Amend the Education Act* (Ont.), [1987] 1 S.C.R. 1148, at p.1207, the *Canadian Charter of Rights and Freedoms* "cannot be interpreted as rendering unconstitutional distinctions that are expressly permitted by the *Constitution Act, 1867*." That case concerned the application of s.15 of the *Charter* to s.93 of the *Constitution Act, 1867*. Although the case is not directly on point with the issues arising in this appeal, in my view, Estey J.'s comment provides support for the position that constitutional provisions enacted later in time are not to be read as impliedly amending the earlier enacted provisions. (See Peter W. Hogg, *Constitutional Law of Canada* (3rd ed. 1992), at p. 1183.) Nor are later provisions of the constitution applicable in terms of the interpretation of earlier provisions. On that reasoning, s. 35(1) is inapplicable to the provision of the *NRTA* that protects the right of aboriginal persons to hunt for food.

13   That is not to say, however, that the principles underlying the interpretation of s. 35(1) have no relevance to the determination of whether a particular legislative enactment has an acceptable purpose and whether it constitutes an acceptable limitation on the rights granted by the *NRTA*. There is no method provided in the *NRTA* whereby government measures that may impinge upon the rights the same document grants to Indians can be scrutinized. It is clear, however, that the *NRTA* does require a balancing of rights. The right of the province to legislate with respect to conservation must be bal-

anced against the right granted to the Indians to hunt for food. Thus, it falls to the Court to develop a test through which this task can be accomplished. In *Sparrow*, this Court developed principles for balancing the constitutionally protected right to fish for food against the federal government's power to pass laws for conservation. Although the *Sparrow* test was developed in the context of s.35(1), the basic thrust of the test, to protect aboriginal rights but also to permit governments to legislate for legitimate purposes where the legislation is a justifiable infringement on those protected rights, applies equally well to the regulatory authority granted to the provinces under para.12 of the *NRTA* as to federal power to legislate in respect of Indians.

14   In this way, the *Sparrow* test is applied to the *NRTA* by analogy, with the result that the Court will have a means by which to ensure that the rights in the *NRTA* are protected, but that provincial governments are also provided with some flexibility in terms of their ability to affect those rights for the purpose of legislating in relation to conservation. As Cory J. points out, the criteria set out in *Sparrow* do not purport to be exhaustive and are to be applied flexibly. In applying them in this context, it is important to bear in mind that what is being justified is the exercise of a power granted to the provinces, which power is made subject to the right to hunt for food. Both are contained in a constitutional document. The application of the *Sparrow* criteria should be consonant with the intention of the framers as to the reconciliation of these competing provisions.

15   I agree with Cory J. that, in the absence of evidence with respect to justification, there must be a new trial and I would dispose of the appeal as suggested by him.

16   The constitutional question and answers are as follows:

If Treaty 8 confirmed to the Indians of the Treaty 8 Territory the right to hunt throughout the tract surrendered, does the right continue to exist or was it extinguished and replaced by para. 12 of the *Natural Resources Transfer Agreement, 1930* (*Constitution Act, 1930*, 20–21 George V, c. 26 (U.K.)), and if the right continues to exist, could that right be exercised on the lands in question and, if so, was the right impermissibly infringed upon by s. 26(1) or s. 27(1) of the *Wildlife Act*, S.A. 1984, c. W-9.1, given Treaty 8 and s. 35(1) of the *Constitution Act, 1982*?

17   The right to hunt for food referred to in Treaty No. 8 was merged in the *NRTA* which is the sole source of the right.

18   Sections 26(1) and 27(1) of the *Wildlife Act* did not infringe the constitutional rights of Mr. Badger or Mr. Kiyawasew to hunt for food.

19   Mr. Ominayak was exercising his constitutional right to hunt for food. Section 26(1) of the *Wildlife Act* is a *prima facie* infringement of his right to hunt for food under *NRTA* and is invalid unless justified.

20   CORY J. (LA FOREST, L'HEUREUX-DUBÉ, GONTHIER, and IACOBUCCI JJ. concurring):— Three questions must be answered on this appeal. First, do Indians who have status under Treaty No. 8 have the right to hunt for food on privately owned land which lies within the territory surrendered under that Treaty? Secondly, have the hunting rights set out in Treaty No. 8 been extinguished or modified as a result of the provisions of para.12 of the *Natural Resources Transfer Agreement, 1930* (*Constitution Act, 1930*, Schedule 2)? Thirdly, to what extent, if any, do s.26(1) and s.27(1) of the *Wildlife Act*, S.A. 1984, c.W-9.1, apply to the appellants? . . .

21   Each of the three appellants was charged with an offence under the *Wildlife Act*. Their trials and appeals have proceeded together.

22   . . . All three appellants, Cree Indians with status under Treaty No. 8, were hunting for food upon lands falling within the tracts surrendered to Canada by the Treaty.

23   The lands in question were all privately owned. . . .

37   On this appeal, the extent of the existing right to hunt for food possessed by Indians who are members of bands which were parties to Treaty No. 8 must be determined. The analysis should proceed through three stages. First, it is necessary to decide what effect para. 12 of the *NRTA* had upon the rights enunciated in Treaty No. 8. After resolving which instrument sets out the right to hunt for food, it is necessary to examine the limitations which are inherent in that right. It must be remembered that, even by the terms of Treaty No. 8, the Indians' right to hunt for food was circumscribed by both geographical limitations and by specific forms of government regulation. Second, consideration must then be given to the question of whether the existing right to hunt for food can be exercised on privately owned land. Third, it is necessary to determine whether the impugned sections of the provincial *Wildlife Act* come within the specific types of regulation which have, since 1899, limited and defined the scope of the right to hunt for food. If they do, those sections do not infringe upon an existing treaty right and will be constitutional. If not, the sections may constitute an infringement of the Treaty rights guaranteed by Treaty No. 8, as modified by the *NRTA*. In this case the impugned provisions should be considered in accordance with the principles set out in *R. v. Sparrow*, [1990] 1 S.C.R. 1075, to determine whether they constitute a prima facie infringement of the Treaty rights as modified, and if so, whether the infringement can be justified. . . .

The Existing Right to Hunt for Food . . .

39   Treaty No. 8 is one of eleven numbered treaties concluded between the federal government and various Indian bands between 1871 and 1923. Their objective was to facilitate the settlement of the West. Treaty No. 8, made on June 21, 1899, involved the surrender of vast tracts of land in what is now northern Alberta, northeastern British Columbia, northwestern Saskatchewan and part of the Northwest Territories. In exchange for the land, the Crown made a number of commitments, for example, to provide the bands with reserves, education, annuities, farm equipment, ammunition, and relief in times of famine or pestilence. However, it is clear that for the Indians the guarantee that hunting, fishing and trapping rights would continue was the essential element which led to their signing the treaties. The report of the Commissioners who negotiated Treaty No. 8 on behalf of the government underscored the importance to the Indians of the right to hunt, fish and trap. The Commissioners wrote:

> There was expressed at every point the fear that the making of the treaty would be followed by the curtailment of the hunting and fishing privileges. . . .
>
> We pointed out . . . that the same means of earning a livelihood would continue after the treaty as existed before it, and that the Indians would be expected to make use of them. . . .
>
> Our chief difficulty was the apprehension that the hunting and fishing privileges were to be curtailed. The provision in the treaty under which ammunition and twine is to be furnished went far in the direction of quieting the fears of the Indians, for they admitted that it would be unreasonable to furnish the means of hunting and fishing if laws were to be enacted which would make hunting and fishing so restricted as to render it impossible to

make a livelihood by such pursuits. But over and above the provision, *we had to solemnly assure them that only such laws as to hunting and fishing as were in the interest of the Indians and were found necessary in order to protect the fish and fur-bearing animals would be made, and that they would be as free to hunt and fish after the treaty as they would be if they never entered into it*. [Emphasis added.]

40   Treaty No. 8, then, guaranteed that the Indians "shall have the right to pursue their usual vocations of hunting, trapping and fishing". The Treaty, however, imposed two limitations on the right to hunt. First, there was a geographic limitation. The right to hunt could be exercised "throughout the tract surrendered . . . saving and excepting such tracts as may be required or taken up from time to time for settlement, mining, lumbering, trading or other purposes". Second, the right could be limited by government regulations passed for conservation purposes.

Impact of Paragraph 12 of the NRTA

Principles of Interpretation

41   At the outset, it may be helpful to once again set out some of the applicable principles of interpretation. First, it must be remembered that a treaty represents an exchange of solemn promises between the Crown and the various Indian nations. It is an agreement whose nature is sacred. See *R. v. Sioui*, [1990] 1 S.C.R. 1025, at p.1063; *Simon v. The Queen*, [1985] 2 S.C.R. 387, at p.401. Second, the honour of the Crown is always at stake in its dealing with Indian people. Interpretations of treaties and statutory provisions which have an impact upon treaty or aboriginal rights must be approached in a manner which maintains the integrity of the Crown. It is always assumed that the Crown intends to fulfil its promises. No appearance of "sharp dealing" will be sanctioned. See *Sparrow, supra*, at pp.1107–8 and 1114; *R. v. Taylor* (1981), 34 O.R. (2d) 360 (Ont. C.A.), at p.367. Third, any ambiguities or doubtful expressions in the wording of the treaty or document must be resolved in favour of the Indians. A corollary to this principle is that any limitations which restrict the rights of Indians under treaties must be narrowly construed. See *Nowegijick v. The Queen*, [1983] 1 S.C.R. 29, at p.36; *Simon, supra*, at p.402; *Sioui, supra*, at p.1035; and *Mitchell v. Peguis Indian Band*, [1990] 2 S.C.R. 85, at pp. 142–43. Fourth, the onus of proving that a treaty or aboriginal right has been extinguished lies upon the Crown. There must be "strict proof of the fact of extinguishment" and evidence of a clear and plain intention on the part of the government to extinguish treaty rights. See *Simon, supra*, at p.406; *Sioui, supra*, at p.1061; *Calder v. Attorney-General of British Columbia*, [1973] S.C.R. 313, at p.404.

42   These principles of interpretation must now be applied to this case.

Interpreting the NRTA

43   The issue at this stage is whether the *NRTA* extinguished and replaced the Treaty No. 8 right to hunt for food. It is my conclusion that it did not. . . .

45   It has been held that the *NRTA* had the clear intention of both limiting and expanding the treaty right to hunt. In *Frank v. The Queen*, [1978] 1 S.C.R. 95, consideration was given to the differences between Treaty No. 6 (which, for this purpose, has a hunting rights clause similar to that in Treaty No. 8) and para.12 of the *NRTA*. Dickson J., as he then was, held at p.100:

The essential differences, for present purposes, between the Treaty and the Agreement are

(i) under the former the hunting rights were at large while under the latter the right is limited to hunting for food and (ii) under the former the rights were limited to about one-third of the Province of Alberta, while under the latter they extend to the entire province.

And at p.101, he stated:

The Appellate Division . . . held that para. 12 of the Natural Resources Transfer Agreements of Alberta and Saskatchewan did two things: (i) it enlarged the areas in which Alberta and Saskatchewan Indians could respectively hunt and fish for food; (ii) it limited their rights to hunt and fish otherwise than for food by making those rights subject to provincial game laws. I would agree that such is the effect of para.12.

To the same effect, see *R. v. Wesley*, [1932] 2 W.W.R. 337 (Alta. S.C. App. Div.), at p.344, as adopted in *Prince* v. *The Queen*, [1964] S.C.R. 81, at p.84.

46   This Court most recently considered the effect the *NRTA* had upon treaty rights in *Horseman, supra*. There, it was held that para.12 of the *NRTA* evidenced a clear intention to extinguish the treaty protection of the right to hunt *commercially*. However, it was emphasized that the right to hunt *for food* continued to be protected and had in fact been expanded by the *NRTA*. At page 933, this appears:

Although the Agreement did take away the right to hunt commercially, *the nature of the right to hunt for food was substantially enlarged. The geographical areas in which the Indian people could hunt was widely extended. Further, the means employed by them in hunting for their food was placed beyond the reach of provincial governments.* For example, they may hunt deer with night lights and with dogs, methods which are or may be prohibited for others. *Nor are the Indians subject to seasonal limitations as are all other hunters.* That is to say, they can hunt ducks and geese in the spring as well as the fall, just as they may hunt deer at any time of the year. *Indians are not limited with regard to the type of game they may kill.* That is to say, while others may be restricted as to the species or sex of the game they may kill, the Indians may kill for food both does and bucks; cock pheasants and hen pheasants; drakes and hen ducks. [Emphasis added.]

See also *Cardinal* v. *Attorney General of Alberta*, [1974] S.C.R. 695, at p.722; and *Myran* v. *The Queen*, [1976] 2 S.C.R. 137, at p.141. I might add that *Horseman, supra,* is a recent decision which should be accepted as resolving the issues which it considered. The decisions of this Court confirm that para.12 of the *NRTA* did, to the extent that its intent is clear, modify and alter the right to hunt for food provided in Treaty No. 8.

47   Pursuant to s.1 of the *Constitution Act, 1930*, there can be no doubt that para.12 of the *NRTA* is binding law. It is the legal instrument which currently sets out and governs the Indian right to hunt. However, the existence of the *NRTA* has not deprived Treaty No. 8 of legal significance. Treaties are sacred promises and the Crown's honour requires the Court to assume that the Crown intended to fulfil its promises. Treaty rights can only be amended where it is clear that effect was intended. It is helpful to recall that Dickson J. in *Frank, supra*, observed at p.100 that, while the *NRTA* had partially amended the scope of the Treaty hunting right, "*of equal importance* was the desire to re-state and reassure to the treaty Indians the continued enjoyment of the right to hunt and fish for food" (emphasis added). I believe that these words support my conclusion that the Treaty No. 8 right to hunt has only been altered or modified by the *NRTA to the extent that* the *NRTA* evinces a clear intention to effect such a modification. This position has been repeatedly confirmed in the decisions referred to earlier. Unless there is a direct conflict

between the *NRTA* and a treaty, the *NRTA* will not have modified the treaty rights. Therefore, the *NRTA* language which outlines the right to hunt for food must be read in light of the fact that this aspect of the treaty right continues in force and effect.

48   Like Treaty No. 8, the *NRTA* circumscribes the right to hunt for food with respect to both the geographical area within which this right may be exercised as well as the regulations which may properly be imposed by the government. The geographical limitations must now be considered.

Geographical Limitations on the Right to Hunt for Food
49   Under the *NRTA*, Indians may exercise a right to hunt for food "on all unoccupied Crown lands and on any other lands to which the said Indians may have a right of access". In the present appeals, the hunting occurred on lands which had been included in the 1899 surrender but were now privately owned. Therefore, it must be determined whether these privately owned lands were "other lands" to which the Indians had a "right of access" under the Treaty.

50   At this stage, three preliminary points should be made. First, the "right of access" in the *NRTA* does not refer to a general right of access but, rather, it is limited to a right of access *for the purposes of hunting*: R. v. *Mousseau*, [1980] 2 S.C.R. 89, at p.97; R. v. *Sutherland*, [1980] 2 S.C.R. 451, at p.459. For example, everyone can travel on public highways, but this general right of access cannot be read as conferring upon Indians a right to hunt on public highways.

51   Second, because the various treaties affected by the *NRTA* contain different wording, the extent of the treaty right to hunt on privately owned land may well differ from one treaty to another. While some treaties contain express provisions with respect to hunting on private land, others, such as Treaty No. 8, do not. Under Treaty No. 8, the right to hunt for food could be exercised "throughout the tract surrendered" to the Crown "saving and excepting such tracts as may be required or taken up from time to time for settlement, mining, lumbering, trading or other purposes." Accordingly, if the privately owned land is not "required or taken up" in the manner described in Treaty No. 8, it will be land to which the Indians had a right of access to hunt for food.

52   Third, the applicable interpretative principles must be borne in mind. Treaties and statutes relating to Indians should be liberally construed and any uncertainties, ambiguities or doubtful expressions should be resolved in favour of the Indians. In addition, when considering a treaty, a court must take into account the context in which the treaties were negotiated, concluded and committed to writing. The treaties, as written documents, recorded an agreement that had already been reached orally and they did not always record the full extent of the oral agreement: see Alexander Morris, *The Treaties of Canada with the Indians of Manitoba and the North-West Territories* (1880), at pp.338–42; *Sioui, supra*, at p. 1068; *Report of the Aboriginal Justice Inquiry of Manitoba* (1991); Jean Friesen, *Grant me Wherewith to Make my Living* (1985). The treaties were drafted in English by representatives of the Canadian government who, it should be assumed, were familiar with common law doctrines. Yet, the treaties were not translated in written form into the languages (here Cree and Dene) of the various Indian nations who were signatories. Even if they had been, it is unlikely that the Indians, who had a history of communicating only orally, would have understood them any differently. As a result, it is well settled that the words in the treaty must not be interpreted in their strict technical sense

nor subjected to rigid modern rules of construction. Rather, they must be interpreted in the sense that they would naturally have been understood by the Indians at the time of the signing. This applies, as well, to those words in a treaty which impose a limitation on the right which has been granted. See *Nowegijick, supra*, at p.36; *Sioui, supra*, at pp. 1035–36 and 1044; *Sparrow, supra*, at p. 1107; and *Mitchell, supra*, where LaForest J. noted the significant difference that exists between the interpretation of treaties and statutes which pertain to Indians.

53   The evidence led at trial indicated that in 1899 the Treaty No. 8 Indians would have understood that land had been "required or taken up" when it was being put to a use which was incompatible with the exercise of the right to hunt. Historian John Foster gave expert evidence in this case. His testimony indicated that, in 1899, Treaty No. 8 Indians would not have understood the concept of private and exclusive property ownership separate from actual land use. They understood land to be required or taken up for settlement when buildings or fences were erected, land was put into crops, or farm or domestic animals were present. Enduring church missions would also be understood to constitute settlement. These physical signs shaped the Indians' understanding of settlement because they were the manifestations of exclusionary land use which the Indians had witnessed as new settlers moved into the West. The Indians' experience with the Hudson's Bay Company was also relevant. Although that company had title to vast tracts of land, the Indians were not excluded from and in fact continued hunting on these lands. In the course of their trading, the Hudson's Bay Company and the Northwest Company had set up numerous posts that were subsequently abandoned. The presence of abandoned buildings, then, would not necessarily signify to the Indians that land was taken up in a way which precluded hunting on them. Yet, it is dangerous to pursue this line of thinking too far. The abandonment of land may be temporary. Owners may return to reoccupy the land, to undertake maintenance, to inspect it or simply to enjoy it. How "unoccupied" the land was at the relevant time will have to be explored on a case-by-case basis.

54   An interpretation of the Treaty properly founded upon the Indians' understanding of its terms leads to the conclusion that the geographical limitation on the existing hunting right should be based upon a concept of visible, incompatible land use. This approach is consistent with the oral promises made to the Indians at the time the Treaty was signed, with the oral history of the Treaty No. 8 Indians, with earlier case law and with the provisions of the Alberta *Wildlife Act* itself.

55   The Indian people made their agreements orally and recorded their history orally. Thus, the verbal promises made on behalf of the federal government at the times the treaties were concluded are of great significance in their interpretation. Treaty No. 8 was initially concluded with the Indians at Lesser Slave Lake. . . .

56   Commissioner Laird told the Indians that the promises made to them were to be similar to those made with other Indians who had agreed to a treaty. Accordingly, it is significant that the earlier promises also contemplated a limited interference with Indians' hunting and fishing practices. See, for example, Alexander Morris, *The Treaties of Canada with the Indians of Manitoba and the North-West Territories, supra*. In negotiating Treaty No. 1, the Lieutenant Governor of Manitoba, A. G. Archibald, made the following statement to the Indians, at p.29:

When you have made your treaty you will still be free to hunt over much of the land included in the treaty. Much of it is rocky and unfit for cultivation, much of it that is wooded is beyond the places where the white man will require to go, at all events for some time to come. *Till these lands are needed for use you will be free to hunt over them, and make all the use of them which you have made in the past. But when lands are needed to be tilled or occupied, you must not go on them any more. There will still be plenty of land that is neither tilled nor occupied where you can go and roam and hunt as you have always done*, and, if you wish to farm, you will go to your own reserve where you will find a place ready for you to live on and cultivate. [Emphasis added.]

With respect to Treaty No. 4, Lt. Gov. Morris made the following statement to the Indians, at p.96:

We have come through the country for many days and we have seen hills and but little wood and in many places little water, and it may be a long time before there are many white men settled upon this land, and you will have the right of hunting and fishing just as you have now *until the land is actually taken up.* [Emphasis added.]

With respect to Treaty No. 6, Lt. Gov. Morris stated at p.218:

You want to be at liberty to hunt as before. I told you we did not want to take that means of living from you, you have it the same as before, only this, *if a man, whether Indian or Half-breed, had a good field of grain, you would not destroy it with your hunt.* [Emphasis added.] . . .

58   Accordingly, the oral promises made by the Crown's representatives and the Indians' own oral history indicate that it was understood that land would be taken up and occupied in a way which precluded hunting when it was put to a visible use that was incompatible with hunting. Turning to the case law, it is clear that the courts have also accepted this interpretation and have concluded that whether or not land has been taken up or occupied is a question of fact that must be resolved on a case-by-case basis.

59   Most of the cases which have considered the geographical limitations on the right to hunt have been concerned with situations where the hunting took place on Crown land. In those cases, it was held that Crown lands were only "occupied" or "taken up" when they were actually put to an active use which was incompatible with hunting. For example, *R. v. Smith*, [1935] 2 W.W.R. 433 (Sask. C.A.), considered whether Indians had a right to hunt for food on a game preserve located on Crown land. There, in my view, it was correctly observed at p.436 that "it is proper to consult th[e] treaty in order to glean from it whatever may throw some light on the meaning to be given to the words" in the *NRTA*. It was sensibly held at p.437 that the Indians did not have a right of access to hunt on the game preserve because to do so would be incompatible with the fundamental purpose of establishing a preserve: "a game preserve would be one in name only if the Indians, or any other class of people, were entitled to shoot in it". See also *R. v. Mirasty*, [1942] 1 W.W.R. 343 (Police Ct.), in which Crown land was taken up for a forest and game preserve; and *Mousseau, supra*, in which Crown land was taken up for a public road. However, the courts have recognized an existing treaty right to hunt on Crown land taken up as a forest because hunting for food is not incompatible with that particular land use: *R. v. Strongquill*, [1953] 8 W.W.R. (N.S.) 247 (Sask. C.A.). Finally, where limited hunting by non-Indians is permitted on Crown land taken up as a wildlife management area or a fur conservation area, the courts have held that Indians continue to have an unlimited right of access for the purposes of hunting for food: *Strongquill, supra*, at pp. 267 and 271; *Sutherland, supra*, at pp. 460 and 464–65; and *Moosehunter v. The Queen*, [1981] 1 S.C.R. 282, at p.292.

60   A second but shorter line of cases has considered whether Indians have a treaty right of access to hunt on privately owned lands. While various factual situations have been considered, the courts have not settled the question as to whether the Treaty No. 8 right to hunt for food extends to privately owned land which is not put to visible use. . . .

62   In *Horse, supra,* the accused persons were hunting on privately owned land without the owner's permission. This Court stated repeatedly that Treaty No.6 did not afford the accused a right of access to hunt on "*occupied* private lands" (see pp.198, 204 and 209– 10). In *Horse, supra,* the private lands were not posted, but they were sown to hay and grain and, thus, were visibly and actively used for farming. In light of these facts, there was no need to consider what was encompassed by the term "occupied private land". The use of the land was so readily apparent that it clearly fell within the category of occupied land. Similarly, in *Mousseau, supra,* at p.97, this Court indicated that Indians had a right to hunt on: (a) all unoccupied Crown lands; (b) any occupied Crown land to which they had a right of access by statute, common law or otherwise; and (c) "any *occupied private lands* to which the Indians have a right of access by custom, usage, or consent of the owner or occupier, for the purpose of hunting, trapping, or fishing". However, that case involved hunting on a public highway which was clearly occupied Crown land. Although *Mousseau, supra,* summarized this Court's position on that point, the question of hunting on unoccupied private land was neither then, nor previously, before the Court. As a result, in both *Horse, supra,* and *Mousseau, supra,* the question of whether the Treaty protected a right of access to unoccupied private lands—private lands which had not been taken up for settlement or other purposes—was left unresolved.

63   One case which has specifically considered the treaty right to hunt on unoccupied private land is *R. v. Bartleman* (1984), 55 B.C.L.R. 78 (B.C.C.A.). There, the accused was charged with using ammunition which was prohibited under the provincial *Wildlife Act.* He had been hunting on uncultivated bush land. No livestock or buildings were present, no fence surrounded the land, and no signs had been posted. He claimed that, on the basis of his Treaty hunting right, the provincial legislation did not apply to him. His hunting rights were set out in the 1852 North Saanich Indian Treaty (quoted in *Bartleman,* at p.87) which provided that the Indians "are at liberty to hunt over the unoccupied lands, and to carry on our fisheries as formerly". The B.C. Court of Appeal held that it was necessary to interpret the right on the basis of what the Indians would have understood in 1852 by the words of the Treaty. It held that the Treaty right to hunt could be exercised where to do so would not interfere with the actual use being made of the privately owned land. At page 97 this was written:

> ... the hunting must take place on land that is unoccupied in the sense that the particular form of hunting that is being undertaken does not interfere with the actual use and enjoyment of the land by the owner or occupier.

64   The Court of Appeal found that hunting was not incompatible with the minimal level of use to which the land was being put.

65   The "visible, incompatible use" approach, which focuses upon the use being made of the land, is appropriate and correct. Although it requires that the particular land use be considered in each case, this standard is neither unduly vague nor unworkable.

66   In summary, then, the geographical limitation on the right to hunt for food is derived from the terms of the particular treaty if they have not been modified or altered

by the provisions of para. 12 of the *NRTA*. In this case, the geographical limitation on the right to hunt for food provided by Treaty No. 8 has not been modified by para.12 of the *NRTA*. Where lands are privately owned, it must be determined on a case-by-case basis whether they are "other lands" to which Indians had a "right of access" under the Treaty. If the lands are occupied, that is, put to visible use which is incompatible with hunting, Indians will not have a right of access. Conversely, if privately owned land is unoccupied and not put to visible use, Indians, pursuant to Treaty No. 8, will have a right of access in order to hunt for food. The facts presented in each of these appeals must now be considered.

67   The first is Mr. Badger. He was hunting on land covered with second growth willow and scrub. Although there were no fences or signs posted on the land, a farm house was located only one quarter of a mile from the place the moose was killed. The residence did not appear to have been abandoned. Second, Mr. Kiyawasew was hunting on a snow-covered field. Although there was no fence, there were run-down barns nearby and signs were posted on the land. Most importantly, the evidence indicated that in the fall, a crop had been harvested from the field. In the situations presented in both cases, it seems clear that the land was visibly being used. Since the appellants did not have a right of access to these particular tracts of land, their treaty right to hunt for food did not extend to hunting there. As a result, the limitations on hunting set out in the *Wildlife Act* did not infringe upon their existing right and were properly applied to these two appellants. The appeals of Mr. Badger and Mr. Kiyawasew must, therefore, be dismissed.

68   However, Mr. Ominayak's appeal presents a different situation. He was hunting on uncleared muskeg. No fences or signs were present. Nor were there any buildings located near the site of the kill. Although it was privately owned, it is apparent that this land was not being put to any visible use which would be incompatible with the Indian right to hunt for food. Accordingly, the geographical limitations upon the Treaty right to hunt for food did not preclude Mr. Ominayak from hunting upon this parcel of land. This, however, does not dispose of his appeal. It remains to be seen whether the existing right to hunt was in any other manner circumscribed by a form of government regulation which is permitted under the Treaty.

Permissible Regulatory Limitations on the Right to Hunt for Food
69   Pursuant to the provisions of s.88 of the *Indian Act*, provincial laws of general application will apply to Indians. This is so except where they conflict with aboriginal or treaty rights, in which case the latter must prevail: *Kruger* v. *The Queen*, [1978] 1 S.C.R. 104, at pp.114–15; *Simon, supra*, at pp.411–14; *Sparrow, supra*, at p.1109. In any event, the regulation of Indian hunting rights would ordinarily come within the jurisdiction of the Federal government and not the Province. However, the issue does not arise in this case since we are dealing with the right to hunt provided by Treaty No. 8 as modified by the *NRTA*. Both the Treaty and the *NRTA* specifically provided that the right would be subject to regulation pertaining to conservation.

70   Treaty No. 8 provided that the right to hunt would be "subject to such regulations as may from time to time be made by the Government of the country". In the West, a wide range of legislation aimed at conserving game had been enacted by the government beginning as early as the 1880s. Acts and regulations pertaining to conservation measures continued to be passed throughout the entire period during which the numbered treaties

were concluded. In *Horseman, supra,* the aim and intent of the regulations was recognized. At page 935, I noted:

> Before the turn of the century the federal game laws of the Unorganized Territories provided for a total ban on hunting certain species (bison and musk oxen) in order to preserve both the species and the supply of game for Indians in the future. See The *Unorganized Territories' Game Preservation Act,* 1894, S.C. 1894, c.31, ss.2, 4 to 8 and 26. Even then the advances in firearms and the more efficient techniques of hunting and trapping, coupled with the habitat loss and the over-exploitation of game, (undoubtedly by Europeans more than by Indians), had made it essential to impose conservation measures to preserve species and to provide for hunting for future generations. Moreover, beginning in 1890, provision was made in the federal *Indian Act* for the Superintendent General to make the game laws of Manitoba and the Unorganized Territories applicable to Indians. See *An Act further to amend "The Indian Act" chapter forty-three of the Revised Statutes,* S.C. 1890, c.29, s.10. A similar provision was in force in 1930. See *Indian Act,* R.S.C. 1927, c.98, s.69.

In light of the existence of these conservation laws prior to signing the Treaty, the Indians would have understood that, by the terms of the Treaty, the government would be permitted to pass regulations with respect to conservation. This concept was explicitly incorporated into the *NRTA* in a modified form providing for Provincial regulatory authority in the field of conservation. Paragraph 12 of the *NRTA* begins by stating its purpose:

> 12. In order to secure to the Indians of the Province the continuance of the supply of game and fish for their support and subsistence, Canada agrees that the *laws respecting game in force in the Province from time to time shall apply to the Indians.* . . . [Emphasis added.]

It follows that by the terms of both the Treaty and the *NRTA,* provincial game laws would be applicable to Indians so long as they were aimed at conserving the supply of game. However, the provincial government's regulatory authority under the Treaty and the *NRTA* did not extend beyond the realm of conservation. It is the constitutional provisions of para.12 of the *NRTA* authorizing provincial regulations which make it unnecessary to consider s.88 of the *Indian Act* and the general application of provincial regulations to Indians.

71   The licensing provisions contained in the *Wildlife Act* are in part, but not wholly, directed towards questions of conservation. At first blush, then, they may seem to form part of the permissible government regulation which can establish the boundaries of the existing right to hunt for food. However, the partial concern with conservation does not automatically lead to the conclusion that s. 26(1) is permissible regulation. It must still be determined whether the manner in which the licensing scheme is administered conflicts with the hunting right provided under Treaty No. 8 as modified by the *NRTA.*

72   This analysis should take into account the wording of the Treaty and the *NRTA.* I believe this to be appropriate since the object will be to determine first whether there has been a *prima facie* infringement of the Treaty No. 8 right to hunt as modified by the *NRTA* and secondly if there is such an infringement whether it can be justified. In essence, we are dealing with a modified treaty right. This, I believe, follows from the principle referred to earlier that treaty rights should only be considered to be modified if a clear intention to do so has been manifested, in this case, by the *NRTA.* Further, the solemn promises made in the treaty should be altered or modified as little as possible. The *NRTA* clearly intended to modify the right to hunt. It did so by eliminating the right to hunt commercially and by preserving and extending the right to hunt for food. The

Treaty right thus modified pertains to the right to hunt for food which prior to the Treaty was an aboriginal right.

73   For reasons that I will amplify later, it seems logical and appropriate to apply the recently formulated *Sparrow* test in these circumstances. I would add that it can properly be inferred that the concept of reasonableness forms an integral part of the *Sparrow* test. It follows that this concept should be taken into account in the consideration of the justification of an infringement. As a general rule the criteria set out in *Sparrow, supra*, should be applied. However, the reasons in *Sparrow, supra*, make it clear that the suggested criteria are neither exclusive nor exhaustive. It follows that additional criteria may be helpful and applicable in the particular situation presented.

Conflict Between the Wildlife Act and Rights Under Treaty No.8
74   It has been recognized that aboriginal and treaty rights are not absolute. The reasons in *Sparrow, supra*, made it clear that aboriginal rights may be overridden if the government is able to justify the infringement.

75   In *Sparrow, supra*, certain criteria were set out pertaining to justification at pp. 1111 and following. While that case dealt with the infringement of aboriginal rights, I am of the view that these criteria should, in most cases, apply equally to the infringement of treaty rights.

76   There is no doubt that aboriginal and treaty rights differ in both origin and structure. Aboriginal rights flow from the customs and traditions of the native peoples. To paraphrase the words of Judson J. in *Calder, supra*, at p. 328, they embody the right of native people to continue living as their forefathers lived. Treaty rights, on the other hand, are those contained in official agreements between the Crown and the native peoples. Treaties are analogous to contracts, albeit of a very solemn and special, public nature. They create enforceable obligations based on the mutual consent of the parties. It follows that the scope of treaty rights will be determined by their wording, which must be interpreted in accordance with the principles enunciated by this Court.

77   This said, there are also significant aspects of similarity between aboriginal and treaty rights. Although treaty rights are the result of mutual agreement, they, like aboriginal rights, may be unilaterally abridged. See *Horseman, supra*, at p.936; *R. v. Sikyea,* [1964] 2 C.C.C. 325 (N.W.T.C.A.), at p.330, aff'd [1964] S.C.R. 642; and *Moosehunter, supra*, at p.293. It follows that limitations on treaty rights, like breaches of aboriginal rights, should be justified.

78   In addition, both aboriginal and treaty rights possess in common a unique, *sui generis* nature. See *Guerin* v. *The Queen*, [1984] 2 S.C.R. 335, at p.382; *Simon, supra*, at p.404. In each case, the honour of the Crown is engaged through its relationship with the native people. As Dickson C.J. and LaForest J. stated at p.1110 in *Sparrow, supra*:

> By giving aboriginal rights constitutional status and priority, Parliament and the provinces have sanctioned challenges to social and economic policy objectives embodied in legislation to the extent that aboriginal rights are affected. Implicit in this constitutional scheme is the obligation of the legislature to satisfy the test of justification. *The way in which a legislative objective is to be attained must uphold the honour of the Crown and must be in keeping with the unique contemporary relationship, grounded in history and policy, between the Crown and Canada's aboriginal peoples. The extent of legislative or regulatory impact on an existing aboriginal right may be scrutinized so as to ensure recognition and affirmation.* [Emphasis added.]

79   The wording of s.35(1) of the *Constitution Act, 1982* supports a common approach to infringements of aboriginal and treaty rights. It provides that "[t]he existing aboriginal and treaty rights of the aboriginal peoples of Canada are hereby recognized and affirmed". In *Sparrow, supra*, Dickson C.J. and La Forest J. appeared to acknowledge the need for justification in the treaty context. They said this at pp. 1118–19 in relation to *R.* v. *Eninew* (1984), 12 C.C.C. (3d) 365 (Sask. C.A.), a case which considered the effect of the Migratory Birds Convention Act on rights guaranteed under Treaty No. 10:

> As we have pointed out, management and conservation of resources is indeed an important and valid legislative objective. Yet, the fact that the objective is of a "reasonable" nature cannot suffice as constitutional recognition and affirmation of aboriginal rights. *Rather, the regulations enforced pursuant to a conservation or management objective may be scrutinized according to the justificatory standard outlined above.* [Emphasis added.]

80   This standard of scrutiny requires that the Crown demonstrate that the legislation in question advances important general public objectives in such a manner that it ought to prevail. In *R.* v. *Agawa* (1988), 65 O.R. (2d) 505 (C.A.), at p.524, Blair J.A. recognized the need for a balanced approach to limitations on treaty rights, stating:

> ... Indian treaty rights are like all other rights recognized by our legal system. The exercise of rights by an individual or group is limited by the rights of others. Rights do not exist in a vacuum and the exercise of any right involves a balancing with the interests and values involved in the rights of others. This is recognized in s.1 of the *Canadian Charter of Rights and Freedoms* which provides that limitation of Charter rights must be justified as reasonable in a free and democratic society.

81   Dickson C.J. and La Forest J. arrived at a similar conclusion in *Sparrow, supra*, at pp.1108–9.

82   In summary, it is clear that a statute or regulation which constitutes a *prima facie* infringement of aboriginal rights must be justified. In my view, it is equally if not more important to justify *prima facie* infringements of treaty rights. The rights granted to Indians by treaties usually form an integral part of the consideration for the surrender of their lands. For example, it is clear that the maintenance of as much of their hunting rights as possible was of paramount concern to the Indians who signed Treaty No. 8. This was, in effect, an aboriginal right recognized in a somewhat limited form by the treaty and later modified by the *NRTA*. To the Indians, it was an essential element of this solemn agreement.

83   It will be remembered that the *NRTA* modified the Treaty right to hunt. It did so by eliminating the right to hunt commercially but enlarged the geographical areas in which the Indian people might hunt in all seasons. The area was to include all unoccupied Crown land in the province together with any other lands to which the Indians may have a right of access. Lastly, the province was authorized to make laws for conservation. Specifically:

> 12. In order to secure to the Indians of the Province the continuance of the supply of game and fish for their support and subsistence, Canada agrees that the laws respecting game in force in the Province from time to time shall apply to the Indians within the boundaries thereof, provided, however, that the said Indians shall have the right, which the Province hereby assures to them, of hunting, trapping and fishing game and fish for food at all seasons of the year on all unoccupied Crown lands and on any other lands to which the said Indians may have a right of access.

84   The *NRTA* only modifies the Treaty No. 8 right. Treaty No. 8 represents a solemn promise of the Crown. For the reasons set out earlier, it can only be modified or altered to the extent that the *NRTA* clearly intended to modify or alter those rights. The Federal government, as it was empowered to do, unilaterally enacted the *NRTA*. It is unlikely that it would proceed in that manner today. The manner in which the *NRTA* was unilaterally enacted strengthens the conclusion that the right to hunt which it provides should be construed in light of the provisions of Treaty No. 8.

85   It follows that any *prima facie* infringement of the rights guaranteed under Treaty No. 8 or the *NRTA* must be justified. How should the infringement of a treaty right be justified? Obviously, the challenged limitation must be considered within the context of the treaty itself. Yet, the recognized principles to be considered and applied in justification should generally be those set out in *Sparrow, supra*. There may well be other factors that should influence the result. The *Sparrow* decision itself recognized that it was not setting a complete catalogue of factors. Nevertheless, these factors may serve as a rough guide when considering the infringement of treaty rights.

Prima Facie Infringement of the Treaty Right to hunt as modified by the NRTA
86   The licensing provisions of the *Wildlife Act* address two objectives: public safety and conservation. These objectives, in and of themselves, are not unconstitutional. However, it is evident from the wording of the Act and its regulations that the manner in which the licensing scheme is set up results in a *prima facie* infringement of the Treaty No. 8 right to hunt as modified by the *NRTA*. The statutory scheme establishes a two-step licensing process. The public safety component is the first one that is engaged.

87   Under s.15(1)(c) of the *Wildlife Act*, the Lieutenant Governor in Council may pass regulations which "specify training and testing qualifications required for the obtaining and holding of a licence or permit". . . .

88   Standing on its own, the requirement that all hunters take gun safety courses and pass hunting competency tests makes eminently good sense. This protects the safety of everyone who hunts, including Indians. It has been held on a number of occasions that aboriginal or treaty rights must be exercised with due concern for public safety. *Myran, supra*, dealt with two Indians charged with hunting without due regard for the safety of others, contrary to the provisions of the *Manitoba Wildlife Act*. The accused argued that they were immune from the Act on the basis of their right to hunt for food guaranteed under the *Manitoba Natural Resources Act* (parallel to the *NRTA*). Dickson J. (as he then was) for the Court found at pp.141–42 that:

> I think it is clear from *Prince and Myron* that an Indian of the Province is free to hunt or trap game in such numbers, at such times of the year, by such means or methods and with such contrivances, as he may wish, provided he is doing so in order to obtain food for his own use and on unoccupied Crown lands or other lands to which he may have a right of access. *But that is not to say that he has the right to hunt dangerously and without regard for the safety of other persons in the vicinity.* [Emphasis added.] . . .

89   That decision was subsequently affirmed by this Court in *Sutherland, supra*, and *Moosehunter, supra*. See to the same effect *R. v. Napoleon*, [1986] 1 C.N.L.R. 86 (B.C.C.A.) and *R. v. Fox*, [1994] 3 C.N.L.R. 132 (Ont. C.A.). Accordingly, it can be seen that reasonable regulations aimed at ensuring safety do not infringe aboriginal or treaty rights to hunt for food. Similarly these regulations do not infringe the hunting rights guaranteed

by Treaty No. 8 as modified by the *NRTA*.

90   While the general safety component of the licensing provisions may not constitute a *prima facie* infringement, the conservation component appears to present just such an infringement. Provincial regulations for conservation purposes are authorized pursuant to the provisions of the *NRTA*. However, the routine imposition upon Indians of the specific limitations that appear on the face of the hunting licence may not be permissible if they erode an important aspect of the Indian hunting rights. This Court has held on numerous occasions that there can be no limitation on the method, timing and extent of Indian hunting under a Treaty. I would add that a Treaty as amended by the *NRTA* should be considered in the same manner. *Horseman, supra,* clearly indicated that such restrictions conflicted with the treaty right. Moreover, in *Simon, supra,* this appears at p.413:

> The section clearly places seasonal limitations and licensing requirements, for the purposes of wildlife conservation, on the right to possess a rifle and ammunition for the purposes of hunting. The restrictions imposed in this case conflict, therefore, with the appellant's right to possess a firearm and ammunition in order to exercise his free liberty to hunt over the lands covered by the Treaty. As noted, it is clear that under s.88 of the Indian Act provincial legislation cannot restrict native treaty rights. If conflict arises, the terms of the treaty prevail.

91   The *Simon* case dealt with Provincial regulations which the government attempted to justify under s.88 of the *Indian Act*. By contrast, in this case, para. 12 of the *NRTA* specifically provides that the provincial government may make regulations for conservation purposes, which affect the Treaty rights to hunt. Accordingly, Provincial regulations pertaining to conservation will be valid so long as they are not clearly unreasonable in their application to aboriginal people.

92   Under the present licensing scheme, an Indian who has successfully passed the approved gun safety and hunting competency courses would not be able to exercise the right to hunt without being in breach of the conservation restrictions imposed with respect to the hunting method, the kind and numbers of game, the season and the permissible hunting area, all of which appear on the face of the licence. Moreover, while the Minister may determine how many licences will be made available and what class of licence these will be, no provisions currently exist for "hunting for food" licences.

93   At present, only sport and commercial hunting are licensed. It is true that the regulations do provide for a subsistence hunting licence. See Alta. Reg. 50/87, s.25; Alta. Reg. 95/87, s.7. However, its provisions are so minimal and so restricted that it could never be considered a licence to hunt for food as that term is used in Treaty No. 8 and as it is understood by the Indians. Accordingly, there is no provision for a licence which does not contain the facial restrictions set out earlier. Finally, there is no provision which would guarantee to Indians preferential access to the limited number of licences, nor is there a provision that would exempt them from the licence fee. As a result, Indians, like all other Albertans, would have to apply for a hunting licence from the same limited pool of licences. Further, if they were fortunate enough to be issued a licence, they would have to pay a licensing fee, effectively paying for the privilege of exercising a treaty right. This is clearly in conflict with both the Treaty and *NRTA* provisions.

94   The present licensing system denies to holders of treaty rights as modified by the *NRTA* the very means of exercising those rights. Limitations of this nature are in direct conflict with the treaty right. Therefore, it must be concluded that s.26(1) of the *Wildlife*

Act conflicts with the hunting right set out in Treaty No. 8 as modified by the *NRTA*.

95   Accordingly, it is my conclusion that the appellant, Mr. Ominayak, has established the existence of a *prima facie* breach of his treaty right. It now falls to the government to justify that infringement.

Justification

96   In my view justification of provincial regulations enacted pursuant to the *NRTA* should meet the same test for justification of treaty rights that was set out in *Sparrow*. The reason for this is obvious. The effect of para. 12 of the *NRTA* is to place the Provincial government in exactly the same position which the Federal Crown formerly occupied. Thus the Provincial government has the same duty not to infringe unjustifiably the hunting right provided by Treaty No. 8 as modified by the *NRTA*. Paragraph 12 of the *NRTA* provides that the province may make laws for a conservation purpose, subject to the Indian right to hunt and fish for food. Accordingly, there is a need for a means to assess which conservation laws will if they infringe that right, nevertheless be justifiable. The *Sparrow* analysis provides a reasonable, flexible and current method of assessing conservation regulations and enactments. . . .

98   In the present case, the government has not led any evidence with respect to justification. In the absence of such evidence, it is not open to this Court to supply its own justification. Section 26(1) of the *Wildlife Act* constitutes a *prima facie* infringement of the appellant Mr. Ominayak's treaty right to hunt. Yet, the issue of conservation is of such importance that a new trial must be ordered so that the question of justification may be addressed. . . .

100   It is evident from these reasons that the constitutional question should be answered as follows. The hunting rights confirmed by Treaty No. 8 were modified by para. 12 of the *NRTA* to the extent indicated in these reasons. Paragraph 12 of the *NRTA* provided for a continuing right to hunt for food on unoccupied land.

101   Mr. Badger and Mr. Kiyawasew were hunting on occupied land to which they had no right of access under Treaty No. 8 or the *NRTA*. Accordingly, ss. 26(1) and 27(1) of the *Wildlife Act* do not infringe their constitutional right to hunt for food.

102   However, Mr. Ominayak was exercising his constitutional right on land which was unoccupied for the purposes of this case. Section 26(1) of the *Wildlife Act* constitutes a *prima facie* infringement of his Treaty right to hunt for food. As a result of their conclusions, the issue of justification was not considered by the courts below. Therefore, in his case, a new trial must be ordered so that the issue of justification may be addressed. . . .

103   The appeals of Mr. Badger and Mr. Kiyawasew are dismissed.

104   The appeal of Mr. Ominayak is allowed and a new trial directed so that the issue of the justification of the infringement created by s.26(1) of the *Wildlife Act* and any regulations passed pursuant to that section may be addressed.

R. v. Marshall (1999)

[1999] 3 S.C.R. 456 (S.C.C.). Lamer C.J. and L'Heureux-Dubé, Gonthier, Cory, McLachlin, Iacobucci, and Binnie JJ., September 17, 1999.

1   BINNIE J. (LAMER C.J., L'HEUREUX-DUBÉ, CORY, and IACOBUCCI, JJ. concurring)—

... the appellant and a companion, both Mi'kmaq Indians, slipped their small outboard motorboat into the coastal waters of Pomquet Harbour, Antigonish County, Nova Scotia to fish for eels. They landed 463 pounds, which they sold for $787.10, and for which the appellant was arrested and prosecuted. ...

4   I would allow this appeal because nothing less would uphold the honour and integrity of the Crown in its dealings with the Mi'kmaq people to secure their peace and friendship, as best the content of those treaty promises can now be ascertained. In reaching this conclusion, I recognize that if the present dispute had arisen out of a modern commercial transaction between two parties of relatively equal bargaining power, or if, as held by the courts below, the short document prepared at Halifax under the direction of Governor Charles Lawrence on March 10, 1760 was to be taken as being the "entire agreement" between the parties, it would have to be concluded that the Mi'kmaq had inadequately protected their interests. However, the courts have not applied strict rules of interpretation to treaty relationships. In *R. v. Denny* (1990), 55 C.C.C. (3d) 322, and earlier decisions cited therein, the Nova Scotia Court of Appeal has affirmed the Mi'kmaq aboriginal right to fish for food. The appellant says the treaty allows him to fish for trade. In my view, the 1760 treaty does affirm the right of the Mi'kmaq people to continue to provide for their own sustenance by taking the products of their hunting, fishing and other gathering activities, and trading for what in 1760 was termed "necessaries". This right was always subject to regulation. The Crown does not suggest that the regulations in question accommodate the treaty right. The Crown's case is that no such treaty right exists. Further, no argument was made that the treaty right was extinguished prior to 1982, and no justification was offered by the Crown for the several prohibitions at issue in this case. Accordingly, in my view, the appellant is entitled to an acquittal.

Analysis

5   The starting point for the analysis of the alleged treaty right must be an examination of the specific words used in any written memorandum of its terms. In this case, the task is complicated by the fact the British signed a series of agreements with individual Mi'kmaq communities in 1760 and 1761 intending to have them consolidated into a comprehensive Mi'kmaq treaty that was never in fact brought into existence. ... Despite some variations among some of the documents, Embree Prov. Ct. J. was satisfied that the written terms applicable to this dispute were contained in a Treaty of Peace and Friendship entered into by Governor Charles Lawrence on March 10, 1760, which in its entirety provides as follows:

> Treaty of Peace and Friendship concluded by [His Excellency Charles Lawrence] Esq. Govr and Comr. in Chief in and over his Majesty's Province of Nova Scotia or Accadia with Paul Laurent chief of the LaHave tribe of Indians at Halifax in the Province of N.S. or Acadia.
>
> I, Paul Laurent do for myself and the tribe of LaHave Indians of which I am Chief do acknowledge the jurisdiction and Dominion of His Majesty George the Second over the Territories of Nova Scotia or Accadia and we do make submission to His Majesty in the most perfect, ample and solemn manner.
>
> And I do promise for myself and my tribe that I nor they shall not molest any of His Majesty's subjects or their dependents, in their settlements already made or to be hereafter made or in carrying on their Commerce or in any thing whatever within the Province of His said Majesty or elsewhere and if any insult, robbery or outrage shall happen to be commit-

ted by any of my tribe satisfaction and restitution shall be made to the person or persons injured.

That neither I nor any of my tribe shall in any manner entice any of his said Majesty's troops or soldiers to desert, nor in any manner assist in conveying them away but on the contrary will do our utmost endeavours to bring them back to the Company, Regiment, Fort or Garrison to which they shall belong.

That if any Quarrel or Misunderstanding shall happen between myself and the English or between them and any of my tribe, neither I, nor they shall take any private satisfaction or Revenge, but we will apply for redress according to the Laws established in His said Majesty's Dominions.

That all English prisoners made by myself or my tribe shall be sett at Liberty and that we will use our utmost endeavours to prevail on the other tribes to do the same, if any prisoners shall happen to be in their hands.

And I do further promise for myself and my tribe that we will not either directly nor indirectly assist any of the enemies of His most sacred Majesty King George the Second, his heirs or Successors, nor hold any manner of Commerce traffick nor intercourse with them, but on the contrary will as much as may be in our power discover and make known to His Majesty's Governor, any ill designs which may be formed or contrived against His Majesty's subjects. *And I do further engage that we will not traffick, barter or Exchange any Commodities in any manner but with such persons or the managers of such Truck houses as shall be appointed or Established by His Majesty's Governor at Lunenbourg or Elsewhere in Nova Scotia or Accadia.*

And for the more effectual security of the due performance of this Treaty and every part thereof I do promise and Engage that a certain number of persons of my tribe which shall not be less in number than two prisoners shall on or before September next reside as Hostages at Lunenburg or at such other place or places in this Province of Nova Scotia or Accadia as shall be appointed for that purpose by His Majesty's Governor of said Province which Hostages shall be exchanged for a like number of my tribe when requested.

And all these foregoing articles and every one of them made with His Excellency C. L., His Majesty's Governor I do promise for myself and on of sd part — behalf of my tribe that we will most strictly keep and observe in themost solemn manner.

In witness whereof I have hereunto putt my mark and seal at Halifax in Nova Scotia this day of March one thousand

Paul Laurent

I do accept and agree to all the articles of the forgoing treaty in Faith and Testimony whereof I have signed these present I have caused my seal to be hereunto affixed this day of march in the 33 year of His Majesty's Reign and in the year of Our lord—1760

Chas Lawrence [Emphasis added.]

6   The underlined portion of the document, the so-called "trade clause", is framed in negative terms as a restraint on the ability of the Mi'kmaq to trade with non-government individuals. A "truckhouse" was a type of trading post. The evidence showed that the promised government truckhouses disappeared from Nova Scotia within a few years and by 1780 a replacement regime of government licensed traders had also fallen into disuse while the British Crown was attending to the American Revolution. The trial judge, Embree Prov. Ct. J., rejected the Crown's argument that the trade clause amounted to nothing more than a negative covenant. He found, at para. 116, that it reflected a grant to the Mi'kmaq of the positive right to "bring the products of their hunting, fishing and gathering to a truckhouse to trade". The Court of Appeal ((1997), 159 N.S.R. (2d) 186) found that the trial judge misspoke when he used the word "right". It held that the trade clause does not grant the Mi'kmaq any rights. Instead, the trade clause represented a

"mechanism imposed upon them to help ensure that the peace was a lasting one, by obviating their need to trade with enemies of the British" (p. 208). When the truckhouses disappeared, said the court, so did any vestiges of the restriction or entitlement, and that was the end of it.

7   The appellant's position is that the truckhouse provision not only incorporated the alleged right to trade, but also the right to pursue traditional hunting, fishing and gathering activities in support of that trade. It seems clear that the words of the March 10, 1760 document, standing in isolation, do not support the appellant's argument. The question is whether the underlying negotiations produced a broader agreement between the British and the Mi'kmaq, memorialized only in part by the Treaty of Peace and Friendship, that would protect the appellant's activities that are the subject of the prosecution. I should say at the outset that the appellant overstates his case. In my view, the treaty rights are limited to securing "necessaries" (which I construe in the modern context, as equivalent to a moderate livelihood), and do not extend to the open-ended accumulation of wealth. The rights thus construed, however, are, in my opinion, treaty rights within the meaning of s. 35 of the *Constitution Act, 1982*, and are subject to regulations that can be justified under the *Badger* test (*R. v. Badger*, [1996] 1 S.C.R 771). . . .

Evidentiary Sources

9   The Court of Appeal took a strict approach to the use of extrinsic evidence when interpreting the Treaties of 1760–61. . . . I think this approach should be rejected for at least three reasons.

10   Firstly, even in a modern commercial context, extrinsic evidence is available to show that a written document does not include all of the terms of an agreement. Rules of interpretation in contract law are in general more strict than those applicable to treaties, yet Professor Waddams states in *The Law of Contracts* (3rd ed. 1993), at para. 316:

> The parol evidence rule does not purport to exclude evidence designed to show whether or not the agreement has been "reduced to writing", or whether it was, or was not, the intention of the parties that it should be the exclusive record of their agreement. Proof of this question is a pre-condition to the operation of the rule, and all relevant evidence is admissible on it. This is the view taken by Corbin and other writers, and followed in the Second Restatement.

. . .

11   Secondly, even in the context of a treaty document that purports to contain all of the terms, this Court has made clear in recent cases that extrinsic evidence of the historical and cultural context of a treaty may be received even absent any ambiguity on the face of the treaty. MacKinnon A.C.J.O. laid down the principle in *Taylor and Williams, supra*, at p. 236:

> . . . if there is evidence by conduct or otherwise as to how the parties understood the terms of the treaty, then such understanding and practice is of assistance in giving content to the term or terms.

The proposition is cited with approval in *Delgamuukw v. British Columbia*, [1997] 3 S.C.R. 1010, at para. 87, and *R. v. Sioui*, [1990] 1 S.C.R. 1025, at p. 1045.

12   Thirdly, where a treaty was concluded verbally and afterwards written up by representatives of the Crown, it would be unconscionable for the Crown to ignore the oral

terms while relying on the written terms, *per* Dickson J. (as he then was) in *Guerin* v. The *Queen*, [1984] 2 S.C.R. 335. Dickson J. stated for the majority, at p. 388:

> Nonetheless, the Crown, in my view, was not empowered by the surrender document to ignore the oral terms which the Band understood would be embodied in the lease. The oral representations form the backdrop against which the Crown's conduct in discharging its fiduciary obligation must be measured. They inform and confine the field of discretion within which the Crown was free to act. After the Crown's agents had induced the Band to surrender its land on the understanding that the land would be leased on certain terms, it would be unconscionable to permit the Crown simply to ignore those terms.

The *Guerin* case is a strong authority in this respect because the surrender there could only be accepted by the Governor in Council, who was not made aware of any oral terms. The surrender could not have been accepted by the departmental officials who were present when the Musqueam made known their conditions. Nevertheless, the Governor in Council was held bound by the oral terms which "the Band understood would be embodied in the lease" (p. 388). In this case, unlike *Guerin*, the Governor did have authority to bind the Crown and was present when the aboriginal leaders made known their terms.

13   The narrow approach applied by the Court of Appeal to the use of extrinsic evidence apparently derives from the comments of Estey J. in *R.* v. *Horse*, [1988] 1 S.C.R. 187, where, at p. 201, he expressed some reservations about the use of extrinsic materials, such as the transcript of negotiations surrounding the signing of Treaty No. 6, except in the case of ambiguity. (Estey J. went on to consider the extrinsic evidence anyway, at p. 203.) Lamer J., as he then was, mentioned this aspect of *Horse* in *Sioui, supra*, at p. 1049, but advocated a more flexible approach when determining the existence of treaties. Lamer J. stated, at p. 1068, that "[t]he historical context, which has been used to demonstrate the existence of the treaty, may equally assist us in interpreting the extent of the rights contained in it".

14   Subsequent cases have distanced themselves from a "strict" rule of treaty interpretation, as more recently discussed by Cory J., in *Badger, supra*, at para. 52:

> . . . *when considering a treaty, a court must take into account the context in which the treaties were negotiated, concluded and committed to writing. The treaties, as written documents, recorded an agreement that had already been reached orally and they did not always record the full extent of the oral agreement*: see Alexander Morris, *The Treaties of Canada with the Indians of Manitoba and the North-West Territories* (1880), at pp. 338–42; *Sioui, supra*, at p. 1068; *Report of the Aboriginal Justice Inquiry of Manitoba* (1991); Jean Friesen, *Grant me Wherewith to Make my Living* (1985). The treaties were drafted in English by representatives of the Canadian government who, it should be assumed, were familiar with common law doctrines. Yet, the treaties were not translated in written form into the languages (here Cree and Dene) of the various Indian nations who were signatories. Even if they had been, it is unlikely that the Indians, who had a history of communicating only orally, would have understood them any differently. *As a result, it is well settled that the words in the treaty must not be interpreted in their strict technical sense nor subjected to rigid modern rules of construction.* [Emphasis added.]

"Generous" rules of interpretation should not be confused with a vague sense of after-the-fact largesse. The special rules are dictated by the special difficulties of ascertaining what in fact was agreed to. The Indian parties did not, for all practical purposes, have the opportunity to create their own written record of the negotiations. Certain assumptions are therefore made about the Crown's approach to treaty making (honourable) which the

Court acts upon in its approach to treaty interpretation (flexible) as to the existence of a treaty (*Sioui, supra*, at p. 1049), the completeness of any written record (the use, e.g., of context and implied terms to make honourable sense of the treaty arrangement: *Simon* v. *The Queen*, [1985] 2 S.C.R. 387, and *R.* v. *Sundown*, [1999] 1 S.C.R. 393), and the interpretation of treaty terms once found to exist (*Badger*). The bottom line is the Court's obligation is to "choose from among the various possible interpretations of the common intention [at the time the treaty was made] the one which best reconciles" the Mi'kmaq interests and those of the British Crown (*Sioui, per* Lamer J., at p. 1069 (emphasis added)). In *Taylor and Williams, supra*, the Crown conceded that points of oral agreement recorded in contemporaneous minutes were included in the treaty (p. 230) and the court concluded that their effect was to "preserve the historic right of these Indians to hunt and fish on Crown lands" (p. 236). The historical record in the present case is admittedly less clear-cut, and there is no parallel concession by the Crown. . . .

Findings of Fact by the Trial Judge

18   The appellant admitted that he did what he was alleged to have done on August 24, 1993. The only contentious issues arose on the historical record and with respect to the conclusions and inferences drawn by Embree Prov. Ct. J. from the documents, as explained by the expert witnesses. The permissible scope of appellate review in these circumstances was outlined by Lamer C.J. in *R.* v. *Van der Peet*, [1996] 2 S.C.R. 507, at para. 82:

> In the case at bar, Scarlett Prov. Ct. J., the trial judge, made findings of fact based on the testimony and evidence before him, and then proceeded to make a determination as to whether those findings of fact supported the appellant's claim to the existence of an aboriginal right. The second stage of Scarlett Prov. Ct. J.'s analysis—his determination of the scope of the appellant's aboriginal rights on the basis of the facts as he found them—is a determination of a question of law which, as such, mandates no deference from this Court. The first stage of Scarlett Prov. Ct. J.'s analysis, however—the findings of fact from which that legal inference was drawn—do mandate such deference and should not be overturned unless made on the basis of a "palpable and overriding error".

19   In the present case, the trial judge, after a careful and detailed review of the evidence, concluded at para. 116:

> I accept as inherent in these treaties that the British recognized and accepted the existing Mi'kmaq way of life. Moreover, it's my conclusion that the British would have wanted the Mi'kmaq to continue their hunting, fishing and gathering lifestyle. The British did not want the Mi'kmaq to become a long-term burden on the public treasury although they did seem prepared to tolerate certain losses in their trade with the Mi'kmaq for the purpose of securing and maintaining their friendship and discouraging their future trade with the French. *I am satisfied that this trade clause in the 1760–61 Treaties gave the Mi'kmaq the right to bring the products of their hunting, fishing and gathering to a truckhouse to trade.* [Emphasis added.]

The treaty document of March 10, 1760 sets out a restrictive covenant and does not say anything about a positive Mi'kmaq right to trade. In fact, the written document does not set out any Mi'kmaq rights at all, merely Mi'kmaq "promises" and the Governor's acceptance. I cannot reconcile the trial judge's conclusion, at para. 116, that the treaties "gave the Mi'kmaq the right to bring the products of their hunting, fishing and gathering to a truckhouse to trade", with his conclusion at para. 112 that:

> The written treaties with the Mi'kmaq in 1760 and 1761 which are before me contain,

and fairly represent, all the promises made and all the terms and conditions mutually agreed to.

It was, after all, the aboriginal leaders who asked for truckhouses "for the furnishing them with necessaries, in Exchange for their Peltry" in response to the Governor's inquiry "Whether they were directed by their Tribes, to propose any other particulars to be Treated upon at this Time". It cannot be supposed that the Mi'kmaq raised the subject of trade concessions merely for the purpose of subjecting themselves to a trade restriction. As the Crown acknowledges in its factum, "The restrictive nature of the truckhouse clause was British in origin". The trial judge's view that the treaty obligations are all found within the four corners of the March 10, 1760 document, albeit generously interpreted, erred in law by failing to give adequate weight to the concerns and perspective of the Mi'kmaq people, despite the recorded history of the negotiations, and by giving excessive weight to the concerns and perspective of the British, who held the pen. (See *Badger*, at para. 41, and *Sioui*, at p. 1036.) The need to give balanced weight to the aboriginal perspective is equally applied in aboriginal rights cases: *Van der Peet*, at paras. 49–50; *Delgamuukw*, at para. 81.

20   While the trial judge drew positive implications from the negative trade clause (reversed on this point by the Court of Appeal), such limited relief is inadequate where the British-drafted treaty document does not accord with the British-drafted minutes of the negotiating sessions and more favourable terms are evident from the other documents and evidence the trial judge regarded as reliable. Such an overly deferential attitude to the March 10, 1760 document was inconsistent with a proper recognition of the difficulties of proof confronted by aboriginal people, a principle emphasized in the treaty context by *Simon*, at p. 408, and *Badger*, at para. 4, and in the aboriginal rights context in *Van der Peet*, at para. 68, and *Delgamuukw*, at paras. 80–82. The trial judge interrogated himself on the scope of the March 10, 1760 text. He thus asked himself the wrong question. His narrow view of what constituted "the treaty" led to the equally narrow legal conclusion that the Mi'kmaq trading entitlement, such as it was, terminated in the 1780s. Had the trial judge not given undue weight to the March 10, 1760 document, his conclusions might have been very different. . . .

23   I take the following points from the matters particularly emphasized by the trial judge at para. 90 following his thorough review of the historical background:

1. The 1760–61 treaties were the *culmination* of more than a *decade* of intermittent hostilities between the British and the Mi'kmaq. Hostilities with the French were also prevalent in Nova Scotia throughout the 1750's, and the Mi'kmaq were constantly allied with the French against the British.
2. The use of firearms for hunting had an important impact on Mi'kmaq society. The Mi'kmaq remained dependant on others for gun powder and the primary sources of that were the French, Acadians and the British.
3. The French frequently supplied the Mi'kmaq with food and European trade goods. By the mid-18th century, the Mi'kmaq were accustomed to, and in some cases relied on, receiving various European trade goods [including shot, gun powder, metal tools, clothing cloth, blankets and many other things]. . . .
6. The British wanted peace and a safe environment for their current and future settlers. Despite their recent victories, they did not feel completely secure in Nova Scotia. [emphasis in original] . . .

25   . . . It is apparent that the British saw the Mi'kmaq trade issue in terms of peace, as the Crown expert Dr. Stephen Patterson testified, "people who trade together do not

fight, that was the theory". Peace was bound up with the ability of the Mi'kmaq people to sustain themselves economically. Starvation breeds discontent. The British certainly did not want the Mi'kmaq to become an unnecessary drain on the public purse of the colony of Nova Scotia or of the Imperial purse in London, as the trial judge found. To avoid such a result, it became necessary to protect the traditional Mi'kmaq economy, including hunting, gathering and fishing. A comparable policy was pursued at a later date on the west coast where, as Dickson J. commented in *Jack* v. *The Queen*, [1980] 1 S.C.R. 294, at p. 311:

> What is plain from the pre-Confederation period is that the Indian fishermen were encouraged to engage in their occupation and to do so for both food and barter purposes.

The same strategy of economic aboriginal self-sufficiency was pursued across the prairies in terms of hunting: see *R.* v. *Horseman*, [1990] 1 S.C.R. 901 *per* Wilson J., at p. 919, and Cory J., at p. 928.

26   The trial judge concluded that in 1760 the British Crown entered into a series of negotiations with communities of first nations spread across what is now Nova Scotia and New Brunswick. These treaties were essentially "adhesions" by different Mi'kmaq communities to identical terms because, as stated, it was contemplated that they would be consolidated in a more comprehensive and all-inclusive document at a later date, which never happened. The trial judge considered that the key negotiations took place not with the Mi'kmaq people directly, but with the St. John River Indians, part of the Maliseet First Nation, and the Passamaquody First Nation, who lived in present-day New Brunswick.

27   The trial judge found as a fact, at para. 108, that the relevant Mi'kmaq treaty did "make peace upon the *same* conditions" (emphasis added) as the Maliseet and Passamaquody. Meetings took place between the Crown and the Maliseet and the Passamaquody on February 11, 1760, twelve days before these bands signed their treaty with the British and eighteen days prior to the meeting between the Governor and the Mi'kmaq representatives, Paul Laurent of LaHave and Michel Augustine of the Richibucto region, where the terms of the Maliseet and Passamaquody treaties were "communicated" and accepted. . . .

29   The genesis of the Mi'kmaq trade clause is therefore found in the Governor's earlier negotiations with the Maliseet and Passamaquody First Nations. . . .

30   It is true, as my colleague points out at para. 97, that the British made it clear from the outset that the Mi'kmaq were not to have any commerce with "any of His Majesty's Enemies". A Treaty of Peace and Friendship could not be otherwise. The subject of trading with the British government as distinguished from British settlers, however, did not arise until after the Indians had first requested truckhouses. The limitation to government trade came as a response to the request for truckhouses, not the other way around.

31   At a meeting of the Governor's Council on February 16, 1760 (less than a week later), the Council and the representatives of the Indians proceeded to settle the prices of various articles of merchandise . . . Prices of "necessaries" for purchase at the truckhouse were also agreed, . . . The British took a liberal view of "necessaries". . . . At trial the Crown expert and the defence experts agreed that fish could be among the items that the Mi'kmaq would trade.

32   In furtherance of this trade arrangement, the British established six truckhouses following the signing of the treaties in 1760 and 1761, including Chignecto, Lunenburg, St. John, Windsor, Annapolis and "the Eastern Battery" along the coast from Halifax. The existence of advantageous terms at the truckhouses was part of an imperial peace strategy. As Governor Lawrence wrote to the Board of Trade on May 11, 1760, "the greatest advantage from this [trade] Article . . . is the friendship of these Indians". The British were concerned that matters might again become "troublesome" if the Mi'kmaq were subjected to the "pernicious practices" of "unscrupulous traders". The cost to the public purse of Nova Scotia of supporting Mi'kmaq trade was an investment in peace and the promotion of ongoing colonial settlement. The strategy would be effective only if the Mi'kmaq had access both to trade and to the fish and wildlife resources necessary to provide them with something to trade.

33   Accordingly, on March 21, 1760, the Nova Scotia House of Assembly passed *An Act to prevent any private Trade or Commerce with the Indians*, 34 Geo. II, c. 11. In July 1761, however, the "Lords of Trade and Plantation" (the Board of Trade) in London objected and the King disallowed the Act as a restraint on trade that disadvantaged British merchants. This coincided with exposure of venality by the local truckhouse merchants. . . .

34   By 1762, Garrish was removed and the number of truckhouses was reduced to three. By 1764, the system itself was replaced by the impartial licensing of private traders approved by the London Board of Trade's "Plan for the Future Management of Indian Affairs", but that eventually died out as well, as mentioned earlier.

35   In my view, all of this evidence, reflected in the trial judgment, demonstrates the inadequacy and incompleteness of the written memorial of the treaty terms by selectively isolating the restrictive trade covenant. Indeed, the truckhouse system offered such advantageous terms that it hardly seems likely that Mi'kmaq traders had to be compelled to buy at lower prices and sell at higher prices. At a later date, they objected when truckhouses were abandoned. The trade clause would not have advanced British objectives (peaceful relations with a self-sufficient Mi'kmaq people) or Mi'kmaq objectives (access to the European "necessaries" on which they had come to rely) unless the Mi'kmaq were assured at the same time of continuing access, implicitly or explicitly, to wildlife to trade. This was confirmed by the expert historian called by the Crown, as set out below.

(ii) *The Expert Evidence*

36   The courts have attracted a certain amount of criticism from professional historians for what these historians see as an occasional tendency on the part of judges to assemble a "cut and paste" version of history: G. M. Dickinson and R. D. Gidney, "History and Advocacy: Some Reflections on the Historian's Role in Litigation", *Canadian Historical Review*, LXVIII (1987), 576; D. J. Bourgeois, "The Role of the Historian in the Litigation Process", *Canadian Historical Review*, LXVII (1986), 195; R. Fisher, "Judging History: Reflections on the Reasons for Judgment in Delgamuukw v. B.C.", *B.C. Studies*, XCV (1992), 43; A. J. Ray, "Creating the Image of the Savage in Defence of the Crown: The Ethnohistorian in Court", *Native Studies Review*, VI (1990), 13.

37   While the tone of some of this criticism strikes the non-professional historian as intemperate, the basic objection, as I understand it, is that the judicial selection of facts and quotations is not always up to the standard demanded of the professional historian,

which is said to be more nuanced. Experts, it is argued, are trained to read the various historical records together with the benefit of a protracted study of the period, and an appreciation of the frailties of the various sources. The law sees a finality of interpretation of historical events where finality, according to the professional historian, is not possible. The reality, of course, is that the courts are handed disputes that require for their resolution the finding of certain historical facts. The litigating parties cannot await the possibility of a stable academic consensus. The judicial process must do as best it can. In this particular case, however, there was an unusual level of agreement amongst all of the professional historians who testified about the underlying expectations of the participants regarding the treaty obligations entered into by the Crown with the Mi'kmaq. I set out, in particular, the evidence of the Crown's expert, Dr. Stephen Patterson, who spent many days of testimony reviewing the minutiae of the historical record. While he generally supported the Crown's narrow approach to the interpretation of the Treaty, which I have rejected on points of law, he did make a number of important concessions to the defence in a relatively lengthy and reflective statement which should be set out in full:

Q. I guess it's fair to say that the British would have understood that the Micmac lived and survived by hunting and fishing and gathering activities.

A. Yes, of course.

Q. And that in this time period, 1760 and '61, fish would be amongst the items they would have to trade. And they would have the right under this treaty to bring fish and feathers and furs into a truckhouse in exchange for commodities that were available.

A. Well, it's not mentioned but it's not excluded. So I think it's fair to assume that it was *permissible.*

Q. Okay. It's fair to say that it's an assumption on which the trade truckhouse clause is based.

A. That the truckhouse clause is based on the *assumption that natives will have a variety of things to trade, some of which are mentioned and some not. Yes, I think that's fair.*

Q. Yes. And wouldn't be out of line to call that a right to fish and a right to bring the fish or furs or feathers or fowl or venison or whatever they might have, into the truckhouses to trade.

A. *Ah, a right.* I think the implication here is that there is a *right to trade* under a certain form of regulation—

Q. Yes.

A. —that's laid down. And if you're saying *right to fish,* I've assumed that in recognizing the Micmac by treaty, the British were recognizing them as the people they were. They understood how they lived and that that meant that *those people had a right to live in Nova Scotia in their traditional ways.* And, to me, that implies that the British were accepting that the Micmac would continue to be a hunting and gathering people, that they would fish, that they would hunt to support themselves. I don't see any problem with that.

It seems to me that *that's implicit* in the thing. Even though it doesn't say it, and I know that there seems to, in the 20th century, be some reluctance to see the value of the 1760 and 1761 treaties because they're not so explicit on these matters, but I personally don't see the hang-up. Because it strikes me that there is a recognition that the Micmac are a people and they have the right to exist. And that has—carries certain implications with it.

More than this, the very fact that there is a truckhouse and that the truckhouse does list some of the things that natives are expected to trade, implies that the British are condoning or recognizing that this is the way that natives live. *They do live by hunting and, therefore, this is the produce of their hunting. They have the right to trade it.*

Q. And you have, in fact, said that in your May 17th, 1994 draft article.

A. That's correct.

Q. Yeah. And you testified to that effect in the *Pelletier* case, as well.

A. Well, my understanding of this issue, Mr. Wildsmith, has developed and grown with my close reading of the material. *It's the position that I come to accept as being a reasonable interpretation of what is here in these documents.* [Emphasis added.]

38   The trial judge gave effect to this evidence in finding a right to bring fish to the truckhouse to trade, but he declined to find a treaty right to fish and hunt to obtain the wherewithal to trade, and concluded that the right to trade expired along with the truckhouses and subsequent special arrangements. The Court of Appeal concluded, at p. 207, that Dr. Patterson used the word "right" interchangeably with the word "permissible", and that the trade clause gave rise to no "rights" at all. I think the view taken by the courts below rather underestimates Dr. Patterson. No reason is given for doubting that Dr. Patterson meant what he said about the common understanding of the parties that he considered at least implicit in this particular treaty arrangement. He initially uses the words "permissible" and "assumption", but when asked specifically by counsel about a "right" to fish and to trade fish, he says, "Ah, a right" (emphasis added), then, weighing his words carefully, he addresses a "right to fish" and concludes that "by treaty" the British did recognize that the Mi'kmaq "had a *right* to live in Nova Scotia in their traditional ways" (emphasis added) which included hunting and fishing and trading their catch for necessaries. (Trading was traditional. The trial judge found, at para. 93, that the Mi'kmaq had already been trading with Europeans, including French and Portugese fishermen, for about 250 years prior to the making of this treaty.) Dr. Patterson said his opinion was based on the historic documents produced in evidence. He said that this was "the position that I come to accept as being a reasonable interpretation of what is here *in these documents*" (emphasis added). Dr. Patterson went on to emphasize that the understanding of the Mi'kmaq would have been that these treaty rights were subject to regulation, which I accept.

39   Dr. Patterson's evidence regarding the assumptions underlying and "implicit" in the treaty were generally agreed with by the defence experts, Dr. John Reid and Dr. William Wicken. . . .

40   In my view, the Nova Scotia judgments erred in concluding that the only enforceable treaty obligations were those set out in the written document of March 10, 1760, whether construed flexibly (as did the trial judge) or narrowly (as did the Nova Scotia Court of Appeal). The findings of fact made by the trial judge taken as a whole demonstrate that the concept of a disappearing treaty right does justice neither to the honour of the Crown nor to the reasonable expectations of the Mi'kmaq people. It is their common intention in 1760—not just the terms of the March 10, 1760 document—to which effect must be given.

Ascertaining the Terms of the Treaty

41   Having concluded that the written text is incomplete, it is necessary to ascertain the treaty terms not only by reference to the fragmentary historical record, as interpreted by the expert historians, but also in light of the stated objectives of the British and Mi'kmaq in 1760 and the political and economic context in which those objectives were reconciled.

42   I mentioned earlier that the Nova Scotia Court of Appeal has held on several occa-

sions that the "peace and friendship" treaties with the Mi'kmaq did not extinguish aboriginal hunting and fishing rights in Nova Scotia: *R. v. Isaac* (1975), 13 N.S.R. (2d) 460, *R. v. Cope* (1981), 132 D.L.R. (3d) 36, *Denny, supra*. We are not here concerned with the exercise of such a right. . . .

43   The law has long recognized that parties make assumptions when they enter into agreements about certain things that give their arrangements efficacy. Courts will imply a contractual term on the basis of presumed intentions of the parties where it is necessary to assure the efficacy of the contract, e.g., where it meets the "officious bystander test": . . . Here, if the ubiquitous officious bystander had said, "This talk about truckhouses is all very well, but if the Mi'kmaq are to make these promises, will they have the right to hunt and fish to catch something to trade at the truckhouses?", the answer would have to be, having regard to the honour of the Crown, "of course". If the law is prepared to supply the deficiencies of written contracts prepared by sophisticated parties and their legal advisors in order to produce a sensible result that accords with the intent of both parties, though unexpressed, the law cannot ask less of the honour and dignity of the Crown in its dealings with First Nations. The honour of the Crown was, in fact, specifically invoked by courts in the early 17th century to ensure that a Crown grant was effective to accomplish its intended purpose: . . .

44   An example of the Court's recognition of the necessity of supplying the deficiencies of aboriginal treaties is *Sioui, supra*, where Lamer J. considered a treaty document that stated simply (at p. 1031) that the Huron tribe "are received upon the same terms with the Canadians, being allowed the free Exercise of their Religion, their Customs, and Liberty of trading with the English". Lamer J. found that, in order to give real value and meaning to these words, it was necessary that a territorial component be supplied, as follows, at p. 1067:

> The treaty gives the Hurons the freedom to carry on their customs and their religion. No mention is made in the treaty itself of the territory over which these rights may be exercised. There is also no indication that the territory of what is now Jacques-Cartier park was contemplated. However, *for a freedom to have real value and meaning*, it must be possible to exercise it somewhere. [Emphasis added.]

Similarly, in *Sundown, supra*, the Court found that the express right to hunt included the implied right to build shelters required to carry out the hunt. See also *Simon, supra*, where the Court recognized an implied right to carry a gun and ammunition on the way to exercise the right to hunt. These cases employed the concept of implied rights to support the meaningful exercise of express rights granted to the first nations in circumstances where no such implication might necessarily have been made absent the *sui generis* nature of the Crown's relationship to aboriginal people. While I do not believe that in ordinary commercial situations a right to trade implies any right of access to things to trade, I think the honour of the Crown requires nothing less in attempting to make sense of the result of these 1760 negotiations.

Rights of the Other Inhabitants

45   My colleague, McLachlin J., takes the view that, subject to the negative restriction in the treaty, the Mi'kmaq possessed only the liberty to hunt, fish, gather and trade "enjoyed by other British subjects in the region" (para. 103). The Mi'kmaq were, in effect, "citizens minus" with no greater liberties but with greater restrictions. I accept that in

terms of the *content* of the hunting, fishing and gathering activities, this may be true. There is of course a distinction to be made between a liberty enjoyed by all citizens and a right conferred by a specific legal authority, such as a treaty, to participate in the same activity. Even if this distinction is ignored, it is still true that a general right enjoyed by all citizens can nevertheless be made the subject of an enforceable treaty promise. In *Taylor and Williams, supra*, at p. 235, the treaty was found to include a term that "[t]he Rivers are open to all & you have an *equal right* to fish & hunt on them", and yet, despite the reference to equal rather than preferential rights, "the historic right of these Indians to hunt and fish" was found to be incorporated in the treaty, *per* MacKinnon A.C.J.O., at p. 236. . . .

47   The Crown objects strongly to any suggestion that the treaty conferred "*preferential* trading rights". I do not think the appellant needs to show *preferential* trading rights. He only has to show *treaty* trading rights. The settlers and the military undoubtedly hunted and fished for sport or necessaries as well, and traded goods with each other. The issue here is not so much the content of the rights or liberties as the level of legal protection thrown around them. A treaty could, to take a fanciful example, provide for a right of the Mi'kmaq to promenade down Barrington Street, Halifax, on each anniversary of the treaty. Barrington Street is a common thoroughfare enjoyed by all. There would be nothing "special" about the Mi'kmaq use of a common right of way. The point is that the treaty rights-holder not only has the *right* or liberty "enjoyed by other British subjects" but may enjoy special treaty *protection* against interference with its exercise. So it is with the trading arrangement. . . .

48   Until enactment of the *Constitution Act, 1982*, the treaty rights of aboriginal peoples could be overridden by competent legislation as easily as could the rights and liberties of other inhabitants. The hedge offered no special protection, as the aboriginal people learned in earlier hunting cases such as *Sikyea* v. *The Queen*, [1964] S.C.R. 642, and *R.* v. *George*, [1966] S.C.R. 267. On April 17, 1982, however, this particular type of "hedge" was converted by s. 35(1) into sterner stuff that could only be broken down when justified according to the test laid down in *R.* v. *Sparrow*, [1990] 1 S.C.R. 1075, at pp. 1112 *et seq.*, as adapted to apply to treaties in *Badger, supra, per* Cory J., at paras. 75 *et seq.* See also *R.* v. *Bombay*, [1993] 1 C.N.L.R. 92 (Ont. C.A.). The fact the content of Mi'kmaq rights under the treaty to hunt and fish and trade was no greater than those enjoyed by other inhabitants does not, unless those rights were extinguished prior to April 17, 1982, detract from the higher *protection* they presently offer to the Mi'kmaq people.

The Honour of the Crown

49   This appeal puts to the test the principle, emphasized by this Court on several occasions, that the honour of the Crown is always at stake in its dealings with aboriginal people. . . .

50   This principle that the Crown's honour is at stake when the Crown enters into treaties with first nations dates back at least to this Court's decision in 1895, *Province of Ontario* v. *Dominion of Canada and Province of Quebec; In re Indian Claims* (1895), 25 S.C.R. 434. In that decision, Gwynne J. (dissenting) stated, at pp. 511–12:

> . . . what is contended for and must not be lost sight of, is that the British sovereigns, ever since the acquisition of Canada, have been pleased to adopt the rule or practice of entering

into agreements with the Indian nations or tribes in their province of Canada, for the cession or surrender by them of what such sovereigns have been pleased to designate the Indian title, by instruments similar to these now under consideration to which they have been pleased to give the designation of "treaties" with the Indians in possession of and claiming title to the lands expressed to be surrendered by the instruments, and further that *the terms and conditions expressed in those instruments as to be performed by or on behalf of the Crown, have always been regarded as involving a trust graciously assumed by the Crown to the fulfilment of which with the Indians the faith and honour of the Crown is pledged*, and which trust has always been most faithfully fulfilled as a treaty obligation of the Crown. [Emphasis added.]

See also *Ontario Mining Co.* v. *Seybold* (1901), 32 S.C.R. 1, at p. 2. . . .

52   I do not think an interpretation of events that turns a positive Mi'kmaq trade demand into a negative Mi'kmaq covenant is consistent with the honour and integrity of the Crown. Nor is it consistent to conclude that the Lieutenant Governor, seeking in good faith to address the trade demands of the Mi'kmaq, accepted the Mi'kmaq suggestion of a trading facility while denying any treaty protection to Mi'kmaq access to the things that were to be traded, even though these things were identified and priced in the treaty negotiations. This was not a commercial contract. The trade arrangement must be interpreted in a manner which gives meaning and substance to the promises made by the Crown. In my view, with respect, the interpretation adopted by the courts below left the Mi'kmaq with an empty shell of a treaty promise.

Contradictory Interpretations of the Truckhouse Clause

53   The appellant argues that the Crown has been in breach of the treaty since 1762, when the truckhouses were terminated, or at least since the 1780s when the replacement system of licensed traders was abandoned. This argument suffers from the same quality of unreasonableness as does the Crown's argument that the treaty left the Mi'kmaq with nothing more than a negative covenant. It was established in *Simon, supra*, at p. 402, that treaty provisions should be interpreted "in a flexible way that is sensitive to the evolution of changes in normal" practice, and *Sundown, supra*, at para. 32, confirms that courts should not use a "frozen-in-time" approach to treaty rights. The appellant cannot, with any show of logic, claim to exercise his treaty rights using an outboard motor while at the same time insist on restoration of the peculiar 18th century institution known as truckhouses.

54   The Crown, on the other hand, argues that the truckhouse was a time-limited response to a temporary problem. As my colleague McLachlin J. sets out at para. 96, the "core" of the treaty was said to be that "[t]he Mi'kmaq agreed to forgo their trading autonomy and the general trading rights they possessed as British subjects, and to abide by the treaty trade regime. The British, in exchange, undertook to provide the Mi'kmaq with stable trading outlets where European goods were provided at favourable terms while the exclusive trade regime existed". My disagreement with that view, with respect, is that the aboriginal people, as found by the trial judge, relied on European powder, shot and other goods and pushed a trade agenda with the British because their alternative sources of supply had dried up; the real inhibition on trade with the French was not the treaty but the absence of the French, whose military had retreated up the St. Lawrence and whose settlers had been expelled; there is no suggestion in the negotiating records that the truckhouse system was a sort of transitional arrangement expected to be temporary, it only

became temporary because the King unexpectedly disallowed the enabling legislation passed by the Nova Scotia House of Assembly; and the notion that the truckhouse was merely a response to a trade restriction overlooks the fact the truckhouse system offered very considerable financial benefits to the Mi'kmaq which they would have wanted to exploit, restriction or no restriction. The promise of access to "necessaries" through trade in wildlife was the key point, and where a right has been granted, there must be more than a mere disappearance of the mechanism created to facilitate the exercise of the right to warrant the conclusion that the right itself is spent or extinguished.

55   The Crown further argues that the treaty rights, if they exist at all, were "subject *ab initio* to regulation ". The effect, it is argued, is that no *Badger* justification would be required. The Crown's attempt to distinguish *Badger* is not persuasive. *Badger* dealt with treaty rights which were specifically expressed in the treaty (at para. 31) to be "subject to such regulations as may from time to time be made by the Government of the country." Yet the Court concluded that a *Sparrow*-type justification was required.

56   My view is that the surviving substance of the treaty is not the literal promise of a truckhouse, but a treaty right to continue to obtain necessaries through hunting and fishing by trading the products of those traditional activities subject to restrictions that can be justified under the *Badger* test.

The Limited Scope of the Treaty Right
57   The Crown expresses the concern that recognition of the existence of a constitutionally entrenched right with, as here, a trading aspect, would open the floodgates to uncontrollable and excessive exploitation of the natural resources. Whereas hunting and fishing for food naturally restricts quantities to the needs and appetites of those entitled to share in the harvest, it is argued that there is no comparable, built-in restriction associated with a trading right, short of the paramount need to conserve the resource. The Court has already addressed this issue in *R. v. Gladstone*, [1996] 2 S.C.R. 723, *per* Lamer C.J., at paras. 57–63, L'Heureux-Dubé J., at para. 137, and McLachlin J., at para. 164; *Van der Peet, supra, per* L'Heureux-Dubé J., at para. 192, and *per* McLachlin J., at para. 279; *R. v. N.T.C. Smokehouse Ltd.*, [1996] 2 S.C.R. 672, *per* L'Heureux-Dubé J., at para. 47; and *Horseman, supra, per* Wilson J., at p. 908, and Cory J., at pp. 928–29. The ultimate fear is that the appellant . . . could lever the treaty right into a factory trawler in Pomquet Harbour gathering the available harvest in preference to all non-aboriginal commercial or recreational fishermen. (This is indeed the position advanced by the intervener the Union of New Brunswick Indians.) This fear (or hope) is based on a misunderstanding of the narrow ambit and extent of the treaty right.

58   The recorded note of February 11, 1760 was that "there might be a Truckhouse established, for the furnishing them with *necessaries*" (emphasis added). What is contemplated therefore is not a right to trade generally for economic gain, but rather a right to trade for necessaries. The treaty right is a regulated right and can be contained by regulation within its proper limits.

59   The concept of "necessaries" is today equivalent to the concept of what Lambert J.A., in *R. v. Van der Peet* (1993), 80 B.C.L.R. (2d) 75, at p. 126, described as a "moderate livelihood". Bare subsistence has thankfully receded over the last couple of centuries as an appropriate standard of life for aboriginals and non-aboriginals alike. A moderate livelihood includes such basics as "food, clothing and housing, supplemented by a few ameni-

ties", but not the accumulation of wealth (*Gladstone, supra*, at para. 165). It addresses day-to-day needs. This was the common intention in 1760. It is fair that it be given this interpretation today.

60   The distinction between a commercial right and a right to trade for necessaries or sustenance was discussed in *Gladstone, supra*, where Lamer C.J., speaking for the majority, held that the Heiltsuk of British Columbia have "an aboriginal right to sell herring spawn on kelp to an extent best described as commercial" (para. 28). This finding was based on the evidence that "tons" of the herring spawn on kelp was traded and that such trade was a central and defining feature of Heiltsuk society. McLachlin J., however, took a different view of the evidence, which she concluded supported a finding that the Heiltsuk derived only sustenance from the trade of the herring spawn on kelp. "Sustenance" provided a manageable limitation on what would otherwise be a free-standing commercial right. . . .

In this case, equally, it is not suggested that Mi'kmaq trade historically generated "wealth which would exceed a sustenance lifestyle". Nor would anything more have been contemplated by the parties in 1760.

61   Catch limits that could reasonably be expected to produce a moderate livelihood for individual Mi'kmaq families at present-day standards can be established by regulation and enforced without violating the treaty right. In that case, the regulations would accommodate the treaty right. Such regulations would not constitute an infringement that would have to be justified under the *Badger* standard. . . .

63   All of these regulations place the issuance of licences within the absolute discretion of the Minister. . . .

64   . . . [T]here is nothing in these regulations which gives direction to the Minister to explain how she or he should exercise this discretionary authority in a manner which would respect the appellant's treaty rights. This Court has had the opportunity to review the effect of discretionary licensing schemes on aboriginal and treaty rights: *Badger*, . . . *R. v. Nikal*, . . . *R. v. Adams*, . . . and *R. v. Côté*. . . . The test for infringement under s. 35(1) of the *Constitution Act, 1982* was set out in *Sparrow*. . . .

Cory J. in *Badger, supra*, at para. 79, found that the test for infringement under s. 35(1) of the *Constitution Act, 1982* was the same for both aboriginal and treaty rights, and thus the words of Lamer C.J. in *Adams*, although in relation to the infringement of aboriginal rights, are equally applicable here. There was nothing at that time which provided the Crown officials with the "sufficient directives" necessary to ensure that the appellant's treaty rights would be respected. To paraphrase *Adams*, at para. 51, under the applicable regulatory regime, the appellant's exercise of his treaty right to fish and trade for sustenance was exercisable only at the absolute discretion of the Minister. Mi'kmaq treaty rights were not accommodated in the Regulations because, presumably, the Crown's position was, and continues to be, that no such treaty rights existed. In the circumstances, the purported regulatory prohibitions against fishing without a licence . . . do *prima facie* infringe the appellant's treaty rights under the Treaties of 1760–61 and are inoperative against the appellant unless justified under the *Badger* test.

65   Further, the appellant was charged with fishing during the close season with improper nets, contrary to s. 20 of the *Maritime Provinces Fishery Regulations*. Such a regulation is also a *prima facie* infringement, as noted by Cory J. in *Badger, supra*, at para. 90:

"This Court has held on numerous occasions that there can be no limitation on the method, timing and extent of Indian hunting under a Treaty", apart, I would add, from a treaty limitation to that effect.

66   The appellant caught and sold the eels to support himself and his wife. Accordingly, the close season and the imposition of a discretionary licensing system would, if enforced, interfere with the appellant's treaty right to fish for trading purposes, and the ban on sales would, if enforced, infringe his right to trade for sustenance. In the absence of any justification of the regulatory prohibitions, the appellant is entitled to an acquittal.

Disposition

67   The constitutional question stated by the Chief Justice on February 9, 1998, as follows:

> Are the prohibitions on catching and retaining fish without a licence, on fishing during the close time, and on the unlicensed sale of fish, contained in ss. 4(1)(a) and 20 of the *Maritime Provinces Fishery Regulations* and s. 35(2) of the *Fishery (General) Regulations*, inconsistent with the treaty rights of the appellant contained in the Mi'kmaq Treaties of 1760–61 and therefore of no force or effect or application to him, by virtue of ss. 35(1) and 52 of the *Constitution Act, 1982?*

should be answered in the affirmative. I would therefore allow the appeal and order an acquittal on all charges.

R. v. Marshall (reconsideration) (1999)

[1999] 3 S.C.R. 533 (reconsideration) (S.C.C.). Lamer C.J. and L'Heureux-Dubé, Gonthier, McLachlin, Iacobucci and Binnie JJ., November 17, 1999.

The following is the judgment delivered by

1   THE COURT — The intervener, the West Nova Fishermen's Coalition (the "Coalition"), applies for a rehearing to have the Court address the regulatory authority of the Government of Canada over the east coast fisheries together with a new trial to allow the Crown to justify for conservation or other purposes the licensing and closed season restriction on the exercise of the appellant's treaty right, and for an order that the Court's judgment, dated September 17, 1999, [1999] 3 S.C.R. 456, be stayed in the meantime. The application is opposed by the Crown, the appellant Marshall and the other interveners.

2   Those opposing the motion object in different ways that the Coalition's motion rests on a series of misconceptions about what the September 17, 1999 majority judgment decided and what it did not decide. These objections are well founded. The Court did not hold that the Mi'kmaq treaty right cannot be regulated or that the Mi'kmaq are guaranteed an open season in the fisheries. Justification for conservation or other purposes is a separate and distinct issue at the trial of one of these prosecutions. It is up to the Crown to decide whether or not it wishes to support the applicability of government regulations when prosecuting an accused who claims to be exercising an aboriginal or treaty right.

3   The Attorney General of Canada, in opposing the Coalition's motion, acknowledges that the Crown did not lead any evidence at trial or make any argument on the appeal that the licensing and closed season regulations which restricted the exercise of the

treaty right were justified in relation to the eel fishery. Accordingly, the issue whether these restrictions could have been justified in this case formed no part of the Court's majority judgment of September 17, 1999, and the constitutional question posed in this prosecution was answered on that basis. . . .

5   The Coalition argues that the native and non-native fishery should be subject to the same regulations. In fact, as pointed out in the September 17, 1999 majority judgment, natives and non-natives were subject to the unilateral regulatory authority of successive governments from 1760–61 to 1982. Until adoption of the *Constitution Act, 1982*, the appellant would clearly have been subject to regulations under the federal *Fisheries Act* and predecessor enactments in the same way and to the same extent as members of the applicant Coalition unless given a regulatory exemption as a matter of government policy.

6   As further pointed out in the September 17, 1999 majority judgment, the framers of the Constitution caused existing aboriginal and treaty rights to be entrenched in s. 35 of the *Constitution Act, 1982*. This gave constitutional status to rights that were previously vulnerable to unilateral extinguishment. The constitutional language necessarily included the 1760–61 treaties, and did not, on its face, refer expressly to a power to regulate. Section 35(1) simply says that "[t]he existing aboriginal and treaty rights of the aboriginal peoples of Canada are hereby recognized and affirmed". In subsequent cases, some aboriginal peoples argued that, as no regulatory restrictions on their rights were expressed in plain language in the Constitution, none could be imposed except by constitutional amendment. On the other hand, some of the Attorneys General argued that as aboriginal and treaty rights had always been vulnerable to unilateral regulation and extinguishment by government, this vulnerability was itself part of the rights now entrenched in s. 35 of the *Constitution Act, 1982*. In a series of important decisions commencing with *R. v. Sparrow*, [1990] 1 S.C.R. 1075, which arose in the context of the west coast fishery, this Court affirmed that s. 35 aboriginal and treaty rights are subject to regulation, provided such regulation is shown by the Crown to be justified on conservation or other grounds of public importance. A series of tests to establish such justification was laid out. These cases were referred to in the September 17, 1999 majority judgment, but the applicable principles were not elaborated because justification was not an issue which the Crown chose to make part of this particular prosecution, and therefore neither the Crown nor the defence had made submissions respecting the government's continuing powers of regulation. The Coalition recognizes that it is raising a new issue. It submits "that it is plain in the Reasons for Judgment, and in the earlier decisions of the Provincial Court of Nova Scotia at trial and of the Nova Scotia Court of Appeal on initial appeal, that that issue [of regulatory justification] has been neither considered nor decided". . . .

Status of the West Nova Fishermen's Coalition

9   Those in opposition challenge the status of the Coalition to bring this application. It is argued that the Coalition, being an intervener, does not have the rights of a party to ask for a rehearing. . . . While it would only be in exceptional circumstances that the Court would entertain an intervener's application for a rehearing, the extended definition of "party" in s. 1 of the Rules gives the Court the jurisdiction to do so. Not only are there no such exceptional circumstances here, but also the Coalition's motion violates the basis on which interveners are permitted to participate in an appeal in the first place, which is that interveners accept the record as defined by the Crown and the defence. Moreover, in

so far as the Coalition's questions are capable of being answered on the trial record in this case, the responses are already evident in the September 17, 1999 majority judgment and the prior decisions of this Court therein referred to. . . .

10   The Coalition requests a rehearing on the following issues:

1   Whether the Appellant is entitled to have been acquitted on a charge of unlicensed sale of fish, contrary to s. 35(2) of the *Fishery (General) Regulations*, in the absence of a new (or further) trial on the issue of whether that Regulation is or can be justified by the government of Canada;

2   Whether the Appellant is entitled to have been acquitted on a charge of out-of-season fishing, contrary to Item 2 of Schedule III of the *Maritime Provinces Fishery Regulations*, in the absence of a new (or further) trial on the issue of whether those Regulations are or can be justified by the government of Canada;

3   Whether the government of Canada has power to regulate the exercise by Mi'kmaq persons, including the Appellant, of their treaty right to fish through the imposition of licensing requirements;

4   Whether the government of Canada has power to regulate the exercise by Mi'kmaq persons, including the Appellant, of their treaty right to fish through the imposition of closed seasons;

5   In any event, what is the scope of regulatory power possessed by the government of Canada for purposes of regulating the treaty right; and

6   . . . pursuant to section 27 of the *Rules of the Supreme Court of Canada*, [requests] an Order that [the Court's] judgment pronounced herein on the 17th day of September, 1999 be stayed pending disposition of the rehearing of the appeal, if ordered.

11   These questions, together with the Coalition's request for a stay of judgment, reflect a basic misunderstanding of the scope of the Court's majority reasons for judgment dated September 17, 1999. As stated, this was a prosecution of a private citizen. It required the Court to determine whether certain precise charges relating to the appellant's participation in the eel fishery could be sustained. The majority judgment of September 17, 1999 was limited to the issues necessary to dispose of the appellant's guilt or innocence.

12   An order suspending the effect of a judgment of this Court is infrequently granted, especially where (as here) the parties have not requested such an order. This was not a reference to determine the general validity of legislative and regulatory provisions, as was the case, for example, in *Reference re Manitoba Language Rights*, [1985] 1 S.C.R. 721, at p. 780, where the Court suspended its declaration of invalidity of Manitoba enactments until "the expiry of the minimum period required for translation, re-enactment, printing and publishing". Nor was this a case where the Court was asked to grant declaratory relief with respect to the invalidity of statutory provisions, as in *M.* v. *H.*, [1999] 2 S.C.R. 3, . . .

13   Here the Crown elected to test the treaty issue by way of a prosecution, which is governed by a different set of rules than is a reference or a declaratory action. This appeal was directed solely to the issue whether the Crown had proven the appellant guilty as charged. . . .

14   As stated in para. 56 of the September 17, 1999 majority judgment, the treaty right was "to continue to obtain necessaries through hunting and fishing by trading the products of those traditional activities *subject to restrictions that can be justified under the Badger test*" (emphasis added). . . . The Crown, as stated, did not offer any evidence or argument justifying the licensing and closed season restrictions (referred to in the statute and regulations as a "close time") on the appellant's exercise of the collective treaty right, such as (for example) a need to conserve and protect the eel population. The eel population may not in fact require protection from commercial exploitation. Such was the assertion of the Native Council of Nova Scotia in opposition to the Coalition's motion: . . .

. . . The majority judgment delivered on September 17, 1999, therefore directed the acquittal of the appellant on the evidence brought against him. The issue of justification was not before the Court and no judgment was made about whether or not such restrictions could have been justified in relation to the eel fishery had the Crown led evidence and argument to support their applicability.

Grounds on Which the Coalition Seeks a Rehearing

1   Whether the Appellant is entitled to have been acquitted on a charge of unlicensed sale of fish, contrary to s. 35(2) of the Fishery (General) Regulations, in the absence of a new (or further) trial on the issue of whether that Regulation is or can be justified by the government of Canada

15   The appellant, as any other citizen facing a prosecution, is entitled to know in a timely way the case he has to meet, and to be afforded the opportunity to answer it. The Coalition seeks a new trial on a new issue. The September 17, 1999 majority decision specifically noted at para. 4 that the treaty right

> . . . *was always subject to regulation*. The Crown does not suggest that the regulations in question accommodate the treaty right. The Crown's case is that no such treaty right exists. Further, no argument was made that the treaty right was extinguished prior to [enactment of the *Constitution Act, 1982*], *and no justification was offered by the Crown for the several prohibitions at issue in this case.* [Emphasis added.]

. . . As stated, the Crown here opposes a rehearing and opposes a new trial. The issues of concern to the Coalition largely relate to the lobster fishery, not the eel fishery, and, if necessary, can be raised and decided in future cases that involve the specifics of the lobster fishery. It is up to the Crown to initiate enforcement action in the lobster and other fisheries if and when it chooses to do so.

2.   Whether the Appellant is entitled to have been acquitted on a charge of out-of-season fishing, contrary to Item 2 of Schedule III of the Maritime Provinces Fishery Regulations, in the absence of a new (or further) trial on the issue of whether those Regulations are or can be justified by the government of Canada

16   The Coalition argues that a rehearing and a further trial are necessary because of "uncertainty" about the authority of the government to manage the fisheries. The Attorney General of Canada, acting on behalf of the federal government which regulates the fisheries, opposes the Coalition's position. . . .

18   The September 17, 1999 majority judgment further pointed out that the accused will be required to demonstrate (as the appellant did here) that the regulatory regime significantly restricts the exercise of the treaty right. The majority judgment concluded on this point, at para. 64, that:

In the circumstances, the purported regulatory prohibitions against fishing without a licence (*Maritime Provinces Fishery Regulations*, s. 4(1)(a)) and of selling eels without a licence (*Fishery (General) Regulations*, s. 35(2)) *do prima facie* infringe the appellant's treaty rights under the Treaties of 1760–61 and are inoperative against the appellant *unless justified under the Badger test*. [Emphasis added.]

19   At the end of the day, it is always open to the Minister (as it was here) to seek to justify the limitation on the treaty right because of the need to conserve the resource in question or for other compelling and substantial public objectives, as discussed below. Equally, it will be open to an accused in future cases to try to show that the treaty right was intended in 1760 by both sides to include access to resources other than fish, wildlife and traditionally gathered things such as fruits and berries. The word "gathering" in the September 17, 1999 majority judgment was used in connection with the types of the resources traditionally "gathered" in an aboriginal economy and which were thus reasonably in the contemplation of the parties to the 1760–61 treaties. While treaty rights are capable of evolution within limits, as discussed below, their subject matter (absent a new agreement) cannot be wholly transformed. Certain unjustified assumptions are made in this regard by the Native Council of Nova Scotia on this motion about "the effect of the economic treaty right on forestry, minerals and natural gas deposits offshore". The Union of New Brunswick Indians also suggested on this motion a need to "negotiate an integrated approach dealing with all resources coming within the purview of fishing, hunting and gathering which includes harvesting from the sea, the forests and the land". This extended interpretation of "gathering" is not dealt with in the September 17, 1999 majority judgment, and negotiations with respect to such resources as logging, minerals or offshore natural gas deposits would go beyond the subject matter of this appeal.

20   The September 17, 1999 majority judgment did not rule that the appellant had established a treaty right "to gather" anything and everything physically capable of being gathered. The issues were much narrower and the ruling was much narrower. No evidence was drawn to our attention, nor was any argument made in the course of this appeal, that trade in logging or minerals, or the exploitation of off-shore natural gas deposits, was in the contemplation of either or both parties to the 1760 treaty; nor was the argument made that exploitation of such resources could be considered a logical evolution of treaty rights to fish and wildlife or to the type of things traditionally "gathered" by the Mi'kmaq in a 1760 aboriginal lifestyle. It is of course open to native communities to assert broader treaty rights in that regard, but if so, the basis for such a claim will have to be established in proceedings where the issue is squarely raised on proper historical evidence, as was done in this case in relation to fish and wildlife. Other resources were simply not addressed by the parties, and therefore not addressed by the Court in its September 17, 1999 majority judgment. As acknowledged by the Union of New Brunswick Indians in opposition to the Coalition's motion, "there are cases wending their way through the lower courts dealing specifically with some of these potential issues such as cutting timber on Crown lands".

21   The fact the Crown elected not to try to justify a closed season on the eel fishery at issue in this case cannot be generalized, as the Coalition's question implies, to a conclusion that closed seasons can never be imposed as part of the government's regulation of the Mi'kmaq limited commercial "right to fish". A "closed season" is clearly a potentially available management tool, but its application to treaty rights will have to be justified for conservation or other purposes. In the absence of such justification, an accused who es-

tablishes a treaty right is ordinarily allowed to exercise it. As suggested in the expert evidence filed on this motion by the Union of New Brunswick Indians, the establishment of a closed season may raise very different conservation and other issues in the eel fishery than it does in relation to other species such as salmon, crab, cod or lobster, or for that matter, to moose and other wildlife. The complexities and techniques of fish and wildlife management vary from species to species and restrictions will likely have to be justified on a species-by-species basis. Evidence supporting closure of the wild salmon fishery is not necessarily transferable to justify closure of an eel fishery.

22   Resource conservation and management and allocation of the permissible catch inevitably raise matters of considerable complexity both for Mi'kmaq peoples who seek to work for a living under the protection of the treaty right, and for governments who seek to justify the regulation of that treaty right. The factual context, as this case shows, is of great importance, and the merits of the government's justification may vary from resource to resource, species to species, community to community and time to time. As this and other courts have pointed out on many occasions, the process of accommodation of the treaty right may best be resolved by consultation and negotiation of a modern agreement for participation in specified resources by the Mi'kmaq rather than by litigation. La Forest J. emphasized in *Delgamuukw* v. *British Columbia*, [1997] 3 S.C.R. 1010 (a case cited in the September 17, 1999 majority decision), at para. 207:

> On a final note, I wish to emphasize that the best approach in these types of cases is a process of negotiation and reconciliation that properly considers the complex and competing interests at stake.

23   The various governmental, aboriginal and other interests are not, of course, obliged to reach an agreement. In the absence of a mutually satisfactory solution, the courts will resolve the points of conflict as they arise case by case. The decision in this particular prosecution is authority only for the matters adjudicated upon. The acquittal ought not to be set aside to allow the Coalition to address new issues that were neither raised by the parties nor determined by the Court in the September 17, 1999 majority judgment.

3. Whether the government of Canada has power to regulate the exercise by Mi'kmaq persons, including the Appellant, of their treaty right to fish through the imposition of licensing requirements

24   The government's power to regulate the treaty right is repeatedly affirmed in the September 17, 1999 majority judgment. In addition to the reference at para. 4 of the majority decision, already mentioned, that the treaty right "was always subject to regulation", the majority judgment further stated, at para. 7:

> In my view, the treaty rights are limited to securing "necessaries" (which I construe in the modern context, as equivalent to a moderate livelihood), and do not extend to the open-ended accumulation of wealth. The rights thus construed, however, are, in my opinion, treaty rights within the meaning of s. 35 of the *Constitution Act, 1982*, and are subject to regulations that can be justified under the *Badger* test. . . . [Emphasis added.]

. . .

At para. 58, the limited nature of the right was reiterated:

> What is contemplated therefore is not a right to trade generally for economic gain, but rather a right to trade for necessaries. *The treaty right is a regulated right and can be contained by regulation within its proper limits.* [Emphasis added.]

At para. 64, the majority judgment again referred to regulation permitted by the *Badger* test. The Court was thus most explicit in confirming the regulatory authority of the federal and provincial governments within their respective legislative fields to regulate the exercise of the treaty right subject to the constitutional requirement that restraints on the exercise of the treaty right have to be justified on the basis of conservation or other compelling and substantial public objectives, discussed below.

25   With all due respect to the Coalition, the government's general regulatory power is clearly affirmed. It is difficult to believe that further repetition of this fundamental point after a rehearing would add anything of significance to what is already stated in the September 17, 1999 majority judgment.

26   As for the specific matter of licences, the conclusion of the majority judgment was not that licensing schemes as such are invalid, but that the imposition of a licensing restriction on the appellant's exercise of the treaty right had not been justified for conservation or other public purposes. The Court majority stated at para. 64:

> . . . under the applicable regulatory regime, the appellant's exercise of his treaty right to fish and trade for sustenance was exercisable only at the absolute discretion of the Minister. Mi'kmaq treaty rights were not accommodated in the Regulations because, presumably, the Crown's position was, and continues to be, that no such treaty rights existed. In the circumstances, the purported regulatory prohibitions . . . are inoperative against the appellant *unless justified under the Badger test*. [Emphasis added.]

27   Although no evidence or argument was put forward to justify the licensing requirement in this case, a majority of the Court nevertheless referred at para. 64 of its September 17, 1999 decision to *R. v. Nikal*, . . . where Cory J., for the Court, dealt with a licensing issue as follows, at paras. 91 and 92:

> With respect to licensing, the appellant [aboriginal accused] takes the position that once his rights have been established, anything which affects or interferes with the exercise of those rights, no matter how insignificant, constitutes a *prima facie* infringement. It is said that a licence by its very existence is an infringement of the aboriginal right since it infers that government permission is needed to exercise the right and that the appellant is not free to follow his own or his band's discretion in exercising that right.
>
> This position cannot be correct. It has frequently been said that rights do not exist in a vacuum, and that the rights of one individual or group is [*sic*] necessarily limited by the rights of another. The ability to exercise personal or group rights is necessarily limited by the rights of others. The government must ultimately be able to determine and direct the way in which these rights should interact. Absolute freedom in the exercise of even a *Charter* or constitutionally guaranteed aboriginal right has never been accepted, nor was it intended. Section 1 of the *Canadian Charter of Rights and Freedoms* is perhaps the prime example of this principle. Absolute freedom without any restriction necessarily infers a freedom to live without any laws. Such a concept is not acceptable in our society.

28   The justification for a licensing requirement depends on facts. The Crown in this case declined to offer evidence or argument to support the imposition of a licensing requirement in relation to the small-scale commercial eel fishery in which the appellant participated.

4. Whether the government of Canada has power to regulate the exercise by Mi'kmaq persons, including the Appellant, of their treaty right to fish through the imposition of closed seasons

29   The regulatory device of a closed season is at least in part directed at conservation

of the resource. Conservation has always been recognized to be a justification of paramount importance to limit the exercise of treaty and aboriginal rights in the decisions of
this Court cited in the majority decision of September 17, 1999, including *Sparrow,
supra*, and *Badger, supra*. As acknowledged by the Native Council of Nova Scotia in opposition to the Coalition's motion, "Conservation is clearly a first priority and the Aboriginal peoples accept this". Conservation, where necessary, may require the complete shut-
down of a hunt or a fishery for aboriginal and non-aboriginal alike.

30   In this case, the prosecution of the appellant was directed to a "closed season" in the
eel fishery which the Crown did not try to justify, and that is the precise context in which
the majority decision of September 17, 1999 is to be understood. No useful purpose
would be served for those like the Coalition who are interested in justifying a closed
season in the lobster fishery if a rehearing or a new trial were ordered in this case, which
related only to the closed season in the eel fishery.

*5. In any event, what is the scope of regulatory power possessed by the government of Canada
    for purposes of regulating the treaty right?*

31   On the face of it, this question is not raised by the subject matter of the appeal, nor
is it capable of being answered on the factual record. As framed, it is so broad as to be
incapable of a detailed response. In effect, the Coalition seeks to transform a prosecution
on specific facts into a general reference seeking an advisory opinion of the Court on a
broad range of regulatory issues related to the east coast fisheries. As was explained in
Reference re Secession of Quebec, [1998] 2 S.C.R. 217, the Court's jurisdiction to give
advisory opinions is exceptional and can be invoked only by the Governor in Council
under s. 53 of the *Supreme Court Act*, R.S.C., 1985, c. S-26. In this instance, the Governor in Council has not sought an advisory opinion from the Court and the Attorney
General of Canada opposes the Coalition's attempt to initiate what she calls a "private
reference".

32   Mention has already been made of "the *Badger* test" by which governments may
justify restrictions on the exercise of treaty rights. The Court in *Badger* extended to treaties the justificatory standard developed for aboriginal rights in *Sparrow, supra*. Cory J. set
out the test, in *Badger, supra*, at para. 97 . . .

33   The majority judgment of September 17, 1999 did not put in doubt the validity of
the *Fisheries Act* or any of its provisions. What it said, in para. 66, was that, "the close
season and the imposition of a discretionary licensing system would, if enforced, interfere
with the appellant's treaty right to fish for trading purposes, and the ban on sales would,
if enforced, infringe his right to trade for sustenance. *In the absence of any justification of
the regulatory prohibitions, the appellant is entitled to an acquittal*" (emphasis added). Section 43 of the Act sets out the basis of a very broad regulatory authority over the fisheries
which may extend to the native fishery where justification is shown: . . .

  (Pursuant to this regulatory power, the Governor in Council had, in fact, adopted the
Aboriginal Communal Fishing Licences Regulations, discussed below.) Although s. 7(1) of
the *Fisheries Act* purports to grant the Minister an "absolute discretion" to issue or not to
issue leases and licences, this discretion must be read together with the authority of the
Governor in Council under s. 43(f) to make regulations "respecting the issue, suspension
and cancellation of licences and leases". Specific criteria must be established for the exercise by the Minister of his or her discretion to grant or refuse licences in a manner that

recognizes and accommodates the existence of an aboriginal or treaty right. In *R.* v. *Adams*, [1996] 3 S.C.R. 101, also cited in the September 17, 1999 majority judgment, the Chief Justice stated as follows at para. 54:

> In light of the Crown's unique fiduciary obligations towards aboriginal peoples, Parliament may not simply adopt an unstructured discretionary administrative regime which risks infringing aboriginal rights in a substantial number of applications in the absence of some explicit guidance. If a statute confers an administrative discretion which may carry significant consequences for the exercise of an aboriginal right, *the statute or its delegate regulations must outline specific criteria for the granting or refusal of that discretion* which seek to accommodate the existence of aboriginal rights. In the absence of such specific guidance, the statute will fail to provide representatives of the Crown with sufficient directives to fulfil their fiduciary duties, and the statute will be found to represent an infringement of aboriginal rights under the *Sparrow* test. [Emphasis added.]

While *Adams* dealt with an aboriginal right, the same principle applies to treaty rights.

34   The *Aboriginal Communal Fishing Licences Regulations*, SOR/93-332, referred to in the September 17, 1999 majority judgment, deal with the food fishery. These regulations provide specific authority to impose conditions where justified respecting the species and quantities of fish that are permitted to be taken or transported; the locations and times at which landing of fish is permitted; the method to be used for the landing of fish and the methods by which the quantity of the fish is to be determined; the information that a designated person or the master of a designated vessel is to report to the Minister or a person specified by the licence holder, prior to commencement of fishing; the locations and times of inspections of the contents of the hold and the procedure to be used in conducting those inspections; the maximum number of persons or vessels that may be designated to carry on fishing and related activities; the maximum number of designated persons who may fish at any one time; the type, size and quantity of fishing gear that may be used by a designated person; and the disposition of fish caught under the authority of the licence. The Governor in Council has the power to amend the *Aboriginal Communal Fishing Licences Regulations* to accommodate a limited commercial fishery as described in the September 17, 1999 majority judgment in addition to the food fishery.

35   Despite the limitations on the Court's ability in a prosecution to address broader issues not at issue between the Crown and the defence, the majority judgment of September 17, 1999 nevertheless referred to the Court's principal pronouncements on the various grounds on which the exercise of treaty rights may be regulated. These include the following grounds:

36   (a) *The treaty right itself is a limited right.* The September 17, 1999 majority judgment referred to the "narrow ambit and extent of the treaty right" (para. 57). In its written argument, the Coalition says that the only regulatory method specified in that judgment was a limit on the quantities of fish required to satisfy the Mi'kmaq need for necessaries. This is not so. What the majority judgment said is that the Mi'kmaq treaty right does not extend beyond the quantities required to satisfy the need for necessaries. The Court stated at para. 61 of the September 17, 1999 majority judgment:

> Catch limits that could reasonably be expected to produce a moderate livelihood for individual Mi'kmaq families at present-day standards can be established by regulation and enforced *without violating the treaty right*. In that case, the regulations would accommodate the treaty right. Such regulations would <u>*not*</u> constitute an infringement that would have to

be justified under the *Badger* standard. [Emphasis by underlining added.]

37   In other words, regulations that do no more than reasonably define the Mi'kmaq treaty right in terms that can be administered by the regulator and understood by the Mi'kmaq community that holds the treaty rights do not impair the exercise of the treaty right and therefore do not have to meet the *Badger* standard of justification.

38   Other limitations apparent in the September 17, 1999 majority judgment include the local nature of the treaties, the communal nature of a treaty right, and the fact it was only hunting and fishing resources to which access was affirmed, together with tradition- ally gathered things like wild fruit and berries. With regard to the Coalition's concern about the fishing rights of its members, para. 38 of the September 17, 1999 majority judgment noted the trial judge's finding that the Mi'kmaq had been fishing to trade with non-natives for over 200 years prior to the 1760–61 treaties. The 1760–61 treaty rights were thus from their inception enjoyed alongside the commercial and recreational fishery of non-natives. Paragraph 42 of the September 17, 1999 majority judgment recognized that, unlike the scarce fisheries resources of today, the view in 1760 was that the fisheries were of "limitless proportions". . . .

The Mi'kmaq treaty right to participate in the largely unregulated commercial fishery of 1760 has evolved into a treaty right to participate in the largely regulated commercial fishery of the 1990s. The notion of equitable sharing seems to be endorsed by the Coali- tion, which refers in its written argument on the motion to "the equal importance of the fishing industry to both Mi'kmaq and non-Mi'kmaq persons". In its Reply, the Coalition says that it is engaged in discussions "with representatives of the Acadia and Bear River Bands in southwestern Nova Scotia and takes pride that those discussions have been productive and that there is reason to hope that they will lead to harmonious and mutu- ally beneficial participation in the commercial lobster fishery by members of those Bands". Equally, the Mi'kmaq treaty right to hunt and trade in game is not now, any more than it was in 1760, a *commercial* hunt that must be satisfied before non-natives have access to the same resources for recreational or commercial purposes. The emphasis in 1999, as it was in 1760, is on assuring the Mi'kmaq equitable access to identified resources for the purpose of earning a moderate living. In this respect, a treaty right differs from an abo- riginal right which in its origin, by definition, was exclusively exercised by aboriginal people prior to contact with Europeans.

39   Only those regulatory limits that take the Mi'kmaq catch *below* the quantities rea- sonably expected to produce a moderate livelihood or other limitations that are not in- herent in the limited nature of the treaty right itself have to be justified according to the *Badger* test.

40   (b) *The paramount regulatory objective is the conservation of the resource. This respon- sibility is placed squarely on the Minister and not on the aboriginal or non-aboriginal users of the resource.* The September 17, 1999 majority decision referred to *Sparrow, supra,* which affirmed the government's paramount authority to act in the interests of conservation. This principle was repeated in *R. v. Gladstone,* . . . *Nikal,* . . . *Adams,* . . . *R. v. Côté,* . . . and *Delgamuukw,* . . . all of which were referred to in the September 17, 1999 majority judgment.

41   (c) *The Minister's authority extends to other compelling and substantial public objec- tives which may include economic and regional fairness, and recognition of the historical reli-*

ance upon, and participation in, the fishery by non-aboriginal groups. The Minister's regulatory authority is not limited to conservation. This was recognized in the submission of the appellant Marshall in opposition to the Coalition's motion. He acknowledges that "it is clear that limits may be imposed to conserve the species/stock being exploited and to protect public safety". Counsel for the appellant Marshall goes on to say: "Likewise, Aboriginal harvesting preferences, *together with non-Aboriginal regional/community dependencies,* may be taken into account in devising regulatory schemes" (emphasis added). In *Sparrow, supra,* at p. 1119, the Court said "We would not wish to set out an exhaustive list of the factors to be considered in the assessment of justification." It is for the Crown to propose what controls are justified for the management of the resource, and why they are justified. In *Gladstone, supra* (cited at para. 57 of the September 17, 1999 majority judgment), the Chief Justice commented on the differences between a Native food fishery and a Native *commercial* fishery, . . . at para. 75. . . .

. . . The aboriginal right at issue in *Gladstone, supra,* was by definition exercised exclusively by aboriginal people prior to contact with Europeans. As stated, no such exclusivity ever attached to the treaty right at issue in this case. Although we note the acknowledgement of the appellant Marshall that "non-Aboriginal regional/community dependencies ... may be taken into account in devising regulatory schemes", and the statements in *Gladstone, supra,* which support this view, the Court again emphasizes that the specifics of any particular regulatory regime were not and are not before us for decision.

42 In the case of any treaty right which may be exercised on a commercial scale, the natives constitute only one group of participants, and regard for the interest of the non-natives, as stated in *Gladstone, supra,* may be shown in the right circumstances to be entirely legitimate. Proportionality is an important factor. In asking for a rehearing, the Coalition stated that it is the lobster fishery "in which the Applicant's members are principally engaged and in which, since release of the Reasons for Judgment, controversy as to exercise of the treaty right has most seriously arisen". In response, the affidavit evidence of Dr. Gerard Hare, a fisheries biologist of some 30 years' experience, was filed. The correctness of Dr. Hare's evidence was not contested in reply by the Coalition. Dr. Hare estimated that the non-native lobster fishery in Atlantic Canada, excluding Newfoundland, sets about 1,885,000 traps in inshore waters each year and "[t]o put the situation in perspective, the recent Aboriginal commercial fisheries appear to be minuscule in comparison". It would be significant if it were established that the combined aboriginal food and limited commercial fishery constitute only a "minuscule" percentage of the non-aboriginal commercial catch of a particular species, such as lobster, bearing in mind, however, that a fishery that is "minuscule" on a provincial or regional basis could nevertheless raise conservation issues on a local level if it were concentrated in vulnerable fishing grounds.

43 (d) *Aboriginal people are entitled to be consulted about limitations on the exercise of treaty and aboriginal rights.* The Court has emphasized the importance in the justification context of consultations with aboriginal peoples. Reference has already been made to the rule in *Sparrow, supra,* at p. 1114, repeated in *Badger, supra,* at para. 97, that:

> The special trust relationship and the responsibility of the government vis-à-vis aboriginals must be the first consideration in determining whether the legislation or action in question can be justified.

The special trust relationship includes the right of the treaty beneficiaries to be consulted about restrictions on their rights, although, as stated in *Delgamuukw, supra*, at para. 168:

> The nature and scope of the duty of consultation will vary with the circumstances.

This variation may reflect such factors as the seriousness and duration of the proposed restriction, and whether or not the Minister is required to act in response to unforeseen or urgent circumstances. As stated, if the consultation does not produce an agreement, the adequacy of the justification of the government's initiative will have to be litigated in the courts.

44   (e) The Minister has available for regulatory purposes the full range of resource management tools and techniques, provided their use to limit the exercise of a treaty right can be justified. If the Crown establishes that the limitations on the treaty right are imposed for a pressing and substantial public purpose, after appropriate consultation with the aboriginal community, and go no further than is required, the same techniques of resource conservation and management as are used to control the non-native fishery may be held to be justified. Equally, however, the concerns and proposals of the native communities must be taken into account, and this might lead to different techniques of conservation and management in respect of the exercise of the treaty right.

45   In its written argument on this appeal, the Coalition also argued that no treaty right should "operate to involuntarily displace any non-aboriginal existing participant in any commercial fishery", and that "neither the authors of the Constitution nor the judiciary which interprets it are the appropriate persons to mandate who shall and shall not have access to the commercial fisheries". The first argument amounts to saying that aboriginal and treaty rights should be recognized only to the extent that such recognition would not occasion disruption or inconvenience to non-aboriginal people. According to this submission, if a treaty right would be disruptive, its existence should be denied or the treaty right should be declared inoperative. This is not a legal principle. It is a political argument. What is more, it is a political argument that was expressly rejected by the political leadership when it decided to include s. 35 in the *Constitution Act, 1982*. The democratically elected framers of the *Constitution Act, 1982* provided in s. 35 that "[t]he existing aboriginal and treaty rights of the aboriginal peoples of Canada are hereby recognized and affirmed" (emphasis added). It is the obligation of the courts to give effect to that national commitment. No useful purpose would be served by a rehearing of this appeal to revisit such fundamental and incontrovertible principles. . . .

46   At no stage of this appeal, either before or after September 17, 1999, has any government requested a stay or suspension of judgment. The Coalition asks for the stay based on its theory that the ruling created broad gaps in the regulatory scheme, but for the reasons already explained, its contention appears to be based on a misconception of what was decided on September 17, 1999. The appellant should not have his acquittal kept in jeopardy while issues which are much broader than the specifics of his prosecution are litigated. The request for a stay of the acquittal directed on September 17, 1999, is therefore denied.

A Stay of the Broader Effect of the September 17, 1999 Majority Judgment

47   In the event the respondent Attorney General of Canada or the intervener Attorney General for New Brunswick should determine that it is in the public interest to apply for a stay of the effect of the Court's recognition and affirmation of the Mi'kmaq treaty right

in its September 17, 1999 majority judgment, while leaving in place the acquittal of the appellant, the Court will entertain argument on whether it has the jurisdiction to grant such a stay, and if so, whether it ought to do so in this case.

Disposition

48   The Coalition's motion is dismissed with costs.

Robinson Treaty (Lake Superior) (1850)

Robinson Treaty (Lake Superior)
With the Ojibewa Indians of Lake Superior
conveying certain lands to the Crown

THIS AGREEMENT *made and entered into on the seventh day of September, in the year of Our Lord one thousand eight hundred and fifty, at Sault Ste. Marie, in the Province of Canada between the Honourable* WILLIAM BENJAMIN ROBINSON, *of the one part on behalf of* HER MAJESTY THE QUEEN, *and* JOSEPH PEANDECHAT, JOHN IUINWAY, MISHE-MUCKQUA, TOTOMENCIE, *Chiefs, and* JACOB WARPELA, AHMUTCHIWA GABOU, MICHEL SHELAGESHICK, MANITSHAINSE, *and* CHIGINANS, *principal men of the* OJIBEWA *Indians inhabiting the Northern Shore of Lake Superior, in the said Province of Canada, from Batchewana Bay to Pigeon River, at the western extremity of said Lake, and inland throughout that extent to the height of land which separates the territory covered by the charter of the Honourable the Hudson's Bay Company from the said tract, and also the Islands in the said Lake within the boundaries of the British possessions therein, of the other part, witnesseth:*

THAT for and in consideration of the sum of two thousand pounds of good and lawful money of Upper Canada, to them in hand paid, and for the further perpetual annuity of five hundred pounds, the same to be paid and delivered to the said Chiefs and their Tribes at, convenient season of each summer, not later than the first day of August at the Honorable the Hudson's Bay Company's Posts of Michipicoton and Fort William, they the said chiefs and principal men do freely, fully and voluntarily surrender, cede, grant and convey unto Her Majesty, Her heirs and successors forever, all their right, title and interest in the whole of the territory above described, save and except the reservations set forth in the schedule hereunto annexed, which reservations shall be held and occupied by the said Chiefs and their Tribes in common, for the purpose of residence and cultivation,—and should the said Chiefs and their respective Tribes at any time desire to dispose of any mineral or other valuable productions upon the said reservations, the same will be at their request sold by order of the Superintendent General of the Indian Department for the time being, for their sole use and benefit, and to the best advantage.

And the said William Benjamin Robinson of the first part, on behalf of Her Majesty and the Government of this province, hereby promises and agrees to make the payments as before mentioned; and further to allow the said chiefs and their tribes the full and free privilege to hunt over the territory now ceded by them, and to fish in the waters thereof as they have heretofore been in the habit of doing, saving and excepting only such portions of the said territory as may from time to time be sold or leased to individuals, or companies of individuals, and occupied by them with the consent of the provincial Government. The parties of the second part further promise and agree that they will not sell, lease, or otherwise dispose of any portion of their reservations without the consent of the

Superintendent General of Indian Affairs being first had and obtained; nor will they at any time hinder or prevent persons from exploring or searching for mineral or other valuable productions in any part of the territory hereby ceded to Her Majesty as before mentioned. The parties of the second part also agree that in case the Government of this province should before the date of this agreement have sold, or bargained to sell, any mining locations or other property on the portions of the territory hereby reserve for their use and benefit, then and in that case such sale, or promise of sale, shall be forfeited, if the parties interested desire it, by the Government, and the amount accruing therefrom shall be paid to the tribe to whom the reservation belongs. The said William Benjamin Robinson on behalf of Her Majesty, who desires to deal liberally and justly with all Her subjects, further promises and agrees that in case the territory hereby ceded by the parties of the second part shall at any future period produce an amount which will enable the Government of this Province without incurring loss to increase the annuity hereby secured to them, then, and in that case, the same shall be augmented from time to time, provided that the amount paid to each individual shall not exceed the sum of one pound provincial currency in any one year, or such further sum as Her Majesty may be graciously pleased to order; and provided further that the number of Indians entitled to the benefit of this Treaty shall amount to two thirds of their present numbers (which is twelve hundred and forty) to entitle them to claim the full benefit thereof, and should their numbers at any future period not amount to two thirds of twelve hundred and forty, the annuity shall be diminished in proportion to their actual numbers.

Schedule of Reservations made by the above named and subscribing Chiefs and principal men. . . .

Treaty No. 6 (1876)*

Between
Her Majesty the Queen
and the
Plains and Wood Cree Indians
and
other tribes of Indians
at
Fort Carlton, Fort Pitt and Battle River

ARTICLES OF A TREATY made and concluded near Carlton on the 23rd day of August, and on the 28th day of said month, respectively, and near Fort Pitt on the 9th day of September, in the year of Our Lord one thousand eight hundred and seventy-six, between Her Most Gracious Majesty the Queen of Great Britain and Ireland, by Her Commissioners, the Honourable Alexander Morris, Lieutenant-Governor of the Province of Manitoba and the North-West Territories, and the Honourable James McKay, and the Honourable William Joseph Christie, of the one part, and the Plain and Wood Cree Tribes of Indians, and the other Tribes of Indians, inhabitants of the country within the limits hereinafter defined and described, by their Chiefs, chosen and named as hereinafter mentioned, of the other part.

Whereas the Indians inhabiting the said country have, pursuant to an appointment made by the said commissioners, been convened at meetings at Fort Carlton, Fort Pitt

* Signed in 1876, Treaty No. 6 covers the parts of Saskatchewan and Alberta.

and Battle River, to deliberate upon certain matters of interest to Her Most Gracious Majesty, of the one part, and the said Indians of the other;

And whereas the said Indians have been notified and informed by Her Majesty's said Commissioners that it is the desire of Her Majesty to open up for settlement, immigration and such other purposes as to Her Majesty may seem meet, a tract of country, bounded and described as hereinafter mentioned, and to obtain the consent thereto of Her Indian subjects inhabiting the said tract, and to make a treaty and arrange with them, so that there may be peace and good will between them and Her Majesty, and that they may know and be assured of what allowance they are to count upon and receive from Her Majesty's bounty and benevolence;

And whereas the Indians of the said tract, duly convened in council as aforesaid, and being requested by Her Majesty's Commissioners to name certain Chiefs and head men, who should be authorized, on their behalf, to conduct such negotiations and sign any treaty to be founded thereon, and to become responsible to Her Majesty for their faithful performance by their respective bands of such obligations as shall be assumed by them, the said Indians have thereupon named for that purpose, that is to say, representing:—the Indians who make the treaty at Carlton, the several Chiefs and Councillors who have subscribed hereto, and representing the Indians who make the treaty at Fort Pitt, the several Chiefs and Councillors who have subscribed hereto;

And thereupon, in open council, the different bands having presented their Chiefs to the said Commissioners as the Chiefs and head men, for the purposes aforesaid, of the respective bands of Indians inhabiting the said district hereinafter described;

And whereas, the said Commissioners then and there received and acknowledged the persons so represented, as Chiefs and head men, for the purposes aforesaid, of the respective bands of Indians inhabiting the said district hereinafter described;

And whereas the said Commissioners have proceeded to negotiate a treaty with the said Indians, and the same has been finally agreed upon and concluded as follows, that is to say:

The Plain and Wood Cree Tribes of Indians, and all other the Indians inhabiting the district hereinafter described and defined, do hereby cede, release, surrender and yield up to the Government of the Dominion of Canada for Her Majesty the Queen and Her successors forever, all their rights, titles and privileges whatsoever, to the lands included within the following limits, that is to say:

Commencing at the mouth of the river emptying into the north-west angle of Cumberland Lake, thence westerly up the said river to its source, thence on a straight line in a westerly direction to the head of Green Lake, thence northerly to the elbow in the Beaver River, thence down the said river northerly to a point twenty miles from the said elbow; thence in westerly direction, keeping on a line generally parallel with the said Beaver River (above the elbow), and about twenty miles distance therefrom, to the source of the said river; thence northerly to the north-easterly point of the south shore of Red Deer Lake, continuing westerly along the said shore to the western limit thereof and thence due west to the Athabaska River, thence up the said river, against the stream, to the Jasper House, in the Rocky Mountains; thence on a course south-easterly, following the easterly range of the Mountains, to the source of the main branch of the Red Deer River; thence down the said river, with the stream, to the junction therewith of the outlet of the river, being the outlet of the Buffalo Lake; thence due east twenty miles; thence on a straight line south-eastwardly to the mouth of the said Red Deer River on the south branch of the Saskatchewan River; thence eastwardly and northwardly, following on the boundaries of the tracts conceded by the several Treaties numbered Four and Five, to the place of beginning;

And also all their rights, titles and privileges whatsoever, to all other lands, wherever situated, in the North-West Territories, or in any other Province or portion of Her Majesty's Dominions, situated and being within the Dominion of Canada.

The tract comprised within the lines above described, embracing an area of 121,000 square miles, be the same more or less;

To have and to hold the same to Her Majesty the Queen and Her successors forever;

And Her Majesty the Queen hereby agrees and undertakes to lay aside reserves for farming lands, due respect being had to lands at present cultivated by the said Indians, and other reserves for the benefit of the said Indians, to be administered and dealt with for them by Her Majesty's Government of the Dominion of Canada, provided all such reserves shall not exceed in all one square mile for each family of five, or in that proportion for larger or smaller families, in manner following, that is to say:—

That the Chief Superintendent of Indian Affairs shall depute and send a suitable person to determine and set apart the reserves for each band, after consulting with the Indians thereof as to the locality which may be found to be most suitable for them;

Provided, however, that Her Majesty reserves the right to deal with any settlers within the bounds of any lands reserved for any band as She shall deem fit, and also that the aforesaid reserves of lands or any interest therein, maybe sold or otherwise disposed of by Her Majesty's Government for the use and benefit of the said Indians entitled thereto, with their consent first had and obtained; and with a view to show the satisfaction of Her Majesty with the behaviour and good conduct of Her Indians, She hereby, through Her Commissioners, makes them a present of twelve dollars for each man, woman and child belonging to the bands here represented, in extinguishment of all claims heretofore preferred;

And further, Her Majesty agrees to maintain schools for instruction in such reserves hereby made, as to Her Government of the Dominion of Canada may seem advisable, whenever the Indians of the reserve shall desire it;

Her Majesty further agrees with Her said Indians that within the boundary of Indian reserves, until otherwise determined by Her Government of the Dominion of Canada, no intoxicating liquor shall be allowed to be introduced or sold, and all laws now in force or hereafter to be enacted to preserve Her Indian subjects inhabiting the reserves or living elsewhere within Her North-West Territories from the evil influence of the use of intoxicating liquors, shall be strictly enforced;

Her Majesty further agrees with Her said Indians that they, the said Indians, shall have right to pursue their avocations of hunting and fishing throughout the tract surrendered as hereinbefore described, subject to such regulations as may from time to time be made by Her Government of Her Dominion of Canada, and saving and excepting such tracts as may from time to time be required or taken up for settlement, mining, lumbering or other purposes by Her said Government of the Dominion of Canada, or by any of the subjects thereof, duly authorized therefor, by the said Government;

It is further agreed between Her Majesty and Her said Indians, that such sections of the reserves above indicated as may at any time be required for public works or buildings of what nature soever, may he appropriated for that purpose by Her Majesty's Government of the Dominion of Canada, due compensation being made for the value of any improvements thereon;

And further, that Her Majesty's Commissioners shall, as soon as possible after the execution of this treaty, cause to be taken, an accurate census of all the Indians inhabiting the tract above described, distributing them in families, and shall in every year ensuing the date hereof, at some period in each year, to be duly notified to the Indians, and at a place or places to be appointed for that purpose within the territory ceded, pay to each Indian person the sum of $5 per head yearly;

It is further agreed between Her Majesty and the said Indians, that the sum of $1500.00 per annum, shall be yearly and every year expended by Her Majesty in the purchase of ammunition and twine for nets for the use of the said Indians, in manner following, that is to say:—In the reasonable discretion as regards the distribution thereof, among the Indians inhabiting the several reserves, or otherwise included herein, of Her Majesty's Indian Agent having the supervision of this treaty;

It is further agreed between Her Majesty and the said Indians that the following articles shall be supplied to any band of the said Indians who are now cultivating the soil, or who shall hereafter commence to cultivate the land, that is to say:— Four hoes for every family actually cultivating, also two spades per family as aforesaid; one plough for every three families as aforesaid, one harrow for every three families as aforesaid; two scythes, and one whetstone and two hay forks and two reaping-hooks for every family as aforesaid; and also two axes, and also one cross-cut saw, and also one hand-saw, one pit-saw, the necessary files, one grindstone and one auger for each band; and also for each Chief for the use of his band, one chest of ordinary carpenter's tools; also for each band enough of wheat, barley, potatoes and oats to plant the land actually broken up for cultivation by such band; also for each band, four oxen, one bull and six cows, also one boar and two sows, and one handmill when any band shall raise sufficient grain therefor; all the aforesaid articles to be given once for all for the encouragement of the practice of agriculture among the Indians;

It is further agreed between Her Majesty and the said Indians, that each Chief, duly recognized as such, shall receive an annual salary of $25 per annum; and each subordinate officer, not exceeding four for each band, shall receive $15 per annum; and each such Chief and subordinate officer as aforesaid, shall also receive, once every three years, a suitable suit of clothing, and each Chief shall receive, in recognition of the closing of the treaty, a suitable flag and medal, and also, as soon as convenient, one horse, harness and waggon;

That in the event hereafter of the Indians comprised within this treaty being overtaken by any pestilence, or by a general famine, the Queen, on being satisfied and certified thereof by Her Indian Agent or Agents, will grant to the Indians assistance of such character and to such extent as Her Chief Superintendent of Indian Affairs shall deem necessary and sufficient to relieve the Indians from the calamity that shall have befallen them;

That during the next three years, after two or more of the reserves hereby agreed to be set apart to the Indians, shall have been agreed upon and surveyed, there shall be granted to the Indians included under the Chiefs adhering to the treaty at Carlton, each spring, the sum of $1000 to be expended for them by Her Majesty's Indian Agents, in the purchase of provisions for the use of such of the band as are actually settled on the reserves and are engaged in cultivating the soil, to assist them in such cultivation;

That a medicine chest shall be kept at the house of each Indian Agent for the use and benefit of the Indians, at the direction of such Agent;

That with regard to the Indians included under the Chiefs adhering to the treaty at Fort Pitt, and to those under Chiefs within the treaty limits who may hereafter give their adhesion hereto (exclusively, however, of the Indians of the Carlton region) there shall, during three years, after two or more reserves shall have been agreed upon and surveyed, be distributed each spring among the bands cultivating the soil on such reserves, by Her Majesty's Chief Indian Agent for this treaty in his discretion, a sum not exceeding $1000, in the purchase of provisions for the use of such members of the band as are actually settled on the reserves and engaged in the cultivation of the soil, to assist and encourage them in such cultivation;

That in lieu of waggons, if they desire it, and declare their option to that effect, there shall be given to each of the Chiefs adhering hereto, at Fort Pitt or elsewhere hereafter (exclusively of those in the Carlton district) in recognition of this treaty, as soon as the same can be conveniently transported, two carts, with iron bushings and tires;

And the undersigned Chiefs on their own behalf, and on behalf of all other Indians inhabiting the tract within ceded, do hereby solemnly promise and engage to strictly observe this treaty, and also to conduct and behave themselves as good and loyal subjects of Her Majesty the Queen;

They promise and engage that they will in all respects obey and abide by the law, and they will maintain peace and good order between each other, and also between themselves and other tribes of Indians, and between themselves and others of Her Majesty's subjects, whether Indians or whites, now inhabiting or hereafter to inhabit any part of the said ceded tracts, and that they will not molest the person or property of any inhabitant of such ceded tracts, or the property of Her Majesty the Queen, or interfere with or trouble any person passing or travelling through the said tracts or any part thereof; and that they will aid and assist the officers of Her Majesty in bringing to justice and punishment any Indian offending against the stipulations of this treaty or infringing the laws in force in the country so ceded.

In Witness Whereof, Her Majesty's said Commissioners and the said Indian Chiefs have hereunto subscribed and set their hands, at or near Fort Carlton, on the day and year aforesaid, and near Fort Pitt on the day above aforesaid.

Signed by the Chiefs within named in the presence of the following witnesses, the same having been first read and explained by Peter Erasmus, Peter Ballendine and the Rev. John McKay. . . .

Report of the Commissioners for Treaty No. 8

September 22, 1899 (Ottawa: Queen's Printer, 1966).

Winnipeg, Manitoba, 22nd September, 1899.

The Honourable
    Clifford Sifton,
        Superintendent General of Indian Affairs,
            Ottawa.

Sir,—We have the honour to transmit herewith the treaty which, under the Commission issued to us on the 5th day of April last, we have made with the Indians of the provisional district of Athabasca and parts of the country adjacent thereto, as described in the treaty and shown on the map attached. . . .

We met the Indians on the 20th, and on the 21st the treaty was signed.

As the discussions at the different points followed on much the same lines, we shall confine ourselves to a general statement of their import. There was a marked absence of the old Indian style of oratory. Only among the Wood Crees were any formal speeches made, and these were brief. The Beaver Indians are taciturn. The Chipewyans confined themselves to asking questions and making brief arguments. They appeared to be more adept at cross-examination than at speech-making, and the Chief at Fort Chipewyan displayed considerable keenness of intellect and much practical sense in pressing the claims of his band. They all wanted as liberal, if not more liberal, terms than were granted to the Indians of the plains. Some expected to be fed by the Government after the making of treaty, and all asked for assistance in seasons of distress and urged that the old and indigent who were no longer able to hunt and trap and were consequently often in distress should be cared for by the Government. They requested that medicines be furnished. At Vermilion, Chipewyan and Smith's Landing, an earnest appeal was made for the services of a medical man. There was expressed at every point the fear that the making of the treaty would be followed by the curtailment of the hunting and fishing privileges, and many were impressed with the notion that the treaty would lead to taxation and enforced military service. They seemed desirous of securing educational advantages for their children, but stipulated that in the matter of schools there should be no interference with their religious beliefs.

We pointed out that the Government could not undertake to maintain Indians in idleness; that the same means of earning a livelihood would continue after treaty as existed before it, and that the Indians would be expected to make use of them. We told them that the Government was always ready to give relief in cases of actual destitution, and that in seasons of distress they would without any special stipulation in the treaty receive such assistance as it was usual to give in order to prevent starvation among Indians in any part of Canada; and we stated that the attention of the Government would be called to the need of some special provision being made for assisting the old and indigent who were unable to work and [were] dependent on charity for the means of sustaining life. We promised that supplies of medicines would be put in the charge of persons selected by the Government at different points, and would be distributed free to those of the Indians who might require them. We explained that it would be practically impossible for the Government to arrange for regular medical attendance upon Indians so widely scattered over such an extensive territory. We assured them, however, that the Government would always be ready to avail itself of any opportunity of affording medical service just as it provided that the physician attached to the Commission should give free attendance to all Indians whom he might find in need of treatment as he passed through the country.

Our chief difficulty was the apprehension that the hunting and fishing privileges were to be curtailed. The provision in the treaty under which ammunition and twine is to be furnished went far in the direction of quieting the fears of the Indians, for they admitted that it would be unreasonable to furnish the means of hunting and fishing if laws were to be enacted which would make hunting and fishing so restricted as to render it impossible to make a livelihood by such pursuits. But over and above the provision, we had to solemnly assure them that only such laws as to hunting and fishing as were in the interest of the Indians and were found necessary in order to protect the fish and fur-bearing animals would be made, and that they would be as free to hunt and fish after the treaty as they would be if they never entered into it.

We assured them that the treaty would not lead to any forced interference with their mode of life, that it did not open the way to the imposition of any tax, and that there was no fear of enforced military service. We showed them that, whether treaty was made or not, they were subject to the law, bound to obey it, and liable to punishment for any infringements of it. We pointed out that the law was designed for the protection of all, and must be respected by all the inhabitants of the country, irrespective of colour or origin; and that, in requiring them to live at peace with white men who came into the country, and not to molest them in person or in property, it only required them to do what white men were required to do as to the Indians.

As to education, the Indians were assured that there was no need of any special stipulation, as it was the policy of the Government to provide in every part of the country, as far as circumstances would permit, for the education of Indian children, and that the law, which was as strong as a treaty, provided for non-interference with the religion of the Indians in schools maintained or assisted by the Government. . . .

In addition to the annuity, which we found it necessary to fix at the figures of Treaty Six, which covers adjacent territory, the treaty stipulates that assistance in the form of seed and implements and cattle will be given to those of the Indians who may take to farming, in the way of cattle and mowers to those who may devote themselves to cattle-raising, and that ammunition and twine will be given to those who continue to fish and hunt. The assistance in farming and ranching is only to be given when the Indians actually take to these pursuits, and it is not likely that for many years there will be a call for any considerable expenditure under these heads. The only Indians of the territory ceded who are likely to take to cattle-raising are those about Lesser Slave Lake and along the Peace River, where there is quite an extent of ranching country; and although there are stretches of cultivable land in those parts of the country, it is not probable that the Indians will, while present conditions obtain, engage in farming further than the raising of roots in a small way, as is now done to some extent. In the main, the demand will be for ammunition and twine, as the great majority of the Indians will continue to hunt and fish for a livelihood. It does not appear likely that the conditions of the country on either side of the Athabasca and Slave Rivers or about Athabasca Lake will be so changed as to affect hunting or trapping, and it is safe to say that so long as the fur-bearing animals remain, the great bulk of the Indians will continue to hunt and to trap.

The Indians are given the option of taking reserves or land in severalty. As the extent of the country treated for made it impossible to define reserves or holdings, and as the Indians were not prepared to make selections, we confined ourselves to an undertaking to have reserves and holdings set apart in the future, and the Indians were satisfied with the promise that this would be done when required. There is no immediate necessity for the general laying out of reserves or the allotting of land. It will be quite time enough to do this as advancing settlement makes necessary the surveying of the land. Indeed, the Indians were generally averse to being placed on reserves. It would have been impossible to have made a treaty if we had not assured them that there was no intention of confining them to reserves. We had to very clearly explain to them that the provision for reserves and allotments of land were made for their protection, and to secure to them in perpetuity a fair portion of the land ceded, in the event of settlement advancing. . . .

The Indians with whom we treated differ in many respects from the Indians of the organized territories. They indulge in neither paint nor feathers, and never clothe themselves in blankets. Their dress is of the ordinary style and many of them are well clothed. In the summer they live in teepees, but many of them have log houses in which they live in winter. The Cree language is the chief language of trade, and some of the Beavers and Chipewyans speak it in addition to their own tongues. All the Indians we met were with rare exceptions professing Christians, and showed evidences of the work which missionaries have carried on among them for many years. A few of them have had their children avail themselves of the advantages afforded by boarding schools established at different missions. None of the tribes appear to have any very definite organization. They are held together mainly by the language bond. The chiefs and headmen are simply the most efficient hunters and trappers. They are not law-makers and leaders in the sense that the chiefs and headmen of the plains and of old Canada were. The tribes have no very distinctive characteristics, and as far as we could learn no traditions of any import. The Wood Crees are an off-shoot of the Crees of the South. The Beaver Indians bear some resemblance to the Indians west of the mountains. The Chipewyans are physically the superior tribe. The Beavers have apparently suffered most from scrofula and phthisis, and there are marks of these diseases more or less among all the tribes.

Although in manners and dress the Indians of the North are much further advanced in civilization than other Indians were when treaties were made with them, they stand as much in need of the protection afforded by the law to aborigines as do any other Indians of the country, and are as fit subjects for the paternal care of the Government. . . .

We desire to express our high appreciation of the valuable and most willing service rendered by Inspector Snyder and the corps of police under him, and at the same time to testify to the efficient manner in which the members of our staff performed their several duties. The presence of a medical man was much appreciated by the Indians, and Dr. West, the physician to the Commission, was most assiduous in attending to the great number of Indians who sought his services. We would add that the Very Reverend Father Lacombe, who was attached to the Commission, zealously assisted us in treating with the Crees.

The actual number of Indians paid was:—

7 Chiefs at $32	$224 00
23 Headmen at $22	506 00
2,187 Indians at $12	26,974 00
	Total: $26,974 00

A detailed statement of the Indians treated with and of the money paid is appended. We have the honour to be, sir,
Your obedient servants,
DAVID LAIRD,
J. H. ROSS,
J. A. J. MCKENNA.
Indian Treaty Commissioners.

SELECTED BIBLIOGRAPHY

Aronson, S. "The Authority of the Crown to Make Treaties with Indians" [1993] 2 C.N.L.R. 1.
Barkwell, P. "The Medicine Chest Clause in Treaty No. 6" [1981] 4 C.N.L.R. 1.
Bell, C. "*R.* v. *Badger*: One Step Forward and Two Steps Back?" (1997) 8 Const. Forum 21.
Canada, DIAND. *Living Treaties, Lasting Agreements: Report of the Task Force to Review Comprehensive Claims Policy* (Ottawa: DIAND, 1985).
Cardinal, H. *The Unjust Society: The Tragedy of Canada's Indians* (Edmonton: Hurtig, 1969).
Fumoleau, R. *As Long As This Land Shall Last: A History of Treaty 8 and Treaty 11 1870–1939*

(Toronto: McClelland and Stewart, 1973).

Grammond, S. "Aboriginal Treaties and Canadian Law" (1994) 20 Queen's L.J. 57.

Green, L.C. "Legal Significance of Treaties Affecting Canada's Indians" (1972) 1 Anglo–Am. L. Rev. 119.

Henderson, W., & D. Ground. "Survey of Aboriginal Land Claims" (1994) 26:1 Ottawa L. Rev. 187.

Indian Treaties and Surrenders Volumes 1 to 3 (1891, 1912; reprint Saskatoon: Fifth House, 1992, 1993).

Isaac, T. *Aboriginal and Treaty Rights in the Maritimes: The Marshall Decisions and Beyond* (Saskatoon: Purich Publishing Ltd., 2001).

———. "The Courts, Government and Public Policy: The Significance of *R.* v. *Marshall*" (2000) 63:2 Sask. L.R. 701.

———. "The *Marshall* Decision and Governments' Duty to Regulate" (2001) 22:5 Policy Options 50.

Knoll, D. "Treaty and Aboriginal Hunting Rights" [1979] 1 C.N.L.R. 1.

Lysyk, K. "The Unique Constitutional Position of the Canadian Indian" (1967) 45 Can. Bar Rev. 513.

Morris, A. *The Treaties of Canada with the Indians of Manitoba and the North-West Territories* (1880; reprint, Saskatoon: Fifth House, 1991).

Paul, D. *We Were Not the Savages: A Micmac Perspective on the Collision of European and Aboriginal Civilization* (Halifax: Nimbus, 1993).

Price, R., ed. *The Spirit of the Alberta Indian Treaties.* Montreal: Institute for Research on Public Policy, 1980.

Savino, V., & E. Schumacher. "'Whenever the Indians of the Reserve Should Desire It': An Analysis of the First Nation Treaty Right to Education" [1992] 21:3 Man. L.J. 476.

Treaty 7 Elders and Tribal Council. *The True Spirit and Original Intent of Treaty 7* (Montreal & Kingston: McGill-Queen's University Press, 1996).

Venne, S. "Understanding Treaty 6: An Indigenous Perspective" in M. Asch, ed. *Aboriginal and Treaty Rights in Canada* (Vancouver: U.B.C. Press, 1997) 173.

Wildsmith, B. "Pre-Confederation Treaties" in B. Morse, ed. *Aboriginal Peoples and the Law* (Ottawa: Carleton University Press, 1985).

Woodward, J. Chapter 21 in *Native Law* (Toronto: Carswell, 1989) looseleaf, 403–16.

Zlotkin, N. "Post-Confederation Treaties" in B. Morse, ed. *Aboriginal Peoples and the Law* (Ottawa: Carleton University Press, 1985).

Chapter 3

FEDERAL, PROVINCIAL, AND TERRITORIAL POWERS AND DUTIES

INTRODUCTION

Parliament and the provincial and territorial legislatures have enacted a variety of legislation and regulations concerning Aboriginal people. This chapter reviews (*a*) the application of federal, provincial, and territorial authority respecting Aboriginal people, (*b*) the Crown's duty to consult and accommodate Aboriginal people, and (*c*) the fiduciary relationship between the Crown and Aboriginal people.

FEDERAL AUTHORITY

Subsection 91(24) of the *Constitution Act, 1867* (s. 91(24))[1] assigns exclusive legislative authority[2] to Parliament over "Indians, and Lands reserved for the Indians." Beginning in 1868[3] and culminating with the present *Indian Act*,[4] Parliament has exercised such exclusive legislative authority by enacting legislation dealing specifically with Indians and lands reserved for them, including the *Indian Oil and Gas Act*[5] and the *First Nations Land Management Act*.[6] Regulations such as the *Indian Mining Regulations*,[7] the *Indian Oil and Gas Regulations*,[8] and the *Indian Timber Regulations*,[9] among others,[10] complete the statutory and regulatory regime exercised by Parliament respecting Indians and lands reserved for them. The Department of Indian Affairs and Northern Development (DIAND) oversees the federal government's responsibilities respecting Indians and administers the *Indian Act*.[11]

---

[1] *Constitution Act, 1867* (U.K.), 30 & 31 Vict., c. 3, reprinted in R.S.C. 1985, App. II, No. 5.

[2] See *Re Waters and Water Powers*, [1929] S.C.R. 200.

[3] *An Act providing for the organization of the department of the Secretary of State of Canada, and for the management of Indian and Ordnance Lands*, S.C. 1868, c. 42. The first federal statute that dealt substantively and exclusively with Indians was the *Indian Act*, S.C. 1876, c. 18.

[4] *Indian Act*, R.S.C. 1985, c. I–5.

[5] *Indian Oil and Gas Act*, R.S.C. 1985, c. I–7. This act regulates the exploitation of oil and gas reserves on Indian reserve lands.

[6] *First Nations Land Management Act*, S.C. 1999, c. 24.

[7] *Indian Mining Regulations*, C.R.C. c. 956 (1978).

[8] *Indian Oil and Gas Regulations*, S.O.R./94-753 (1995).

[9] *Indian Timber Regulations*, C.R.C. c. 961 (1978).

[10] Other regulations enacted under the *Indian Act* include *Disposal of Forfeited Goods and Chattels Regulations*, C.R.C., c. 948 (1978); *Indian Band Council Borrowing Regulations*, C.R.C., c. 949 (1978); *Indian Band Council Procedure Regulations*, C.R.C., c. 950 (1978); *Indian Band Election Regulations*, C.R.C., c. 952 (1978); *Indian Band Revenue Moneys Regulations*, C.R.C., c. 953 (1978); *Indian Estates Regulations*, C.R.C., c. 954 (1978); *Indian Referendum Regulations*, C.R.C., c. 957 (1978); *Indian Reserve Traffic Regulations*, C.R.C., c. 959 (1978); *Indian Reserve Waste Disposal Regulations*, C.R.C., c. 960 (1978); and *Indian Bands Council Method of Election Regulations*, SOR/90–46.

[11] *Department of Indian Affairs and Northern Development Act*, R.S.C. 1985, c. I-6.

Indian Act

First enacted in 1876 and amended many times since then,[12] the *Indian Act* addresses almost every aspect of Indian life and governance. The Act is a mix of paternalism and assimilation and is seen by many as being antiquated. The original objectives of the Act were to:

1. assimilate Indians into mainstream Canadian society;

2. control Indians' relationship with the federal Crown;[13] and

3. protect a small amount of Canada's land base for the exclusive use and benefit of Indians.[14]

The 1886 *Indian Act*[15] stated that "Every Indian or person who engages in or assists in celebrating the Indian festival known as 'Potlatch' . . . is guilty of a misdemeanor." A revised version of this section was repealed by the 1951 *Indian Act*.[16] The potlatch ritual, including ceremonial feasting, has special significance for Indians along the Pacific coast of Canada. The 1869 Act[17] introduced the concept of enfranchisement and permitted Indians to relinquish their Indian status. Section 17 of this Act provided that enfranchised Indians ". . . shall no longer be deemed Indians within the meaning of the laws relating to Indians. . . ." Subsection 86(1) stated:

> Any Indian who may be admitted to the degree of Doctor of Medicine, or to any other degree by any University of Learning, or who may be admitted in any Province of the Dominion to practice law . . . or who may enter Holy Orders . . . shall *ipso facto* become and be enfranchised under this Act.[18]

This provision, and others like it, prevented Indians from pursuing higher education while retaining their Indian status.

The Act contains various rights and restrictions applicable to Indians registered as such under the Act and establishes the reserve land system. There are more than 2,300 reserves in Canada for more than six hundred Indian bands totalling approximately 2.7 million hectares of land. "Reserves" are lands that: (1) are set aside for the use and benefit of Indians, (2) are governed by the Act, and (3) have been established using a variety of mechanisms including:

---

[12] See S. Venne, ed., *Indian Acts and Amendments 1868–1975: An Indexed Collection* (Saskatoon: University of Saskatchewan Native Law Centre, 1981); *The Indian Act and Amendments 1970–1993: An Indexed Collection* (Saskatoon: University of Saskatchewan Native Law Centre, 1993); and T. Isaac, *Pre-1868 Legislation Concerning Indians* (Saskatoon: University of Saskatchewan Native Law Centre, 1993).

[13] K. Jamieson, "Sex Discrimination and the *Indian Act*" in J.R. Ponting, ed., *Arduous Journey: Canadian Indians and Decolonization* (Toronto: McLelland and Stewart, 1986) at 117 summarizes three primary functions of the *Indian Act*:

> (1) "civilizing" the Indians—that is, assimilating them (and their lands) into Eurocanadian citizenry; (2) while accomplishing this, the ever more efficient, "better management" of Indians and their lands was always a goal to be pursued and, following on this, an important element in better management was controlling expenditure and resources; (3) to accomplish this efficiency it became important to define who was an Indian and who was not.

[14] Even the protection of Indian lands was not certain under the Act. For example, in British Columbia, reserve lands were unilaterally cut back in size in the early twentieth century; see the *British Columbia Indian Lands Settlement Act*, S.C. 1920, c. 51.

[15] *Indian Act*, S.C. 1886, c. 43, s. 114.

[16] *Indian Act*, S.C. 1951, c. 29.

[17] *An Act for the gradual enfranchisement of Indians, the better management of Indians affairs, and to extend the provisions of the Act 31ˢᵗ Victoria, Chapter 42*, S.C. 1869, c. 6.

[18] This section became s. 111 of the *Indian Act*, R.S.C. 1906, c. 81, and eventually was repealed by S.C. 1919–1920, c. 50, s. 3.

a) the setting aside of land by agreement of the federal and provincial governments;[19]

b) by authority of the federal Royal prerogative, as used in the northern territories;[20]

c) lands purchased by the Crown for use by Indians, such as those reserves established in the Maritimes;

d) by way of formal federal executive instrument usually in the form of an order-in-council; and

e) by establishing reserves out of lands over which treaties do not apply, such as in British Columbia.

Certain rights attach to reserve land, such as the tax exemption for property owned by an Indian or an Indian band that is situated on a reserve.[21] In addition, property owned by an Indian or Indian band that is situated on a reserve cannot be seized by a non-Indian.[22] Although s. 89 of the Act protects Indian property from seizure, it also makes it difficult for Indians to obtain loans because their on-reserve property, including all reserve lands, cannot be used as collateral. This is a significant barrier to economic development on reserves.

Amendments to the *Indian Act*

The *Indian Act* has been amended many times over the years, with a number of failed attempts. On June 15, 1969, after months of consultation with Aboriginal people, the then Minister of DIAND, Jean Chrétien, presented a White Paper to Parliament entitled "Statement of the Government of Canada on Indian Policy, 1969." In effect, it called for a repeal of the *Indian Act* and would have:

1. ended the federal statutory responsibility for Indians;

2. terminated Indians' special legal status;

3. dismantled DIAND;

4. ended federal fiscal transfers to the provinces; and

5. transferred directly to Indians control over reserve land with the goal of eliminating the federal Crown's fiduciary role.

The White Paper was rejected by Aboriginal people and the general public and was ultimately set aside by the Government of Canada.

On December 12, 1996, Bill C-79, the *Indian Act Optional Modification Act,* was introduced into the House of Commons. The bill was to provide Indian bands more control to govern and to provide less control to the Minister and government officials. To simplify the process of approval in other matters, the Minister rather than the governor in council, would have had the authority to grant management and control of reserve lands and to control, manage, and expend revenue moneys to Indian band governments. It also lengthened the term of office for chiefs and councillors under the Act's electoral system to three years from two years.[23] This bill died primarily because Indian bands and the federal

---

[19] See *Ontario Mining Co.* v. *Seybold*, [1903] A.C. 73 at 82–83 (J.C.P.C.).

[20] *Hay River* v. *R.* (1979), 101 D.L.R. (3d) 184 at 186 (F.C.T.D.).

[21] *Indian Act, supra* note 4 at s. 87.

[22] *Ibid.* at s. 89.

[23] This would have been particularly helpful for governance on-reserve since, under the existing system of two-

government could not agree on the amendments.

On January 7, 1998, the Minister of DIAND and the federal Interlocutor for Métis and Non-Status Indians[24] released the federal government's response to the Report of the Royal Commission on Aboriginal Peoples in a report entitled *Gathering Strength—Canada's Aboriginal Action Plan*. Proposals in *Gathering Strength* included: (*a*) a $350-million fund to support community-based healing to deal with the aftermath of abuse in the residential school system, (*b*) a commitment to develop further Aboriginal governance options, including capacity-building and the creation of an entity to assist Aboriginal groups to negotiate and implement self-government, (*c*) a commitment to develop a new fiscal relationship with Aboriginal people, and (*d*) a platform for the development of a strong Aboriginal human resource and economic base. Along with acknowledging the federal government's role in the residential school system and the death of Métis leader Louis Riel, *Gathering Strength's* "Statement of Reconciliation" affirmed that the "Government of Canada . . . formally expresses to all Aboriginal people in Canada our profound regret for past actions of the federal government which have contributed to these difficult pages in the history of our relationship together."[25]

On April 30, 2001 the Minister launched another initiative to update the *Indian Act*, primarily with respect to governance. The First Nations Governance Initiative was intended to assist in designing a new statutory framework for Indian governance including: (*a*) updating electoral and voting systems for reserve-based governments,[26] (*b*) balancing the interests of on- and off-reserve Indian band members, and (*c*) enhancing the resources available to band councils to operate effective governments. The initiative has been met with a great deal of concern by Indian leaders across Canada.

As part of the initiative, Bill C-61 was introduced into the House of Commons on July 14, 2002 and reintroduced as Bill C-7. The *First Nations Governance Act*, is the federal government's attempt to modernise the *Indian Act* and provide more accountability to Indian people by their reserve-based governments. For example, s. 5 of Bill C-7 calls for the introduction of leadership selection codes by Indian bands that would ensure that guidelines respecting band council elections are put in writing, including those Indian bands that presently operate by custom election. Bill C-7 also contains provisions regarding the establishment of codes for financial management and accountability by Indian bands and for administration of government, dealing with matters such as conflicts of interest, access to information, privacy, and standards regarding the frequency of, and notice relating to, Indian band meetings.

Although the notion of more authority and control over their own lives is appealing to many Indians, other Indians also feel comfortable with the federal government providing a check on the actions of chiefs and councils. A mechanism is needed by which Indian bands can exercise as much control over their lives as possible, but in a manner that provides as much accountability and transparency as possible, not only to their own Indian constituents but also to public governments in Canada respecting the expenditure

year terms, many chiefs and councils do not have enough time to implement their mandate.

[24] Note that DIAND (Indian and Northern Affairs Canada) does not have responsibility for the Métis and non-status Indians. The federal government maintains that it does not have legislative authority over the Métis and non-status Indians, thereby attempting to limit the federal government's fiduciary and fiscal responsibilities for these Aboriginal people.

[25] Canada, Department of Indian Affairs and Northern Development, *Gathering Strength—Canada's Aboriginal Action Plan* (Ottawa: Minister of Public Works and Government Services Canada, 1997), 4–5.

[26] See *Corbiere v. Canada (Min. of Indian and Northern Affairs)*, [1999] 2 S.C.R. 203.

by Indian bands of public funds. At the time of writing, Bill C-7 was the target of extensive criticism from Aboriginal and non-Aboriginal people.[27]

Jurisdiction Respecting "Indians" and "Aboriginal People"

The *Indian Act* applies to all registered Indians and Indian band governments across
Canada, with a few exceptions.[28] As of 2001, there were more than 690,000 registered
Indians in Canada.[29] The Act defines the term "Indian" for the purposes of the Act and
establishes a register to record the names of qualified individuals.[30] Individuals coming
within the statutory definition of Indians are known as "status" or "registered" Indians.
Registered Indians may live on Indian reserves and are entitled to the privileges provided
for in the Act.

The *Indian Act* states that an Indian is a person who is registered as an "Indian" under
the Act, or who may be entitled to such registration.[31] Courts have held that corporations
wholly owned by Indians are not "Indians" for the purposes of the Act.[32] Subsection
91(24) provides that Indians and the Inuit[33] and their lands are within the jurisdiction of
Parliament. The Inuit come within the meaning of "Indians" for the purposes of s. 91(24),
but not within the meaning of "Indian" under the *Indian Act*, and therefore the *Indian
Act* does not apply to them.[34] The Métis and those Indians who are not registered under
the *Indian Act* are not subject to the Act. It is unclear whether the Métis (those of mixed
Indian and non-Indian descent) are considered "Indians" for the purposes of s. 91(24).
The jurisdictional responsibility for Indians is particularly important for the federal and
provincial governments because it is an important factor in determining which level of
government is financially responsible for the provision of services.

"Aboriginal people" is not only a term commonly used to define the Indian, Métis,
and Inuit peoples of Canada, but is also the term used in s. 35 of the *Constitution Act,
1982*[35] and in s. 25 of the *Canadian Charter of Rights and Freedoms*.[36] Subsection 35(2) of
the *Constitution Act, 1982* defines Aboriginal peoples as being the "Indian, Inuit and
Métis peoples of Canada." Approximately 3 percent[37] of the population of Canada, or
about one million people, identify themselves as being of Aboriginal origin. However,
"Aboriginal origin" does not denote the vast cultural differences that exist not only be-

---

[27] For example, see the Canadian Bar Association, "Submission on Bill C-7—*First Nations Governance Act*"
(CBA, National Aboriginal Law Section, February 2003); see also *Federation of Saskatchewan Indians* v. *Canada*,
[2003] 2 C.N.L.R. 131 (F.C.T.D.).
[28] Those Indian bands that have signed modern treaties are almost entirely excluded from the Act, but usually
with the exception that the registration provisions of the Act continue to apply. Also, some Indian bands have
alternative governance arrangements that are outside the Act, such as the Sechelt Indian Band of British Columbia. See the *Sechelt Indian Band Self-Government Act*, S.C. 1986, c. 27.
[29] Canada, Indian and Northern Affairs, *Basic Departmental Data 2002* (DIAND: March 2003).
[30] See L. Gilbert, *Entitlement to Indian Status and Membership Codes in Canada* (Toronto: Carswell, 1996).
[31] *Indian Act, supra* note 4 at s. 2(1).
[32] See *Four B. Manufacturing Ltd.* v. *U.G.W.*, [1980] 1 S.C.R. 1031; *Re Stony Plain Indian Reserve No. 135*,
[1982] 1 C.N.L.R. 133 (Alta. C.A.); *Kinookimaw Beach Assn.* v. *R.*, [1979] 4 C.N.L.R. 101 (Sask. C.A.); and
Western Industrial Contractors Ltd. v. *Sarcee Development Ltd.*, [1979] 2 C.N.L.R. 107 (Alta. C.A.).
[33] See *Re Eskimos*, [1939] S.C.R. 104.
[34] *Ibid.*; s. 4(1) of the Act states that the term "Indian" as used in the Act "does not include any person of the
race of aborigines commonly referred to as Inuit."
[35] *Constitution Act, 1982*, Schedule B to the *Canada Act 1982* (U.K.), 1982, c. 11, as am. by the *Constitution
Amendment Proclamation 1983*, R.S.C. 1985, App. II, No. 46, adding ss. 35(3) and 35(4).
[36] *Ibid.*, Part 1.
[37] Canada, Statistics Canada, *2001 Census of Canada: Population reporting an Aboriginal identity, by mother
tongue, provinces and territories* (April 25, 2003).

tween Métis, Inuit, and Indian peoples, but also between groups and tribes within these groups. Although the term "Aboriginal peoples" has a legal definition within the *Constitution Act, 1982*, by itself, the term does not encompass all the legal categories affecting Aboriginal people.[38] The term "Native" was used predominantly throughout the 1970s and 1980s to make reference to Aboriginal people. Many use the term "First Nation" to refer to Indian bands. The term "Indian bands" is used throughout this text because it is legally defined by the Act, while the term "First Nation," with the exception of the *First Nations Land Management Act,* is not.[39]

There is also a distinction between treaty and non-treaty Indians. Treaty Indians are those Indians who can trace their ancestry to Indians who signed treaties in Canada, whereas non-treaty Indians cannot. To confuse matters even more, a person can be a treaty Indian and not be registered or registrable under the Act. This means that although a person may be entitled to rights under a treaty, they may not be entitled to rights as an Indian under the Act. Another group are those Aboriginal people who are beneficiaries under land claims agreements or modern treaties, but who may not be registrable under the Act.

At the national level, the Assembly of First Nations[40] represents registered Indian interests, while the Congress of Aboriginal Peoples[41] represents the interests of non-registered Indians, some urban Indians, and some Métis. The Métis National Council[42] represents national Métis interests, while the Inuit Tapirisat of Canada[43] represents the interests of the Inuit nationally.

On April 17, 1985, the so-called Bill C-31 amendments to the *Indian Act* came into force and modernized the Indian membership and registration provisions of the Act. Prior to Bill C-31, the Act: (*a*) provided that Indian status was passed on through the male line; (*b*) allowed for no or little Indian involvement in determining and managing the membership of Indian bands and "Indian" registration; and (*c*) discriminated against Indian women on the basis of their sex. In the latter case, registered Indian women who married non-Indian men lost their Indian status and their right to live on reserve, among other benefits. Conversely, registered Indian men who married non-Indian women retained their Indian status and in addition passed Indian status along to their wives. Although the new membership regime has sought to clarify and modernize the older membership and status provisions, it is complex and has not clarified the issue of who has a right to reside on reserve lands.[44]

Reserve Lands

Subsection 91(24) of the *Constitution Act, 1867* also confers on Parliament the exclusive legislative authority respecting "Lands reserved for the Indians." This component of s. 91(24)

---

[38] See Thomas Isaac, "The Power of Constitutional Language: The Case Against Using 'Aboriginal Peoples' As a Referent for First Nations" (1993) 19:1 Queen's L.J. 415; C. Chartier, "'Indian': An Analysis of the Term Used in Section 91(24) of the British North America Act, 1867" (1978–79) 43 Sask. L. Rev. 37; and P. Chartrand, "'Terms of Division': Problems of 'Outside-Naming' for Aboriginal People in Canada" (1991) 2:2 Journal of Indigenous Stud. 1.

[39] Subsection 2(1) of the FNLMA, *supra* note 6, defines "first nation" as a "band named in the schedule" to the FNLMA.

[40] Assembly of First Nations, online: <http://www.afn.ca>.

[41] Congress of Aboriginal Peoples, online: <http://www.abo-peoples.org>.

[42] Metis National Council, online: <http://www.metisnation.ca>.

[43] Inuit Tapirisat of Canada, online: <http://www.tapirisat.ca>.

[44] For a more detailed discussion of this issue, see chapter 8, "Aboriginal Women."

not only includes those lands formally designated as reserves (relatively small commu-nity-based segments of land), but also lands recognized as reserves under the *Royal Procla-mation of 1763*[45] and all lands that remain subject to Aboriginal title. This grant of legis-lative power to Parliament, however, does not necessarily carry with it proprietary rights. Underlying title to the land remains with the Crown in right of the provinces, with the exception of the northern territories.

The *Indian Act* governs the use and development of Indian reserve lands and resources. Lands that have been reserved for an Indian band under the Act are held by the federal Crown in trust for the use and benefit of a band. The Act imposes stringent restrictions on the transfer of any land that is "reserve" land, which is defined in s. 2(1) of the Act as follows:

(a) A tract of land, the legal title to which is vested in Her Majesty, that has been set apart by Her Majesty for the use and benefit of a band, and

(b) Except for section 18(2), sections 20 to 25, 28, 36 to 38, 42, 44, 46, 48 to 51, 58 and 60 and the Regulations made under any of those provisions, includes designated lands.

Any land in which the legal title is vested in the Crown for the use and benefit of an Indian band is considered to be reserve land for the purposes of the Act.[46] Although reserves are defined in the Act, no legislative provisions exist regarding the creation or expansion of reserves. Reserve status is created by the governor in council (usually by an order-in-council), through the exercise of the Crown's royal prerogative. The creation and expansion of reserves is guided by the Additions to Reserves Policy of DIAND.[47]

In *Ross River Dena Council Band* v. *Canada*,[48] the Supreme Court of Canada consid-ered whether a reserve had been created with respect to a parcel of land that is now the Indian band's village. Although LeBel J., for the majority, held that no reserve had been created, he set out a number of principles to guide courts in considering whether a reserve had been created in various circumstances:

Thus, in the Yukon Territory as well as elsewhere in Canada, there appears to be no single procedure for creating reserves, although an Order-in-Council has been the most common and undoubtedly best and clearest procedure used to create reserves. (See: *Canadian Pacific Ltd.* v. *Paul*, [1988] 2 S.C.R. 654, at pp. 674–75; . . .) Whatever method is employed, the Crown must have had an intention to create a reserve. This intention must be possessed by Crown agents holding sufficient authority to bind the Crown. For example, this intention may be evidenced either by an exercise of executive authority such as an Order-in-Council, or on the basis of specific statutory provisions creating a particular reserve. Steps must be taken in order to set apart land. The setting apart must occur for the benefit of Indians. And, finally, the band concerned must have accepted the setting apart and must have started to make use of the lands so set apart. Hence, the process remains fact-sensitive. The evalu-ation of its legal effect turns on a very contextual and fact-driven analysis. Thus, this analy-sis must be performed on the basis of the record.[49]

---

[45] *Royal Proclamation of 1763*, R.S.C. 1985, App. II, No. 1.

[46] Reserve lands can extend beyond the formal boundaries of an Indian reserve, such as severalty lands as noted in the March 27, 2000 agreement of the McLeod Lake Indian Band when it adhered to Treaty No. 8; see *Chingee* v. *B.C.*, [2003] 1 C.N.L.R. 24 (B.C.S.C.).

[47] Indian and Northern Affairs Canada, *Communications Toolkit for First Nations on Additions to Reserves* (Dec 30, 2002), online: Additions To Reserve—Indian and Northern Affairs Canada <http://www.ainc-inac.gc.ca/pr/pub/atr/atr19_e.html>.

[48] *Ross River Dena Council Band* v. *Canada*, [2002] 2 S.C.R. 816.

[49] *Ibid.*, at para. 67.

Ross River is significant because the above-noted indicia of what constitutes a setting aside of land for the purposes of creating a reserve are so broad and fact-dependent that it leaves open for debate many other lands set aside for Indian bands as being "reserves" for the purposes of the Act.

Section 38 of the *Indian Act* confirms that an Indian band may not directly transfer or lease reserve lands and prohibits any conveyance of title or the granting of any interest in reserve lands unless the lands have been absolutely surrendered to the Crown or unless otherwise permitted by the Act.

Under the *Indian Act*, reserves, including designated land (temporarily surrendered as reserve land, usually for development purposes or leases), allow Indians to protect personal property from seizure by creditors. A creditor (other than an Indian or an Indian band) may not seize the assets of an Indian situated on a reserve. However, an exception to the general prohibition against seizure of Indian property on a reserve is provided for in the case where the secured party maintains a right of possession or a right of title in the chattel seized.[50]

Sections 37 to 41 of the *Indian Act* regulate surrenders (selling) and designations (leasing) of reserve land. Although certain procedural steps must be followed, essentially the Indian band turns the reserve land over to the Minister, either absolutely or conditionally, for the purposes of leasing or selling the land to a third party on behalf of the band. There is an outstanding legal issue regarding the effect of a surrender and whether surrendered Indian land remains within federal jurisdiction under s. 91(24). While some decisions suggest that absolute surrenders of reserve land equate to federal jurisdiction no longer applying,[51] other decisions suggest that surrendered lands remain subject to federal jurisdiction.[52]

In *Osoyoos Indian Band* v. *Oliver (Town)*,[53] the Supreme Court of Canada considered an appeal by the Osoyoos Indian Band concerning whether the Band had the authority to assess and impose a tax on a piece of property that crossed the Band's reserve land. At issue was whether the land in question was "in the reserve" within the meaning of s. 83(1)(a) of the Act, which states:

> Without prejudice to the powers conferred by section 81, the council of a band may, subject to the approval of the Minister, make by-laws for any or all of the following purposes, namely,
>
> (a) subject to subsections (2) and (3), taxation for local purposes of land, or interests in land, in the reserve, including rights to occupy, possess or use land in the reserve;

Osoyoos concerned the interpretation to be given to a 1957 order-in-council made under s. 35 of the *Indian Act* granting an interest in the reserve land at issue to the Province of British Columbia. The Court allowed the appeal and held that the order-in-council was ambiguous as to the nature of interest transferred and therefore did not evince a clear and plain intention to extinguish the Band's interest in the reserve land. The Court commented on the connection between the Aboriginal interest in reserve land and the nature of Aboriginal title, and stated that "[a]lthough the two interests are not identical,

---

[50] Subsection 89(2) of the Act states "A person who sells to a band or a member of a band a chattel under an agreement whereby the right of property or right of possession thereto remains wholly or in part in the seller may exercise his rights under the agreement notwithstanding that the chattel is situated on a reserve."

[51] *R.* v. *Smith*, [1983] 1 S.C.R. 554.

[52] *Surrey* v. *Peace Arch Ent. Ltd.* (1970), 74 W.W.R. 380 (B.C.C.A.).

[53] *Osoyoos Indian Band* v. *Oliver (Town)*, [2001] 3 S.C.R. 746.

they are fundamentally similar."[54] The Court also held that the Aboriginal interests in reserve land and in Aboriginal title include similar interests: both are inalienable except to the Crown, both are rights of use and occupation, both are held communally, and both are distinct from normal proprietary interests.[55] On the issue of the communal nature of reserve lands, it is important to note that reserve lands can be held (but not owned) individually.[56] Also, considering the different sources of reserve land, overly general similarities between reserve land and Aboriginal title are difficult to understand (i.e., a reserve that is not based at all on a claim of Aboriginal title).

Section 89 of the *Indian Act* contains the general prohibition against the mortgage or seizure of property belonging to Indians on reserve lands. Depending upon the circumstances and nature of the security interest, creditors, with some success, assign their debts to an Indian, thereby allowing the Indian to seize the property on reserve.[57] Subsection 89(1.1) provides an exception to the seizure exemption for leasehold interests in designated lands. Subsections 89(1) and (1.1) of the Act state:

> (1) Subject to this Act, the real and personal property of an Indian or a band situated on a reserve is not subject to charge, pledge, mortgage, attachment, levy, seizure, distress or execution in favour or at the instance of any person other than an Indian or a band.

> (1.1) Notwithstanding subsection (1), a leasehold interest in designated lands is subject to charge, pledge, mortgage, attachment, levy, seizure, distress and execution.

This prohibition in s. 89(1) of the Act is relevant only to security interests in the real or personal property of an "Indian." The Act does not regulate the personal property of a non-Indian which is situated on reserve lands. However, questions arise over whether the leasehold interests of non-Indians over reserve lands held by individual Indians can be mortgaged in a form that can be executed upon. As well, in light of: (*a*) the general purpose behind the Act to protect Indian reserve lands, (*b*) the express exemption from s. 89(1) of the Act for leasehold interests in designated lands pursuant to s. 89(1.1) of the Act, and (*c*) the general prohibition against seizure of Indian reserve lands in ss. 29 and 89(1) of the Act, questions remain about whether mortgaged leasehold interests held by non-Indians on non-designated reserve lands may be subject to the seizure, mortgage, and execution restrictions in ss. 29 and 89(1) of the Act. The better view probably is that a mortgaged leasehold interest, as a distinct estate, between non-Indians is not captured by the Act, since the lease and the mortgage are not the property of Indians. However, s. 89(1.1) creates uncertainty in this conclusion.

First Nations Land Management Act

On June 17, 1999, the *First Nations Land Management Act*[58] was proclaimed into law. The Act allows Indian bands named in the schedule to the Act to be legally responsible for managing their reserve land according to an agreement between the Indian bands and DIAND, and to be subject to the *First Nations Land Management Act* rather than the

---

[54] *Ibid.* at para. 41; see *R. v. Guerin*, [1984] 2 S.C.R. 335 at p. 379; *Delgamuukw v. B.C.*, [1997] 3 S.C.R. 1010 at paras. 116–21.

[55] *Osoyoos, supra* note 53 at para. 42.

[56] Subsection 20(2) of the Act allows for individual Indians to be granted an interest in reserve lands: "The Minister may issue to an Indian who is lawfully in possession of land in a reserve a certificate, to be called a Certificate of Possession, as evidence of his right to possession of the land described therein."

[57] For example, see *Ferguson Gifford v. Lax Kw'Alaams Band*, [2000] 2 C.N.L.R. 30 (B.C.S.C.).

[58] FNLMA, *supra* note 6; the FNLMA is available online: <http://laws.justice.gc.ca/en/F-11.8>.

Indian Act. Under this optional scheme, each Indian band that signs a framework agreement with the federal government must also pass a land code, approved by the members of that Indian band, setting out the process for dealing with their reserve land interests. The Indian bands must also deal with such matters as the division of marital property on a reserve.[59] To date, fourteen Indian bands have signed the framework agreement: Westbank, Musqueam, Lheidli T'enneh, N'quatqua, Squamish, Siksika, Muskoday, Cowessess, Opaskwayak Cree, Nipissing, Mississaugas of Scugog Island, Chippewas of Mnjikaning, Chippewas of Georgina Island, and Saint Mary's. More Indian bands have made a request to be subject to the *First Nations Land Management Act.*

Constitution Act, 1982[60]

Federal legislation, acts, or decisions that infringe existing Aboriginal or treaty rights recognized and affirmed by s. 35(1) of the *Constitution Act, 1982* (s. 35(1)) are of no force or effect to the extent of the infringement, unless such infringement can be justified. The extent to which s. 35(1) applies to federal or provincial legislation is unclear, particularly respecting the extent to which Aboriginal self-government may impact upon federal or provincial jurisdiction. In *R. v. Sparrow,*[61] the Supreme Court of Canada stated that "rights that are recognized and affirmed are not absolute."[62] Federal legislative powers continue to exist, including the power to legislate on matters relating to "Indians, and Lands reserved for the Indians" under s. 91(24). In *R. v. Simon,* the Court stated that, "under s. 88 of the *Indian Act,* when the terms of a treaty come into conflict with federal legislation, the latter prevails, subject to whatever may be the effect of s. 35 of the *Constitution Act, 1982.*"[63]

The impact of s. 35(1) on ministerial discretionary authority was at issue in the Supreme Court of Canada decision of *R. v. Adams.*[64] *Adams* concerned a Mohawk Indian who was charged with fishing without a licence. The federal Minister of Fisheries and Oceans possessed authority to issue a special licence to permit the catching of fish for food. The licence requirement was held to be an infringement of the Mohawk's Aboriginal rights that could not be justified:

> [T]he regulatory scheme subjects the exercise of the appellant's Aboriginal rights to a pure act of Ministerial discretion, and sets out no criteria regarding how that discretion is to be exercised. . . . [T]he scheme both imposes undue hardship on the appellant and interferes with his preferred means of exercising his rights.[65]

Ministerial discretionary authority must be set out in statutes and regulations in a clear manner and with direction detailing how the discretionary authority is to be used when it could affect existing Aboriginal and treaty rights.

In the Supreme Court of Canada decision of *R. v. Van der Peet,*[66] Lamer C.J., writing for the majority, stated that the Crown's sovereignty must be reconciled with the fact that Aboriginal people were here before European settlement. The rights recognized and affirmed by s. 35 of the *Constitution Act, 1982* must be "directed towards the reconciliation

[59] *Ibid.* s. 17.
[60] *Constitution Act, 1982, supra* note 35.
[61] *R. v. Sparrow,* [1990] 1 S.C.R. 1075.
[62] *Ibid.* at 1109.
[63] *R. v. Simon,* [1985] 2 S.C.R. 387 at 411.
[64] *R. v. Adams,* [1996] 3 S.C.R. 101.
[65] *Ibid.* at para. 52.
[66] *R. v. Van der Peet,* [1996] 2 S.C.R. 507.

of the pre-existence of Aboriginal societies with the sovereignty of the Crown."[67] Notwithstanding the need for reconciliation between Aboriginal societies and the sovereignty of the Crown, the Court has affirmed the exclusive authority of Parliament to legislate with respect to Indians and their lands. In the SCC decision of *Delgamuukw* v. *B.C.*,[68] Lamer C.J. stated:

> [T]he exclusive power to legislate in relation to "Indians, and Lands reserved for the Indians" has been vested with the federal government by virtue of s. 91(24). . . . That head of jurisdiction . . . encompasses within it the exclusive power to extinguish Aboriginal rights, including Aboriginal title.[69]

Parliament's authority to extinguish Aboriginal rights and Aboriginal title is only relevant pre-April 17, 1982, when the *Constitution Act, 1982* came into effect. After April 17, 1982, the Crown could no longer unilaterally extinguish existing Aboriginal rights, Aboriginal title, or treaty rights.

PROVINCIAL AUTHORITY

Although Indians and their lands are within the exclusive legislative authority of Parliament, provincial laws may apply to Indians in certain circumstances. Practically, provincial governments are cautious to legislate in areas that may have a direct impact upon Indians or reserve lands. This is primarily because of the constitutional parameters imposed by s. 91(24) of the *Constitution Act, 1867*, and provincial concerns regarding taking financial responsibility for a federal head of power; namely, Indians and their lands.

An early twentieth century British Columbia Supreme Court decision held that provincial legislative authority ended at the boundary to an Indian reserve, thus promoting the notion that Indian reserves were "federal enclaves" outside provincial jurisdiction.[70] This has been overturned by the Supreme Court of Canada in *Cardinal* v. *A.-G. of Alberta*,[71] and was reaffirmed by the Court in *Four B Manufacturing. Ltd.* v. *UGW.*[72]

Section 88, *Indian Act*

Provincial laws of general application apply to Indians and their lands in two ways:

1. they can apply of their own effect (*ex proprio vigore*), so long as they do not interfere with Parliament's jurisdiction over Indians and their lands and are not inconsistent with any other federal law; and

2. by way of s. 88 of the *Indian Act*, whereby provincial laws of general application can apply to Indians, even though they affect "Indianness,"[73] so long as they are not contrary to the Act or any other federal legislation.

Section 88 of the *Indian Act* incorporates by reference provincial laws of general appli-

---

[67] *Ibid.* at para. 31.
[68] *Delgamuukw* v. *B.C.*, [1997] 3 S.C.R. 1010.
[69] *Ibid.* at para. 173.
[70] *R.* v. *Jim* (1915), 22 B.C.R. 106 (B.C.S.C.).
[71] *Cardinal* v. *A.-G. of Alberta*, [1974] S.C.R. 695.
[72] *Four B Manufacturing. Ltd.* v. *UGW* (1980), 102 D.L.R. (3d) 385 (S.C.C.) at 398–99.
[73] "Indianness" has not been thoroughly defined by the courts. However, the term probably refers to those elements of being an Indian that set Indians apart from other Canadians. Beetz J. in *R.* v. *Dick*, [1985] 2 S.C.R. 309 at 323, stated: "laws which had crossed the line of general application were laws which, either overtly or colourably, single out Indians for special treatment and impair their status as Indians."

cation into federal law, subject to the terms of any treaty. Laws of general application are those laws that are "provincial in scope"[74] and that are not in relation to one class of citizens (e.g., Indians[75]).

Section 88 of the Act essentially provides that: (*a*) provincial legislatures do not stray into federal jurisdiction with respect to Indians and their lands, (*b*) there is no legislative vacuum for Indians, and (*c*) provincial laws of general application are subject to the terms of any treaty.[76] Because treaty rights are constitutionally recognized and affirmed by s. 35(1) of the *Constitution Act, 1982,* such rights can have the effect of making certain parts of provincial laws of no force or effect, to the extent that such laws infringe existing treaty rights, and such laws cannot otherwise be justified.

The Supreme Court of Canada has held that the provincial laws to which Indians are subject must be general in nature and cannot relate exclusively or directly to Indians. In *Kruger*, Dickson J. stated:

> There are two indicia by which to discern whether or not a provincial enactment is a law of general application. . . . If the Act does not extend uniformly throughout the territory, the inquiry is at an end. . . . If the law does extend uniformly throughout the jurisdiction, the intention and effects of the enactment need to be considered. The law must not be in relation to one class of citizens in object and purpose. . . . There are few laws which have a uniform impact. The line is crossed, however, when an enactment, though "in relation to" another matter, by its effect, impairs the status or capacity of a particular group.[77]

The Supreme Court of Canada has since expanded its interpretation of "laws of general application." Provincial legislation can impair the status and capacity of an Indian without necessarily singling out an Indian. In *R. v. Dick,*[78] the Court held that although the British Columbia *Wildlife Act*[79] prevented year-round hunting and affected the accused Indian, who wished to hunt to maintain or follow a traditional way of life, the Act did not single out Indians and, therefore, was *intra vires* the province. *Dick's* interpretation of s. 88 of the *Indian Act* has been reaffirmed by the Supreme Court in *Derrickson* v. *Derrickson*[80] and *R. v. Francis.*[81]

In *R. v. Francis*, the Supreme Court of Canada held that the term "treaty" in s. 88 of the *Indian Act* does not include international treaties, such as the Jay Treaty (a 1794 treaty between Great Britain and the United States), but refers only to treaties made with Indians.[82] Although the Indian treaties are not international treaties and are not formally implemented in Canadian law, except to the extent that they are mentioned in s. 88 of the *Indian Act*, Indian treaties are nevertheless enforceable, both before and after April 17, 1982.[83]

---

[74] *R. v. George,* [1966] 2 S.C.R. 267 at 281.
[75] *Kruger and Manuel* v. *R.,* [1978] 1 S.C.R. 104 at 110.
[76] See *R. v. White and Bob,* [1965] S.C.R. vi; *R. v. Simon,* [1985] 2 S.C.R. 387; *R. v. Sioui,* [1990] 1 S.C.R. 1025.
[77] *Kruger, supra* note 75.
[78] *R. v. Dick,* [1985] 2 S.C.R. 309; see also, *Derrickson* v. *Derrickson,* [1986] 1 S.C.R. 285.
[79] *Wildlife Act,* R.S.B.C. 1979, c. 433, ss. 3, 8.
[80] *Derrickson* v. *Derrickson, supra* note 78.
[81] *R. v. Francis,* [1988] 1 S.C.R. 1025.
[82] *R. v. Francis,* [1956] S.C.R. 618. For a commentary on *R. v. Francis* see K. Lysyk, "The Unique Constitutional Position of the Canadian Indian" (1967) 45 Can. Bar Rev. 513 at 527–28. The Ontario Court of Appeal held in *R. v. Vincent,* [1993] 2 C.N.L.R. 165; leave to appeal to S.C.C. dismissed [1993] 4 C.N.L.R. vi, that the Jay Treaty was not a treaty for the purposes of s.35(1).
[83] See *R. v. Wesley,* [1932] 4 D.L.R. 774 (Alta. C.A.); *R. v. Prince,* [1964] S.C.R. 81; *R. v. Agawa,* [1988] 3 C.N.L.R. 73 (Ont. C.A.).

The basic rule is that provincial laws of general application apply to Indians and lands reserved for Indians.[84] For example, in *R. v. Francis*,[85] the Supreme Court of Canada held that provincial traffic laws apply to Indians driving vehicles on Indian reserves. In British Columbia, provincial legislation protecting heritage objects, including Aboriginal cultural artifacts, does not affect "Indianness."[86] However, provincial laws which purport to define the extent of Indian access to land for hunting purposes[87] are *ultra vires*, or not within the jurisdiction of the provinces, because they single out Indians.

Although the basic rule is that provincial laws apply to Indians,[88] this rule is subject to a number of conditions. First, provincial legislation must not single out Indians and lands reserved for Indians because in so doing it would infringe upon an area of exclusive federal jurisdiction.[89] In *Kitkatla Band v. B.C. (Min. of Small Business, Tourism and Culture)*,[90] Le Bel J. for the Supreme Court of Canada stated that the "mere mention of the word 'aboriginal' in a statutory provision does not render it *ultra vires* the province."[91] Second, provincial laws must not affect "an integral part of primary federal jurisdiction over Indians and Lands reserved for the Indians."[92] Third, the provinces of Alberta, Saskatchewan, and Manitoba are subject to the Natural Resources Transfer Agreements (1930),[93] which provide that provincial laws cannot deprive Indians of their right to take game and fish for food.[94] Fourth, if a provincial law of general application is inconsistent with a federal law in its application to Indians or to lands reserved for Indians, then the doctrine of federal paramountcy applies, which provides that where there is an inconsistency or a conflict between federal and provincial laws, the federal law prevails. Finally, a provincial law, like a federal law, may be declared by a court to be of no force or effect if it infringes an existing Aboriginal or treaty right recognized and affirmed by s. 35(1) of the *Constitution Act, 1982*.[95]

However, while a provincial law must not single out Indians, provincial laws can have a disproportionate effect on Indians. In *Kruger*,[96] Dickson J. stated "the fact that a law may have graver consequence to one person than to another does not, on that account

---

[84] For discussion see: P. Hughes, "Indians and Lands Reserved for the Indians: Off Limits to the Provinces?" (1983) 21 Osgoode Hall L.J. 82.
[85] *Francis, supra* note 81.
[86] *Kitkatla Band v. B.C. (Min. of Small Business, Tourism and Culture)*, [2000] 2 C.N.L.R. 36 (B.C.C.A.), aff'd [2002] 2 S.C.R. 146.
[87] *R. v. Sutherland*, [1980] 2 S.C.R. 451; *R. v. Moosehunter*, [1981] 1 S.C.R. 282.
[88] *Kitkatla Band v. B.C. (Min. of Small Business, Tourism and Culture)*, [2002] 2 S.C.R. 146, para. 66.
[89] *Sutherland, supra* note 87; *R. v. Dick, supra* note 78; *Leighton v. B.C.*, [1989] 3 C.N.L.R. 136 (B.C.C.A.).
[90] *Kitkatla, supra* note 88.
[91] *Ibid.* at para. 66. For example, British Columbia has enacted the *Indian Cut-off Lands Dispute Act*, R.S.B.C. 1996, c. 218 and the *First Peoples' Heritage, Language and Culture Act*, R.S.B.C. 1996, c. 174. Alberta has enacted the *First Nations Sacred Ceremonial Objects Repatriation Act*, R.S.A. 2000, c. F-14. The Northwest Territories has enacted the *Aboriginal Custom Adoption Recognition Act*, S.N.W.T. 1994, c. 26. Nova Scotia has enacted the *Mi'kmaq Education Act*, S.N.S. 1998, c. 17. Ontario has enacted the *Indian Welfare Services Act*, R.S.O. 1990, c. I.4.
[92] *Four B Manufacturing v. UGW, supra* note 32 at 1047.
[93] *Constitution Act, 1930*, R.S.C. 1985, App. II, No. 8.
[94] See, for example, *R. v. Horseman*, [1990] 1 S.C.R. 901.
[95] In *R. v. Perry*, [1996] 2 C.N.L.R. 167 (Ont. Gen. Div.), the Court held that the Government of the Province of Ontario's distinction between registered and non-registered Indians in its *Interim Enforcement Policy* violated s. 15 (equality provision) of the Charter and was *ultra vires* Ontario because of Parliament's jurisdiction in s. 91(24). The Court interpreted the policy to provide that where the terms "status" or "non-status" are used, the term "Aboriginal" is to be used in its place.
[96] *Kruger, supra* note 75.

alone make the law other than one of general application."[97] A likely exception to the singling out rule is the duty on provinces to provide guidance to statutory decision-makers when Aboriginal or treaty rights may be affected or in respect of guidance dealing with consultation and accommodation with Aboriginal people.[98]

In *Kitkatla*, the Supreme Court of Canada considered whether provincial legislation that dealt with Aboriginal culturally modified trees and their protection was within provincial jurisdiction. The Court held that the overall effect of the legislation in question was to improve the protection of Aboriginal culture and safeguard the "presence and the memory of the cultural objects"[99] of Aboriginal people, without jeopardizing the identity and core values of the affected Aboriginal people. The impugned provisions in *Kitkatla* had disproportionate effects on Aboriginal people because Aboriginal people have produced the majority of heritage objects in British Columbia. The provisions of the impugned legislation, while disproportionately affecting Aboriginal people, apply to all people in British Columbia and do not, therefore, "single out" Indians. The Court stated that there was a lack of evidence to support any finding that the impugned legislation impaired the status or capacity of Indians.[100]

On the issue of whether provincial laws of general application apply to the use of reserve lands, the Alberta Court of Appeal affirmed in *Re Stony Plain*[101] that once reserve land is surrendered and title is transferred in fee simple, it is: (*a*) no longer a reserve within the meaning of the Act, (*b*) no longer land "reserved for the Indians" for the purposes of s. 91(24), and (*c*) subject to provincial legislative jurisdiction. However, when the fee simple title to the surrendered land is held by the grantee in trust for the benefit of the Indian band and its members, no band interest is ceded and the land remains in the reserve. If the terms of a surrender provide that the Crown in right of Canada retains title to the surrendered land, then the Indian band affected retains landlord rights, including the right of reversion. The Court stated that a corporation, such as those wholly owned by Indians, cannot be an "Indian" for the purposes of either the Act or s. 91(24). Finally, the Court held that where provincial legislation affects the use, enjoyment of, and interests in reserve lands, provincial legislation is inapplicable to those lands. If reserve lands are surrendered for leasing purposes, the reversion is held by the Indians and provincial legislation limiting reversion will not be applicable. Surrendered land remains land "reserved for the Indians" and, therefore, remains within federal authority.

In *Delgamuukw*,[102] the Supreme Court of Canada reaffirmed that provincial laws of general application that do not affect "Indianness" apply by way of their own force. Laws that affect "Indianness" must depend on s. 88 of the *Indian Act*, which referentially incorporates provincial legislation into federal law.[103] Furthermore, s. 91(24) confirms the exclusive authority of Parliament to extinguish Aboriginal rights and title[104] prior to April 17, 1982. The right to extinguish Aboriginal rights and title was not held by the provinces. In *R. v. Côté*,[105] the Court stated:

---

[97] *Ibid.* at 110.

[98] See text accompanying footnotes 65, 114, 115, 236, and 237.

[99] *Kitkatla, supra* note 88 at para. 78.

[100] *Ibid.* at para. 70.

[101] *Re Stony Plain, supra* note 32.

[102] *Delgamuukw, supra* note 68.

[103] *Ibid.* at para. 37.

[104] *Ibid.* at para. 173.

[105] *R. v. Côté*, [1996] 3 S.C.R. 139.

[O]n the face of s. 88, treaty rights appear to enjoy a broader protection from contrary provincial law under the *Indian Act* than under the *Constitution Act, 1982*. Once it has been demonstrated that a provincial law infringes "the terms of [a] treaty", the treaty would arguably prevail under s. 88 even in the presence of a well-grounded justification. The statutory provision does not *expressly* incorporate a justification requirement analogous to the justification stage included in the *Sparrow* framework. But the precise boundaries of the protection of s. 88 remains a topic for future consideration. I know of no case which has authoritatively discounted the potential existence of an *implicit* justification stage under s. 88. In the near future, Parliament will no doubt feel compelled to re-examine the existence and scope of this statutory protection in light of these uncertainties and in light of the parallel constitutionalization of treaty rights under s. 35(1).[106] [emphasis in original]

Although interesting, it is doubtful that a statutory provision can trump the constitutional test used to determine whether an infringement of s. 35(1) can be justified.

A number of commentators have argued that s. 88 of the *Indian Act* is of "doubtful constitutional validity."[107] The primary basis for this argument appears to rest on the lack of reference to Aboriginal rights and title in the section, thereby suggesting that provincial laws of general application cannot affect matters central or incidental to the exercise of Aboriginal rights or to the nature of Aboriginal title.[108] These positions also appear to rely on Lamer C.J.'s reasons in *Delgamuukw* respecting the lack of provincial authority to extinguish Aboriginal rights. While there is no reference to either Aboriginal rights or title in s. 88, this reference is not required. Before April 17, 1982, it was necessary to make reference to treaty rights expressly, otherwise they could be overridden by ordinary legislation. After April 17, 1982, any reference to treaty rights, Aboriginal rights, or Aboriginal title is redundant to the extent that these rights are constitutionally recognized and affirmed within s. 35 of the *Constitution Act, 1982* and have become part of the Constitution of Canada, to which all federal and provincial laws are subject.

Neither s. 91(24) nor s. 35(1) erode provincial legislative authority,[109] except to confirm that: (*a*) provinces cannot legislate in areas of exclusive federal jurisdiction, and (*b*) provincial jurisdiction is subject to existing Aboriginal and treaty rights in s. 35(1), subject to being justified.[110]

In *Delgamuukw*, the Supreme Court of Canada confirmed that the Province of British Columbia did not possess the authority to extinguish Aboriginal rights after 1871, either under its own jurisdiction or by operation of s. 88 of the *Indian Act*:[111]

---

[106] *Ibid.* at para. 87.

[107] See B. Slattery, "First Nations and the Constitution: A Question of Trust" (1992) 71 Can. Bar Rev. 261 at 285; K. McNeil, "Aboriginal Title and Section 88 of the *Indian Act*" (2000) 34:1 U.B.C. Law Rev. 159; and K. Wilkins, "'Still Crazy After All These Years': Section 88 of the Indian Act at Fifty" (2000) 38:2 Alta. L. Rev. 458 at 503.

[108] In *Delgamuukw, supra* note 68 at para. 183, Lamer C.J. wrote: "I see nothing in the language of the provision [s. 88] which even suggests the intention to extinguish aboriginal rights. Indeed, the explicit reference to treaty rights in s. 88 suggests that the provision was clearly not intended to undermine aboriginal rights."

[109] Aboriginal rights may be infringed by federal (see *Sparrow, supra* note 61) and provincial (see *Côté, supra* note 105) governments; see also *Delgamuukw, supra* note 68 at para 160.

[110] In *Côté, supra* note 105 at para. 74, the Supreme Court of Canada noted:
[I]t is quite clear that the Sparrow test applies where a provincial law is alleged to have infringed an aboriginal or treaty right in a manner which cannot be justified. . . . The text and purpose of s. 35(1) do not distinguish between federal and provincial laws which restrict aboriginal or treaty rights, and they should both be subject to the same standard of constitutional scrutiny.

[111] *Delgamuukw, supra* note 68 at paras. 172–83.

I conclude with two remarks. First, even if the point were not settled, I would have come to the same conclusion. The judges in the court below noted that separating federal jurisdiction over Indians from jurisdiction over their lands would have a most unfortunate result—the government vested with primary constitutional responsibility for securing the welfare of Canada's aboriginal peoples would find itself unable to safeguard one of the most central of native interests—their interest in their lands. Second, although the submissions of the parties and my analysis have focused on the question of jurisdiction over aboriginal title, in my opinion, the same reasoning applies to jurisdiction over any aboriginal right which relates to land. . . . Those relationships with the land, however, may be equally fundamental to aboriginal peoples and, for the same reason that jurisdiction over aboriginal title must vest with the federal government, so too must the power to legislate in relation to other aboriginal rights in relation to land. . . . [T]he Court has held that s. 91(24) protects a "core" of Indianness from provincial intrusion, through the doctrine of interjurisdictional immunity. It follows, at the very least, that this core falls within the scope of federal jurisdiction over Indians. That core, for reasons I will develop, encompasses aboriginal rights, including the rights that are recognized and affirmed by s. 35(1). Laws which purport to extinguish those rights therefore touch the core of Indianness which lies at the heart of s. 91(24), and are beyond the legislative competence of the provinces to enact. The core of Indianness encompasses the whole range of aboriginal rights that are protected by s. 35(1). Those rights include rights in relation to land; that part of the core derives from s. 91(24)'s reference to "Lands reserved for the Indians". But those rights also encompass practices, customs and traditions which are not tied to land as well; that part of the core can be traced to federal jurisdiction over "Indians". Provincial governments are prevented from legislating in relation to both types of aboriginal rights.[112]

Lamer C.J.'s reasons are interesting in that they focus on the provincial authority to extinguish Aboriginal rights and title and to *legislate* with respect to Aboriginal rights and title. Lamer C.J.'s reasons do not contradict earlier Supreme Court of Canada decisions with respect to the provincial authority to interfere and infringe existing Aboriginal and treaty rights, when justified according to the legal test set out by the Court.

The Court's discussion of s. 91(24) in *Delgamuukw* and provincial jurisdiction can be better understood by analyzing existing Aboriginal rights and treaty rights possessing two distinct elements: constitutional and jurisdictional. The *constitutional* element provides that existing Aboriginal rights and treaty rights are "recognized and affirmed" and serve as a check on the exercise of federal and provincial authority. Within this element, both the federal and provincial governments, within their respective jurisdictions, must consider, and may justifiably infringe, existing Aboriginal and treaty rights. This has been confirmed by the Court in its decisions dealing with s. 35(1).[113]

Parliament retains exclusive authority to legislate with respect to Aboriginal and treaty rights. This is the *jurisdictional* element of Aboriginal and treaty rights and is important when examining whether Aboriginal and treaty rights have been extinguished (prior to April 17, 1982), since only Parliament possessed that authority. Although these two elements are related, they are distinct. Both elements exist within both s. 91(24) and s. 35(1) and are consistent with the efforts of the Supreme Court of Canada to balance existing Aboriginal and treaty rights with the constitutional authority of Parliament and the provincial legislatures.

Based on the Court's direction to date, provincial legislatures can enact legislation to maintain the honour of the Crown and the Crown's duty to consult, respecting matters

[112] *Ibid.* at paras. 176–78.
[113] *Sparrow, supra* note 61; *R. v. Badger*, [1996] 1 S.C.R. 771; *Côté, supra* note 105; *Delgamuukw, supra* note 68.

that may interfere with and infringe the exercise of Aboriginal and treaty rights. Such legislation would have to be precise and carefully drafted so as not to intrude upon federal jurisdiction, but it is necessary in light of the Court's direction for provincial governments to consult Aboriginal people. The Court affirmed this direction, in part, in *R. v. Marshall* (reconsideration),[114] where the Court stated the following with respect to the Crown's regulatory authority:

> The Court was thus most explicit in confirming the regulatory authority of the federal *and provincial governments* within their respective legislative fields to regulate the exercise of the treaty right [Emphasis added].[115]

Upon examining the Court's understanding and definition of s. 35(1) and the operative words "recognized and affirmed," it becomes clear why Crown decisions and actions that infringe justifiably existing Aboriginal and treaty rights are also designed to attempt a "balancing" of interests between the rights of Aboriginal people and other Canadians. In *R. v. Badger*[116] the Court cited with approval the Ontario Court of Appeal decision of *R. v. Agawa*,[117] where Blair J.A. stated: "Rights do not exist in a vacuum and the exercise of any right involves a balancing with the interests and values involved in the rights of others."

Any understanding of the reasoning of the Supreme Court of Canada regarding the Crown's ability to regulate and justify its actions and decisions with respect to Aboriginal people must begin with *Sparrow*:

> While it [constitutional protection] does not promise immunity from government regulation in a society that, in the twentieth century, is increasingly more complex, interdependent and sophisticated, and where exhaustible resources need protection and management, it does hold the Crown to a substantive promise.[118]

Authority of Provincial Adjudicative Bodies[119]

In *Paul v. B.C. (Forest Appeals Commission)*,[120] the British Columbia Court of Appeal examined the authority of provincial adjudicative bodies to consider Aboriginal rights and title in their deliberations. Thomas Paul, a registered Indian under the *Indian Act*, was charged with illegally cutting and removing Crown timber without timber marks, contrary to the *Forest Practices Code of British Columbia Act* and the *Forest Act*. On June 11, 2003, the Supreme Court of Canada unanimously allowed the appeal from the bench, and released its written reasons on October 3, 2003.[121]

The District Manager concluded that Paul contravened the code and the *Forest Act*. Paul appealed the decision to an Administrative Review Panel. The panel agreed with the District Manager. Paul argued that he possessed an existing Aboriginal right to harvest

[114] *R. v. Marshall* (reconsideration), [1999] 3 S.C.R. 533.

[115] *Ibid.* at para. 24.

[116] *Badger, supra* note 113 at para. 80.

[117] *R. v. Agawa, supra* note 83 at 89–90.

[118] *Sparrow, supra* note 61 at 1110.

[119] See Thomas Isaac, "Provincial Jurisdiction, Adjudicative Authority and Aboriginal Rights: A Comment on *Paul* v. *B.C. (Forest Appeals Commission)*" (January 2002) 60:1 The Advocate 77–88.

[120] *Paul* v. *B.C. (Forest Appeals Commission)*, [2001] 4 C.N.L.R. 210 (B.C.C.A.), appeal allowed by the S.C.C., 2003 SCC 55. For application of *Paul*, see *Katlodeeche First Nation* v. *Canada and the Canada Industrial Relations Board*, (Dock.: S-0001-CV-2002000104), December 12, 2003 (N.W.T.S.C.).

[121] *Paul* v. *B.C. (Forest Appeals Commission)* 2003 SCC 55.

timber for house construction and that the District Manager and panel did not possess the adjudicative jurisdiction necessary to consider his Aboriginal rights. Paul claimed that these rights were protected within s. 35(1) and were unjustifiably infringed.

The Forest Appeals Commission adjourned its proceedings to allow the parties to bring an action in the British Columbia Supreme Court, but stated that it nevertheless had the authority to consider Aboriginal interests. Paul appealed the Commission's decision regarding its jurisdiction to adjudicate on Aboriginal rights. Pitfield J. allowed Paul to bring a petition to quash the Commission's decision regarding its jurisdiction and a prohibition order and declaration preventing the Commission from considering and determining questions related to Paul's Aboriginal rights. While the Commission had the authority to determine questions of Aboriginal rights in the course of carrying out its functions under the *Forest Practices Code,* the District Manager and the Administrative Review Panel did not. Paul appealed the Commission's decision.

The Court of Appeal allowed the appeal, with Huddart J.A. writing a dissent. Lambert J.A. stated two questions facing the Court:

1. whether the B.C. Legislative Assembly possessed the constitutional capacity to confer on the Commission the jurisdiction to decide questions of Aboriginal rights and title in the context of deciding appeals under the Forest Practices Code; and

2. whether the B.C. Legislative Assembly, if it possessed the constitutional authority to do so, conferred the necessary jurisdiction on the Commission.

Lambert J.A. stated that "any conferral of quasi-judicial adjudicative jurisdiction on the District Manager, the Administrative Review Panel, or the . . . Commission over questions of Aboriginal title and Aboriginal rights by the British Columbia Legislature would be unconstitutional."[122]

The British Columbia Court of Appeal decision in *Paul* placed provincial governments in a difficult position when attempting to fulfil their constitutional obligation to consider potential impacts to the rights of Aboriginal people, and represented a misunderstanding of the guidance by the Supreme Court of Canada respecting provincial jurisdiction vis-à-vis Aboriginal rights generally.

The Supreme Court of Canada affirmed that provinces have the legislative authority to empower administrative tribunals with the capacity to consider questions respecting Aboriginal rights when carrying out a valid provincial mandate. Importantly, the Court also stated that the power of provincial boards to adjudicate in areas of federal legislative competence "fits comfortably within the general constitutional and judicial architecture of Canada."[123] This confirmation of the general law of Canada providing guidance to a question of Aboriginal law is instructive and demonstrates that Aboriginal law does not exist and will not be developed in a legal vacuum.

The Court also noted that while provincial boards may consider questions of Aboriginal rights, their decisions are not legally binding precedents and their collective weight over time will not amount to an "authoritative body of common law."[124] The raising of a defence of Aboriginal right does not oust a provincial board's jurisdiction.

In order to determine if a provincial board has the authority to determine questions of Aboriginal rights, the appropriate test to be applied is the standard test: has the board in

---

[122] *Paul, supra* note 120 at para. 80 (B.C.C.A.).

[123] *Paul, supra* note 121 at para. 21.

[124] *Ibid.* at para. 31.

question been given the authority to decide questions of law? Bastarache J., for the Court, wrote:

> With respect, I think that the majority of the Court of Appeal misunderstood the scope of the doctrine of interjurisdictional immunity. . . . The majority of the Court of Appeal applied the doctrine in the context of an adjudicative, not legislative, function. The effect of the Code is not to alter the substance of any federal rule or aboriginal right, but rather to prescribe that Indians charged under the Code will first raise an Aboriginal rights defence before the Commission, as opposed to before a superior court judge.[125]

Finally, from a more practical perspective, the Crown's duty to consult Aboriginal people must mean *something*. If, after a provincial government consulted and considered the existence of potential Aboriginal rights or title in relation to its decision or act, its own adjudicative bodies could not consider such due diligence, what then would the purpose of such consultation achieve? The duty to consult by provincial governments must also entail an element of provincial jurisdiction. Presumably, provincial governments are obligated to consult regarding those acts or decisions that may interfere with the exercise of existing Aboriginal rights or title that are within their legislative competence. It follows that this consultation must be with respect to provincial governments having the authority to act or decide in areas of provincial jurisdiction that may impact upon such rights or title, subject to adequate consultation as may be determined by provincial adjudicative bodies.

Natural Resources Transfer Agreements

Unlike the other provinces, Manitoba, Saskatchewan, and Alberta did not initially own their public lands and natural resources as provided for in ss. 109 and 117 of the *Constitution Act, 1867*.[126] The federal Crown retained ownership of Crown lands and natural resources in the prairie provinces to facilitate federal policies with respect to immigration, land settlement, and railway development. In 1929 and 1930, the federal government signed the Natural Resources Transfer Agreements (NRTAs) with the three prairie provinces to give them ownership of natural resources and Crown lands, and the NRTAs were given constitutional effect by the *Constitution Act, 1930*.[127]

The NRTAs also present a limitation on the applicability of provincial legislation to Indians.[128] The following clause is found in the Alberta (para. 12), Saskatchewan (para. 12), and Manitoba (para. 13) NRTAs:

> In order to secure to the Indians of the Province the continuance of the supply of game and fish for their support and subsistence, Canada agrees that the laws respecting game in force in the Province from time to time shall apply to the Indians within the boundaries thereof, provided, however, that the said Indians shall have the right, which the Province hereby assures to them of hunting, trapping and fishing game for food at all seasons of the year on

---

[125] *Ibid.* at para. 6.
[126] The Crown in right of Canada retains ownership of most public lands and their natural resources in the Northwest Territories, Nunavut, and the Yukon Territory.
[127] *Constitution Act, 1930, supra* note 93.
[128] Cory J. for a majority of the Supreme Court of Canada in *R. v. Horseman, supra* note 94 at 934 cited with approval Laskin J.'s dissenting judgment in *Cardinal* v. *A.G. of Alberta*, [1974] S.C.R. 695 at 722 on the true effect of para. 12 of the NRTA. Laskin J.'s dissent reads, in part:

> > [Section 12] is concerned rather with Indians as such, and with guaranteeing to them a continuing right to hunt, trap and fish for food regardless of provincial game laws which would otherwise confine Indians in parts of the Province that are under provincial administration. *Although inelegantly expressed, s.12 does not expand provincial legislative power but contracts it.* . . . There is hence, by virtue of the sanction of the *British North America Act, 1930*, a limitation upon provincial authority regardless of whether or not Parliament legislates [emphasis added].

all unoccupied Crown lands and on any other lands to which the said Indians may have a right of access.

This clause in the NRTAs clearly expands the right to hunt, trap, and fish to the entire province on "all unoccupied Crown lands," limits the right to "for food" only, and allows such rights to be exercised "at all seasons of the year."

In *R. v. Horse*,[129] the Supreme Court of Canada held that para. 12 of the Saskatchewan NRTA must be given a broad and liberal interpretation and any ambiguity in the phrase "right of access" must be resolved in favour of the Indians. The Court affirmed that Indians have no right of access to the private lands in question. *R. v. Horseman*[130] gave a broader interpretation to the Alberta NRTA. The Court held that the Indian commercial right to hunt guaranteed by Treaty No. 8 in 1899 was "merged and consolidated" by para. 12 of the Alberta NRTA and that the Indians' hunting rights were now limited to those specified by the NRTA. *Horseman* also confirmed that the treaty right to hunt for food was expanded by the NRTA to include all of Alberta, not just the lands covered by the terms of Treaty No. 8.

Paragraph 12 of the NRTA provides that Canada and Saskatchewan recognize that Indians have special hunting, fishing, and trapping rights and that the Indians are dependent on game and fish for food. The passage applies only to provincial legislation, however; federal legislation respecting migratory birds, inland fisheries, and the sea coast continue to apply, subject to s. 35(1).

The primary purpose of para. 12 of the NRTA was first stated by McGillivray J. of the Alberta Supreme Court, Appellate Division, in *R. v. Wesley*:[131]

> It seems to me that the language of s. 12 is unambiguous and the intention of Parliament to be gathered therefrom clearly is to assure to the Indians a supply of game in the future for their support and subsistence by requiring them to comply with the game laws of the Province, subject however to the express and dominant proviso that care for the future is not to deprive them of the right to satisfy their present need for food by hunting and trapping game, using the word "game" in its broadest sense, at all seasons on unoccupied Crown lands or other lands to which they may have a right of access.

The Supreme Court of Canada adopted this statement in *R. v. Sutherland*.[132] Indians are guaranteed the right to take game and fish "for food" during all seasons of the year on unoccupied Crown lands; provincial laws to the contrary are inapplicable to Indians. The words "for food" are a restriction on the hunting and fishing rights conferred by the NRTA. The NRTAs restricted the rights of those Indians who may have had a treaty right to fish and hunt for commercial purposes. Since the NRTAs apply only to the prairie provinces, they do not apply to Treaty No. 8 territory in the Northwest Territories and British Columbia.

Paragraph 12 of Saskatchewan's NRTA "merges and consolidates" Treaty No. 6 hunting rights.[133] Section 35 of the *Constitution Act, 1982* neither expands nor constricts rights that were affected by para. 12 of the NRTA.[134] In *R. v. McIntyre*,[135] the Saskatchewan

---

[129] *R. v. Horse*, [1988] 1 S.C.R. 187.

[130] *Horseman, supra* note 94.

[131] *Wesley, supra* note 83.

[132] *Sutherland, supra* note 87 at 462.

[133] *Moosehunter, supra* note 87; *R. v. Horse*, [1984] 4 C.N.L.R. 99 at 106 (Sask. C.A.); *R. v. Bird*, [1992] 1 C.N.L.R. 119 (Sask. Prov. Ct.).

[134] See *Badger, supra* note 113.

[135] *R. v. McIntyre*, [1992] 3 C.N.L.R. 113 (Sask. C.A.).

Court of Appeal held that para. 12 of the NRTA "merges and consolidates" Treaty No. 10 hunting rights. The Court of Appeal affirmed that Saskatchewan has the authority, established in *R.* v. *Strongquill*[136] and confirmed by the Supreme Court of Canada in *R.* v. *Sutherland*,[137] to create game preserves. The Supreme Court also noted that Saskatchewan has the right to create road corridor game preserves provided they were established for *bona fide* reasons.[138] The Alberta Court of Queen's Bench in *R.* v. *Alexson*[139] held that leased grazing land was not "unoccupied Crown land" or "other lands" within para. 12 of the NRTA. Thus, treaty Indians must obtain the permission of leaseholders before hunting on leased lands.

Provincial Ability to Justifiably Infringe Rights

One criticism levelled against the Supreme Court of Canada has been that the Court has allowed provincial governments to infringe Aboriginal and treaty rights, even though such rights are at the heart of federal jurisdiction over Indians and their lands as set out in s. 91(24) of the *Constitution Act, 1867*.[140] Additionally, the Court has also appeared to place non–constitutionally protected interests on an equal footing with existing Aboriginal and treaty rights by claiming that Aboriginal and treaty rights may be *balanced* with other competing public interests.[141] How can provincial legislatures legislate in areas of federal jurisdiction and how can non–constitutionally protected interests be balanced with existing Aboriginal and treaty rights? The answer lies within s. 35(1) of the *Constitution Act, 1982* itself and the definition that the Court attributed to the phrase "recognized and affirmed."

Prior to *Sparrow*,[142] commentators in this area were preoccupied with understanding the meaning of s. 35 of the *Constitution Act, 1982* and what its effects would be. *Sparrow* was the first decision in which the Supreme Court of Canada gave its unanimous views on the meaning of s. 35(1)[143] and noted that "rights that are recognized and affirmed are not absolute."[144] The Court also stated that the words "recognized and affirmed" place "some restraint on the exercise of sovereign power"[145] and "gives a measure of control over government conduct and a strong check on legislative power."[146] The Court concluded that although existing Aboriginal and treaty rights are not subject to s. 1[147] of the Charter, this does not mean that any law or regulation affecting Aboriginal rights will "automatically be of no force or effect".[148] Also, the rights in the Charter are defined in absolute

---

[136] *R.* v. *Strongquill*, [1953] 2 D.L.R. 264 (Sask. C.A.).

[137] *Sutherland, supra* note 87.

[138] *R.* v. *Wolverine*, [1989] 3 C.N.L.R. 181 (Sask. C.A.).

[139] *R.* v. *Alexson*, [1990] 4 C.N.L.R. 28 (Alta. Q.B.).

[140] See *Delgamuukw, supra* note 68 at para. 178; see K. McNeil, "Aboriginal Title and the Division of Powers: Rethinking Federal and Provincial Jurisdiction" (2000) 61:2 Sask. L. Rev. 431.

[141] See for example, K. McNeil, "How can Infringements of the Constitutional Rights of Aboriginal Peoples be Justified?" (1997) 8:2 Const. Forum 33.

[142] *Sparrow, supra* note 61.

[143] *Ibid.* at 1082; the Supreme Court of Canada stated: "This appeal requires this Court to explore for the first time the scope of s.35(1) . . .".

[144] *Ibid.* at 1109.

[145] *Ibid.* at 1109.

[146] *Ibid.* at 1110.

[147] Section 1 of the Charter reads: "The *Canadian Charter of Rights and Freedoms* guarantees the rights and freedoms set out in it subject only to such reasonable limits prescribed by law as can be demonstrably justified in a free and democratic society."

[148] *Sparrow, supra* note 61 at 1109.

terms as "rights," except for the application of s. 1 of the Charter, and the rights contained within the Charter are "guaranteed" rather than "recognized and affirmed." Legislation interfering with existing Aboriginal and treaty rights will be valid if it can be justified according to the legal test set out by the Court in *Sparrow* and other judicial decisions.

Williamson J. in *Campbell* v. *British Columbia (A.G.)*[149] commented on the division of federal and provincial powers in considering an application by a number of members of the Opposition of the Legislative Assembly of British Columbia who sought a declaration that the Nisga'a Final Agreement is, in part, inconsistent with the Constitution of Canada. Such inconsistency was based on the argument that the agreement: (*a*) granted to the Nisga'a Nation legislative jurisdiction within the exhaustive division of powers in ss. 91 and 92 of the *Constitution Act, 1867*; (*b*) conferred authority on the Nisga'a Nation that interferes with the concept of royal assent; and (*c*) violated the voting rights of non-Nisga'a living on Nisga'a lands, contrary to s. 3 of the Charter.

Williamson J. dismissed the application and noted that ss. 91 and 92 of the *Constitution Act, 1867* do not exhaust the distribution of all legislative powers between Parliament and the provincial legislatures. Land claims agreements, contemplated by s. 35(3) of the *Constitution Act, 1982*, may include self-government provisions. Williamson J. noted that the issue of royal assent relating to the Nisga'a legislative powers contemplated by the Nisga'a Final Agreement cannot be described as "a profound constitutional upheaval"[150] and that the powers of the Nisga'a government are not "absolute or sovereign"[151] in nature.

Campbell was not appealed. Although interesting, *Campbell* is probably not as helpful as the general question implicitly raised in the case: What is the practical impact of negotiated, constitutionally protected, and legally complex and lengthy agreements and treaties on the existing division of powers, and on the exercise of those powers, by federal and provincial governments?

In *Lovelace* v. *Ontario*,[152] the Supreme Court of Canada held that a casino initiative between the Government of Ontario and a number of Indian band governments, excluding Métis and other Aboriginal involvement, was not *ultra vires* the province. Ontario's authority to engage in this initiative came from its constitutional spending power. Nothing in the casino partnership affected s. 91(24) of the *Constitution Act, 1867,* nor did it affect "Indianness." Writing for the majority, Iacobucci J. stated:

> In my opinion there is nothing in the casino program affecting the core of the s. 91(24) federal jurisdiction. The Ontario government is simply using the definition of band found in the federal *Indian Act.* The province has done nothing to impair the status or capacity of the appellants as aboriginal peoples. Furthermore, in *Pamajewon* . . . [[1996] 2 S.C.R. 821] this Court found that gambling, or the regulation of gambling activities, is not an aboriginal right. Consequently, this casino program cannot have the effect of violating the rights affirmed by s. 35(1) of the *Constitution Act, 1982,* and does not approach the core of aboriginality. I agree with the Ontario Court of Appeal, therefore, that the casino program falls within the provincial spending power, and the province did not act in any way to encroach upon federal jurisdiction.[153]

---

[149] *Campbell* v. *British Columbia (A.G.)*, [2000] 4 C.N.L.R. 1 (B.C.S.C.).
[150] *Ibid.* at para. 149.
[151] *Ibid.* at para. 183.
[152] *Lovelace* v. *Ontario*, [2000] 1 S.C.R. 950.
[153] *Ibid.* at para. 111.

Thus, provincial governments can use terms such as "band" as descriptive terms in their legislation and can also enter freely into agreements with Aboriginal people, depending upon the circumstances, without fear of such action being *ultra vires.*

GOVERNMENTAL RESPONSIBILITIES

Courts in Canada have provided some direction to governments as to how they can improve their regulatory regimes in respect of the rights of Aboriginal people:

1. Discretionary authority conferred by statute on a Crown representative must outline specific criteria for the granting or refusal of that discretion when existing Aboriginal or treaty rights may be affected.[154]

2. Where the discretionary authority of a Crown representative is exercised and where existing Aboriginal or treaty rights may be affected, governments must be able to explain their decisions in a justifiable and transparent manner;.

3. Regulations that, at their core, interfere with and infringe existing Aboriginal or treaty rights, such as hunting or fishing rights, must be drafted in a manner that is clear and unambiguous in their meaning and intent; that is, if the goal is safety, conservation, or some other compelling public interest, then it should be stated clearly within the regulation.

4. Where it is clear that regulations may interfere with and infringe existing Aboriginal or treaty rights, the regulations should provide for a meaningful consideration of these rights and a mechanism to indicate that such consideration has occurred.

5. Reasonable attempts should be made to reach accommodation or negotiated settlements with Aboriginal people when their rights are affected.

6. Regulations that "accommodate" existing Aboriginal and treaty rights—for example, the setting of catch limits that provide for a "moderate livelihood" for Mi'kmaq Indians (the issue in *Marshall)*—do not require justification since they would not infringe any rights; how this principle would apply to rights other than fishing is unclear.

The above are a few examples of what could be done to meet the Supreme Court of Canada's standard of justification imposed on governments. While these suggestions require a wholesale re-examination of thousands of pages of laws, regulations, and policies, this is the onus that the courts have placed on governments. These suggestions also appear to confirm that governments not only need to coordinate their efforts internally in respect of Aboriginal land and other interests, but should also work closely with other governments in Canada to develop a truly coordinated and legally correct approach. This also requires a fundamental shift in how governments are currently undertaking their litigation strategies and consultation efforts respecting Aboriginal people and their rights. It is important to note that while these suggestions may appear to impede governmental authority, the opposite is true. By re-tooling the existing regulatory regime, fewer laws and decision-making processes will be overturned or deemed inapplicable due to interference with existing Aboriginal and treaty rights.

---

[154] See text accompanying notes 64 and 65.

TERRITORIAL AUTHORITY

Unlike the provinces, the Yukon Territory, the Northwest Territories, and Nunavut are creatures of Parliament and therefore do not possess independent constitutional status akin to the provincial legislatures and Parliament. The federal statutes establishing the Yukon Territory, the Northwest Territories, and Nunavut can be amended by Parliament. Both the *Northwest Territories Act*[155] and the *Yukon Act*[156] allow for the respective commissioners in council of each territory and the governor in council to enact ordinances (legislation) and make regulations dealing specifically with Indian and Inuit people in a narrow range of matters.

The creation of Nunavut on April 1, 1999 marked Canada's first major jurisdictional realignment since Newfoundland joined Confederation in 1949. The creation of Nunavut was the direct result of the Nunavut Land Claims Agreement, which obliged the federal government to put legislation before Parliament to create the new territory. This it did in 1993 in the *Nunavut Act*.[157] Nunavut, which has a publicly elected government, is unique in that it is the result of a land claims agreement with the Inuit, who represent approximately 85 percent of Nunavut's population. Section 25 of the *Nunavut Act* allows the Nunavut legislature to make laws for the purpose of the implementing the Nunavut Land Claims Agreement or any other land claim agreement designated by the governor in council.

Section 18 of the *Northwest Territories Act* and s. 19 of the *Yukon Act*[158] provide that the territorial legislatures may make laws regarding the preservation of game in the territories and that such laws are applicable to Indians and the Inuit. However, such laws cannot restrict or prohibit Indians or Inuit from hunting for food on unoccupied Crown land unless the game has been declared by the governor in council as game that is in danger of becoming extinct.

Subsection 22(2) of the *Northwest Territories Act* provides that "all laws of general application in force in the Territories are, except where otherwise provided, applicable to the Inuit in the Territories." The purpose of this section is unclear since the territorial governments are delegated forms of government receiving their authority to govern from Parliament, which has jurisdiction over the Inuit under s. 91(24) of the *Constitution Act, 1867*. In *Re Noah Estate*,[159] Sissons J. stated that the purpose of then s. 17(2) (now s. 22(2)) of the *Northwest Territories Act*:[160]

> was to make legislation of the Territorial Council of the Northwest Territories in relation to preservation of game into federal legislation relating to Indians and Eskimos and of general application [and] . . . to authorize the abrogation, abridgment or infringement of the hunting rights of the Eskimos and other rights of the Eskimos by the Territorial Government.[161]

Laws of general application in the Northwest Territories are subject to: (*a*) federal

---

[155] *Northwest Territories Act*, R.S.C. 1985, c. N-27.
[156] *Yukon Act*, S.C. 2002, c. 7, which received Royal Assent on 26 March 2002, came into effect on 1 April 2003, and replaced the *Yukon Act*, R.S.C. 1985, c. Y-2.
[157] *Nunavut Act*, S.C. 1993, c. 28.
[158] Section 19 has been substantially amended by the *Yukon First Nations Land Claims Settlement Act*, S.C. 1994, c. 34, s. 20, and that amendment will come into force on the first day on which the final agreements of all Yukon Indian bands are given effect.
[159] *Re Noah Estate* (1961), 32 D.L.R. (2d) 185 (N.W.T. Terr. Ct.).
[160] *Northwest Territories Act*, R.S.C. 1952, c. 331, s. 17(2), as am. by S.C. 1960 c. 20, s. 2.
[161] *Re Noah, supra* note 159 at 203.

legislative authority, (*b*) s. 35 of the *Constitution Act, 1982*, and (*c*) rights set out in land claims agreements that are considered to be "treaty rights" within the meaning of ss. 35(1) and 35(3) of the *Constitution Act, 1982*. Territorial common law has been interpreted as including some Inuit customary law. For example, in *Re Katies Adoption Petition,*[162] Sissons J. held that customary Inuit adoptions were in accordance with the laws of the Northwest Territories. In *Re Deborah,*[163] the Northwest Territories Court of Appeal stated that the territorial legislation regarding adoptions was never intended to restrict the applicability of Inuit customary law.[164]

The *Yukon Act* and the *NWT Act* authorize the Minister of DIAND to enter into agreements with Indians and Inuit for the herding, control, management, administration, sale, slaughter, and protection of reindeer in the territories.

In *Bruce* v. *Yukon Territory (Commissioner),*[165] Lilles J. of the Yukon Territorial Court held that the terms "band community" and "band council," which were specifically mentioned in a territorial law, were merely descriptive terms of a geographical area and not necessarily restricted to Indians. The terms were used to reflect the social and political reality of the geographical area and were not used in the constitutional sense. This reflects the unique nature of government in Canada's North, where most communities are mixed Indian/non-Indian or Inuit/non-Inuit.

The new *Yukon Act*[166] came into effect on April 1, 2003 and is part of the federal government's commitment to the Government of the Yukon and Yukon Indian bands to transfer the responsibilities of the Minister of DIAND respecting land and resource management in the Yukon Territory to the Government of the Yukon. The devolution of land and resource management powers is a critical element of the new *Yukon Act*. The new act also amended s. 19 (s. 22 under the new Act) of the *Yukon Act* noted above by modernizing the language of the section and by making reference to the Inuvialuit Final Agreement[167] and the *Yukon First Nations Land Claims Settlement Act*.[168]

CONSULTATION AND ACCOMMODATION

Introduction

The Crown's duty to consult and accommodate Aboriginal people constitutes a relatively complex legal doctrine that is not yet fully developed and understood in Canadian law. However, an analysis of the applicable case law and the relationship between the judicial commentary on Crown consultation and accommodation with Aboriginal people and the doctrines of general administrative law provide a basis for understanding the Crown's duties in this respect. This analysis can also provide guidance on how the law in this area appears to be developing.[169]

---

[162] *Re Katies Adoption Petition* (1961), 32 D.L.R. (2d) 686 (N.W.T. Terr. Ct.).
[163] *Re Deborah* (1972), 28 D.L.R. (3d) 483 (N.W.T.C.A.).
[164] For further discussion, see N. Zlotkin, "Judicial Recognition of Aboriginal Customary Law in Canada: Selected Marriage and Adoption Cases" [1984] 4 C.N.L.R. 1.
[165] *Bruce* v. *Yukon Territory (Commissioner)*, [1994] 3 C.N.L.R. 25 (Y. Terr. Ct.).
[166] *Supra* note 156.
[167] Inuvialuit Final Agreement, (Ottawa: Indian Affairs and Northern Development, 1984).
[168] *Supra* note 158.
[169] See generally: Thomas Isaac and Anthony Knox, "The Crown's Duty to Consult Aboriginal People" (2003) 41:1 Alta. L. Rev. 49–77; and Thomas Isaac, "The Crown's Duty to Consult and Accommodate Aboriginal People" (November 2003) 61:6 The Advocate 865–880.

The decisions of the Supreme Court of Canada in *Sparrow*,[170] *Delgamuukw*,[171] and others[172] confirm that the duty of the Crown to consult requires a fundamental shift in the way the Crown has traditionally interacted with Aboriginal people. As a result of *Delgamuukw* and other judicial decisions, some governments have attempted to enhance their consultation policies and mechanisms.[173] However, Crown-Aboriginal consultation regimes have not yet resulted in the necessary stability with respect to governmental decision-making and predictability.

Sources of the Crown's Duty to Consult and Accommodate

The Crown's duty to consult and accommodate Aboriginal people has arisen primarily from judicial analysis of the justification test relating to Crown infringements of Aboriginal and treaty rights. However, both Aboriginal case law and Canadian law generally suggest at least three other sources for the Crown's duty to consult and accommodate: (1) the right of all persons under Canadian law to be dealt with by the Crown in a manner that is, with few exceptions, procedurally fair, reasonable, and in accordance with general administrative law; (2) the "honour of the Crown," which can only be properly served in circumstances in which the Crown considers the Aboriginal perspective and demonstrably addresses such perspective in Crown decision-making; and (3) the requirement of the Crown, as a fiduciary, to consult with and consider the views of, its Aboriginal beneficiaries in circumstances that are subject to such fiduciary relationship.[174]

In *Delgamuukw* the Supreme Court of Canada began its discussion of the Crown's duty to consult by noting that the fiduciary relationship between the Crown and Aboriginal people *may* be satisfied "by the involvement of aboriginal peoples in decisions taken with respect to their lands."[175] Note the use of the word "involvement" and not, for example, the word "approval" or "veto," and the use of the word "may" and not "must." This demonstrates the Court's attempt to set out an analytical framework for interpreting existing Aboriginal and treaty rights that is, on the one hand, not absolute[176] but, on the other hand, affords these rights adequate and fair treatment by governments.

Triggering the Duty to Consult

The Supreme Court of Canada has made reference to the duty to consult within the context of the justification analysis of s. 35(1) of the *Constitution Act, 1982*, thereby requiring Aboriginal and treaty rights to be *proven* (or existing) prior to the duty to consult and accommodate being engaged. In *Sparrow*, the Court held that consultation forms an important component of the Crown's justification analysis when justifying as infringement of an existing Aboriginal or treaty right. Dickson C.J. stated that whether the Aboriginal group at issue had been consulted is one of the further questions courts are to ask when determining whether the Crown's infringement of an Aboriginal or treaty right is

---

[170] *Sparrow, supra* note 61 at 1113, 1119.

[171] *Delgamuukw, supra* note 68 at para. 68.

[172] *Marshall* (reconsideration), *supra* note 114, at paras. 43–44; *R. v. Nikal*, [1996] 1 S.C.R. 1013 at para. 110; *Van der Peet, supra* note 66 at para. 311, McLachlin J. dissenting); *Mikisew Cree First Nation* v. *Canada (Min. of Canadian Heritage)*, [2002] 1 C.N.L.R. 169 at para. 130 (F.C.T.D.); and *Nunavik Inuit* v. *Canada (Min. of Canadian Heritage)*, [1998] 4 C.N.L.R. 68 at paras. 107–9 (F.C.T.D.).

[173] For example, see British Columbia's Aboriginal consultation policy at <http://srmwww.gov.bc.ca/cpp/docs/ConsultationPolicyFN.pdf>.

[174] *Wewaykum Indian Band* v. *Canada*, [2002] 4 S.C.R. 245 (S.C.C.).

[175] *Delgamuukw, supra* 68 at para. 168.

[176] Aboriginal and treaty rights, while recognized and affirmed by s. 35(1), have been repeatedly held by the

justified.[177] Within this context, the duty to consult is seen as a duty that arises once an existing Aboriginal or treaty right is deemed to be existing or not extinguished within the meaning of s. 35(1).

In *Ontario (Min. of Municipal Affairs and Housing)* v. *Trans-Canada Pipelines Ltd.*,[178] the Ontario Court of Appeal affirmed that consultation is not an independent right held by Aboriginal people but, rather, it attaches to already existing Aboriginal and treaty rights.[179] Similarly, in commenting on *Sparrow*,[180] *Badger*,[181] and *Delgamuukw*,[182] the Ontario Court of Appeal in *Trans-Canada Pipelines* also noted that

> what these cases decide is that the duty of the Crown to consult with First Nations is a legal requirement that assists the court in determining whether the Crown is constitutionally justified in engaging in a particular action that has been found to *prima facie* infringe an existing Aboriginal or treaty right of a First Nation. It is only after the First Nation has established such infringement through an appropriate hearing that the duty of the Crown to consult with First Nations becomes engaged as a factor for the court to consider in the justificatory phase of the proceeding.[183]

However, the British Columbia Court of Appeal in both *Taku River Tlingit First Nation* v. *Ringstad*[184] and *Haida Nation* v. *B.C. (Min. of Forests)*[185] has held that the duty to consult can arise in the absence of a proven Aboriginal right. Both decisions affirmed that the duty to consult can be engaged in cases where an Aboriginal right appears only *prima facie* to be existing and such purported right is threatened by infringement. These decisions are currently under appeal to the Supreme Court of Canada.

The British Columbia Court of Appeal has held that the duty to consult and to accommodate does not arise solely from the s. 35(1) justification test, but that it also arises from the "broader fiduciary footing of the Crown's relationship with the Indian peoples who are under its protection."[186] However, in light of the Supreme Court of Canada decision of *Wewaykum*,[187] the conclusion of the British Columbia Court of Appeal likely needs modification to read "honour of the Crown" and not "fiduciary" because *Wewaykum* clearly dispels any notion of a "universal" Crown/Aboriginal *sui generis* fiduciary relationship.

Engagement of the Crown's duty to consult based on the honour of the Crown resembles the general duty of the Crown to treat all its subjects fairly when acting or determining issues likely to have an impact upon them. As a result, Canadian governments are well advised to adopt a broad approach when fulfilling their duty to consult and accommodate Aboriginal people in order to ensure that potentially infringing Crown actions can withstand judicial scrutiny under s. 35(1) of the *Constitution Act, 1982*. In *R.* v. *Côté*,[188]

Supreme Court of Canada not to be absolute. See *Sparrow, supra* note 61 at 1119.

[177] *Sparrow, supra* note 61 at 1119.

[178] *Ontario (Min. of Municipal Affairs and Housing)* v. *Trans-Canada Pipelines Ltd.*, [2000] 3 C.N.L.R. 153 (Ont. C.A.).

[179] *Ibid.* at para. 112.

[180] *Sparrow, supra* note 61.

[181] *Badger, supra* note 113.

[182] *Delgamuukw, supra* note 68.

[183] *Trans-Canada Pipelines, supra* note 178 at para. 119.

[184] *Taku River Tlingit First Nation* v. *Ringstad*, [2002] 2 C.N.L.R. 312 (B.C.C.A.).

[185] *Haida Nation* v. *B.C. (Min. of Forests)*, [2002] 2 C.N.L.R. 121, (B.C.C.A.); see also *Gitxsan First Nation* v. *B.C. (Min. of Forests)*, [2003] 2 C.N.L.R. 142 (B.C.S.C.).

[186] *Ibid.*, *Haida* at para. 55.

[187] *Wewaykum, supra* note 174.

[188] *Côté, supra* note 105.

the Supreme Court of Canada stated that

> Section 35(1) only lays down the constitutional minimums that governments must meet in their relations with aboriginal peoples with respect to aboriginal and treaty rights. Subject to constitutional constraints, governments may choose to go beyond the standard set by s.35(1).[189]

Clearly, in determining the appropriate content of consultation and accommodation, governments should look to the courts for guidance but remain unfettered to develop fair procedures in the spirit of such general guidance. To ensure that Crown decisions can withstand judicial scrutiny under s. 35(1) of the *Constitution Act, 1982*, the Crown may have to go beyond the minimum standards set by s. 35(1) and the general guidance of the courts relating to Crown consultation and accommodation, as the appropriate standard will vary along the spectrum noted above according to the circumstances. Reasonable *bona fide* attempts of consultation and accommodation are required. However, First Nations cannot frustrate[190] such reasonable *bona fide* attempts, and cannot use unreasonable positions to thwart government from making decisions or acting in cases where such attempts have not resulted in an agreement.

The logic of requiring some form of consultation in the face of a *prima facie* claim of rights is that in order for the Crown's consultation with Aboriginal people to be meaningful, it should precede, not follow, an infringement. No Aboriginal group has yet judicially proven Aboriginal title and few Aboriginal rights have been proven. In most foreseeable cases, Crown consultation must occur before any reasonable ability by the Aboriginal group to prove judicially their claimed Aboriginal rights or title.[191] However, the degree to which consultation and particularly accommodation may occur must be dependent upon the degree to which such rights have been proven. For example, in a *prima facie* case of Aboriginal title, the procedural requirements of consultation may apply. However, the application of the substantive elements of accommodation, such as compensation or, depending on the circumstances, mitigation, may be entirely inappropriate. Thus, the use of a *prima facie* case of Aboriginal title, for example, cannot, by its very nature, provide the degree of rights and entitlement of proven Aboriginal title. To suggest otherwise runs contrary to all of the Supreme Court's decisions to date in this area which clearly require rights to be *proven*. Where the line is drawn between the two is challenging, but likely is in the proximity of the procedural requirements of consultation, and not the substantive requirements dealing with accommodation. The challenge for governments, and where judicial direction is required, is the weight to be given to *prima facie* and not *proven* Aboriginal rights or title claims, and the extent, if any, of accommodation required. Finally, simply because accommodation may not be required to meet the minimum standard when *prima facie* s. 35(1) rights are concerned, governments may, nevertheless, want to exceed this minimum threshold in appropriate circumstances.

Thus, referring back to the suggestion that there are at least four sources to the Crown's duty to consult and accommodate Aboriginal people, these four sources can be categorized into two subcategories: universal and restricted. The universal duty of the Crown to consult and accommodate Aboriginal people arises from: (*a*) the Crown's general duty to all of its subjects to treat them fairly; and (*b*) the "honour of the Crown." The restricted

---

[189] *Ibid.*, at para. 83.
[190] *Trans-Canada Pipelines, supra* note 178.
[191] *Halfway River First Nation* v. *B.C. (Min. of Forests)*, [1999] 4 C.N.L.R. 1 at 44 (B.C.C.A.) at para. 161.

duty to consult and accommodate arises from: (*a*) in appropriate circumstances that trigger a "fiduciary relationship," a duty by the Crown (the fiduciary) to consult with Aboriginal people (the beneficiary); and (*b*) the justification test used under s. 35(1) of the *Constitution Act, 1982*. The subcategorization of the sources of the Crown's duty to consult and accommodate are helpful because the degree and extent of the duty is invariably higher under the restricted subcategory than it is under the universal subcategory.

Nature of the Duty to Consult

In *Delgamuukw*, the Supreme Court of Canada focused on accommodation and consultation within the context of the justification test and provided the Court's most substantive comment to date on the issue. Lamer C.J. stressed the importance of consultation by the Crown with Aboriginal people respecting decisions, actions, and legislation of the Crown that may infringe aboriginal title:

> There is always a duty of consultation. . . . The nature and scope of the duty of consultation will vary with the circumstances. In occasional cases, when the breach is less serious or relatively minor, it will be no more than a duty to discuss important decisions that will be taken with respect to lands held pursuant to aboriginal title. Of course, even in these rare cases when the minimum acceptable standard is consultation, this consultation must be in good faith, and with the intention of substantially addressing the concerns of the aboriginal peoples whose lands are at issue. In most cases, it will be significantly deeper than mere consultation. Some cases may even require the full consent of an aboriginal nation, particularly when provinces enact hunting and fishing regulations in relation to aboriginal lands.[192]

This excerpt from *Delgamuukw* establishes the emergence of three general categories of consultation with Aboriginal people emerging:

1. The narrow category of "occasional," "rare," or "mere consultation" that must occur to address the concerns of Aboriginal people. "Mere consultation" would appear to mean talking together for mutual understanding. It also implies discussion and the sharing of information between the Crown and its representatives and affected Aboriginal people, with the Crown responding to the concerns raised by the Aboriginal group concerned.

2. In most cases, something "significantly deeper than mere consultation" will be required. While this category appears to involve Aboriginal participation by way of input into the decision-making process, it clearly does not extend into the third described level of consultation, which seems to resemble negotiations requiring the consent of both parties or perhaps adjudication. This broad middle ground of Crown consultation with Aboriginal people seems primarily to be concerned with the Crown's duty to accommodate the interests of Aboriginal people.

3. The other narrow category on the consultation spectrum may require the "consent" of the Aboriginal group involved. This last category, on its face, appears limited to proven Aboriginal title and it is not clear as to what indicia might be established to require such Aboriginal consent.

These three categories of consultation correspond closely with the categories that flow from the duty of procedural fairness in Anglo-Canadian administrative law. Like Lamer C.J. in *Delgamuukw*, de Smith in his well-known text, *Judicial Review of Administrative*

---

[192] *Delgamuukw, supra* note 68 at para. 168.

Action,[193] states that "mere consultation" is at the lower end of fair procedures.[194] In a striking parallel to Lamer C.J., de Smith notes that a full hearing is at the other end of the administrative law spectrum. Between these poles is the bulk of the content of procedural fairness, including the entitlement to make written and oral representations and to have such representations meaningfully considered. Such meaningful consideration, within the context of Aboriginal consultation, includes attempting accommodation of Aboriginal people's interests, mitigating the negative effects of infringements on Aboriginal and treaty rights, and attempting negotiated solutions, where appropriate.

In *Marshall* (reconsideration), the Supreme Court of Canada suggested that agreements between Aboriginal people and the Crown can satisfy the requirement to maintain the special trust relationship between the Crown and Aboriginal people.[195] Such agreements would be consistent with the Crown acting "honourably," which appears to be another core element of the Crown's duty to consult and accommodate. This suggests that agreements between industry and Aboriginal groups, which are becoming quite common in many parts of Canada, should have some degree of Crown sanction and involvement so as to ensure their applicability to any judicial determination of consultation and accommodation within the meaning of s. 35(1) of the *Constitution Act, 1982*.

Consultation and accommodation in the Aboriginal context is different from the consultation required in general administrative law, in that it responds to the special Crown responsibility to and relationship with Aboriginal people by requiring that adequate consultation and accommodation possess both a procedural and a substantive element.

Procedurally, if their constitutional rights are to be infringed, Aboriginal people must be given an opportunity to have their views heard and considered in a manner entirely analogous to that required by general administrative law and procedural fairness. In effect, bad procedure can render a correct decision unenforceable.[196]

Substantively, Aboriginal people must have their rights accommodated, which can include mitigation of harmful impacts on Aboriginal rights, minimal impairment of Aboriginal rights, providing compensation, or attempting negotiated solutions. If consultation and accommodation do not produce a Crown decision that is accepted by the affected Aboriginal group as an appropriate basis for justifiable infringement, the adequacy of such justification may be judicially determined according to the justification test discussed above.[197] In this respect, the "consent" of *Delgamuukw* and the "judicial hearing" of de Smith seem to be closely related. Only correct procedures and substantively correct decisions will uphold the justification of an infringement of Aboriginal or treaty rights in the courts.

The principles of accommodation and prioritization are closely related to the concept of consultation. The Supreme Court of Canada in *R. v. Gladstone*[198] stated that the following questions are relevant to whether the Crown has granted priority to, and has accommodated, Aboriginal rights:

1. whether the government has accommodated the exercise of the Aboriginal right;

[193] Stanley de Smith, The Lord Woolf & Jeffrey Jowell, *Judicial Review of Administrative Action*, 5th ed. (London: Sweet & Maxwell, 1995), 377–84.

[194] *Ibid.* at 431.

[195] *Marshall* (reconsideration), *supra* note 114 at para 43.

[196] *Nunavut Tunngavik Inc. v. Canada (Min. of Fisheries and Oceans)*, [2000] 3 C.N.L.R. 136 (F.C.T.D.); aff'd [2001] 1 C.N.L.R. iv (F.C.A.); see also Isaac, and Isaac and Knox, *supra* note 169.

[197] *Marshall* (reconsideration), *supra* note 114 at para. 43.

[198] *R. v. Gladstone*, [1996] 2 S.C.R. 723.

2. whether the objectives of government by enacting a particular regulatory scheme reflect the need to consider the Aboriginal priority;

3. the extent of participation in the fishery, in the case of fishing rights, by Aboriginal people relative to their proportion of the population;

4. how government has accommodated different Aboriginal rights (i.e., the right to fish for food and the right to fish commercially);

5. how important the right is to the economic and material well-being of the Aboriginal group claiming the right; and

6. the criteria used by government to allocate the particular resources at issue.[199]

Apart from the issue of priority, other questions raised under this component of the *Sparrow* justification analysis include:[200]

1. Has there been as little infringement as possible in order to effect the desired result?

2. In expropriation, has fair compensation been paid?

3. Has the Aboriginal group been consulted with respect to the conservation measures used, or at least have they been informed of these conservation measures?

The British Columbia Court of Appeal noted in *Halfway River First Nation* v. *B.C. (Min. of Forests)* that the "fact that adequate notice of an intended decision may have been given, does not mean that the requirement for adequate consultation has also been met."[201] In *Delgamuukw*, Lamer C.J. described the concept of priority as applied to Aboriginal title:

> [I]f the Crown's fiduciary duty requires that aboriginal title be given priority, then it is the altered approach to priority that I laid down in *Gladstone* which should apply. . . . [T]his might entail, for example, that governments accommodate the participation of aboriginal peoples in the development of the resources of British Columbia.[202]

Interestingly, the above excerpt from *Delgamuukw* is one paragraph before Lamer C.J.'s discussion of consultation and Aboriginal title. This excerpt provides a basis for the Supreme Court of Canada's overall analytical thrust of balancing the rights of Aboriginal people with the ability of governments to govern. While different words are used, such as "accommodation," "priority," and "consultation," they all seek a non-absolute or flexible interpretation of existing Aboriginal and treaty rights that is fair and balanced.

Consultation in the Aboriginal context can be said to possess both procedural and substantive elements. Procedurally, Aboriginal people must be given an opportunity to have their views heard and considered, in a manner similar to that required by the law relating to procedural fairness. Substantively, accommodation of Aboriginal and treaty rights must be attempted, including: (*a*) mitigation of harmful impacts on Aboriginal rights, (*b*) minimal impairment of Aboriginal rights, and (*c*) attempting negotiated solutions. If consultation does not produce an agreement, the adequacy of the Crown's justification and consultation efforts may be litigated in the courts.[203]

---

[199] *Ibid.* at para. 64.
[200] *Sparrow, supra* note 61 at 1119; *Badger, supra* note 113 at para. 84; *Gladstone, supra* note 198 at para. 55.
[201] *Halfway River, supra* note 190 at 44.
[202] *Delgamuukw, supra* note 68 at para. 167.
[203] *Marshall* (reconsideration), *supra* note 114 at para. 43.

In *Sparrow*, the Supreme Court of Canada affirmed its general approach regarding the Crown's fiduciary obligations to Aboriginal people first outlined in *R. v. Guerin*[204] by stating that the scrutiny to be applied to federal and provincial legislative authority under s. 35(1) of the *Constitution Act, 1982* is in keeping with "the concept of holding the Crown to a high standard of honourable dealing."[205] This forms a core element of the duty to consult: honourable dealing with Aboriginal people by the Crown.

Duty of Aboriginal People Not to Frustrate Consultation

Aboriginal people have an obligation not to frustrate attempts by the Crown to consult with them. In *Halfway River*,[206] the British Columbia Court of Appeal considered the duty owed by the Ministry of Forests to consult with the Halfway River First Nation over various cutting decisions made by the ministry. The Court of Appeal commented on the nature of the Crown's duty to consult within the context of Treaty No. 8 and affirmed that the ministry had a duty to consult Halfway River First Nation prior to making decisions that may affect Aboriginal and treaty rights. It was noted that the ministry failed to take all reasonable efforts to consult with, and inform itself about, Halfway River First Nation. The Court of Appeal also stated that the ministry failed to the give Halfway River First Nation relevant information relating to decisions being made.

While relevant information must be provided to Aboriginal people in a timely manner and their representations taken seriously by government, Aboriginal people also have a duty not to frustrate or obstruct the consultation process by refusing to participate in it or by placing unreasonable conditions on government:

> The fact that adequate notice of an intended decision may have been given, does not mean that the requirement for adequate consultation has also been met. The Crown's duty to consult imposes on it a positive obligation to reasonably ensure that Aboriginal peoples are provided with all necessary information in a timely way so that they have an opportunity to express their interests and concerns, and to ensure that their representations are seriously considered and, wherever possible, demonstrably integrated into the proposed plan of action. . . . There is a reciprocal duty on Aboriginal peoples to express their interests and concerns once they have had an opportunity to consider the information provided by the Crown, and to consult in good faith by whatever means are available to them. They cannot frustrate the consultation process by refusing to meet or participate, or by imposing unreasonable conditions.[207]

This statement is interesting in that it clearly places a duty not only on the Crown, but also on Aboriginal people. Aboriginal people, in becoming attuned to what rights they possess by way of treaty, Aboriginal title, or otherwise, must also be attuned to the corresponding duties. Thus, like public governments, Aboriginal people need to develop processes by which they manage government consultation and referrals. Aboriginal people will also want to become engaged in establishing the appropriate administrative, legal, and other mechanisms necessary to fully respond to governments' consultation requests. This necessary work can be a daunting task for many Indian bands who do not have adequate resources.

---

[204] *R. v. Guerin*, [1984] 2 S.C.R. 335.

[205] *Sparrow, supra* note 61 at 1109.

[206] *Halfway River, supra* note 190.

[207] *Ibid.* 44; the Ontario Court of Appeal felt that the onus on Indian bands not to frustrate the consultation process as enunciated in *Halfway River* had "considerable merit"; see *Trans-Canada Pipelines, supra* note 178 at para. 123 (Ont. C.A.)

In *Kelly Lake Cree Nation* v. *B.C.*,[208] the Crown was found not to have an obligation to consult, and if there was such an obligation, it was met when the Kelly Lake Cree Nation failed to provide any response to the Crown's letter following discussions between the Crown and the Indian band. The British Columbia Supreme Court also noted that the decision-maker for the Crown in this case took into consideration potential Aboriginal and treaty rights that may be affected:

> The process of consultation cannot be viewed in a vacuum and must take into account the general process by which government deals with First Nations people, including any discussions between resource developers such as Amoco and First Nations people. . . . It was submitted that the SFN [Saulteau First Nation] were without the resources to provide information unless requested. The evidence, while establishing that this community of First Nations is of limited means does not establish a community incapable of providing the information sought. . . . In conclusion, while the SFN as represented by Chief Cameron are adamant in their opposition to this project, they have been afforded the fulfilment of the duty upon the Crown to be consulted. Any responsibility for the absence of consultation lies with their own representatives.[209]

This so-called requirement not to "frustrate" the consultation process is simply another example of the courts imposing a level of reasonableness on the overall relationship between the Crown and Aboriginal people and their rights.

Another issue is whether there is a legal requirement on the part of the Crown to fund consultation processes involving Aboriginal people. From the perspective of achieving certainty and stability with respect to dealing with these matters, it would seem that governments have an interest in ensuring that their consultation guidelines and schemes are fully implemented. This may require the expenditure of resources, which can be justified in light of the growing litigation costs relating to these matters and the increasing degree of business uncertainty that has been created and will exist until all parties trust the consultation process to be objectively fair.

To Whom is the Duty Owed?

Courts have generally referred to the Crown's duty to consult being owed to the group or to the First Nation, rather than to individual Indians. For example, in *Halfway River First Nation* v. *B.C. (Min. of Forests)*,[210] Dorgan J., affirmed by the British Columbia Court of Appeal,[211] stated that the Crown has a duty to "undertake reasonable consultation with a First Nation which may be affected by its decision."[212] The Supreme Court of Canada in *Delgamuukw*[213] also described the Crown's duty to consult as being with the Aboriginal group. Aboriginal and treaty rights are communal in nature, even though they may be exercised by individuals of the group.[214]

There remains an outstanding legal issue of whether Indian bands possess the capacity to bring an action and be sued in their own right.[215] Nothing prevents an individual from

---

[208] *Kelly Lake Cree Nation* v. *B.C. (Min. of Energy and Mines)*, [1999] 3 C.N.L.R. 126 (B.C.S.C.).

[209] *Ibid.* at paras. 154, 244, 252.

[210] *Halfway River First Nation* v. *B.C. (Min. of Forests)*, [1997] 4 C.N.L.R. 45 (B.C.S.C.).

[211] *Supra* note 190.

[212] *Halfway River, supra* note 210 at 71.

[213] *Delgamuukw, supra* note 68 at para. 168.

[214] *Sparrow, supra* note 61 at 1112; *Delgamuukw, supra* note 68 at 1082–83.

[215] For example, in *Mintuck* v. *Valley River Band No. 63A*, [1976] 4 W.W.R. 543 at 553–54 (Man. Q.B.), Soloman J. raised some doubt as to whether an Indian band could bring an action in its own name. Some courts have held that Indian bands possess such capacity; see *Canadian Pacific Railway* v. *Paul*, [1984] 3

bringing an action as a representative for a larger group of Indians. To avoid any ambiguity, some counsel for Aboriginal people commonly bring forward representative actions.[216] Individual Indians may be able to bring claims on their own behalf with respect to the breach of treaty rights. Presumably this could also apply to consultation, but does not necessarily mean a successful result.

Assuming that individual Indians can initiate claims for breach of the duty to consult, the issue is whether the consultation with the representatives of the Indian band would satisfy a court that adequate consultation had occurred. Barring any unusual circumstances, a court should find that such consultation with duly authorized representatives of an Indian band (its chief and councillors, for example) is adequate to satisfy the duty to consult. This consultation not only makes practical sense, but is also founded upon the law relating to the negotiation of Indian treaties.

In *Pawis* v. *The Queen*,[217] Marceau J. of the Federal Court, Trial Division, expressly dealt with the issue of whether a claim arising from an 1850 treaty between the Crown and the representatives of the Ojibway Indians could be raised by individual Ojibway Indians or by their representatives:

> Although each individual Ojibway Indian was to benefit from the Treaty, it seems to me that the language used therein *precludes the idea that each individual was a party to the contract* and had therefore the status to sue personally and individually for an alleged breach thereof. Since the Treaty was negotiated and entered into with the Ojibway Indians taken as a group, it seems to me that *an action based on the Treaty, alleging breach of the promises subscribed therein toward the group, could only be instituted by the contracting party itself, that is to say, the group.*[218] [emphasis added.]

In circumstances where individuals are raising specific concerns not addressed by the representatives or agents of the Indian band (i.e., identifying culturally modified trees that were not identified by the Indian band representatives or agents), reliance upon the direction provided by the duly authorized representative or agent of the Indian band should suffice. However, depending upon the circumstances, there may be instances where the prudent action is to receive the information being offered by the individual. Circumstances where this might be the appropriate response could include those areas where the information received by the Indian band is known to be weak or not complete.

Accommodation

The terms "accommodate" and "accommodation" have been defined as:

> [A]dapt, harmonize, reconcile . . . an adjustment or adaptation to suit a special or different purpose . . . a convenient agreement; a settlement or compromise.[219]

As part of the Supreme Court of Canada's attempt to balance governmental authority with Aboriginal and treaty rights, accommodation should serve as a tool for government to "adjust," "adapt," and "compromise" in the face of infringements to existing Aboriginal and treaty rights. The concept of accommodation has been raised by the Court in many of its decisions respecting s. 35(1) of the *Constitution Act, 1982*, including *Sparrow*,

---

C.N.L.R. 42 (N.B.C.A.).

[216] *Martin* v. *B.C.*, [1986] 3 C.N.L.R. 84 (B.C.S.C.), aff'd. *Oregan Jack Creek Indian Band* v. *C.N.R.*, [1990] 2 C.N.L.R. 85 at 93–94 (B.C.C.A.).

[217] *Pawis* v. *The Queen* (1979), 102 D.L.R. (3d) 603 (F.C.T.D.).

[218] *Ibid.* at 612.

[219] R.E. Allen, ed., *The Concise Oxford Dictionary of Current English,* 8th ed. (Oxford: Clarendon Press, 1990) 8.

wherein the Court stressed the need to balance competing societal interests with Aboriginal and treaty rights.[220] In its 1990 decision of *R. v. Sioui*,[221] the Court stated that the Crown bears the burden of proving that its occupancy of certain lands "cannot be accommodated to reasonable exercise of the Hurons' rights."[222] In *Côté*[223] the Court stated the following with respect to its discussion of the s. 35(1) justification test:

> [T]he courts must examine whether the infringement unduly restricts the aboriginal right in question, and whether the restriction can be accommodated with the Crown's special fiduciary relationship with First Nations.[224]

In *Gladstone*[225] the Court, in discussing questions relevant to whether the government has granted priority to Aboriginal rights-holders, stated that such questions relate to compensation, consultation, and "whether the government has accommodated the exercise of the aboriginal right" and how the government "has accommodated different aboriginal rights in a particular fishery (food *versus* commercial rights, for example)".[226] Furthermore, in *Gladstone*, the Court confirmed that the Crown can rebut the inference of an infringement of an Aboriginal right if it can demonstrate that the regulatory scheme in question "viewed as a whole, accommodates the collective aboriginal right in question."[227]

In *Delgamuukw*,[228] the Court stated the following in respect of accommodation and Aboriginal title:

> Under the second part of the justification test, these legislative objectives are subject to accommodation of the aboriginal peoples' interests. This accommodation must always be in accordance with the honour and good faith of the Crown. Moreover, when dealing with a generalized claim over vast tracts of land, accommodation is not a simple matter of asking whether licences have been fairly allocated in one industry, or whether conservation measures have been properly implemented for a specific resource. Rather, the question of accommodation of "aboriginal title" is much broader than this. Certainly, one aspect of accommodation in this context entails notifying and consulting aboriginal peoples with respect to the development of the affected territory. Another aspect of accommodation is fair compensation.[229]

In respect of treaty rights, the Court held in *R. v. Marshall*[230] that regulations that allowed for fishing to produce a moderate livelihood could accommodate the treaty right.[231] In *Marshall* (reconsideration)[232] the Court stated:

> As this and other courts have pointed out on many occasions, the process of accommodation of the treaty right may best be resolved by consultation and negotiation.[233]

In *Mitchell v. Minister of National Revenue*[234] the Supreme Court of Canada cited its

---

[220] *Sparrow, supra* note 61 at 1109, 1110, 1118, 1119.

[221] *Sioui, supra* note 76.

[222] *Ibid.* at 1072.

[223] *Côté, supra* note 105.

[224] *Ibid.* at 189.

[225] *Gladstone, supra* note 198.

[226] *Ibid.* at 768.

[227] *Ibid.* at 818.

[228] *Delgamuukw, supra* note 68.

[229] *Ibid.* at para. 203.

[230] *R. v. Marshall*, [1999] 3 S.C.R. 456.

[231] *Ibid.* at para. 61; see also paras. 64, 111–14.

[232] *Marshall* (reconsideration), *supra* note 114.

[233] *Ibid.* at para. 22; see also paras. 13, 15, 26, 27, 33, 36.

[234] *Mitchell v. Minister of National Revenue*, [2001] 1 S.C.R. 911.

decision in *Delgamuukw* wherein it stated that "accommodation must be done in a manner that does not strain 'the Canadian legal and constitutional structure'." The Crown's ability to accommodate, in certain circumstances, must be prescribed by legislation,[235] in particular, where a minister of the Crown, in exercising discretionary authority, seeks to accommodate Aboriginal and treaty rights. In *Marshall*, the Court referred with approval to the following statement from *Adams*[236] regarding the need for administrative discretionary authority that may affect Aboriginal and treaty rights to be given sufficient statutory guidance:

> In light of the Crown's unique fiduciary obligations towards Aboriginal peoples, *Parliament may not simply adopt an unstructured discretionary administrative regime which risks infringing Aboriginal rights in a substantial number of applications in the absence of some explicit guidance.* If a statute confers an administrative discretion which may carry significant consequences for the exercise of an Aboriginal right, the statute or its delegate regulations must outline specific criteria for the granting or refusal of that discretion which seek to accommodate the existence of Aboriginal rights. In the absence of such specific guidance, the statute will fail to provide representatives of the Crown with sufficient directives to fulfill their fiduciary duties, and the statute will be found to represent an infringement of Aboriginal rights under the *Sparrow* test. [emphasis in original]

This illustrates the need for governments across Canada to legislate clear guidance to assist discretionary decision-makers in accommodating existing Aboriginal and treaty rights. The Supreme Court of Canada expressly stated that an administrative regime that may infringe Aboriginal or treaty rights must provide express guidance to ministers of the Crown and other government decision-makers when exercising decision-making authority. Such express guidance must include specific criteria to grant or refuse that discretion which seeks to accommodate the existence of Aboriginal rights.

A review of legislation across Canada indicates that no government/legislature has implemented this express requirement set out by the Supreme Court of Canada. The only example that may be close to the Court's requirement can be found in the *Manitoba Fishery Regulation*.[237] Section 13.2 of the regulation states that the Minister of Fisheries and Oceans (or the director) shall consider the following factors before varying a close time for a fishery: whether such variance of the close time (*a*) will infringe any existing treaty or Aboriginal right; (*b*) is reasonably necessary for conservation; and (*c*) respects the priority of the holders of a treaty or Aboriginal right.

Case Law: Procedural Errors

Cheslatta Carrier Nation v. *B.C.*[238] provides an example of where the Crown failed to meet its duty to consult. The government of British Columbia possessed insufficient information to assess adequately the potential impact on Aboriginal rights and, therefore, did not allow the Cheslatta Carrier Nation to mount a proper defence to the proposed action. This British Columbia Supreme Court decision was based primarily on the statutory duty to consult outlined in British Columbia's *Environmental Assessment Act*.

In *Trans-Canada Pipelines Ltd.*,[239] the Ontario Court of Appeal considered an order made by a commission under the *Municipality Act* to amalgamate a number of townships

---

[235] See note 98.
[236] *Marshall, supra* note 230 at para. 64; see *Adams, supra* note 64 at para. 54.
[237] *Manitoba Fishery Regulation*, SOR/87-509; SOR 98/247, 5.6.
[238] *Cheslatta Carrier Nation* v. *B.C.*, [1998] 3 C.N.L.R. 1 (B.C.S.C.).
[239] *Trans-Canada Pipelines, supra* note 178.

into a single municipality. A number of First Nations sought a declaration that the order infringed hunting, fishing, and trapping rights guaranteed in Treaty No. 9 and could impede future land claims negotiations. The lower court allowed the applications for judicial review. The Court of Appeal allowed the appeal and confirmed the original order creating a single municipality. One argument upon which the lower court rested its decision and the Court of Appeal addressed considerably was the issue of whether the Crown failed to consult with the affected First Nations. The Court held that although the commission had failed to consult with the affected First Nations, it did not lose its jurisdiction. The *Municipality Act* placed no *statutory* duty on the commission to consult. The Court also held that the Crown's duty to consult Aboriginal people is only engaged when a particular action of the Crown has been found to infringe an existing Aboriginal or treaty right.[240] This contradicts the British Columbia Court of Appeal decisions, discussed earlier, in *Taku River*[241] and *Haida*, where a good *prima facie* case regarding the potential existence of Aboriginal rights was sufficient to engage the Crown's duty to consult Aboriginal people.[242]

In *Liidlii Kue First Nation* v. *Canada*,[243] the Federal Court, Trial Division considered an application by the Liidlii Kue First Nation seeking a declaration that the Crown breached its fiduciary duty to consult them prior to issuing a land use permit (by a land use administrator). The Court refused to grant the declaratory relief and sent the matter back to a different land use administrator. The Court confirmed that there exists a *constitutional* duty to consult those exercising the Treaty No. 11 rights to hunt, trap, and fish on unoccupied Crown lands and that the Crown's duty to consult, and the standard required, will vary from case to case.

Consultation must be "adequate" considering the circumstances in order to support the justification of a governmental infringement of an Aboriginal or treaty right. Litigation may well be the only means by which the parties involved can conclude whether the level of consultation in a particular case was adequate. Not only is consultation a critical component for any government conducting its business, especially when this business may infringe the rights of Aboriginal people, but it is also a key component to a government seeking to justify an infringement of Aboriginal and treaty rights. There is no clear and consistent definition of what "adequate" consultation means. Rather, the determination of what is adequate consultation depends on a case-by-case analysis, which is consistent with general procedural fairness and administrative law. "Appropriate" would seem ultimately to depend upon what is reasonable in the circumstances.

Duty to be Fair

The duty to consult can be broken down into two distinct but interconnected administrative law concepts: (1) the duty to provide a fair *process*, and (2) the duty to provide a fair *decision*. The process is the act of consulting, including notice, information gathering and distribution, discussions with Aboriginal people, and consideration and understanding of the issues and concerns of Aboriginal people. The decision is that part of a government action in which it decides to do or sanction a particular activity that may have an impact upon Aboriginal and treaty rights. Like the process, the decision must be seen as being transparent, considered, and arrived at in a manner that ensures that the rights of

---

[240] *Ibid.* at para. 119.
[241] *Taku River, supra* note 184.
[242] *Haida, supra* note 185.
[243] *Liidlii Kue First Nation* v. *Canada*, [2000] 4 C.N.L.R. 123 (F.C.T.D.).

Aboriginal people were "taken seriously."[244]

At one end of the procedural fairness spectrum in general administrative law is "mere consultation." At the other end is a hearing or a trial. Between these extremes is a substantive body of law directing decision-makers on how to act and deal fairly in a broad range of circumstances. An important point, and one that is particularly relevant to consultation with Aboriginal people, is that "procedural fairness does not, however, guarantee that the exercise of the opportunity to make representations will automatically result in the representations made being accepted."[245] This is supported in the Aboriginal legal context by the fact that existing Aboriginal rights and treaty rights are not absolute, but may be infringed if governments can justify the infringement, in accordance with the tests set out by the courts.

The concept of "reasonableness" forms an integral part of the duty to consult under s. 35(1) of the *Constitution Act, 1982*. In. *R. v. Nikal*, Cory J. stated:

> It can, I think, properly be inferred that the concept of reasonableness forms an integral part of the *Sparrow* test for justification. . . . So too in the aspects of information and consultation the concept of reasonableness must come into play. For example, . . . a request for consultations cannot simply be denied. So long as every reasonable effort is made to inform and to consult, such efforts would suffice to meet the justification requirement.[246]

The British Columbia Supreme Court has held that there is a duty of procedural fairness when decisions are made that may affect claimed Aboriginal rights.[247] Based on the case law to date and the preceding discussion, the Crown's duty to consult Aboriginal people also appears to require:

a) a genuine invitation to give advice;[248]

b) a genuine consideration of that advice;

c) the provision of sufficient information and time to the Aboriginal party being consulted;

d) that no unreasonable timelines be imposed, considering the relevant circumstances;

e) the government to explain clearly its positions;

f) the Aboriginal concern to be genuinely considered and addressed;

g) Aboriginal people are dealt with reasonably and their rights taken seriously;

h) there be no "sharp dealing"; and

i) that *bona fide* attempts to accommodate the interests of Aboriginal people be made in the face of interference with Aboriginal and treaty rights.

---

[244] *Sparrow, supra* note 61 at 1119.

[245] de Smith, *supra* note 193 at 376.

[246] *R. v. Nikal, supra* note 172 at para. 110.

[247] *Westbank First Nation* v. *B.C. (Min. of Forests)*, [2001] 1 C.N.L.R. 361 (B.C.S.C.); see also *Union of Nova Scotia Indians* v. *Canada*, [1997] 4 C.N.L.R. 280 at 294–303 (F.C.T.D.).

[248] See *R. v. Secretary of State for Social Services*, [1986] 1 All E.R. 164 (Q.B.); see also *Fletcher* v. *Min. of Town & Country Planning*, [1997] 2 All E.R. 496 at 500.

Ministerial Discretionary Authority

Many instances of consultation between the Crown and Aboriginal people involve the use of ministerial discretionary authority. In *Adams*[249] and *Marshall* (reconsideration),[250] the Supreme Court of Canada stated clearly that where a minister of the Crown exercises discretionary authority that may have an impact upon Aboriginal or treaty rights, then any such legislation setting out such ministerial discretionary authority must provide for consideration of potential interference with Aboriginal and treaty rights. Yet, notwithstanding this clear direction from the Court, few substantive amendments with respect to ministerial discretionary authority have been made to any federal or provincial legislation.[251]

The issue of the exercise of ministerial discretionary authority was considered in *Nunavut Tunngavik Inc. v. Canada (Min. of Fisheries and Oceans)*.[252] The issue concerned a decision of the Minister of Fisheries and Oceans regarding turbot quotas affecting an area within the Nunavut Land Claims Agreement. Nunavut Tunngavik Inc. argued that the minister failed to consider the advice of the Nunavut Wildlife Management Board (NWMB), which is constituted under the Nunavut Land Claims Agreement. Campbell J. held that the agreement states that there must be "meaningful inclusion of the NWMB in the Governmental decision-making process before any decisions are made."[253] The concept of meaningful inclusion is on its face a component of consultation and, in this case, within the terms of a treaty. Campbell J. held that the minister could not simply receive and examine the advice and recommendations given by the NWMB. He concluded that the relationship between the minister and the NWMB was intended to be "mandatory, close, cooperative and highly respectful".[254] Government must take a proactive stance when "considering" Aboriginal interests and advice with respect to decisions and actions that may adversely affect Aboriginal people.

The Federal Court of Appeal, while agreeing with the trial court's conclusion to set aside the minister's decision, referred the matter back to the minister for reconsideration. The Court of Appeal focused on whether the minister gave special consideration to the adjacency and economic dependence principles required by the Nunavut Land Claims Agreement or misconstrued these principles in their application. The Court also rejected a number of the trial judge's conclusions regarding the interpretation given to the relevant provisions of the Nunavut Land Claims Agreement. The Court stressed that it would not "second guess" the minister,[255] but balanced this by noting that "the Minister's discretion in section 7 of the *Fisheries Act* is no longer absolute when the exercise of that discretion affects the wildlife and the marine areas of the [Nunavut Settlement Area] and the wildlife management."[256]

Nunavut Tunngavik Inc. again challenged the authority of the Minister of Fisheries and Oceans in the decision of *Nunavut Tunngavik Inc. v. Canada (Min. of Fisheries and Oceans)*.[257] In that decision, Blais J. dismissed a similar application by Nunavut Tunnga-

---

[249] *Adams, supra* note 64.
[250] *Marshall* (reconsideration), *supra* note 114 at para. 33.
[251] See note 173.
[252] *Nunavut Tunngavik Inc. v. Canada (Min. of Fisheries and Oceans)*, [1997] 4 C.N.L.R. 193 (F.C.T.D.).
[253] *Ibid.* at 211.
[254] *Ibid.* at 210.
[255] [2000] 3 C.N.L.R. 114 at 132 (F.C.A.).
[256] *Ibid.* at 122.
[257] *Nunavut Tunngavik Inc., supra* note 196.

vik Inc. that the minister erred in failing to apply the principles set out in the Nunavut Land Claims Agreement:

> The authority of the NWMB was in the nature of advice and recommendations and the minister did look into it. It was within the Minister's discretion and within the limits of the Agreement to take into consideration a number of factors including growth and decline in stock. . . . Finally, in view of the situation that prevails in the Atlantic affecting every eastern province and territory with respect to the Atlantic fishery, the end result provided by the Minister's decision on quota allocation can not be seen as unfair in view of the important decline in stock.[258]

The difference in this case is the clear evidence that: (*a*) the minister took into account all of the relevant considerations; (*b*) the minister communicated clearly that such consideration occurred; and (*c*) there was a clear paper trail of the minister receiving and considering the applicable advice. The Federal Court of Appeal affirmed the trial court's decision and stated:

> [B]ecause of the classically polycentric nature of the allocation of a fixed quota among competing group of fishers, the proper standard of review of the exercise of the Minister's discretion is patent unreasonableness. The Minister's decision easily withstands that test. The decision has a rational basis, because it was open to the Minister to determine the quota by reference to quotas historically allocated for turbot fishing in Davis Strait, rather than to the allocation of quotas in other zones in the Atlantic fishery.[259]

Nunavut Tunngavik Inc.'s leave to appeal application to the Supreme Court of Canada was dismissed.

These decisions are noteworthy because they clearly demonstrate, with a particular focus on the proper exercise of ministerial discretionary authority, how a lack of proper consultation with Nunavut Tunngavik Inc. had an impact upon the minister's authority. The *Nunavut Tunngavik* decisions also demonstrate how a lack of administrative due process by government can be rectified to meet the standard required by, and owed to, Aboriginal people. In the second *Nunavut Tunngavik Inc.* decision, the minister's decision regarding turbot quotas was able to withstand judicial scrutiny under s. 35(1) and of the Crown's fiduciary relationship with Aboriginal people. This was due, in part, to the Crown ensuring that the basic administrative law and procedural fairness processes were put in place and fully implemented.

Consultation and Industry

The case law from the Supreme Court of Canada strongly suggests that any constitutional duty to consult rests solely with the Crown[260] and not with private interests such as resource companies, other industries, or municipal governments. Federal and provincial governments must be diligent, however, to ensure that their decisions, activities, and legislation adequately account for and consider Aboriginal interests that may be affected by their actions.[261] Industry and third-party consultation with Aboriginal people has been based on governmental delegation (as in environmental review processes), or by way of voluntary actions by industry (as in mutually profitable joint-development or impact and benefit agreements).

---

[258] *Ibid.* at paras. 91, 92, 94 (F.C.T.D.).

[259] *Ibid.* at para. 4 (F.C.A.).

[260] See *Sparrow, supra* note 61; *Delgamuukw, supra* note 68 at para. 168; *Marshall* (reconsideration), *supra* note 114 at para. 43.

[261] *Kruger* v. *R.*, [1985] 3 C.N.L.R. 15 at 98 (F.C.A.).

In a number of important resource developments, the Crown has informally delegated many of the procedural elements of its duty to consult to industry. Such delegation is merely doing what is reasonable in order to effect an appropriate consultation. Both federal and provincial governments have, in many instances, left industry to negotiate critical relationships with Aboriginal people in respect of access to natural resources with a minimum of guidance and certainty that the negotiated settlement is a solid, long-term foundation for substantial investment and stability.

This should not prevent industry from exceeding the minimum standard required in order to continue to enter into economic and impact and benefit agreements with Aboriginal groups. However, the need for government to become engaged in a clear and meaningful way with these industry initiatives is important to ensure that such negotiated agreements have the requisite legal certainty that only the Crown can provide. In order to achieve its objectives, industry needs to be in contact with government, reminding and guiding government of its key role, and assisting it in doing what is appropriate to balance the interests of industry and Aboriginal people.

THE FIDUCIARY RELATIONSHIP

Introduction

Generally, fiduciary obligations arise from relationships such as those between lawyer and client, parent and child, or doctor and patient,[262] or can arise from the circumstances of a specific situation.[263] Although writing in dissent in *Frame* v. *Smith*,[264] Wilson J. provided a general articulation of a fiduciary obligation,[265] which was adopted subsequently by the majority of the Supreme Court of Canada:[266]

> A few commentators have attempted to discern an underlying fiduciary principle but, given the widely divergent contexts emerging from the case law, it is understandable that they have differed in their analyses. . . . [citations omitted] Yet there are common features discernible in the contexts in which fiduciary duties have been found to exist and these common features do provide a rough and ready guide to whether or not the imposition of a fiduciary obligation on a new relationship would be appropriate and consistent.
>
> Relationships in which a fiduciary obligation have been imposed seem to possess three general characteristics:
>
> (1) The fiduciary has scope for the exercise of some discretion or power.
>
> (2) The fiduciary can unilaterally exercise that power or discretion so as to affect the beneficiary's legal or practical interests.
>
> (3) The beneficiary is peculiarly vulnerable to or at the mercy of the fiduciary holding the discretion or power.[267]

Although the above excerpt from Wilson J. is useful in a general sense, the fiduciary relationship between the Crown and Aboriginal people has developed into a unique body of law that is difficult to generalize. The Courts have characterized the relationship be-

---

[262] See *Norberg* v. *Wynrib*, [1992] 2 S.C.R. 226.
[263] *Lac Minerals Ltd.* v. *International Corona Resources Ltd.*, [1989] 2 S.C.R. 574.
[264] *Frame* v. *Smith*, [1987] 2 S.C.R. 99.
[265] *Ibid.* at 136.
[266] *Lac Minerals, supra* note 263 at para. 32.
[267] *Frame* v. *Smith, supra* note 264 at 136.

tween Aboriginal people and the Crown as a special fiduciary or trust relationship.[268] This special relationship arises from numerous sources, including the historical, political, legal, and socio-economic relationship the federal Crown has had with Aboriginal people, the *Royal Proclamation of 1763*,[269] treaties, and legislation.[270]

The Supreme Court of Canada has discussed the fiduciary relationship between the Crown and Aboriginal people in a number of decisions: *Guerin*,[271] *Sparrow*,[272] *Gladstone*,[273] *Van der Peet*,[274] *Adams*,[275] *Delgamuukw*,[276] and *Wewaykum Indian Band* v. *Canada*.[277] While the historic and primary relationship with Aboriginal people has been with the federal Crown, the provincial Crowns may, in appropriate circumstances, also have a fiduciary relationship with Aboriginal people.[278]

R. v. *Guerin* (1984)

The first Supreme Court of Canada decision to deal with the Crown's fiduciary relationship with Aboriginal people in a substantive manner was *Guerin*.[279] In October 1957, the Musqueam Indian Band surrendered 162 acres of reserve land situated in Vancouver, British Columbia to the federal Crown pursuant to ss. 37–41 of the *Indian Act*.[280] The surrender enabled the Musqueam to secure a lease with a golf club. The terms and conditions of the lease were not part of the surrender but, rather, were discussed between federal officials and the Musqueam. The Crown executed the lease on terms that were not as favourable as the terms originally agreed upon orally with the Musqueam. The Crown did not have the Musqueam's permission to change the terms of the lease, nor did it provide a copy of the lease to the Musqueam until 1970. The Musqueam instituted an action against the Crown for breach of trust.

---

[268] For a general discussion of fiduciary obligations see *ibid.*; *Lac Minerals Ltd.* v. *International Corona Resources Ltd.*, *supra* note 263; *Canson Enterprises Ltd.* v. *Boughton and Co.*, [1991] 3 S.C.R. 543.

[269] *Royal Proclamation, supra* note 45. Indians are referred to in the *Royal Proclamation of 1763*, and in many of the treaties, as being "under the protection" of the Crown.

[270] In *Roberts* v. *Canada*, [1989] 1 S.C.R. 322 at 337, Wilson J. for the Supreme Court of Canada stated that the relevant provisions of the *Indian Act* "codify the preexisting duties of the Crown toward the Indians."

[271] *Guerin, supra* note 204.

[272] *Sparrow, supra* note 61.

[273] *Gladstone, supra* note 198.

[274] *Van der Peet, supra* note 66.

[275] *Adams, supra* note 64.

[276] *Delgamuukw, supra* note 68.

[277] *Wewaykum, supra* note 174.

[278] For example, in *R.* v. *Smith, supra* note 51, Estey J., for the majority, was considering a band's release of its interests in land and how such a release could give rise to differences between the parties to the release. Estey J. quotes with approval Street J. from *Ontario Mining Co. Ltd.* v. *Seybold*, [1901] 32 O.R. 301 at 565 (Ont. Div. Ct.):

> The surrender was undoubtedly burdened with the obligation imposed by the treaty to select and lay aside special portions of the tract . . . for the special use and benefit of the Indians. The Provincial Government could not without plain disregard of justice take advantage of the surrender and refuse to perform the condition attached to it.

See also *Cree Regional Authority* v. *Robinson*, [1991] 4 C.N.L.R. 84 at 106, (F.C.T.D.) and *Ontario (A.G.)* v. *Bear Island Foundation*, [1991] 2 S.C.R. 570 at 575. In *Bear Island*, the court noted that the "Crown has failed to comply with some of its obligations . . . and thereby breached its fiduciary obligations to the Indians." What is interesting in *Bear Island* is that the federal Crown was not the subject of the litigation, but rather it was the provincial Crown of Ontario.

[279] *Guerin, supra* note 204. For commentary see John Hurley, "The Crown's Fiduciary Duty and Indian Title: *Guerin* v. *The Queen*" (1985) 30 McGill L.J. 559.

[280] *Indian Act*, R.S.C. 1952, c. 149; now R.S.C. 1985, c. I–5.

Guerin consisted of three sets of reasons (eight judges took part in the decision, but some simply concurred with the other judges). Seven of the eight judges held that the Crown has a fiduciary duty respecting Indians lands. Dickson J. wrote for the majority:

> [T]he nature of Indian title and the framework of the statutory scheme established for disposing of Indian land places upon the Crown an equitable obligation, enforceable by the courts, to deal with the land for the benefit of the Indians. This obligation does not amount to a trust in the private law sense. It is rather a fiduciary duty. If however, the Crown breaches this fiduciary duty it will be liable to the Indians in the same way and to the same extent as if such a trust were in effect.[281]

Quebec (A.G.) v. *Canada (National Energy Board)* (1994)

In *Quebec (A.G.)* v. *Canada (National Energy Board)*,[282] the Supreme Court of Canada considered a decision of the National Energy Board (NEB) regarding the granting of licences to Hydro-Quebec to sell electricity to the United States. The NEB granted licences subject to two conditions relating to the successful completion of the environmental assessment of future power generation facilities.[283] The appellants, the Grand Council of the Crees (of Québec) and the Cree Regional Authority, claimed that:

a) the NEB did not properly conduct a regional social cost-benefit review;

b) the NEB was not *procedurally* fair by not disclosing fully the NEB's assumptions and the basis upon on which the cost-benefit review was based;

c) the NEB owed the appellants a fiduciary duty in the exercise of its decision-making authority and that this duty was not fulfilled;

d) the decision of the NEB affected the appellants' Aboriginal rights and the NEB was therefore required to meet the justification test for infringements to Aboriginal rights under s. 35(1) of the *Constitution Act, 1982*; and

e) the NEB failed to follow the requirements of the *National Energy Board Act*,[284] among other regulations.

The Federal Court of Appeal rejected the appellants' arguments but allowed the appeal by Hydro-Quebec and Quebec, and concluded that the NEB had exceeded its jurisdiction by imposing the two environmental assessment conditions. The two conditions were severed from the licence.

The Supreme Court of Canada unanimously allowed the appeal and restored the original decision of the NEB. Iacobucci J. began the Court's analysis by examining whether the NEB failed to carry out the social cost-benefit review properly. Iacobucci J. considered the appellants' claim that, by virtue of their status as Aboriginal people, the NEB owed them a fiduciary duty extending to the decision-making process used by the NEB in considering applications for export licences. The appellants' argument was based primarily on the fact that the NEB is an agent of the federal government and a creation of Parliament and simply exercises delegated powers granted to it by Parliament. Therefore, the NEB should also hold the same fiduciary obligations to Aboriginal people as does

---

[281] *Guerin, supra* note 204 at 376.
[282] *Quebec (A.G.)* v. *Canada (National Energy Board)*, [1994] 1 S.C.R. 159.
[283] *Re applications under the National Energy Board Act by Hydro-Québec for Exports to the Vermont Joint Owners and New York Power Authority*, NEB Dec. No. EH-3-89, [1991] 2 C.N.L.R. 70 (NEB).
[284] *National Energy Board Act*, R.S.C. 1985, c. N-7, as am. S.C. 1990, c. 7.

Parliament and the Crown. The appellants characterized the scope of the fiduciary obligations in two ways:

1. that it includes the duty to ensure the full and fair participation of the appellants in the hearing process; and

2. to take into account Aboriginal people's best interests when making decisions.[285]

On the issue of the fiduciary relationship between the federal Crown and Aboriginal people, Iacobucci J. stated:

> Nonetheless, it must be remembered that not every aspect of the relationship between fiduciary and beneficiary takes the form of a fiduciary obligation: *Lac Minerals Ltd.* v. *International Corona Resources Ltd.*, [1989] 2 S.C.R. 574. The nature of the relationship between the parties defines the scope, and the limits, of the duties that will be imposed. The courts must be careful not to compromise the independence of quasi-judicial tribunals and decision-making agencies by imposing upon them fiduciary obligations which require that their decisions be made in accordance with a fiduciary duty.[286]

Thus, the fiduciary relationship between Aboriginal people and the Crown is not static. Rather, it must be examined on a case-by-case basis in order to determine the scope and parameters of the fiduciary duties that flow from the fiduciary relationship:

> [T]he fiduciary relationship between the Crown and the appellants does not impose a duty on the Board to make its decisions in the best interests of the appellants, or to change its hearing process so as to impose super added requirements of disclosure. When the duty is defined in this manner, such tribunals no more owe this sort of fiduciary duty than do the courts. Consequently, no such duty existed in relation to the decision-making function of the Board.[287]

Iacobucci J. considered the appellants' claim that the decision of the NEB is subject to the justification analysis of an infringement to an Aboriginal right under s. 35(1) of the *Constitution Act, 1982* outlined in *Sparrow*. The respondents argued that with the signing of the James Bay and Northern Quebec Agreement in 1975, as incorporated in the *James Bay and Northern Quebec Native Claims Settlement Act*,[288] the appellants ceded all Aboriginal rights except those that were set out in the agreement, and therefore, the s. 35(1) justification analysis was unnecessary:

> [I]t is not possible to evaluate realistically the impact of the decision of the Board on the rights of the appellants without reference to the *James Bay Act*. . . . [E]ven assuming that the decision of the Board is one that has, *prima facie*, an impact on the aboriginal rights of the appellants, and that the appellants are correct in arguing that, for the Board to justify its interference, it must, at a minimum, conduct a rigorous, thorough, and proper cost-benefit review, I find, for the reasons expressed above, that the review carried out in this case was not wanting in this respect.[289]

Iacobucci J. found that the NEB did not exceed its jurisdiction under the NEB Act by considering the environmental effects of the construction of future generating facilities as they relate to the proposed export licence. Iacobucci J. found that the conditions imposed by the NEB relate to the contemplated environmental review and regulation in the fed-

---

[285] *Hydro-Quebec, supra* note 282 at 183.
[286] *Ibid.*
[287] *Ibid.* at 184.
[288] *James Bay and Northern Québec Native Claims Settlement Act*, S.C. 1976–77, c. 32.
[289] *Hydro-Quebec, supra* note 282 at 186.

eral sphere. By proceeding in this way, the full environmental effects of the proposals would be known to the NEB before the construction of the project was to proceed and before the decision to grant the licenses was irrevocable.[290] Iacobucci J. concluded that the original order of the NEB should be restored.

The Supreme Court of Canada specifically discussed Aboriginal rights in a separate section of *Hydro-Quebec*, distinct from the issue of fiduciary duty. With respect to the decisions of the NEB being subject to the analysis required by s. 35(1), Iacobucci J. stated:

> It is obvious that the Board must exercise its decision-making function, including the interpretation and application of its governing legislation, in accordance with the dictates of the Constitution, including s. 35(1) of the *Constitution Act, 1982*. Therefore, it must first be determined whether this particular decision of the Board . . . could have the effect of interfering with the existing aboriginal rights of the appellants so as to amount to a *prima facie* infringement of s. 35(1)."[291]

This passage confirms that NEB decisions are subject to s. 35(1) and can infringe existing Aboriginal and treaty rights. An infringement of an Aboriginal right under s. 35(1) can be justified by government using the justification analysis set out by the Supreme Court of Canada initially in *Sparrow*.[292] A central component of the justification of an infringement of a s. 35(1) right is the duty to consult. Any acts or decisions of the NEB that may adversely affect Aboriginal rights trigger the duty to consult.

The duty to consult does not, if carried out properly and fairly, undermine the quasi-judicial role of the NEB. Nothing prevents a quasi-judicial tribunal or decision-making agency from consulting with Aboriginal people, so long as it is properly authorized and constituted and deals with the possibility of an apprehension of bias. This explains the SCC's careful and considered reasoning in *Hydro-Quebec* when it limited its comments regarding the fiduciary relationship between the Crown and Aboriginal people to the specific elements discussed above, because these elements would directly interfere with the NEB's ability to act in a quasi-judicial manner. This is further supported by the Court's characterization of these elements as "utmost good faith."

Other Fiduciary-Related Case Law

The Federal Court of Appeal has held that when reserve land is taken by surrender under the threat of expropriation and the use for which the land was taken, even if it is to be used for government purposes, is not known, there is an obligation of the fiduciary (the Crown) to ensure that the land will revert back to the Indian band once it is no longer needed. Otherwise, the Crown must find some other mechanism that provides the least possible impairment of the rights of the Indian band.[293]

In *Blueberry River Indian Band* v. *R.*,[294] the Supreme Court of Canada held that the federal government breached its fiduciary duties to an Indian band resulting from the

---

[290] *Ibid.* at 199.

[291] *Ibid.* at 185.

[292] *Sparrow, supra* note 61.

[293] *Semiahmoo Indian Band* v. *Canada*, [1998] 1 C.N.L.R. 250 (Fed. C.A); this is also supported by the SCC's decision in *Osoyoos, supra* note 53.

[294] *Blueberry River Indian Band* v. *R.*, [1995] 4 S.C.R. 344; see also J.P. Salembier, "Crown Fiduciary Duty, Indian Title and the Lost Treasure of I.R. 172: The Legacy of *Apsassin* v. *The Queen (Blueberry River)*", [1996] 3 C.N.L.R. 1, and O.B. Griffiths, "Case Comment on *Blueberry River:* Is the Crown Fiduciary Obligation in the Currents of Change?", [1996] 3 C.N.L.R. 25.

surrender of two parcels of reserve land and related mineral rights. The Court held that DIAND failed to exercise its statutory power, which in this case would have mitigated the Indian band's loss. As a trustee of the Indian band's land, the department was under a fiduciary obligation to deal with the land and surrender in the "best interests" of the Indian band. Finally, the Indian band was entitled to receive compensation based on what a reasonable price would have been for the land, rather than placing an obligation on the department to secure the best possible price for the land.

In *Sparrow*, Dickson C.J. stated:

> [T]he Government has the responsibility to act in a fiduciary capacity with respect to aboriginal peoples. The relationship between the Government and aboriginals is trust-like, rather than adversarial, and contemporary recognition and affirmation of aboriginal rights must be defined in light of this historic relationship.[295]

The *Sparrow* statement on the fiduciary relationship is significant in that it signifies a burden on the ability of federal, provincial, and territorial governments to exercise their legislative authority.

In *Van der Peet* the Supreme Court of Canada stated:

> The Crown has a fiduciary obligation to aboriginal peoples with the result that in dealings between the government and aboriginals the honour of the Crown is at stake. Because of this fiduciary relationship, and its implication of the honour of the Crown, treaties, s.35(1), and other statutory and constitutional provisions protecting the interests of aboriginal peoples, must be given a generous and liberal interpretation.[296]

Thus, legislation, treaties, and constitutional provisions, including s. 35(1) of the *Constitution Act, 1982*, must be interpreted generously and liberally when considering the rights of Aboriginal people.

In *Adams*, Lamer C.J. stated that regulations that confer unfettered and unstructured discretionary authority on a minister may violate the Crown's fiduciary duty towards Aboriginal people:

> In light of the Crown's unique fiduciary obligations towards Aboriginal peoples, Parliament may not simply adopt an unstructured discretionary administrative regime which risks infringing Aboriginal rights in a substantial number of applications in the absence of some explicit guidance. If a statute confers an administrative discretion which may carry significant consequences for the exercise of an Aboriginal right, the statute or its delegate regulations must outline specific criteria for the granting or refusal of that discretion which seek to accommodate the existence of Aboriginal rights. In the absence of such specific guidance, the statute will fail to provide representatives of the Crown with sufficient directives to fulfil their fiduciary duties, and the statute will be found to represent an infringement of Aboriginal rights under the *Sparrow* test.[297]

In order to protect the integrity of a minister's decision, the regulation or statute setting out the ministerial discretionary authority must ensure that the minister considers the impact of decisions on the rights of Aboriginal people.

The Crown's fiduciary duty to Aboriginal people does not appear to extend to non-government entities. In *Lax Kw'Alaams Band of Indians* v. *Hudson's Bay Co.*,[298] the British

---

[295] *Sparrow, supra* note 61 at 1108.
[296] *Van der Peet, supra* note 66 at para. 24.
[297] *Adams, supra* note 64 at para. 54.
[298] *Lax Kw'Alaams Band of Indians* v. *Hudson's Bay Co.*, [1999] 1 C.N.L.R. 90, (1998), 159 D.L.R. (4th) 526 (B.C.S.C.), add. reasons (5 November 1998; Doc. Prince Rupert SC1359) (B.C.S.C.).

Columbia Supreme Court held that land purchased by the Hudson's Bay Company directly from the Lax Kw'Alaams Band was not being held in trust by the Company for the Band.

Although most of the litigation to date relating to the fiduciary obligations of the Crown relate to the federal Crown, some litigation has dealt specifically with the provincial Crown and has implied a fiduciary obligation on the provincial Crown.[299] However, no express distinction has yet been made by the Supreme Court of Canada between the federal and provincial Crowns vis-à-vis a general fiduciary obligation. Although there may be specific fiduciary duties for which the federal Crown is accountable because of its unique relationship to Indians under s. 91(24) to which a provincial Crown would not be held, the general fiduciary obligations outlined in *Sparrow, Guerin,* and others apply to provincial governments as well.[300] This is consistent with the Court's direction to governments that the rights of Aboriginal people be "taken seriously."[301]

In *Osoyoos,*[302] the Supreme Court of Canada considered the fiduciary duty of the Crown when lands are removed from their reserve status. The Court noted that the fiduciary duty of the Crown is not restricted to issues regarding the surrender of reserve land but is also imposed upon the Crown to expropriate or grant only "the minimum interest required in order to fulfil that public purpose, thus ensuring a minimal impairment of the use and enjoyment of Indian lands by the band."[303] Commenting further on this fiduciary duty with respect to expropriation of reserve land, the Court stated that the Crown acts in the public interest when determining whether an expropriation involving Indian reserve land is necessary in order to fulfil some public purpose. At this stage, no fiduciary duty exists. However, the Court also stated that once the decision to expropriate has been made, the fiduciary duty of the Crown is raised and requires the Crown to expropriate any interest that will fulfil the public purpose in a manner that preserves the Indian interest in the reserve land to the greatest extent practicable.[304] The Court stated:

> The duty to impair minimally Indian interests in reserve land not only serves to balance the public interest and the Indian interest, it is also consistent with the policy behind the rule of general inalienability in the *Indian Act* which is to prevent the erosion of the native land base: *Opetchesaht Indian Band* v. *Canada,* [1997] 2 S.C.R. 119, at para. 52.[305]

The Court concluded in *Osoyoos* that the Crown's fiduciary duty must be to protect the use and enjoyment of Indian interest in expropriated reserve lands to the greatest extent practicable. This includes the duty to protect the Indian interest to such an extent that it preserves an Indian band's jurisdiction to tax the land pursuant to s. 83(1)(c) of the *Indian Act* and therefore the band's continued ability to earn income from the reserve land.[306]

---

[299] See note 278.

[300] See *Perry* v. *Ontario,* [1998] 2 C.N.L.R. 79 (Ont. C.A.) at para. 88. In *Gitanyow First Nation* v. *Canada,* [1999] 3 C.N.L.R. 89 (B.C.S.C.) at para 49, Williamson J. stated: "the fiduciary obligations of the Crown remain whether they are dealing with the Crown of colonial times, or are dealing with the Crown in Right of Canada or the Crown in Right of British Columbia."

[301] *Sparrow, supra* note 61 at 1119.

[302] *Osoyoos, supra* note 53.

[303] *Ibid.* at para. 52.

[304] *Ibid.* at para. 53.

[305] *Ibid.* at para. 54.

[306] *Ibid.* at para. 55.

Wewaykum Indian Band v. *Canada* (2002)

One of the more significant Supreme Court of Canada decisions to date respecting the nature of the Crown's fiduciary relationship with Aboriginal people is *Wewaykum*.[307] *Wewaykum* clearly confirms the existence of such a fiduciary duty but clarifies that such a duty is not an attribute of the relationship between the Crown and Aboriginal people in *all* circumstances. While *Wewaykum* is not surprising in light of the originally stated jurisprudential basis of the Crown's fiduciary duty to Aboriginal people, it places limits on a doctrine that has often been invoked, but has now been shown not to be infinitely flexible.

Unlike the facts of other Supreme Court decisions dealing with the Crown's fiduciary duty to Aboriginal people, such as *Guerin* and *Blueberry River*, the facts of *Wewaykum* reveal no material mishandling of Aboriginal interests by the Crown.

Wewaykum concerned applications by two Indian bands of the same First Nation, each of which claimed the other's reserve land that had been in the possession of the respective incumbent bands since the end of the nineteenth century. The Cape Mudge Band claimed Reserve No. 11, held by the Campbell River Band, and Campbell River claimed Reserve No. 12, held by Cape Mudge. Although each band sought formal declaration of trespass, possession, and injunctive relief against the other band, they acknowledged that they would both be satisfied with financial compensation from the federal Crown. The bands based their claims on various breaches of the federal Crown's fiduciary duty to Aboriginal people purportedly resulting from clerical errors by Crown officials in the early twentieth century.

Campbell River claimed that a 1907 resolution whereby Cape Mudge ceded its proprietary interest in Reserve No. 11 was valid, whereas Cape Mudge argued that such resolution was invalid because it failed to follow properly the surrender provisions of the *Indian Act*. Campbell River also argued that it was entitled to Reserve No. 12 based on the written records of the Department of Indian Affairs and Northern Development. On such records, there are ditto marks indicating that Reserve No. 12 was allocated to Campbell River. The trial judge concluded that these ditto marks were a "simple slip"[308] that contradicted the intention of the parties with respect to the allocation of Reserve No. 12 to Cape Mudge.

After surveying Indian reserve creation in British Columbia since colonial times, Binnie J. concluded, on behalf of a unanimous panel of nine justices of the Supreme Court, that there was

> . . . no doubt on the evidence that when the federal Crown received the B.C. Order-in-Council 1036 . . . it intended to set apart each of the contested reserves for the beneficial use and occupation of the present incumbent. The claim of each appellant band to *both* reserves is misconceived.[309]

Binnie J. rejected Cape Mudge's argument on the basis that: (*a*) arguments between sister bands over the allocation of reserve land should not be framed as a "surrender," (*b*) the land designated as Reserve No. 11 was not properly designated as a "reserve" within the meaning of the *Indian Act* and was still provincial Crown land, and (*c*) in any event, the surrender provisions of the *Indian Act* were suspended by proclamation at the time.[310]

---

[307] *Wewaykum*, *supra* note 174.
[308] *Ibid.* at para. 43.
[309] *Ibid.* at para. 19.
[310] *Ibid.* at para. 40.

Binnie J. stated that, in this case, "substance not form prevails"[311] and, therefore, Cape Mudge should retain Reserve No. 12. Additionally, in 1936 and 1937 the chief and principal men of both bands signed declarations confirming the "ditto mark error" and acknowledging that Reserve Nos. 11 and 12 belong to each incumbent band and that there was no dispute between them.[312]

Binnie J. stated that three areas required consideration: (1) the scope of the fiduciary duty of the Crown in the processes of creating Indian reserves; (2) whether the acts of government officials in this case constituted a breach of any fiduciary duty; and (3) what equitable remedies are available to remedy such breaches, if any.[313]

Binnie J. held that no fiduciary duty had been breached and no equitable relief was available either by way of injunction or compensation. The error that occurred in noting which band held which reserve was simply a clerical one and did not invoke any fiduciary principles. In any event, all claims made by the bands were barred by the expiry of the applicable limitation periods. Binnie J. noted that the thirty-year limitation period, set out in the *Limitations Act*,[314] "is subject to very limited exceptions, none of which apply here."[315] In addition, it was held that the Crown could use the defences of laches and acquiescence to defeat equitable claims by Aboriginal people.

Binnie J. discussed the legal development of the Crown's fiduciary relationship with Aboriginal people and focused on the concept of the Crown's political trust or "trust in the higher sense."[316] He noted that since the Court's decision in *Guerin*[317] Canadian courts "have experienced a flood of 'fiduciary duty' claims by Indian bands across a whole spectrum of possible complaints."[318]

Binnie J. said that invocation of the Crown's fiduciary duty to Aboriginal people as a "source of plenary Crown liability"[319] "overshoots the mark."[320] He confirmed that the general law relating to fiduciary relationships applies to the relationship between the Crown and Aboriginal people.[321] This general law includes the general equitable principles described in *Guerin* and *Blueberry River* that trigger the existence of fiduciary duties in a private law context, and the principle that not all obligations between the parties to a fiduciary relationship are themselves fiduciary.

Wewaykum adds greatly to understanding the Crown's fiduciary relationship with Aboriginal people by outlining the following conclusions:[322]

1. The content of the Crown's fiduciary duty to Aboriginal people will vary with the nature and importance of the interest sought to be protected and does not provide general indemnity.

2. Prior to reserve creation, the Crown exercises a public law function under the *Indian Act* that is subject to judicial supervision. At this stage, a fiduciary relationship

---

[311] *Ibid.* at para. 53.
[312] *Ibid.* at paras. 59-60.
[313] *Ibid.* para. 5.
[314] *Limitations Act*, S.B.C. 1975, c. 37, s. 8.
[315] *Wewaykum, supra* note 174 at para. 132.
[316] *Ibid.* at para. 73.
[317] *Guerin, supra* note 204; *Blueberry River, supra* note 294; *Hydro-Quebec, supra* note 282.
[318] *Wewaykum, supra* note 174 at para. 82.
[319] *Ibid.* at para. 81.
[320] *Ibid.*
[321] *Ibid.* at para 83.
[322] *Ibid.* at para. 86.

may arise but the law limits the Crown's duty to the basic obligations of loyalty, good faith, appropriate full disclosure, and acting with ordinary prudence in the best interests of the Aboriginal beneficiaries.

3. The content of the Crown's fiduciary duty to Aboriginal people expands once a reserve is created in order to protect and preserve the band's quasi-proprietary interest in protecting the reserve land from exploitation.

4. The public law duty of the Crown does not exclude the creation of a fiduciary relationship in the nature of a private law duty. However, such private law fiduciary duty by the Crown to Aboriginal people "depends on identification of a cognizable Indian interest, and the Crown's undertaking of discretionary control in relation thereto."[323]

5. In *Wewaykum*, it was held that each band lacked beneficial interest in the other band's reserve and therefore equitable remedies are not available.

6. Binnie J. explained the fiduciary duty of the Crown to Aboriginal people as primarily a duty to prevent an exploitative bargain, as discussed by Wilson J. in *Guerin*,[324] and consistent with *Blueberry River*[325] and *R. v. Lewis*.[326] This means that the Crown must exercise "ordinary diligence" to avoid the destruction of a band's quasi-property interest in its reserve land by an exploitative bargain with third parties or the Crown. The Crown will also have other fiduciary responsibilities respecting its administrative control over reserve lands and band assets.[327]

One of the most important statements by Binnie J. in *Wewaykum* was that "substance not form prevails" in this matter.[328] This simple statement conveys the approach the Supreme Court of Canada appears to apply to its recent analysis of the law as applicable to Aboriginal people.[329] The two bands agreed, many years earlier, that each band was entitled to the reserve that it currently possessed and that their respective claims were really paper claims against the federal Crown for compensation due to a clerical error. Neither band suffered any actual compensable loss. "Substance over form" dictated that the Court would look beyond the Crown's "clerical error" and determine the matter based on its substantive merits.

The decision that the general law of Canada respecting fiduciaries applies to the Crown's fiduciary duty to Aboriginal people, and that obligations between the parties in a fiduciary relationship are not necessarily fiduciary in nature, is an important clarification of the doctrine of the Crown's fiduciary duty to Aboriginal people.

Wewaykum and other recent Supreme Court of Canada decisions respecting Aboriginal and treaty rights confirm:

1. Placing reasonable limits on the exercise and interpretation of Aboriginal and treaty rights;

---

[323] *Ibid.* at para. 85.
[324] *Guerin, supra* note 204.
[325] *Blueberry River, supra* note 294.
[326] *R. v. Lewis*, [1996] 1 S.C.R. 921.
[327] *Wewaykum, supra* note 174 at para. 77.
[328] *Ibid.* at paras. 59–60.
[329] For example, see Thomas Isaac, "The Meaning of Subsection 35(1) of the *Constitution Act, 1982*: A Comment on *Mitchell* v. *Min. of National Revenue*" (November 2002) 60:6, The Advocate 835–65.

2. Placing limits on the application of the Crown's fiduciary duty to Aboriginal people, akin to the standards normally applicable under general Canadian fiduciary law; namely, not every duty in a fiduciary relationship is fiduciary in nature;

3. A clearer definition of the Crown's fiduciary relationship with Aboriginal people;

4. The proposition that the Crown's fiduciary duty to Aboriginal people is best used in the case of exploitative bargains and with the administrative responsibilities of the Crown in dealing with reserve land and band assets; and

5. Holding Aboriginal groups to a reasonable standard more consistent with the rules governing Canadian law, in this case, the application of limitation periods.

These are important developments in that they demonstrate a move by the Supreme Court of Canada away from merely defining Aboriginal and treaty rights in an expansive way, to now applying such rights within the context of the Canadian legal system that, by implication, demands a balanced, nonabsolute, and case-by-case approach.

CONCLUSION

Prior to 1982, Aboriginal and treaty rights were vulnerable to modification or extinguishment by the federal Crown. Since the 1982 recognition and affirmation of existing Aboriginal and treaty rights in s. 35(1), the legal and constitutional status of the rights of Aboriginal people has had a dramatic effect on Canadian law. The rights of Aboriginal people cannot now be unilaterally modified or extinguished by the federal Crown. Since 1982, federal, provincial, and territorial legislation is subject to s. 35(1), and if a law or government action interferes with the exercise of an existing Aboriginal or treaty right, that law or act must be justified in order for the law to remain applicable.

The Crown's duty to consult and accommodate Aboriginal people is important because of the central role it plays in understanding how the Crown should govern and balance the competing broader societal and public policy issues with the rights of Aboriginal people. In recent years, there has been much discussion surrounding "consultation" and "accommodation," the role these concepts play in enabling the Crown to justify infringements of Aboriginal and treaty rights, and how such concepts fit into the developing framework of the Crown's relationship with Aboriginal people and, more generally, Aboriginal law.

The concepts of accommodation and consultation are best understood together, and based on the case law to date, form "catch-all" concepts that place procedural and substantive duties on the Crown when the Crown makes decisions or acts in a manner that affects existing Aboriginal and treaty rights. The concepts of accommodation and consultation are not new and represent a logical progression in understanding the Crown's duty to be fair generally and to fulfill its special responsibilities to Aboriginal people. Although the Supreme Court of Canada has not yet fully analysed the Crown's duty to accommodate and consult Aboriginal people, it appears that both concepts work together, forming a complete package in respect of the Crown's obligations to Aboriginal people when infringing their rights.

The Crown's fiduciary relationship with Aboriginal people has also undergone a dramatic change with respect to its meaning and effect. The jurisprudence relating to the Crown's fiduciary relationship with Aboriginal people has clearly affirmed that the Crown will be held to a high standard in all of its dealings concerning Aboriginal people and their lands when such dealings trigger the Crown's fiduciary duties. However, *Wewyakum* clearly imposes limits on the ability of Aboriginal people to invoke the fiduciary doctrine in a general sense.

CASES AND MATERIALS

FEDERAL AUTHORITY

Constitution Act, 1867
30 and 31 Vict. c. 3 (U.K.), R.S.C. 1985, App. II, No. 5.

VI. Distribution Of Legislative Powers
Powers of the Parliament

91. It shall be lawful for the Queen, by and with the Advice and Consent of the Senate and House of Commons, to make laws for the Peace, Order, and good Government of Canada, in relation to all Matters not coming within the Classes of Subjects by this Act assigned exclusively to the Legislatures of the Provinces; and for greater Certainty, but not so as to restrict the Generality of the foregoing Terms of this Section, it is hereby declared that (notwithstanding anything in this Act) the exclusive Legislative Authority of the parliament of Canada extends to all Matters coming within the Classes of Subjects next herein-after enumerated; that is to say,— . . .

    24. Indians, and Lands reserved for the Indians.

Selected provisions of the *Indian Act*
R.S.C. 1985, c. I–5.*

Reserves . . .

18. (1) Subject to this Act, reserves are held by Her Majesty for the use and benefit of the respective bands for which they were set apart; and subject to this Act and to the terms of any treaty or surrender, the Governor in Council may determine whether any purpose for which lands in a reserve are used or are to be used is for the use and benefit of the band.

    (2) The Minister may authorize the use of lands in a reserve for the purpose of Indian schools, the administration of Indian affairs, Indian burial grounds, Indian health projects or, with the consent of the council of the band, for any other purpose for the general welfare of the band, and may take any lands in a reserve required for such purposes, but where an individual Indian, immediately prior to such taking, was entitled to the possession of such lands, compensation for such use shall be paid to the Indian, in such amount as may be agreed between the Indian and the Minister, or, failing agreement, as may be determined in such manner as the Minister may direct. . . .

* ss. 81–83, see pages 475–77; s. 88, see page 243; ss. 83, 87, 89, 90, see pages 340–41.

Surrenders And Designations . . .

37. (1) Lands in a reserve shall not be sold nor title to them conveyed until they have been absolutely surrendered to Her Majesty pursuant to subsection 38(1) by the band for whose use and benefit in common the reserve was set apart.

    (2) Except where this Act otherwise provides, lands in a reserve shall not be leased nor an interest in them granted until they have been surrendered to Her Majesty pursuant to subsection 38(2) by the band for whose use and benefit in common the reserve was set apart. . . .

38. (1) A band may absolutely surrender to Her Majesty, conditionally or unconditionally, all of the rights and interests of the band and its members in all or part of a reserve.

    (2) A band may, conditionally or unconditionally, designate by way of a surrender to Her Majesty that is not absolute, any right or interest of the band and its members in all or part of a reserve, for the purpose of its being leased or a right or interest therein being granted. . . .

39. (1) An absolute surrender or designation is void unless
    (a) it is made to Her Majesty;
    (b) it is assented to by a majority of the electors of the band
        (i) at a general meeting of the band called by the council of the band
        (ii) at a special meeting of the band called by the Minister for the purpose of considering a proposed absolute surrender or designation, or
        (iii) by a referendum as provided in the regulations; and
    (c) it is accepted by the Governor in Council.

    (2) Where a majority of the electors of a band did not vote at a meeting or referendum called pursuant to subsection (1), the Minister may, if the proposed absolute surrender or designation was assented to by a majority of the electors who did vote, call another meeting by giving thirty days notice thereof or another referendum as provided in the regulations.

    (3) Where a meeting is called pursuant to subsection (2) and the proposed absolute surrender or designation is assented to at the meeting or referendum by a majority of the electors voting, the surrender or designation shall be deemed, for the purposes of this section, to have been assented to by a majority of the electors of the band.

    (4) The Minister may, at the request of the council of the band or whenever he considers it advisable, order that a vote at any meeting under this section shall be by secret ballot.

    (5) Every meeting under this section shall be held in the presence of the superintendent or some other officer of the Department designated by the Minister.

40. A proposed absolute surrender or designation that is assented to by the band in accordance with section 39 shall be certified on oath by the superintendent or other officer who attended the meeting and by the chief or a member of the council of the band and then submitted to the Governor in Council for acceptance or refusal. . . .

41. An absolute surrender or designation shall be deemed to confer all rights that are

necessary to enable Her Majesty to carry out the terms of the surrender or designation. . . .

57. The Governor in Council may make regulations

    (a) authorizing the Minister to grant licences to cut timber on surrendered lands, or, with the consent of the council of the band, on reserve lands;

    (b) imposing terms, conditions and restrictions with respect to the exercise of rights conferred by licences granted under paragraph (a);

    (c) providing for the disposition of surrendered mines and minerals underlying lands in a reserve;

    (d) prescribing the penalty not exceeding one hundred dollars or imprisonment for a term of three months, or both, that may be imposed on summary conviction for violation of any regulation made under this section; and

    (e) providing for the seizure and forfeiture of any timber or minerals taken in violation of any regulation made under this section. . . .

60. (1) The Governor in Council may at the request of a band grant to the band the right to exercise such control and management over lands in the reserve occupied by the band as the Governor in Council considers desirable.

(2) The Governor in Council may at any time withdraw from a band a right conferred upon the band under subsection (1).

Management of Indian Moneys

61. (1) Indian moneys shall be expended only for the benefit of the Indians or bands for whose use and benefit in common the moneys are received or held, and subject to this Act and to the terms of any treaty or surrender, the Governor in Council may determine whether any purpose for which Indian moneys are used or are to be used is for the use and benefit of the band.

(2) Interest upon Indian moneys held in the Consolidated Revenue Fund shall be allowed at a rate to be fixed from time to time by the Governor in Council. . . .

Treaty Money

72. Moneys that are payable to Indians or to Indian bands under a treaty between Her Majesty and the band and for the payment of which the Government of Canada is responsible, may be paid out of the Consolidated Revenue Fund.

Regulations

73. (1) The Governor in Council may make regulations

    (a) for the protection and preservation of fur-bearing animals, fish and other game on reserves;

    (b) for the destruction of noxious weeds and prevention of the spreading or prevalence of insects, pests or diseases that may destroy or injure vegetation on Indian reserves;

    (c) for the control of the speed, operation and parking of vehicles on roads within reserves;

    (d) for the taxation, control and destruction of dogs and for the protection of sheep on reserves;

    (e) for the operation, supervision and control of pool rooms, dance halls and other places of amusement on reserves;

(f) to prevent, mitigate and control the spread of diseases on reserves, whether or not the diseases are infectious or communicable;

(g) to provide medical treatment and health services for Indians;

(h) to provide compulsory hospitalization and treatment for infectious disease among Indians;

(i) to provide for the inspection of premises on reserves and the destruction, alteration or renovation thereof;

(j) to prevent overcrowding of premises on reserves used as dwellings;

(k) to provide for sanitary conditions in private premises on reserves as well as in public places on reserves;

(l) for the construction and maintenance of boundary fences; and

(m) for empowering and authorizing the council of a band to borrow money for band projects or housing purposes and providing for the making of loans out of moneys so borrowed to members of the band for housing purposes.

(2) The Governor in Council may prescribe the penalty, not exceeding a fine of one thousand dollars or imprisonment for a term not exceeding three months, or both, that may be imposed on summary conviction for violation of a regulation made under subsection (1).

(3) The Governor in Council may make orders and regulations to carry out the purposes and provisions of this Act.

Re Eskimos

[1939] S.C.R. 104 (S.C.C.). April 5, 1939.

Excerpts from *Re Eskimos* can be found at pages 317–20.

PROVINCIAL AUTHORITY

Section 88, *Indian Act*

R.S.C. 1985, c. I–5.

Legal Rights . . .

88. Subject to the terms of any treaty and any other Act of the Parliament of Canada, all laws of general application from time to time in force in any province are applicable to and in respect of Indians in the province, except to the extent that such laws are inconsistent with this Act or any order, rule, regulation or by-law, made thereunder, and except to the extent that such laws make provision for any matter for which provision is made by or under the Act.

R. v. Dick (1985)

[1985] 2 S.C.R. 309 (S.C.C.). Dickson C.J., Beetz, Estey, McIntyre, and Chouinard JJ., October 31, 1985.

BEETZ J.:— . . . Appellant and respondent appear to agree in substance as to the issues raised by this appeal, save one. But they express them differently and I find it preferable to rephrase them as follows:

1. Is the practice of year-round foraging for food so central to the Indian way of life of the

Alkali Lake Shuswap that it cannot be restricted by ss. 3(1) and 8(1) of the *Wildlife Act*, R.S. B.C. 1979, c .433 [rep. by S. B.C. 1982, c. 57, s. 123] without impairment of their status and capacity as Indians, and invasion of the federal field under para. 91(24) of the *Constitution Act, 1867*?

2. If the answer to the first question is in the affirmative and, consequently, the *Wildlife Act* cannot apply *ex proprio vigore* to the appellant, then is this Act a law of general application referentially incorporated into federal law by s. 88 of the *Indian Act*

3. Does this appeal raise a question of law alone for the purpose of s. 114 of the *Offence Act*, R.S.B.C. 1979, c. 305?

The third issue was raised only by respondent.

In addition, a constitutional question was stated by the Chief Justice:

> Are ss. 3(1)(c) and 8(1) of the *Wildlife Act*, R.S.B.C. 1979, c .433, constitutionally inapplicable in the circumstances of this case on the ground that the restriction imposed by such sections affects the appellant qua Indian and therefore may only be enacted by the Parliament of Canada pursuant to s. 91(24) of the *Constitution Act, 1867*? . . .

Another issue had been raised by appellant in the Court of Appeal, namely whether the County Court Judge had erred in holding that the manner of administration of the *Wildlife Act* by provincial officials,—somewhat misleadingly referred to as the policy of the Act—had not significantly changed since the judgment of this Court in *Kruger and Manuel* v. *R.* [1978] 1 S.C.R. 104, ... But the Court of Appeal, following *R. v. Haines* (1981), 34 B.C.L.R. 148, ... , [1982] 2 C.N.L.R. 135, unanimously held that this issue was not a "ground that involved a question of law alone". While appellant referred in his factum to the policy of the provincial government not to issue sustenance permits for out of season hunting by Indians who regularly depend on hunting for their food, I did not understand him to press this matter in this Court as a distinct issue. . . .

Appellant's main submission which was apparently presented in the Court of Appeal as an alternative argument, is that the *Wildlife Act* strikes at the core of Indianness, that the question stated in the first issue should accordingly be answered in the affirmative and the *Wildlife Act*, while valid legislation, should be read down so as not to apply to Appellant in the circumstances of the case at bar. . . .

The reasons of Lambert J.A., dissenting, are quite elaborate. For the greater part, they expound the similarities and differences between the case at bar and *Kruger and Manuel* and his understanding of the tests adopted in the latter case to determine whether a law is one of general application, a matter to which I will return in dealing with the second issue. But he used the same tests to answer the question stated in the first issue, namely whether the application of the *Wildlife Act* to appellant would regulate him *qua* Indian. Here is what he wrote in *R. v. Dick*, 3 C.C.C. (3d) 481 at p. 492 (B.C.C.A.), [1983] 2 C.N.L.R. 134 at pp. 144–45:

> . . . it seems to me that the same tests as are applied to determine whether the application of a provincial law to a particular group of Indians in a particular activity is the application of a law of general application, should also be applied to determine whether the application of provincial law to a particular group of Indians in a particular activity is the legislation in relation to Indians in their Indianness. . . .

And, before concluding at p. 495 [p. 147 C.N.L.R.] Lambert J.A. wrote:

> Indeed, I would add that if the facts in this case do not place the killing of the deer within the central core of Indianness, if there is one, or within the boundary that outlines the status

and capacities of the Alkali Lake Band, then it is difficult to imagine other facts that would do so.

In *Cardinal* v. *Attorney General of Alberta*, [1974] S.C.R. 695 at p. 706, it had already been held, apart from any evidence, that provincial game laws do not relate to Indians *qua* Indians. In the case at bar, there was considerable evidence capable of supporting the conclusions of Lambert J.A. to the effect that the *Wildlife Act* did impair the Indianness of the Alkali Lake Band, as well as the opposite conclusions of the courts below.

I am prepared to assume, without deciding, that Lambert J.A. was right on this point and that the appellant's submission on the first issue is well taken. . . .

On the basis of this assumption and subject to the question of referential incorporation which will be dealt with in the next chapter, it follows that the *Wildlife Act* could not apply to the appellant *ex proprio vigore*, and, in order to preserve its constitutionality, it would be necessary to read it down to prevent its applying to appellant in the circumstances of this case. . . .

In holding that the tests adopted by this Court in *Kruger and Manuel* to determine whether a law is one of general application are the same tests which should be applied to determine whether the application of the *Wildlife Act* to appellant would regulate him in his Indianness, Lambert J.A. fell into error, in my respectful opinion. And this error resulted from a misapprehension of what was decided in *Kruger and Manuel* as to the nature of a law of general application.

The tests which Lambert J.A. applied in reviewing the evidence in his above quoted reasons are perfectly suitable to determine whether the application of the *Wildlife Act* to the appellant would have the effect of regulating him *qua* Indian, with the consequential necessity of a reading down if it did; but, apart from legislative intent and colourability, they have nothing to do with the question whether the *Wildlife Act* is a law of general application. On the contrary, it is precisely because the *Wildlife Act* is a law of general application that it would have to be read down were it not for s. 88 of the *Indian Act*. If the special impact of the *Wildlife Act* on Indians had been the very result contemplated by the legislature and pursued by it as a matter of policy, the Act could not be read down because it would be in relation to Indians and clearly *ultra vires*. . . .

Lambert J.A. then emphasized the importance of the effect of the legislation as opposed to its purpose. At p. 489 [p. 142 C.N.L.R.] *R.* v. *Dick*, 3 C.C.C. (3d) 481 (B.C.C.A.), [1983] 2 C.N.L.R. 134, of his reasons he wrote:

> . . . evidence about the motives of individual members of the Legislature or even about the more abstract "intention of the legislature" or "legislative purpose of the enactment" is not relevant. What is relevant is evidence about the effect of the legislation. In fact, evidence about its "application".

With all due deference, it seems to me that the correct view is the reverse one and that what Dickson J., as he then was, referred to in *Kruger and Manuel* when he mentioned laws which had crossed the line of general application were laws which, either overtly or colourably, single out Indians for special treatment and impair their status as Indians. Effect and intent are both relevant. Effect can evidence intent. But in order to determine whether a law is not one of general application, the intent, purpose or policy of the legislation can certainly not be ignored: they form an essential ingredient of a law which discriminates between various classes of persons as opposed to a law of general application. This in my view is what Dickson J. meant when in the above quoted passage, he wrote:

It would have to be shown that the policy of such an Act was to impair the status and capacities of Indians.

I am reinforced in this view by the fact that at p. 113 S.C.R., Dickson J. quoted with approval the following passage of Davey J.A. in *R. v. White and Bob* (1965), 52 W.W.R. 193, at p. 198:

> Secs. 8 and 15 of the *Game Act* specifically exempt Indians from the operation of certain provisions of the Act, and from that I think it clear that the other provisions are intended to be of general application and to include Indians. If these general sections are sufficiently clear to show an intention to abrogate or qualify the contractual rights of hunting notoriously reserved to Indians by agreements such as Ex. 8, they would, in my opinion, fail in that purpose because that would be legislation in relation to Indians that falls within parliament's exclusive legislative authority under sec. 91(24) of the *B.N.A. Act, 1867*, 30 & 31 Vict., ch. 3 and also because that would conflict with sect. 87 of the *Indian Act* passed under that authority. . . .

It has already been held in *Kruger and Manuel* that on its face, and in form, the *Wildlife Act* is a law of general application. In the previous chapter, I have assumed that its application to appellant would have the effect of regulating the latter *qua* Indian. However, it has not been demonstrated, in my view, that this particular impact has been intended by the provincial legislator. While it is assumed that the *Wildlife Act* impairs the status or capacity of appellant, it has not been established that the legislative policy of the *Wildlife Act* singles out Indians for special treatment or discriminates against them in any way.

I accordingly conclude that the *Wildlife Act* is a law of general application within the meaning of s. 88 of the *Indian Act*.

It remains to decide whether the *Wildlife Act* has been referentially incorporated to federal laws by s. 88 of the *Indian Act*.

In *Kruger and Manuel*, Dickson J. wrote at p. 115:

> There is in the legal literature a juridical controversy respecting whether s. 88 referentially incorporates provincial laws of general application or whether such laws apply to Indians *ex proprio vigore*. The issue was considered by this Court in *Natural Parents* v. *Superintendent of Child Welfare*, [1976] 2 S.C.R. 751.

This controversy has so far remained unresolved in this Court.

I believe that a distinction should be drawn between two categories of provincial laws. There are, on the one hand, provincial laws which can be applied to Indians without touching their Indianness, like traffic legislation; there are on the other hand, provincial laws which cannot apply to Indians without regulating them *qua* Indians.

Laws of the first category, in my opinion, continue to apply to Indians *ex proprio vigore* as they always did before the enactment of s. 88 in 1951, then numbered s. 87—Statutes of Canada, 1951 c. 29, s. 87—and quite apart from s. 88—*Vide Rex* v. *Hill* (1980), 15 O.L.R. 406 where an Indian was convicted of unlawful practice of medicine contrary to a provincial medical act, and *Rex* v. *Martin* (1917–18), 41 O.L.R. 79 where an Indian was convicted of unlawful possession of intoxicating liquor, contrary to a provincial temperance act.

I have come to the view that it is to the laws of the second category that s. 88 refers. I agree with what Laskin C.J. wrote in the *Natural Parents* case at p. 763:

> When s. 88 refers to "all laws of general application from time to time in force in any

province" it cannot be assumed to have legislated a nullity but, rather, to have in mind provincial legislation which, per se, would not apply to Indians under the Indian Act unless given force by federal reference.

I am fully aware of the contention that it is enough to give force to the several opening provisions of s. 88, which, respectively, make the "provincial" reference subject to the terms of any treaty and any other federal Act and subject also to inconsistency with the *Indian Act* and orders, rules, regulations or by-laws thereunder. That contention would have it that s. 88 is otherwise declaratory. On this view, however, it is wholly declaratory save perhaps in its reference to "the terms of any treaty", a strange reason, in my view, to explain all the other provisions of s. 88. I think too that the concluding words of s. 88, "except to the extent that such laws make provision for any matter for which provision is made by or under this Act" indicate clearly that Parliament is indeed effecting incorporation by reference.

I also adopt the suggestion expressed by Professor Lysyk, as he then was in "The Unique Constitutional Position of the Canadian Indian" (1967) 45 *Can. Bar Rev.* 513 at p. 552:

> Provincial laws of general application will extend to Indians whether on or off reserves. It has been suggested that the constitution permits this result without the assistance of section 87 of the *Indian Act*, and that the only significant result of that section is, by expressly embracing all laws of general application (subject to the exceptions stated in the section), to contemplate extension of particular laws which otherwise might have been held to be so intimately bound up with the essential capacities and rights inherent in Indian status as to have otherwise required a conclusion that the provincial legislation amounted to an inadmissible encroachment upon section 91(24) of the *British North America Act*.

The word "all" in s. 88 is telling but, as was noticed by the late Chief Justice, the concluding words of s. 88 are practically decisive: it would not be open to Parliament in my view to make the *Indian Act* paramount over provincial laws simply because the *Indian Act* occupied the field. Operational conflict would be required to this end. But Parliament could validly provide for any type of paramountcy of the *Indian Act* over other provisions which it alone could enact, referentially or otherwise. It is true that the paramountcy doctrine may not have been as precise in 1951 as it has become, at a later date, but it is desirable to adopt a construction of s. 88 which accords with established constitutional principles. . . .

I accordingly conclude that, in view of s. 88 of the *Indian Act*, the *Wildlife Act* applied to appellant even if, as I have assumed, it has the effect of regulating him *qua* Indian. . . .

I would answer the constitutional question as follows:

> Ss. 3(1) and 8(1) of the *Wildlife Act*, R.S.B.C. 1979 c. 433, being laws of general application in the Province of British Columbia, are applicable to the Appellant either by referential incorporation under s. 88 of the *Indian Act*, R.S.C. 1970 c. I–6, or of their own force. . . .

I would dismiss the appeal and make no order as to costs.

Kitkatla Band v. B.C. *(Min. of Small Business, Tourism and Culture)* (2002)

[2002] 2 S.C.R. 146 (S.C.C.). McLachlin C.J. and Gonthier, Iacobucci, Major, Binnie, Arbour and LeBel J.J., March 28, 2002.

LEBEL J.— . . .

1   This case concerns a constitutional challenge to the application of provincial legislation on the protection of cultural heritage property. The dispute relates to culturally

modified trees or CMTs. These trees have often been altered by aboriginal people as part of their traditional use and have cultural, historical and scientific importance for a number of First Nations in British Columbia. In the opinion of the appellants, legislation authorizing the removal or modification of these cultural objects would fall beyond the scope of provincial legislative powers. Hence, the *Heritage Conservation Act*, R.S.B.C. 1996, c. 187 ("the Act"), should be struck down in part to the extent that it allows for the alteration and destruction of native cultural objects. For the reasons which are set out below, I am of the view that this appeal should fail because the impugned legislation falls within the provincial jurisdiction on property and civil rights within the province, as the British Columbia Court of Appeal held.

II. The Origins of the Case

2   The dispute arose during the process of administrative review and authorization of logging operations in British Columbia. The respondent, International Forest Products Limited ("Interfor"), had long held a forest licence over land in the central coast of British Columbia which included an area known as the Kumealon. Provincial forestry legislation required Interfor, as the holder of a forest licence, to propose sequential forest development plans. The legislation also granted the public some participatory rights in the creation of these plans. Interfor provided direct notification of its development plans to the appellant Kitkatla Band ("the Band") since early 1994, but these plans never specifically identified the Kumealon area. The appellants claimed aboriginal rights in this area and had been engaged in treaty negotiations with the province. In early 1998, aware of its obligations under the Act, Interfor hired a firm of archaeologists in order to report on the impact of future logging operations in an area that included the Kumealon. Coincidentally, it appears, the appellants expressed an interest in the Kumealon at roughly the same time. Interfor was alerted to this claim, and, shortly thereafter, the firm it hired contacted the Band in order to ascertain their views. The Band designated two persons for this purpose. Interfor was concerned with the possible presence of native heritage sites and objects including CMTs in the area to be harvested. The archaeologist eventually reported the presence of a significant number of these trees in seven cutblocks Interfor intended to harvest.

3   Meanwhile, Interfor applied to the respondent, the Minister of Small Business, Tourism and Culture ("the Minister"), for a site alteration permit under s. 12 of the Act, to authorize the cutting and processing of CMTs during logging operations. The Minister forwarded Interfor's application to the Band, along with a cover letter requesting its written submissions on the application. No submissions were received by the deadline. One week later, on March 31, 1998, and without having considered a single archaeological report, the Minister issued a site alteration permit.

4   At this stage, the Band commenced proceedings to challenge the legality of the permit. They began judicial review proceedings. These proceedings raised administrative law arguments asserting that the Minister had failed to address all relevant issues — and had violated his fiduciary obligations towards the appellants by failing to provide them with proper notification and the opportunity to consult — before issuing the permit. The Band also challenged the Act as being *ultra vires* the province.

5   The administrative law challenge succeeded. A judgment of the British Columbia Supreme Court ordered the Minister to reconsider the part of its decision which affected

the CMTs, after giving the Band an adequate opportunity to be consulted and to make representations. At the same time, the trial court dismissed the constitutional challenge.

6   The Minister went through the reconsideration process. During this process, the Band asserted a claim of aboriginal rights in the continued existence of the CMTs. It petitioned for an order in the nature of prohibition, to restrain the Minister from granting the site alteration permit. The Minister took the position that this issue fell outside the scope of the permit granting procedure and should be left to the courts. Wilson J. agreed with the Minister and dismissed the petition. In the end, the Minister issued a site alteration permit in accordance with the CMTs management plan proposed by Interfor which provided that all fallen CMTs should be preserved together with 76 of 116 trees still standing in the cutblocks. This led to the present appeal. Meanwhile, the Band launched another judicial review application on the basis that the Minister should have considered native rights in the permit granting procedure. This new challenge also failed. . . .

Heritage Conservation Act, R.S.B.C. 1996, c. 187

8   For greater certainty, no provision of this Act and no provision in an agreement entered into under section 4 abrogates or derogates from the aboriginal and treaty rights of a first nation or of any aboriginal peoples.

12   (1) In this section, except subsection (6), and in sections 13(4) and 14(4), "minister" includes a person authorized in writing by the minister for the purposes of the section.

(2) The minister may
(a) issue a permit authorizing an action referred to in section 13, or
(b) refuse to issue a permit for an action that, in the opinion of the minister, would be inconsistent with the purpose of the heritage protection of the property.

13   (1) Except as authorized by a permit issued under section 12 or 14, a person must not remove, or attempt to remove, from British Columbia a heritage object that is protected under subsection (2) or which has been removed from a site protected under subsection (2).

(2) Except as authorized by a permit issued under section 12 or 14, or an order issued under section 14, a person must not do any of the following:
(a) damage, desecrate or alter a Provincial heritage site or a Provincial heritage object or remove from a Provincial heritage site or Provincial heritage object any heritage object or material that constitutes part of the site or object;
(b) damage, desecrate or alter a burial place that has historical or archaeological value or remove human remains or any heritage object from a burial place that has historical or archaeological value;
(c) damage, alter, cover or move an aboriginal rock painting or aboriginal rock carving that has historical or archaeological value;
(d) damage, excavate, dig in or alter, or remove any heritage object from, a site that contains artifacts, features, materials or other physical evidence of human habitation or use before 1846; . . .

(4) The minister may, after providing an opportunity for consultation with the first

nation whose heritage site or object would be affected,

(a) define the extent of a site protected under subsection (2), or

(b) exempt a site or object from subsection (2) on any terms and conditions the minister considers appropriate if the minister considers that the site or object lacks sufficient heritage value to justify its conservation. . . .

V. Constitutional Questions

30   On January 22, 2001, the Chief Justice stated the following constitutional questions:

1) Is s. 12(2)(a) in respect of the subject matter of s. 13(2)(c) and (d) of the *Heritage Conservation Act* in pith and substance law in relation to Indians or Lands reserved for the Indians, or alternatively, is the law in relation to property, and, therefore, within the exclusive legislative competence of the Province under s. 92(13) of the *Constitution Act, 1867?*

2) If the impugned provisions of the *Heritage Conservation Act* are within provincial jurisdiction under s. 92(13) of the *Constitution Act, 1867* do they apply to the subject matter of s. 13(2)(c) and (d) of the *Heritage Conservation Act?*

3) If the impugned provisions do not apply to the appellants *ex proprio vigore*, do they nonetheless apply by virtue of s. 88 of the *Indian Act? . . .*

41   Thus, the main issues have been clearly framed by the parties and in the constitutional questions. The Court must first consider the pith and substance of the legislation. Three sub-questions must be discussed in this respect. First, do ss. 12(2)(a) and 13(2)(c) and (d) intrude into a federal head of power, and to what extent? Then, if they do intrude, are they nevertheless part of a valid legislative scheme? At the next step of the analysis, it should be considered whether the impugned provisions are sufficiently integrated with the scheme. If the answer is yes, we may turn to consider the doctrine of interjurisdictional immunity and, if need be, s. 88 of the *Indian Act*. Before I move on to these, I will review the heritage conservation scheme adopted by the province of British Columbia and discuss some evidentiary issues relevant to the rights claimed by the appellants.

C. Heritage Conservation Legislation in British Columbia

42   The *Heritage Conservation Act* is designed to grant a broad protection to the cultural heritage of British Columbia in a very comprehensive manner. The history of the province means that its cultural heritage is in the vast majority of cases an aboriginal one, often going back to pre-contact times and prior to the establishment of the first non-native settlements and the creation of the British colonies on Vancouver Island and on the mainland. The Act was adopted to conserve and protect all forms of cultural property, objects and artifacts as well as sites in British Columbia which have heritage value to the province as a whole, to a community or to an aboriginal people, as appears for example in the definition of "heritage object" in the Act: "heritage object, means, whether designated or not, personal property that has heritage value to British Columbia, a community or an aboriginal people".

43   The Act attempts to address the importance of the cultural heritage of First Nations in various ways. Section 4 provides for agreements with First Nations with respect to the preservation of aboriginal sites and artifacts. Section 8 states a key interpretive principle in the interpretation and implementation of the Act which is designed to pro-

tect aboriginal and treaty rights of First Nations:

> For greater certainty, no provision of this Act and no provision in an agreement entered into under section 4 abrogates or derogates from the aboriginal and treaty rights of a first nation or of any aboriginal peoples.

44   Native concerns must be weighed at most steps of the administrative procedures created for the application of the Act. For example, prior to the designation of lands as a heritage site, notice must be given to the First Nations within whose traditional territory they lie. Section 13 grants broad protection against any alteration of sites or things in use before 1846, which will usually be part of the cultural heritage of First Nations in British Columbia (see s. 13(2)(d)).

45   The Act considers First Nations' culture as part of the heritage of all residents of British Columbia. It must be protected, not only as an essential part of the collective material memory which belongs to the history and identity of First Nations, but also as part of the shared heritage of all British Columbians. The Act grants protection where none existed before. At the same time, heritage conservation schemes such as the Act here must strike a balance between conservation and other societal interests, which may require the destruction of heritage objects or sites after a careful review by the Minister. Time and nature, as well as mishaps and unforeseen events, may destroy or render the conservation of a site or thing an impossibility. Other needs and concerns may arise and require an assessment of the nature and importance of a site or cultural object. Conservation schemes must thus also provide for removal and destruction. This is what is at issue here. Is the power to order the alteration or even destruction of a cultural object beyond provincial powers when it affects native cultural objects?

D. Evidentiary Problems

46   Constitutional questions should not be discussed in a factual vacuum. Even in a division of powers case, rights must be asserted and their factual underpinnings demonstrated. In this case, the appellants assert that the importance of the CMTs goes to the core of their cultural values and identity. This assertion grounds their claim that the impugned provisions of the Act impinge on a federal head of power. Because of this assertion, the nature and quality of the evidence offered will have to be assessed and discussed. Even if this case remains a division of powers case, the comments of McLachlin C.J. on evidentiary standards and problems in aboriginal law cases in *Mitchell* v. *M.N.R.*, [2001] 1 S.C.R. 911, 2001 SCC 33, remain highly apposite. In such cases, oral evidence of aboriginal values, customs and practices is necessary and relevant. It should be assessed with understanding and sensitivity to the traditions of a civilization which remained an essentially oral one before and after the period of contact with Europeans who brought their own tradition of reliance on written legal and archival records. Nevertheless, this kind of evidence must be evaluated like any other. Claims must be established on a balance of probabilities, by persuasive evidence (*Mitchell, supra*, at para. 39, per McLachlin C.J.). "Sparse, doubtful and equivocal evidence cannot serve as the foundation for a successful claim . . ." (*Mitchell*, at para. 51, *per* McLachlin C.J.).

47   These comments on the use of evidence must be kept in mind during a review of the evidence in this case. The appellants attempted to downplay the importance and relevance of this issue by stressing that this Court was not faced with a claim of aboriginal rights or title. As stated above, facts must be established in order to demonstrate in this

case that there exists a conflict between federal and provincial legislative powers. In this respect, the factual basis of the claim looks weak.

48   The appellants' claim in this case is concerned with what archaeologists refer to as culturally modified trees (CMTs). From the evidence, large numbers of CMTs are found in British Columbia. Thousands are reported and registered every year in British Columbia in the archaeology branch of the ministry. For ministry purposes, CMTs are trees which bear the marks of past aboriginal intervention occurring as part of traditional aboriginal use. Bark may have been stripped from them. Pieces or chunks of wood may have been removed from the trees to make tools or build canoes. Sap or pitch may have been collected from the trees. It would appear that the identification of CMTs is an involved process. Sometimes, the modifications found on trees result from the work of nature. On the other hand, modifications may have been made by non-native persons. Therefore, in order to identify true CMTs, archaeologists have developed complex "field" guidelines. In certain cases, these guidelines will prove incapable to the task, and it will be necessary to take a sample or even fell a particular tree to determine whether it is a CMT. In this appeal, the CMTs that the archaeologists were able to identify were generally categorized as either "bark-stripped trees" or "aboriginally-logged trees".

49   In addition, there is one matter that, as of now, lies beyond the ken from any archaeological expert. Even if there is evidence of native intervention, it is next to impossible to tell which aboriginal group modified them (see Braidwood J.A., at para. 30). In this case, in particular, the trees are found in an area covered by the conflicting claims of the Band and another group, the Lax Kw'alaams, which, like the appellants, also belong to the Tsimshian Tribal Council. This second group has agreed with the forestry management plan proposed by Interfor, and approved by the Minister.

50   The appellants, in support of their claim, assert that the preservation of the CMTs as living trees is required in order to safeguard evidence of their cultural heritage including the work, activities and endeavours of their forebears. Indeed, they argue that the CMTs constitute the only physical record of their heritage. Unfortunately, the evidence supporting these claims is sparse. Aside from an affidavit sworn by the appellant Chief Hill, there is very little evidence as to the extent to which these trees in the Kumealon had been related to or incorporated into the culture of the Band. In this respect, according to other evidence, the firm of archeologists hired by Interfor identified these CMTs and brought their existence to the attention of the appellants. The constitutional questions must be reviewed in the context of this factual record, with its particular weaknesses. I will now turn to the constitutional issues.

E. The Division of Powers Issue

51   The constitution of Canada does not include an express grant of power with respect to "culture" as such. Most constitutional litigation on cultural issues has arisen in the context of language and education rights. However, provinces are also concerned with broader and more diverse cultural problems and interests. In addition, the federal government affects cultural activity in this country through the exercise of its broad powers over communications and through the establishment of federally funded cultural institutions. Consequently, particular cultural issues must be analyzed in their context, in relation to the relevant sources of legislative power. In this case, the issues raised by the parties concern the use and protection of property in the province. The Act imposes limitations on

property rights in the province by reason of their cultural importance. At first blush, this would seem to be a provincial matter falling within the scope of s. 92(13) of the *Constitution Act, 1867*. This view will have to be tested through a proper pith and substance analysis, in order to establish the relationship between the impugned provisions and the federal power on Indian affairs.

F. The Pith and Substance of the Provisions of the Heritage Conservation Act

52   The beginning of any division of powers analysis is a characterization of the impugned law to determine the head of power within which it falls. This process is commonly known as "pith and substance analysis": see the comments of Lamer C.J. in *R. v. Swain*, [1991] 1 S.C.R. 933, at pp. 998. By thus categorizing the impugned provision, one is able to determine whether the enacting legislature possesses the authority under the constitution to do what it did.

53   A pith and substance analysis looks at both (1) the purpose of the legislation as well as (2) its effect. First, to determine the purpose of the legislation, the Court may look at both intrinsic evidence, such as purpose clauses, or extrinsic evidence, such as Hansard or the minutes of parliamentary committees.

54   Second, in looking at the effect of the legislation, the Court may consider both its legal effect and its practical effect. In other words, the Court looks to see, first, what effect flows directly from the provisions of the statute itself; then, second, what "side" effects flow from the application of the statute which are not direct effects of the provisions of the statute itself: see *R. v. Morgentaler*, [1993] 3 S.C.R. 463, at pp. 482–83. Iacobucci J. provided some examples of how this would work in *Global Securities Corp. v. British Columbia (Securities Commission)*, [2000] 1 S.C.R. 494, 2000 SCC 21, at para. 23 . . .

55   There is some controversy among the parties to this case as to the appropriate approach to the pith and substance analysis where what is challenged is not the Act as a whole but simply one part of it. The appellants tend to emphasize the characterization of the impugned provisions outside the context of the Act as a whole. The respondents and interveners take the opposite view, placing greater emphasis on the pith and substance of the Act as a whole. The parties also disagree as to the order in which the analysis should take place: the appellants favour looking at the impugned provisions first, while the respondents and interveners tend to prefer to look at the Act first.

. . .

G. Purpose of the Provisions Test

59   The first stage of the analysis requires a characterization of the impugned provisions in isolation, looking at both their purpose and effect. . . .

60   Paragraphs (c) and (d) of s. 13(2) have as their purpose the protection of certain aboriginal heritage objects from damage, alteration, or removal. In other words, the purpose of these paragraphs is heritage conservation, specifically the heritage of the aboriginal peoples of British Columbia. The protection extends to all aboriginal rock paintings or aboriginal rock carvings that have historical or archaeological value, as well as to heritage objects, including artifacts, features, materials or other physical evidence of human habitation or use before 1846, which in effect consists almost entirely of aboriginal cultural artifacts.

61   Paragraph (a) of s. 12(2), on the other hand, provides the minister responsible for the operation of the Act as a whole with the discretion to grant a permit authorizing one of the actions prohibited under s. 13(2)(c) and (d). In other words, this paragraph provides a tempering of the absolute protection otherwise provided by s. 13(2)(c) and (d).

62   The purpose of such a provision seems obvious when one considers the nature of heritage conservation legislation generally and its specific application in the context of British Columbia. No heritage conservation scheme can provide absolute protection to all objects or sites that possess some historical, archaeological, or cultural value to a society. To grant such an absolute protection would be to freeze a society at a particular moment in time. It would make impossible the need to remove, for example, buildings or artifacts of heritage value which, nevertheless, create a public health hazard or otherwise endanger lives. In other cases, the value of preserving an object may be greatly outweighed by the benefit that could accrue from allowing it to be removed or destroyed in order to accomplish a goal deemed by society to be of greater value. It cannot be denied that ss. 12(2)(a) and 13(2)(c) could sometimes affect aboriginal interests. As will be seen below, these provisions form part of a carefully balanced scheme. As recommended by the Court in *Delgamuukw, supra,* it is highly sensitive to native cultural interests. At the same time, it appears to strike an appropriate balance between native and non-native interests. Native interests must be carefully taken into account at every stage of a procedure under the Act. The Act clearly considers them as an essential part of the interests to be preserved and of the cultural heritage of British Columbia as well as of all First Nations.

63   Consequently, any heritage conservation scheme inevitably includes provisions to make exceptions to the general protection the legislation is intended to provide. Such a permissive provision strikes a balance among competing social goals.

H. Effect of the Provisions

64   Having looked at the purpose of these provisions, I turn now to consider their effects. Sections 12(2)(a) and 13(2)(c) and (d) grant the Minister a discretion to allow the alteration or removal of aboriginal heritage objects. We have no evidence before us with respect to the total number of aboriginal heritage objects which may be covered by this legislation. Nor do we have any evidence as to how often the Minister has exercised the discretion to permit the removal or destruction of aboriginal heritage objects of whatever type. We know only that, in the present case, the permit granted to the respondent Interfor allowed it to cut 40 out of about 120 standing CMTs within seven identified cutblocks. Thus, the practical effect, in this case anyway, is to permit the destruction of what are alleged to be Kitkatla heritage objects (although there is no specific proof here that the 40 CMTs in question were indeed the products of Kitkatla ancestors) while protecting 80 CMTs from alteration and removal. In addition, all CMTs allowed to be logged must be catalogued and an archival record of them must be retained. In other words, the effect here is the striking of a balance between the need and desire to preserve aboriginal heritage with the need and desire to promote the exploitation of British Columbia's natural resources.

I. Effect on Federal Powers

65   Given this analysis of the purpose and effect of the legislation in order to characterize the impugned provisions, the Court must then determine whether the pith and substance of ss. 12(2)(a) and 13(2)(c) and (d) fall within a provincial head of power or if,

rather, they fall within a federal head of power. If the Court characterizes these provisions as a heritage conservation measure that is designed to strike a balance between the need to preserve the past while also allowing the exploitation of natural resources today, then they would fall squarely within the provincial head of power in s. 92(13) of the *Constitution Act, 1867* with respect to property and civil rights in the province.

66   On the other hand, one cannot escape the fact that the impugned provisions directly affect the existence of aboriginal heritage objects, raising the issue of whether the provisions are in fact with respect to Indians and lands reserved to Indians, a federal head of power under s. 91(24) of the *Constitution Act, 1867*. In considering this question, the Court must assess a number of factors. First, the Court must remember the basic assumption that provincial laws can apply to aboriginal peoples; First Nations are not enclaves of federal power in a sea of provincial jurisdiction: see *Cardinal* v. *Attorney General of Alberta*, [1974] S.C.R. 695. The mere mention of the word "aboriginal" in a statutory provision does not render it ultra vires the province.

67   Second, it is clear that legislation which singles out aboriginal people for special treatment is ultra vires the province: see *Four B Manufacturing Ltd.* v. *United Garment Workers of America*, [1980] 1 S.C.R. 1031. For example, a law which purported to affect the Indian status of adopted children was held to be ultra vires the province: see *Natural Parents* v. *Superintendent of Child Welfare*, [1976] 2 S.C.R. 751. Similarly, laws which purported to define the extent of Indian access to land for the purpose of hunting were ultra vires the provinces because they singled out Indians: see *Sutherland, supra*; *Moosehunter* v. *The Queen*, [1981] 1 S.C.R. 282. Further, provincial laws must not impair the status or capacity of Indians: see *Kruger* v. *The Queen*, [1978] 1 S.C.R. 104, at p. 110; *Dick, supra*, at pp. 323–24.

68   Nevertheless, "singling out" should not be confused with disproportionate effect. Dickson J. (as he then was) said in *Kruger, supra*, at p. 110, that "the fact that a law may have graver consequence to one person than to another does not, on that account alone, make the law other than one of general application".

69   In the present case, the impugned provisions cannot be said to single out aboriginal peoples, at least from one point of view. The provisions prohibit everyone, not just aboriginal peoples, from the named acts, and require everyone, not just aboriginal peoples, to seek permission of the Minister to commit the prohibited acts. In that respect, the impugned provisions treat everyone the same. The impugned provisions' disproportionate effects can be attributed to the fact that aboriginal peoples have produced by far the largest number of heritage objects in British Columbia. These peoples have been resident in British Columbia for thousands of years; other British Columbians arrived in the last two hundred years.

70   A more serious objection is raised with respect to the issue of whether permitting the destruction of aboriginal heritage objects impairs the status or capacity of Indians. The appellants' submission seeks to situate these cultural interests, along with aboriginal rights, at the "core of Indianness", *Delgamuukw, supra*, at para. 181. However, as pointed out above, little evidence has been offered by the appellants with respect to the relationship between the CMTs and Kitkatla culture in this area. The appellants argue that aboriginal heritage objects constitute a major portion of their identity and culture in a way that non-aboriginal heritage objects do not go to the centre of non-aboriginal identity.

Consequently, they argue, aboriginal people are singled out for more severe treatment. I would reject this argument. Because British Columbia's history is dominated by aboriginal culture, fewer non-aboriginal objects and sites receive protection than aboriginal objects and sites. The Act provides a shield, in the guise of the permit process, against the destruction or alteration of heritage property. When one considers the relative protection afforded aboriginal and non-aboriginal heritage objects, the treatment received by both groups is the same, and indeed is more favourable, in one sense to aboriginal peoples.

71   In any case, it should be remembered that the Act cannot apply to any aboriginal heritage object or site which is the subject of an established aboriginal right or title, by operation of s. 35(1) of the *Constitution Act, 1982* and by operation of s. 8 of the *Heritage Conservation Act* (and, by implication, s. 12(7) of that Act which states that a permit does not grant a right to alter or remove an object without the consent of the party which has title to the object or site on which the object is situated). The Act is tailored, whether by design or by operation of constitutional law, to not affect the established rights of aboriginal peoples, a protection that is not extended to any other group. On the whole, then, I am of the opinion that ss. 12(2)(a) and 13(2)(c) and (d) of the Act are valid provincial law and that they do not single out aboriginal peoples or impair their status or condition as Indians. . . .

J. Paramountcy and Federal Powers

74   The doctrine of paramountcy does not appear applicable in this case, as no valid federal legislation occupies the same field. There are provisions in the *Indian Act* with respect to aboriginal heritage conservation, but they are confined to objects on reserve lands. As I noted above, the *Heritage Conservation Act* does not apply to aboriginal heritage objects or sites which are the subject of an established aboriginal right or title by virtue both of s. 35(1) of the *Constitution Act, 1982* and s. 8 of the Act itself, which is declaratory of that fact. In any case, the CMTs in question in this case are not located on an Indian reserve but on Crown land.

75   I thus find that there is no intrusion on a federal head of power. It has not been established that these provisions affect the essential and distinctive core values of Indianness which would engage the federal power over native affairs and First Nations in Canada. They are part of a valid provincial legislative scheme. The legislature has made them a closely integrated part of this scheme. The provisions now protect native interests in situations where, before, land owners and business undertakings might have disregarded them, absent evidence of a constitutional right.

76   The Act purports to give the provincial government a means of protecting heritage objects while retaining the ability to make exceptions where economic development or other values outweigh the heritage value of the objects. In the British Columbia context, this generally means that the provincial government must balance the need to exploit the province's natural resources, particularly its rich abundance of lumber, in order to maintain a viable economy that can sustain the province's population, with the need to preserve all types of cultural and historical heritage objects and sites within the province. Given the overwhelming prevalence of aboriginal heritage objects in the province and, in this particular case, the ubiquitous nature of CMTs, legislation which sought to permit the striking of this balance but which did not attempt to extend this to aboriginal heritage objects and sites would inevitably fall very far short of its goal, if in fact it would not in most respects gut the purposes of the Act.

77   Given this conclusion, it will not be useful to discuss the doctrine of interjurisdictional immunity. It would apply only if the provincial legislation went to the core of the federal power. (See *Ordon Estate* v. *Grail*, [1998] 3 S.C.R. 437, at para. 81; *Delgamuukw, supra*, at paras. 177–78, *per* Lamer C.J.) In these circumstances, no discussion of the principle governing the application of s. 88 of the Indian Act would be warranted.

VII. Conclusion and Disposition

78   Heritage properties and sites may certainly, in some cases, turn out to be a key part of the collective identity of people. In some future case, it might very well happen that some component of the cultural heritage of a First Nation would go to the core of its identity in such a way that it would affect the federal power over native affairs and the applicability of provincial legislation. This appeal does not raise such issues, based on the weak evidentiary record and the relevant principles governing the division of powers in Canada. In the circumstances of this case, the overall effect of the provision is to improve the protection of native cultural heritage and, indeed, to safeguard the presence and the memory of the cultural objects involved in this litigation, without jeopardizing the core values defining the identity of the appellants as Indians. For these reasons, I would dismiss the appeal, without costs. The constitutional questions should be answered as follows:

1 Is s. 12(2)(a) in respect of the subject matter of s. 13(2)(c) and (d) of the *Heritage Conservation Act* in pith and substance law in relation to Indians or Lands reserved for the Indians, or alternatively, is the law in relation to property, and, therefore, within the exclusive legislative competence of the Province under s. 92(13) of the *Constitution Act, 1867*?

   Answer: Section 12(2)(a) in respect of the subject matter in s. 13(2)(c) and (d) of the *Heritage Conservation Act* is in pith and substance law within the legislative competence of the Province under s. 92(13) of the *Constitution Act, 1867*.

2 If the impugned provisions of the *Heritage Conservation Act* are within provincial jurisdiction under s. 92(13) of the *Constitution Act, 1867* do they apply to the subject matter of s. 13(2)(c) and (d) of the *Heritage Conservation Act*?

   Answer: Yes.

3 If the impugned provisions do not apply to the appellants *ex proprio vigore*, do they nonetheless apply by virtue of s. 88 of the *Indian Act*?

   Answer: No need to answer.

Appeal dismissed.

NATURAL RESOURCES TRANSFER AGREEMENTS

Constitution Act, 1930

R.S.C. 1985, App. II, No. 8 (formerly the *British North America Act, 1930*, 20–21 George V, c. 26 (U.K.).

An Act to confirm and give effect to certain agreements entered into between the Government of the Dominion of Canada and the Governments of the Provinces of Manitoba, British Columbia, Alberta and Saskatchewan respectively. . . .

(3) Saskatchewan

Memorandum of Agreement . . .

Transfer of Public Lands Generally

1. In order that the Province may be in the same position as the original Provinces of Confederation are in virtue of section one hundred and nine of the *British North America Act, 1867*, the interest of the Crown in all Crown lands, mines, minerals (precious and base) and royalties derived therefrom within the Province, and all sums due or payable for such lands, mines, minerals or royalties, shall from and after the coming into force of this agreement and subject as therein otherwise provided, belong to the province subject to any trusts existing in respect thereof, and to any interest other than that of the Crown in the same, and the said lands, mines, minerals and royalties shall be administered by the Province for the purposes thereof, subject, until the Legislature of the Province otherwise provides, to the provisions of any Act of the Parliament of Canada relating to such administration; and payment received by Canada in respect of any such lands, mines, minerals or royalties before the coming into force of this agreement shall continue to belong to Canada whether paid in advance or otherwise, it being the intention that, except as herein otherwise specially provided, Canada shall not be liable to account to the Province for any payment made in respect of any of the said lands, mines, minerals, or royalties before the coming into force of this agreement, and that the Province shall not be liable to account to Canada for any such payment made thereafter.

2. The Province will carry out in accordance with the terms thereof every contract to purchase or lease any Crown lands, mines or minerals and every other arrangement whereby any person has become entitled to any interest therein as against the Crown, and further agrees not to affect or alter any term of any such contract to purchase, lease or other arrangement by legislation or otherwise, except either with the consent of all the parties thereto other than Canada or in so far as any legislation may apply generally to all similar agreements relating to lands, mines or minerals in the Province or to interests therein, irrespective of who may be the parties thereto. . . .

Indian Reserves

10. All lands included in Indian reserves within the Province, including those selected and surveyed but not yet confirmed, as well as those confirmed, shall continue to be vested in the Crown and administered by the Government of Canada for the purposes of Canada, and the Province will from time to time, upon the request of the Superintendent General of Indian Affairs, set aside, out of the unoccupied Crown lands hereby transferred to its administration, such further areas as the said Superintendent General may, in agreement with the appropriate Minister of the Province, select as necessary to enable Canada to fulfil it obligations under the treaties with the Indians of the Province, and such areas shall thereafter be administered by Canada in the same way in all respects as if they had never passed to the Province under the provisions hereof.

R. v. Horse (1988)

[1988] 1 S.C.R. 187 (S.C.C.). Beetz, Estey, McIntyre, Lamer, Wilson, Le Dain, and L'Heureux-Dubé JJ., January 28, 1988.

Estey J.:— . . . Each of the appellants was charged with an offence under s. 37 of the

Saskatchewan Wildlife Act, S.S. 1979, c. W–13.1, which prohibits the use of a spotlight for the purpose of hunting any wildlife. . . .

Each of the appellants was convicted at Provincial Court by Seniuk Prov. Ct. J. . . . An appeal to the Saskatchewan Queen's Bench was allowed and the convictions were set aside by Dielschneider J. . . . The Crown appealed this judgment and the Saskatchewan Court of Appeal restored the convictions. . . .

To succeed the appellants must demonstrate a right in law to hunt on these privately owned lands and to do notwithstanding the regulation of hunting under the provincial statute.

The right of access to the land in issue for the purpose of hunting is alleged to derive from the *Wildlife Act* itself, or from the provisions of Treaty No. 6, or from custom and usage. If such a right exists in law then the appellants claim immunity from prosecution by means of provisions of the Natural Resources Transfer Agreement, as confirmed by the *Constitution Act, 1930* (U.K.), 20 & 21 Geo. 5, c. 26 (reprinted in R.S.C. 1970, App. II, No. 25), or under the Indian Act, R.S.C. 1970, c. I–6, s. 88. They also rely on s. 35(1) of the *Constitution Act, 1982.*

In my view, the appellants were properly convicted under s. 37 of the *Wildlife Act* and the appeal must be dismissed.

1. The Natural Resources Transfer Agreement

In 1929 and 1930 agreements were entered into between each of the provinces of Alberta, Manitoba and Saskatchewan and the Canadian government for the primary purpose of effecting a transfer of control of natural resources and Crown lands from the Dominion government to the Prairie provinces. They were confirmed by legislation enacted in each of the provinces, and by the Parliament of Canada. The United Kingdom Parliament, by enacting the *Constitution Act, 1930*, gave these agreements the force of law.

Paragraph 12 of the Saskatchewan agreement, with which we are here concerned, provides:

> 12. In order to secure to the Indians of the Province the continuance of the supply of game and fish for their support and subsistence, Canada agrees that the laws respecting game in force in the Province from time to time shall apply to the Indians within the boundaries thereof, provided, however, that the said Indians shall have the right, which the Province hereby assures to them of hunting, trapping and fishing game and fish for food at all seasons of the year *on all unoccupied Crown lands and on any other lands to which the said Indians may have a right of access.* [emphasis added]

This appeal concerns the category "other lands" which on the facts here, means privately owned lands. . . .

(a) Statutory Rights

The appellants claim that s. 38 of the *Wildlife Act* creates a statutory right of access to private lands. They also contend that the Act contemplates that private lands will be used for hunting by reason of the fact that reference is made to an owner giving consent to hunting on his or her land. Section 38 provides in part:

> 38. (1) Where there are legible signs, of a size specified in the regulations, prominently placed along the boundaries of any land so as to provide reasonable notice bearing the words "No Trespassing", "No Hunting", "No Shooting" or words or symbols to like effect, no person shall hunt any wildlife within the boundaries of such land except with the consent of the owner or occupant.

(2) Subject to this Act and the regulations, where there are legible signs of the size specified in the regulations prominently placed along the boundaries of any land so as to provide reasonable notice of instructions concerning the method of hunting or the use of vehicles connected with hunting, no person shall hunt any wildlife on such land except in accordance with the posted instructions.

(6) Nothing in this section limits or affects any rights or remedies of an owner or occupier of land for trespass at common law, and, where he has not erected or placed signs along the boundaries of his land in accordance with subsection (1) or (2), that fact alone is not to be deemed to imply consent by him to entry upon his land or to imply a right of access to his land for the purpose of hunting.

These provincial provisions came before the court in *Prince and Myron* v. *The Queen*, [1964] S.C.R. 81, with reference to similar legislation in the province of Manitoba. The Manitoba legislation prescribed a notice procedure whereby land could be protected from hunting. The notice requirement stemmed from the following provision in the Manitoba legislation:

76.(1) No person shall hunt any bird or any animal mentioned in this Part if it is upon or over any land with regard to which notice has been given under this Part, without having obtained the consent of the owner or lawful occupant thereof.

From this provision the Manitoba Court of Appeal concluded that in the absence of signs posted as prescribed Indians had a right of access to occupied private land for the purpose of hunting. (See *R.* v. *Prince* (1962), 40 W.W.R. 234).

This court in *Myron* v. *The Queen, supra,* and later in *McKinney* v. *The Queen*, [1980] 1 S.C.R. 401, [1981] 2 C.N.L.R. 113 took occasion to "reserve" the Manitoba court's conclusion in *Prince, supra,* with reference to right of access to private lands. In commenting upon the earlier Manitoba Court of Appeal decision in *Prince, supra,* Dickson J. (as he then was) in *Myron, supra,* stated (p. 145):

I would have grave doubt that this can be the law. Section 40 of *The Wildlife Act* (of Manitoba) does not deal with interests in property. It is intended, I would have thought, to create a separate offence under the provincial statute in respect of posted lands and not to confer entry rights in respect of unposted lands. . . . With great respect, in my opinion the majority of the Manitoba Court of Appeal in *Prince and Myron* v. *The Queen* may have erred in their view of the import of s. 76 of *The Game and Fisheries Act,* the antecedent of s. 40, in failing to appreciate the importance of s. 76(4) reading: 76.(4) Nothing in this section limits or affects the remedy at common law of any such owner or occupant for trespass.

Dickson J., in dealing with substantially the same legislation as that now before the court in this appeal, then concluded (p. 146):

. . . that in Manitoba at the present time hunters enter private property with no greater rights than other trespassers; that they have no right of access except with the owner's permission; and, lacking permission, are subject to civil action for trespass and prosecution. . . .

It is noted that the foregoing extracts from the *Myron* judgment, *supra,* were not necessary in resolving these issues arising in that appeal. These comments came before this court in *McKinney* v. *The Queen, supra,* where Chief Justice Laskin stated (at p. 401) [p. 113 C.N.L.R.]:

We adopt as a correct statement of the law what was said *obiter* by Dickson J. in *Myron, Meeches et al.* v. *The Queen,* at p. 145. We agree with the Manitoba Court of Appeal that *R.* v. *Prince* was wrongly decided.

The opposite result to that reached in this court in the combination of *Myron* and *McKinney, supra,* was reached by the Saskatchewan Court of Appeal in *R. v. Tobacco,* [1981] 1 W.W.R. 545, 4 Sask. R. 380, [1980] 3 C.N.L.R. 81. That case, however, was predicated upon the then *Saskatchewan Wildlife Act* which did not include the above-mentioned provision in the *Manitoba Wildlife Act* dealing with the rights of an owner at common law or by statute for trespass in respect of his land. As can be seen from the excerpts from the present Saskatchewan statute, *supra,* subs. (6) of s. 38 contains a provision preserving the rights of an owner or occupant at common law for trespass and accordingly the *Tobacco* case is of no application here.

Additionally, the appellants seek to establish a statutory right of access by reason of the *Wildlife Act* as the result of judicial decisions in this court in *R. v. Sutherland,* [1980] 2 S.C.R. 451, [1980] 3 C.N.L.R. 71, and *Moosehunter* v. *The Queen,* [1981] 1 S.C.R. 282, [1981] 1 C.N.L.R. 61. In *Sutherland* the right to hunt accorded to the public generally by the province was limited to enumerated animals. The court concluded that once any hunting was allowed to the general public, Indians under paragraph 13 of the Manitoba agreement enjoyed unlimited hunting rights. *Moosehunter, supra* was to the same effect. It should be noted that in those two cases the court was not dealing with privately owned land but with Crown lands in respect of which the Crown in the right of the province has granted to all persons a limited right to hunt. In *Sutherland, supra,* the court stated through Dickson J., as he then was, at p. 459 [p. 76 C.N.L.R.]:

> It is arguable that where the Crown has validly occupied lands, there is *prima facie* no right of access, as is the case with land occupied by private owners, save and except that right of access the Crown confers on the public and/or Indians, as occupant of the land. In the Management Area the Crown has granted public access to hunt, but *on certain terms.* The province cannot deny access to Indians while granting it to the public, but the province can deny access for purposes of hunting which binds Indians and non-Indians alike.

It is a long jump to move from the concept of "a limited right to hunt" to unlimited hunting by Indians on private land by reason of the right of the owner of the private land in general law to grant or withhold access to anybody for any purpose. The mere capacity in the owner to grant right of access for hunting to friends or licensees or invitees is not a limited right of hunting in the sense that Indians therefore, without consent, can proceed upon the land for the purpose of hunting.

The appellants have not, by either submission or approach, succeeded in establishing that the *Wildlife Act* accords to them a statutory right of access for the purpose of hunting on private lands.

(b) Custom or Usage
Admitting, only for the purpose of examining the rights of appellants, that Indians and/or others may by custom or usage acquire a right of access to lands for hunting, there is no evidence or material adduced in these proceedings which demonstrate the existence of any such right by custom or usage arising in the appellants. In my view this renders this appeal a wholly unsatisfactory basis upon which to determine the argument of access based on custom. I agree with the view expressed by Vancise J.A. in the Saskatchewan Court of Appeal below where he stated [pp. 105–106 C.N.L.R.]:

> In this case the respondent sought to argue issues such as custom and usage, implied consent, right of access to surrendered lands under the treaties and access for the purpose of pursuing the avocation of hunting and fishing on which there was no evidence before the court. If the parties wish to argue these matters on an agreed statement of facts the state-

ment should contain sufficient factual information and underpinning to allow a full and complete arguing of the issues and evidence should be called to establish factual underpinning.

In view of the total absence of the necessary evidence it cannot be determined whether the appellants have a right of access based on custom or usage.

2. Treaty No. 6

The appellants argue that the terms of the treaty give them a right to hunt for food on private land. If such a right exists under the treaty then they contend that it is protected by both paragraphs 2 and 12 of the *Natural Resources Transfer Agreement*. Paragraph 2 reads:

> 2. The Province will carry out in accordance with the terms thereof every contract to purchase or lease any Crown lands, mines or minerals and every other arrangement whereby any person has become entitled to any interest therein as against the Crown, and further agrees not to affect or alter any term of any such contract to purchase, lease or other arrangement by legislation or otherwise, except either with the consent of all the parties thereto other than Canada or in so far as any legislation may apply generally to all similar agreements relating to lands, mines or minerals in the Province or to interests therein, irrespective of who may be the parties thereto.

They also invoke s. 35(1) of the *Constitution Act, 1982* which provides:

> 35.(1) The existing aboriginal and treaty rights of the aboriginal peoples of Canada are hereby recognized and affirmed.

Finally, s. 88 of the *Indian Act* is invoked to protect treaty rights from application of the *Wildlife Act*. . . .

The operative provision of Treaty No. 6 is as follows:

> Her Majesty further agrees with her said Indians that they, the said Indians, shall have right to pursue their avocations of hunting and fishing throughout the tract surrendered as hereinbefore described, subject to such regulations as may from time to time be made by her Government of her Dominion of Canada, and *saving and excepting such tracts as may from time to time be required or taken up for settlement*, mining, lumbering or other purposes by her said Government of the Dominion of Canada, or by any of the subjects thereof, duly authorized therefor, by the said Government . . . [emphasis added]

The comparable provision in Treaty No. 7 was considered in *R.* v. *Little Bear* (1958), 25 W.W.R. 580 (Alta. Dist. Ct.) (affirmed (1958), 26 W.W.R. 335 (Alta. C.A.)). On the facts in that case the accused Indian had consent from the private owner of the lands to hunt and thus he came under the protection of paragraph 12 in the Alberta Natural Resources Transfer Agreement.

The trial judge in *Little Bear, supra*, also considered whether Treaty No. 7 gave the accused a right of access to privately owned land. The judge considered the hunting rights proviso in the treaty which is in all material respects the same as the clause at issue here in Treaty No. 6, *supra*. At page 583 this ground of argument is rejected by Turcotte D.C.J.

> It is clear that, without more, the treaty of 1877 did not give Little Bear the right to kill a deer on the Wellman land, because the Wellsan land "had been taken up for settlement by one of Her Majesty's subjects duly authorized thereof by the said Government."

It is evident that the clause relating to hunting rights in Treaty No. 6 should be given the same interpretation as the court in *Little Bear, supra*, gave to the comparable clause in Treaty No. 7. . . .

In summary then the terms of the treaty are clear and unambiguous: the right to hunt preserved in Treaty No. 6 did not extend to land occupied by private owners. When the passages from the negotiations sought to be introduced by the appellants are viewed in the context of the various treaties covered in the Morris text it becomes clear that while the Indians were entitled to continue their mode of life by hunting, the preservation of that right did not include the grant of access to lands privately owned and occupied by settlers. Settlement of these lands was the goal of the government along with the intention of including, where possible, the nomadic Indian population at least to the extent that some of them would turn to agriculture with government assistance as their principal source of sustenance and survival. The extraneous material which properly should be examined when ambiguity in the treaty is encountered, in any case supports and does not contradict the unambiguous terms of the treaty. . . .

I would note in closing that the appellants, in their factum, presented an argument that s. 38(6) of the *Wildlife Act*, as amended by the *Wildlife Amendment Act*, 1982, S.S. 1982–83, c. 20, s. 7, is inoperative by virtue of s. 88 of the *Indian Act, supra*. The submission must be rejected for two reasons. Firstly, it cannot be said that the amendment of s. 38 (6) affects the appellants' status as treaty Indians because, for the reasons given above, the treaty did not give to the appellants a right of access to the lands in question. Secondly, the appellants have not demonstrated, in my view, that the purpose or the effect of the amendment is to deprive them, as Indians, of the right of access. The decisions of this court in *Dick* v. *The Queen*, [1985] 2 S.C.R. 309, . . . [1985] 4 C.N.L.R, 55, and *Kruger* v. *The Queen*, [1978] 1 S.C.R. 104, . . . are determinative of this argument in my opinion.

For the reasons given above I do not believe that the appellants have established that they had a right of access to occupied private lands on any of the grounds put forward. Having failed on this point, the appellants are not immune from the provisions of the *Wildlife Act* and thus they were properly convicted of the offences for which they were found guilty at trial. I would dismiss this appeal and restore the orders of the trial Judge with respect to conviction and sentence.

YUKON AND THE NORTHWEST TERRITORIES

Northwest Territories Act
R.S.C. 1985, c. N–27.

Government

Legislative Powers of Commissioner in Council . . .

Game Ordinances

18. (1) Notwithstanding section 17 but subject to subsection (3), the Commissioner in Council may make ordinances for the government of the Territories in relation to the preservation of game in the Territories that are applicable to and in respect of Indians and Inuit.

(2) Any ordinances made by the Commissioner in Council in relation to the preservation of game in the Territories, unless the contrary intention appears therein, are applicable to and in respect of Indians and Inuit.

(3) Nothing in subsections (1) and (2) shall be construed as authorizing the Com-

missioner in Council to make ordinances restricting or prohibiting Indians or Inuit from hunting for food, on unoccupied Crown lands, game other than game declared by the Governor in Council to be game in danger of becoming extinct. . . .

Laws Applicable to the Territories

22. (2) All laws of general application in force in the Territories are, except where otherwise provided, applicable to and in respect of Inuit in the Territories. . . .

Reindeer

45. The Governor in Council may make regulations

    (a) authorizing the Minister to enter into agreements with Indians or Inuit, or persons with Indian or Inuit blood living the life of an Indian or Inuk, for the herding of reindeer that are the property of Her Majesty, which agreements, if deemed advisable by the Minister, shall include provisions for the transfer of such portions of the herds as may be therein specified to the herders on satisfactory completion of the agreements;

    (b) for the control, management, administration and protection of reindeer in the Territories, whether they are the property of Her Majesty or otherwise;

    (c) for the sale of reindeer and the slaughter or other disposal of surplus reindeer and the carcasses thereof; and

    (d) controlling or prohibiting the transfer or shipment by any means of reindeer or their carcasses or parts thereof, whether they are the property of Her Majesty or otherwise, from any place in the Territories to any other place within or outside the Territories.

*Yukon Act**
R.S.C. 1985, c. Y–2.

Government

Legislative Powers of Commissioner in Council . . .

Game Ordinances

19. (1) Notwithstanding section 18 but subject to subsection (3), the Commissioner in Council may make ordinances for the government of the Territory, in relation to the preservation of game in the Territory, that are applicable to and in respect of Indians and Inuit.

(2) Any ordinances made by the Commissioner in Council in relation to the preservation of game in the Territory, unless the contrary intention appears therein, are applicable to and in respect of Indians and Inuit.

(3) Nothing in subsections (1) and (2) shall be construed as authorizing the Commissioner in Council to make ordinances restricting or prohibiting Indians or Inuit from hunting for food, on unoccupied Crown lands, game other than game declared

---

* Section 19 has been amended by s. 20 of the *Yukon First Nations Land Claims Settlement Act*, S.C. 1994, c. 34. Section 20 of that act provides that the amended ss. 19(1), (2), and (4) of the *Yukon Act* come into force on the first day on which the final agreements of all fourteen Yukon First Nations are given effect. Note that those provisions are not yet in force at the time of publication.

by the Governor in Council to be game in danger of becoming extinct. . . .

20 (1) Subsection 19(1) of the Yukon Act is replaced by the following:*

19 (1) Notwithstanding section 18, the Commissioner in Council may make ordinances for the government of the Territory, in relation to the preservation of game in the Territory, that are applicable to and in respect of Indians and Inuit.

(2) Subsection 19(3) of the Act is repealed.

(3) Section 19 of the Act is amended by adding the following after subsection (3):

(4) After a first nation's final agreement within the meaning of the Yukon First Nations Land Claims Settlement Act, is given effect by or under that Act, subsection (3) does not apply in respect of
    (a) hunting by persons eligible to be enrolled under the agreement; or
    (b) hunting by any person in the first nation's traditional territory as identified in the agreement.

(4) Subsection 19(4) of the Act, as enacted by subsection (3), is repealed.

Section 22 of the Yukon Act, which came into force on April 1, 2003, is as follows:

22. (1) Despite subsection 20(1), any law of the Legislature in relation to the conservation of wildlife, unless the contrary intention appears in it, applies to and in respect of Indians and Inuit.

(2) Nothing in paragraph 18(1)(m) or subsection (1) shall be construed as authorizing the Legislature to make laws restricting or prohibiting Indians and Inuit from hunting for food on unoccupied public real property, other than a species that is declared by order of the Governor in Council to be in danger of becoming extinct. This subsection does not apply to laws that implement the Agreement given effect by the Western Arctic (Inuvialuit) Claims Settlement Act.

(3) After a final agreement referred to in section 4 or 5 of the Yukon First Nations Land Claims Settlement Act is given effect by or under that Act, subsection (2) does not apply in respect of persons eligible to be enrolled under the agreement or the traditional territory identified in it.

Laws Applicable to Territory

23. (2) All laws of general application in force in the Territory are, except where otherwise provided, applicable to and in respect of Inuit in the Territory. . . .

Reindeer

48. The Governor in Council may make regulations
    (a) authorizing the Minister to enter into agreements with Indians or Inuit, or persons with Indian or Inuit blood living the life of an Indian or Inuk, for the herding of reindeer that are the property of Her Majesty, which agreements, if deemed advisable by the Minister, shall include provisions for the transfer of such portions of the herds as may be therein specified to the herders on satisfactory completion of the agreements;
    (b) for the control, management, administration and protection of reindeer in the Territory, whether they are the property of Her Majesty or otherwise;

(c) for the sale of reindeer and the slaughter or other disposal of surplus reindeer and the carcasses thereof; and

(d) controlling or prohibiting the transfer or shipment by any means of reindeer or their carcasses or parts thereof, whether they are the property of Her Majesty or otherwise, from any place in the Territory to any other place within or outside the Territory.

THE FIDUCIARY RELATIONSHIP

R. v. Guerin (1984)

[1984] 2 S.C.R. 335 (S.C.C.). Laskin C.J.C. (took no part in the judgment), Dickson, Beetz, Chouinard, Lamer, Estey, Wilson, Ritchie, and McIntyre JJ., November 1, 1984.

DICKSON J. (BEETZ, CHOUINARD and LAMER JJ. concurring):— . . . The gist of the present action is a claim that the federal Crown was in breach of its trust obligations in respect of the leasing of approximately 162 acres of reserve land to the Shaughnessy Heights Golf Club of Vancouver. The band alleged that a number of the terms and conditions of the lease were different from those disclosed to them before the surrender vote and that some of the lease terms were not disclosed to them at all. The band also claimed failure on the part of the federal crown to exercise the requisite degree of care and management as a trustee. . . .

The issue of the Crown's liability was dealt with in the courts below on the basis of the existence or non-existence of a trust. In dealing with the different consequences of a "true" trust, as opposed to a "political" trust, Le Dain J. noted that the Crown could be liable only if it were subject to an "equitable obligation enforceable in a court of law". I have some doubt as to the cogency of the terminology of "higher" and "lower" trusts, but I do agree that the existence of an equitable obligation is the *sine qua non* for liability. Such an obligation is not, however, limited to relationships which can be strictly defined as "trusts". As will presently appear, it is my view that the Crown's obligations vis-à-vis the Indians cannot be defined as a trust. That does not, however, mean that the Crown owes no enforceable duty to the Indians in the way in which it deals with Indian land.

In my view, the nature of Indian title and the framework of the statutory scheme established for disposing of Indian land places upon the Crown an equitable obligation, enforceable by the courts, to deal with the land for the benefit of the Indians. This obligation does not amount to a trust in the private law sense. It is rather a fiduciary duty. If, however, the Crown breaches this fiduciary duty it will be liable to the Indians in the same way and to the same extent as if such a trust were in effect.

The fiduciary relationship between the Crown and the Indians has its roots in the concept of aboriginal, native or Indian title. The fact that Indian bands have a certain interest in lands does not, however, in itself give rise to a fiduciary relationship between the Indians and the Crown. The conclusion that the Crown is a fiduciary depends upon the further proposition that the Indian interest in the land is inalienable except upon surrender to the Crown.

An Indian band is prohibited from directly transferring its interest to a third party. Any sale or lease of land can only be carried out after a surrender has taken place, with the Crown then acting on the band's behalf. The Crown first took this responsibility upon itself in the *Royal Proclamation of 1763*. . . . It is still recognized in the surrender provisions of the *Indian Act*. The surrender requirement, and the responsibility it entails, are the source of a distinct fiduciary obligation owed by the Crown to the Indians. In order to explore the character of this obligation, however, it is first necessary to consider the basis of aboriginal title and the nature of the interest in land which it represents. . . .

(c) The Crown's Fiduciary Obligation

The concept of fiduciary obligation originated long ago in the notion of breach of confidence, one of the original heads of jurisdiction in Chancery. In the present appeal its relevance is based on the requirement of a "surrender" before Indian land can be alienated.

The *Royal Proclamation of 1763* provided that no private person could purchase from the Indians any lands that the Proclamation had reserved to them, and provided further that all purchases had to be by and in the name of the Crown, in a public assembly of the Indians held by the governor or commander-in-chief of the colony in which the lands in question lay. As Lord Watson pointed out in *St. Catherine's Milling,* supra, at p. 54, this policy with respect to the sale or transfer of the Indians' interest in land has been continuously maintained by the British Crown, by the governments of the colonies when they became responsible for the administration of Indian affairs, and, after 1867, by the federal government of Canada. Successive federal statutes, predecessors to the present *Indian Act*, have all provided for the general inalienability of Indian reserve land except upon surrender to the Crown, the relevant provisions in the present Act being ss. 37–41.

The purpose of this surrender requirement is clearly to interpose the Crown between the Indians and prospective purchasers or lessees of their land, so as to prevent the Indians from being exploited. This is made clear in the Royal Proclamation itself, which prefaces the provision making the Crown an intermediary with a declaration that [at p. 128] "great Frauds and Abuses have been committed in purchasing Lands of the Indians, to the great Prejudice of our Interests, and to the great Dissatisfaction of the said Indians . . .". Through the confirmation in the *Indian Act* of the historic responsibility which the Crown has undertaken, to act on behalf of the Indians so as to protect their interests in transactions with third parties, Parliament has conferred upon the Crown a discretion to decide for itself where the Indians' best interests really lie. This is the effect of s. 18(1) of the Act.

This discretion on the part of the Crown, far from ousting, as the Crown contends, the jurisdiction of the courts to regulate the relationship between the Crown and the Indians, has the effect of transforming the Crown's obligation into a fiduciary one. Professor Ernest J. Weinrib maintains in his article "The Fiduciary Obligation" (1975), 25 U.T.L.J. 1, at p. 7, that "the hallmark of a fiduciary relation is that the relative legal positions are such that one party is at the mercy of the other's discretion". Earlier, at p. 4, he puts the point in the following way:

> [Where there is a fiduciary obligation] there is a relation in which the principal's interests can be affected by, and are therefore dependent on, the manner in which the fiduciary uses the discretion which has been delegated to him. The fiduciary obligation is the law's blunt tool for the control of this discretion.

I make no comment upon whether this description is broad enough to embrace all fiduciary obligations. I do agree, however, that where by statute, agreement, or perhaps by unilateral undertaking, one party has an obligation to act for the benefit of another, and that obligation carries with it a discretionary power, the party thus empowered becomes a fiduciary. Equity will then supervise the relationship by holding him to the fiduciary's strict standard of conduct.

It is sometimes said that the nature of fiduciary relationships is both established and exhausted by the standard categories of agent, trustee, partner, director, and the like. I do not agree. It is the nature of the relationship, not the specific category of actor involved that gives rise to the fiduciary duty. The categories of fiduciary, like those of negligence, should not be considered closed: see, e.g., *Laskin* v. *Bache & Co.*, [1972] 1 O.R. 465, 23 D.L.R. (3d) 385 at 392 (C.A.); *Goldex Mines Ltd.* v. *Revill*; *Probe Mines Ltd.* v. *Goldex Mines Ltd.* (1974), 7 O.R. (2d) 216, 54 D.L.R. (3d) 672 at 224 (C.A.).

It should be noted that fiduciary duties generally arise only with regard to obligations originating in a private law context. Public law duties, the performance of which requires the exercise of discretion, do not typically give rise to a fiduciary relationship. As the "political trust" cases indicate, the Crown is not normally viewed as a fiduciary in the exercise of its legislative or administrative function. The mere fact, however, that it is the Crown which is obligated to act on the Indians' behalf does not of itself remove the Crown's obligation from the scope of the fiduciary principle. As was pointed out earlier, the Indians' interest in land is an independent legal interest. It is not a creation of either the legislative or executive branches of government. The Crown's obligation to the Indians with respect to that interest is therefore not a public law duty. While it is not a private law duty in the strict sense either, it is nonetheless in the nature of a private law duty. Therefore, in this *sui generis* relationship, it is not improper to regard the Crown as a fiduciary.

Section 18(1) of the *Indian Act* confers upon the Crown a broad discretion in dealing with surrendered land. In the present case, the document of surrender, set out in part earlier in these reasons, by which the Musqueam band surrendered the land at issue, confirms this discretion in the clause conveying the land to the Crown "in trust to lease . . . upon such terms as the Government of Canada may deem most conducive to our Welfare and that of our people." When, as here, an Indian band surrenders its interest to the Crown, a fiduciary obligation takes hold to regulate the manner in which the Crown exercises its discretion in dealing with the land on the Indians' behalf.

I agree with Le Dain J. that before surrender the Crown does not hold the land in trust for the Indians. I also agree that the Crown's obligation does not somehow crystallize into a trust, express or implied, at the time of surrender. The law of trusts is a highly developed, specialized branch of the law. An express trust requires a settlor, a beneficiary, a trust corpus, words of settlement, certainty of object and certainty of obligation. Not all of these elements are present here. Indeed, there is not even a trust corpus. As the *Smith* decision, *supra,* makes clear, upon unconditional surrender the Indians' right in the land disappears. No property interest is transferred which could constitute the trust res, so that even if the other indicia of an express or implied trust could be made out, the basic requirement of a settlement of property has not been met. Accordingly, although the nature of Indian title coupled with the discretion vested in the Crown are sufficient to give rise to a fiduciary obligation, neither an express nor an implied trust arises upon surrender.

Nor does surrender give rise to a constructive trust. As was said by this court in *Pettkus* v. *Becker*, [1980] 2 S.C.R. 834 at 847, "The principle of unjust enrichment lies at the heart of the constructive trust". . . . Any similarity between a constructive trust and the Crown's fiduciary obligation to the Indians is limited to the fact that both arise by operation of law; the former is an essentially restitutionary remedy, while the latter is not. In the present case, for example, the Crown has in no way been enriched by the surrender transaction, whether unjustly or otherwise, but the fact that this is so cannot alter either the existence or the nature of the obligation which the Crown owes.

The Crown's fiduciary obligation to the Indians is therefore not a trust. To say as much is not to deny that the obligation is trust-like in character. As would be the case with a trust, the Crown must hold surrendered land for the use and benefit of the surrendering band. The obligation is thus subject to principles very similar to those which govern the law of trusts concerning, for example, the measure of damages for breach. The fiduciary relationship between the Crown and the Indians also bears a certain resemblance to agency, since the obligation can be characterized as a duty to act on behalf of the Indian bands who have surrendered lands, by negotiating for the sale or lease of the land to third parties. But just as the Crown is not a trustee for the Indians, neither is it their agent; not only does the Crown's authority to act on the band's behalf lack a basis in contract, but the band is not a party to the ultimate sale or lease, as it would be if it were the Crown's principal. I repeat, the fiduciary obligation which is owed to the Indians by the Crown is *sui generis*. Given the unique character both of the Indians' interest in land and of their historical relationship with the Crown, the fact that this is so should occasion no surprise.

The discretion which is the hallmark of any fiduciary relationship is capable of being considerably narrowed in a particular case. This is as true of the Crown's discretion vis-à-vis the Indians as it is of the discretion of trustees, agents, and other traditional categories of fiduciary. The *Indian Act* makes specific provision for such narrowing in ss. 18(1) and 38(2). A fiduciary obligation will not, of course, be eliminated by the imposition of conditions that have the effect of restricting the fiduciary's discretion. A failure to adhere to the imposed conditions will simply itself be a *prima facie* breach of the obligation. In the present case both the surrender and the Order-in-Council accepting the surrender referred to the Crown leasing the land on the band's behalf. Prior to the surrender the band had also been given to understand that a lease was to be entered into with the Shaughnessy Heights Golf Club upon certain terms, but this understanding was not incorporated into the surrender document itself. The effect of these so-called oral terms will be considered in the next section.

(d) Breach of the Fiduciary Obligation

The trial judge found that the Crown's agents promised the band to lease the land in question on certain specified terms and then, after surrender, obtained a lease on different terms. The lease obtained was much less valuable. As already mentioned, the surrender document did not make reference to the "oral" terms. I would not wish to say that those terms had nonetheless somehow been incorporated as conditions into the surrender. They were not formally assented to by a majority of the electors of the band, nor were they accepted by the Governor in Council, as required by s. 39(1)(b) and (c). I agree with Le Dain J. that there is no merit in the appellants' submission that for purposes of s. 39 a surrender can be considered independently of its terms. This makes no more sense than would a claim that a contract can have an existence which in no way depends on the terms and conditions that comprise it.

Nonetheless, the Crown, in my view, was not empowered by the surrender document to ignore the oral terms which the band understood would be embodied in the lease. The oral representations form the backdrop against which the Crown's conduct in discharging its fiduciary obligation must be measured. They inform and confine the field of discretion within which the Crown was free to act. After the Crown's agents had induced the band to surrender its land on the understanding that the land would be leased on certain terms, it would be unconscionable to permit the Crown simply to ignore those terms.

When the promised lease proved impossible to obtain, the Crown, instead of proceeding to lease the land on different, unfavourable terms, should have returned to the band to explain what had occurred and seek the band's counsel on how to proceed. The existence of such unconscionability is the key to a conclusion that the Crown breached its fiduciary duty. Equity will not countenance unconscionable behaviour in a fiduciary, whose duty is that of utmost loyalty to his principal.

While the existence of the fiduciary obligation which the Crown owes to the Indians is dependent on the nature of the surrender process, the standard of conduct which the obligation imports is both more general and more exacting than the terms of any particular surrender. In the present case the relevant aspect of the required standard of conduct is defined by a principle analogous to that which underlies the doctrine of promissory or equitable estoppel. The Crown cannot promise the band that it will obtain a lease of the latter's land on certain stated terms, thereby inducing the band to alter its legal position by surrendering the land, and then simply ignore that promise to the band's detriment: see, e.g., *Central London Property Trust Ltd.* v. *High Trees House Ltd.*, [1947] 1 K.B. 130; *Robertson* v. *Min. of Pensions*, [1949] 1 K.B. 227 (C.A.).

In obtaining without consultation a much less valuable lease than that promised, the Crown breached the fiduciary obligation it owed the band. It must make good the loss suffered in consequence. . . .

I would therefore allow the appeal, set aside the judgment in the Federal Court of Appeal and reinstate without variation the trial judge's award, with costs to the present appellants in all courts.

ESTEY J. (concurring in the result): . . . The *Indian Act*, R.S.C. 1952, c. 149 [now R.S.C. 1970, c. I-6], as amended, the Constitution, the pre-Confederation laws of the colonies in British North America, and the *Royal Proclamation of 1763* [see R.S.C. 1970, App. II] all reflect a strong sense of awareness of the community interest in protecting the rights of the native population in those lands to which they had a longstanding connection. One common feature in all these enactments is reflected in the present-day provision in the *Indian Act*, s. 37, which requires anyone interested in acquiring ownership or some lesser interest in lands set aside for native populations, from a willing grantor, to do so through the appropriate level of government, now the federal government. This section has already been set out by my colleagues. In the elaborate provisions in the *Indian Act*, there are many alternative ways of protecting the interests of the Indians and of reflecting the community interest in that protection. The statute and the cases make provision for a surrender of the Indian interest in Indian lands as defined in the Act. And cases such as *St. Catherine's* indicate the extent to which the Indian band must go in order to sever entirely the connection of the native population from the lands in question. This type of surrender would be better described as a release, in the modern lexicon.

Unfortunately, the statute employs the word "surrender" in another connotation. In order to deal with what has been found to be the personal interest of the Indian population in Indian lands, the Act requires the band to "surrender" the land to the Crown in the right of Canada in order to effect the proposed alternate use of the land for the benefit of the Indians. The Act, in short, does not require the Indian to limit his interest in Indian lands to present and continuous occupation. The band may vicariously occupy the lands, or part of such lands, through the medium of a lease or licence. The marketing of the personal interest is not only permitted by the statute, but the machinery is provided for the proper exploitation of this interest by the Indians, subject always to compliance with the statute: vide *St. Ann's Island Shooting Fishing Club Ltd.* v. *R.*, [1950] S.C.R. 211. The step to be taken by the Indian band in seeking to avail itself of the benefits of their right of possession in this manner is, unhappily, also referred to in the statute and in the cases as a "surrender" of the lands and their interest therein to the Crown. This is not a release in the sense of that term in the general law. Indeed, it is quite the opposite. It is a retention of interest and the exploitation of that interest in the manner and to the extent permitted by statute law. The Crown becomes the appointed agent of the Indians to develop and exploit, under the direction of the Indians and for their benefit, the usufructuary interest as described in *St. Catherine's.* . . .

The fact that the agent is prescribed by statute in no way detracts in law from the legal capacity of the agent to act as such. The further consideration that the principal (the Indian band as holder of the personal interest in the land) is constrained by statute to act through the agency of the Crown, in no way reduces the rights of the instructing principal to call upon the agent to account for the performance of the mandate. The measure of damages applied by the learned trial judge is in no way affected by ascribing the resultant rights in the plaintiff to a breach of agency. Indeed, it is consonant with the purpose of the statutory agency as prescribed by Parliament, now and historically, that the agent (the Crown), in all its actions, shall serve only the interests of the native population whose rights alone are the subject of the protective measures of the statute. If anything, the principal in this relationship is more secure in his rights than in the absence of a statutorily prescribed agency. The principal is restricted in the selection of the agent, but the agent is nowhere protected in the statute from the consequences in law of a breach of that agency. . . . this appeal should be allowed with costs.

WILSON J. (concurring in the result) (RITCHIE AND MCINTYRE JJ. concurring): . . .

Wewaykum Indian Band v. *Canada* (2002)

[2002] 4 S.C.R. 245. McLachlin C.J. and L'Heureux-Dubé, Gonthier, Iacobucci, Major, Bastarache, Binnie, Arbour and Bell JJ., December 6, 2002.

. . .

72   If, as we affirm, neither band emerged from the reserve-creation process with both reserves, the issue arises whether this outcome establishes in the case of either appellant band a breach of fiduciary duty on the part of the federal Crown.

73   Prior to its watershed decision in *Guerin, supra,* this Court had generally character-ized the relationship between the Crown and Indian peoples as a "political trust" or "trust in the higher sense". In *St. Catherine's Milling and Lumber Co.* v. *The Queen* (1887), 13 S.C.R. 577, decided just prior to Ashdown Green's trip to Campbell River, Taschereau J. of this Court described the Crown's obligation towards aboriginal people as a "sacred political obligation, *in the execution of which the state must be free from judicial control*" ((p. 649) emphasis added). Over 60 years later, in *St. Ann's Island Shooting and Fishing Club Ltd.* v. *The King*, [1950] S.C.R. 211, Rand J. stated at p. 219:

> The language of the statute [Indian Act] embodies the accepted view that these aborigenes are, in effect, wards of the State, whose care and welfare are a *political trust* of the highest obligation. [Emphasis added.]

74   The enduring contribution of *Guerin* was to recognize that the concept of political trust did not exhaust the potential legal character of the multitude of relationships be-tween the Crown and aboriginal people. A quasi-proprietary interest (e.g., reserve land)

could not be put on the same footing as a government benefits program. The latter will generally give rise to public law remedies only. The former raises considerations "in the nature of a private law duty" (*Guerin*, at p. 385). Put another way, the existence of a public law duty does not exclude the possibility that the Crown undertook, in the discharge of that public law duty, obligations "in the nature of a private law duty" towards aboriginal peoples.

75   In *Calder* v. *Attorney General of British Columbia*, [1973] S.C.R. 313, the Court had recognized for the first time in the modern era that the Indian interest in their ancestral lands constituted a legal interest that predated European settlement. Recognition of aboriginal rights could not, therefore, be treated merely as an act of grace and favour on the part of the Crown. These propositions, while brought to the fore in Canadian law relatively recently, are not new. Marshall C.J. of the United States ruled as early as 1823 that the legal rights of Indians in the lands they traditionally occupied prior to European colonization both predated and survived the claims to sovereignty made by various European nations in the territories of the North American continent: *Johnson* v. *M'Intosh*, 21 U.S. (8 Wheat.) 543 (1823), at pp. 573–74; *Guerin, supra*, at pp. 377–78; *Mitchell* v. *M.N.R.*, [2001] 1 S.C.R. 911, 2001 SCC 33, at paras. 141–46. . . .

78   The *Guerin* concept of a *sui generis* fiduciary duty was expanded in *R.* v. *Sparrow*, [1990] 1 S.C.R 1075, to include protection of the aboriginal people's pre-existing and still existing aboriginal and treaty rights within s. 35 of the *Constitution Act, 1982*. In that regard, it was said at p. 1108:

> The *sui generis* nature of Indian title, and the historic powers and responsibility assumed by the Crown constituted the source of such a fiduciary obligation. In our opinion, *Guerin*, together with *R.* v. *Taylor and Williams* (1981), 34 O.R. (2d) 360, ground a general guiding principle for s. 35(1). That is, the Government has the responsibility to act in a fiduciary capacity with respect to aboriginal peoples. The relationship between the Government and aboriginals is trust-like, rather than adversarial, and contemporary recognition and affirmation of aboriginal rights must be defined in light of this historic relationship. [Emphasis added.]

See also: *Quebec (Attorney General)* v. *Canada (National Energy Board)*, [1994] 1 S.C.R. 159, at p. 185. . . .

81   But there are limits. The appellants seemed at times to invoke the "fiduciary duty" as a source of plenary Crown liability covering all aspects of the Crown-Indian band relationship. This overshoots the mark. The fiduciary duty imposed on the Crown does not exist at large but in relation to specific Indian interests. In this case we are dealing with land, which has generally played a central role in aboriginal economies and cultures. Land was also the subject matter of *Ross River* ("the lands occupied by the Band"), *Blueberry River* and *Guerin* (disposition of existing reserves). Fiduciary protection accorded to Crown dealings with aboriginal interests in land (including reserve creation) has not to date been recognized by this Court in relation to Indian interests other than land outside the framework of s. 35(1) of the *Constitution Act, 1982*.

82   Since *Guerin*, Canadian courts have experienced a flood of "fiduciary duty" claims by Indian bands across a whole spectrum of possible complaints, for example:

    (i)   to structure elections (*Batchewana Indian Band (Non-resident members)* v. *Batchewana Indian Band*, [1997] 1 F.C. 689 (C.A.), at para. 60; subsequently dealt with in this Court on other grounds);

(ii)   to require the provision of social services (*Southeast Child & Family Services* v. *Canada (Attorney General)*, [1997] 9 W.W.R. 236 (Man. Q.B.));

(iii) to rewrite negotiated provisions (*B.C. Native Women's Society* v. *Canada*, [2000] 1 F.C. 304 (T.D.));

(iv)   to cover moving expenses (*Paul* v. *Kingsclear Indian Band* (1997), 137 F.T.R. 275); *Mentuck* v. *Canada*, [1986] 3 F.C. 249 (T.D.); *Deer* v. *Mohawk Council of Kahnawake*, [1991] 2 F.C. 18 (T.D.));

(v)   to suppress public access to information about band affairs (*Chippewas of the Nawash First Nation* v. *Canada (Minister of Indian and Northern Affairs)* (1996), 116 F.T.R. 37, aff'd (1999), 251 N.R. 220 (F.C.A.); *Montana Band of Indians* v. *Canada (Minister of Indian and Northern Affairs)*, [1989] 1 F.C. 143 (T.D.); *Timiskaming Indian Band* v. *Canada (Minister of Indian and Northern Affairs)* (1997), 132 F.T.R. 106);

(vi)   to require legal aid funding (*Ominayak* v. *Canada (Minister of Indian Affairs and Northern Development)*, [1987] 3 F.C. 174 (T.D.));

(vii) to compel registration of individuals under the Indian Act (rejected in *Tuplin* v. *Canada (Indian and Northern Affairs)* (2001), 207 Nfld. & P.E.I.R. 292 (P.E.I.T.D.));

(viii) to invalidate a consent signed by an Indian mother to the adoption of her child (rejected in *G. (A.P.)* v. *A. (K.H.)* (1994), 120 D.L.R. (4th) 511 (Alta. Q.B.)).

83   I offer no comment about the correctness of the disposition of these particular cases on the facts, none of which are before us for decision, but I think it desirable for the Court to affirm the principle, already mentioned, that not all obligations existing between the parties to a fiduciary relationship are themselves fiduciary in nature (*Lac Minerals, supra*, at p. 597), and that this principle applies to the relationship between the Crown and aboriginal peoples. It is necessary, then, to focus on the particular obligation or interest that is the subject matter of the particular dispute and whether or not the Crown had assumed discretionary control in relation thereto sufficient to ground a fiduciary obligation. . . .

85   I do not suggest that the existence of a public law duty necessarily excludes the creation of a fiduciary relationship. The latter, however, depends on identification of a cognizable Indian interest, and the Crown's undertaking of discretionary control in relation thereto in a way that invokes responsibility "in the nature of a private law duty", as discussed below.

N. Application of Fiduciary Principles to Indian Lands

86   For the reasons which follow, it is my view that the appellant bands' submissions in these appeals with respect to the existence and breach of a fiduciary duty cannot succeed:

1 The content of the Crown's fiduciary duty towards aboriginal peoples varies with the nature and importance of the interest sought to be protected. It does not provide a general indemnity.

2 Prior to reserve creation, the Crown exercises a public law function under the *Indian Act*—which is subject to supervision by the courts exercising public law rem-

edies. At that stage a fiduciary relationship may also arise but, in that respect, the Crown's duty is limited to the basic obligations of loyalty, good faith in the discharge of its mandate, providing full disclosure appropriate to the subject matter, and acting with ordinary prudence with a view to the best interest of the aboriginal beneficiaries.

3   Once a reserve is created the content of the Crown's fiduciary duty expands to include the protection and preservation of the band's quasi-proprietary interest in the reserve from exploitation.

4   In this case, as the appellant bands have rightly been held to lack any beneficial interest in the other band's reserve, equitable remedies are not available either to dispossess an incumbent band that is entitled to the beneficial interest, or to require the Crown to pay "equitable" compensation for its refusal to bring about such a dispossession.

5   Enforcement of equitable duties by equitable remedies is subject to the usual equitable defences, including laches and acquiescence. . . .

92   This is not to suggest that a fiduciary duty has no role to play in these circumstances. It is to say, however, that caution must be exercised. As stated, even in the traditional trust context not all obligations existing between the parties to a well-recognized fiduciary relationship are themselves fiduciary in nature: *Lac Minerals, supra,* per Sopinka J., at pp. 597 *et seq.* Moreover, as pointed out by La Forest J. in *McInerney v. MacDonald,* [1992] 2 S.C.R. 138, not all fiduciary relationships and not all fiduciary obligations are the same: "These are shaped by the demands of the situation" (p. 149). Thus, for example, the singular demands of the administration of justice drive and "shape" the content of the fiduciary relationship between solicitor and client: *R. v. Neil,* 2002 SCC 70. These observations are of particular importance in a case where the fiduciary is also the government, as the Court in *Guerin* fully recognized (p. 385). (In the case of rival bands asserting overlapping claims to s. 35 aboriginal title over the same land, for example, the Crown is caught truly and unavoidably in the middle, but that is not the case here.)

93   The starting point in this analysis, therefore, is the Indian bands' interest in specific lands that were subject to the reserve-creation process for their benefit, and in relation to which the Crown constituted itself the exclusive intermediary with the province. The task is to ascertain the content of the fiduciary duty in relation to those specific circumstances.

95   In this case the intervention of the Crown was positive, in that the federal government sought to create reserves for the appellant bands out of provincial Crown lands to which these particular bands had no aboriginal or treaty right. As explained, the people of the Laich-kwil-tach First Nation arrived in the Campbell River area at about the same time as the early Europeans (1840–1853). Government intervention from 1871 onwards was designed to protect members of the appellant bands from displacement by the other newcomers.

96   When exercising ordinary government powers in matters involving disputes between Indians and non-Indians, the Crown was (and is) obliged to have regard to the interest of all affected parties, not just the Indian interest. The Crown can be no ordinary fiduciary; it wears many hats and represents many interests, some of which cannot help but be conflicting: *Samson Indian Nation and Band v. Canada,* [1995] 2 F.C. 762 (C.A.). As the Campbell River Band acknowledged in its factum, "[t]he Crown's position as

fiduciary is necessarily unique" (para. 96). In resolving the dispute between Campbell River Band members and the non-Indian settlers named Nunns, for example, the Crown was not solely concerned with the band interest, nor should it have been. The Indians were "vulnerable" to the adverse exercise of the government's discretion, but so too were the settlers, and each looked to the Crown for a fair resolution of their dispute. At that stage, *prior to reserve creation,* the Court cannot ignore the reality of the conflicting demands confronting the government, asserted both by the competing bands themselves and by non-Indians. As Dickson J. said in *Guerin, supra,* at p. 385:

> It should be noted that fiduciary duties generally arise only with regard to obligations originating in a private law context. Public law duties, the performance of which requires the exercise of discretion, do not *typically* give rise to a fiduciary relationship. [Emphasis added.]

. . .

103   While courts applying principles of equity rightly insist on flexibility to deal with the unforeseeable and infinite variety of circumstances and interests that may arise, and which will fall to be decided under equitable rules, it must be said that the bold attempt of the appellant bands to extend their claim to fiduciary relief on the present facts is overly ambitious. . . .

105   The various technical arguments arrayed by the bands are, in any event, singularly inappropriate in a case where they seek equitable remedies. As noted, each band has, over the past 65 or more years, reasonably relied on the repeated declarations and disclaimers of its sister band, and on the continuance of the *status quo,* to reside on and improve its reserve.

106   Reserves Nos. 11 and 12 were formally created when the federal Crown obtained administration and control of the subject lands in 1938. At that time, as outlined above, the appellant bands had manifested on several occasions their acknowledgement that the beneficial interest in Reserve No. 11 resided in the Campbell River Band and the beneficial interest in Reserve No. 12 resided in the Cape Mudge Band. The equitable remedies sought by the appellant bands necessarily address the disposition of the *beneficial* or equitable interest. The trial judge found as a fact (although not using these precise terms) that the equitable interests are reflected in the *status quo.* A mandatory injunction is not available to dispossess the rightful incumbent. Nor is there any requirement on the Crown to pay equitable compensation to a claimant band to substitute for an equitable or beneficial interest that does not belong to it. . . .

110   The doctrine of laches is applicable to bar the claims of an Indian band in appropriate circumstances: *L'Hirondelle* v. *The King* (1916), 16 Ex. C.R. 193; *Ontario (Attorney General)* v. *Bear Island Foundation* (1984), 49 O.R. (2d) 353 (H.C.), at p. 447 (aff'd on other grounds (1989), 68 O.R. (2d) 394 (C.A.), aff'd [1991] 2 S.C.R. 570); *Chippewas of Sarnia Band* v. *Canada (Attorney General)* (2000), 51 O.R. (3d) 641 (C.A.). There are also dicta in two decisions of this Court considering, without rejecting, arguments that laches may bar claims to aboriginal title: *Smith* v. *The Queen,* [1983] 1 S.C.R. 554, at p. 570; *Guerin, supra,* at p. 390.

111   It seems to me both branches of the doctrine of laches and acquiescence apply here, namely: (i) where "the party has, by his conduct done that which might fairly be regarded as equivalent to a waiver", and (ii) such conduct "results in circumstances that make the prosecution of the action unreasonable" *(M. (K.)* v. *M. (H.), supra,* at pp. 76 and 78).

Conduct equivalent to a waiver is found in the declaration, representations and failure to assert "rights" in circumstances that required assertion, as previously set out. Unreasonable prosecution arises because, relying on the status quo, each band improved the reserve to which it understood its sister band made no further claim. All of this was done with sufficient knowledge "of the underlying facts relevant to a possible legal claim" *(M. (K.) v. M. (H.), supra*, at p. 79).

112   I conclude therefore that the claims of the appellant bands were rightly rejected on their merits by the trial judge.

SELECTED BIBLIOGRAPHY

Bartlett, R. *Indian Reserves and Aboriginal Lands in Canada: A Homeland* (Saskatoon: Native Law Centre, University of Saskatchewan, 1990).
———. "Provincial Jurisdiction and Resource Development on Indian Reserve Lands" (1986) Managing Resources 189.
Griffiths, O.B. "Case Commentary on Blueberry River: Is the Crown Fiduciary Obligation in the Currents of Change?" [1996] 3 C.N.L.R. 25.
Hughes, P. "Indians and Lands Reserved for the Indians: Off-limits to the Provinces" (1983) 21 Osgoode Hall L.J. 82.
Hurley, J. "The Crown's Fiduciary Duty and Indian Title: *Guerin* v. *The Queen*" (1985) 30 McGill L.J. 559.
Isaac T. *Pre-1868 Legislation Concerning Indians* (Saskatoon: University of Saskatchewan Native Law Centre, 1993).
———. "Provincial Jurisdiction, Adjudicative Authority and Aboriginal Rights. A Comment on *Paul* v. *B.C. (Forest Appeals Commission)*" (January 2002) 60:I The Advocate 77–88.
———. "The Crown's Duty to Consult and Accommodate Aboriginal People" (November 2003) 61:6 The Advocate 865–880.
Isaac T. & T. Knox. "The Crown's Duty to Consult Aboriginal People" (2003) 41 Alta. L. Rev. 49–77.
Johnston, D. "A Theory of Crown Trust Towards Aboriginal People" (1986) 30 Ottawa L. Rev. 307.
Lawrence, S. & P. Macklem. "From Consultation to Reconciliation: Aboriginal Rights and the Crown's Duty to Consult" (2000) 70 Can. Bar Rev. 252.
Notzke, C. *Aboriginal Peoples and Natural Resources in Canada* (Toronto: Captus University Publications, 1994).
Rotman, L.I. *Parallel Paths: Fiduciary Doctrine and the Crown-Native Relationship in Canada* (Toronto: University of Toronto Press, 1996).
Ryder, B. "The Demise and Rise of the Classical Paradigm in Canadian Federalism: Promoting Autonomy for the Provinces and First Nations" (1991) 36 McGill L.J. 308.
Salembier, J.P. "Crown Fiduciary Duty, Indian Title and the Lost Treasure of I.R. 172: The Legacy of *Apsassin* v. *The Queen (Blueberry River)*" [1996] 3 C.N.L.R. 1.
Sanders, D. "The Application of Provincial Laws" in B. Morse, ed. *Aboriginal Peoples and the Law: Indian, Metis and Inuit Rights in Canada* (Ottawa: Carleton University Press, 1985).
Slattery, B. "Understanding Aboriginal Rights" [1987] 66 Can. Bar Rev. 727.
Venne, S., ed. *Indian Acts and Amendments 1868–1975: An Indexed Collection* (Saskatoon: Native Law Centre, University of Saskatchewan, 1981).
Weaver, S.M. *Making Canadian Indian Policy: The Hidden Agenda 1968–1970* (Toronto: University of Toronto Press, 1981).

Chapter 4

THE MÉTIS AND INUIT

INTRODUCTION

"Aboriginal peoples" include the Indian, Métis, and Inuit peoples of Canada. Aboriginal legal jurisprudence, however, has focused primarily on Indians, although a large portion of this jurisprudence continues to apply to the Métis and Inuit. While there have been some judicial decisions respecting the Métis, relatively few judicial decisions have dealt substantively with the rights of the Inuit, except for a few case relating to the 1993 Nunavut Land Claims Agreement.

THE MÉTIS

Definition of "Métis"

The 2001 census revealed that approximately 290,000 people in Canada identify as being Métis.[1] Historically, the Métis were those people who possessed both Indian and European ancestry and lived a distinct Métis lifestyle. The Alberta *Métis Settlements Act*[2] defines Métis as meaning "a person of aboriginal ancestry who identifies with Métis history and culture."

Until recently there has been a confusing range of definitions used to describe the Métis that has caused confusion among the national Métis community itself. In many ways, the problem with a sole definition of who are "Métis" is indicative of the broader issue of the Métis struggle to have their rights recognized.[3] James Frideres outlined the dilemma of defining the Métis in the following manner:

> The Métis are a unique people in Canadian society. Originally they grew out of the symbiotic relationship that existed between Natives and the European immigrants to the New World. Yet it was the later government implementation of a complex set of social and political acts that ultimately determined their status as a separate ethnic group.[4]

The complex historical reality that has faced the Métis is discussed later in this chapter, however a large part of this problem relates to the allocation of land and the recognition of the Métis as a distinct Aboriginal people.

---

[1] Canada, Statistics Canada, *2001 Census of Population—Aboriginal Identity*; see also P. Chartrand, ed., *Who Are Canada's Aboriginal Peoples?* (Saskatoon: Purich Publishing, 2002).

[2] *Métis Settlements Act*, S.A. 1990, c. M–14.3, s. 1.

[3] In *R. v. Castonguay*, [2003] 1 C.N.L.R. 177 (N.B. Prov. Ct.), the New Brunswick Provincial Court held that an accused, claiming to be Métis, did not produce sufficient evidence to allow the Court to conclude that he was Métis. The Court stated that a Métis is a person who: (a) has some ancestral family connection to Métis, (b) self-identifies as a Métis, and (c) is accepted by the Métis community. See also *R. v. Daigle*, [2003] 3 C.N.L.R. 232 (N.B. Prov. Ct.).

[4] J. Frideres, *Native Peoples in Canada: Contemporary Conflicts*, 3d ed. (Scarborough: Prentice-Hall, 1988), 295.

In *R.* v. *Powley*[5] the Supreme Court of Canada stated that the Métis referred to in s. 35(1) of the *Constitution Act, 1982*[6] (s. 35(1)) are "distinctive peoples who, in addition to their mixed ancestry, developed their own customs, way of life, and recognizable group identity separate from their Indian or Inuit and European forebears."[7] The Supreme Court of Canada stated that there are three broad factors that provide the indicia of Métis identity for the purpose of claiming Métis rights under s. 35(1): (1) self-identification as a member of the Métis community, (2) the existence of evidence of an ancestral connection to an historic Métis community (which does not include a minimum "blood quantum" component"), and (3) the claimant must demonstrate that they are accepted by a modern Métis community.[8]

The Supreme Court of Canada has not yet determined whether the Métis are included within the meaning of "Indians" in s. 91(24)[9] of the *Constitution Act, 1867*[10] (s. 91(24)). Subsection 35(2) of the *Constitution Act, 1982* defines the Aboriginal people of Canada as including the Métis, in addition to Indians and the Inuit.[11] In *Re Eskimos* (1939),[12] the Supreme Court of Canada affirmed that the Inuit are "Indians" for the purposes of s. 91(24), but made no reference to the Métis. However, the following excerpt from *Re Eskimos* provides some basis for an interpretation of s. 91(24) that could include the Métis. Kerwin and Canon JJ. state that the term "Indians" in s. 91(24) is defined as "all the present and future aborigine native subjects of the proposed Confederation."[13] Academic commentary on whether the Métis are included within the meaning of s. 91(24) is mixed.[14]

At the federal level, the Privy Council Office is responsible for Métis issues, rather than the Department of Indian and Northern Affairs Canada (DIAND). The Métis and non-status Indians also have a separate federal cabinet voice: the Federal Interlocutor for Métis and Non-Status Indians. This separation is an attempt to limit the extent of federal legislative and financial responsibility for the Métis. The federal government has stated that the Métis, although one of the Aboriginal peoples of Canada, are not within its exclusive legislative jurisdiction under s. 91(24), but are primarily a provincial responsi-

---

[5] *R.* v. *Powley*, 2003 SCC 43 (S.C.C.).

[6] *Constitution Act, 1982*, Schedule B of the *Canada Act 1982* (U.K.), 1982, c. 11 as am. by the *Constitution Amendment Proclamation 1983*, R.S.C. 1985, App. II, No. 46, (add. ss. 35(3) and 35(4)).

[7] *Powley, supra* note 5.

[8] *Ibid.* paras. 31–34.

[9] In *R.* v. *Blais*, [1998] 4 C.N.L.R. 103 (Man. Q.B.), the Manitoba Court of Queen's Bench held that Métis are not included in the reference to "Indians" in s. 91(24) of the *Constitution Act, 1867*. On appeal, the Supreme Court of Canada did not deal with the s. 91(24) argument, but did conclude that the Métis did not come within the meaning of "Indians" as used in para. 13 of the 1930 *Natural Resources Transfer Agreement; R.* v. *Blais*, 2003 SCC 44 (S.C.C.), para. 36.

[10] *Constitution Act, 1867* (U.K.), 30 & 31 Vict., c. 3 (R.S.C. 1985, App. II, No. 5).

[11] Subsection 35(2) of the *Constitution Act, 1982* states: "In this Act, "aboriginal peoples of Canada" includes the Indian, Inuit and Métis peoples of Canada."

[12] *Re Eskimos*, [1939] S.C.R. 104.

[13] *Ibid.* at 118, 119, 121.

[14] See B. Schwartz, "The Métis and s.91(24): The Legal History" and "The Métis and s.91(24): Policy Aspects" in *First Principles: Constitutional Reform with respect to the Aboriginal Peoples of Canada 1982–1984* (Kingston: Institute of Intergovernmental Relations, Queen's University, 1985) wherein Schwartz argues that the terms "Indian" and "half-breed" were used deliberately to distinguish between two different groups, with different rights. Clem Chartier has argued for a broader interpretative approach which would see these two terms being used historically together in the context of s. 91(24) and federal responsibility. See also C. Chartier, "Indians: An Analysis of the Term Used in s .91(24) of the BNA Act, 1867" (1978–1979) 43 Sask. L. Rev. 39.

bility. Métis people are represented nationally by the Métis National Council[15] and the Congress of Aboriginal Peoples,[16] and also at the provincial and territorial level by other local organizations.

Métis History

Distinct Métis communities began to appear toward the end of the eighteenth century,[17] and the Métis presence as a distinct group increased throughout the 1800s in western Canada. In 1869, the Hudson Bay Company's interest in Rupert's Land was sold to the Dominion of Canada for cash and one-twentieth of the territory's fertile land. The Métis resisted this transfer of land and in October 1868 they formed a National Métis Committee and demanded an independent status for the Métis Nation. The Métis established a provisional government headed by Louis Riel. While Sir John A. Macdonald wanted to recognize elements of the Métis demands concerning political status (a separate province), language (English and French as official languages for the new province), and land (provincial control of public lands), he feared that a separate Métis province would impede his ambitious immigration policy for the West.

Macdonald's compromise was the 1870 *Manitoba Act*,[18] which created the province of Manitoba. The Act affirmed Métis retention of 1.4 million acres in the Red River area. The 1879 *Dominion Lands Act*[19] provided that the delegated powers of the Governor in Council included satisfying "any claims existing in connection with the extinguishment of the Indian title, preferred by half-breeds resident in the North-West Territories outside the limits of Manitoba."

Notwithstanding these assurances, the Métis were dispossessed of this land grant. Between 1876 and 1884, two-thirds of the Métis people moved out of Manitoba. Petitions made by the Métis throughout the latter part of the nineteenth century were virtually ignored by the federal government, even though it was negotiating ambitiously with Indians in western Canada. Riel formed a second government at Batoche in 1885 and again demanded self-government and land tenure for the Métis. This ended in a battle that ended with Riel being hung for treason on 16 November 1885.

After the 1885 resistance by the Métis, many Métis began moving north and west into what are now Alberta, northeastern British Columbia, and the Northwest Territories. The *Manitoba Act, 1870* and the *Dominion Lands Act* allowed for the distribution of land to the Métis, known as scrip. Scrip was provided to the Métis on an individual basis and not communally in groups like Indian reserve land. Many Métis found that their scrip was virtually impossible to redeem, and often sold their scrip for much less than what it was worth.

The 1995 report by the Honourable A.C. Hamilton to the Minister of DIAND on alternatives to extinguishment[20] focused on the need for the federal government to deal with the issue of Métis people and their rights:

> I do not wish to enter into the debate as to who qualifies to be a Métis. It is obvious however

---

[15] Metis National Council, online: <http://metisnation.ca>.

[16] Congress of Aboriginal Peoples, online: <http://www.abo-peoples.org>.

[17] The Métis defeated settlers at the Battle of Seven Oaks in 1816, where the Métis leader Cuthbert Grant, Jr. unfurled the Métis Nation flag.

[18] *Manitoba Act*, S.C. 1870, c. 3; R.S.C. 1985, App. II, No. 8.

[19] *Dominion Lands Act*, S.C. 1879, c. 31, s. 125(e) (re-enacted S.C. 1883, c. 17, s. 81).

[20] Hon. A.C. Hamilton, *Canada and Aboriginal Peoples: A New Partnership* (Ottawa: Minister of Public Works and Government Services Canada, 1995).

that there are certainly Métis in Canada, and that due to their constitutional recognition, they have rights as Aboriginal peoples.

The federal government has given some recognition to Métis rights by agreeing that they be involved in comprehensive claims negotiations in the Northwest Territories where some have signed treaties in conjunction with the Dene. The federal government is also providing funding to the Labrador Métis Association to research its claim. In any event, a determination should be made as to whether the federal government's Comprehensive Land Claims Policy is available to deal with the Métis or whether some other approach may be necessary.[21]

The Royal Commission on Aboriginal Peoples (RCAP) stated the following with respect to the historical treatment of the Métis:

> The federal government's suppression and neglect of Métis aspirations was demonstrated most dramatically by its military destruction of Batoche in 1885, in response to the Saskatchewan Métis' desperate step of asking Louis Riel to form a second provisional government based there. . . . While the federal government dithered in coming to grips with Métis and Indian grievances, Riel proceeded to form a provisional government. Under the leadership of Gabriel Dumont, a military force of plainsmen was also formed, but the federal government countered by sending a strong military expedition to the north-west in the spring of 1885. The Métis forces were crushed at Batoche, and Riel was hanged, after being convicted of treason, at Regina on 16 November 1885.[22]

The question of jurisdiction over "Indians" in s. 91(24) and Métis rights has yet to be resolved. The courts have determined that Parliament has authority respecting Indians and the Inuit within s. 91(24). The inclusion of the Métis within the meaning of s. 91(24) would assist the Métis in having their rights recognized, strengthen their negotiating position and also allow them to receive benefits directly from the federal government. As a result, the federal government has attempted to distance itself from the Métis. The federal government has taken little responsibility for Métis outside the Northwest Territories and the Yukon Territory.[23] Likewise, most provincial governments, with the notable exceptions of Alberta and Saskatchewan with their Métis-specific legislation, have been reluctant to take a lead role with respect to the Métis since they argue that the Métis fall under federal jurisdiction.

Métis Legislation in Alberta

Alberta is one of two provinces with legislation dealing expressly with the Métis, including Métis local government and approximately 1.25 million acres of settlement land. Proclaimed into force on 1 November 1990, the Alberta *Métis Settlements Act*[24] provides a system of local government and, combined with other legislation, a land base for the Métis and their respective settlements. The Alberta legislation establishes Settlement Corporations and the General Council as legal entities. The Settlement Corporations deal with matters relating to local government and the needs of each community, whereas the General Council deals with issues that affect the settlements collectively. The legislation was developed cooperatively between the government of Alberta and the Alberta

---

[21] *Ibid.* at 32–34.
[22] Royal Commission on Aboriginal Peoples, *Report of the Royal Commission on Aboriginal Peoples*, "Looking Forward, Looking Back," vol. 1 (Ottawa: Ministry of Supply & Services, 1996) 154.
[23] There are exceptions; see for example the members of the "half-breed adhesion" to Treaty No. 3 (1873).
[24] *Métis Settlements Act*, R.S.A. 2000, c. M-14; and *Métis Settlements Land Protection Act*, R.S.A. 2000, c. M-16.

Federation of Métis Settlements.[25] The *Constitution of Alberta Amendment Act*[26] provides for certainty of tenure to the lands in question and has the effect of ensuring that the Métis legislation has some permanency.

Métis Legislation in Saskatchewan

The government of Saskatchewan proclaimed *The Métis Act*[27] on 28 January 2002. *The Métis Act*:

1. Recognizes the culture, history, and significance of the Métis in Saskatchewan;[28]

2. Confirms the establishment of a bilateral process between the Métis and the government of Saskatchewan to work on issues such as land, harvesting, governance, and capacity building;[29] and

3. Establishes the "Métis Nation-Saskatchewan Secretariat Inc." as the administrative body of the Métis Nation of Saskatchewan.[30]

The Métis Act states in its preamble that nothing in it is to be construed as altering or affecting the position of the government of Saskatchewan that legislative authority in relation to the Métis rests with Parliament under s. 91(24).

Métis Rights

The *Manitoba Act, 1870*[31] conferred certain rights to the "half-breeds."[32] These rights are codified in s. 31 of the *Manitoba Act, 1870*. The *Dominion Lands Act*[33] provided that "any claims existing in connection with the extinguishment of the Indian title, preferred by half-breeds resident in the North-West Territories outside of the limits of Manitoba" be satisfied. Both Acts recognize a degree of Métis interest in the land.[34]

In 1874, the "half-breeds" or Métis of Rainy River signed an adhesion to Treaty No. 3 (1873). It states that in return for surrendering "all claim, right, title or interest which they, by virtue of their Indian blood, have or possess," they received reserve lands, in addition to annuities and other items under the terms of Treaty No. 3.

The Manitoba Métis Federation and individual Métis sought a declaration that various federal and provincial statutes and orders-in-council enacted during the 1870s and 1880s were unconstitutional because they had the effect of depriving the Métis of land to which they were entitled under the *Manitoba Act, 1870*. In *Manitoba Métis Federation Inc. v. Canada* (1988),[35] the Manitoba Court of Appeal dealt with an application by the federal government to have the statement of claim of the Manitoba Métis Federation struck because there was no cause of action. In deciding the procedural issue, both the Manitoba Court of Appeal and the Supreme Court of Canada provided some substantive

[25] For an in-depth discussion of Métis governance and dispute resolution in Alberta see C. Bell, *Contemporary Métis Justice: The Settlement Way* (Saskatoon: University of Saskatchewan Native Law Centre, 1999).
[26] *Constitution of Alberta Amendment Act*, S.A. 1990, c. C–22.2.
[27] *Métis Act*, S.S. 2001, c. M-14.01.
[28] *Ibid*. s. 2.
[29] *Ibid*. s. 3(1).
[30] *Ibid*. s. 5.
[31] *Manitoba Act*, R.S.C. 1985, App. II, No. 8.
[32] Although it is a term that many find objectionable, it is used here only in the interests of historical accuracy.
[33] *Dominion Lands Act*, *supra* note 19.
[34] See D.N. Sprague, "Métis Land Claims" in K. Coates, ed. *Aboriginal Land Claims in Canada: A Regional Perspective* (Toronto: Copp Clark Pitman, 1997).
[35] *Manitoba Métis Federation Inc. v. A.-G. Canada*, [1990] 1 S.C.R. 279.

statements about the nature of Métis title and rights.

A majority of the Court of Appeal agreed with the federal Attorney-General and held that the impugned legislation did not negatively affect Métis rights. Section 31 of the *Manitoba Act* did not create a communal interest in the land for Métis, but rather individual rights. Thus, the Manitoba Métis Federation did not have a cause of action. O'Sullivan J.A. dissented and held that s. 35 of the *Constitution Act, 1982* recognizes and affirms Métis rights and that the *Manitoba Act, 1870* was not merely a statute, but represented a treaty negotiated between the Crown and the Métis people.

The Supreme Court of Canada unanimously disagreed with the Manitoba Court of Appeal and held that the Métis application for a declaration did not have a "plain and obvious" conclusion or outcome that was "beyond doubt." The issue of whether certain pieces of legislation violated Métis rights recognized by the *Manitoba Act, 1870* is a justiciable issue and can be brought before the courts.

In Alberta, paragraph 12 of the 1930 Natural Resources Transfer Agreement (NRTA)[36] has been interpreted broadly to follow the language of the 1927 *Indian Act*[37] which included defining an Indian as someone with Indian blood and who lived the Indian mode of life. In *R. v. Desjarlais*,[38] the Alberta Court of Queen's Bench held that a person of mixed Indian and European ancestry could be entitled to the benefits of paragraph 12 of the NRTA so long as they followed an "Indian mode of life."[39]

In *R. v. Blais*[40] a unanimous Supreme Court of Canada affirmed the Manitoba Court of Appeal decision[41] and held that the use of the term "Indians" in paragraph 13 of the NRTA (Manitoba) cannot be read to include the Métis. Paragraph 13 of the NRTA provides that Indians have a right to hunt for food on unoccupied Crown land at any time of the year. *Blais* concerned a Manitoba Métis who was convicted of hunting deer out of season for food on unoccupied Crown land. The Supreme Court, in affirming the Court of Appeal decision, upheld the conviction and prevented the convicted Métis from relying on paragraph 13 as a basis for a Métis right to hunt for food.

In *R. v. Morin*,[42] the Saskatchewan Court of Queen's Bench considered a trial court judgment that affirmed that the Métis of northwest Saskatchewan had an Aboriginal right to fish within a specified area, that this right had not been extinguished by the taking of scrip, and that the requirements of the *Saskatchewan Fishery Regulations* for obtaining a fishing licence were unjustified infringements of the Métis right to fish. The Court upheld the trial decision and found that the Métis had established their right to fish for food. The trial decision[43] held that the Métis and Indians of northwest Saskatchewan are two "similarly situated" groups of people who were not being similarly treated. The Métis were required to purchase their fishing licences, whereas Indians could obtain them at no cost.

In *R. v. Grumbo*,[44] the Saskatchewan Court of Appeal considered whether a Métis

---

[36] Natural Resources Transfer Agreement; *Constitution Act, 1930*, R.S.C. 1985, App. II, No. 26 (20 & 21 Geo. V, c. 26 (U.K.)).

[37] *Indian Act*, R.S.C. 1927, c. 98, s. 2(h).

[38] *R. v. Desjarlais*, [1996] 3 C.N.L.R. 113 (Alta. Q.B.).

[39] See also *R. v. Ferguson*, [1994] 1 C.N.L.R. 117 (Alta. Q.B.).

[40] *R. v. Blais*, 2003 SCC 44 (S.C.C.).

[41] *R. v. Blais*, [2001] 3 C.N.L.R. 187 (Man. C.A.).

[42] *R. v. Morin*, [1998] 1 C.N.L.R. 182 (Sask. Q.B.).

[43] [1996] 3 C.N.L.R. 157 (Sask. Prov. Ct.).

[44] *R. v. Grumbo*, [1998] 3 C.N.L.R. 172 at 184 (Sask. C.A.); for commentary, see L.N. Chartrand, "Are We Métis or Are We Indians? A Commentary on *R. v. Grumbo*" (1999-2000) 31 Ottawa L. Rev. 267–81.

person convicted of illegal possession of wildlife was an "Indian" for the purposes paragraph 12 of the NRTA and thereby possessed certain rights to hunt. Although the Court did not resolve the issue, they did not dismiss the possibility. Instead, the Court stated that some fundamental questions needed to be answered, including whether the Métis people are an Aboriginal people distinct from Indians and, if they are, whether they possess a form of Aboriginal title or a right to hunt in Saskatchewan and whether this right was affected by the NRTA.

In *R. v. Watier*,[45] Goliath Prov. Ct. J. held that the *Wildlife Regulations, 1981*, which made it an offence to possess a deer carcass without an approved seal, did not offend s. 15(1) of the *Canadian Charter of Rights and Freedoms* ("Charter").[46] The charged Métis hunter claimed that since Indians were not subject to the regulation at issue, it discriminated against the charged, as an Aboriginal person. Goliath Prov. Ct. J. concluded by stating:

> The differential treatment of the defendant in this case arises not from the singling out of any person or group for denial of benefits for imposition of burdens, but from the constitutionally-guaranteed rights enjoyed by Indians and by some differently-situated Aboriginal hunters. . . .[47]

In *R. v. Muswagon*,[48] Jewers J. of the Manitoba Court of Appeal commented on the existence of Métis hunting and fishing Aboriginal rights in Manitoba:

> Aboriginals and Métis living in Manitoba may very well have inherent rights to hunt and fish for food in all seasons; many, if not all, treaty Indians certainly have that right under the various Indian treaties applicable in this province.

In *R. v. McPherson*,[49] Schulman J. of the Manitoba Court of Queen's Bench affirmed that where provincial laws of general application have been found inapplicable to Aboriginal people because these laws conflict with treaty rights or federal legislation in relation to Indians, the legislation should be read down so as not to apply to such Aboriginal peoples. Schulman J. affirmed Gregoire J.'s decision of the Manitoba Provincial Court, which held that the two Métis persons charged under the *Wildlife Act*[50] for hunting moose out of season possessed hunting rights protected by s. 35(1) and that these rights could be limited for conservation purposes pursuant to the justification analysis set out by the Supreme Court of Canada in *R. v. Sparrow*.[51] Using the *Sparrow* analysis, the Court held that the impugned sections of the *Wildlife Act* failed to protect Métis rights, due to a lack of consultation with the Métis and a lack of priority for Métis hunting rights.[52]

In the Supreme Court of Canada decision of *R. v. Van der Peet*,[53] Lamer C.J., for the majority, made a number of comments regarding the Métis, although the case itself had nothing to do with Métis rights:

[45] *R. v. Watier*, [2000] 2 C.N.L.R. 269 (Sask. Prov. Ct.).
[46] Part I of the *Constitution Act, 1982, supra* note 6.
[47] *Watier, supra* note 45 at para. 24.
[48] *R. v. Muswagon*, [1992] 4 C.N.L.R. 159 at 163 (Man. Q.B.).
[49] *R. v. McPherson*, [1994] 2 C.N.L.R. 137 (Man. Q.B.).
[50] *Wildlife Act*, R.S.M. 1987, c. W130, s. 26.
[51] *R. v. Sparrow*, [1990] 1 S.C.R. 1075.
[52] Also see *R. v. Ferguson, supra* note 39, which held that a Métis person could be considered an "Indian" for the purposes of para. 12 of the NRTA, and *R. v. Chevrier*, [1989] 1 C.N.L.R. 128 (Ont. Dist. Ct.), which held that a "mixed blood" person could exercise treaty hunting rights even though she or he was not entitled to be registered as an "Indian" under the *Indian Act*.
[53] *R. v. Van der Peet*, [1996] 2 S.C.R. 507.

Although s. 35 includes the Métis within its definition of "aboriginal peoples of Canada", and thus seems to link their claims to those of other Aboriginal peoples under the general heading of "aboriginal rights", the history of the Métis, and the reasons underlying their inclusion in the protection given by s. 35, are quite distinct from those of other Aboriginal peoples in Canada. As such, the manner in which the Aboriginal rights of other Aboriginal peoples are defined is not necessarily determinative of the manner in which the Aboriginal rights of the Métis are defined.[54]

This statement is one of the most substantive from the Supreme Court of Canada respecting Métis rights. However, many questions remain unanswered; for example, if Métis rights are to be understood differently, does that mean that they are to be understood in a way that will make them less authoritative than other Aboriginal rights? Is there a priority among Indian, Métis, and Inuit rights when such rights conflict with each other? Lamer C.J.'s statement in *Van der Peet* has undoubtedly raised concerns for those advocating an expansive approach to interpreting Métis rights.

Lovelace v. Ontario (2000)

In *Lovelace v. Ontario*,[55] the Supreme Court of Canada considered the constitutionality of the exclusion of non-Indian Aboriginal communities, primarily Métis, from negotiating and sharing in the proceeds of the First Nations Fund. The First Nations Fund resulted from the 1993 Ontario–Ontario First Nations Agreement to partner in the development of the Ontario's first reserve-based commercial casino.

Lovelace considered the scope of federal jurisdiction regarding the Métis and non-registered Indians and the proper interpretation of s. 15 of the Charter. The Supreme Court of Canada concluded that the province of Ontario did not act *ultra vires* in partnering the casino initiative with registered Indians and Indian bands, to the exclusion of other Aboriginal people. The exclusion of non-registered Indians and other Aboriginal communities did not act to define or impair the "Indianness" of the appellants since Ontario was simply exercising its constitutional spending power in making the casino arrangements.

The Court concluded that s. 15(1) of the Charter[56] applies just as powerfully to targeted ameliorative programs as s. 15(2).[57] Subsection 15(2) provides interpretative assistance in the development of the discrimination analysis in s. 15(1) of the Charter.

The Court confirmed that the Métis have the same need of amelioration of social, cultural, and economic conditions in their communities as the Indian bands that are part of the First Nations Fund. Since the program at issue was partnered, it must be distinguished from a universal or generally comprehensive benefits program. Nothing in the program affects the core of federal jurisdiction under s. 91(24). The Ontario government simply used the definition of band found in the Act and did nothing to impair the status or capacity of the appellants as "Aboriginal people." *Lovelace* suggests that governments can discriminate *within* the overall group of Aboriginal people between Indian and Métis people.

---

[54] *Ibid.* at para. 67; see also *Powley, supra* note 5 at para. 16.

[55] *Lovelace* v. *Ontario*, [2000] 1 S.C.R. 950.

[56] Subsection 15(1) of the Charter states: "Every individual is equal before and under the law and has the right to the equal protection and benefit of the law without discrimination and, in particular, without discrimination based on race, national or ethnic origin, colour."

[57] Subsection 15(2) of the Charter states: " Subsection (1) does not preclude any law, program or activity that has as its object the amelioration of conditions of disadvantaged individuals or groups including those that are disadvantaged because of race, national or ethnic original, colour, religion, sex, age or mental or physical disability."

R. v. *Powley* (2003)

In *Powley*[58] a unanimous Supreme Court of Canada confirmed that Métis rights are recognized and affirmed in s. 35(1). *Powley* concerned two respondents of Métis descent and members of the historic Métis community in Sault Ste. Marie. They shot and killed a moose and claimed, as a defence, that they possessed a right to hunt for food under s. 35(1). They were charged with hunting and possession of moose without a licence contrary to ss. 46 and 47(1) of Ontario's *Game and Fish Act*.[59] The trial judge, the Ontario Superior Court of Justice, and the Ontario Court of Appeal dismissed appeals by the Crown of the trial judge's acquittal. The Crown argued that the Powleys did not possess Métis rights to hunt for food under s. 35(1). Alternatively, the Crown argued that if the Powleys did possess Métis hunting rights, any infringement of these rights was justified for the purposes of conservation, equitable sharing of scarce resources, and social and economic benefits. Finally, the Crown argued that if the appeal was dismissed, the judgment should be stayed for one year, so as to allow the Crown to implement the changes that would be required.

The Supreme Court of Canada began its analysis of *Powley* by affirming that a modified version of the test to prove Aboriginal rights (the *Van der Peet* test, discussed in chapter 6) applies to the Métis as well. The central modification imposed by the Court in the *Van der Peet* test is to replace the "pre-contact" focus with a "pre-control" focus; that is, prior to effective European control.[60]

In *Powley*, the Court held that the proper characterization of the claimed Métis right was a right to hunt for food near Sault Ste. Marie, not a right to hunt mouse for food.[61] The Court upheld the lower court decisions respecting the distinctive Métis community of Sault Ste. Marie and that such a community existed, even if not always formally designated as such.[62]

The Court discussed the meaning of the term "Métis" and who is included within the meaning of that term as used in s. 35(1) and discussed earlier in this chapter.[63] The Court confirmed that the Métis are distinct Aboriginal peoples within the meaning of s. 35(1) and that three indicia guide the determination of who is a "Métis": (1) self-identification, (2) ancestral connection to a historic Métis community, and (3) acceptance by a modern Métis community.[64]

The Court also held that subsistence hunting and fishing was an important aspect of Métis life and such activities/rights were not extinguished.[65] The Court concluded by stating that the Métis community in and around Sault Ste. Marie have an Aboriginal right to hunt for food under s. 35(1).

Powley is a significant decision for Métis nationally. It sets out a clear definition of who is a Métis for the purposes of s. 35(1) and affirms that the *Van der Peet* test, as modified, applies to Métis rights claims.

[58] *Powley, supra* note 5.
[59] *Game and Fish Act*, R.S.O. 1990, c. G.1; now the *Fish and Wildlife Conservation Act*, 1997, S.O. 1997, c. 41.
[60] *Powley, supra* note 5 at paras. 18, 36.
[61] *Ibid.* at para. 20.
[62] *Ibid.* at para. 26.
[63] See commentary referred to in notes 5 to 8.
[64] *Powley, supra* note 5 at paras. 30–34.
[65] The Supreme Court of Canada affirmed that the doctrine of extinguishment applies equally to Métis and First Nations claims. *Ibid.* para. 46.

THE INUIT

Definition of "Inuit"

Historically, the Inuit (formerly known as Eskimos) have inhabited the central and eastern portions of northern Canada. Approximately forty-five thousand people identified as being Inuit in the 2001 census.[66] The Inuit primarily reside in Nunavut, the Northwest Territories (the "NWT"), northern Labrador, and northern Quebec. The claims of the Labrador Inuit and Inuit of northern Québec (Makavik) are discussed in Chapter 2.

The Inuit come within the legislative authority of Parliament pursuant to s. 91(24). In *Re Eskimos*,[67] the Supreme Court of Canada unanimously decided that the term "Indians" in s. 91(24) included the Inuit, bringing the Inuit within the legislative authority of Parliament. Subsection 35(2) of the *Constitution Act, 1982* includes the Inuit as one of the Aboriginal peoples of Canada, along with the Métis and Indians. Although the responsibility of Indian and Northern Affairs Canada, the Inuit are not governed by specific federal legislation (unlike Indians registered under the Act). Subsection 4(1) of the *Indian Act* provides: "A reference in this Act to an Indian does not include any person of the race of aborigines commonly referred to as Inuit."

Nunavut Land Claims Agreement (1993)

In May 1993 the Nunavut Land Claims Agreement[68] was signed between Canada (the government of the Northwest Territories being part of the federal team) and the Tunngavik Federation of Nunavut, on behalf of the Inuit of the Nunavut settlement area and now known as Nunavut Tunngavik Inc. The agreement settles the Inuit's comprehensive claim over a large portion of the central Northwest Territories and the eastern Arctic. The Tunngavik Federation of Nunavut claim covered more than two million square kilometres.[69]

The Inuit Tapirisat of Canada (representing the Inuit nationally) had initially submitted the claim to the federal government in February 1976. The claim was amended and resubmitted in December 1977. The Inuit proposals for a new territory made little progress during 1978 and 1979. By 1980, negotiations resumed on the understanding that the issue of a new territory would be negotiated outside of the comprehensive claims framework. The Inuit Tapirisat of Canada was replaced by the Tunngavik Federation of Nunavut as the negotiating vehicle for the Inuit in 1982. Although a number of sub-agreements were in place by 1986, it was not until 30 April 1990, that the agreement-in-principle was signed.

The Nunavut Land Claims Agreement provided that the Inuit receive title to approximately 351,000 square kilometres of land, including nearly 37,000 square kilometres of land over which they have mineral rights. The Inuit will receive more than $1 billion, to be paid over fourteen years. A Nunavut Wildlife Management Board (NWMB), with equal public and Inuit representation, was also established under the agreement to manage and regulate access to wildlife within the Nunavut Settlement Area, which stretched approximately 2 million square kilometres). While ultimate authority over wildlife rests

---

[66] *Supra* note 1.

[67] *Re Eskimos, supra* note 12.

[68] Nunavut Land Claims Agreement (Ottawa: DIAND, 1993). En. by *Nunavut Land Claims Agreement Act,* S.C. 1993, c. 29.

[69] For an historical perspective, see R.Q. Duffy, *The Road to Nunavut: The Progress of the Eastern Arctic Inuit Since the Second World War* (Kingston & Montreal: McGill-Queen's University Press, 1988).

with the Nunavut government, the NWMB is a key decision-making entity within the Nunavut Settlement Area, with advisory authority respecting the waters adjacent to the area. The Inuit are guaranteed equal representation on a number of administrative boards responsible for land management, environmental and socio-economic reviews, wildlife management, and water use.

Nunavut was created on 1 April 1999. It comprises approximately 20 per cent of Canada's total area, has twenty-six communities, and has a population of approximately 27,000, about 85 per cent of whom are Inuit.

Robert Bone provides a succinct summary of Nunavut:

> [T]he Nunavut agreement recognized the Inuit's aspirations for a territorial homeland and thereby set the stage for the establishment of the Territory of Nunavut. While all residents of Nunavut have equal rights, the demographic reality is that 85 of every 100 of its inhabitants are Inuit, making the territory a vehicle through which their political aspirations can be expressed. Demography and politics have forged Nunavut into a unique political entity within Canada. Territorial government policies and programs reflect Inuit aspirations, beliefs and values. Two examples of this are: (a) the principle of decentralization that ensures that government is close to the people; and (b) the principle of promoting the Inuktitut language and culture.
>
> The Legislative Assembly is 19 MLAs. . . . There are no political parties. The Premier and Ministers are elected by the Assembly to the Executive Council or Cabinet.[70]

The Nunavut Land Claims Agreement, like other land claims agreements, includes the following provision, in which the Inuit agreed to:

> [c]ede, release and surrender to Her Majesty in Right of Canada, all their aboriginal claims, rights, title and interests, if any, in and to lands and waters anywhere within Canada and adjacent offshore areas within the sovereignty or jurisdiction of Canada.[71]

In addition, the Inuit agreed not to assert any legal action against Canada based on Aboriginal rights, claims, title, or interests.

The Nunavut Land Claims Agreement was considered in *Nunavut Tunngavik Inc.* v. *Canada (Min. of Fisheries and Oceans)*[72] and *Nunavik Inuit* v. *Canada.*[73] (See chapter 2 for a discussion of these decisions.)

In *Kadlak v. Nunavut (Min. of Sustainable Development),*[74] an Inuit applicant sought judicial review of a decision by the Minister of Sustainable Development to disallow the NWMB's decision related to hunting polar bears. The minister's decision was quashed and the matter was referred back to the minister. Kilpatrick J. stated:

> Section 35(1) . . . does not promise that the rights under the Nunavut Land Claims Agreement will be immune from all forms of government regulation. It does require the Territorial and Federal Crown to justify any decision that impacts adversely upon the promises made and rights conferred in the Land Claims Settlement.[75]

---

[70] Robert M. Bone, "The Three Territories: An Introduction", *The Canadian North: Embracing Change* (Montréal, QC: Centre for Research and Information on Canada, June 2002), 8.

[71] Kevin A. Gray, "The Nunavut Land Claims Agreement and the Future of the Eastern Arctic: The Uncharted Path to Effective Self-Government" (1994) 52:2 U. Tor. Fac. L. Rev. 300.

[72] *Nunavut Tunngavik Inc.* v. *Canada (Min. of Fisheries and Oceans),* [1997] 4 C.N.L.R. 193 (F.C.T.D.).

[73] *Nunavik Inuit* v. *Canada (Min. of Canadian Heritage),* [1998] 4 C.N.L.R. 68 (F.C.T.D.).

[74] *Kadlak* v. *Nunavut (Min. of Sustainable Development),* [2001] 1 C.N.L.R. 147 (Nun. Ct. J.).

[75] *Ibid.* at para. 22.

Kilpatrick J. confirmed that status of existing Canadian law as it applies to the Nunavut Land Claims Agreement. While the agreement provides a substantive basis for protecting the treaty rights of the Inuit, those rights, like any rights, are not absolute but remain subject to federal and provincial authority, justifiable, as the case may be.

CONCLUSION

The situation of the Métis and the Inuit are, in some ways, at extreme ends of a spectrum. While the Métis continue to struggle to have their constitutional rights recognized by governments, the Inuit of Nunavut possess treaty rights, constitutionally recognized and affirmed, as set out in the Nunavut Land Claims Agreement, as do the Inuit of Labrador in the Labrador Inuit Land Claim Agreement. Just as their situations are different, so too are their legal challenges. The Inuit will likely strive for more clarity around what constitutional recognition and affirmation in s. 35(1) means in light of the rights contained in the Nunavut Land Claims Agreement and other land claims agreements they have negotiated. Métis legal issues will likely continue to revolve around hunting, fishing, and trapping rights and self-government. In both cases, important legal questions remain outstanding.

CASES AND MATERIALS

THE MÉTIS

Manitoba Act, 1870
ss. 30–32, R.S.C. 1985, App. II, No. 8.

30. All ungranted or waste lands in the Province shall be, from and after the date of the said transfer, vested in the Crown, and administered by the Government of Canada for the purposes of the Dominion, subject to, and except and so far as the same may be affected by, the conditions and stipulations contained in the agreement for the surrender of Rupert's Land by the Hudson's Bay Company to Her Majesty.

31. And whereas, it is expedient, towards the extinguishment of the Indian Title to the lands in the Province, to appropriate a portion of such ungranted lands, to the extent of one million four hundred thousand acres thereof, for the benefit of the families of the half-breed residents, it is hereby enacted, that, under regulations to be from time to time made by the Governor General in Council, the Lieutenant-Governor shall select such lots or tracts in such parts of the Province as he may deem expedient, to the extent aforesaid, and divide the same among the children of the half-breed heads of families residing in the Province at the time of the said transfer to Canada, and the same shall be granted to the said children respectively, in such mode and on such conditions as to settlement and otherwise, as the Governor General in Council may from time to time determine. . . .

32. For the quieting of titles, and assuring to the settlers in the province the peaceable possession of the lands now held by them, it is enacted as follows:
    1. All grants of land in freehold made by the Hudson's Bay Company up to the

eighth day of March, in the year 1869, shall, if required by the owner, be confirmed by grant from the Crown.

2. All grants of estates less than freehold in land made by the Hudson's Bay Company up to the eighth day of March aforesaid, shall, if required by the owner, be converted into an estate in free-hold by grant from the Crown.

3. All titles by occupancy with the sanction and under the license and authority of the Hudson's Bay Company up to the eighth day of March aforesaid, of land in that part of the Province in which the Indian Title has been extinguished, shall, if required by the owner, be converted into an estate in freehold by grant from the Crown.

4. All persons in peaceable possession of tracts of land at the time of the transfer to Canada, in those parts of the Province in which the Indian Title has not been extinguished, shall have the right of pre-emption of the same, on such terms and conditions as may be determined by the Governor in Council.

5. The Lieutenant-Governor is hereby authorized, under regulations to be made from time to time by the Governor General in Council, to make all such provisions for ascertaining and adjusting, on fair and equitable terms, the rights of Common, and rights of cutting Hay held and enjoyed by the settlers in the Province, and for the commutation of the same by grants of land from the Crown.

Constitution Act, 1982
s. 35(2).

(2) In this Act, "aboriginal peoples of Canada" includes the Indian, Inuit and Métis peoples of Canada.

Manitoba Metis Federation Inc. v. A.-G. of Canada

(*sub nom. Dumont v. A.-G. Canada*), [1988] 3 C.N.L.R. 39 (Man. C.A.). O'Sullivan, Huband, Philp, Twaddle, and Lyon JJ.A., June 17, 1988.

TWADDLE J.A.:— The plaintiffs challenge the constitutional validity of several pieces of federal legislation enacted between 1871 and 1886. They say the legislation was unconstitutional because it altered provisions of the *Manitoba Act*, S.C. 1870, c. 3, contrary to the prohibition against such alteration contained in the *Constitution Act, 1871* (U.K. c. 28). The Attorney General of Canada seeks to abort the challenge on the ground, amongst others, that the validity of the impugned legislation is a matter of academic interest only.

The learned judge in Motions Court, who dismissed the Attorney General's application to strike out the claim, understood the plaintiffs' claim to be that the allegedly invalid legislation had deprived the plaintiffs' forebears of a community of interest in land which, but for the legislation, would have been inherited by the plaintiffs as the descendants of those to whom the community of interest was given. Based on this understanding of the plaintiffs' case, the learned judge dismissed the application to strike out the claim. It is from the order dismissing his application that the Attorney General of Canada now appeals. . . .

Doubts having been expressed as to the authority of the Parliament of Canada to establish the Province of Manitoba, the United Kingdom Parliament enacted the *Constitution Act, 1871*, which retroactively validated the *Manitoba Act*. Section 6 of the *Constitution Act, 1871* provided:

6. Except as provided by the third section of this Act, it shall not be competent for the Parliament of Canada to alter the provisions of the last-mentioned Act of the said Parliament in so far as it relates to the Province of Manitoba, or of any other Act hereafter establishing new Provinces in the said Dominion, subject always to the right of the Legislature of the Province of Manitoba to alter from time to time the provisions of any law respecting the qualification of electors and members of the Legislative Assembly and to make laws respecting elections in the said Province.

Subsequent legislation enacted by the Parliament of Canada and by the Governor General in Council regulated the allocation of land to half-breed children and the making of claims to land under s. 32 of the *Manitoba Act*. The plaintiffs allege that the subsequent legislation went beyond mere regulation. They say that it altered or embellished the original statutory provisions. They also say that this alteration or embellishment was contrary to the provisions of s. 6 of the *Constitution Act, 1871*.

I must say that, when I read the impugned legislation, I do not find provisions which can readily be regarded as alterations to the original enactment. Indeed, one of the impugned statutes actually conferred additional rights on individual half-breeds (S.C. 1874, c. 20). I do not find it necessary, however, to decide this appeal on the basis that the plaintiffs do not have a reasonable cause of action. It is my view that this appeal can be decided on the question of whether the issue which the plaintiffs wish to raise is justifiable.

Before turning to that question, let me make it clear that, for the purpose of this appeal, I assume the truth of all allegations of fact contained in the statement of claim. Those allegations include the allegation that all half-breeds of 1870 were "Métis"; that the Métis of 1870 were a distinct people; and that all their descendants are included within the undefined group of persons constitutionally recognized today as "the Métis people." These allegations which I assume as true also include the allegation that some half-breeds of 1870 did not receive, or were deprived of, constitutionally entrenched rights and the allegation that their loss of those rights was a result of the impugned legislation. . . . It is, in any event, impossible to construe s. 31 of the *Manitoba Act* as conferring on half-breed children generally a community of interest in the 1,400,000 acres appropriated for the benefit of the families of half-breed residents. The section makes it quite clear that the land was to he divided "among the children of the half-breed heads of families residing in the Province" and "granted to the said children respectively." . . .

The *Constitution Act, 1982* recognized the Métis as an aboriginal people. The enactment also recognized the existing aboriginal rights of the Métis, whatever they were. The proclamation of 1984 recognized the future rights which the Métis might acquire by way of a land claims agreement. The federal government has expressed a willingness to negotiate a settlement of the claim. Once it has been settled, the rights which the agreement confers on the Métis will be part of the Constitution of Canada Until then, the federal government is obliged to do no more than negotiate with the Métis in good faith.

The legal basis of the land claim is a matter of great uncertainty. Unlike the Nishga Indian Tribe in *Calder* v. *Attorney-General of British Columbia*, [1973] S.C.R. 313, 34 D.L.R. (3d) 145, the Métis people did not occupy a clearly defined area of land and only on one side of their families can they show descent from persons who inhabited the land from time immemorial. Even if they had aboriginal rights prior to July 15, 1870, these rights may have been extinguished by the *Manitoba Act* or its subsequent validation. The issue of extinguishment divided the Supreme Court of Canada in the *Calder* case. It cannot be assumed that it will be resolved in favour of the Métis.

The federal government will be influenced in its negotiations with the Métis by many considerations. As well as by the Métis claim to legal rights, the federal government will be influenced by social and political considerations and by the historical circumstances which have resulted in the Métis being an aboriginal people without a land base. Those historical circumstances include the effects of the impugned legislation on the land holdings of individual Métis. The federal government will be able to consider those effects regardless of the legislation's constitutional validity. . . .

For these reasons, I am of the opinion that the appeal should be allowed, the order made in Motions Court set aside and an order made striking out the plaintiffs' claim against the Attorney General of Canada. . . .

O'SULLIVAN J.A.: (dissenting) . . . The problem confronting us is how can the rights of the Métis people as a people be asserted. Must they turn to international bodies or to the conscience of humanity to obtain redress for their grievances as a people, or is it possible for us at the request of their representatives, to recognize their people claims as justiciable?

Whatever may have been the case prior to 1982, I think it is indisputable that the Canadian Constitution recognizes the existence of aboriginal peoples of Canada and that the Métis are an aboriginal people. . . .

I know there is a school of thought that says that the framers of the Constitution were of the view that the Métis people as such had no rights and that a cruel deception was practised on them and on the Queen whose duty it is to respect the treaties and understandings that she has entered into with her Métis people. But I do not subscribe to this school of thought.

In my opinion, it is impossible in our jurisprudence to have rights without a remedy and the rights of the Métis people must be capable of being asserted by somebody. If not by the present plaintiffs, then by whom?

It must be noted that the existence of the Métis people is asserted in the Constitution as of the present, not simply as of the past. Each individual plaintiff can, I think, prove indisputably his membership in the Métis nation. Their genealogical records are unparalleled in modern societies. See Sprague and Frye, *The Genealogy of the First Métis Nation* (1983). In any event, the question of their membership in this nation should not be called into question at the preliminary stage of a motion to strike out.

I may say in parenthesis that I find it most extraordinary that as I understand it the federal government should be funding a lawsuit which the government's Attorney General is simultaneously attempting to kill at birth.

One of the difficulties in enforcing the rights of native peoples is that they are difficult to define in common-law terms. Even the question of membership in a people may provide perplexing issues. But that a half-breed people existed as a people in the western plains of British North America in 1869 can hardly be doubted by those familiar with the history of this country. The half-breeds formed the overwhelming majority of the population of the Red River colony and had achieved such a degree of self-awareness as a people that with the acquiescence of Donald A. Smith and under the chairmanship of Judge Black they were able to form a provisional government which maintained law and order for many months in 1870. This provisional government may not have been recognized by some of the Canadian settlers in Ruperts' land, but it was recognized by the British government which entered into negotiations with delegates appointed by the convention that sanctioned and elected the provisional government.

The *Manitoba Act* sanctioned by Imperial legislation, is not only a statute; it embodies a treaty which was entered into between the delegates of the Red River settlement and the

Imperial authority. Although some historians have suggested that concessions made to the Métis were "granted" by Macdonald, the truth is that the negotiations proceeded in the presence of Imperial delegates. . . .

It has been accepted by everyone that the aboriginal rights could not be lost save by the consent of those who enjoyed them. If the Métis people did not give up their aboriginal rights by agreeing to accept the provisions of the *Manitoba Act* in lieu thereof, then the aboriginal rights of this people must still subsist.

But when they state the rights given to them under the *Manitoba Act* were given to them as a people and not simply as individuals, they are met with incomprehension.

As I understand the claim of the plaintiffs they say that the rights which the Métis were led to expect they had as a result of their agreement to give up their aboriginal titles were never honoured and they are seeking in a variety of ways to assert their grievances as a result.

One of the things which stands in the way of their claim is that the federal and provincial legislatures and governments have passed a series of statutes and regulations which were designed to have the effect, and did have the effect, of rendering nugatory the scheme which the Métis representatives had negotiated.

That scheme envisioned the developing of tracts of land en bloc to the extent of 1,400,000 acres in Manitoba. The people say they expected to have the land surveyed and allotted in such a way as to enable the half-breeds to continue their way of life which was not to live in isolated square sections, but in communities with community resources, with provision not only for individual cultivation but also for common pasturage and hunting. This point of view was put clearly enough in the negotiations by one of the delegates, Msgr. Ritchot, in the following words as set out in his diary for May 2, 1870:

> We continued to claim 1,500,000 acres and we agreed on the mode of distribution as follows: the land will be chosen throughout the province by each lot and in several different lots and in various places, if it is judged to be proper by the local legislature which ought itself to distribute these parcels of lands to heads of families in proportion to the number of children existing at the time of the distribution; that these lands should then be distributed among the children by their parents or guardians, always under the supervision of the above-mentioned local legislature which could pass laws to ensure the continuance of these lands in the Métis families. [W.L. Morton, *Manitoba: The Birth of a Province*]

The governments knew well how to allot land in such a way as to enable a community to live as such. They were able to accommodate the Mennonites by the eastern reserve and the western reserve and they were able to accommodate the French-Canadians on Pembina mountain. There, settlers were not given land at random; land was allotted only to persons who shared common values.

Many of the Métis themselves proved how possible it was to allot land in accordance with their customs by themselves setting up settlements on the banks of the Saskatchewan after it became clear to them that the government's understanding of the "treaty" they made was different from theirs. As to these settlements, reference may be made to Beal and Macleod, *Prairie Fire* (Toronto 1984).

The plaintiffs want court declarations nullifying the laws which, according to them, amended and changed the *Manitoba Act* in an unconstitutional way. . . .

Since constitutional facts can only be ascertained by a process quite foreign to the ordinary trial procedures, it may be that justice with regard to minorities can only be attained by the creation of constitutional courts or by developing within the existing court system a special process for dealing with constitutional facts. A time-honoured method of dealing with the kind of claim now before us is the Royal Commission and that may be at the present time the best way to deal with the claim of the Métis.

Nevertheless, I think it is important to accept that the claims asserted by the plaintiffs in the present action are justiciable and not merely political. The plaintiffs have status to assert their claims in the Court of Queen's Bench. I am sure the judge assigned to try the case will have a difficult time and will have to be able to adapt the process of the court to suit the nature of the case. But, in the end, in my opinion it is in the development of law to deal with claims of "peoples" that lies the best hope of achieving justice and harmony in a world full of minority groups.

Dumont v. A.-G. of Canada

(*sub nom. Manitoba Metis Fed.* v. *A.-G. Canada*), [1990] 1 S.C.R. 279 (S.C.C.). Dickson C.J., Wilson, La Forest, Sopinka, Gonthier, Cory, and McLachlin JJ., March 2, 1990.

DICKSON C.J.C. (orally):—We are all of the view that this appeal succeeds. The judgment of the Court will be delivered by Mme. Justice Wilson.

WILSON J. (orally):—The members of the Court are all of the view that the test laid down in *Attorney General of Canada* v. *Inuit Tapirisat*, [1980] 2 S.C.R. 735 for striking out a statement of claim is not met in this case. It cannot be said that the outcome of the case is "plain and obvious" or "beyond doubt".

Issues as to the proper interpretation of the relevant provisions of the *Manitoba Act* of 1870 and the *Constitution Act* of 1871 and the effect of the impugned ancillary legislation upon them would appear to be better determined at trial where a proper factual base can be laid.

The Court is of the view also that the subject matter of the dispute, inasmuch as it involves the constitutionality of legislation ancillary to the *Manitoba Act*, is justiciable in the courts and that declaratory relief may be granted in the discretion of the court in aid of extra-judicial claims in an appropriate case.

We see no reason, therefore, why the action should not proceed to trial. The appeal is accordingly allowed and the order of the Court of Appeal striking out the appellants' claim against the Attorney General of Canada is set aside.

R. v. Powley

2003 SCC 43 (S.C.C.). McLachlin C.J., Gonthier, Iacobucci, Major, Bastarache, Binnie, Arbour, Le Bel, and Deschamps JJ., September 19, 2003.

THE COURT—

I. Introduction

1   This case raises the issue of whether members of the Métis community in and around Sault Ste. Marie enjoy a constitutionally protected right to hunt for food under the s. 35 of the *Constitution Act, 1982*. We conclude that they do. . . .

6   The facts are not in dispute. The Powleys freely admit that they shot, killed, and took possession of a bull moose without a hunting license. However, they argue that, as Métis, they have an aboriginal right to hunt for food in the Sault Ste. Marie area that cannot be infringed by the Ontario government without proper justification. Because the Ontario government denies the existence of any special Métis right to hunt for food, the Powleys argue that subjecting them to the moose hunting provisions of the Game and Fish Act violates their rights under s. 35(1) of the *Constitution Act, 1982*, and cannot be justified.

7   The trial court, Superior Court, and Court of Appeal agreed with the Powleys. They found that the members of the Métis community in and around Sault Ste. Marie have an aboriginal right to hunt for food that is infringed without justification by the Ontario hunting regulations. Steve and Roddy Powley were therefore acquitted of unlawfully hunting and possessing the bull moose. Ontario appeals from these acquittals.

8   The question before us is whether ss. 46 and 47(1) of the *Game and Fish Act,* which prohibit hunting moose without a licence, unconstitutionally infringe the respondents' aboriginal right to hunt for food, as recognized in s. 35(1) of the *Constitution Act, 1982.*

II. Analysis . . .

10   The term "Métis" in s. 35 does not encompass all individuals with mixed Indian and European heritage; rather, it refers to distinctive peoples who, in addition to their mixed ancestry, developed their own customs, way of life, and recognizable group identity separate from their Indian or Inuit and European forebears. Métis communities evolved and flourished prior to the entrenchment of European control, when the influence of European settlers and political institutions became pre-eminent. . . .

11   The Métis of Canada share the common experience of having forged a new culture and a distinctive group identity from their Indian or Inuit and European roots. This enables us to speak in general terms of "the Métis". However, particularly given the vast territory of what is now Canada, we should not be surprised to find that different groups of Métis exhibit their own distinctive traits and traditions. This diversity among groups of Métis may enable us to speak of Métis "peoples", a possibility left open by the language of s. 35(2), which speaks of the "Indian, Inuit and Métis peoples of Canada."

12   We would not purport to enumerate the various Métis peoples that may exist. Because the Métis are explicitly included in s. 35, it is only necessary for our purposes to verify that the claimants belong to an identifiable Métis community with a sufficient degree of continuity and stability to support a site-specific aboriginal right. A Métis community can be defined as a group of Métis with a distinctive collective identity, living together in the same geographic area and sharing a common way of life. The respondents here claim membership in the Métis community centred in and around Sault Ste. Marie. It is not necessary for us to decide, and we did not receive submissions on, whether this community is also a Métis "people", or whether it forms part of a larger Métis people that extends over a wider area such as the Upper Great Lakes.

13   Our evaluation of the respondents' claim takes place against this historical and cultural backdrop. The overarching interpretive principle for our legal analysis is a purposive reading of s. 35. The inclusion of the Métis in s. 35 is based on a commitment to recognizing the Métis and enhancing their survival as distinctive communities. The purpose and the promise of s. 35 is to protect practices that were historically important features of these distinctive communities and that persist in the present day as integral elements of their Métis culture.

14   For the reasons elaborated below, we uphold the basic elements of the *Van der Peet* test (*R. v. Van der Peet*, [1996] 2 S.C.R. 507) and apply these to the respondents' claim. However, we modify certain elements of the pre-contact test to reflect the distinctive history and post-contact ethnogenesis of the Métis, and the resulting differences between Indian claims and Métis claims.

A. The *Van der Peet* Test

15   The core question in *Van der Peet* was: "How should the aboriginal rights recognized and affirmed by s. 35(1) of the *Constitution Act, 1982* be defined?" (para. 15, per Lamer C.J.). Lamer C.J. wrote for the majority, at para. 31:

> [W]hat s. 35(1) does is provide the constitutional framework through which the fact that aboriginals lived on the land in distinctive societies, with their own practices, traditions and cultures, is acknowledged and reconciled with the sovereignty of the Crown. The substantive rights which fall within the provision must be defined in light of this purpose; the aboriginal rights recognized and affirmed by s. 35(1) must be directed towards the reconciliation of the pre-existence of aboriginal societies with the sovereignty of the Crown.

16   The emphasis on prior occupation as the primary justification for the special protection accorded aboriginal rights led the majority in *Van der Peet* to endorse a pre-contact test for identifying which customs, practices or traditions were integral to a particular aboriginal culture, and therefore entitled to constitutional protection. However, the majority recognized that the pre-contact test might prove inadequate to capture the range of Métis customs, practices or traditions that are entitled to protection, since Métis cultures by definition post-date European contact. For this reason, Lamer C.J. explicitly reserved the question of how to define Métis aboriginal rights for another day. He wrote at para. 67:

> [T]he history of the Métis, and the reasons underlying their inclusion in the protection given by s. 35, are quite distinct from those of other aboriginal peoples in Canada. As such, the manner in which the aboriginal rights of other aboriginal peoples are defined is not necessarily determinative of the manner in which the aboriginal rights of the Métis are defined. At the time when this Court is presented with a Métis claim under s. 35 it will then, with the benefit of the arguments of counsel, a factual context and a specific Métis claim, be able to explore the question of the purposes underlying s. 35's protection of the aboriginal rights of Métis people, and answer the question of the kinds of claims which fall within s. 35(1)'s scope when the claimants are Métis. The fact that, for other aboriginal peoples, the protection granted by s. 35 goes to the practices, customs and traditions of aboriginal peoples prior to contact, is not necessarily relevant to the answer which will be given to that question.

17   As indicated above, the inclusion of the Métis in s. 35 is not traceable to their pre-contact occupation of Canadian territory. The purpose of s. 35 as it relates to the Métis is therefore different from that which relates to the Indians or the Inuit. The constitutionally significant feature of the Métis is their special status as peoples that emerged between first contact and the effective imposition of European control. The inclusion of the Métis in s. 35 represents Canada's commitment to recognize and value the distinctive Métis cultures, which grew up in areas not yet open to colonization, and which the framers of the *Constitution Act, 1982* recognized can only survive if the Métis are protected along with other aboriginal communities.

18   With this in mind, we proceed to the issue of the correct test to determine the entitlements of the Métis under s. 35 of the Constitution Act, 1982. The appropriate test must then be applied to the findings of fact of the trial judge. We accept *Van der Peet* as the template for this discussion. However, we modify the pre-contact focus of the *Van der Peet* test when the claimants are Métis to account for the important differences between Indian and Métis claims. Section 35 requires that we recognize and protect those customs and traditions that were historically important features of Métis communities prior to the

time of effective European control, and that persist in the present day. This modification is required to account for the unique post-contact emergence of Métis communities, and the post-contact foundation of their aboriginal rights.

(1) Characterization of the Right

19   The first step is to characterize the right being claimed: *Van der Peet, supra*, at para. 76. Aboriginal hunting rights, including Métis rights, are contextual and site-specific. The respondents shot a bull moose near Old Goulais Bay Road, in the environs of Sault Ste. Marie, within the traditional hunting grounds of that Métis community. They made a point of documenting that the moose was intended to provide meat for the winter. The trial judge determined that they were hunting for food, and there is no reason to overturn this finding. The right being claimed can therefore be characterized as the right to hunt for food in the environs of Sault Ste. Marie.

20   We agree with the trial judge that the periodic scarcity of moose does not in itself undermine the respondents' claim. The relevant right is not to hunt moose but to hunt for food in the designated territory.

(2) Identification of the Historic Rights-Bearing Community

21   The trial judge found that a distinctive Métis community emerged in the Upper Great Lakes region in the mid-17th century, and peaked around 1850. We find no reviewable error in the trial judge's findings on this matter, which were confirmed by the Court of Appeal. The record indicates the following: In the mid-17th century, the Jesuits established a mission at Sainte-Marie-du-Sault, in an area characterized by heavy competition among fur traders. In 1750, the French established a fixed trading post on the south bank of the Saint Mary's River. The Sault Ste. Marie post attracted settlement by Métis—the children of unions between European traders and Indian women, and their descendants (A.J. Ray, "An Economic History of the Robinson Treaty Areas Before 1860 (1998) ("Ray Report"), at p. 17. According to Dr. Ray, by the early nineteenth century, "[t]he settlement at Sault Ste. Marie was one of the oldest and most important [Métis settlements] in the upper lakes area" (Ray Report, *supra*, at p. 47). The Hudson Bay Company operated the St. Mary's post primarily as a depot from 1821 onwards (Ray Report, *supra*, at p. 51). Although Dr. Ray characterized the Company's records for this post as "scanty" (Ray Report, *supra*, at p. 51), he was able to piece together a portrait of the community from existing records, including the 1824–25 and 1827–28 post journals of HBC Chief Factor Bethune, and the 1846 report of a government surveyor, Alexander Vidal (Ray Report, *supra*, at pp. 52–53).

22   Dr. Ray's report indicates that the individuals named in the post journals "were overwhelmingly Métis", and that Vidal's report "provide[s] a crude indication of the rate of growth of the community and highlights the continuing dominance of Métis in it" (Ray Report, *supra*, at p. 53). Dr. Victor P. Lytwyn characterized the Vidal report and accompanying map as "clear evidence of a distinct and cohesive Métis community at Sault Ste. Marie," (V.P. Lytwyn, "Historical Report on the Métis Community at Sault Ste. Marie" (1998) ("Lytwyn Report"), at p. 2 while Dr. Ray elaborated: "By the time of Vidal's visit to the Sault Ste. Marie area, the people of mixed ancestry living there had developed a distinctive sense of identity and Indians and Whites recognized them as being a separate people" (Ray Report, *supra*, at p. 56).

23   In addition to demographic evidence, proof of shared customs, traditions, and a collective identity is required to demonstrate the existence of a Métis community that can support a claim to site-specific aboriginal rights. We recognize that different groups of Métis have often lacked political structures and have experienced shifts in their members' self-identification. However, the existence of an identifiable Métis community must be demonstrated with some degree of continuity and stability in order to support a site-specific aboriginal rights claim. Here, we find no basis for overturning the trial judge's finding of a historic Métis community at Sault Ste. Marie. This finding is supported by the record and must be upheld.

(3) Identification of the Contemporary Rights-Bearing Community

24   Aboriginal rights are communal rights: They must be grounded in the existence of a historic and present community, and they may only be exercised by virtue of an individual's ancestrally based membership in the present community. The trial judge found that a Métis community has persisted in and around Sault Ste. Marie despite its decrease in visibility after the signing of the Robinson-Huron Treaty in 1850. While we take note of the trial judge's determination that the Sault Ste. Marie Métis community was to a large extent an "invisible entity" (para. 80) from the mid-19th century to the 1970s, we do not take this to mean that the community ceased to exist or disappeared entirely.

25   Dr. Lytwyn describes the continued existence of a Métis community in and around Sault Ste. Marie despite the displacement of many of the community's members in the aftermath of the 1850 treaties:

> [T]he Métis continued to live in the Sault Ste. Marie region. Some drifted into the Indian Reserves which had been set apart by the 1850 Treaty. Others lived in areas outside of the town, or in back concessions. The Métis continued to live in much the same manner as they had in the past—fishing, hunting, trapping and harvesting other resources for their livelihood.
>
> (Lytwyn Report, p. 31 (emphasis added);
> see also Morrison, "The Robinson Treaties", at p. 201)

26   The advent of European control over this area thus interfered with, but did not eliminate, the Sault Ste. Marie Métis community and its traditional practices, as evidenced by census data from the 1860s through the 1890s. Dr. Lytwyn concluded from this census data that "[a]lthough the Métis lost much of their traditional land base at Sault Ste. Marie, they continued to live in the region and gain their livelihood from the resources of the land and waters" (Lytwyn Report, *supra*, at p. 32). He also noted a tendency for underreporting and lack of information about the Métis during this period because of their "removal to the peripheries of the town," and "their own disinclination to be identified as Métis" in the wake of the Riel rebellions and the turning of Ontario public opinion against Métis rights through government actions and the media (Lytwyn Report, *supra*, at p. 33).

27   We conclude that the evidence supports the trial judge's finding that the community's lack of visibility was explained and does not negate the existence of the contemporary community. There was never a lapse; the Métis community went underground, so to speak, but it continued. Moreover, as indicated below, the "continuity" requirement puts the focus on the continuing practices of members of the community, rather than more generally on the community itself, as indicated below.

28   The trial judge's finding of a contemporary Métis community in and around Sault Ste. Marie is supported by the evidence and must be upheld.

(4) Verification of the Claimant's Membership in the Relevant Contemporary Community
29   While determining membership in the Métis community might not be as simple as verifying membership in, for example, an Indian band, this does not detract from the status of Métis people as full-fledged rights-bearers. As Métis communities continue to organize themselves more formally and to assert their constitutional rights, it is imperative that membership requirements become more standardized so that legitimate rights-holders can be identified. In the meantime, courts faced with Métis claims will have to ascertain Métis identity on a case-by-case basis. The inquiry must take into account both the value of community self-definition, and the need for the process of identification to be objectively verifiable. In addition, the criteria for Métis identity under s. 35 must reflect the purpose of this constitutional guarantee: to recognize and affirm the rights of the Métis held by virtue of their direct relationship to this country's original inhabitants and by virtue of the continuity between their customs and traditions and those of their Métis predecessors. This is not an insurmountable task.

30   We emphasize that we have not been asked, and we do not purport, to set down a comprehensive definition of who is Métis for the purpose of asserting a claim under s. 35. We therefore limit ourselves to indicating the important components of a future definition, while affirming that the creation of appropriate membership tests *before* disputes arise is an urgent priority. As a general matter, we would endorse the guidelines proposed by Vaillancourt J. and O'Neill J. in the courts below. In particular, we would look to three broad factors as indicia of Métis identity for the purpose of claiming Métis rights under s. 35: self-identification, ancestral connection, and community acceptance.

31   First, the claimant must *self-identify* as a member of a Métis community. This self-identification should not be of recent vintage: While an individual's self-identification need not be static or monolithic, claims that are made belatedly in order to benefit from a s. 35 right will not satisfy the self-identification requirement.

32   Second, the claimant must present evidence of an *ancestral connection* to a historic Métis community. This objective requirement ensures that beneficiaries of s. 35 rights have a real link to the historic community whose practices ground the right being claimed. We would not require a minimum "blood quantum", but we would require some proof that the claimant's ancestors belonged to the historic Métis community by birth, adoption, or other means. Like the trial judge, we would abstain from further defining this requirement in the absence of more extensive argument by the parties in a case where this issue is determinative. In this case, the Powleys' Métis ancestry is not disputed.

33   Third, the claimant must demonstrate that he or she is *accepted by the modern community* whose continuity with the historic community provides the legal foundation for the right being claimed. Membership in a Métis political organization may be relevant to the question of community acceptance, but it is not sufficient in the absence of a contextual understanding of the membership requirements of the organization and its role in the Métis community. The core of community acceptance is past and ongoing participation in a shared culture, in the customs and traditions that constitute a Métis community's identity and distinguish it from other groups. This is what the community membership criterion is all about. Other indicia of community acceptance might include

evidence of participation in community activities and testimony from other members about the claimant's connection to the community and its culture. The range of acceptable forms of evidence does not attenuate the need for an objective demonstration of a solid bond of past and present mutual identification and recognition of common belonging between the claimant and other members of the rights-bearing community.

34   It is important to remember that, no matter how a contemporary community defines membership, only those members with a demonstrable ancestral connection to the historic community can claim a s. 35 right. Verifying membership is crucial, since individuals are only entitled to exercise Métis aboriginal rights by virtue of their ancestral connection to and current membership in a Métis community.

35   In this case, there is no reason to overturn the trial judge's finding that the Powleys are members of the Métis community that arose and still exists in and around Sault Ste. Marie. We agree with the Court of Appeal that, in the circumstances of this case, the fact that the Powleys' ancestors lived on an Indian reserve for a period of time does not negate the Powleys' Métis identity. As the Court of Appeal indicated, "E. B. Borron, commissioned in 1891 by the province to report on annuity payments to the Métis, was of the view that Métis who had taken treaty benefits remained Métis and he recommended that they be removed from the treaty annuity lists" (Sharpe J.A., at para. 139). We emphasize that the individual decision by a Métis person's ancestors to take treaty benefits does not necessarily extinguish that person's claim to Métis rights. It will depend, in part, on whether there was a collective adhesion by the Métis community to the treaty. Based on the record, it was open to the trial judge to conclude that the rights of Powleys' ancestors did not merge into those of the Indian band.

(5) Identification of the Relevant Time Frame
36   As indicated above, the pre-contact aspect of the *Van der Peet* test requires adjustment in order to take account of the post-contact ethnogenesis of the Métis and the purpose of s. 35 in protecting the historically important customs and traditions of these distinctive peoples. While the fact of prior occupation grounds aboriginal rights claims for the Inuit and the Indians, the recognition of Métis rights in s. 35 is not reducible to the Métis' Indian ancestry. The unique status of the Métis as an Aboriginal people with post-contact origins requires an adaptation of the pre-contact approach to meet the distinctive historical circumstances surrounding the evolution of Métis communities.

37   The pre-contact test in *Van der Peet* is based on the constitutional affirmation that aboriginal communities are entitled to continue those practices, customs and traditions that are integral to their distinctive existence or relationship to the land. By analogy, the test for Métis practices should focus on identifying those practices, customs and traditions that are integral to the Métis community's distinctive existence and relationship to the land. This unique history can most appropriately be accommodated by a post contact but pre-control test that identifies the time when Europeans effectively established political and legal control in a particular area. The focus should be on the period after a particular Métis community arose and before it came under the effective control of European laws and customs. This pre-control test enables us to identify those practices, customs and traditions that predate the imposition of European laws and customs on the Métis.

38   We reject the appellant's argument that Métis rights must find their origin in the pre-contact practices of the Métis' aboriginal ancestors. This theory in effect would deny

to Métis their full status as distinctive rights-bearing peoples whose own integral practices are entitled to constitutional protection under s. 35(1). The right claimed here was a practice of both the Ojibway and the Métis. However, as long as the practice grounding the right is distinctive and integral to the pre-control Métis community, it will satisfy this prong of the test. This result flows from the constitutional imperative that we recognize and affirm the aboriginal rights of the Métis, who appeared after the time of first contact. . . .

40   The historical record indicates that the Sault Ste. Marie Métis community thrived largely unaffected by European laws and customs until colonial policy shifted from one of discouraging settlement to one of negotiating treaties and encouraging settlement in the mid-19th century. The trial judge found, and the parties agreed in their pleadings before the lower courts, that "effective control [of the Upper Great Lakes area] passed from the Aboriginal peoples of the area (Ojibway and Métis) to European control" in the period between 1815 and 1850 (para. 90). The record fully supports the finding that the period just prior to 1850 is the appropriate date for finding effective control in this geographic area, which the Crown agreed was the critical date in its pleadings below.

(6) Determination of Whether the Practice is Integral to the Claimants' Distinctive Culture
41   The practice of subsistence hunting and fishing was a constant in the Métis community, even though the availability of particular species might have waxed and waned. The evidence indicates that subsistence hunting was an important aspect of Métis life and a defining feature of their special relationship to the land (Peterson, *supra*, at p. 41; Lytwyn Report, *supra*, at p. 6). A major part of subsistence was the practice at issue here, hunting for food. . . .

44   This evidence supports the trial judge's finding that hunting for food was integral to the Métis way of life at Sault Ste. Marie in the period just prior to 1850.

(7) Establishment of Continuity Between the Historic Practice and the Contemporary Right Asserted
45   Although s. 35 protects "existing" rights, it is more than a mere codification of the common law. Section 35 reflects a new promise: a constitutional commitment to protecting practices that were historically important features of particular aboriginal communities. A certain margin of flexibility might be required to ensure that aboriginal practices can evolve and develop over time, but it is not necessary to define or to rely on that margin in this case. Hunting for food was an important feature of the Sault Ste. Marie Métis community, and the practice has been continuous to the present. Steve and Roddy Powley claim a Métis aboriginal right to hunt for food. The right claimed by the Powleys falls squarely within the bounds of the historical practice grounding the right.

(8) Determination of Whether or not the Right was Extinguished
46   The doctrine of extinguishment applies equally to Métis and to First Nations claims. There is no evidence of extinguishment here, as determined by the trial judge. The Crown's argument for extinguishment is based largely on the Robinson-Huron Treaty of 1850, from which the Métis as a group were explicitly excluded.

(9) If There is a Right, Determination of Whether There is an Infringement
47   Ontario currently does not recognize any Métis right to hunt for food, or any

"special access rights to natural resources" for the Métis whatsoever (appellant's record, at p. 1029). This lack of recognition, and the consequent application of the challenged provisions to the Powleys, infringe their aboriginal right to hunt for food as a continuation of the protected historical practices of the Sault Ste. Marie Métis community.

(10) Determination of Whether the Infringement is Justified

48   The main justification advanced by the appellant is that of conservation. Although conservation is clearly a very important concern, we agree with the trial judge that the record here does not support this justification. If the moose population in this part of Ontario were under threat, and there was no evidence that it is, the Métis would still be entitled to a priority allocation to satisfy their subsistence needs in accordance with the criteria set out in *R. v. Sparrow*, [1990] 1 S.C.R. 1075. While preventative measures might be required for conservation purposes in the future, we have not been presented with evidence to support such measures here. The Ontario authorities can make out a case for regulation of the aboriginal right to hunt moose for food if and when the need arises. On the available evidence and given the current licensing system, Ontario's blanket denial of any Métis right to hunt for food cannot be justified.

49   The appellant advances a subsidiary argument for justification based on the alleged difficulty of identifying who is Métis. As discussed, the Métis identity of a particular claimant should be determined on proof of self-identification, ancestral connection, and community acceptance. The development of a more systematic method of identifying Métis rights-holders for the purpose of enforcing hunting regulations is an urgent priority. That said, the difficulty of identifying members of the Métis community must not be exaggerated as a basis for defeating their rights under the Constitution of Canada.

50   While our finding of a Métis right to hunt for food is not species-specific, the evidence on justification related primarily to the Ontario moose population. The justification of other hunting regulations will require adducing evidence relating to the particular species affected. In the immediate future, the hunting rights of the Métis should track those of the Ojibway in terms of restrictions for conservation purposes and priority allocations where threatened species may be involved. In the longer term, a combination of negotiation and judicial settlement will more clearly define the contours of the Métis right to hunt, a right that we recognize as part of the special aboriginal relationship to the land. . . .

52   The initial stay expired on February 23, 2002, and more than a year has passed since that time. The Court of Appeal's decision has been the law of Ontario in the interim, and chaos does not appear to have ensued. We see no compelling reason to issue an additional stay. We also note that it is particularly important to have a clear justification for a stay where the effect of that stay would be to suspend the recognition of a right that provides a defence to a criminal charge, as it would here.

III. Conclusion

53   Members of the Métis community in and around Sault Ste. Marie have an aboriginal right to hunt for food under s. 35(1). This is determined by their fulfillment of the requirements set out in *Van der Peet*, modified to fit the distinctive purpose of s. 35 in protecting the Métis.

54   The appeal is dismissed with costs to the respondents. The cross-appeal is dismissed.

55   The constitutional question is answered as follows:

Are ss. 46 and 47(1) of the Game and Fish Act, R.S.O. 1990, c. G.1, as they read on October 22, 1993, of no force or effect with respect to the respondents, being Métis, in the circumstances of this case, by reason of their aboriginal rights under s. 35 of the Constitution Act, 1982?
Answer: Yes.

R. v. Blais

2003 SCC 44 (S.C.C.). McLachlin C.J., Gonthier, Iacobucci, Major, Bastarache, Binnie, Arbour, LeBel and Deschamps, JJ., September 19, 2003.

THE COURT—

I. Introduction

1   This case raises the issue of whether the Métis are "Indians" under the hunting rights provisions of the Manitoba *Natural Resources Transfer Agreement*, incorporated as Schedule (1) to the *Constitution Act, 1930* (the "*NRTA*"). We conclude that they are not.

2   On February 10, 1994, Ernest Blais and two other men went hunting for deer in the District of Piney, in the Province of Manitoba. At that time, deer hunting was prohibited in that area by the terms of the wildlife regulations passed pursuant to The *Wildlife Act* of Manitoba, R.S.M. 1987, c. W130, s. 26, as amended by S.M. 1989–90, c. 27, s. 13. Mr. Blais was charged with unlawfully hunting deer out of season.

3   The requisite elements of the offence were conceded at trial. However, the appellant asserted two defences that would have entitled him to acquittal. Both defences were based on his identity as a Métis. First, the appellant argued that, as a Métis, he had an aboriginal right to hunt for food under s. 35 of the *Constitution Act, 1982*. Second, he claimed a constitutional right to hunt for food on unoccupied Crown lands by virtue of para. 13 of the *NRTA*. . . .

5   The trial judge rejected both of the appellant's defences and entered a conviction on August 22, 1996 ([1997] 3 C.N.L.R. 109). The appellant appealed the conviction to the Manitoba Court of Queen's Bench ([1998] 4 C.N.L.R. 103) and to the Manitoba Court of Appeal ([2001] 3 C.N.L.R. 187). His appeals were based solely on the defence that, as a Métis, he is immune from conviction under the *Wildlife Act* regulations in so far as they infringe on his right to hunt for food under para. 13 of the *NRTA*. Both courts rejected this defence and upheld the appellant's conviction.

6   Because we agree that para. 13 of the *NRTA* cannot be read to include the Métis, we would dismiss this appeal. We make no findings with respect to the existence of a Métis right to hunt for food in Manitoba under s. 35 of the *Constitution Act, 1982*, since the appellant chose not to pursue this defence.

II. Analysis

7   Mr. Blais is a "Métis", a member of a distinctive community descended from unions between Europeans and Indians or Inuit. This is agreed by the parties and was con-

firmed by the trial judge. There is no basis for disturbing this finding, particularly as the appellant satisfies the criteria of self-identification, ancestral connection, and community acceptance set out in *R. v. Powley*, 2003 SCC 43. The question is whether, as a Métis, he is entitled to benefit from this hunting provision for "Indians".

8   Paragraph 13 of the *NRTA* reads:

> In order to secure to the Indians of the Province the continuance of the supply of game and fish for their support and subsistence, Canada agrees that the laws respecting game in force in the Province from time to time shall apply to the Indians within the boundaries thereof, provided, however, that the said Indians shall have the right, which the Province hereby assures to them, of hunting, trapping and fishing game and fish for food at all seasons of the year on all unoccupied Crown lands and on any other lands to which the said Indians may have a right of access.
>
> This provision consists of a stipulation and an exception. The stipulation is that "the laws respecting game in force in the Province from time to time shall apply to the <u>Indians</u>" (emphasis added). The exception is the continuing right of the Indians to hunt, trap and fish for food on unoccupied Crown lands "provided, however, that the *said Indians* shall have the right, which the Province hereby assures to them, of hunting, trapping and fishing game and fish for food at all seasons of the year on all unoccupied Crown lands and on any other lands to which the said Indians may have a right of access" (emphasis added).

9   The issue, as stated, is whether the exception addressed to "Indians" applies to the Métis. As we explain in *Powley*, *supra*, at para. 10, the term "Métis" does not designate all individuals with mixed heritage; "rather, it refers to distinctive peoples who, in addition to their mixed ancestry, developed their own customs, way of life, and recognizable group identity separate from their Indian or Inuit and European forebears". Members of Métis communities in the prairie provinces collectively refer to themselves as the "Métis Nation", and trace their roots to the western fur trade: *Report of the Royal Commission on Aboriginal Peoples* (1996), vol. 4, at p. 203 ("*RCAP Report*"). Other Métis communities emerged in eastern Canada: *RCAP Report*; see *Powley*, at para. 10. The sole question before us is whether the appellant, being a Métis, is entitled to benefit from the protection accorded to "Indians" in the *NRTA*. He can claim this benefit only if the term "Indians" in para. 13 encompasses the Métis. . . .

16   Against this background, we turn to the issue before us: whether "Indians" in para. 13 of the *NRTA* include the Métis. The starting point in this endeavour is that a statute— and this includes statutes of constitutional force—must be interpreted in accordance with the meaning of its words, considered in context and with a view to the purpose they were intended to serve: see E.A. Driedger, *Construction of Statutes* (2nd ed. 1983), at p. 87. As P.-A. Côté stated in the third edition of his treatise, "Any interpretation that divorces legal expression from the context of its enactment may produce absurd results" (*The Interpretation of Legislation in Canada* (3rd ed. 2000), at p. 290.

17   The *NRTA* is a constitutional document. It must therefore be read generously within these contextual and historical confines. A court interpreting a constitutionally guaranteed right must apply an interpretation that will fulfill the broad purpose of the guarantee and thus secure "for individuals the full benefit of the [constitutional] protection": *R. v. Big M Drug Mart Ltd.*, [1985] 1 S.C.R. 295, at p. 344. "At the same time it is important not to overshoot the actual purpose of the right or freedom in question, but to recall that the [constitutional provision] was not enacted in a vacuum, and must therefore ... be placed in its proper linguistic, philosophic and historical contexts": *Big M Drug Mart*,

supra, at p. 344. This is essentially the approach the Court used in 1939 when the Court examined the historical record to determine whether the term "Indians" in s. 91(24) of the *British North America Act* includes the Inuit (*Reference as to Whether "Indians" in s. 91 (24) of the British North America Act, 1867 (U.K.), includes Eskimo inhabitants of the Province of Quebec*, [1939] S.C.R. 104).

18   Applied to this case, this means that we must fulfill—but not "overshoot"—the purpose of para. 13 of the *NRTA*. We must approach the task of determining whether Métis are included in "Indians" under para. 13 by looking at the historical context, the ordinary meaning of the language used, and the philosophy or objectives lying behind it.

(1) Historical Context

19   The *NRTA* was not a grant of title, but an administrative transfer of the responsibilities that the Crown acknowledged at the time towards "the Indians within the boundaries" of the Province—a transfer with constitutional force. In ascertaining which group or groups the parties to the *NRTA* intended to designate by the term "Indians", we must look at the prevailing understandings of Crown obligations and the administrative regimes that applied to the different Aboriginal groups in Manitoba. The record suggests that the Métis were treated as a different group from "Indians" for purposes of delineating rights and protections.

20   The courts below found, and the record confirms, that the Manitoba Métis were not considered wards of the Crown. This was true both from the perspective of the Crown, and from the perspective of the Métis. . . .

22   The *Manitoba Act, 1870* used the term "half-breed" to refer to the Métis, and set aside land specifically for their use: *Manitoba Act, 1870*, S.C. 1870, c. 3 s. 31 (reprinted in R.S.C. 1985. App. II, No. 8). While s. 31 states that this land is being set aside "towards the extinguishment of the Indian Title to the lands in the Province", this was expressly recognized at the time as being an inaccurate description. . . .

23   Other evidence in the record corroborates this view. For example, at trial, the expert witness Dr. G. Ens attached to his report a book written by Lieutenant-Governor A. Morris entitled *The Treaties of Canada with the Indians of Manitoba and the North-West Territories*, published in 1880. The book includes an account of negotiations between the Governor and an Indian Chief who expresses the concern that his mixed-blood offspring might not benefit from the proposed treaty. The Governor explains, at p. 69: "I am sent here to treat with the Indians. In Red River, where I came from, and where there is a great body of Half-breeds, they must be either white or Indian. If Indians, they get treaty money; if the Half-breeds call themselves white, they get land". This statement supports the view that Indians and Métis were widely understood as distinct groups for the purpose of determining their entitlements vis-à-vis the colonial administration.

24   It could be argued that the ability of individual Métis to identify themselves with Indian bands and to claim treaty rights on this basis weighs against a view of the two groups as entirely distinct. However, the very fact that a Métis person could "choose" either an Indian or a white identity supports the view that a Métis person was not considered Indian in the absence of an individual act of voluntary association. . . .

26   Placing para. 13 in its proper historical context does not involve negating the rights of the Métis. Paragraph 13 is not the only source of the Crown's or the Province's obliga-

tions towards Aboriginal peoples. Other constitutional and statutory provisions are better suited, and were actually intended, to fulfill this more wide-ranging purpose. The sole issue before us is whether the term "Indians" in the NRTA includes the Métis. The historical context of the *NRTA* suggests that it does not.

(2) Language

27   The common usage of the term "Indian" in 1930 also argues against a view of this term as encompassing the Métis. Both the terms "Indian" and "half-breed" were used in the mid-nineteenth century. Swail J. cites a North American census prepared by the Hudson's Bay Company in 1856–57 (pp. 146–47). The census records 147,000 "Indians", and breaks this down into various groups, including "The Plain Tribes", "The Esquimaux", "Indians settled in Canada", and so forth. A separate line indicates the number of "Whites and half-breeds in Hudson's Bay Territory", which is estimated at 11,000, for a total of 158,000 "souls". This document illustrates that the "Whites and half-breeds" were viewed as an identifiable group, separate and distinct from the Indians.

28   The Red River Métis distinguished themselves from the Indians. For example, the successive Lists of Rights prepared by Métis leaders at the time of the creation of the Province of Manitoba excluded "the Indians" from voting. This provision could not plausibly have been intended to disenfranchise the Métis, who were the authors of the Lists and the majority of the population. The Third and Fourth Lists of Rights emphasized the importance of concluding treaties "between Canada and the different Indian tribes of the Province," with the "advice and cooperation of the Local Legislature" (appellant's record, at pp. 272 and 275). The Local Legislature was, at that time, a Métis-dominated body, underscoring the Métis' own view of themselves and the Indians as fundamentally distinct. . . .

30   . . . Quite apart from formal rules of statutory construction, common sense dictates that the content of a provision will in some way be related to its heading. Paragraph 13 falls under the heading "Indian Reserves." Indian reserves were set aside for the use and benefit of Status Indians, not for the Métis. The placement of para. 13 in the part of the *NRTA* entitled "Indian Reserves", along with two other provisions that clearly do not apply to the Métis, supports the view that the term "Indian" as used throughout this part was not seen as including the Métis. This placement weighs against the argument that we should construe the term "Indians" more broadly than otherwise suggested by the historical context of the *NRTA* and the common usage of the term at the time of the *NRTA*'s enactment.

31   We find no basis in the record for overturning the lower courts' findings that, as a general matter, the terms "Indian" and "half-breed" were used to refer to separate and distinguishable groups of people in Manitoba from the mid-19th century through the period in which the *NRTA* was negotiated and enacted.

(3) The NRTA*'s Objectives*

32   The purpose of para. 13 of the *NRTA* is to ensure respect for the Crown's obligations to "Indians" with respect to hunting rights. It was enacted to protect the hunting rights of the beneficiaries of Indian treaties and the Indian Act in the context of the transfer of Crown land to the provinces. It took away the right to hunt commercially while protecting the right to hunt for food and expanding the territory upon which this

could take place: see *Frank, supra,* at p. 100; *Moosehunter, supra,* at p. 285; *Horseman, supra,* at pp. 931–32; and *Badger, supra,* at para. 45. . . .

33   The protection accorded by para. 13 was based on the special relationship between Indians and the Crown. Underlying this was the view that Indians required special protection and assistance. Rightly or wrongly, this view did not extend to the Métis. The Métis were considered more independent and less in need of Crown protection than their Indian neighbours, as Wright J. confirmed. Shared ancestry between the Métis and the colonizing population, and the Métis' own claims to a different political status than the Indians in their Lists of Rights, contributed to this perception. The stark historic fact is that the Crown viewed its obligations to Indians, whom it considered its wards, as different from its obligations to the Métis, who were its negotiating partners in the entry of Manitoba into Confederation.

34   This perceived difference between the Crown's obligations to Indians and its relationship with the Métis was reflected in separate arrangements for the distribution of land. Different legal and political regimes governed the conclusion of Indian treaties and the allocation of Métis scrip. Indian treaties were concluded on a collective basis and entailed collective rights, whereas scrip entitled recipients to individual grants of land. While the history of scrip speculation and devaluation is a sorry chapter in our nation's history, this does not change the fact that scrip was based on fundamentally different assumptions about the nature and origins of the government's relationship with scrip recipients than the assumptions underlying treaties with Indians.

35   The historical context of the *NRTA,* the language of the section, and the purpose that led to its inclusion in the *Constitution Act, 1930* support the lower courts' conclusion that para. 13 does not encompass the Métis.

D. Appellant's Counter-Arguments

(1) Continuity of Language

36   The appellant asks us to impose a "continuity of language" requirement on the Constitution as a whole in order to support his argument that the term "Indians" in the *NRTA* includes the Métis. We do not find this approach persuasive. To the contrary, imposing a continuity requirement would lead us to conclude that "Indians" and "Métis" are different, since they are separately enumerated in s. 35(2) of the *Constitution Act, 1982.* We emphasize that we leave open for another day the question of whether the term "Indians" in s. 91(24) of the *Constitution Act, 1867* includes the Métis—an issue not before us in this appeal. . . .

3) The "Living Tree" Principle

39   We decline the appellant's invitation to expand the historical purpose of para. 13 on the basis of the "living tree" doctrine enunciated by Viscount Sankey with reference to the 1867 British North America Act: *Edwards* v. *Attorney-General for Canada,* [1930] A.C. 124, at p. 136. The appellant, emphasizing the constitutional nature of para. 13, argues that this provision must be read broadly as providing solutions to future problems. He argues that, regardless of para. 13's original meaning, contemporary values, including the recognition of the Crown's fiduciary duty towards Aboriginal peoples and general principles of restitutive justice, require us to interpret the word "Indians" as including the Métis.

40   This Court has consistently endorsed the living tree principle as a fundamental tenet of constitutional interpretation. Constitutional provisions are intended to provide "a continuing framework for the legitimate exercise of governmental power": *Hunter* v. *Southam Inc.*, [1984] 2 S.C.R. 145, per Dickson J. (as he then was), at p. 155. But at the same time, this Court is not free to invent new obligations foreign to the original purpose of the provision at issue. The analysis must be anchored in the historical context of the provision. As emphasized above, we must heed Dickson J.'s admonition "not to overshoot the actual purpose of the right or freedom in question, but to recall that the Charter was not enacted in a vacuum, and must therefore ... be placed in its proper linguistic, philosophic and historical contexts": *Big M Drug Mart, supra*, at p. 344; see *Côté, supra*, at p. 265. Dickson J. was speaking of the Charter, but his words apply equally to the task of interpreting the *NRTA*. Similarly, Binnie J. emphasized the need for attentiveness to context when he noted in *R. v. Marshall*, [1999] 3 S.C.R. 456, at para. 14, that "'[g]enerous' rules of interpretation should not be confused with a vague sense of after-the-fact largesse." Again the statement, made with respect to the interpretation of a treaty, applies here.

41   We conclude that the term "Indians" in para. 13 of the *NRTA* does not include the Métis, and we find no basis for modifying this intended meaning. This in no way precludes a more liberal interpretation of other constitutional provisions, depending on their particular linguistic, philosophical and historical contexts.

III. Conclusion

42   We find no reason to disturb the lower courts' findings that neither the Crown nor the Métis understood the term "Indians" to encompass the Métis in the decades leading up to and including the enactment of the *NRTA*. Paragraph 13 does not provide a defence to the charge against the appellant for unlawfully hunting deer out of season. We do not preclude the possibility that future Métis defendants could argue for site-specific hunting rights in various areas of Manitoba under s. 35 of the *Constitution Act, 1982*, subject to the evidentiary requirements set forth in *Powley, supra*. However, they cannot claim immunity from prosecution under the Manitoba wildlife regulations by virtue of para. 13 of the *NRTA*.

43   The appeal is dismissed. Each party shall bear its own costs.

44   The constitutional question is answered as follows:

Is the appellant Ernest Lionel Joseph Blais, being a Métis, encompassed by the term "Indians" in para. 13 of the Natural Resources Transfer Agreement, 1930, as ratified by the Manitoba *Natural Resources Act,* (1930) 20–21 Geo. V, c. 29 (Can.) and confirmed by the *Constitution Act (1930)*, 20–21 Geo. V, c. 26 (U.K.), and therefore rendering s. 26 of the *Wildlife Act* of Manitoba unconstitutional to the extent that it infringes upon the appellant's right to hunt for food for himself and his family?
    Answer: No.

Constitution of Alberta Amendment Act
1990, S.A. c. C–22.2.

WHEREAS the Metis were present when the Province of Alberta was established and they and the land set aside for their use form a unique part of the history and culture of the Province; and

WHEREAS it is desired that the Metis should continue to have a land base to provide for the preservation and enhancement of Metis culture and identity and to enable the Metis to attain self-governance under the laws of Alberta and, to that end, Her Majesty in right of Alberta is granting title to land to the Metis Settlements General Council; and

WHEREAS Her Majesty in right of Alberta has proposed the land so granted be protected by the Constitution of Canada, but until that happens it is proper that the land be protected by the constitution of the Province; and

WHEREAS section 45 of the Constitution Act, 1982 empowers the legislature of a province, subject to section 41 of that Act, to amend the constitution of the province; and

WHEREAS nothing in this Act, the Metis Settlements Land Protection Act, the Metis Settlements Accord Implementation Act or the Metis Settlements Act is to be construed so as to abrogate or derogate from any aboriginal rights referred to in section 35 of the Constitution Act, 1982;

NOW THEREFORE HER MAJESTY, by and with the advice and consent of the Legislative Assembly of Alberta, enacts as follows:

Constitution amended

1   The constitution of Alberta is amended by this Act.

Definition

2   In this Act, "Metis settlement land" means land held in fee simple by the Metis Settlements General Council under letters patent from Her Majesty in right of Alberta.

Expropriation

3   The fee simple estate in Metis settlement land, or any interest in it less than fee simple, may not be acquired through expropriation by Her Majesty in right of Alberta or any person, but an interest less than fee simple may be acquired in that land in a manner permitted by the *Metis Settlements Land Protection Act*.

Exemption from seizure

4   The fee simple estate in Metis settlement land is exempt from seizure and sale under court order, writ of execution or any other process whether judicial or extra-judicial.

Restriction on Legislative Assembly

5   The Legislative Assembly may not pass any Bill that would
   (a) amend or repeal the Metis Settlements Land Protection Act,
   (b) alter or revoke letters patent granting Metis settlement land to the Metis Settlements General Council, or
   (c) dissolve the Metis Settlements General Council or result in its being composed of persons who are not settlement members, without the agreement of the Metis Settlements General Council.

Application of laws
6   Nothing in this Act shall be construed as limiting

   (a) the application of the laws of Alberta to, or

(b) the jurisdiction of the Legislature to enact laws in and for Alberta applicable to, the Metis settlement land and any activities on or in respect of that land, except to the extent necessary to give effect to this Act.

Power to affect Act

7 A Bill that would amend or repeal this Act may be passed by the Legislative Assembly of Alberta only after a plebiscite of settlement members under the Election Act where a majority of the members of each settlement vote in favour of the subject-matter of the Bill.

Repeal

8 Notwithstanding section 7, this Act may be repealed by the Legislature after the Metis settlement land is protected by the Constitution of Canada.

Coming into force

7 This Act comes into force on Proclamation.

*Metis Settlements Act**
R.S.A. 2000, c. M-14 (Alberta).

. . .

2 (2) Each settlement consists of the persons who are settlement members of that settlement. . . .

3 (1) Subject to this Act, a settlement has the rights, powers and privileges of a natural person.

(2) A settlement council may carry out the following activities only if it is permitted to do so under subsection (3):
(a) engage in commercial activities,
(b) make investments other than those described in Schedule 2,
(c) lend money,
(d) borrow money,
(e) guarantee the repayment of a loan by a lender to someone other than the settlement, or
(f) guarantee the payment of interest on a loan by a lender to someone other than the settlement.

(3) A settlement council may do some or all of the activities described in subsection (2) if
(a) a regulation passed under section 239 or 240 approves the activity, or
(b) the activity is
(i) authorized by a General Council Policy, and
(ii) permitted by a settlement by-law. . .

8 (1) Each settlement has a settlement council composed of 5 councillors.

(2) A settlement council is a continuing body. . . .

---

* Proclaimed on November 1, 1990, the *Metis Settlements Act* is part of a package of Alberta legislation that seeks to provide a governance and land tenure regime for Métis in Alberta.

10 (1) At the organizational meeting of a settlement council after an annual election, the councillors must elect a settlement chairman from among themselves. . . .

12 (1) An annual election must be held for each settlement council.

Election procedure

13 (1) Councillors must be elected to a settlement council in accordance with the *Local Authorities Election Act* and this Act.

(2) If there is inconsistency between this Act and the *Local Authorities Election Act*, this Act prevails.

(3) If the *Local Authorities Election Act* or this Act cannot be applied to an election under this Act, the Minister may make regulations governing the matter.

Eligibility to vote

14 No person is eligible to vote at an annual election or by-election unless that person
   (a) is a settlement member,
   (b) has resided in the settlement area for the 12 months immediately preceding election day, or any lesser period prescribed in a settlement by-law, and
   (c) has his or her principal residence in the settlement area on election day. . . .

50 (1) Except where the context otherwise requires, the by-law making authority of a settlement council is confined to the geographic area of the settlement. . . .

51 A settlement council may make by-laws respecting
   (a) the matters set out in Schedule 1;
   (b) the matters described or referred to elsewhere in this Act and in other enactments. . . .

72 (1) A by-law or resolution that is inconsistent with this Act or any other enactment is of no effect to the extent of the inconsistency, unless it is a by-law or resolution to implement a General Council Policy on hunting, trapping, fishing or gathering.

(2) A by-law or resolution that is inconsistent with a General Council Policy is of no effect to the extent of the inconsistency.

Regulations

73 The Minister may, in accordance with section 240, make regulations
   (a) respecting an administrative and employment policy to be followed by the settlement council and its employees;
   (b) respecting payments to be made to councillors, settlement employees and representatives of a settlement. . . .

74 (1) A person may apply to a settlement council for membership in a settlement only if
   (a) the applicant is a Metis and at least 18 years old, and
   (b) the applicant
       (i) has previously been a settlement member or a member of a settlement association under the former Act, or
       (ii) has lived in Alberta for the 5 years immediately preceding the date of application. . . .

75 (1) An Indian registered under the *Indian Act* (Canada) or a person who is registered as an Inuk for the purposes of a land claims settlement is not eligible to apply for membership or to be recorded as a settlement member unless subsection (2) applies.

(2) An Indian registered under the *Indian Act* (Canada) or a person who is registered as an Inuk for the purposes of a land claims settlement may be approved as a settlement member if

(a)   the person was registered as an Indian or an Inuk when less than 18 years old,

(b)   the person lived a substantial part of his or her childhood in the settlement area,

(c)   one or both parents of the person are, or at their death were, members of the settlement, and

(d)   the person has been approved for membership by a settlement by-law specifically authorizing the admission of that individual as a member of the settlement.

(3) If a person who is registered as an Indian under the *Indian Act* (Canada) is able to apply to have his or her name removed from registration, subsection (2) ceases to be available as a way to apply for or to become a settlement member. . . .

76 Every application for membership in a settlement must be sent to the settlement office and must be accompanied by

(a)   a statutory declaration that

  (i)   the applicant has Canadian aboriginal ancestry, describing the facts on which the declaration is based, and

  (ii) the applicant identifies with Métis history and culture;

(b)   one or more of the following:

  (i)   genealogical records as evidence that the applicant has aboriginal ancestry;

  (ii) a statutory declaration of at least 2 Métis who are recognized as Métis elders that the applicant has aboriginal ancestry, describing the facts on which the declaration is made;

  (iii) such other evidence satisfactory to the settlement council that the applicant has aboriginal ancestry; . . .

214 (1) The Metis Settlements General Council is established as a corporation.

(2) The General Council consists of the councillors of all the settlement councils and the officers of the General Council. . . .

239 (1) A regulation to be made in accordance with this section may be made, amended or repealed only if the General Council requests the Minister to make the regulation.

(2) The Minister may make, amend or repeal a regulation without a request under subsection (1) if the regulation, amendment or repeal is required to protect the public interest.

(3) Before making, amending or repealing a regulation under subsection (1) or (2), the Minister must

(a)   provide the General Council with notice in writing and a copy of the proposed regulation, and

(b)   give due consideration to written suggestions about the regulation that are received from the General Council within 45 days of the notice. . . .

240 (1) A regulation to be made in accordance with this section may be made, amended or repealed only if the General Council or a settlement council requests the Minister to make the regulation.

(2) The Minister may make, amend or repeal a regulation without a request under subsection (1) if the regulation, amendment or repeal is required to protect the public interest. . .

Schedule 1

By-Laws

By-law Making Authority of Settlement Councils
General governance

1   A settlement council may make by-laws for the general governance of the settlement area. . . .

2   A settlement council may make by-laws for the internal management of the settlement, including. . . .

3   A settlement council may make by-laws
    (a) describing the circumstances when a settlement member who is on an authorized leave of absence is not considered to be a resident of the settlement area;
    (b) respecting the establishment of holidays in a settlement area;
    (c) describing the persons who have a right to live on patented land in addition to those described in section 92;
    (d) respecting those matters that may, by this or any other enactment, be subject to a settlement by-law.

Health, safety and welfare

4   A settlement council may make by-laws to promote the health, safety and welfare of the residents of the settlement area.

Public order and safety

5   A settlement council may make by-laws respecting public order and safety, including by-laws
    (a) prohibiting or regulating the discharge of firearms as defined in section 84(1) of the Criminal Code (Canada);
    (b) prohibiting or regulating activities or conduct offensive to or not in the public interest as determined by the council;
    (c) establishing curfews for children who are not accompanied by a parent or appropriate guardian and providing for penalties in respect of parents or guardians whose children contravene the by-law.

Fire protection

6   A settlement council may make by-laws to prevent and extinguish fires, preserve life and property and protect persons from injury or destruction by fire, including. . . .

Nuisances and pests

7   A settlement council may make by-laws
    (a) prohibiting unsightly or untidy land or buildings or anything on land that is

unsightly or untidy;
(b) prohibiting or regulating noise generally or during specified periods throughout or in designated areas of the settlement area;
(c) requiring or providing for the removal or burning of trees or shrubs that may interfere with settlement works or utilities;
(d) regulating or controlling activities for the purpose of eliminating or mitigating animal or insect pests and diseases.

Animals

8   A settlement council may make by-laws
(a) preventing the leading, riding and driving of cattle or horses in any public place;
(b) prohibiting or regulating the running at large of dogs and other animals. . . .
(c) regulating the keeping by any person of poultry or wild or domestic animals;
(d) prohibiting the keeping by any person of poultry or wild or domestic animals in any specified part or parts of the settlement area when, in the opinion of the council, that keeping is likely to cause a nuisance;
(e) preventing cruelty to animals.

Airports

9   A settlement council, subject to any Act of the Parliament of Canada, may make by-laws establishing, controlling, operating or maintaining an airport, aerodrome or seaplane base.

Posters and advertising

10   A settlement council may make by-laws (a) prohibiting or regulating the posting or exhibition of pictures, posters or other material; ....

Refuse disposal

11   (1) A settlement council may make by-laws
(a) defining "refuse" for the purpose of this section and the by-laws;
(b) prohibiting or regulating the placement or depositing of refuse;
(c) regulating the activities or use of waste disposal sites established by the settlement council;
(d) establishing and regulating a system for the collection and disposal of refuse. . . .

Public health

12   A settlement council may make by-laws
(a) respecting the health of the residents of the settlement area and against the spread of diseases;
(b) regulating and controlling the use of wells, springs and other sources of water for the settlement area and preventing the contamination of it or of any water in the settlement area;
(c) compelling the removal of dirt, filth or refuse or any other obstruction from public rights of way or private roads by the person depositing it and providing for its removal at the expense of that person if he or she fails to remove it;
(d) compelling the removal from any place within the settlement area of anything considered dangerous to the health or lives of the inhabitants.

Parks and recreation

13 A settlement council may make by-laws respecting the regulating of activities and equipment in
    (a) parks or recreation areas;
    (b) trailer courts or mobile home parks;
    (c) campgrounds;
    (d) exhibition or rodeo grounds.

Control of business

14 (1) A settlement council may make by-laws to control and regulate businesses, industries and activities carried on in the settlement area, including . . .

Sewerage system fees

16 (1) A settlement council may by by-law impose a service charge payable by all persons occupying property connected to the sewerage system of the settlement. . . .

17 A settlement council may by by-law impose special levies for the purposes of providing recreation and community services and facilities to residents, and may provide for the charging of admissions or the raising of funds as the council may decide.

Planning, land use and development by-laws

18 A settlement council may make by-laws
    (a) establishing a general plan for land use and development in a settlement area;
    (b) prohibiting or regulating and controlling the use and development of land and buildings in the settlement area;
    (c) authorizing the settlement council, or a person designated by it, to prohibit the development or use of land or buildings if there are inadequate arrangements for access to, and for utilities and other services to, the land or buildings.

By-laws under a General Council Policy

19 If there is a General Council Policy in effect, a settlement council may, in accordance with that Policy, make by-laws
    (a) prohibiting persons who are not settlement members from hunting, trapping, gathering or fishing in the settlement area;
    (b) prescribing the terms and conditions under which a person or class of person is permitted to occupy, hunt, trap, gather or fish in the settlement area;
    (c) prescribing the manner in which and the terms and conditions subject to which a settlement member may acquire
        (i) the right to trap, hunt or gather in the settlement area;
        (ii) the right to fish in a marsh, pond, lake, stream or creek in the settlement area and the circumstances under which that right may be suspended, limited or revoked;
    (d) as to the use by settlement members of a part of the land allocated for occupation by a settlement council in respect of which no person has the exclusive right of occupation;
    (e) respecting the cutting of timber on all or part of the settlement area, . . .

Métis Act
S.S. 2001, c. M-14.01 (Saskatchewan).

WHEREAS the existing Aboriginal rights of Métis people are protected pursuant to section 35 of the Constitution Act, 1982;

AND WHEREAS the Government of Saskatchewan wishes to work in partnership with the Government of Canada and the Métis people to promote and strengthen the capacity for Métis governance of Métis institutions and communities;

AND WHEREAS, pursuant to section 14.1 of *The Interpretation Act, 1995*, nothing in this Act is to be construed as abrogating or derogating from the existing Aboriginal rights of Métis people mentioned in section 35 of the Constitution Act, 1982;

AND WHEREAS nothing in this Act is to be construed as altering or affecting the position of the Government of Saskatchewan that legislative authority in relation to Métis people rests with the Government of Canada pursuant to section 91(24) of the *Constitution Act, 1867*;

THEREFORE HER MAJESTY, by and with the advice and consent of the Legislative Assembly of Saskatchewan, enacts as follows:

Part I
Short Title

Short title

1 This Act may be cited as The Métis Act.

Part II
Recognition of Métis Contributions

Recognition of Métis contributions

2 The purpose of this Part is to recognize the contributions of the Métis people to the development and prosperity of Canada, including:
   (a) the rich and evolving history of the Métis people;
   (b) the cultural distinctiveness of the Métis communities and traditional ways of life of the Métis people;
   (c) the importance of the languages of the Métis people, including the Michif language, to Canada's culture and heritage;
   (d) the distinctive culture and cultural legacy of the Métis people, as symbolized by the Métis flag, the Métis sash, the Red River cart, the fiddle and the Red River jig;
   (e) the significance of the Métis farms and the Batoche historic site;
   (f) the honourable and invaluable service of the Métis veterans during the two World Wars and the Korean War and in many peace-keeping missions around the world;
   (g) the importance of Métis entrepreneurs to Canada's economy, beginning in the 18th Century with the historic involvement of the Métis in the North West fur trade;
   (h) the leadership role of Métis institutions in providing educational, social and health services to Métis people, and the contribution of those institutions to the delivery of those services; and

(i)   the important contribution of the Métis Nation – Saskatchewan in representing the needs and aspirations of the Métis people.

Part III
Bilateral Process

Bilateral process

3   (1) The Government of Saskatchewan and the Métis Nation – Saskatchewan will work together through a bilateral process to address issues that are important to the Métis people, including the following:
(a)   capacity building;
(b)   land;
(c)   harvesting;
(d)   governance.

(2) Where the Government of Saskatchewan and the Métis Nation – Saskatchewan consider it appropriate, they may enter into a memorandum of understanding that reflects the discussions resulting from the bilateral process mentioned in subsection (1).

Part IV
Métis Nation – Saskatchewan Secretariat Inc.

. . .

MNS Secretariat Inc. established

5   (1) The Métis Nation – Saskatchewan Secretariat Inc. is established pursuant to this Act as a body corporate without share capital.

(2) The Corporation is the administrative body by which the policies and programs of the Métis Nation – Saskatchewan may be carried out and administered.

Powers

6   Subject to this Act, the corporation has the capacity, rights, powers and privileges of a natural person.

Board of directors

7   (1) The board of directors consists of three persons who are members of the Provincial Métis Council of the Métis Nation – Saskatchewan.

(2) The board of directors shall direct and manage the activities and affairs of the corporation.

(3) The board of directors shall formalize its decisions by resolution or bylaw.

Bylaws

8   Bylaws shall be made for the governance the proper administration of the corporation's activities, affairs, property and interests. . . .

THE INUIT

Indian Act
R.S.C. 1985, c. I–5, s. 4(1).

4.   (1) A reference in this Act to an Indian does not include any person of the race of aborigines commonly referred to as Inuit. . . .

Re Eskimos
[1939] S.C.R. 104 (S.C.C.). Duff C.J.C., Cannon, Crocket, Davis, Kerwin, and Hudson JJ., April 5, 1939

SIR LYMAN P. DUFF C.J.C.:—The reference with which we are concerned arises out of a controversy between the Dominion and the Province of Quebec touching the question whether the Eskimo inhabitants of that Province are "Indians" within the contemplation of head no. 24 of s. 91 of the *B.N.A. Act* which is in these words, "Indians and Lands Reserved for Indians"; and under the reference we are to pronounce upon that question. Among the inhabitants of the three Provinces, Nova Scotia, New Brunswick and Canada that, by the immediate operation of the *B.N.A. Act* became subject to the constitutional enactments of that statute there were few, if any, Eskimo. But the *B.N.A. Act* contemplated the eventual admission into the Union of other parts of British North America as is explicitly declared in the preamble and for which provision is made by s. 146 thereof.

The Eskimo population of Quebec, with which we are now concerned, inhabits (in the northern part of the Province) a territory that in 1867 formed part of Rupert's Land; and the question we have to determine is whether these Eskimo, whose ancestors were aborigines of Rupert's Land in 1867 and at the time of its annexation to Canada, are Indians in the sense mentioned.

In 1867 the Eskimo population of what is now Canada, then between four and five thousand in number, occupied, as at the present time, the northern littoral of the continent from Alaska to, and including part of, the Labrador coast within the territories under the control of the Hudson's Bay Co., that is to say, in Rupert's Land and the North-Western Territory which, under the authority given by s. 146 of the *B.N.A. Act* were acquired by Canada in 1871. In addition to these Eskimo in Rupert's Land and the North-Western Territory, there were some hundreds of them on that part of the coast of Labrador (east of Hudson Strait) which formed part of, and was subject to the Government of, Newfoundland. The *B.N.A. Act* is a statute dealing with British North America, and, in determining the meaning of the word "Indians" in the statute, we have to consider the meaning of that term as applied to the inhabitants of British North America. In 1867 more than half of the Indian population of British North America were within the boundaries of Rupert's Land and the North-Western Territory; and of the Eskimo population nearly 90% were within those boundaries. It is, therefore, important to consult the reliable sources of information as to the usage of the term "Indian" in relation to the Eskimo in those territories. Fortunately, there is evidence of the most authoritative character furnished by the Hudson's Bay Co. itself.

It will be recalled that the Hudson's Bay Co., besides being a trading company, possessed considerable powers of government and administration. Some years before the passing of the *B.N.A. Act* complaints having been made as to the manner in which these responsibilities had been discharged, a committee of the House of Commons in 1856 and 1857 investigated the affairs of the company. Among the matters which naturally engaged the attention of the Committee was the company's relations with and conduct towards the aborigines; and for the information of the Committee a census was prepared and produced before it by the officers of the company showing the Indian populations under its rule throughout the whole of the North American continent. This census was accompanied by a map showing the "location" of the various tribes and was included in the Report of the Committee; and was made an appendix to the Committee's Report which was printed and published by the order of the House of Commons. It is indisputable that in the census and in the map the "Esquimaux" fall under the general designation "Indians" and that, indeed, in these documents, "Indians" is used as synonymous with "aborigines." The map bears this description, "An Aboriginal Map of North America denoting the boundaries and locations of various Indian Tribes." Among these "Indian Tribes" the Eskimo are shown inhabiting the northern littoral of the continent from Labrador to Russian America. In the margin of the map are tables. Two are of great significance. The first of these is headed "Statement of the Indian Tribes of the Hudson's Bay Territories." The tribes "East of the Rocky Mountains" are given as "Blackfeet and Sioux groups comprising eight tribes, Algonquins comprising twelve tribes" and "Esquimaux."

The second is headed "Indian Nations once dwelling East of the Mississippi." The list is as follows:

Algonquin	Uchee (extinct)	Kolooch
Dahcotah or Sioux	Natches (extinct)	Athabascan
Huron Iroquois	Mobilian	Sioux
Catawba (extinct)	Esquimaux	Iroquois
Cherokee		

The census concludes with a summary which is in these words: The Indian Races shown in detail in the foregoing census may be classified as follows:

Thickwood Indians on the east side of the Rocky Mountains	35,000
The Plain Tribes (Blackfeet, etc.)	25,000
The Esquimaux	4,000
Indians settled in Canada	3,000
Indian in British Oregon and on the North West Coast	80,000
Total Indians	147,000
Whites and half-breeds in Hudson's Bay Territory	11,000
Souls	158,000

. . . The B.N.A. Act came into force on July 1, 1867, and, in December of that year, a joint address to Her Majesty was voted by the Senate and House of Commons of Canada praying that authority might be granted to the Parliament of Canada to legislate for the future welfare and good government of these regions and expressing the willingness of Parliament to assume the duties and obligations of government and legislation as regards those territories. In the Resolution of the Senate expressing the willingness of that body to concur in the joint address is this paragraph: "Resolved that upon the transference of the Territories in question to the Canadian Government, it will be the duty of the Government to make adequate provisions for the protection of the Indian Tribes, whose interest and well being are involved in the transfer."

By Order-in-Council of June 23, 1870, it was ordered that from and after July 15, 1870, the North-West Territory and Rupert's Land should be admitted into, and become part of, the Dominion of Canada and that, from that date, the Parliament of Canada should have full power and authority to legislate for the future welfare and good government of the territory. As regards Rupert's Land, such authority had already been conferred upon the Parliament of Canada by s. 5 of the Rupert's Land Act of 1868.

The vast territories which by these transactions became part of the Dominion of Canada and were brought under the jurisdiction of the Parliament of Canada were inhabited largely, indeed almost entirely, by aborigines. It appears to me to be a consideration of great weight in determining the meaning of the word "Indians" in the *B.N.A. Act* that, as we have seen, the Eskimo were recognized as an Indian tribe by the officials of the Hudson's Bay Co. which, in 1867, as already observed, exercised powers of government and administration over this great tract; and that, moreover, this employment of the term "Indians" is evidenced in a most unequivocal way by documents prepared by those officials and produced before the Select Committee of the House of Commons which were included in the Report of that Committee which, again, as already mentioned, was printed and published by the order of the House. It is quite clear from the material before us that this Report was the principal source of information as regards the aborigines in those territories until some years after Confederation.

I turn now to the Eskimo inhabiting the coast of Labrador beyond the confines of the Hudson's Bay territories and within the boundaries and under the Government of Newfoundland. As regards these, the evidence appears to be conclusive that, for a period beginning about 1760 and extending down to a time subsequent to the passing of the B.N.A. Act, they were by governors, commanders-in-chief of the fleet and other naval officers, ecclesiastics, missionaries and traders who came into contact with them, known and classified as Indians.

First of the official documents. In 1762, General Murray, then Governor of Quebec, who afterwards became first Governor of Canada, in an official report of the state of the Government of Quebec deals under the sixth heading with "Indian nations residing within the government." He introduces the discussion with this sentence: "In order to discuss this point more clearly I shall first take notice of the Savages on the North shore of the River St. Lawrence from the Ocean upwards, and then of such as inhabit the South side of the same River, as far as the present limits of the Government extend on either side of it."

In the first and second paragraphs he deals with the "Savages" on the North Shore and he says: "The first to be met with on this are the Esquimaux." In the second paragraph he deals with the Montagnais who inhabited a "vast tract" of country from Labrador to the Saguenay.

It is clear that here the Eskimo are classified under the generic term Indian. They are called "Savages," it is true, but so are the Montagnais and so also the Hurons settled at Jeune Lorette. It is useful to note that he speaks in the first paragraph of the Esquimaux as "the wildest and most untamable of any" and mentions that they are "emphatically styled by the other Nations, Savages."

Then there are two reports to His Majesty by the Lords of Trade. The first, dated June 8,1763, discusses the trade carried on by the French on the coast of Labrador. It is said that they carried on "an extensive trade with the Esquimaux Indians in Oyl, Furs, & ca. [sic] (in which they allowed Your Majesty's Subjects no Share)."

In the second, dated April 16, 1765, in dealing with complaints on the part of the Court of France respecting the French fishery on the coast of Newfoundland and in the Gulf of St. Lawrence, their observations on these complaints are based upon information furnished by Commodore Palliser who had been entrusted with the superintendency of the Newfoundland fishery and the Government of the island. In this report, this sentence occurs: "The sixth and last head of complaint contained in the French Ambassador's letter is, that a captain of a certain French vessel was forbid by your Majesty's Governor from having commerce with the Esquimaux Indians"; and upon that it is observed that the Governor "is to be commended for having forbid the subjects of France to trade or treat with these Indians." "These Indians" are spoken of as inhabitants ". . .who are under the protection of and dependent upon your Majesty."

Then there is a series of proclamations by successive Governors and Commanders-in-Chief in Newfoundland, the first of which was that of Sir Hugh Palliser of July 1, 1764. . . .

There are other official documents. In a report in 1798 by Captain Crofton, addressed to Admiral Waldegrave, Governor and Commander-in-Chief of Newfoundland, the phrase "Esquimaux Indians" occurs several times and the Eskimo are plainly treated as coming under the designation "Indians." A report to Lord Dorchester, Governor and Commander-in-Chief of Quebec, Nova Scotia, New Brunswick and their dependencies, in 1788, upon an application by George Cartwright for a grant of land at Touktoke Bay on the coast of Labrador by a special Committee of the Council appointed to consider the same refers to the applicant's exertions in "securing friendly intercourse with the Esquimaux Indians and his success in bringing about a friendly intercourse between that nation and the Mountaineers."

Evidence as to subsequent official usage is adduced in a letter of 1824 from the Advocate General of Canada to the Assistant Civil Secretary on some matter of a criminal prosecution in which "Esquimaux Indians" are concerned; and in a report of 1869 by Judge Pinsent of the Court of Labrador to the Governor of Newfoundland in which this sentence occurs: "In this number about 300 Indians and half-breeds of the Esquimaux and Mountaineer races are included." . . .

Nor do I think that the fact that British policy in relation to the Indians, as evidenced in the Instructions to Sir Guy Carleton and the Royal Proclamation of 1763, did not contemplate the Eskimo (along with many other tribes and nations of British North American aborigines) as within the scope of that policy is either conclusive or very useful in determining the question before us. For that purpose, for construing the term "Indians" in the B.N.A. Act in order to ascertain the scope of the provisions of that Act defining the powers of the Parliament of Canada, the Report of the Select Committee of the House of Commons in 1857 and the documents relating to the Labrador Eskimo are, in my opinion, far more trust-worthy guides.

Nor can I agree that the context (in head no. 24) has the effect of restricting the term "Indians." If "Indians" standing alone in its application to British North America denotes the aborigines, then the fact that there were aborigines for whom lands had not been reserved seems to afford no good reason for limiting the scope of the term "Indians" itself.

For these reasons I think the question referred to us should be answered in the affirmative. . . .

SELECTED BIBLIOGRAPHY

Bell, C. *Alberta's Métis Settlement Legislation: An Overview of Ownership and Management of Settlement Lands* (Regina: Canadian Plains Research Center, University of Regina, 1994).

———. "Who are the Métis People in Section 35(2)?" (1991) 29:2 Alta. L. Rev. 351.

———. "Métis Self-Government: The Alberta Settlement Model" in J. Hylton, ed. *Aboriginal Self-Government in Canada*, 2d ed. (Saskatoon: Purich Publishing, 1999).

Chartier, C. "'Indian': An Analysis of the Term as used in Section 91(24) of the British North America Act, 1867" (1978–79) 43 Sask. L. Rev. 37.

————. "Aboriginal Self-Government and the Métis Nation" in J. Hylton, ed. *Aboriginal Self-Government in Canada*, 2d ed. (Saskatoon: Purich Publishing, 1999).

Chartrand, L. "Métis Identity and Citizenship" (2001, Nov.) 12 W.R.L.S.I. 5.

Chartrand, P. *Manitoba's Métis Settlement Scheme of 1870* (Saskatoon: Native Law Centre, University of Saskatchewan, 1991).

————. "Aboriginal Rights: The Dispossession of the Métis" (1991) 29 Osgoode Hall L.J. 457.

————, ed. *Who Are Canada's Aboriginal Peoples? Recognition, Definition and Jurisdiction* (Saskatoon: Purich Publishing, 2002).

Cumming, P. "Canada's North and Native Rights" in B. Morse, ed. *Aboriginal Peoples and the Law: Indian, Métis and Inuit Rights in Canada* (Ottawa: Carleton University Press, 1985).

Flanagan, T. "The Case Against Métis Aboriginal Rights" in M. Boldt et al., eds. *The Quest For Justice: Aboriginal Peoples and Aboriginal Rights* (Toronto: University of Toronto Press, 1985).

Frideres, J. "The Métis" in *Native Peoples in Canada: Contemporary Conflicts*, 3d ed. (Scarborough: Prentice-Hall, 1988).

Gray, K.R. "The Nunavut Land Claims Agreement and the Future of the Canadian Arctic: The Uncharted Path to Effective Self-Government" (Spring 1994) 52:1 U. T. Fac. L. Rev. 300.

Hardy, R. "Métis Rights in the Mackenzie River District of the Northwest Territories" [1980] 1 C.N.L.R. 1.

Hunt, C.D. "Knowing the North: The Law and its Institutions" [1986] 4 C.N.L.R. 1.

Isaac, T. "The Nunavut Agreement-in-Principle and Section 35 of the Constitution Act, 1982" (1992) 21:3 Man. L. J. 390.

Kersey, A. "Comment: The Nunavut Agreement: A Model for Preserving Indigenous Rights" (Fall, 1994) 11 Ariz. J. Int'l & Comp. Law 429.

Lester, G.S. "The Territorial Rights of the Inuit of the Canadian Northwest Territories: A Legal Argument." Unpublished Ph.D. dissertation (Toronto: York University, 1981).

Merritt, J. et al. *Nunavut: Political Choices and Manifest Destiny* (Ottawa: Canadian Arctic Resources Committee, 1989).

Purich, D. *The Inuit and Their Land: The Story of Nunavut* (Toronto: Lorimer, 1992).

————. *The Métis* (Toronto: Lorimer, 1988).

Rodon, T. "Co-management and self-determination in Nunavut" (1998) 22:2 Polar Geography 119–35.

Sprague, D.N. "Métis Land Claims" in K. Coates, ed. *Aboriginal Land Claims in Canada: A Regional Perspective* (Toronto: Copp Clark Pitman, 1997).

Chapter 5

TAXATION

INTRODUCTION

The taxation of Indians, their reserve lands, and their personal property comes within the legislative authority of Parliament. Under certain circumstances, the present *Indian Act*[1] permits Indians to be exempt from paying income, consumptive, and other taxes. The Indian tax exemption was codified in Canadian law before Confederation, with legislation of Upper Canada in 1850 and 1859 providing for Indians to be exempt from taxation.[2] These tax exemptions are presently codified in s. 87 of the Act and do not apply to the Métis, Inuit, and other Aboriginal people not registered as Indians under the Act. The authority to levy taxes is, however, becoming an increasingly important aspect of Aboriginal self-government and autonomy.

INDIAN TAX EXEMPTION – SECTION 87, *INDIAN ACT*[3]

Introduction

The statutory tax exemption for Indians is set out in s. 87 of the *Indian Act,* and is supported by s. 81(1)(a) of the *Income Tax Act,*[4] which states that an exemption from taxation is provided for "an amount that is declared to be exempt from income tax by any other enactment of the Parliament of Canada."[5] Section 87 of the *Indian Act* states:

> 87. (1) Notwithstanding any other Act of Parliament or any Act of legislation of a province, but subject to section 83, the following property is exempt from taxation, namely,
>
> (a) the interest of an Indian or a band in reserve lands or surrendered lands; and

---

[1] *Indian Act,* R.S.C. 1985, c. I-5.

[2] *An Act for the protection of the Indians in Upper Canada from imposition, and the property occupied or enjoyed by them from trespass and injury,* S. Prov. C., 1850, c. 74, s. IV, and *An Act to prevent trespasses to Public and Indian Lands,* C.S.U.C. 1859, c. 81, s. 23, as found in Thomas Isaac, *Pre-1868 Legislation Concerning Indians* (Saskatoon: University of Saskatchewan Native Law Centre, 1993).

[3] See the *Canadian Tax Journal* (2000) 48:4, 1181–1251); 48:5, 1468–1644); 48:6, 1815–48) for articles on the issue of taxation, Aboriginal people, and self-government.

[4] *Income Tax Act,* R.S.C. 1985 (5th Supp.), c. 1.

[5] The CCRA's Income Tax Interpretation Bulletin (IT-397R, 23 February 1990) states:
STATUTORY EXEMPTIONS
Indian Act . . .
2. The Indian Act is considered to exempt from taxation the income of a status Indian if that income has a *situs* on a reserve (*Nowegijick* 83 CTC 20; 83 DTC 5041). In addition, the Indian Remission Order (PC 1985-2446) currently exempts status Indians on certain income not sited on a reserve if that income is derived from the performance of services on a reserve.

(b) the personal property of an Indian or a band situated on a reserve.

(2) No Indian or band is subject to taxation in respect of the ownership, occupation, possession or use of any property mentioned in paragraph (1)(a) or (b) or is otherwise subject to taxation in respect of any such property.

(3) No succession duty, inheritance tax or estate duty is payable on the death of any Indian in respect of any property mentioned in paragraphs (1)(a) or (b) or the succession thereto if the property passes to an Indian, nor shall any such property be taken into account in determining the duty payable under the *Dominion Succession Duty Act*, . . . or the tax payable under the *Estate Tax Act*, . . . on or in respect of other property passing to an Indian.

The Act's tax exemption does not exempt Indians from all forms of taxation. Only those Indian or Indian band interests in reserve or surrendered reserve lands, and the personal property of an Indian or Indian band that is situated on a reserve, are exempt from taxation. As the Supreme Court of Canada stated in *Mitchell* v. *Peguis Indian Band*,[6] "Indians who acquire and deal in property outside lands reserved for their use, deal with it on the same basis as all other Canadians." The Supreme Court held that the purpose of the Indian tax provisions in the Act was not to remedy the economically disadvantaged position of Indians but rather to protect their interest in reserve lands from seizure:

One must guard against ascribing an overly broad purpose to ss. 87 and 89. These provisions are not intended to confer privileges on Indians in respect of any property they may acquire and possess, wherever situated. Rather, their purpose is simply to insulate the property interests of Indians in their reserve lands from the intrusions and interference of the larger society so as to ensure that Indians are not dispossessed of their entitlements.[7]

Under the federal *Income Tax Act*, Indians are required to file tax returns even though they may be exempt from paying any tax.[8] The Métis and the Inuit are not entitled to claim any tax exemption benefit based on s. 87 of the Act. To date, governments in Canada only recognize the Indian tax exemption found in s. 87 of the Act, rather than arguments for such exemption based on Aboriginal or treaty rights.

R. v. *Williams* (1992) – Connecting Factors Test

The meaning of "property situated on reserve" within s. 87(1) of the Act was considered by the Supreme Court of Canada in *R.* v. *Nowegijick*.[9] The Court held that employment income was a simple debt and the *situs* of the employer was the determining factor in whether the property was exempt. In order for an Indian's property to be tax exempt, the *situs* of the employer had to be "on reserve," as provided for by the Act, even if the work itself was done off-reserve.

In *R.* v. *Williams*,[10] the Court modified *Nowegijick* and held that the mere *situs* of the employer or source of income was not sufficient in order to determine that the property/income was situated on reserve. Rather, in order to determine the *situs* of intangible personal property, courts must consider various "connecting factors" that bind the property to one location or another. The Court noted three important factors to be considered:

[6] *Mitchell* v. *Peguis Indian Band*, [1990] 2 S.C.R. 85 at p. 131.
[7] *Ibid.* at 133.
[8] *R.* v. *Point* (1957), 22 W.W.R. 527 (B.C.C.A.).
[9] *R.* v. *Nowegijick*, [1983] 1 S.C.R. 29.
[10] *R.* v. *Williams*, [1992] 1 S.C.R. 877.

1. the purpose of the exemption under the Act;

2. the character of the property in question; and

3. the nature of the taxation of that property.

This test is more flexible and less predictable than the 1983 *Nowegijick* test in determining whether the s. 87 tax exemption applies to income. For example, under *Williams* the location of the employer (e.g., head office) is simply one of a number of factors used to determine the *situs* of the work performed.

On February 16, 1993, the Canada Customs and Revenue Agency (CCRA, formerly Revenue Canada) released an interpretation of *Williams*, of which the following is a summary:

1. Although *Williams* dealt specifically with unemployment insurance benefits, it applies to all other forms of income. All applicable connecting factors must be examined to determine whether or not income is tax exempt.

2. An employer situated on a reserve is not enough, by itself, to warrant a tax exemption. The primary factor of connecting income to the reserve is where the duties of the employee are performed. The location of the employer will continue to be a factor, but other factors must also be considered.

3. The tax exemption applies to (*a*) employment income for duties performed entirely on a reserve, (*b*) employment income for duties performed entirely off-reserve but where the employer and the Indian reside on-reserve, (*c*) employment income for duties, most of which, are performed on-reserve and either the employer or the Indian resides on-reserve, (*d*) unemployment, pension, or retiring benefits received in relation to exempt employment income, and (*e*) the exemption shall be pro-rated where duties are performed on and off a reserve.

A detailed set of guidelines respecting the Act's tax exemption and employment income was released by CCRA in June 1994 and is set out in the materials section of this chapter. *Williams* redefined the tax exemption, which was formerly deemed to apply, for example, where a head office was simply located on reserve, while the substantive business of the employer was off-reserve, with all affected parties living off-reserve. *Williams* ensures that a connection must be made between the *situs* of the employment income and the performance of the duties related to the income in order for the tax exemption to apply.

Application of *Williams*[11]

The Tax Court of Canada applied *Williams* in *Recalma* v. *Canada*.[12] The Court considered whether income earned by investments purchased at an on-reserve bank branch was exempt from income tax pursuant to s. 87 of the *Indian Act*. In applying *Williams,* the Court noted that the investment income was the personal property of registered Indians

[11] See also *Monias* v. *Canada*, [2001] 4 C.N.L.R. 194 (Fed. C.A.), leave to appeal to S.C.C. dismissed [2002] 2 C.N.L.R. iv (S.C.C.) (employment income); *Akiwenzie* v. *Canada*, [2003] 2 C.N.L.R. 1 (T.C.C.) (employment income); *Sero* v. *Canada*, [2001] 4 C.N.L.R. 307 (T.C.C.) (bank deposits); *Folster* v. *R.* (1997), 97 D.T.C. 5315 (Fed. C.A.) (employment income); *Naphonse* v. *R.*, [2001] 3 C.N.L.R. 178 (T.C.C.) (employment income); *Brant* v. *Min. of National Revenue*, [1992] 2 C.T.C. 2635 (T.C.C.) (family allowance payments), *Matthew* v. *Min. of National Revenue*, [1999] 3 C.T.C. 2547 (T.C.C.) (employee of DIAND); and *Southwind* v. *Canada*, [1998] 2 C.N.L.R. 233 (F.C.A.) (business income).

[12] *Recalma* v. *Canada*, [1997] 4 C.N.L.R. 272 (T.C.C.), aff'd [1998] 3 C.N.L.R. 279 (F.C.A.).

and applied the following connecting elements in order to determine the *situs* of the investment income:

1. the residence of the registered Indians;

2. the origin and location of the capital used to buy the securities;

3. the location of the bank branch where the securities were bought;

4. the location where the investment was used;

5. the location of the investment instruments;

6. the location where the investment income payment was made; and

7. the nature of the securities, including the residence of the issuer, the location of the issuer's income-generating activity from which the investment was made, and the location of the issuer's property in the event of a default that could result in a potential seizure.

After examining these factors, the court determined that all of the transactions associated with the investment instruments occurred off-reserve. Because the only action that took place on-reserve was the purchase, the investment income was deemed to be located off-reserve and therefore subject to income tax. As a result, CCRA has stated:

> [G]iven the *Recalma* decision, if the investment income stream for a financial instrument involves an entity located off-reserve, that investment income will not qualify as personal property situated on a reserve. Rather, the income is considered to be earned in the economic mainstream.
>
> In conclusion, it is our view that the decision supports the position that income earned in the economic mainstream is so strongly connected to a location off reserve that it will generally outweigh other factors that may indicate the income is connected to a location on reserve.[13]

In *Shilling* v. *Canada (Min. of National Revenue)*,[14] the Federal Court of Appeal considered an appeal by the Crown from a decision of the Trial Division. Shilling, a registered Indian who worked at a health agency off-reserve, was hired through an employment agency located on-reserve. At trial, the Court held that the location of the employer was the most significant factor in the *Williams* connecting factors test and held that the tax exemption applied to Shilling.

The Federal Court of Appeal held that location of employment is an important but not the only factor to determine the *situs* of employment income. Because there were no other significant factors connecting Shilling's employment income to a reserve, the income was not situated on reserve and accordingly not exempt from taxation under s. 87(1)(b) of the *Indian Act*:

> It follows that Ms. Shilling's employment is to be regarded as in the "commercial mainstream". This conclusion may appear counter-intuitive when applied to a Native person who identifies with her Band and First Nation, and is working with a social agency delivering programmes to assist Native people. . . . However, in the context of determining the

[13] Canada Customs and Revenue Agency. *Income Tax—Technical News*, No. 9 (10 February 1997), online: <http://www.ccra-adrc.gc.ca/E/pub/tp/itnews-9/itnews-9-e.html>.
[14] *Shilling* v. *Canada (Min. of National Revenue)*, [2001] 3 C.N.L.R. 332 (F.C.A.), leave to appeal to S.C.C. dismissed, [2002] 2 C.N.L.R. iv (S.C.C.).

location of intangible property for the purpose of section 87, "commercial mainstream" is to be contrasted with "integral to the life of a reserve". . . . The purpose of the tax exemption in paragraph 87(1)(b) is not to address the general economically disadvantaged position of Indians in Canada.[15]

Shilling confirmed that the mere location of the employer as a factor of the *Williams* connecting elements test is insufficient to link the income derived therefrom to a reserve. There must be evidence demonstrating that there are significant aspects of the employer's business occurring on reserve or there are some other relevant factors that connect the employment to the reserve.

The use of the tax exemption set out in s. 87 of the *Indian Act* to benefit an Indian band and life for Indians on Indian reserves is not an "independent, free-standing connecting factor."[16] Indians who hold and deal with property in the commercial mainstream must do so on the same basis as other Canadians, regardless if their activity may be related to a traditional activity, such as fishing.[17]

In *Amos v. Canada*,[18] the Federal Court of Appeal considered an appeal from the Tax Court of Canada which affirmed a decision by the Minister of National Revenue refusing the Indian appellants the use of the s. 87 tax exemption on income earned on reserve. The Indian appellants resided on reserve and worked for a pulp mill that was located partially on land leased from an Indian band and partially on non-reserve land. The pulp mill was located on the non-reserve land, while the leased reserve land was used for fuel and mill wood chip storage. The Court held that although the appellants did not work on the leased reserve lands, it was agreed by all parties that the uses made of the leased reserve land were connected to the employment of the appellants:

> [T]his employment was directly related to the realization by the Band and its members of their entitlements to the reserve land and, in accordance with the purpose of the tax exemption in section 87, the government should not be able through income taxation to erode income from such use, direct or indirect, of their land as is found in this case.[19]

This confirms that the courts are willing to take a broad approach in examining the *situs* of employment to determine what constitutes "on-reserve" employment.

The CCRA stated that as a result of *Williams*, the location of a savings account on reserve, by itself, would not be sufficient to exempt the interest income earned thereon:

> Where a bank account is considered to be situated at a location on reserve, this is one factor to weigh in determining whether interest earned on deposits in that account is exempt from taxation. There could be other factors that would connect the income to a location off reserve. For instance, an Indian may live off reserve and earn only taxable income, and use an automated teller machine located off reserve to deposit funds into a bank account located on reserve. In this example, it is our view that the interest income would be taxable, notwithstanding that the head office of the financial institution may be located on reserve. On the other hand, where an Indian lives on reserve, earns only tax-exempt income, and deposits funds into a bank account located on reserve, the income will be exempt from taxation. Revenue Canada has always maintained the view that term deposits, bankers' acceptances and government treasury bills are not located on reserve and not exempt.[20]

---

[15] *Ibid.* at paras. 64, 65; see also *Naponse v. Canada*, [2001] 3 C.N.L.R. 178 (T.C.C.).

[16] *Bell* v. *Canada*, [2000] 3 C.N.L.R. 32 (F.C.A.) at para. 40.

[17] *Ibid.* at para. 45.

[18] *Amos* v. *Canada*, [2000] 3 C.N.L.R. 1 (F.C.A.), rev'g [1999] 1 C.N.L.R. 7 (T.C.C.); see also *Dykstra v. Monture*, [2000] 3 C.N.L.R. 59 (Ont. Sup. Ct.), at paras. 22–24.

[19] *Ibid.* at para. 7.

[20] Canada, Canada Customs and Revenue Agency, *Income Tax – Technical News* (No. 7, February 21, 1996).

Paramount Location Test

Section 87 of the *Indian Act* prevents the taxation of personal property situated on reserve. The term "situated" includes the ownership, occupation, possession, and use of property. Electricity[21] delivered to a reserve and motor vehicles[22] purchased on a reserve are personal property within the meaning of s.87 and are exempt from taxation. The phrase "situated on reserve" means situated at the time of delivery. The paramount location of property is established by examining the pattern of use and safekeeping regarding the property. If the paramount location is on reserve, then the property is tax exempt even with respect to its off-reserve use.[23]

The New Brunswick Court of Appeal applied the "paramount location test" in *Union of New Brunswick Indians* v. *New Brunswick*.[24] The Court of Appeal considered whether personal property purchased off-reserve by an Indian or Indian band but intended for ownership, consumption, or use on a reserve fell within the meaning of the words "situated on reserve" in s. 87(1) and therefore are not subject to New Brunswick's Social Services and Education Tax (a sales tax). The paramount location test requires that the primary location of a good must be determined according to its normal pattern of use and safekeeping. The Court held that the purchase of goods destined for use and consumption on a reserve by an Indian or an Indian band are not subject to provincial sales tax and that delivery to the reserve is unnecessary for the application of s. 87.[25]

The Supreme Court of Canada overturned the Court of Appeal's decision. McLachlin J. (as she then was) stated for the majority that s. 87 of the Act applied only to goods physically located on-reserve and whose paramount location is on-reserve when the tax attaches to the goods. McLachlin J. also held that the tax, when imposed on a retail sale, is a sales tax and not a consumption tax. The "paramount location test" cannot be applied to sales taxes on tangible goods because the only relevant factor is the place of sale. The location of the goods for consumption is irrelevant.

GST and Other Federal Taxes

Pursuant to *G.S.T. Technical Information Bulletin, B–039R* of November 25, 1993, the federal Goods and Services Tax (GST) is not payable respecting on-reserve purchases of goods by registered Indians and bands, on-reserve purchases of services by registered Indians where the benefit is realized primarily on reserve, or for off-reserve purchases of goods delivered to a reserve and purchased by registered Indians.

Neither the Act's s. 87 exemption nor the Jay Treaty (a 1794 treaty between Great Britain and the United States proposing a duty exemption for Indians who crossed what is now the United States/Canada border) have been accepted by the courts to establish an exemption from customs or excise taxes. Customs duties apply as soon as goods cross the border. The Jay Treaty was not enacted in Canada by domestic legislation and is not in force.[26] In *Mitchell* v. *Canada (Min. of Nat. Rev.)*,[27] the Supreme Court of Canada held

[21] *R.* v. *Brown*, [1979] 3 C.N.L.R. 67 (B.C.C.A.).

[22] *Danes* v. *B.C.*; *Watts* v. *B.C.*, [1985] 2 C.N.L.R. 18 (B.C.C.A.).

[23] *Leighton* v. *B.C.*, [1989] 3 C.N.L.R. 136 (B.C.C.A.). Cited with approval by La Forest J. in *Peguis, supra* note 6 at 132, 133.

[24] *Union of New Brunswick Indians* v. *New Brunswick*, [1997] 1 C.N.L.R. 213 (B.C.C.A.), rev'd [1998] 1 S.C.R. 1161 295 (S.C.C.).

[25] For another example of the application of the paramount location test, see *Petro-Canada Inc.* v. *Fort Nelson Indian Band*, [1993] 1 C.N.L.R. 72 (B.C.S.C.).

[26] *R.* v. *Francis*, [1956] S.C.R. 618.

[27] *Mitchell* v. *Canada (Min. of Nat. Rev.)*, [2001] 1 S.C.R. 911.

that the Mohawks of Akwesasne do not possess an Aboriginal right to bring goods across the Canada–United States border free from paying customs duties and taxes.

Corporations wholly owned by Indian band councils may be exempt from paying tax on income earned anywhere if they are deemed to be municipalities within the meaning of the federal *Income Tax Act,* which provides that municipalities are tax exempt. The Tax Court of Canada confirmed this in *Otineka Development Corp. Ltd.* v. *Canada.*[28] In *Kinookimaw Beach Assoc.* v. *Saskatchewan,*[29] the Saskatchewan Court of Appeal refused to allow the personal tax exemption to be applied to corporate entities, regardless of whether they were owned by registered Indians.

Indians cannot use the Act as a shield to being subject to bankruptcy legislation. Thus, on-reserve assets can be taken into account in considering the disposition to be made on a bankrupt's application for a discharge.[30]

INDIAN BAND TAXATION AUTHORITY

Subsection 83(1)(a) and other sections of the *Indian Act* were amended by Parliament on June 2, 1988,[31] by the so-called Kamloops amendment to allow Indian bands to enact property tax by-laws applicable to reserve lands that had been conditionally surrendered. The original wording of s. 83(1)(a) of the Act limited band councils to enact by-laws related to the assessment and taxation of interests "in land in the reserve of persons lawfully in possession thereof." This language could have been interpreted to restrict the property taxation authority of Indian bands to only Indian interests, rather than extended to include non-Indian interests, such as those on conditionally surrendered or designated lands. Subsection 83(1)(a) of the Act states:

> Without prejudice to the powers conferred by section 81, the council of a band may, subject to the approval of the Minister, make by-laws for any or all of the following purposes, namely, (a) subject to subsections (2) and (3), taxation for local purposes of land, or interests in land, in the reserve, including rights to occupy, possess or use land in the reserve. . . .

Additionally, s. 83(3) of the Act also contains provisions for an appeal procedure for assessments made under the authority of an Indian band's taxation by-law; approval of the taxation by-law by the Minister of the Department of Indian Affairs and Northern Development (DIAND) is also required. The appeal mechanism is important to non-Indian leaseholders of Indian land since they do not vote in Indian band council elections. In January 1989 the Minister of DIAND established the Indian Taxation Advisory Board which, among other tasks, provides recommendations to the Minister respecting the approval of Indian band's taxation by-laws and to promote the exercise of these tax powers generally.[32] With these new taxation powers comes the issue of determining what lands remain "in the reserve" for the purposes of Indian band taxation under s. 83(1)(c) of the *Indian Act.*

In *St. Mary's Indian Band* v. *Cranbrook,*[33] the British Columbia Court of Appeal confirmed that the transfer of a fee simple absolute removes land from a reserve. *St. Mary's*

[28] *Otineka Development Corp. Ltd.* v. *Canada*, [1994] 2 C.N.L.R. 83 (T.C.C.). Revenue Canada did not appeal this decision.
[29] *Kinookimaw Beach Assoc.* v. *Saskatchewan*, [1979] 4 C.N.L.R. 101 (Sask. C.A.).
[30] *Davey (Re)*, [2000] 3 C.N.L.R. 48 (Ont. Sup. Ct.); see also *Dykstra* v. *Monture, supra* note 18.
[31] Bill C-115, an *Act to Amend the Indian Act*, R.S.C. 1985 (4th Supp.), c. 17.
[32] See online: <http://www.itab.ca>.
[33] *St. Mary's Indian Band* v. *Cranbrook*, [1997] 2 S.C.R. 657.

concerned whether "surrendered" lands come within the legal definition of a "reserve" under the *Indian Act* and, if so, whether surrendered lands would be subject to the property tax jurisdiction of the Indian band under s. 83(1)(a) of the Act. The Supreme Court of Canada affirmed *St. Mary's* and stated the following with respect to the application of real property concepts to questions involving reserve lands:

> The reason the Court has said that common law real property concepts do not apply to native lands is to prevent native intentions from being frustrated by an application of formalistic and arguably alien common law rules. Even in a case such as this where the Indian band received full legal representation prior to the surrender transaction, we must ensure that form not trump substance.[34]

In *St. Mary's*, the Supreme Court of Canada also provided a succinct summary of the distinction between reserve lands surrendered for sale and reserve lands surrendered for purposes other than for sale, such as a lease:

> [T]he *sui generis* nature of native land rights means that we do not apply technical land transfer requirements to the surrender of Indian lands. It does not mean, however, that this Court should resolve this case without reference to the ordinary rules of statutory interpretation. Indeed, it is my view that the Court can dispose of this appeal by simple reference to the Kamloops Amendments themselves. Although the Kamloops Amendments were intended to clarify the status of reserve lands surrendered *for lease,* they were never intended to draw lands surrendered *for sale* into the definition of reserve. Parliament has always considered lands surrendered for sale to have been surrendered absolutely.[35]

In the Federal Court, Trial Division decision of *Canadian Pacific Ltd.* v. *Matsqui Indian Band*,[36] Teitelbaum J. held that a determinable fee in reserve lands removed the lands from the reserve for the purposes of taxation while the fee continued. Décary J. of the Federal Court of Appeal stated the following with respect to the interpretative approach to be taken when examining a railway company's interest in reserve lands:

> In order to determine the nature and extent of a railway company's interest in reserve lands— and, by the same token, the nature and extent of what was taken away from a band—resort must be had "to the language of the statutes, to any agreements between the original parties and to subsequent actions and declarations of the parties" (*Canadian Pacific Ltd.* v. *Paul* [[1998] 2 S.C.R. 654], para. 25 [these reasons] at 665).[37]

Marceau J. A. stated the following regarding the difference between Indian bands and municipalities with respect to taxation authority:

> Finally, it appears to me quite inappropriate to apply to the Indian Bands' new by-law powers the principles of interpretation developed in municipal law. There is a big difference between municipalities and Indian Bands in that the existence of the Indian groupings is not like that of municipal units, wholly dependant on an act of Government authority, and the rationale behind the granting of taxation powers to both such bodies is clearly not the same. The devolved taxation powers of municipalities exists, to my mind, only to further governmental objectives of efficiency in operation and administration. The recent granting of taxation powers to Indian Bands has a much broader and humane objective, which can only be seen in the context of furthering the ability of natives to govern themselves and

[34] *Ibid.* at 668.
[35] *Ibid.* at 670–71.
[36] *Canadian Pacific Ltd.* v. *Matsqui Indian Band* (1996), 134 D.L.R. (4th) 555 at 581 (F.C.T.D.), aff'd (1998), 162 D.L.R. (4th) 649 (F.C.A.), leave to appeal to S.C.C. refused, [1998] 1 S.C.R. vii.
[37] *Ibid.* at 662, para. 32 (F.C.A.).

thus, to a certain extent, invokes rights and responsibilities that predate all Indian Acts. It would be wrong, in my view, to subject both sets of rules to the same standard of inflexibility, rigidity and limitation.[38]

The Supreme Court of Canada decision of *Westbank First Nation* v. *B.C. Hydro and Power Authority*[39] held that s. 125 of the *Constitution Act, 1867*[40] prevents Indian bands from applying assessment and taxation by-laws to agents of the provincial Crown. *Westbank* concerned the levying of taxes on B.C. Hydro by the Westbank First Nation for B.C. Hydro's use and occupation of certain reserve lands to build transmission and distribution lines, which also provided electricity to residents of the Westbank First Nation. The taxes were held to be taxation within the meaning of s. 91(3) of the *Constitution Act, 1867* and not within provincial jurisdiction.

Section 83 of the *Indian Act* empowers an Indian band to impose taxation for local purposes of land or interests in land. In *Matsqui Indian Band* v. *Canadian Pacific Ltd.*[41] the Supreme Court of Canada considered an Indian band that imposed a tax on Canadian Pacific Ltd. pursuant to its bylaw made under s. 83 of the Act. The bylaw provided that an appeal of the assessment could be made to a tribunal constituted under the bylaw. CP applied for judicial review of the assessment in the Federal Court, thereby avoiding the tribunal. The Court confirmed the right of appeal to the Federal Court for judicial review, notwithstanding that a purpose behind s. 83 of the Act is to promote Aboriginal self-government and control over taxation. Lamer C.J., for the majority, wrote:

> Moreover, while I agree that the larger context of Aboriginal self-government informs the determination of whether the statutory appeal procedures established by the appellants constitute an adequate alternative remedy for the respondents, I cannot agree with Sopinka J.'s conclusion that this context is relevant to the question of whether the bands' tribunals give rise to a reasonable apprehension of bias at an institutional level. In my view, principles of natural justice apply to the bands' tribunals as they would apply to any tribunal performing similar functions. The fact that the tribunals have been constituted within the context of a federal policy promoting Aboriginal self-government does not, in itself, dilute natural justice. The Indian Taxation Advisory Board, which intervened before this Court on behalf of the appellant bands, has itself determined that appeal tribunals constituted under s. 83(3) of the *Indian Act* must comply with the principles of natural justice. I would cite the following excerpt from the Board's Introduction to Real Property Taxation on Reserve (1990), at p. 23, a manual designed to assist Aboriginal bands in establishing their taxation tribunals: "Subsection 83(3) of the *Indian Act* requires taxation by-laws to provide 'an appeal procedure in respect of assessments made for the purposes of taxation.' A statutory right of appeal is fundamental to any tax assessment process for two reasons. First, the nature of the assessment process is such that an assessment decision is made only on the strength of an assessor's judgment, without any prior hearing providing input from the party assessed. Second, a fundamental rule of the common law relating to administrative procedures, like assessments, is that everyone has a right to a hearing where matters are involved affecting that person's liberty or property rights. This rule is derived from the principles of natural justice, which are fundamental principles of administrative law that basically ensure (i) a person's right to a hearing and (ii) that the person is heard by an impartial tribunal. . . . The *Indian Act* does not detail the types of appeal processes that councils should establish in their taxation by-laws. However, whatever appeal mechanisms are put in place they will have to

---

[38] *Canadian Pacific Ltd.* v. *Matsqui Indian Band* (1999), 176 D.L.R. (4th) 35 at para. 29.
[39] *Westbank First Nation* v. *B.C. Hydro and Power Authority*, [1999] 3 S.C.R. 134.
[40] Section 125 of the *Constitution Act, 1867* states: "No Lands or Property belonging to Canada or any Province shall be liable to Taxation."
[41] *Matsqui Indian Band* v. *Canadian Pacific Ltd.*, [1995] 1 S.C.R. 85.

adhere to the principles of natural justice, since, as mentioned above, the appeal is in effect a subsequent hearing. . . ." With respect, I do not believe that either *Nowegijick* v. *The Queen*, [1983] 1 S.C.R. 29, or *Mitchell* v. *Peguis Indian Band*, [1990] 2 S.C.R. 85, the cases cited by Sopinka J., support the view that the policy of Aboriginal self-government is relevant to a determination of whether the appellant Band's taxation tribunals comply with the principles of natural justice.[42]

Lands surrendered absolutely (subject to a condition subsequent, which is a right not connected to an interest in the land) do not become "designated lands" as defined by the *Indian Act*. As such, these lands do not become part of reserve lands and, therefore, may be subject to municipal taxes. These lands do not fall within the authority of Indian bands to levy taxes pursuant to s. 83 of the *Indian Act*.[43]

Osoyoos Indian Band v. *Oliver (Town)* (2001)

In *Osoyoos Indian Band* v. *Oliver (Town)*,[44] Iacobucci J., for the majority of the Supreme Court of Canada, considered whether lands expropriated for public purposes under s. 35 of the *Indian Act* were still "in the reserve" for the purposes of s. 83(1)(c) of the Act.

The Osoyoos Indian Band enacted a by-law pursuant to s. 83(1)(a) of the Act. The Band then sought to include on its assessment roll the land upon which an irrigation canal was situated. *Osoyoos* concerned an application by the Band's Board of Review seeking the Supreme Court of Canada's opinion on two questions:

> 1. Are lands, taken pursuant to s.35 of the *Indian Act*, "land or interests in land" in a reserve of a Band within the meaning of s.83(1) (a) of the *Indian Act* such that those lands are assessable and taxable pursuant to Band Assessment By-laws and taxable pursuant to Band Taxation By-laws?

> 2. If s.35 of the *Indian Act* authorizes the removal of lands from reserve status, does federal Order in Council 1957-577, by which the Lands were transferred, remove the Lands from reserve status so that they are not assessable and taxable by the Osoyoos Indian Band?[45]

The Government of British Columbia required certain Band reserve lands for the purposes of constructing an irrigation canal. British Columbia purchased the land and, in return, the Governor in Council enacted Order in Council 1957-577 on April 25, 1957, pursuant to s. 35 of the Act, consenting to "the taking of the said lands by the Province of British Columbia and to transfer the administration and control thereof to Her Majesty the Queen in right of the Province of British Columbia."[46] The land was registered by way of a Certificate of Indefeasible Title[47] in the name of the Crown in right of British Columbia.

Iacobucci J. began his analysis by addressing four preliminary issues: (1) the unsatis-

[42] *Ibid.* at para. 74.
[43] *St. Mary's, supra* note 33.
[44] *Osoyoos Indian Band* v. *Oliver (Town)*, [2001] 3 S.C.R. 746; rev'g [1999] 4 C.N.L.R. 91 (B.C.C.A.); aff'g [1998] 2 C.N.L.R. 66 (B.C.S.C.); applied in *BC Tel* v. *Seabird Island Indian Band*, [2002] 4 C.N.L.R. 1 (F.C.A.).
[45] *Ibid.* at para. 13.
[46] *Ibid.* at para. 93.
[47] The British Columbia *Land Title Act*, R.S.B.C., 1996, c. 250, s. 23 allows for the registration of a certificate of indefeasible title and describes it as "conclusive evidence at law and in equity, as against the Crown and all other persons, that the person named in the title is indefeasibly entitled to an estate in fee simple described in the indefeasible title, subject to . . . " certain conditions, such as those contained in the original Crown grant, public right of way, lease, or agreement not exceeding a term of three years, among others.

factory factual basis in the case;[48] (2) the *sui generis* nature of the Aboriginal interest in reserve land;[49] (3) the meaning of, and interpretation given to, s. 83 of the Act;[50] and (4) the content of the Crown's fiduciary duty within the context of s. 35 of the Act.[51] Iacobucci J. stated that there was a significant lack of evidence in this case and the Court should be "cautious in taking away interests in land in the absence of a complete evidentiary record."[52] This lack of evidence, particularly for older OICs, may not be unusual. Iacobucci J. stated that the Aboriginal interest in reserve land and Aboriginal title included some common features in that they are: (1) inalienable except to the Crown; (2) both are rights of use and occupation; and (3) both are held communally.

Iacobucci J. stated that there are three implications that flow from the Aboriginal interests in reserve lands that are important within the context of this decision. First, the traditional common law principles relating to property law may not be helpful in understanding Aboriginal interests in reserve land and, as such, the transfer of reserve land at issue in this case cannot be regarded as a "regular, commercial transaction."[53] Second, the intervention of the Crown is required to add or replace reserve land and therefore reserve land does not fit within the traditional reasoning that underlines the process of expropriation in exchange for compensation based on market value.[54] This may be questioned as the Crown is required to ensure that adequate compensation for such transactions is made available or somehow negotiated. Third, the Aboriginal interest in reserve land is more than a fungible commodity in that the Aboriginal interest in reserve land will normally have an important cultural component to it. Based on these principles and based on the fact that the Crown owes a fiduciary duty to Indians, he held that the Crown must demonstrate a clear and plain intention to remove land from a reserve.[55]

As stated by the Supreme Court of Canada in other decisions,[56] Iacobucci J. confirmed that s. 83(1)(a) of the *Indian Act* should be given a "broad reading."[57] As a result, unless the entire interest of an Indian band is removed from expropriated Indian reserve land, expropriated Indian reserve land remains reserve land for the purposes of s. 83(1)(a) of the Act, and both easements and rights to use or occupy such land by entities that are not members of the Indian band are subject to taxation by the Indian band.

Iacobucci J. continued by stating that the Crown's intent to extinguish the Aboriginal interest in reserve land must be "clear and plain."[58] Section 35 of the *Indian Act* authorizes the taking or use of a range of interests in reserve land including and up to a fee simple interest. Section 35(3) of the Act authorizes the Governor in Council to grant or transfer only those lands that could be taken within the relevant statutory authority of the enabling expropriation legislation, in this case the British Columbia *Water Act*. The *Water Act* only permitted the granting of an interest in the land that was "reasonably required" for the purposes of the irrigation canal. The evidence before the Court was insufficient to provide a clear answer as to what type of interest would be reasonably required for the purposes of the irrigation canal.

[48] *Osoyoos, supra* note 44 at paras. 38–40.
[49] *Ibid.* at paras. 41–47.
[50] *Ibid.* at paras. 48–50.
[51] *Ibid.* at paras. 51–55.
[52] *Ibid.* at para. 40.
[53] *Ibid.* at para. 44.
[54] *Ibid.* at para. 45.
[55] *Ibid.* at para. 47.
[56] *Nowegijick, supra* note 9; *Peguis, supra* note 6.
[57] *Osoyoos, supra* note 44 at para. 49.
[58] *Ibid.* at para. 56.

Iacobucci J. stated that four principles should guide the interpretation of the Order in Council. First, the Crown must demonstrate a clear and plain intention to extinguish the Aboriginal interest in reserve land. Second, the interpretation or application that impairs the Indian interest in the land as little as possible should be preferred over other interpretations or applications. Third, the Court will presume that the Crown acted *intra vires* in making the transfer of land at issue in this case, in that the Governor in Council is presumed to have transferred only those interests that were "reasonably required" for the purposes of the irrigation canal. Fourth, a departure from the traditional common law property rules in relation to dealing with Indian reserve land is justified based on the *sui generis* nature of the Aboriginal interests in reserve land, meaning that the transfer of land in this case should not be regarded as a regular or commercial transaction and that a non-technical approach to interpreting the Order in Council is appropriate.

There was sufficient ambiguity within the language of the Order in Council that a definitive interpretation of it was not possible. *Osoyoos* confirmed that if an interest akin to a fee simple is to be taken from reserve lands, there must be a clear and plain intention on the part of the Crown to do so, there cannot be any ambiguity in the instrument of authorization affecting the transfer and there must be minimal impairment of the Indians' use and benefit of the reserve land, consistent with the Crown's fiduciary obligation to Indians. *Osoyoos* is consistent with the earlier Supreme Court of Canada decision of *St. Mary's*,[59] which held that the transfer of a fee simple interest removes land from "reserve" status, and the Federal Court of Appeal decision of *Matsqui*,[60] which concluded that a determinable fee in reserve lands removed the lands from the taxation authority of an Indian band.

SUBSECTION 90(1), *INDIAN ACT*

Subsection 90(1) of the *Indian Act* expands the application of the Act's s. 87 tax exemption by defining personal property as follows:

For the purposes of sections 87 and 89, personal property that was

(a) purchased by Her Majesty with Indian moneys or moneys appropriated by Parliament for the use and benefit of Indians or bands, or
(b) given to Indians or to a band under a treaty or agreement between a band and Her Majesty,

shall be deemed always to be situated on a reserve.

The Crown need not purchase property directly in order for s. 90(1) of the Act to apply. Band purchases made with moneys provided by loans from the Crown fall within the meaning of s. 90(1).[61]

In *Peguis*, "Her Majesty" in s. 90(1) of the *Indian Act* was held to be limited to the federal Crown. The exemptions and privileges in ss. 87 and 89 of the Act apply solely in respect of property that the federal Crown transfers to Indians; they do not apply to purely private commercial transactions unless that property is situated on-reserve. La Forest J. (with Sopinka and Gonthier JJ.) noted:

The historical record that so clearly reveals a cogent rationale for protecting the personal

[59] *St. Mary's Indian Band* v. *Cranbrook (City)*, [1996] 2 C.N.L.R. 222 (B.C.C.A.).
[60] *Matsqui*, (F.C.A.), *supra* note 36.
[61] *Kingsclear Indian Band* v. *J.E. Brooks & Ass. Ltd.*, [1992] 2 C.N.L.R. 46 (N.B.C.A.).

property that enures to Indians by operation of treaty obligations regardless of situs, is silent as to any reason why personal property that Indians bands acquire from the provincial Crowns should receive the same extraordinary level of protection. ...I would, therefore, limit application of the term "Her Majesty" as used in s. 90(1)(b) to the federal Crown.[62]

Peguis also stands for the proposition that a liberal construction should be given to legislation affecting Indians and that any doubts as to the meaning of legislation should be resolved in favour of the Indians.

PROVINCIAL TAXES

Provincial taxes are not payable when Indians purchase property that is on reserve at the time the property passes.[63] An exception to this rule applies to those Indian bands that have been granted the authority to enact by-laws respecting the taxation of tobacco products purchased by Indians on reserve.[64] Although not self-government agreements in the strict sense, some Indian bands have entered into agreements with the federal government to impose tax on alcohol, fuel, and tobacco products.[65]

Provinces cannot impair the ability of Indians to take advantage of the Act's s. 87 tax exemption by attempting to apply provincial tax to Indian property that has a reserve as its paramount location.[66]

Some Indians bands have entered into agreements with the provinces and territories whereby consumptive goods, such as tobacco[67] and gasoline, are sold tax-free to Indian reserve retailers based on an approximate amount of the volume of these products sold to registered Indians. The remaining portion of the volume sold to Indian reserve retailers is sold with the provincial/territorial taxes applied. In other instances, Indian reserve retailers purchase consumptive goods that include all applicable provincial/territorial taxes. These goods are then sold to registered Indians "tax-free," and the Indian reserve retailers apply for a refund of the original tax paid.

In *Tseshaht Band* v. *British Columbia*,[68] the British Columbia Court of Appeal held that the provincial refund and quota system to regulate the sale of tobacco and gasoline products was *intra vires*. Notwithstanding *Tseshaht*, the law regarding the extent and application of provincial and territorial taxation regimes on consumptive goods to registered Indians remains unclear.[69]

---

[62] *Peguis, supra* note 6 at 140, 142.
[63] *Johnson* v. *Nova Scotia (A.G.)*, [1990] 2 C.N.L.R. 62 (N.S.C.A.), leave to appeal dismissed, [1991] 1 C.N.L.R. vi (S.C.C.); *Danes* v. *B.C.*; *Watts* v. *B.C., supra* note 22.
[64] See *Large* v. *Canada (Min. of Justice)* (1997), 155 D.L.R. (4th) 704 (B.C.S.C.); see the *Budget Implementation Act, 2000*, S.C. 2000, c. 14.
[65] Those Indian bands that may impose such taxes pursuant to the *Budget Implementation Act, 2000, ibid.* are: Cowichan Band, also known as Cowichan Tribes; Westbank First Nation; Kamloops Band; Sliammon Band; Osoyoos Band; Adams Lake Band; Tsawout First Nation; Chemainus First Nation; Dakota Tipi Band, also known as Dakota Tipi First Nation; Waywayseecappo First Nation Treaty Four—1874; Opaskwayak Cree Nation; Buffalo Point First Nation; Tobique Band, also known as Maliseet Nation at Tobique; and Tzeachten First Nation.
[66] *Leighton, supra* note 23; *Mission (District)* v. *Dewdney/Alouette Assessor Area No. 13*, [1992] 1 C.N.L.R. 66 (B.C.S.C.).
[67] See *R.* v. *MacLaurin*, [2000] 2 C.N.L.R. 216 (Man. Q.B.), restrictions on possession of tobacco upheld.
[68] *Tseshaht Band* v. *British Columbia*, [1992] 4 C.N.L.R. 171 (B.C.C.A.); leave to appeal to S.C.C. granted, [1993] 2 C.N.L.R. vi (S.C.C.), discontinued [1995] 3 C.N.L.R. iv.
[69] See, for example, *Bomberry* v. *Ontario*, [1989] 3 C.N.L.R. 27 (Ont. Div. Ct.), aff'd (1993), 107 D.L.R. (4th) 448 (Ont. C.A.).

In order to prevent double taxation, British Columbia enacted the *Indian Self-Government Enabling Act,*[70] which allows for the provincial and municipal governments to withdraw from taxing reserve lands when an Indian band enacts a taxation by-law.

In Nova Scotia, the *Revenue Act*[71] requires that a wholesaler be licensed and collect for the government the tax payable on tobacco products. In *Union of Nova Scotia Indians* v. *Nova Scotia (A.G.),*[72] the Nova Scotia Court of Appeal considered an appeal from a Mi'Kmaq Indian seeking a declaration that all Indians in Nova Scotia have the right as wholesale/retail vendors to purchase tobacco products on Indian reserves anywhere in Canada, transport those products to Indian reserves in Nova Scotia, and sell those products to other registered Indians, without being registered as a wholesale/retail vendor or collecting tax or otherwise complying with the *Revenue Act.* The basis for this declaration was s. 87 of the *Indian Act.* The Court dismissed the Mi'Kmaq appeal and held that the *Revenue Act* is a constitutionally valid law of general application and, as such, applies to the importation and sale of all tobacco products in Nova Scotia:

> It is immaterial that the product is imported from a reserve outside the province by Indians for sale solely to Indians on reserves in Nova Scotia. Those cases did not turn solely on the fact that sales were also being made to non-Indians. No authorities have been cited for the proposition that Indians are free to trade between reserves exempt from restrictions imposed by provincial laws of general application. With respect, the decisions of the Supreme Court of Canada in *Francis* v. *The Queen*, [1956] S.C.R. 618 . . . do not support the claim that Indians have the right to purchase and transport tobacco products from reserve to reserve for the purpose of resale.[73]

In *Union of New Brunswick Indians* v. *New Brunswick,*[74] the Supreme Court of Canada confirmed:

1. Retail sales taxes, as defined by New Brunswick's *Social Services and Education Tax Act,*[75] are sales taxes and not consumptive taxes.[76]

2. The "paramount location test" does not apply to sales taxes on tangible goods, since it is the place of sale alone that guides the application of the sales tax. "The location of the property after the sale and the imposition of the tax is irrelevant."[77]

3. The "point of sale" test allows those Indians living off-reserve to purchase goods tax-free on reserves, regardless of where the goods are ultimately used, while it also allows those Indians living on-reserve to establish their own retail outlets in a competitive manner. The "point of sale" approach also allows for band governments to impose taxes on the sale of goods on reserve thus "creating a tax base for Aboriginal governments."[78]

Municipal governments have no authority to tax on reserves that are within municipal

---

[70] *Indian Self-Government Enabling Act*, R.S.B.C. 1996, c. 219.
[71] *Revenue Act*, S.N.S 1995–96, c.17.
[72] *Union of Nova Scotia Indians* v. *Nova Scotia (A.G.)*, [1999] 1 C.N.L.R. 277 (N.S.C.A.), leave to appeal to S.C.C. dismissed, [1998] S.C.C.A. 451 (S.C.C.).
[73] *Ibid.* at para. 24.
[74] *Union of New Brunswick Indians* v. *New Brunswick*, [1998] 1 S.C.R. 1161.
[75] *Social Services and Education Tax Act*, R.S.N.B., 1973, c. S-10, ss. 4, 5.
[76] *Supra* note 74.
[77] *Ibid.* at para. 35.
[78] *Ibid.* at paras. 43–45.

boundaries.[79] The application of municipal licences on reserves raises different issues. In *Surrey* v. *Peace Arch Ent. Ltd.*,[80] the British Columbia Court of Appeal confirmed that municipalities may not enact or enforce zoning by-laws respecting reserve lands within municipal boundaries.

TREATIES AND LAND CLAIMS AGREEMENTS[81]

No historic treaties expressly provide for tax exemptions for Indians. The reports of the treaty commissioners for a number of treaties make reference to verbal promises and assurances made to Indians that were not explicitly outlined in the language of the treaties. One such assurance related to taxation can be found in the 1899 report of the Treaty Commissioners in respect of Treaty No. 8:

> There was expressed at every point the fear that the making of the Treaty would be followed by the curtailment of the hunting and fishing privileges, and many were impressed with the notion that the Treaty would lead to taxation and enforced military service.
>
> We assured them that the Treaty would not lead to any forced interference with their mode of life, that it did not open the way to the imposition of any tax, and that there was no fear of enforced military service.

The Supreme Court of Canada in *Peguis*[82] cited the above passage as evidence that the signatories to Treaty No. 8 were promised an exemption from taxation regarding their treaty entitlements.

Some Aboriginal people argue that they possess treaty and Aboriginal rights that exempt them from taxation.[83] While the issue of an Aboriginal right to be exempt from taxation remains active, there appears to be a lack of substantive law supporting such a proposition.[84]

In *Benoit* v. *Canada*,[85] the Federal Court, Trial Division considered an action brought by a number of Treaty No. 8 (1899) beneficiary representatives who claimed that Treaty No. 8 included a treaty right not to have any tax imposed upon them at any time, for any reason. Campbell J. agreed with the plaintiffs and held that the evidence, including a treaty report written by the Crown's representative, clearly demonstrated that there was a promise made to the signatories of Treaty No. 8 and that in order for the honour of the Crown to be maintained, the Crown must recognize and fulfil the tax assurance as it was understood by the Aboriginal signatories. Campbell J. also concluded that this treaty right was never extinguished and that the Crown cannot justify its infringement.[86]

---

[79] *Campbell River* v. *Naknakim*, [1984] 2 C.N.L.R. 85 (B.C. Prov. Ct.); *Keewatin Tribal Council* v. *Thompson (City)*, [1989] 3 C.N.L.R. 121 (Man. Q.B.).

[80] *Surrey* v. *Peace Arch Ent. Ltd.* (1970), 74 .W.W.R. 380 (B.C.C.A.).

[81] For a good discussion of this issue see R.A. Brown & R.C. Strother, *The Taxation and Financing of Aboriginal Businesses in Canada,* looseleaf (Toronto: Carswell, 1998), chapter 11.

[82] *Peguis, supra* note 6 at 136.

[83] In the *Report of Commissioners for Treaty No. 8* (22 September 1899), the Hon. Clifford Sifton wrote: "We assured them [the Indians] that the treaty would not lead to any forced interference with their mode of life, that it did not open the way to the imposition of any tax" (Ottawa: DIAND, 1966) 6.

[84] For example, *R.* v. *Johnson*, [1994] 1 C.N.L.R. 129 (N.S.C.A.), noted that nothing in the Treaty of 1752 exempts Indians from paying tobacco taxes. *R.* v. *Poitras*, [1994] 3 C.N.L.R. 157 (Sask. Q.B.), held that Treaty No. 4 does not exempt Indians from paying tobacco taxes.

[85] *Benoit* v. *Canada*, [2002] 2 C.N.L.R. 1 (F.C.T.D.).

[86] *Ibid.* at paras. 333, 335.

The Federal Court of Appeal[87] overturned the trial court decision and concluded:

> . . . there is insufficient evidence to support the view that the Aboriginal signatories understood that they would be exempted from taxation at any time and for any reason. . . .

1. The Treaty is silent with respect to a promise exempting the Aboriginal signatories from taxation.

2. The documentary evidence relating to the Treaty, save for the Commissioners' Report, is also silent with respect to such a promise.

3. The Treaty Commissioners did not make such a promise and were not so authorized by the Canadian Government.

4. The Commissioners' Report, when received in Ottawa, did not give rise to any complaints or objections on the part of the Government, whose instructions to the Commissioners were that they should not go beyond the previous treaties.

5. The previous numbered treaties did not contain any promise of a tax exemption.

6. Drs. Irwin and McCormack, experts called by the respondents, both testified that their historical and anthropological research did not lead them to any written source which would support the view that the Aboriginal signatories understood that they had been exempted from tax.

7. The extensive 1946 submissions to the Joint Committee by the various Treaty 8 bands did not raise the issue of an unfulfilled tax promise.

8. Defenders of the Aboriginal signatories, such as Bishop Breynat and Father Fumoleau, did not voice any complaints with regard to an unfulfilled tax promise.

9. The TARR interviews do not support the view that a promise was made exempting the Aboriginal signatories from taxation.[88]

In *Pictou* v. *Canada*,[89] the Federal Court of Appeal considered an appeal by a number of Mi'kmaq Indians who operated gas bar/convenience stores on reserve lands from a decision of the Tax Court of Canada, which confirmed a GST assessment for failing to collect and remit on sales to non-Indian consumers. The primary Mi'kmaq arguments focused on the basis that: (*a*) they hold a treaty right not to pay taxes as a result of the Treaties of 1760–61 and s. 35(1) of the *Constitution Act, 1982*,[90] (*b*) they had a right to be consulted in respect of the imposition of the *Excise Tax Act*, and (*c*) such breach of the duty to consult was also a breach of a fiduciary relationship between the Mi'kmaq and the Crown.

The Federal Court of Appeal affirmed that:

1. the Mi'kmaq did not establish a treaty right to trade in the goods at issue;

2. any treaty-protected trade right of the Mi'kmaq does not include the sale of products to non-Indians;

3. there is nothing in the record to suggest that the Mi'kmaq would be exempt forever

---

[87] *Benoit* v. *Canada*, [2003] 3 C.N.L.R. 20, 2003 FCA 236 (F.C.A.).

[88] *Ibid.* at para. 116.

[89] *Pictou* v. *Canada*, [2003] 2 C.N.L.R. 213 (Fed. C.A.); aff'g [2001] 1 C.N.L.R. 230 (T.C.C.), leave to appeal to S.C.C. dismissed [2003] 3 C.N.L.R. iv (S.C.C.).

[90] *Constitution Act, 1982*, Schedule B to the *Canada Act 1982* (U.K.), 1982, c. 11, as am. by the *Constitution Amendment Proclamation 1983*, R.S.C. 1985, App. II, No. 46, adding ss. 35(3) and 35(4).

from the application of laws applicable to trading goods with non-Indians;

4. there is evidence to suggest that the Crown promised or is obligated to consult with the Mi'kmaq prior to imposing on them any new legislative burdens, such as the *Excise Tax Act*; and

5. the Crown does not have a fiduciary duty to consult the Mi'kmaq prior to enacting the *Excise Tax Act* or before assessing the Mi'kmaq for failure to collect and remit the applicable taxes.

Land claims agreements and modern treaties also deal with the issue of Aboriginal taxation. The financial components of the land claims agreements settled to date have been exempt from taxation. For example, s. 25.3.1 of the James Bay and Northern Quebec Agreement (1975)[91] provides that the capital amounts are not subject to taxation under the *Income Tax Act* as capital gains or as income. This provision is similar to that included in the Northeastern Quebec Agreement (1978).[92] Other land claims agreements have similar provisions.[93]

The authority of Indian bands and other Aboriginal governments to impose taxes is a cornerstone to the development of a substantive form of self-government. Of course, with taxation comes the responsibility of providing essential and basic community services. The Nisga'a Final Agreement provides that the Nisga'a Central Government may make laws with respect of direct taxation of Nisga'a citizens on Nisga'a lands for Nisga'a government purposes. The agreement also provides that s. 87 of the *Indian Act* will no longer apply to Nisga'a citizens after a twelve-year period, the first such example of phasing out the Act exemption. Chapter 16, ss. 5–9 of the NFA provides that s. 87 of the Act will not apply to Nisga'a citizens in respect of (*a*) transaction taxes after the eighth anniversary, and (*b*) all other taxes after the twelfth anniversary, of the effective date of the Nisga'a Final Agreement.

Section 20.6 of the Teslin Tlingit Council Final Agreement[94] provides that s. 87 of the *Indian Act* no longer applies to an interest in reserve or surrendered land in the Yukon Territory, or to personal property situated on-reserve in and out of the Yukon Territory to any Indian, Yukon First Nation, or an Indian band covered by the agreement. Section 20.6.0 of the Umbrella Final Agreement provides that on the third anniversary of the effective date of the settlement legislation, s. 87 of the Act will not apply to Yukon reserve lands, Yukon Indian bands, or Indians in the Yukon with respect to those Yukon First Nations that have ratified final agreements. In *Carcross/Tagish First Nation* v. *Canada*,[95] the Federal Court of Appeal confirmed that the Umbrella Final Agreement has no legal significance of its own and that the tax exemption in s. 87 continues to apply to Yukon Indian bands until they ratify a final agreements, as contemplated by the Umbrella Final Agreement.

[91] Canada Department of Indian Affairs and Northern Development, *James Bay and Northern Quebec Agreement* (Ottawa: Supply and Services, 1976).
[92] Canada, Department of Indian Affairs and Northern Development, *Northeastern Quebec Agreement* (Ottawa: Supply and Services, 1978).
[93] Inuvialuit Final Agreement (1984), s. 15(11); Gwich'in Final Agreement (1992), s. 11.2.1; Sahtu Dene and Metis Final Agreement (1993), s. 11.2.1; Umbrella Final Agreement—Council for Yukon Indians (1993), s. 20.3.1; Nunavut Land Claims Agreement (1993), s. 30.1.1; and Nisga'a Final Agreement (2000), c. 16, s. 18.
[94] Canada, Department of Indian Affairs and Northern Development, *Teslin Tlingit Council Final Agreement* (Ottawa: DIAND, 1993).
[95] *Carcross/Tagish First Nation* v. *Canada*, [2001] 4 C.N.L.R. 49 (F.C.A.).

The new *First Nations Goods and Services Tax Act*[96] provides authority for interested and eligible First Nations to levy sales tax on their lands. The tax is payable by both Aboriginal and non-Aboriginal people and applies in the same manner, and at the same rate, as the current goods and services tax or federal component of the harmonized sales tax. The obligation to pay the First Nations goods and services tax arises despite current tax exemptions under s. 87 of the *Indian Act* or other similar exemptions made by Parliament.

Even where the tax powers of a First Nation are limited by other federal legislation, the First Nation may, if listed in the schedule provided with this Act, enact a tax law under the authority of s. 4(1) of the *First Nations Goods and Services Tax Act*.

4.   (1) Subject to this section, the governing body of a first nation that is listed in the schedule and that is a band or has the power to enact laws that has been recognized or granted under any other Act of Parliament or under an agreement that has been given effect by any other Act of Parliament may enact a law that imposes

(a) a tax in respect of a taxable supply made on the lands of the first nation;

(b) a tax in respect of the bringing of tangible personal property onto the lands of the first nation from a place in Canada; and

(c) a tax in respect of an imported taxable supply made on the lands of the first nation.

Before a First Nations goods and services tax law comes into effect, the First Nation governing body must provide the Minister of Finance with a copy of the law, as well as negotiate an administration agreement with the Minister.

The *First Nations Goods and Services Tax Act* is intended to operate seamlessly with the current GST tax scheme. A First Nations goods and services tax applies to the supply of goods and services on First Nation lands in the same manner as GST applies off those lands. Moreover, s. 13 prevents double taxation. Any GST/HST that would otherwise apply, is retracted if a First Nations goods and services tax applies to the same goods and services.

CONCLUSION

The authority of Indian bands to tax their members and purchases on their reserve lands is key to the future of Aboriginal self-government[97] and self-sufficiency. While the Indian Act's s. 87 tax exemption provides some benefit to a limited number of beneficiaries, in the long term, the elimination of the tax exemption, balanced with an increased ability for Aboriginal governments to raise their own revenue and be ultimately accountable for the decisions they make, may result in an improvement in the social and economic welfare of Aboriginal Canadians.

[96] *First Nations Goods and Services Tax Act*, s. 67 of the *Budget Implementation Act, 2003*, S.C. 2003, c. 15.

[97] A claim of sovereign status will not exempt an Indian band's company from paying taxes; see *Canada (M.N.R.)* v. *Ochapowace Ski Resort Inc.*, [2002] 4 C.N.L.R. 76 (Sask. Prov. Ct.).

CASES AND MATERIALS

Indian Act, Sections 83, 87, 89, 90
R.S.C. 1985, c. I-5.

83. (1) Without prejudice to the powers conferred by section 81, the council of a band may, subject to the approval of the Minister, make by-laws for any or all of the following purposes, namely,

(a) subject to subsections (2) and (3), taxation for local purposes of land, or interests in land, in the reserve, including rights to occupy, possess or use land in the reserve;

      (a.1)   the licensing of businesses, callings, trades and occupations; . . .

(f) the raising of money from band members to support band projects; and

(g) with respect to any matter arising out of or ancillary to the exercise of powers under this section.

(2) An expenditure made out of moneys raised pursuant to subsection (1) must be so made under the authority of a by-law of the council of the band.

(3) A by-law made under paragraph (1)(a) must provide an appeal procedure in respect of assessments made for the purposes of taxation under that paragraph.

(4) The Minister may approve the whole or a part only of a by-law made under subsection (1). . . .

87. (1) . . . Notwithstanding any other Act of Parliament or any Act of the legislature of a province, but subject to section 83, the following property is exempt from taxation, namely,

(a) the interest of an Indian or a band in reserve lands or surrendered lands; and

(b) the personal property of an Indian or band situated on a reserve.

(2) No Indian or band is subject to taxation in respect of the ownership, occupation, possession or use of any property mentioned in paragraph (1)(a) or (b) or is otherwise subject to taxation in respect of any such property.

(3) No succession duty, inheritance tax or estate duty is payable on the death of any Indian in respect of any property mentioned in paragraphs (1)(a) or (b) or the succession thereto if the property passes to an Indian, nor shall any such property be taken into account in determining the duty payable under the Dominion Succession Duty Act, being chapter 89 of the Revised Statutes of Canada, 1952, or the tax payable under the Estate Tax Act, on or in respect of other property passing to an Indian. . . .

89. (1) . . . Subject to this Act, the real and personal property of an Indian or a band situated on a reserve is not subject to charge, pledge, mortgage, attachment, levy, seizure, distress or execution in favour or at the instance of any person other than an Indian or a band.

(1.1) . . . Notwithstanding subsection (1), a leasehold interest in designated lands is subject to charge, pledge, mortgage, attachment, levy, seizure, distress and execution.

(2) . . . A person who sells to a band or a member of a band a chattel under an agreement whereby the right of property or right of possession thereto remains wholly or in part in the seller, may exercise his rights under the agreement notwithstanding that the chattel is situated on a reserve.

90. (1) . . . For the purposes of sections 87 and 89, personal property that was
    (a) purchased by Her Majesty with Indian moneys or moneys appropriated by Parliament for the use and benefit of Indians or bands, or
    (b) given to Indians or to a band under a treaty or agreement between a band and Her Majesty, shall be deemed always to be situated on a reserve.

(2) Every transaction purporting to pass title to any property that is by this section deemed to be situated on a reserve or any interest in such property, is void unless the transaction is entered into with the consent of the Minister or is entered into between members of a band or between the band and a member thereof.

(3) Every person who enters into any transaction that is void by virtue of subsection (2) is guilty of an offence, and every person who, without the written consent of the Minister, destroys personal property that is by this section deemed to be situated on a reserve, is guilty of an offence.

R. v. Nowegijick

[1983] 1 S.C.R. 29 (S.C.C.). Ritchie, Dickson, Beetz, Estey, McIntyre, Chouinard, and Lamer JJ., January 25, 1983.

DICKSON J.:—The question is whether the appellant, Gene A. Nowegijick, a registered Indian can claim by virtue of the *Indian Act*, R.S.C. 1970, c. I-6, an exemption from income tax for the 1975 taxation year. . . .

Mr. Nowegijick is an Indian within the meaning of the *Indian Act* and a member of the Gull Bay (Ontario) Indian Band. During the 1975 taxation year Mr. Nowegijick was an employee of the Gull Bay Development Corporation, a company without share capital, having its head office and administrative offices on the Gull Bay Reserve. All the directors, members and employees of the Corporation live on the Reserve and are registered Indians.

During 1975 the Corporation in the course of its business conducted a logging operation 10 miles from the Gull Bay Reserve. Mr. Nowegijick was employed as a logger and remunerated on a piece-work basis. He was paid bi-weekly by cheque at the head office of the Corporation on the Reserve.

During 1975, Mr. Nowegijick maintained his permanent dwelling on the Gull Bay Reserve. Each morning he would leave the Reserve to work on the logging operations, and return to the Reserve at the end of the working day. . . .

The short but difficult question to be determined is whether the tax sought to be imposed under the *Income Tax Act*, S.C. 1970-71-72, c. 63 upon the income of Mr. Nowegijick can be said to be "in respect of" "any" personal property situated upon a reserve. . . .

Construction of Section 87 of the Indian Act

Indians are citizens and, in affairs of life not governed by treaties or the *Indian Act*, they are subject to all of the responsibilities including payment of taxes, of other Canadian citizens.

It is legal lore that, to be valid, exemptions to tax laws should be clearly expressed. It seems to me, however, that treaties and statutes relating to Indians should be liberally construed and doubtful expressions resolved in favour of the Indian. If the statute contains language which can reasonably be construed to confer tax exemption that construction, in my view, is to be favoured over a more technical construction which might be available to deny exemption. In *Jones* v. *Meehan,* 175 U.S. 1, it was held that "Indian treaties must be construed, not according to the technical meaning of their words, but in the sense in which they would naturally be understood by the Indians".

There is little in the cases to assist in the construction of s. 87 of the *Indian Act.* In *R.* v. *The National Indian Brotherhood* (1978), 78 D.T.C. 6488 [[1978] C.N.L.B. (No. 4) 107] the question was as to situs, an issue which does not arise in the present case. The appeal related to the failure of the National Indian Brotherhood to deduct and pay over to the Receiver General for Canada the amount which the defendant was required by the *Income Tax Act* and regulations to deduct from the salaries of its Indian employees. The salaries in question were paid to the employees in Ottawa by cheque drawn on an Ottawa bank. Thurlow A.C.J. said at p. 6491 [pp. 113–4 C.N.L.R.]:

> I have already indicated that it is my view that the exemption provided for by subsection 87 does not extend beyond the ordinary meaning of the words and expressions used in it. There is no legal basis, notwithstanding the history of the exemption, and the special position of Indians in Canadian society, for extending it by reference to any notional extension of reserves or of what may be considered as being done on reserves. The issue, as I see it, assuming that the taxation imposed by the *Income Tax Act* is taxation of individuals in respect of property and that a salary or a right to salary is property, is whether the salary which the individual Indian received or to which he was entitled was "personal property" of the Indian "situated on a reserve". . . .

A tax on income is in reality a tax on property itself. If income can be said to be property I cannot think that taxable income is any less so. Taxable income is by definition, s. 2(2) of the *Income Tax Act,* "his income for the year minus the deductions permitted by Division C." Although the Crown in paragraph 14 of its factum recognizes that "salaries" and "wages" can be classified as "personal property" it submits that the basis of taxation is a person's "taxable" income and that such taxable income is not "personal property" but rather a "concept", that results from a number of operations. This is too fine a distinction for my liking. If wages are personal property it seems to me difficult to say that a person taxed "in respect of" wages is not being taxed in respect of personal property. It is true that certain calculations are needed in order to determine the quantum of tax but I do not think this in any way invalidates the basic proposition.

The words "in respect of" are, in my opinion, words of the widest possible scope. They import such meanings as "in relation to", "with reference to" or "in connection with". The phrase "in respect of" is probably the widest of any expression intended to convey some connection between two related subject matters.

Crown counsel submits that the effect of s. 87 of the *Indian Act* is to exempt what can properly be classified as "direct taxation on property" and the judgment of Jackett C.J. in *Minister of National Revenue* v. *Iroquois of Caughnawaga (Caughnawaga Indian Band),* [1977] 2 F.C. 269 [[1977] C.N.L.B. (No. 1) 15] is cited. The question in that case was whether the employer's share of unemployment insurance premiums was payable in respect of persons employed by an Indian band at a hospital operated by the band on a reserve. It was argued that the premiums were "taxation" on "property" within s. 87 of the

Indian Act. Chief Justice Jackett held that even if the imposition by statute on an employer of liability to contribute to the cost of a scheme of unemployment insurance were "taxation" it would not, in the view of the Chief Justice, be taxation on "property" within the ambit of s. 87. The Chief Justice continued at p. 271:

> From one point of view, all taxation is directly or indirectly taxation on property; from another point of view, all taxation is directly or indirectly taxation on persons. It is my view, however, that when section 87 exempts "personal property of an Indian or band situated on a reserve" from "taxation", its effect is to exempt what can properly be classified as direct taxation on property. The courts have had to develop jurisprudence as to when taxation is taxation on property and when it is taxation on persons for the purposes of section 92(2) of *The British North America Act,* 1867, and there would seem to be no reason why such jurisprudence should not be applied to the interpretation of section 87 of the *Indian Act.* See, for example, with reference to section 92(2), *Provincial Treasurer of Alberta* v. *Kerr,* [1933] A.C. 710. . . .

With respect, I do not agree with Chief Justice Jackett that the effect of s. 87 of the *Indian Act* is only to exempt what can properly be classified as direct taxation on property. Section 87 provides that "the personal property of an Indian . . . on a reserve" is exempt from taxation; but it also provides that "no Indian . . . is . . . subject to taxation in respect of any such property". The earlier words certainly exempt certain property from taxation; but the latter words also exempt certain persons from taxation in respect of such property. As I read it, s. 87 creates an exemption for both persons and property. It does not matter then that the taxation of employment income may be characterized as a tax on persons, as opposed to a tax on property.

We must, I think, in these cases, have regard to substance and the plain and ordinary meaning of the language used, rather than to forensic dialectics. I do not think we should give any refined construction to the section. A person exempt from taxation in respect of any of his personal property would have difficulty in understanding why he should pay tax in respect of his wages. And I do not think it is a sufficient answer to say that the conceptualization of the *Income Tax Act* renders it so.

I conclude by saying that nothing in these reasons should be taken as implying that no Indian shall ever pay tax of any kind. Counsel for the appellant and counsel for the intervenants do not take that position. Nor do I. We are concerned here with personal property situated on a reserve and only with property situated on a reserve. . . .

Mitchell v. Peguis Indian Band

[1990] 2 S.C.R. 85 (S.C.C.). Dickson C.J., Lamer, Wilson, La Forest, L'Heureux-Dubé, Sopinka, and Gonthier JJ., June 21, 1990.

LA FOREST J. (SOPINKA and GONTHIER JJ., concurring):—I have had the advantage of reading the reasons of the Chief Justice. I agree with his proposed disposition of this case, but I do so for quite different reasons. With respect, I am unable to agree with his approach and, in particular, with his adoption of the trial judge's interpretation of s. 90(1)(b) of the *Indian Act,* R.S.C. 1970, c. I-6 [now R.S.C. 1985, c. I-5].

The Chief Justice has summarized the facts and the judicial history and I need not repeat them. In broad terms, the issue to be determined involves funds in the hands of the Government of Manitoba which it agreed to pay to the respondent Indians in settlement of a claim for the return of taxes paid by the Indians to Manitoba Hydro in respect of sales of electricity on reserves. The question is whether those funds may be garnisheed by the appellants who are suing the Indians for fees for representing the Indians in negotiating the settlement.

Both the trial judge [reported [1983] 4 C.N.L.R. 50, [1983] 5 W.W.R. 117] and the Court of Appeal [reported [1985] 2 C.N.L.R. 90, [1986] 2 W.W.R 477] held the funds were not subject to garnishment. These decisions, as the Chief Justice has noted, were based on the interpretation given by those courts to s. 90(1)(b) of the *Indian Act*. In my respectful view, this interpretation not only goes beyond the clear terms and purposes of the Act, but flies in the face of the historical record and has serious implications for Indian policy that are harmful both for government and native people. . . .

As is clear from the comments of the Chief Justice in *Guerin v. The Queen*, [1984] 2 S.C.R, 335 at 383, [1985] 1 C.N.L.R. 120 at 136, these legislative restraints on the alienability of Indian lands are but the continuation of a policy that has shaped the dealings between the Indians and the European settlers since the time of the *Royal Proclamation of 1763*. The historical record leaves no doubt that native peoples acknowledged the ultimate sovereignty of the British Crown, and agreed to cede their traditional homelands on the understanding that the Crown would thereafter protect them in the possession and use of such lands as were reserved for their use; see the comments of Professor Slattery in his article "Understanding Aboriginal Rights" (1987), 66 *Can. Bar Rev.* 727 at 753. The sections of the *Indian Act* relating to the inalienability of Indian lands seek to give effect to this protection by interposing the Crown between the Indians and the market forces which, if left unchecked, had the potential to erode Indian ownership of these reserve lands. This Court, in its recent decision of *Canadian Pacific Ltd.* v. *Paul*, [1988] 2 S.C.R. 654, [1989] 1 C.N.L.R. 47, alluded to this point when it noted, at p. 677 [pp. 59–60 C.N.L.R.], that the feature of inalienability was adopted as a protective measure for the Indian population lest it be persuaded into improvident transactions.

I take it to be obvious that the protections afforded against taxation and attachment by ss. 87 and 89 of the *Indian Act* go hand-in-hand with these restraints on the alienability of land. I noted above that the Crown, as part of the consideration for the cession of Indian lands, often committed itself to giving goods and services to the natives concerned. Taking but one example, by terms of the "numbered treaties" concluded between the Indians of the prairie regions and part of the Northwest Territories, the Crown undertook to provide Indians with assistance in such matters as education, medicine and agriculture, and to furnish supplies which Indians could use in the pursuit of their traditional vocations of hunting, fishing, and trapping. The exemptions from taxation and distraint have historically protected the ability of Indians to benefit from this property in two ways. First, they guard against the possibility that one branch of government, through the imposition of taxes, could erode the full measure of the benefits given by that branch of government entrusted with the supervision of Indian affairs. Secondly, the protection against attachment ensures that the enforcement of civil judgments by non-natives will not be allowed to hinder Indians in the untrammelled enjoyment of such advantages as they had retained or might acquire pursuant to the fulfillment by the Crown of its treaty obligations. In effect, these sections shield Indians from the imposition of the civil liabilities that could lead, albeit through an indirect route, to the alienation of the Indian land base through the medium of foreclosure sales and the like; see Brennan J.'s discussion of the purpose served by Indian tax immunities in the American context in *Bryan v. Itasca County*, 426 U.S. 373 (1976), at p. 391.

In summary, the historical record makes it clear that ss. 87 and 89 of the *Indian Act*, the sections to which the deeming provision of s. 90 applies, constitute part of a legislative "package" which bears the impress of an obligation to native peoples which the Crown has recognized at least since the signing of the *Royal Proclamation of 1763*. From that time on, the Crown has always acknowledged that it is honour-bound to shield Indians from any efforts by non-natives to dispossess Indians of the property which they hold *qua* Indians, i.e., their land base and the chattels on that land base.

It is also important to underscore the corollary to the conclusion I have just drawn. The fact that the modern-day legislation, like its historical counterparts, is so careful to underline that exemptions from taxation and distraint apply only in respect of personal property situated on reserves demonstrates that the purpose of the legislation is not to remedy the economically disadvantaged position of Indians by ensuring that Indians may acquire, hold, and deal with property in the commercial mainstream on different terms than their fellow citizens. An examination of the decisions bearing on these sections confirms that Indians who acquire and deal in property outside lands reserved for their use, deal with it on the same basis as all other Canadians. . . .

In support of my view that Indians will have perceived that their treaty benefits were given unconditionally, I would point to the following extract from the report of the Treaty Commissioners in respect of Treaty No. 8. The passage is eloquent testimony to the fact that native peoples feared that the imposition of taxes would seriously interfere with their ability to maintain a traditional way of life on the lands reserved for their use, and, additionally, leaves no doubt that Indians were promised that their entitlements would be exempt from taxation:

> There was expressed at every point the fear that the making of the Treaty would be followed by the curtailment of the hunting and fishing privileges, and many were impressed with the notion that the Treaty would lead to taxation and enforced military service.
>
> We assured them that the Treaty would not lead to any forced interference with their mode of life, that it did not open the way to the imposition of any tax, and that there was no fear of enforced military service. [Treaty No. 8, 1899 (Queen's Printer, Ottawa), as quoted in R. Bartlett, *Indians and Taxation in Canada*, 2d ed. (Saskatoon, Sask.: University of Saskatchewan Native Law Centre, 1987), p. 5]

In summary, I conclude that an interpretation of s. 90(1)(b), which sees its purpose as limited to preventing non-natives from hampering Indians from benefitting in full from the personal property promised Indians in treaties and ancillary agreements, is perfectly consistent with the tenor of the obligations that the Crown has always assumed vis-à-vis the protection of native property.

Section 90(1)(b) as including the Provincial Crowns

I turn next to the second of the two alternative readings of "Her Majesty" in s. 90(1)(b). If this term is meant to include the provincial Crowns, the exemptions and privileges of ss. 87 and 89 will apply to a much wider range of personal property. In effect, it would follow inexorably that the notional situs of s. 90(1)(b) will extend these protections to any and all personal property that could enure to Indians through the whole range of agreements that might be concluded between an Indian band and Her Majesty in right of a province.

As I see it, if one is to reject the interpretation advanced above, that s. 90(1)(b) refers solely to property which enures to Indians from the federal Crown through operation of the treaties and ancillary agreements, there is no basis in logic for the further assumption that some, but not all agreements, between Indian bands and provincial Crowns would be contemplated by the provision. Section 90(1)(b) does not qualify the term "agreement," and if one interprets "Her Majesty" as including the provincial Crown, it must follow as a matter of due course that s. 90(1)(b) takes in all agreements that could be concluded between an Indian band and a provincial Crown.

It follows inexorably that if an Indian band, pursuant to a purely commercial agreement with a provincial Crown, acquires personal property, that property will be exempt from taxation and distraint, regardless of its *situs*. Moreover, the protections of ss. 87 and 89 would apply in respect of any subsequent dealings by the Indian band respecting that property, even if those dealings were confined to ordinary commercial matters. This would have broad ramifications, and I cannot accept the notion that Parliament, in fulfilling its constitutional responsibility over Indian affairs, intended that the protective envelope of ss. 87 and 89 should apply on such a broad scale.

My conclusion rests on the fact that such a result cannot be reconciled with the scope of the protections that the Crown has traditionally extended to the property of natives. As I stated earlier, a review of the obligations that the Crown has assumed in this area shows that it has done no more than seek to shield the property of Indians that has an immediate and discernible nexus to the occupancy of reserve lands from interference at the hands of non-natives. The legislation has always distinguished between property situated on reserves and property Indians hold outside reserves. There is simply no evidence that the Crown has ever taken the position that it must protect property simply because that property is held by an Indian as opposed to a non-native. . . .

There can be no doubt, on a reading of s. 90(1)(b), that it would not apply to any personal property that an Indian band might acquire in connection with an ordinary commercial agreement with a private concern. Property of that nature will only be protected once it can be established that it is situated on a reserve. Accordingly, any dealings in the commercial mainstream in property acquired in this manner will fall to be regulated by the laws of general application. Indians will enjoy no exemptions from taxation in respect of this property, and will be free to deal with it in the same manner as any other citizen. In addition, provided the property is not situated on reserve lands, third parties will be free to issue execution on this property. I think it would be truly paradoxical if it were to be otherwise. As the Chief Justice has pointed out in *Nowegijick* v. *The Queen*, [1983] 1 S.C.R. 29 at 36, [1983] 2 C.N.L.R. 89 at 93–94:

> Indians are citizens and, in affairs of life not governed by treaties or the *Indian Act*, they are subject to all of the responsibilities, including payment of taxes, of other Canadian citizens.

But, in my respectful view, the implications flowing from the interpretation the trial judge advanced of s. 90(1)(b) go counter to this statement, for as I have pointed out earlier, as a logical consequence of that interpretation, any time Indians acquired personal property in an agreement with a provincial Crown, even one of a purely commercial character, the exemptions and protections of ss. 87 and 89 would apply in respect of that particular asset, regardless of *situs*. . . .

I conclude that the statutory notional *situs* of s. 90(1)(b) is meant to extend solely to personal property which enures to Indians through the discharge by "Her Majesty" of her treaty or ancillary obligations. Pursuant to s. 91(24) of the *Constitution Act, 1867*, it is of course "Her Majesty" in right of Canada who bears the sole responsibility for conferring any such property on Indians, and I would, therefore, limit application of the term "Her Majesty" as used in s. 90(1)(b) to the federal Crown. . . .

Moreover, I would question the conclusion that interpreting "Her Majesty" as including the provincial Crowns in the context of s. 90(1)(b) is tantamount to resolving the ambiguity of the meaning of this term in favour of the Indians. Section 87 and 89, as I have shown above, have been crafted so as to place obstacles in the way of non-natives who would presume to dispossess Indians of personal property that is situated on reserves. But when Indians deal in the general marketplace, the protections conferred by these sections have the potential to become powerful impediments to their engaging successfully in commercial matters. Access to credit is the lifeblood of commerce, and I find it very difficult to accept that Indians would see any advantage, when seeking credit, in being precluded from putting forth in pledge property they may acquire from provincial Crowns. Indians, I would have thought, would much prefer to have free rein to conduct their affairs as all other fellow citizens when dealing in the commercial mainstream.

To elaborate, if Indians are to be unable to pledge or mortgage such personal property as they acquire in agreements with provincial Crowns, businessmen will have a strong incentive to avoid dealings with Indians. This is simply because the fact that Indians will be liable to be distrained in respect of some classes of property, and not in respect of others, will introduce a level of complexity in business dealings with Indians that is not present in other transactions. I think it safe to say that businessmen place a great premium on certainty in their commercial dealings, and that, accordingly, the greatest possible incentive to do business with Indians would be the knowledge that business may be conducted with them on exactly the same basis as with any other person. Any special considerations, extraordinary protections or exemptions that Indians bring with them to the marketplace introduce complications and would seem guaranteed to frighten off potential business partners.

In summary, while I of course endorse the applicability of the canons of interpretation laid down in *Nowegijick*, it is my respectful view that the interpretation proposed in this particular instance takes one beyond the confines of the fair, large and liberal, and can, in fact, be seen to involve the resolution of a supposed ambiguity in a manner most unfavourable to Indian interests. . . .

I would dismiss the appeal with costs throughout.

Wilson J. (Lamer and L'Heureux-Dubé JJ., concurring): . . .

Dickson C.J.: . . .

The Applicable Interpretive Principles

I should say at the outset that I find the reasons and reasoning of Morse J. persuasive. In particular, he was correct in resorting to the principle enunciated by this Court in *Nowegijick* v. *The Queen*, [1983] 1 S.C.R. 29 at 36, [1983] 2 C.N.L.R. 89 at 94, when he found it necessary to resolve interpretive difficulties. In *Nowegijick* the Court had the following to say:

> It is legal lore that, to be valid, exemptions to tax laws should be clearly expressed. It seems to me, however, that treaties and statutes relating to Indians should be liberally construed and doubtful expressions resolved in favour of the Indians. If the statute contains language which can reasonably be construed to confer tax exemption that construction, in my view, is to be favoured over a more technical construction which might be available to deny exemption. In *Jones* v. *Meehan*, 175 U.S. 1 (1899), it was held that Indian treaties "must . . . be construed, not according to the technical meaning of [their] words . . . but in the sense in which they would naturally be understood by the Indians."

Two elements of liberal interpretation can be found in this passage: (1) ambiguities in the interpretation of treaties and statutes relating to Indians are to be resolved in favour of the Indians, and (2) aboriginal understandings of words and corresponding legal concepts in Indian treaties are to be preferred over more legalistic and technical constructions. In some cases, the two elements are indistinguishable, but in other cases the interpreter will only be able to perceive that there is an ambiguity by first invoking the second element.

The appellants maintain that the *Nowegijick* principle should not govern the present appeal. Rather, it is asserted that the normal principle that derogations from the civil rights of a creditor should be strictly construed, is applicable. The appellants attempt to distinguish *Nowegijick* in part by saying that the case was concerned with trying to resolve a conflict between the State and an Indian, in which case it was appropriate to resolve any ambiguity against the author of the doubt. The appellants are in effect arguing that *Nowegijick* is not applicable when it is a private citizen or other civil party, and not the State (the author of the doubt or ambiguity) who will lose out if the Act is interpreted in favour of aboriginal litigants.

I cannot accept that the comments in *Nowegijick* were implicitly limited in this way. The *Nowegijick* principles must be understood in the context of this Court's sensitivity to the historical and continuing status of aboriginal peoples in Canadian society. The above-quoted statement is clearly concerned with interpreting a statute or treaty with respect to the persons who are its *subjects*—Indians—not with interpreting a statute in favour of Indians simply because it is the State that is the other interested party. It is Canadian society at large which bears the historical burden of the current situation of native peoples and, as a result, the liberal interpretive approach applies to any statute relating to Indians, even if the relationship thereby affected is a private one. Underlying *Nowegijick* is an appreciation of societal responsibility, and a concern with remedying disadvantage, if only in the somewhat marginal context of treaty and statutory interpretation.

In oral argument, the appellants also sought to distinguish *Nowegijick* on the basis that the case dealt only with laws touching upon the particular status or qualities of Indians, thus providing a policy basis for the interpretive principle. *Nowegijick* dealt with tax exemptions under s. 87 of the Act, while this case deals with exemptions from garnishment ("attachment") under s. 89. Both provisions reflect the policy of the Act that Indians should be protected from the operation of laws which otherwise might allow Indians to be dispossessed of their property. In *Nowegijick*, the Court was concerned with whether a provincial law was applicable to Indians as a law of general application (s. 88, *Indian Act*). The only limitation to the principle articulated in *Nowegijick* was that the treaties or statutes must relat[e] to Indians" for the liberal interpretive principle to apply. The *Indian Act* is the quintessential Act relating to Indians and the interpretation of any provision in it is, therefore, subject to the *Nowegijick* principle.

I would finally note that the appellants' argument to the effect that as against a private party the Court should not create privileges where Parliament has not explicitly done so, even if accepted, would not avail them in this case. Section 89(1) provides that a non-Indian cannot attach personal property of an Indian in certain circumstances. It clearly contemplates that Indians will be favoured vis-à-vis non-Indians. Therefore, it would be inconsistent with *Nowegijick* to interpret s. 90, which extends s. 89's protection, in a restrictive manner. . . .

The Main Issue—The Meaning of "Her Majesty" . . .

The divisibility of the Crown in the sense just noted does not determine the interpretation to be given, to the words "Her Majesty." Even if the Court of Appeal had been correct as a matter of constitutional law regarding indivisibility of the Crown, this would not necessarily have determined the correct statutory interpretation of "Her Majesty" in s. 90(1)(b): see, for example, *Nickel Rim Mines Ltd.* v. *Attorney General for Ontario*, [1967] S.C.R. 672, 63 D.L.R. (2d) 668 in which Spence J. (in Chambers) interpreted "Her Majesty" in s. 105 of the *Supreme Court Act*, R.S.C. 1952, c. 259, as including both the federal and provincial Crowns despite his constitutional premise that "[t]here is only one Crown although there are two separate statutory purses" (at p. 674). Instead, Morse J.'s approach commends itself in all material respects (at pp. 127–28 W.W.R.) [p. 59 C.N.L.R.]:

> In the *Interpretation Act of Canada* (s. 28) it is provided that "'Her Majesty,' 'His Majesty,' 'the Queen,' 'the King' or 'the Crown' means the Sovereign of the United Kingdom, Canada, and Her other Realms and Territories, and Head of the Commonwealth." In *A.G. Que.* v. *Nipissing Ry. Co.*, [1926] A.C. 715 . . . , it was held by the Privy Council that s. 189 of the *Railway Act*, 1919 (Can.), c. 68, which empowered any railway company, with the consent of the Governor General, to take Crown lands for the use of the railway, applied to provincial Crown lands as well as to Dominion Crown lands. It was also held that the enactment was constitutionally valid by reason of the exclusive power to legislate in respect of interprovincial railways reserved to the Dominion Parliament by ss. 91(29) and 92(10) of the *B.N.A. Act, 1867* (now the *Constitution Act, 1867*).
>
> Giving a liberal construction to the words "Her Majesty" and resolving any doubt in favour of the defendants, I think that the words include Her Majesty in right of the Province of Manitoba.

In my view, the trial judge adopted the correct approach. "Her Majesty" can refer to the province; the question is whether it does so refer. . . .

Nowegijick directs the courts to resolve any "doubtful expression" in favour of the Indian where more than one reasonable interpretation is available. There is no doubt in my mind that it is fully in keeping with Nipissing and Nickel Rim Mines to turn to the *Nowegijick* principle in this case, given the ambiguity that exists. In each of those cases, it was found necessary to resort to some further argument beyond the text itself in order to determine the issue. In light of Nipissing and Nickel Rim Mines, I would turn, to *Nowegijick* for the resolution of the ambiguity here and would accordingly choose an interpretation that favours the Indians. I would, therefore, find that "Her Majesty" includes the provincial Crown.

This interpretation is also supported by the second aspect of the *Nowegijick* principle, namely that aboriginal understanding of words and corresponding legal concepts in Indian treaties are to be preferred over more legalistic and technical constructions. This concern with aboriginal perspective, albeit in a different context, led a majority of this Court in *Guerin* v. *The Queen*, [1984] 2 S.C.R. 335, [1985] 1 C.N.L.R. 120, to speak of the Indian interest in land as a *sui generis* interest, the nature of which cannot be totally captured by a lexicon derived from European legal systems.

While this appeal does not involve the interpretation of a treaty, I find it helpful to consider the aboriginal perspective in illustrating the ambiguity of "Her Majesty" in s. 90(1)(b). *Nowegijick* dictates taking a generous liberal approach to interpretation. In my opinion, reference to the notion of "aboriginal understanding," which respects the unique culture and history of Canada's aboriginal peoples, is an appropriate part of that approach. In the context of this appeal, the aboriginal understanding of "the Crown" or "Her Majesty" is rooted in pre-Confederation realities. The recent case of *Guerin* took as its fundamental premise the unique character both of the Indians' interest in land and of *the historical relationship with the Crown.* (at p. 387 S.C.R. [p. 139 C.N.L.R.] emphasis added.) That relationship began with pre-Confederation contact between the historic occupiers of North American lands (the aboriginal peoples) and the European colonizers (since 1763, "the Crown"), and it is this relationship between aboriginal peoples and the Crown that grounds the distinctive fiduciary obligation on the Crown. On its facts, *Guerin* only dealt with the obligation of the federal Crown arising upon surrender of land by Indians and it is true that, since 1867, the Crown's role has been played, as a matter of the federal division of powers, by Her Majesty in right of Canada, with the *Indian Act* representing a confirmation of the Crown's historic responsibility for the welfare and interests of these peoples. However, the Indians' relationship with the Crown or sovereign has never depended on the particular representatives of the Crown involved. From the aboriginal perspective, any federal-provincial divisions that the Crown has imposed on itself are internal to itself and do not alter the basic structure of Sovereign-Indian relations. This is not to suggest that aboriginal peoples are outside the sovereignty of the Crown, nor does it call into question the divisions of jurisdiction in relation to aboriginal peoples in federal Canada.

One can over-emphasize the extent to which aboriginal peoples are affected only by the decisions and actions of the federal Crown. Part and parcel of the division of powers is the incidental effects doctrine according to which a law in relation to a matter within the competence of one level of government may validity affect a matter within the competence of the other; as recently stated in *Alberta Government Telephones* v. *Canada (Canadian Radio-television and Telecommunications Commission)*, [1989] 2 S.C.R. 225 at p. 275, "Canadian federalism has evolved in a way which tolerates overlapping federal and provincial legislation in many respects. . . ." As long as Indians are not affected *qua* Indians, a provincial law may affect Indians, and significantly so in terms of everyday life. Section 88 of the *Indian Act* greatly increases the extent to which the provinces can affect Indians by acknowledging the validity of laws of general application, unless they are supplanted by treaties or federal law. This fluidity of responsibility across lines of jurisdiction accords well with the fact that the newly entrenched s. 35 of the *Constitution Act, 1982*, applies to all levels of government in Canada.

I conclude, therefore, that "Her Majesty" in s. 90(1)(b) of the *Indian Act* is to be interpreted as referring to both the federal and provincial Crowns. . . .

Conclusion

I find that the Court of Appeal was correct in the disposition of this case and the trial judge was correct in his reasoning and interpretation of the elements of s. 90(1)(b). "Her Majesty" in s. 90(1)(b) of the *Indian Act* refers to both the federal and provincial Crowns. Therefore, the moneys in question are protected from garnishment by virtue of s. 89(1) of the Act. The scope of this protection is defined according to the terms of the Act. General commercial transactions involving Indians are not meant to be limited by this interpretation. In this case, the substance of the appellants' claim has, of course, not been determined, and it is clearly open to the appellants to continue legal action. In the circumstances, however, the appellants are prevented from garnishing moneys owed to the respondents by the provincial Crown.

I would dismiss the appeal with costs in this Court and both courts below.

R. v. Williams

[1992] 1 S.C.R. 877 (S.C.C.). La Forest, L'Heureux-Dubé, Sopinka, Gonthier, Cory, McLachlin, and Stevenson JJ., April 16, 1992.

GONTHIER J.:—At issue in this case is the situs of unemployment insurance benefits received by an Indian for the purpose of the exemption from taxation provided by s. 87 of the *Indian Act*, R.S.C. 1970, c. I-6 (now R.S.C. 1985. c. I-5).

1. Facts and Procedural History

The appellant received a notice of assessment by the Minister of National Revenue which included in his income, for the taxation year 1984, certain unemployment insurance benefits. The appellant contested the assessment. His objection was overruled by the Minister of National Revenue. The appellant appealed to the Federal Court, Trial Division: [1989] 2 F.C. 318. . . . The appeal proceeded on the basis of an agreed statement of facts.

At all material times, the appellant was a member of the Penticton Indian Band and resided on the Penticton Indian Reserve No. 1. In 1984 he received regular unemployment insurance benefits for which he qualified because of his former employment with a logging company situated on the reserve, and his employment by the band in a "NEED Project" on the reserve. In both cases, the work was performed on the reserve, the employer was located on the reserve, and the appellant was paid on the reserve. During his employment, contributions to the unemployment insurance scheme were paid both by the appellant and his employers.

All of the regular unemployment insurance benefits were paid by federal government cheques mailed from the Canada Employment and Immigration Commission's regional computer centre in Vancouver. (While the instruments of payment may not technically have been cheques, this is of no consequence in this appeal.) . . .

3. Framing the Issues

In order to decide the basis upon which a situs is to be assigned to the unemployment insurance benefits in this case, it is necessary to explore the purposes of the exemption from taxation in s. 87 of the *Indian Act*, the nature of the benefits in question, and the manner in which the incidence of taxation falls upon the benefits to be taxed.

A. The Nature and Purpose of the Exemption from Taxation

The question of the purpose of ss. 87, 89 and 90 has been thoroughly addressed by La Forest J. in the case of *Mitchell* v. *Peguis Indian Band*, [1990] 2 S.C.R. 85. . . . La Forest J. expressed the view that the purpose of these sections was to preserve the entitlements of Indians to their reserve lands and to ensure that the use of their property on their reserve lands was not eroded by the ability of governments to tax or creditors to seize. The corollary of this conclusion was that the purpose of the sections was not to confer a general economic benefit upon the Indians. . . .

La Forest J. also noted that the protection from seizure is a mixed blessing, in that it removes the assets of an Indian on a reserve from the ordinary stream of commercial dealings (at pp. 146–47 [S.C.R., p. 66 C.N.L.R.]).

Therefore, under the Indian Act, an Indian has a choice with regard to his personal property. The Indian may situate this property on the reserve, in which case it is within the protected area and free from seizure and taxation, or the Indian may situate this property off the reserve, in which case it is outside the protected area, and more fully available for ordinary commercial purposes in society. Whether the Indian wishes to remain within the protected reserve system or integrate more fully into the larger commercial world is a choice left to the Indian.

The purpose of the *situs* test in s. 87 is to determine whether the Indian holds the property in question as part of the entitlement of an Indian *qua* Indian on the reserve. Where it is necessary to decide amongst various methods of fixing the location of the relevant property, such a method must be selected having regard to this purpose.

B. Nature of Benefit and the Incidence of Taxation

Section 56 of the *Income Tax Act* is the section which taxes income from unemployment insurance benefits. That section specifies that unemployment insurance benefits which are "received by the taxpayer in the year" are to be included in computing the income of a taxpayer. The parties have approached this question on the basis that what is being taxed is a debt owing from the Crown to the taxpayer on account of unemployment insurance which the taxpayer has qualified for. This is not precisely true, since the liability for taxation arises not when the debt (if that is what it is) arises, but rather when it is paid, and the money is received by the taxpayer. However, it is true that the taxation does not attach to the money in the hands of the taxpayer, but instead to the receipt by the taxpayer of the money. Thus the incidence of taxation in the case of unemployment insurance benefits is on the taxpayer in respect of the transaction, that is, the receipt of the benefit.

This Court's decision in *Nowegijick* v. *The Queen*, [1983] 1 S.C.R. 29, [1983] 2 C.N.L.R. 89, . . . stands for the proposition that the receipt of salary income is personal property for the purpose of the exemption from taxation provided by the *Indian Act*. I can see no difference between salary income and income from unemployment insurance benefits in this regard, therefore I hold that the receipt of income from unemployment insurance benefits is also personal property for the purposes of the *Indian Act*.

Nowegijick also stands for the proposition that the inclusion of personal property in the calculation of a taxpayers income gives rise to a tax in respect of that personal property within the meaning of the *Indian Act,* despite the fact that the tax is on the person rather than on the property directly.

Therefore, most of the requirements of s. 87 of the *Indian Act* have clearly been met in this case. The receipt of unemployment insurance benefits is personal property. That property is owned by an Indian. The Indian is being taxed in respect of that property, since it is being included in his income for the purpose of income taxation. The remaining question is whether the property in question is situated on a reserve.

Since it is the receipt of the benefit that is taxed, the simplest argument would be that the *situs* of the receipt of the benefit is where it is received, which would generally be the residence of the taxpayer. However, the *Income Tax Act* qualifies "received" by "in the year." This suggests that the notion of "receipt" in the *Income Tax Act* has more to do with when the income is received, rather than where. Thus, aside from the fact that the incidence of taxation falls upon the transaction itself, rather than the money in the hands of the employer or the taxpayer, little ought to be made of the notion of receipt in this context.

C. Comments on the "Residence of the Debtor" Test

The factor identified in previous cases as being of primary importance to determine the situs of this kind of property is the residence of the debtor, that is, the person paying the income. This was clearly stated by Thurlow A.C.J. in *The Queen* v. *National Indian Broth-*

erhood, [1979] 1 F.C. 103 at p. 109, 92 D.L.R. (3d) 333, ...:

> A chose in action such as the right to a salary in fact has no situs. But where for some purpose the law has found it necessary to attribute a *situs*, in the absence of anything in the contract or elsewhere to indicate the contrary, the *situs* of a simple contract debt has been held to be the residence or place where the debtor is found. See Cheshire, *Private International Law,* seventh edition, pp. 420 *et seq.*

This conclusion was cited with approval by this Court in *Nowegijick* v. *The Queen, supra,* at p. 34 [S.C.R., p. 92 C.N.L.R.]:

> The Crown conceded in argument, correctly in my view, that the situs of the salary which Mr. Nowegijick received was sited on the reserve because it was there that the residence or place of the debtor, the Gull Bay Development Corporation, was to be found and it was there that the wages were payable. See Cheshire and North, *Private International Law* (10th ed., 1979) at pp. 536 *et seq.* and also the judgment of Thurlow A.C.J. in *R.* v. *National Indian Brotherhood,* [1979] 1 F.C. 103 particularly at pp. 109 *et seq.*

The only justification given in these cases for locating the situs of a debt at the residence of the debtor is that this is the rule applied in the conflict of laws. The rationale for this rule in the conflict of laws is that it is at the residence of the debtor that the debt may normally be enforced. Cheshire and North, *Private International Law* (11th ed. 1987), quote Atkin L.J. to this effect in *New York Life Insurance Co.* v. *Public Trustee,* [1924] 2 Ch. 101 (C.A.), at p. 119:

> . . . the reason why the residence of the debtor was adopted as that which determined where the debt was situate was because it was in that place where the debtor was that the creditor could, in fact, enforce payment of the debt.

Dicey and Morris adopt the same explanation in *The Conflict of Laws* (11th ed. 1987), vol. 2, at p. 908, as does Castel in *Canadian Conflict of Laws* (2nd ed. 1986), at p. 401. This may be reasonable for the general purposes of conflicts of laws. However, one must inquire as to its utility for the purposes underlying the exemption from taxation in the *Indian Act.* . . .

In resolving this question, it is readily apparent that to simply adopt general conflicts principles in the present context would be entirely out of keeping with the scheme and purposes of the *Indian Act* and *Income Tax Act.* The purposes of the conflict of laws have little or nothing in common with the purposes underlying the *Indian Act.* It is simply not apparent how the place where a debt may normally be enforced has any relevance to the question whether to tax the receipt of the payment of that debt would amount to the erosion of the entitlements of an Indian *qua* Indian on a reserve. The test for *situs* under the *Indian Act* must be constructed according to its purposes, not the purposes of the conflict of laws. Therefore, the position that the residence of the debtor exclusively determines the *situs* of benefits such as those paid in this case must be closely reexamined in light of the purposes of the *Indian Act.* It may be that the residence of the debtor remains an important factor, or even the exclusive one. However, this conclusion cannot be directly drawn from an analysis of how the conflict of laws deals with such an issue.

4. The Proper Test

Because the transaction by which a taxpayer receives unemployment insurance benefits is not a physical object, the method by which one might fix its *situs* is not immediately apparent. In one sense, the difficulty is that the transaction has no *situs.* However, in another sense, the problem is that it has too many. There is the *situs* of the debtor, the *situs* of the creditor, the *situs* where the payment is made, the *situs* of the employment which created the qualification for the receipt of income, the *situs* where the payment will be used, and no doubt others. The task is then to identify which of these locations is the relevant one, or which combination of these factors controls the location of the transaction.

The appellant suggests that in deciding the *situs* of the receipt of income, a court ought to balance all of the relevant "connecting factors" on a case by case basis. Such an approach would have the advantage of flexibility, but it would have to be applied carefully in order to avoid several potential pitfalls. It is desirable, when construing exemptions from taxation, to develop criteria which are predictable in their application, so that the taxpayers involved may plan their affairs appropriately. This is also important as the same criteria govern an exemption from seizure.

Furthermore, it would be dangerous to balance connecting factors in an abstract manner, divorced from the purpose of the exemption under the *Indian Act*. A connecting factor is only relevant in so much as it identifies the location of the property in question for the purposes of the *Indian Act*. In particular categories of cases, therefore, one connecting factor may have much more weight than another. It would be easy in balancing connecting factors on a case by case basis to lose sight of this.

However, an overly rigid test which identified one or two factors as having controlling force has its own potential pitfalls. Such a test would be open to manipulation and abuse, and in focusing on too few factors could miss the purposes of the exemption in the *Indian Act* as easily as a test which indiscriminately focuses on too many.

The approach which best reflects these concerns is one which analyzes the matter in terms of categories of property and types of taxation. For instance, connecting factors may have different relevance with regard to unemployment insurance benefits than in respect of employment income, or pension benefits. The first step is to identify the various connecting factors which are potentially relevant. These factors should then be analyzed to determine what weight they should be given in identifying the location of the property, in light of three considerations: (1) the purpose of the exemption under the *Indian Act;* (2) the type of property in question; and (3) the nature of the taxation of that property. The question with regard to each connecting factor is therefore what weight should be given that factor in answering the question whether to tax that form of property in that manner would amount to the erosion of the entitlement of the Indian *qua* Indian on a reserve.

This approach preserves the flexibility of the case by case approach, but within a framework which properly identifies the weight which is to be placed on various connecting factors. Of course, the weight to be given various connecting factors cannot be determined precisely. However, this approach has the advantage that it preserves the ability to deal appropriately with future cases which present considerations not previously apparent.

A. The Test for the Situs of the Unemployment Insurance Benefits

Unemployment insurance benefits are income replacement insurance, paid when a person is out of work under certain qualifying conditions. While one often refers to unemployment insurance "benefits," the scheme is based on employer and employee premiums. These premiums are themselves tax-deductible for both the employer and employee.

There are a number of potentially relevant connecting factors in determining the location of the receipt of unemployment insurance benefits. The following have been suggested: the residence of the debtor, the residence of the person receiving the benefits, the place the benefits are paid, and the location of the employment income which gave rise to the qualification for the benefits. One's attention is naturally first drawn to the traditional test, that of the residence of the debtor. The debtor in this case is the federal Crown, through the Canada Employment and Immigration Commission. The Commission argues that the residence of the debtor in this case is Ottawa, referring to s. 11 of the *Employment and Immigration Department and Commission Act*, S.C. 1976–77, c. 54 (now R.S.C. 1985, c. E-5, s. 17), which mandates that the head office of the Commission be located in the National Capital Region.

There are, however, conceptual difficulties in establishing the *situs* of a Crown agency in any particular place within Canada. For most purposes, it is unnecessary to establish the *situs* of the Crown. The conflict of laws is interested in *situs* to determine jurisdictional and choice of law questions. With regard to the Crown, no such questions arise, since the Crown is present throughout Canada and may be sued anywhere in Canada. Unemployment insurance benefits are also available anywhere in Canada, to any Canadian who qualifies for them. Therefore, the purposes behind fixing the *situs* of an ordinary person do not apply to the Crown, and in particular do not apply to the Canada Employment and Immigration Commission in respect of the receipt of unemployment insurance benefits.

This does not necessarily mean that the physical location of the Crown is irrelevant to the purposes underlying the exemption from taxation provided by the *Indian Act*. However, it does suggest that the significance of the Crown being the source of the payments at issue in this case may lie more in the special nature of the public policy behind the payments, rather than the Crown's *situs*, assuming it can be fixed. Therefore, the residence of the debtor is a connecting factor of limited weight in the context of unemployment insurance benefits. For similar reasons, the place where the benefits are paid is of limited importance in this context. . . .

The general scheme of taxation with regard to unemployment insurance premiums and benefits bears further examination in this regard. As noted above, unemployment insurance is premium based. The intent of the scheme is that the premiums received will, overall, largely equal the benefits paid out. This is not to say that the scheme is completely self-financing. However, it is more accurate to characterize an unemployment insurance benefit as something paid for through the premiums of employed persons than to characterize it as a benefit granted by the government out of its general revenues.

This becomes important in analyzing the tax implications of the unemployment insurance benefit scheme. The treatment of premiums and benefits for the purposes of taxation is that the premiums paid by employed persons are deductible from their taxable income, whereas the benefits paid to unemployed persons must be included in their taxable income. By allowing premiums to be deducted from taxable income, and mandating that benefits be included in taxable income, the effect of the unemployment insurance scheme on general tax revenue is minimized. The tax revenues lost by the government due to the deductibility of premiums are offset by the revenues gained by the taxation of the benefits. This is not to say that the unemployment insurance scheme has no effect on taxation revenues, since premiums may not precisely equal benefits overall, and the effect of different rates of taxation cannot be ignored. However, it is clear that the scheme established by Parliament was intended, in principle, to minimize the tax implications of unemployment insurance.

Since unemployment insurance benefits are based on premiums arising out of previous employment, not general tax revenue, the connection between the previous employment and the benefits is a strong one. The manner in which unemployment insurance benefits are treated for the purposes of taxation further strengthens this connection, as there is a symmetry of treatment in the taxation of premiums and benefits, since premiums arc tax-deductible and benefits are taxed, thereby minimizing the influence of the unemployment insurance scheme on general tax revenues.

The location of the qualifying employment income is therefore an important factor in establishing whether the taxation of subsequent benefits would erode the entitlements of an Indian qua Indian on the reserve. For in the case of an Indian whose qualifying employment income was on the reserve, the symmetry in the tax implications of premiums and benefits breaks down. For such an Indian, the original employment income was tax-exempt. The taxation paid on the subsequent benefits therefore does more than merely offset the tax saved by virtue of the premiums. Instead, it is an erosion of the entitlements created by the Indian's employment on the reserve.

Furthermore, since the duration and extent of the benefits are tied to the terms of employment during a specified period, it is the location of the qualifying employment income during that period that is relevant.

Having regard to the importance of the location of the qualifying employment income as a factor in identifying the location of the unemployment insurance benefits, the remaining factor of the residence of the recipient of the benefits at the time of their receipt is only potentially significant if it points to a location different from that of the qualifying employment.

B. The Situs of the Appellant's Unemployment Insurance Benefits
In the present case, the residence of the appellant when he received the benefits was on the reserve.

It has been assumed by the parties that the previous employment of the appellant which gave rise to the qualification for unemployment insurance benefits was also located on the reserve, since the two employers in question were located on the reserve. This question must be reexamined in light of our determination that this conclusion cannot safely be drawn from the principles of the conflict of laws.

However, this would not be an appropriate case in which to develop a test for the *situs* of the receipt of employment income. All the potential connecting factors with respect to the qualifying employment of the appellant point to the reserve. The employer was located on the reserve, the work was performed on the reserve, the appellant resided on the reserve, and he was paid on the reserve. A test for the *situs* of employment income could therefore only be developed in an abstract vacuum in this case, since there is no real controversy of relevant factors pulling in opposite directions. The same would be true of any consideration of the weight, if any, to be given to the residence of the appellant upon receipt of the benefits as this was also on the reserve.

Furthermore, as can be seen from our discussion of the test for the *situs* of unemployment insurance benefits, the creation of a test for the location of intangible property under the *Indian Act* is a complex endeavour. In the context of unemployment insurance we were able to focus on certain features of the scheme and its taxation implications in order to establish one factor as having particular importance. It is not clear whether this would be possible in the context of employment income, or what features of employment income and its taxation should be examined to that end.

. . . [T]he employment of the appellant by which he qualified for unemployment insurance benefits was clearly located on the reserve, no matter what the proper test for the *situs* of employment income is determined to be. Because the qualifying employment was located on the reserve, so too were the benefits subsequently received. The question of the relevance of the residence of the recipient of the benefits at the time of receipt does not arise in this case since it was also on the reserve. . . .

Determining the *situs* of intangible personal property requires a court to evaluate various connecting factors which tie the property to one location or another. In the context of the exemption from taxation in the *Indian Act*, there are three important considerations: the purpose of the exemption; the character of the property in question; and the incidence of taxation upon that property. Given the purpose of the exemption, the ultimate question is to what extent each factor is relevant in determining whether to tax the particular kind of property in a particular manner would erode the entitlement of an Indian *qua* Indian to personal property on the reserve.

With regard to the unemployment insurance benefits received by the appellant, a particularly important factor is the location of the employment which gave rise to the qualification for the benefits. In this case, the location of the qualifying employment was on the reserve, therefore the benefits received by the appellant were also located on the reserve. The question of the relevance of the residence of the recipient of the benefits at the time of receipt does not arise in this case.

The appeal is therefore allowed and the cross-appeal dismissed, with costs throughout. The matter is referred back to the Minister of National Revenue to be reassessed on the basis that all of the unemployment benefits in question are exempt from taxation.

Indian Act Exemption for Employment Income: Guidelines.

CCRA, June 1994. (See also the CCRA's Income Tax—Technical New Issue No. 2, December 30, 1994, for an additional summary.)

Guideline 1

When at least 90% of the duties of an employment are performed on a reserve, all of the income of an Indian from that employment will usually be exempt from income tax. . . .

Proration Rule

When less than 90% of the duties of an employment are performed on a reserve and the employment income is not exempted by another guideline, the exemption is to be prorated. The exemption will apply to the portion of the income related to the duties performed on the reserve. . . .

Guideline 2

When:
- The employer is resident on a reserve; and
- The Indian lives on a reserve;

all of the income of an Indian from an employment will usually be exempt from income tax. . . .

Guideline 3

When:
- More than 50% of the duties of an employment are performed on a reserve; and

- The employer is resident on a reserve, or the Indian lives on a reserve;

all of the income of an Indian from an employment will usually be exempt from income tax. . . .

Guideline 4

When:

- The employer is resident on a reserve; and
- The employer is:
  - an Indian band which has a reserve, or a tribal council representing one or more Indian bands which have reserves, or
  - an Indian organization controlled by one or more such bands or tribal councils, if the organization is dedicated exclusively to the social, cultural, educational, or economic development of Indians who for the most part live on reserves; and
- the duties of the employment are in connection with the employer's non-commercial activities carried on exclusively for the benefit of Indians who for the most part live on reserves;

all of the income of an Indian from an employment will usually be exempt from income tax. . . .

Employment Related Income

The receipt of unemployment insurance benefits, retiring allowances, Canada Pension Plan payments, Quebec Pension Plan payments, registered pension plan benefits or wage loss replacement plan benefits will usually be exempt from income tax when received as a result of employment income that was exempt from tax. If a portion of the employment income was exempt, then a similar portion of these amounts will be exempt. . . .

Meaning of Terms Used

"Employer is resident on a reserve" means that the reserve is the place where the central management and control over the employer organization is actually located. . . .

GST/HST Technical Information Bulletin B-039R
November 25, 1993.

Introduction

This bulletin summarizes the policy concerning the treatment of Indian purchases under the Goods and Services Tax (GST)

. . .

The treatment of Indian purchases under the GST is consistent with the *Indian Act* under which personal property of an Indian or an Indian band situated on a reserve and their interests in reserves or designated lands are not subject to tax.

. . .

Certificate of Indian Status Card

The Certificate of Indian Status identification card is issued by the Department of Indian Affairs and Northern Development to eligible Indians. The certificates are laminated identifications that display the Canadian maple leaf logo, followed immediately by Indian and Northern Affairs Canada. The certificate may also bear the photograph and description of the individual, a registry number, the name of the band to which the individual belongs, and the family number.

. . .

An Indian must present proof of registration under the *Indian Act* to a vendor in order to acquire property or services on reserve without paying the GST. Revenue Canada, Customs, Excise and Taxation, will accept as proof of registration under the *Indian Act* the Certificate of Indian Status identification card. . . .

Purchases by Indians, Indian Bands and Band Empowered Entities

Property

On Reserve

Indians, Indian bands, or unincorporated band-empowered entities may acquire property on reserve without paying the GST, provided they have the appropriate documentation to show the vendor.

Acquisitions of property on reserve by non-Indians will be subject to the normal GST rules.

Normally, corporations are considered to be separate legal persons from either an Indian or an Indian band and would not be eligible for relief from the GST. However, the tax will not apply to incorporated band-empowered entities purchasing for band management activities.

Off Reserve

Indians, Indian bands and unincorporated band-empowered entities, as well as incorporated band-empowered entities purchasing for band management activities, may acquire property off reserve without paying the GST, provided
• they have the appropriate documentation to show the vendor; and
• the property is delivered to a reserve by the vendor or the vendor's agent.

However, if the purchaser uses his or her own vehicle to transport the property to the reserve, the acquisition is subject to the normal GST rules.

Note: There is an exception for remote stores. . . .

Importations

Importations by Indians, Indian bands or band-empowered entities are subject to the normal import rules, that is, they are taxable at seven per cent unless they are specifically zero-rated. GST on imported goods is collected by Canada Customs under the authority of the *Customs Act* at the time of importation.

Importations of goods are subject to the GST even in those instances where, after importation, the property is delivered to a reserve by the vendor's agent or by Canada Post.

Services

Individual Indians

• **Services for property.** If a service is performed totally on reserve and the property is situated on reserve at that time, *the GST will not apply.*
• **Services for individuals.** If the service is performed totally on reserve for an Indian who is on reserve at the time the service is performed, e.g., a haircut given on reserve, *the service will not be subject to the GST.*
• **Transportation services.** *GST will apply to these services, unless* both the origin and the destination are on a reserve. For example, a taxi service operating within the boundaries of a reserve would not charge GST on that reserve fare.

Individual Indians must pay the seven per cent GST on all taxable services that are not performed or occur totally on reserve, unless the services are purchased for real property interests on reserve.

Services are subject to the normal GST rules when they are provided to non-Indians on reserve.

Indian Bands and Band-Empowered Entities

Services acquired on or off reserve by an Indian band or band-empowered entity for band management activities or for real property on reserve are not subject to GST.

Exception: Indian bands and band-empowered entities will pay the GST on off-reserve purchases of transportation, short-term accommodation, meals and entertainment. However, the band or the band-empowered entity may file a General Rebate application to recover the GST paid on these purchases when these services are purchased for management activities or for real property located on reserve.

Other Rebate: Indian bands and band-empowered entities are entitled to file the applicable Public Service Body Rebate for a partial rebate on the remaining GST that was paid. Please note that band funding of Indian non-profit organizations will be considered equivalent to government funding to qualify for the 50 per cent GST rebate to non-profit organizations.

Vendor Documentation

Vendors must keep adequate evidence that sales for which no GST was payable were made to Indians, Indian bands or band-empowered entities.

Individual Indians

When the purchaser is an individual Indian, vendors must maintain adequate evidence that a sale was made to an Indian, as registered under the *Indian Act.* Revenue Canada will accept as adequate evidence, notation on the invoice or other sales document which is retained by the vendor, of the nine or ten digit registry number or the band name and family number (commonly referred to as the band number/treaty number).

Indian Bands and Band-Empowered Entities

When the purchaser is an Indian band or band-empowered entity, a certificate must be provided and retained by the vendor that the property is being acquired by an Indian band or band-empowered entity or that the services are being acquired for band management activities. . . .

Off-Reserve Purchases of Property Delivered to a Reserve

Along with the individual's *Certificate of Indian Status* card number *or* the certification by the Indian band or band-empowered entity, the vendor is required to maintain proof of delivery (e.g., waybill, postal receipt, freight bill, etc.), indicating the destination of the property to a reserve.

Delivery

If the store from which property has been acquired is not located on a reserve, then the property must be delivered to a reserve for the purchase to be relieved from the GST.

The property must be delivered by either the vendor or an agent of the vendor.

If these conditions or the provisions for remote stores . . . are not met, the normal GST rules apply.

Vendor

Where property is delivered to a reserve in the vendor's own vehicle, the vendor must maintain proof that delivery was made to a reserve. This will be indicated on the invoice of the vendor and the vendor's internal records, e.g., mileage log, dispatch records. Such proof must be maintained in addition to the proof of Indian status or certification by an Indian band or band-empowered entity.

Normal GST rules will apply where an Indian, Indian band or band-empowered entity who is the purchaser takes possession of the property off a reserve and delivers the property to a reserve in his or her own vehicle.

Vendor's Agent

Where the property is delivered by the vendor's agent to a reserve, the vendor must maintain:

- proof of Indian status or certification by the band or band-empowered entity; and
- proof of delivery being made to the reserve (e.g., a waybill, postal receipt showing a reserve address, etc.).

An agent of the vendor includes an individual or company under contract to the vendor for making deliveries (e.g., postal services, trains, boats, couriers, etc.). The vendor would normally bear all the risks of the agent during the course of the delivery as if these risks were the vendor's own, unless specifically covered in the agency agreement.

A carrier who is under contract with the recipient is not regarded as the agent of the vendor. In addition, undertakings by purchasers of property to deliver the property to themselves as agents of the vendor are not acceptable to the Department.

Sales By Indians, Indian Bands and Band-Empowered Entities

Businesses owned by Indians, Indian bands or band-empowered entities whose annual sales of property and services are more than $30,000, are required to register for the GST. Like other businesses, once registered, they must collect the tax on their sales of property and services (unless the sales are made to Indians, bands or band-empowered entities under conditions in which the GST is not payable), claim input tax credits for the GST paid on purchases made in carrying out their business and remit the balance to Revenue Canada Excise/GST.

Businesses, whether owned by Indians or non-Indians, selling property or services to Indians must include their taxable sales to Indians, *even if no GST was charged,* in their calculation of annual revenue to determine if they must register for the GST. Sales of property and services taxable at seven per cent are considered to be tax relieved when sold to Indians, Indian bands or band-empowered entities . . .; however, they are still considered taxable sales.

Incorporated businesses owned by Indians must pay the GST on their purchases of taxable goods and services. Incorporated band-empowered entities are not required to pay GST on property acquired for use in band management activities and GST will not apply when services are acquired for band management activities or for real property on reserve.

Sole proprietorships and partnerships owned by Indians receive the same treatment on purchases as individual Indians. If they are registered for the GST, they, like all other businesses, must collect the GST on their sales of taxable property and services (unless they are made to Indians, bands or band-empowered entities under the conditions in which the GST is not payable) and can recover any GST they do pay on their business purchases by claiming input tax credits.

In the case of purchases made by partnerships, tax relief is available for purchases made in either the Indian purchaser's own name or the partnership name. Where a partnership has both Indian and non-Indian participants, relief from GST will apply fully to the partnership. However, all conditions for the Indian or band partner to receive tax relief on the acquisition must be met, i.e., property must be acquired on reserve or delivered to a reserve and the proper documentation must be maintained.

Remote Stores

Some vendors who are not located on a reserve make a significant portion of their sales to Indians, Indian band and band-empowered entities. In some instances, these vendors are in a remote location and their *regular trading zone* includes a reserve which is not in the immediate vicinity. In such cases, the requirement for goods to be delivered to a reserve by the vendor in remote locations may be difficult to meet, either because of the prohibitive cost or a lack of public transportation.

In recognition of the unique circumstances of both the vendor and purchaser, the requirement for delivery to a reserve will be waived where property is purchased by an Indian, Indian band or band-empowered entity in the following circumstances:

Option 1

Where the regular trading zone of the vendor includes a reserve and,
- the vendor is located in a remote location, and,
- during the previous year, more than 50 per cent of all sales were made to Indians, Indian bands or band-empowered entities,

the requirement that goods be delivered to a reserve by the vendor in order to be relieved from GST will not apply. The regular trading zone means the area in which all or substantially all (90 per cent or more) of a vendor's customers reside.

A vendor is considered to be in a remote location when:
- the vendor is serviced by year-round road access, and is located over 350 kilometres from the nearest community with a population of 5,000 or more, by the most direct route normally travelled in the circumstances; or
- surface transportation is not available year-round on paved or gravelled roads linking the vendor with the nearest established community. An established community means a village, hamlet, town, etc. within which there exist most basic or standard municipal services.

Please note that a vendor in an established community which is not linked by year-round roads to other communities is *not* considered to be in a remote location. Therefore, such a vendor cannot use this option in order to waive the delivery requirement on sales to Indians, Indian bands and band-empowered entities.

Option 2

The requirement for delivery will also be waived where
- the vendor is within 10 kilometres of the reserve; and
- during the previous year, all or substantially all the vendor's sales (90 per cent or more) were made to Indians, Indian bands or band-empowered entities situated on reserve.

For both Option 1 and Option 2, the vendor must continue to keep the required documentation to verify on any given sale that the purchaser was an Indian, Indian band or band-empowered entity. This documentation will be used to verify the percentage of total sales made to Indians, Indian bands and band-empowered entities, and to justify non-payment of the GST on otherwise taxable sales.

Each year, vendors who choose to operate under the special provisions for remote stores must advise the nearest Revenue Canada Excise/GST District Office in writing of their decision to do so.

SELECTED BIBLIOGRAPHY

Bartlett, R. *Indians and Taxation in Canada*, 3d ed. (Saskatoon: University of Saskatchewan Native Law Centre, 1992).

Brown, R.A. & R.C. Strother. *The Taxation and Financing of Aboriginal Businesses in Canada* (Toronto: Carswell, 1998) looseleaf.

Canadian Tax Journal (2000), Vol. 48, No. 4 (pp. 1181–1251), No. 5 (pp. 1468–1644) and No. 6 (pp. 1815–48).

Dockstator, M. "The Nowegijick Case: Implications for Indian Tax Planning" [1985] 4 C.N.L.R. 1.

LeDressay, A. "A Brief Tax(on a me) of First Nations Taxation and Economic Development" in *Sharing the Harvest: The Road to Self-Reliance*, Royal Commission on Aboriginal Peoples (Ottawa: RCAP, 1993).

Morry, H. "Taxation of Aboriginals in Canada" (1992) 21:3 Man. L.J. 426.

Chapter 6

ABORIGINAL RIGHTS AND
THE *CONSTITUTION ACT, 1982*

INTRODUCTION

Prior to 1982, Aboriginal and treaty rights were vulnerable to unilateral federal modification or extinguishment. The 1973 decision of *Calder* v. *B.C. (A.G.)*[1] was a watershed in
that the Supreme Court of Canada formally recognized the existence of Aboriginal title,
but it was not until existing Aboriginal and treaty rights received express constitutional
recognition and affirmation that their legal status became clearer under Canadian law.
On April 17, 1982, the *Constitution Act, 1982*[2] was proclaimed into force, initiating a
new era for the rights of Aboriginal people in Canadian law. In addition to constitutionally recognizing and affirming existing Aboriginal and treaty rights, the *Constitution Act,
1982* contains the *Canadian Charter of Rights and Freedoms*[3] (Charter) and a Canadian-
based amending formula for the Constitution of Canada.

BACKGROUND

In October 1980, Prime Minister Trudeau introduced a proposal to amend the Constitution of Canada, including adding a charter of rights and a new amending procedure,
which made no reference to Aboriginal and treaty rights. However, by the time the Constitution was amended in 1982, ss. 25, 35, and 37 were added to the *Constitution Act,
1982,* which included express references to Aboriginal people. Section 37[4] of the *Constitution Act, 1982* required the Prime Minister to convene a constitutional conference on
matters affecting Aboriginal people within one year after the coming into force of the
Constitution Act, 1982. In March 1983 this conference was held and resulted in changes[5]
to s. 25 of the Charter[6] and s. 35[7] and added s. 35.1, which required that before any
constitutional amendment is made to s. 91(24) of the *Constitution Act, 1867*[8] (s. 91(24)),
to s. 25 of the Charter, or to Part II (including s. 35 of the *Constitution Act, 1982*), a

---

[1] *Calder* v. *B.C. (A.G.),* [1973] S.C.R. 313.
[2] *Constitution Act, 1982,* Schedule B of the *Canada Act 1982* (U.K.), 1982, c. 11 as am. by the *Constitution
Amendment Proclamation 1983,* R.S.C. 1985, App. II, No. 46, [am. ss. 25(b) and add. ss. 35(3), 35(4), 35.1,
37.1 and 54.1].
[3] *Canadian Charter of Rights and Freedoms,* Part I of the *Constitution Act, 1982, supra* note 2.
[4] Section 37 of the *Constitution Act,* 1982 was automatically repealed on 18 April 1983 by operation of s. 54
of the *Constitution Act, 1982.*
[5] *Constitutional Amendment Proclamation, supra* note 2.
[6] Section 25 of the Charter was amended by replacing the phrase "land claims settlement" with "land claims
agreements or may be so acquired."
[7] Section 35 of the *Constitution Act, 1982* was amended by adding subsections (3) and (4).
[8] *Constitution Act, 1867* (U.K.), 30 and 31 Vict., c. 3, reprinted in R.S.C. 1985, App. II, No. 5.

constitutional conference involving the Premiers and the Prime Minister would be convened and representatives of the Aboriginal people of Canada would be invited to participate. Finally, s. 37.1 was also added by the 1983 amendments, requiring two additional constitutional conferences to be held, with Aboriginal issues to be included on the agenda of each.[9] The Government of Canada, nine provincial governments (Quebec excepted), the two territorial governments, and the four national Aboriginal organizations agreed to the constitutional amendments. Subsequent Aboriginal constitutional conferences in 1984, 1985, and 1987, focusing mainly on self-government, failed to produce any further constitutional amendments.[10]

In March 1987, Prime Minister Mulroney and the ten Premiers agreed on the Meech Lake Constitutional Accord,[11] which proposed to recognize Quebec as a distinct society but did not include any reference to the rights of Aboriginal people. The Meech Lake Accord was not enacted because it did not receive the consent of the Legislatures of Newfoundland and Manitoba. In 1992, a Canada-wide referendum was held respecting the Charlottetown Accord, which proposed, among other items, that Aboriginal governments comprise a distinct and separate order of government, alongside the federal and provincial governments, and that the inherent right of self-government be constitutionally entrenched.[12] The Canadian electorate did not approve the Charlottetown Accord.

SECTION 25, *CANADIAN CHARTER OF RIGHTS AND FREEDOMS*

Section 25 of the Charter states:

> The guarantee in this Charter of certain rights and freedoms shall not be construed so as to abrogate or derogate from any aboriginal, treaty or other rights or freedoms that pertain to the aboriginal peoples of Canada including (a) any rights or freedoms that have been recognized by the Royal Proclamation of October 7, 1763; and (b) any rights or freedoms that now exist by way of land claims agreements or may be so acquired.

Section 25, the only provision of the Charter that makes express reference to Aboriginal people, does not create any new rights for Aboriginal people, but protects Aboriginal and treaty rights from being abrogated or derogated by Charter rights. The Supreme Court of Canada has confirmed that s. 25 is representative of one of Canada' core constitutional values—the protection of the rights of minorities—and is "a non-derogation clause in favour of the rights of aboriginal people."[13] In effect, s. 25 prevents other rights and freedoms guaranteed in the Charter from having a negative effect on existing Aboriginal and treaty rights.

[9] Section 37.1 was repealed on 18 April 1987 by s. 54.1 of the *Constitution Act, 1982.*

[10] See R.E. Gaffney, G.P. Gould & A.J. Semple, *Broken Promises: The Aboriginal Constitutional Conferences* (Fredericton: N.B. Association of Metis and Non-Status Indians, 1984); N. Zlotkin, *Unfinished Business: Aboriginal Peoples and the 1983 Constitutional Conference* (Kingston: Institute of Intergovernmental Relations, Queen's University, 1983); N. Zlotkin, "The 1983 and 1984 Constitutional Conferences: Only the Beginning", [1984] 3 C.N.L.R. 3; D. Hawkes, *Aboriginal Peoples and Constitutional Reform: What Have We Learned?* (Kingston: Institute of Intergovernmental Relations, Queen's University, 1989); B. Schwartz, *First Principles: Constitutional Reform with Respect to the Aboriginal Peoples of Canada 1982–1984* (Kingston: Queen's University, Institute of Intergovernmental Relations, 1986).

[11] See P. Hogg, *Meech Lake Constitutional Accord Annotated* (Toronto: Carswell, 1988).

[12] See Thomas Isaac, "The 1992 Charlottetown Accord and First Nations People: Guiding the Future" (1992) 8:2 Native Studies Rev. 109.

[13] *Reference re: Secession of Quebec*, [1998] 2 S.C.R. 217 at para. 82.

The purpose of s. 25 can be found in an examination of the other provisions of the Charter that could be interpreted as having an impact upon or modifying the rights of Aboriginal people. For example, s. 15(1) provides that every individual is equal before the law and is entitled to equal protection and benefit of the law without discrimination, based on a number of criteria, including race. Subsection 15(1) could be interpreted as having an impact upon Aboriginal and treaty rights since such rights, by their very nature, are distinguishable from the rights held by non-Aboriginal Canadians. Thus, statutes such as the *Indian Act*[14] could, but for s. 25, be held to be constitutionally invalid and discriminatory, contrary to the Charter.[15]

The New Brunswick Court of Appeal in *Augustine and Augustine v. R.; Barlow v. R.*[16] cited with approval the following statement from Peter Hogg's *Constitutional Law of Canada*:

> [Section 25] does not create any new rights, or even fortify existing rights. It is simply a saving provision, included to make clear that the Charter is not to be construed as derogating from "any aboriginal, treaty or other rights or freedoms that pertain to the aboriginal peoples of Canada". In the absence of s. 25, it would perhaps have been arguable that rights attaching to groups defined by race were invalidated by s. 15 (the equality clause) of the Charter.[17]

"Abrogate" means to repeal or abolish.[18] "Derogate" means to take away or detract from.[19] Thus, the terminology of s. 25 suggests that Charter rights cannot be construed so as to abolish or detract from Aboriginal, treaty, or other rights and freedoms of Aboriginal people. Section 25 does not include the word "existing" as used in s. 35(1). Although this could mean that s. 25 continues to apply to Aboriginal and treaty rights that did not exist as of April 17, 1982, the likely better interpretation is that the Aboriginal and treaty rights to which s. 25 refers means only those rights that exist and are recognized and affirmed by s. 35(1). As a result, the reference in s. 25 to "aboriginal and treaty rights" should likely be read as incorporating those *existing* Aboriginal and treaty rights recognized and affirmed by s. 35(1). Section 25 also expressly recognizes the rights set out in the *Royal Proclamation of 1763*,[20] although the effect of such recognition has not yet been judicially considered.

The interplay between the individual rights and freedoms accorded to all Canadians, including Aboriginal people, by the Charter and the distinct collective rights that Aboriginal people also possess is an important question that remains to be fully judicially considered.[21] The discourse of Aboriginal rights is often associated with the language of

---

[14] *Indian Act*, R.S.C. 1985, c. I-5.

[15] See also Bruce Wildsmith, *Aboriginal Peoples and Section 25 of the Canadian Charter of Rights and Freedoms*, (Saskatoon: University of Saskatchewan Native Law Centre, 1988) at 2; W. Pentney, "The Rights of the Aboriginal Peoples of Canada and the *Constitution Act, 1982*; Part I: The Interpretive Prism of Section 25" (1988) 22:1 U.B.C. L. Rev. 21; K. McNeil, "The Constitution Act, 1982, Sections 25 and 35," [1988] 1 C.N.L.R. 1; K. McNeil, "Aboriginal Government and the *Canadian Charter of Rights and Freedoms* (1996) 34:1 Osgoode Hall L. J. 61–99.

[16] *Augustine and Augustine v. R.; Barlow v. R.*, [1987] 1 C.N.L.R. 20 at 44 (N.B.C.A.).

[17] Peter Hogg, *Constitutional Law of Canada*, 2d ed. (Toronto: Carswell, 1985); this statement was in his 3rd ed. (1992), 27.9, p. 694, and altered slightly in his 4th ed. (1997) 27.9, pp. 700–1.

[18] *The Concise Oxford Dictionary of Current English*, 8th ed., ed. by. R.E. Allen (Oxford: Clarendon Press, 1990) 4.

[19] *Ibid. at* 314.

[20] *Royal Proclamation of 1763*, R.S.C. 1985, App. II, No. 1.

[21] The Charter has been used successfully by Aboriginal people to protect their individual rights and freedoms;

the collective or the group, and can limit the discussion of individual rights. Thus, a balanced approach to the interpretation of the Constitution is required to ensure that one set of the rights does not overshadow another set of rights.

The reference to "other rights and freedoms" in s. 25 could arguably have the effect of protecting Aboriginal rights or freedoms that are not otherwise constitutionally recognized and affirmed by s. 35(1), such as those contained in the *Indian Act* or other federal statutes.[22] If this is the case, then it is possible that s. 25 is more than an "interpretive prism,"[23] and could become a mechanism by which statutory rights or freedoms are somewhat insulated from the Charter application. However, it is not clear that the provisions of the *Indian Act,* for example, would be included. The words "rights" and "freedoms" are notably absent from the Act. Likewise, including statutory provisions within the meaning of s. 25 is not necessary since Parliament has the exclusive constitutional authority to legislate with respect to Indians and their lands, as set out in s. 91(24). While parts of the Act may be discriminatory by violating s. 15(1) of the Charter, it can perhaps be constitutionally justified, without s. 25, on the basis of s. 1 of the Charter as being "demonstrably justified in a free and democratic society," and on the basis of s. 91(24). This conclusion is based on the Act not containing "other rights and freedoms" for the purposes of s. 25. This is supported, in part, by L'Heureux-Dubé J.'s dissenting reasons in relation to s. 25 in *Corbiere v. Canada (Min. of Indian and Northern Affairs).*[24] She noted that a mere reference to Aboriginal people in a statute, on its own, is not sufficient to bring the statute or the reference within the scope of s. 25.[25]

It is not clear what "other rights and freedoms" Aboriginal people may possess that are not already covered by s. 25. This could simply be an all-inclusive reference to ensure that nothing is missed. It could also be a reference to those rights and freedoms set out, for example, in federal and provincial human rights legislation. This would ensure that the anti-discriminatory protection provided for in such human rights legislation would work for the benefit of Aboriginal people without fear of being trumped by the Charter. The case law suggests that the Charter applies to Indian band governments under the *Indian Act.*[26]

---

for example see: *Bearshirt* v. *Canada*, [1987] 2 C.N.L.R. 55 (Alta. Q.B.) (s. 2(a), freedom of religion and conscience); *R.* v. *Skead*, [1984] 4 C.N.L.R. 108 (Alta. Prov. Ct.) (s. 2(b), freedom of expression and assembly); *R.* v. *Daniels*, [1990] 4 C.N.L.R. 51 (Sask. Q.B.), rev'd on other grounds (1991), 93 Sask. R. 144 (Sask. C.A.), lv. to app. refused [1992] 1 S.C.R. vii (s. 7, life, liberty and security of the person); *R.* v. *Noltcho*, [1987] 1 C.N.L.R. 108 (Sask. Prov. Ct.), *Douglas* v. *R.*, [1984] 3 C.N.L.R. 65 (B.C. Co. Ct.), and *R.* v. *Jackson*, [1992] 4 C.N.L.R. 121 (Ont. Prov. Ct.) (s. 8, reasonable search or seizure); *R.* v. *Bird*, [1991] 2 C.N.L.R. 96 (Sask. Q.B.) and *R.* v. *Angnatuk*, [2000] 2 C.N.L.R. 81 (C.Q. (Crim. Div.)), aff'd [2001] 4 C.N.L.R. 257 (Que. C.A.) (s. 11(b), trial within a reasonable time); *R.* v. *Pratt*, [1986] 1 C.N.L.R. 123 (Sask. Prov. Ct.), *R.* v. *Herman*, [1986] 1 C.N.L.R. 72 (Sask. Prov. Ct.), *R.* v. *Chief*, [1990] 1 C.N.L.R. 92 (Y.T.C.A.), and *R.* v. *McGillivary*, [1991] 3 C.N.L.R. 130 (Sask. C.A.) (s. 12, cruel and unusual treatment or punishment); *R.* v. *Punch*, [1986] 2 C.N.L.R. 114 (N.W.T.S.C.), *R.* v. *Perry*, [1996] 2 C.N.L.R. 167 (Ont. Ct. (Gen. Div.)), *Willier* v. *Alberta (Liquor Control Bd.)*, [1996] 3 C.N.L.R. 233 (Alta. Liq. Lic. App. Council), *R.* v. *Morin*, [1996] 3 C.N.L.R. 157 (Sask. Prov. Ct.), *Scrimbitt* v. *Sakimay Indian Band Council*, [2000] 1 C.N.L.R. 205 (F.C.T.D.), and *Corbiere* v. *Canada (Min. of Indian and Northern Affairs)*, [1999] 2 S.C.R. 203 (s. 15(1), equality rights).

[22] See Pentney, *supra* note 15 at 55–57, and McNeil (1996), *supra* note 15 at 89–90.

[23] See Pentney, *supra* note 15.

[24] *Corbiere* v. *Canada (Min. of Indian and Northern Affairs)*, [1999] 2 S.C.R. 203.

[25] *Ibid.* at para. 52.

[26] For a summary of such case law, see *Horse Lake First Nation* v. *Horseman*, [2003] 2 C.N.L.R. 180 (Alta. Q.B.) at paras. 20–28.

Judicial Application of Section 25

Few courts have considered s. 25. In *Steinhauer* v. *R.*,[27] the Alberta Court of Queen's Bench held that s. 25 acts as a shield and does not add to Aboriginal rights. In *Corbiere*,[28] the Supreme Court of Canada considered an action by the off-reserve members of the Batchewana Band in Ontario, who comprise approximately 70 percent of the band's total membership. The majority of the off-reserve band members were re-registered under the *Indian Act* as a result of Bill C-31 amendments.[29] The off-reserve band members claimed that their exclusion from voting in band elections under s. 77(1) of the *Indian Act* violated s. 15(1) of the Charter. The Court agreed, with McLachlin J. (as she then was) and Bastarache J. stating that the Court was not prepared to deal with s. 25 since a case for its application in the matter under appeal had not been made.[30]

L'Heureux-Dubé J., writing the dissent in *Corbiere*, outlined some considerations to be taken into account when examining s. 25. She stated that the reference to "other rights and freedoms that pertain to the aboriginal peoples of Canada" in s. 25 was a reference to more than those existing Aboriginal and treaty rights recognized and affirmed by s. 35(1) and could include statutory rights, that is, rights outlined in legislation:[31]

> I emphasize, however, that as I will discuss below, the contextual approach to s. 15 requires that the equality analysis of provisions relating to Aboriginal people must always proceed with consideration of and respect for Aboriginal heritage and distinctiveness, recognition of Aboriginal and treaty rights, and with emphasis on the importance for Aboriginal Canadians of their values and history.[32]

L'Heureux-Dubé J. also wrote:

> Section 25 is triggered when s. 35 Aboriginal or treaty rights are in question, or when the relief requested under a *Charter* challenge could abrogate or derogate from "other rights or freedoms that pertain to the aboriginal peoples of Canada." This latter phrase indicates that the rights included in s. 25 are broader than those in s. 35, and may include statutory rights. However, the fact that legislation relates to Aboriginal people cannot alone bring it within the scope of the "other rights or freedoms" included in s. 25.[33]

The simple fact that a statute makes reference to Aboriginal people, then, is not enough, on its own, to automatically bring the statute and the reference to Aboriginal people within the scope of s. 25. This statement supports the earlier analysis that any statutory provision relating to Aboriginal people that is to be included within the scope of s. 25 must make express reference to a right or freedom.

In *Shubenacadie Indian Band* v. *Canada*,[34] the Federal Court of Appeal reaffirmed that s. 25 is a shield that "protects the rights mentioned therein from being adversely affected by other Charter rights"[35] and that it can "only be evoked as a defence if it had been found that the appellant's conduct had violated s. 15(1) of the Charter."[36]

---

[27] *Steinhauer* v. *R.*, [1985] 3 C.N.L.R. 187 at 191 (Alta. Q.B.).

[28] *Corbiere, supra* note 24.

[29] In 1985, Parliament enacted Bill C-31 to bring the Act into conformity with the Charter and ensured equality of treatment to Indian women and men with respect to membership under the Act.

[30] *Corbiere, supra* note 24 at para. 20.

[31] *Ibid.* at para. 52.

[32] *Ibid.* at paras. 53–54.

[33] *Ibid.* at para. 52.

[34] *Shubenacadie Indian Band* v. *Canada (Human Rights Commission)*, [2000] 4 C.N.L.R. 275 (F.C.A.) at para. 20.

[35] *Ibid.* at para. 43.

[36] *Ibid.*

In *Friends of Democracy* v. *Northwest Territories (A.G.)*,[37] de Weerdt J. of the Northwest Territories Supreme Court considered an application for a declaration that certain sections of the Northwest Territories *Legislative Assembly and Executive Council Act* were void in that they violated s. 3 (right to vote) of the Charter. The Legislative Assembly declined a proposal by the Electoral Boundaries Commission to add two electoral districts to represent under-represented voters in Yellowknife. Intervenors, representing Aboriginal people in the area, argued against the application, stating that nothing should affect the *status quo* respecting the distribution of electoral districts in the Legislative Assembly until ongoing land claim and self-government negotiations with Aboriginal people were complete. They argued that s. 25 implicitly supported this position. In allowing the application, in part, de Weerdt J. stated:

> I remain unpersuaded that section 3 of the Charter is in any sense to be understood as qualified by section 25 of the Charter . . . given the evidence before the court in this application. It is entirely unacceptable that such a fundamental right of citizenship as that recognized and guaranteed in section 3 of the Charter . . . should be held in suspense, and thus be withheld, during government negotiations over the future of self-government of aboriginal or other groups which might yet take decades to bring to a conclusion.[38]

In denying leave to appeal, the Northwest Territories Court of Appeal stated:

> While our decision should not be taken to mean or to imply that the rights of the interveners as set out in ss. 35 and 25 are unimportant quite to the contrary, the interveners have not satisfied us on the material before us that leave to appeal ought to be granted.[39]

In *R. v. Redhead*,[40] Oliphant J. of the Manitoba Court of Queen's Bench dismissed an application by an Aboriginal person charged with second degree murder for an order that he was entitled, based on an Aboriginal right, to have his trial held in his home community and have jury members selected from among its residents. The Court held that the Government of Manitoba did not violate the applicant's rights under ss. 7, 11(d), 15(1), or 25, of the Charter. In dismissing the application, the Court stated that the Aboriginal applicant:

> can place no reliance whatsoever on s. 25 of the *Charter*. That section does not confer new rights upon aboriginal people. It merely confirms certain rights held by aboriginal people prior to the inception of the *Charter*. There is absolutely no evidence before me that the rights claimed here . . . were conferred upon aboriginal people prior to the inception of the *Charter*.[41]

In *R. v. F (A)*,[42] Strach J. of the Ontario Court of Justice–General Division, considered an application by an Aboriginal person charged with sexual assault against another Aboriginal person at the Sandy Lake First Nation. The applicant asserted a constitutional right to be tried by a jury of his cultural peers rather than the process set out in the Ontario *Juries Act*. In dismissing the application, Strach J. stated:

> Section 25 confers no new substantive rights or freedoms upon aboriginal peoples. . . . Section 25 simply means that the rights and freedoms given generally to the people of Canada

---

[37] *Friends of Democracy* v. *N.W.T. (A.G.)* (1999), 171 D.L.R. (4th) 551 (N.W.T.S.C.).
[38] *Ibid.* at para. 26.
[39] *Friends of Democracy* v. *N.W.T. (A.G.)* (1999), 176 D.L.R. (4th) 661, at para. 13 (N.W.T.C.A.).
[40] *R. v. Redhead*, [1996] 3 C.N.L.R. 217 (Man. Ct. Q.B.).
[41] *Ibid.* at para. 84.
[42] *R. v. Fiddler*, [1994] 4 C.N.L.R. 99 (Ont. Ct. (Gen. Div.)).

shall not be construed so as to override aboriginal rights. . . . In my view, aboriginal rights are not being impaired; none are being overridden.[43]

All three decisions, *Friends of Democracy, Redhead,* and *Fiddler,* are similar in that the Aboriginal claimants in each case did not provide sufficient evidence to support a claim that they possessed a right or freedom, as Aboriginal people, within the meaning of s. 25. To date, the judicial decisions in which s. 25 has been considered are often based on poor facts and weak evidence to demonstrate the existence of Aboriginal and treaty rights, or "other rights and freedoms," for the purposes of s. 25, or, more generally, have not had s. 25 as their primary focus.[44]

In *Campbell* v. *British Columbia,*[45] the Liberal Party of British Columbia challenged the Nisga'a Final Agreement. One argument raised was that the provisions of the agreement that prevented non-Nisga'a from voting in Nisga'a elections violated s. 3 of the Charter (the right to vote). Williamson J. of the British Columbia Supreme Court rejected this argument:

> [O]ne must keep in mind that the communal nature of Aboriginal rights is on the face of it at odds with the European/North American concept of individual rights articulated in the *Charter.* . . . [T]he purpose of this section is to shield the distinctive position of Aboriginal peoples in Canada from being eroded or undermined by provisions of the *Charter.*[46]

Williamson J. answered the questions surrounding s. 25 and the Charter in an absolute manner by stating that s. 25, in protecting treaty rights from abrogation or derogation by Charter rights, protects the Nisga'a Final Agreement from any limitations that may be imposed on it by the Charter. However, Williamson J. also noted that while it was argued that the Nisga'a Final Agreement violates the rights of non-Nisga'a citizens set out in s. 7 (right to life, liberty, and security of the person) and s. 15(1) of the Charter, no evidence was submitted that they have "actually been denied some right"[47] under the Charter. Thus, the question could not be answered with respect to the circumstances of the case.

Section 25 is likely supplemental to s. 15(2) of the Charter in that s. 15(2) underscores the fundamental purpose behind s. 25.[48] Subsection 15(2) states that any affirmative action program to assist people based on race is not precluded simply because of the anti-discriminatory provisions in s. 15(1). Section 25 is not limited merely to s. 15(1) but is directed toward *all* rights and freedoms guaranteed by the Charter. The Ontario Court of Justice (Provincial Division) held in *R.* v. *Willocks*[49] that s. 25 does not prevent a court from examining Aboriginal alternative justice programs in light of s. 15 of the Charter.

SECTION 35, *CONSTITUTION ACT, 1982*

"Aboriginal rights" are those rights held by Aboriginal people that relate to activities that are an element of a practice, custom, or tradition integral to the distinctive culture of the Aboriginal group claiming such rights, and that have not otherwise been extinguished

---

[43] *Ibid.* at p. 129.
[44] See also *R.* v. *David,* [2000] O.J. No. 561 (Ont. Sup. Ct.) at para. 11.
[45] *Campbell* v. *British Columbia (A.G.),* [2000] 4 C.N.L.R. 1 (B.C.S.C.).
[46] *Ibid.* at paras. 155 and 158.
[47] *Ibid.* at para. 165.
[48] *R.* v. *Nicholas and Bear,* [1989] 2 C.N.L.R. 131 (N.B.Q.B.).
[49] *R.* v. *Willocks,* [1994] 1 C.N.L.R. 167 (Ont. Ct. J. (Prov. Div.)).

prior to April 17, 1982, or by treaty.[50] "Aboriginal title" is a subcategory of Aboriginal rights and encompasses the right to exclusive use and occupation of the land for a variety of purposes and that those protected uses must not be irreconcilable with the nature of the Aboriginal group's attachment to such land.[51] "Treaty rights" are those rights that are contained in treaties entered into between the Crown and Aboriginal people and can include specific rights such as those relating to hunting, fishing, and trapping. Although some treaties date back to the eighteenth century, modern treaties or land claims agreements have been concluded beginning in the 1970s.

Prior to s. 35(1), Aboriginal rights and treaty rights could be unilaterally modified or extinguished by the federal Crown. Parliament's authority over "Indians, and lands reserved for the Indians" is set out in s. 91(24). Section 35 of the *Constitution Act, 1982* states:

(1) The existing aboriginal and treaty rights of the aboriginal peoples of Canada are hereby recognized and affirmed.

(2) In this Act, "aboriginal peoples of Canada" includes the Indian, Inuit and Métis peoples of Canada.

(3) For greater certainty, in subsection (1) "treaty rights" includes rights that now exist by way of land claims agreements or may be so acquired.

(4) Notwithstanding any other provision of this Act, the aboriginal and treaty rights referred to in subsection (1) are guaranteed equally to male and female persons.

Through a series of decisions including *R. v. Sparrow*,[52] *R. v. Badger*,[53] *R. v. Van der Peet*,[54] *Delgamuukw*,[55] and *R. v. Marshall*,[56] the Supreme Court of Canada has set out the meaning and significance of the constitutional recognition and affirmation of Aboriginal rights and treaty rights in s. 35(1). This body of case law has resulted in federal and provincial laws, acts, or decisions that interfere with and infringe existing Aboriginal and treaty rights being subject to such rights, unless the laws, acts, or decisions can be justified by the Crown. Subsection 35(1) has been described by the Supreme Court of Canada as a "solemn commitment [by the Crown] that must be given meaningful content"[57] and s. 35(1) calls for a "just settlement for aboriginal peoples."[58] The Court set out an analysis to determine if s. 35(1) has been infringed by a government regulation, act, or decision. The analysis is composed of two elements: (1) the infringement test, and (2) the justification analysis.

The Infringement Test

The first question to be asked is whether the federal[59] or provincial[60] legislation in question has the effect of "interfering" with an existing Aboriginal right or treaty right. If

[50] *R. v. Van der Peet*, [1996] 2 S.C.R. 507 at para. 46.
[51] *Delgamuukw* v. *B.C.*, [1997] 3 S.C.R. 1010 at para. 159.
[52] *R. v. Sparrow*, [1990] 1 S.C.R. 1075.
[53] *R. v. Badger*, [1996] 1 S.C.R. 771.
[54] *Van der Peet, supra* note 50.
[55] *Delgamuukw, supra* note 51.
[56] *R. v. Marshall*, [1999] 3 S.C.R. 456 and *R. v. Marshall* (reconsideration refused), [1999] 3 S.C.R. 533.
[57] *Sparrow, supra* note 52 at 1108.
[58] *Ibid.* at 1106.
[59] *Ibid.* at 1108.
[60] *R. v. Côté*, [1996] 3 S.C.R. 139 at para. 74; and *Delgamuukw, supra* note 51 at para. 160.

there is an interference with an existing Aboriginal or treaty right, there is a *prima facie* infringement of s. 35(1). Questions to be asked to determine whether the legislation, act, or decision in question interferes with an existing Aboriginal and treaty right include:

1. Is the limitation imposed by the regulation/legislation unreasonable?[61]

2. Does the regulation/legislation impose undue hardship on the Aboriginal people affected? This can include asking whether, in the case of the exercise of ministerial discretionary authority, that authority is adequately described and takes into consideration the potential existence of Aboriginal and treaty rights.[62]

3. Does the regulation deny the holders of the right their preferred means of exercising their right?[63] and

4. Does the regulation unnecessarily infringe the interests protected by the right?

The onus to prove the infringement of an Aboriginal right or treaty right rests with the group or person challenging the legislation at issue.[64]

The Justification Test

If there has been interference with an existing Aboriginal right or treaty right, there is a *prima facie* infringement of s. 35(1). The analysis then moves to the justification test, which shifts the onus to the Crown to demonstrate that the infringement is justified.[65] The purpose of this justification analysis is to determine what constitutes a legitimate and justifiable infringement of an existing Aboriginal and treaty right.[66] The justification test requires a case-by-case analysis.[67] This is significant because the results in Aboriginal legal decisions can vary and are hardly predictable. It underscores that while the courts have been useful in articulating general principles and guidelines to deal with the adjudication of Aboriginal and treaty rights, no generalizations can be made. With such a dependence on the courts and case-by-case analyses, it is no wonder the courts have not hesitated in promoting negotiations rather than litigation to settle these issues.[68]

The Supreme Court of Canada has stated that the objective of Parliament, provincial governments, and their respective agencies must be examined to determine the merits of the government's justification, and that the merits will vary from resource to resource, species to species, community to community, and from time to time.[69] Valid legislative

---

[61] *Sparrow, supra* note 52 at 1112.

[62] *Sparrow, ibid.; R. v. Adams*, [1996] 3 S.C.R. 101; *Côté, supra* note 60 at para. 76. In *Côté*, user fees for parks were not considered an "undue hardship" and not an infringement of s. 35(1) (see *Côté* at para. 78).

[63] *Sparrow, ibid.* In *Badger, supra* note 53 at para. 89, the Supreme Court of Canada held that hunting regulations enacted for safety purposes did not deny the holders of their preferred means of hunting and did not infringe s. 35(1).

[64] *Sparrow, supra* note 52 at 1112; see also *R. v. Gladstone*, [1996] 2 S.C.R. 723 at para. 39.

[65] See *R. v. Guimond*, [2001] 2 C.N.L.R. 195 (Man. Prov. Ct.) at paras. 186–224. An example of where the federal Department of Fisheries and Oceans met the justification test can be found in *R. v. Aleck*, [2001] 2 C.N.L.R. 118 (B.C. Prov. Ct.).

[66] *Sparrow, supra* note 52 at 1112–13; *Badger, supra* note 53 at paras. 82, 96; *Côté, supra* note 60 at para. 81; *Gladstone, supra* note 64 at para. 54; and *Delgamuukw, supra* note 51 at para. 161.

[67] *Delgamuukw, supra* note 51 at para. 165.

[68] In *Delgamuukw, supra* note 51 at para. 186, Lamer C.J. stated: "Ultimately, it is through negotiated settlements, with good faith and give and take on all sides, reinforced by the judgments of this Court, that we will achieve what I stated in *Van der Peet [supra* note 50 at para. 31] to be a basic purpose of s.35(1)—'the reconciliation of the pre-existence of aboriginal societies with the sovereignty of the Crown.' Let us face it, we are all here to stay."

[69] *Marshall* (reconsideration), *supra* note 56 at para. 22.

objectives can justify an infringement of a s. 35(1) right, and include: conserving and managing a natural resource,[70] preventing harm to the general populous and Aboriginal people (ensuring safety),[71] other "compelling and substantial" objectives,[72] "important general public objectives," limits placed on existing Aboriginal and treaty rights where the objectives furthered are of "sufficient importance to the broader community as a whole,"[73] economic and regional fairness, and, in the case of fishing, the historical reliance upon and participation in the fishery by non-Aboriginal people.[74] In *Delgamuukw*, the Court stated that the following objectives are valid for justifying an infringement under s. 35(1):

> [D]evelopment of agriculture, forestry, mining, and hydroelectric power, the general economic development of the interior of British Columbia, protection of the environment or endangered species, the building of infrastructure and the settlement of foreign populations.[75]

As the above excerpt from *Delgamuukw* illustrates, the range of justifiable legislative objectives is fairly broad.

If a valid legislative objective for the infringement is found, the infringement is not finally determined to be justified unless the infringement is consistent with the honour of the Crown and the fiduciary and trust relationship that exists between Aboriginal people and the Crown.[76] The Crown's fiduciary relationship with Aboriginal people must be the first consideration to determine whether legislation is justified.

The issue of prioritizing Aboriginal and treaty rights over the rights of others is a consideration within the honour of the Crown. With internally limited Aboriginal rights, such as the right to fish for food, with the food component being an internal limitation, the order of priority is as follows: conservation first, Indian food fishing, non-Indian food fishing, non-Indian commercial fishing, and non-Indian sports fishing.[77] Where an Aboriginal right has no internal limitation, this notion of priority must be modified.[78] Some questions relevant to whether government has granted priority to Aboriginal rights include:

1. whether the government has accommodated the exercise of the Aboriginal right;

2. whether the objectives of government by enacting a particular regulatory scheme reflect the need to consider the Aboriginal priority;

3. the extent of participation in the fishery, in the case of fishing rights, by Aboriginal people relative to their proportion of the population;

4. how government has accommodated different Aboriginal rights (i.e., the right to

[70] *Sparrow, supra* note 52 at 1113; *Adams, supra* note 62 at para. 57, *Delgamuukw, supra* note 51 at para. 161; and *Marshall* (reconsideration), *supra* note 56 at paras. 21, 26.
[71] *Sparrow, ibid.;* and *Badger, supra* note 53 at para. 89.
[72] *Sparrow, ibid.; Adams, supra* note 62 at para. 56; *Delgamuukw, supra* note 51 at para. 161; and *Gladstone, supra* note 64 at para. 72; Sport fishing has been found by the Supreme Court of Canada as not being a "compelling and substantive objective." See *Adams, supra* note 62 at para. 58; *Côté, supra* note 60 at para. 52; and *Marshall* (reconsideration), *supra* note 56 at para. 26.
[73] *Gladstone, supra* note 64 at para. 73.
[74] *Ibid.* at para. 75; *Delgamuukw, supra* note 51 at para. 161; and *Marshall* (reconsideration), *supra* note 56 at para. 41.
[75] *Delgamuukw, supra* note 51 at para. 165.
[76] *Sparrow, supra* note 52 at 1114; *Gladstone, supra* note 64 at para. 54; and *Delgamuukw, supra* note 51 at para. 162.
[77] *Sparrow, supra* note 52 at 1116, *Adams, supra* note 62 at para. 59, *Gladstone, supra* note 64 at para. 54 and *Delgamuukw, supra* note 51 at para. 163.
[78] *Gladstone, supra* note 64 at para. 59.

fish for food and the right to fish commercially);

5. how important the right is to the economic and material well-being of the Aboriginal group claiming the right; and

6. the criteria used by government to allocate the particular resources at issue.[79]

Apart from the issue of priority, other questions to be asked under this component of the justification analysis include:[80]

1. Has there been as little infringement as possible in order to effect the desired result?

2. In expropriation, has fair compensation been paid?

3. Has the Aboriginal group been consulted with respect to the conservation measures used, or at least have they been informed of these conservation measures?

It is important to note that while existing Aboriginal and treaty rights can create a significant burden on the Crown, these rights are not absolute.[81] Governments continue to possess the authority to enact legislation and make decisions within their respective jurisdictional areas and can infringe Aboriginal and treaty rights, if the infringement can be justified in accordance with the test described above. If consultation does not produce an agreement, the adequacy of the government's justification may be litigated in the courts.[82] Consultation is discussed in detail in chapter 3.

In *R. v. Denny*,[83] the Nova Scotia Court of Appeal considered the appeal of three Mi'kmaq convicted of offences contrary to the *Fisheries Act*. The Court overturned the lower court conviction and acquitted the three Mi'kmaq. The Court held that the Mi'kmaq possessed an Aboriginal right to fish for food in the waters in question (Indian Brook and Afton River). The Court concluded that constitutionally guaranteed Aboriginal rights are not violated by the legislative exercise of reasonable regulation, such as conservation of the fisheries resource. Once conservation is taken into consideration though, the Mi'kmaq would be entitled to fish to satisfy their food needs.[84] The Supreme Court of Canada affirmed this view of Aboriginal rights and their priority in *Sparrow*.[85]

By virtue of s. 52[86] of the *Constitution Act, 1982*, s. 35 is part of the supreme law of Canada, thereby superseding federal, provincial, and territorial legislation inconsistent with its provisions:

> By virtue of s. 52(1), the Constitution of Canada is superior to all other laws in force in Canada, whatever their origin; federal statutes, provincial statutes, pre-confederation statutes, received statutes, imperial statutes and common law; all of these laws must yield to inconsistent provisions of the Constitution of Canada. Section 52(1) provides an explicit basis for judicial review of legislation in Canada, for, whenever a court finds that a law is inconsistent with the Constitution of Canada, the court must hold that law to be invalid ("of no force or effect").[87]

[79] *Ibid.* at para. 64.

[80] *Sparrow, supra* note 52 at 1119; *Badger, supra* note 53 at para. 84; and *Gladstone, supra* note 64 at para. 55.

[81] *Sparrow, supra* note 52 at 1109.

[82] *Marshall* (reconsideration), *supra* note 56 at para. 43.

[83] *R. v. Denny*, [1990] 2 C.N.L.R. 115 (N.S.C.A.).

[84] *Ibid.* at 133.

[85] *Sparrow, supra* note 52.

[86] Subsection 52(1) of the *Constitution Act, 1982* states: "(1) The Constitution of Canada is the supreme law of Canada, and any law that is inconsistent with the provisions of the Constitution is, to the extent of the inconsistency, of no force or effect."

[87] Peter Hogg, *Constitutional Law of Canada*, 4th ed. (Toronto: Carswell, 1997) 3.4, p. 53.

The effect of Aboriginal and treaty rights being constitutionally recognized and affirmed is that they become part of the supreme law of Canada and have made the legislative authority of the federal, provincial, and territorial governments subject to their fair treatment. Aboriginal rights are not created by s. 35(1). Aboriginal people hold these rights "by reason of the fact that aboriginal peoples were once independent, self-governing entities in possession of most of the lands now making up Canada."[88]

The Meaning of Subsection 35(1)

Sparrow[89] was the first decision from the Supreme Court of Canada to deal substantively with s. 35(1). Ronald Sparrow, a member of the Musqueam Indian Band of British Columbia, was charged and convicted at trial under s. 61(1) of the *Fisheries Act*[90] for fishing with a drift net that was longer than that permitted under the band's food fishing licence. Sparrow admitted that the facts constituted an offence but defended his action on the basis that he was exercising an existing Aboriginal right to fish and that the drift net length restriction was inconsistent with s. 35(1) and was, therefore, invalid.

The Supreme Court of Canada held that "existing" means the rights that were in existence when the *Constitution Act, 1982* came into effect on April 17, 1982. The word "existing" means unextinguished;[91] "existing aboriginal rights" require an interpretation that is flexible so as "to permit their [aboriginal rights] evolution over time."[92] The Court noted that "existing" means that rights are "affirmed in a contemporary form rather than in their primeval simplicity and vigour."[93]

On the issue of Crown sovereignty and legislative power and Aboriginal title, the Court stated: "[T]here was from the outset never any doubt that sovereignty and legislative power, and indeed the underlying title, to such lands vested in the Crown."[94] The Court noted that the interpretation of "recognized and affirmed" is derived from "general principles of constitutional interpretation"[95] and that s. 35 shall be interpreted in a "purposive way." That is, it shall be given a "generous, liberal interpretation."[96] The Court then cited its earlier decision of *R. v. Nowegijick*,[97] wherein it stated: "[T]reaties and statutes relating to Indians should be liberally construed and doubtful expressions resolved in favour of the Indians."[98]

The Court outlined the infringement and justification test, discussed above, to determine whether an Aboriginal right had been infringed and whether federal or provincial legislation justified such infringement. Although s. 35(1) is not part of the Charter and its s. 1 limitation clause,[99] the justificatory analysis in *Sparrow* is similar to that of the

---

[88] Brian Slattery, "The Constitutional Guarantee of Aboriginal and Treaty Rights" (1983) 8 Queen's L.J. 232 at 242.

[89] *Sparrow, supra* note 52.

[90] *Fisheries Act*, R.S.C. 1970, c. F–14, ss. 34, 61(1); now R.S.C. 1985, c. F–14, ss. 43, 79.

[91] *Sparrow, supra* note 52 at 1092.

[92] *Ibid.* at 1093.

[93] Brian Slattery, "Understanding Aboriginal Rights" (1988) 66 Can. Bar Rev. 782, as cited in *Sparrow, supra* note 52.

[94] *Sparrow, supra* note 52 at 1103.

[95] *Ibid.* at 1106.

[96] *Ibid.*

[97] *R. v. Nowegijick*, [1983] 1 S.C.R. 29.

[98] *Sparrow, supra* note 52 at 1107.

[99] Section 1 of the Charter reads: "The *Canadian Charter of Rights and Freedoms* guarantees the rights and freedoms set out in it subject only to such reasonable limits prescribed by law as can be demonstrably justified in a free and democratic society." See *Van der Peet, supra* note 50 at para. 71.

Charter's s. 1 analysis as outlined in *R. v. Oakes*.[100] In order for a Charter right to be limited by s. 1 of the Charter, two criteria must be met. First, the legislation in question must be of sufficient importance to warrant an override of a constitutional right. Second, the limitations imposed must be reasonably and demonstrably justified using a three-part proportionality test:

1. The measures must be designed to achieve the desired objective.

2. The measures must impair rights as little as possible.

3. The proportionality between the effects of the measures and the objectives desired must be of sufficient importance.[101]

Sparrow's "valid legislative objective" test is similar to the "sufficient importance" requirement in *Oakes*. The *Oakes* proportionality test mirrors aspects of the *Sparrow* justificatory analysis in that *Sparrow* asks if the limitation is unreasonable, does it impose undue hardship, and does it deny to the holder of the right his or her preferred means of exercising that right.[102]

Delgamuukw[103] also set out a justification analysis concerning when and how Aboriginal title may be infringed and affirms that the *Sparrow* justificatory principles also operate with respect to Aboriginal title. Lamer C.J. notes that Aboriginal title is not absolute and must be balanced with the fact that Aboriginal societies are part of the broader Canadian social, economic, and political environment. To this end, activities that support economic development generally, among other things, may be justified when examined on a case-by-case basis. The Supreme Court of Canada's decision of *Delgamuukw* also strengthens the argument that compensation may be payable to an Aboriginal group when its Aboriginal title has been breached.[104]

Since *Sparrow*, *Van der Peet*[105] has clarified further the nature of rights protected by s. 35 of the *Constitution Act, 1982* and affirmed that Aboriginal title is a subcategory of Aboriginal rights. Lamer C.J. wrote that "Aboriginal rights and Aboriginal title are related concepts, Aboriginal title is a sub-category of Aboriginal rights which deals solely with claims of rights to land."[106] *Van der Peet* also confirmed that Aboriginal rights are derived from the historical reality that Aboriginal people were in Canada first, prior to European contact. The doctrine of Aboriginal rights exists, and is recognized and affirmed by s. 35(1), because of one simple fact: when Europeans arrived in North America, Aboriginal people were already here, living in communities on the land, and participating in distinctive cultures, as they had done for centuries.[107]

Supreme Court of Canada decisions since *Sparrow* have placed a number of significant limitations on the exercise of Aboriginal and treaty rights, and have stated broad principles to justify their infringement. The Court has clearly outlined for governments the

---

[100] *R. v. Oakes*, [1986] 1 S.C.R. 103. The *Oakes* test has since been expanded and modified by numerous Supreme Court of Canada decisions.

[101] *Ibid.* at 139.

[102] See the 1996 British Columbia Court of Appeal decisions of *R. v. Samson*, [1996] 2 C.N.L.R. 184 (B.C.C.A.), and *R. v. Jack*, [1996] 2 C.N.L.R. 113 (B.C.C.A.), wherein the primary issue dealt with the application of the *Sparrow* justificatory analysis. In both cases, government failed to meet the burden imposed by *Sparrow*.

[103] *Delgamuukw, supra* note 51.

[104] See commentary on *Delgamuukw* in chap. 1; see also *ibid.* at paras. 165–69.

[105] *Van der Peet, supra* note 50; see commentary by D.W. Elliot, "Fifty Dollars of Fish: A Comment on *R. v. Van der Peet*" (1997), 35:3 Alta. Law Rev.

[106] *Van der Peet, supra* note 50 at para. 74.

[107] *Ibid.* at para. 30.

types of objectives that can justify the infringement of Aboriginal rights and title. These objectives include conservation and resource management[108] and other purposes or objectives[109] and must be for a "compelling and substantial" objective.[110] *Gladstone* further expanded upon these purposes and held that there are broad range of objectives that can justify the infringement of Aboriginal rights:

> Because, however, distinctive Aboriginal societies exist within, and are a part of, a broader social, political and economic community, over which the Crown is sovereign, there are circumstances in which, in order to pursue objectives of compelling and substantial importance to that community as a whole (. . . Aboriginal societies are a part of that community), some limitation of those rights will be justifiable. . . . [L]imits placed on those rights are, where the objectives . . . are of sufficient importance to the broader community . . . *equally* a necessary part of that reconciliation.[111]

Gladstone epitomizes the Supreme Court of Canada's interpretation of the constitutional protection afforded to Aboriginal and treaty rights in s. 35(1). The Court's understanding of "reconciliation," for example, means that Aboriginal rights are not to be interpreted in an absolute manner but rather within the context of Canadian sovereignty, also affirmed by the Constitution.

In *Gladstone*, the Court also noted that objectives such as economic and regional fairness and the historical reliance of non-Aboriginal people on the fishery, for example, satisfy the *Sparrow* justificatory standard.[112]

Subsection 35(1) and Evidence—*Mitchell* (2001)

The June 16, 2001 Supreme Court of Canada decision of *Mitchell* v. *Minister of National Revenue*[113] focuses on the evidentiary burden being placed on Aboriginal groups wanting to prove such rights. *Mitchell* concerns Grand Chief Mitchell, a Mohawk of Akwesasne, Quebec, who crossed the international border from the United States into Canada. He had in his possession some blankets, bibles, motor oil, food, and other items, all of which had been purchased in the United States. He claimed that he possessed Aboriginal and treaty rights that exempted him from paying duty on the goods. All of the goods brought across the border, with the exception of the motor oil, were gifts to be given to the Mohawk community of Tyendinaga, Ontario. The motor oil was placed in a store in the Akwesasne territory for resale. In September 1989, Chief Mitchell was served with a Notice of Ascertained Forfeiture claiming $361.64 for unpaid duties, taxes, and penalties.

McKeown J. of the Federal Court, Trial Division held that Chief Mitchell possessed an existing Aboriginal right, but not a treaty right, to pass freely across the Canada–United States border. The Federal Court of Appeal affirmed the trial court judgment and found that the Mohawks possessed an Aboriginal right to bring goods into Canada duty free, subject to limitations based on the evidence of the traditional range of Mohawk trading.

The Supreme Court of Canada held that the Mohawks do not possess an Aboriginal right to bring goods across the Canada–United States border free from paying customs duties and taxes. McLachlin C.J. for the majority began by summarizing the nature of

---

[108] See note 72.
[109] See *Sparrow, supra* note 52 at 1113; *Marshall* (reconsideration), *supra* note 56 at paras. 21, 26; and *Badger, supra* note 53 at para. 80.
[110] *Ibid.*; and *R.* v. *N.T.C. Smokehouse Ltd.*, [1996] 2 S.C.R. 672 at para. 97.
[111] *Gladstone, supra* note 64 at para. 73.
[112] *Ibid.* at para 75.
[113] *Mitchell* v. *Minister of National Revenue*, [2001] 1 S.C.R. 911.

Aboriginal rights in Canadian law and stated that with the enactment of s. 35(1), common law Aboriginal rights were elevated to constitutional status.[114] McLachlin C.J. stated that practices, traditions, and customs that are marginal or incidental to an Aboriginal society's cultural identity are excluded as "rights" for the purposes of s. 35(1); by implication, s. 35(1) emphasizes practices, traditions, and customs that are "vital to the life, culture and identity of the aboriginal society in question."[115] McLachlin C.J. stated that the claimed Aboriginal right must be characterized in the proper context and must not be distorted to fit the desired result:

> It must be neither artificially broadened nor narrowed. An overly narrow characterization risks the dismissal of valid claims and an overly broad characterization risks distorting the right by neglecting the specific culture and history of the claimant's society. . . .[116]

McLachlin C.J. stated that the trial judge characterized the Aboriginal right being claimed as including the right to engage in "small, noncommercial scale trade."[117] McLachlin C.J. also noted that the characterization of the Aboriginal right does not necessarily require internal limitations such as narrowing the claim so as not to include the right to pass freely across the border but rather simply to trade and stated that internal limitations are unnecessary since Aboriginal rights, once established, can encompass other rights that are necessary for the meaningful exercise of these rights.[118] The right claimed in *Mitchell* is "the right to bring goods across the St. Lawrence River for the purposes of trade."[119]

McLachlin C.J. stated that rights contained in s. 35(1) should not be "rendered illusory by imposing an impossible burden of proof" on those claiming such rights.[120] This flexible approach with the continued operation of "general evidentiary principles."[121] The Court affirmed, as in *Marshall*,[122] that "'[g]enerous rules of interpretation should not be confused with a vague sense of after-the-fact largesse."[123] With this general sense of bal-

---

[114] *Ibid.* at para. 11. While this meant that Aboriginal rights fell under the constitutional recognition and affirmation of s. 35(1) and could not be unilaterally abrogated by government decisions or actions, governments did retain the jurisdiction to interfere and infringe Aboriginal rights for justifiable reasons in the pursuit of substantial and compelling public objectives. See *Gladstone, supra* note 64 and *Delgamuukw, supra* note 51.

[115] *Mitchell, supra* note 113 at para. 12; see also *Van der Peet, supra* note 50 at paras. 54–59.

[116] *Mitchell, supra* note 113 at para. 15; see also *R. v. Pamajewon,* [1996] 2 S.C.R. 821.

[117] *Mitchell, supra* note 113 at para. 21; McLachlin C.J. stated that there are practical difficulties inherent in defining "small, non-commercial scale trade" and notes that many small acts of trading can add up to more significant or major trade. It is therefore more accurate to simply characterize the right as a right to trade *simpliciter.*

[118] *Ibid.* at para. 22. In this case, the Supreme Court of Canada noted that if any finding of a trading right was made, it should also confirm a mobility right since the right to trade necessarily encompasses the right to physical access to the territory in question.

[119] *Ibid.* at para. 25.

[120] *Ibid.* at para. 27; at para. 30 the Supreme Court of Canada stated:

> [F]lexible adaptation of traditional rules of evidence to the challenge of doing justice in aboriginal claims is but an application of the time-honoured principle that the rules of evidence are not "cast in stone, nor are they enacted in a vacuum" (*R. v. Levogiannis* [1993] 4 S.C.R. 475, at p. 487). Rather, they are animated by broad, flexible principles, applied purposively to promote truth-finding and fairness. The rules of evidence should facilitate justice, not stand in its way. Underlining the diverse rules on the admissibility of evidence are three simple ideas. First, the evidence must be useful in the sense of tending to prove a fact relevant to the issues in the case. Second, the evidence must be reasonably reliable; unreliable evidence may hinder the search for the truth more than help it. Third, even useful and reasonably reliable evidence may be excluded in the discretion of the trial judge if its probative value is overshadowed by its potential for prejudice.

[121] *Ibid.* at para. 38.

[122] *Marshall, supra* note 56 at para. 14.

[123] *Mitchell, supra* note 113 at para. 39.

ance between the general rules regarding evidence and the special nature of Aboriginal rights litigation, the Court focused its attention on the evidence to consider whether it demonstrated an ancestral Mohawk practice of trading north of the St. Lawrence River.

McLachlin C.J. held that the findings of fact by the trial and appellate courts in *Mitchell* represented a "palpable and overriding error."[124] She examined the evidence and concluded that it did not support the findings of fact made by the trial judge and found a number of apparent inconsistencies between what the trial judge inferred evidence to mean and what the evidence actually supported. One example is Mitchell's evidence that cited D.K. Richter's book[125] to support the existence of the claimed Aboriginal right. Richter's book was referenced by Sexton J.A., writing for the majority in the Federal Court of Appeal decision, and held that Richter's book demonstrated, supported by McKeown J., that there was "clear archaeological evidence of North–South trade across what is now the Canada–United States border."[126] McLachlin C.J. examined this statement, made reference to Richter's book, and concluded that the opposite was more accurate. Richter supports an East–West trade access, not directly from the North as implied by the Court of Appeal and McKeown J. Additionally, McLachlin C.J. noted that while Richter's book may support the thesis of precontact existence of a North–South trade route, "it refutes the direct involvement of the Mohawks in this trade."[127] The evidence was summarized as being sparse, doubtful, and hardly compelling.[128] The Court concluded that an ancestral practice of transporting goods across the St. Lawrence River for the purposes of trade was not established and based this conclusion directly on the lack of substantive evidence presented to the Court.

McLachlin C.J. continued, however, by also noting that even if the trial judge's findings of precontact trade relations between the Mohawk and the Aboriginal groups of the St. Lawrence River were established, the evidence did not establish this northerly trade as a "defining feature" of the Mohawk culture.[129] It was clear that if such trade did not exist, it would not have "fundamentally altered" the Mohawk culture and that the trade was not something that "made the society what it was."[130]

The Crown argued that even if a Mohawk practice of cross-border trade was established, it would be barred from recognition as Aboriginal right within the meaning of s. 35(1) because it would be incompatible with the Crown's sovereign interest in regulating its borders. McLachlin C.J. noted that this argument is based on the doctrine of continuity and sovereign incompatibility. McLachlin C.J. did not rule out the possibility of a successful Crown argument in this respect; however, no comment was offered. Binnie J., writing in dissent, discussed in detail the concept of sovereign incapability, which posits that Aboriginal rights, as part of the common law, ought not to be incompatible with, or unconscionable towards, the Crown's sovereignty. The idea of incompatibility with Crown sovereignty was a defining feature of sovereign succession and therefore a limitation on the parameters of Aboriginal rights.[131]

A critical problem for McLachlin C.J. in *Mitchell* was that the evidence relied upon by

---

[124] *Ibid.* at para. 51.
[125] D.K. Richter, *The Ordeal of the Longhouse: The Peoples of the Iroquois League In the Era of European Colonization*. Chapel Hill, N.C.: University of North Carolina Press, 1992.
[126] *Mitchell, supra* note 113 at para. 43 (para. 50 of F.C.A. decision).
[127] *Ibid.* at para. 46.
[138] *Ibid.* at paras. 47 and 51.
[129] *Ibid.* at para. 54.
[130] *Ibid.* at para. 60, referencing *Van der Peet, supra* note 50 at para. 55.
[131] *Ibid.* at paras. 153–54.

the trial and appellate courts was exceedingly weak. *Delgamuukw* contemplated that there would be instances where a trial judge may err in making findings of fact and that appellate intervention does "not proceed automatically."[132] The test for whether an appellate court should intervene to correct the error was set out by the Supreme Court of Canada in *Schwartz* v. *Canada*[133] and cited by the Supreme Court of Canada in *Delgamuukw*: in order for appellate intervention, the error must be sufficiently serious that it was "overriding and determinative in the assessment of the balance of probabilities with respect to that factual issue."[134] In *Mitchell*, the Supreme Court of Canada made such an assessment of the lower courts' treatment of the evidence:

> [A] consciousness of the special nature of aboriginal claims does not negate the operation of general evidentiary principles. While evidence adduced in support of aboriginal claims must not be undervalued, neither should it be interpreted or weighed in a manner that fundamentally contravenes the principles of evidence law, which, as they relate to the valuing of evidence, are often synonymous with the "general principles of common sense" . . . Placing "due weight" on the aboriginal perspective, or ensuring its supporting evidence an "equal footing" with more familiar forms of evidence, means precisely what these phrases suggest: *equal* and *due* treatment. While the evidence presented by aboriginal claimants should not be undervalued "simply because that evidence does not conform precisely with the evidentiary standards that would be applied in, for example, a private law torts case" (*Van der Peet, supra* at para. 68), neither should it be artificially strained to carry more weight than it can reasonably support. If this is an obvious proposition, it must nonetheless be stated.[135]

McLachlin C.J. found that the evidence in *Mitchell* did not support the claims being made. Even so, *Mitchell* is a practical application of the evidentiary principles set out in *Van der Peet* and *Delgamuukw* and is wholly consistent with earlier Supreme Court of Canada commentary on the treatment of evidence in Aboriginal rights cases. *Mitchell* is also significant for what it did not say. Unlike its predecessors, *Mitchell* did not focus on explaining the "principles" or "theories" surrounding Aboriginal rights adjudication. With the exception of Binnie J., the Court focused on the practical application of legal principles to the facts and evidence at issue, and chose *not* to send the matter back to trial, as it did in *Sparrow*, or affirm a right but not articulate how governments will practically deal with such affirmation, as it did in *Delgamuukw*, with respect to Aboriginal title.

Mitchell adds to the growing list of appropriate justifications that may be applied to limit or curtail the application of Aboriginal rights. In *Mitchell*, the limiting factor was the applicability and weakness of the evidence provided. However, Binnie J. (along with Major J.) discussed "sovereign incompatibility" as an appropriate limitation on the scope of Aboriginal rights:

> Yet the language of s. 35(1) cannot be construed as a wholesale repudiation of the common law. The subject matter of the constitutional provision is "existing" aboriginal and treaty rights and they are said to be "recognized and affirmed" not wholly cut loose from either their legal or historical origins. One of the defining characteristics of sovereign succession and therefore a limitation on the scope of aboriginal rights, . . . was the notion of incompatibility with the new sovereignty.[136]

This is partly a re-articulation of *Sparrow* in that the recognition and affirmation of Abo-

---

[132] *Delgamuukw, supra* note 51 at para. 88.

[133] *Schwartz* v. *Canada*, [1996] 1 S.C.R. 254 at 281.

[134] *Delgamuukw, supra* note 51 at para. 88.

[135] *Mitchell, supra* note 113 at paras. 38 and 39.

[136] *Ibid.* at para. 150.

riginal rights are subject to internal and external limiting factors. Internally, the phrase "recognized and affirmed" is distinct from an outright guarantee, as found, for example, in the Charter.[137] Externally, those Aboriginal and treaty rights that exist are subject to infringement by federal and provincial governments, if they can be justified. Binnie J. suggested that Aboriginal and treaty rights are also limited in their applicability by virtue of them being "incompatible" with Canadian sovereignty—such as a right to create and maintain a military, distinct from Canada.[138] Although Binnie J. suggested that the principle of sovereign compatibility is a limitation on the exercise of rights recognized and affirmed by s. 35(1), he also stated that it should be "sparingly applied."[139]

Establishing Aboriginal Rights—The *Van der Peet* Test

In *Van der Peet,* Lamer C.J., for the majority, outlined the test for identifying Aboriginal rights in s. 35(1). The Supreme Court of Canada noted that any test aimed at identifying Aboriginal rights must be directed at the practices, traditions, and customs central to the Aboriginal people concerned, prior to their contact with Europeans. In order to be an Aboriginal right protected by s. 35(1), an activity must be an "element of a practice, custom or tradition integral to the distinctive culture of the Aboriginal group claiming the right."[140] The Court outlined ten factors to be considered in determining whether or not an activity is "integral to a distinctive culture":

1. The Aboriginal perspective must be taken into account, keeping in mind that, at the same time, the right being claimed must be put forward in a manner "cognizable to the Canadian and legal constitutional structure."[141]

2. The Aboriginal claim should be characterized precisely. In doing so, consideration should be given to the nature of the action performed pursuant to the claimed Aboriginal right; the nature of government regulation or limitation on the activity; and the Aboriginal traditions, customs, or practices being relied upon to establish the right.[142]

3. The practice, custom, or tradition being relied upon must be significantly central to the Aboriginal society in question. With respect to this factor, Lamer C.J. stated that in order for an activity to be significantly central it should be a "defining feature of the culture in question."[143]

4. The period of time in which a court should look to establish whether or not an

[137] Charter, *supra* note 3.
[138] Binnie J., in *Mitchell, supra* note 113 at para. 153, used the military as such an example, noting the following with respect to the Mohawks' warrior tradition:

> However, important as they may have been to the Mohawk identity as a people, it could not be said, in my view, that pre-contact warrior activities gave rise under successor regimes to a *legal right* under s.35(1) to engage in military adventures on Canadian territory. Canadian sovereign authority has, as one of its inherent characteristics, a monopoly on the *lawful* use of military force within its territory. . . . This example, remote as it is from the particular claim advanced in this case, usefully illustrates the principled limitation flowing from sovereign incompatibility in the s.35(1) analysis.

[139] *Mitchell, supra* note 113 at para. 154.
[140] *Van der Peet, supra* note 50 at para. 46. In *R.* v. *Jacobs,* [1999] 3 C.N.L.R. 239 (B.C.S.C.) at paras. 116–27, Macauley J. noted that not all registered Indians are necessarily "Aboriginal" for the purposes of claiming an Aboriginal right, and vice-versa. Only "Aboriginal" people can claim Aboriginal rights and those individuals, for example, that may be accepted by an Aboriginal community may not necessarily be entitled to claim Aboriginal rights.
[141] *Van der Peet, supra* note 50 at para. 49.
[142] *Ibid.* at para. 53.
[143] *Ibid.* at para. 59.

activity is protected as an Aboriginal right is that period prior to European contact. Those existing practices, customs, or traditions that can be shown to have their origin in pre-contact Aboriginal societies will be eligible for protection as Aboriginal rights, subject to other factors.[144] This continuity with pre-contact times is critical. As Lamer C.J. wrote:

> Where an Aboriginal community can demonstrate that a particular practice, custom or tradition is integral to its distinctive culture today, and that this practice, custom or tradition has continuity with the practices, customs and traditions of pre-contact times, that community will have demonstrated that the practice, custom or tradition is an Aboriginal right for the purposes of s.35(1).[145]

5. The evidentiary demands of proving an Aboriginal right must be considered in the broader perspective of the special nature of Aboriginal rights in Canadian law and the evidentiary difficulties inherent in proving Aboriginal rights prior to European contact.

6. Aboriginal rights must be dealt with on a case-by-case basis; a general approach to Aboriginal rights is not appropriate.

7. The practice, custom, or tradition being claimed as an Aboriginal right must exist independently and cannot be incidental to another practice, custom, or tradition. An incidental or secondary practice, custom, or tradition does not qualify for protection as an Aboriginal right.

8. The custom, practice, or tradition must be distinctive, but not necessarily distinct. "Distinct" implies unique, whereas "distinctive" implies an activity that is a distinguishing characteristic.[146]

9. European influence on Aboriginal culture is relevant only where it can be shown that the practice, custom, or tradition is integral only because of such influence.

10. Courts must consider both the relationship of Aboriginal peoples to the land and the Aboriginal peoples' distinctive cultures and societies.[147]

Perhaps the most striking feature of the *Van der Peet* test is that it appears that a right can be proven without it necessarily being linked to a particular piece of land. Thus, whereas in the past, the link to land has been a critical feature and a necessary component to proving Aboriginal rights, the focus now appears to be what Aboriginal societies did in the past. McLachlin J., in her dissent, summarized the issue succinctly:

> [A]nything which can be said to be part of the aboriginal culture would qualify as an aboriginal right protected by the *Constitution Act, 1982*. This would confer constitutional protection on a multitude of activities, ranging from the trivial to the vital.[148]

Delgamuukw[149] further exemplifies this point wherein the Court further stressed that Aboriginal rights are not dependent on the use and occupation of land or on Aboriginal title.[150]

---

[144] *Ibid.* at para. 62.
[145] *Ibid.* at para. 63.
[146] *Ibid.* at para. 71.
[147] *Ibid.* at para. 74.
[148] *Ibid.* at para. 256.
[149] *Delgamuukw, supra* note 51.
[150] *Ibid.* at paras. 137–38.

R. v. *Gladstone* (1996)

In *Gladstone*,[151] the Supreme Court of Canada held that the Heiltsuk people of British Columbia possessed an Aboriginal right to trade in herring spawn on kelp, protected under s. 35(1), because this activity was a central and significant feature of their society. This activity, best described as commercial in nature, existed amongst the Heiltsuk prior to European contact. Because of the commercial nature of this right, after the conservation objectives had been achieved over the resource, the government was not obligated to give the Heiltsuk a priority right to fishery, as was the case in *Sparrow* when dealing with fishing for food rights. Rather, the government must allocate the resource in a way that is respectful of the fact that the Aboriginal rights have priority over other interests in the fishery.[152] Issues to be considered by government when allocating a resource in this manner include: the extent of the participation by Aboriginal peoples in the fishery relative to their percentage of the population generally affected; how the government has accommodated different Aboriginal rights in a particular fishery (for example, food versus commercial); how important the fishery is to the economic well-being of the band; and what other factors the government considered when allocating commercial licences in the area. The Supreme Court of Canada noted that these factors are not an exhaustive list.[153] *Gladstone* demonstrated that despite all of the judicial reasoning on s. 35(1) in recent years, there remains a fundamental vagueness (in this case with respect to the test for being a "priority") that is dependent on a case-by-case analysis.

In *Adams*,[154] the Supreme Court of Canada applied the *Van der Peet* test regarding activities that are integral to the distinctive culture of the Aboriginal group claiming Aboriginal rights. *Adams* concerned an appeal of a number of Mohawks from convictions under the *Quebec Fishery Regulations*[155] and the *Fisheries Act* for fishing for food without a proper licence. The Court considered whether the *Quebec Fishery Regulations* were of no force or effect because of Aboriginal rights possessed by the Mohawk under s. 35(1). The question centred around whether a claim to an Aboriginal right to fish must rest on a claim to Aboriginal title to the area where the fishing occurred. In applying *Van der Peet*, the Court held that the licence requirement infringed the appellant's Aboriginal right to fish for food and that the regulatory scheme was dependant upon ministerial discretion that had no criteria attached to its application. Applying *Van der Peet*, the Court determined that although the Mohawks' claim to occupancy over the area in question was weak, the claim with respect to their use of the lands and waters in question, that is their distinct practices in the area, was strong. Thus, although a link to land may be critical to support Aboriginal rights, a link to a particular piece of land and associated Aboriginal title is not necessary for a claim of Aboriginal rights. In *Marshall* (1999) the Court cited with approval the *Van der Peet* test outlined in *Adams* as it applied to licensing schemes. In *Adams*, the Court stated:

> In light of the Crown's unique fiduciary obligations towards Aboriginal peoples, Parliament may not simply adopt an unstructured discretionary administrative regime which risks infringing Aboriginal rights in a substantial number of applications in the absence of some explicit guidance. If a statute confers an administrative discretion which may carry signifi-

---

[151] *Gladstone, supra* note 64.
[152] *Ibid.* at paras. 61 and 62.
[153] *Ibid.* at para. 64.
[154] *Adams, supra* note 62.
[155] *Quebec Fishery Regulations*, 1990, SOR/90-214.

cant consequences for the exercise of an Aboriginal right, the statute or its delegate regulations must outline specific criteria for the granting or refusal of that discretion which seek to accommodate the existence of Aboriginal rights. In the absence of such specific guidance, the statute will fail to provide representatives of the Crown with sufficient directives to fulfill their fiduciary duties, and the statute will be found to represent an infringement of Aboriginal rights under the *Sparrow* test.[156]

R. v. Côté (1996)

In *Côté*,[157] the Supreme Court of Canada again considered the *Van der Peet* criteria. This Quebec case dealt with Algonquin Indians who had entered a controlled harvest zone by way of a vehicle without paying the required fee and had fished there without a valid licence. *Côté* affirmed that although French law did not explicitly recognize the existence of a unique Aboriginal interest in the land, it also did not explicitly state that such an interest did not exist. Thus, the French Crown may not have assumed full title over the lands occupied by Aboriginal people because they dealt with the Aboriginal peoples as sovereign nations. As in *Adams,* the Court had difficulty with the extent of the minister's discretionary authority to issue a licence. The requirement of a licence, in light of the undisciplined nature of the minister's discretionary authority, infringed in an unjustifiable manner the appellant's Aboriginal right to fish for food. The imposition of a fee to enter the controlled zone using a vehicle, although a condition on the exercise of the right, did not amount to an infringement. The fee was not revenue-generating in nature but rather was used to improve transportation within the land in question.

Both *Adams* and *Côté* underscore that governments must ensure that the use of ministerial discretionary authority is clearly articulated and justified. The courts have not said that discretionary authority *per se* is unacceptable when dealing with Aboriginal rights. Rather, the courts have focused on those provisions that grant a great degree of authority with few or no criteria under which the authority is to be carried out. Governments must be prepared to explain their decisions and how they reached them, as they must in any administrative law or procedural fairness context.

The Supreme Court of Canada also applied the *Van der Peet* test in *R. v. N.T.C. Smokehouse Ltd.*[158] *Smokehouse* concerned whether the exchange of fish at potlatches and at other traditional ceremonies constituted a right to engage in the commercial selling of fish. The court held, based on the evidence, that the exchange of fish at these ceremonies was incidental to the ceremonies and did not possess any independent significance. Thus, the exchange of fish was not an integral part of the Aboriginal group's distinctive culture.

SUBSECTION 35(3), *CONSTITUTION ACT, 1982*[159]

Subsection 35(3) of the *Constitution Act, 1982* states:

> For greater certainty, in subsection (1) "treaty rights" includes rights that now exist by way of land claims agreements or may be so acquired.

Subsection 35(3) of the *Constitution Act, 1982* provides that rights included in land

---

[156] *Adams, supra* note 52 at para. 54.
[157] *Côté, supra* note 60.
[158] *R. v. N.T.C. Smokehouse Ltd., supra* note 110.
[159] See discussion in chapter 2. See Thomas Isaac, "The *Constitution Act, 1982* and the Constitutionalization of Aboriginal Self-Government in Canada: *Cree-Naskapi (of Quebec) Act*", [1991] 1 C.N.L.R. 1.

claims agreements are "treaty rights" for the purposes of s. 35(1). The effect of this provision is noteworthy because it transforms the rights in land claims agreements or modern treaties from being merely contractual or legislative in nature to being part of the Constitution of Canada and thus potentially able to supersede federal, provincial, or territorial legislation. More problematic, however, is that it remains unclear what is a "right" protected under a land claims agreement or modern treaty, such as the Nisga'a Final Agreement in British Columbia. Put another way, are only those provisions labelled as "rights" protected by s. 35(1), or are other provisions protected as well?[160]

Although they are not explicitly constitutionally protected in s. 35, self-government arrangements, such as those reached in the Yukon Territory, with the Sechelt Indian Band, or contemplated by the Meadow Lake First Nations, are significant. Save for some unreasonable exercise of Crown authority, these types of agreements satisfy some practical concerns of the communities to which they apply. Even with respect to their constitutional status, some questions arise:

> An aspect of s.35(3) common to all three drafts was that it encompassed rights under future land claims agreements. It thus removed the doubt—or maybe established for the first time—that *in general*, treaties entered into after April 17, 1982, receive whatever protection s.35(1) affords to its contents. Question: is an agreement on self-government a "treaty"? I have no recollection of anyone discussing this possibility at the March '83 Conference. In the fall of 1983 the *Penner Report* suggested that Indian First Nations governments be established by an agreement making process between the federal government and Indian governments. Could any of those agreements acquire the constitutional protection of s.35(3)? If the answer is yes, then by expanding the scope of s.35(1) to include post-April 17, 1982 agreements, s.35(3) may have provided a mechanism whereby Indian self-government in Canada can receive constitutional recognition and protection. Chapter XXI analyzes the legal position in some detail. For now, I will only say that the effect that s.35(3) may have on the constitutional position of aboriginal self-government may be one of the most important outcomes of the March '83 Conference—even if that effect did not occur to many, or even any, of the participants.[161]

From a textual perspective, s. 35(3) makes reference to "rights" rather than to land claims agreements, thereby operating to recognize and affirm only the *rights* in such agreements and not the entire agreements themselves. Also, s. 35(3) does not limit the type of rights that may be included in land claims agreements; such rights under s. 35(3) could be much broader than those rights that relate to land use or customary activities of Aboriginal people, which has traditionally comprised Aboriginal and historical treaty rights.

Another interesting textual element to s. 35(3) is that it makes reference to rights that exist "by way of" land claims agreements, rather than rights that are contained in such agreements. Thus, this language could catch rights that are not in a land claim agreement itself, but owe their existence to such agreement, such as self-government agreements.

In *R. v. Kapp*[162] Kitchen J. of the British Columbia Provincial Court considered whether the *Aboriginal Communal Fishing Licences Regulations*[163] (regulated commercial Aboriginal fishery) was unconstitutional. The accused in this case were non-Aboriginal fishers. Kitchen J. held:

[160] B. Schwartz, *supra* note 10 at 81–82.
[161] *Ibid.*
[162] *R. v. Kapp*, 2003 BCPC 0279 (B.C. Prov. Ct.).
[163] *Aboriginal Communal Fishing Licences Regulations*, SOR/93-332, as am.

. . . I conclude that the pilot sales fishery draws a distinction and defines two groups on the basis of whether or not individuals have a bloodline connection to the Musqueam, Burrard or Tsawwassen Bands. This is analogous to a racial distinction. The group without the bloodline connection is subjected to differential treatment by having a benefit withheld—their right to participate as equals in the public commercial fishery. This has the effect of promoting the view that these individuals are less capable, less worthy of recognition, and less valuable as members of Canadian society. It also promotes the view that they are not as equally deserving of concern, respect and consideration as the members of the three bands.

This disadvantage was not pre-existing; it was caused by the implementation of the pilot sales program, which has been held out as having an ameliorative purpose. I conclude it does not serve such a purpose. Although probably well intentioned, the program was misconceived, illogical, and ineffective in any way in dealing with any disadvantages the three bands may experience. The pilot sales program therefore offends the provisions of Section 15 of the Charter of Rights and Freedoms and violates the rights of the accused thereunder.

. . . Racial discrimination in our society takes on many guises. Any racial group may be the victim. The Aboriginal people in Canada have obviously been the victims of racial dynamics and discrimination that have disadvantaged them in many ways. This discrimination has been sometimes subtle, but always insidious. Ameliorative programs are necessary to remedy this, but they must be carefully crafted to balance the interests of all members of society. The pilot sales program has not met this standard; the program was misguided in conception and has been insensitively implemented and maintained.

The most troubling aspect of this discrimination is that it is government sponsored. The government should be setting an example for the rest of society, but unfortunately, this has not been our history. We have had many shameful examples of legislated racial discrimination including laws to keep Orientals from working in the coal mines and on the railways in the early 1900's, legislation to phase out and exclude the Japanese from the commercial fishery in the 1920's, and legislation interning and confiscating the property of Japanese fishers in the 1940's. After such a sad history, our governments should be much more sympathetic to these issues than has been the case here. When racial discrimination or a semblance of it is identified, any continuance of it should not be permitted. The application is denied, and the charges are stayed, effective immediately.[164]

Although substantially alone in respect of similar decisions, *Kapp* raises critical issues, particularly for Canadian governments who are mandated to *balance* the rights of Aboriginal people with the rights of other Canadians.

INDIVIDUAL AND COLLECTIVE RIGHTS

In *Thomas v. Norris*,[165] Hood J. of the British Columbia Supreme Court considered whether a claimed Aboriginal right to participate in spirit dancing included the right of a group of Aboriginal people to assault, batter, and imprison an individual against their will. *Thomas* provides an interesting fact situation to analyze potential conflicts between individual and collective Aboriginal rights.

The Indian defendants, who were found guilty, argued that the collective rights of Aboriginal people under s. 35(1) overrode the rights of Thomas, a registered Indian. Hood J. decided that s. 35(1) was not applicable and held that if spirit dancing was an Aboriginal right that was practised prior to the assertion of British sovereignty and the

---

[164] *Kapp, supra* note 162 at paras. 203, 204, 234, 235.
[165] *Thomas v. Norris*, [1992] 2 C.N.L.R. 139 (B.C.S.C.); see Thomas Isaac, "Individual Versus Collective Rights: Aboriginal People and the Significance of *Thomas v. Norris*" (1992) 21:3 Man. Law J. 618–30.

introduction of English law, there are aspects of the right that were "contrary to English common law."[166] The use of force, assault, battery, and wrongful imprisonment would not have survived the introduction of English law.

> If spirit dancing generally was in existence in April of 1982 when the *Constitution Act, 1982*, came into force, the impugned aspects of it, to which I have referred, had been expressly extinguished. . . . It has never been the law of this Province that any person, or group of persons, Indians or non-Indians, had the right to subject another person to assault, battery or false imprisonment, and violate that person's original rights, with impunity. . . . The assumed aboriginal right . . . is not absolute and the Supreme Court of Canada reaffirmed this in *Sparrow*. Like most freedoms or rights it is, and must be, limited by laws, both civil and criminal, which protect those who may be injured by the exercise of that practise.[167]

Three issues were raised and considered by the British Columbia Supreme Court in *Thomas*: (1) did the defendants assault, batter, and falsely imprison the plaintiff, including the defences asserted (lack of intent and consent on the part of the plaintiff); (2) is spirit dancing a protected existing Aboriginal right under s. 35(1), thus rendering inoperative the infringing common law of assault, battery, and false imprisonment; and (3) if successful, to what damages is the plaintiff entitled?

Hood J. held that the plaintiff was battered, assaulted, and unlawfully imprisoned when he was seized by the defendants, carried into the Long House, and detained there for four or five days, all of which was done without the plaintiff's consent or acquiescence.[168] Hood J. considered whether spirit dancing was a protected Aboriginal right under s. 35(1) and he adopted the plaintiff's submission that the defendants cannot use s. 25 to protect the right to spirit dance from infringing upon the plaintiff's common law rights. The Court noted that while the Charter applies to the common law, it does not apply to actions between private parties unless government intervention, in some manner, is involved.[169] The right to spirit dance was put forward by the defence not as a constitutional or common law freedom of religion but, rather, solely as an Aboriginal right under s. 35(1) and thus, outside of the application of the Charter.

Hood J. concluded that the evidence submitted was insufficient to establish that spirit dancing is an existing Aboriginal right under s. 35(1). He stated that even if he were to hold that spirit dancing fell within the category of existing Aboriginal rights, the evidence provided did not support the inclusion of "spirit dancing" as a protected right and one that was practised at the material times, namely, the mid-1800s when British sovereignty was asserted. Assuming that spirit dancing is a protected Aboriginal right under s. 35(1), Hood J. concluded that the defendants cannot succeed:

> Placing the aboriginal right at its highest level it does not include civil immunity for coercion, force, assault, unlawful confinement, or any other unlawful tortious conduct on the part of the defendants, in forcing the plaintiff to participate in their tradition. While the plaintiff may have special rights and status in Canada as an Indian, the "original" rights and freedoms he enjoys can be no less than those enjoyed by fellow citizens, Indian and non-

[166] *Thomas, supra* note 165 at 160.
[167] *Ibid.*
[168] *Ibid.* at 150.
[169] See *RWDSU* v. *Dolphin Delivery*, [1986] 2 S.C.R. 573; s. 32(1) of the Charter reads: "This Charter applies (a) to the Parliament and government of Canada in respect of all matters within the authority of Parliament including all matters relating to the Yukon Territory and Northwest Territories; and (b) to the legislature and government of each province in respect of all matters within the authority of the legislature of each province."

Indian alike. He lives in a free society and his rights are inviolable. He is free to believe in, and to practise, any religion or tradition, if he chooses to do so. He cannot be coerced or forced to participate in one by any group purporting to exercise their collective rights in doing so. His freedoms and rights are not "subject to the collective rights of the aboriginal nation to which he belongs."[170]

The limitation of collective rights is legitimate when the personal safety of an individual is concerned. A value judgment is made that certain individual rights ought not to be tampered with by any other rights, including the communal rights of Aboriginal people. Some Aboriginal groups protested *Thomas*, calling it "a complete denial of their constitutionally protected rights."[171]

At the heart of this conflict is the notion that collective rights and individual rights are mutually exclusive.[172] The plaintiff was entitled to certain rights as a member of a group, namely Aboriginal people, but was also entitled to certain individual rights *within* the group to ensure his own personal security. Thus, his individual rights supersede the rights of the collective when his personal security is threatened. Aboriginal people can practise their rights to the extent that they do not inflict harm upon other people, Aboriginal and non-Aboriginal alike. This type of rights application does not restrict the practice of spirit dancing except to the extent that it is practised upon involuntary participants.[173]

Thomas affirms that Aboriginal people can possess collective and individual rights. The necessity for Aboriginal collective rights can be found, to some degree, in the need to protect the well-being of individual Aboriginal persons. Therefore, if Aboriginal communities and Aboriginal rights are exercised in a manner that does not protect the well-being of their individual members, the justification for collective rights is questionable. Aboriginal individuals are as entitled to have their individual rights protected as all other Canadians. There must be a rational balance of collective and individual rights, as in so many other areas of law.

CONCLUSION

Through s. 35(1), the Supreme Court of Canada has attempted to place reasonable parameters on the exercise of existing Aboriginal and treaty rights. Nowhere on the globe are rights expressed in absolute terms; they must always be subject to reasonable limitations, varying only in degree. At the same time, governmental authority is also being held accountable so as to require justification of legislation and decisions that infringe existing Aboriginal and treaty rights.

The general principles surrounding existing Aboriginal and treaty rights have been set out by the Supreme Court of Canada in a series of decisions and will undoubtedly continue to be refined. As these principles are applied to specific fact situations utilizing a case-by-case approach, it is becoming clear that the evidentiary burden on Aboriginal

---

[170] *Thomas, supra* note 165 at 162.

[171] Robert Matas, "Native rite ruled subject to law," *The Globe and Mail* (8 February 1992) A6.

[172] For a general discussion, see L. McDonald, "Can Collective and Individual Rights Coexist?" 22 Melbourne Univ. L. Rev. 310.

[173] Richard Simeon makes a similar point in "Sharing Power: How Can First Nations Government Work?" in F. Cassidy, ed., *Aboriginal Self-Determination* (Lantzville, B.C.: Oolichan Books, 1991), 99 at 103: "[I]t is clear that the assertion that there is a fundamental dichotomy between individual and group rights is false. In fact, it is by virtue of our membership in a larger community, and through the protection of its institutions, that we have rights at all. Community is implicit in rights. Conversely, the only justification for community is that its strength and vitality is essential to the well-being, indeed the rights, of each of its members."

people is high. It is also becoming clear that government has a high degree of latitude, when their jurisdiction is properly exercised and decisions are procedurally and substantively fair, to justifiably interfere with and infringe Aboriginal and treaty rights. The real question remaining for governments is what mechanisms they will establish to fulfil their constitutional obligations to Aboriginal people but also to protect their respective areas of legislative jurisdiction.

CASES AND MATERIALS

Sections 35, 37(1), 37.1 and 52(1), *Constitution Act, 1982*
Schedule B of the *Canada Act 1982* (U.K.), 1982, c. 11

Part II Rights of the Aboriginal Peoples Of Canada

35. (1) The existing aboriginal and treaty rights of the aboriginal peoples of Canada are hereby recognized and affirmed.

(2) In this Act, "aboriginal peoples of Canada" includes the Indian, Inuit and Métis peoples of Canada.

(3) For greater certainty, in subsection (1) "treaty rights" includes rights that now exist by way of land claims agreements or may be so acquired.

(4) Notwithstanding any other provision of this Act, the aboriginal and treaty rights referred to in subsection (1) are guaranteed equally to male and female persons.

35.1 The government of Canada and the provincial governments are committed to the principle that, before any amendment is made to Class 24 of section 91 of the "Constitution Act, 1867", to section 25 of this Act or to this Part,
(a) constitutional conference that includes in its agenda an item relating to the proposed amendment, composed of the Prime Minister of Canada and the first ministers of the provinces, will be convened by the Prime Minister of Canada; and
(b) the Prime Minister of Canada will invite representatives of the aboriginal peoples of Canada to participate in the discussions on that item.

Part IV Constitutional Conference

37. (1) A constitutional conference composed of the Prime Minister of Canada and the first ministers of the provinces shall be convened by the Prime Minister of Canada within one year after this Part comes into force.

(2) The conference convened under subsection (1) shall have included in its agenda an item respecting constitutional matters that directly affect the aboriginal peoples of Canada, including the identification and definition of the rights of those peoples to be included in the Constitution of Canada, and the Prime Minister of Canada shall invite representatives of those peoples to participate in the discussions on that item.

(3) The Prime Minister of Canada shall invite elected representatives of the governments of the Yukon Territory and the Northwest Territories to participate in the discussions on any item on the agenda of the conference convened under subsection (1) that, in the opinion of the Prime Minister, directly affects the Yukon Territory and the Northwest Territories.

Part IV.I Constitutional Conferences

37.1 (1) In addition to the conference convened in March 1983, at least two constitutional conferences composed of the Prime Minister of Canada and the first ministers of the provinces shall be convened by the Prime Minister of Canada, the first within three years after April 17, 1982 and the second within five years after that date.

(2) Each conference convened under subsection (1) shall have included in its agenda constitutional matters that directly affect the aboriginal peoples of Canada, and the Prime Minister of Canada shall invite representatives of those peoples to participate in the discussions on those matters.

(3) The Prime Minister of Canada shall invite elected representatives of the governments of the Yukon Territory and the Northwest Territories to participate in the discussions on any item on the agenda of a conference convened under subsection (1) that, in the opinion of the Prime Minister, directly affects the Yukon Territory and the Northwest Territories.

(4) Nothing in this Section shall be construed so as to derogate from subsection 35(1). . . .

52. (1) The Constitution of Canada is the supreme law of Canada, and any law that is inconsistent with the provisions of the Constitution is, to the extent of the inconsistency, of no force or effect...

SECTION 35

R. v. *Sparrow*

[1990] 1 S.C.R. 1075 (S.C.C.). Dickson C.J., Lamer, Wilson, La Forest, L'Heureux-Dubé, McIntyre (took no part in the judgement), Sopinka JJ., May 31, 1990

DICKSON C.J. and LA FOREST J.:—This appeal requires this Court to explore for the first time the scope of s. 35(1) of the *Constitution Act, 1982*, and to indicate its strength as a promise to the aboriginal peoples of Canada. Section 35(1) is found in Part II of that Act, entitled "Rights of the Aboriginal Peoples of Canada," and provides as follows:

> 35.(1) The existing aboriginal and treaty rights of the aboriginal peoples of Canada are hereby recognized and affirmed.

The context of this appeal is the alleged violation of the terms of the Musqueam food fishing licence which are dictated by the *Fisheries Act*, R.S.C. 1970, c. F-14 (R.S.C. 1985, c. F-14), and the regulations under that Act. The issue is whether Parliament's power to regulate fishing is now limited by s. 35(1) of the *Constitution Act, 1982*, and, more specifically, whether the net length restriction in the licence is inconsistent with that provision.

Facts

The appellant, a member of the Musqueam Indian Band, was charged under s. 61(1) of the *Fisheries Act* of the offence of fishing with a drift net longer than that permitted by the terms of the Band's Indian food fishing licence. The fishing which gave rise to the charge took place on May 25, 1984 in Canoe Passage which is part of the area subject to the Band's licence. The licence, which had been issued for a one-year period beginning March 31, 1984, set out a number of restrictions including one that drift nets were to be limited to 25 fathoms in length. The appellant was caught with a net which was 45 fathoms in length. He has throughout admitted the facts alleged to constitute the offence, but has defended the charge on the basis that he was exercising an existing aboriginal right to fish and that the net length restriction contained in the Band's licence is inconsistent with s. 35(1) of the *Constitution Act, 1982* and therefore invalid. . . .

Leave to appeal to this Court was then sought and granted. On November 24, 1987, the following constitutional question was stated:

> Is the net length restriction contained in the Musqueam Indian Band Indian Food Fishing Licence dated March 30, 1984, issued pursuant to the *British Columbia Fishery (General) Regulations* and the *Fisheries Act,* R.S.C. 1970, c. F-14, inconsistent with s. 35(1) of the *Constitution Act, 1982*?

The appellant appealed on the ground that the Court of Appeal erred (1) in holding that s. 35(1) of the *Constitution Act, 1982* protects the aboriginal right only when exercised for food purposes and permits restrictive regulation of such rights whenever "reasonably justified as being necessary for the proper management and conservation of the resource or in the public interest," and (2) in failing to find the net length restriction in the Band's food fish licence was inconsistent with s. 35(1) of the *Constitution Act, 1982*.

The respondent Crown cross-appealed on the ground that the Court of Appeal erred in holding that the aboriginal right had not been extinguished before April 17, 1982, the date of commencement of the *Constitution Act, 1982*, and in particular in holding that, as a matter of fact and law, the appellant possessed the aboriginal right to fish for food. In the alternative, the respondent alleged, the Court of Appeal erred in its conclusions respecting the scope of the aboriginal right to fish for food and the extent to which it may be regulated, more particularly in holding that the aboriginal right included the right to take fish for the ceremonial purposes and societal needs of the Band and that the Band enjoyed a constitutionally protected priority over the rights of other people engaged in fishing. Section 35(1), the respondent maintained, did not invalidate legislation passed for the purpose of conservation and resource management, public health and safety and other overriding public interests such as the reasonable needs of other user groups. Finally, it maintained that the conviction ought not to have been set aside or a new trial directed because the appellant failed to establish a *prima facie* case that the reduction in the length of the net had unreasonably interfered with his right by preventing him from meeting his food fish requirements. According to the respondent, the Court of Appeal had erred in shifting the burden of proof to the Crown on the issue before the appellant had established a *prima facie* case. . . .

The Regulatory Scheme

The *Fisheries Act,* s. 34, confers on the Governor in Council broad powers to make regulations respecting the fisheries. . . .

Contravention of the Act and the regulations is made an offence under s. 61(1) under which the appellant was charged.

Acting under its regulation-making powers, the Governor in Council enacted the *British Columbia Fishery (General) Regulations*, SOR/84-248. Under these Regulations (s. 4), everyone is, *inter alia*, prohibited from fishing without a licence, and then only in areas and at the times and in the manner authorized by the Act or regulations. That provision also prohibits buying, selling, trading or bartering fish other than those lawfully caught under the authority of a commercial fishing licence. . . .

The Regulations make provision for issuing licences to Indians or a band "for the sole purpose of obtaining food for that Indian and his family and for the band," and no one other than an Indian is permitted to be in possession of fish caught pursuant to such a licence. Subsection 27(1) and (4) of the Regulations read:

> 27.(1) In this section "Indian food fish licence" means a licence issued by the Minister to an Indian or a band for the sole purpose of obtaining food for that Indian and his family or for the band. . . .
>
> (4) No person other than an Indian shall have in his possession fish caught under the authority of an Indian food fish licence.

As in the case of other licences issued under the Act, such licences may, by s. 12 of the Regulations, be subjected to restrictions regarding the species and quantity of fish that may be taken, the places and times when they may be taken, the manner in which they are to be marked and, most important here, the type of gear and equipment that may be used . . . .

Pursuant to these powers, the Musqueam Indian Band, on March 31, 1984, was issued an Indian food fishing licence as it had since 1978 "to fish for salmon for food for themselves and their family" in areas which included the place where the offence charged occurred, the waters of Ladner Reach and Canoe Passage therein described. The licence contained time restrictions as well as the type of gear to be used, notably "One Drift net twenty-five (25) fathoms in length."

The appellant was found fishing in the waters described using a drift net in excess of 25 fathoms. He did not contest this, arguing instead that he had committed no offence because he was acting in the exercise of an existing aboriginal right which was recognized and affirmed by s. 35(1) of the Constitution Act, 1982.

Analysis

We will address first the meaning of "existing" aboriginal rights and the content and scope of the Musqueam right to fish. We will then turn to the meaning of "recognized and affirmed," and the impact of s. 35(1) on the regulatory power of Parliament.

"Existing"

The word "existing" makes it clear that the rights to which s. 35(1) applies are those that were in existence when the *Constitution Act, 1982* came into effect. This means that extinguished rights are not revived by the *Constitution Act, 1982*. A number of courts have taken the position that "existing" means being in actuality in 1982: *R. v. Eninew* (1983), [1984] 2 C.N.L.R. 122 at 124 . . . (Sask. Q.B.), affd. [1984] 2 C.N.L.R. 126 . . . (Sask. C.A.). See also *Attorney-General for Ontario v. Bear Island Foundation* (1984), [1985] 1 C.N.L.R. 1 . . . (H.C.); *R. v. Hare and Debassige*, [1985] 3 C.N.L.R. 139 . . . (Ont. C.A.); *Re Steinhauer v. The Queen*, [1985] 3 C.N.L.R. 187 (Alta. Q.B.); *Martin v. The Queen*, (1985), 65 N.B.R. (2d) 21, 167 A.P.R. 21 (N.B.Q.B.); *R. v. Agawa*, [1988] 3 C.N.L.R. 73. . . .

Further, an existing aboriginal right cannot be read so as to incorporate the specific manner in which it was regulated before 1982. The notion of freezing existing rights would incorporate into the Constitution a crazy patchwork of regulations. Blair J.A. in *Agawa, supra* had this to say about the matter, at p. 214 [p. 87 C.N.L.R.]:

> Some academic commentators have raised a further problem which cannot be ignored. The Ontario Fishery Regulations contain detailed rules which vary for different regions in the province. Among other things, the Regulations specify seasons and methods of fishing, species of fish which can be caught and catch limits. Similar detailed provisions apply under the comparable fisheries Regulations in force in other provinces. These detailed provisions might be constitutionalized if it were decided that the existing treaty rights referred to in s. 35(1) were those remaining after regulation at the time of the proclamation of the *Constitution Act, 1982.*

As noted by Blair J.A., academic commentary lends support to the conclusion that "existing" means "unextinguished" rather than exercisable at a certain time in history. Professor Slattery, "Understanding Aboriginal Rights" (1987), 66 *Can. Bar Rev.* 726, at pp. 781–82, has observed the following about reading regulations into the rights:

> This approach reads into the Constitution the myriad of regulations affecting the exercise of aboriginal rights, regulations that differed considerably from place to place across the country. It does not permit differentiation between regulations of long-term significance and those enacted to deal with temporary conditions, or between reasonable and unreasonable restrictions. Moreover, it might require that a constitutional amendment be enacted to implement regulations more stringent than those in existence on 17 April 1982. This solution seems unsatisfactory. . . .

The arbitrariness of such an approach can be seen if one considers the recent history of the federal regulation in the context of the present case and the fishing industry. If the *Constitution Act, 1982* had been enacted a few years earlier, any right held by the Musqueam Band, on this approach, would have been constitutionally subjected to the restrictive regime of personal licences that had existed since 1917. Under that regime, the Musqueam catch had by 1969 become minor or nonexistent. In 1978 a system of band licences was introduced on an experimental basis which permitted the Musqueam to fish with a 75 fathom net for a greater number of days than other people. Under this regime, from 1977 to 1984, the number of Band members who fished for food increased from 19 persons using 15 boats, to 64 persons using 38 boats, while 10 other members of the Band fished under commercial licences. Before this regime, the Band's food fish requirement had basically been provided by Band members who were licensed for commercial fishing. Since the regime introduced in 1978 was in force in 1982, then, under this approach, the scope and content of an aboriginal right to fish would be determined by the details of the Band's 1978 licence.

The unsuitability of the approach can also be seen from another perspective. Ninety-one other tribes of Indians, comprising over 20,000 people (compared with 540 Musqueam on the reserve and 100 others off the reserve) obtain their food fish from the Fraser River. Some or all of these bands may have an aboriginal right to fish there. A constitutional patchwork quilt would be created if the constitutional right of these bands were to be determined by the specific regime available to each of those bands in 1982.

Far from being defined according to the regulatory scheme in place in 1982, the phrase "existing aboriginal rights" must be interpreted flexibly so as to permit their evolution over time. To use Professor Slattery's expression, in "Understanding Aboriginal Rights", *supra*, at p. 782, the word "existing" suggests that those rights are "affirmed in a contemporary form rather than in their primeval simplicity and vigour." Clearly, then, an approach to the constitutional guarantee embodied in s. 35(1) which would incorporate "frozen rights" must be rejected.

The Aboriginal Right

We turn now to the aboriginal right at stake in this appeal. The Musqueam Indian Reserve is located on the north shore of the Fraser River close to the mouth of that river and within the limits of the City of Vancouver. There has been a Musqueam village there for hundreds of years. This appeal does not directly concern the reserve or the adjacent waters, but arises out of the Band's right to fish in another area of the Fraser River known as Canoe Passage in the South Arm of the river, some 16 kilometres (about 10 miles) from the reserve. The reserve and those waters are separated by the Vancouver International Airport and the Municipality of Richmond.

The evidence reveals that the Musqueam have lived in the area as an organized society long before the coming of European settlers, and that the taking of salmon was an integral part of their lives and remains so to this day. Much of the evidence of an aboriginal right to fish was given by Dr. Suttles, an anthropologist, supported by that of Mr. Grant, the Band administrator. The Court of Appeal thus summarized Dr. Suttles' evidence, *R. v. Sparrow*, 9 B.C.L.R. (2d) 300, [1987] 1 C.N.L.R. 145 (B.C.C.A.) at pp. 307–308 [pp. 151–52 C.N.L.R.]:

> Dr. Suttles was qualified as having particular qualifications in respect of the ethnography of the Coast Salish Indian people of which the Musqueams were one of several tribes. He thought that the Musqueam had lived in their historic territory, which includes the Fraser River estuary, for at least 1,500 years. That historic territory extended from the north shore of Burrard Inlet to the south shore of the main channel of the Fraser River including the waters of the three channels by which that river reaches the ocean. As part of the Salish people, the Musqueam were part of a regional social network covering a much larger area but, as a tribe, were themselves an organized social group with their own name, territory and resources. Between the tribes there was a flow of people, wealth and food. No tribe was wholly self-sufficient or occupied its territory to the complete exclusion of others.

Dr. Suttles described the special position occupied by the salmon fishery in that society. The salmon was not only an important source of food but played an important part in the system of beliefs of the Salish people, and in their ceremonies. The salmon were held to be a race of beings that had, in "myth times," established a bond with human beings requiring the salmon to come each year to give their bodies to the humans who, in turn, treated them with respect shown by performance of the proper ritual. Towards the salmon, as toward other creatures, there was an attitude of caution and respect which resulted in effective conservation of the various species.

While the trial for a violation of penal prohibition may not be the most appropriate setting in which to determine the existence of an aboriginal right, and the evidence was not extensive, the correctness of the finding of fact of the trial judge "that Mr. Sparrow was fishing in ancient tribal territory where his ancestors had fished from time immemorial in that part of the mouth of the Fraser River for salmon" is supported by the evidence and was not contested. The existence of the right, the Court of Appeal tells us, "was not the subject of serious dispute." It is not surprising, then, that, taken with other circumstances, that court should find that "the judgment appealed from was wrong in . . . failing to hold that Sparrow at the relevant time was exercising an existing aboriginal right."

In this Court, however, the respondent contested the Court of Appeal's finding, contending that the evidence was insufficient to discharge the appellant's burden of proof upon the issue. It is true that for the period from 1867 and 1961 the evidence is scanty. But the evidence was not disputed or contradicted in the courts below and there is evidence of sufficient continuity of the right to support the Court of Appeal's finding, and we would not disturb it.

What the Crown really insisted on, both in this Court and the courts below, was that the Musqueam Band's aboriginal right to fish had been extinguished by regulations under the *Fisheries Act.* . . .

See also *Attorney-General of Ontario* v. *Bear Island Foundation, supra,* at pp. 439–40 [pp. 80–81 C.N.L.R.]. That in Judson J.'s view was what had occurred in *Calder, supra,* where, as he saw it, a series of statutes evinced a unity of intention to exercise a sovereignty inconsistent with any conflicting interest, including aboriginal title. But Hall J. in that case stated (at p. 404) that "the onus of proving that the Sovereign intended to extinguish the Indian title lies on the respondent and *that intention must be 'clear and plain'*" (emphasis added). The test of extinguishment to be adopted, in our opinion, is that the Sovereign's intention must be clear and plain if it is to extinguish an aboriginal right.

There is nothing in the *Fisheries Act* or its detailed regulations that demonstrates a clear and plain intention to extinguish the Indian aboriginal right to fish. The fact that express provision permitting the Indians to fish for food may have applied to all Indians and that for an extended period permits were discretionary and issued on an individual rather than a communal basis in no way shows a clear intention to extinguish. These permits were simply a manner of controlling the fisheries, not defining underlying rights.

We would conclude then that the Crown has failed to discharge its burden of proving extinguishment. In our opinion, the Court of Appeal made no mistake in holding that the Indians have an existing aboriginal right to fish in the area where Mr. Sparrow was fishing at the time of the charge. This approach is consistent with ensuring that an aboriginal right should not be defined by incorporating the ways in which it has been regulated in the past.

The scope of the existing Musqueam right to fish must now be delineated. The anthropological evidence relied on to establish the existence of the right suggests that, for the Musqueam, the salmon fishery has always constituted an integral part of their distinctive culture. Its significant role involved not only consumption for subsistence purposes, but also consumption of salmon on ceremonial and social occasions. The Musqueam have always fished for reasons connected to their cultural and physical survival. As we stated earlier, the right to do so may be exercised in a contemporary manner. . . .

Government regulations governing the exercise of the Musqueam right to fish, as described above, have only recognized the right to fish *for food* for over a hundred years. This may have reflected the existing position. However, historical policy on the part of the Crown is not only incapable of extinguishing the existing aboriginal right without clear intention, but is also incapable of, in itself, delineating that right. The nature of government regulations cannot be determinative of the content and scope of an existing aboriginal right. Government policy *can* however, regulate the exercise of that right, but such regulation must be in keeping with s. 35(1).

In the courts below, the case at bar was not presented on the footing of an aboriginal right to fish for commercial or livelihood purposes. Rather, the focus was and continues to be on the validity of a net length restriction affecting the appellant's *food fishing licence.*

We therefore adopt the Court of Appeal's characterization of the right for the purpose of this appeal, and confine our reasons to the meaning of the constitutional recognition and affirmation of the existing aboriginal right to fish for food and social and ceremonial purposes.

"Recognized and Affirmed"

We now turn to the impact of s. 35(1) of the *Constitution Act, 1982* on the regulatory power of Parliament and on the outcome of this appeal specifically. . . .

It is worth recalling that while British policy towards the native population was based on respect for their right to occupy their traditional lands, a proposition to which the Royal Proclamation of 1763 bears witness, there was from the outset never any doubt that sovereignty and legislative power, and indeed the underlying title, to such lands vested in the Crown: see *Johnson* v. *M'Intosh* (1823), 8 Wheaton 543 (U.S.S.C.); see also the Royal Proclamation itself (R.S.C. 1985, App. II, No. 1, pp. 4-6); *Calder, supra, per* Judson J. at p. 328, Hall J. at pp. 383, 403. And there can be no doubt that over the years the rights of the Indians were often honoured in the breach (for one instance in a recent case in this Court, see *Canadian Pacific Ltd.* v. *Paul*, [1988] 2 S.C.R. 654, [1989] 1 C.N.L.R. 47). As MacDonald J. stated in *Pasco* v. *Canadian National Railway Co.*, [1986] 1 C.N.L.R. 35 at 37, 69 B.C.L.R. 76 (B.C.S.C.): "We cannot recount with much pride the treatment accorded to the native people of this country."

For many years, the rights of the Indians to their aboriginal lands—certainly as legal rights—were virtually ignored. The leading cases defining Indian rights in the early part of the century were directed at claims supported by the Royal Proclamation or other legal instruments and even these cases were essentially concerned with settling legislative jurisdiction or the rights of commercial enterprises. For fifty years after the publication of Clement's *The Law of the Canadian Constitution* (3rd ed. 1916), there was a virtual absence of discussion of any kind of Indian rights to land even in academic literature. By the late 1960s, aboriginal claims were not even recognized by the federal government as having any legal status. Thus the *Statement of the Government of Canada on Indian Policy* 1969, although well meaning, contained the assertion (at p. 11) that "aboriginal claims to land . . . are so general and undefined that it is not realistic to think of them as specific claims capable of remedy except through a policy and program that will end injustice to the Indians as members of the Canadian community." In the same general period, the James Bay development by Quebec Hydro was originally initiated without regard to the right of the Indians who lived there, even though these were expressly protected by a constitutional instrument; see the *Quebec Boundary Extension Act*, 1912, S.C. 1912, c. 45. It took a number of judicial decisions and notably the *Calder* case in this Court (1973) to prompt a reassessment of the position being taken by government.

In the light of its reassessment of Indian claims following *Calder*, the federal government on August 8, 1973 issued "a statement of policy" regarding Indian lands. By it, it sought to "signify the Government's *recognition and acceptance* of its continuing responsibility under the *British North America Act* for Indians and lands reserved for Indians," which it regarded "as an historic evolution dating back to the *Royal Proclamation of 1763*, which, whatever differences there may be about its judicial interpretation, stands as a basic declaration of the Indian people's interests in land in this country." [Emphasis added.] See S*tatement made by the Honourable Jean Chrétien, Minister of Indian Affairs and Northern Development on Claims of Indian and Inuit People*, August 8, 1973. The remarks about these lands were intended "as an expression of acknowledged responsibility." But the statement went on to express, for the first time, the government's willingness to negotiate regarding claims of aboriginal title, specifically in British Columbia, Northern Quebec, and the Territories, and this without regard to formal supporting document. "The Government," it stated, "is now ready to negotiate with authorized representatives of these native peoples on the basis that where their traditional interest in the lands concerned can be established, an agreed form of compensation or benefit will be provided to native peoples in return for their interest."

It is obvious from its terms that the approach taken towards aboriginal claims in the 1973 statement constituted an expression of a policy, rather than a legal position; see also Canada, Department of Indian Affairs and Northern Development, *In All Fairness: A Native Claims Policy—Comprehensive Claims* (1981), pp. 11–12; Slattery, "Understanding Aboriginal Rights" (1987), 66 Can. Bar. Rev. 726 at 730. As recently as *Guerin* v. *The Queen*, [1984] 2 S.C.R. 335, [1985] 1 C.N.L.R. 120 . . ., the federal government argued in this Court that any federal obligation was of a political character.

It is clear, then, that s. 35(1) of the *Constitution Act, 1982*, represents the culmination of a long and difficult struggle in both the political forum and the courts for the constitutional recognition of aboriginal rights. The strong representations of native associations and other groups concerned with the welfare of Canada's aboriginal people made the adoption of s. 35(1) possible and it is important to note that the provision applies to the Indians, the Inuit and the Métis. Section 35(1), at the least, provides a solid constitutional base upon which subsequent negotiations can take place. It also affords aboriginal peoples constitutional protection against provincial legislative power. We are, of course, aware that this would, in any event, flow from the *Guerin* case, *supra*, but for a proper understanding of the situation, it is essential to remember that the *Guerin* case was decided after the commencement of the *Constitution Act, 1982*. In addition to its effect on aboriginal rights, s. 35(1) clarified other issues regarding the enforcement of treaty rights (see Sanders, "Pre-existing Rights: The Aboriginal Peoples of Canada," in Beaudoin and Ratushny, eds., *The Canadian Charter of Rights and Freedoms*, 2nd ed., esp. at p. 730).

In our opinion, the significance of s. 35(1) extends beyond these fundamental effects. Professor Lyon in "An Essay on Constitutional Interpretation" (1988), 26 *Osgoode Hall L.J.* 95, says the following about s. 35(1), at p. 100:

> ... the context of 1982 is surely enough to tell us that this is not just a codification of the case law on aboriginal rights that had accumulated by 1982. Section 35 calls for a just settlement for aboriginal peoples. It renounces the old rules of the game under which the Crown established courts of law and denied those courts the authority to question sovereign claims made by the Crown.

The approach to be taken with respect to interpreting the meaning of s. 35(1) is derived from general principles of constitutional interpretation, principles relating to aboriginal rights, and the purposes behind the constitutional provision itself. Here, we will sketch the framework for an interpretation of "recognized and affirmed" that, in our opinion, gives appropriate weight to the constitutional nature of these words.

In *Reference re Manitoba Language Rights*, [1985] 1 S.C.R. 721, this Court said the following about the perspective to be adopted when interpreting a constitution, at p. 745:

> The Constitution of a country is a statement of the will of the people to be governed in accordance with certain principles held as fundamental and certain prescriptions restrictive of the powers of the legislature and government. It is, as s. 52 of the *Constitution Act, 1982*

declares, the "supreme law" of the nation, unalterable by the normal legislative process, and unsuffering of laws inconsistent with it. The duty of the judiciary is to interpret and apply the laws of Canada and each of the provinces, and it is thus our duty to ensure that the constitutional law prevails.

The nature of s. 35(1) itself suggests that it be construed in a purposive way. When the purposes of the affirmation of aboriginal rights are considered, it is clear that a generous, liberal interpretation of the words in the constitutional provision is demanded. When the Court of Appeal below was confronted with the submission that s. 35 has no effect on aboriginal or treaty rights and that it is merely a preamble to the parts of the *Constitution Act, 1982*, which deal with aboriginal rights, it said the following at p. 322 [p. 168 C.N.L.R.]:

> This submission gives no meaning to s. 35. If accepted, it would result in denying its clear statement that existing rights are hereby recognized and affirmed, and would turn that into a mere promise to recognize and affirm those rights sometime in the future. . . . To so construe s. 35(1) would be to ignore its language and the principle that the Constitution should be interpreted in a liberal and remedial way. We cannot accept that that principle applies less strongly to aboriginal rights than to the rights guaranteed by the Charter particularly having regard to the history and to the approach to interpreting treaties and statutes relating to Indians required by such cases as *Nowegijick* v. *R.* [1983] 1 S.C.R. 29. . . .

In *Nowegijick* v. *The Queen*, [1983] 1 S.C.R. 29 at 36, [1983] 2 C.N.L.R. 89 at 94 . . ., the following principle that should govern the interpretation of Indian treaties and statutes was set out:

> … treaties and statutes relating to Indians should be liberally construed and doubtful expression resolved in favour of the Indians.

In *R.* v. *Agawa, supra*, Blair J.A. stated that the above principle should apply to the interpretation of s. 35(1). He added the following principle to be equally applied, at pp. 215–16 [p. 89 C.N.L.R.]:

> The second principle was enunciated by the late Associate Chief Justice MacKinnon in *R.* v. *Taylor and Williams* (1981), 34 O.R. (2d) 360, [1981] 3 C.N.L.R. 114. He emphasized the importance of Indian history and traditions as well as the perceived effect of a treaty at the time of its execution. He also cautioned against determining Indian rights "in a vacuum." The honour of the Crown is involved in the interpretation of Indian treaties and, as a consequence, fairness to the Indians is a governing consideration. He said at p. 367 [p. 123 C.N.L.R.]: "The principles to be applied to the interpretation of Indian treaties have been much canvassed over the years. In approaching the terms of a treaty quite apart from the other considerations already noted, the honour of the Crown is always involved and no appearance of 'sharp dealing' should be sanctioned."

This view is reflected in recent judicial decisions which have emphasized the responsibility of Government to protect the rights of Indians arising from the special trust relationship created by history, treaties and legislation: see *Guerin* v. *The Queen*, [1984] 2 S.C.R. 335; 13 D.L.R. (4th) 321, [1985] 1 C.N.L.R. 120.

In *Guerin, supra*, the Musqueam Band surrendered reserve lands to the Crown for lease to a golf club. The terms obtained by the Crown were much less favourable than those approved by the Band at the surrender meeting. This Court found that the Crown owed a fiduciary obligation to the Indians with respect to the lands. The *sui generis* nature of Indian title, and the historic powers and responsibility assumed by the Crown constituted the source of such a fiduciary obligation. In our opinion, *Guerin*, together with *R.*

v. *Taylor and Williams* (1981), 34 O.R. (2d) 360, [1981] 3 C.N.L.R. 114, ground a general guiding principle for s. 35(1). That is, the Government has the responsibility to act in a fiduciary capacity with respect to aboriginal peoples. The relationship between the Government and aboriginals is trust-like, rather than adversarial, and contemporary recognition and affirmation of aboriginal rights must be defined in light of this historic relationship.

We agree with both the British Columbia Court of Appeal below and the Ontario Court of Appeal that the principles outlined above, derived from *Nowegijick, Taylor and Williams* and *Guerin*, should guide the interpretation of s. 35(1). As commentators have noted, s. 35(1) is a solemn commitment that must be given meaningful content (*Lyon, supra*; William Pentney, "The Rights of the Aboriginal Peoples of Canada in the Constitution Act, 1982, Part II, Section 35: The Substantive Guarantee" (1987) 22 *U.B.C. L. Rev.* 207; Schwartz, "Unstarted Business: Two Approaches to Defining s. 35—'What's in the Box?' and 'What Kind of Box?'," Ch. XXIV, in *First Principles, Second Thoughts* (Montreal: Institute for Research on Public Policy, 1986); Slattery, *supra*; and Slattery, "The Hidden Constitution: Aboriginal Rights in Canada" (1984), 32 *Am. J. of Comp. Law* 361).

In response to the appellant's submission that s. 35(1) rights are more securely protected than the rights guaranteed by the Charter, it is true that s. 35(1) is not subject to s. 1 of the Charter. In our opinion, this does not mean that any law or regulation affecting aboriginal rights will automatically be of no force or effect by the operation of s. 52 of the *Constitution Act, 1982*. Legislation that affects the exercise of aboriginal rights will nonetheless be valid, if it meets the test for justifying an interference with a right recognized and affirmed under s. 35(1).

There is no explicit language in the provision that authorizes this Court or any court to assess the legitimacy of any government legislation that restricts aboriginal rights. Yet, we find that the words "recognition and affirmation" incorporate the fiduciary relationship referred to earlier and so import some restraint on the exercise of sovereign power. Rights that are recognized and affirmed are not absolute. Federal legislative powers continue, including, of course, the right to legislate with respect to Indians pursuant to s. 91(24) of the *Constitution Act, 1867*. These powers must, however, now be read together with s. 35(1). In other words, federal power must be reconciled with federal duty and the best way to achieve that reconciliation is to demand the justification of any government regulation that infringes upon or denies aboriginal rights. Such scrutiny is in keeping with the liberal interpretive principle enunciated in *Nowegijick, supra* and the concept of holding the Crown to a high standard of honourable dealing with respect to the aboriginal peoples of Canada as suggested by *Guerin* v. *The Queen, supra*.

We refer to Professor Slattery's "Understanding Aboriginal Rights," *supra*, with respect to the task of envisioning a s. 35(1) justificatory process. Professor Slattery, at p. 782, points out that a justificatory process is required as a compromise between a "patchwork" characterization of aboriginal rights whereby past regulations would be read into a definition of the rights, and a characterization that would guarantee aboriginal rights in their original form unrestricted by subsequent regulation. We agree with him that these two extreme positions must be rejected in favour of a justificatory scheme.

Section 35(1) suggests that while regulation affecting aboriginal rights is not precluded, such regulation must be enacted according to a valid objective. Our history has shown, unfortunately all too well, that Canada's aboriginal peoples are justified in worrying about government objectives that may be superficially neutral but which constitute *de facto* threats to the existence of aboriginal rights and interests. By giving aboriginal rights constitutional status and priority, Parliament and the provinces have sanctioned challenges to social and economic policy objectives embodied in legislation to the extent that aboriginal rights are affected. Implicit in this constitutional scheme is the obligation of the legislature to satisfy the test of justification. The way in which a legislative objective is to be attained must uphold the honour of the Crown and must be in keeping with the unique contemporary relationship, grounded in history and policy, between the Crown and Canada's aboriginal peoples. The extent of legislative or regulatory impact on an existing aboriginal right may be scrutinized so as to ensure recognition and affirmation.

The constitutional recognition afforded by the provision therefore gives a measure of control over government conduct and a strong check on legislative power. While it does not promise immunity from government regulation in a society that, in the twentieth century, is increasingly more complex, interdependent and sophisticated, and where exhaustible resources need protection and management, it does hold the Crown to a substantive promise. The government is required to bear the burden of justifying any legislation that has some negative effect on any aboriginal right protected under s. 35(1).

In these reasons, we will outline the appropriate analysis under s. 35(1) in the context of a regulation made pursuant to the *Fisheries Act*. We wish to emphasize the importance of context and a case-by-case approach to s. 35(1). Given the generality of the text of the constitutional provision, and especially in light of the complexities of aboriginal history, society and rights, the contours of a justificatory standard must be defined in the specific factual context of each case.

Section 35(1) and the Regulation of the Fisheries
Taking the above framework as guidance, we propose to set out the test for *prima facie* interference with an existing aboriginal right and for the justification of such an interference. With respect to the question of the regulation of the fisheries, the existence of s. 35(1) of the *Constitution Act, 1982*, renders the authority of *R. v. Derricksan*, [1976] 2 S.C.R. V, inapplicable. In that case, Laskin C.J., for this Court, found that there was nothing to prevent the *Fisheries Act* and the Regulations from subjecting the alleged aboriginal right to fish in a particular area to the controls thereby imposed. As the Court of Appeal in the case at bar noted, the *Derricksan* line of cases established that, before April 17, 1982, the aboriginal right to fish was subject to regulation by legislation and subject to extinguishment. The new constitutional status of that right enshrined in s. 35(1) suggests that a different approach must be taken in deciding whether regulation of the fisheries might be out of keeping with constitutional protection.

The first question to be asked is whether the legislation in question has the effect of interfering with an existing aboriginal right. If it does have such an effect, it represents a *prima facie* infringement of s. 35(1). Parliament is not expected to act in a manner contrary to the rights and interests of aboriginals, and, indeed, may be barred from doing so by the second stage of s. 35(1) analysis. The inquiry with respect to interference begins with a reference to the characteristics or incidents of the right at stake. Our earlier observations regarding the scope of the aboriginal right to fish are relevant here. Fishing rights are not traditional property rights. They are rights held by a collective and are in keeping with the culture and existence of that group. Courts must be careful, then, to avoid the application of traditional common law concepts of property as they develop their understanding of what the reasons for judgment in *Guerin, supra*, at p. 382 [p. 136 C.N.L.R.], referred to as the "sui generis" nature of aboriginal rights. (See also Little Bear, "A Concept of Native Title," [1982] 5 *Can. Legal Aid Bul.* 99.)

While it is impossible to give an easy definition of fishing rights, it is possible, and, indeed, crucial, to be sensitive to the aboriginal perspective itself on the meaning of the rights at stake. For example, it would be artificial to try to create a hard distinction between the right to fish and the particular manner in which that right is exercised.

To determine whether the fishing rights have been interfered with such as to constitute a *prima facie* infringement of s. 35(1), certain questions must be asked. First, is the limitation unreasonable? Second, does the regulation impose undue hardship? Third, does the regulation deny to the holders of the right their preferred means of exercising that right? The onus of proving a *prima facie* infringement lies on the individual or group challenging the legislation. In relation to the facts of this appeal, the regulation would be found to be a *prima facie* interference if it were found to be an adverse restriction on the Musqueam exercise of their right to fish for food. We wish to note here that the issue does not merely require looking at whether the fish catch has been reduced below that needed for the reasonable food and ceremonial needs of the Musqueam Indians. Rather the test involves asking whether either the purpose or the effect of the restriction on net length unnecessarily infringes the interests protected by the fishing right. If, for example, the Musqueam were forced to spend undue time and money per fish caught or if the net length reduction resulted in a hardship to the Musqueam in catching fish, then the first branch of the s. 35(1) analysis would be met.

If a *prima facie* interference is found, the analysis moves to the issue of justification. This is the test that addresses the question of what constitutes legitimate regulation of a constitutional aboriginal right. The justification analysis would proceed as follows. First, is there a valid legislative objective? Here the court would inquire into whether the objective of Parliament in authorizing the department to enact regulations regarding fisheries is valid. The objective of the department in setting out the particular regulations would also be scrutinized. An objective aimed at preserving s. 35(1) rights by conserving and managing a natural resource, for example, would be valid. Also valid would be objectives purporting to prevent the exercise of s. 35(1) rights that would cause harm to the general populace or to aboriginal peoples themselves, or other objectives found to be compelling and substantial.

The Court of Appeal below held, at p. 331 [p. 178 C.N.L.R.] that regulations could be valid if reasonably justified as "necessary for the proper management and conservation of the resource or in the public interest". . . . We find the "public interest" justification to be so vague as to provide no meaningful guidance and so broad as to be unworkable as a test for the justification of a limitation on constitutional rights.

The justification of conservation and resource management, on the other hand, is surely uncontroversial. In *Kruger* v. *The Queen*, [1978] 1 S.C.R. 104, [1977] 4 W.W.R. 300, the applicability of the B.C. *Wildlife Act*, S.B.C. 1966, c. 55, to the appellant members of the Penticton Indian Band was considered by this Court. In discussing that Act, the following was said about the objective of conservation (at p.112):

> Game conservation laws have as their policy the maintenance of wildlife resources. It might be argued that without some conservation measures the ability of Indians or others to hunt for food would become a moot issue in consequence of the destruction of the resource. The presumption is for the validity of a legislative enactment and in this case the presumption has to mean that in the absence of evidence to the contrary the measures taken by the British Columbia Legislature were taken to maintain an effective resource in the Province for its citizens and not to oppose the interests of conservationists and Indians in such a way as to favour the claims of the former.

While the "presumption" of validity is now outdated in view of the constitutional status of the aboriginal rights at stake, it is clear that the value of conservation purposes for government legislation and action has long been recognized. Further, the conservation and management of our resources is consistent with aboriginal beliefs and practices, and, indeed, with the enhancement of aboriginal rights.

If a valid legislative objective is found, the analysis proceeds to the second part of the justification issue. Here, we refer back to the guiding interpretive principle derived from *Taylor and Williams* and *Guerin, supra*. That is, the honour of the Crown is at stake in dealings with aboriginal peoples. The special trust relationship and the responsibility of the government vis-à-vis aboriginals must be the first consideration in determining whether the legislation or action in question can be justified.

The problem that arises in assessing the legislation in light of its objective and the responsibility of the Crown is that the pursuit of conservation in a heavily used modern fishery inevitably blurs with the efficient allocation and management of this scarce and valued resource. The nature of the constitutional protection afforded by s. 35(1) in this context demands that there be a link between the question of justification and the allocation of priorities in the fishery. The constitutional recognition and affirmation of aboriginal rights may give rise to conflict with the interests of others given the limited nature of the resource. There is a clear need for guidelines that will resolve the allocational problems that arise regarding the fisheries. We refer to the reasons of Dickson J. in *Jack* v. *The Queen*, [1980] 1 S.C.R. 294, [1979] 2 C.N.L.R. 25, for such guidelines.

In *Jack*, the appellants' defence to a charge of fishing for salmon in certain rivers during a prohibited period was based on the alleged constitutional incapacity of Parliament to legislate such as to deny the Indians their right to fish for food. They argued that Art. 13 of the British Columbia Terms of Union imposed a constitutional limitation on the federal power to regulate. While we recognize that the finding that such a limitation had been imposed was not adopted by the majority of this Court, we point out that this case concerns a different constitutional promise that asks this Court to give a meaningful interpretation to recognition and affirmation. That task requires equally meaningful guidelines responsive to the constitutional priority accorded aboriginal rights. We therefore repeat the following passage from *Jack*, at p. 313 [p. 41 C.N.L.R.]:

> Conservation is a valid legislative concern. The appellants concede as much. Their concern is in the allocation of the resource after reasonable and necessary conservation measures have been recognized and given effect to. They do not claim the right to pursue the last living salmon until it is caught. Their position, as I understand it, is one which would give effect to an order of priorities of this nature: (i) conservation; (ii) Indian fishing; (iii) non-Indian commercial fishing; or (iv) non-Indian sports fishing; the burden of conservation measures should not fall primarily upon the Indian fishery.
>
> I agree with the general tenor of this argument. . . . With respect to whatever salmon are to be caught, then priority ought to be given to the Indian fishermen, subject to the practical difficulties occasioned by international waters and the movement of the fish themselves. But any limitation upon Indian fishing that is established for a valid conservation purpose overrides the protection afforded the Indian fishery by art. 13, just as such conservation measures override other taking of fish.

The constitutional nature of the Musqueam food fishing rights means that any allocation of priorities after valid conservation measures have been implemented must give top priority to Indian food fishing. If the objective pertained to conservation, the conservation plan would be scrutinized to assess priorities. While the detailed allocation of maritime resources is a task that must be left to those having expertise in the area, the Indians' food requirements must be met first when that allocation is established. The significance of giving the aboriginal right to fish for food top priority can be described as follows. If, in a given year, conservation needs required a reduction in the number of fish to be caught such that the number equalled the number required for food by the Indians, then all the fish available after conservation would go to the Indians according to the constitutional nature of their fishing right. If, more realistically, there were still fish after the Indian food requirements were met, then the brunt of conservation measures would be borne by the practices of sport fishing and commercial fishing.

The decision of the Nova Scotia Court of Appeal in *Denny, Paul and Sylliboy* v. *The Queen*, unreported rendered March 5, 1990 [now reported [1990] 2 C.N.L.R. 115] addresses the constitutionality of the Nova Scotia Micmac Indians' right to fish in the waters of Indian Brook and the Afton River, and does so in a way that accords with our understanding of the constitutional nature of aboriginal rights and the link between allocation and justification required for government regulation of the exercise of the rights. Clarke C.J.N.S., for a unanimous court, found that the Nova Scotia Fishery Regulations enacted pursuant to the federal *Fisheries Act* were in part inconsistent with the constitutional rights of the appellant Micmac Indians. Section 35(1) of the *Constitution Act, 1982*, provided the appellants with the right to a top priority allocation of any surplus of the fisheries resource which might exist after the needs of conservation had been taken into account. With respect to the issue of the Indians' priority to a food fishery, Clarke C.J.N.S. noted that the official policy of the federal government recognizes that priority. He added the following, at pp. 22–23 [p. 131 C.N.L.R.]:

> I have no hesitation in concluding that factual as well as legislative and policy recognition must be given to the existence of an Indian food fishery in the waters of Indian Brook, adjacent to the Eskasoni Reserve, and the waters of the Afton River after the needs of conservation have been taken into account...

To afford user groups such as sports fishermen (anglers) a priority to fish over the legitimate food needs of the appellants and their families is simply not appropriate action on the part of the federal government. It is inconsistent with the fact that the appellants have for many years, and continue to possess an aboriginal right to fish for food. The appellants have, to employ the words of their counsel, a "right to share in the available resource." This constitutional entitlement is second only to conservation measures that may be undertaken by federal legislation. . . .

As we have pointed out, management and conservation of resources is indeed an important and valid legislative objective. Yet, the fact that the objective is of a "reasonable" nature cannot suffice as constitutional recognition and affirmation of aboriginal rights. Rather, the regulations enforced pursuant to a conservation or management objective may be scrutinized according to the justificatory standard outlined above.

We acknowledge the fact that the justificatory standard to be met may place a heavy burden on the Crown. However, government policy with respect to the British Columbia fishery, regardless of s. 35(1), already dictates that, in allocating the right to take fish, Indian food fishing is to be given priority over the interests of other user groups. The constitutional entitlement embodied in s. 35(1) requires the Crown to ensure that its regulations are in keeping with that allocation of priority. The objective of this requirement is not to undermine Parliament's ability and responsibility with respect to creating and administering overall conservation and management plans regarding the salmon fishery. The objective is rather to guarantee that those plans treat aboriginal peoples in a way ensuring that their rights are taken seriously.

Within the analysis of justification, there are further questions to be addressed, depending on the circumstances of the inquiry. These include the questions of whether there has been as little infringement as possible in order to effect the desired result; whether, in a situation of expropriation, fair compensation is available; and, whether the aboriginal group in question has been consulted with respect to the conservation measures being implemented. The aboriginal peoples, with their history of conservation-consciousness and interdependence with natural resources, would surely be expected, at the least, to be informed regarding the determination of an appropriate scheme for the regulation of the fisheries.

We would not wish to set out an exhaustive list of the factors to be considered in the assessment of justification. Suffice it to say that recognition and affirmation requires sensitivity to and respect for the rights of aboriginal peoples on behalf of the government, courts and indeed all Canadians.

Application to this Case—Is the Net Length Restriction Valid?

The Court of Appeal below found that there was not sufficient evidence in this case to proceed with an analysis of s. 35(1) with respect to the right to fish for food. In reviewing the competing expert evidence, and recognizing that fish stock management is an uncertain science, it decided that the issues at stake in this appeal were not well adopted to being resolved at the appellate court level. . . .

In conclusion, we would dismiss the appeal and the cross-appeal and affirm the Court of Appeal's setting aside of the conviction. We would accordingly affirm the order for a new trial on the questions of infringement and whether any infringement is nonetheless consistent with s. 35(1), in accordance with the interpretation set out here.

For the reasons given above, the constitutional question must be answered as follows:

Question

Is the net length restriction contained in the Musqueam Indian Band Indian Food Fishing Licence dated March 30, 1984, issued pursuant to the *British Columbia Fishery (General) Regulations* and the *Fisheries Act*, R.S.C. 1970, c. F-14, inconsistent with s. 35(1) of the *Constitution Act, 1982*?

Answer

This question will have to be sent back to trial to be answered according to the analysis set out in these reasons.

R. v. Van der Peet

[1996] 2 S.C.R. 507 (S.C.C.). Lamer C.J., La Forest, L'Heureux-Dubé, Sopinka, Gonthier, Cory, McLachlin, Iacobucci, and Major JJ., August 21, 1996

LAMER C.J. (LA FOREST, SOPINKA, GONTHIER, CORY, IACOBUCCI and MAJOR JJ. concurring):—

Introduction

1   This appeal, along with the companion appeals in *R. v. N.T.C. Smokehouse Ltd.*, [1996] 2 S.C.R. 672, and *R. v. Gladstone*, [1996] 2 S.C.R. 723, raises the issue left unresolved by this Court in its judgment in *R. v. Sparrow*, [1990] 1 S.C.R. 1075: How are the Aboriginal rights recognized and affirmed by s. 35(1) of the *Constitution Act, 1982* to be defined?

2   In *Sparrow*, Dickson C.J. and La Forest J., writing for a unanimous Court, outlined the framework for analyzing s. 35(1) claims. First, a court must determine whether an applicant has demonstrated that he or she was acting pursuant to an Aboriginal right. Second, a court must determine whether that right has been extinguished. Third, a court must determine whether that right has been infringed. Finally, a court must determine whether the infringement is justified. In *Sparrow,* however, it was not seriously disputed that the Musqueam had an Aboriginal right to fish for food, with the result that it was unnecessary for the Court to answer the question of how the rights recognized and affirmed by s. 35(1) are to be defined. It is this question and, in particular, the question of whether s. 35(1) recognizes and affirms the right of the Sto:lo to sell fish, which must now be answered by this Court.

3   In order to define the scope of Aboriginal rights, it will be necessary first to articulate the purposes which underpin s. 35(1), specifically the reasons underlying its recognition and affirmation of the unique constitutional status of Aboriginal peoples in Canada. Until it is understood why Aboriginal rights exist, and are constitutionally protected, no definition of those rights is possible. As Dickson J. (as he then was) said in *R.* v. *Big M Drug Mart Ltd.*, [1985] 1 S.C.R. 295, at p. 344, a constitutional provision must be understood "in the light of the interests it was meant to protect". This principle, articulated in relation to the rights protected by the *Canadian Charter of Rights and Freedoms*, applies equally to the interpretation of s. 35(1). . . .

5   The appellant Dorothy Van der Peet was charged under s. 61(1) of the *Fisheries Act*, R.S.C. 1970, c. F-14, with the offence of selling fish caught under the authority of an Indian food fish licence, contrary to s. 27(5) of the British Columbia Fishery (General) Regulations, SOR/84-248. At the time at which the appellant was charged s. 27(5) read:

> 27. . . .
> (5) No person shall sell, barter or offer to sell or barter any fish caught under the authority of an Indian food fish licence. . . .

13   Leave to appeal to this Court was granted on March 10, 1994. The following constitutional question was stated:

> Is s. 27(5) of the *British Columbia Fishery (General) Regulations*, SOR/84-248, as it read on September 11, 1987, of no force or effect with respect to the appellant in the circumstances of these proceedings, in virtue of s. 52 of the *Constitution Act, 1982*, by reason of the Aboriginal rights within the meaning of s. 35 of the *Constitution Act, 1982*, invoked by the appellant? . . .

16   In her factum the appellant argued that the majority of the Court of Appeal erred because it defined the rights in s. 35(1) in a fashion which "converted a Right into a Relic"; such an approach, the appellant argued, is inconsistent with the fact that the Aboriginal rights recognized and affirmed by s. 35(1) are rights and not simply Aboriginal practices. The appellant acknowledged that Aboriginal rights are based in Aboriginal societies and cultures, but argued that the majority of the Court of Appeal erred because it defined Aboriginal rights through the identification of pre-contact activities instead of as pre-existing legal rights.

17   While the appellant is correct to suggest that the mere existence of an activity in a particular Aboriginal community prior to contact with Europeans is not, in itself, sufficient foundation for the definition of Aboriginal rights, the position she would have this

Court adopt takes s. 35(1) too far from that which the provision is intended to protect. Section 35(1), it is true, recognizes and affirms existing Aboriginal rights, but it must not be forgotten that the rights it recognizes and affirms are Aboriginal.

18   In the liberal enlightenment view, reflected in the American Bill of Rights and, more indirectly, in the Charter, rights are held by all people in society because each person is entitled to dignity and respect. Rights are general and universal; they are the way in which the "inherent dignity" of each individual in society is respected: *R. v. Oakes*, [1986] 1 S.C.R. 103, at p. 136; *R. v. Big M Drug Mart Ltd., supra*, at p. 336.

19   Aboriginal rights cannot, however, be defined on the basis of the philosophical precepts of the liberal enlightenment. Although equal in importance and significance to the rights enshrined in the Charter, Aboriginal rights must be viewed differently from Charter rights because they are rights held only by Aboriginal members of Canadian society. They arise from the fact that Aboriginal people are Aboriginal. As academic commentators have noted, Aboriginal rights "inhere in the very meaning of Aboriginality", Michael Asch and Patrick Macklem, "Aboriginal Rights and Canadian Sovereignty: An Essay on R. v. Sparrow" (1991), 29 *Alta. L. Rev.* 498, at p. 502; they are the rights held by "Indians *qua* Indians", Brian Slattery, "Understanding Aboriginal Rights" (1987), 66 *Can. Bar Rev.* 727, at p. 776.

20   The task of this Court is to define Aboriginal rights in a manner which recognizes that Aboriginal rights are *rights* but which does so without losing sight of the fact that they are rights held by Aboriginal people because they are *Aboriginal*. The Court must neither lose sight of the generalized constitutional status of what s. 35(1) protects, nor can it ignore the necessary specificity which comes from granting special constitutional protection to one part of Canadian society. The Court must define the scope of s. 35(1) in a way which captures both the Aboriginal and the rights in Aboriginal rights.

21   The way to accomplish this task is, as was noted at the outset, through a purposive approach to s. 35(1). It is through identifying the interests that s. 35(1) was intended to protect that the dual nature of Aboriginal rights will be comprehended. In *Hunter* v. *Southam Inc.*, [1984] 2 S.C.R. 145, Dickson J. explained the rationale for a purposive approach to constitutional documents. Courts should take a purposive approach to the Constitution because constitutions are, by their very nature, documents aimed at a country's future as well as its present; the Constitution must be interpreted in a manner which renders it "capable of growth and development over time to meet new social, political and historical realities often unimagined by its framers": *Hunter, supra*, at p. 155. A purposive approach to s. 35(1), besides ensuring that the provision is not viewed as static and only relevant to current circumstances, will ensure that the recognition and affirmation it offers are consistent with the fact that what it is recognizing and affirming are "rights". Further, because it requires the court to analyze a given constitutional provision "in the light of the interests it was meant to protect" (*Big M Drug Mart Ltd., supra*, at p. 344), a purposive approach to s. 35(1) will ensure that that which is found to fall within the provision is related to the provision's intended focus: Aboriginal people and their rights in relation to Canadian society as a whole.

22   In *Sparrow, supra*, Dickson C.J. and La Forest J. held at p. 1106 that it was through a purposive analysis that s. 35(1) must be understood:

The approach to be taken with respect to interpreting the meaning of s. 35(1) is derived from general principles of constitutional interpretation, principles relating to Aboriginal rights, and *the purposes behind the constitutional provision itself.* [Emphasis added.]

In that case, however, the Court did not have the opportunity to articulate the purposes behind s. 35(1) as they relate to the scope of the rights the provision is intended to protect. Such analysis is now required to be undertaken.

General Principles Applicable to Legal Disputes Between Aboriginal Peoples and the Crown
23   Before turning to a purposive analysis of s. 35(1), however, it should be noted that such analysis must take place in light of the general principles which apply to the legal relationship between the Crown and Aboriginal peoples. In *Sparrow, supra,* this Court held at p. 1106 that s. 35(1) should be given a generous and liberal interpretation in favour of Aboriginal peoples:

> When the purposes of the affirmation of Aboriginal rights are considered, *it is clear that a generous, liberal interpretation of the words in the constitutional provision is demanded.* [Emphasis added.]

24   This interpretive principle, articulated first in the context of treaty rights—*Simon* v. *The Queen,* [1985] 2 S.C.R. 387, at p. 402; *Nowegijick* v. *The Queen,* [1983] 1 S.C.R. 29, at p. 36; *R.* v. *Horseman,* [1990] 1 S.C.R. 901, at p. 907; *R.* v. *Sioui,* [1990] 1 S.C.R. 1025, at p. 1066—arises from the nature of the relationship between the Crown and Aboriginal peoples. The Crown has a fiduciary obligation to Aboriginal peoples with the result that in dealings between the government and Aboriginals the honour of the Crown is at stake. Because of this fiduciary relationship, and its implication of the honour of the Crown, treaties, s. 35(1), and other statutory and constitutional provisions protecting the interests of Aboriginal peoples, must be given a generous and liberal interpretation: *R.* v. *George,* [1966] S.C.R. 267, at p. 279. This general principle must inform the Court's analysis of the purposes underlying s. 35(1), and of that provision's definition and scope.

25   The fiduciary relationship of the Crown and Aboriginal peoples also means that where there is any doubt or ambiguity with regards to what falls within the scope and definition of s. 35(1), such doubt or ambiguity must be resolved in favour of Aboriginal peoples. In *R.* v. *Sutherland,* [1980] 2 S.C.R. 451, at p. 464, Dickson J. held that paragraph 13 of the Memorandum of Agreement between Manitoba and Canada, a constitutional document, should be interpreted so as to resolve any doubts in favour of the Indians, the beneficiaries of the rights assured by the paragraph. This interpretive principle applies equally to s. 35(1) of the *Constitution Act, 1982* and should, again, inform the Court's purposive analysis of that provision.

Purposive Analysis of Section 35(1) …
27   When the court identifies a constitutional provision's purposes, or the interests the provision is intended to protect, what it is doing in essence is explaining the rationale of the provision; it is articulating the reasons underlying the protection that the provision gives. With regards to s. 35(1), then, what the court must do is explain the rationale and foundation of the recognition and affirmation of the special rights of Aboriginal peoples; it must identify the basis for the special status that Aboriginal peoples have within Canadian society as a whole.

28   In identifying the basis for the recognition and affirmation of Aboriginal rights it must be remembered that s. 35(1) did not create the legal doctrine of Aboriginal rights;

Aboriginal rights existed and were recognized under the common law: *Calder* v. *Attorney-General of British Columbia*, [1973] S.C.R. 313. At common law Aboriginal rights did not, of course, have constitutional status, with the result that Parliament could, at any time, extinguish or regulate those rights: *Kruger v. The Queen*, [1978] 1 S.C.R. 104, at p. 112; *R. v. Derriksan* (1976), 71 D.L.R. (3d) 159 (S.C.C.), [1976] 2 S.C.R. v; it is this which distinguishes the Aboriginal rights recognized and affirmed in s. 35(1) from the Aboriginal rights protected by the common law. Subsequent to s. 35(1) Aboriginal rights cannot be extinguished and can only be regulated or infringed consistent with the justificatory test laid out by this Court in *Sparrow, supra*.

29   The fact that Aboriginal rights pre-date the enactment of s. 35(1) could lead to the suggestion that the purposive analysis of s. 35(1) should be limited to an analysis of why a pre-existing legal doctrine was elevated to constitutional status. This suggestion must be resisted. The pre-existence of Aboriginal rights is relevant to the analysis of s. 35(1) because it indicates that Aboriginal rights have a stature and existence prior to the constitutionalization of those rights and sheds light on the reasons for protecting those rights; however, the interests protected by s. 35(1) must be identified through an explanation of the basis for the legal doctrine of Aboriginal rights, not through an explanation of why that legal doctrine now has constitutional status.

30   In my view, the doctrine of Aboriginal rights exists, and is recognized and affirmed by s. 35(1), because of one simple fact: when Europeans arrived in North America, Aboriginal peoples *were already here*, living in communities on the land, and participating in distinctive cultures, as they had done for centuries. It is this fact, and this fact above all others, which separates Aboriginal peoples from all other minority groups in Canadian society and which mandates their special legal, and now constitutional, status.

31   More specifically, what s. 35(1) does is provide the constitutional framework through which the fact that Aboriginals lived on the land in distinctive societies, with their own practices, traditions and cultures, is acknowledged and reconciled with the sovereignty of the Crown. The substantive rights which fall within the provision must be defined in light of this purpose; the Aboriginal rights recognized and affirmed by s. 35(1) must be directed towards the reconciliation of the pre-existence of Aboriginal societies with the sovereignty of the Crown.

32   That the purpose of s. 35(1) lies in its recognition of the prior occupation of North America by Aboriginal peoples is suggested by the French version of the text. For the English "existing Aboriginal and treaty rights" the French text reads "*[l]es droits existants-ancestraux ou issus de traités*". The term "*ancestral*", which *Le Petit Robert 1* (1990) dictionary defines as "*[q]ui a appartenu aux ancêtres*, qu'on tient des ancêtres", suggests that the rights recognized and affirmed by s. 35(1) must be temporally rooted in the historical presence—the ancestry—of Aboriginal peoples in North America.

33   This approach to s. 35(1) is also supported by the prior jurisprudence of this Court. In *Calder, supra*, the Court refused an application by the Nishga for a declaration that their Aboriginal title had not been extinguished. There was no majority in the Court as to the basis for this decision; however, in the judgments of both Judson J. and Hall J. (each speaking for himself and two others) the existence of Aboriginal title was recognized. Hall J. based the Nishga's Aboriginal title in the fact that the land to which they were claiming title had "been in their possession from time immemorial" (*Calder, supra*, at p. 375).

Judson J. explained the origins of the Nishga's Aboriginal title as follows, at p. 328:

> Although I think that it is clear that Indian title in British Columbia cannot owe its origin to the Proclamation of 1763, *the fact is that when the settlers came, the Indians were there, organized in societies and occupying the land as their forefathers had done for centuries. This is what Indian title means* and it does not help one in the solution of this problem to call it a "personal or usufructuary right". What they are asserting in this action is that they had a right to continue to live on their lands as their forefathers had lived and that this right has never been lawfully extinguished. [Emphasis added.]

The position of Judson and Hall JJ. on the basis for Aboriginal title is applicable to the Aboriginal rights recognized and affirmed by s. 35(1). Aboriginal title is the aspect of Aboriginal rights related specifically to Aboriginal claims to land; it is the way in which the common law recognizes Aboriginal land rights. As such, the explanation of the basis of Aboriginal title in *Calder, supra,* can be applied equally to the Aboriginal rights recognized and affirmed by s. 35(1). Both Aboriginal title and Aboriginal rights arise from the existence of distinctive Aboriginal communities occupying "the land as their forefathers had done for centuries" (p. 328).

34   The basis of Aboriginal title articulated in *Calder, supra,* was affirmed in *Guerin v. The Queen,* [1984] 2 S.C.R. 335. The decision in *Guerin* turned on the question of the nature and extent of the Crown's fiduciary obligation to Aboriginal peoples; because, however, Dickson J. based that fiduciary relationship, at p. 376, in the "concept of Aboriginal, native or Indian title," he had occasion to consider the question of the existence of Aboriginal title. In holding that such title existed, he relied, at p. 376, on *Calder, supra,* for the proposition that "Aboriginal title as a legal right *derived from the Indians' historic occupation and possession of their tribal lands*". [Emphasis added.]

35   The view of Aboriginal rights as based in the prior occupation of North America by distinctive Aboriginal societies, finds support in the early American decisions of Marshall C.J. Although the constitutional structure of the United States is different from that of Canada, and its Aboriginal law has developed in unique directions, I agree with Professor Slattery both when he describes the Marshall decisions as providing "structure and coherence to an untidy and diffuse body of customary law based on official practice" and when he asserts that these decisions are "as relevant to Canada as they are to the United States"— "Understanding Aboriginal Rights", *supra,* at p. 739. I would add to Professor Slattery's comments only the observation that the fact that Aboriginal law in the United States is significantly different from Canadian Aboriginal law means that the relevance of these cases arises from their articulation of general principles, rather than their specific legal holdings. . . .

42   ...

> *The challenge of defining aboriginal rights stems from the fact that they are rights peculiar to the meeting of two vastly dissimilar legal cultures;* consequently there will always be a question about which legal culture is to provide the vantage point from which rights are to be defined. . . . a morally and politically defensible conception of aboriginal rights will incorporate both legal perspectives. [Emphasis added.]

Similarly, Professor Slattery has suggested that the law of Aboriginal rights is "neither English nor Aboriginal in origin: it is a form of intersocietal law that evolved from long-standing practices linking the various communities" (Brian Slattery, "The Legal Basis of

Aboriginal Title", in Frank Cassidy, ed., *Aboriginal Title in British Columbia: Delgamuukw v. The Queen* (1992), at pp. 120–21) and that such rights concern "the status of native peoples living under the Crown's protection, and the position of their lands, customary laws, and political institutions" ("Understanding Aboriginal Rights", *supra*, at p. 737).

43   The Canadian, American and Australian jurisprudence thus supports the basic proposition put forward at the beginning of this section: the Aboriginal rights recognized and affirmed by s. 35(1) are best understood as, first, the means by which the Constitution recognizes the fact that prior to the arrival of Europeans in North America the land was already occupied by distinctive Aboriginal societies, and as, second, the means by which that prior occupation is reconciled with the assertion of Crown sovereignty over Canadian territory. The content of Aboriginal rights must be directed at fulfilling both of these purposes; the next section of the judgment, as well as that which follows it, will attempt to accomplish this task.

The Test for Identifying Aboriginal Rights in Section 35(1)
44   In order to fulfil the purpose underlying s. 35(1)—i.e., the protection and reconciliation of the interests which arise from the fact that prior to the arrival of Europeans in North America Aboriginal peoples lived on the land in distinctive societies, with their own practices, customs and traditions—the test for identifying the Aboriginal rights recognized and affirmed by s. 35(1) must be directed at identifying the crucial elements of those pre-existing distinctive societies. It must, in other words, aim at identifying the practices, traditions and customs central to the Aboriginal societies that existed in North America prior to contact with the Europeans.

45   In *Sparrow, supra*, this Court did not have to address the scope of the Aboriginal rights protected by s. 35(1); however, in their judgment at p. 1099 Dickson C.J. and La Forest J. identified the Musqueam right to fish for food in the fact that:

> The anthropological evidence relied on to establish the existence of the right suggests that, for the Musqueam, the salmon fishery has always constituted *an integral part of their distinctive culture*. Its significant role involved not only consumption for subsistence purposes, but also consumption of salmon on ceremonial and social occasions. The Musqueam have always fished for reasons connected to their cultural and physical survival. [Emphasis added.]

The suggestion of this passage is that participation in the salmon fishery is an Aboriginal right because it is an "integral part" of the "distinctive culture" of the Musqueam. This suggestion is consistent with the position just adopted; identifying those practices, customs and traditions that are integral to distinctive Aboriginal cultures will serve to identify the crucial elements of the distinctive Aboriginal societies that occupied North America prior to the arrival of Europeans.

46   In light of the suggestion of *Sparrow, supra*, and the purposes underlying s. 35(1), the following test should be used to identify whether an applicant has established an Aboriginal right protected by s. 35(1): in order to be an Aboriginal right an activity must be an element of a practice, custom or tradition integral to the distinctive culture of the Aboriginal group claiming the right.

47   I would note that this test is, in large part, consistent with that adopted by the judges of the British Columbia Court of Appeal. Although the various judges disagreed on such crucial questions as how the right should be framed, the relevant time at which

the Aboriginal culture should be examined and the role of European influences in limiting the scope of the right, all of the judges agreed that Aboriginal rights must be identified through the practices, customs and traditions of Aboriginal cultures. Macfarlane J.A. held at para. 20 that Aboriginal rights exist where "the right had been exercised . . . for a sufficient length of time to become *integral to the aboriginal society*" (emphasis added); Wallace J.A. held at para. 78 that Aboriginal rights are those practices "traditional and integral to the native society"...; Lambert J.A. held at para. 131 that Aboriginal rights are those "custom[s], tradition[s], or practice[s] . . . which formed a*n integral part of the distinctive culture of the aboriginal people in question*" (emphasis added). While, as will become apparent, I do not adopt entirely the position of any of the judges at the Court of Appeal, their shared position that Aboriginal rights lie in those practices, customs and traditions that are integral is consistent with the test I have articulated here.

Factors to be Considered in Application of the Integral to a Distinctive Culture Test

48   The test just laid out—that Aboriginal rights lie in the practices, customs and traditions integral to the distinctive cultures of Aboriginal peoples—requires further elaboration with regards to the nature of the inquiry a court faced with an Aboriginal rights claim must undertake. I will now undertake such an elaboration, concentrating on such questions as the time period relevant to the court's inquiry, the correct approach to the evidence presented, the specificity necessary to the court's inquiry, the relationship between Aboriginal rights and the rights of Aboriginal people as Canadian citizens, and the standard that must be met in order for a practice, custom or tradition to be said to be "integral".

Courts must take into account the perspective of Aboriginal peoples themselves

49   In assessing a claim for the existence of an Aboriginal right, a court must take into account the perspective of the Aboriginal people claiming the right. In *Sparrow, supra*, Dickson C.J. and La Forest J. held, at p. 1112, that it is "crucial to be sensitive to the Aboriginal perspective itself on the meaning of the rights at stake". It must also be recognized, however, that that perspective must be framed in terms cognizable to the Canadian legal and constitutional structure. As has already been noted, one of the fundamental purposes of s. 35(1) is the reconciliation of the pre-existence of distinctive Aboriginal societies with the assertion of Crown sovereignty. Courts adjudicating Aboriginal rights claims must, therefore, be sensitive to the Aboriginal perspective, but they must also be aware that Aboriginal rights exist within the general legal system of Canada. To quote again Walters, at p. 413: "a morally and politically defensible conception of Aboriginal rights will incorporate both [Aboriginal and non-Aboriginal] legal perspectives". The definition of an Aboriginal right must, if it is truly to reconcile the prior occupation of Canadian territory by Aboriginal peoples with the assertion of Crown sovereignty over that territory, take into account the Aboriginal perspective, yet do so in terms which are cognizable to the non-Aboriginal legal system.

50   It is possible, of course, that the Court could be said to be "reconciling" the prior occupation of Canada by Aboriginal peoples with Crown sovereignty through either a narrow or broad conception of Aboriginal rights; the notion of "reconciliation" does not, in the abstract, mandate a particular content for Aboriginal rights. However, the only fair and just reconciliation is, as Walters suggests, one which takes into account the Aboriginal perspective while at the same time taking into account the perspective of the common

law. True reconciliation will, equally, place weight on each.

Courts must identify precisely the nature of the claim being made in determining whether an Aboriginal claimant has demonstrated the existence of an Aboriginal right
51. Related to this is the fact that in assessing a claim to an Aboriginal right a court must first identify the nature of the right being claimed; in order to determine whether a claim meets the test of being integral to the distinctive culture of the Aboriginal group claiming the right, the court must first correctly determine what it is that is being claimed. The correct characterization of the appellant's claim is of importance because whether or not the evidence supports the appellant's claim will depend, in significant part, on what, exactly, that evidence is being called to support.

52   I would note here by way of illustration that, in my view, both the majority and the dissenting judges in the Court of Appeal erred with respect to this aspect of the inquiry. The majority held that the appellant's claim was that the practice of selling fish "on a commercial basis" constituted an Aboriginal right and, in part, rejected her claim on the basis that the evidence did not support the existence of such a right. With respect, this characterization of the appellant's claim is in error; the appellant's claim was that the practice of selling fish was an Aboriginal right, not that selling fish "on a commercial basis" was. It was, however, equally incorrect to adopt, as Lambert J.A. did, a "social" test for the identification of the practice, tradition or custom constituting the Aboriginal right. The social test casts the Aboriginal right in terms that are too broad and in a manner which distracts the court from what should be its main focus-the nature of the Aboriginal community's practices, customs or traditions themselves. The nature of an applicant's claim must be delineated in terms of the particular practice, custom or tradition under which it is claimed; the significance of the practice, custom or tradition to the Aboriginal community is a factor to be considered in determining whether the practice, custom or tradition is integral to the distinctive culture, but the significance of a practice, custom or tradition cannot, itself, constitute an Aboriginal right.

53   To characterize an applicant's claim correctly, a court should consider such factors as the nature of the action which the applicant is claiming was done pursuant to an Aboriginal right, the nature of the governmental regulation, statute or action being impugned, and the practice, custom or tradition being relied upon to establish the right. In this case, therefore, the Court will consider the actions which led to the appellant's being charged, the fishery regulation under which she was charged and the practices, customs and traditions she invokes in support of her claim.

54   It should be acknowledged that a characterization of the nature of the appellant's claim from the actions which led to her being charged must be undertaken with some caution. In order to inform the court's analysis the activities must be considered at a general rather than at a specific level. Moreover, the court must bear in mind that the activities may be the exercise in a modern form of a practice, custom or tradition that existed prior to contact, and should vary its characterization of the claim accordingly.

In order to be integral a practice, custom or tradition must be of central significance to the Aboriginal society in question
55   To satisfy the integral to a distinctive culture test the Aboriginal claimant must do more than demonstrate that a practice, custom or tradition was an aspect of, or took place

in, the Aboriginal society of which he or she is a part. The claimant must demonstrate that the practice, custom or tradition was a central and significant part of the society's distinctive culture. He or she must demonstrate, in other words, that the practice, custom or tradition was one of the things which made the culture of the society distinctive—that it was one of the things that truly *made the society what it was.*

56   This aspect of the integral to a distinctive culture test arises from fact that Aboriginal rights have their basis in the prior occupation of Canada by distinctive Aboriginal societies. To recognize and affirm the prior occupation of Canada by distinctive Aboriginal societies it is *to what makes those societies distinctive* that the court must look in identifying Aboriginal rights. The court cannot look at those aspects of the Aboriginal society that are true of every human society (e.g., eating to survive), nor can it look at those aspects of the Aboriginal society that are only incidental or occasional to that society; the court must look instead to the defining and central attributes of the Aboriginal society in question. It is only by focusing on the aspects of the Aboriginal society that make that society distinctive that the definition of Aboriginal rights will accomplish the purpose underlying s. 35(1).

57   Moreover, the Aboriginal rights protected by s. 35(1) have been said to have the purpose of reconciling pre-existing Aboriginal societies with the assertion of Crown sovereignty over Canada. To reconcile Aboriginal societies with Crown sovereignty it is necessary to identify the distinctive features of those societies; it is precisely those distinctive features which need to be acknowledged and reconciled with the sovereignty of the Crown.

58   As was noted earlier, Lambert J.A. erred when he used the significance of a practice, custom or tradition as a means of identifying what the practice, custom or tradition is; however, he was correct to recognize that the significance of the practice, custom or tradition is important. The significance of the practice, custom or tradition does not serve to identify the nature of a claim of acting pursuant to an Aboriginal right; however, it is a key aspect of the court's inquiry into whether a practice, custom or tradition has been shown to be an integral part of the distinctive culture of an Aboriginal community. The significance of the practice, custom or tradition will inform a court as to whether or not that practice, custom or tradition can be said to be truly integral to the distinctive culture in question.

59   A practical way of thinking about this problem is to ask whether, without this practice, custom or tradition, the culture in question would be fundamentally altered or other than what it is. One must ask, to put the question affirmatively, whether or not a practice, custom or tradition is a defining feature of the culture in question.

The practices, customs and traditions which constitute Aboriginal rights are those which have continuity with the practices, customs and traditions that existed prior to contact

60   The time period that a court should consider in identifying whether the right claimed meets the standard of being integral to the Aboriginal community claiming the right is the period prior to contact between Aboriginal and European societies. Because it is the fact that distinctive Aboriginal societies lived on the land prior to the arrival of Europeans that underlies the Aboriginal rights protected by s. 35(1), it is to that pre-contact period that the courts must look in identifying Aboriginal rights.

61   The fact that the doctrine of Aboriginal rights functions to reconcile the existence

of pre-existing Aboriginal societies with the sovereignty of the Crown does not alter this position. Although it is the sovereignty of the Crown that the pre-existing Aboriginal societies are being reconciled with, it is to those pre-existing societies that the court must look in defining Aboriginal rights. It is not the fact that Aboriginal societies existed prior to Crown sovereignty that is relevant; it is the fact that they existed *prior to the arrival of Europeans in North America*. As such, the relevant time period is the period prior to the arrival of Europeans, not the period prior to the assertion of sovereignty by the Crown.

62   That this is the relevant time should not suggest, however, that the Aboriginal group claiming the right must accomplish the next to impossible task of producing conclusive evidence from pre-contact times about the practices, customs and traditions of their community. It would be entirely contrary to the spirit and intent of s. 35(1) to define Aboriginal rights in such a fashion so as to preclude in practice any successful claim for the existence of such a right. The evidence relied upon by the applicant and the courts may relate to Aboriginal practices, customs and traditions post-contact; it simply needs to be directed at demonstrating which aspects of the Aboriginal community and society have their origins pre-contact. It is those practices, customs and traditions that can be rooted in the pre-contact societies of the Aboriginal community in question that will constitute Aboriginal rights.

63   I would note in relation to this point the position adopted by Brennan J. in *Mabo*, *supra*, where he holds, at p. 60, that in order for an Aboriginal group to succeed in its claim for Aboriginal title it must demonstrate that the connection with the land in its customs and laws has continued to the present day:

> … when the tide of history has washed away any real acknowledgment of traditional law and any real observance of traditional customs, the foundation of native title has disappeared. A native title which has ceased with the abandoning of laws and customs based on tradition cannot be revived for contemporary recognition.

The relevance of this observation for identifying the rights in s. 35(1) lies not in its assertion of the effect of the disappearance of a practice, custom or tradition on an Aboriginal claim (I take no position on that matter), but rather in its suggestion of the importance of considering the continuity in the practices, customs and traditions of Aboriginal communities in assessing claims to Aboriginal rights. It is precisely those present practices, customs and traditions which can be identified as having continuity with the practices, customs and traditions that existed prior to contact that will be the basis for the identification and definition of Aboriginal rights under s. 35(1). Where an Aboriginal community can demonstrate that a particular practice, custom or tradition is integral to its distinctive culture today, and that this practice, custom or tradition has continuity with the practices, customs and traditions of pre-contact times, that community will have demonstrated that the practice, custom or tradition is an Aboriginal right for the purposes of s. 35(1).

64   The concept of continuity is also the primary means through which the definition and identification of Aboriginal rights will be consistent with the admonition in *Sparrow*, *supra*, at p. 1093, that the phrase "'existing Aboriginal rights' must be interpreted flexibly so as to permit their evolution over time". The concept of continuity is, in other words, the means by which a "frozen rights" approach to s. 35(1) will be avoided. Because the practices, customs and traditions protected by s. 35(1) are ones that exist today, subject

only to the requirement that they be demonstrated to have continuity with the practices, customs and traditions which existed pre-contact, the definition of Aboriginal rights will be one that, on its own terms, prevents those rights from being frozen in pre-contact times. The evolution of practices, customs and traditions into modern forms will not, provided that continuity with pre-contact practices, customs and traditions is demonstrated, prevent their protection as Aboriginal rights.

65   I would note that the concept of continuity does not require Aboriginal groups to provide evidence of an unbroken chain of continuity between their current practices, customs and traditions, and those which existed prior to contact. It may be that for a period of time an Aboriginal group, for some reason, ceased to engage in a practice, custom or tradition which existed prior to contact, but then resumed the practice, custom or tradition at a later date. Such an interruption will not preclude the establishment of an Aboriginal right. Trial judges should adopt the same flexibility regarding the establishment of continuity that, as is discussed, *infra*, they are to adopt with regards to the evidence presented to establish the prior-to-contact practices, customs and traditions of the Aboriginal group making the claim to an Aboriginal right.

66   Further, I would note that basing the identification of Aboriginal rights in the period prior to contact is not inconsistent with the fact that s. 35(2) of the *Constitution Act, 1982* includes within the definition of "aboriginal peoples of Canada" the Métis people of Canada.

67   Although s. 35 includes the Métis within its definition of Aboriginal peoples of Canada, and thus seems to link their claims to those of other Aboriginal peoples under the general heading of Aboriginal rights, the history of the Métis, and the reasons underlying their inclusion in the protection given by s. 35, are quite distinct from those of other Aboriginal peoples in Canada. As such, the manner in which the Aboriginal rights of other Aboriginal peoples are defined is not necessarily determinative of the manner in which the Aboriginal rights of the Métis are defined. At the time when this Court is presented with a Métis claim under s. 35 it will then, with the benefit of the arguments of counsel, a factual context and a specific Métis claim, be able to explore the question of the purposes underlying s. 35's protection of the Aboriginal rights of Métis people, and answer the question of the kinds of claims which fall within s. 35(1)'s scope when the claimants are Métis. The fact that, for other Aboriginal peoples, the protection granted by s. 35 goes to the practices, customs and traditions of Aboriginal peoples prior to contact, is not necessarily relevant to the answer which will be given to that question. It may, or it may not, be the case that the claims of the Métis are determined on the basis of the pre-contact practices, customs and traditions of their Aboriginal ancestors; whether that is so must await determination in a case in which the issue arises.

Courts must approach the rules of evidence in light of the evidentiary difficulties inherent in adjudicating Aboriginal claims

68   In determining whether an Aboriginal claimant has produced evidence sufficient to demonstrate that her activity is an aspect of a practice, custom or tradition integral to a distinctive Aboriginal culture, a court should approach the rules of evidence, and interpret the evidence that exists, with a consciousness of the special nature of Aboriginal claims, and of the evidentiary difficulties in proving a right which originates in times where there were no written records of the practices, customs and traditions engaged in.

The courts must not undervalue the evidence presented by Aboriginal claimants simply because that evidence does not conform precisely with the evidentiary standards that would be applied in, for example, a private law torts case.

Claims to Aboriginal rights must be adjudicated on a specific rather than general basis
69   Courts considering a claim to the existence of an Aboriginal right must focus specifically on the practices, customs and traditions of the particular Aboriginal group claiming the right. In the case of *Kruger, supra*, this Court rejected the notion that claims to Aboriginal rights could be determined on a general basis. This position is correct; the existence of an Aboriginal right will depend entirely on the practices, customs and traditions of the *particular Aboriginal community claiming the right*. As has already been suggested, Aboriginal rights are constitutional rights, but that does not negate the central fact that the interests Aboriginal rights are intended to protect relate to the specific history of the group claiming the right. Aboriginal rights are not general and universal; their scope and content must be determined on a case-by-case basis. The fact that one group of Aboriginal people has an Aboriginal right to do a particular thing will not be, without something more, sufficient to demonstrate that another Aboriginal community has the same Aboriginal right. The existence of the right will be specific to each Aboriginal community.

For a practice, custom or tradition to constitute an Aboriginal right it must be of independent significance to the Aboriginal culture in which it exists
70   In identifying those practices, customs and traditions that constitute the Aboriginal rights recognized and affirmed by s. 35(1), a court must ensure that the practice, custom or tradition relied upon in a particular case is independently significant to the Aboriginal community claiming the right. The practice, custom or tradition cannot exist simply as an incident to another practice, custom or tradition but must rather be itself of integral significance to the Aboriginal society. Where two customs exist, but one is merely incidental to the other, the custom which is integral to the Aboriginal community in question will qualify as an Aboriginal right, but the custom that is merely incidental will not. Incidental practices, customs and traditions cannot qualify as Aboriginal rights through a process of piggybacking on integral practices, customs and traditions.

The integral to a distinctive culture test requires that a practice, custom or tradition be distinctive; it does not require that that practice, custom or tradition be distinct
71   The standard which a practice, custom or tradition must meet in order to be recognized as an Aboriginal right is *not* that it be *distinct* to the Aboriginal culture in question; the Aboriginal claimants must simply demonstrate that the practice, custom or tradition is *distinctive*. A tradition or custom that is distinct is one that is unique—"different in kind or quality, unlike" (*Concise Oxford Dictionary*, 9th ed). A culture with a distinct tradition must claim that in having such a tradition it is different from other cultures; a claim of distinctness is, by its very nature, a claim relative to other cultures or traditions. By contrast, a culture that claims that a practice, custom or tradition is *distinctive*—"distinguishing, characteristic"—makes a claim that is not relative; the claim is rather one about the culture's own practices, customs or traditions considered apart from the practices, customs or traditions of any other culture. It is a claim that this tradition or custom makes the culture *what it is*, not that the practice, custom or tradition is different from the practices, customs or traditions of another culture. The person or community claim-

ing the existence of an Aboriginal right protected by s. 35(1) need only show that the particular practice, custom or tradition which it is claiming to be an Aboriginal right is distinctive, not that it is distinct.

72   That the standard an Aboriginal community must meet is distinctiveness, not distinctness, arises from the recognition in *Sparrow, supra*, of an Aboriginal right to fish for food. Certainly no Aboriginal group in Canada could claim that its culture is "distinct" or unique in fishing for food; fishing for food is something done by many different cultures and societies around the world. What the Musqueam claimed in *Sparrow, supra*, was rather that it was fishing for food which, in part, made Musqueam culture what it is; fishing for food was characteristic of Musqueam culture and, therefore, a distinctive part of that culture. Since it was so it constituted an Aboriginal right under s. 35(1).

The influence of European culture will only be relevant to the inquiry if it is demonstrated that the practice, custom or tradition is only integral because of that influence

73   The fact that Europeans in North America engaged in the same practices, customs or traditions as those under which an Aboriginal right is claimed will only be relevant to the Aboriginal claim if the practice, custom or tradition in question can only be said to exist because of the influence of European culture. If the practice, custom or tradition was an integral part of the Aboriginal community's culture prior to contact with Europeans, the fact that that practice, custom or tradition continued after the arrival of Europeans, and adapted in response to their arrival, is not relevant to determination of the claim; European arrival and influence cannot be used to deprive an Aboriginal group of an otherwise valid claim to an Aboriginal right. On the other hand, where the practice, custom or tradition arose solely as a response to European influences then that practice, custom or tradition will not meet the standard for recognition of an Aboriginal right.

Courts must take into account both the relationship of Aboriginal peoples to the land and the distinctive societies and cultures of Aboriginal peoples

74   As was noted in the discussion of the purposes of s. 35(1), Aboriginal rights and Aboriginal title are related concepts; Aboriginal title is a sub-category of Aboriginal rights which deals solely with claims of rights to land. The relationship between Aboriginal title and Aboriginal rights must not, however, confuse the analysis of what constitutes an Aboriginal right. Aboriginal rights arise from the prior occupation of land, but they also arise from the prior social organization and distinctive cultures of Aboriginal peoples on that land. In considering whether a claim to an Aboriginal right has been made out, courts must look at both the relationship of an Aboriginal claimant to the land and at the practices, customs and traditions arising from the claimant's distinctive culture and society. Courts must not focus so entirely on the relationship of Aboriginal peoples with the land that they lose sight of the other factors relevant to the identification and definition of Aboriginal rights.

75   With these factors in mind I will now turn to the particular claim made by the appellant in this case to have been acting pursuant to an Aboriginal right.

Application of the Integral to a Distinctive Culture Test to the Appellant's Claim

76   The first step in the application of the integral to a distinctive culture test requires the court to identify the precise nature of the appellant's claim to have been exercising an Aboriginal right. In this case the most accurate characterization of the appellant's position

is that she is claiming *an Aboriginal right to exchange fish for money or for other goods*. She is claiming, in other words, that the practices, customs and traditions of the Sto:lo include as an integral part the exchange of fish for money or other goods.

77   That this is the nature of the appellant's claim can be seen through both the specific acts which led to her being charged and through the regulation under which she was charged. Mrs. Van der Peet sold 10 salmon for $50. Such a sale, especially given the absence of evidence that the appellant had sold salmon on other occasions or on a regular basis, cannot be said to constitute a sale on a "commercial" or market basis. These actions are instead best characterized in the simple terms of an exchange of fish for money. It follows from this that the Aboriginal right pursuant to which the appellant is arguing that her actions were taken is, like the actions themselves, best characterized as an Aboriginal right to exchange fish for money or other goods.

78   Moreover, the regulations under which the appellant was charged prohibit all sale or trade of fish caught pursuant to an Indian food fish licence. As such, to argue that those regulations implicate the appellant's Aboriginal right requires no more of her than that she demonstrate an Aboriginal right to the exchange of fish for money (sale) or other goods (trade). She does not need to demonstrate an Aboriginal right to sell fish commercially.

79   The appellant herself characterizes her claim as based on a right "to sufficient fish to provide for a moderate livelihood". In so doing the appellant relies on the "social" test adopted by Lambert J.A. at the British Columbia Court of Appeal. As has already been noted, however, a claim to an Aboriginal right cannot be based on the significance of an Aboriginal practice, custom or tradition to the Aboriginal community in question. The definition of Aboriginal rights is determined through the process of determining whether a particular practice, custom or tradition is integral to the distinctive culture of the Aboriginal group. The *significance* of the practice, custom or tradition is relevant to the determination of whether that practice, custom or tradition is integral, but cannot itself constitute the claim to an Aboriginal right. As such, the appellant's claim cannot be characterized as based on an assertion that the Sto:lo's use of the fishery, and the practices, customs and traditions surrounding that use, had the significance of providing the Sto:lo with a moderate livelihood. It must instead be based on the actual practices, customs and traditions related to the fishery, here the custom of exchanging fish for money or other goods.

80   Having thus identified the nature of the appellant's claim, I turn to the fundamental question of the integral to a distinctive culture test: Was the practice of exchanging fish for money or other goods an integral part of the specific distinctive culture of the Sto:lo prior to contact with Europeans? In answering this question it is necessary to consider the evidence presented at trial, and the findings of fact made by the trial judge, to determine whether the evidence and findings support the appellant's claim that the sale or trade of fish is an integral part of the distinctive culture of the Sto:lo.

81   It is a well-settled principle of law that when an appellate court reviews the decision of a trial judge that court must give considerable deference to the trial judge's findings of fact, particularly where those findings of fact are based on the trial judge's assessment of the testimony and credibility of witnesses. In *Stein* v. *The Ship "Kathy K"*, [1976] 2 S.C.R. 802, Ritchie J., speaking for the Court, held at p. 808 that absent a "palpable and overrid-

ing error" affecting the trial judge's assessment of the facts, an appellate court should not substitute its own findings of fact for those of the trial judge:

> These authorities are not to be taken as meaning that the findings of fact made at trial are immutable, but rather that they are not to be reversed unless it can be established that the learned trial judge made some palpable and overriding error which affected his assessment of the facts. While the Court of Appeal is seized with the duty of re-examining the evidence in order to be satisfied that no such error occurred, it is not, in my view, a part of its function to substitute its assessment of the balance of probability for the findings of the judge who presided at the trial.

This principle has also been followed in more recent decisions of this Court: *Beaudoin-Daigneault* v. *Richard*, [1984] 1 S.C.R. 2, at pp. 8–9; *Laurentide Motels Ltd.* v. *Beauport (City)*, [1989] 1 S.C.R. 705, at p. 794; *Hodgkinson* v. *Simms*, [1994] 3 S.C.R. 377, at p. 426. In the recently released decision of *Schwartz* v. *Canada*, [1996] 1 S.C.R. 254, La Forest J. made the following observation at para. 32, with which I agree, regarding appellate court deference to findings of fact:

> Unlimited intervention by appellate courts would greatly increase the number and the length of appeals generally. Substantial resources are allocated to trial courts to go through the process of assessing facts. The autonomy and integrity of the trial process must be preserved by exercising deference towards the trial courts' findings of fact. . . . This explains why the rule applies not only when the credibility of witnesses is at issue, although in such a case it may be more strictly applied, but also to all conclusions of fact made by the trial judge. . . .

I would also note that the principle of appellate court deference has been held to apply equally to findings of fact made on the basis of the trial judge's assessment of the credibility of the testimony of expert witnesses, *N.V. Bocimar S.A.* v. *Century Insurance Co. of Canada*, [1987] 1 S.C.R. 1247, at pp. 1249–50.

82   In the case at bar, Scarlett Prov. Ct. J., the trial judge, made findings of fact based on the testimony and evidence before him, and then proceeded to make a determination as to whether those findings of fact supported the appellant's claim to the existence of an Aboriginal right. The second stage of Scarlett Prov. Ct. J.'s analysis—his determination of the scope of the appellant's Aboriginal rights on the basis of the facts as he found them— is a determination of a question of law which, as such, mandates no deference from this Court. The first stage of Scarlett Prov. Ct. J.'s analysis, however—the findings of fact from which that legal inference was drawn—do mandate such deference and should not be overturned unless made on the basis of a "palpable and overriding error". This is particularly the case given that those findings of fact were made on the basis of Scarlett Prov. Ct. J.'s assessment of the credibility and testimony of the various witnesses appearing before him.

83   In adjudicating this case Scarlett Prov. Ct. J. obviously did not have the benefit of direction from this Court as to how the rights recognized and affirmed by s. 35(1) are to be defined, with the result that his legal analysis of the evidence was not entirely correct; however, that Scarlett Prov. Ct. J. was not entirely correct in his legal analysis of the facts as he found them *does not mean that he made a clear and palpable error in reviewing the evidence and making those findings of fact*. Indeed, a review of the transcript and exhibits submitted to this Court demonstrate that Scarlett Prov. Ct. J. conducted a thorough and compelling review of the evidence before him and committed no clear and palpable error which would justify this Court, or any other appellate court, in substituting its findings

of fact for his. Moreover, I would note that the appellant, while disagreeing with Scarlett Prov. Ct. J.'s legal analysis of the facts, made no arguments suggesting that in making findings of fact from the evidence before him Scarlett Prov. Ct. J. committed a palpable and overriding error.

84   Scarlett Prov. Ct. J. carefully considered all of the testimony presented by the various witnesses with regards to the nature of Sto:lo society and came to the following conclusions at p. 160:

> Clearly, the Sto:lo fish for food and ceremonial purposes. Evidence presented did not establish a regularized market system in the exchange of fish. Such fish as were exchanged through individual trade, gift, or barter were fish surplus from time to time. Natives did not fish to supply a market, there being no regularized trading system, nor were they able to preserve and store fish for extended periods of time. A market as such for salmon was not present but created by European traders, primarily the Hudson's Bay Company. At Fort Langley the Sto:lo were able to catch and deliver fresh salmon to the traders where it was salted and exported. This use was clearly different in nature and quantity from Aboriginal activity. Trade in dried salmon with the fort was clearly dependent upon Sto:lo first satisfying their own requirements for food and ceremony.
>
> This court was not satisfied upon the evidence that Aboriginal trade in salmon took place in any regularized or market sense. Oral evidence demonstrated that trade was incidental to fishing for food purposes. Anthropological and archaeological evidence was in conflict. This Court accepts the evidence of Dr. Stryd and John Dewhurst [sic] in preference to Dr. Daly and therefore, accepts that the Sto:lo were a band culture as opposed to tribal. While bands were guided by siem or prominent families, no regularized trade in salmon existed in Aboriginal times. Such trade as took place was either for ceremonial purposes or opportunistic exchanges taking place on a casual basis. Such trade as did take place was incidental only. Evidence led by the Crown that the Sto:lo had no access to salt for food preservation is accepted.
>
> Exchange of fish was subject to local conditions of availability, transportation and preservation. It was the establishment by the Hudson's Bay Company at the fort at Langley that created the market and trade in fresh salmon. Trade in dried salmon in Aboriginal times was, as stated, minimal and opportunistic.

I would add to Scarlett Prov. Ct. J.'s summation of his findings only the observation, which does not contradict any of his specific findings, that the testimony of the experts appearing before him indicated that such limited exchanges of salmon as took place in Sto:lo society were primarily linked to the kinship and family relationships on which Sto:lo society was based. For example, under cross-examination Dr. Daly described trade as occurring through the "idiom" of maintaining family relationships:

> The medium or the idiom of much trade was the idiom of kinship, of providing hospitality, giving gifts, reciprocating in gifts. . . .

Similarly, Mr. Dewhirst testified that the exchange of goods was related to the maintenance of family and kinship relations.

85   The facts as found by Scarlett Prov. Ct. J. do not support the appellant's claim that the exchange of salmon for money or other goods was an integral part of the distinctive culture of the Sto:lo. As has already been noted, in order to be recognized as an Aboriginal right, an activity must be of central significance to the culture in question—it must be something which makes that culture what it is. The findings of fact made by Scarlett Prov. Ct. J. suggest that the exchange of salmon for money or other goods, while certainly

taking place in Sto:lo society prior to contact, was not a significant, integral or defining feature of that society.

86   First, Scarlett Prov. Ct. J. found that, prior to contact, exchanges of fish were only "incidental" to fishing for food purposes. As was noted above, to constitute an Aboriginal right, a custom must itself be integral to the distinctive culture of the Aboriginal community in question; it cannot be simply incidental to an integral custom. Thus, while the evidence clearly demonstrated that fishing for food and ceremonial purposes was a significant and defining feature of the Sto:lo culture, this is not sufficient, absent a demonstration that the exchange of salmon was itself a significant and defining feature of Sto:lo society, to demonstrate that the exchange of salmon is an integral part of Sto:lo culture.

87   For similar reasons, the evidence linking the exchange of salmon to the maintenance of kinship and family relations does not support the appellant's claim to the existence of an Aboriginal right. Exchange of salmon as part of the interaction of kin and family is not of an independent significance sufficient to ground a claim for an Aboriginal right to the exchange of fish for money or other goods.

88   Second, Scarlett Prov. Ct. J. found that there was no "regularized trading system" amongst the Sto:lo prior to contact. The inference drawn from this fact by Scarlett Prov. Ct. J., and by Macfarlane J.A. at the British Columbia Court of Appeal, was that the absence of a market means that the appellant could not be said to have been acting pursuant to an Aboriginal right because it suggests that there is no Aboriginal right to fish commercially. This inference is incorrect because, as has already been suggested, the appellant in this case has only claimed a right to exchange fish for money or other goods, not a right to sell fish in the commercial marketplace; the significance of the absence of regularized trading systems amongst the Sto:lo arises instead from the fact that it indicates that the exchange of salmon was not widespread in Sto:lo society. Given that the exchange of salmon was not widespread it cannot be said that, prior to contact, Sto:lo culture was defined by trade in salmon; trade or exchange of salmon took place, but the absence of a market demonstrates that this exchange did not take place on a basis widespread enough to suggest that the exchange was a defining feature of Sto:lo society.

89   Third, the trade engaged in between the Sto:lo and the Hudson's Bay Company, while certainly of significance to the Sto:lo society of the time, was found by the trial judge to be qualitatively different from that which was typical of the Sto:lo culture prior to contact. As such, it does not provide an evidentiary basis for holding that the exchange of salmon was an integral part of Sto:lo culture. As was emphasized in listing the criteria to be considered in applying the "integral to" test, the time relevant for the identification of Aboriginal rights is prior to contact with European societies. Unless a post-contact practice, custom or tradition can be shown to have continuity with pre-contact practices, customs or traditions, it will not be held to be an Aboriginal right. The trade of salmon between the Sto:lo and the Hudson's Bay Company does not have the necessary continuity with Sto:lo culture pre-contact to support a claim to an Aboriginal right to trade salmon. Further, the exchange of salmon between the Sto:lo and the Hudson's Bay Company can be seen as central or significant to the Sto:lo primarily as a result of European influences; activities which become central or significant because of the influence of European culture cannot be said to be Aboriginal rights.

90   Finally, Scarlett Prov. Ct. J. found that the Sto:lo were at a band level of social

organization rather than at a tribal level. As noted by the various experts, one of the central distinctions between a band society and a tribal society relates to specialization and division of labour. In a tribal society there tends to be specialization of labour—for example, specialization in the gathering and trade of fish—whereas in a band society division of labour tends to occur only on the basis of gender or age. The absence of specialization in the exploitation of the fishery is suggestive, in the same way that the absence of regularized trade or a market is suggestive, that the exchange of fish was not a central part of Sto:lo culture. I would note here as well Scarlett Prov. Ct. J.'s finding that the Sto:lo did not have the means for preserving fish for extended periods of time, something which is also suggestive that the exchange or trade of fish was not central to the Sto:lo way of life.

91   For these reasons, then, I would conclude that the appellant has failed to demonstrate that the exchange of fish for money or other goods was an integral part of the distinctive Sto:lo society which existed prior to contact. The exchange of fish took place, but was not a central, significant or defining feature of Sto:lo society. The appellant has thus failed to demonstrate that the exchange of salmon for money or other goods by the Sto:lo is an Aboriginal right recognized and affirmed under s. 35(1) of the *Constitution Act, 1982*.

The Sparrow Test
92   Since the appellant has failed to demonstrate that the exchange of fish was an Aboriginal right of the Sto:lo, it is unnecessary to consider the tests for extinguishment, infringement and justification laid out by this Court in *Sparrow, supra.*

VI. Disposition

93   Having concluded that the Aboriginal rights of the Sto:lo do not include the right to exchange fish for money or other goods, I would dismiss the appeal and affirm the decision of the Court of Appeal restoring the trial judge's conviction of the appellant for violating s. 61(1) of the *Fisheries Act.* There will be no order as to costs.

94   For the reasons given above, the constitutional question must be answered as follows:

Question
Is s. 27(5) of the *British Columbia Fishery (General) Regulations*, SOR/84-248, as it read on September 11, 1987, of no force or effect with respect to the appellant in the circumstances of these proceedings, in virtue of s. 52 of the *Constitution Act, 1982*, by reason of the Aboriginal rights within the meaning of s. 35 of the *Constitution Act, 1982*, invoked by the appellant?

Answer
No.

L'Heureux-Dubé J. (dissenting) ...
McLachlin J. (dissenting) ...

R. v. *Gladstone*

[1996] 2 S.C.R. 723 (S.C.C.). Lamer C.J., La Forest, L'Heureux-Dubé, Sopinka, Gonthier, Cory, McLachlin, Iacobucci, and Major JJ., August 21, 1996

LAMER C.J. (SOPINKA, GONTHIER, CORY, IACOBUCCI and MAJOR JJ. concurring):— ...

1   Donald and William Gladstone, the appellants, are members of the Heiltsuk Band. The appellants were charged under s. 61(1) of the *Fisheries Act*, R.S.C. 1970, c. F-14, with the offences of offering to sell herring spawn on kelp caught under the authority of an Indian food fish licence, contrary to s. 27(5) of the *British Columbia Fishery (General) Regulations*, SOR/84-248 and of attempting to sell herring spawn on kelp not caught under the authority of a Category J herring spawn on kelp licence, contrary to s. 20(3) of the *Pacific Herring Fishery Regulations*, SOR/84-324. Only the charges arising under s. 20(3) of the *Pacific Herring Fishery Regulations* are still at issue in this appeal. . . .

17   . . . The appellants appealed on the basis that the courts below were in error in holding that the actions of the appellants were sufficient to constitute an attempt to sell in law. The appellants also appealed on the basis that, given that the evidence presented at trial demonstrated the extent and significance of Heiltsuk trading activities, the Court of Appeal erred in holding that the appellants do not have an Aboriginal right to trade and sell herring spawn on kelp. The appellants argued further that because the regulations constituted a total ban on the sale of any herring spawn on kelp, the Court of Appeal erred in not finding a *prima facie* infringement of the appellants' Aboriginal rights. Finally, the appellants argued that the Crown did not adduce sufficient evidence to support its assertion that the regulations fulfilled a conservation objective and that the Crown had failed to fulfil its fiduciary obligation to the Heiltsuk Band, with the result that the Court of Appeal erred in finding that any infringement which did exist was justified. . .

18   Before turning to the heart of the appellants' case—the argument that their convictions constitute an unjustifiable infringement of the Aboriginal rights recognized and affirmed by s. 35(1)—it is necessary to dispose of their argument that the facts do not demonstrate an "attempt to sell" as required by s. 20(3) of the *Pacific Herring Fishery Regulations*. The basis of the appellants' position is that because the Crown only provided evidence to show that the appellants asked Mr. Hirose if he was "interested" in herring spawn on kelp, without providing any evidence that the appellants had discussed the quantity, quality, price or delivery date of the herring spawn on kelp with Mr. Hirose, the Crown only demonstrated that the appellants had engaged in preparation for an attempt to sell; the Crown did not demonstrate that the appellants had actually attempted to sell herring spawn on kelp to Mr. Hirose.

19   This argument is without merit. In *R. v. Deutsch*, [1986] 2 S.C.R. 2, Le Dain J., writing for a unanimous Court on this issue, discussed the distinction between an attempt and mere preparation at pp. 22–23:

> It has been frequently observed that no satisfactory general criterion has been, or can be, formulated for drawing the line between preparation and attempt, and that the application of this distinction to the facts of a particular case must be left to common sense judgment. . . Despite academic appeals for greater clarity and certainty in this area of the law I find myself in essential agreement with this conclusion.
>
> In my opinion the distinction between preparation and attempt is essentially a qualitative one, involving the relationship between the nature and quality of the act in question and the nature of the complete offence, although consideration must necessarily be given,

in making that qualitative distinction, to the relative proximity of the act in question to what would have been the completed offence, in terms of time, location and acts under the control of the accused remaining to be accomplished.

In this case the facts as found by the trial judge clearly demonstrate that the appellants attempted to sell herring spawn on kelp to Mr. Hirose. The appellants arranged for the shipment of the herring spawn on kelp to Vancouver, they took a sample of the herring spawn on kelp to Mr. Hirose's store and they specifically asked Mr. Hirose if he was "interested" in herring spawn on kelp. The appellants' actions have sufficient proximity to the acts necessary to complete the offence of selling herring spawn on kelp to move those actions beyond mere preparation to an actual attempt. I would note here that the appellants have not disputed the facts as found by the trial judge and that the courts below were unanimous in finding that the actions of the appellant were sufficient to amount to an attempt to sell.

Section 35(1) of the Constitution Act, 1982

20   In *Sparrow, supra*, Dickson C.J. and La Forest J., writing for a unanimous court, held that an analysis of a claim under s. 35(1) has four steps: first, the court must determine whether an applicant has demonstrated that he or she was acting pursuant to an Aboriginal right; second, a court must determine whether that right was extinguished prior to the enactment of s. 35(1) of the *Constitution Act, 1982*; third, a court must determine whether that right has been infringed; finally, a court must determine whether that infringement was justified.

21   This judgment will undertake the analysis required for the four steps of the *Sparrow* framework, taking into account the elaboration of that framework in the cases of *R. v. Van der Peet*, [1996] 2 S.C.R. 507, *R. v. N.T.C. Smokehouse Ltd.*, [1996] 2 S.C.R. 672, and *R. v. Nikal*, [1996] 1 S.C.R. 1013, all of which were heard contemporaneously with this appeal. I will also undertake to clarify the *Sparrow* framework as is required in order to apply that framework to the different circumstances of this appeal.

Definition

22   This appeal, like those heard contemporaneously in *N.T.C. Smokehouse* and *Van der Peet*, requires the Court to consider the scope of the Aboriginal rights recognized and affirmed by s. 35(1) of the *Constitution Act, 1982*. In this case it must be determined whether the appellants Donald and William Gladstone can, on the basis of the test laid out in *Van der Peet*, claim to have been acting pursuant to an Aboriginal right when they attempted to sell herring spawn on kelp to Seaborn Enterprises. In *Van der Peet* the Court held, at para. 46, that to be recognized as an Aboriginal right an activity must be "an element of a practice, custom or tradition integral to the distinctive culture of the Aboriginal group claiming the right". Thus, the appellants in this case must demonstrate that their attempt to sell herring spawn on kelp was an element of a practice, custom, or tradition integral to the distinctive culture of the Heiltsuk Band.

23   The first step in applying the *Van der Peet* test is the determination of the precise nature of the claim being made, taking into account such factors as the nature of the action said to have been taken pursuant to an Aboriginal right, the government regulation argued to infringe the right, and the practice, custom or tradition relied upon to establish the right. At this stage of the analysis the Court is, in essence, determining what

the appellants will have to demonstrate to be an Aboriginal right in order for the activities they were engaged in to be encompassed by s. 35(1). There is no point in the appellants' being shown to have an Aboriginal right unless that Aboriginal right includes the actual activity they were engaged in; this stage of the *Van der Peet* analysis ensures that the Court's inquiry is tailored to the actual activity of the appellants.

24   This case, like *N.T.C. Smokehouse*, potentially creates problems at the characterization stage. The actions of the appellants, like the actions of the members of the Sheshaht and Opetchesaht bands in *N.T.C. Smokehouse,* appear to be best characterized as the commercial exploitation of herring spawn on kelp. By contrast, the regulations under which the appellants were charged, like the regulations at issue in *N.T.C. Smokehouse,* prohibit all sale or trade in herring spawn on kelp without a Category J licence, appear, therefore, to be best characterized as aimed at the exchange of herring spawn on kelp for money or other goods, regardless of whether the extent or scale of that sale or trade could reasonably be characterized as commercial in nature. The means to resolve this difficulty in characterization, as was the case in *N.T.C. Smokehouse*, is by addressing both possible characterizations of the appellants' claim. This judgment will thus consider first, whether the appellants can demonstrate that the Heiltsuk Band has an Aboriginal right to exchange herring spawn on kelp for money or other goods and will then go on to consider, second, whether the appellants have demonstrated the further Aboriginal right of the Heiltsuk Band to sell herring spawn on kelp to the commercial market.

25   The second step in the *Van der Peet* test requires the Court to determine whether the practice, custom or tradition claimed to be an Aboriginal right was, prior to contact with Europeans, an integral part of the distinctive Aboriginal society of the particular Aboriginal people in question. The Court must thus, as has just been noted, determine in this case whether the exchange of herring spawn on kelp for money or other goods, and/or the sale or trade of herring spawn on kelp in the commercial marketplace, were, prior to contact, defining features of the distinctive culture of the Heiltsuk.

26   The facts as found by the trial judge, and the evidence on which he relied, support the appellants' claim that exchange of herring spawn on kelp for money or other goods was a central, significant and defining feature of the culture of the Heiltsuk prior to contact. Moreover, those facts support the appellants' further claim that the exchange of herring spawn on kelp on a scale best characterized as commercial was an integral part of the distinctive culture of the Heiltsuk. In his reasons Lemiski Prov. Ct. J. summarized his findings of fact as follows:

> It cannot be disputed that hundreds of years ago, the Heiltsuk Indians regularly harvested herring spawn on kelp as a food source. The historical/anthropological records readily bear this out.
>   *I am also satisfied that this Band engaged in inter-tribal trading and barter of herring spawn on kelp.* The exhibited Journal of Alexander McKenzie [sic] dated 1793 refers to this trade and the defence lead [sic] evidence of several other references to such trade.
>   The Crown conceded that there may have been some incidental local trade but questions its extent and importance. *The very fact that early explorers and visitors to the Bella Bella region noted this trading has to enhance its significance.* All the various descriptions of this trading activity are in accord with common sense expectations. Obviously one would not expect to see balance sheets and statistics in so primitive a time and setting. [Emphasis added.]

27   There was extensive evidence presented at trial to support Lemiski Prov. Ct. J.'s findings. . .

28   In *Van der Peet*, at para. 61, this Court held that a claimant to an Aboriginal right need not provide direct evidence of pre-contact activities to support his or her claim, but need only provide evidence which is "directed at demonstrating which aspects of the Aboriginal community and society have their origins pre-contact. It is those practices, customs and traditions that can be rooted in the pre-contact societies of the Aboriginal community in question that will constitute Aboriginal rights". In *Van der Peet* this was described as the requirement of "continuity"-the requirement that a practice, custom or tradition which is integral to the Aboriginal community now be shown to have continuity with the practices, customs or traditions which existed prior to contact. The evidence presented in this case, accepted by the trial judge and summarized above, is precisely the type of evidence which satisfies this requirement. The appellants have provided clear evidence from which it can be inferred that, prior to contact, Heiltsuk society was, in significant part, based on such trade. The Heiltsuk were, both before and after contact, traders of herring spawn on kelp. Moreover, while to describe this activity as "commercial" prior to contact would be inaccurate given the link between the notion of commerce and the introduction of European culture, the extent and scope of the trading activities of the Heiltsuk support the claim that, for the purposes of s. 35(1) analysis, the Heiltsuk have demonstrated an Aboriginal right to sell herring spawn on kelp to an extent best described as commercial. The evidence of Dr. Lane, and the diary of Dr. Tolmie, point to trade of herring spawn on kelp in "tons". While this evidence relates to trade post-contact, the diary of Alexander Mackenzie provides the link with pre-contact times; in essence, the sum of the evidence supports the claim of the appellants that commercial trade in herring spawn on kelp was an integral part of the distinctive culture of the Heiltsuk prior to contact.

29   I would note that the significant difference between the situation of the appellants in this case, and the appellants in *Van der Peet* and *N.T.C. Smokehouse*, lies in the fact that for the Heiltsuk Band trading in herring spawn on kelp was not an activity taking place as an incident to the social and ceremonial activities of the community; rather, trading in herring spawn on kelp was, in itself, a central and significant feature of Heiltsuk society. In *Van der Peet* and *N.T.C. Smokehouse* the findings of fact at trial suggested that whatever trade in fish had taken place prior to contact was purely incidental to the social and ceremonial activities of the Aboriginal societies making the claim; here the evidence suggests that trade in herring spawn on kelp was not an incidental activity for the Heiltsuk but was rather a central and defining feature of Heiltsuk society.

Extinguishment, Infringement and Justification

30   The appellants have demonstrated that they were acting pursuant to an Aboriginal right to trade herring spawn on kelp on a commercial basis. I will therefore turn to the other three stages of the *Sparrow* analysis, that is, to the questions of whether the right under which the appellants were acting has been extinguished, whether that right was infringed by the actions of the government and, finally, whether that infringement was justified.

Extinguishment

31   The test for determining when an Aboriginal right has been extinguished was laid

out by this Court in *Sparrow*. Relying on the judgment of Hall J. in *Calder* v. *Attorney-General of British Columbia*, [1973] S.C.R. 313, the Court in *Sparrow* held at p. 1099 that "[t]he test of extinguishment to be adopted, in our opinion, is that the Sovereign's intention must be clear and plain if it is to extinguish an Aboriginal right". Further, the Court held that the mere fact that a right had, in the past, been regulated by the government, and its exercise subject to various terms and conditions, was not sufficient to extinguish the right. The argument that it did so (*Sparrow*, at p. 1097)

> confuses regulation with extinguishment. That the right is controlled in great detail by the regulations does not mean that the right is thereby extinguished.

The regulations relied on by the Crown in that case were, the Court held at p. 1099 . . ., "simply a manner of controlling the fisheries, not defining underlying rights".

32   The reasoning used to reject the Crown's argument in *Sparrow* applies equally to the Crown's argument in this case. To understand why this is so it will be necessary to review the legislation relied upon by the Crown in its argument that the Heiltsuk's right to harvest herring spawn on kelp on a commercial basis was extinguished prior to 1982.

33   There are two types of legislative action relied upon by the Crown: the provisions of the *Fisheries Act* which, prior to 1955, prohibited the destruction of the "fry of food fishes", and the provisions of the fisheries regulations relating directly to the herring spawn fishery. The former are exemplified by s. 39 of the *Fisheries Act* of 1927 which stated that "The fry of food fishes shall not be at any time destroyed"; identical provisions existed in the 1932 and 1952 *Fisheries Acts*. The latter first appeared in 1955. In 1955 the 1954 *British Columbia Fishery Regulations* were amended by SOR/55-260, s. 3, by the addition of a new s. 21A:

> 21A. No person shall take or collect by any means herring, eggs from herring spawning areas, and no person shall buy, sell, barter, process or traffic in herring eggs so taken; but an Indian may at any time take or collect herring eggs from spawning areas for use as food by Indians and their families but for no other purpose.

Similar prohibitions on the harvest and sale of herring spawn continued until 1974 (SOR/74-50, s. 9). At that time the section was amended . . .

This regulatory scheme remained in place until 1980 when the provision (which had been transferred to s. 17 of the *Pacific Herring Fishery Regulations*, C.R.C., c. 825) was amended by SOR/80-876, s. 8 to read

> 17. No person shall
>
> (a) take or collect herring roe except under authority of a licence issued pursuant to the Pacific Fishery Registration and Licensing Regulations; or
> (b) possess herring roe unless it was so taken or collected.

According to the submissions of the Crown, no further modifications to this regulatory scheme took place prior to the enactment of the *Constitution Act, 1982*.

34   None of these regulations, when viewed individually or as a whole, can be said to express a clear and plain intention to extinguish the Aboriginal rights of the Heiltsuk Band. While to extinguish an Aboriginal right the Crown does not, perhaps, have to use language which refers expressly to its extinguishment of Aboriginal rights, it must demonstrate more than that, in the past, the exercise of an Aboriginal right has been subject to

a regulatory scheme. In this instance, the regulations and legislation regulating the herring spawn on kelp fishery prior to 1982 do not demonstrate any consistent intention on the part of the Crown. At various times prior to 1982 Aboriginal peoples have been entirely prohibited from harvesting herring spawn on kelp, allowed to harvest herring spawn on kelp for food only, allowed to harvest herring spawn on kelp for sale with the written permission of the regional director and allowed to take herring roe pursuant to a licence granted under the *Pacific Fishery Registration and Licensing Regulations*. Such a varying regulatory scheme cannot be said to express a clear and plain intention to eliminate the Aboriginal rights of the appellants and of the Heiltsuk Band. As in *Sparrow*, the Crown has only demonstrated that it controlled the fisheries, not that it has acted so as to delineate the extent of Aboriginal rights.

35   The Crown also argued, however, that even if the regulations do not extinguish the appellants' Aboriginal rights, their rights were extinguished by the enactment of Order in Council, P.C. 2539, of September 11, 1917. Regulation 2539 reads as follows:

> *Whereas it is represented that since time immemorial, it has been the practice of the Indians of British Columbia to catch salmon by means of spears and otherwise after they have reached the upper non-tidal portions of the rivers;*
>
> *And whereas while after commercial fishing began it became eminently desirable that all salmon that succeeded in reaching the upper waters should be allowed to go on to their spawning beds unmolested, in view of the great importance the Indians attached to their practice of catching salmon they have been permitted to do so for their own food purposes only,* and to this end subsection 2 of section 8 of the Special Fishery Regulations for British Columbia provides as follows: -
>
>> 2. Indians may, at any time, with the permission of the Chief Inspector of Fisheries, catch fish to be used as food for themselves and their families, but for no other purpose; but no Indian shall spear, trap or pen fish on their spawning grounds, or in any place leased or set apart for the natural or artificial propagation of fish, or in any other place otherwise specially reserved.
>
> And whereas notwithstanding this concession, great difficulty is being experienced in preventing the Indians from catching salmon in such waters for commercial purposes and recently, an Indian was convicted before a local magistrate for a violation of the above quoted regulation, the evidence being that he had been found fishing and subsequently selling fish. The case was appealed and the decision of the magistrate reversed, it being held that there was no proof that the fish caught by the Indian were those sold by him;
>
> And whereas it is further represented that it is practically impossible for the Fishery Officers to keep fish that may be caught by the Indians in non-tidal waters, ostensibly for their own food purposes, under observation from the time they are caught until they are finally disposed of in one way or another;
>
> And whereas the Department of the Naval Service is informed that the Indians have concluded that this regulation is ineffective, and this season arrangements are being made by them to carry on fishing for commercial purposes in an extensive way;
>
> And whereas it is considered to be in the public interest that this should be prevented and the Minister of the Naval Service, after consultation with the Department of Justice on the subject, recommends that action as follows be taken;
>
> Therefore His Excellency the Governor General in Council, under the authority of section 45 of the Fisheries Act, 4-5 George V, Chapter 8, is pleased to order and it is hereby ordered as follows:-
>
> Subsection 2 of section 8 of the Special Fishery Regulations for the Province of British Columbia, adopted by Order in Council of the 9th February, 1915, is hereby rescinded,

and the following is hereby enacted and substituted in lieu thereof:—

> 2. An Indian may, at any time, with the permission of the Chief Inspector of Fisheries, catch fish to be used as food for himself and his family, but for no other purpose. The Chief Inspector of Fisheries shall have the power in any such permit (a) to limit or fix the area of the waters in which such fish may be caught; (b) to limit or fix the means by which, or the manner in which such fish may be caught, and (c) to limit or fix the time in which such permission shall be operative. An Indian shall not fish for or catch fish pursuant to the said permit except in the waters by the means or in the manner and within the time limit expressed in the said permit, and any fish caught pursuant to any such permit shall not be sold or otherwise disposed of and a violation of the provisions of the said permit shall be deemed to be a violation of these regulations… [Emphasis added]

The language of the Regulation suggests that the government had two purposes in enacting the amendment to the existing scheme: first, the government wished to ensure that conservation goals were met so that salmon reached their "spawning grounds"; second, the government wished to pursue those goals in a manner which would ensure that the special protection granted to the Indian food fishery would continue. The government attempted to meet these goals by making it clear that no special protection was being granted to the Indian commercial fishery and that, instead, the Indian commercial fishery would be subject to the general regulatory system governing commercial fishing in the province.

36   Under the *Sparrow* test for extinguishment, this Regulation cannot be said to have extinguished the Aboriginal right to fish commercially held by the appellants in this case. The government's purpose was to ensure that conservation goals were met, and that the Indian food fishery's special protection would continue; its purpose was not to eliminate Aboriginal rights to fish commercially. It is true that through the enactment of this regulation the government placed Aboriginal rights to fish commercially under the general regulatory scheme applicable to commercial fishing, and therefore did not grant the Aboriginal commercial fishery special protection of the kind given to Aboriginal food fishing; however, the failure to recognize an Aboriginal right, and the failure to grant special protection to it, do not constitute the clear and plain intention necessary to extinguish the right.

37   That the government did not in fact have this intention becomes clear when one looks at the general regulatory scheme of which this Regulation is one part. First, Aboriginal people were not prohibited, and have never been prohibited since the scheme was introduced in 1908, from obtaining licences to fish commercially under the regulatory scheme applicable to commercial fishing. Second, and more importantly, *the government has, at various times, given preferences to Aboriginal commercial fishing.* For example, the government has provided for greatly reduced licensing fees for Aboriginal fishers and has attempted to encourage Aboriginal participation in the commercial fishery. I would note the statistics cited by the interveners the British Columbia Fisheries Survival Coalition and British Columbia Wildlife Federation to the effect that, in 1929, of the 13,860 commercial salmon licences issued 3,632 were held by Aboriginal people and that, during and after World War II, there was a "substantial fleet of Indian-owned and operated seine boats, as well as gill-netters and trollers". The interveners assert that, today, Aboriginal participation in the commercial fishery is at a considerably higher percentage than the percentage of Aboriginal people in the population as a whole. Such substantial encour-

agement of the Aboriginal commercial fishery is not, in my view, consistent with the assertion that through enacting a Regulation aimed at ensuring conservation of the fishery in a manner which continues the special protection given to the Aboriginal food fishery, the government had the clear and plain intention to extinguish the Aboriginal rights to fish commercially held by some Aboriginal peoples in the province.

38   Finally, I would note that the Regulation is of an entirely different nature than the document relied on for a finding of extinguishment in *R.* v. *Horseman*, [1990] 1 S.C.R. 901, at p. 933, (per Cory J.) and *R.* v. *Badger*, [1996] 1 S.C.R. 771, at para. 46 (*per* Cory J.). Section 12 of the *Natural Resources Transfer Agreement* (*NRTA*), the provision at issue in those cases, is a provision in a constitutional document, the enactment of which provides for a permanent settlement of the legal rights of the Aboriginal groups to whom it applies. The Regulation, by contrast, was merely a statutory document dealing with an immediate conservation concern and was subject to amendment through nothing more elaborate than the normal legislative process. The *NRTA* was aimed at achieving a permanent clarification of the province's legislative jurisdiction and of the legal rights of Aboriginal peoples within the province; the Regulation was aimed at dealing with the immediate problems caused by the fact that an insufficient number of salmon were reaching their spawning grounds. The intention of the government in enacting the Regulation must, as a consequence, be viewed quite differently from its intention in enacting the *NRTA*, with the result that while the NRTA can be seen as evincing the necessary clear and plain intention to extinguish Aboriginal rights to hunt commercially in the province to which it applies, the Regulation cannot be seen as evincing the necessary clear and plain intention to extinguish Aboriginal rights to fish commercially in British Columbia.

Infringement

39   *Sparrow* also lays out the test for determining whether or not the government has infringed the Aboriginal rights of the appellants (at pp. 1111–12):

> The first question to be asked is whether the legislation in question has the effect of interfering with an existing aboriginal right. If it does have such an effect, it represents a *prima facie* infringement of s. 35(1). Parliament is not expected to act in a manner contrary to the rights and interests of aboriginals, and, indeed, may be barred from doing so by the second stage of s. 35(1) analysis. . .
>
> To determine whether the fishing rights have been interfered with such as to constitute a *prima facie* infringement of s. 35(1) certain questions must be asked. First, is the limitation unreasonable? Second, does the regulation impose undue hardship? Third, does the regulation deny to the holders of the right their preferred means of exercising that right? The onus of proving a prima facie infringement lies on the individual or group challenging the legislation.

The test as laid out in *Sparrow* is determined to a certain extent by the factual context in which it was articulated; the Court must take into account variations in the factual context of the appeal which affect the application of the test.

40   At the infringement stage, the primary distinction between the factual context of *Sparrow*, and the context of this appeal, is that the regulation impugned in *Sparrow*—a net length restriction—was challenged independently of the broader fisheries management scheme of which it was a part. In this case, while the appellants' constitutional challenge is focused on a single regulation—s. 20(3) of the *Pacific Herring Fishery Regulations*—the scope of the challenge is much broader than the terms of s. 20(3). The appel-

lants' arguments on the points of infringement and justification effectively impugn the entire approach taken by the Crown to the management of the herring spawn on kelp fishery.

41   The fact that the appellants' challenge to the legislation is broader than that of the appellant in *Sparrow* arises from the difference in the nature of the regulation being challenged. Restrictions on net length have an impact on an individual's ability to exercise his or her Aboriginal rights, and raise conservation issues, which can be subject to constitutional scrutiny independent of the broader regulatory scheme of which they are a part. The Category J licence requirement, on the other hand, cannot be scrutinized for the purposes of either infringement or justification without considering the entire regulatory scheme of which it is a part. The requirement that those engaged in the commercial fishery have licences is, as will be discussed in more detail below, simply a constituent part of a larger regulatory scheme setting the amount of herring that can be caught, the amount of herring allotted to the herring spawn on kelp fishery and the allocation of herring spawn on kelp amongst different users of the resource. All the aspects of this regulatory scheme potentially infringe the rights of the appellants in this case; to consider s. 20(3) apart from this broader regulatory scheme for the herring fishery would distort the Court's inquiry.

42   The significance of this difference for the *Sparrow* test is that the questions asked by this Court in *Sparrow* must, in this case, be applied not simply to s. 20(3) but also to the other aspects of the regulatory scheme of which s. 20(3) is one part. In order to do this it will be necessary to consider, in some detail, the regulatory scheme being challenged by the appellants in this case. Before doing so, however, I have one further comment with regards to the test for infringement laid out by this Court in *Sparrow*.

43   The *Sparrow* test for infringement might seem, at first glance, to be internally contradictory. On the one hand, the test states that the appellants need simply show that there has been a *prima facie* interference with their rights in order to demonstrate that those rights have been infringed, suggesting thereby that any meaningful diminution of the appellants' rights will constitute an infringement for the purpose of this analysis. On the other hand, the questions the test directs courts to answer in determining whether an infringement has taken place incorporate ideas such as unreasonableness and "undue" hardship, ideas which suggest that something more than meaningful diminution is required to demonstrate infringement. This internal contradiction is, however, more apparent than real. The questions asked by the Court in *Sparrow* do not define the concept of *prima facie* infringement; they only point to factors which will indicate that such an infringement has taken place. Simply because one of those questions is answered in the negative will not prohibit a finding by a court that a *prima facie* infringement has taken place; it will just be one factor for a court to consider in its determination of whether there has been a *prima facie* infringement.

44   I now turn to the regulatory scheme challenged by the appellants in this case. I will consider this scheme both as it exists now and in terms of its historical development. The reason for this is that some aspects of the scheme challenged by the appellants go back to the introduction of the commercial herring spawn on kelp fishery in the early 1970s; as such, in order to scrutinize those aspects it is necessary to consider the regulation of the herring fishery from its inception.

45   The commercial herring spawn on kelp and herring roe fisheries, in the form in which they exist today, developed in British Columbia in the early 1970s. Prior to that time herring was exploited primarily for the purpose of reducing the fish to oil. The shift in the use of the herring fishery resulted from a confluence of factors; in particular, extensive overfishing had radically depleted the herring stock (in 1965 the reduction fishery was shut down indefinitely) in response to which the Department of Fisheries and Oceans shifted from a policy of taking the maximum sustainable yield of the herring stock each year to a policy of exploiting the herring fishery so as to maximize the economic and social benefits derived from that fishery for the people of Canada. As part of this policy shift the Department of Fisheries and Oceans encouraged the growth of a commercial herring spawn on kelp fishery. Because herring spawn on kelp is eaten as part of the traditional celebration of the new year in Japan, an export market for this product existed; the herring industry and the Department of Fisheries and Oceans believed that this market could be exploited lucratively. . .

51   To summarize, the government's scheme for regulating the herring spawn on kelp fishery can be divided into four constituent parts: (1) the government determines the amount of the herring stock that will be harvested in a given year; (2) the government allots the herring stock to the different herring fisheries (herring roe, herring spawn on kelp and other herring fisheries); (3) the government allots the herring spawn on kelp fishery to various user groups (commercial users and the Indian food fishery); and, (4) the government allots the commercial herring spawn on kelp licences.

52   Because each of these constituent parts has a different objective, and each involves a different pattern of government action, at the stage of justification it will be necessary to consider them separately; however, at the infringement stage the government scheme can be considered as a whole. The reason for this is that at the infringement stage it is the cumulative effect on the appellants' rights from the operation of the regulatory scheme that the court is concerned with. The cumulative effect of the regulatory scheme on the appellants' rights is, simply, that the total amount of herring spawn on kelp that can be harvested by the Heiltsuk Band for commercial purposes is limited. Thus, in order to demonstrate that there has been a *prima facie* infringement of their rights, the appellants must simply demonstrate that limiting the amount of herring spawn on kelp that they can harvest for commercial purposes constitutes, on the basis of the test laid out in *Sparrow*, a *prima facie* interference with their Aboriginal rights.

53   In light of the questions posed by this Court in *Sparrow*, it seems clear that the appellants have discharged their burden of demonstrating a *prima facie* interference with their Aboriginal rights. Prior to the arrival of Europeans in North America, the Heiltsuk could harvest herring spawn on kelp to the extent they themselves desired, subject only to such limitations as were imposed by any difficulties in transportation, preservation and resource availability, as well as those limitations that they thought advisable to impose for the purposes of conservation; subsequent to the enactment of the regulatory scheme described above the Heiltsuk can harvest herring spawn on kelp for commercial purposes only to the limited extent allowed by the government. To use the language of Cory J. in *R. v. Nikal*, *supra*, at para. 104, the government's regulatory scheme "clearly impinge[s]" upon the rights of the appellant and, as such, must be held to constitute a *prima facie* infringement of those rights.

Justification

54   In *Sparrow*, Dickson C.J. and La Forest J. articulated a two-part test for determining whether government actions infringing Aboriginal rights can be justified. First, the government must demonstrate that it was acting pursuant to a valid legislative objective (at p. 1113): . . . Second, the government must demonstrate that its actions are consistent with the fiduciary duty of the government towards Aboriginal peoples. This means, Dickson C.J. and La Forest J. held, that the government must demonstrate that it has given the Aboriginal fishery priority in a manner consistent with this Court's decision in *Jack* v. *The Queen*, [1980] 1 S.C.R. 294, at p. 313, where Dickson J. (as he then was) held that the correct order of priority in the fisheries is "(i) conservation; (ii) Indian fishing; (iii) non-Indian commercial fishing; or (iv) non-Indian sports fishing". . .

55   Dickson C.J. and La Forest J. also held at p. 1119 that the Crown's fiduciary duty to Aboriginal peoples would require the Court to ask, at the justification stage, such further questions as:

> . . . whether there has been as little infringement as possible in order to effect the desired result; whether, in a situation of expropriation, fair compensation is available; and, whether the aboriginal group in question has been consulted with respect to the conservation measures being implemented. . .
>
> We would not wish to set out an exhaustive list of the factors to be considered in the assessment of justification. Suffice it to say that recognition and affirmation requires sensitivity to and respect for the rights of aboriginal peoples on behalf of the government, courts and indeed all Canadians.

56   As was noted with regards to the question of infringement, the framework for analysing Aboriginal rights laid out in *Sparrow* depends to a considerable extent on the legal and factual context of that appeal. In this case, where, particularly at the stage of justification, the context varies significantly from that in *Sparrow*, it will be necessary to revisit the *Sparrow* test and to adapt the justification test it lays out in order to apply that test to the circumstances of this appeal.

57   Two points of variation are of particular significance. First, the right recognized and affirmed in this case—to sell herring spawn on kelp commercially—differs significantly from the right recognized and affirmed in *Sparrow*—the right to fish for food, social and ceremonial purposes. That difference lies in the fact that the right at issue in *Sparrow* has an inherent limitation which the right recognized and affirmed in this appeal lacks. The food, social and ceremonial needs for fish of any given band of Aboriginal people are internally limited—at a certain point the band will have sufficient fish to meet these needs. The commercial sale of the herring spawn on kelp, on the other hand, has no such internal limitation; the only limits on the Heiltsuk's need for herring spawn on kelp for commercial sale are the external constraints of the demand of the market and the availability of the resource. This is particularly so in this case where the evidence supports a right to exchange fish on a genuinely commercial basis; the evidence in this case does not justify limiting the right to harvest herring spawn on kelp on a commercial basis to, for example, the sale of herring spawn on kelp for the purposes of obtaining a "moderate livelihood". Even Lambert J.A., who used the moderate livelihood standard in dissent in the *R.* v. *Van der Peet* (1993), 80 B.C.L.R. (2d) 75, and *R.* v. *N.T.C. Smokehouse Ltd.* (1993), 80 B.C.L.R. (2d) 158, did not so confine the rights of the appellants in this case, defining their right at para. 79 as the right to "harvest herring spawn deposited on kelp

. . . for the purposes of trade in quantities measured in tons, subject only to the need for conservation of the resource". I do not necessarily endorse this characterization; however, it supports the basic point that the Aboriginal right in this case is, unlike the right at issue in *Sparrow*, without internal limitation.

58   The significance of this difference for the *Sparrow* test relates to the position taken in that case that, subject to the limits of conservation, Aboriginal rights holders must be given priority in the fishery. In a situation where the Aboriginal right is internally limited, so that it is clear when that right has been satisfied and other users can be allowed to participate in the fishery, the notion of priority, as articulated in *Sparrow*, makes sense. In that situation it is understandable that in an exceptional year, when conservation concerns are severe, it will be possible for Aboriginal rights holders to be alone allowed to participate in the fishery, while in more ordinary years other users will be allowed to participate in the fishery after the Aboriginal rights to fish for food, social and ceremonial purposes have been met.

59   Where the Aboriginal right has no internal limitation, however, what is described in *Sparrow* as an exceptional situation becomes the ordinary: in the circumstance where the Aboriginal right has no internal limitation, the notion of priority, as articulated in *Sparrow*, would mean that where an Aboriginal right is recognized and affirmed that right would become an exclusive one. Because the right to sell herring spawn on kelp to the commercial market can never be said to be satisfied while the resource is still available and the market is not sated, to give priority to that right in the manner suggested in *Sparrow* would be to give the right-holder exclusivity over any person not having an Aboriginal right to participate in the herring spawn on kelp fishery.

60   In my view, such a result was not the intention of *Sparrow*. The only circumstance contemplated by *Sparrow* was where the Aboriginal right was internally limited; the judgment simply does not consider how the priority standard should be applied in circumstances where the right has no such internal limitation. That this is the case can be seen by a consideration of the judgment of *Jack, supra*, which was relied upon by Dickson C.J. and La Forest J. in their articulation of the notion of priority. While *Jack* undoubtedly stands for the proposition for which it was cited, it is interesting to note that in that case, Dickson J. specifically distinguished at p. 313 between food and commercial fishing:

> [The appellants'] position, as I understand it, is one which would give effect to an order of priorities of this nature: (i) conservation; (ii) Indian fishing; (iii) non-Indian commercial fishing; or (iv) non-Indian sports fishing; the burden of conservation measures should not fall primarily upon the Indian fishery.
>   I agree with the general tenor of this argument. Article 13 calls for distinct protection of the Indian fishery, in that pre-Confederation policy gave the Indians a priority in the fishery. *That priority is at its strongest when we speak of Indian fishing for food purposes, but somewhat weaker when we come to local commercial purposes.* [Emphasis added.]

In *Sparrow* it was obviously not necessary for Dickson C.J. and La Forest J. to address the distinction suggested by Dickson J. (as he then was) in *Jack*; that such a distinction exists suggests, however, that *Sparrow* should not be seen as the final word on the question of priority, at least where the Aboriginal right in question does not have the internal limitation which the right actually at issue in *Sparrow* did.

61   The basic insight of *Sparrow*—that Aboriginal rights holders have priority in the

fishery—is a valid and important one; however, the articulation in that case of what priority means, and its suggestion that it can mean exclusivity under certain limited circumstances, must be refined to take into account the varying circumstances which arise when the Aboriginal right in question has no internal limitations.

62   Where the Aboriginal right is one that has no internal limitation then the doctrine of priority does not require that, after conservation goals have been met, the government allocate the fishery so that those holding an Aboriginal right to exploit that fishery on a commercial basis are given an exclusive right to do so. Instead, the doctrine of priority requires that the government demonstrate that, in allocating the resource, it has taken account of the existence of Aboriginal rights and allocated the resource in a manner respectful of the fact that those rights have priority over the exploitation of the fishery by other users. This right is at once both procedural and substantive; at the stage of justification the government must demonstrate both that the process by which it allocated the resource and the actual allocation of the resource which results from that process reflect the prior interest of Aboriginal rights holders in the fishery.

63   The content of this priority—something less than exclusivity but which nonetheless gives priority to the Aboriginal right—must remain somewhat vague pending consideration of the government's actions in specific cases. Just as the doctrine of minimal impairment under s. 1 of the *Canadian Charter of Rights and Freedoms* has not been read as meaning that the courts will impose a standard "least drastic means" requirement on the government in all cases, but has rather been interpreted as requiring the courts to scrutinize government action for reasonableness on a case-by-case basis (see, for example, *Irwin Toy Ltd.* v. *Quebec (Attorney General)*, [1989] 1 S.C.R. 927, at pp. 993–94; *Stoffman* v. *Vancouver General Hospital*, [1990] 3 S.C.R. 483, at pp. 526–27, *McKinney* v. *University of Guelph*, [1990] 3 S.C.R. 229, at pp. 285–86, *R.* v. *Butler*, [1992] 1 S.C.R. 452, at pp. 504–5), priority under *Sparrow's* justification test cannot be assessed against a precise standard but must rather be assessed in each case to determine whether the government has acted in a fashion which reflects that it has truly taken into account the existence of Aboriginal rights. Under the minimal impairment branch of the *Oakes* test *(R.* v. *Oakes,* [1986] 1 S.C.R. 103), where the government is balancing the interests of competing groups, the court does not scrutinize the government's actions so as to determine whether the government took the least rights-impairing action possible; instead the court considers the reasonableness of the government's actions, taking into account the need to assess "conflicting scientific evidence and differing justified demands on scarce resources" (*Irwin Toy, supra*, at p. 993). Similarly, under *Sparrow's* priority doctrine, where the Aboriginal right to be given priority is one without internal limitation, courts should assess the government's actions not to see whether the government has given exclusivity to that right (the least drastic means) but rather to determine whether the government has taken into account the existence and importance of such rights.

64   That no blanket requirement is imposed under the priority doctrine should not suggest, however, that no guidance is possible in this area, or that the government's actions will not be subject to scrutiny. Questions relevant to the determination of whether the government has granted priority to Aboriginal rights holders are those enumerated in *Sparrow* relating to consultation and compensation, as well as questions such as whether the government has accommodated the exercise of the Aboriginal right to participate in the fishery (through reduced licence fees, for example), whether the government's objec-

tives in enacting a particular regulatory scheme reflect the need to take into account the priority of Aboriginal rights holders, the extent of the participation in the fishery of Aboriginal rights holders relative to their percentage of the population, how the government has accommodated different Aboriginal rights in a particular fishery (food versus commercial rights, for example), how important the fishery is to the economic and material well-being of the band in question, and the criteria taken into account by the government in, for example, allocating commercial licences amongst different users. These questions, like those in *Sparrow*, do not represent an exhaustive list of the factors that may be given priority to Aboriginal rights holders; they give some indication, however, of what such an inquiry should look like.

65   Before turning to the second relevant difference between this case and *Sparrow*, I would note one or two points in favour of the interpretation of priority just adopted. As was emphasized in this Court's decision in *Van der Peet*, Aboriginal rights are highly fact specific—the existence of an Aboriginal right is determined through consideration of the particular distinctive culture, and hence of the specific practices, customs and traditions, of the Aboriginal group claiming the right. The rights recognized and affirmed by s. 35(1) are not rights held uniformly by all Aboriginal peoples in Canada; the nature and existence of Aboriginal rights vary in accordance with the variety of Aboriginal cultures and traditions which exist in this country. As a result, governments must not only make decisions about how to allocate fish between Aboriginal rights holders and those who do not enjoy such rights, but must also make decisions as to how to allocate fish both between different groups of Aboriginal rights holders and between different Aboriginal rights. The government must, for example, make decisions as to how to allocate fish between those Aboriginal peoples with the Aboriginal right to fish for food, social and ceremonial purposes, and those Aboriginal peoples who have Aboriginal rights to sell fish commercially; it must also decide, where more than one Aboriginal group has a right to sell fish commercially, how much fish each group will have access to.

66   The existence of such difficult questions of resource allocation supports the position that, where a right has no adequate internal limitations, the notion of exclusivity of priority must be rejected. Certainly the holders of such Aboriginal rights must be given priority, along with all others holding Aboriginal rights to the use of a particular resource; however, the potential existence of other Aboriginal rights holders with an equal claim to priority in the exploitation of the resource, suggests that there must be some external limitation placed on the exercise of those Aboriginal rights which lack internal limitation. Unless the possibility of such a limitation is recognized, it is difficult to see how the government will be able to make decisions of resource allocation amongst the various parties holding prioritized rights to participate in the fishery. And while this does not lead automatically to the conclusion that, as between Aboriginal rights holders and those who do not hold such rights, the notion of exclusivity must be rejected, it does point to some of the difficulties inherent in the recognition of such a concept in the context of this and similar cases.

67   It should also be noted that the Aboriginal rights recognized and affirmed by s. 35(1) exist within a legal context in which, since the time of the Magna Carta, there has been a common law right to fish in tidal waters that can only be abrogated by the enactment of competent legislation:

    . . . the subjects of the Crown are entitled as of right not only to navigate but to fish in the high seas and tidal waters alike. . . .

    [I]t has been unquestioned law that since Magna Charta [sic] no new exclusive fishery could be created by Royal grant in tidal waters, and that no public right of fishing in such waters, then existing, can be taken away without competent legislation. [*Attorney-General of British Columbia v. Attorney General of Canada*, [1914] A.C. 153 (J.C.P.C.), at pp. 169–70, per Viscount Haldane.]

While the elevation of common law Aboriginal rights to constitutional status obviously has an impact on the public's common law rights to fish in tidal waters, it was surely not intended that, by the enactment of s. 35(1), those common law rights would be extinguished in cases where an Aboriginal right to harvest fish commercially existed. As was contemplated by *Sparrow*, in the occasional years where conservation concerns drastically limit the availability of fish, satisfying Aboriginal rights to fish for food, social and ceremonial purposes may involve, in that year, abrogating the common law right of public access to the fishery; however, it was not contemplated by *Sparrow* that the recognition and affirmation of Aboriginal rights should result in the common law right of public access in the fishery ceasing to exist with respect to all those fisheries in respect of which exist an Aboriginal right to sell fish commercially. As a common law, not constitutional, right, the right of public access to the fishery must clearly be second in priority to Aboriginal rights; however, the recognition of Aboriginal rights should not be interpreted as extinguishing the right of public access to the fishery.

68   That this should not be the case becomes particularly clear when it is remembered that, as was noted above, the existence of Aboriginal rights varies amongst different Aboriginal peoples, with the result that the notion of priority applies not only between Aboriginals and other Canadians, but also between those Aboriginal peoples who have an Aboriginal right to use the fishery and those who do not. For Aboriginal peoples like the Sheshaht, Opetchesaht and the Sto:lo, the fact that they were unable to demonstrate that their Aboriginal rights include the right to sell fish on a commercial basis should not mean, if another Aboriginal group is able to establish such a right, that the rights they hold in common with other Canadians—to participate in the commercial fishery—are eliminated. This could not have been intended by the enactment of s. 35(1).

69   I now turn to the second significant difference between this case and *Sparrow*. In *Sparrow*, while the Court recognized at p. 1113 that, beyond conservation, there could be other "compelling and substantial" objectives pursuant to which the government could act in accordance with the first branch of the justification test, the Court was not required to delineate what those objectives might be. Further, in delineating the priority requirement, and the relationship between Aboriginal rights-holders and other users of the fishery, the only objective considered by the Court was conservation. This limited focus made sense in *Sparrow* because the net-length restriction at issue in that case was argued by the Crown to have been necessary as a conservation measure (whether it was necessary as such was not actually decided in that case); in this case, however, while some aspects of the government's regulatory scheme arguably relate to conservation—setting the total allowable catch at 20% of the estimated herring stock, requiring the herring roe fishery to bear the brunt of variations in the herring stock because it is more environmentally destructive—other aspects of the government's regulatory scheme bear little or no relation to issues of conservation. Once the overall level of the herring catch has been established, and allocated to the different herring fisheries, *it makes no difference in terms of conservation who is allowed to catch the fish*. Conservation of the fishery is simply not affected

once, after the herring spawn on kelp fishery is set at 2,275 tons, 224 tons or 2,275 tons is allocated to the commercial fishery or to some other use. This is not to suggest that these decisions are unimportant or made pursuant to unimportant objectives, but simply that, whatever objectives the government is pursuing in making such decisions, conservation is not (or is only marginally) one of them. As such, it is necessary in this case to consider what, if any, objectives the government may pursue, other than conservation, which will be sufficient to satisfy the first branch of the *Sparrow* justification standard.

70   Considering this question is made more difficult in this case because, as will be discussed below, almost no evidence has been provided to this Court about the objectives the government was pursuing in allocating the herring resource as it did. Absent some concrete objectives to assess, it is difficult to identify the objectives other than conservation that will meet the "compelling and substantial" standard laid out in *Sparrow*. That being said, however, it is possible to make some general observations about the nature of the objectives that the government can pursue under the first branch of the *Sparrow* justification test.

71   In *Oakes, supra*, Dickson C.J. observed at p. 136 that it is not only the case that the rights and freedoms protected by the *Charter* must be understood through the purposes underlying the protection of those rights, but that the limitations on rights allowed under s. 1 of the *Charter* must, similarly, be understood through the purposes underlying the *Charter*:

> A second contextual element of interpretation of s. 1 is provided by the words "free and democratic society". Inclusion of these words as the final standard of justification for limits on rights and freedoms refers the Court to the very purpose for which the *Charter* was originally entrenched in the Constitution. . . The underlying values and principles of a free and democratic society are the genesis of the rights and freedoms guaranteed by the *Charter* and the ultimate standard against which a limit on a right or freedom must be shown, despite its effect, to be reasonable and demonstrably justified.

Although the Aboriginal rights recognized by s. 35(1) are, as was noted in *Van der Peet*, fundamentally different from the rights in the *Charter*, the same basic principle—that the purposes underlying the rights must inform not only the definition of the rights but also the identification of those limits on the rights which are justifiable—applies equally to the justification analysis under s. 35(1).

72   In *Van der Peet* the purposes underlying s. 35(1)'s recognition and affirmation of Aboriginal rights were identified, at para. 39, as

> first, the means by which the constitution recognizes the fact that prior to the arrival of Europeans in North America the land was already occupied by distinctive aboriginal societies, and, as, second, the means by which that prior occupation is reconciled with the assertion of Crown sovereignty over Canadian territory.

In the context of the objectives which can be said to be compelling and substantial under the first branch of the *Sparrow* justification test, the import of these purposes is that the objectives which can be said to be compelling and substantial will be those directed at either the recognition of the prior occupation of North America by Aboriginal peoples or—and at the level of justification it is this purpose which may well be most relevant—at the reconciliation of Aboriginal prior occupation with the assertion of the sovereignty of the Crown.

73   Aboriginal rights are recognized and affirmed by s. 35(1) in order to reconcile the existence of distinctive Aboriginal societies prior to the arrival of Europeans in North America with the assertion of Crown sovereignty over that territory; they are the means by which the critical and integral aspects of those societies are maintained. Because, however, distinctive Aboriginal societies exist within, and are a part of, a broader social, political and economic community, over which the Crown is sovereign, there are circumstances in which, in order to pursue objectives of compelling and substantial importance to that community as a whole (taking into account the fact that Aboriginal societies are a part of that community), some limitation of those rights will be justifiable. Aboriginal rights are a necessary part of the reconciliation of Aboriginal societies with the broader political community of which they are part; limits placed on those rights are, where the objectives furthered by those limits are of sufficient importance to the broader community as a whole, equally a necessary part of that reconciliation.

74   The recognition of conservation as a compelling and substantial goal demonstrates this point. Given the integral role the fishery has played in the distinctive cultures of many Aboriginal peoples, conservation can be said to be something the pursuit of which can be linked to the recognition of the existence of such distinctive cultures. Moreover, because conservation is of such overwhelming importance to Canadian society as a whole, including Aboriginal members of that society, it is a goal the pursuit of which is consistent with the reconciliation of Aboriginal societies with the larger Canadian society of which they are a part. In this way, conservation can be said to be a compelling and substantial objective which, provided the rest of the *Sparrow* justification standard is met, will justify governmental infringement of Aboriginal rights.

75   Although by no means making a definitive statement on this issue, I would suggest that with regards to the distribution of the fisheries resource after conservation goals have been met, objectives such as the pursuit of economic and regional fairness, and the recognition of the historical reliance upon, and participation in, the fishery by non-Aboriginal groups, are the type of objectives which can (at least in the right circumstances) satisfy this standard. *In the right circumstances, such objectives are in the interest of all Canadians and, more importantly, the reconciliation of Aboriginal societies with the rest of Canadian society may well depend on their successful attainment.*

76   I now turn to the application of the *Sparrow* justification test to the government regulatory scheme challenged in this case. As has already been noted, the government's regulatory scheme has four constituent parts, which, for ease of reference, I will reiterate here: (1) the government determines the amount of the herring stock that will be harvested in a given year; (2) the government allots the herring stock to the different herring fisheries (herring roe, herring spawn on kelp and other herring fisheries); (3) the government allots the herring spawn on kelp fishery to various user groups (commercial users and the Indian food fishery); and, (4) the government allots the commercial herring spawn on kelp licences.

77   Other than with regards to the first aspect of the government's regulatory scheme, the evidence and testimony presented in this case is insufficient for this Court to make a determination as to whether the government's regulatory scheme is justified. The trial in this case concluded on May 7, 1990, several weeks prior to the release of this Court's judgment in *Sparrow*. Perhaps as a result of this fact, the testimony, evidence and argument presented at the trial simply do not contain the information that is necessary for

this Court to assess whether, in allocating the 40,000 tons of herring allotted to the herring fishery, the government has either acted pursuant to a compelling and substantial objective or has acted in a manner consistent with the fiduciary obligation it owes to Aboriginal peoples. It is not that the Crown has failed to discharge its burden of demonstrating that the scheme for allocating the 20% of the herring stock was justified; it is simply that the question of whether or not that scheme of allocation was justified was not addressed at trial, at least in the sense necessary for this Court to decide the question of whether, under the *Sparrow* test, it was justified.

78   The lack of evidence is problematic with regards to both aspects of the *Sparrow* analysis. First, in so far as an evaluation of the government's objective is concerned, no witnesses testified, and no documents were submitted as evidence, with regards to the objectives pursued by the government in allocating the herring, and the herring spawn on kelp, amongst different user groups. As was noted above, there was evidence presented about the selection criteria used by the Department of Fisheries and Oceans in allocating herring spawn on kelp licences in 1975; however, no evidence was presented as to how or why those selection criteria were chosen or applied. Also, the evidence does not indicate whether those selection criteria changed over time (not all licences were allocated in 1975) or whether the emphasis placed on the different criteria varied. Clear evidence was presented at trial demonstrating that setting the total herring catch at 20% was directed at conservation, but no evidence was presented regarding the objectives sought to be attained in allocating that 20% amongst different user groups.

79   Second, with regards to priority, there is no evidence as to how much (if any) Aboriginal participation there is in the herring roe fishery or as to whether there are any existing Aboriginal rights to participate in the herring roe fishery, whether for food or commercial purposes. Whether the allocation of herring between the herring roe and herring spawn on kelp fishery meets the *Sparrow* test for priority will depend in part on the existence (or non-existence) of such rights. There is, similarly, no evidence as to whether other Aboriginal rights in the herring spawn on kelp fishery exist—whether for food or commercial purposes—and as to the number of such rights holders there might be.

80   Other evidentiary problems exist with regards to the priority analysis. There is no evidence as to how, between the different Aboriginal bands holding Category J licences, allocation decisions are made. There is no evidence as to how, or to whom, the remaining 2,051 tons of herring spawn on kelp is allocated after the 224 tons of herring spawn on kelp is allocated to Category J licences. There is also no evidence as to how many Aboriginal groups live in the region of the herring spawn on kelp fishery, what percentage Aboriginal peoples are of the population in that region, and the size of the Heiltsuk Band relative to other Aboriginal groups and the general population in the region.

81   In the courts below, the judges considering the justification issue avoided the difficulties created by the inadequacy of the evidentiary record in two ways: they either held that the nature of the appellants' actions rendered the government's actions justifiable (the approach of the trial judge) or they held that the allocation of 60% of Category J licences to Aboriginal groups demonstrated that the government's regulatory scheme was justifiable. The problem with the first of these approaches is that the nature of the appellants' actions is not relevant to the inquiry into the constitutionality of the regulation under which they were charged. The problem with the second approach is that the fact that 60% of the Category J licences were held by Aboriginal people does not demon-

strate, in itself, that the licences were allocated in a manner which took into account the existence of Aboriginal rights. It is, perhaps, consistent with that having taken place, but absent some further evidence as to how or why this result was reached, about the percentage of Aboriginal people in relation to the population of the British Columbia coast as a whole, and about the other allocation issues in the herring roe and herring spawn on kelp fisheries, the fact that 60% of the Category J licences are held by Aboriginal peoples does not, on its own, serve to justify the government's actions.

82   Obviously a new trial will not necessarily provide complete and definitive answers to all of these questions; however, given that the parties simply did not address the justifiability of the government scheme, other than the setting of the herring catch at 20% of the total herring stock, a new trial will almost certainly provide the court with better information than currently exists. Prior to *Sparrow* it was not clear what the government, or parties challenging government action, had to demonstrate in order to succeed in s. 35(1) cases; this lack of clarity undoubtedly contributed to the deficiency of the evidentiary record in this case. A new trial on the question of justification will remedy this deficiency.

83   A new trial is not, however, necessary with regards to the first aspect of the government's scheme; the evidentiary record clearly demonstrates that this aspect of the government's scheme was justified. Witnesses testified as to the conservation objectives of setting the stock at 20% and as to the difficulties encountered by the herring fishery when the catch was set at much higher levels, as was the case in the 1960s. Moreover, the defence witness Dr. Gary Vigers testified that "fisheries management is full of uncertainty"; in the context of such uncertainty this Court must grant a certain level of deference to the government's approach to fisheries management.

84   Although the evidence regarding consultation is somewhat scanty, and more will hopefully be presented at a new trial on the justification issue, there is some evidence to suggest that the government was cognizant of the views of Aboriginal groups with regards to the herring fishery. The correspondence between the Native Brotherhood and the Department is indicative of the existence of such consultation. Finally, the setting of the herring catch at 20% of the fishable herring stock, because aimed at conservation, and not affecting the priority of Aboriginal *versus* non-Aboriginal users of the fishery, is consistent with the priority scheme as laid out in *Sparrow* and as elaborated in this judgment.

V. Disposition

85   In the result, the appeal is allowed and a new trial directed on the issue of guilt or innocence and, with regards to the constitutionality of s. 20(3), on the issue of the justifiability of the government's allocation of herring.

86   For the reasons given above, the constitutional question must be answered as follows:

Question:

Is s. 20(3) of the *Pacific Herring Fishery Regulations,* SOR/84-324, as it read on April 28, 1988, of no force or effect with respect to the appellants in the circumstances of these proceedings, in virtue of s. 52 of the *Constitution Act, 1982,* by reason of the Aboriginal rights within the meaning of s. 35 of the *Constitution Act, 1982,* invoked by the appellants?

Answer:

This question will have to be sent back to trial to be answered in accordance with the analysis set out in these reasons. . .

LA FOREST J. (dissenting) …

L'HEUREUX-DUBÉ J. (concurring with result of Lamer C.J.) …

R. v. *Adams*

[1996] 3 S.C.R. 101 (S.C.C.). Lamer C.J., La Forest, L'Heureux-Dubé, Sopinka, Gonthier, Cory, McLachlin, Iacobucci, and Major JJ., October 3, 1996

LAMER C.J. (LA FOREST, SOPINKA, GONTHIER, CORY, MCLACHLIN, IACOBUCCI and MAJOR JJ., concurring):—…

1   This appeal and the appeal of *R.* v. *Côté*, [1996] 3 S.C.R. 139, have been released simultaneously and should be read together in light of the closely related issues raised by both cases.

2   The appellant, a Mohawk, was charged with the regulatory offence of fishing without a licence in Lake St. Francis in the St. Régis region of Quebec. He challenges his conviction on the basis that he was exercising an Aboriginal right to fish as recognized and affirmed by s. 35(1) of the *Constitution Act, 1982*.

3   In resolving this appeal and the appeal in *Côté*, this Court must answer the question of whether Aboriginal rights are necessarily based in Aboriginal title to land, so that the fundamental claim that must be made in any Aboriginal rights case is to Aboriginal title, or whether Aboriginal title is instead one subset of the larger category of Aboriginal rights, so that fishing and other Aboriginal rights can exist independently of a claim to Aboriginal title.

4   In the trilogy of *R.* v. *Van der Peet*, [1996] 2 S.C.R. 507, *R.* v. *N.T.C. Smokehouse Ltd.*, [1996] 2 S.C.R. 672, and *R.* v. *Gladstone*, [1996] 2 S.C.R. 723, this Court had opportunity to consider the question of the scope of the Aboriginal rights recognized and affirmed by s. 35(1). This case and *Côté* will require the application of the principles articulated in those cases to the question of the relationship between Aboriginal title and the other Aboriginal rights, particularly fishing rights, recognized and affirmed by s. 35(1). Furthermore, these two related appeals involve the claim of an Aboriginal right to fish within the historical boundaries of New France. As such, this Court must answer the question of whether, under the principles of the *Van der Peet* trilogy, the constitutional protection of s. 35(1) extends to Aboriginal practices, customs, and traditions which may not have achieved legal recognition under the colonial regime of New France prior to the transition to British sovereignty in 1763. . .

5   The appellant, George Weldon Adams, is a Mohawk who lives on the St. Regis (Akwesasne) Reserve. He was charged with fishing for perch without a licence contrary to s. 4(1) of the *Quebec Fishery Regulations*, C.R.C., c. 852. . .

24   Leave to appeal to this Court was granted on December 9, 1993 ([1993] 4 S.C.R. v). On June 22, 1994 the following constitutional question was stated:

> Is s. 4(1) of the *Quebec Fishery Regulations*, as they read on May 7, 1982, of no force or effect with respect to appellant in the circumstances of these proceedings in virtue of s. 52 of the *Constitution Act, 1982* by reason of the Aboriginal rights within the meaning of s. 35 of the

Constitution Act, 1982 invoked by appellant?

The appellant appealed on the basis that the Court of Appeal erred in holding that Aboriginal fishing rights could not exist where there was no Aboriginal title; more-over, the appellant argued that on the facts of this case such a fishing right had been shown to exist. The appellant appealed on the further basis that the Court of Appeal erred in holding that the Mohawks did not have Aboriginal title to the fishing area; the appellant argued that such title did exist and that an Aboriginal right to fish arose as an incident to that title.

V. Analysis

Aboriginal Title and Aboriginal Rights

25   As was noted at the outset, the fundamental question to be answered in this case is as to whether a claim to an Aboriginal right to fish must rest in a claim to Aboriginal title to the area in which the fishing took place. In other words, this Court must determine whether Aboriginal rights are inherently based in Aboriginal title to the land, or whether claims to title to the land are simply one manifestation of a broader-based conception of Aboriginal rights. The reasons of this Court in *Van der Peet* demonstrate that it is the latter characterization of the relationship between Aboriginal rights and Aboriginal title that is correct.

26   In *Van der Peet*, at para. 43, Aboriginal rights were said to be best understood as:

> ... first, the means by which the Constitution recognizes the fact that prior to the arrival of Europeans in North America the land was already occupied by distinctive aboriginal socie-ties, and as, second, the means by which that prior occupation is reconciled with the asser-tion of Crown sovereignty over Canadian territory.

From this basis the Court went on to hold, at para. 46, that Aboriginal rights are identi-fied through the following test:

> ... in order to be an Aboriginal right an activity must be an element of a practice, custom or tradition integral to the distinctive culture of the Aboriginal group claiming the right.

What this test, along with the conceptual basis which underlies it, indicates, is that while claims to Aboriginal title fall within the conceptual framework of Aboriginal rights, Aboriginal rights do not exist solely where a claim to Aboriginal title has been made out. Where an Aboriginal group has shown that a particular practice, custom or tradition taking place on the land was integral to the distinctive culture of that group then, *even if they have not shown that their occupation and use of the land was sufficient to support a claim of title to the land*, they will have demonstrated that they have an Aboriginal right to engage in that practice, custom or tradition. The *Van der Peet* test protects activities which were integral to the distinctive culture of the Aboriginal group claiming the right; it does not require that that group satisfy the further hurdle of demonstrating that their connec-tion with the piece of land on which the activity was taking place was of a central signifi-cance to their distinctive culture sufficient to make out a claim to Aboriginal title to the land. *Van der Peet* establishes that s. 35 recognizes and affirms the rights of those peoples who occupied North America prior to the arrival of the Europeans; that recognition and affirmation is not limited to those circumstances where an Aboriginal group's relation-ship with the land is of a kind sufficient to establish title to the land.

27   To understand why Aboriginal rights cannot be inexorably linked to Aboriginal

title it is only necessary to recall that some Aboriginal peoples were nomadic, varying the location of their settlements with the season and changing circumstances. That this was the case does not alter the fact that nomadic peoples survived through reliance on the land prior to contact with Europeans and, further, that many of the practices, customs and traditions of nomadic peoples that took place on the land were integral to their distinctive cultures. The Aboriginal rights recognized and affirmed by s. 35(1) should not be understood or defined in a manner which excludes some of those the provision was intended to protect.

28   Moreover, some Aboriginal peoples varied the location of their settlements both before and after contact. The Mohawks are one such people; the facts accepted by the trial judge in this case demonstrate that the Mohawks did not settle exclusively in one location either before or after contact with Europeans. That this is the case may (although I take no position on this point) preclude the establishment of Aboriginal title to the lands on which they settled; however, it in no way subtracts from the fact that, wherever they were settled before or after contact, *prior to contact the Mohawks engaged in practices, customs or traditions on the land which were integral to their distinctive culture. . .*

30   The recognition that Aboriginal title is simply one manifestation of the doctrine of Aboriginal rights should not, however, create the impression that the fact that some Aboriginal rights are linked to land use or occupation is unimportant. Even where an Aboriginal right exists on a tract of land to which the Aboriginal people in question do not have title, that right may well be site specific, with the result that it can be exercised only upon that specific tract of land. For example, if an Aboriginal people demonstrates that hunting on a specific tract of land was an integral part of their distinctive culture then, even if the right exists apart from title to that tract of land, the Aboriginal right to hunt is nonetheless defined as, and limited to, the right to hunt on the specific tract of land. A site-specific hunting or fishing right does not, simply because it is independent of Aboriginal title to the land on which it took place, become an abstract fishing or hunting right exercisable anywhere; it continues to be a right to hunt or fish on the tract of land in question.

Aboriginal Rights and The Colony of New France

31   The respondent raises another important question concerning the doctrine of Aboriginal rights under s. 35(1). The Aboriginal right to fish claimed in this instance relates to a tract of territory, specifically Lake St. Francis, which falls within the boundaries of New France prior to 1763. The respondent argues that this claimed right should be rejected as the French colonial regime never legally recognized the existence of Aboriginal title or any incident Aboriginal right to fish prior to the commencement of British sovereignty.

32   Under the British law governing colonization, the Crown assumed ownership of newly discovered territories subject to an underlying interest of Indigenous peoples in the occupation and use of such territories. By contrast, it is argued that under the French regime of colonization, the French monarch assumed full and complete ownership of all newly discovered territories upon discovery and symbolic possession. In the absence of a specific concession, colonists and Aboriginal peoples were only entitled to enjoy the use of the land through the grace and charity of the French monarch, but not by any recognized legal right. . .

33   For the reasons developed in *Côté, supra,* this argument must be rejected. The respondent's characterization of the status of Aboriginal rights under French colonial law is open to question, although, as in *Côté,* I need not decide the point here. What is important is that, as explained in *Van der Peet, supra,* the purpose of the entrenchment of s. 35(1) was to extend constitutional protection to the practices, customs and traditions central to the distinctive culture of Aboriginal societies prior to contact with Europeans. If the exercise of such practices, customs and traditions effectively continued following contact in the absence of specific extinguishment, such practices, customs and traditions are entitled to constitutional recognition subject to the infringement and justification test outlined in *Sparrow, supra,* and more recently, in *Gladstone, supra.* The fact that a particular practice, custom or tradition continued following the arrival of Europeans, but in the absence of the formal gloss of legal recognition from the European colonizers, should not undermine the protection accorded to Aboriginal peoples. Section 35(1) would fail to achieve its noble purpose of preserving the integral and defining features of distinctive Aboriginal societies if it only protected those defining features which were fortunate enough to have received the legal approval of British and French colonizers.

The Van der Peet Test
34   I now turn to the claim made by the appellant in this case. The appellant argues that the Mohawks have an Aboriginal right to fish in Lake St. Francis. In order to succeed in this argument the appellant must demonstrate that, pursuant to the test laid out by this Court in *Van der Peet,* fishing in Lake St. Francis was "an element of a practice, custom or tradition integral to the distinctive culture" of the Mohawks. For the reasons given below, I am of the view that the appellant has satisfied this test. Given that this is so, it will be unnecessary to address the appellant's argument that the Mohawks have Aboriginal title to the lands in the fishing area that gives rise to an incidental right to fish there. The appellant himself rests his claim primarily on the existence of a free-standing Aboriginal right to fish in Lake St. Francis; since I accept this argument it is unnecessary to consider any subsidiary arguments the appellant makes.

35   The first stage in the application of the *Van der Peet* test requires the Court to determine the precise nature of the claim being made, taking into account such factors as the nature of the action said to have been done pursuant to an Aboriginal right, the government regulation argued to infringe the right, and the practice, custom or tradition relied upon to establish the right.

36   In this case, the appellant's claim is best characterized as a claim for the right to fish for food in Lake St. Francis. First, Francis Lickers, a biologist working for the St. Regis band, testified at trial that the "Indians used perch *for food* in the winter and caught the fish during summer in order to store it for the winter" (emphasis added). There was no suggestion that the perch caught by the appellant was to be used for any purpose other than to meet the food requirements of the appellant and his band. Second, the regulation under which the appellant was charged prohibits all fishing without a licence, whether for food or any other purpose; the only manner in which an Indian food fishing licence can be issued is by an act of ministerial discretion under s. 5(9) of the Regulations, a provision which the appellant challenges the constitutional validity of. The breadth of this scheme, and the limits it places on the Aboriginal food fishery, support the characterization of the appellant's essential challenge as to the prohibition of food fishing. Finally, all the evidence presented at trial to support the appellant's claim was directed at demonstrating

that it was a custom of the Mohawks to rely on the perch in Lake St. Francis for food. The evidence was not directed towards demonstrating any other use of the fish, for example use for ceremonial or commercial purposes.

37   The second stage of the *Van der Peet* analysis requires the Court to determine whether the activity claimed to be an Aboriginal right is part of a practice, custom or tradition which was, prior to contact with Europeans, an integral part of the distinctive Aboriginal society of the Aboriginal people in question. The Court must determine in this case, therefore, whether fishing for food in Lake St. Francis was a central, significant or defining feature of the distinctive culture of the Mohawks.

38   In making this determination the normal approach of this Court—and that followed in *Van der Peet, N.T.C. Smokehouse Ltd.* and *Gladstone*—is to rely on the findings of fact made by the trial judge and to assess whether those findings of fact (if not made as a result of a clear and palpable error) support the claim that an activity is an aspect of a practice, custom or tradition integral to the distinctive culture of the Aboriginal people in question. In this case, however, in deciding that the appellant had an Aboriginal right to fish in Lake St. Francis, the trial judge did not explicitly articulate the findings of fact on which this decision was based. With regards to this question the trial judge said at pp. 139–40:

> [TRANSLATION] In addition to their rights over their lands, the Mohawks have always had and have always exercised a right of hunting and fishing on the St. Lawrence River and in particular on Lake St. Francis in this part situated in the southwest area of this lake and where there are numerous islands and very vast marshes.
> This right of hunting and fishing is distinct from the right of use of their lands. This right can be exercised over vast territories and even over lands belonging to the Crown. . .
> This was a hunting and fishing territory situated in the immediate neighbourhood of their village and which is part of an easily identifiable whole.

The trial judge thus came to a clear legal conclusion on the issue of whether the Mohawks have an Aboriginal right to fish in the area but did not articulate the facts on which this legal conclusion is based. In his consideration of the Aboriginal title issue Barrette Ct. S.P.J. did articulate his findings of fact regarding the Mohawks' historical presence on the lands of the fishing area; however, these findings do not relate specifically to, and nor are they determinative of, the question of whether the reliance on fish in the St. Lawrence River and Lake St. Francis as a source of food was a significant part of the life of the Mohawks prior to contact.

39   That the trial judge did not make explicit findings of fact on this question is not surprising given that he was writing entirely without any guidance from this Court on the factual basis necessary for determining whether an Aboriginal right under s. 35(1) has been demonstrated; however, that he did not do so means that in this appeal the Court cannot rely entirely on his reasons to determine whether the Mohawks have demonstrated the existence of an Aboriginal right to fish for food in Lake St. Francis. That the Court cannot do so is not, however, fatal to the appeal. At trial testimony was received from two expert witnesses: Dr. Bruce Trigger for the appellant and Dr. Rénald Parent for the respondent. The testimony of these two witnesses, despite being contradictory in some respects, provides a sufficient basis for this Court to review, and to uphold, the trial judge's conclusion that the Mohawks have a right to fish for food in Lake St. Francis. . .

44   The general picture presented by the testimony of Parent and Trigger, when consid-

ered together, is that prior to 1603 it is unclear which Aboriginal peoples made use of the St. Lawrence Valley, although there is evidence to suggest that at that time the lands were occupied in part by a group of Iroquois unrelated to the Mohawks. From 1603 to the 1650s the area was the subject of conflict between various Aboriginal peoples, including the Mohawks. During this period the Mohawks clearly fished for food in the St. Lawrence River, either because the Mohawks exercised military control over the region and adopted the territory as fishing and hunting grounds, or because the Mohawks conducted military campaigns in the region during which they were required to rely on the fish in the St. Lawrence River and Lake St. Francis for sustenance.

45   This general picture, regardless of the uncertainty which arises because of the witnesses' conflicting characterizations of the Mohawks' control and use over this area from 1603 to 1632, supports the trial judge's conclusion that the Mohawks have an Aboriginal right to fish for food in Lake St. Francis. Either because reliance on the fish in the St. Lawrence River for food was a necessary part of their campaigns of war, or because the lands of this area constituted Mohawk hunting and fishing grounds, the evidence presented at trial demonstrates *that fishing for food in the St. Lawrence River and, in particular, in Lake St. Francis, was a significant part of the life of the Mohawks from a time dating from at least 1603 and the arrival of Samuel de Champlain into the area.* The fish were not significant to the Mohawks for social or ceremonial reasons; however, they were an important and significant source of subsistence for the Mohawks.

46   This conclusion is sufficient to satisfy the *Van der Peet* test. The arrival of Samuel de Champlain in 1603, and the consequent establishment of effective control by the French over what would become New France, is the time which can most accurately be identified as "contact" for the purposes of the *Van der Peet* test. The evidence presented clearly demonstrates that from that time fishing for food in the fishing area was a significant part of the Mohawks' life. Further, where there is evidence that *at the point of contact* a practice was a significant part of a group's culture (in this case fishing for food in the fishing area) then the Aboriginal group will have demonstrated that the practice was a significant part of the Aboriginal group's culture prior to contact. No Aboriginal group will ever be able to provide conclusive evidence of what took place prior to contact (and here the witnesses agree that it is unclear which Aboriginal peoples were fishing in the fishing area prior to 1603); evidence that *at contact* a custom was a significant part of their distinctive culture should be sufficient to demonstrate that *prior to contact* that custom was also a significant part of their distinctive culture. The appellant here has clearly demonstrated that at the time of contact fishing in the St. Lawrence River and Lake St. Francis for food was a significant part of the life of the Mohawks. This is sufficient to demonstrate that it was so prior to contact.

47   As part of the second stage of the *Van der Peet* analysis, there must be "continuity" between Aboriginal practices, customs and traditions that existed prior to contact and a particular practice, custom or tradition that is integral to Aboriginal communities today: *Van der Peet, supra*, at para. 63; *Gladstone, supra*, at para. 28. This part of the *Van der Peet* test has been met as well. The evidence of numerous witnesses at the trial proves the existence of continuity. Francis Henry Lickers, a biologist, testified that according to the Mohawk, the practice of fishing had been going on for years and years. Reverend Thomas Eagan, a Jesuit Pastor at St. Regis, testified that before the establishment of the village of Akwesasne and while living at Akwesasne, the Mohawks used the area for hunting and

fishing. This was the way of life of their ancestors, and these practices continued into the present. Chief Lawrence Francis testified that hunting and fishing have been practised by the Mohawks since time immemorial, and that the practice of fishing has not been interrupted. It was no doubt this testimony which led Barrette Ct. S.P.J. to make the finding of fact at trial that the Mohawks had and had always exercised a right to fish on the St. Lawrence River and in particular on Lake St. Francis.

Extinguishment

48   Having accepted the appellant's claim that he was exercising an Aboriginal right to fish in the fishing area, the Court must now consider whether, prior to 1982, that right was extinguished. In *Sparrow, supra*, the Court held that in order for an Aboriginal right to be extinguished the Crown must demonstrate a "clear and plain intention" for such extinguishment. In this case, the Crown rests its argument that such an intention has been demonstrated on two events: the submersion of the lands constituting the fishing area in 1845 as part of the construction of the Beauharnois canal and the 1888 surrender agreement entered into between the Mohawks and the Crown in which the lands around the fishing area were surrendered to the Crown, in exchange for $50,000 in compensation.

49   While these events may be adequate to demonstrate a clear and plain intention in the Crown to extinguish any Aboriginal *title to the lands* of the fishing area, neither is sufficient to demonstrate that the Crown had the clear and plain intention of extinguishing the appellant's Aboriginal *right to fish for food* in the fishing area. The enlargement of the body of water on which the appellant has the Aboriginal right to fish for food does not relate to the existence of that right, let alone demonstrate a clear and plain intention to extinguish it. The surrender of lands, because of the fact that title to land is distinct from the right to fish in the waters adjacent to those lands, equally does not demonstrate a clear and plain intention to extinguish a right. The surrender agreement dealt only with the Mohawks proprietary interest to the lands in question; it did not deal with the freestanding aboriginal right to fish for food which existed in the waters adjacent to those lands. There is no evidence to suggest what the parties to the surrender agreement, including the Crown, intended with regards to the right of the Mohawks to fish in the area; absent such evidence the *Sparrow* test for extinguishment cannot be said to have been met.

Infringement and Justification

50   Given that the appellant was exercising an existing Aboriginal right to fish for food when he was fishing in Lake St. Francis, the next question this Court must address is whether s. 4(1) of the *Quebec Fishery Regulations* constituted an infringement of the appellant's Aboriginal rights and, if it did so, whether that infringement was justified. In order to answer this question the nature of the impact on the appellant's rights from the operation of the provision must be determined, taking into account the broader regulatory scheme of which the provision is a part.

51   The basic structure of the government's regulatory scheme, in terms of its application to the appellant, is as follows: under s. 4(1) of the *Regulations* fishing is prohibited absent a licence of the type described in Schedule III. Under Schedule III licences are available for sport and commercial fishing only; the Schedule does not allow for the issuance of licences for Aboriginal food fishing. Under s. 5(9) of the *Regulations* the Minister

may, at his discretion, issue a special permit to an Indian or Inuk authorizing them to fish for their own subsistence. In essence, under the regulatory scheme as it currently exists, the appellant's exercise of his Aboriginal right to fish for food is exercisable only at the discretion of the Minister.

52   This scheme infringes the Aboriginal rights of the appellant under the test for infringement laid out in *Sparrow*. In *Sparrow* the Court held at p. 1112 that to determine whether an Aboriginal right has been infringed the Court must consider the following questions:

> First, is the limitation unreasonable? Second, does the regulation impose undue hardship? Third, does the regulation deny to the holders of the right their preferred means of exercising that right?

In this instance, the regulatory scheme subjects the exercise of the appellant's Aboriginal rights to a pure act of Ministerial discretion, and sets out no criteria regarding how that discretion is to be exercised. For this reason, I find that the scheme both imposes undue hardship on the appellant and interferes with his preferred means of exercising his rights.

53   In a normal setting under the *Canadian Charter of Rights and Freedoms*, where a statute confers a broad, unstructured administrative discretion which may be exercised in a manner which encroaches upon a constitutional right, the court should not find that the delegated discretion infringes the *Charter* and then proceed to a consideration of the potential justifications of the infringement under s. 1. Rather, the proper judicial course is to find that the discretion must subsequently be exercised in a manner which accommodates the guarantees of the *Charter*. See *Slaight Communications Inc.* v. *Davidson*, [1989] 1 S.C.R. 1038, at pp. 1078–79; *R.* v. *Swain*, [1991] 1 S.C.R. 933, at pp. 1010–11; and *Schachter* v. *Canada*, [1992] 2 S.C.R. 679, at p. 720.

54   I am of the view that the same approach should not be adopted in identifying infringements under s. 35(1) of the *Constitution Act, 1982*. In light of the Crown's unique fiduciary obligations towards Aboriginal peoples, Parliament may not simply adopt an unstructured discretionary administrative regime which risks infringing Aboriginal rights in a substantial number of applications in the absence of some explicit guidance. If a statute confers an administrative discretion which may carry significant consequences for the exercise of an Aboriginal right, the statute or its delegate regulations must outline specific criteria for the granting or refusal of that discretion which seek to accommodate the existence of Aboriginal rights. In the absence of such specific guidance, the statute will fail to provide representatives of the Crown with sufficient directives to fulfil their fiduciary duties, and the statute will be found to represent an infringement of Aboriginal rights under the *Sparrow* test. . .

56   Moreover, the Crown has failed to adduce evidence sufficient to demonstrate that this infringement was justified. Under *Sparrow*, in order to demonstrate that an infringement of an Aboriginal right is justified the Crown must demonstrate, first, that the infringement took place pursuant to a compelling and substantial objective and that, second, the infringement is consistent with the Crown's fiduciary obligation to Aboriginal peoples. On the evidence presented in this case the Crown has satisfied neither of these criteria. I would note here, and adopt, the description of the Crown's evidence regarding the regulatory scheme given by Proulx J.A. at the Court of Appeal at pp. 127–28:

> [TRANSLATION] Far from proving that perch fishing for food would have harmful ecological

effects (the witness did not even know the incidence of sport fishing on conservation), the evidence tends instead to prove *the existence of a policy that essentially favours sport fishing, to the detriment of those wanting to fish for food.*

... [I]t appears to me that what has been shown instead in the case at bar is that sport fishing is the major concern, after conservation [emphasis added].

What counts as a compelling and substantial objective for the purposes of limiting s. 35(1) rights was recently discussed by this Court in *Gladstone*. The lack of evidence in that case precluded us from determining whether the government's regulatory scheme was justified. We therefore did not have to definitively determine what particular objectives, beyond conservation, do or do not meet the test of justification set out in *Sparrow*. Nevertheless, we made some general observations about the kinds of objectives which might be compelling and substantial enough to justify governmental infringements on Aboriginal rights.

57   As with limitations of the rights enshrined in the *Charter*, limits on the Aboriginal rights protected by s. 35(1) must be informed by the same purposes which underlie the decision to entrench those rights in the Constitution to be justifiable: *Gladstone, supra*, at para. 71. Those purposes are the recognition of the prior occupation of North America by Aboriginal peoples, and the reconciliation of prior occupation by Aboriginal peoples with the assertion of Crown sovereignty: *Van der Peet*, at para. 39, *Gladstone*, at para. 72. Measures which are aimed at conservation clearly accord with both these purposes, and can therefore serve to limit Aboriginal rights, as occurred in *Sparrow*.

58   I have some difficulty in accepting, in the circumstances of this case, that the enhancement of sports fishing *per se* is a compelling and substantial objective for the purposes of s. 35(1). While sports fishing is an important economic activity in some parts of the country, in this instance, there is no evidence that the sports fishing that this scheme sought to promote had a meaningful economic dimension to it. On its own, without this sort of evidence, the enhancement of sports fishing accords with neither of the purposes underlying the protection of Aboriginal rights, and cannot justify the infringement of those rights. It is not aimed at the recognition of distinct Aboriginal cultures. Nor is it aimed at the reconciliation of Aboriginal societies with the rest of Canadian society, since sports fishing, without evidence of a meaningful economic dimension, is not "of such overwhelming importance to Canadian society as a whole" (*Gladstone*, at para. 74) to warrant the limitation of Aboriginal rights.

59   Furthermore, the scheme does not meet the second leg of the test for justification, because it fails to provide the requisite priority to the Aboriginal right to fish for food, a requirement laid down by this Court in *Sparrow*. As we explained in *Gladstone*, the precise meaning of priority for Aboriginal fishing rights is in part a function of the nature of the right claimed. The right to fish for food, as opposed to the right to fish commercially, is a right which should be given first priority after conservation concerns are met. . .

60   In the result the appeal is allowed and the appellant's conviction is set aside.

61   For the reasons given above, the constitutional question must be answered as follows:

Question:
Is s. 4(1) of the *Quebec Fishery Regulations*, as they read on May 7, 1982, of no force or effect with respect to appellant in the circumstances of these proceedings in virtue of s. 52

of the *Constitution Act, 1982* by reason of the Aboriginal rights within the meaning of s. 35 of the *Constitution Act, 1982* invoked by appellant?

Answer:
Yes... .

SECTION 25

Canadian Charter of Rights and Freedoms, Section 25

General

25. The guarantee in this Charter of certain rights and freedoms shall not be construed so as to abrogate or derogate from any aboriginal, treaty or other rights or freedoms that pertain to the aboriginal peoples of Canada including
    (a) any rights or freedoms that have been recognized by the Royal Proclamation of October 7, 1763; and
    (b) any rights or freedoms that now exist by way of land claims agreements or may be so acquired....

A.-G. of Ontario v. *Bear Island Foundation*
[1985] 1 C.N.L.R. 1 at 85 (Ont. S.C.). Steele J., December 11, 1984

Section 25 of the *Constitution Act, 1982* provides that no guarantee of rights and freedoms set out in the Charter shall be construed so as to abrogate or derogate from any aboriginal, treaty or other rights that pertain to the aboriginal peoples of Canada, including any rights or freedoms that have been recognized by the Royal Proclamation and any rights or freedoms that may have been acquired by way of land claims settlements. Obviously, this section means that the rights and freedoms given generally to the people of Canada shall not be construed so as to override aboriginal rights. It has nothing to do with the question of what aboriginal and treaty rights are protected by the *Constitution Act, 1982*, that question being specifically dealt with in section 35. I cannot interpret section 25 to be a limitation upon what was dealt with in section 35. The Parliaments of the United Kingdom and Canada knew full well that many aboriginal rights that existed in 1763 had been interfered with over the centuries by the statutes and actions of the United Kingdom, Canada and Ontario. If the Parliaments had intended to reverse all of those encroachments and reinstate aboriginal rights to the state they were in when enjoyed in 1763, the Parliaments would have clearly said so, rather than inserting the word "existing" in the *Constitution Act, 1982*. The reference in section 25 cannot, by inference, move the clock back over 200 years, nor was it intended so to do.

SELECTED BIBLIOGRAPHY

Asch, M. & P. Macklem. "Aboriginal Rights and Canadian Sovereignty: An Essay on *R.* v. *Sparrow*" (1991) 26:2 Alta. L. Rev. 502.
Binnie, W.I.C. "The Sparrow Doctrine: Beginning of the End or End of the Beginning?" (1991) 15 Queen's L.J. 217.
Elliot, D.W. "In the Wake of Sparrow" (1991) 40 U.N.B.L.J. 23.

———. "Fifty Dollars of Fish: A Comment on *R.* v. *Van der Peet*" (1997) 35:3 Alta. L.R.

Gaffney, R.E., G.P. Gould & A.J. Semple. *Broken Promises: The Aboriginal Constitutional Conferences* (Fredericton: Association of Metis and Non-Status Indians, 1984).

Isaac, T. "The Meaning of Subsection 31(1) of the *Constitution Act, 1982*: A Comment on *Mitchell* v. *Min. of Nat. Rev.*" (November 2002) 60:6 The Advocate 853.

———. "Canadian Charter of Rights and Freedoms: The Challenge of the Individual and Collective Rights of Aboriginal People" (2003) 29:1 Win. Yrbk. Acc. Just.

———. "Individual Versus Collective Rights: Aboriginal People and the Significance of Thomas v. Norris" (1992) 21:3 Man. L.J. 618.

———. "The Honour of the Crown: Aboriginal Rights and the *Constitution Act, 1982*; The Significance of *R.* v. *Sparrow*" (1992) 13:1 Policy Options/Politiques 22.

———. "The *Constitution Act, 1982* and the Constitutionalization of Aboriginal Self-Government in Canada: The Cree-Naskapi (of Quebec) Act" [1991] 1 C.N.L.R. 1.

———. "Balancing Rights: The Supreme Court of Canada, *R.* v. *Sparrow*, and the Future of Aboriginal Rights" (1993) 13:2 Can. J. Nat. S. 1999.

———. "Understanding the *Sparrow* Decision" (1991) 16:2 Queen's L. J. 377.

Pentney, W. "The Rights of the Aboriginal Peoples of Canada and the Constitution Act, 1982; Part I: The Interpretive Prism of Section 25" (1988) 22:1 U.B.C. L. Rev. 21.

Scwartz, B. *First Principles, Second Thoughts: Aboriginal Peoples, Constitutional Reform and Canadian Statecraft* (Kingston: Institute for Intergovernmental Relations, Queen's University, 1985).

Slattery, B. "The Constitutional Guarantee of Aboriginal and Treaty Rights" (1983) 8 Queen's L.J. 232.

———. "First Nations and the Constitution: A Question of Trust" (1992) 71 Can. Bar Rev. 261.

Wildsmith, B. *Aboriginal Peoples and Section 25 of the Canadian Charter of Rights and Freedoms* (Saskatoon: University of Saskatchewan Native Law Centre, 1988).

Zlotkin, N. *Unfinished Business: Aboriginal Peoples and the 1983 Constitutional Conference* (Kingston: Institute of Intergovernmental Relations, Queen's University, 1983).

———. "The 1983 and 1984 Constitutional Conferences: Only the Beginning" [1984] 3 C.N.L.R. 3.

Chapter 7

SELF-GOVERNMENT

INTRODUCTION

"Aboriginal self-government" is an often-used term with as many meanings as there are Aboriginal groups in Canada. For some Aboriginal people "self-government" means sovereignty outside of Canada; for others it means a legislated and delegated form of government (Sechelt Indian Band); others use the term to describe constitutionally protected forms of Aboriginal governance such as those provided for in modern treaties like the 1999 Nisga'a Final Agreement.[1]

The concept of self-government has been an important national issue for Aboriginal people, particularly since the early 1980s. Some Aboriginal people have argued that they possess an "inherent right of self-government" and that this inherent right best expresses their self-governing aspirations. The "inherent" nature of the right of self-government is that such a right should not be based on any express constitutional provision or agreement, but rather inheres in Aboriginal peoples' residual sovereignty. The inherent right of self-government continues to be a focal point for many Aboriginal people as they pursue self-government negotiations. The inherent right of self-government took a central place in the constitutional process and self-government discussions during the 1992 round of constitutional discussions resulting in the proposed Charlottetown Accord. The Accord proposed the constitutional entrenchment of the inherent Aboriginal right of self-government and the recognition that Aboriginal governments comprise a distinct and separate order of government, alongside the federal and provincial governments, within Canada. The Royal Commission on Aboriginal Peoples (RCAP), in both its specific report on self-government and its general report, also focused a great deal on questions surrounding Aboriginal self-government.[2] For British Columbia, self-government remains a central issue in the treaty negotiations currently under way there.

DEFINING SELF-GOVERNMENT

Defining self-government presents legal and political difficulties. Federal and provincial governments fear its meaning could be expanded too broadly; Aboriginal people fear a restrictive interpretation. Nevertheless, all parties agree that "self-government" expresses the desire of Aboriginal people for control over their lives, for self-reliance, and for the accountability of their leadership to their own people and not to Parliament or the provincial or territorial legislatures.

There are also practical problems inherent in attempting to define an issue as complex

[1] Nisga'a Final Agreement (2000), c. 11; en. by the *Nisga'a Final Agreement Act*, S.C. 2000, c. 7.
[2] Royal Commission on Aboriginal Peoples, *Partners in Confederation: Aboriginal Peoples, Self-Government, and the Constitution* (Ottawa: Supply and Services Canada, 1993) and *Report of the Royal Commission on Aboriginal People* (Ottawa: Supply and Services Canada, 1996).

as governance. There are a number of different Aboriginal traditions and perspectives on the issue, and self-government will undoubtedly take on different political characteristics in a variety of distinct circumstances. For example, for the Inuit of Nunavut, who comprise approximately 85 percent of the population in that area, a territorial form of public government, complemented by distinct management boards established under the 1993 Nunavut Land Claims Agreement[3] has delivered to the Inuit a powerful form of self-government, albeit in the form of a public government.

The issue of governance goes beyond what is set out in a single document to accommodate the day-to-day realities of managing a society in a highly complex and interdependent world. Thus, although municipal governments in Canada are, strictly speaking, creatures of provincial legislation, they are for most Canadians an important and probably the most direct governing element in their daily lives. Similarly, many of the boards that exist in northern Canada as a result of several land claims agreements are not simply administrative structures but have the force of constitutionally recognized and affirmed land claims agreements behind them. These boards make decisions about such issues as renewable resources and water that affect the lives of many people and activities in Canada's North.[4]

The 1983 report of the House of Commons Special Committee on Self-Government (Penner Report)[5] recommended that

> full legislative and policy-making powers on matters affecting Indian people, and full control over the territory and resources within the boundaries of Indian lands, should be among the powers of Indian First Nation governments.[6]

Although the Penner Report recommended significant legislative authority for Aboriginal communities, it tempered its recommendations by stating that the "exact scope of jurisdiction should be decided by negotiation" and that the areas of jurisdiction "must be worked out through agreement."[7]

Governance is a broad concept, and cannot be determined by merely examining whether or not a government possesses jurisdictional authority. Governance could mean exclusive constitutionally protected legislative authority, or it may simply mean consulting a group regarding decisions that affect them. In between are numerous mechanisms that can achieve many governance aspirations, including the ability of a group of people to effect change and have control over their lives. Perhaps the real answer to the self-government question in Canada is not to look to a single model or to a single type of authority as forming the whole of self-government. Rather, perhaps what is needed is a broad-based approach that incorporates constitutional and delegated forms of government, complemented by appropriate co-management regimes.

Royal Commission on Aboriginal Peoples

In August 1993, RCAP released a report entitled *Partners in Confederation: Aboriginal Peoples, Self-Government, and the Constitution,*[8] which examined the argument that s. 35(1)

---

[3] Nunavut Land Claims Agreement (1993), en. by the *Nunavut Land Claims Agreement Act,* S.C. 1993, c. 29.
[4] For example, the Nunavut Land Claims Agreement established the Nunavut Wildlife Management Board (Art. 5.2), the Nunavut Planning Commission (Art. 11.4), the Nunavut Impact Review Board (Art. 12.2), and the Nunavut Water Board (Art. 13.2), among others.
[5] Canada, House of Commons, Report of the Special Committee on Indian Self-Government, *Indian Self-Government in Canada* (Ottawa: Queen's Printer, 1983) (Chairman: Keith Penner).
[6] *Ibid.* at 64.
[7] *Ibid.*
[8] RCAP, *Partners, supra* note 2; For commentary, see C. Bell, "Comments on Partners in Confederation: A

of the *Constitution Act, 1982*[9] contains an existing right of self-government and that there-fore the right of self-government does not require any explicit constitutional recognition. RCAP argued that the inherent right of self-government is recognized by both federal constitutional common law and by s. 35 of the *Constitution Act, 1982* and stated that although the right is inherent in its origin, it is, nevertheless, a right held under Canadian law. This means that it can be exercised only within the "framework of Confederation." RCAP proposed that the inherent right could be implemented immediately (in certain core areas) by Aboriginal governments without either court action or self-government agreements. However, like the courts, RCAP singled out negotiation as probably being the best means of implementing the right. RCAP suggested that a "middle path" would be more appropriate, whereby the right of self-government would be viewed "organi-cally." RCAP used the term "organic" to mean something that is not static but is, rather, flexible and capable of growing in clarity and substance.

The organic model of self-government affirms that Aboriginal governments retain the right to exercise jurisdiction over certain "core subject areas" on a defined land base. Such core subject areas would include matters vital to the life and welfare of a community that do not have a major effect on adjacent jurisdictions or communities. The outer limits of Aboriginal jurisdiction within the inherent right would be governed by three guiding principles:

1. Aboriginal governments would hold the same jurisdiction now held by Parliament under s. 91(24) of the *Constitution Act, 1867*;[10]

2. Where conflict arises between federal and Aboriginal laws, Aboriginal laws would prevail, except where the federal laws meet the justificatory analysis addressed in *R. v. Sparrow*;[11] and

3. The interaction between Aboriginal and provincial laws would be regulated by the rules that govern the relationship between federal and provincial legislation.

RCAP's argument could be interpreted to mean that Aboriginal governments possess a large part of federal and provincial jurisdiction, which would fundamentally alter the existing division of powers in Canada between the federal and provincial governments. Determining the scope of the "outer limits" of Aboriginal jurisdiction would require the establishment of a dispute-resolution mechanism to ensure the principles of negotiation were maintained. Even if that were done, decisions of the Supreme Court of Canada and several Court of Appeal decisions respecting the meaning of s. 35(1) make it appear un-likely that s. 35(1) protects the type of "inherent right of self-government" envisioned by RCAP.

In late 1996, RCAP released its comprehensive report on self-government.[12] The rec-ommendations made by RCAP are many, but of particular interest is the summary of recommendations found in volume 5.

Report on Self-Government by the Royal Commission on Aboriginal Peoples" (1993) 27:2 U.B.C. Law Rev. 361.
[9] *Constitution Act, 1982*, Schedule B to the *Canada Act 1982* (U.K.), 1982, c. 11, as am. by the *Constitution Amendment Proclamation 1983*, R.S.C. 1985, App. II, No. 46, adding ss. 35(3) and 35(4).
[10] *Constitution Act, 1867* (U.K.), 30 & 31 Vict., c. 3, reprinted in R.S.C. 1985, App. II, No. 5.
[11] *R. v. Sparrow*, [1990] 1 S.C.R. 1075.
[12] *Report on the Royal Commission on Aboriginal Peoples, supra* note 2. The report comprises more than three thousand pages in five volumes focusing on land, governance, treaties, history generally, women's issues, elders and youth, Métis, and off-reserve Indians.

SOURCE OF SELF-GOVERNMENT

The debate surrounding the source of the right of self-government centres around two questions: where does the right of self-government originate, and has it been extinguished? The Supreme Court of Canada appears to support the view that Aboriginal governments historically were self-governing. In *R. v. Sioui*,[13] the Court cited with approval the following passage from the United States Supreme Court decision of *Worcester* v. *Georgia*:[14]

> Such was the policy of Great Britain towards the Indian nations inhabiting the territory from which she excluded all other Europeans; such her claims, and such her practical exposition of the charters she had granted: *she considered them as nations capable of maintaining the relations of peace and war; of governing themselves, under her protection; and she made treaties with them, the obligation of which she acknowledged.*[15] [Emphasis by Lamer J.]

This passage affirms the view that Aboriginal governments were historically seen as, at the least, semi-sovereign entities capable of governing their internal affairs. The Supreme Court of Canada also offered favourable comments regarding Aboriginal autonomy in *Sioui*: "The British Crown recognized that the Indians had certain ownership rights over their land. . . . It also allowed them autonomy in their internal affairs, intervening in this area as little as possible."[16]

Some argue[17] that an inherent right of self-government exists at common law and has been constitutionally recognized and affirmed in s. 35(1). Others maintain that the inherent right of self-government, strictly defined, has been extinguished, although it existed at one time. Although the courts have acknowledged some historical degree of sovereignty enjoyed by Aboriginal people, the Supreme Court of Canada seems clear on its views of Aboriginal self-government and Canadian sovereignty. In *Sparrow*, the Supreme Court of Canada stated:

> [T]here was from the outset never any doubt that sovereignty and legislative power, and indeed the underlying title, to such lands vested in the Crown. . . . Rights that are recognized and affirmed are not absolute. Federal legislative powers continue, including, of course, the right to legislate with respect to Indians pursuant to s.91(24).[18]

Subsection 35(1) does not create new Aboriginal or treaty rights. Brian Slattery has stated that these rights are held by Aboriginal people ". . . by reason of the fact that aboriginal peoples were once independent, self-governing entities in possession of most of the lands now making up Canada."[19] In *Mitchell* v. *Peguis Indian Band*,[20] La Forest J. of the Supreme Court of Canada stated:

> The historical record leaves no doubt that native peoples acknowledged the ultimate sover-

---

[13] *R. v. Sioui*, [1990] 1 S.C.R. 1025.

[14] *Worcester* v. *Georgia* (1832), 6 Peters 515 (U.S.S.C.), at 548–49.

[15] *Sioui, supra* note 13 at 1053–54.

[16] *Ibid.* at 1055.

[17] Bruce Clark, *Native Liberty, Crown Sovereignty* (Montreal & Kingston: McGill-Queen's University Press, 1990). Also see Michael Asch, "Aboriginal Self-Government and the Construction of Canadian Constitutional Identity" (1992) 30:2 Alta. L. Rev. 456; Patrick Macklem, "First Nations, Self-Government and the Borders of the Canadian Legal Imagination" (1991) 36 McGill L.J. 382; S. Nakatsuru, "A Constitutional Right of Indian Self-Government" (1985) 43 U.T. Fac. L. Rev. 72; RCAP, *Partners, supra* note 2; and Thomas Isaac, "The Storm Over Aboriginal Self-Government: Section 35 of the *Constitution Act, 1982* and the Redefinition of the Inherent Right of Aboriginal Self-Government," [1992] 2 C.N.L.R. 6.

[18] *Sparrow, supra* note 11 at 1103, 1109.

[19] Brian Slattery, "The Constitutional Guarantee of Aboriginal and Treaty Rights" (1983) 8 Queen's L.J. 232 at 242.

[20] *Mitchell* v. *Peguis Indian Band*, [1990] 2 S.C.R. 85.

eignty of the British Crown, and agreed to cede their traditional homelands on the understanding that the Crown would thereafter protect them in the possession and use of such lands as were reserved for their use.[21]

Thus, self-government, at least within the existing constitutional framework, means something other than possession of the underlying title of Aboriginal lands in Canada and means something other than the sovereignty now exercised by Parliament and provincial, and to a lesser degree, territorial legislatures.

If the right of self-government is inherent, a constitutional arrangement, such as the Charlottetown Accord, may be unnecessary to the extent that the right of self-government is already recognized and not contingent upon federal, provincial, or territorial recognition. However, if the right of self-government is contingent—that is, if it depends upon some form of recognition by the federal, provincial, and territorial governments or the courts for its existence—then the right may be subject to considerable limitations. The distinction between the two approaches signifies a fundamental element in the debate over self-government.

Sparrow contains several important principles respecting Aboriginal rights and assists in understanding the relationship between Aboriginal rights and an inherent right of self-government. For example, the Supreme Court of Canada speaks of a "flexible interpretation" of Aboriginal rights so as to permit their "evolution." This is further supported by the purposive approach adopted by the Court, which calls for a liberal and generous interpretation of Aboriginal rights. The affirmation of the principles in *R. v. Nowegijick*[22] that treaties and statutes relating to Indians be construed in favour of Indians also supports the position that Aboriginal people possess some degree of internal sovereignty.

In *Sparrow,* the Supreme Court of Canada noted that sovereignty and underlying title to the land vests in the Crown. However, the issue of underlying title may not necessarily rule out a favourable interpretation from the Court in the future on internal Aboriginal sovereignty on reserve and other Aboriginal lands over distinct areas of jurisdiction.

JUDICIAL COMMENTARY

Although there are now a number of Supreme Court of Canada decisions dealing directly with s. 35(1), such as *Sparrow, R. v. Van der Peet,*[23] *R. v. Adams,*[24] *R. v. Pamajewon,*[25] *Delgamuukw* v. *B.C.,*[26] and *R. v. Marshall,*[27] there is a general lack of substantive judicial commentary dealing with Aboriginal self-government. These decisions speak only to the regulation of rights and the means of dealing with s. 35 generally. They do not deal with ongoing relationships between Aboriginal governments and the federal, provincial, and territorial governments. *Sparrow,*[28] *Delgamuukw,*[29] and *R. v. Marshall* (reconsideration)[30] do, however, clearly state that negotiations are the best way of resolving the broader issue of Aboriginal rights generally, including self-government arrangements.

---

[21] *Ibid.* at 130.
[22] *R. v. Nowegijick,* [1983] 1 S.C.R. 29.
[23] *R. v. Van der Peet,* [1996] 2 S.C.R. 507.
[24] *R. v. Adams,* [1996] 3 S.C.R. 101.
[25] *R. v. Pamajewon,* [1996] 2 S.C.R. 821.
[26] *Delgamuukw* v. *B.C.,* [1997] 3 S.C.R. 1010.
[27] *R.* v. *Marshall,* [1999] 3 S.C.R. 456.
[28] *Sparrow, supra* note 11 at 1105.
[29] *Delgamuukw, supra* note 26 at paras. 186, 207.
[30] *R. v. Marshall* (reconsideration), [1999] 3 S.C.R. 533 at para. 22.

Delgamuukw v. *B.C.*

In *Delgamuukw*,[31] the British Columbia Court of Appeal considered the application of Gitksan and Wet'suwet'en hereditary chiefs for a declaration affirming their ownership of approximately 57,000 square kilometres of British Columbia, including their right to govern their traditional territory and to receive compensation for the loss of land and resources. In 1993, the Court of Appeal overturned a considerable portion of the earlier lower court decision and held that the Gitksan and Wet'suwet'en peoples possess unextinguished nonexclusive Aboriginal rights, other than a right of ownership, over much of their traditional territory. On the issue of self-government, Macfarlane J.A. stated:

> [T]here is no question the Gitksan and Wet'suwet'en people had an organized society. It is pointless to argue that such a society was without traditions, rules and regulations. Insofar as those continue to exist there is no reason why those traditions may not continue so long as members of the Indian community agree to adhere to them. But those traditions, rules, and regulations cannot operate if they are in conflict with the laws of the Province or of Canada. In 1871, when British Columbia joined Confederation, legislative power was divided between Canada and the provinces. The division exhausted the source of such power. Any form of Indian self-government, then existing, was superseded by the *Constitution Act, 1867*, as adopted by the Province in 1871.[32]

Lambert J.A. in his dissenting judgment concluded:

> I would declare that the present Aboriginal rights of self-government and self-regulation of the Gitksan and Wet'suwet'en peoples, would include rights of self-government and self-regulation exercisable through their own institutions to preserve and enhance their social, political, cultural, linguistic and spiritual identity.[33]

Macfarlane J.A.'s majority judgment likely represents the prevailing views, including the Supreme Court of Canada, on the issue of whether Aboriginal people have retained a right of self-government. Only a decision by the Supreme Court of Canada on self-government specifically will settle this ambiguity. (The Court did not deal with self-government in its 1997 decision of *Delgamuukw*.) Lambert J.A.'s judgment can be read restrictively in that self-government and self-regulation are exercisable only to "preserve and enhance" the identity of Aboriginal people. It remains to be seen whether self-government and self-regulation could include legislative authority akin to that held by the provinces or Parliament. To date, the courts have not dealt substantively or convincingly with whether, and to what extent, the right of self-government is extinguished. However, in *R. v. Williams*,[34] the British Columbia Court of Appeal agreed with the trial court decision that any possibility that Aboriginal self-government authority remained unextinguished was terminated by the British Columbia Terms of Union of 1871[35] and by the *Constitution Act, 1867*, wherein all legislative powers were divided between the federal and provincial governments. The fact that Indians are subjects of the Crown either by treaty[36] or otherwise[37] sets a limiting context within which self-government could exist, by means other than negotiated agreements, in Canada.

---

[31] *Delgamuukw* v. *B.C.*, [1993] 5 C.N.L.R. (B.C.C.A.).

[32] *Ibid.* at 76.

[33] *Ibid.* at 250.

[34] *R.* v. *Williams*, [1995] 2 C.N.L.R. 229 (B.C.C.A.).

[35] *British Columbia Terms of Union*, R.S.C. 1985, App. II, No. 10.

[36] See *Logan* v. *Styres* (1959), 20 D.L.R. (2d) 416 (Ont. H.C.).

[37] See *Pawis* v. *R.*, [1979] 2 C.N.L.R. 52 (F.C.T.D.).

R. v. Pamajewon (1996)

In *Pamajewon*,[38] the Supreme Court of Canada affirmed the Ontario Court of Appeal's convictions of a number of Aboriginal people under the *Criminal Code of Canada*[39] concerning charges related to illegal gaming activities. The Supreme Court affirmed a number of principles that are useful in exploring how courts may interpret an Aboriginal right of self-government. First, assuming that s. 35(1) may encompass a right of self-government, the claim of such a right is no different from any other claim for an Aboriginal right under s. 35(1) and must therefore be held to the same legal standard (such as that laid out in *Van der Peet* and presumably other relevant tests such as *Sparrow*).

In *Pamajewon*, the appellants claimed the right to operate casinos and regulate high-stakes gambling on reserve, describing this as a "broad right to manage the use of their reserve lands."[40] The Court noted that this right is not specific enough for the *Van der Peet* test, which requires that the asserted right must be examined in light of the specific history and culture of the Aboriginal group claiming the right, having regard to the specific circumstances of the case. This position was reaffirmed by the Supreme Court in its decision in *Delgamuukw*,[41] wherein Lamer C.J. noted "rights to self-government, if they existed, cannot be framed in excessively general terms."[42] Second, the Court held that based on the evidence presented, high-stakes gambling was not an activity that formed an integral part of the distinctive cultures of the Shawanaga and Eagle Lake First Nations. The Court focused on the need for specificity in analyzing any Aboriginal right to self-government, if such a right exists within the rubric of s. 35(1). The onus to demonstrate this level of specificity is placed on the Aboriginal group claiming such a right.

Campbell v. B.C.

In *Campbell* v. *B.C.*,[43] the British Columbia Supreme Court considered an application seeking an order that the Nisga'a Final Agreement[44] is, in part, inconsistent with Constitution of Canada and therefore, in part, of no force or effect. The applicant argued that the agreement was inconsistent because it purports to bestow upon the governing body of the Nisga'a Nation legislative authority inconsistent with the division of powers granted to Parliament and the legislative assemblies of the provinces by ss. 91 and 92 of the *Constitution Act, 1867*. The Court held that the assertion of sovereignty by the British Crown did not necessarily extinguish the right of Aboriginal people to govern themselves. Any Aboriginal right to self-government could be extinguished after Confederation and before 1982 by federal legislation or it could be replaced or modified by the negotiation of a treaty. Post-1982, such rights could not be extinguished, but may be defined and given meaning by way of a treaty.

The Court held that the Nisga'a Final Agreement defined the content of Aboriginal self-government expressly. The *Constitution Act, 1867* did not distribute all legislative power to Parliament and the provincial Legislatures. The *Constitution Act, 1867* did not purport to and does not end what remains of the royal prerogative or Aboriginal and treaty rights, including the diminished but not extinguished power of self-government

---

[38] *Pamajewon, supra* note 25.
[39] *Criminal Code of Canada*, R.S.C. 1985, c. C-46.
[40] *Pamajewon, supra* note 25 at para. 27.
[41] *Delgamuukw, supra* note 26.
[42] *Ibid.* at para. 170.
[43] *Campbell* v. *B.C. (A.G.)*, [2000] 4 C.N.L.R. 1 (B.C.S.C.).
[44] *NFA, supra* note 1.

which remained with the Nisga'a in 1982. Section 35 of the *Constitution Act, 1982* recognized and affirmed a constitutionally limited form of self-government that remained with the Nisga'a after the assertion of sovereignty; the Nisga'a Final Agreement and settlement legislation give that limited right definition. The Nisga'a government is subject both to the limitations set out in the Nisga'a Final Agreement itself and to the limited guarantee of the rights recognized and affirmed by s. 35 of the *Constitution Act, 1982.*

Based on the jurisprudence to date, it seems clear that there will not be legal recognition of a general overriding right of self-government. Rather, if the right exists at all, the Supreme Court of Canada seems focused on limiting that right to specific activities of governance, as it has done with other Aboriginal rights. Neither is the overarching supremacy of Canadian sovereignty generally being questioned by the courts. Demonstrating the substantive right of self-government envisioned by many Indian bands and Aboriginal people in Canada will be subject to a high standard in the legal system. Like treaty-making, discussed in chapter 2, negotiation is probably the best means for Aboriginal people to achieve self-government.

THE GOVERNMENT OF CANADA'S INHERENT RIGHT OF SELF-GOVERNMENT POLICY

In 1995, the Government of Canada released its policy guide and approach to implementing the inherent right of self-government in Canada.[45] The policy was first outlined in the Liberals' 1993 election platform, *Creating Opportunity: The Liberal Plan for Canada* (the "Red Book"), and it articulates the government's commitment to recognizing "the inherent right of self-government as an existing right within s. 35 of the *Constitution Act, 1982.*"[46]

The guide emphasizes the Government's preference for negotiation over litigation, which it indicates should be the last resort in sorting out the issue of self-government. The guide states that any Aboriginal governments or institutions exercising the inherent right of self-government will do so within the framework of the Constitution of Canada, and that Aboriginal laws, jurisdictions, and authorities should work harmoniously with the powers exercised by other governments in Canada. The *Canadian Charter of Rights and Freedoms*[47] will apply to Aboriginal governments and their institutions. A "cookie-cutter" or "one-size-fits-all" approach to self-government will not work in Canada. Rather, negotiations must proceed within a generally agreed upon framework but must allow for case-by-case circumstances to be considered.

The guide further states that Aboriginal governments could be responsible for matters such as: internal constitutions and governing structures, membership, marriage, adoption[48] and child welfare, education,[49] health, social services, enforcement of Aboriginal laws and policing, property rights, natural resources management, agriculture, hunting, fishing, and trapping on Aboriginal lands, direct taxation and property taxes of Aboriginal governments' members, housing, local transportation, and the licensing of businesses. The government's position is based on the premise that Aboriginal jurisdiction extends to

---

[45] *Federal Policy Guide: Aboriginal Self-Government* (Ottawa: Minister of Public Works and Government Services Canada, 1995).

[46] *Creating Opportunity: The Liberal Plan for Canada* (1993) 1.

[47] *Canadian Charter of Rights and Freedoms,* Part I of the *Constitution Act, 1982, supra* note 9.

[48] The Northwest Territories has recognized Aboriginal customary adoptions in the *Aboriginal Custom Adoption Recognition Act*, S.N.W.T. 1994, c. 26.

[49] See the *Mi'Kmaq Education Act*, S.C. 1998, c. 24.

matters that are "internal to the group, integral to its distinct Aboriginal culture, and essential to its operation as a government or institution."[50] However, the degree of authority to be held by Aboriginal governments over these areas is unclear. This is especially true since most of the areas of jurisdiction "on the table" are provincial in nature.

Primary law-making authority would remain with the federal and provincial governments with respect to matters such as divorce, labour and training, administration of justice, penitentiaries and parole, environmental protection and assessment, fisheries and migratory birds co-management, gaming, and emergency preparedness. The federal government would be willing to negotiate only some degree of Aboriginal involvement in these areas because these areas of jurisdiction may go beyond matters that are integral to an Aboriginal culture. Finally, there are matters that are not on the table for negotiation with Aboriginal governments. These include areas related to Canadian sovereignty, defence and external relations, currency, criminal law, aeronautics, the postal service, and navigation and shipping.

Although formal federal acknowledgement of the right of Aboriginal people to govern themselves was a watershed, by itself the policy has little weight. The real test will come at the negotiating table.

The vast majority of the issues that the federal government has put on the table are provincial and territorial in nature. Most of the core federal powers are not open to negotiation and the provincial and territorial governments may well be unwilling to discuss these areas of jurisdiction. This underscores how important it is for the federal, provincial, and territorial governments to work together if the issue of Aboriginal governance is to be settled. Without cooperation between the public governments in Canada, many Aboriginal governments will continue to find themselves squeezed out by the respective interests being brought to the table by non-Aboriginal governments.

Politics aside, a central test for the policy will be a financial one. Although the federal government stresses that provincial and territorial governments must share the financial burden of making the policy work, it is the federal government that will be responsible for establishing financing mechanisms for Aboriginal people that serve the country as a whole. As provincial and territorial transfer payments continue to be reduced by Ottawa, the pressure on Ottawa by the territorial and provincial governments to deal with the Aboriginal financing issue will mount. Without federal leadership on the financing issue, the likelihood of success on the issue of self-government is low.

An example of how the lack of appropriate fiscal resources directly affects the ability of Aboriginal governments to exercise their authority, at whatever level or in whatever form, can be found in the Naskapi Band's presentation to the Cree-Naskapi Commission regarding the implementation of the *Cree-Naskapi (of Quebec) Act*[51] in northern Quebec. The Naskapi Band stated that it was "reluctant to adopt certain by-laws in the knowledge that the Band has no funds budgeted for the costs of prosecuting offenders under those by-laws."[52] The Mistassini Band noted, in the same process:

> A related problem to this incredible lack of the basic elements of a viable justice system is our inability to properly and fully enforce our by-laws. Without the ability to enforce our by-laws, the powers and rights granted under the Act are rendered nugatory.[53]

[50] *Creating Opportunity, supra* note 46 at 5.
[51] *Cree-Naskapi (of Quebec) Act (CNA)*, S.C. 1984, c. 46.
[52] Cree-Naskapi Commission, Special Hearing on Implementation of the *Cree-Naskapi (of Quebec) Act* (Hull: 28 October 1986), 218.
[53] *Ibid.*, 29 October 1986, p. 31.

IMPLEMENTING SELF-GOVERNMENT

A number of examples of self-government exist in Canada today. Since it was created in 1999, Nunavut has provided the eastern Arctic with a public government that is predominately populated by Inuit. The Métis Settlements of Alberta have their own legislative base and have been governing themselves successfully for many years. Although riddled with problems, the *Indian Act*[54] provides for a system of Indian band governance, including governance by custom. The Sechelt Band of British Columbia, the Cree and Naskapi Bands of northern Quebec, and eight Yukon First Nations have federal legislation and agreements that guide their governance. Finally, the Nisga'a Final Agreement, signed in 1999, provides for a form of self-government, with a land base, that forms part of a constitutionally recognized and affirmed treaty in British Columbia.

On July 26, 2003, the Governments of Canada and British Columbia and the Lheidli T'enneh First Nation, which has approximately three hundred members, signed an agreement in principle under the British Columbia treaty process. The agreement in principle provides for a governance agreement, but this and any final agreement will not alter federal and provincial laws continuing to apply to the Lheidli T'enneh First Nation. The Lheidli T'enneh's law-making authority will be concurrent with federal and provincial authority. The governance agreement will not form part of the final agreement and will, therefore, likely not receive the constitutional recognition afforded to any final agreement under s. 35(1).

On April 16, 2003 the Gwich'in Tribal Council, the Inuvialuit Regional Corporation, and the Governments of Canada and the Northwest Territories signed the Gwich'in and Inuvialuit Self-government Agreement-in-Principle. The agreement in principle contains twenty-nine chapters and provides for new law-making and administrative powers for new and restructured governments in the Beaufort-Delta region, including community governments (Aboriginal and public combined), Inuvialuit government, Gwich'in government, and a regional government. The AIP is a step to fulfil the commitment to negotiate self-government arising from the 1984 Inuvialuit Final Agreement and the 1992 Gwich'in Comprehensive Land Claim Agreement.

On August 25, 2003, the Dogrib Treaty 11 Council, and the Governments of Canada and the Northwest Territories signed the Tlicho Agreement. The agreement is the first combined land claim and self-government comprehensive land claim agreement in the Northwest Territories. The agreement created a Tlicho Government which will have the authority to enact laws in relation to its governance structure, Tlicho lands, the protection of the Tlicho language and culture, the practice of traditional medicine, heritage resources on Tlicho lands, adoption of Tlicho children by a Tlicho citizen, education, wills and estates of Tlicho citizens, and child and family services, among other areas.[55] The Government of the Northwest Territories will establish "core principles" respecting such areas as social assistance and child and family services; Tlicho Government standards in such areas must be "compatible" with these core principles. With respect to conflicts between the laws of the Tlicho Government and those of Canada and the Northwest Territories, Canada's laws prevail, whereas those of the Northwest Territories do not.[56]

---

[54] *Indian Act*, R.S.C. 1985, c. I-5.
[55] See chapter 7 of the Tlicho Agreement.
[56] See chapter 8 of the Tlicho Agreement.

Indian Act

Indian band councils, which are the legal delegated governing bodies constituted under the *Indian Act*, carry out four basic functions, as acknowledged in *Whitebear Indian Council v. Carpenter's Provincial Council of Saskatchewan*:[57] (1) municipal government, (2) acting as an agent of the Minister of the Department of Indian Affairs and Northern Development, (3) acting as an instrument of communication between the band members and other governments, and (4) acting in an advisory capacity to the Minister.[58] Sections 81, 83, and 85.1 of the Act constitute the by-law–making authority of Indian band councils. Section 81 states that a band council may make by-laws for a variety of purposes so long as the by-laws are not inconsistent with the Act or any regulation made by the Minister or by the Governor in Council.

The courts have interpreted s. 81 of the Act to mean that band by-laws have no effect outside of the reserve,[59] just as municipal by-laws have no effect outside of a municipality. In many ways, the powers conferred under s. 81 of the Act resemble those of a municipality. In *Re Stacey and Montour* (1982),[60] the Quebec Court of Appeal stated:

> [Section 81 powers are] powers to regulate, and to regulate only "administrative statutes". In other words, a band council has, in this area, the same sort of legislative powers as those possessed by the council of a municipal corporation.

Subsection 82(2) allows the Minister to disallow any bylaw made pursuant to s. 81. The Minister is not required to give reasons for the disallowance and is not required to give notice to the band that a by-law is disallowed.[61] Section 83 of the Act confers, subject to the approval of the Minister, the power to make by-laws relating to taxation for local purposes, licensing of businesses, appointment of officials to conduct business, remunerating chief and council in such amounts as are approved by the Minister, enforcement of payment of amounts duly raised, raising of money from band members to support band projects, and any ancillary matters arising out of this section. Section 85.1 of the Act permits band councils to make by-laws relating to the prohibition of the sale, barter, supply, or manufacturing of intoxicants on the reserve.

Regardless of the limited authority that the *Indian Act* confers on band councils, the legislation is still essentially paternalistic in that the Minister can disallow any by-law and the fundamental purpose of the Act remains to control Indians. The federal Department of Indian Affairs and Northern Development ("DIAND") has delegated some of its authority, but even these

> delegated federal powers under the *Indian Act* are not a path to full Indian government as much as they are a path leading towards bands and tribal councils increasing their capacity to implement INAC programs, which are designed and funded in a centralized fashion and are based on principles that deny the essential spirit of Indian government.[62]

For most Aboriginal governments, control over service delivery is not enough to meet their aspirations for self-government. In addition, they want the authority to determine

---

[57] *Whitebear Indian Council* v. *Carpenter's Provincial Council of Saskatchewan*, [1982] 3 C.N.L.R. 181 (Sask. C.A.).
[58] *Ibid.* at 186.
[59] *R.* v. *Sam*, [1986] 1 C.N.L.R. 129 (B.C. Prov. Ct.).
[60] *Re Stacey and Montour*, [1982] 3 C.N.L.R. 158 (Que. C.A.) at 166.
[61] See *Twinn* v. *Canada (Minister of Indian Affairs and Northern Development)*, [1988] 1 C.N.L.R. 159 (F.C.T.D.).
[62] Frank Cassidy and Robert Bish, *Indian Government: Its Meaning in Practice* (Montreal: The Institute for Research on Public Policy, 1989) 50.

the substance of the programs they deliver to their people. They want autonomous legislative and jurisdictional authority. The *Indian Act* severely restricts the ability of Indians to manage their own affairs and to determine their destiny. The Act is paternalistic and remains the single largest impediment to Aboriginal self-government and Aboriginal social and economic development.

Possession and allocation of reserve lands are important components to an Aboriginal governance regime and presently involve a large degree of ministerial authority. The band council must seek ministerial approval in order to allocate land, and the Minister has the final authority to secure possession of reserve land. Moreover, the power of the band council to manage reserves and surrendered or designated lands under ss. 53–60 of the *Indian Act* is delegated by the Minister to the band council. The same is true for the authority of the band council to manage Indian moneys.

In addition to the ministerial powers, the *Indian Act* provides for a wide range of regulatory powers held by the Governor in Council. Section 73 of the Act contains a lengthy list of regulations that can be enacted by the Governor in Council. Note that these regulations supersede a band by-law passed by a band council pursuant to s. 81 of the Act.

Some modest attempts have been made by Indian and Northern Affairs Canada to limit the control of the *Indian Act* over communities. For example, the 1994 Manitoba Framework Agreement provides for a ten-year process to dismantle the department's regional presence in Manitoba and transfer its responsibilities to Indian bands in that province. As well, the department has proposed extensive changes to modernize the *Indian Act* with the *First Nations Governance Act*.[63]

Legal Status of Indian Band Councils

The precise legal status of Indian bands remains unclear. Some cases suggest that a band is neither a legal person nor a corporation; other cases suggest a more liberal approach.[64] Bill C-61, the *First Nations Governance Act*, proposed to clarify this by expressly providing that band councils are natural persons and are capable of entering into contracts, being sued, and other related functions.[65]

At present, Indian band councils are distinct entities; they are capable of being sued[66] and have been found to be similar to municipal forms of government.[67] In *Tawich Development Corporation* v. *Que. (D.M. of Revenue)*,[68] the Quebec Court of Appeal affirmed a lower court decision that held that the Wemindji Band was not a municipality for the purpose of s. 985 of Quebec's *Taxation Act*.[69] Although the Wemindji Band was consti-

---

[63] *First Nations Governance Act*, (2002), Bill C-61, s. 15.

[64] *R. v. Cochrane*, [1997] 3 W.W.R. 660 (Man. Co. Ct.), and *R. v. Peter Ballantyne Band*, [1987] 1 C.N.L.R. 67 (Sask. Q.B.), held that a band is neither a natural nor a legal person and is not a corporation. However, some recent cases have held that a band can sue and be sued and is a legal entity with legal rights and obligations, notwithstanding that it may not be a "legal person." See *Springhill Lumber Ltd.* v. *Lake St. Martin Indian Band*, [1986] 2 C.N.L.R. 179 (Man. Q.B.), and *Clow Darling Ltd.* v. *Big Trout Lake Band of Indians*, [1990] 4 C.N.L.R. 7 (Ont. Dist. Ct.).

[65] *Supra* note 63.

[66] *Kucey* v. *Peter Ballantyne Band Council*, [1987] 3 C.N.L.R. 68 (Sask. C.A.).

[67] *Isolation Sept-Iles Inc.* c. *Montagnais de Sep-Iles ef Maliotenam*, [1989] 2 C.N.L.R. 49 (Que. Sup. Ct.). The delegated nature of an Indian band council's authority was discussed in *Mohawks of the (Bay of Quinte) Tyendincga Mohawk Territory (Re)*, [2001] 1 C.N.L.R. 195 (Can. Indust. Rels. Bd.) at paras. 28–29.

[68] *Tawich Development Corporation* v. *Que. (D.M. of Revenue)*, [2000] 3 C.N.L.R. 383 (Que. C.A.).

[69] *Taxation Act*, R.S.Q. c. I-3.

tuted as an incorporated local government pursuant to the *Cree-Naskapi (of Quebec) Act*,[70] nowhere does the *Cree-Naskapi (of Quebec) Act* constitute an Indian band as a municipal corporation. The Court concluded that a municipality cannot be constituted by judicial means.

In *Canadian Pacific Ltd. v. Matsqui Indian Band*,[71] Marceau J.A. of the Federal Court of Appeal stated the following with respect to the difference between an Indian band and a municipality, within the context of taxation authority:

> [I]t appears to me quite inappropriate to apply to Indian Bands' new by-law powers the principles of interpretation developed in municipal law. There is a big difference between municipalities and Indian Bands in that the existence of the Indian groupings is not like that of municipal units, wholly dependant on an act of Government authority, and the rationale behind the granting of taxation powers to both such bodies is clearly not the same. The devolved taxation powers of municipalities exists, to my mind, only to further governmental objectives of efficiency in operation and administration. The recent granting of taxation powers to Indian Bands has a much broader and humane objective, which can only be seen in the context of furthering the ability of natives to govern themselves and thus, to a certain extent, invokes rights and responsibilities that predate all Indian Acts. It would be wrong, in my view, to subject both sets of rules to the same standard of inflexibility, rigidity and limitation.[72]

Cree Naskapi (of Quebec) Act

One of the earliest modern examples of negotiated self-government is the *Cree-Naskapi (of Quebec) Act*, enacted in 1984.[73] The *Cree-Naskapi (of Quebec) Act* resulted from the 1975 James Bay and Northern Quebec Agreement,[74] which permitted the Quebec government to proceed with the James Bay hydroelectric project. In return for ceding most of their land, the Cree, Inuit, and subsequently the Naskapi received certain environmental, land-use, and government rights. For the purposes of this chapter, the most notable provision of the agreement is outlined in s. 9.0.1. It imposed an obligation on Parliament to enact legislation providing for local government for the Cree, and subsequently the Naskapi.[75] The *Cree-Naskapi (of Quebec) Act* provides the Cree and Naskapi with by-law–making authority similar to that held by most municipalities. These powers, outlined in s. 45 of the Act, include the authority to make by-laws relating to the administration of band affairs and internal management, public order, taxation for local purposes, and local services, including fire protection.

A major weakness of the *Cree-Naskapi (of Quebec) Act* is that it does not confer independent legislative authority on the Cree and Naskapi Bands; however, they possess local government-type powers that are inextricably tied to a constitutionally protected treaty. These bands do not have the power to create their own constitutions. Although the Minister does not have a general disallowance power for by-laws made under the *Cree-Naskapi*

---

[70] *CNA, supra* note 51.

[71] *Canadian Pacific Ltd. v. Matsqui Indian Band*, [2000] 1 C.N.L.R. 21 (F.C.A.).

[72] *Ibid.* at para. 29.

[73] *CNA, supra* note 51.

[74] James Bay and Northern Quebec Agreement (JBNQA) (Quebec: Editeur official du Québec, 1976).

[75] Section 9.0.1 of the JBNQA provides: "Subject to all other provisions of the Agreement, there shall be recommended to Parliament special legislation concerning local government for the James Bay Crees on Category IA lands allocated to them." The corresponding text and section for the Naskapi Band is s. 7.1 of the Northeastern Quebec Agreement (Ottawa: DIAND, 1984).

(of Quebec) Act, the Minister may disallow or create by-laws relating to local taxation, hunting and trapping, elections, special band meetings, land registry system, long-term borrowing, band expropriation, and fines and penalties for breaking band by-laws. The Cree and Naskapi Bands remain subject to Parliament and to the Quebec National Assembly, as the case may be.[76]

The Cree and Naskapi do not retain their traditional rights and title to the land. The agreement states that the Cree "cede, release, surrender and convey all their Native claims, rights, title and interest"[77] in the land. All the bands are separate corporate entities under their umbrella regional organization, the Cree Regional Authority. The *Cree-Naskapi (of Quebec) Act* outlines permissible forms of government. Each community must have a band council that follows a prescribed set of rules and orders.[78] Band by-laws and resolutions must be enacted according to the procedures set out in the Act and elections must be carried out in the prescribed manner (with election by-laws being subject to ministerial approval).[79]

In *Eastmain Band* v. *Gilpin*,[80] Lavergne P.C.J. of the Quebec Provincial Court noted that the *Cree-Naskapi (of Quebec) Act*, by way of s. 35(3) of the *Constitution Act, 1982*, maintains the "proposition that the Crees hold some sort of residual sovereignty as regards their local governments." Indeed, in the Court of Quebec decision of *Tawich Development Corp.* v. *Dep. Min. of Revenue of Que.*,[81] the Court found that the Cree Nation of Wemindji, a band under the auspices of the James Bay and Northern Quebec Agreement and an incorporated local government under the *Cree-Naskapi (of Quebec) Act*, was not a municipality for the purposes of the *Taxation Act*.[82] The band did not exercise delegated authority. Rather its authority comes from a treaty (the James Bay and Northern Quebec Agreement) and the band thus has a *sui generis* form of government.

The Quebec Superior Court has stated that the *Cree-Naskapi (of Quebec) Act* must be interpreted in a reasonable manner and that acknowledges that:

> Parliament allowed the band councils to exercise the powers of a local government authority . . . which one could compare to the powers of a municipality. Thus, s. 45(1) [of the *Cree-Naskapi (of Quebec) Act*] confers on the Cree bands the power to make by-laws of a local nature. They only have the powers which the statute gives them. There are no residual powers. Each power must be based on an explicit empowering provision (*R.* v. *Lewis*, [1996] 1 S.C.R. 921, *per* Iacobucci J., pp. 958–59).[83]

The *Cree-Naskapi (of Quebec) Act*, while perhaps not a model for other parts of Canada, is unique in being both a federal statute and a key result of a constitutionally recognized and affirmed land claim agreement.

---

[76] This conclusion is not absolute. For example, in *Chisasibi Band* v. *Barbara Chewanish* (1986) (Que. Prov. Ct., No. 640-27-000099-842) 27, Ouellet J. held the following:

> [I]t would seem to me that the Band Council constitutes an autonomous level of government when it exercises the powers conferred upon it by the *Cree-Naskapi (of Quebec) Act*. As long as it remains within the powers so conferred, the Band Council represents a level of government independent from the Canadian Parliament and the Quebec legislature.

[77] JBNQA, *supra* note 74 at s. 21.
[78] CNA, *supra* note 51 at ss. 25–39.
[79] *Ibid.* at ss. 49–57, 63–78.
[80] *Eastmain Band* v. *Gilpin*, [1987] 3 C.N.L.R. 54 (Que. Prov. Ct.) at 67.
[81] *Tawich Development Corp.* v. *D.M. of Revenue of Que.*, [1997] 2 C.N.L.R. 189 (C.Q.).
[82] *Supra* note 69.
[83] *Cree Nation of Chisasibi* v. *CALP*, [2000] 1 C.N.L.R. 91 (Que. Sup. Ct.) at paras. 211, 212.

Sechelt Indian Band Self-Government Act

The *Sechelt Indian Band Self-Government Act*[84] came into force in October 1986 and provides a form of Aboriginal government for the Sechelt Band of British Columbia. The Act establishes a municipal form of government and delegates legislative authority to the band council in areas similar to those provided to the Cree and Naskapi bands. Although the band is no longer under the auspices of the *Indian Act*, except where a void in legislation has not yet been filled by the Sechelt Band Council, it still possesses only delegated authority. The Act can be amended or repealed by Parliament since it remains federal legislation. The band also possesses the authority to enact its own constitution. The Sechelt Band Council is also involved in the British Columbia treaty process, which, if successful, can only increase their authority and governance stature.

In terms of natural resources, Indian bands do not own the natural resources on their land and are still subject to the *Indian Oil and Gas Act*,[85] which provides for little band involvement. As well, both the *British Columbia Indian Reserves Mineral Resources Act*[86] and the *Indian Reserves Minerals Resources Act*[87] apply to the Sechelt Indian Band. These examples are particularly important considering the dependence of many governments on the exploitation of natural resources. Ownership and control of natural resources are significant for many Indian nations that have vast mineral deposits, timber reserves, or oil and gas reserves.

The *Sechelt Indian Band Self-Government Act* replaces, for the most part, the *Indian Act*, as it applies to Sechelt lands and members. The Act "enable[s] the Sechelt Indian Band to exercise and maintain self-government on Sechelt lands and to obtain control over and the administration of the resources and services available to its members."[88]

It also raises questions about the nature of land tenure and government. The Act provides that Sechelt lands shall be held in fee simple.[89] Usually the Crown holds the lands in trust for the use and benefit of Indians. The issue of fee simple title is noteworthy in that it signifies what title does not vest in the band; namely radical or sovereign title.[90] Ultimate title still resides with the federal or provincial Crown. Nevertheless, fee simple title enables the Sechelt Band to engage in a much broader economic development strategy by offering security for investors.

The Cree and Naskapi Bands and the Sechelt Indian Band are not autonomous governments that exercise jurisdiction and authority at the same level as the federal and provincial governments. They are improvements over the *Indian Act* system, but they do not represent autonomous orders of government in Canada because they are subject to the ultimate legislative authority of either one of the other two orders of government. The federal and provincial governments continue to play a major role in the allocation and level of funding, the establishment of spending priorities, and the ability of the band governments to operate on a day-to-day level. It is unclear exactly what realm these band

[84] *Sechelt Indian Band Self-Government Act*, S.C. 1986, c. 27.
[85] *Indian Oil and Gas Act*, R.S.C. 1985, c. I-7.
[86] *British Columbia Indian Reserves Mineral Resources Act*, S.C. 1943–1944, c. 9.
[87] *Indian Reserves Minerals Resources Act*, R.S.B.C. 1979, c. 192.
[88] *Supra* note 84, s. 4.
[89] *Ibid.* at ss. 23(1), which reads: "The title to all lands that were, . . . reserves, . . . of the *Indian Act* Sechelt band is hereby transferred in fee simple to the Band."
[90] A.M. Sinclair in *Introduction to Real Property Law*, 3d ed. (Toronto: Butterworths, 1987) 9, writes: "The Crown at the top owns the land. At the base is O who owns a fee simple (a 'bundle' of rights) in relation to that land. He then may easily dispose of some of these rights. This leaves totally undisturbed the ownership of the land; that's up above."

governments do occupy. In the case of the Cree and Naskapi, their forms of government are tied directly to constitutionally protected land claims agreements, and they have been described by some courts as being *sui generis* in nature.

Meadow Lake First Nations

On January 22, 2001 the Meadow Lake Tribal Council and the Governments of Canada and Saskatchewan signed a tripartite agreement in principle establishing the provincial role in self-government negotiations among the parties. The Meadow Lake Tribal Council and Canada also signed a comprehensive agreement in principle, which sets out the terms for finalizing a self-government agreement among the parties. The final agreement will be negotiated within the context of existing treaties and will not affect the treaty rights of the Meadow Lake First Nations. The Meadow Lake First Nations, under the final agreement, would have the authority to enact laws in a wide variety of areas and would be able to delegate this law-making authority to a regional body, such as the Meadow Lake Tribal Council. Meadow Lake First Nations laws would operate concurrently with federal and provincial laws and the final agreement would set out a process regarding how conflicts between laws would be resolved.

Mohawks of Kanesatake

On June 14, 2001, the *Kanesatake Interim Land Base Governance Act*[91] became law. The Act gives legal effect to an agreement between the Mohawks of Kanesatake and the Government of Canada that recognizes an interim land base for the Mohawks of Kanesatake as s. 91(24) or federal lands, but not lands under the administration of the Act. The Act sets out the legal basis upon which the Mohawks of Kanesatake can establish and implement laws over an array of areas. The Act also provides that before jurisdiction can be exercised, the Mohawks of Kanesatake must adopt a land governance code dealing with matters such as rights of appeal, accountability, and land assessment.[92]

The Act also addresses a matter of importance to many non-Aboriginal local governments: harmonization between local communities and Aboriginal governments. The Act states that before the Mohawks of Kanesatake can make any law dealing with land use or establishing land use standards, they must enter into a harmonization agreement with the Municipality of Oka.[93]

Nisga'a Final Agreement

On August 4, 1998, the Governments of British Columbia and Canada and the Nisga'a initialled the Nisga'a Final Agreement. Discussed in chapter 2, the agreement outlines an extensive array of land, economic, and governance provisions. The agreement, including all of the governance powers, is a treaty and a land claims agreement within the meaning of ss. 25 and 35 of the *Constitution Act, 1982*.[94] Although the Nisga'a Final Agreement does not specify what is to be constitutionally recognized and affirmed, it does state that the Nisga'a Nation has a "right to self-government, and the authority to make laws, as set out in this Agreement."[95] Thus, for the first time in Canada, a treaty has been constitu-

---

[91] *Kanesatake Interim Land Base Governance Act*, S.C. 2001, c. 8.
[92] *Ibid.*, see ss. 7 and 9.
[93] *Ibid.*, see ss. 12–13.
[94] Nisga'a Final Agreement, c. 2, s. 1.
[95] *Ibid.* c. 11, s. 1.

tionally protected and has constitutionally "recognized and affirmed" an Aboriginal right of self-government.

Yukon Territory

In 1993, the Yukon government, the federal government, and the Council for Yukon Indians signed an umbrella final agreement and final agreements for four Yukon First Nations: the Vuntut Gwitchin First Nation, the Champagne and Aishihik First Nations, the Teslin Tlingit Council, and the First Nation of Nacho Nyak Dun. Each First Nation also signed separate self-government agreements negotiated under the framework of the umbrella final agreement. Since 1993, four other Yukon First Nations have signed self-government agreements. The *Yukon First Nations Self-Government Act*[96] was proclaimed into force on February 14, 1995, and is the federal enabling legislation for the self-government agreements.

The Yukon self-government agreements replace the Act, with the exception of determining who is an Indian. Although delegated, the Yukon self-government agreements[97] provide a wide range of legislative authority to applicable Yukon First Nations and offer a new approach to self-government within a comprehensive claims framework, particularly with respect to powers of taxation.[98]

CONCLUSION

To date the courts have offered a restrictive interpretation of s. 35 and the right of self-government. Unless the courts take a more liberal view of whether a right of self-government exists and has not been extinguished, negotiation may be the only forum for Aboriginal people to address the issue.

On the issue of sovereignty, Binnie J. in *Mitchell* v. *Canada (Min. of National Revenue)*,[99] stated the following vis-à-vis self-government:

> In terms of sovereign incompatibility, it is a conclusion that the respondent's claim relates to national interests that all of us have in common rather than to distinctive interests that for some purposes differentiate an Aboriginal community. In my view, reconciliation of these interests in this particular case favours an affirmation of our collective sovereignty. . . .
>
> In reaching that conclusion, however, I do not wish to be taken as either foreclosing or endorsing any position on the compatibility or incompatibility of *internal* self-governing institutions of First Nations with Crown sovereignty, either past or present. I point out in this connection that the sovereign incompatibility principle has not prevented the United States (albeit with its very different constitutional framework) from continuing to recognize forms of *internal* Aboriginal self-government which it considers to be expressions of residual Aboriginal sovereignty. The concept of a "domestic dependent nation" was introduced by Marshall C.J. in *Cherokee Nation* v. *Georgia*, 30 U.S. (5 Pet.) 1 (1831), at p. 17. . . .
>
> I refer to the U.S. law only to alleviate any concern that addressing aspects of the sover-

---

[96] *Yukon First Nations Self-Government Act*, S.C. 1994, c. 35.

[97] The Yukon self-government agreements are also discussed in chapter 2.

[98] The *Umbrella Agreement* makes it clear that self-government agreements are not accorded constitutional protection. Subsection 24.12.1 reads: "Agreements entered into pursuant to this chapter and any legislation enacted to implement such agreements shall not be construed to be treaty rights within the meaning of section 35 of the *Constitution Act, 1982.*" This clause is mirrored in the individual First Nations' final agreements (see, for example, s. 24.12.1 of the Teslin Tlingit Council Final Agreement).

[99] *Mitchell* v. *Canada (Min. of National Revenue)*, [2001] 1 S.C.R. 911.

eignty issue in the context of a claim to an international trading and mobility right would prejudice one way or the other a resolution of the much larger and more complex claim of First Nations in Canada to *internal* self-governing institutions. The United States has lived with internal tribal self-government within the framework of external relations determined wholly by the United States government without doctrinal difficulties since *Johnson* v. *M'Intosh*, 21 U.S. (8 Wheat.) 543 (1823), was decided almost 170 years ago.[100]

Although Aboriginal governments focus on jurisdiction, it is only one element of a successful governance regime. Without adequate fiscal resources and a land base, jurisdiction can be extremely limited. Finding innovative governance arrangements for urban Aboriginal governments will be particularly challenging. With jurisdiction comes a serious responsibility to ensure that the necessary democratic systems of governance are in place, and that the necessary checks and balances on power are easily identified and accessible. These systems require fiscal resources and infrastructure, and the majority of Aboriginal groups in Canada may not have the population base to support them on their own. Land claims agreements have provided a very useful tool to a number of Aboriginal groups in establishing autonomous governments outside of the *Indian Act* system. In other instances, Aboriginal governments have been served by focusing on practical arrangements, with all the necessary safeguards, so that their interests and objectives are met, rather than focusing on more abstract mechanisms such as jurisdictional authority.

CASES AND MATERIALS

R. v. Sioui

[1990] 1 S.C.R. 1025 (S.C.C.).

LAMER J.:— . . . I consider that, instead, we can conclude from the historical documents that both Great Britain and France felt that the Indian nations had sufficient independence and played a large enough role in North America for it to be a good policy to maintain relations with them very close to those maintained between sovereign nations.

The mother countries did everything in their power to secure the alliance of each Indian nation and to encourage nations allied with the enemy to change sides. When these efforts met with success, they were incorporated in treaties of alliance or neutrality. This clearly indicates that the Indian nations were regarded in their relations with the European nations which occupied North America as independent nations. The papers of Sir William Johnson (*The Papers of Sir William Johnson*, 14 vol.), who was in charge of Indian affairs in British North America, demonstrate the recognition by Great Britain that nation-to-nation relations had to be conducted with the North American Indians. As an example, I cite an extract from a speech by Sir Johnson at the Onondaga Conference held in April 1748, attended by the Five nations:

> Brethren of the five Nations I will begin upon a thing of a long standing, our first *Brothership*. My Reason for it is, I think there are several among you who seem to forget it; It may seem strange to you how I a *Foreigner* should know this, But I tell you I found out some of the old

---

[100] *Ibid.* at paras. 164, 165, 169.

Writings of our Forefathers which was thought to have been lost and in this old valuable Record I find, that our first *Friendship* Commenced at the Arrival of the first great Canoe or Vessel at Albany . . . [Emphasis added] (*The Papers of Sir William Johnson*, vol. 1, 1921, at p. 157)

As the Chief Justice of the United States Supreme Court said in 1832 in *Worcester* v. *State of Georgia*, 31 U.S. (6 Pet.) 515 (1832), at pp. 548–49, about British policy towards the Indians in the mid-eighteenth century:

> Such was the policy of Great Britain towards the Indian nations inhabiting the territory from which she excluded all other Europeans; such her claims, and such her practical exposition of the charters she had granted: *she considered them as nations capable of maintaining the relations of peace and war: of governing themselves, under her protection: and she made treaties with them, the obligation of which she acknowledged.* [Emphasis added.]

Further, both the French and the English recognized the critical importance of alliances with the Indians, or at least their neutrality, in determining the outcome of the war between them and the security of the North American colonies.

R. v. Sparrow

[1990] 1 S.C.R. 1075 (S.C.C.).

. . . It is worth recalling that while British policy towards the native population was based on respect for their right to occupy their traditional lands, a proposition to which the *Royal Proclamation of 1763* bears witness, there was from the outset never any doubt that sovereignty and legislative power, and indeed the underlying title, to such lands vested in the Crown: see *Johnson* v. *M'Intosh* (1823); . . . see also the Royal Proclamation . . . [and] *Calder*. . . . And there can be no doubt that over the years the rights of the Indians were often honoured in the breach (for one instance in a recent case in this Court, see *Canadian Pacific Ltd.* v. *Paul*, [1989] 1 C.N.L.R. 47). As MacDonald J. stated in *Pasco* v. *Canadian National Railway Co.*, [1986] 1 C.N.L.R. 35 at 37, (B.C.S.C.): "We cannot recount with much pride the treatment accorded to the native people of this country."

. . .

There is no explicit language in the provision that authorizes this Court or any court to assess the legitimacy of any government legislation that restricts aboriginal rights. Yet, we find that the words "recognition and affirmation" incorporate the fiduciary relationship referred to earlier and so import some restraint on the exercise of sovereign power. Rights that are recognized and affirmed are not absolute. Federal legislative powers continue, including, of course, the right to legislate with respect to Indians pursuant to s. 91(24) of the *Constitution Act, 1867*. These powers must, however, now be read together with s. 35(1). In other words, federal power must be reconciled with federal duty and the best way to achieve that reconciliation is to demand the justification of any government regulation that infringes upon or denies aboriginal rights. . . .

R. v. Pamajewon

[1996] 2 S.C.R. 821 (S.C.C.). Lamer C.J., La Forest, L'Heureux-Dubé, Sopinka, Gonthier, Cory, McLachlin, Iacobucci, and Major JJ., August 22, 1996.

LAMER C.J. (LA FOREST, SOPINKA, GONTHIER, CORY, MCLACHLIN, IACOBUCCI and MAJOR JJ., concurring)—. . .

1   This appeal raises the question of whether the conduct of high stakes gambling by

the Shawanaga and Eagle Lake First Nations falls within the scope of the Aboriginal rights recognized and affirmed by s. 35(1) of the *Constitution Act, 1982*. . . .

3   The appellants Pamajewon and Jones are members of the Shawanaga First Nation. On March 29, 1993, both were found guilty of the offence of keeping a common gaming house contrary to s. 201(1) of the *Criminal Code*, R.S.C., 1985, c. C-46. Section 201(1) of the *Criminal Code* reads:

> 201. (1) Every one who keeps a common gaming house or common betting house is guilty of an indictable offence and liable to imprisonment for a term not exceeding two years.

4   The charges arose out of the high stakes bingo and other gambling activities which took place on the Shawanaga First Nation Reservation between September 11, 1987 and October 6, 1990. Throughout this period Jones was Chief of the Shawanaga First Nation and Pamajewon was a member of the Shawanaga Band Council.

5   Gambling on the reservation took place pursuant to the authority of the Shawanaga First Nation lottery law. This lottery law, enacted by the Band Council in August 1987, was not a by-law passed pursuant to s. 81 of the *Indian Act*, R.S.C., 1985, c. I-5.

6   The Shawanaga First Nation did not have a provincial licence authorizing its gambling activities. The band had met with the Ontario Lottery Corporation but had refused the Corporation's offer of a gambling licence on the basis that such a licence was unnecessary because the band had an inherent right of self-government.

7   At trial the appellants Pamajewon and Jones were convicted. Their convictions were upheld by the Ontario Court of Appeal.

Gardner, Pitchenese and Gardner
8   The appellants Arnold Gardner, Jack Pitchenese and Allan Gardner are all members of the Eagle Lake First Nation. On November 19, 1993 they were found guilty of conducting a scheme for the purpose of determining the winners of property, contrary to s. 206(1)(*d*) of the Code. Section 206(1)(*d*) of the Code reads:

> 206. (1) Every one is guilty of an indictable offence and liable to imprisonment for a term not exceeding two years who . . .
>
> (*d*) conducts or manages any scheme, contrivance or operation of any kind for the purpose of determining who, or the holders of what lots, tickets, numbers or chances, are the winners of any property so proposed to be advanced, lent, given, sold or disposed of. . . .

9   At the time they were charged Arnold Gardner was Chief of the Eagle Lake Band and chairman of the bingo committee. Jack Pitchenese managed the bingo operations. Allan Gardner was the chief bingo caller.

10   The gambling activities on the Eagle Lake Reserve were conducted pursuant to the Eagle Lake First Nation Band Council's lottery law, enacted in March 1985. This lottery law was not a by-law passed pursuant to s. 81 of the *Indian Act*.

11   The Eagle Lake First Nation did not have a provincial licence authorizing its gambling operations; the band had refused to negotiate with the Ontario Lottery Commission, even though it was approached for this purpose by the Ministry of Consumer and Commercial Relations. The band would not negotiate because it asserted the right to be self-regulating in its economic activities.

12   The appellants Gardner, Pitchenese and Gardner were convicted at trial. Their convictions were upheld by the Ontario Court of Appeal. . . .

20   Leave to appeal to this Court was granted on June 1, 1995, [1995] 2 S.C.R. viii. On July 6, 1995 the following constitutional question was stated:

> Are s. 201, s. 206 or s. 207 of the *Criminal Code*, separately or in combination, of no force or effect with respect to the appellants, by virtue of s. 52 of the *Constitution Act, 1982* in the circumstances of these proceedings, by reason of the aboriginal or treaty rights within the meaning of s. 35 of the *Constitution Act, 1982* invoked by the appellants?

21   The appellants appealed on the basis that the Court of Appeal erred in restricting Aboriginal title to rights that are activity and site specific and in concluding that self-government only extends to those matters which were governed by ancient laws or customs. The appellant argued further that the Court of Appeal erred in concluding that the Code extinguished self-government regarding gaming and in not addressing whether the Code's gaming provisions unjustifiably interfered with the rights recognized and affirmed by s. 35(1) of the *Constitution Act, 1982*. . . .

23   The resolution of the appellants' claim in this case rests on the application of the test, laid out by this Court in *R. v. Van der Peet*, [1996] 2 S.C.R. 507, for determining the Aboriginal rights recognized and affirmed by s. 35(1) of the *Constitution Act, 1982*. The appellants in this case are claiming that the gambling activities in which they took part, and their respective bands' regulation of those gambling activities, fell within the scope of the Aboriginal rights recognized and affirmed by s. 35(1). *Van der Peet*, supra, lays out the test for determining the practices, customs and traditions which fall within s. 35(1) and, as such, provides the legal standard against which the appellants' claim must be measured.

24   The appellants' claim involves the assertion that s. 35(1) encompasses the right of self-government, and that this right includes the right to regulate gambling activities on the reservation. Assuming without deciding that s. 35(1) includes self-government claims, the applicable legal standard is nonetheless that laid out in *Van der Peet*, supra. Assuming s. 35(1) encompasses claims to Aboriginal self-government, such claims must be considered in light of the purposes underlying that provision and must, therefore, be considered against the test derived from consideration of those purposes. This is the test laid out in *Van der Peet*, supra. In so far as they can be made under s. 35(1), claims to self-government are no different from other claims to the enjoyment of Aboriginal rights and must, as such, be measured against the same standard.

25   In *Van der Peet, supra,* the test for identifying Aboriginal rights was said to be as follows, at para. 46:

> in order to be an aboriginal right an activity must be an element of a practice, custom or tradition integral to the distinctive culture of the aboriginal group claiming the right.

In applying this test the Court must first identify the exact nature of the activity claimed to be a right and must then go on to determine whether, on the evidence presented to the trial judge, and on the facts as found by the trial judge, that activity could be said to be (*Van der Peet*, at para. 59) "a defining feature of the culture in question" prior to contact with Europeans.

26   I now turn to the first part of the *Van der Peet* test, the characterization of the appellants' claim. In *Van der Peet, supra*, the Court held at para. 53 that:

To characterize an applicant's claim correctly, a court should consider such factors as the nature of the action which the applicant is claiming was done pursuant to an Aboriginal right, the nature of the governmental regulation, statute or action being impugned, and the practice, custom or tradition being relied upon to establish the right.

When these factors are considered in this case it can be seen that the correct characterization of the appellants' claim is that they are claiming the right to participate in, and to regulate, high stakes gambling activities on the reservation. The activity which the appellants organized, and which their bands regulated, was high stakes gambling. The statute which they argue violates those rights prohibits gambling subject only to a few very limited exceptions (laid out in s. 207 of the Code). Finally, the applicants rely in support of their claim on the fact that the "Ojibwa people . . . had a long tradition of public games and sporting events, which pre-dated the arrival of Europeans". Thus, the activity in which the appellants were engaged and which their bands regulated, the statute they are impugning, and the historical evidence on which they rely, all relate to the conduct and regulation of gambling. As such, the most accurate characterization of the appellants' claim is that they are asserting that s. 35(1) recognizes and affirms the rights of the Shawanaga and Eagle Lake First Nations to participate in, and to regulate, gambling activities on their respective reserve lands.

27   The appellants themselves would have this Court characterize their claim as to "a broad right to manage the use of their reserve lands". To so characterize the appellants' claim would be to cast the Court's inquiry at a level of excessive generality. Aboriginal rights, including any asserted right to self-government, must be looked at in light of the specific circumstances of each case and, in particular, in light of the specific history and culture of the Aboriginal group claiming the right. The factors laid out in *Van der Peet*, and applied, *supra*, allow the Court to consider the appellants' claim at the appropriate level of specificity; the characterization put forward by the appellants would not allow the Court to do so.

28   I now turn to the second branch of the *Van der Peet* test, the consideration of whether the participation in, and regulation of, gambling on the reserve lands was an integral part of the distinctive cultures of the Shawanaga or Eagle Lake First Nations. The evidence presented at both the Pamajewon and Gardner trials does not demonstrate that gambling, or that the regulation of gambling, was an integral part of the distinctive cultures of the Shawanaga or Eagle Lake First Nations. In fact, the only evidence presented at either trial dealing with the question of the importance of gambling was that of James Morrison, who testified at the Pamajewon trial with regards to the importance and prevalence of gaming in Ojibwa culture. While Mr. Morrison's evidence does demonstrate that the Ojibwa gambled, it does not demonstrate that gambling was of central significance to the Ojibwa people. Moreover, his evidence in no way addresses the extent to which this gambling was the subject of regulation by the Ojibwa community. His account is of informal gambling activities taking place on a small-scale; he does not describe large-scale activities, subject to community regulation, of the sort at issue in this appeal.

29   I would note that neither of the trial judges in these cases relied upon findings of fact regarding the importance of gambling to the Ojibwa; however, upon review of the evidence I find myself in agreement with the conclusion arrived at by Osborne J.A. when he said first, at p. 400, that there "is no evidence to support a conclusion that gambling generally or high stakes gambling of the sort in issue here, were part of the First Nations'

historic cultures and traditions, or an aspect of their use of their land" and, second, at p. 400, that "there is no evidence that gambling on the reserve lands generally was ever the subject matter of Aboriginal regulation". . . .

30   Given this evidentiary record, it is clear that the appellants have failed to demonstrate that the gambling activities in which they were engaged, and their respective bands' regulation of those activities, took place pursuant to an Aboriginal right recognized and affirmed by s. 35(1) of the *Constitution Act, 1982.* . . .

31   These are my reasons for dismissing the appeal and for affirming the decision of the Court of Appeal upholding the trial judge's conviction of the various appellants for violating ss. 201 and 206 of the Code. . . .

32   For the reasons given above, the constitutional question must be answered as follows: . . . No. . . .

*Indian Act**
R.S.C. 1985, c. I-5

Powers of the Council . . .

81. (1) The council of a band may make by-laws not inconsistent with this Act or with any regulation made by the Governor in Council or the Minister, for any or all of the following purposes, namely,

   (a) to provide for the health of residents on the reserve and to prevent the spreading of contagious and infectious diseases;

   (b) the regulation of traffic;

   (c) the observance of law and order;

   (d) the prevention of disorderly conduct and nuisances;

   (e) the protection against and prevention of trespass by cattle and other domestic animals, the establishment of pounds, the appointment of pound-keepers, the regulation of their duties and the provision for fees and charges for their services;

   (f) the construction and maintenance of watercourses, roads, bridges, ditches, fences and other local works;

   (g) the dividing of the reserve or a portion thereof into zones and the prohibition of the construction or maintenance of any class of buildings or the carrying on of any class of business, trade or calling in any such zone;

   (h) the regulation of the construction, repair and use of buildings, whether owned by the band or by individual members of the band;

   (i) the survey and allotment of reserve lands among the members of the band and the establishment of a register of Certificates of Possession and Certificates of Occupation relating to allotments and the setting apart of reserve lands for common use, if authority therefor has been granted under section 60;

   (j) the destruction and control of noxious weeds;

   (k) the regulation of bee-keeping and poultry raising;

   (l) the construction and regulation of the use of public wells, cisterns, reservoirs and other water supplies;

* Selected provisions of ss. 81–83 of the *Indian Act* relating to powers of a band council.

(m)   the control and prohibition of public games, sports, races, athletic contests and other amusements;

(n)   the regulation of the conduct and activities of hawkers, peddlers or others who enter the reserve to buy, sell or otherwise deal in wares or merchandise;

(o)   the preservation, protection and management of fur-bearing animals, fish and other game on the reserve;

(p)   the removal and punishment of persons trespassing upon the reserve or frequenting the reserve for prohibited purposes;

(p.1) the residence of band members and other persons on the reserve;

(p.2) to provide for the rights of spouses or common-law partners and children who reside with members of the band on the reserve with respect to any matter in relation to which the council may make by-laws in respect of members of the band;

(p.3) to authorize the Minister to make payments out of capital or revenue moneys to persons whose names were deleted from the Band List of the band;

(p.4) to bring subsection 10(3) or 64.1(2) into effect in respect of the band;

(q)   with respect to any matter arising out of or ancillary to the exercise of powers under this section; and

(r)   the imposition on summary conviction of a fine not exceeding one thousand dollars or imprisonment for a term not exceeding thirty days, or both, for violation of a by-law made under this section.

(2) Where any by-law of a band is contravened and a conviction entered, in addition to any other remedy and to any penalty imposed by the by-law, the court in which the conviction has been entered, and any court of competent jurisdiction thereafter, may make an order prohibiting the continuation or repetition of the offence by the person convicted.

(3) Where any by-law of a band passed is contravened, in addition to any other remedy and to any penalty imposed by the by-law, such contravention may be restrained by court action at the instance of the band council.

82. (1) A copy of every by-law made under section 81 shall be forwarded by mail by the chief or a member of the council of the band to the Minister within four days after it is made.

(2) A by-law made under section 81 comes into force forty days after a copy thereof is forwarded to the Minister pursuant to subsection (1), unless it is disallowed by the Minister within that period, but the Minister may declare the by-law to be in force at any time before the expiration of that period. . . .

83. (1) Without prejudice to the powers conferred by section 81, the council of a band may, subject to the approval of the Minister, make by-laws for any or all of the following purposes, namely,

(a)   subject to subsections (2) and (3), taxation for local purposes of land, or interests in land, in the reserve, including rights to occupy, possess or use land in the reserve;

(a.1) the licensing of businesses, callings, trades and occupations;

(b)   the appropriation and expenditure of moneys of the band to defray band expenses;

(c)   the appointment of officials to conduct the business of the council, prescribing their duties and providing for their remuneration out of any moneys raised pursuant to paragraph (a);

(d)   the payment of remuneration, in such amount as may be approved by the Minister, to chiefs and councillors, out of any moneys raised pursuant to paragraph (a);

(e)   the enforcement of payment of amounts that are payable pursuant to this section, including arrears and interest;

(e.1) the imposition and recovery of interest on amounts that are payable pursuant to this section, where those amounts are not paid before they are due, and the calculation of that interest;

(f)   the raising of money from band members to support band projects; and

(g)   with respect to any matter arising out of or ancillary to the exercise of powers under this section.

(2)   An expenditure made out of moneys raised pursuant to subsection (1) must be so made under the authority of a by-law of the council of the band.

(3)   A by-law made under paragraph (1)(a) must provide an appeal procedure in respect of assessments made for the purposes of taxation under that paragraph.

(4)   The Minister may approve the whole or a part only of a by-law made under subsection (1).

(5)   The Governor in Council may make regulations respecting the exercise of the by-law making powers of bands under this section.

(6)   A by-law made under this section remains in force only to the extent that it is consistent with the regulations made under subsection (5). R.S.C. 1985 (4th Supp.), c. 17. s. 10. . . .

Whitebear Band Council v. *Carpenters' Provincial Council of Saskatchewan*

[1982] 3 C.N.L.R. 181 (Sask. C.A.). Bayda C.J.S., MacDonald and Cameron JJ.A., April 6, 1982.

CAMERON J.A.:— . . . As municipal councils are the "creatures" of the legislatures of the provinces, so Indian band councils are the "creatures" of the Parliament of Canada. Parliament, in exercising the exclusive jurisdiction conferred upon it by s. 91(24) of the *B.N.A. Act* to legislate in relation to "Indians, and Lands reserved for the Indians", enacted the *Indian Act*, R.S.C. 1970, c. I-6, which provides—among its extensive provisions for Indian status, civil rights, assistance, and so on, and the use and management of Indian reserves—for the election of a chief and 12 councillors by and from among the members of an Indian band resident on an Indian reserve. These elected officials constitute Indian band councils, who in general terms are intended by Parliament to provide some measure—even if rather rudimentary—of local government in relation to life on Indian reserves and to act as something of an intermediary between the band and the Minister of Indian Affairs.

More specifically, s. 81 of the Act clothes Indian band councils with such powers and duties in relation to an Indian reserve and its inhabitants are usually associated with a rural municipality and its council: a band council may enact by-laws for the regulation of traffic, the construction and maintenance of public works, zoning, the control of public games and amusements and of hawkers and peddlers, the regulation of the construction, repair and use of buildings, and so on. Hence a band council exercises—by way of delegation from Parliament—these and other municipal and governmental powers in relation to the reserve whose inhabitants have elected it.

I think it worth noting that the *Indian Act* contemplates a measured maturing of self-government on Indian reserves. Section 69 of the Act empowers the Governor in Council to "permit" a band to manage and spend its revenue moneys—pursuant to regulation by the Governor in Council—and by s. 83 the Governor in Council may declare that a band "has reached an advance stage of development", in which event the band council may, with the approval of the minister, raise money by way of assessment and taxation of reserve lands and the licensing of reserve businesses. Until then, the band council derives its funds principally from the government of Canada.

The Governor in Council has made no declaration under s. 83 of the Act declaring the Whitebear Band Council to have reached an advanced stage of development; however, the Whitebear Band Council is the subject of an order of the Governor in Council made pursuant to s. 69 of the Act, and has been empowered to control, manage and expend in whole or in part its revenue moneys in accordance with the regulations made pursuant to this section, which require it to establish, as it has done, an account with a recognized financial institution, under the authority of three persons, two of whom are members of the band. The chief and Mr. Paul, both members of the council, were given this authority.

In addition to their municipal and governmental function, band councils are also empowered by the *Indian Act* to perform an advisory role, and in some cases to exercise a power of veto with respect to certain activities of the minister in relation to the reserve, including the spending of Indian moneys, both capital and revenue, and the use and possession of reserve lands.

Moreover, in light of the provisions of the single contribution agreement and some of the terms of the consolidated contribution agreement, it appears that in practice Indian band councils from time to-time act as agents of the Minister of Indian Affairs and representatives of the members of the reserve with respect to the implementation of certain federal government programs designed for Indian reserves and their residents—a complementary role consistent with their function.

In summary, an Indian band council is an elected public authority, dependent on Parliament for its existence, powers and responsibilities, whose essential function it is to exercise municipal and government power—delegated to it by Parliament—in relation to the Indian reserve whose inhabitants have elected it; as such, it is to act from time to time as the agent of the minister and the representative of the band with respect to the administration and delivery of certain federal programs for the benefit of Indians on Indian reserves, and to perform an advisory, and in some cases a decisive, role in relation to the exercise by the minister of certain of his statutory authority relative to the reserve. . . .

As I have observed, the primary function of an Indian band council is to provide a measure of self-government by Indians on Indian reserves. In enacting by-laws pursuant to their power to do so, and in performing generally their local government function, an Indian band council is doing that which Parliament is exclusively empowered to do pursuant to s. 92(24) of the *B.N.A. Act* but which Parliament, through the *Indian Act,* has delegated band councils to do. In this sense, the function of an Indian band council is very much federal. So too, in my opinion, are their associated functions—acting at once as the representative body of the inhabitants of the reserve and the agent of the minister with regard to federal programs for reserves and their residents—and participating in certain of the decisions of the minister in relation to the reserve. Given this, the provisions of the *Indian Act* to which I have referred and the origin and nature, purpose and function of an Indian band council, I am satisfied that the power generally to regulate the labour relations of a band council and its employees, engaged in those activities contemplated by the *Indian Act*, forms an integral part of primary federal jurisdiction in relation to "Indians, and Lands reserved for the Indians" pursuant to s. 91(24) of the *B.N.A. Act.* . . .

Sechelt Indian Band Self-Government Act
S.C. 1986, c. 27.

An act relating to self-government for the Sechelt Indian Band. . . .

3. For greater certainty, nothing in this Act shall be construed so as to abrogate or derogate from any existing aboriginal or treaty rights of the members of the Sechelt Indian Band, or any other aboriginal peoples of Canada, under section 35 of the Constitution Act, 1982.

Purposes of Act

4. The purposes of this Act are to enable the Sechelt Indian Band to exercise and maintain self-government on Sechelt lands and to obtain control over and the administration of the resources and services available to its members.

Sechelt Indian Band

5. (1) The Sechelt Indian Band is hereby established to replace the Indian Act Sechelt band.

    (2) The Indian Act Sechelt Band ceases to exist, and all its rights, titles, interests, assets, obligations and liabilities, including those of its band council, vest in the Sechelt Indian Band established under subsection (1).

Capacity and Powers of Band

6. The Band is a legal entity and has, subject to this Act, the capacity, rights, powers and privileges of a natural person and, without restricting the generality of the foregoing, may
    (a) enter into contracts or agreement;
    (b) acquire and hold property or any interest therein, and sell or otherwise dispose of that property or interest;
    (c) expend or invest moneys;
    (d) borrow money;
    (e) sue or be sued; and
    (f) do such other things as are conducive to the exercise of its rights, powers and privileges.

7. The powers and duties of the Band shall be carried out in accordance with its constitution.

Sechelt Indian Band Council

8. The Sechelt Indian Band Council shall be the governing body of the Band, and its

members shall be elected in accordance with the constitution of the Band.

9. The Band shall act through the Council in exercising its powers and carrying out its duties and functions.

Band Constitution

10. (1) The constitution of the Band shall be in writing and may
    (a) establish the composition of council, the terms of office and tenure of its members and procedures relating to the election of council members
    (b) establish the procedures or processes to be followed by Council in exercising the Band's powers and carrying out its duties
    (c) provide for a system of financial accountability of the council to the members of the Band, including audit arrangements and the publication of financial reports
    (d) include a membership code for the Band;
    (e) establish rules and procedures relating to the holding of referenda referred to in section 12 or subsection 21(3) or provided for in the constitution of the Band;
    (f) establish rules and procedures to be followed in respect of the disposition of rights and interests in the Sechelt lands;
    (g) set out specific legislative powers of the Council selected from among the general class of matters set out in section 14; and
    (h) provide for any other matters relating to the government of the Band, its members or Sechelt lands.

(2) A membership code established in the constitution of the Band shall respect rights to membership in the *Indian Act* Sechelt band acquired under the *Indian Act* immediately prior to the establishment of that code. . . .

Legislative Powers of Council

14. (1) The Council has, to the extent that it is authorized by the constitution of the Band to do so, the power to make laws in relation to matters coming within any of the following classes of matters:
    (a) access to and residence on Sechelt lands;
    (b) zoning and land use planning in respect of Sechelt lands;
    (c) expropriation, for community purposes, of interests in Sechelt lands by the Band;
    (d) the use, construction, maintenance, repair and demolition of buildings and structures on Sechelt lands;
    (e) taxation, for local purposes, of interests in Sechelt lands, and of occupants and tenants of Sechelt land in respect of their interests in those lands, including assessment, collection and enforcement procedures and appeals relating thereto;
    (f) the administration and management of property belonging to the Band;
    (g) education of Band members on Sechelt lands;
    (h) social and welfare services with respect to Band members, including, without restricting the generality of the foregoing, the custody and placement of children of Band members;
    (i) health services on Sechelt lands;
    (j) the preservation and management of natural resources on Sechelt lands;
    (k) the preservation, protection and management of fur-bearing animals, fish and

game on Sechelt lands;

(l)   public order and safety on Sechelt lands;

(m)   the construction, maintenance and management of roads and the regulation of traffic on Sechelt lands;

(n)   the operation of businesses, professions and trades on Sechelt lands;

(o)   the prohibition of the sale, barter, supply, manufacture or possession of intoxicants on Sechelt lands and any exceptions to a prohibition of possession;

(p)   subject to subsection (2), the imposition on summary conviction of fines or imprisonment for the contravention of any law made by the Band government;

(q)   the devolution, by testate or intestate succession, of real property of Band members on Sechelt lands and personal property of Band members ordinarily resident on Sechelt lands;

(r)   financial administration of the Band;

(s)   the conduct of Band elections and referenda;

(t)   the creation of administrative bodies and agencies to assist in the administrative of the affairs of the Band; and

(u)   matters related to the good government of the Band, its members or Sechelt lands.

(2) A law made in respect of the class of matters set out in paragraph (1)(p) may specify a maximum fine or a maximum term of imprisonment or both, but the maximum fine may not exceed two thousand dollars and the maximum term of imprisonment may not exceed six months.

(3) For greater certainty, the Council has the power to adopt any laws of British Columbia as its own law if it is authorized by the constitution to make laws in relation to the subject-matter of those laws.

(4) A law made by the Council may require the holding of a licence or permit and may provide for the issuance thereof and fees therefor. . . .

15. The Council may exercise any legislative power granted to it by or pursuant to an Act of the legislature of British Columbia. . . .

Transfer of Lands

23 (1) The title to all lands that were, immediately prior to the coming into force of this section, reserves, within the meaning of the Indian Act, of the Indian Act Sechelt band is hereby transferred in fee simple to the Band, subject to the rights, interests and conditions referred to in section 24.

(2) In subsection (1), "reserves" includes surrendered lands, within the meaning of the Indian Act, that have not been sold or the title to which has not been otherwise transferred.

(3) All rights and interests of the Indian Act Sechelt band in respect of the lands referred to in subsection (1) cease to exist on the coming into force of this section. . . .

Sechelt Lands

31. For greater certainty, Sechelt lands are lands reserved for the Indians within the meaning of Class 24 of section 91 of the *Constitution Act, 1867.*

Application of the Indian Act

35. (1) Subject to section 36, the *Indian Act* applies, with such modifications as the circumstances require, in respect of the Band, its members, the Council and Sechelt lands except to the extent that the *Indian Act* is inconsistent with this Act, the constitution of the Band or a law of the Band.

(2) For greater certainty, the *Indian Act* applies for the purpose of determining which members of the Band are "Indians" within the meaning of the Act.

(3) For greater certainty, section 87 of the *Indian Act* applies, with such modifications as the circumstances require, in respect of the Band and its members who are Indians within the meaning of that Act, subject to any laws made by the Council in relation to the class of matters set out in paragraph 14(1)(e).

36. The Governor in Council may, on the advice of the Minister, by order declare that the Indian Act or any provision thereof does not apply to
(a)   the Band or its members, or
(b)   any portion of Sechelt lands,
and may, on the advice of the Minister, by order revoke any such order.

Application of Laws of Canada

37. All federal laws of general application in force in Canada are applicable to and in respect of the Band, its members and Sechelt lands, except to the extent that those laws are inconsistent with this Act.

Application of Laws of British Columbia

38. Laws of general application of British Columbia apply to or in respect of the members of the Band except to the extent that those laws are inconsistent with the terms of any treaty, this or any other Act of Parliament, the constitution of the Band or a law of the Band. . . .

Cree-Naskapi (of Quebec) Act
S.C. 1984, c. 18.

Application of Indian Act

5. Except for the purpose of determining which of the Cree beneficiaries and Naskapi beneficiaries are "Indians" within the meaning of the *Indian Act*, the *Indian Act* does not apply to Cree bands or the Naskapi band, nor does it apply on or in respect of Category IA or IA-N land.

Band By-Laws and Resolutions

6. A by-law of a band made under this Act may have application within the following territorial limits:
(a)   that band's Category IA or IA-N; and
(b)   Category III land situated within the perimeter of that band's Category IA or IA-N land and the ownership of which was ceded by letters patent or by any other method
   (i)   prior to November 11, 1975, in the case of Category III land within the perimeter of Category IA land, or

(ii)   prior to January 31, 1978, in the case of Category III land within the perimeter of Category IA-N land. . . .

Regulations

10. The Governor in Council may make regulations.
(a)   prescribing anything that by this Act is to be prescribed; and
(b)   generally for carrying out the purposes and provisions of this Act.

Incorporation by Reference of Provincial Laws

11. (1)   For the purpose of applying the portion of paragraph 5.1.13 of the *James Bay and Northern Quebec Agreement* and of paragraph 5.1.13 of the *Northeastern Quebec Agreement* dealing with the leasing of lands and the granting of real rights to non-Natives, the Governor in Council may make regulations for the purpose of making provincial law in force in the Province applicable to leasehold interests or other real rights in Category IA or IA-N land granted to non-beneficiaries for periods exceeding five years, including any renewal thereof.

(2)   For the purposes of subsection (1), a non beneficiary is a person who is not
(a   a Cree beneficiary, Naskapi beneficiary or Inuk of Fort George;
(b)   a corporation or other body established pursuant to either of the Agreements;
(c)   a corporation or other body the majority of whose shareholders or members are Cree beneficiaries, Naskapi beneficiaries or Inuit of Fort George; or
(d)   a corporation or other body in which Cree beneficiaries, Naskapi beneficiaries or Inuit of Fort George participate, as shareholders or members or otherwise, and that is prescribed.

Part I Local Government

. . .

Objects and Powers of Bands

21. The objects of a band are
(a)   to act as the local government authority on its Category IA or IA-N land;
(b)   to use, manage, administer and regulate its Category IA or IA-N land and the natural resources thereof;
(c)   to control the disposition of rights and interests in its Category IA or IA-N land and in the natural resources thereof;
(d)   to regulate the use of buildings on its Category IA-N land;
(e)   to use, manage and administer its moneys and other assets;
(f)   to promote the general welfare of its members of the band;
(g)   to promote and carry out community development and charitable works in the community;
(h)   to establish and administer services, programs and projects for members of the band, other residents of Category IA and IA-N land and residents of the Category III land referred to in paragraph 6(b);
(i)   to promote and preserve the culture, values and traditions of the Crees or Naskapis, as the case may be; and
(j)   to exercise the powers and carry out the duties conferred or imposed on the band or on its predecessor Indian Act band by any Act of Parliament or regulations made thereunder, and by the Agreements.

22. (1) A band has, subject to this Act and the regulations, the capacity, rights, powers and privileges of a natural person.

(2) A band shall not engage, directly or indirectly, in any commercial activity, except in so far as it is related to

(a) the management or administration of
   (i)   its Category IA or IA-N land or the natural resources thereof, or
   (ii) its buildings or other immovable assets on its Category IA or IA-N land; or
(b) the provision of public services to or in respect of its Category IA or IA-N land or residents thereof.

(3) Notwithstanding subsection (2), a band may own shares in corporations that carry on commercial activities. . . .

By-Laws Respecting Local Government

45. (1) Subject to this section, a band may make by-laws of a local nature for the good government of its Category IA or IA-N land and of the inhabitants of such land, and for the general welfare of the members of the band, and, without limiting the generality of the foregoing, may make by-laws respecting

(a) the administration of band affairs and the internal management of the band;
(b) the regulation of buildings for the protection of public health and safety, including the construction, maintenance, repair and demolition of buildings;
(c) health and hygiene, including
   (i)   the prevention of overcrowding of residences,
   (ii) the sanitary condition of public and private property,
   (iii) the control or prohibition of activities or undertakings that constitute a danger to public health,
   (iv) the construction, operation and regulation of waste disposal systems and the collection, removal and disposal of waste generally, and
   (v)   subject to the laws of the Province, the establishment, maintenance and operation of cemeteries;
(d) public order and safety, including
   (i)   the establishment, maintenance and operation of fire departments;
   (ii) the discharge of firearms or of arms discharged by compressed air or any other means,
   (iii) the keeping of animals,
   (iv) curfews,
   (v)   the prohibition of the sale or exchange of alcoholic beverages,
   (vi) the possession or consumption of alcoholic beverages in public places, and
   (vii) the control of public games, sports, races, athletic contests and other amusements;
(e) the protection of the environment, including natural resources;
(f) the prevention of pollution;
(g) the definition of nuisances and the control and prohibition of nuisances;
(h) the taxation for local purposes, otherwise than by means of an income tax,
   (i)   of interests in its Category IA or IA-N land, except those of Canada and Quebec, and
   (ii) of occupants and tenants of its Category IA or IA-N land, except Canada and Quebec,

subject to subsections (2) and (3) and subject to and in accordance with regulations made under subsection (4);

(i)   subject to subsection (5), the establishment, maintenance and operation of local services relating to water, sewers, fire protection, recreation, cultural activities, roads, garbage removal and disposal, lighting, heating, power, transportation, communications or snow removal, and respecting user charges for any such service;

(j)   roads, traffic and transportation, including
    (i)   the operation and speed of vehicles,
    (ii)   the maintenance, construction and operation of roads,
    (iii)   the regulation of traffic of all kinds,
    (iv)   the transportation of dangerous substances, and
    (v)   the establishment, maintenance and operation of wharves, harbours, drydocks and other landing places;

(k)   the operation of businesses and the carrying on of trades; and

(l)   parks and recreation.

(2)   A band

(a)   may not make taxation by-laws other than those described in paragraph (1)(h); and

(b)   may not make by-laws under paragraph (1)(h) until there are in force regulations made under (4).

(3)   A by-law made under paragraph (1)(h) must be approved by the electors of the band at a special band meeting or referendum at which at least ten per cent of the electors of the band voted on the matter.

(4)   The Governor in Council may make regulations respecting the exercise, pursuant to paragraph (1)(h), of a band's power of taxation, including, without restricting the generality of the foregoing, regulations respecting

(a)   assessments and the determination of tax rates;

(b)   contestation of assessments;

(c)   collection of taxes;

(d)   contestation of taxation; and

(e)   enforcement procedures.

(5)   A by-law described in paragraph (1)(i) respecting a user charge for a service may differentiate on an equitable basis between different categories of users and different categories of land that benefit from the service, but

(a)   may not delegate to anyone the power to prescribe user charges or user charge rates but must itself prescribe the user charges or the user charge rates; and

(b)   may not prescribe user charges or user charge rates that exceed the total actual or anticipated cost of providing the service.

(6)   A band may accept payment of a tax referred to in paragraph (1)(h)or a user charge referred to in paragraph (1)(i) in a form other than money.

46.   (1) A band may make by-laws respecting land and resource use and planning, including, without limiting the generality of the foregoing, by-laws respecting

(a)   the inventory, use and management of its Category IA or IA-N land and the natural resources thereof;

(b) the adoption of land use plans and resource use plans in relation to its Category IA or IA-N land; and

(c) use permits relating to its Category IA or IA-N land and buildings located thereon, and the conditions relating to the issuance, suspension or revocation of such permits. . . .

47. (1) A band may make by-laws respecting zoning, including, without limiting the generality of the foregoing, by-laws respecting

(a) the division of all or part of its Category IA or IA-N land into zones for the purpose of regulating the use of the land, natural resources thereof and buildings; and

(b) the implementation of a land use plan or resource use plan referred to in subsection 46(1) that was approved by the electors of the band under subsection 46(2). . . .

48. (1) Subject to this section, a band may make by-laws respecting hunting, fishing and trapping and the protection of wildlife, including, without limiting the generality of the foregoing, by-laws respecting

(a) the exercise of the right to harvest referred to in section 24 of the James Bay and Northern Quebec Agreement and in An Act respecting hunting and fishing rights in the James Bay and New Quebec territories (Quebec);

(b) matters described in section 85 and 86 of that Act;

(c) residence requirements relating to sport hunting and sport fishing by persons other than Cree or Naskapi beneficiaries, as contemplated by section 37 of that Act; and

(d) the right of persons of Cree or Naskapi ancestry to harvest for personal use, as contemplated by sections 38 and 38.1 of that Act. . . .

Residence Rights

103.(1) The following persons have the right to reside on the Category IA or IA-N land of a band:

(a) a member of that band;

(b) the member's consort, within the meaning of section 174; and

(c) the family to the first degree of a person described in paragraph (a) or (b). . . .

Rights Of Bands, Quebec and Others in Relation to Category Ia And Ia-N Land

109.(1) Quebec retains the bare ownership of Category IA and IA-N land.

(2) Subject to this Act, a band has the exclusive use and benefit of its Category IA or IA-N land and the natural resources thereof, and may administer, manage, control, use and enjoy that land and the natural resources thereof for community, commercial, industrial, residential or other purposes, as if it were the owner thereof. . . .

Mineral, Subsurface and Mining Rights

113.(1) Subject to this Act, Quebec retains the ownership of all mineral rights and subsurface rights on Category IA and IA-N land.

(2) Subject to subsection (3), after November 11, 1975 (in the case of Category IA land) or January 31, 1978 (in the case of Category IA-N land) no mineral right or subsurface right on Category IA or IA-N land of a band may be granted or exercised

and no mineral or other subsurface material or substance may be mined or extracted from such land without the consent of the band and payment to the band of compensation agreed to by the band. . . .

Part XIV Tax Exemptions

187.(1) In this Part, "Indian" means
   (a) in subsection (2), a Cree beneficiary or Naskapi beneficiary who is an Indian as defined in the Indian Act; and
   (b) in section 188, an Indian as defined in the *Indian Act.*

(2) For the purposes of this Part, personal property
   (a) that became the property of a band by virtue of section 13 or 15 and had been purchased by Canada with money appropriated by Parliament,
   (b) that is purchased by Canada after the coming into force of this Part with money appropriated by parliament for the use and benefit of Indians or bands, or
   (c) that is given, after the coming into force of this Part, to Indians or to a band under a treaty or agreement between a band and Canada shall be deemed always to be situated on Category IA or IA-N land.

188.(1) Notwithstanding any other Act of Parliament or of the legislature of any province, but subject to any by-laws of a band made pursuant to paragraph 45(1)(h), the following property is exempt from taxation:
   (a) the interest of an Indian or a band in Category IA or IA-N land; and
   (b) the personal property of an Indian or a band on Category IA or IA-N land. . . .

Eastmain Band v. *Gilpin* *

[1987] 3 C.N.L.R. 54 (Que. Prov. Ct.). Lavergne P.C.J., April 1, 1987.

LAVERGNE P.C.J.:— . . . The *Cree-Naskapi (of Quebec) Act*, assented to on June 14, 1984, gave substance to Canada's pledge under article 9.0.1 of the Agreement. In fact, the Act emanates from this pledge. The preamble to the Act stresses the wishes already formulated in the Agreement and the approving legislation, and confirms the will to give the Crees and Naskapis an organized and efficient local government regime, the management and control of Category IA lands, and the power to ensure the safeguard of their individual and collective rights. Without a doubt, the Act includes a wide range of powers similar to those given the municipalities governed by the *Cities and Towns Act* (R. S. Q. , c. C-19) and the *Municipal Code of Quebec* (R.S.Q., c.C-27.1). The *Cree-Naskapi (of Quebec) Act* includes provisions reflecting the legislator's will to ensure the right for the Crees to set their own standards of behaviour according to their social needs.

Under ss. 7 and 8 of this Act, the band councils may require the holding of a licence permit, and prohibit an activity. According to s. 9, the *Statutory Instruments Act* (S.C. 1970–71–72, c. 38) does not apply to resolutions or by-laws of bands made under the *Cree-Naskapi (of Quebec) Act.* Section 3 provides that where there is any inconsistency between the *Cree-Naskapi (of Quebec) Act* and any other federal act, the former Act will prevail. Section 4 stipulates that provincial laws do not apply where they are inconsistent with by-laws made by band councils. Finally, under s. 5, the *Indian Act* does not apply to

---

* Gilpin was charged for allowing his child to be in breach of a curfew, contrary to a band by-law enacted under the *Cree-Naskapi (of Quebec) Act*, S.C. 1983-84, c. 18, s. 45(1)(d)(iv). This decision deals with the accused's motion challenging the validity of the band council to adopt the by-law.

Cree and Naskapi bands, except for the purpose of determining Indian status within the meaning of the Indian Act.

The subjects and powers of bands are described at ss. 21(a) to 21(j). Section 21(f) reads:

21. The objects of a band are . . .

(f) to promote the general welfare of the members of the band;

When interpreting the validity of a by-law, the objective of the organization described in the law should be taken into account. This method of interpretation was recognized by a majority of Supreme Court justices in *CKOY Ltd.* v. *R.* ((1979) 1 S.C.R. 2). In the case at bar, s. 45(1)(d)(iv) authorizes the bands to make by-laws respecting curfew. There is good reason to wonder whether the Eastmain Council, for the good of its members' general welfare, could avail itself of s. 21(f) to introduce discrimination in its curfew by-law. There is room for doubt in the light of the reasons given by Beetz J. in the *Arcade Amusements* case.

Nevertheless, the Court believes that this case does not concern statutory instruments within the meaning generally accepted in public law, because of the spirit reflected by the Agreement and the ensuing legislation.

Native rights have been given constitutional recognition. Section 35(1) of the *Constitution Act, 1982* stipulates:

The existing aboriginal and treaty rights of the aboriginal peoples of Canada are hereby recognized and affirmed.

And as though to remove all ambiguity as to whether or not the James Bay Agreement was a treaty, the proclamation of 1983 amending the Constitution (O.G. part. III, August 10, 1984, p. 1581) added a third paragraph to s. 35:

(3) For greater certainty, in subsection (1) "treaty rights" includes rights that now exist by way of land claims agreements or may be so acquired.

Similarly, s-s. 1 of s. 52 of the *Constitution Act, 1982* states:

The Constitution of Canada is the supreme law of Canada, and any law that is inconsistent with the provisions of the Constitution is, to the extent of the inconsistency, of no force or effect.

Since patriation of the Constitution had raised some bad feelings among the Natives because they were not consulted, s. 35.1 was added by the proclamation of 1983. This section provided for an agreement to invite the Native peoples of Canada to be present when amendments were to be made to s. 91(24) of the *Constitution Act, 1867* giving the federal Parliament jurisdiction over the Indians and lands set aside for Indians, as well as to ss. 35 and 35.1 of the *Constitution Act, 1982*.

Therefore, the Crees' rights conferred and recognised by the James Bay agreement as regards Category IA lands, have been made constitutional. These rights were given legislative approval by the *Cree Naskapi (of Quebec) Act* as promised in the Agreement. That being the case, it seems that the federal Parliament cannot adopt laws encroaching upon the rights conferred upon the Crees and the Naskapis under the *Cree Naskapi (of Quebec) Act*, without violating the Constitution. Such laws would be inoperative as they would be inconsistent with the rights guaranteed the Natives by s. 35(3) of the *Constitution Act, 1982* (s. 52). Any change to the Natives' existing rights would be legal only if brought about by a constitutional amendment.

Consequently, subordination, which is one of the essential characteristics of regulatory power in our juridical system, does not apply to the case at bar. Band councils' regulatory power is not subjected to the will of the federal Parliament, because this power is included in the rights guaranteed by the Constitution. In the Court's opinion the right of a local administration to make by-laws is part of those guaranteed rights. The federal Parliament could not adopt a law taking away from the band councils the power to regulate curfews, for instance. This situation is unique in Canada. The constitutional amendment proclaims the permanence and stability of the James Bay Cree population and, therefore, undoubtedly confers upon it a particular status. Since the Constitution prevents Parliament from adopting laws encroaching upon the guaranteed rights regarding Category IA lands, it would be rather strange were this same Parliament to retain the right to delegate to Cree bands the power to make discriminatory by-laws. It would be illogical and inconsistent to transfer a power irrevocably, subject only to a constitutional amendment, and retain a right to supervise the manner in which this power is exercised.

Respect for those fundamental freedoms which mainly motivated the principle of non-discrimination in matters of regulatory power, except when expressly stipulated in the enabling law, is safeguarded by s. 15 of the *Charter of Human Rights and Freedoms*.

The Court concludes that the principle of non-discrimination in the exercise of regulatory power does not apply to this case. The above-mentioned texts must be interpreted, by necessary implication, as conferring the Cree bands full power to legislate within specified fields, according to community needs identified by themselves.

In this perspective, the Court agrees with the proposition that the Crees hold some sort of residual sovereignty as regards their local governments.

Therefore, the Court: Declares the Eastmain Band Curfew By-Law legal, and dismissed the preliminary motion submitted by the accused.

Waskaganish Band v. *Blackned*

[1986] 3 C.N.L.R. 168. (Que. Prov. Ct.). Ouellet J., March 18, 1986.

OUELLET J.:— . . . Under these circumstances, it would seem to me that the band council constitutes an autonomous level of government when it exercises the powers conferred upon it by the *Cree-Naskapi (of Quebec) Act*. As long as it remains within the powers so conferred, the band council represents a level of government independent from the Canadian Parliament and the Quebec legislature. Its members are the elected representatives of the community who, in giving them their mandate, invest them with the powers granted to the band under the Treaty Convention and especially the *Cree-Naskapi (of Quebec) Act*. It is to the band members that the council is accountable for its administration and the exercise of its powers, and not to Parliament, of which it is not an agent. . . .

It is therefore obvious to me that Parliament's intention was to create a level of local government for the Cree communities. Such local government would be invested with the powers of local administration generally conferred upon municipalities as well as certain other powers coming under the provincial legislatures, in the case of non-Indians, and of the federal parliament itself, in the case of Indians. . . .

Nisga'a Final Agreement

between the Governments of British Columbia and Canada and the Nisga'a Nation. Enacted federally by the *Nisga'a Final Agreement Act*, S.C. 2000, c. 7 and provincially by the *Nisga'a Final Agreement Act*, S.B.C. 1999, c. 2.

Chapter 11—Nisga'a Government

Self-Government

1. The Nisga'a Nation has the right to self-government, and the authority to make laws, as set out in this Agreement.

Recognition of Nisga'a Lisims Government and Nisga'a Village Governments

2. Nisga'a Lisims Government and Nisga'a Village Governments, as provided for under the Nisga'a Constitution, are the governments of the Nisga'a Nation and the Nisga'a Villages, respectively.

3. Except as may otherwise be agreed to by the relevant Parties in respect of particular matters, Nisga'a Lisims Government is responsible for intergovernmental relations between the Nisga'a Nation on the one hand, and Canada or British Columbia, or both, on the other hand.

4. The exercise of Nisga'a Government jurisdiction and authority set out in this Agreement will evolve over time.

Legal Status and Capacity

5. The Nisga'a Nation, and each Nisga'a Village, is a separate and distinct legal entity, with the capacity, rights, powers, and privileges of a natural person, including to:

    a. enter into contracts and agreements;

    b. acquire and hold property or an interest in property, and sell or otherwise dispose of that property or interest;

    c. raise, spend, invest, or borrow money;

    d. sue and be sued; and do other things ancillary to the exercise of its rights, powers and privileges.

6. The rights, powers, and privileges of the Nisga'a Nation, and of each Nisga'a Village, will be exercised in accordance with:

    a. this Agreement;

    b. the Nisga'a Constitution; and

    c. Nisga'a laws.

7. The Nisga'a Nation will act through Nisga'a Lisims Government in exercising its rights, powers, and privileges and in carrying out its duties, functions, and obligations.

8. Each Nisga'a Village will act through its Nisga'a Village Government in exercising its rights, powers, and privileges and in carrying out its duties, functions, and obligations.

Nisga'a Constitution

9. The Nisga'a Nation will have a Nisga'a Constitution, consistent with this Agreement, which will:

    a. provide for Nisga'a Lisims Government and Nisga'a Village Governments, including their duties, composition, and membership;

    b. provide that this Agreement sets out the authority of Nisga'a Government to make laws;

    c. assign to Nisga'a Lisims Government and Nisga'a Village Governments the rights, powers, privileges, and responsibilities under this Agreement that are not specifically assigned to Nisga'a Lisims Government;

d. provide for the enactment of laws by Nisga'a Government;

e. provide for challenging the validity of Nisga'a laws;

f. provide for the creation, continuation, amalgamation, dissolution, naming, or renaming of:

    i.   Nisga'a Villages on Nisga'a Lands, and

    ii. Nisga'a Urban Locals;

g. provide for Nisga'a Urban Locals, or other means by which Nisga'a citizens residing outside of the Nass Area may participate in Nisga'a Lisims Government;

h. provide for the establishment of Nisga'a Public Institutions;

i. provide for the role of the Nisga'a elders, Simgigat and Sigidimhaanak, in providing guidance and interpretation of the Ayuuk to Nisga'a Government;

j. provide that in the event of an inconsistency or conflict between the Nisga'a Constitution and the provisions of any Nisga'a law, the Nisga'a law is, to the extent of the inconsistency or conflict, of no force or effect;

k. require that Nisga'a Government be democratically accountable to Nisga'a citizens, and, in particular:

    i.   that elections for Nisga'a Lisims Government and each Nisga'a Village Government be held at least every five years, and

    ii. that, subject to residency, age, and other requirements set out in the Nisga'a Constitution or Nisga'a law, all Nisga'a citizens are eligible to vote in Nisga'a elections and to hold office in Nisga'a Government;

l. require a system of financial administration comparable to standards generally accepted for governments in Canada, through which Nisga'a Lisims Government will be financially accountable to Nisga'a citizens, and Nisga'a Village Governments will be financially accountable to Nisga'a citizens of those Nisga'a Villages;

m. require conflict of interest rules that are comparable to standards generally accepted for governments in Canada;

n. provide conditions under which the Nisga'a Nation or a Nisga'a Village may:

    i.   dispose of the whole of its estate or interest in any parcel of Nisga'a Lands or Nisga'a Fee Simple Lands, and

    ii. from the whole of its estate or interest, create or dispose of any lesser estate or interest in any parcel of Nisga'a Lands or Nisga'a Fee Simple Lands;

o. recognize and protect rights and freedoms of Nisga'a citizens;

p. provide that every Nisga'a participant who is a Canadian citizen or permanent resident of Canada is entitled to be a Nisga'a citizen;

q. provide for Nisga'a Government during the period from the effective date until the date on which the office holders elected in the first Nisga'a elections take office;

r. provide for amendment of the Nisga'a Constitution; and

s. include other provisions, as determined by the Nisga'a Nation.

10. The Nisga'a Constitution, as approved in accordance with the Ratification Chapter, comes into force on the effective date.

11. The Nisga'a Constitution will initially include an amending procedure requiring that an amendment be approved by at least 70% of Nisga'a citizens voting in a referendum.

Nisga'a Government Structure

12. Each Nisga'a Village Government consists of elected members as set out in the Nisga'a Constitution.

13. On the effective date, there are three Nisga'a Urban Locals, as set out in the Nisga'a Constitution, known as:

    a. Greater Vancouver Urban Local;

    b. Terrace Urban Local; and

    c. Prince Rupert/Port Edward Urban Local.

14. Nisga'a Lisims Government consists of the following members, as set out in the Nisga'a Constitution:

    a. at least three officers elected by the Nisga'a Nation in a general election;

    b. the elected members of the Nisga'a Village Governments; and

    c. at least one representative elected by the Nisga'a citizens of each Nisga'a Urban Local. . . .

Appeal and Review of Administrative Decisions

16. Nisga'a Government will provide appropriate procedures for the appeal or review of administrative decisions of Nisga'a Public Institutions.

17. The Supreme Court of British Columbia has jurisdiction in respect of applications for judicial review of administrative decisions of Nisga'a Institutions exercising a statutory power of decision under Nisga'a law, but no application for judicial review of those decisions may be brought until all procedures for appeal or review provided by Nisga'a Government and applicable to that decision have been exhausted.

Register of Laws

18. Nisga'a Lisims Government will:

    a. maintain a public registry of Nisga'a laws in the English language and, at the discretion of Nisga'a Lisims Government, in the Nisga'a language;

    b. provide Canada and British Columbia with a copy of a Nisga'a law as soon as practicable after that law is enacted; and

    c. establish procedures for the coming into force and publication of Nisga'a laws.

Relations With Individuals Who Are Not Nisga'a Citizens

19. Nisga'a Government will consult with individuals who are ordinarily resident within Nisga'a Lands and who are not Nisga'a citizens about Nisga'a Government decisions that directly and significantly affect them.

20. Nisga'a Government will provide that individuals who are ordinarily resident within Nisga'a Lands and who are not Nisga'a citizens may participate in a Nisga'a Public Institution, if the activities of that Nisga'a Public Institution directly and significantly affect them.

21. The means of participation under paragraph 20 will be:
    a. a reasonable opportunity to make representations to the Nisga'a Public Institution in respect of activities that significantly and directly affect them;
    b. if the members of a Nisga'a Public Institution are elected:
        i. the ability to vote for or become members of the Nisga'a Public Institution, or
        ii. a guaranteed number of members, with the right to vote, on the Nisga'a Public Institution; or
    c. other comparable measures.

22. Nisga'a Government will provide that individuals who are ordinarily resident within Nisga'a Lands and who are not Nisga'a citizens may avail themselves of the appeal or review procedures referred to in paragraph 16.

23. Nisga'a Government may appoint individuals who are not Nisga'a citizens as members of Nisga'a Public Institutions. . . .

Legislative Jurisdiction and Authority

General

32. In the event of an inconsistency or conflict between this Agreement and the provisions of any Nisga'a law, this Agreement prevails to the extent of the inconsistency or conflict.

33. Nisga'a Lisims Government and Nisga'a Village Governments, respectively, have the principal authority, as set out in, and in accordance with, this Agreement, in respect of Nisga'a Government, Nisga'a citizenship, Nisga'a culture, Nisga'a language, Nisga'a Lands, and Nisga'a assets.

Nisga'a Government

34. Nisga'a Lisims Government may make laws in respect of the administration, management and operation of Nisga'a Government, including:
    a. the establishment of Nisga'a Public Institutions, including their respective powers, duties, composition, and membership;
    b. powers, duties, responsibilities, remuneration, and indemnification of members, officials, employees, and appointees of Nisga'a Institutions;
    c. the establishment of Nisga'a Corporations, but the registration or incorporation of the Nisga'a Corporations must be under federal or provincial laws;
    d. the delegation of Nisga'a Government authority, but the authority to make laws may be delegated only to a Nisga'a Institution;
    e. financial administration of the Nisga'a Nation, Nisga'a Villages, and Nisga'a Institutions; and
    f. elections, by-elections, and referenda.

35. Each Nisga'a Village Government may make laws in respect of the administration, management, and operation of that Nisga'a Village Government, including:
    a. the establishment of Nisga'a Public Institutions of that Nisga'a Village Government, including their respective powers, duties, composition, and membership;
    b. powers, duties, responsibilities, remuneration, and indemnification of members,

officials, employees, and appointees of Nisga'a Public Institutions referred to in subparagraph (a); and

c. the delegation of the Nisga'a Village Government's authority, but the authority to make laws may be delegated only to a Nisga'a Institution.

36. In the event of an inconsistency or conflict between a Nisga'a law under paragraphs 34 or 35 and a federal or provincial law, the Nisga'a law prevails to the extent of the inconsistency or conflict.

37. Nisga'a Lisims Government may make laws in respect of the creation, continuation, amalgamation, dissolution, naming, or renaming of:

a. Nisga'a Villages on Nisga'a Lands; and

b. Nisga'a Urban Locals.

38. In the event of an inconsistency or conflict between a Nisga'a law under paragraph 37 and a federal or provincial law, the Nisga'a law prevails to the extent of the inconsistency or conflict.

Nisga'a Citizenship

39. Nisga'a Lisims Government may make laws in respect of Nisga'a citizenship. The conferring of Nisga'a citizenship does not:

a. confer or deny rights of entry into Canada, Canadian citizenship, the right to be registered as an Indian under the Indian Act, or any of the rights or benefits under the Indian Act; or

b. except as set out in this Agreement or in any federal or provincial law, impose any obligation on Canada or British Columbia to provide rights or benefits.

40. In the event of an inconsistency or conflict between a Nisga'a law under paragraph 39 and a federal or provincial law, the Nisga'a law prevails to the extent of the inconsistency or conflict.

Culture and Language

41. Nisga'a Lisims Government may make laws to preserve, promote, and develop Nisga'a culture and Nisga'a language, including laws to authorize or accredit the use, reproduction, and representation of Nisga'a cultural symbols and practices, and the teaching of Nisga'a language.

42. Except as provided for by federal or provincial law, Nisga'a Lisims Government jurisdiction under paragraph 41 to make laws in respect of Nisga'a culture and Nisga'a language does not include jurisdiction to make laws in respect of intellectual property, the official languages of Canada or the prohibition of activities outside of Nisga'a Lands. . . .

Nisga'a Property in Nisga'a Lands

44. Nisga'a Lisims Government may make laws in respect of:

a. the use and management of Nisga'a Lands owned by the Nisga'a Nation, a Nisga'a Village, or a Nisga'a Corporation;

b. the possession of Nisga'a Lands owned by the Nisga'a Nation, a Nisga'a Village, or a Nisga'a Corporation, including the granting of rights of possession in Nisga'a Lands and any conditions or restrictions on those rights;

c. the disposition of an estate or interest of the Nisga'a Nation, a Nisga'a Village or a Nisga'a Corporation, in any parcel of Nisga'a Lands, including: . . .

d. the conditions on, and restrictions subject to which, the Nisga'a Nation, a Nisga'a Village or a Nisga'a Corporation may create or dispose of its estates or interests in any parcel of Nisga'a Lands;

e. the conditions or restrictions, to be established at the time of the creation or disposition of an estate or interest of the Nisga'a Nation, a Nisga'a Village or a Nisga'a Corporation in any parcel of Nisga'a Lands, in respect of that and any subsequent disposition;

f. the reservation or exception of interests, rights, privileges, and titles from any creation or disposition of an estate or interest of the Nisga'a Nation, a Nisga'a Village, or Nisga'a Corporation in Nisga'a Lands; and

g. other similar matters relating to the property interests of the Nisga'a Nation, Nisga'a Villages, and Nisga'a Corporations in Nisga'a Lands.

45. In the event of an inconsistency or conflict between a Nisga'a law under paragraph 44 and a federal or provincial law, the Nisga'a law prevails to the extent of the inconsistency or conflict.

46. Nisga'a laws under paragraph 44(c) in respect of estates or interests that are recognized and permitted by federal or provincial laws of general application will be consistent with federal and provincial laws of general application in respect of those estates or interests, other than the provincial Torrens system and any federal land title or land registry laws.

Regulation, Administration and Expropriation of Nisga'a Lands
47. Nisga'a Lisims Government may make laws in respect of:

a. the use, management, planning, zoning, and development of Nisga'a Lands;

b. regulation, licensing, and prohibition of the operation on Nisga'a Lands of businesses, professions, and trades, including the imposition of licence fees or other fees, other than laws in respect of the accreditation, certification, or professional conduct of professions and trades; and

c. other similar matters related to the regulation and administration of Nisga'a Lands.

48. Each Nisga'a Village Government may make laws in respect of the matters referred to in paragraph 47, to apply on their respective Nisga'a Village Lands.

49. In the event of an inconsistency or conflict between a Nisga'a law under paragraph 47 or 48 and a federal or provincial law, the Nisga'a law prevails to the extent of the inconsistency or conflict.

50. Nisga'a Lisims Government may make laws in respect of:

a. subject to paragraphs 2, 3, and 4 of the Land Title Chapter, the establishment and operation of a land title or land registry system, in respect of estates, interests, charges, encumbrances, conditions, provisos, restrictions, exceptions, and reservations on or in Nisga'a Lands, including the establishment of a requirement similar to subsection 20(1) of the Land Title Act;

b. designation of any parcel of Nisga'a Lands as Nisga'a Private Lands or Nisga'a Village Lands;

    c. expropriation by Nisga'a Government for public purposes and public works, of estates, or interests in Nisga'a Lands other than:

      i. interests referred to in paragraphs 30 and 41 of the Lands Chapter to which Nisga'a Lands are subject on the effective date,

      ii. subject to paragraphs 35 and 36 of the Lands Chapter, interests referred to in paragraphs 33 and 34 of the Lands Chapter to which Nisga'a Lands are subject on the effective date,

      iii. estates or interests expropriated by Canada in accordance with the Lands Chapter, and

      iv. rights of way acquired by British Columbia or a public utility in accordance with the Roads and Rights of Way Chapter; and

    d. other similar matters related to the regulation and administration of Nisga'a Lands.

51. In the event of an inconsistency or conflict between a Nisga'a law under paragraph 50 and a federal or provincial law, the Nisga'a law prevails to the extent of the inconsistency or conflict.

52. Notwithstanding paragraph 51, in the event of a conflict between a Nisga'a law and a federal law of general application in respect of prospecting for, production of, refining, and handling of uranium or other products capable of releasing atomic energy, the federal law prevails to the extent of the conflict. Nothing in this paragraph is intended to require the production of uranium or other products capable of releasing atomic energy. . . .

Public Order, Peace, and Safety

59. Nisga'a Lisims Government may make laws in respect of the regulation, control, or prohibition of any actions, activities, or undertakings on Nisga'a Lands, or on submerged lands within Nisga'a Lands, other than actions, activities, or undertakings on submerged lands that are authorized by the Crown, that constitute, or may constitute, a nuisance, a trespass, a danger to public health, or a threat to public order, peace, or safety.

60. A Nisga'a Village Government may make laws in respect of the regulation, control, or prohibition of any actions, activities, or undertakings on the Nisga'a Village Lands of that Nisga'a Village, or on submerged lands within those Nisga'a Village Lands, other than actions, activities, or undertakings on those submerged lands that are authorized by the Crown, that constitute, or may constitute, a nuisance, a trespass, a danger to public health, or a threat to public order, peace, or safety.

61. For greater certainty, Nisga'a Government authority does not include authority in respect of criminal law.

62. In the event of a conflict between a Nisga'a law under paragraph 59 or 60 and a federal or provincial law of general application, the federal or provincial law prevails to the extent of the conflict. . . .

Buildings, Structures, and Public Works

69. Subject to the Roads and Rights of Way Chapter, Nisga'a Lisims Government may make laws in respect of the design, construction, maintenance, repair, and demolition of buildings, structures, and public works on Nisga'a Lands.

70. Subject to the Roads and Rights of Way Chapter, a Nisga'a Village Government may

make laws in respect of the matters referred to in paragraph 69, to apply on the Nisga'a Village Lands of that Nisga'a Village.

71. In the event of a conflict between a Nisga'a law under paragraph 69 or 70 and a federal or provincial law of general application, the federal or provincial law prevails to the extent of the conflict.

Traffic and Transportation

72. A Nisga'a Village Government may make laws in respect of the regulation of traffic and transportation on Nisga'a Roads within its village, to the same extent as municipal governments have authority in respect of the regulation of traffic and transportation in municipalities in British Columbia.

73. Nisga'a Lisims Government may make laws in respect of the regulation of traffic and transportation on Nisga'a Roads, other than Nisga'a Roads within Nisga'a villages, to the same extent as municipal governments have authority in respect of the regulation of traffic and transportation in municipalities in British Columbia.

74. In the event of a conflict between a Nisga'a law under paragraphs 72 or 73 and a federal or provincial law of general application, the federal or provincial law prevails to the extent of the conflict.

Solemnization of Marriages

75. Nisga'a Lisims Government may make laws in respect of solemnization of marriages within British Columbia, including prescribing conditions under which individuals appointed by Nisga'a Lisims Government may solemnize marriages.

76. In the event of a conflict between a Nisga'a law under paragraph 75 and a federal or provincial law of general application, the federal or provincial law prevails to the extent of the conflict.

77. Individuals appointed by Nisga'a Lisims Government to solemnize marriages:

   a. will be registered by British Columbia as persons authorized to solemnize marriages; and

   b. have the authority to solemnize marriages under British Columbia law and Nisga'a law, and have all the associated rights, duties and responsibilities of a marriage commissioner under the provincial Marriage Act.

Social Services

78. Nisga'a Lisims Government may make laws in respect of the provision of social services by Nisga'a Government to Nisga'a citizens, other than the licensing and regulation of facility-based services off Nisga'a Lands.

79. In the event of a conflict between a Nisga'a law under paragraph 78 and a federal or provincial law of general application, the federal or provincial law prevails to the extent of the conflict.

80. If Nisga'a Lisims Government makes laws under paragraph 78, at the request of any Party, the Parties will negotiate and attempt to reach agreements in respect of exchange of information, avoidance of double payments, and related matters.

81. At the request of any Party, the Parties will negotiate and attempt to reach agreements for administration and delivery by Nisga'a Government of federal and provincial social services and programs for all individuals residing within Nisga'a Lands.

Those agreements will include a requirement that Nisga'a citizens and individuals who are not Nisga'a citizens be treated equally in the provision of those social services and programs.

Health Services

82. Nisga'a Lisims Government may make laws in respect of health services on Nisga'a Lands.

83. In the event of a conflict between a Nisga'a law under paragraph 82 and a federal or provincial law of general application, the federal or provincial law prevails to the extent of the conflict.

84. Notwithstanding paragraph 83, in the event of an inconsistency or conflict between a Nisga'a law determining the organization and structure for the delivery of health services on Nisga'a Lands, and a federal or provincial law, the Nisga'a law prevails to the extent of the inconsistency or conflict.

85. At the request of any Party, the Parties will negotiate and attempt to reach agreements for Nisga'a Lisims Government delivery and administration of federal and provincial health services and programs for all individuals residing within Nisga'a Lands. Those agreements will include a requirement that Nisga'a citizens and individuals who are not Nisga'a citizens be treated equally in the provision of those health services and programs.

Aboriginal Healers

86. Nisga'a Lisims Government may make laws in respect of the authorization or licensing of individuals who practice as aboriginal healers on Nisga'a Lands, but, this authority to make laws does not include the authority to regulate products or substances that are regulated under federal or provincial laws of general application.

87. In the event of an inconsistency or conflict between a Nisga'a law under paragraph 86 and a federal or provincial law, the Nisga'a law prevails to the extent of the inconsistency or conflict.

88. Any Nisga'a law under paragraph 86 will include measures in respect of competence, ethics and quality of practice that are reasonably required to protect the public.

Child and Family Services

89. Nisga'a Lisims Government may make laws in respect of child and family services on Nisga'a Lands, provided that those laws include standards comparable to provincial standards intended to ensure the safety and well-being of children and families.

90. Notwithstanding any laws made under paragraph 89, if there is an emergency in which a child on Nisga'a Lands is at risk, British Columbia may act to protect the child and, in those circumstances, unless British Columbia and Nisga'a Lisims Government otherwise agree, British Columbia will refer the matter back to Nisga'a Lisims Government after the emergency.

91. In the event of an inconsistency or conflict between a Nisga'a law under paragraph 89 and a federal or provincial law, the Nisga'a law prevails to the extent of the inconsistency or conflict.

92. At the request of Nisga'a Lisims Government, Nisga'a Lisims Government and British Columbia will negotiate and attempt to reach agreements in respect of child and

family services for Nisga'a children who do not reside on Nisga'a Lands.

93. Laws of general application in respect of reporting of child abuse apply on Nisga'a Lands.

Child Custody

94. Nisga'a Government has standing in any judicial proceedings in which custody of a Nisga'a child is in dispute, and the court will consider any evidence and representations in respect of Nisga'a laws and customs in addition to any other matters it is required by law to consider.

95. The participation of Nisga'a Government in proceedings referred to in paragraph 94 will be in accordance with the applicable rules of court and will not affect the court's ability to control its process.

Adoption

96. Nisga'a Lisims Government may make laws in respect of the adoption of Nisga'a children, provided that those laws:

   a. expressly provide that the best interests of the child be the paramount consideration in determining whether an adoption will take place; and

   b. require Nisga'a Lisims Government to provide British Columbia and Canada with records of all adoptions occurring under Nisga'a laws.

97. Nisga'a law applies to the adoption of a Nisga'a child residing off Nisga'a Lands if:

   a. the parent, parents, or guardian of the child consent to the application of Nisga'a law to the adoption; or

   b. a court dispenses with the requirement for the consent referred to in subparagraph (a), in accordance with the criteria that would be used by that court in an application to dispense with the requirement for a parent or guardian's consent to an adoption.

98. If the Director of Child Protection, or a successor to that position, becomes the guardian of a Nisga'a child, the Director will:

   a. provide notice to Nisga'a Lisims Government that the Director is the guardian of the Nisga'a child;

   b. provide notice to Nisga'a Lisims Government of any plan for the Nisga'a child's care that could result in an application to adopt the Nisga'a child; and

   c. consent to the application of Nisga'a law to the adoption of that child, unless it is determined under provincial law that there are good reasons to believe it is in the best interests of the child to withhold consent.

99. In the event of an inconsistency or conflict between a Nisga'a law under paragraph 96 and a federal or provincial law, the Nisga'a law prevails to the extent of the inconsistency or conflict.

Pre-school to Grade 12 Education

100. Nisga'a Lisims Government may make laws in respect of pre-school to grade 12 education on Nisga'a Lands of Nisga'a citizens, including the teaching of Nisga'a language and culture, provided that those laws include provisions for:

   a. curriculum, examination, and other standards that permit transfers of students between school systems at a similar level of achievement and permit admission of students to the provincial post-secondary education systems;

b. certification of teachers, other than for the teaching of Nisga'a language and culture, by:

    i.   a Nisga'a Institution, in accordance with standards comparable to standards applicable to individuals who teach in public or independent schools in British Columbia, or

    ii. a provincial body having the responsibility to certify individuals who teach in public or independent schools in British Columbia; and

c. certification of teachers, for the teaching of Nisga'a language and culture, by a Nisga'a Institution, in accordance with standards established under Nisga'a law.

101. In the event of an inconsistency or conflict between a Nisga'a law under paragraph 100 and a federal or provincial law, the Nisga'a law prevails to the extent of the inconsistency or conflict.

102. If Nisga'a Lisims Government makes laws under paragraph 100, at the request of Nisga'a Lisims Government or British Columbia, those Parties will negotiate and attempt to reach agreements concerning the provision of Kindergarten to Grade 12 education to:

a. persons other than Nisga'a citizens residing within Nisga'a Lands; and

b. Nisga'a citizens residing off Nisga'a Lands.

Post-Secondary Education

103. Nisga'a Lisims Government may make laws in respect of post-secondary education within Nisga'a Lands, including:

a. the establishment of post-secondary institutions that have the ability to grant degrees, diplomas or certificates;

b. the determination of the curriculum for post-secondary institutions established under Nisga'a law;

c. the accreditation and certification of individuals who teach or research Nisga'a language and culture; and

d. the provision for and coordination of all adult education programs.

104. Nisga'a laws in respect of post-secondary education will include standards comparable to provincial standards in respect of:

a. institutional organizational structure and accountability;

b. admission standards and policies;

c. instructors' qualifications and certification;

d. curriculum standards sufficient to permit transfers of students between provincial post-secondary institutions; and

e. requirements for degrees, diplomas, or certificates.

105. In the event of an inconsistency or conflict between a Nisga'a law under paragraph 103 and a federal or provincial law, the Nisga'a law prevails to the extent of the inconsistency or conflict.

106. Nisga'a Lisims Government may operate and provide post-secondary education serv-

ices outside Nisga'a Lands in accordance with federal and provincial laws.

107. Nisga'a Lisims Government may prescribe the terms and conditions under which Nisga'a post-secondary institutions may enter into arrangements with other institutions or British Columbia to provide post-secondary education outside Nisga'a Lands.

Gambling and Gaming

108. British Columbia will not licence or approve gambling or gaming facilities on Nisga'a Lands other than in accordance with any terms and conditions established by Nisga'a Government that are not inconsistent with federal and provincial laws of general application.

109. Any change in federal or provincial legislation or policy that permits the involvement of aboriginal peoples in the regulation of gambling and gaming will, with the consent of Nisga'a Lisims Government, apply to Nisga'a Government.

Intoxicants

110. Nisga'a Government may make laws in respect of the prohibition of, and the terms and conditions for, the sale, exchange, possession, or consumption of intoxicants on Nisga'a Lands.

111. In the event of a conflict between a Nisga'a law under paragraph 110 and a federal or provincial law of general application, the federal or provincial law prevails to the extent of the conflict.

112. The Nisga'a Nation, its agents and assignees have:

a. the exclusive right to sell liquor on Nisga'a Lands in accordance with laws of general application; and

b. the right to purchase liquor from the British Columbia Liquor Distribution Branch, or its successors, in accordance with federal and provincial laws of general application. . . .

Devolution of Cultural Property

115. In paragraphs 116 to 119, "cultural property" means:

a. ceremonial regalia and similar personal property associated with a Nisga'a chief or clan; and

b. other personal property that has cultural significance to the Nisga'a Nation.

116. Nisga'a Lisims Government may make laws in respect of devolution of the cultural property of a Nisga'a citizen who dies intestate. In the event of an inconsistency or conflict between a Nisga'a law under this paragraph and a federal or provincial law, the Nisga'a law prevails to the extent of the inconsistency or conflict.

117. Nisga'a Lisims Government has standing in any judicial proceeding in which:

a. the validity of the will of a Nisga'a citizen; or

b. the devolution of the cultural property of a Nisga'a citizen is at issue, including any proceedings under wills variation legislation.

118. Nisga'a Lisims Government may commence an action under wills variation legislation in British Columbia in respect of the will of a Nisga'a citizen that provides for a devolution of cultural property. . . .

Other Areas of Legislative Jurisdiction

121. In addition to the laws that Nisga'a Government may make under this Chapter, Nisga'a Government may make laws in respect of matters within Nisga'a Government jurisdiction as set out in, and in accordance with, this Agreement.

Emergency Preparedness

122. Nisga'a Lisims Government, with respect to Nisga'a Lands, has the rights, powers, duties, and obligations of a local authority under federal and provincial legislation in respect of emergency preparedness and emergency measures.

123. Nisga'a Lisims Government may make laws in respect of its rights, powers, duties, and obligations under paragraph 122. In the event of a conflict between a Nisga'a law under this paragraph and a federal or provincial law of general application, the federal or provincial law prevails to the extent of the conflict.

124. For greater certainty, Nisga'a Lisims Government may declare a state of local emergency, and exercise the powers of a local authority in respect of local emergencies in accordance with federal and provincial laws in respect of emergency measures, but any declaration and any exercise of those powers is subject to the authority of Canada and British Columbia set out in those federal and provincial laws.

125. Nothing in this Agreement affects the authority of:

a. Canada to declare a national emergency; or

b. British Columbia to declare a provincial emergency in accordance with federal and provincial laws of general application.

Other Matters

126. For greater certainty, the authority of Nisga'a Government to make laws in respect of a subject matter as set out in this Agreement includes the authority to make laws and to do other things as may be necessarily incidental to exercising its authority.

127. Nisga'a Government may make laws and do other things that may be necessary to enable each of the Nisga'a Nation, a Nisga'a Village, and Nisga'a Government to exercise its rights, or to carry out its responsibilities, under this Agreement.

128. Nisga'a Government may provide for the imposition of penalties, including fines, restitution, and imprisonment for the violation of Nisga'a laws, within the limits set out for summary conviction offences in the Criminal Code of Canada or the British Columbia Offence Act.

129. Nisga'a Government may adopt federal or provincial laws in respect of matters within Nisga'a Government jurisdiction as set out in this Agreement. . . .

SELECTED BIBLIOGRAPHY

Asch, M. "Aboriginal Self-Government and the Construction of Canadian Constitutional Identity" (1992) 30:2 Alta. L. Rev. 465.

Barron, F.L. & J. Garcia, eds. *Urban Indian Reserves* (Saskatoon: Purich Publishing Ltd., 1999).

Borrows, J. "A Genealogy of Law: Inherent Sovereignty and First Nations Self-Government" (1992) 30 Osgoode Hall L.J. 2.

Cassidy, F. & R. Bish. *Indian Government: Its Meaning in Practice* (Montreal: The Institute for Research on Public Policy, 1989).

Doerr, A. "Building New Orders of Government—The Future of Aboriginal Self-Government" (1997) 40:2 Can. Pub. Admin. 274.

Isaac, T. "The Storm Over Aboriginal Self-Government: Section 35 of the *Constitution Act, 1982* and the Redefinition of the Inherent Right of Aboriginal Self-Government" [1992] 2 C.N.L.R. 6.

Macklem, P. "First Nations, Self-Government and the Borders of the Canadian Legal Imagination" (1991) 36 McGill L.J. 382.

Morse, B.W. "Permafrost Rights: Aboriginal Self-Government and the Supreme Court in *R. v. Pamajewon*" (September 1997) 42 McGill L.J. 1011.

Nakatsuru, S. "A Constitutional Right of Indian Self-Government" (1985) 43 U.T. Fac. L. Rev. 72.

Olynyk, J. "Approaches to Sorting Out Jurisdiction in a Self-Government Context" (1995) 53 U.T. Fac. L. Rev. 235.

Royal Commission on Aboriginal Peoples. *Partners in Confederation: Aboriginal Peoples, Self-Government and the Constitution*. Ottawa: RCAP, 1993.

Chapter 8

ABORIGINAL WOMEN

INTRODUCTION[1]

Aboriginal women have suffered discrimination, particularly due to the profound effect the *Indian Act*[2] and its governmental regimes has had on the lives of many Aboriginal women. Aboriginal women continue to face discrimination as members of a visible minority group—Aboriginal people—and discrimination as a result of their gender:

> [N]ative females suffer multiple jeopardy on the basis of a number of objective indicators of social and economic well-being. The fact that Indians as a group are and Indian females in particular suffer the greatest disadvantage suggests that Indian status, with its historical trappings of colonial dependency, does indeed create additional barriers to economic and social health. The position of Indian women with respect to labour-force participation and income, suggests that they are the most severely handicapped in their exchange relations with employers.[3]

At a minimum, the dual discrimination that Aboriginal women face places them in a vulnerable position both within mainstream society that holds certain stereotypes of Aboriginal people and women, and within their own communities.

Canada's 1982 constitutional amendments sought to ensure gender equality. Subsection 35(4) of the *Constitution Act, 1982*[4] states:

> Notwithstanding any other provision of this Act, the Aboriginal and treaty rights referred to in subsection (1) are guaranteed equally to male and female persons.

Subsection 35(4) of the *Constitution Act, 1982* ensures equal treatment for Aboriginal women in the application of Aboriginal and treaty rights, in addition to the antidiscrimination language of s. 15(1) of the *Canadian Charter of Rights and Freedoms*[5] ("Charter"). This special protection is necessary in part because of the negative and disruptive effects that the *Indian Act* system of government has on traditional Aboriginal societies.

---

[1] Readers should also reference *Report of the Royal Commission on Aboriginal Peoples*, "Women's Perspectives," vol. 2 (Ottawa: RCAP, 1996), c. 2; T. Isaac, "Dually Disadvantaged and Historically Forgotten?: Aboriginal Women and the Inherent Right of Aboriginal Self-Government" (1992) 21:3 Man. L.J. 453; K. Faith, "Aboriginal Women" in *Unruly Women: The Politics of Confinement and Resistance* (Vancouver: Press Gang Publishers, 1993), 186–203; and J. Silman, ed., *Enough is Enough* (Toronto: Women's Press, 1987).
[2] *Indian Act*, R.S.C. 1985, c. I-5.
[3] G.M. Gerber, "Multiple Jeopardy: A Socio-Economic Comparison of Men and Women Among the Indian, Metis and Inuit Peoples of Canada" (1990) 22:3 Canadian Ethnic Studies 80.
[4] *Constitution Act, 1982*, Schedule B to the *Canada Act 1982* (U.K.), 1982, c. 11, as am. by the *Constitution Amendment Proclamation 1983*, R.S.C. 1985, App. II, No. 46, adding ss. 35(3) and 35(4).
[5] *Canadian Charter of Rights and Freedoms*, Part I of the *Constitution Act, 1982, ibid.*

Members of the Iroquois Confederacy, which occupied parts of what is now the state of New York, southern Quebec, and Ontario, were governed by a matriarchal system (which continues to this day).

> [Iroquois women] played a profound role in Iroquois political life. . . . The basic unit of government was the "hearth", which consisted of a mother and her children. Each hearth was part of a wider group called an otiianer, and two or more otiianers constituted a clan. The word otiianer specifically referred to the female heirs to the chieftainship titles of the League. The otiianer women selected one of the males within the group to fill any of the fifty seats in the League. . . . Iroquois political philosophy was rooted in the concept that all life was spiritually unified with the natural environment and other forces surrounding people. . . . Iroquois youth were trained to enter a society that was egalitarian, with power more evenly distributed between male and female, young and old.[6]

In an attempt to ensure gender equality in the legislative realm, it was proposed that the Nunavut Legislative Assembly be constituted so as to ensure an equal number of men and women. On May 26, 1997, residents of the eastern Northwest Territories, which became Nunavut on April 1, 1999, voted by plebiscite on whether one man and one woman should represent each electoral district in the first Nunavut Legislative Assembly. The people of Nunavut rejected the proposal by a vote of 57 percent against and 43 percent in favour.[7]

HISTORICAL DISCRIMINATION

The first comprehensive legislation concerning Indians was enacted by the Parliament of Canada in 1869.[8] Prior to European contact, many Aboriginal women possessed something akin to the right to vote and had significant influence in decision-making in their communities. The 1869 Act imposed many changes on the traditional ways in which Indian women were treated. Upon the death of an Indian male, his goods and possessions passed to his children and not to his spouse. The female spouse was excluded because her care was seen as being the responsibility of the children. Band councils were to be elected, which is non-traditional to many Indian tribes, and the group entitled to elect councillors was restricted to adult males. Females and children had no substantive role in elections and government. Section 6 of the 1869 Act provided that any Indian women who married a non-Indian lost her status as an Indian under the Act. Her children also lost their status. In this manner, the 1869 Act promoted assimilation. Finally, an Indian woman who married an Indian man from another band lost her status (and so did her children) to her own band and automatically became a member of the male's band. The 1869 Act affirmed the principle that, like European women, Indian women should be subject to their husbands and that by law, the children belonged to him.

The first act to bear the name *Indian Act* was enacted in 1876 and embodied all of the above-mentioned provisions. The 1876 Act expanded the definition of "Indian" by promoting the legitimacy of descent through the male line. Although some of the above provisions vanished with time, the requirement that Indian women lost their status upon

[6] D. Grinde & B. Johansen, *Exemplar of Liberty: Native America and the Evolution of Democracy* (Los Angeles: University of California Press, 1991) 27–28.
[7] Lisa Young, "Gender equal legislation: Evaluating the Proposed Nunavut electoral system." (1997) 23:3 Can. Pub. Policy 306–15.
[8] *An Act for the gradual enfranchisement of Indians, the better management of Indian affairs, and to extend the provisions of the Act 31st Victoria, Chapter 42*, S.C. 1869, c. 6.

marrying non-Indian men was not abolished until 1985.

The 1869 Act, and subsequent legislation, had a profound impact on generations of Aboriginal women. In their report on the Manitoba justice system and Aboriginal people,[9] Hamilton and Sinclair discussed the effects of a dysfunctional justice system on Aboriginal women:

> Aboriginal women and their children suffer tremendously as victims in contemporary Canadian society. They are the victims of racism, of sexism and of unconscionable levels of domestic violence. The justice system has done little to protect them from any of these assaults. At the same time, Aboriginal women have an even higher rate of over-representation in the prison system than Aboriginal men. In community after community, Aboriginal women brought these disturbing facts to our attention. We believe the plight of Aboriginal women and their children must be a priority for any changes in the justice system. . . .
>
> The victimization of Aboriginal women accelerated with the introduction after Confederation of residential schools for Aboriginal children. Children were removed from their families and homes at a young age, some to return eight to 10 years later, some never to return. The ability to speak Aboriginal languages and the motivation to do so were severely undermined. Aboriginal students were taught to devalue everything Aboriginal and value anything Euro-Canadian. . . .
>
> Aboriginal women traditionally played a prominent role in the consensual decision-making process of their communities. The *Indian Act* created the chief and council system of local government. The local Indian agent chaired the meetings of the chief and council, and had the power to remove the chief and council from office. Aboriginal women were denied any vote in the new system imposed by the Indian Affairs administration. As a result, they were stripped of any formal involvement in the political process.
>
> The segregation of Aboriginal women, both from wider society and from their traditional role as equal and strong members of tribal society, continues to the present day. This is due partly to the fact that the effects of past discrimination have resulted in the poor socio-economic situation applicable to most Aboriginal women, but it is also attributable to the demeaning image of Aboriginal women that has developed over the years. North American society has adopted a destructive and stereotypical view of Aboriginal women.[10]

INDIAN STATUS UNDER THE *INDIAN ACT*

A major issue of concern for many Indian women has been the status accorded to them under the Act, the ease with which the Crown could remove their status, and the impact of this lost status on everything from involvement in band governance to the provision of basic services.

The term "Indian status" refers to those persons who are registered as Indians pursuant to the Act. Under s. 10 of the Act,[11] Indian bands control their own membership. The practical result of this authority is that there may be persons who are members of a band but who are not registered, and persons who are registered but who are not members of a band.

Another peculiarity of the Act is that there are Aboriginal persons who self-identify as

---

[9] A.C. Hamilton & C.M. Sinclair, *The Justice System and Aboriginal People: Report of the Aboriginal Justice Inquiry*, vol. 1 (Winnipeg: Queen's Printer, 1991) at 475–507.

[10] *Ibid.* at 475, 478–79.

[11] Subsection 10(1) of the *Indian Act* provides:

> A band may assume control of its own membership if it establishes membership rules for itself in writing in accordance with this section and if, after the band has given appropriate notice of its intention to assume control of its own membership, a majority of the electors of the band gives its consent to the band's control of its own membership. . . .

being Indians but who are not registerable under the Act.[12] Likewise, there are persons who are registered under the Act who are not of Aboriginal ancestry. What eventually became s. 12(1)(b) of the Act[13] provided that Indian women who married non-Indian men lost their Indian status and could no longer receive the benefits accorded to registered Indians. Indian men who married non-Indian women, however, retained their registration; the non-Indian women they married gained status, as did their children. The Act institutionalized discrimination in many ways:

> Section 12(1)(b) is not an aberration; it reflects the main thesis in the membership system of the *Indian Act* which is determining membership on the basis of kinship and not on the basis of race. . . . The *Indian Act* focused on nuclear family units, and to ensure that all members of the nuclear family unit could reside on the reserve or not reside on the reserve, it was determined that the units should be single status units. To achieve that, the male was used as the head of the household to determine status for all members of the nuclear family unit. This of course did not coincide with traditional Indian kinship systems, which were not always patrilineal, nor did it align itself with another characteristic of Indian kinship systems which is that they did not focus on nuclear family units but on extended family units.[14]

Discrimination under the *Indian Act*

In *R. v. Drybones*,[15] the Supreme Court of Canada considered s. 94(b) of the *Indian Act,* which provided that it was an offence for an Indian to be intoxicated off a reserve. The Court held that the use of the racial classification of "Indian" in s. 94 violated the equality guarantee set out in the *Canadian Bill of Rights.*[16] The *Bill of Rights* had the effect of limiting the extent to which the *Indian Act* could discriminate against Indians. *Drybones* was the first and only decision by the Court to hold that a federal statute was inconsistent with the *Bill of Rights*, which created high hopes for the *Bill of Rights*. However, the Supreme Court of Canada decision of *A.-G. of Canada* v. *Lavell and Bedard*[17] quickly dampened such hopes.

Lavell and Bedard concerned whether s. 12(1)(b) of the Act violated the "equality before the law" provision in the *Bill of Rights. Lavell and Bedard* is similar to *Drybones* in that they both deal with the definition of equality under the *Bill of Rights.* Section 12(1)(b) of the Act denied an Indian woman who married a non-Indian her Indian status, including her right to hold property and live on an Indian reserve. A male Indian who married a non-Indian retained his Indian status.

The Court held, five to four, that s. 12(1)(b) of the Act did not constitute a violation of equality before the law. Ritchie J., writing for the majority, wrote that the Act might discriminate against women, but so long as the provision applied equally to all women

[12] In *R. v. Fowler* (1993), 134 N.B.R. (2d) 361 at 367 (N.B. Prov. Ct.), the New Brunswick Provincial Court held that an accused's right to hunt was protected by the treaties of 1725–26, even though the accused was not registered under the Act: "This evidence all shows that the defendant's ancestors were members of the St. Mary's Band and Oromocto Band. It further demonstrates that non-registration is not to be equated with non-entitlement." See also *R. v. Chevrier*, [1989] 1 C.N.L.R. 128 (Ont. Dist. Ct.).
[13] *Indian Act*, R.S.C. 1970, c. I-6.
[14] Canada, House of Commons, Standing Committee on Indian Affairs and Northern Development, *Minutes of Proceedings and Evidence of the Sub-Committee on Indian Women and the Indian Act* (14 September 1982, 5:13).
[15] *R. v. Drybones*, [1970] S.C.R. 282.
[16] *Canadian Bill of Rights*, S.C. 1960, c. 44; R.S.C. 1985, App. III.
[17] *A.-G. of Canada* v. *Lavell and Bedard*, [1974] S.C.R. 1349.

affected, there was no violation of equality before the law. It is difficult to reconcile *Lavell and Bedard* with *Drybones*, which Ritchie J. also wrote. *Lavell and Bedard* left Aboriginal women in a precarious position not only for what the decision said respecting s. 12(1)(b) of the Act, but also because it gave the more general message that Aboriginal women could not achieve true equality through the judicial system.

Bill C-31

The issue surrounding s. 12(1)(b) of the Act took on an international stature when Sandra Lovelace, an Indian woman divorced from her non-Indian male spouse, tried unsuccessfully for three years to obtain housing for herself and for her son on her home reserve in New Brunswick. Lovelace petitioned the United Nations Human Rights Committee to examine s. 12(1)(b) in light of its discriminatory effects on Indian women. In July 1981, the committee issued its final decision on the matter and declared that s. 12(1)(b) was inconsistent with the *International Covenant on Civil and Political Rights*.[18] However, because the committee's decision had no direct domestic legal impact, it took until 1985 before the Act was amended.[19]

After much public pressure, including the negative decision by the United Nations Human Rights Committee, Parliament passed Bill C-31, an *Act to Amend the Indian Act*,[20] to bring the Act into accord with the Charter[21] to ensure equality of treatment to Indian men and women. Changes were made to the Act to recognize the right of Aboriginal governments to control their own membership. The amendments also abolished the concept of "enfranchisement," which permitted Indians to give up their Indian status and band membership for a number of reasons.

Under Bill C-31 Indian women who lost their Indian status and band membership because of sexual discrimination under s. 12 of the Act were once again eligible to have their Indian status and band membership restored. As well, children of reinstated women were accorded the right to have their status and band membership restored.

The positive effects of Bill C-31 are obvious. Bands received increased control over membership and the Act was brought into accord with the equality provisions of the Charter. Women and their children regained their status as Indians.[22] To date, more than 114,000 individuals have gained registered Indian status. Many bands have objected to the change, however, for economic reasons:

> Many band/tribal councils opposed Bill C-31 on grounds that their ancestral heritage (i.e. reserve lands and treaty benefits, etc.) is inadequate to provide their present membership with an acceptable standard of living. Therefore, they could not accommodate additional members. This resulted in a squabble among blood heirs over their ancestral heritage. The squabble over this heritage is complicated by "privatization," that is, the Indian Act provision under which communal benefits (assets and entitlements) are being transferred into individual benefits. The Indian elite class, which benefits disproportionately from privatization, is motivated by a powerful class-based interest to protect their bloated share of band/

[18] Adopted and opened for signature, ratification an accession by General Assembly Resolution 2200 A (XXI) of 16 December 1966. Entered into force on 23 March 1976.
[19] A. Bayefsky, "The Human Rights Committee and the Case of Sandra Lovelace" (1982) 20 International Yearbook of International Law 244.
[20] *An Act to Amend the Indian Act*, S.C. 1985, c. 31 (28 June 1985).
[21] Charter, *supra* note 5.
[22] Canada, Indian and Northern Affairs, *Impacts of the 1985 Amendments to the Indian Act (Bill C-31) Summary Report* (Ottawa: 1990).

tribal assets from potential diminishment by claims from any additional "heirs."[23]

This class and power struggle continues to be played out on a number of reserves across Canada.

Bill C-31[24] has resulted in the creation of three types of registered Indians: (1) those individuals registered under s. 6(1) who can pass registration entitlement on to all of their children, regardless of whom they marry; (2) those individuals registered under s. 6(2) of the Act who can pass registration entitlement to their children only if they marry another registered Indian; and (3) those individuals who are not registered under the Act and whose children will be entitled to be registered only if the child's other parent is registered under s. 6(1) of the Act. If a child has one parent registered under s. 6(2) of the Act and the other parent is a non-Indian, that child will not be entitled to registration under the Act.

Parents' Registration		Child's Registration
6(1) + 6(1)	=	6(1)
6(1) + 6(2)	=	6(1)
6(1) + non-Indian	=	6(2)
6(2) + non-Indian	=	non-Indian

These rules are complicated by the ability of Indian bands to enact their own membership rules, thereby eradicating the former connection between registration and band membership. It is now possible to be a registered Indian but not be a member of an *Indian Act* band, and vice-versa.[25]

The s. 6(2) provisions will have, over time, a dramatic effect on the number of Indians registered or registrable as such under the Act as more and more Aboriginal people become urbanized and mix with mainstream society.

SECTION 25 OF THE CHARTER AND GENDER EQUALITY

Section 25 appears not to have an impact upon the application of s. 28 of the Charter, which provides that the rights set out in the Charter apply equally to male and female persons. Section 28 begins by stating: "Notwithstanding *anything* in this Charter. . . ." This is an absolute statement and no such language is found in s. 25, which limits itself to rights and freedoms guaranteed by the Charter. Also noteworthy is that s. 28 makes reference to rights that are "referred to" in the Charter, whereas s. 25 speaks to rights guaranteed in the Charter. Presumably, then, s. 28 also applies to the rights and freedoms set out in the *Proclamation*, land claims agreements, and "other rights and freedoms."

The gender equality guarantee in s. 15(1) of the Charter, supported by the interpretive principle set out in s. 28 of the Charter, appears to be absolute. Thus, the Charter ensures

[23] Menno Boldt, *Surviving as Indians: The Challenge of Self-Government* (Toronto: University of Toronto Press, 1993) 212–13.
[24] For discussion regarding decisions made by the Registrar of the Indian Register in respect of Bill C-31 applicants, see: *Canada (Registrar, Indian Register)* v. *Sinclair*, [2001] 4 C.N.L.R. 11 (F.C.T.D.); and *Canada (Min. des Affaires et du Nord)* c. *McKenzie*, [2001] 4 C.N.L.R. 41 (Que. Sup. Ct.).
[25] For discussion see D.N. Sprague, "The New Math of the New *Indian Act*: 6(2)=6(2)=(6)1" (1995) 10:1 Native Studies Rev. 47–60.

that Aboriginal, treaty, and other rights and freedoms of Aboriginal people as may be determined apply equally to female and male persons. This is further supported by s. 35(4) of the *Constitution Act, 1982* which provides that the existing Aboriginal and treaty rights recognized and affirmed by s. 35(1) of the *Constitution Act, 1982* are guaranteed equally to female and male persons.

Like s. 25, s. 28 of the Charter is an interpretive section and does not grant rights *per se*. Sections 15 and 28 of the Charter outline in precise language the equal protection afforded male and female persons. The Native Women's Association of Canada (NWAC) has expressed concerns regarding the existing Charter provisions, including s. 25, to the extent that s. 25 may be used to derogate or abrogate from individual rights held by Aboriginal women. In a 1991 discussion paper NWAC suggested that an additional paragraph be added to s. 25 which would read:

> Notwithstanding anything is this Charter, all rights and freedoms of the Aboriginal people of Canada are guaranteed equally to male and female Aboriginal persons.[26]

While the above proposal for the amendment of s. 25 is interesting and would not result in any substantive change to the Charter, it is not clear that such a clause is necessary. While s. 25 refers to "certain rights and freedoms" in the Charter, s. 28 reads "notwithstanding anything in this Charter." The result is that s. 25 refers to the rights guaranteed in the Charter, whereas s. 28 of the Charter speaks to *anything* in Charter. Since s. 28 does not guarantee rights, it is not affected by s. 25.

The Quebec Native Women's Association has stated:

> It must be clearly understood that we have never questioned the collective rights of our Nations, but we strongly believe that as citizens of these Nations, we are also entitled to protection. We maintain that the individual rights of Native citizens can be recognized while affirming collective rights. This is why we would like to be in a position to rely on a Charter guaranteeing the rights and freedoms of all Native Citizens. The only model that we have at the present time is the Canadian Charter of Rights and Freedoms.[27]

The protection of individual rights, such as those of Aboriginal women, does not imply the weakening of collective rights. The two types of rights can coexist.

It may be concluded that s. 25 is designed to balance the potential impact of s. 15(1) of the Charter on Aboriginal and treaty rights. The equality guarantees set out in s. 15(1) of the Charter could be interpreted in a manner that would negate any positive application of the rights of Aboriginal people recognized and affirmed by s. 35(1). Additionally, s. 25 could protect the *Indian Act* from the Charter's application in that s. 25 also incorporates "other rights and freedoms" of Aboriginal people. If "other rights and freedoms" includes statutory provisions, such as those contained in the Act, then s. 25 could have the effect of limiting the Charter's application to provisions of the Act that conflict with the Charter. However, even if this is the case, s. 28 of the Charter, protecting the equality of male and female persons, would continue to apply. Notwithstanding the potential that s. 25 could protect the Act, it is not clear that "other rights and freedoms" includes statutory provisions. It would be counter to the purposes and objectives of the Charter to allow an interpretive clause to exclude a statute from the Charter's application. It would

---

[26] Native Women's Association of Canada, *Native Women and Self-Government: A Discussion Paper* (Ottawa: N.W.A.C., 1991) at 14.

[27] Quebec Native Women's Association, *Presentation to Hearing on the First Nations Constitutional Circle* (Montreal: 5 February 1992).

also appear to be contrary to the language of s. 25 to allow a statute, such as the *Indian Act*, to receive the benefits of s. 25, even though the Act or the statute contains no "rights" or "freedoms" *per se*.

The Supreme Court of Canada has adopted a "purposive" approach to interpreting the Charter[28] which seeks to understand the purpose behind a Charter right and to ensure that the right is interpreted in a manner consistent with its purpose. Since the purpose of any particular Charter right is not absolute, this provides the courts with latitude in interpreting the Charter. A purposive approach is similar to a generous approach. The normal effect of the purposive approach will be to "narrow the scope of the right."[29] Assuming that a purposive approach would also be applied to an interpretative provision of the Charter, s. 25 could be interpreted in a narrow manner to preserve the rights of individuals, in the face of Aboriginal or treaty rights to the contrary.

Section 25 of the Charter allows for Aboriginal people to be treated differently, based on their rights, without fear that their rights will be diminished by way of s. 1 of the Charter (reasonable limitations) and by s. 15(1) of the Charter (equality rights), for example. However, s. 25 is not limited to these two provisions but rather, applies to all rights and freedoms set out in the Charter. Section 25 fulfils the purpose it was intended to perform: protecting the collective rights of Aboriginal people from encroachment by the individual rights set out in the Charter. Individual rights must be protected along with collective rights. Ultimately, it is only at the level of the individual that either set of rights can be exercised. Indian band governments are likely subject to the Charter.[30]

CORBIERE v. *CANADA* (1993)

The Federal Court, Trial Division decision of *Corbiere* v. *Canada*[31] concerned an action by off-reserve members of the Batchewana Indian Band in Ontario, who comprise approximately 70 percent of the band's total membership. The majority of the off-reserve band members were re-registered under the *Indian Act* as a result of Bill C-31 amendments. As such, *Corbiere* is important for Aboriginal women because it is directly linked to their registration under the Act and their ability to affect governance on reserve. The off-reserve Batchewana Indian Band members claimed that their exclusion from voting in band elections under s. 77(1) of the Act violated s. 15(1) of the Charter. The Court held that the provisions denying non-resident band members the right to vote (in matters relating to communal property) violated s. 15 of the Charter and could not be justified by s. 1.

The Federal Court of Appeal affirmed the Trial Court judgment but altered the remedy.[32] The Court applied the *Van der Peet*[33] test and concluded that there was not enough evidence to establish that the exclusion of non-resident band members from voting is an Aboriginal right protected by s. 35 of the *Constitution Act, 1982* nor is it one of the "other

---

[28] For example, see *Hunter* v. *Southam*, [1984] 2 S.C.R. 145 at 156; *R.* v. *Big M Drug Mart*, [1985] 1 S.C.R. 295 at 344; and *Re B.C. Motor Vehicle Act*, [1985] 2 S.C.R. 486 at 499.

[29] Peter Hogg, *Constitutional Law of Canada*, 4th ed. (Toronto: Carswell, 1997) 820.

[30] For a summary of judicial commentary on this point see *Horse Lake First Nation* v. *Horseman*, [2003] 2 C.N.L.R. 193 (Alta. Q.B.) at paras. 20–29.

[31] *Corbiere* v. *Canada*, [1994] 1 C.N.L.R. 71 (F.C.T.D.); for commentary see T. Isaac, "Case Commentary: *Corbiere* v. *Canada*" [1994] 1 C.N.L.R. 55.

[32] *Batchewana Indian Band* v. *Canada* (sub. nom. *Corbiere* v. *Canada*), [1997] 3 C.N.L.R. 21 (F.C.A.); leave to appeal to S.C.C. granted 24 April 1997.

[33] *R.* v. *Van der Peet*, [1996] 2 S.C.R. 507.

rights or freedoms" referenced by s. 25 of the Charter. Instead of affirming the invalidity of s. 77(1) in its entirety as the Trial Court did, the Court of Appeal severed the words "and is ordinarily resident on the reserve" from s. 77(1) as it applies to the Batchewana Indian Band and ordered a constitutional exemption.

The Supreme Court of Canada[34] held that s. 77(1) of the Act violated the equality provisions set out in s. 15 of the Charter. Specifically, the use of the words "ordinarily resident on reserve" in s. 77(1) of the Act had the effect of prohibiting band members who lived off reserve from voting in band council elections. The Court also noted that on- and off-reserve members need not possess exactly the same voting rights, since some decisions may be primarily related to on-reserve matters, for example. L'Heureux-Dube J. stated:

> A considerable number of the band members who live off-reserve recently gained or re-gained this status under Bill C-31. . . . Many of those affected are women, and the descend-ants of women, who lost their Indian status because they married men who did not have Indian status. . . . Aboriginal women who married outside their band became members of their husband's band. See, for example, *The Indian Act*, S.C. 1951, c. 29, ss. 12 and 14, now repealed. Legislation depriving Aboriginal women of Indian status has a long history. The involuntary loss of status by Aboriginal women and children began in Upper and Lower Canada with the passage of *An Act to encourage the gradual Civilization of the Indian Tribes in the Province, and to amend the Laws respecting Indians*, S. Prov. C. 1857, 20 Vict., c. 26. A woman whose husband "enfranchised" had her status removed along with his. This legisla-tion introduced patriarchal concepts into many Aboriginal societies which did not exist before. . . . As the Royal Commission on Aboriginal Peoples stated in *Perspectives and Reali-ties*, [. . . Volume 4 of the RCAP's 1996 Report], at p. 26:
>
> In the pre-Confederation period, concepts were introduced that were foreign to Abo-riginal communities and that, wittingly or unwittingly, undermined Aboriginal cultural values. In many cases, the legislation displaced the natural, community-based and self-iden-tification approach to determining membership—which included descent, marriage, resi-dency, adoption and simple voluntary association with a particular group—and thus dis-rupted complex and interrelated social, economic and kinship structures. Patrilineal descent of the type embodied in the *Gradual Civilization Act*, for example, was the least common principle of descent in Aboriginal societies, but through these laws, it became predominant. From this perspective, the *Gradual Civilization Act* was an exercise in government control in deciding who was and was not an Indian.
>
> This continued in the *Gradual Enfranchisement Act*, S.C. 1869, c. 6. This legislation, for the first time, instituted the policy that women who married men without Indian status lost their own status, and their children would not receive status. The rationale for these poli-cies, given at the time, focussed on concerns about control over reserve lands, and the need to prevent non-Indian men from gaining access to them (*Perspectives and Realities*, supra, at p. 27). These policies were continued and expanded upon with the passage of the *Indian Act* in 1876, and amendments to it in subsequent years, particularly a major revision that took place in 1951.[35]

As a result of *Corbiere*, the Indian Band Election Regulations and the Indian Referen-dum Regulations were amended to enable mail-in ballots to accommodate off-reserve residents.[36]

---

[34] *Corbiere v. Canada (Min. of Indian and Northern Affairs)*, [1999] 2 S.C.R. 203.

[35] *Ibid.* at paras. 85–86.

[36] The *Indian Band Election Regulations*, C.R.C. 1978, c. 952 and the *Indian Referendum Regulations*, C.R.C. 1978, c. 957 were amended on 19 October 2000 (SOR/2000-391) to allow for voting by off-reserve band members without compelling their attendance on the reserve to vote, e.g., the use of mail-in ballots.

MARITAL PROPERTY

The courts have focused on examining the division of marital property as a constitutional division of powers issue, rather than an issue of fairness and equity for Aboriginal women. For example, in *Derrickson* v. *Derrickson*,[37] the Supreme Court of Canada considered whether Part 3 of British Columbia's *Family Relations Act*,[38] dealing with the division of family assets upon marital breakdown, applied to reserve lands held by Indians. The appellant Indian wife brought a petition of divorce, including a division of the family assets pursuant to the *Family Relations Act*. The Court held that matters involving reserve land, such as their possession under Certificates of Possession by Indians, fall within the exclusive authority of Parliament and that provincial legislation does not apply. To resolve this matter, the Court affirmed that in lieu of dividing property on reserve, a court can make an order for compensation for the purpose of adjusting the division of the family assets between spouses.[39]

No amendments have been made to the *Indian Act* to allow for equitable principles to apply in the division of family assets resulting from a marital breakdown. Some have argued that Indian women have borne the brunt of this legislative void.[40] Thus, while courts can make attempts to balance the division of property upon marital breakdown, Aboriginal women cannot rely on the significant advancements made in provincial marital law that ensure equal and fair treatment of the female spouse's contribution to the marriage.

The *First Nations Land Management Act*[41] provides that a First Nation will establish rules and procedures in their land code to govern the use, occupation, possession of, and interests in First Nation land upon the breakdown of a marriage. Section 17 of the Act provides that such rules and procedures to govern the breakdown of a marriage shall be in accordance with the Final Agreement which provides that all male and female members, whether living on- or off-reserve, shall have the right to vote on whether to approve the Land Code.[42]

NATIVE WOMEN'S ASSN. OF CANADA v. *CANADA* (1994)

In *Native Women's Assn. of Canada* v. *Canada*,[43] the Supreme Court of Canada considered whether NWAC was entitled to funding similar to that provided to the other national Aboriginal organizations (the Inuit Tapirisat of Canada, the Metis National Council, the Assembly of First Nations, and the Native Council of Canada) to participate in the 1992 constitutional discussions which led to the 1992 Charlottetown Accord. The Court held that the federal government's decision not to provide equal funding and participation to NWAC in the constitutional review did not violate their rights under ss. 2(b) and 28 of the Charter. The freedom of expression under s. 2(b) of the Charter does not guarantee any particular means of expression or place a positive obligation upon the federal govern-

---

[37] *Derrickson* v. *Derrickson*, [1986] 1 S.C.R. 285; see also *Paul* v. *Paul*, [1986] 1 S.C.R. 306.

[38] *Family Relations Act*, R.S.B.C. 1979, c. 121.

[39] *Derrickson, supra* note 37; see, for example, *George* v. *George*, [1993] 2 C.N.L.R. 112 (B.C.S.C.).

[40] See M. Montour, "Iroquois Women's Rights with Respect to Matrimonial Property on Indian Reserves", [1987] 4 C.N.L.R. 1; and M.E. Turpel, "Home/Land" (1991) 10 Can. J. of Family Law 17.

[41] *First Nations Land Management Act*, S.C. 1999, c. 24.

[42] Framework Agreement on First Nation Land Management, 12 February 1996, s. 7.

[43] *Native Women's Assn. of Canada* v. *Canada*, [1994] 3 S.C.R. 627.

ment to consult anyone. The Court also held that s. 35 of the *Constitution Act, 1982* was inapplicable because the right of Aboriginal people to participate in constitutional discussions does not derive from any existing Aboriginal or treaty right under s. 35. NWAC's primary argument was that the decision to fund these primarily male-dominated groups had the effect of leaving out the voices of Aboriginal women in the constitutional process. The Court rejected this claim due to a lack of evidence.

CANADIAN HUMAN RIGHTS ACT

The *Canadian Human Rights Act*[44] applies to all those matters coming within the legislative authority of Parliament. Section 67 of the Act states:

> Nothing in this Act affects any provision of the *Indian Act* or any provision made under or pursuant to that Act.

While s. 67 of the *Human Rights Act* appears to provide an absolute bar to applying the Act on reserve, such is not the case. While provisions of the *Indian Act* that are discriminating in nature may not come within the ambit of the *Human Rights Act* as a result of s. 67, activities and by-laws of Indian bands may continue to be subject to the *Human Rights Act*. For example, in *Canada (Human Rights Commission)* v. *Gordon Band Council*,[45] the Federal Court of Appeal held that the band council was immune from a claim of discrimination under the *Human Rights Act* because the acts of the band council in question were set out in s. 20 of the Act:

> That is not to say that Indians can never have recourse to the *Canadian Human Rights Act*. Challenges under that statute were successful in *Desjarlais* and in *Shubenacadie Indian Band* v. *Canada (Human Rights Commission)*, [1998] 2 F.C. 198 . . . (T.D.), affirmed by the Federal Court of Appeal . . . 187 D.L.R. (4th) 741, [2000] 4 C.N.L.R. 275. In neither case was the *Indian Act* the source of the authority to make the challenged decision.[46]

Application of the *Canadian Human Rights Act* to Aboriginal governments, by culturally sensitive tribunals, would advance accountability and fairness within reserve-based governments. Under Bill C-7, the *First Nations Governance Act*, s. 67 of the *Canadian Human Rights Act* would be repealed.[47] As the Canadian Human Rights Commission stated in its January 28, 2003 presentation to the Standing Committee on Aboriginal Affairs, Northern Development and Nature Resources:

> Section 67 has created an objectionable situation: First Nations' people are the only citizens of Canada that do not have full access to a human rights complaints system to resolve complaints of discrimination. All citizens should have this right, it is part of our citizenship.
>
> Members of First Nations' communities, like other people in Canada, encounter situations in which they believe their rights have been breached. Arguably denying the right to complain to the CHRC is contrary to the equal protection provision of section 15 of the Charter as well as international human rights standards such as the United Nations International Covenant on Civil and Political Rights.[48]

---

[44] *Canadian Human Rights Act*, R.S.C. 1985, c. H-6.
[45] *Canada (Human Rights Commission)* v. *Gordon Band Council*, [2001] 1 C.N.L.R. 1 (F.C.A.).
[46] *Ibid.* at para. 31.
[47] *First Nations Governance Act*, (2002), Bill C-7, ss. 41–42.
[48] Canadian Human Rights Commission, *Submission to the Standing Committee on Aboriginal Affairs, Northern Development and Natural Resources*, Bill C-7; *First Nations Governance Act* (Ottawa: 28 January 2003).

Courtois v. *Canada*

A Canadian Human Rights Tribunal decision underscores some of the problems that women reinstated by Bill C-31 have encountered upon returning to their home reserves. In *Courtois* v. *Canada*,[49] Louise Courtois and Marie-Jeanne Raphael, Indian women reinstated under Bill C-31, complained to the Canadian Human Rights Commission that they and their children were being discriminated against by the Department of Indian Affairs and Northern Development in that the department was not permitting their children to have access to the Pointe-Bleue band-controlled school. The discrimination related to a moratorium declared by the band council pursuant to s. 11(2) of the *Indian Act,* which suspended for two years the provision of services to reinstated Indian women. The department agreed with the band council's decision. Both women filed complaints of discrimination against the department on the grounds of sex and marital status under the *Canadian Human Rights Act.*[50]

The Human Rights Tribunal concluded that the department's proposal to educate the children of reinstated Indian women off reserve had the effect of creating distinctions between band and non-band members on the basis of sex and marital status. The tribunal held that the "moratorium was clearly aimed at women reinstated by Bill C-31."[51] The department should have "taken action to ensure school service was provided to children of reinstated women at Pointe-Bleue."[52]

In *Barry* v. *Garden River Band*,[53] the respondent Garden River Indian Band decided to distribute $1 million of a land claim settlement to its members on a per capita basis. The Band also decided to deduct $1,000 from the share of women who gained Indian status by way of Bill C-31 and refused to pay the children of these women who were born prior to April 17, 1985. The Ontario Court of Appeal held that: (*a*) an express trust was created when the Band decided to distribute the $1 million, (*b*) the Band, as a trustee, breached its duty by failing to treat all Band members equally, and (*c*) the Band's women and children were entitled to their full share of the per capita distribution.[54]

In *Scrimbitt* v. *Sakimay Indian Band Council*,[55] Mackay J. of the Federal Court, Trial Division considered an application by an Indian woman reinstated under Bill C-31 for judicial review of a decision by the Sakimay Indian Band Council refusing her the right to vote in band council elections. Mackay J. held that the band council violated its own membership code and s. 77 of the Act, which provides a right to vote to all band members. Mackay J. also held that the denial of the right to vote violated the applicant's right to equal protection and equal benefit of the law under s. 15(1) of the Charter:

> [T]he limitation on the applicant's rights, i.e., the refusal of her right to vote in 1997 elections, was not prescribed by law. Whether the basis for it was, as claimed, the Band's policy, the Band custom or the Band council's economic concerns, it is not an infringement permitted by s. 1 of the *Charter.*[56]

---

[49] *Courtois* v. *Canada*, [1991] 1 C.N.L.R. 40 (Can. H.R.T.). In *Jacobs* v. *Mohawk Council of Kahnawake*, [1998] 3 C.N.L.R. 68 (Can. H.R.T.), a Canadian human rights tribunal held that the Mohawk Council of Kahnawake discriminated against a number of individuals and their children on the basis that they were registrants under Bill C-31.

[50] *Supra* note 44.

[51] *Courtois, supra* note 49 at 41.

[52] *Ibid.*

[53] *Barry* v. *Garden River Band* (1997), 33 O.R. (3d) 782, [1997] 4 C.N.L.R. 28 (Ont. C.A.).

[54] See also *Moon* v. *Campbell River Indian Band*, [1997] 1 C.N.L.R. 77 (F.C.T.D.), aff'd (1999) 176 D.L.R. (4th) 254 (F.C.A.).

[55] *Scrimbitt* v. *Sakimay Indian Band Council*, [2000] 1 C.N.L.R. 205 (F.C.T.D.).

[56] *Ibid.* at para. 70.

CONCLUSION

Although the Bill C-31 amendments may have brought some clarity with respect to Aboriginal women's entitlement to registration under the Act, substantial issues remain to be resolved with respect to the rights of reinstated Aboriginal women to live on reserve lands and receive band entitlements as registered Indians. In many ways, this issue is closely related to governance generally and may be best resolved through self-government negotiations, assuming Aboriginal women have their voice heard. Likewise, the issue of marital property and the application of provincial family law legislation generally needs to be resolved in a manner that is in keeping with the individual rights protected under the Charter, the legal developments in this area, and in a manner that is culturally sensitive.

CASES AND MATERIALS

RELEVANT LEGISLATIVE AND CONSTITU-TIONAL PROVISIONS

Indian Act, Subsections 12(1) and (2)*
R.S.C. 1970, c. I-6.

12. (1) The following persons are not entitled to be registered, namely,
    (a) a person who
        (i) has received or has been allotted half-breed lands or money scrip,
        (ii) is a descendant of a person described in subparagraph (i),
        (iii) is enfranchised, or
        (iv) is a person born of a marriage entered into after the 4th day of September 1951 and has attained the age of twenty-one years, whose mother and whose father's mother are not persons described in paragraph 11(1)(a), (b) or (d) or entitled to be registered by virtue of paragraph 11(1)(e),
        unless, being a woman, that person is the wife or widow of a person described in section 11, and
    (b) a woman who married a person who is not an Indian, unless that woman is subsequently the wife or widow of a person described in section 11.

(2) The addition to a Band List of the name of an illegitimate child . . . may be protested at any time within twelve months after the addition, and if upon the protest it is decided that the father of the child was not an Indian, the child is not entitled to be registered under that paragraph.

Selected provisions of the *Indian Act*
R.S.C. 1985, c. I-5, relating to membership criteria and the Bill C-31 amendments.

. . . INDIAN REGISTER . . .

5. (1) There shall be maintained in the Department an Indian Register in which shall

* Section 12 was repealed by S.C. 1985, c. 27, s. 4.

be recorded the name of every person who is entitled to be registered as an Indian under this Act.

(2) The names in the Indian Register immediately prior to April 17, 1985 shall constitute the Indian Register on April 17, 1985.

(3) The Registrar may at any time add to or delete from the Indian Register the name of any person who, in accordance with this Act, is entitled or not entitled, as the case may be, to have his name included in the Indian Register.

(4) The Indian Register shall indicate the date on which each name was added thereto or deleted therefrom.

(5) The name of a person who is entitled to be registered is not required to be recorded in the Indian Register unless an application for registration is made to the Registrar.

6. (1) Subject to section 7, a person is entitled to be registered if
    (a) that person was registered or entitled to be registered immediately prior to April 17, 1985;
    (b) that person is a member of a body of persons that has been declared by the Governor in Council on or after April 17, 1985 to be a band for the purposes of this Act;
    (c) the name of that person was omitted or deleted from the Indian Register, or from a Band List prior to September 4, 1951, under subparagraph 12(1)(a)(iv), paragraph 12(1)(b) or subsection 12(2) or under subparagraph 12(1)(a)(iii) pursuant to an order made under subsection 109(2), as each provision read immediately prior to April 17, 1985, or under any former provision of this Act relating to the same subject-matter as any of those provisions;
    (d) the name of that person was omitted or deleted from the Indian Register, or from a Band List prior to September 4, 1951, under subparagraph 12(1)(a)(iii) pursuant to an order made under subsection 109(1), as each provision read immediately prior to April 17, 1985, or under any former provision of this Act relating to the same subject-matter as any of those provisions;
    (e) the name of that person was omitted or deleted from the Indian Register, or from a Band List prior to September 4, 1951,
       (i) under section 13, as it read immediately prior to September 4, 1951, or under any former provision of this Act relating to the same subject-matter as that section, or
       (ii) under section 111, as it read immediately prior to July 1, 1920, or under any former provision of this Act relating to the same subject-matter as that section; or
    (f) that person is a person both of whose parents are or, if no longer living, were at the time of death entitled to be registered under this section.

(2) Subject to section 7, a person is entitled to be registered if that person is a person one of whose parents is or, if no longer living, was at the time of death entitled to be registered under subsection (1).

(3) For the purposes of paragraph (1)(f) and subsection (2),
    (a) a person who was no longer living immediately prior to April 17, 1985 but who

was at the time of death entitled to be registered shall be deemed to be entitled to be registered under paragraph (1)(a); and

(b) a person described in paragraph (1)(c), (d), (e), or (f) or subsection (2) who was no longer living on April 17, 1985 shall be deemed to be entitled to be registered under that provision.

7. (1) The following persons are not entitled to be registered:

(a) a person who was registered under paragraph 11(1)(f), as it read immediately prior to April 17,1985, or under any former provision of this Act relating to the same subject-matter as that paragraph, and whose name was subsequently omitted or deleted from the Indian Register under this Act or

(b) a person who is the child of a person who was registered or entitled to be registered under paragraph 11(1)(f), as it read immediately prior to April 17, 1985, or under any former provision of this Act relating to the same subject-matter as that paragraph, and is also the child of a person who is not entitled to be registered.

(2) Paragraph (1)(a) does not apply in respect of a female person who was, at any time prior to being registered under paragraph 11(1)(f) entitled to be registered under any other provision of this Act.

(3) Paragraph (1)(f) does not apply in respect of the child of a female person who was, at any time prior to being registered under paragraph 11(1)(f), entitled to be registered under any other provision of this Act.

Band Lists . . .

8. There shall be maintained in accordance with this Act for each band a Band List in which shall be entered the name of every person who is a member of that band. . . .

9. (1) Until such time as a band assumes control of its Band List, the Band List of that band shall be maintained in the Department by the Registrar.

(2) The names in a Band List of a band immediately prior to April 17,1985 shall constitute the Band List of that band on April 17, 1985.

(3) The Registrar may at any time add to or delete from a Band List maintained in the Department the name of any person who, in accordance with this Act, is entitled or not entitled, as the case may be, to have his name included in that List.

(4) A Band List maintained in the Department shall indicate the date on which each name was added thereto or deleted therefrom.

(5) The name of a person who is entitled to have his name entered in a Band List maintained in the Department is not required to be entered therein unless an application for entry therein is made to the Registrar. . . .

10. (1) A band may assume control of its own membership if it establishes membership rules for itself in writing in accordance with this section and if, after the band has given appropriate notice of its intention to assume control of its own membership, a majority of the electors of the band gives its consent to the band's control of its own membership.

(2) A Band may, pursuant to the consent of a majority of the electors of the band,

(a) after it has given appropriate notice of its intention to do so establish membership rules for itself; and

(b) provide for a mechanism for reviewing decisions on membership.

(3) Where the council of a band makes a by-law under paragraph 81(p. 4) bringing this subsection into effect in respect of the band, the consents required under subsection: (1) and (2) shall be given by a majority of the members of the band who are of the full age of eighteen years.

(4) Membership rules established by a band under this section may not deprive any person who had the right to have his name entered in the Band List for that band, immediately prior to the time the rules were established, of the right to have his name so entered by reason only of a situation that existed or an action that was taken before the rules came into force.

(5) For greater certainty, subsection (4) applies in respect of a person who was entitled to have his name entered in the Band List under paragraph 11(1)(c) immediately before the band assumed control of the Band List if that person does not subsequently cease to be entitled to have his name entered in the Band List.

(6) Where the conditions set out in subsection (1) have been met with respect to a band, the council of the band shall forthwith give notice to the Minister in writing that the band is assuming control of its own membership and shall provide the Minister with a copy of the membership rules for the band.

(7) On receipt of a notice from the council of a band under subsection (6), the Minister shall, if the conditions set out in subsection (1) have been complied with, forthwith

(a) give notice to the band that it has control of its own membership; and

(b) direct the Registrar to provide the band with a copy of the Band List maintained in the Department.

(8) Where a band assumes control of its membership under this section, the membership rules established by the band shall have effect from the day on which notice is given to the Minister under subsection (6), and any additions to or deletions from the Band List of the band by the Registrar on or after that day are of no effect unless they are in accordance with the membership rules established by the band.

(9) A band shall maintain its own Band List from the date on which a copy of the Band List is received by the band under paragraph (7)(b), and, subject to section 13.2, the Department shall have no further responsibility with respect to that Band List from that date.

(10) A band may at any time add to or delete from a Band List maintained by it the name of any person who, in accordance with the membership rules of the band, is entitled or not entitled, as the case may be, to have his name included in that list.

(11) A Band List maintained by a band shall indicate the date on which each name was added thereto or deleted therefrom.

11. (1) Commencing on April 17, 1985, a person is entitled to have his name entered in a Band List maintained in the Department for a band if

(a) the name of that person was entered in the Band List for that band, or that person was entitled to have his name entered in the Band List for that band, immediately prior to April 17, 1985;

(b)   that person is entitled to be registered under paragraph 6(1)(b) as a member of that band;

(c)   that person is entitled to be registered under paragraph 6(1)(c) and ceased to be a member of that band by reason of the circumstances set out in that paragraph; or

(d)   that person was born on or after April 17,1985 and is entitled to he registered under paragraph 6(1)(f) and both parents of that person are entitled to have their names entered in the Band List or, if no longer living, were at the time of death entitled to have their names entered in the Band List.

(2)   Commencing on the day that is two years after the day that an Act entitled An Act to amend the Indian Act, introduced in the House of Commons on February 28, 1985, is assented to, or on such earlier day as may be agreed to under section 13.1, where a band does not have control of its Band List under this Act, a person is entitled to have his name entered in a Band List maintained in the Department for the band

(a)   if that person is entitled to be registered under paragraph 6(1)(d) or (e) and ceased to be a member of that band by reason of the circumstances set out in that paragraph; or

(b)   if that person is entitled to be registered under paragraph 6(1)(f) or subsection 6(2) and a parent referred to in that provision is entitled to have his name entered in the Band List or, if no longer living, was at the time of death entitled to have his name entered in the Band List.

(3)   For the purposes of paragraph (1)(d) and subsection (2),

(a)   a person whose name was omitted or deleted from the Indian Register or a band list in the circumstances set out in paragraph 6(1)(c), (d) or (e) who was no longer living on the first day on which the person would otherwise be entitled to have the person's name entered in the Band List of the band of which the person ceased to be a member shall be deemed to be entitled to have the person's name so entered; and

(b)   a person described in paragraph 2(b) shall be deemed to be entitled to have the person's name entered in the Band List in which the parent referred to in that paragraph is or was, or is deemed by this section to be, entitled to have the parent's name entered.

(4)   Where a band amalgamates with another band or is divided so as to constitute new bands, any person who would otherwise have been entitled to have his name entered in the Band List of that band under this section is entitled to have his name entered in the Band List of the amalgamated band or the new band to which he has the closest family ties, as the case may be.

12.   Commencing on the day that is two years after the day that an Act entitled An Act to amend the Indian Act, introduced in the House of Commons on February 28, 1985, is assented to, or on such earlier day as may be agreed to under section 13.1, any person who

(a)   is entitled to be registered under section 6, but is not entitled to have his name entered in the Band List maintained in the Department under section 11, or

(b)   is a member of another band, is entitled to have his name entered in the Band List maintained in the Department for a band if the council of the admitting band consents.

13. Notwithstanding sections 11 and 12, no person is entitled to have his name entered at the same time in more than one Band List maintained in the Department.

13.1 (1) A band may, at any time prior to the day that is two years after the day that an Act entitled An Act to amend the Indian Act, introduced in the House of Commons on February 28, 1985, is assented to, decide to leave the control of its Band List with the Department if a majority of the electors of the band gives its consent to that decision.

(2) Where a band decides to leave the control of its Band List with the Department under subsection (1) the council of the band shall forthwith give notice to the Minister in writing to that effect.

(3) Notwithstanding a decision under subsection (1), a band may, at any time after that decision is taken, assume control of its Band List under section 10.

13.2 (1) A band may, at any time after assuming control of its Band List under section 10, decide to return control of the Band List to the Department if a majority of the electors of the band gives its consent to that decision.

(2) Where a band decides to return control of its Band List to the Department under subsection (1), the council of the band shall forthwith give notice to the Minister in writing to that effect and shall provide the Minister with a copy of the Band List and a copy of all the membership rules that were established by the band under subsection 10(2) while the band maintained its own Band List.

(3) Where a notice is given under subsection (2) in respect of a Band List, the maintenance of that Band List shall be the responsibility of the Department from the date on which the notice is received and from that time the Band List shall be maintained in accordance with the membership rules set out in section 11.

13.3 A person is entitled to have his name entered in a Band List maintained in the Department pursuant to section 13.2 if that person was entitled to have his name entered, and his name was entered, in the Band List immediately before a copy of it was provided to the Minister under subsection 13.2(2), whether or not that person is also entitled to have his name entered in the Band List under section 11.

Canadian Charter of Rights and Freedoms

Equality Rights

15. (1) Every individual is equal before and under the law and has the right to the equal protection and equal benefit of the law without discrimination and, in particular, without discrimination based on race, national or ethnic origin, colour, religion, sex, age or mental or physical disability. . . .

General

25. The guarantee in this Charter of certain rights and freedoms shall not be construed so as to abrogate or derogate from any aboriginal, treaty or other rights or freedoms that pertain to the aboriginal peoples of Canada including
    (a) any rights or freedoms that have been recognized by the Royal Proclamation of October 7, 1763; and
    (b) any rights or freedoms that now exist by way of land claims agreements or may be so acquired. . . .

28. Notwithstanding anything in this Charter, the rights and freedoms referred to in it are guaranteed equally to male and female persons. . . .

Constitution Act, 1982

Part II Rights of the Aboriginal Peoples of Canada

35.(1)   The existing aboriginal and treaty rights of the aboriginal peoples of Canada are hereby recognized and affirmed. . . .

(4) Notwithstanding any other provision of this Act, the aboriginal and treaty rights referred to in subsection (1) are guaranteed equally to male and female persons.

CASES

A.-G. of Canada v. *Lavell and Bedard; Isaac et al.* v. *Bedard*

[1974] S.C.R. 1349 (S.C.C.). Fauteux C.J.C., Abbott, Martland, Judson, Ritchie, Hall, Spence, Pigeon, and Laskin JJ., August 27, 1973.

[FAUTEUX, MARTLAND, JUDSON JJ. concur with RITCHIE J.]
ABBOTT (dissenting) . . .
RITCHIE, J.:—I have had the advantage of reading the reasons for judgment prepared for delivery by my brother Laskin.

These appeals, which were heard together, are from two judgments holding that the provisions of s. 12(1)(b) of the *Indian Act*, R.S.C. 1970, c. 1-6, are rendered inoperative by s. 1(b) of the *Canadian Bill of Rights*, R.S.C. 1970, App. III, as denying equality before the law to the two respondents.

Both respondents were registered Indians and "Band" members within the meaning of s. 11(b) of the *Indian Act* when they elected to marry non-Indians and thereby relinquished their status as Indians in conformity with the said s. 12(1)(b) which reads as follows:

12(1) The following persons are not entitled to be registered, namely,

(b) a woman who married a person who is not an Indian, unless that woman is subsequently the wife or widow of a person described in section 11.

It is contended on behalf of both respondents that s. 12(1)(b) of the Act should be held to be inoperative as discriminating between Indian men and women and as being in conflict with the provisions of the *Canadian Bill of Rights* and particularly s. 1 thereof which provides:

1.   It is hereby recognized and declared that in Canada there have existed and shall con-

tinue to exist without discrimination by reason of race, national origin, colour, religion or sex, the following human rights and fundamental freedoms, namely,

(b) the right of the individual to equality before the law and the protection of the law; . . .

In my opinion the exclusive legislative authority vested in Parliament under s. 91(24) could not have been effectively exercised without enacting laws establishing the qualifications required to entitle persons to status as Indians and to the use and benefit of Crown "lands reserved for Indians". The legislation enacted to this end was, in my view, necessary for the implementation of the authority so vested in Parliament under the Constitution.

To suggest that the provisions of the Bill of Rights have the effect of making the whole *Indian Act* inoperative as discriminatory is to assert that the Bill has rendered Parliament powerless to exercise the authority entrusted to it under the Constitution of enacting legislation which treats Indians living on reserves differently from other Canadians in relation to their property and civil rights. The proposition that such a wide effect is to be given to the Bill of Rights was expressly reserved by the majority of this Court in the case of *R. v. Drybones* (1969), 9 D.L.R. (3d) 473 at pp. 485–6, to which reference will hereafter be made, and I do not think that it can be sustained.

What is at issue here is whether the Bill of Rights is to be construed as rendering inoperative one of the conditions imposed by Parliament for the use and occupation of Crown lands reserved for Indians. These conditions were imposed as a necessary part of the structure created by Parliament for the internal administration of the life of Indians on reserves and their entitlement to the use and benefit of Crown lands situate thereon, they were thus imposed in discharge of Parliament's constitutional function under s. 91(24) and in my view can only be changed by plain statutory language expressly enacted for the purpose. It does not appear to me that Parliament can be taken to have made or intended to make such a change by the use of broad general language directed at the statutory proclamation of the fundamental rights and freedoms enjoyed by all Canadians, and I am therefore of opinion that the Bill of Rights had no such effect. . . .

The contention that the Bill of Rights is to be construed as overriding all of the special legislation imposed by Parliament under the *Indian Act* is, in my view, fully answered by Pigeon, J., in his dissenting opinion in the *Drybones* case where he said, at pp. 489–90:

> If one of the effects of the *Canadian Bill of Rights* is to render inoperative all legal provisions whereby Indians as such are not dealt with in the same way as the general public, the conclusion is inescapable that parliament, by the enactment of the Bill, has not only fundamentally altered the status of the Indians in that indirect fashion but has also made any future use of federal legislative authority over them subject to the requirement of expressly declaring every time "that the law shall operate notwithstanding the *Canadian Bill of Rights*". I find it very difficult to believe that Parliament so intended when enacting the Bill. If a virtual suppression of federal legislation over Indians as such was meant, one would have expected this important change to be made explicitly, not surreptitiously, so to speak.

That it is membership in the band which entitles an Indian to the use and benefit of lands on the reserve is made plain by the provisions of ss. 2 and 18 of the *Indian Act*. . . .

In my view the meaning to be given to the language employed in the Bill of Rights is the meaning which it bore in Canada at the time when the Bill was enacted, and it follows that the phrase "equality before the law" is to be construed in light of the law existing in Canada at that time. In considering the meaning to be attached to "equality before the law" as those words occur in s. 1(b) of the Bill, I think it important to point out that in my opinion this phrase is not effective to invoke the egalitarian concept exemplified by the 14th Amendment of the U.S. Constitution as interpreted by the Courts of that country: see *R. v. Smythe* (1971), 19 D.L.R. (3d) 480, 3 C.C.C. (2d) 366, [1971] S.C.R. 680, per Fauteux, C.J.C., at pp. 482 and 484–5. I think rather that, having regard to the language employed in the second paragraph to the preamble to the Bill of Rights, the phrase "equality before the law" as used in s. 1 is to be read in its context as a part of "the rule of law" to which overriding authority is accorded by the terms of that paragraph. . . .

"Equality before the law" in this sense is frequently invoked to demonstrate that the same law applies to the highest official of Government as to any other ordinary citizen, and in this regard Professor F. R. Scott, in delivering the Plaunt Memorial Lectures on Civil Liberties and Canadian Federalism (1959), speaking of the case of *Roncarelli* v. *Duplessis* (1959), 16 D.L.R. (2d) 689, [1959] S.C.R. 121, had occasion to say:

> . . . it is always a triumph for the law to show that it is applied equally to all without fear or favour. This is what we mean when we say that all are equal before the law.

The relevance of these quotations to the present circumstances is that "equality before the law" as recognized by Dicey as a segment of the rule of law, carries the meaning of equal subjection of all classes to the ordinary law of the land as administered by the ordinary Courts, and in my opinion the phrase "equality before the law" as employed in s. 1(b) of the Bill of Rights is to be treated as meaning equality in the administration or application of the law by the law enforcement authorities and the ordinary Courts of the land. This construction is, in my view, supported by the provisions of paras. (a) to (g) of s. 2 of the Bill which clearly indicate to me that it was equality in the administration and enforcement of the law with which Parliament was concerned when it guaranteed the continued existence of "equality before the law".

Turning to the *Indian Act* itself, it should first be observed that by far the greater part of that Act is concerned with the internal regulation of the lives of Indians on reserves and that the exceptional provisions dealing with the conduct of Indians off reserves and their contracts with other Canadian citizens fall into an entirely different category.

It was, of course necessary for Parliament, in the exercise of s. 91(24) authority, to first define what Indian meant, and in this regard s. 2(1) of the Act provides that: "Indian" means a person who pursuant to this Act is registered as an Indian or is entitled to be registered as an Indian. It is therefore clear that registration is a necessary prerequisite to Indian status. . . .

The *Drybones* case can, in my opinion, have no application to the present appeals as it was in no way concerned with the internal regulation of the lives of Indians on reserves or their right to the use and benefit of Crown lands thereon, but rather deals exclusively with the effect of the Bill of Rights on a section of the *Indian Act* creating a crime with attendant penalties for the conduct by Indians off a reserve in an area where non-Indians, who were also governed by federal law, were not subject to any such restriction.

The fundamental distinction between the present case and that of *Drybones,* however, appears to me to be that the impugned section in the latter case could not be enforced without denying equality of treatment in the administration and enforcement of the law before the ordinary Courts of the land to a racial group, whereas no such inequality of treatment between Indian men and women flows as a necessary result of the application of s. 12(1)(b) of the *Indian Act.*

To summarize the above, I am of opinion:

1. that the Bill of Rights is not effective to render inoperative legislation, such as s. 12(1)(b) of the *Indian Act,* passed by the Parliament of Canada in discharge of its

constitutional function under s. 91(24) of the *British North America Act, 1867*, to specify how and by whom Crown lands reserved for Indians are to be used;

2. that the Bill of Rights does not require federal legislation to be declared inoperative unless it offends against one of the rights specifically guaranteed by s. 1, but where legislation is found to be discriminatory, this affords an added reason for rendering it ineffective;

3. that equality before the law under the Bill of Rights means equality of treatment in the enforcement and application of the laws of Canada before the law enforcement authorities and the ordinary Courts of the land, and no such inequality is necessarily entailed in the construction and application of s. 12(1)(b).

I would allow the appeal of the *Attorney-General of Canada* v. *Lavell*, reverse the judgment of the Federal Court of Appeal and restore the decision of judge B.W. Grossberg. . . .

On the appeal of *Isaac et al.* v. *Bedard*, a question was raised in this Court as to the jurisdiction of the trial Court. In view of the conclusion reached on the merits, no decision is now necessary on that question. The appeal to this Court should be allowed, the judgment at trial should be reversed and the action dismissed. . . .

HALL and SPENCE, JJ., concur with LASKIN, J. . . .

PIGEON, J.: I agree in the result with Ritchie, J. I certainly cannot disagree with the view I did express in *R.* v. *Drybones* . . . that the enactment of the *Canadian Bill of Rights* was not intended to effect a virtual suppression of federal legislation over Indians. My difficulty is Laskin, J.'s strongly reasoned opinion that, unless we are to depart from what was said by the majority in *Drybones*, these appeals should be dismissed because, if discrimination by reason of race makes certain statutory provisions inoperative, the same result must follow as to statutory provisions which exhibit discrimination by reason of sex. In the end, it appears to me that, in the circumstances, I need not reach a firm conclusion on that point. Assuming the situation is such as Laskin, J., says, it cannot be improper for me to adhere to what was my dissenting view, when a majority of those who did not agree with it in respect of a particular section of the *Indian Act*, R.S.C. 1970, c. I-6, now adopt it for the main body of this important statute.

I would observe that this result does not conflict with any of our decisions subsequent to *Drybones*. In no case was the *Canadian Bill of Rights* given an invalidating effect over prior legislation. . . .

LASKIN, J. (dissenting): . . . In my opinion, unless we are to depart from what was said in *Drybones*, both appeals now before us must be dismissed. I had no disposition to reject what was decided in *Drybones*; and on the central issue of prohibited discrimination as catalogued in s. 1 of the *Canadian Bill of Rights*, it is, in my opinion, impossible to distinguish *Drybones* from the two cases in appeal. If, as in *Drybones*, discrimination by reason of race makes certain statutory provisions inoperative, the same result must follow as to statutory provisions which exhibit discrimination by reason of sex.

I would dismiss both appeals. . . .

Human Rights Committee Decision; re: Sandra Lovelace

Lovelace v. *Canada*, [1981] 2 H.R.L.J. 158 (U.N.H.R.C.).

. . . The Human Rights Committee, in the examination of the communication before it, has to proceed from the basic fact that Sandra Lovelace married a non-Indian on 23

May 1970 and consequently lost her status as a Maliseet Indian under Section 12(1)(b) of the *Indian Act.* This provision was—and still is—based on a distinction de jure on the ground of sex. However, neither its application to her marriage as the cause of her loss of Indian status nor its effects could at that time amount to a violation of the Covenant, because this instrument did not come into force for Canada until 19 August 1976. Moreover, the Committee is not competent, as a rule, to examine allegations relating to events having taken place before the entry into force of the Covenant and the Optional Protocol. Therefore, as regards Canada it can only consider alleged violations of human rights occurring on or after 19 August 1976. In the case of a particular individual claiming to be a victim of a violation, it cannot express its view on the law in the abstract, without regard to the date on which this law was applied to the alleged victim. In the case of Sandra Lovelace it follows that the Committee is not competent to express any view on the original cause of her loss of Indian status, i.e. the *Indian Act* as applied to her at the time of her marriage in 1970.

11. The Committee recognizes, however, that the situation may be different if the alleged violations, although relating to events occurring before 19 August 1976, continue, or have effects which themselves constitute violations, after that date. In examining the situation of Sandra Lovelace in this respect, the Committee must have regard to all relevant provisions of the Covenant. It has considered, in particular, the extent to which the general provisions in articles 2 and 3 as well as the rights in articles 12(1), 17(1), 23(1), 24, 26 and 27, may be applicable to the facts of her present situation.

12. The Committee first observes that from 19 August 1976 Canada had undertaken under article 2(1) and (2) of the Covenant to respect and ensure to all individuals within its territory and subject to its jurisdiction, the rights recognized in the Covenant without distinction of any kind such as sex, and to adopt the necessary measures to give effect to these rights. Further, under article 3, Canada undertook to ensure the equal right of men and women to the enjoyment of these rights. These undertakings apply also to the position of Sandra Lovelace. The Committee considers, however, that it is not necessary for the purposes of her communication to decide their extent in all respects. The full scope of the obligation of Canada to remove the effects or inequalities caused by the application of existing laws to past events, in particular as regards such matters as civil or personal status, does not have to be examined in the present case, for the reasons set out below.

13.1 The Committee considers that the essence of the present complaint concerns the continuing effect of the *Indian Act,* in denying Sandra Lovelace legal status as an Indian, in particular because she cannot for this reason claim a legal right to reside where she wishes to, on the Tobique Reserve. This fact persists after the entry into force of the Covenant, and its effects have to be examined, without regard to their original cause. Among the effects referred to on behalf of the author (quoted in paragraph 9.9, above, and listed (1) to (9)), the greater number, ((1) to (8)), relate to the *Indian Act* and other Canadian rules in fields which do not necessarily adversely affect the enjoyment of rights protected by the Covenant. In this respect the significant matter is her last claim, that "the major loss to a person ceasing to be an Indian is the loss of the cultural benefits of living in an Indian community, the emotional ties to home, family, friends and neighbours, and the loss of identity".

13.2 Although a number of provisions of the Covenant have been invoked by Sandra Lovelace, the Committee considers that the one which is most directly applicable to the complaint is article 27, which reads as follows:

> In those States in which ethnic, religious or linguistic minorities exist, persons belonging to such minorities shall not be denied the right, in community with the other members of their group, to enjoy their own culture, to profess and practise their own religion, or to use their own language.

> It has to be considered whether Sandra Lovelace, because she is denied the legal right to reside on the Tobique Reserve, has by that fact been denied the right guaranteed by article 27 to persons belonging to minorities, to enjoy their own culture and to use their own language in community with other members of their group.

14. The rights under article 27 of the Covenant have to be secured to "persons belonging" to the minority. At present Sandra Lovelace does not qualify as an Indian under Canadian legislation. However, the Indian Act deals primarily with a number of privileges which, as stated above, do not as such come within the scope of the Covenant therefore have to be distinguished. Persons who are born and brought up on a reserve, who have kept ties with their community and wish to maintain these ties must normally be considered as belonging to that minority within the meaning of the Covenant. Since Sandra Lovelace is ethnically a Maliseet Indian and has only been absent from her home reserve for a few years during the existence of her marriage, she is, in the opinion of the Committee, entitled to be regarded as "belonging" to this minority and to claim the benefits of article 27 of the Covenant. The question whether these benefits have been denied to her, depends on how far they extend.

15. The right to live on a reserve is not as such guaranteed by article 27 of the Covenant. Moreover, the *Indian Act* does not interfere directly with the functions which are expressly mentioned in that article. However, in the opinion of the Committee the right of Sandra Lovelace to access to her native culture and language "in community with the other members" of her group, has in fact been, and continues to be interfered with, because there is no place outside the Tobique Reserve where such a community exists. On the other hand, not every interference can be regarded as a denial of rights within the meaning of article 27. Restrictions on the right to residence, by way of national legislation, cannot be ruled out under article 27 of the Covenant. This also follows from the restrictions to article 12(1) of the Covenant set out in article 12(3). The Committee recognizes the need to define the category of persons entitled to live on a reserve, for such purposes as those explained by the Government regarding protection of its resources and preservation of the identity of its people. However, the obligations which the Government has since undertaken under the Covenant must also be taken into account.

16. In this respect, the Committee is of the view that statutory restrictions affecting the right to residence on a reserve of a person belonging to the minority concerned, must have both a reasonable and objective justification and be consistent with the other provisions of the Covenant, read as a whole. Article 27 must be construed and applied in the light of the other provisions mentioned above, such as articles 12, 17 and 23 in so far as they may be relevant to the particular case, and also the provisions against discrimination, such as articles 2, 3 and 26, as the case may be. It is not necessary, however, to determine in any general manner which restrictions may be justified under the Covenant, in particular as a result of marriage, because the cir-

cumstances are special in the present case.

17. The case of Sandra Lovelace should be considered in the light of the fact that her marriage to a non-Indian has broken up. It is natural that in such a situation she wishes to return to the environment in which she was born, particularly as after the dissolution of her marriage her main cultural attachment again was to the Maliseet band. Whatever may be the merits of the *Indian Act* in other respects, it does not seem to the Committee that to deny Sandra Lovelace the right to reside on the reserve is reasonable, or necessary to preserve the identity of the tribe. The Committee therefore concludes that to prevent her recognition as belonging to the band is an unjustifiable denial of her rights under article 27 of the Covenant, read in the context of the other provisions referred to.

18. In view of this finding, the Committee does not consider it necessary to examine whether the same facts also show separate breaches of the other rights invoked. The specific rights most directly applicable to her situation are those under article 27 of the Covenant. The rights to choose one's residence (article 12), and the rights aimed at protecting family life and children (articles 17, 23 and 24) are only indirectly at stake in the present case. The facts of the case do not seem to require further examination under those articles. The Committee's finding of a lack of a reasonable justification for the interference with Sandra Lovelace's rights under article 27 of the Covenant also makes it unnecessary, as suggested above (paragraph 12), to examine the general provisions against discrimination (articles 2, 3 and 26) in the context of the present case, and in particular to determine their bearing under inequalities predating the coming into force of the Covenant for Canada.

19. Accordingly, the Human Rights Committee, acting under article 5(4) of the Optional Protocol to the *International Covenant on Civil and Political Rights,* is of the view that the facts of the present case, which establish that Sandra Lovelace has been denied the legal right to reside on the Tobique Reserve, disclose a breach by Canada of article 27 of the Covenant.

Native Women's Association of Canada v. *Canada*

[1994] 3 S.C.R. 627 (S.C.C.). Lamer C.J., La Forest, L'Heureux-Dubé, Sopinka, Gonthier, Cory, McLachlin, Iacobucci, and Major JJ., October 27, 1994.

Sopinka J.:—This case raises the issue of the extent to which the freedom of expression and equality provisions of the *Canadian Charter of Rights and Freedoms* require that government funding be provided to various groups in order to promote the representation of certain interests at constitutional reform discussions. Specifically, where the Government of Canada provides funding to certain Aboriginal groups, alleged to be male-dominated, does s. 2(b) in combination with s. 28 of the Charter oblige the Government of Canada to provide equal funding to an association claiming to represent the interests of female Aboriginal persons so that they may also express their views at the constitutional discussions? Alternatively, is this result mandated by s. 15 of the Charter or s. 35 of the *Constitution Act, 1982*? This case also invites consideration of whether there is any violation of the Charter if the Government of Canada refuses to extend an invitation to a group representing the interests of Aboriginal women to come to the table to discuss possible constitutional reform.

Subsidiary issues are also raised concerning the justiciability of the Charter matters as well as the jurisdiction of the Federal Court of Appeal to grant the remedy of a declaration when it was not specifically requested at the Trial Division.

Following a review of the facts, I will briefly analyze the issue of the jurisdiction of the Federal Court of Appeal. I will next embark on a discussion of the main focus of this appeal regarding the alleged violations of the Charter. In light of my conclusion that there was no Charter violation in this case, it will be unnecessary to address the issue concerning justiciability. Therefore, for the purposes of this appeal, I will assume that the matters raised herein are justiciable. . . .

The substance of the complaint is that by financing the four recipient Aboriginal groups with respect to the constitutional renewal discussions, the Government of Canada assisted the propagation of the view that the Charter should not apply to Aboriginal self-government. The respondents allege that by funding male-dominated groups and failing to provide equal funding to NWAC, the Government of Canada violated their freedom of expression and right to equality. The respondents' application was dismissed by the Federal Court, Trial Division . . . [and] [T]he Federal Court of Appeal. . . .

Canadian Charter of Rights and Freedoms
2. Everyone has the following fundamental freedoms: . . .
   (b) freedom of thought, belief, opinion and expression, including freedom of the press and other media of communication; . . .
15. (1) Every individual is equal before and under the law and has the right to the equal protection and equal benefit of the law without discrimination and, in particular, without discrimination based on race, national or ethnic origin, colour, religion, sex, age or mental or physical disability.
28. Notwithstanding anything in this Charter, the rights and freedoms referred to in it are guaranteed equally to male and female persons. . . .

The conclusions reached in *Haig* v. *Canada,* [1993] 2 S.C.R. 995 have application to the case at bar. Similar to a referendum, the Government of Canada was engaging in a consultative process to secure the public opinion with respect to potential constitutional amendments. To further this goal, a parallel process of consultation was established within the Aboriginal community. It cannot be claimed that NWAC has a constitutional right to receive government funding aimed at promoting participation in the constitutional conferences. The respondents conceded as much in paragraph 91 of their factum as well as in oral argument. Furthermore, the provision of funding and the invitation to participate in constitutional discussions facilitated and enhanced the expression of Aboriginal groups. It did not stifle expression.

However, the respondents rely on *Haig* for the proposition that the Government cannot provide a platform of expression in a discriminatory fashion or in a way which otherwise violates the Charter. They state that this result is clearly mandated by s. 28 of the Charter. The following passage from the reasons of L'Heureux-Dubé J., at pp. 1041–42, is relied on:

> In my view, though a referendum is undoubtedly a platform for expression, s. 2(b) of the Charter does not impose upon a government, whether provincial or federal, any positive obligation to consult its citizens through the particular mechanism of a referendum. Nor does it confer upon all its citizens the right to express their opinions in a referendum. A government is under no constitutional obligation to extend this platform of expression to *anyone,* let alone to *everyone.* A referendum as a platform of expression is, in my view, a matter of legislative policy and not of constitutional law.
> The following caveat is, however, in order here. *While s. 2(b) of the Charter does not*

include the right to any particular means of expression, where a government chooses to provide one, it must do so in a fashion that is consistent with the Constitution. The traditional rules of Charter scrutiny continue to apply. Thus, while the government may extend such a benefit to a limited number of persons, it may not do so in a discriminatory fashion, and particularly not on ground prohibited under s. 15 of the Charter.

I would add that issues of expression may on occasion be strongly linked to issues of equality. In *Schachter v. Canada*, [1992] 2 S.C.R. 679, the Court said that s. 15 of the Charter is indeed a hybrid of positive and negative protection, and that a government may be required to take positive steps to ensure the equality of people or groups who come within the scope of s. 15. It might well be that, in the context of a particular equality claim, those positive steps may involve the provision of means of expression to certain groups or individuals. However, despite obvious links between various provisions of the Charter, I believe that, should such situations arise, it would be preferable to address them within the boundaries of s. 15, without unduly blurring the distinctions between different Charter guarantees.

Therefore, *Haig* establishes the principle that generally the government is under no obligation to fund or provide a specific platform of expression to an individual or a group. However, the decision in Haig leaves open the possibility that, in certain circumstances, positive governmental action may be required in order to make the freedom of expression meaningful. Furthermore, in some circumstances where the government does provide such a platform, it must not do so in a discriminatory fashion contrary to the Charter. It is this last proposition upon which the respondents rely in conjunction with s. 28 of the Charter to support their position that their rights under s. 2(b) of the Charter were violated in that they did not receive an equal platform to express their views.

At this point, I should add that it cannot be said that every time the Government of Canada chooses to fund or consult a certain group, thereby providing a platform upon which to convey certain views, that the Government is also required to fund a group purporting to represent the opposite point of view. Otherwise, the implications of this proposition would be untenable. For example, if the Government chooses to fund a women's organization to study the issue of abortion to assist in drafting proposed legislation, can it be argued that the Government is bound by the Constitution to provide equal funding to a group purporting to represent the rights of fathers? If this was the intended scope of s. 2(b) of the Charter, the ramifications on government spending would be far reaching indeed. . . .

Therefore, while it may be true that the Government cannot provide a particular means of expression that has the effect of discriminating against a group, it cannot be said that merely by consulting an organization, or organizations, purportedly representing a male or female point of view, the Government must automatically consult groups representing the opposite perspective. It will be rare indeed that the provision of a platform or funding to one or several organizations will have the effect of suppressing another's freedom of speech.

Although it appears that the respondents' arguments relate more closely to an equality argument under s. 15 of the Charter, the respondents devoted much of their energy addressing s. 2(b). In either case, regardless of how the arguments are framed, it will be seen that the evidence does not support the conclusions urged by the respondents. . . .

I am in complete agreement with the intervener AFN's submissions that there was no evidence before the Federal Court of Appeal, nor before this Court, that AFN or the other funded groups advocated "male-dominated Aboriginal self-governments". Nor was there any evidence to suggest that AFN, NCC, ITC or MNC were less representative of the viewpoint of women with respect to the Constitution. The main argument of NWAC in this regard is that only they were advocating the inclusion of the Charter in any negotiated form of Aboriginal self-government. The evidence clearly discloses that of the four funded groups at least MNC also supported its inclusion. Furthermore, NCC did not oppose application of the Charter, rather it desired that each Aboriginal self government be free to determine the issue for itself. ITC was also willing to consider application of the Charter. Thus, it was not exclusively the position of NWAC that the Charter be maintained.

Furthermore, in a letter dated March 2, 1992 (exhibit A to the supplementary affidavit of Gail Stacey-Moore), the Minister Responsible for Constitutional Affairs wrote the following:

> The national Aboriginal associations do represent both men and women from their communities. I encourage you to work within your communities to ensure your views are heard and represented through those associations.

Thus, in the opinion of the Government of Canada as well, the funded organizations were not perpetuating only a male-dominated point of view. Although this is certainly not determinative, it is indicative that a minister of the Crown who was familiar with the position and views advanced by them regarded the four national organizations as bona fide representatives of Aboriginal persons. . . .

The evidence is also indicative of the fact that Aboriginal women, including members of NWAC, did have a direct voice regarding the position of the funded groups with respect to the constitutional discussions. NWAC participated in the parallel process set up by the four national Aboriginal organizations to discuss constitutional reform. For example, the respondent Stacey-Moore and other women secured positions on the Constitutional Working Group of the AFN. The respondent McIvor was the NWAC representative to the AFN Constitutional Commission, while Jane Gottfriedson, President of the British Columbia Native Women's Society (affiliated with NWAC) was appointed to the NCC Constitutional Commission. As well, on March 13, 14 and 15, 1992, an Aboriginal Conference on the Constitution was held in Ottawa. After a sustained effort, NWAC secured eight official seats and four observers out of a total of 184 delegates.

Furthermore, NWAC also received some of the Government funding under the Contribution Agreements, as all four groups were required to direct a portion of the funds received specifically to address women's issues. AFN and NCC each supplied $130,000 to NWAC. ITC contributed $170,000 to its women's organization, Pauktuutit, for research and other work related to constitutional affairs and more funding was expected. Pauktuutit, as the representative of Inuit women, was actively involved in the constitutional process.

Rather than illustrate that the funded groups advocated male-dominated Aboriginal self-government, the evidence discloses that the four funded groups made efforts to include the viewpoint of women. As well, there was no evidence to suggest that NWAC enjoyed any higher level of support amongst Aboriginal women as compared to the funded Aboriginal groups.

(c) Conclusions on Sections 2(b) and 28 of the Charter

The freedom of expression guaranteed by s. 2(b) of the Charter does not guarantee any particular means of expression or place a positive obligation upon the Government to consult anyone. The right to a particular platform or means of expression was clearly rejected by this Court in *Haig*. The respondents had many opportunities to express their views through the four Aboriginal groups as well as directly to the Government, for example, through the Beaudoin-Dobbie Commission. NWAC even took the opportunity to express its concerns directly to the Minister Responsible for Constitutional Affairs and received a response, albeit one that did not satisfy NWAC.

Even assuming that in certain extreme circumstances, the provision of a platform of expression to one group may infringe the expression of another and thereby require the Government to provide an equal opportunity for the expression of that group, there was no evidence in this case to suggest that the funding or consultation of the four Aboriginal groups infringed the respondents' equal right of freedom of expression. The four Aboriginal groups invited to discuss possible constitutional amendments are all *bona fide* national representatives of Aboriginal people in Canada and, based on the facts in this case, there was no requirement under s. 2(b) of the Charter to also extend an invitation and funding directly to the respondents.

Although I would hope that it is evident from these reasons, I wish to stress that nothing stated in them is intended to detract in any way from any contention by or on behalf of Aboriginal women that they face racial arid sexual discrimination which impose serious hurdles to their equality.

(3) Section 15(1) Of The Charter: Equality Rights

It seems that the respondents' contentions regarding ss. 2(b) and 28 of the Charter are better characterized as a s. 15 Charter argument. As L'Heureux-Dubé J. stated in *Haig, supra,* the allegations that a platform of expression has been provided on a discriminatory basis are preferably dealt with under s. 15.

The respondents contend that the refusal to fund NWAC and invite them to be equal participants at the round of constitutional discussions violated their rights under s. 15(1) of the Charter due to the under-inclusive nature of the Government's decision. Again relying on *Haig* in their factum, the respondents submit that an equality claim may involve the provision of means of expression to certain groups or individuals.

I have concluded that the arguments of the respondents with respect to s. 15 must also fail. The lack of an evidentiary basis for the arguments with respect to ss. 2(b) and 28 is equally applicable to any arguments advanced under s. 15(1) of the Charter in this case. I agree with the Court of Appeal that s. 15(1) is of no assistance to the respondents.

(4) Section 35 of the Charter: Existing Aboriginal and Treaty Rights

I also agree with the conclusions of the Court of Appeal with respect to the inapplicability of s. 35 of the *Constitution Act, 1982* to the present case. The right of the Aboriginal people of Canada to participate in constitutional discussions does not derive from any existing Aboriginal or treaty right protected under s. 35. Therefore, s. 35(4) of the *Constitution Act, 1982,* which guarantees Aboriginal and treaty rights referred to in s. 35(1) equally to male and female persons, is of no assistance to the respondents. . . .

I respectfully disagree with the conclusion of the Federal Court of Appeal that the failure to provide funding to the respondents and invite them as equal participants in the constitutional discussions violated their rights under ss. 2(b) and 28 of the Charter.

I am, however, in agreement with the Federal Court of Appeal that s. 15(1) of the Charter and s. 35 of the *Constitution Act, 1982* have no application in this case.

Therefore, I would allow the appeal, set aside the declaration made by the Federal Court of Appeal and restore the judgment of Walsh D.J. with costs to the appellant both here and in the Court of Appeal if demanded. . . .

L'HEUREUX-DUBÉ J.: . . . I cannot agree with my colleague when be states that *Haig* "establishes the principle that generally the government is under no obligation to fund or provide a specific platform of expression to an individual or a group". In my view, *Haig* rather stands for the proposition that the government *in that particular case* was under no constitutional obligation to provide for the right to a referendum under 9. 2(b) of the Charter, but that if and when the government does decide to provide a specific platform of expression, it must do so in a manner consistent with the Charter.

This Court has always fostered a broad approach to the interpretation of 2(b) of the Charter, freedom of expression being a important aspect of the healthy functioning of the democratic process (see, *Inter alia: Irwin Toy Ltd.* v. *Québec (Attorney General)*, [1989] 1 S.C.R. 927). Haig is consistent with this approach in that it underlines the possible consequences of disparate financing of viewpoints and the importance of promoting a variety of views. It is also recognised in *Haig*, at p. 1037, "that a philosophy of non-interference may not *in all circumstances* guarantee the optimal functioning of the marketplace of ideas". (Emphasis added.)

The approach in *Haig* is one that in fact affords significant relevance to circumstances, and this is why I am of the view that in certain ones, funding or consultation may be mandated by the Constitution by virtue of the fact that when the government does decide to facilitate the expression of views, it must do so in a manner that is mindful of the Charter. In this respect, one must note that the circumstances in which the government may be held to a positive obligation in terms of providing a specific platform of expression invariably depend on the nature of the evidence presented by the parties.

In the present case, the evidence demonstrates that the complainant organization was not prevented from expressing its views, albeit not in the way it would have desired. I would therefore agree that on its facts, this case does not give rise to a positive obligation analogous to the type referred to in *Haig* since not providing the complainant organization with the funding and constitutional voice requested did not amount to a breach of its freedom of expression. However, I cannot resist reiterating that pursuant to *Haig*, had the government extended such a platform of expression to other organizations in a manner that had the effect of violating the complainant organization's freedom of expression, this would most definitely have amounted to a breach of 2(b) of the Charter. In other words, the outcome of the present case should in no way be interpreted as limiting the proposition for which *Haig* stands for.

In the result, I would allow the appeal. . . .

McLACHLIN J.: [concurs with judgment of Sopinka J.]

Corbiere v. *Canada (Min. of Indian and Northern Affairs)*

[1999] 2 S.C.R. 203 (S.C.C.). Lamer C.J., L'Heureux-Dube, Gonthier, Cory, McLachlin, Iacobucci, Major, Bastarache and Binnie JJ., May 20, 1999.

The judgment of Lamer C.J. and Cory, McLachlin, Major and Bastarache JJ. was delivered by

1   McLACHLIN AND BASTARACHE JJ. — We have read the reasons for judgment of Justice L'Heureux-Dubé. We believe that this case can be resolved on simpler grounds. We will therefore briefly outline the reasoning upon which we base our own decision.

2   L'Heureux-Dubé J. has set out in detail the facts in this case as well as a description of its judicial history. We adopt this factual background.

3   The narrow issue raised in this appeal is whether the exclusion of off-reserve members of an Indian band from the right to vote in band elections pursuant to s. 77(1) of the *Indian Act,* R.S.C., 1985, c. I-5, is inconsistent with s. 15(1) of the *Canadian Charter of Rights and Freedoms.* There is no need for us to describe the steps applicable to a s. 15(1) analysis. They have been affirmed with great precision by Iacobucci J. in *Law v. Canada (Minister of Employment and Immigration),* [1999] 1 S.C.R. 497.

4   The first step is to determine whether the impugned law makes a distinction that denies equal benefit or imposes an unequal burden. The *Indian Act's* exclusion of off-reserve band members from voting privileges on band governance satisfies this requirement.

5   The next step is to determine whether the distinction is discriminatory. The first inquiry is whether the distinction is made on the basis of an enumerated ground or a ground analogous to it. The answer to this question will be found in considering the general purpose of s. 15(1), i.e. to prevent the violation of human dignity through the imposition of disadvantage based on stereotyping and social prejudice, and to promote a society where all persons are considered worthy of respect and consideration.

6   We agree with L'Heureux-Dubé J. that Aboriginality-residence (off-reserve band member status) constitutes a ground of discrimination analogous to the enumerated grounds. However, we wish to comment on two matters: (1) the suggestion by some that the same ground may or may not be analogous depending on the circumstances; and (2) the criteria that identify an analogous ground.

7   The enumerated grounds function as legislative markers of suspect grounds associated with stereotypical, discriminatory decision making. They are a legal expression of a general characteristic, not a contextual, fact-based conclusion about whether discrimination exists in a particular case. As such, the enumerated grounds must be distinguished from a finding that discrimination exists in a particular case. Since the enumerated grounds are only indicators of suspect grounds of distinction, it follows that decisions on these grounds are not always discriminatory; if this were otherwise, it would be unnecessary to proceed to the separate examination of discrimination at the third stage of our analysis discussed in *Law, supra,* per Iacobucci J.

8   The same applies to the grounds recognized by the courts as "analogous" to the grounds enumerated in s. 15. To say that a ground of distinction is an analogous ground is merely to identify a type of decision making that is suspect because it often leads to discrimination and denial of substantive equality. Like distinctions made on enumerated grounds, distinctions made on analogous grounds may well not be discriminatory. But this does not mean that they are not analogous grounds or that they are analogous grounds only in some circumstances. Just as we do not speak of enumerated grounds existing in one circumstance and not another, we should not speak of analogous grounds existing in one circumstance and not another. The enumerated and analogous grounds stand as constant markers of suspect decision making or potential discrimination. What varies is whether they amount to discrimination in the particular circumstances of the case.

9   We therefore disagree with the view that a marker of discrimination can change

from case to case, depending on the government action challenged. It seems to us that it is not the ground that varies from case to case, but the determination of whether a distinction on the basis of a constitutionally cognizable ground is discriminatory. Sex will always be a ground, although sex-based legislative distinctions may not always be discriminatory. To be sure, *R. v. Turpin*, [1989] 1 S.C.R. 1296, suggested that residence might be an analogous ground in certain contexts. But in view of the synthesis of previous cases suggested in *Law, supra*, it is more likely that today the same result, dismissal of the claim, would be achieved either by finding no analogous ground or no discrimination in fact going to essential human dignity.

10   If it is the intention of L'Heureux-Dubé J.'s reasons to affirm contextual dependency of the enumerated and analogous grounds, we must respectfully disagree. If "Aboriginality-residence" is to be an analogous ground (and we agree with L'Heureux-Dubé J. that it should), then it must always stand as a constant marker of potential legislative discrimination, whether the challenge is to a governmental tax credit, a voting right, or a pension scheme. This established, the analysis moves to the third stage: whether the distinction amounts, in purpose or effect, to discrimination on the facts of the case.

11   Maintaining the distinction in *Law, supra*, between the enumerated or analogous ground analysis and the third-stage contextual discrimination analysis, offers several advantages. Both stages are concerned with discrimination and the violation of the presumption of the equal dignity and worth of every human being. But they approach it from different perspectives. The analogous grounds serve as jurisprudential markers for suspect distinctions. They function conceptually to identify the sorts of claims that properly fall under s. 15. By screening out other cases, they avoid trivializing the s. 15 equality guarantee and promote the efficient use of judicial resources. And they permit the development over time of a conceptual jurisprudence of the sorts of distinctions that fall under the s. 15 guarantee, without foreclosing new cases of discrimination. A distinction on an enumerated or analogous ground established, the contextual and fact-specific inquiry proceeds to whether the distinction amounts to discrimination in the context of the particular case.

12   Our second concern relates to the manner in which a new analogous ground may be identified. In our view, conflation of the second and third stages of the *Law* framework is to be avoided. To be sure, *Law* is meant to provide a set of guidelines and not a formalistic straitjacket, but the second and third stages are unquestionably distinct: the former asks whether the distinction is on the basis of an enumerated or analogous ground, the latter whether that distinction on the facts of the case affronts s. 15. Affirmative answers to both inquiries are a precondition to establishing a constitutional claim.

13   What then are the criteria by which we identify a ground of distinction as analogous? The obvious answer is that we look for grounds of distinction that are analogous or like the grounds enumerated in s. 15—race, national or ethnic origin, colour, religion, sex, age, or mental or physical disability. It seems to us that what these grounds have in common is the fact that they often serve as the basis for stereotypical decisions made not on the basis of merit but on the basis of a personal characteristic that is immutable or changeable only at unacceptable cost to personal identity. This suggests that the thrust of identification of analogous grounds at the second stage of the *Law* analysis is to reveal grounds based on characteristics that we cannot change or that the government has no legitimate interest in expecting us to change to receive equal treatment under the law. To

put it another way, s. 15 targets the denial of equal treatment on grounds that are actually immutable, like race, or constructively immutable, like religion. Other factors identified in the cases as associated with the enumerated and analogous grounds, like the fact that the decision adversely impacts on a discrete and insular minority or a group that has been historically discriminated against, may be seen to flow from the central concept of immutable or constructively immutable personal characteristics, which too often have served as illegitimate and demeaning proxies for merit-based decision making.

14   L'Heureux-Dubé J. ultimately concludes that "Aboriginality-residence" as it pertains to whether an Aboriginal band member lives on or off the reserve is an analogous ground. We agree. L'Heureux-Dubé J.'s discussion makes clear that the distinction goes to a personal characteristic essential to a band member's personal identity, which is no less constructively immutable than religion or citizenship. Off-reserve Aboriginal band members can change their status to on-reserve band members only at great cost, if at all.

15   Two brief comments on this new analogous ground are warranted. First, reserve status should not be confused with residence. The ordinary "residence" decisions faced by the average Canadians should not be confused with the profound decisions Aboriginal band members make to live on or off their reserves, assuming choice is possible. The reality of their situation is unique and complex. Thus no new water is charted, in the sense of finding residence, in the generalized abstract, to be an analogous ground. Second, we note that the analogous ground of off-reserve status or Aboriginality-residence is limited to a subset of the Canadian population, while s. 15 is directed to everyone. In our view, this is no impediment to its inclusion as an analogous ground under s. 15. Its demographic limitation is no different, for example, from pregnancy, which is a distinct, but fundamentally interrelated form of discrimination from gender. "Embedded" analogous grounds may be necessary to permit meaningful consideration of intra-group discrimination.

16   Having concluded that the distinction made by the impugned law is made on an analogous ground, we come to the final step of the s. 15(1) analysis: whether the distinction at issue in this case in fact constitutes discrimination. In plain words, does the distinction undermine the presumption upon which the guarantee of equality is based— that each individual is deemed to be of equal worth regardless of the group to which he or she belongs?

17   Applying the applicable Law factors to this case—pre-existing disadvantage, correspondence and importance of the affected interest—we conclude that the answer to this question is yes. The impugned distinction perpetuates the historic disadvantage experienced by off-reserve band members by denying them the right to vote and participate in their band's governance. Off-reserve band members have important interests in band governance which the distinction denies. They are co-owners of the band's assets. The reserve, whether they live on or off it, is their and their children's land. The band council represents them as band members to the community at large, in negotiations with the government, and within Aboriginal organizations. Although there are some matters of purely local interest, which do not as directly affect the interests of off-reserve band members, the complete denial to off-reserve members of the right to vote and participate in band governance treats them as less worthy and entitled, not on the merits of their situation, but simply because they live off-reserve. The importance of the interest affected is underlined by the findings of the Royal Commission on Aboriginal Peoples, *Report of the*

Royal Commission on Aboriginal Peoples (1996), vol. 1, *Looking Forward, Looking Back,* at pp. 137–91. The Royal Commission writes in vol. 4, *Perspectives and Realities,* at p. 521:

> Throughout the Commission's hearings, Aboriginal people stressed the fundamental importance of retaining and enhancing their cultural identity while living in urban areas. Aboriginal identity lies at the heart of Aboriginal peoples' existence; maintaining that identity is an essential and self-validating pursuit for Aboriginal people in cities.

And at p. 525:

> Cultural identity for urban Aboriginal people is also tied to a land base or ancestral territory. For many, the two concepts are inseparable. . . . Identification with an ancestral place is important to urban people because of the associated ritual, ceremony and traditions, as well as the people who remain there, the sense of belonging, the bond to an ancestral community, and the accessibility of family, community and elders.

18   Taking all this into account, it is clear that the s. 77(1) disenfranchisement is discriminatory. It denies off-reserve band members the right to participate fully in band governance on the arbitrary basis of a personal characteristic. It reaches the cultural identity of off-reserve Aboriginals in a stereotypical way. It presumes that Aboriginals living off-reserve are not interested in maintaining meaningful participation in the band or in preserving their cultural identity, and are therefore less deserving members of the band. The effect is clear, as is the message: off-reserve band members are not as deserving as those band members who live on reserves. This engages the dignity aspect of the s. 15 analysis and results in the denial of substantive equality.

19   The conclusion that discrimination exists at the third stage of the *Law* test does not depend on the composition of the off-reserve band members group, its relative homogeneity or the particular historical discrimination it may have suffered. It is the present situation of the group relative to that of the comparator group, on-reserve band members, that is relevant. All parties have accepted that the off-reserve group comprises persons who have chosen to live off-reserve freely, persons who have been forced to leave the reserve reluctantly because of economic and social considerations, persons who have at some point been expelled then restored to band membership through Bill C-31 (An Act to amend the Indian Act, S.C. 1985, c. 27), and descendants of these people. It is accepted that off-reserve band members are the object of discrimination and constitute an underprivileged group. It is also accepted that many off-reserve band members were expelled from the reserves because of policies and legal provisions which were changed by Bill C-31 and can be said to have suffered double discrimination. But Aboriginals living on reserves are subject to the same discrimination. Some were affected by Bill C-31. Some left the reserve and returned. The relevant social facts in this case are those that relate to off-reserve band members as opposed to on-reserve band members. Even if all band members living off-reserve had voluntarily chosen this way of life and were not subject to discrimination in the broader Canadian society, they would still have the same cause of action. They would still suffer a detriment by being denied full participation in the affairs of the bands to which they would continue to belong while the band councils are able to affect their interests, in particular by making decisions with respect to the surrender of lands, the allocation of land to band members, the raising of funds and making of expenditures for the benefit of all band members. The effect of the legislation is to force band members to choose between living on the reserve and exercising their political rights, or living off-reserve and renouncing the exercise of their political rights.

The political rights in question are related to the race of the individuals affected, and to their cultural identity. As mentioned earlier, the differential treatment resulting from the legislation is discriminatory because it implies that off-reserve band members are lesser members of their bands or persons who have chosen to be assimilated by the mainstream society.

20   We have been asked to consider the possible application of s. 25 of the *Charter*. This section provides that rights accorded in the *Charter* must not be construed as abrogating or derogating from the rights of Aboriginals. We agree with L'Heureux-Dubé J. that given the limited argument on this issue, it would be inappropriate to articulate general principles pertaining to s. 25 in this case. Suffice it to say that a case for its application has not been made out here.

21   Having found that s. 77(1) is discriminatory, we must address the s. 1 argument of the appellants. The applicable test was recently described by Iacobucci J. in *Egan* v. *Canada*, [1995] 2 S.C.R. 513, at para. 182. We are satisfied that the restriction on voting is rationally connected to the aim of the legislation, which is to give a voice in the affairs of the reserve only to the persons most directly affected by the decisions of the band council. It is admitted that although all band members are subject to some decisions of the band council, most decisions would only impact on members living on the reserve. The restriction of s. 15 rights is however not justified under the second branch of the s. 1 test; it has not been demonstrated that s. 77(1) of the Indian Act impairs the s. 15 rights minimally. Even if it is accepted that some distinction may be justified in order to protect legitimate interests of band members living on the reserve, it has not been demonstrated that a complete denial of the right of band members living off-reserve to participate in the affairs of the band through the democratic process of elections is necessary. Some parties and interveners have mentioned the possibility of a two-tiered council, of reserved seats for off-reserve members of the band, of double-majority votes on some issues. The appellants argue that there are important difficulties and costs involved in maintaining an electoral list of off-reserve band members and in setting up a system of governance balancing the rights of on-reserve and off-reserve band members. But they present no evidence of efforts deployed or schemes considered and costed, and no argument or authority in support of the conclusion that costs and administrative convenience could justify a complete denial of the constitutional right. Under these circumstances, we must conclude that the violation has not been shown to be demonstrably justified.

22   With regard to remedy, the Court of Appeal was of the view that it would be preferable to grant the Batchewana Band a permanent constitutional exemption rather than to declare s. 77(1) of the *Indian Act* to be unconstitutional and without effect generally. With respect, we must disagree. The remedy of constitutional exemption has been recognized in a very limited way in this Court, to protect the interests of a party who has succeeded in having a legislative provision declared unconstitutional, where the declaration of invalidity has been suspended; see *Schachter* v. *Canada*, [1992] 2 S.C.R. 679, at pp. 715–17; *Rodriguez* v. *British Columbia (Attorney General)*, [1993] 3 S.C.R. 519, at p. 577. We do not think this is a case where a possible expansion of the constitutional exemption remedy should be considered. There is no evidence of special circumstances upon which this possibility might be raised. The evidence before the Court is that there are off-reserve members of most if not all Indian bands in Canada that are affected by s. 77(1) of the Indian Act, and no evidence of other rights that may be relevant in examin-

ing the effect of s. 77(1) with regard to any band other than the Batchewana Band. If another band could establish an Aboriginal right to restrict voting, as suggested by the Court of Appeal, that right would simply have precedence over the terms of the Indian Act; this is not a reason to restrict the declaration of invalidity to the Batchewana Band.

23   Where there is inconsistency between the *Charter* and a legislative provision, s. 52 of the *Constitution Act, 1982* provides that the provision shall be rendered void to the extent of the inconsistency. We would declare the words "and is ordinarily resident on the reserve" in s. 77(1) of the Indian Act to be inconsistent with s. 15(1) but suspend the implementation of this declaration for 18 months. We would not grant a constitutional exemption to the Batchewana Band during the period of suspension, as would normally be done according to the rule in *Schachter*. The reason for this is that in the particular circumstances of this case, it would appear to be preferable to develop an electoral process that will balance the rights of off-reserve and on-reserve band members. We have not overlooked the possibility that legislative inaction may create new problems. Such claims will fall to be dealt with on their merits should they arise.

24   We would therefore dismiss the appeal and modify the remedy by striking out the words "and is ordinarily resident on the reserve" in s. 77(1) of the *Indian Act* and suspending the implementation of the declaration of invalidity for 18 months, with costs to the respondents. We would answer the restated constitutional questions as follows:

1.   Do the words "and is ordinarily resident on the reserve" contained in s. 77(1) of the *Indian Act,* R.S.C., 1985, c. I-5, contravene s. 15(1) of the *Canadian Charter of Rights and Freedoms,* either generally or with respect only to members of the Batchewana Indian Band?

Yes, in their general application.

2.   If the answer to question 1 is in the affirmative, is s. 77(1) of the *Indian Act* demonstrably justified as a reasonable limit pursuant to s. 1 of the *Canadian Charter of Rights and Freedoms?*

No.

The reasons of L'Heureux-Dubé, Gonthier, Iacobucci and Binnie JJ. were delivered by L'Heureux-Dubé J. . . .

26   The chiefs and councils of *Indian Act* bands, pursuant to the definition of "council of the band" in s. 2(1), are chosen following the band's custom, or, if an order in council has been made under s. 74(1), by the procedures set out in the Act, including s. 77(1). The trial judge found that the policy of the Department of Indian and Northern Affairs Canada is that a band will not be deleted from the order in council placing it under the election procedures of the *Indian Act* unless the band council and the current "electors" so approve, either through a plebiscite or at a public meeting. Certain other conditions must also be met. The most recent order in council, the *Indian Bands Council Elections Order,* SOR/97-138, which came into effect on March 4, 1997, provides that 288 bands select their leadership in accordance with the Indian Act. This number represents just under half of the *Indian Act* bands in Canada. . . .

30   The number of Batchewana Band members has risen dramatically since 1985, and at the same time the percentage of band members living on the reserves has dramatically fallen. In 1985, 71.1 percent of the 543 registered members of the band lived on-reserve.

In 1991, only 32.8 percent of the 1,426 registered members lived on the reserves. The parties agree that this trend is continuing. This dramatic increase in the number of off-reserve members occurred largely because of the passage of An Act to amend the *Indian Act*, S.C. 1985, c. 27 ("Bill C-31"), by Parliament. This legislation restored Indian status to most of those who had lost this status because of the operation of certain sections of the Indian Act, as well as to the descendants of such people. Prior to this legislation, women with Indian status who married non-Indian men lost their status, and their children did not get status, though men who married non-Indian women, and their children, maintained Indian status. Registered Indians who voluntarily "enfranchised" also lost Indian status. For the Batchewana Band, approximately 85 percent of the growth in band membership consisted of people who were reinstated to Indian status and band membership because of Bill C-31. Similar trends may be seen in many other bands. . . .

A. Should the Section 15 Analysis Focus Only on the Batchewana Band?

45   A preliminary question is whether the s. 15(1) analysis should focus on the Batchewana Band in particular, or on the legislation as it applies in general, to all bands affected by s. 77(1). At trial, the focus was on the particular situation of the Batchewana Band, since the respondents asked only for a constitutional exemption applying to their band.

46   However, examining only the circumstances of the Batchewana Band in the s. 15(1) analysis would be to presume that the appropriate remedy is a constitutional exemption. As the guardians of the rights in the *Charter*, it is courts' duty to ensure that a remedy is given that is commensurate with the extent of the violation that has been found, and to determine the appropriate remedy. Before considering any question of constitutional exemption, therefore, the general application of the legislation, and the available evidence relating to that general application, should be examined. Only if there is no evidence of general invalidity will it be necessary to consider the specific circumstances of the Batchewana Band and, therefore, the doctrine of constitutional exemption. . . .

50   Here, the constitutional question that was served on the appropriate parties pursuant to Rule 32, though it did contain the words "with respect only to members of the Batchewana Indian Band", constituted notice to all attorneys general that the constitutional validity of the residency requirement for voting contained in the *Indian Act* was at issue. The remedy preferred by the federal Crown in this case, if there is to be one, is for a general declaration to be made rather than a constitutional exemption, and this was argued in its factum and oral argument. As emphasized above, the issues relating to the general application of s. 77(1) were argued and discussed before us and in the Federal Court of Appeal by the parties and by interveners. Despite the wording of the question, it was clear that this Court, when analysing the situation of the Batchewana Band, might set down principles that would apply to other bands. I do not believe, therefore, that any substantive prejudice has been caused to attorneys general or anyone else by the wording of the question, or that they would reasonably have made a different decision about exercising their right to intervene. In the circumstances, therefore, I will restate the constitutional questions as follows:

1.   Do the words "and is ordinarily resident on the reserve" contained in s. 77(1) of the *Indian Act*, R.S.C., 1985, c. I-5, contravene s. 15(1) of the *Canadian Charter of Rights and Freedoms, either* generally or with respect only to members of the Batchewana Indian Band?

2 . If the answer to question 1 is in the affirmative, is s. 77(1) of the *Indian Act* demonstrably justified as a reasonable limit pursuant to s. 1 of the *Canadian Charter of Rights and Freedoms?* . . .

C. Section 15(1) Analysis

(1) The Section 15(1) Framework

5   In *Law v. Canada (Minister of Employment and Immigration)*, [1999] 1 S.C.R. 497, Iacobucci J. discussed the framework within which s. 15(1) analysis must be carried out. As set out in para. 88 of *Law*, an inquiry into whether legislation violates s. 15(1) involves three broad inquiries:

(A) Does the impugned law (a) draw a formal distinction between the claimant and others on the basis of one or more personal characteristics, or (b) fail to take into account the claimant's already disadvantaged position within Canadian society resulting in substantially differential treatment between the claimant and others on the basis of one or more personal characteristics?

(B) Is the claimant subject to differential treatment based on one or more enumerated and analogous grounds? and

(C) Does the differential treatment discriminate, by imposing a burden upon or withholding a benefit from the claimant in a manner which reflects the stereotypical application of presumed group or personal characteristics, or which otherwise has the effect of perpetuating or promoting the view that the individual is less capable or worthy of recognition or value as a human being or as a member of Canadian society, equally deserving of concern, respect, and consideration?

56   At all three of these stages, it must be recognized that the focus of the inquiry is purposive and contextual (see, e.g., *Law, supra,* at para. 41). A court considering a discrimination claim must examine the legislative, historical, and social context of the distinction, the reality and experiences of the individuals affected by it, and the purposes of s. 15(1).

(2) First Stage: Differential Treatment

57   The first stage of inquiry is easily satisfied in the present case. Section 77(1) of the *Indian Act* draws a distinction between band members who live on-reserve and those who live off-reserve, by excluding the latter from the definition of "elector" within the band. This constitutes differential treatment.

(3) Second Stage: Analogous Grounds

58   The differential treatment in this case is based on the status of holding membership in an *Indian Act* band, but living off that band's reserve. This combination of traits does not fall under one of the enumerated or already recognized analogous grounds. The fundamental consideration at the second stage, if the ground is not enumerated or already recognized as analogous, is whether recognition of the basis of differential treatment as an analogous ground would further the purposes of s. 15(1): *Law, supra,* at para. 93. These purposes are, as stated at para. 51 of *Law:*

[T]o prevent the violation of essential human dignity and freedom through the imposition of disadvantage, stereotyping, or political or social prejudice, and to promote a society in which all persons enjoy equal recognition at law as human beings or as members of Canadian society, equally capable and equally deserving of concern, respect and consideration.

59   The analysis at the analogous grounds stage involves considering whether differential treatment of those defined by that characteristic or combination of traits has the potential to violate human dignity in the sense underlying s. 15(1): *Egan* v. *Canada*, [1995] 2 S.C.R. 513, at para. 171, per Cory J. In *Law*, the concept of human dignity as it relates to s. 15(1) was described by Iacobucci J., at para. 53, as follows:

> Human dignity means that an individual or group feels self-respect and self-worth. It is concerned with physical and psychological empowerment and integrity. Human dignity is harmed by unfair treatment premised on personal traits or circumstances which do not relate to individual needs, capacities, or merits. It is enhanced by laws which are sensitive to the needs, capacities, and merits of different individuals, taking into account the context underlying their differences. Human dignity is harmed when individuals and groups are marginalized, ignored, or devalued, and is enhanced when laws recognize the full place of all individuals and groups within Canadian society. Human dignity within the meaning of the equality guarantee does not relate to the status or position of an individual in society *per se*, but rather concerns the manner in which a person legitimately feels when confronted with a particular law.

The analogous grounds inquiry, like the other two stages of analysis, must be undertaken in a purposive and contextual manner: *Law, supra,* at para. 41. The "nature and situation of the individual or group at issue, and the social, political, and legal history of Canadian society's treatment of that group" must be considered: *Law, supra,* at para. 93. As stated by Wilson J. in *Andrews, supra,* at p. 152, cited with approval in *Law* at para. 29, the determination of whether a ground qualifies as analogous under s. 15(1):

> . . . is not to be made only in the context of the law which is subject to challenge but rather in the context of the place of the group in the entire social, political and legal fabric of our society. While legislatures must inevitably draw distinctions among the governed, such distinctions should not bring about or reinforce the disadvantage of certain groups and individuals by denying them the rights freely accorded to others. . . .

62   Here, several factors lead to the conclusion that recognizing off-reserve band member status as an analogous ground would accord with the purposes of s. 15(1). From the perspective of off-reserve band members, the choice of whether to live on- or off-reserve, if it is available to them, is an important one to their identity and personhood, and is therefore fundamental. It involves choosing whether to live with other members of the band to which they belong, or apart from them. It relates to a community and land that have particular social and cultural significance to many or most band members. Also critical is the fact that as discussed below during the third stage of analysis, band members living off-reserve have generally experienced disadvantage, stereotyping, and prejudice, and form part of a "discrete and insular minority" defined by race and place of residence. In addition, because of the lack of opportunities and housing on many reserves, and the fact that the *Indian Act*'s rules formerly removed band membership from various categories of band members, residence off the reserve has often been forced upon them, or constitutes a choice made reluctantly or at high personal cost. For these reasons, the second stage of analysis has been satisfied, and "off-reserve band member status" is an analogous ground. It will hereafter be recognized as an analogous ground in any future case involving this combination of traits. I note that in making this determination, I

make no findings about "residence" as an analogous ground in contexts other than as it affects band members who do not live on the reserve of the band to which they belong.

(4) Third Stage of Analysis

63   At the third stage, the appropriate focus is on how, in the context of the legislation and Canadian society, the particular differential treatment impacts upon the people affected by it. This requires examining whether the legislation conflicts with the purposes of s. 15(1): to recognize all individuals and groups as equally deserving, worthy, and valuable, to remedy stereotyping, disadvantage and prejudice, and to ensure that all are treated as equally important members of Canadian society. Determining whether legislation violates these purposes requires examining the legislation in the context in which it applies, with attention to the interests it affects, and the situation and history in Canadian society of those who are treated differently by it. It must be examined how "a person legitimately feels when confronted with a particular law": *Law, supra,* at para. 53. . . .

65   I would emphasize that the "reasonable person" considered by the subjective-objective perspective understands and recognizes not only the circumstances of those *like* him or her, but also appreciates the situation of others. Therefore, when legislation impacts on various groups, particularly if those groups are disadvantaged, the subjective-objective perspective will take into account the particular experiences and needs of all of those groups.

66   Before turning to the specific contextual factors enumerated by Iacobucci J. in *Law,* it is worth mentioning one additional factor important to the particular circumstances of this appeal. Section 77(1) implicates, in a direct way that does not affect other Canadians, the interests of two groups who have generally experienced "pre-existing disadvantage, vulnerability, stereotyping, or prejudice": *Law, supra,* at para. 63. All band members affected by this legislation, whether on-reserve or off-reserve, have been affected by the legacy of stereotyping and prejudice against Aboriginal peoples.

67   When analysing a claim that involves possibly conflicting interests of minority groups, one must be especially sensitive to their realities and experiences, and to their values, history, and identity. This is inherent in the nature of a subjective-objective analysis, since a court is required to consider the perspective of someone possessed of similar characteristics to the claimant. Thus, in the case of equality rights affecting Aboriginal people and communities, the legislation in question must be evaluated with special attention to the rights of Aboriginal peoples, the protection of the Aboriginal and treaty rights guaranteed in the Constitution, the history of Aboriginal people in Canada, and with respect for and consideration of the cultural attachment and background of all Aboriginal women and men. It must also always be remembered that s. 15(1) provides for the "unremitting protection" of the right to equality, in whatever context the analysis takes place, whether there is one disadvantaged or minority group affected or more than one: see *Andrews, supra,* at p. 175; *R. v. Turpin,* [1989] 1 S.C.R. 1296, at p. 1326. In addition, it must be recalled that all the circumstances must always be evaluated from the perspective of a person with similar characteristics to the claimant, fully informed of the circumstances.

68   I am aware, of course, that issues have been raised about the constitutionality of distinctions created by the *Indian Act* between band members and non-band members

within the Aboriginal community. One such issue was dealt with in Bill C-31, discussed below. While the discussion of context which follows necessarily touches on the experiences of Aboriginal peoples generally, the decision in this case relates only to the constitutionality of the voting distinctions made within bands themselves by s. 77(1) of the *Indian Act.*

69   Since equality is a comparative concept, the analysis must consider the person relative to whom the claimant is being treated differentially: *Law, supra,* at para. 56. I accept the claimants' argument that the comparison here is between band members living on- and off-reserve, since these are the two groups whom the legislation treats differentially on its face. This denies the benefit of voting for band leadership to members of bands affected by s. 77(1) who do not live on a reserve. Because of the groups involved, the Court must also be attentive to the fact that there may be unique disadvantages or circumstances facing on-reserve band members. However, no evidence has been presented that would suggest that the legislation, in purpose or effect, ameliorates the position of band members living on-reserve, and therefore I find it unnecessary to consider the third contextual factor outlined in *Law.* I turn now to the particular contextual factors outlined in *Law* which may indicate that the legislation conflicts with the purposes of s. 15(1).

(a) *Disadvantage, Vulnerability, Stereotyping, and Prejudice . . .*
72   Second, off-reserve band members experience particular disadvantages compared to those living on-reserve because of their separation from the reserve. They are apart from communities to which many feel connection, and have experienced racism, culture shock, and difficulty maintaining their identity in particular and serious ways because of this fact. Third, it should be noted that the context is one in which, due to various factors, Aboriginal women, who can be said to be doubly disadvantaged on the basis of both sex and race, are among those particularly affected by legislation relating to off-reserve band members, because of their history and circumstances in Canadian and Aboriginal society.

(b) *Relationship Between the Basis of the Differential Treatment and the Claimant's Characteristics or Circumstances*
73   The second factor set out by Iacobucci J. examines the relationship between the basis on which the differential treatment occurs and the characteristics of the claimant and others, with the goal of recognizing the human dignity and right to full participation in society of all of them. Some distinctions may correspond to the needs, capacities, or circumstances of a group in a manner that does not affect their human dignity or that of others, viewed from a subjective-objective perspective *(Law, supra,* at paras. 69–71).

74   In the case at bar, considering this factor involves examining the legislative context surrounding the distinction at issue. The voting rights at issue affect other sections of the legislation; it must be determined how the functions of electors and powers of the band council chosen by them relate to the needs, circumstances, and human dignity of the band members included and excluded by the voting scheme. In my opinion, if the powers of electors or the chief and council they vote for affect issues that are purely local, and do not affect the interests of off-reserve band members, the differential treatment between band members contained in s. 77(1) cannot be considered to violate the right to substantive equality of the off-reserve members. Such differential treatment would relate to the different positions and needs of the two groups and could not be said, in my opinion, to stereotype off-reserve members or suggest they are less deserving, worthy, or important

band members from the perspective of someone affected by them. However, if the powers of the electors and the band council affect the interests and needs of both groups, this will be an indicator that the differential treatment is more likely to be discriminatory.

75   The band council chosen by the electors has by-law making powers under s. 81(1), which include the regulation of traffic on the reserve, control over the observance of law and order, and other such powers. Strayer J., the trial judge, found that these powers are mostly of a local nature, related to the governance of the reserve itself, and he suggested that they primarily affect residents. I would agree, in general, with this characterization, and I would add to the list of provisions affecting primarily local functions the powers contained in s. 85.1. However, I would note that several paragraphs of s. 81(1) affect in a particular way all band members, irrespective of residence on the reserve. Section 81(1)(*i*) allows the band council to allot land on the reserve, where this authority has been given by the Governor in Council. Sections 81(1)(*p*) and 81(1)(*p.1*) allow by-laws relating to residence and trespass on the reserve, which may affect the ability of non-residents to use the facilities and land on the reserve, and return to live there. The ability to live on the reserve, or to participate in activities on reserve lands if they desire, has been shown to be important to non-residents, and these functions of the band council affect their circumstances and needs directly and in a fundamental way. . . .

76   Section 83 gives the council power to make money by-laws, which include taxation of land on the reserve, licensing of businesses, appropriation of moneys to defray band expenses, and payment of remuneration to chiefs and councillors. These powers, in my opinion, are a mixture of functions that affect residents on the reserve only, and also all members of the band. While the taxation of land and businesses on the reserve and the licensing of businesses are primarily local functions, appropriation of money for various band purposes and the amounts to be paid to chiefs and councillors are matters in which all band members have an interest. In addition, under s. 83(1)(*f*), the band may make by-laws relating to "the raising of money from band members to support band projects" which may have the potential to affect all band members.

77   Although the band council's powers under ss. 81(1) and 83(1) are similar, in many ways, to those of a municipality, the exclusion of non-residents from voting rights affects other powers of the band council that relate to the needs of all members of the band, whether or not they are ordinarily resident on the reserve. Section 64(1) allows the expenditure by the Minister, with the band council's consent, of the band's capital moneys for various purposes, including distributions per capita to members of the band, and construction of new housing. The band's capital moneys come from the sale of surrendered lands or capital assets of the band (s. 62), assets that belong, collectively, to *all* members of the band. As found by Strayer J., all band members have important interests in these expenditures. Similarly, under s. 66(1), the Minister, with the approval of the band council, can make orders appropriating the band council's revenue moneys; the band council may be authorized to do so under s. 69. Expenditures by the band council may include matters like education, creation of new housing, creation of facilities on reserves, and other matters that may affect off-reserve band members' economic interest in its assets and the infrastructure that will be available to help them return to the reserve if they wish. Finally, s. 39(1)(b) requires the consent of a majority of "electors" of the band for the surrender of band lands. The definition of "elector" in s. 2(1) excludes band members who are disqualified from voting in band elections, so the wording of s. 77(1)

excludes off-reserve members from voting on the question of whether the lands they own in common will be surrendered.

78   The wording of s. 77(1), therefore, gives off-reserve band members no voice in electing a band council that, among other functions, spends moneys derived from land owned by all members, and money provided to the band council by the government to be spent on all band members. The band council also determines who can live on the reserve and what new housing will be built. The legislation denies those in the position of the claimants a vote in decisions about whether the reserve land owned by all members of the band will be surrendered. In addition, members who live in the vicinity of the reserve, as shown by the evidence of several of the plaintiffs in this case, may take advantage of services controlled by the band council such as schools or recreational facilities. Moreover, as a practical matter, representation of Aboriginal peoples in processes such as land claims and self-government negotiations often takes place through the structure of *Indian Act* bands. The need for and interest in this representation is shared by all band members, whether they live on- or off-reserve. Therefore, although in some ways, voting for the band council and chief relates to functions affecting reserve members much more directly than others, in other ways it affects all band members. Since interests are affected that are unrelated to the basis upon which the differential treatment is made (off-reserve residence status), considering the principle of respect for human dignity and substantive equality, this is an important indicator that the differential treatment is discriminatory.

(c) *Nature of the Affected Interest*
79   The fourth contextual factor which was described by Iacobucci J. in *Law, supra*, at paras. 74–75, and which is of particular importance in this case, is the nature of the affected interest. In general, the more important and significant the interest affected, the more likely it will be that differential treatment affecting this interest will amount to a discriminatory distinction within the meaning of s. 15(1).

80   Several social and legislative facts are important to analysing this contextual factor. The first is the important financial interest that non-residents have in the affairs of the band. As I outlined in the previous section, the band council must give consent for expenditures of the band's capital and revenue moneys. The band's electors also control decisions about the surrender of band lands which are owned collectively by all band members. Second, the band council controls the allotment of land and by-laws relating to trespass and residence, which affect in important ways the ability to return and live on the reserve. Third, the council makes decisions about the availability of services that may be important to non-residents, particularly those who may live near the reserve. Also important is the role of band leadership in the work of the Assembly of First Nations and other Aboriginal organizations at the regional, national and international levels. All these factors show that the *functions and powers* of the band council have important significance for the lives of off-reserve band members. Denying them voting rights when band leadership is chosen through a system of democracy affects significant interests they have in band governance.

81   The importance many band members place on maintaining a connection to their cultural roots is also particularly significant. Maintaining one's cultural identity will mean different things to different off-reserve band members, but to many it will entail an identification of interests with their band. When band leadership is chosen through a demo-

cratic system, one of the most powerful expressions of identification with that band is through the exercise of voting. When certain band members are not given any say in that system, the denial of that voice affects their belonging and connection to the band of which they are members.

82   Moreover, the band council has the power to affect directly the cultural interests of those off-reserve band members who identify with their band and reserve. The Royal Commission on Aboriginal Peoples stated that sources of traditional Aboriginal culture include "contact with the land, elders, Aboriginal languages and spiritual ceremonies" *(Perspectives and Realities, supra,* at p. 522). As outlined in the previous section, the band council has many powers affecting access to the reserve, management of the reserve lands, and the expenditure of money for the welfare of the band. Furthermore, the "electors" of the band can vote on the surrender of band lands. The band council therefore has considerable power to safeguard, develop and promote the sources of traditional Aboriginal culture and to affect the access of off-reserve band members to these sources.

83   Historical circumstances that have had and continue to have repercussions for the members of this group add to the reasons why the interest affected by this legislation is of important societal significance for those in the position of the claimants. Indeed, the creation of the group of off-reserve Aboriginal people can be seen as a consequence, in part, of historic policies toward Aboriginal peoples. The Royal Commission on Aboriginal Peoples describes the relationship between the federal government and Aboriginal peoples during the period from the early 1800s to 1969 as one of "displacement and assimilation" *(Report of the Royal Commission on Aboriginal Peoples,* vol. 1, *Looking Forward, Looking Back,* at pp. 137–91).

84   Maintaining a connection with the band of which they are members is of particular importance to those in the position of the claimants because they often live apart from reserves due to factors that are likely largely beyond their control. Lack of land, what are often scarce job opportunities on reserves, and the need to go far from the community for schooling, are among the reasons that members left the reserve in the past, and continue to leave. There are also particular issues affecting Aboriginal women's migration: *Perspectives and Realities, supra,* at pp. 573–76. The fact that those affected or their ancestors may well have had no choice but to leave the reserve signals that the interest in keeping a connection with the band of which they are members is particularly important to them because the separation from other members of the band and the reserve may well have been undesired or unchosen.

85   A considerable number of the band members who live off-reserve recently gained or regained this status under Bill C-31. This legislation modified sections of the *Indian Act* that denied Indian status to various categories of band members, though not all those who were restored to status became members of a band. It is, therefore, helpful to examine the history of the legislation that removed Indian status from them or from their ancestors. I must emphasize that this discussion is in no way related to the constitutionality of Bill C-31, in general or in the context of particular bands. Rather, I refer to it for the purpose of examining the context underlying the current legislative distinction and showing why the interest affected is an important one for band members.

86   Many of those affected are women, and the descendants of women, who lost their Indian status because they married men who did not have Indian status (see Indian and

Northern Affairs Canada, *Impacts of the 1985 Amendments to the Indian Act (Bill C-31): Summary Report (1990))*. Aboriginal women who married outside their band became members of their husband's band. See, for example, *The Indian Act*, S.C. 1951, c. 29, ss. 12 and 14, now repealed. Legislation depriving Aboriginal women of Indian status has a long history. The involuntary loss of status by Aboriginal women and children began in Upper and Lower Canada with the passage of *An Act to encourage the gradual Civilization of the Indian Tribes in the Province, and to amend the Laws respecting Indians*, S. Prov. C. 1857, 20 Vict., c. 26. A woman whose husband "enfranchised" had her status removed along with his. This legislation introduced patriarchal concepts into many Aboriginal societies which did not exist before: see Public Inquiry into the Administration of Justice and Aboriginal People, *Report of the Aboriginal Justice Inquiry of Manitoba* (1991), vol. 1, *The Justice System and Aboriginal People*, at pp. 476–79. As the Royal Commission on Aboriginal Peoples stated in *Perspectives and Realities, supra*, at p. 26:

> In the pre-Confederation period, concepts were introduced that were foreign to Aboriginal communities and that, wittingly or unwittingly, undermined Aboriginal cultural values. In many cases, the legislation displaced the natural, community-based and self-identification approach to determining membership—which included descent, marriage, residency, adoption and simple voluntary association with a particular group — and thus disrupted complex and interrelated social, economic and kinship structures. Patrilineal descent of the type embodied in the Gradual Civilization Act, for example, was the least common principle of descent in Aboriginal societies, but through these laws, it became predominant. From this perspective, the *Gradual Civilization Act* was an exercise in government control in deciding who was and was not an Indian.

This continued in the *Gradual Enfranchisement Act*, S.C. 1869, c. 6. This legislation, for the first time, instituted the policy that women who married men without Indian status lost their own status, and their children would not receive status. The rationale for these policies, given at the time, focussed on concerns about control over reserve lands, and the need to prevent non-Indian men from gaining access to them *(Perspectives and Realities, supra*, at p. 27). These policies were continued and expanded upon with the passage of the *Indian Act* in 1876, and amendments to it in subsequent years, particularly a major revision that took place in 1951.

87   The 1951 legislation was challenged under the *Canadian Bill of Rights*, S.C. 1960, c. 44 (reprinted in R.S.C., 1985, App. III), in *Attorney General of Canada v. Lavell*, [1974] S.C.R. 1349. The majority of this Court, using an approach to equality that was later rejected in *Andrews, supra*, held that the provisions did not violate the right to equality in the *Canadian Bill of Rights* and that even if they did, they could not be struck down as inconsistent with it.

88   These were not the only people who lost their status. The enfranchisement provisions of the *Indian Act* were designed to encourage Aboriginal people to renounce their heritage and identity, and to force them to do so if they wished to take a full part in Canadian society. In order to vote or hold Canadian citizenship, status Indians had to "voluntarily" enfranchise. They were then given a portion of the former reserve land in fee simple, and they lost their Indian status. At various times in history, status Indians who received higher education, or became doctors, lawyers, or ministers were automatically enfranchised. Those who wanted to be soldiers in the military during the two World Wars were required to enfranchise themselves and their whole families, and those who left the country for more than five years without permission also lost Indian status. (See L. Gil-

bert, *Entitlement to Indian Status and Membership Codes in Canada* (1996), at pp. 23–30.)

89   This history shows that Aboriginal policy, in the past, often led to the denial of status and the severing of connections between band members and the band. It helps show why the interest in feeling and maintaining a sense of belonging to the band free from barriers imposed by Parliament is an important one for all band members, and especially for those who constitute a significant portion of the group affected, who have been directly affected by these policies and are now living away from reserves, in part, because of them.

90   All these facts emphasize the importance, for band members living off-reserve, of having their voices included when band leadership is chosen through a process of common suffrage as set out in this legislation. They show why the interest in s. 77(1) is a fundamental one, and why the denial of voting rights in this context has serious consequences from the perspective of those affected. They show why there is not only economic, but also important societal significance to the interests affected by the differential treatment contained in s. 77(1): *Law, supra,* at para. 74.

(d) Conclusions on the Third Stage of Analysis

91   In summary, therefore, a contextual view of the people affected and the differential treatment in question leads to the conclusion that this legislative distinction conflicts with the purposes of s. 15(1). The people affected by this distinction, in general, are vulnerable and disadvantaged. They experience stereotyping and disadvantage as Aboriginal people and band members living away from reserves. They form part of a "discrete and insular minority" defined by race and residence, and it is more likely that further disadvantage will have a discriminatory impact upon them. Second, the distinction in question does not correspond with the characteristics or circumstances of the claimants and on-reserve band members in a manner which "respects and values their dignity and difference": *Law, supra,* at para. 28. The powers of the band council affect cultural, political, and financial interests and needs that are shared by band members living on and off the reserve. Third, the nature of the interests affected is fundamental. Given the form of representative democracy provided for in the *Indian Act,* failure to give any voice in that process to certain members of the band affects an important attribute of membership, and places a barrier between them and a community which has particular importance to them. The council and electors also make decisions about important financial, cultural, and political interests of the members that have important significance within the band and Canadian society. Finally, the interest affected is also significant because of the ways in which, in the past, ties between band members and the band or reserve have been involuntarily or reluctantly severed. Those affected or their parents may have left the reserve for many reasons that do not signal a lack of interest in the reserve given the various historical circumstances surrounding reserve communities in Canada such as an often inadequate land base, a serious lack of economic opportunities and housing, and the operation of past Indian status and band membership rules imposed by Parliament.

92   In the context of this vulnerable group, and these important interests, this distinction reinforces the stereotype that band members who do not live on reserves are "less Aboriginal", and less valuable members of their bands than those who do. A reasonable person in the position of the claimants, fully apprised of the context, would see the differential treatment contained in s. 77(1) as suggesting that off-reserve band members are less worthy or valuable as band members and members of Canadian society, and giving them

less concern, respect and consideration than band members living on reserves. Based upon this finding of discriminatory impact, the third stage of analysis, the identification of discrimination based on a violation of substantive equality and human dignity in the circumstances of this case, has been satisfied.

93   The factors discussed above outline the context surrounding the differential treatment contained in s. 77(1) of the *Indian Act*. This case involves people who have generally experienced significant historical disadvantage, and interests that are particularly important to those affected by the legislation. Taken together, they lead to a finding that from a subjective-objective perspective, the differential treatment in question violates off-reserve band members' equality rights. Yet neither of these factors should be seen as essential to my conclusions. I would also note that my discussion of the general history of off-reserve band members does not suggest that the conclusion that this legislation violates s. 15(1) would not apply to a band affected by s. 77(1) whose off-reserve members had a different composition or history from that of the general population of off-reserve band members in Canada. Every case of alleged discrimination, of course, must be considered in its own legislative and social context to determine whether it violates the constitutional rights of those affected, but in this case, both the general disadvantage and vulnerability of those affected, and the importance to all band members of the affected interests are compelling factors in my conclusions at the third stage of analysis.

94   The above analysis also does not suggest that any distinction between on-reserve and off-reserve band members would be stereotypical, interfere with off-reserve members' dignity, or conflict with the purposes of s. 15(1). There are clearly important differences between on-reserve and off-reserve band members, which Parliament could legitimately recognize. Taking into account, recognizing, and affirming differences between groups in a manner that respects and values their dignity and difference are not only legitimate, but necessary considerations in ensuring that substantive equality is present in Canadian society. The current powers of the band council, as discussed earlier, include some powers that are purely local, affecting matters such as taxation on the reserve, the regulation of traffic, etc. In addition, those living on the reserve have a special interest in many decisions made by the band council. For example, if the reserve is surrendered, they must leave their homes, and this affects them in a direct way it does not affect non-residents. Though non-residents may have an important interest in using them, educational or recreational services on the reserve are more likely to serve residents, particularly if the reserve is isolated or the non-residents live far from it. Many other examples can be imagined.

95   Recognizing non-residents' right to substantive equality in accordance with the principle of respect for human dignity, therefore, does not require that non-residents have identical voting rights to residents. Rather, what is necessary is a system that recognizes non-residents' important place in the band community. It is possible to think of many ways this might be done, while recognizing, respecting, and valuing the different positions, needs, and interests of on-reserve and off-reserve band members. One might be to divide the "local" functions which relate purely to residents from those that affect all band members and have different voting regimes for these functions. A requirement of a double majority, or a right of veto for each group might also respect the full participation and belonging of non-residents. There might be special seats on a band council for non-residents, which give them meaningful, but not identical, rights of participation. The

solution may be found in the customary practices of Aboriginal bands. There may be a separate solution for each band. Many other possibilities can be imagined, which would respect non-residents' rights to meaningful and effective participation in the voting regime of the community, but would also recognize the somewhat different interests of residents and non-residents. However, without violating s. 15(1), the voting regime cannot, as it presently does, completely deny non-resident band members participation in the electoral system of representation. Nor can that participation be minimal, insignificant, or merely token.

96   Therefore, I conclude that the present wording of s. 77(1) violates the right to equality without discrimination of the off-reserve members of bands affected by it. This finding is a general one, and is in no way related to the specific situation of the Batchewana Band. Since the provision has been found to be discriminatory as it applies to all bands affected by it, there is no need to consider the specific circumstances of the Batchewana Band.

D. Section 1 . . .

98   Throughout the s. 1 analysis, it must be remembered that it is the right to substantive equality and the accompanying violation of human dignity that has been infringed when a violation of s. 15(1) has been found. Even when the interests of various disadvantaged groups are affected, s. 15(1) mandates that government decisions must be made in a manner that respects the dignity of all of them, recognizing all as equally capable, deserving, and worthy of recognition. The fact that various minorities or vulnerable groups may have competing interests cannot alone constitute a justification for treating any of them in a substantively unequal manner, nor can it relieve the government of its burden to justify a violation of a Charter right on a balance of probabilities: see *Thomson Newspapers Co.* v. *Canada (Attorney General)*, [1998] 1 S.C.R. 877, at para. 88, per Bastarache J. . . .

100   Therefore, it is the objective of the restriction of voting rights to band members ordinarily resident on the reserve that must be considered in this case, although this must be considered along with the purpose of the *Indian Act* as a whole for a complete understanding of the broader scheme of the legislation. It must be remembered that in the case of equality rights, the legislative objective must be sufficiently pressing and substantial to justify a law that has been found to violate the essential human dignity and freedom of those possessed of similar characteristics to the claimants. In this case, Parliament's objective is properly classified as ensuring that those with the most immediate and direct connection with the reserve have a special ability to control its future. This objective, in my opinion, is pressing and substantial. It accords with *Charter* values, by recognizing the important dignity and autonomy interest in one's home and livelihood, and the connection band members feel to their land. Through this provision, Parliament is also moderating the interests of groups with different and possibly conflicting interests.

101   Turning to the proportionality analysis, restricting the vote to those living on the reserve is rationally connected to Parliament's objective. Although both band members living on- and off-reserve have interests in many of the functions determined by voting rights, those living on the reserve do have a more direct interest in many of the band council's functions. In terms of the "local" functions of the band council, they are the only people with an interest. In relation to functions that affect the future of the land or

the building of facilities on the reserve, on-reserve band members, in general, have a more direct interest in the decisions of the band council. Decisions about reserve lands affect their current living space, and a decision to surrender the reserve would mean that they would be forced to move from their homes and, in many cases, from their source of earning a livelihood. This statement is not meant to suggest that non-residents would be more likely to surrender the reserve or to make decisions that are not in the interest of the band as a whole, but rather to recognize that those who live on the reserve have particular interests in the land, given current circumstances.

102   By ensuring that only those who live on the reserve can vote in relation to all of the band council's functions, s. 77(1) gives them control over the future directions that the band will take, and over decisions about the reserve land on which they live. Excluding non-residents from voting is connected to the objective because, by denying all others a vote, the legislation ensures that those with the most direct and immediate interest, residents, maintain voting control over the decisions that will affect the future of the reserve.

103   However, those seeking to uphold this law have not demonstrated that a *complete* exclusion of non-residents from the right to vote, which violates their equality rights, constitutes a minimal impairment of these rights. Indeed, they have not shown that *any* infringement of the respondents' equality rights is necessary to achieve this purpose. As I outlined earlier, the guarantee of equality does not require that on- and off-reserve band members be treated the same, and respecting the rights of dignity and belonging of off-reserve band members need not mean ignoring the particular interest of residents in decisions affecting the reserve. I discussed several possible solutions above, which would respect the dignity of off-reserve band members, but would not stereotype them or otherwise violate their right to substantive equality. The appellants have not shown why solutions like special majorities, representative band councils not based directly on population, dividing the local functions from the broader powers of the band council, or other solutions that would not have the effect of suggesting off-reserve band members are less worthy of concern, respect, and consideration could not accomplish this objective.

104   The appellant Her Majesty the Queen suggests that the current model meets the criterion of minimal impairment because of the administrative difficulties and costs involved in setting up, for example, a two-tiered council where one tier would deal with local issues and the other with issues affecting all band members, or in maintaining a voter's list and conducting elections where the electorate may be widely dispersed. Even assuming that such costs could legitimately constitute a s. 1 justification, these arguments are unconvincing. It must be remembered that the burden of justifying limitations on constitutional rights is upon the government. The government has presented no evidence to show that a system that would respect equality rights is particularly expensive or difficult to implement. Rather, there are many possible solutions that would not be difficult to administer, but would require a creative design of an electoral system that would balance the rights involved. Change to any administrative scheme so it accords with equality rights will always entail financial costs and administrative inconvenience. The refusal to come up with new, different, or creative ways of designing such a system, and to find cost-effective ways to respect equality rights cannot constitute a minimal impairment of these rights. Though the government argues that these costs should not be imposed on small communities such as the Batchewana Band, the possible failure, in the future, of the government to provide Aboriginal communities with additional resources necessary

to implement a regime that would ensure respect for equality rights cannot justify a violation of constitutional rights in its legislation.

105 Since this legislation does not minimally impair the respondents' equality rights, I agree with Strayer J. and the Court of Appeal that it is not justified under s. 1 of the *Charter.* . . .

SELECTED BIBLIOGRAPHY

Bayefsky, A. "The Human Rights Committee and the Case of Sandra Lovelace" (1982) 20 Can. Y.B. Int'l Law 244.

Boldt, M. *Surviving as Indians: The Challenge of Self-Government* (Toronto: University of Toronto Press, 1993).

Faith, K. "Aboriginal Women" in *Unruly Women: The Politics of Confinement and Resistance* (Vancouver: Press Gang Publishers, 1993) 186–203.

Gilbert, L. *Entitlement to Indian Status and Membership Codes in Canada* (Toronto: Carswell, 1996).

Greschner, D. "Aboriginal Women, the Constitution and Criminal Justice" (1992) U.B.C. L. Rev. 338.

Isaac, T. "Dually Disadvantaged and Historically Forgotten?: Aboriginal Women and the Inherent Right of Aboriginal Self-Government" (1992) 21:3 Man. L. J. 453.

———. "Case Commentary: *Corbiere* v. *Canada*" [1994] 1 C.N.L.R. 55.

———. "Case Commentary: Self-Government, Indian Women and their Rights of Reinstatement under the *Indian Act:* A Comment on *Sawridge Band* v. *Canada*" [1995] 4 C.N.L.R. 1.

Jordan, E. "Residual Sex Discrimination in the Indian Act: Constitutional Remedies" (Fall 1995) 11 J. L. & Soc. Pol'y 213.

Montour, M. "Iroquois Women's Rights with Respect to Matrimonial Property on Indian Reserves" (1987) 4 C.N.L.R. 1.

Monture, P. "Reflecting on Flint Women" in R. Devlin, ed. *Canadian Perspectives on Legal Theory* (Toronto: Edmond Montgomery, 1991).

Moss, W. "Indigenous Self-Government and Sexual Equality under the *Indian Act:* Resolving Conflicts Between Collective and Individual Rights" (1990) 15 Queen's L.J. 279.

———. "Indigenous Self-Government in Canada and Sexual Equality under the *Indian Act:* Resolving Conflicts Between Collective and Individual Rights" (1990) 15:2 Queen's L.J. 281.

Sanders, D. "Indian Status: A Women's Issue or an Indian Issue" (1984) 3 C.N.L.R. 30.

Silman, J., ed. *Enough Is Enough: Aboriginal Women Speak Out* (Toronto: Women's Press, 1987).

INDEX

See Table of Cases starting on page xi for index to specific legal cases.